Government Contract Law

Government Contract Law

Second Edition

Charles Tiefer
PROFESSOR
UNIVERSITY OF BALTIMORE SCHOOL OF LAW

William A. Shook
PARTNER
PRESTON GATES ELLIS & ROUVELAS MEEDS LLP
WASHINGTON, D.C.

CAROLINA ACADEMIC PRESS
Durham, North Carolina

Library of Congress Cataloging-in-Publication Data

Tiefer, Charles.
    Government contract law : cases and materials / by Charles Tiefer and William A.
Shook. -- 2nd ed.
        p. cm.
    ISBN 0-89089-437-X
        1. Public contracts -- United States -- Cases. I. Shook, William A., 1952-II. Title.

KF848.T54 2003
346.7302'3--dc22

                                                                    2003062561

CAROLINA ACADEMIC PRESS

700 Kent Street
Durham, North Carolina 27701
Telephone (919) 489-7486
Fax (919) 493-5668
www.cap-press.com

Printed in the United States of America

Contents

Foreword

Government contracting law matters. It directs a large, legally structured portion of the overlapping worlds of government and business. As a field of practice, it puts new lawyers to work where they can do their country, the economy, and themselves much good, taking on the challenges of a very sophisticated legal mini-world. As a subject, it is both intensely practical and intellectually stimulating. There is no point in memorizing or otherwise dully plodding away at government contract law, for it is too vast, too complex, and too rapidly changing to yield to young lawyers unless they apply to it their very highest capacities.

Surprisingly, at the present time, no current one-volume casebook exists for learning government contract law. The authors themselves learned from, and taught from, important previous casebooks, including John W. Whelan, *Cases and Materials on Federal Government Contracts* (1985)(with 1989 supplement). They owe a large debt to Professor Whelan, who kindly shared course and other materials with Professor Tiefer. Professor William Kovacic also assisted by providing his course syllabus and many insights into the subject. Other intellectual debts are owed to Donald P. Arnavas & William J. Ruberry, *Government Contract Guidebook* (2d ed. 1994)(with annual supplements), and to *Government Contract Law: The Deskbook for Procurement Professionals*, which is the assembled government contracting law course outlines for the Judge Advocate General's School. Each of these books, in its way, provided illumination. However, they are either more than one volume in length, not casebooks, or not current. Today, there is a great need for a current one-volume casebook primarily to support law students or others learning the subject by the casebook method.

As for the two authors, Charles Tiefer, Associate Professor at University of Baltimore Law School, annually teaches a course in government contract law. He served as Solicitor and Deputy General Counsel of the U.S. House of Representatives in 1984-95. William Shook heads the government procurement practice at the firm of Preston Gates Ellis & Rouvelas Meeds in Washington, D.C. He came to that position after serving from 1979 through 1985 on various congressional investigations committees that focused on government contracting procedures and abuses. Since coming to Preston Gates, he has lectured across the country regarding government contract law. It has been an effective, thought-provoking, and pleasant collaboration, with one party bringing the academic perspective, and the other, successful and extensive experience with a broad range of issues in practice, and both sharing the unique Congressional perspective that is so important to this area of statutory law.

Professor Tiefer acknowledges the assistance of his colleagues at the University of Baltimore Law School with whom he has had valuable discussions of the work, including Dean John Sebert, himself an expert in contract law; Associate Dean Steven Davison, who, with memories of his own fine environmental law book, eased this one's path; Michael Meyerson, Steve Shapiro, and Fred Brown, who sat in on course sessions and gave important advice on their improvement; and Robert Lande, Michele Gilligan, Eric Easton, Barbara Babb, Jack Lynch, Dick Bourne, Lynn McLain, Larry Katz, and Elizabeth Samuels, all of whom gave advice and support over the years of development. Helping in countless ways were his wife, Hillary Burchuk, who leant both support and her own insights into the workings of government and business from her years in advanced practice in both public and private sectors; his sister, Dr. Leonore Tiefer, whose own best-selling books on sexual psychology, alas, could only have some of their aspects of interest smoothly melded into this book; and his mother, Rosalind Tiefer, a teacher of American history devoted to all subjects, like this one, that are, at bottom, best understood from that history.

Working diligently on this edition have been three academic assistants at the University of Baltimore Law School: Lori Sherwood, Elinor Walker, and Heather Akeshurst-Krause. Each conducted research and wrote memoranda, which served as draft notes for the casebook on a number of advanced subjects. Each brought diligence, skill, freshness, and insight, and a special invaluable contribution for a casebook-in-preparation that only the law student can provide, namely, the deepest and most sincere sympathy for the readers and the matching sensitivity to what might smooth their path. Principal credit for the skilled word processing on the book, including the patient massaging of many very raw sources into polished form, goes to Maria Jameson. Additional invaluable rounds of expert word processing at the galleys stage came from Pam Labbe and Mary Heywood-Peterson, both of whom put in intense and ingenious efforts to keep the book on schedule. The author was also greatly assisted by Barbara Jones, ace juggler of a thousand projects.

Also helping have been Emily Greenburg, Joshua Arenberg, Robin Klein, Will Tress, and Robert Pool, who miraculously retrieved library and computer resources, often from the most unexpected and inaccessible sources. And much help came from the students of government contracting law classes, who cheerfully learned the subject from predecessor materials and whose diplomatic yet urgent requests for improvement in those materials spurred the book's progress.

Keith Sipe at Carolina Academic Press provided a high level of enthusiasm and professional counsel in getting the book to completion. He helped to visualize the book when it was only imminent in the minds of the authors, and still quite encumbered with their uncertainties, and used his own confidence to bring it forth. Kristin Strange, the editor, performed Herculean labors to make the text read more smoothly and interestingly.

William Shook acknowledges the significant help, by his forebearance, of Stratton Shook, who somewhat willingly agreed to excuse his father from his otherwise mandatory attendance at various sporting and school events; his ability to excel in his elementary school studies as well as his dedication to good sportsmanship and intelligent performance on the athletic field have been a source of constant inspiration and pleasure. And without Peggy Shook, who as spouse and mother has excelled at the fine art of helpful support, even when it involved the author's extended and regular teaching trip absences, the author's contribution to this project would not have been possible.

A deep sense of gratitude is also owed to his partners at Preston Gates who not only fully supported this project, but who, over the years, have provided the best of professional environments in which it could be initiated and accomplished. Firm Chairman

Emanuel Rouvelas, Managing Partner Jonathan Blank, and Litigation Department Chairman Stanley Gorinson have, through both their direct example and assistance, provided the core professionalism that makes the practice of law pleasurable.

Thanks must also go to Richard Wall, Robert Gustin, and Chris Pockney of Ernst & Young LLP who have shared the teaching podium on countless occasions and have educated the author not only in the fine details of government contracting pricing and accounting but the manner in which such details can be enjoyably imparted to others. Hopefully some of their fine teaching examples are imparted throughout the pages of this text.

Everyone mentioned has contributed to this book.

Charles Tiefer
William A. Shook
Washington, D.C.
June, 1999

Note for the Second Edition

The rapid developments in government contract law of the late 1990s and 2000s call for a second edition. There seems little point in attempting to list all those developments; no chapter has gone without updating with new cases and notes. Two entirely new chapters have come to the book: Chapter 3 as to the new contracting methods such as commercial contracting; and Chapter 12 as to ethics. Chapters 2 and 11, as to acquisition and remedy procedures, respectively, have adapted to the major developments such as, respectively, the reforms of the competitive proposals method, the new jurisdiction of the Court of Federal Claims, and the end of the regular bid protest jurisdiction of the district courts.

The authors extend their gratitude for the support from their families and colleagues. William Shook again acknowledges the significant help of Stratton Shook, provided in the first edition by a supportive son, and for this one, by a dynamic young man. William Shook adds an acknowledgement of his partners at Preston Gates who have entrusted him with the chair of the Government Contracts group at the firm and who continue to suport his literary efforts. Charles Tiefer acknowledges, in addition to the irreplaceable encouragement of his wife, Hillary Burchuk, now also two energetic and joyous new helpers who came into the world since that first edition, Max David Tiefer and Roy Bernard Tiefer. Mostly, our colleagues helping with the first edition continue to be the ones helping with this one. In addition, a fresh source of fine secretarial assistance was Kisme Scott. Charles Tiefer adds an acknowledgement of the assistance of the new Dean of the University of Baltimore Law School, Gilbert Holmes, and the new Associate Dean, Donald Stone, both strong encouragers of scholarship. Keith Sipe at Carolina Academic Press continues as the source of publishing vision and professional counsel in bringing this new edition to maturity.

Charles Tiefer
William A. Shook
Washington, D.C.
August, 2003

Copyright Acknowledgments

We gratefully acknowledge the permission granted by authors, publishers, and organizations to reprint portions of the following copyrighted materials:

Arnavas, Donald P., & Ruberry, William J., GOVERNMENT CONTRACT GUIDE-BOOK 2d ed. 1994). Published by Federal Publications, Inc. Reprinted by permission.

Coburn, George, *Enlarged Bid Protest Jurisdiction of the United States Court of Federal Claims, The Procurement Lawyer*, Fall 1997. Published by the American Bar Association. Reprinted by permission.

Judge Advocate General's School, U.S. Army in Charlottesville, Virginia, Materials from the Contract Attorney's Courses (1995-1998). Reprinted with approval.

Livingston, Scott A., *Fair Treatment for Contractors Doing Business With the State of Maryland*, 15 University of Baltimore Law Review 215 (1986). Reprinted by permission.

Massengale, Eugene W., FUNDAMENTALS OF FEDERAL CONTRACT LAW (1991). Published by Quorum Books. Reprinted by permission.

Tiefer, Charles, *"Budgetized" Health Entitlements and the Fiscal Constituion in Congress's 1995-1996 Budget Battle*, 33 Harvard Journal on Legislation 411 (1996). Reprinted by permission.

Tiefer, Charles and Stroman, Ronald, *Congressional Intent and Commercial Products, The Procurement Lawyer*, Spring 1997. Published by the American Bar Association. Reprinted by permission.

Government Contract Law

Chapter 1

Government Contracting Doctrines

A. Introduction: The Challenge of the Different Culture of Government Contracting

Government contracting law has grown in interest and attraction for law students (and others who would study this casebook). Federal government contracting law directs the federal government's procurement of goods and services. It thereby governs an area of practice which accords a large role for lawyers because the federal government binds itself, and its contractors, by much more elaborate law than the comparatively simple law governing how private parties contract with each other. This has long been true.

Today, though, studying federal government contracting law has increased value. Most states model their state and local procurement, to a considerable degree, on federal government law. Aspects of government procurement law apply to the large amount of health care expenditures covered by Medicare and Medicaid and to other government programs such as government grants and loans. Finally, selected aspects of government contract law apply to, or influence contractual relations with, the subcontractors, suppliers, and others who aid those who contract directly with the government. Combining all these, government contracting law shapes legal work for procurement amounting to many hundreds of billions of dollars of commerce with intensive needs for lawyering.

Moreover, government contracting law presents a unique opportunity, being situated at the complex and ambiguous boundary zone between public and private law. On one side, government contract law draws on concepts familiar to students grounded in the introductory contracts course of the first year of law school, with its common law origins. Government contract formation law draws on the familiar concepts of offer and acceptance; government contract rules for accurate statements draw on the familiar concepts of mistake and fraud; government contract administration draws on the familiar concepts of interpretation, conditions, and excuse; government contract termination draws on the familiar concepts of breach and remedy.

However, government contract law deserves respectful attention for the large number of new concepts. Basic (private) contract law remains largely true to its common law roots, even when codified and, in the process, modified, by such developments as the Uniform Commercial Code. In contrast, government contract law ultimately derives only to a limited degree from court-made law, as distinguished from the overriding importance of statutes, regulations, and standard clauses. Today, the federal code of government contract rules, known as the Federal Acquisition Regulation (the "FAR"), more than any body of adjudications, answers the largest number of legal questions in government contract law.

Basic contract law contrasts with government contract law as to the economic "culture" in which they play the legal role. Basic contract law exists in the culture of the private economy, with its transactions between private parties, and its law made by those private parties, that is, its "private" law. It governs symmetric transactions in which the parties on both sides not only have solely private, not public, powers and responsibilities, but also solely economic, not governmental, motivations and interests. In contract, government contract law involves governmental powers and responsibilities, and, looking at the surrounding "culture," also governmental motivations and interests. The presence of governmental agencies and their contracting officers on one side of the transaction brings in an entire culture of public law. Contracting officers do not act from pure economic self-interest, as a private contracting party does; they implement public policymaking, meaning that they must find their way through the sometimes clear, but sometimes mysterious, mix of instructions that govern the public world. Their instructions come from the elected Congress and President, the appointed heads of departments, the senior civil service above them, and the fellow governmental employees who are their colleagues and assistants. Their public law culture sets them apart in every respect from the private commercial world: in institutions, motives, rules, ethics, and language. Sometimes they even act in a particularly special sub-culture within the public world, such as military contracting officers whose procurement activity derives its shape in part from the unique military culture.

Hence, for learning this different culture and its different language, a casebook becomes just as vital a learning tool for government contract law as for basic (private) contract law. The cases supply the vital context that a reading of dry regulations would not: like a newspaper story, they tell, in discussing the legal issue, what is being purchased, by whom, when, where, and how. They place the new vocabulary, especially the wealth of acronyms from ACOs and the ASPR to TINA and the VABCA, in comprehensible surroundings. Their stories show the interaction of the special motivations of government officials and government contractors, thereby revealing the meaning and purpose infusing the clauses, rules, and statutes.

So, this book depends heavily on its cases, not in defiance of the difference between the statutory origins of government contract law and the common law origins of private contract law, but in recognition and acknowledgement of that difference. The cases are needed to show the government contract culture, as well as its black-letter law. If government contract law were just another common law subject, similar to basic contract law but with different rules, perhaps then the graduate of a course in basic contract law could learn the differences from an abstraction of the specific rules in a Restatement or codification. As an entirely different culture, government contracting requires the contextual richness of cases to effectively transmit understanding.

Accordingly, this chapter starts with a case chosen not so much for its particular point of law, as to illustrate the different culture of government contracting. The chapter then continues with cases and discussion about the three doctrinal areas that most distinguish government contract law: the limited authority of government employees; the source of the law in statutes, regulations, and standard clauses; and, the role of public budgets as a separate formal constraint on contracting. Finally, the chapter uses some state materials to illustrate the similarities and differences between federal and state government contracting law.

As for the particular case that starts this chapter, the opinion has many passages of remarkably clear, helpful exposition of government contract law. Deriving full benefit from these involves a major effort that is its own reward: a first chance, in the context of a relatively comprehensible opinion, to encounter the differentiating aspects of government contract law. So, in reading the case, try not to rush past, or to glide over, the following new aspects; instead, begin acclimating to them, making it much easier to deal with them when they recur in subsequent opinions:

1. The government procurement context. In this first case the context consists of the government buying medical care for military dependents. The plaintiff sells those medical services to an Army hospital commanded by Colonel James Henry. Readers must learn how that context works from the opinion, unless for some unusual reason they may have independent knowledge of the context of military health care.

For example, some of the plaintiff's dealings concern Colonel Henry. But other of the plaintiff's dealings concern the "fiscal intermediary," the Associated Group. This reflects how government procurement works in this context. Colonel Henry, as the hospital commander who buys the services, makes some decisions. However, the Army has set up its medical system so that the plaintiff sends its bills not to Colonel Henry, but to a fiscal intermediary, namely, the Associated Group, which processes them on behalf of the Army. So, the Associated Group makes some decisions. It is a challenge for the reader without any previous background to come to understand the major different roles in this opinion assigned by this Army medical care procurement system to Colonel Henry and to the Associated Group. A host of persons or entities in the Department of Defense also have cameo roles in this opinion.

2. Acronyms. A reader of this opinion would usefully keep a chart as to what each of the following stands for: TMM, CHAMPUS, MOU, MEI, and CDA. Only CDA will recur later on, but the habit of dealing with acronyms as they arise will stand a reader of government contract law in good stead. Government contract law involves learning precisely this specialized new language.

3. Specialized procedures. The opinion's citation tells that this decision comes from the United States Court of Appeals for the Federal Circuit, a specialized tribunal. Almost immediately, the opinion's first sentence tells that the appeal comes up from the Court of Federal Claims, another specialized tribunal. Later, the "Procedural History" section indicates that the case began as a claim under the Contract Disputes Act ("CDA"), a specialized procedure. None of this will seem familiar from a course in basic contract law, which commonly gets litigated in general nonspecialized tribunals and begins without preliminary formalities like a claim under a special "Disputes Act." Yet all these specialized aspects will prove recurrent and important as the course proceeds. It will probably require reading several other cases occurring more or less the same way before beginning to feel at home with these specialized procedures.

4. Statutes. The opinion's "Background" section begins with Congress establishing this military health plan by statute. This statute, and other statutes, play a large part in the law of this opinion. Quite evidently, the health care system for military dependents, and the law regarding that system, did not arise by descent from the common law. It started with Congressional enactments, signified by the citation to 10 U.S.C. §1071-1106, where the U.S.C. is the United States Code, the codification of federal statutes.

5. Regulations. Fairly quickly, it turns out that the details of the rate-setting dispute in this case between the Army and the medical provider (TMM) concern regulations. The Department of Defense, it seems, has provided the detailed law regarding this health care system in such regulations. Unless the readers have taken administrative law, this may be their first encounter with extensive resort to federal regulations. These regulations are signified by citation to 32 C.F.R. §199, where the C.F.R. is the Code of Federal Regulations, the codification of federal regulations. The wording of the regulations resolves this case. It is decisive. It is the law. So the opinion has an important lesson: regulations may make slow reading because of the concentrated style in which they are written, but they are where the law is.

Total Medical Management, Inc., Plaintiff-Appellee, v. The United States, Defendant-Appellant

No. 96-5013. United States Court of Appeals,
Federal Circuit. Jan. 16, 1997.

Before ARCHER, Chief Judge, MICHEL and RADER, Circuit Judges.

MICHEL, Circuit Judge.

The United States ("government") appeals from the November 2, 1994 order of the United States Court of Federal Claims, No. 92-838C, granting summary judgment of contractual liability against the government in favor of Total Medical Management, Inc. ("TMM"). The order became final when, on August 31, 1995, the trial court entered judgment in TMM's favor in the amount of $57,197.50, plus interest. The appeal was submitted for our decision following oral argument on July 2, 1996. We hold that, because the applicable base reimbursement rate in this local contract conflicts with valid national regulations, the contract is void as beyond the authority of the government signatory. As such, we reverse and remand with instructions to dismiss for failure to state a claim upon which relief can be granted.

BACKGROUND

In 1956, Congress established a health plan for dependents of members of the uniformed services. This plan allowed for the provision of medical care at civilian medical facilities for those who could not be cared for at military medical facilities. See Dependents' Medical Care Act, Pub.L. No. 84-569, 70 Stat. 250 (1956) (codified as amended at 10 U.S.C. §§1071-1106) ("Act"). This plan has been implemented through the Civilian Health and Medical Program of the Uniformed Services ("CHAMPUS"). 10 U.S.C. §1072(4) (1994). The plan allows military hospitals and private health care companies to create facility-sharing arrangements. Specifically, according to section 1096(a) of the Act,

> The Secretary of Defense may enter into an agreement providing for the sharing of resources between facilities of the uniformed services and facilities of a civilian health care provider or providers that the Secretary contracts with under section 1079, 1086, or 1097 of this title if the Secretary determines that such an agreement would result in the delivery of health care to which covered beneficiaries are entitled under this chapter in a more effective, efficient, or economical manner.

10 U.S.C. §1096(a) (1994). The Secretary of Defense has implemented this general power granted by Congress by encouraging military hospital commanders to enter into

facility-sharing partnership agreements, upon approval of the Director of CHAMPUS and the Surgeon General of the appropriate military department, with private health care companies. See Department of Defense Instruction 6010.12, "Military-Civilian Health Services Partnership Program" (Oct. 22, 1987); 32 C.F.R. §199.1(p) (1995) (permitting entry into agreements under "Military-Civilian Health Services Partnership Program"). These partnership agreements are typically memorialized in "Memoranda of Understanding" ("MOUs") or "Memoranda of Agreement" ("MOAs"). This arrangement saves the government the expense of reimbursement for treatment in expensive civilian medical facilities. This additional expense would otherwise be billed to CHAMPUS.

Instead of billing patients, the private health care companies that have entered into MOUs file claim forms with a fiscal intermediary (in TMM's case, the Associated Group) that processes and pays the claims. Prior to February 1989, the reimbursement rate scheme was as follows:

The allowable charge for authorized care shall be the lower of:

(A) The billed charge for the service;

(B) The prevailing charge level that does not exceed the amount equivalent to the 80th percentile of billed charges made for similar services in the same locality during the base period.

32 C.F.R. §199.14(h)(1)(i) (1989).

Effective February 1, 1989, Congress modified the CHAMPUS payment rules. Department of Defense Appropriations Act of 1989, Pub.L. No. 100-463, §8019, 102 Stat. 2270. The new reimbursement scheme is:

The allowable charge for authorized care shall be the lowest of the amounts identified...:

(A) The billed charge for the service.

(B) The prevailing charge level that does not exceed the amount equivalent to the 80th percentile of billed charges made for similar services in the same locality during the base period.

* * *

(C) For charges from physicians and other individual professional providers, the fiscal year 1988 prevailing charges adjusted by the Medicare Economic Index (MEI), as the MEI is applied to Medicare prevailing charge levels.

32 C.F.R. §199.14(g)(1) (1990). The CHAMPUS Operating Manual and the Code of Federal Regulations both reflected this change in the reimbursement scheme, thus putting all program participants on constructive notice that the MEI could limit the reimbursement amount. 44 U.S.C. §1507 (1994).

On November 10, 1988, TMM entered into an MOU with Ireland Army Hospital in Fort Knox, Kentucky, to provide internal medicine services for CHAMPUS beneficiaries. The MOU contained the following provision relating to reimbursement rates for services provided under the agreement:

...Billing rates are as follows:

(1) CHAMPUS eligibles at 75% of current CHAMPUS prevailing rate for outpatient services (current as of date of billing).

(2) All others (primarily active duty military) at 75% of current CHAMPUS prevailing rate for all outpatient services.

(3) All inpatient services at 80% of current CHAMPUS prevailing rate.

By letter dated February 10, 1989, the Associated Group informed TMM that the Internal Medicine MOU had been approved. In addition, the letter noted that "all payments are based on the CHAMPUS allowable charge methodology; payment for a procedure will not exceed the area prevailing charge." Similarly, the letter indicated that "Partnership claims will be processed in the same manner as CHAMPUS claims and are subject to program and policy limitations....Payments may not exceed the CHAMPUS prevailing fees."

* * *

In 1990, the Associated Group began reimbursing TMM according to the limitation imposed by the use of the MEI. On February 22, 1990, TMM sent a letter to Colonel James Henry, the Commander at the Fort Knox hospital, reporting that the MEI had been used in determining the amount that TMM was reimbursed for certain medical services. TMM pointed out that the Internal Medicine MOU called for reimbursement based upon "75% of the current CHAMPUS prevailing rate" and made no mention of the use of the MEI to limit payments.

Colonel Henry conveyed TMM's concern to the Army Health Services Command. In his letter, Colonel Henry sought clarification regarding the MEI limitation. The Associated Group prepared a response and sent it to CHAMPUS on May 10, 1990. This response indicated that the payments made by the Associated Group were in accordance with the MEI limitation in the CHAMPUS regulations. CHAMPUS then sent a response to the Army.

TMM and the Army re-executed the * * * MOUs at the end of each of the initial two year terms * * * The re-executed contracts were silent as to the MEI limitation. On February 22, 1991, the Associated Group sent a letter to TMM stating:

> Per the agreement, the reimbursement of your Parntership claims will be based on a single percentage of the * * * prevailing charge or the maximum allowable prevailing charge (also called the Medicare Economic Index adjusted prevailing charge), whichever is lower) * * * *

* * *

PROCEDURAL HISTORY

On April 10, 1992, TMM sent a claim under the Contract Disputes Act ("CDA") for $52,746.28 to Colonel Thomas Clements at Ireland Army Community Hospital. This amount was calculated as the difference between the actually reimbursed MEI rate and TMM's calculation of the contract rate.

* * *

TMM filed a complaint against the government in the Court of Federal Claims on December 8, 1992.

* * *

On July 11, 1994, the parties filed cross-motions for summary judgment on the issue of liability. On November 2, 1994, the trial court granted TMM's summary judgment motion and denied the government's motion. In a ruling from the bench, the trial judge held that liability turned on the meaning of the term "current CHAMPUS prevailing rate" used in the MOU. The judge agreed with TMM that this was the same as the "current CHAMPUS prevailing charge" as used in 32 C.F.R. §199.14 (1990), rather than the "allowable rate," which, under the CHAMPUS regulations, would have included the MEI limitation.

DISCUSSION

* * *

There is no question that TMM pleaded the existence of a valid contract here. The proper question, despite the government's label, is one of the merits: whether TMM failed to state a claim upon which relief can be granted. Id.

The requirements for a valid contract with the United States are: a mutual intent to contract including offer, acceptance, and consideration; and authority on the part of the government representative who entered or ratified the agreement to bind the United States in contract. Thermalon Indus., Ltd. v. United States, 34 Fed.Cl. 411, 414 (1995) (citing City of El Centro v. United States, 922 F.2d 816, 820 (Fed.Cir.1990) and Fincke v. United States, 230 Ct.Cl. 233, 244, 675 F.2d 289, 295 (1982)). In addition, government contracts must comply with statutorily sanctioned regulations. See, e.g., United States v. Amdahl Corp., 786 F.2d 387, 392 (Fed.Cir.1986) (holding that a procurement contract award in conflict with statute and regulation was void ab initio). A contract which is "plainly illegal" is a nullity and void ab initio. John Reiner & Co. v. United States, 163 Ct.Cl. 381, 325 F.2d 438, 440 (1963). A contract is "plainly illegal" when made contrary to statute or regulation either because of some action or statement by the contractor, or when the contractor is on "direct notice that the procedures being followed were violative of such requirements." Amdahl, 786 F.2d at 395 (quoting a decision of the Comptroller General, B-176393, 52 Comp. Gen. 214, 218 (1972) (citing Schoenbrod v. United States, 187 Ct.Cl. 627, 410 F.2d 400 (1969)).

Here, the existence of the negotiated, signed MOUs evidences offer and acceptance. There was also consideration in the mutuality of obligation: TMM is to provide discounted health care services; the Army is to provide support staff and free space in the military hospital.

The Contract Disputes Act defines a contracting officer as:

> any person who, by appointment in accordance with applicable regulations, has the authority to enter into and administer contracts and make determinations and findings with respect thereto. The term also includes the authorized representative of the contracting officer, acting within the limits of his authority.

41 U.S.C. §601(3) (1994). The Secretary of Defense has authority to enter into resource sharing "agreements" with civilian health care providers. 10 U.S.C. §1096 (1994). In Department of Defense Instruction 6010.12, the Secretary authorizes hospital commanders to administer the partnership agreements and to encourage civilian health care providers to participate in them. Hospital commanders may execute an agreement only after submitting it for approval to the Director, CHAMPUS, and the Surgeon General of the appropriate military department. Department of Defense Instruction 6010.12(F)(1). The MOUs here were forwarded to the Associated Group, the CHAMPUS approval designee, and were approved. Therefore, we hold that the MOU was ratified by a government representative with the authority to bind the United States in contract. Thus, we hold all elements for a contract were met by the MOUs.

* * *

However, even though the basic requirements for a government contract are met, the contract is void because the MOUs are in direct conflict with CHAMPUS regulations.

This regulatory scheme in effect at the time each of the contracts was entered into (or renewed), explicitly limited health care provider reimbursement base rates to the lowest of three possibilities: the billed charge, the prevailing charge, or the MEI limited prevailing charge. 32 C.F.R. §199.14(g)(1) (1990). Neither the Secretary of Defense nor any of his designated representatives had the authority to obligate CHAMPUS beyond these base rates set by regulation. The government "is not bound by its agents acting beyond their authority and contrary to regulation." Urban Data Sys., Inc. v. United States, 699 F.2d 1147, 1153 (Fed.Cir.1983) (quoting Yosemite Park & Curry Co. v. United States, 217 Ct.Cl. 360, 582 F.2d 552, 558 (1978)); see also Office of Personnel Management v. Richmond, 496 U.S. 414, 428, 110 S.Ct. 2465, 2473, 110 L.Ed.2d 387 (1990) (agencies' unauthorized statements to citizens cannot obligate the Treasury for the payment of funds). A contractor who enters into an arrangement with an agent of the government bears the risk that the agent is acting outside the bounds of his authority, even when the agent himself is unaware of the limitations on his authority. Federal Crop Ins. Corp. v. Merrill, 332 U.S. 380, 384, 68 S.Ct. 1, 3, 92 L.Ed. 10 (1947).

Furthermore, the illegality was "plain" under the Reiner test. 325 F.2d at 440. TMM was on constructive and actual notice that the CHAMPUS regulatory scheme would be used in determining payment rates. Each of the MOUs was either entered into or renewed after the new regulatory reimbursement scheme went into effect. Also, the Associated Group informed TMM in their approvals of the MOUs that "CHAMPUS allowable charge methodology" would be used in determining reimbursement rates. Since the contracts were "plainly illegal," they were void ab initio. A dismissal on this basis is one for failure to state a claim. Gould, 67 F.3d at 930.

Since the MOUs were void ab initio, TMM failed to state a claim upon which relief can be granted. We therefore reverse and remand with instructions to dismiss for failure to state a claim.

REVERSED AND REMANDED.

Notes and Questions

1. The two sides' opposing theories have surprising simplicity and intrinsic interest, revealed by peeling off the surrounding layers of acronyms and specialized vocabulary. Simple opposing theories underlie the arguments about the wording of statutes, regulations, and contracts. In 1990, Congress by statute, and the Defense Department by regulations, imposed a ceiling on medical rates. That ceiling capped contract rate increases at a level found by adding the "Medicare Economic Index" to the previous year "prevailing charges." Regardless of the precise calculation of that cap, what matters is that Congress intended to cap the increase of federal payments for medical care. However, TMM, the health provider, had a contract without any express mention of this new MEI cap, so it wanted to be paid at what it considers its contract's rate.

What would the health provider argue in such a case, in terms of fairness? What would the government, in opposing that claim, argue back? Evidently the court thinks it irrelevant whether what Congress intends is fair. Why does the court make the case turn on a textual reading of the wording of the statutes, regulations, and contract clauses, as opposed to dwelling on or even mentioning any notions of fairness, justice, or contractor expectations?

2. The government contracts context often reflects particular historical developments that statutes and regulations arise from but say little or nothing explicit about. Even the

best judicial opinions often leave that context relatively undiscussed, although the judges probably understand it well, particularly when, as in this case, the statute and regulation arose within a few years of the case. By statute that became effective in 1990, Congress decided to cap federal payments for medical care. While the opinion does not discuss "why," from your own knowledge, why do you suppose Congress capped medical cost inflation at that time? To what extent does the whole elaborate machinery of government contracting reflected in this opinion exist just so that Congress, for such reasons, can make such decisions?

3. Why is there a system of specialized tribunals and specialized procedures to handle a matter like this? As later cases in this book will reflect, often these matters do go before tribunals of general jurisdiction, one of which is the United States Supreme Court, yet most such matters stay within the administrative and judicial systems of specialized jurisdiction. By the same token, would it be expected that the lawyers working on these issues, either within the government or with the contractors, have specialized training (such as that imparted by studying this casebook)? Is such specialized training more necessary than, say, for some similar issue that might arise if TMM had a contract dispute with a private sector contracting party, like the insurance carrier for some private sector employer's policy for its private employees' dependents?

4. Note the distinction drawn in the opinion between the two types of issues that will come up next in this chapter: the limited authority of government agents and the decisive role of statutes, regulations, and standard clauses. TMM's contract with the government consisted of an MOU, which had been entered for the government when the Associated Group approved it. Did the court analyze whether the Associated Group had the authority to enter the MOU? What determines whether the Associated Group had that authority? The court separately analyzes whether the MOU conflicted with regulations. Evidently the court can separate these two questions, of the government agent's authority and the contract's conflict with regulations. Both these questions involve regulations and a dispute between the two sides on how to view those regulations. What separates the two questions so much that the court rules for one side on one question, and for the other side on the other?

5. Size up how difficult is the legal issue in this case by how the different specialized deciders and tribunals go different ways on it. When the Associated Group entered the MOU, it must have thought the MOU legal. Yet later, the Associated Group and the Army refused what TMM asked. Then, the Court of Federal Claims agreed with TMM, rejecting the position of the Associated Group and the Army. Whereupon on appeal, the Federal Circuit reversed the Court of Federal Claims, accepting the position of the Associated Group and the Army and rejecting TMM's. One moral of the story: it is complicated enough to figure out the answers to such government contracting law questions that practitioners in the field have a great deal to argue about and deal with.

B. Characteristic Doctrines

1. Limited Authority

A key characteristic doctrine of government contracting law concerns the limited authority of the government's agents. As made clear by the leading case, *OPM v. Rich-*

mond, this doctrine has major significance at a number of levels. In the sphere of private contracts and other private interactions, the authority to act has sufficient significance to form an important part of the course taught under the various headings of "agency and partnership," "corporations," and "business organization." That is, in the private sector, whenever forming contracts and similar interactions between any private entities (other than two individuals acting directly for themselves), the legal question arises of the authority of the persons or entities communicating during the contract formation or similar interaction to bind the entities or other individuals that they represent. Concretely, private economic activity regularly turns on whether a corporation, partnership, or other entity is bound when an employee negotiates the contract, or when superior officers higher in the entity sanction it, or, perhaps, only when some central governing body like the corporation's board of directors expressly considers and approves it.

Even compared to the law of authority regarding private entities, the law of the limited authority of government agents has new and intriguing aspects. In the government sector, the issues carry much greater significance than in private sector relations. They go to the heart of the legal nature of the public sphere and, particularly, the public sphere in American law, as distinct from the private sphere. The twin notions underlying the nature of a federal government sphere consist of a Constitution constraining all arms of government and a set of democratic processes making Congress and the President representative institutions of a sovereign body of citizens. These notions make the entire system of government turn on a set of legal doctrines regarding authority, for this is how the Constitution and the representative Congress and President direct and control the actions of the government's employees. In a government contracting interaction, the authority on the private side follows the simple rules of the law of agency. By contract, the authority on the public side follows a much more complex, subtle, and important set of rules, intended to make the Constitution, its statutory implementation, and the activity of the Congress and the President relevant and decisive factors in what the entire government can and cannot do.

Calling this doctrine by its superficial terms, that "estoppel does not run against the government," or that government agents do not have "apparent authority," hardly begin to express the significance of this doctrine. Describing this as an estoppel issue makes it sound like it matters only insofar as some particular defense available in equity, an estoppel, is unavailable. Many government contracting officers could work for an entire career without their actions coming before a court of equity, and they might comfortably carry out an entire lifetime of responsibility without any need to think of the word *estoppel*. Yet rare is the responsible government contracting officer who does not act with considerable familiarity with both the content of some body of constraining regulations or the like (such as departmental or military-service guidelines, agency manuals, bureau instructions, or standard government forms), and an intimate feel for how that substantive body of constraining regulations defines that officer's sphere of activity. In a word, employees must go "by the book." The doctrine of limited authority of government agents defines what they do, carrying far more weight than simply preventing the private persons with whom they interact from raising the particular equitable issue of estoppel.

Thus, one of the great steps in the transition from familiarity with basic contract law to government contracting law is coming to understand the workings of the doctrine of the limited authority of government agents. Administrative law also involves the issues of the discretion of administrative agencies; the government's contracting officers in some respects act as merely another kind of administrator, like a licensing officer or an officer who manages administrative cases. Even from there, it is a new leap from the concept of an administrator's discretion in the regulatory and administrative sphere to the new sphere of contracting activity.

On the one hand, statutes and regulations confine a contracting officer's discretion so that even government officers who believe and act as though they could take a contracting action may turn out unable to do so. Their statements of agreement or advice, and even their signatures on agreements and orders, do not signify that the government who they appear to represent so agrees or so orders. On the other hand, within such contracting officers' sphere of discretion and authority these officers may well be able to take contracting actions which would draw disagreement from their superiors in the government, their colleagues, or even sound-thinking predecessors, colleagues, and successors in their own office. The lawyer practicing government contracting law develops an acute feel for what actions the subordinates of a contracting officer can take, what actions only a fully authorized contracting officer can take, and what actions even a contracting officer cannot take or takes without binding effect.

The high significance of this doctrine puts the leading case on this subject, *OPM v. Richmond*, at the start of today's government contracting course, just as the predecessor Supreme Court opinion, *Federal Crop Insurance Corp v. Merrill*, 332 U.S. 380 (1947)(discussed in a note after the *OPM* case), started government contracting courses from the 1940s to the 1990s. *OPM v. Richmond* develops the issue with emphasis on the Constitution's Appropriations Clause and the body of law regarding public money. That body of law, referred to herein as appropriations law, budget law, or fiscal law, will come up again later in this book.

Note that *OPM v. Richmond* concerns, in one respect, a type of government program that will not arise again in this book, namely a benefits program for disabled government employees. While many ties exist between the subjects of government contracting and government benefits, the line has to be drawn somewhere to keep the subject of government contracting manageable in size. However, the doctrine of the limited authority of government employees applies the same to the law of government contracts and the law of government benefits. Only the particular statutory system of retirement benefits will not recur.

The doctrine of the limited authority of government agents has another important variant: as for those actions which the government can take, even these can only be taken by the particular government agents, acting in the particular way, contemplated by the authorization, and not by other government agents acting in other ways. *Mil-Spec Contractors, Inc. v. United States* exemplifies this doctrinal variant. Just as the doctrine of *OPM v. Richmond* allows the law to define what a government agency can and cannot do, the doctrine in *Mil- Spec* allows the law to define who can do it and how it can be done. This has intriguing implications all throughout government contracting. Relatively few government agents have the authority of full "contracting officers," compared to the larger numbers of those who assist them and who frequently handle virtually all the actual details of contact with contractors. Conversely, questions also arise of the extent to which the superiors of contracting officers, from slightly higher-grade civil servants up to the President, can issue them commands about decisions that statutes put in the contracting officers' own hands, like the decisions to terminate a contract. Contracting decisions are power. In a word, these doctrines determine who has that power.

For further discussion of the issues in this section see: Michael Cameron Pitou, *Equitable Estoppel: Its Genesis, Development and Application in Government Contracting*, 19

Pub. Cont. L.J. 606 (1990); Joel P. Shedd, *Principles of Authority on Contracting Officers in Administration of Government Contracts*, 5 Pub. Cont. L.J. 88 (1972).

Office of Personnel Management, Petitioner v. Charles Richmond

No. 88-1943. Supreme Court of the United States 496 U.S. 414, Argued Feb. 21, 1990. Decided June 11, 1990.

Justice KENNEDY delivered the opinion of the Court.

This case presents the question whether erroneous oral and written advice given by a Government employee to a benefits claimant may give rise to estoppel against the Government and so entitle the claimant to a monetary payment not otherwise permitted by law. We hold that payments of money from the Federal Treasury are limited to those authorized by statute, and we reverse the contrary holding of the Court of Appeals.

I

Not wishing to exceed a statutory limit on earnings that would disqualify him from a disability annuity, respondent Charles Richmond sought advice from a federal employee and received erroneous information. As a result he earned more than permitted by the eligibility requirements of the relevant statute and lost six months of benefits. Respondent now claims that the erroneous and unauthorized advice should give rise to equitable estoppel against the Government, and that we should order payment of the benefits contrary to the statutory terms. Even on the assumption that much equity subsists in respondent's claim, we cannot agree with him or the Court of Appeals that we have authority to order the payment he seeks.

Respondent was a welder at the Navy Public Works Center in San Diego, California. He left this position in 1981 after petitioner, the Office of Personnel Management (OPM), approved his application for a disability retirement. OPM determined that respondent's impaired eyesight prevented him from performing his job and made him eligible for a disability annuity under 5 U.S.C. §8337(a). Section 8337(a) provides this benefit for disabled federal employees who have completed five years of service. The statute directs, however, that the entitlement to disability payments will end if the retired employee is "restored to an earning capacity fairly comparable to the current rate of pay of the position occupied at the time of retirement." §8337(d).

The statutory rules for restoration of earning capacity are central to this case. Prior to 1982, an individual was deemed restored to earning capacity, and so rendered ineligible for a disability annuity, if

> in each of 2 succeeding calendar years the income of the annuitant from wages or self-employment…equals at least 80 percent of the current rate of pay of the position occupied immediately before retirement." 5 U.S.C. §8337(d) (1976 ed.) (emphasis added).

The provision was amended in 1982 by the Omnibus Budget Reconciliation Act, Pub.L. 97-253, 96 Stat. 792, to change the measuring period for restoration of earning capacity from two years to one:

> Earning capacity is deemed restored if in any calendar year the income of the annuitant from wages or self-employment or both equals at least 80 percent of

the current rate of pay of the position occupied immediately before retirement. 5 U.S.C. §8337(d) (emphasis added).

After taking disability retirement for his vision impairment, respondent undertook part-time employment as a schoolbus driver. From 1982 to 1985, respondent earned an average of $12,494 in this job, leaving him under the 80% limit for entitlement to continued annuity payments. In 1986, however, he had an opportunity to earn extra money by working overtime. Respondent asked an employee relations specialist at the Navy Public Works Center's Civilian Personnel Department for information about how much he could earn without exceeding the 80% eligibility limit. Relying upon the terms of the repealed pre-1982 statute, under which respondent could retain the annuity unless his income exceeded the 80% limit in two consecutive years, the specialist gave respondent incorrect advice. The specialist also gave respondent a copy of Attachment 4 to Federal Personnel Manual Letter 831-64, published by OPM, which also stated the former 2-year eligibility rule. The OPM form was correct when written in 1981; but when given to respondent, the form was out of date and therefore inaccurate. Respondent returned to the Navy in January 1987 and again was advised in error that eligibility would be determined under the old 2-year rule.

After receiving the erroneous information, respondent concluded that he could take on the extra work as a schoolbus driver in 1986 while still receiving full disability benefits for impaired vision so long as he kept his income for the previous and following years below the statutory level. He earned $19,936 during 1986, exceeding the statutory eligibility limit. OPM discontinued respondent's disability annuity on June 30, 1987. The annuity was restored on January 1, 1988, since respondent did not earn more than allowed by the statute in 1987. Respondent thus lost his disability payments for a 6-month period, for a total amount of $3,993.

Respondent appealed the denial of benefits to the Merit Systems Protection Board (MSPB). * * * The MSPB denied respondent's petition for review, and respondent appealed to the Court of Appeals for the Federal Circuit.

A divided panel of the Court of Appeals reversed, accepting respondent's contention that the misinformation from Navy personnel estopped the Government, and that the estoppel required payment of disability benefits despite the statutory provision to the contrary. * * *

We granted certiorari, 493 U.S. 806, 110 S.Ct. 46, 107 L.Ed.2d 15 (1989).

II

From our earliest cases, we have recognized that equitable estoppel will not lie against the Government as it lies against private litigants. In Lee v. Munroe & Thornton, 7 Cranch 366, 3 L.Ed. 373 (1813), we held that the Government could not be bound of an agent unless it were clear that the representations were within the scope of the agent's authority. In The Floyd Acceptances, 7 Wall. 666, 19 L.Ed. 169 (1869), we held that the Government could not be compelled to honor bills of exchange issued by the Secretary of War where there was no statutory authority for the issuance of the bills. In Utah Power & Light Co. v. United States, 243 U.S. 389, 408-409, 37 S.Ct. 387, 391, 61 L.Ed. 791 (1917), we dismissed the argument that unauthorized representations by agents of the Government estopped the United States to prevent erection of power houses and transmission lines across a public forest in violation of a statute: "Of this it is enough to say that the United States is neither bound nor estopped by acts of its officers or agents in entering into an arrangement or agreement to do or cause to be done what the law does not sanction or permit."

The principles of these and many other cases were reiterated in Federal Crop Ins. Corporation v. Merrill, 332 U.S. 380, 68 S.Ct. 1, 92 L.Ed. 10 (1947), the leading case in our modern line of estoppel decisions. In Merrill, a farmer applied for insurance under the Federal Crop Insurance Act to cover his wheat farming operations. An agent of the Federal Crop Insurance Corporation advised the farmer that his entire crop qualified for insurance, and the farmer obtained insurance through the Corporation. After the crop was lost, it was discovered that the agent's advice had been in error, and that part of the farmer's crop was reseeded wheat, not eligible for federal insurance under the applicable regulation. While we recognized the serious hardship caused by the agent's misinformation, we nonetheless rejected the argument that his representations estopped the Government to deny insurance benefits. We recognized that "not even the temptations of a hard case" will provide a basis for ordering recovery contrary to the terms of the regulation, for to do so would disregard "the duty of all courts to observe the conditions defined by Congress for charging the public treasury." Id., at 385–386, 68 S.Ct., at 3–4.

Despite the clarity of these earlier decisions, dicta in our more recent cases have suggested the possibility that there might be some situation in which estoppel against the Government could be appropriate. The genesis of this idea appears to be an observation found at the end of our opinion in Montana v. Kennedy, 366 U.S. 308, 81 S.Ct. 1336, 6 L.Ed.2d 313 (1961). In that case, petitioner brought a declaratory judgment action seeking to establish his American citizenship. After discussing petitioner's two statutory claims at length, we rejected the final argument that a consular official's erroneous advice to petitioner's mother that she could not return to the United States while pregnant prevented petitioner from having been born in the United States and thus deprived him of United States citizenship. Our discussion was limited to the observation that in light of the fact that no legal obstacle prevented petitioner's mother from returning to the United States,

> what may have been only the consular official's well-meant advice—'I am sorry, Mrs., you cannot [return to the United States] in that condition'—falls far short of misconduct such as might prevent the United States from relying on petitioner's foreign birth. In this situation, we need not stop to inquire whether, as some lower courts have held, there may be circumstances in which the United States is estopped to deny citizenship because of the conduct of its officials. Id., at 314–315, 81 S.Ct., at 1340–1341.

The proposition about which we did not "stop to inquire" in Kennedy has since taken on something of a life of its own. Our own opinions have continued to mention the possibility, in the course of rejecting estoppel arguments, that some type of "affirmative misconduct" might give rise to estoppel against the Government. See INS v. Hibi, 414 U.S. 5, 8, 94 S.Ct. 19, 21, 38 L.Ed.2d 7 (1973) (per curiam) ("While the issue of whether 'affirmative misconduct' on the part of the Government might estop it from denying citizenship was left open in Montana v. Kennedy, 366 U.S. 308, 314, 315, 81 S.Ct. 1336, 1340, 1341, 6 L.Ed.2d 313 (1961), no conduct of the sort there adverted to was involved here"); Schweiker v. Hansen, 450 U.S. 785, 788, 101 S.Ct. 1468, 1470, 67 L.Ed.2d 685 (1981) (per curiam) (denying an estoppel claim for Social Security benefits on the authority of Merrill, supra, but observing that the Court "has never decided what type of conduct by a Government employee will estop the Government from insisting upon compliance with valid regulations governing the distribution of welfare benefits"); INS v. Miranda, 459 U.S. 14, 19, 103 S.Ct. 281, 283, 74 L.Ed.2d 12 (1982) (per curiam) ("This case does not require us to reach the question we reserved in Hibi, whether affirmative misconduct in a particular case would estop the Government from enforcing the immigration laws"); Heckler v. Community Health Services, 467 U.S., at 60, 104 S.Ct., at 2224 ("We have left the issue open in the past, and do so again today").

The language in our decisions has spawned numerous claims for equitable estoppel in the lower courts. * * *

The Solicitor General proposes to remedy the present confusion in this area of the law with a sweeping rule. As it has in the past, the Government asks us to adopt "a flat rule that estoppel may not in any circumstances run against the Government." Community Health Services, supra, 467 U.S., at 60, 104 S.Ct., at 2224. * * * Petitioner advances as a second basis for this rule the doctrine of separation of powers. Petitioner contends that to recognize estoppel based on the misrepresentations of Executive Branch officials would give those misrepresentations the force of law, and thereby invade the legislative province reserved to Congress. This rationale, too, supports the petitioner's contention that estoppel may never justify an order requiring executive action contrary to a relevant statute, no matter what statute or what facts are involved.

We have recognized before that the "arguments the Government advances for the rule are substantial." Community Health Services, supra, 467 U.S., at 60, 104 S.Ct., at 2224. And we agree that this case should be decided under a clearer form of analysis than "we will know an estoppel when we see one." Hansen, supra, at 792, 101 S.Ct., at 1473 (MAR-SHALL, J., dissenting). But it remains true that we need not embrace a rule that no estoppel will lie against the Government in any case in order to decide this case. We leave for another day whether an estoppel claim could ever succeed against the Government. A narrower ground of decision is sufficient to address the type of suit presented here, a claim for payment of money from the Public Treasury contrary to a statutory appropriation.

III

The Appropriations Clause of the Constitution, Art. I, §9, cl. 7, provides that: "No Money shall be drawn from the Treasury, but in Consequence of Appropriations made by Law." For the particular type of claim at issue here, a claim for money from the Federal Treasury, the Clause provides an explicit rule of decision. Money may be paid out only through an appropriation made by law; in other words, the payment of money from the Treasury must be authorized by a statute. All parties here agree that the award respondent seeks would be in direct contravention of the federal statute upon which his ultimate claim to the funds must rest, 5 U.S.C. §8337. The point is made clearer when the appropriation supporting the benefits sought by respondent is examined. In the same subchapter of the United States Code as the eligibility requirements, Congress established the Civil Service Retirement and Disability Fund. §8348(a)(1)(A). That section states in pertinent part: "The Fund...is appropriated for the payment of...benefits as provided by this subchapter...." (Emphasis added.) The benefits respondent claims were not "provided by" the relevant provision of the subchapter; rather, they were specifically denied. It follows that Congress has appropriated no money for the payment of the benefits respondent seeks, and the Constitution prohibits that any money "be drawn from the Treasury" to pay them.

Our cases underscore the straightforward and explicit command of the Appropriations Clause. "It means simply that no money can be paid out of the Treasury unless it has been appropriated by an act of Congress." Cincinnati Soap Co. v. United States, 301 U.S. 308, 321, 57 S.Ct. 764, 770, 81 L.Ed. 1122 (1937) (citing Reeside v. Walker, 11 How. 272, 291, 13 L.Ed. 693 (1851)). In Reeside, supra, we addressed a claim brought by the holder of a judgment of indebtedness against the United States that the Secretary of the Treasury of the United States should be ordered to enter the claim upon the books of the Treasury so that the debt might be paid. In rejecting petitioner's claim for relief, we stated as an alternative ground for decision that if

> the petition in this case was allowed so far as to order the verdict against the United States to be entered on the books of the Treasury Department, the plaintiff would be as far from having a claim on the Secretary or Treasurer to pay it as now. The difficulty in the way is the want of any appropriation by Congress to pay this claim. It is a well-known constitutional provision, that no money can be taken or drawn from the Treasury except under an appropriation by Congress. See Constitution, art. 1, §9 (1 Stat. at Large, 15).

> However much money may be in the Treasury at any one time, not a dollar of it can be used in the payment of any thing not thus previously sanctioned. Any other course would give to the fiscal officers a most dangerous discretion. Id., at 291.

The command of the Clause is not limited to the relief available in a judicial proceeding seeking payment of public funds. Any exercise of a power granted by the Constitution to one of the other branches of Government is limited by a valid reservation of congressional control over funds in the Treasury. * * *

We have not had occasion in past cases presenting claims of estoppel against the Government to discuss the Appropriations Clause, for reasons that are apparent. Given the strict rule against estoppel applied as early as 1813 in Lee v. Munroe & Thornton, 7 Cranch 366, 3 L.Ed. 373, claims of estoppel could be dismissed on that ground without more. In our cases following Montana v. Kennedy, 366 U.S. 308, 81 S.Ct. 1336, 6 L.Ed.2d 313 (1961), reserving the possibility that estoppel might lie on some facts, we have held only that the particular facts presented were insufficient. As discussed, supra, at 2470–2471, we decline today to accept the Solicitor General's argument for an across-the-board no-estoppel rule. But this makes it all the more important to state the law and to settle the matter of estoppel as a basis for money claims against the Government.

Our decision is consistent with both the holdings and the rationale expressed in our estoppel precedents. Even our recent cases evince a most strict approach to estoppel claims involving public funds. See Community Health Services, 467 U.S., at 63, 104 S.Ct., at 2225 ("Protection of the public fisc requires that those who seek public funds act with scrupulous regard for the requirements of law"). The course of our jurisprudence shows why: Opinions have differed on whether this Court has ever accepted an estoppel claim in other contexts, see id., at 60, 104 S.Ct., at 224 (suggesting that United States v. Pennsylvania Industrial Chemical Corp., 411 U.S. 655, 93 S.Ct. 1804, 36 L.Ed.2d 567 (1973) (PICCO), was decided on estoppel grounds); id., at 68, 104 S.Ct., at 2228 (opinion of REHNQUIST, J.) (PICCO not an estoppel case), but not a single case has upheld an estoppel claim against the Government for the payment of money. And our cases denying estoppel are animated by the same concerns that prompted the Framers to include the Appropriations Clause in the Constitution. As Justice Story described the Clause:

> "The object is apparent upon the slightest examination. It is to secure regularity, punctuality, and fidelity, in the disbursements of the public money. As all the taxes raised from the people, as well as revenues arising from other sources, are to be applied to the discharge of the expenses, and debts, and other engagements of the government, it is highly proper, that congress should possess the power to decide how and when any money should be applied for these purposes. If it were otherwise, the executive would possess an unbounded power over the public purse of the nation; and might apply all its

moneyed resources at his pleasure. The power to control and direct the appropriations, constitutes a most useful and salutary check upon profusion and extravagance, as well as upon corrupt influence and public peculation...." 2 Commentaries on the Constitution of the United States §1348 (3d ed. 1858).

The obvious practical consideration cited by Justice Story for adherence to the requirement of the Clause is the necessity, existing now as much as at the time the Constitution was ratified, of preventing fraud and corruption. We have long ago accepted this ground as a reason that claims for estoppel cannot be entertained where public money is at stake, refusing to "introduce a rule against an abuse, of which, by improper collusions, it would be very difficult for the public to protect itself." Lee, supra, at 370. But the Clause has a more fundamental and comprehensive purpose, of direct relevance to the case before us. It is to assure that public funds will be spent according to the letter of the difficult judgments reached by Congress as to the common good and not according to the individual favor of Government agents or the individual pleas of litigants.

Extended to its logical conclusion, operation of estoppel against the Government in the context of payment of money from the Treasury could in fact render the Appropriations Clause a nullity. If agents of the Executive were able, by their unauthorized oral or written statements to citizens, to obligate the Treasury for the payment of funds, the control over public funds that the Clause reposes in Congress in effect could be transferred to the Executive. If, for example, the President or Executive Branch officials were displeased with a new restriction on benefits imposed by Congress to ease burdens on the fisc (such as the restriction imposed by the statutory change in this case) and sought to evade them, agency officials could advise citizens that the restrictions were inapplicable. Estoppel would give this advice the practical force of law, in violation of the Constitution.

* * *

Respondent points to no authority in precedent or history for the type of claim he advances today. Whether there are any extreme circumstances that might support estoppel in a case not involving payment from the Treasury is a matter we need not address. As for monetary claims, it is enough to say that this Court has never upheld an assertion of estoppel against the Government by a claimant seeking public funds. In this context there can be no estoppel, for courts cannot estop the Constitution. The judgment of the Court of Appeals is

Reversed.

Justice WHITE, with whom Justice BLACKMUN joins, concurring.

I agree that the Government may not be estopped in cases such as this one and therefore join the opinion and judgment of the Court. I write separately to note two limitations to the Court's decision. First, the Court wisely does not decide that the Government may not be estopped under any circumstances. Ante, at 2471. In my view, the case principally relied on by respondent, United States v. Pennsylvania Industrial Chemical Corp., 411 U.S. 655, 93 S.Ct. 1804, 36 L.Ed.2d 567 (1973) (PICCO), may well have been decided on the basis of estoppel. But there is a world of difference between PICCO and this case: In PICCO, the courts were asked to prevent the Government from exercising its lawful discretionary authority in a particular case whereas here the courts have been asked to require the Executive Branch to violate a congressional statute. The Executive Branch does not have the dispensing power on its own, see Kendall v. United States ex rel. Stokes, 12 Pet. 524, 613, 9 L.Ed. 1181 (1838), and should not be granted such a power by judicial authorization.

Second, although the Court states that "[a]ny exercise of a power granted by the Constitution to one of the other branches of Government is limited by a valid reservation of congressional control over funds in the Treasury," ante, at 2472, the Court does not state that statutory restrictions on appropriations may never fall even if they violate a command of the Constitution such as the Just Compensation Clause, cf. Jacobs v. United States, 290 U.S. 13, 54 S.Ct. 26, 78 L.Ed. 142 (1933), or if they encroach on the powers reserved to another branch of the Federal Government. Although Knote v. United States, 95 U.S. 149, 154, 24 L.Ed. 442 (1877), held that the President's pardon power did not extend to the appropriation of moneys in the Treasury without authorization by law for the benefit of pardoned criminals, it did not hold that Congress could impair the President's pardon power by denying him appropriations for pen and paper.

[Other concurring and dissenting opinions are omitted.]

Notes and Questions

1. Cutting off the employee's disability benefits in this case struck the Ninth Circuit as so unfair that the court of appeals strained the law a long way—more, as it turned out, than the Supreme Court would let it—to rule for the employee. Does cutting off the employee's benefits strike you, too, as extremely unfair? The doctrine that estoppel does not run against the government often seems cruel in operation. Some students of the law, particularly those who (to their credit) have been slow to abandon the basic notions of sympathy, fairness, and justice as guidance, may read this case and this doctrine as simply a harsh, mean, even absurdist statement that government contracting law excludes what would otherwise be essential elements of decency without anything in its place. Certainly the Supreme Court does not offer anything particularly sympathetic or emotionally "warm" even as dicta, recognizing that its kindler and gentler past dicta have spawned lower court elaborations that undermine the heart of its doctrine.

Could you portray the argument for the government, that is, for the limited authority of its agents, in ways that would appeal to more widely shared values than just an acceptance that law can sometimes be strict, rigid, and pitiless? The notions of a government of limited powers and of the "rule of law" rather than men, often appeals to libertarian and populist sentiments. The opinion's specific notion of a particularly tight requirement of authorization for decisions about spending appeals to particular libertarian and populist sentiments having to do with who, in Anglo-American democracy, wields the power of the purse. To put it differently, how much is this case about penalizing a (blameless) retired Navy welder as the only way to constrain the power of a (blameworthy) Navy employee relations specialist by rendering the specialist's advice ineffective? Focus on that mistaken Navy employee relations specialist. Even if you are very sympathetic to the welder, do you want that mistaken specialist empowered to override the law as made by a Congress authorized by the Constitution and responsible to the electorate? Tight statutory "pocketbook" control means that to the extent that individuals must yield up their money as taxes, it is spent only pursuant to the formally enacted collective decisions of their elected representatives. This means that Navy specialists, whether in the employee benefits or the artillery-firing departments, cannot act out either their merciful or their martial sentiments without public authorization. You might want Navy specialists to be able to give potent disability benefits advice, even without authorization; would you want them able to start wars that way?

2. Note how the Court draws a distinction between the limited sphere of Government agent decisions directly concerned with public money, for which it makes a strict rule against agent authority, and the sphere of other Government agent decisions, which it carefully does not, for now, address. Consider how this applies technically in government contracting. Some decisions of contracting officers directly concern money: the prices at which procurement occurs, or, many decisions on money that occur with changes, modifications, claims, and terminations. What about the decisions of contracting officers that do not directly concern money, but concern such matters as the timing of what is being provided or the details of reporting and disclosure duties? Suppose the employment specialist's advice had supplanted not a substantive element of the retired welder's right to disability payments, but rather the frequency with which the welder must submit some kind of required report to OPM? *See Joseph DeVito v. United States*, 188 Ct. Cl. 979 (1969)(waiver, by government employee delay, of opportunity to terminate for default).

3. Note the distinction between the doctrines of estoppel and finality. For example, the opinion mentions without further analysis that the retired welder exceeded the eligibility limit during 1986, but OPM did not discontinue his disability annuity until June 30, 1987. Suppose that means the retired welder got benefits to which he was not entitled from January through June of 1987, but, on the other hand, suppose the disability statute makes such payments relatively final so that there is no way to recoup wrong payments. So the welder might have gotten and kept six months of benefits (January through July, 1987) to which he was not entitled. How do you square the retention on finality grounds by the welder of six months of benefits to which he was not entitled, with the Court's reasoning for his not getting, on estoppel grounds, six more months of benefits (July through December)? If it is a constitutional imperative that the taxpayer's money not end up without authorization in the private party's pocket, what is he doing with that six months of benefits?

4. Decisions since OPM v. Richmond have preserved a sphere for estoppel and the similar doctrine of laches. In *Burnside-Ott Aviation Training Ctr., Inc. v. United States*, 985 F.2d 1574, 1581 (Fed. Cir. 1993), the Court remanded the issue of equitable estoppel. It found that the Claims Court improperly relied on *OPM*, when Burnside-Ott's assertion was not based on a statutory entitlement, but rather on a contract with the Navy. However, the *Burnside-Ott* ruling did not negate the relevance of *OPM* when equitable estoppel against the government was sought to prevent conducting a competitive bid process. *Westinghouse Electric Corp. v. United States Dep't of Navy*, 894 F. Supp. 204 (W.D. Pa. 1995), No. 97-346C, 1998 WL 354197, at *11 (Fed. Cl. June 17, 1998). The notion of asserting laches against the government remains unclear since *OPM*. In *JANA, Inc. v. United States*, 936 F.2d 1265 (Fed. Cir. 1991), *cert. denied*, 112 S. Ct. 869 (1992), the Court of Appeals reversed the Claims Court, holding that the government's actions in delaying an audit and the issuance of the contracting officer's assessment of overcharges by the contractor were not unreasonable and inexcusable so as to constitute laches.

5. Note on Federal Crop Ins. Corp. v. Merrill, 332 U.S. 680 (1947). OPM v. Richmond describes the case of FCIC v. Merrill as "the leading case in our modern line of estoppel decisions." In that case, farmers applied for and received federal crop insurance on government advice, and then, after their crop was destroyed by drought, the Court held that erroneous advice by the government's agents did not bind the government to admit coverage. A private insurer would not be allowed to deny coverage in a similar situation. In Merrill, besides the basic logic of the limited authority of government

agents, the Court threw in that the public is "charged with knowledge" of limitations on authority in statutes and in regulations published in the Federal Register, which were incorporated by reference in the crop insurance application. But, Justice Jackson's dissent took on the Federal Register argument, lambasting the "absurdity" of expecting farmers to "peruse this voluminous and dull publication," and doubting, too, "that a reading of technically worded regulations would enlighten" the farmer "much in any event." If disabled navy welders and insurance-obtaining wheat farmers with every appropriate reason to rely on government advice cannot win on this issue, what chance does a government contractor have?

Mil-Spec Contractors, Inc., Plaintiff-Appellant, v. The United States, Defendant-Appellee
No. 87-1203. 835 F.2d 865
United States Court of Appeals, Federal Circuit. Dec. 16, 1987.

Before FRIEDMAN, SMITH, and MAYER, Circuit Judges.

FRIEDMAN, Circuit Judge.

This is an appeal from a decision of the Armed Services Board of Contract Appeals (Board), dismissing a contractor's claim for additional compensation on the ground that an oral agreement to settle the claims constituted an accord and satisfaction. Mil-Spec Contractors, Inc., 87-1 B.C.A. (CCH) ¶19,391 (Sept. 23, 1986). We hold that there was not a valid accord and satisfaction, and therefore reverse and remand.

I

The government awarded to the predecessor of the appellant Mil-Spec Contractors, Inc. (Mil-Spec), a contract to insulate certain buildings on Norton Air Force Base in California. The contract was funded from an Air Force general account for energy conservation. The Air Force allocated approximately $622,000 for the work. The contract price was $581,247, and a contingency fund of $6,000 to $7,000 was available for contract modifications.

After completing the work, Mil-Spec submitted to the government a series of increasing claims for additional costs it allegedly incurred. After Mil-Spec had rejected several of the government's proposals for additional payment, Mr. Hooppaw, the resident contracting officer (who was also the resident engineer), telephoned Mr. Barnes, Mil-Spec's principal officer, in late August or early September 1983. Mr. Hooppaw explained that he could not obtain extra funds for additional payment under the contract because the money came from an appropriation that would expire on September 30, 1983, and that after that date the $6,000–$7,000 in the contingency fund would not be available. Mr. Barnes was advised that if he did not agree to a settlement, "the only other way to get funds is to go to court."

Three days before the funds would expire, Mr. Barnes and Mr. Barker, a negotiator, had several telephone conversations during which they orally agreed upon a settlement. Mr. Barker's notes state that Mr. Barnes

> agreed to drop his proposal of [a] $70,956.00 increase in Contract amount and accept the Government estimate amount of $6,367.00. In doing so, the contractor requested that all remaining funds (less $100.00) be paid to him with this settlement.

Both parties agreed to accept [a] $6367.00 increase in [the] Contract amount as fair and reasonable. The Contract time was extended 87 calendar days to a final completion date of 20 June 1980. The negotiated price of $6367.00 is hereby accepted subject to approval of the Contracting Officer.

The contracting officer, Mr. Hooppaw, then prepared a contract modification (standard form 30), signed it and mailed it to Mr. Barnes for his signature. In the interval, an Internal Revenue Service (IRS) employee had told Mr. Barnes that with a legitimate claim Mr. Barnes could have obtained more than the government had offered. Mr. Barnes telephoned Mr. Hooppaw and stated that he did not accept the government's settlement offer.

On September 30, 1983, the government issued a check for $6,367 to the IRS because of a previously filed tax lien.

Mil-Spec filed with the contracting officer a claim for its alleged additional costs. When the contracting officer failed to decide the claim within a reasonable time, Mil-Spec appealed to the Board. After a hearing, the Board held that the oral settlement agreement constituted an accord and satisfaction, and denied the appeal.

II

The Court of Claims, the decisions of which are binding precedents in this court, South Corp. v. United States, 690 F.2d 1368, 1370 (Fed.Cir.1982), has stated:

The essential elements of an effective accord and satisfaction are proper subject matter, competent parties, meeting of the minds of the parties, and consideration.

Brock & Blevins Co. v. United States, 343 F.2d 951, 955 (Ct.Cl.1965) (quoting Nevada Half Moon Mining Co. v. Combined Metals Reduction Co., 176 F.2d 73, 76 (10th Cir.1949), cert. denied, 338 U.S. 943, 70 S.Ct. 429, 94 L.Ed. 581 (1950)).

Relying on that decision, the Board held:

These essential elements are fully met in this appeal. There is no question concerning either the propriety of subject matter or the competence of the parties. Both parties agree that there was a meeting of the minds and the fact that this was an oral agreement does not change its legal effect. Consideration was shown by the check which the Government issued and which, because of a prior tax lien, was paid to IRS for appellant's account thus diminishing its outstanding delinquent taxes. Appellant agreed to accept that amount for a full settlement of all outstanding claims.

Mil-Spec Contractors, Inc., 87-1 B.C.A. (CCH) ¶19,391 (Sept. 23, 1986).

The ruling of the Board has three fatal flaws: (A) There was no valid oral agreement because Mr. Barker, the negotiator, had no authority to bind the government to the settlement; (B) as the government recognized, the accord and satisfaction constituted a modification of the contract which was required to be in writing and signed by both parties; and (C) the government's "payment" to Mil-Spec of $6,367 by sending a check for that amount to the IRS did not comply with the terms of the oral agreement and therefore did not constitute consideration adequate to support the alleged accord and satisfaction.

A. "It is well established that a purported agreement with the United States is not binding unless the other party can show that the official with whom the agreement was made had authority to bind the Government." S.E.R., Jobs for Progress, Inc. v. United States, 759 F.2d 1, 4 (Fed.Cir.1985) (citations omitted). The oral agreement was a modification of the contract, since it increased the amount the government would pay for the work Mil-Spec had done. Only the contracting officer was authorized to bind the government to such a modification. Cf. 48 C.F.R. §2.101 (1986) ("'Contracting officer' means a person with the authority to enter into, administer, and/or terminate contracts and make related determinations and findings.").

Mr. Barker, who negotiated the oral settlement with Mr. Barnes, was not the contracting officer but only a negotiator. As such, he had no authority to commit the government. As Mr. Barker himself recognized, only the contracting officer had that authority: Mr. Barker's notes of the negotiation and agreement stated that the "negotiated price of $6,367.00" was "accepted subject to approval of the Contracting Officer."

The contracting officer also recognized this fact, since he prepared and signed a form 30 contract modification document that embodied the oral settlement previously negotiated. Unless and until there was a binding modification to which both Mil-Spec and the contracting officer had agreed in writing, there could not be a binding modification of the contract. The oral agreement of September 27, 1983, could not and did not constitute a valid accord and satisfaction. The contracting officer's subsequent approval of the oral agreement, reflected in his signature of the written contract modification form he prepared, did not nunc pro tunc turn the prior oral agreement into a valid contractual commitment that bound the government.

B. The Federal Acquisition Regulations applicable to the contract in this case require that a modification of a contract be in writing and executed by both parties. Federal Acquisition Regulations System, 48 C.F.R. §2.101 (1986), the Definitions section, states in pertinent part:

> "Contract" means a mutually binding legal relationship.... It includes all types of commitments that obligate the Government to an expenditure of appropriated funds and that, except as otherwise authorized, are in writing.... contracts include... bilateral contract modifications.

Pertinent provisions of 48 C.F.R. provide as follows:

§43.101 (1986):

> "Contract modification" means any written change in the terms of a contract (see 43.103).

* * *

> "Supplemental agreement" means a contract modification that is accomplished by the mutual action of the parties.

§43.103 (1986):

> Contract modifications are of the following types:
>
> (a) Bilateral. A bilateral modification (supplemental agreement) is a contract modification that is signed by the contractor and the contracting officer....

§43.301 (1986):

> (a)(1) The Standard Form 30 (SF 30), Amendment of Solicitation/Modification of Contract, shall... be used for—

* * *

> (v) Supplemental agreements (see 43.103);

Thus, any bilateral modification of a contract is a "supplemental agreement," which requires the execution of a written standard form 30.

Mr. Hooppaw, the contracting officer, recognized that the oral settlement agreement that Mr. Barker had negotiated with Mr. Barnes would not be effective until both the contracting officer and Mr. Barnes had signed a written modification agreement. After the oral settlement had been negotiated, Mr. Hooppaw prepared a written modification agreement, signed it, and sent it to Mr. Barnes to sign. If Mr. Hooppaw had believed that the oral settlement itself was a valid agreement that bound both parties to the contract, there would have been no need for him to prepare the form 30 contract modification agreement. All he need have done was to have written a simple letter to Mr. Barnes summarizing and confirming the oral agreement.

In SCM Corp. v. United States, 595 F.2d 595, 598 (1979), the Court of Claims held that where the pertinent regulations required that contract modifications be written, an oral modification that had not been reduced to writing and signed by both parties was ineffective. The situation in SCM was analogous to that in the present case.

In SCM the contractor sought an equitable adjustment of approximately $122,000. The contracting officer and the contractor by telephone agreed to settle the dispute for $55,000. Preparation of the written contract modification provision was delayed because the agency lacked funds to make the payment. When the contracting officer finally sent the written modification, the contractor refused to sign it on the ground that it did not properly reflect the oral agreement.

The contractor then filed suit for the $55,000, alleging a breach of the oral settlement agreement. The Court of Claims rejected the claim on the ground that the governing Armed Services Procurement Regulations, the pertinent provisions of which were similar to the Acquisition Regulations involved in this case, "require that settlements are written contracts to be executed on standard form 30." 595 F.2d at 598. * * *

C. The oral settlement agreement contemplated and provided that the $6,367 would be paid to Mr. Barnes. * * * Although the government may have acted within its legal authority in making payment to the IRS, such payment cannot be said to have been a term of the settlement to which Mr. Barnes agreed.

CONCLUSION

The decision of the Armed Services Board of Contract Appeals is reversed, and the case is remanded to the Board to consider the merits of Mil-Spec's claim.

REVERSED and REMANDED.

Notes and Questions

1. The court does not resolve this case by an absence of offer and acceptance, nor by a requirement of a writing under the Statute of Frauds. Both these rules apply, in appropriate circumstances, to government contracts. Evidently, the agreement between the government negotiator and the government contractor satisfies offer and acceptance and does not require a writing as a matter of basic contract law. Moreover, the court does not suggest that any stronger or higher principles of offer and acceptance, or any stronger or higher form of the Statute of Frauds, applies. What, then, are the issues?

2. Note the importance in the case of Standard Form 30, the classic embodiment of government contract modifications. Basic contract law discusses "formalities." The re-

quirement of consideration and the Statute of Frauds exemplify such formalities: a seller's solemn oral commitment to offer a house for purchase to a buyer thirty days hence for just $100,000 is not binding; the same commitment, for which the buyer pays $100 and receives a written receipt with the key details on it, is binding. Yet, the importance in government contracting law of standard forms and standard clauses dwarfs the importance of formalities in basic contract law. Why? Is there something more than the service of bureaucratic order and convenience?

3. Meeting in this case the contracting officer's "negotiator" begins to suggest the cast of characters in the drama of government contracting. Soon, the cast will include many different kinds of contracting officers to handle different phases of major contracts: the Procuring Contracting Officer ("PCO"), the Administrative Contracting Officer ("ACO"), and, that dreaded creature, the Terminating Contracting Officer ("TCO") (perhaps known to colleagues as "The Terminator" and played in the movies by Arnold Schwarzenegger). A larger population consists of the many representatives and assistants, like the negotiator here, such as technical representatives, legal advisers, and accounting assistants. A recurring question consists of whether a contracting officer can delegate authority to these assistants when the contracting officer plainly expresses her wish to do so, particularly on matters calling for the assistants' specialized expertise and which the contracting officer fears, with reason, will only be hindered in execution by failure to delegate. Would this case have come out differently if the contracting officer gave the negotiator an SF 30 signed in blank? Suppose the contracting officer told both the negotiator and the contractor that the negotiator had full authority to reach agreement within a range of outcomes known to the officer, and the negotiator then did so?

HARBERT/LUMMUS AGRIFUELS PROJECTS, et al., Plaintiffs-Cross Appellants, v. The UNITED STATES, Defendant-Appellant.

Nos. 97-5047, 97-5052. United States Court of Appeals,
Federal Circuit. 142 F.3d 1429 April 21, 1998.

Before SCHALL, Circuit Judge, FRIEDMAN, Senior Circuit Judge, and GAJARSA, Circuit Judge.

GAJARSA, Circuit Judge.

The United States seeks review of the decision of the United States Court of Federal Claims in Harbert/Lummus v. United States, 36 Fed. Cl. 494 (1996), holding that the United States entered into an oral, unilateral contract with Harbert/Lummus to continue guaranteeing future borrowing requests until completion of a construction project and awarding Harbert/Lummus damages for breach of this contract. Harbert/Lummus cross-appeals, seeking review of the trial court's method of calculating these damages and refusal to recognize the existence of a second contract to accelerate the construction and payment schedule. Because the contracting officer lacked the authority to enter into the oral, unilateral contract and did not ratify the contract, we reverse the decision of the trial court regarding the existence of a binding contract in which the Department of Energy ("DOE") promised not to suspend its guarantee and vacate the trial court's damages award.

BACKGROUND

The facts of this case have been set out in great detail in the trial court's decision and will be referred to in this opinion only to the extent necessary for an understanding of the issues that give rise to this appeal. During the oil crisis in the late 1970's, the federal government investigated alternative sources of energy. Congress passed the Biomass Energy and Alcohol Fuels Act of 1980 (the "Act"), which created the Alcohol Fuels Program (the "Program") to encourage private companies to design and build alternative fuel energy plants. The Act created the Office of Alcohol Fuels (the "Program Office") within DOE to administer the Program. Specifically, the Program Office was vested with the power to issue government loan guarantees for up to 90 percent of the cost of construction of ethanol and other alternative fuel plants. The Program Office had no independent contracting authority.

One of these loan guarantees was issued to Agrifuels Refining Corporation ("Agrifuels"), which in turn contracted with Harbert/Lummus to construct an ethanol plant. The funds that Agrifuels needed to construct the plant were provided by lending banks and guaranteed by DOE through a loan guarantee agreement and a loan servicing agreement. Harbert/Lummus was not a party to these contracts and was in contractual privity only with Agrifuels through the construction contract. This construction contract provided for a bonus for Harbert/Lummus for early completion and a penalty for late completion.

* * *

During construction of the plant, Harbert/Lummus stated at a meeting at which all the parties were present that it was not receiving timely payments and that it wanted the accelerated construction schedule to be adopted by the parties. The Deputy Director of the Program Office responded that "DOE was committed to funding the project to completion, and if the contractor completes the project, all the payments would work out in the end." Id. at 506. The Deputy Director did not have authority to bind the government. The trial court found that the CO was present at the same meeting, but did not question the offer and was silent after the offer was made. Id. The trial court found that the CO adopted the Deputy Director's statement by his silence and created a new, binding unilateral offer to Harbert/Lummus that the government would continue its role as guarantor of future borrowing requests by Agrifuels in exchange for Harbert/Lummus' continued work on the project. Id. at 513. When Harbert/Lummus continued work on the project, the trial court held that Harbert/Lummus had accepted DOE's offer, thereby creating a binding contract. Id. at 513–14.

Prior to completion of the plant, the ultimate parent companies of Agrifuels declared bankruptcy, triggering an event of default under the loan agreements between Agrifuels and DOE. DOE eventually decided to stop funding the project and Harbert/Lummus sued for damages for breach of DOE's promise to not withdraw its guarantee until completion of the project. The trial court awarded Harbert/Lummus $2,870,768 in damages for breach of this unilateral contract.

This appeal concerns the alleged formation of two oral contracts. The first contract regards the unilateral offer by the Deputy Director to continue guaranteeing Agrifuels' borrowing requests until completion of the project. The second contract regards the alleged acceptance by DOE of an accelerated construction and payment schedule. With regard to the unilateral contract to continue to guarantee funding, the government argues that the trial court erred in recognizing this contract as binding because (1) the Act and its implementing regulations do not authorize DOE to contract directly with construction contractors, (2) DOE could not enter into this oral contract because of restrictions imposed by statute and regulations, (3) the CO was not delegated the authority to enter into such a contract, and (4) the CO did not ratify the contract. In its cross-appeal, Harbert/Lummus argues that the trial court erred in calculating the damages with respect to DOE's breach of this oral agreement. We need only determine whether the CO had the authority to enter into the oral, unilateral contract and whether he ratified such contract. ***

DISCUSSION

In reviewing judgments of the Court of Federal Claims, we review conclusions of law de novo and findings of fact for clear error. See City of El Centro v. United States, 922 F.2d 816, 819 (Fed. Cir.1990). Because neither party challenges the trial court's findings of fact, we review the trial court's decision with regard to contract formation de novo. See Trauma Serv. Group v. United States, 104 F.3d 1321, 1325 (Fed.Cir.1997) ("In the absence of factual disputes, the question of contract formation is a question of law, reviewable de novo.").

A. The Alleged Contract to Continue Guaranteeing Funding of the Project

It is well established that the government is not bound by the acts of its agents beyond the scope of their actual authority. See Federal Crop Ins. Corp. v. Merrill, 332 U.S. 380, 384, 68 S. Ct. 1, 3, 92 L. Ed. 10 (1947); Trauma Serv. Group, 104 F.3d at 1325. Contractors dealing with the United States must inform themselves of a representative's authority and the limits of that authority. See Federal Crop Ins., 332 U.S. at 384, 68 S. Ct. at 3. Moreover, "anyone entering into an agreement with the Government takes the risk of accurately ascertaining the authority of the agents who purport to act for the Government, and this risk remains with the contractor even when the Government agents themselves may have been unaware of the limitations on their authority." Trauma Serv. Group, 104 F.3d at 1325. The burden was on Harbert/Lummus to prove that the CO had the authority to enter into the oral, unilateral contract. See id. The fact that Harbert/Lummus may have believed that the CO had authority is irrelevant; Harbert/Lummus must prove that the CO had actual authority. Id. For the reasons set forth below, we hold that the CO did not have authority to enter into an oral contract to continue to guarantee funding of the project until its completion.

The CO's authority to commit and bind DOE contractually was specifically conditioned in his delegation of authority as follows:

> [The CO] is hereby delegated the authority, with respect to actions valued at $50 million or less, to approve, execute, enter into, modify, administer, close-out, terminate and take any other necessary and appropriate action (collectively, "Actions") with respect to Financial Incentive awards on behalf of the Department of Energy without the *prior written approval* of or further delegation being necessary from the Director, Office of Procurement Operations (or designee). However, a separate prior written approval of any such action must be given by or concurred in by [the CO] to accompany the action. At that dollar threshold, a specific delegation from the Director, Office of Procurement Operations (or designee) is not required. This delegation shall include the authority to make all required determinations and decisions, except those that are specifically to be made by other authority.

Thus, the CO's delegation of contracting authority contained a separate and independent provision which required that all actions entered into by him be accompanied by his prior, written approval. Harbert/Lummus directs us to nothing in the record that evidences any separate, prior written approval by the CO of the oral, unilateral contract. Accordingly, the CO was not authorized to bind the government in disregard of this explicit provision. Harbert/Lummus argues that the CO had implied authority to enter into the unilateral contract and that such a contract was "necessary and appropriate" with regard to his actions relating to the Financial Incentive awards. These arguments are unpersuasive in light of the express mandate in the delegation that the CO agree to any action by prior, written approval. Harbert/Lummus also argues that, because the government does not dispute the CO's authority to enter into a written contract with Harbert/Lummus to care for the plant after DOE ceased its guarantees, the CO must have had the authority to enter into the oral, unilateral contract because both contracts stemmed from the CO's authority to minimize DOE's expenses with regard to the project. Again, this argument is unpersuasive because it does not address the fact that the unilateral contract was oral and did not contain the required written approval.

As we have held before, agency procedures must be followed before a binding contract can be formed. See American Gen. Leasing, Inc. v. United States, 218 Ct. Cl. 367, 587 F.2d 54, 57–58 (1978) (holding that express oral agreement with government agent was not binding because, among other factors, applicable regulations required contract to be in writing); New Am. Shipbuilders, Inc. v. United States, 871 F.2d 1077, 1080 (Fed. Cir.1989) ("Oral assurances do not produce a contract implied-in-fact until all the steps have been taken that the agency procedure requires; until then, there is no intent to be bound. Thus, it is irrelevant if the oral assurances emanate from the very official who will have authority at the proper time, to sign the contract or grant."). It appears evident that, if Harbert/Lummus had examined the CO's delegation of authority, it could not have reasonably believed it had entered into a binding contract with the government in the absence of the required written approval by the CO. Because there is no evidence of such prior, written approval by the CO of the unilateral contract, we hold that the CO lacked the authority to enter into the oral contract and it is therefore not binding upon the government. See EWG Assocs., Ltd. v. United States, 231 Ct. Cl. 1028, 1030 (1982) (explaining that the government is not estopped from denying the existence of a contract where the acts upon which the contractor relies are unauthorized); see also OPM v. Richmond, 496 U.S. 414, 420–33, 110 S. Ct. 2465, 2469–76, 110 L.Ed.2d 387 (1990) (explaining that the government is not estopped by the unauthorized acts of its agents).

Even if the CO somehow possessed the authority to enter into the oral contract, we hold that he did not ratify it. The trial court found that the Deputy Director, who did not have any contracting authority, actually made the offer to enter into the unilateral contract. Agreements made by government agents without authority to bind the government may be subsequently ratified by those with authority if the ratifying officials have actual or constructive knowledge of the unauthorized acts. See United States v. Beebe, 180 U.S. 343, 354, 21 S.Ct. 371, 375, 45 L.Ed. 563 (1901). The Supreme Court has stated that:

> Where an agent has acted without authority and it is claimed that the principal has thereafter ratified his act, such ratification can only be based upon a full knowledge of all the facts upon which the unauthorized action was taken. This is as true in the case of the government as in that of an individual. Knowledge is necessary in any event.... If there be want of it, though such want arises from the neglect of the principal, no ratification can be based on any act of his. Knowledge of the facts is the essential element of ratification, and must be shown or such facts proved that its existence is a necessary inference from them.

Id. at 354, 21 S.Ct. at 375.

In our case, the trial court merely found that the CO was present when the Deputy Director made the offer and was silent after the offer was made. There was no finding that the CO even heard the statement. This is not sufficient evidence to support a finding of actual knowledge by the CO of the offer. In addition, the facts as found by the trial court do not support imputing to the CO constructive knowledge of the unilateral contract. The mere fact that Harbert/Lummus continued performing its construction activities would not have put the CO on notice of the existence of a new, unilateral contract because Harbert/Lummus had been performing its construction activities before the offer by the Deputy Director in accordance with its construction contract with Agrifuels. In the absence of either actual or constructive knowledge of the unilateral contract, the CO's silence cannot be a ratification of the unilateral contract. Moreover, ratification must also be based on a demonstrated acceptance of the contract. See EWG Assocs., Ltd., 231 Ct.Cl. at 1030. Silence in and of itself is not sufficient to establish a demonstrated acceptance of the contract by the CO. See id. The silence in this case by the CO was not an assent or acceptance of the oral, unilateral contract.

In addition, as previously discussed, the CO's delegation of authority expressly provided that even a ratification by the CO would have to be in writing. In the absence of such a writing, the CO could not have properly demonstrated his acceptance of the contract. Because we find that the government is not bound by this oral contract to guarantee funding of the project to completion, we reverse the decision of the trial court that there was such a contract and we vacate the trial court's damages award with respect to this alleged contract. We therefore need not reach Harbert/Lummus' argument that such damages were improperly calculated.

CONCLUSION

For the foregoing reasons, we reverse the judgment of the trial court with respect to its recognition of a binding oral, unilateral contract between the government and Harbert/Lummus and therefore we vacate the trial court's damages award for breach of this contract. We affirm the judgment of the trial court with respect to its finding that DOE was not contractually bound to an accelerated construction and payment schedule.

Notes and Questions

1. Like the *Mil-Spec* case, this case does not concern an action which the statutes or regulations place beyond any officials' authority, but only concerns who has the available authority to take that action and whether an official with the authority has exercised it through the authorized procedural mechanism. This time, since the CO did have delegated authority to take contracting steps like modifications, and the CO was the official who entered into the alleged oral, unilateral contract, the issue does not concern whether the official had authority but solely whether that official exercised it through the authorized procedures. The opinion discusses why an it considers the CO's action to be unauthorized insofar as the delegation of authority only authorized written actions. Conceptually or practically, does this differ from the Statute of Frauds? How?

This opinion cites a line of cases after American General Leasing, Inc. v. United States, 587 F.2d 54 (Ct. Cl. 1978), that have found various statutes or regulations barring the enforcement of a merely oral contract. The issue continues to get fought over. In a competing line of cases, courts have found that the government entered implied-in-fact contracts without written agreements. See, e.g., PacOrd, Inc. v. United States, 139 F.3d 1320 (9th Cir. 1998). This line of cases was criticized in Arnie Bruce Mason, Note, Implied-in-Fact Contracts Under the Federal Acquisition Regulation: Why PacOrd Got It Wrong, 41 Wm. & Mary L. Rev. 709 (2000).

2. The Alcohol Fuel Programs had contracted, as to a loan guarantee, directly with Agrifuels Refining Corporation. As the construction contractor for Agrifuels, Harbert/Lummus had the status of a subcontractor, as the opinion notes when stating that Harbert/Lummus was only in contractual privity with Agrifuels. The case begins to suggest the subtleties in the relationship between the government, and its subcontractors. As later chapters will discuss, on the one hand, the government keeps its distance from subcontractors on many issues, such as usually not (albeit with exceptions) allowing subcontractors to surmount that barrier of privity for purposes of pressing claims against the government. On the other hand, as this case itself illustrates, often the government has ardent desires regarding what subcontractors do. A subcontractor like Harbert/Lummus may view itself as having the worst of both worlds. Its prime contractor, Agrifuels, went bankrupt, as in the private sector, but then the ultimate party upon whom it depended, the government, invoked the special defenses of the public sector to escape its promises. Is it fair for the subcontractor to view itself as so unfortunate? What are the compensations to a subcontractor for that situation?

3. After the opinion determines that the CO did not have authority to enter this oral contract, the opinion then addresses separately the issue of whether the CO ratified the contract. The extremely high formal requirements for exercise of authority naturally lead to enhanced importance for the possibility, if they are not met, of ratification. Suppose Harbert/Lummus had written a memorandum of confirmation after the meeting, and the Deputy Director wrote back to it, truthfully, that the CO had read and orally agreed with the memorandum. Would that suffice for ratification?

4. For a discussion, see Christopher S. Pugsley, *The Game of "Who Can You Trust?"— Equitable Estoppel Against the Federal Government*, 31 Pub. Cont. L. J. 202 (2001).

2. Law in Statutes, Regulations, and Standard Clauses

In contrast to the common law background of basic (private) contract law, government contract law derives primarily from non-judicial public law sources. In theory, this consists of an evenly layered three-tier legal structure: statute, regulations, and contract clauses. In practice, the layers vary in extent; often Congressional statutes address only in general terms the issues that arise in particular contexts. Regulations, however, tend to be extensive, detailed, and comprehensive. The government contracts themselves can vary: some may be voluminous, resolving a multitude of issues and bringing the whole range of statutory and regulatory law to bear by cues relating to their sources in statutes and regulations. On the other hand, sometimes the government contracts do not contain the clauses that would expressly bring in that whole range of law. Then, the issue is posed of what is known, after a case involving the G.L. Christian company, as the "*Christian* doctrine." The case in this section, *Appeal of University of California, San Francisco*, deals with that doctrine.

It is also useful to get some overview at this point, historically, of the government contracting law statutes and regulations. Readings on this subject are included below. It would not be possible to lay these out completely, for to describe the whole of government contracting statutes and regulations would cram the entire book into this section. At this point, it helps to have a sense of the historic rise of government contracting law from the early 19th century statutes, through the World War I and II development, into the much more elaborate development as large-scale government procurement continued in the post-World War II era. Congressional action continued by a series of "reform" statutes of the 1980s and 1990s, principally the Competition in Contracting Act (1984), the Federal Acquisition Streamlining Act (1994), and the Federal Acquisition Reform Act (1996)

Meanwhile, elaborate sets of agency regulations had developed. From the origins in the regulations of individual military services and individual civilian departments came, in the post-World War II era, consolidation into comprehensive military procurement regulations (the Armed Services Procurement Regulations) and comprehensive civilian procurement regulations (the Federal Procurement Regulations). From these, the Federal Acquisition Regulation, the "FAR," came in 1983 as a comprehensive code of regulations operating throughout the government. It is no exaggeration to say that government contracting law today follows the FAR as much as "code" subjects in private contracting law follow the various articles of the Uniform Commercial Code.

In reading *Appeal of University of California, San Francisco*, do not try at this point to absorb the detailed law of required disclosure of cost and pricing data. We will return to this case in the section discussing that area of law. Rather, without getting into the details of that area of law, the question at this point is simply: is the contract controlled by that set of legal rules when the contract does not contain the clause usually used to indicate that the contract is under those rules (namely, the "Defective Pricing" clause)?

Regulations

From: Government Contract Guidebook Donald P. Arnavas
& William J. Ruberry (Federal Publications Inc. 2d ed. (1994))

Government procurement is procurement by regulation. The informality that often accompanies the solicitation and award of a purely commercial contract is obviously inappropriate where public funds are being expended for public purposes. Because of this, regulations play a key role in Government contracts.

1. Federal Acquisition Regulation

The basic set of regulations relating to federal procurement is the Federal Acquisition Regulation-the FAR. This set of regulations, which went into effect on April 1, 1984, is the primary set of regulations for all federal executive agencies. It is prepared, issued, and maintained by the Secretary of Defense, the Administrator of General Services, and the Administrator of the National Aeronautics and Space Administration.

Prior to the FAR, two sets of regulations governed Government contracts. One was the Defense Acquisition Regulation — the DAR as it was commonly called. The DAR (which was at one time called the Armed Services Procurement Regulation — the ASPR) governed procurements by military agencies. The other pre-FAR set of regulations was called the Federal Procurement Regulations — the FPR — governing procurements by civilian agencies.

The FAR is a massive document. At its most basic level of organization, as found in Chapter 1 of Title 48 in the *Code of Federal Regulations,* it consists of eight "subchapters," which in turn are composed of 53 "parts." Figure 2-1 on the following page lists the parts of the FAR, showing how they are arranged under each of the subchapters. In addition, Appendix A to this volume shows the structure of the FAR to the "subpart" level.

The FAR establishes uniform policies and procedures for procurement of supplies and services (including construction). It applies to all such purchases made within or outside the United States for procurements that obligate appropriated funds.

The FAR is by no means a static document. As already mentioned, it is subject to frequent revision through the coordinated action of the DAR Council and the CAA Council. Revision is accomplished through the issuance of Federal Acquisition Circulars (FACs).

Federal Acquisition Regulation Structure

Subchapter A General

    Part 1-Federal Acquisition Regulations System

    Part 2-Definitions of Words and Terms

    Part 3-Improper Business Practices and Personal Conflicts of Interest

    Part 4-Administrative Matters

Subchapter B: Acquisition Planning

    Part 5-Publicizing Contract Actions

    Part 6-Competition Requirements

    Part 7-Acquisition Planning

    Part 8-Required Sources of Supplies and Services

    Part 9-Contractor Qualifications

    Part 10-Specifications, Standards, and Other Purchase Descriptions

    Part 11-Acquisition and Distribution of Commercial Products

    Part 12-Contract Delivery or Performance

Subchapter C: Contracting Methods and Contract Types

    Part 13-Small Purchase and Other Simplified Purchase Procedures

    Part 14-Sealed Bidding

    Part 15-Contracting by Negotiation

    Part 16-Types of Contracts

    Part 17-Special Contracting Methods

    Part 18-[Reserved]

Subchapter D: Socioeconomic Programs

    Part 19-Small Business and Small Disadvantaged Business Concerns

    Part 20-Labor Surplus Area Concerns

    Part 21-[Reserved]

2. Agency Acquisition Regulations

Agency acquisition regulations are limited to (a) those necessary to implement FAR policies and procedures within the agency and (b) additional policies, procedures, solicitation provisions, or contract clauses that supplement the FAR to satisfy the specific needs of the agency.

Although the various civilian agencies have each issued their own sets of regulations implementing the FAR, the most comprehensive set is the DFARS (the Defense FAR Supplement), which applies to all of the military and DOD agencies. It is organized to correspond to the 53 parts of the FAR and incorporates several appendices and supplements. DOD completely rewrote the DFARS in 1991 to (1) eliminate text and clauses that were unnecessary, (2) eliminate or modify thresholds, certifications, and other regulatory burdens on Contracting Officers and contractors, and (3) rephrase all remaining text and clauses in plain English.

Like the FAR, the DFARS is codified in the *Code of Federal* Regulations (designated as Chapter 2 of Title 48). The civilian agency regulations implementing the FAR are also codified in Title 48.

The DFARS is supplemented from time to time by the issuance of Defense Acquisition Circulars (DACS) or Departmental Letters. A DAC may include-in addition to DFARS-revisions, policies, directives, and informational items. These Circulars can be of significance to contractors. Unless otherwise stated in the DAC, any new provisions, policies, or directives are effective as of the effective date stated in the DAC.

Because the FAR is the key set of procurement regulations, most of the citations in this book will be to the FAR. Occasionally, the DFARS will also be cited.

3. Deviations

Deviations from the FAR are allowed only if they are (a) authorized and (b) approved by a designated official. The same holds true for deviations from the DFARS. Generally, deviations from the FAR consist of use of a contract clause containing language differing from the standard FAR language, use of forms other than prescribed forms, alteration of prescribed forms, or omission of a mandatory contract clause.

G. L. CHRISTIAN AND ASSOCIATES v. The UNITED STATES. Court of Claims

312 F.2d 418 No. 56—59. Jan. 11, 1963.

DAVIS, Judge.

This case, which involves claims totaling $5,156,144.50,grew out of the deactivation of Fort Polk, Louisiana, by the Department of the Army in 1958. At the time when the decision to deactivate Fort Polk was made, a large housing project, which was to consist of 2,000 dwelling units for the use of military personnel at Fort Polk, was being constructed under a contract that had previously been made by the Corps of Engineers * * * The housing contract was terminated by the Corps of Engineers on February 5, 1958, after which numerous claims for damages were submitted to the Government.

* * * *

II

The Government concedes that the claimants are entitled to be made financially whole, at least with respect to all reasonable expenses that they incurred in preparing to perform work under the Fort Polk housing contract, in partially performing that contract from August 1957 to January 1958, and in meeting the situation that arose when the contract was formally terminated by the Government early in February 1958. The controversy revolves around the proper amounts of the claimants' unreimbursed expenses and the legal question whether the claimants are entitled to recover for anticipated profits. At the time work was suspended in January 1958, the project was only 2.036% complete and the work was substantially behind schedule.

The principal legal question is whether the claimants should be permitted to recover for anticipated profits. In this connection, it is settled that, when the Government enters into a contract, it has rights and it ordinarily incurs responsibilities similar to those of a private person who is a party to a contract * * * and if the Government terminates a contract without justification, such termination is a breach of the contract and the Government becomes liable for all the damages resulting from the wrongful act * * *.

The right to recover for anticipated profits arises, however, only if the termination of the contract by the Government is wrongful and constitutes a breach. If the Government has reserved the right to terminate a contract for its convenience and then does so, there is no breach and normally there can be no recovery for the profits * * *

In the present case, although the Fort Polk housing contract did not contain any provision expressly authorizing the Government to terminate the contract for its convenience, the Government contends that the contract should be read as if it did contain such a clause. This argument is largely based upon Section 8.703 of the Armed Services Procurement Regulations. Section 8.703 provided (with an exception which is not pertinent here) that 'the following standard clause shall be inserted in all fixed-price construction contracts amounting to more than $1,000,' and then proceeded to prescribe a detailed termination clause that began with the unequivocal declaration that 'the performance of work under this contract may be terminated by the Government in accordance with this clause in whole, or from time to time in part, whenever the Contracting Officer shall determine that such termination is in the best interest of the Government,' and included a formula which did not encompass anticipated profits. As the Armed Services Procurement Regulations were issued under statutory authority,those regulations, including Section 8.703, had the force and effect of law. See ; Ex parte . If they applied here, there was a legal requirement that the plaintiff's contract contain the standard termination clause and the contract must be read as if it did. * * *

Despite the unusual character of the contract, we have little difficulty in reading the Procurement Regulations, especially the rule requiring the insertion of the standard termination clause, as applying to the present type of agreement * * *

We are not, and should not be, slow to find the standard termination article incorporated, as a matter of law, into plaintiff's contract if the Regulations can fairly be read as permitting that interpretation. The termination clause limits profit to work actually done, and prohibits the recovery of anticipated but unearned profits. That limitation is a deeply ingrained strand of public procurement policy. Regularly since World War I, it has been a major government principle, in times of stress or increased military procurement, to provide for the cancellation of defense contracts when they are no longer needed, as well as for the reimbursement of costs actually incurred before cancellation, plus a reasonable profit on that work—but not to allow anticipated profits. * * * Since World War II, the standard termination clauses promulgated by the Defense Department and its constituent agencies have taken the same tack. Literally thousands of defense contracts and subcontracts have been settled on that basis in the past decades.

This history shows, in our view, that the Defense Department and the Congress would be loath to sanction a large contract which did not provide for power to terminate and at the same time proscribe anticipated profits if termination did occur. Particularly in the field of military housing, tied as it is to changes and uncertainties in installations would it be necessary to take account of a possible termination in advance of completion, and to guard against a common law measure of recovery which had been disallowed for so many years in military procurement. The experienced contractor in this case, for its part, could not have been wholly unaware that there might be a termination for the convenience of the Government, which the defendant would not deem a breach. Although the housing contract does not contain such an express provision, there are at least four references in it (and the accompanying agreements) to a 'termination of the Housing Contract for the convenience of the Government' and to the Government's assumption of certain obligations in that event. These references must have had some meaning. For many years unearned profits have not been paid upon such terminations, and we think it probable, too, that Centex-Zachry knew of that general policy.

For all of these reasons, we believe that it is both fitting and legally sound to read the termination article required by the Procurement Regulations as necessarily applicable to the present contract and therefore as incorporated into it by operation of law.

It follows that Centex-Zachry and its subcontractors cannot recover unearned but anticipated profits. * * *

Appeal of University of California, San Francisco

1996 WL 681971 (V.A.B.C.A.), 97-1 BCA 28,642,
VABCA No. 4661 November 25, 1996.
Opinion is in Chapter 4, Section on
"TINA and Defective Pricing"

Notes and Questions

1. Just how fundamental is the *Christian* doctrine? The *Christian* doctrine, in a nutshell, puts the parties to a government contract as much under the control of standard, "mandatory" government contract clauses when those clauses have been left out of the contract document, as when they have been put in. The opinion in *Appeal of University of California, San Francisco* discusses a number of other cases, harkening back to the original *Christian* decision itself, regarding the reasons for the *Christian* doctrine. Just how fundamental is that doctrine? Consider the following two views, assessing which captures better the place of this doctrine.

On the one hand, the jurisprudence of government contract law could view the *Christian* doctrine as serving some of the same fundamental necessities of the public law sphere as the limited-authority doctrines discussed in *OPM v. Richmond* and *Mil-Spec.* In a government structured by the Constitution and the enactments under it, and controlled by the elected Congress and President, the law governing each government contract cannot be left to the individual discretion of the particular contracting officers involved in the contract's drafting. The power belongs to the Congress, the President, and the formal processes they supervise that produce implementing regulations, not to the individual government officials who draw up particular contracts. Hence, the *Christian* doctrine implements the public law nature of government contracting, by importing into every contract what those higher formally-acting authorities prescribe.

On the other hand, the *Christian* doctrine does not have nearly the historic pedigree, recited in *OPM v. Richmond,* of the rule barring estoppel of the government by the actions of government agents and the limited authority of those agents. The *Christian* doctrine only arose in the post-World War II era. Moreover, while there were, historically, agency regulations and standard government clauses, their comprehensive interaction became more significant in that same post-World War II era. In that sense, it could be argued that the *Christian* doctrine lacks the deep significance of the doctrine discussed in *OPM v. Richmond,* which was well understood by Supreme Court Chief Justice John Marshall and has roots in the text of the Constitution. Rather, the *Christian* doctrine represents a modern innovation, like many of those in administrative law, coordinating the more complex, regulation-dependent system of recent decades. Moreover, the *Christian* doctrine does not apply with the extensive completeness of the *OPM v. Richmond* doctrine. Rather, as the *UCSF* opinion reflects, only a regulation-by-regulation, clause-by-clause assessment will determine whether the *Christian* doctrine applies to particular regulations and clauses.

2. Consider the larger role and responsibility for government contract lawyers this case creates. In private sector contracting, the parties to the contract, and their lawyers, can more or less take care of their concerns by adjusting the drafting of the contractual instrument. By contrast, the private party to a government contract finds himself at the mercy of the entire body of federal regulations. She derives scant comfort from what the instrument itself says, and depending upon her lawyer to know what dangers lurk in the whole Federal Acquisition Regulation.

3. A related issue concerns the type of interpretation principles to apply—the ones for public law, or, the ones for contract clauses. See William E. Slade, A Question of Intent, 7 Fed. Cir. Bar J. 251 (Fall 1997).

4. *OPM v. Richmond* expressed a doctrine that applied regardless of how unfair it seemed to the individual, the retired welder, who had relied to his peril on the advice of a Navy specialist. In the *UCSF* case, the University of California might contend that it was unfair to penalize it for relying on the government officers' omission of a defective pricing clause. Does the University have as much of a fairness argument as the welder did in *OPM v. Richmond*? Does the court weigh fairness arguments in deciding this case? Considering the reasons for the *Christian* doctrine, should it?

3. Budgets

The law of government budgeting warrants a brief mention at this point. Like the other characteristic principles of government contracting in this chapter, it marks part of the network by which the Constitution and statutes, and the Congress and the President, control government contracting interactions. Moreover, budgeting has enormous practical influence in government contracting decisions. Contracting officers have one eye on all the rest of government contracting law as it empowers or constrains them, and the other eye on how much government money they have to spend as this independently empowers or constrains them.

Most government contracting expends appropriated funds in the narrow sense of "appropriation," that is, funds provided by Congress in annually enacted appropriation laws. For example, most of the money for defense procurement comes in the annual Department of Defense Appropriation law. (However, the government also spends large sums for entitlements, such as Medicare, in which the funds are promised by statutes that are not appropriation laws and that are not enacted annually.) Appropriations get decided in an annual budgeting cycle. For example, for the Army to get funds to buy laptop computers, its officials would put a request for those funds in their service's draft budget. The Office of Management and Budget, which is the President's budgeting arm, would approve inclusion of that request in the President's official budget request. Then, the House and Senate Appropriation Committees would consider the laptop request and include the money as they report appropriation bills to their chambers.

Once Congress enacted a Department of Defense appropriation law containing the money corresponding to that request, the money would then be passed out within the government, with the Office of Management and Budget "apportioning" the funds for the Army, and the Army "allotting" the funds to particular matters. Ultimately one of the Army's contracting officers would be formally notified of the availability of funds to be "obligated" by award of a contract. Upon the contractor's delivery and the Army's acceptance of the laptops, the Army would issue a Treasury check to the contractor, drawing down the Army's account in the Treasury, and "liquidating" the contractual obligation.

Many aspects of budgeting will receive attention later. Some particular items warrant mention now. In general, appropriation laws primarily contain bare provisions setting forth amounts of money and their tersely stated objects. Even these bare appropriation provisions contain a great deal of law governing the expenditure of funds. They tell how long the funds remain available, which may be one year, several years, or even longer. And they tell the object for the funds, which may be expressed very broadly, such as a general appropriation of billions of dollars for the Navy's operations and maintenance, or may be expressed very narrowly, such as specific appropriation of a few thousands dollars for a particular improvement in the Library of Congress. Broad appropriations carry non-binding but highly influential guidance in the form of the original detailed budget requests submitted to the Congress, and the committee reports and other legislative history of the appropriation bills within Congress.

Furthermore, appropriation laws can, and do, contain expressive language further governing the expenditure of those funds. Appropriation laws frequently contain limitations that preclude spending the funds for various purposes, from statutory clauses putting an end to a war by forbidding further military expenditures on it to statutory clauses imposing "Buy America" rules by forbidding expending the funds to make purchases from foreign sources. Such law enacted by inclusion in appropriation laws has as much force and effect as any other statute. In fact, a fair portion of the statutory background of government contract law entered the Statutes at Large aboard appropriation laws. For example, the entire Federal Acquisition Reform Act of 1996 got enacted by inclusion in an appropriation law.

A number of government offices serve fiscal and financial purposes, and these interact with the contracting officers and directly or indirectly with the contractors. Departments typically have elaborate financial offices tasked to formulate proposed budgets and to track the obligation and the ultimate expenditure of the enacted funding. A very important agency, the Government Accounting Office ("GAO") headed by the Comptroller General, performs a variety of functions including fiscal investigations. The GAO historically gives advisory opinions about the legality of expenditure of funds. From this general function of the GAO arose its specific function, of great importance in government contracting law, of deciding one particular type of issue regarding contracting, namely, the "bid protest" discussed in the chapters on sealed bidding and negotiated procurements.

Agencies have several types of offices to conduct financial investigations, particularly investigations of government contractors. These include the offices that conduct the large number of regular audits, such as the Defense Contract Audit Agency for military contracts. They also include the Inspector General offices, which look into possible overcharging, fraud, and other contractual abuses.

C. State Procurement

In one sense, no casebook can treat fully the law of procurement by state and local governments, even if the entire casebook focused on that law: since state procurement law derives largely from statutes, regulations, and contract clauses, each state has written its own law. There is no unifying "common law" of state procurement law, and there is no uniform state procurement law adopted in fifty states like the Uniform Commercial Code. No one book could even reproduce, let alone discuss, the specifics of the procurement law in the fifty different state systems and the thousands of local systems.

However, in another sense, simply by dint of discussing federal procurement law a great deal of what would be needed to practice state procurement law will be discussed. There have always been unifying factors between federal and state procurement law. These factors have become increasingly important since the end of World War II and the rise of a uniform, regularized federal system centered upon the Federal Acquisition Regulation as a complete and orderly code. Both state government lawyers and the practitioners with which they deal have tended to bring the federal law that they master into their state contracting.

The two readings in this chapter do not seek to describe comprehensively state procurement law. Rather, they aim to illustrate the mix of carried-over federal law and the retained particularized law of the individual state, that make up the whole of state procurement law. In these readings, look for the following:

First, look at how the structure of state procurement law resembles the structure of federal procurement law. That is, in a way parallel to the sources of federal procurement law, the sources of state procurement law consists of state statutes, state regulations, and state standard contract clauses. Both of the readings discuss Maryland's adoption of a new statutory procurement code in 1980, the adoption of the state procurement regulations (in the "Code of Maryland Regulations" or "COMAR"), and the use of standard Maryland contract clauses. Similar authority limitations and appropriation mechanisms to the federal ones allow the state constitutions and laws, and the state elected legislatures and governors, to direct and control the actions of state officials, including state contracting officers.

Second, look at what makes up the mix of current state procurement law. Part of it consists of borrowings from federal law: the bid protest and contract dispute systems at the state level, for example, resemble the federal ones, as do substantive rules on many subjects from bid bonds to construction contract arrangements for unexpected costs (known as "differing site conditions"). Another part of it consists of modernized state systems codifying, unifying, centralizing, and organizing state procurement arrangements, such as the 1980 system established in Maryland. Modernized state procurement systems often draw on the American Bar Association's Model Procurement Code. A residual part of it consists of continuation of traditional state procurement arrangements, often tied to the particularized governing structure of that state or locality. For example, the Maryland system preserved a central role in the awarding of contracts for the Board of Public Works, a state body consisting of the Governor and a few other state officials. This is a classic state arrangement tying state procurement to the state governing structure, which varies from state to state and has no close federal analogue.

For further discussions of the issues in this section, see: Constance Cushman, *The ABA Model Procurement Code: Implementation, Evolution, and Crisis of Survival*, 25 Pub. Cont. L.J. 173 (1996); Lewis J. Baker, *Procurement Disputes at the State and Local Level: A Hodgepodge of Remedies*, 25 Pub. Cont. L.J. 265 (1996); F. Trowbridge von Baur, *A Personal History of the Model Procurement Code*, 25 Pub. Cont. L.J. 4 (1976).

Kennedy Temporaries v. Comptroller of the Treasury

No. 484 Sept. Term 1983. Court of Special Appeals of Maryland.
468 A.2d 1026, Jan. 4, 1984

Argued before MOYLAN, LISS and WILNER, JJ.

WILNER, Judge.

Appellant bid on a State contract. He was underbid by one of his competitors and therefore did not get the contract. Alleging that the low bidder should have been disqualified because of an insufficient bid bond, appellant eventually commenced a proceeding that has grown in complexity at each successive stage. * * * [W]e shall be obliged to discuss in some detail not only the factual and procedural history of the case but also the procurement law, the regulations issued under it, and some of the procedures mandated by the law and the regulations.

I. The Procurement Law

In 1980, after several years of study, the General Assembly enacted a new procurement code for the State. It took effect July 1, 1981, and is presently codified as Md.Code Ann. art. 21.

The heart of the law is §2-201(a), which states simply that no State agency in the Executive Branch "may enter into a contract for supplies, services, or construction except in accordance with the provisions of this article and the regulations established pursuant to this article." The law then sets forth some basic rules governing the methods by which the State is to select and deal with its suppliers. In title 3, for example, it authorizes five types of source selection (§3-201(a)), establishes a preference for one of them—competitive sealed bidding (§3-201(b)), and requires that when that method is used, "[t]he contract shall be awarded to the responsive and responsible bidder whose bid is...the lowest bid price...." Other sections in title 3 specify qualification standards for bidders (subtitle 4), bond requirements (subtitle 5), and restrictions on certain types of contracts (subtitle 7).

In title 7 (§7-201), the law establishes a specific four-step procedure for resolving disputes relating to both the formation of a contract (i.e., the award of a contract) and a contract already awarded. The first step is the agency procurement officer who, upon timely demand, and "consistent with...all applicable laws and regulations," is authorized to "negotiate and resolve" these disputes, including disputes "concerning the qualification of bidders...and the determination of the successful bidder...." (§7-201(a)). The second step is review of the procurement officer's decision by the agency head, who may "approve or disapprove the procurement officer's decision" and whose determination "is deemed final action by the agency...." (§7-201(c)). The third step is an appeal to the Board of Contract Appeals, an independent entity created by §7-202. The decision of that Board, according to §7-201(d), "is final only subject to judicial review." Judicial review, in accordance with the Administrative Procedure Act, is the fourth and final step. (§7-203).

Subject to these statutory criteria, the essential thrust of the law is to continue overall control over State procurement in the Board of Public Works, where it has resided for at least fifty years, but to permit the Board, by regulation, to delegate part of its control authority to four other State agencies having special procurement responsibilities—the University of Maryland and the Departments of Budget and Fiscal Planning, General Services, and Transportation. These five agencies—but primarily the Board of Public Works—are directed to develop the necessary implementing details and procedures by administrative regulation. We see this in §2-101.

Section 2-101(a) places in the Board of Public Works "power and authority over the procurement, management, and control of all supplies, services, construction, and other items procured by the State." See also Md.Code Ann. art. 78A, §§1B and 10. To carry out the provisions of the statute, the Board "has authority to set policy and to adopt regulations which are consistent with this article," as well as to exercise any authority conferred on the other four specified agencies. Subsection (b) also deals with regulations. It states, in relevant part, that the Board "shall adopt regulations, consistent with this article, governing procedures for the review and approval of procurement contracts...[and] procedures for review of determinations...." The Board is further directed to "ensure that the regulations of the procurement agencies provide for procedures which are consistent with this article and which are substantially the same among the agencies."

The four departmental procurement units derive their special authority from §2-101(c). That section directs each of those agencies to adopt regulations "consistent with this article" concerning a number of things, including "[r]ejection of bids, consideration of alternate bids, and waiver of informalities in bids."

Regulations were, in fact, adopted by the Board and the four other agencies, effective July 1, 1981. They appear in COMAR, Title 21, and include, among other things, procedures and requirements relating to bid bonds (21.06.07), protests (21.10.02), the Board of Contract Appeals (21.02.02 and 21.10.06), and the waiver of minor irregularities and deficiencies in bids (21.05.02.12 and 21.06.02.03). Approval authority over certain types of procurement contracts was delegated to the other four agencies (21.02.01.03-07), but anything not delegated was reserved to the Board of Public Works. With respect to any such contracts (including service contracts exceeding $100,000), the agency procurement officer has no authority to award the contract. His decision, or, upon review, that of the agency head or the Board of Contract Appeals, is in the nature of a recommendation to the Board of Public Works, which alone can approve or reject.

When these various provisions governing the dispute-resolution process and the overall authority of the Board of Public Works are read together harmoniously, as they should be, the legislative intent seems clear that the dispute-resolution process set forth in §7-201 should be completed before the Board of Public Works, as the final approval authority, acts on a disputed matter concerning contract formation, in order that the Board may then act in conformance with the decision reached through that process. That is what §2-201(a) would seem to require; and only in that manner can the prerogatives of the Board under the law be clearly and neatly meshed with the more specific criteria and procedures mandated by the General Assembly.

II. Factual and Procedural Setting

At some point in the early fall of 1981, the Comptroller of the Treasury determined that he would need additional temporary personnel to assist in the processing of income tax returns expected to be received during the winter and spring of 1982. On October 1, 1981, through his procurement officer, John A. Clinton, the Comptroller issued an invitation to about twenty companies to bid on a contract to provide such personnel for the period January 1—June 30, 1982. Enclosed with the invitation was a memorandum describing the bidding process. Paragraph P of that memorandum dealt with bid bonds. Reflecting the provisions of Md.Code Ann. art. 21, §3-504 and COMAR 21.06.07.01 and .02, Paragraph P stated:

> Bids exceeding $25,000 in anticipated price must contain a Bid Bond in an amount equal to at least five percent (5%) of the total amount bid. The preferred bid security is a bond in form satisfactory to the State underwritten by a company licensed to issue bonds in Maryland. The bond shall be in substantially the form contained in Appendix (F). State procurement regulations permit other forms of bid securities. Contact the issuing officer to discuss any other form of bid security. Failure to provide an acceptable bid security with the bid when required shall result in the bid being rejected. (Emphasis in original.)

When the bids were opened on November 17, 1981, it appeared that the two lowest bidders were Bay Services, Inc. at $608,159, and Kennedy Temporaries at $621,502. Bay Services' bid was accompanied by a bid bond, in proper form, in the amount of $30,000, which was $407.95 short of five percent of its bid. Kennedy did not submit a bid bond. Its bid was accompanied by a letter from a branch officer of Maryland National Bank stating, in relevant part:

> As part of the above bid proposal, it is necessary to provide a $50,000.00 'Bid Proposal Bond.'

> Please be advised by this letter that Maryland National Bank guarantees to provide any collateral necessary to the State of Maryland to be held as collateral against performance; should Stephen G. Kennedy's bid be accepted by the State of Maryland.

Mr. Kennedy was in attendance when the bids were opened, and he asked if he could see the amount of the bid bond posted by Bay Services. The procurement officer initially rejected his request—"until we got everything sorted out"—but permitted such an inspection on November 23, 1981. Mr. Kennedy then noticed the shortfall and pointed it out to Ms. Mary Ann Porter, the personnel manager of the Comptroller's office, indicating that, as a result of the deficiency, the Bay Services bid should be rejected. The next day, Mr. Clinton, the procurement officer, called, and Kennedy iterated his complaint to him.

On November 25, 1981, Clinton wrote to Bay Services, pointing out the deficiency in the bid bond and advising that "a question has been raised" with respect to it. Clinton called attention to COMAR 21.05.02.12, permitting him to waive "technicalities or minor regulations [sic, irregularities] in bids," and COMAR 21.06.02.03, defining "minor irregularity" and empowering the procurement officer to "give the bidder…an opportunity to cure any deficiency resulting from a minor informality or irregularity in a bid…or waive the deficiency, whichever is to the advantage of the State."

Obviously regarding the shortage in the bid bond as "minor," Clinton purported to exercise his prerogative under the latter regulation and directed Bay Services to file an additional $500 in approved security by December 1, 1981. A copy of that letter was sent to Kennedy. Two days later—on November 27—Clinton sent another letter to Bay Services, again with a copy to Kennedy. In this letter he abandoned reliance on COMAR 21.05.02.12 and 21.06.02.03 and instead invoked his authority under COMAR 21.06.07.02B. That regulation provides, in relevant part:

> If a bid does not comply with the security requirements of this regulation, the bid shall be rejected as nonresponsive, unless the failure to comply is determined by the procurement officer to be nonsubstantial when:
>
> * * *
>
> (2) The amount of the bid security submitted, though less than the amount required by the invitation for bids, is equal to or greater than the difference in the price stated in the next higher acceptable bid.…

Because the $30,000 bid bond filed by Bay Services was greater in amount than the $13,000 difference between its bid and that of Kennedy, Clinton concluded that the deficiency was "nonsubstantial" and would therefore be excused altogether. He ended the letter with the statement, "your bid bond is accepted without any need for further action."

* * * On December 2, 1981, the matter was taken up by the Board of Public Works which, as we have noted, retained under the law full approval authority over service contracts exceeding $100,000. The transcript of that meeting shows that both Mr. Clinton and Mr. Kennedy appeared and presented their respective views. No mention was made by Mr. Clinton (or by anyone else) of the lack of written protest; but neither did Mr. Kennedy give any indication that he intended to pursue the matter before the Board of Contract Appeals. Clinton maintained that the deficiency in the Bay Services bid bond was non-substantial and argued that "it just doesn't make sense to disqualify a low bidder for a $407 deficiency in a bond and cost the State $13,000." Kennedy, on the other hand, forcefully argued his case—that the statute was there, that it was clear, and that it ought to be applied uniformly—and he seemed clearly to understand that the final resolution of the matter was in the Board's hands. The Board was apparently unimpressed by Kennedy's argument, as it approved the contract with Bay Services that day, although it is not certain from the record when that decision was first communicated to Kennedy.

On December 7, 1981, Kennedy called and left a message for Clinton requesting "the final decision of the Procurement Office." * * *

Clinton received [from Kennedy a] letter on December 30, and responded immediately. He stated first that his recommendation that the contract be awarded to Bay Services, which had been approved by the Board of Public Works, as indicated in his letter of December 9, was his "final recommendation." * * * Nothing further happened until January 15, 1982, when, by letter of that date, Kennedy appealed to the Board of Contract Appeals. * * *

In a decision rendered July 20, 1982—three weeks after the contract with Bay Services had been fully completed—the Board of Contract Appeals concluded that:

* * * In excusing the deficiency in Bay Services' bid bond, Clinton acted in conformance with COMAR 21.06.07.02B. The bond exceeded the difference between the two bids and thus the deficiency could, under the regulation, properly be regarded as "non-substantial." The statute, however, art. 21, §3-504, was explicit. Subsection (b) requires the bid bond to be "in an amount equal to at least 5 percent of the amount of the bid," and subsection (c) states that, if the invitation requires that a bid bond be provided, "a bidder...that does not comply shall be rejected." To the extent that COMAR 21.06.07.02B permitted the waiver of "non-substantial" deficiencies in bid bonds, it was inconsistent with that clear legislative mandate and therefore was void.

In light of those conclusions, the Board "sustained" Kennedy's appeal. * * *

Neither party was satisfied with the Board's decision and thus both appealed to the Circuit Court for Baltimore City. * * *

The court, though agreeing with the Comptroller that the Board of Contract Appeals had no authority to declare COMAR 21.06.07.02B invalid, nonetheless effectively affirmed the Board's decision. The court itself declared the regulation to be "an improper extension of the administrative authority of the Procurement Officer" and thus to be "null and void." It also found, however, that Kennedy's claim for damages was "barred by the doctrine of sovereign immunity."

The court's decision brought no more solace to the parties than that of the Board of Contract Appeals, and we therefore again have cross-appeals. * * *

III. Discussion

A. Precis

We think that the Comptroller's third argument is valid; Kennedy does not qualify as a "responsive" bidder, and thus has no legal status to challenge the award to Bay Services. We believe, in addition, that, even if Kennedy were to be regarded as having such status, by failing to pursue his administrative remedy in conformance with the requirements of §7-201, he has waived his right to complain. * * *

B. Kennedy's Standing As A Responsive Bidder

In Part II, above, we observed that Kennedy's bid was not accompanied by a bid bond. In place of such a bond, it submitted a letter from Maryland National Bank guaranteeing "to provide any collateral necessary to the State of Maryland to be held as collateral against performance," should Kennedy's bid be accepted.

Section 3-504(a), in stating the requirement of a bid bond, provides: "The bid bond shall be provided by a surety company authorized to do business in this State, or the equivalent in cash, or in a form satisfactory to the procurement officer." COMAR 21.06.07.01B expands upon that. It permits, as bid security, a surety bond, a bank check, or a "[p]ledge of securities backed by the full faith and credit of the United States government or bonds issued by the State of Maryland."

A bid bond is a very limited kind of performance bond. It is designed to assure only that a bidder, if successful, will, in fact, enter into the contract he has bid upon, and to provide a secure fund to compensate the State if he fails to do so. The condition of the bond is that the principal will "execute such further contractual documents, if any, and give such bond(s) as may be required by the terms of the bid...." COMAR 21.06.07.03

(Exhibit E). See Board of Education v. Allender, 206 Md. 466, 476, 112 A.2d 455 (1955); Harran Transportation Co. v. Board of Ed., 71 Misc.2d 143, 335 N.Y.S.2d 971 (1972). Its function and its legal effect end once a contract is signed, for at that point the condition of the bond has been satisfied. As the Comptroller points out, the loss accruing from the default by a successful bidder—i.e., his failure to enter into the contract in accordance with his bid—is normally the difference between what the State would have paid absent the default (usually the amount of the defaulter's bid) and what it actually has to pay as the result of the default (generally the next highest bid accepted by the State). That is what a bid bond is intended to secure; and indeed the guarantee of the surety is that, in the event of a default in executing a contract, "the Principal shall pay the State for any cost of procuring the work which exceeds the amount of its bid." COMAR 21.06.07.03 (Exhibit E).

The letter from Maryland National Bank does not, in our judgment, satisfy the bid bond requirement of the statute, the regulation, or the invitation to bid. In the first place, the pledge of collateral was against "performance" should Kennedy's bid be accepted, not specifically against loss occurring by virtue of a default in entering into the contract. Second, it is not clearly a pledge of securities backed by the full faith and credit of the United States or the State of Maryland. If, as Kennedy claims, Mr. Clinton was without authority to waive the $408 deficiency in Bay Services' bond, he surely was without authority to waive this type of deficiency.

C. Protest Requirements—Waiver

The statutory provisions governing the resolution of disputes arising under the procurement law are, as we have said, found in §7-201. * * * The process is more sharply defined in COMAR 21.10.02, which requires, among other things, that a protest "shall be in writing and addressed to the respective procurement officer representing the State agency" (21.10.02.02) and that where the basis of the protest is not apparent before the bid opening, "bid protests shall be filed not later than 7 days after the basis for protest is known or should have been known, whichever is earlier." (21.10.02.03).

Kennedy discovered the basis of his protest on November 23, 1981; to comply strictly with the regulation Kennedy should therefore have filed a written protest with Mr. Clinton by November 30. That clearly was not done, and thus there can be no legitimate claim of compliance by Kennedy with the requirements of the regulation.

Kennedy's response is that, by taking cognizance of his complaint, Clinton effectively waived the seven-day-written-protest requirement, to which the Comptroller rejoins that Clinton had no legal authority to waive that requirement.

* * * We also would note that, even if regarded as merely procedural in nature, the regulation was not that of the Comptroller. It was adopted by the Department of Budget and Fiscal Planning, with the approval of the Governor and the Board of Public Works, and was imposed by those agencies upon the Comptroller's office in the latter's capacity as a procurement agency. Whatever the procurement officer's authority might be to waive a procedural regulation of the Comptroller, we find no authority in the law for him to waive a requirement externally imposed pursuant to clear statutory authority. Such a power would be inconsistent with the whole thrust and scheme of the law. * * *

For all of these reasons, we conclude that Kennedy's appeal to the Board of Contract Appeals should have been dismissed. We shall remand the case to the Circuit Court for Baltimore City for entry of an order to that effect.

JUDGMENT VACATED

Notes and Questions

1. Parse the aspects of *Kennedy Temporaries* that have close federal analogues, and the aspects that are unique to state procurement or to this particular state. Start with the procedures. The issues in *Kennedy Temporaries* received consideration at each of the following levels: the contracting officer, the Board of Public Works, the Board of Contract Appeals, the Circuit Court, and the Court of Special Appeals. Which of these have federal analogues? What is the role of the others?

2. Now, consider the aspects which governed the decision of the appeal: the bid bond requirements, the bidder's "standing" to challenge the award, and the strictness of the timing rules that forbade their waiving by the Board of Contract Appeals. What aspects of this would be identical in a federal contract?

Fair Treatment for Contractors Doing Business with the State of Maryland

15 Univ. of Baltimore L. Rev. 215 Winter, 1986. Scott A. Livingston

I. INTRODUCTION

In 1980, the Maryland General Assembly enacted the Procurement Article, which incorporates into Maryland law the policy of providing fair treatment for persons who deal with the state procurement system. Prior to the Article taking effect in 1981, Maryland did not have a comprehensive statute that regulated procurement of public works by state agencies.

The Article was enacted to provide for a comprehensive and impartial system of procurement. In the opinion of the General Assembly, persons who have a reasonable expectation of fair treatment from the state will compete more vigorously for state contracts. The Procurement Article contains provisions that were designed to implement the fair treatment policy. Specific provisions govern the manner in which the state awards contracts. Other provisions specify mandatory terms for inclusion in contracts and establish a method for resolution of disputes.

This article examines procurement methods used by various state agencies prior to 1981. The article explains the laws that govern state procurement of public works and evaluates the degree to which the Procurement Article has provided fair treatment for contractors working for the state. Section II describes the recent history of Maryland procurement with emphasis on the period immediately preceding 1981. Section II also discusses procurement of architectural and engineering services, use of procurement to achieve socio-economic policy, and development of dispute resolution procedures. Section III examines the methods used to award contracts and resolve disputes under the Procurement Article. In addition, section III discusses cases in which Maryland appellate courts reviewed disputes resolved by a board of contract appeals. In section IV, the author addresses the future of Maryland procurement and presents suggestions for modifying the system in a manner that advances the policies underlying the Procurement Article, especially the policy of promoting fair treatment of contractors doing business with the state.

II. PROCUREMENT PRIOR TO 1981

The history of Maryland is reflected in the history of public works, to borrow a phrase from Victor Hugo. Events of political history, fortunate and otherwise, have influenced legislation governing procurement of public works by the state.

A. How Contracts Were Awarded

1. General

Prior to 1981, the methods state agencies used to award contracts were dictated by the Board of Public Works and the General Assembly. The seminal powers of the Board of Public Works could be circumscribed by the General Assembly; however, the General Assembly did not enact a comprehensive procurement statute limiting the scope of the Board's powers until 1981. Approval by the Board of Public Works usually provided sufficient authorization for a state agency to award a contract.

Instead of enacting a comprehensive procurement statute, the General Assembly enacted legislation that created various executive branch agencies. The enabling legislation for these agencies usually contained provisions that mandated the manner in which the new agencies would conduct procurement. * * *

B. Terms of the Procurement Contract

1. No Uniformity Prior to 1981

Prior to 1981, state law did not require the inclusion of uniform terms in state contracts for procurement of public works construction services. The contract terms differed from agency to agency. It is difficult to say whether the particular terms used reflected the diverse needs of each agency or merely the personal preferences of various procurement officers.

* * *

In the early seventies, [Maryland Department of Transportation, or MDOT] conducted a study of the various clauses used by the modal administrations of MDOT. MDOT found that numerous, often conflicting clauses were contained in boilerplate procurement contracts. In 1976, after several years of study, MDOT adopted its 'General Provisions for Construction Contracts.'

The General Provisions were important for several reasons. First, the terms set out in the General Provisions fairly allocated the risks inherent in public works construction. Second, the General Provisions represented a major effort to coordinate the procurement practices of the agencies in MDOT, the department that enjoyed the largest public works budget in state government. Third, the provisions were modeled so closely on federal clauses that case law construing the federal clauses could be used to provide guidance under Maryland law for interpretation of the terms contained in the General Provisions. Previously, because of the doctrine of sovereign immunity, there had been a dearth of Maryland case law on contract claims against the government.

The sudden application of familiar federal clauses and case law encouraged national competition for state contracts, especially on the Baltimore Metro project. Only a limited number of contractors can procure the finances, equipment, and other resources needed to build subway stations and tunnels. These contractors usually are familiar with the provisions used in standard federal contracts. Familiarity with the provisions enables contractors to anticipate the costs of risks allocated under federal contracts and submit their bids accordingly. Prudent contractors tend to compete less vigorously for contracts that contain unfamiliar or unfair clauses.

2. Socio-Economic Policies

In Maryland, the process used to award procurement contracts for public works incorporates procedures designed to implement socio-economic policies identified by the General Assembly. Public funds are spent on projects in such a way as to encourage certain business practices that appear to be in the public interest. For example, Maryland has enacted legislation designed to encourage the purchase of American-made steel for state public works projects. Among the several socio-economic policies identified by the General Assembly, the one that most drastically affects traditional practices in public works procurement is the Minority Business Enterprise Program.

In order to understand how the Minority Business Enterprise (MBE) policies affected procurement, it is necessary to examine procurement practices prior to 1978. Traditionally, the state awarded public works contracts to the low bidder based on a formal advertisement for sealed bids. The party identified as the low bidder became the prime contractor pursuant to a contract with the state.

When a prime contractor elected to enter into subcontracts for performance of work on a project, the state generally was not involved in the selection of any subcontractor. The prime contractor was responsible for completing the project according to contract specifications; accordingly, he exercised virtually unlimited discretion in the selection of subcontractors.

Prime contractors usually did not subcontract with businesses owned and operated by black individuals. Instead, prime contractors subcontracted with firms that they had dealt with for years, a practice that civil rights advocates found operated to exclude minority firms. The traditional practice of subcontracting with firms that the prime contractor previously had done business with tended to exclude minority businesses from participating in public works projects.

* * *

During its 1978 session, the General Assembly enacted legislation designed to alter the traditional practice of subcontracting on public works projects. The legislation called for state agencies to intervene on behalf of minority businesses in the selection of subcontractors for major public works projects. As indicated in the preamble to the legislation, the General Assembly was 'concerned that minority businesses may experience the effect of past discrimination' in the award of subcontracts on state public works projects. The General Assembly directed MDOT to establish departmental procedures for procuring construction services that encourage minority business participation to the extent of ten percent of the dollar value of contracts exceeding $100,000.

Anticipating the passage of minority business legislation by the General Assembly, MDOT established an MBE Program. MDOT designed the MBE Program in a fashion that implemented the policy of encouraging participation by minority businesses in MDOT construction projects.

* * *

C. Resolution of Disputes

Parties to state public works contracts recognize that disputes commonly, if not invariably, arise regarding the interpretation of contract terms. Inclusion of a 'Disputes

Clause,' which provides a procedure for fairly resolving contract disputes, helps prevent litigation concerning the interpretation of contract terms from impeding completion of public works projects. Prior to 1976, the Disputes Clause provided the principal means that a contractor could use to obtain appropriate compensation from the state in the event of dispute. An examination of the respective positions of the state and the contractor illustrates the manner in which the Disputes Clause functions in the public works construction process.

1. Disputes are Inherent

Disputes are inherent in the construction of public works projects. A tension exists between the state and the contractor who agrees to build a project. Each party is oriented to the contract price, which is a fixed amount reached on the basis of competitive sealed bidding. Not only is the contract price fixed, but it is fixed as the lowest amount offered by any responsible contractor who competitively bid for the project.

The rationale used to justify the practice of awarding the contract to the low bidder is that the practice promotes price competition among those seeking public works contracts. Although it may promote competition, the practice of awarding to the low bidder produces an anomalous effect. As a practical matter, awarding the contract to the lowest responsible bidder forces both the contractor and the state to search intensively for means to protect, if not improve, their positions once the contract price is fixed and performance is begun.

The parties' abilities to improve their respective positions largely depend upon the contractual language that allocates cost risks associated with performance. The contractor, who has underbid his competitors to win the contract, wants to minimize his performance costs. Thus, the contractor interprets the contract language in a manner that enables him to render the minimum performance—at the lowest cost—that complies with the terms of the contract. The state, however, like any owner who hires a contractor, is inclined to demand the maximum possible performance.

Contract price disputes occur because the contract price is fixed low and fixed early—at the time of bid opening. At this point, both the contractor and the state estimate generally, but neither can estimate exactly, how much money it will cost to perform the contract. Hence, the contractor has no extra money in his bid to pay for unforeseen expenses that occur during performance. To maintain its profit position, the contractor is justified in requesting extra compensation when unforeseen expenses arise.

A public works contract generally allocates the construction risks and provides for a contractual means to deal with the risk that a dispute will arise. In the contract, the parties agree to make adjustments to the contract price upon the occurrence of certain events that affect cost or time of performance. For example, if the subsurface conditions at the project site differ materially from those indicated in the plans, the contract price will be adjusted to compensate for increased costs incurred as a result. A contractor who encounters subsurface conditions that differ materially from those indicated in the plans presents to the state a claim for an equitable adjustment. The term 'claim' is thus neutral insofar as it merely signifies the contractor's exercise of a right promised by the state.

The parties recognize in advance that there may be disputes over whether an equitable adjustment is justified. Although each party is oriented to the contract price, both view as advantageous the provision of a contractual procedure for resolving disputes regarding claims for equitable adjustments arising under the contract.

2. Resolution via a Disputes Clause

The procedure that governs the resolution of disputes is set forth in a Disputes Clause. The current Disputes Clause authorizes the state to decide initially the proper interpretation of contract requirements. Generally, the procedure contemplates a three-tiered process. First, a lower- level official in the agency that commissioned the project is authorized to interpret the contract terms. Second, a contractor who is dissatisfied with the interpretation can obtain upper-level administrative review within the agency. While the interpretation is under review, the contractor remains obligated to perform the disputed work. Third, the contractor can appeal the agency's final decision to an outside forum that reviews the agency's decision.

* * *

III. POST-1981 MARYLAND PROCUREMENT SYSTEM

A. Passage of the Procurement Article

The Procurement Article provides an equitable, modern system for the procurement of public works projects. Three important features distinguish the modern system from the procurement practices used by the state prior to 1981. First, the Procurement Article establishes uniform methods for the awarding of all state contracts. The preferred method for awarding contracts for construction of public works is competitive sealed bidding. By using the method of competitive sealed bidding, the state is obligated to award contracts for construction of public works to the lowest responsive and responsible bidder. Second, the Procurement Article establishes specific clauses that must be included in all state construction contracts. The clauses are contained in regulations that have been promulgated to implement the provisions of the Procurement Article. These mandatory clauses are designed to allocate fairly the risks inherent in the construction of public works projects. Third, the Procurement Article establishes the Maryland State Board of Contract Appeals (MSBCA).

* * *

Instead of merely having jurisdiction over disputes regarding contracts entered into by the Department of Transportation, as did MDOT BCA, MSBCA has jurisdiction over disputes relating to any contract entered into by the state. In addition, MSBCA has jurisdiction to hear and decide bid protests, which are disputes relating to the formation of state contracts. Prior to the establishment of MSBCA, bid protests were resolved summarily by the Board of Public Works. The practice of summary resolution of bid protests by the Board of Public Works was altered by the General Assembly because it left the state vulnerable to public criticism of political favoritism.

* * *

V. CONCLUSION

The modern era of Maryland procurement began in 1976 when the General Assembly passed legislation that provided for a partial waiver of the doctrine of sovereign immunity. Shortly thereafter, MDOT created a board of contract appeals, introduced standard clauses for inclusion in procurement contracts, and instituted responsible procedures for contract award. These three safeguards were designed to enhance MDOT's ability to insure fair treatment for contractors.

In 1981, with the passage of the Procurement Article by the General Assembly, the safeguards provided by MDOT became applicable to virtually all state contracts. The policy of fair treatment for contractors doing business with the State of Maryland was incorporated into law. In the future, the policy of providing fair treatment for contractors who do business with the state will continue to be a crucial aspect of Maryland procurement.

Notes and Questions

1. Clearly, state procurement in Maryland went through a major change in 1981. What drove it through that change? What aspects of the pre-1981 system persist?

2. From *Kennedy Temporaries* and this article, how much do you think a lawyer in Maryland who has regular work with the federal procurement system and occasional contact with the Maryland procurement system can handle Maryland state procurement matters? How much do you think a lawyer in California with the same regular work with the federal procurement system and occasional contact with non-Maryland procurement systems can handle Maryland state procurement matters?

3. How "neutral" are the trends in state procurement, such as greater parallelism to the federal system and to the system in other states, and greater codification and regularization? Focus on the aspect that some of these trends encourage non-local vendors to find it easier to compete for state contracts. Consider how these trends fit with powerful trends in the private commercial realm toward reducing other state barriers to a uniform national market (e.g., the shift from statewide banking to nationwide banking) and beyond that, to a global market. Sometimes the nationalization and globalization trends are considered to reduce the power of localities to run their own lives, as when locally-oriented businesses are replaced by national and multinational ones. When a state changes its procurement system to make it more open to non-local vendors, does it "gain" like consumers who get benefits from global vendor competition, or does it "lose" like sovereigns who surrender one of their great powers, the power to promote local values through locally-oriented procurement?

Chapter 2

Sealed Bids and Competitive Proposals

"It gives me great confidence to know that I am going into space aboard a shuttle that was built by the low cost contractor." — Senator Jake Garn (R-UT)

The main line of the evolution of formal competition has run through two methods, sealed bids and competitive proposals. Sealed bids held sway during peacetime until after World War II. It still gets some use, both at the federal and state levels, although especially at the federal level much more of formal competition, by dollar volume, occurs by competitive proposals. Competitive proposals increasingly came to predominate as both defense and civilian procurement involved more complex goods and services. Sealed bids mainly deserves study because many of its concepts and procedures serve as a foundation for understanding all acquisition methods. This chapter starts with the aspects best illustrated in the context of sealed bids, before turning to competitive proposals.

By statute, a federal agency is to solicit sealed bids if: (1) there is sufficient time to solicit, receive, and evaluate the sealed bids; (2) award can be made based only on price and price-related factors; (3) it is not necessary to have discussions with the bidders about their bids; and (4) there is a reasonable expectation of receiving more than one sealed bid. Once, sealed bids were the favored method for protecting the integrity of the procurement system. Such protection was needed to avoid the type of cost overruns and insider deal making that made such popular congressional hearing fodder in the mid-1980s and that led to the wholesale change of procurement law and the enactment of the Competition in Contracting Act.

The problematic reality of trying to make good procurement decisions simply on the basis of price makes sealed bids no longer the most common procurement method, especially for large dollar procurements. In a choice between "sealed bids" and "competitive proposals," sealed bids can almost always be awarded in less time due to the almost rote decision of awarding to the low priced bidder. Similarly, the third factor that is to be considered when making the decision to use sealed bids, the need or lack thereof for discussions with potential contractors, is lessening as the government relies more on commercial items that are designed for general use and not specifically designed to meet specific government needs. Likewise, the fourth factor, the possibility of competition is not really a choice between sealed bids and competitive proposals, but more of a choice between contracting with a single source and use of either of the formal competitive methods.

It is the second factor, award based on price and price-related factors, that keeps sealed bidding from being the favored procurement methodology. As required by the mandates of the Competition in Contracting Act, government contracting officials are required, except in limited circumstances when less than full and open competition is permissible, to use competitive proposals when sealed bids are not appropriate. Competitive proposals are used when the government wants to evaluate offers based on non-price related factors such as the technical capability or the quality of the product being offered, in addition to the price.

In the 1990s, the federal procurement system was influenced by the new concept that almost any procurement decision based simply on price alone will result in less than the best deal for the government. Non-price related factors such as past performance have taken on greater importance in award decisions thus forcing government contracting officers to utilize the more discretionary procurement method of competitive prosposals (RFPs).

A. Sealed Bids

Sealed bidding, principally known by the initials "IFB" for "Invitation for Bids," but also known as "formal advertising," has been around since at least the time of the Civil War. It was at that time that government officials decided that collusion and bias among contractors and federal procurement officials could be lessened by attempting to create the ever-desirable "level playing field" and a system of almost mandatory fairness through equal competition.

The requirements of sealed bidding are quite simple. It starts with the government publicizing an invitation to bid to provide a very specific item (hence the term, formal advertising). In order to give each and every prospective bidder an opportunity to compete for the government's business, invitations for bids are to be widely and visibly publicized. Although electronic bulletin boards and electronic commerce are gaining wider use in the government, traditionally the most widely used system for bids contracts of greater value than $25,000 is the *Commerce Business Daily* (CBD) published by the Department of Commerce. Serious government contractors must read the CBD each day in order to track bid opportunities, a process made considerably easier due to its easy availability on the internet and electronic word searches. Furthermore, public notices must give bidders reasonable time to prepare and submit bids, generally considered to be 30 days.

After processing the bids, the government is to award a firm-fixed-price contract for goods or services to the "responsible" contractor submitting a "responsive" bid that will be most advantageous to the government. By doing business with only "responsible" contractors, the government avoids the false economy of awarding a contract to the lowest-priced, but less reliable bidder, only to incur additional costs associated with untimely deliveries, unsatisfactory performance, or ultimately, contract default. In order to be deemed responsible, a potential contractor (and its subcontractors) must: (1) have adequate financial resources to perform the contract; (2) be able to meet with the required delivery or performance schedule; (3) have a satisfactory performance record (although not having any performance record at all cannot disqualify a bidder); and (4) have a satisfactory record of integrity and business ethics. Potential contractors can run afoul of responsibility issues on grounds spanning all their bids by having committed a fraud or similar offense such as embezzlement, theft, forgery, bribery, falsification or destruction of records, tax evasion, or receiving stolen property and thereby having either the company, individuals within the company, or both, "debarred" from doing business with the government.

The concept of submitting a "responsive" bid goes to the heart of achieving fairness and a level playing field among potential contractors. Unlike the method of "competitive proposals" discussed in the next chapter, sealed bids or IFBs require the contractor's proposed bid to meet each and every mandatory and material requirement of the solicitation and specification of the product or service to be provided. By requiring the government to use specifications which do not include restrictive provisions or conditions except to the extent necessary to satisfy the needs of the government, each prospective contractor is able to determine exactly what it is the government wants, and can therefore compete fairly on price and price-related factors alone for the government's business. Governmental discretion to choose a particular brand name item (e.g. Coke or Pepsi) or a particular contractor is eliminated when the sealed bid solicitation states that the government wants to buy a cola soft drink. At the same time, the offer of 7-Up will disqualify a potential bid as not being responsive to the government solicitation requirements.

For further discussion of the subjects in this part, see: Susan L. Turley, *Wielding the Virtual Gavel—DOD Moves Forward With Reverse Auctions*, 173 Mil. L. Rev. 1 (2002); Steven L. Schooner, *Fear of Oversight: The Fundamental Failure of Businesslike* Government, 50 Am. U. L. Rev. 627 (2001); Girard R. Visconti, *Quiet Falls over Public Bid Protest*, 46 R.I. B.J. 13 (April, 1998); George M. Coburn, *Unfavorable Past Performance Determinations as De Facto Debarments*, Procurement Law., Summer 1996, at 26; Daniel I. Gordon, *Unbalanced Bids*, 24 Pub. Cont. L.J. 1 (1994); William P. Rudland, *Rationalizing the Bid Mistake Rules*, 16 Pub. Cont. L.J. 446 (1987); Colleen A. Preston, *Evaluating Bids Against Cost Limitations*, 15 Pub. Cont. L.J. 463 (1985); Alfred A. Gray, *Responsiveness Versus Responsibility: Policy and Practice in Government Contracts*, 7 Pub. Cont. L.J. 46 (1974).

1. Responsiveness

The issue of responsiveness in sealed bidding goes to the heart of the governmental policy of trying to establish a level playing field for all would-be government contractors. Where price is the only factor to be considered, all other elements of the procurement must be identical in order to give each competitor the very same chance of doing business with the government. This is true whether the government is buying items or, as the following case demonstrates, when the government is selling an item.

Maintaining the requirement that all bidders are on an equal footing also goes a long way in eliminating potential fraudulent activity on the part of either government officials, contractors, or both. Consider the consequences in the following case had one bidder been privately "advised" by a government official that the government would accept contract terms more favorable to the bidder than set forth in the solicitation. Similarly, consider the consequences if a bidder, unsure of the volatility of the marketplace, submitted a bid knowing that she could possibly disavow it simply by adding in a differing term, if the offered price was not consistent with marketplace pricing—in other words, if it turned out not to be a good deal for the contractor.

Toyo Menka Kaisha, Ltd. v. The United States

United States Court of Claims.
597 F.2d 1371. Decided May 16, 1979.

FRIEDMAN, Chief Judge:

This is an action for damages based upon the government's alleged breach of a contract to sell surplus rice to the plaintiff. The contract was awarded through competitive bidding. In a suit by an unsuccessful bidder, the district court held that the contract was invalid and enjoined the government from performing it. The plaintiff has moved for summary judgment, and the government has moved to dismiss the two counts of the petition charging breach of contract. We heard oral argument.

We deny the plaintiff's motion for summary judgment, grant the government's motion, reject as insubstantial a third claim in the petition asserting a taking of plaintiff's property for which just compensation is payable, and dismiss the petition.

I.

The cessation of the Vietnamese War in 1975 found a number of cargoes of American agricultural commodities enroute to Indochina. To prevent these cargoes from being delivered to non-allies, the government seized them under the Foreign Assets Control Regulations. 31 C.F.R. ss 500.101—.809 (1975). Instructions were then issued to the agricultural attaches in the countries where these cargoes were stored to sell them promptly 'as is, where is.' Due to the perishable nature of these cargoes (and possibly from a desire to avoid legal claims from Vietnam), the sale was to occur as quickly as possible.

One of the cargoes so affected was a large quantity of rice, which was deflected to Guam. The agricultural attache in Manila, Glenn Sampson, was designated the contracting officer to sell this rice. Mr. Sampson was not a trained contracting officer but apparently had recently disposed of three other similarly deflected agricultural commodities without incident. The rice was to be sold on a formally advertised basis.

The American Embassy in Manila prepared and circulated an invitation for bids ('invitation') on the rice. The invitation contained a number of detailed 'Terms and Conditions' of sale. It also stated, in conformity with regulations (see 41 C.F.R. §§ 1-2.301, 1-2.404-2, 1-2.405 (1975)), that 'Any oral statement or representation by any representative of the Government, changing or supplementing the Invitation or contract or any Condition thereof, is unauthorized and shall confer no right upon the Bidder or Purchaser,' that modifications which made 'the terms of the otherwise successful bid more favorable to the Government will be considered at any time (they are) received prior to award and may be accepted,' and that the contract would be awarded 'to that responsible Bidder whose bid conforming to the Invitation' was most advantageous to the government.

When those bids were opened on October 8, 1975, plaintiff Toyo Menka Kaisha, Ltd.'s bid of $273,600 was highest, and the bid of $222,163 by Ambyth, Inc., was next highest. There is no dispute that Ambyth's bid conformed to the invitation; Toyo's bid, however, contained a number of conditions that varied from the invitation, and these variations led to the present dispute.

    A. The invitation provided that the purchaser 'must make all arrangements necessary for packing, removal and transportation of property,' must load the property and must remove the property within 10 working days after the award. If further stated that the government would furnish '(n)o assistance' in loading. Toyo's bid, however, was conditioned upon (1) the government's arranging transportation (known as 'fobbing') of the rice between the warehouse and the vessel Toyo would provide; (2) if the vessel were berthed in front of the naval warehouse, Toyo would pay the fobbing charges, which should be less than $5 per metric ton; (3) if the vessel were berthed at the more distant commercial port, Toyo would pay the actual fobbing charges of not more than $20.94 per metric ton; and (4) the government would pay the carrying charges, including any interest to November 20, 1975, with shipment to occur between October 20 and November 20.

B. The invitation stated that the rice was offered for sale 'as is' and 'where is,' and that 'the Government makes no warranty, express or implied, as to…its fitness for any use or purpose.' Toyo's bid provided: (1) the government was to guarantee that the rice was 'surely for human consumption'; (2) the government was to assume the risk of rejection or other claim by 'customs or other authorities' in Hong Kong, where Toyo planned to sell the rice; (3) Toyo's bid covered only 'clean and sound bagged rice' and not 'stained and/or cover tone (sic) bagged rice and/or bags for sweeping rice at warehouse or open yard up to the vessel'; and (4) the government was to bear the risk of any damage to the rice between its removal from the warehouse and its stowage on the vessel (though the invitation stated the price was to be 'FOB warehouse Guam').

C. The invitation stated that the purchaser 'shall pay all customs, duties, taxes and similar charges which may be levied by respective governments' against the purchaser and that the government would 'not be liable for taxes, duties or other assessments imposed by any government…on any property transferred under this contract.' Toyo's bid required the government to pay any export taxes or duties on the rice.

On the day the bids were opened, the contracting officer informed the Foreign Agricultural Service in Washington by Telex that Toyo had qualified its bid, and requested permission to accept the next highest bid if these qualifications could not be satisfactorily negotiated. The next day, October 9, the contracting officer sent a further telex to Washington which detailed every qualification in Toyo's bid, advised that Ambyth probably would protest if the contract were awarded to Toyo, and requested advice on how to proceed. Washington responded to the first telex (which did not detail Toyo's conditions) the following day, October 10. It directed the contracting officer to 'make best effort to resolve problems (with Toyo) while remaining consistent with 'as is, whee (sic) is' and other IFB terms' but 'if unable to complete Toyo Menka's sale, next high bid acceptable to FAS/W if did conforms to IFB.'

Following negotiations between the contracting officer or his assistant and Toyo, the latter agreed to drop those conditions to which the contracting officer objected. The Navy then indicated it wanted three new conditions in the contract: (1) the quantity of rice to be sold was to be increased from 1,800 tons to about 2,000 tons; (2) Toyo must pay in advance the charges for moving the rice from the warehouse to onboard the vessel; and (3) the rice was to be moved on the naval base by the Navy's forwarder (which was similar, if not identical, to one of Toyo's original conditions, supra). Further negotiations ensued. Toyo agreed to these changes, but insisted that its liability for the cost of loading the rice onboard the vessel be limited to $5 per metric ton regardless of from which port the rice was loaded. (The district court found the cost of loading the rice would be $8.50 per metric ton at the naval pier and $34.41 per metric ton at the commercial port.)

On October 14, when all the disagreements had been resolved, the contracting officer advised Toyo's representative that he would not sign the contract until October 16. That representative nevertheless advised Toyo's home office on October 14 that final agreement had been reached. On the next day, but before the signing of the contract, Toyo signed an agreement to sell the rice to a Hong Kong buyer. On October 16, the contracting officer executed the contract in two steps: first he signed the purchase confirmation provided by Toyo, and later in the afternoon he signed the remaining contract documents. Prior to the signing of the latter, Ambyth told the contracting officer that it would file suit to void the contract with Toyo. Toyo claims it never knew of this impending suit.

Later on the same day (October 16), but after the contract had been signed, the contracting officer received from Washington a reply to the October 9 telex, which had detailed Toyo's original conditions and had warned of Ambyth's possible legal action. The reply stated: 'Since Toyo Menka, the highest bidder, offered to buy subject rice with qualifications contrary to tender terms, you are hereby authorized to award the contract to the next highest bidder within the tender terms.'

The contract signed on October 16 contained the following conditions that varied from the invitation: (1) the government was to pay all fobbing charges above $5 per ton; (2) Toyo's bid covered only clean and sound bagged rice; (3) the government was to state that the rice was fit for human consumption; (4) the government was to pay any export taxes or duties on the rice at Guam; (5) the Navy's forwarder was to be used if the vessel to carry the rice were berthed at the naval pier—otherwise a private forwarder would be used.

Following the October 16 signing, Toyo signed a charter contract for a ship to carry the rice from Guam to Hong Kong.

On October 20, Ambyth filed suit in the United States District Court for the Territory of Guam to void the award of the contract to Toyo. It named as defendant only the United States. Although Toyo's officer in charge of completing the contract voluntarily testified in the district court proceeding, neither the parties nor the court sought to make Toyo a party, and Toyo did not attempt to intervene.

After a trial on October 22 and 23, the district court held that Toyo's bid did not conform to the terms, conditions and specifications in the invitation and should have been rejected as nonresponsive. The court determined that the contract with Toyo was null and void ab initio, permanently enjoined the government from performing the contract and ordered that another invitation for bids be issued and that the rice be properly sold.

After new bids were submitted, the rice was resold on November 10 to Toyo for $403,000, which was $129,400 more than the price under the original contract.

In the present suit Toyo seeks damages based upon the government's alleged breach of either the contract signed on October 16 or a contract implied-in-fact that resulted from the course of dealings between Toyo and the government.

II.

The parties have argued at length a number of contentions. The government's basic contention is that this suit constitutes an impermissible collateral attack upon the judgment of the District Court for Guam that held that contract null and void. Toyo responds that it is not bound by that judgment because it was not a party to that suit, and that because of Toyo's absence from the case, the district court lacked jurisdiction to determine the validity of the contract. On the merits, Toyo claims that its bid substantially conformed to the invitation, so that a valid contract resulted; and that in any event the government is estopped from asserting the invalidity of the contract. Alternatively, it argues that if the original contract was invalid, it may recover on a theory of quantum meruit based upon an implied-in-fact contract.

We find it unnecessary to resolve most of these contentions since we conclude (1) that the contracting officer had no authority to enter into the original contract because Toyo's bid was not responsive to the invitation, and (2) that since none of the expenditures Toyo made in anticipation of performing the original contract conferred in any benefits upon the United States, Toyo cannot recover in quantum meruit.

III.

Where a government contract is awarded under competitive bidding, 'deviations (from advertised specifications) may be waived by the contracting officer provided they do not go to the substance of the bid or work an injustice to other bidders. A substantial deviation is defined as one which affects either the price, quantity, or quality of the article offered.' Prestex Inc. v. United States, 320 F.2d 367, 372, 162 Ct.Cl. 620, 627 (1963) (footnote omitted). See also Mid-West Construction, Ltd. v. United States, 387 F.2d 957, 961, 181 Ct.Cl. 774, 781 (1967); Albano Cleaners, Inc. v. United States, 455 F.2d 556, 559, 197 Ct.Cl. 450, 455 (1972). Cf. United States v. Ellicott, 223 U.S. 524, 32 S.Ct. 334, 56 L.Ed. 535 (1912). Federal Procurement Regulations incorporate these principles.[1]

In terms, these regulations apply to procurement rather than to disposal of property, which the present case involves. The general government regulations covering the disposal of personal property provide that except for negotiated sales 'property shall be sold by competitive bid sale after advertising.§ 41 C.F.R. s 101— 45.304 —1 (1975). Since the Federal Procurement Regulations reflect fundamental policies regarding the letting of government contracts involving personal property, it is appropriate to draw upon them in determining the governing requirements when government property is 'sold by competitive bid sale after advertising,' as was done in this case.

When the issue of the 'responsiveness of the accepted bid arises after the award, the court should ordinarily impose the binding stamp of nullity only when the illegality is plain' and should 'uphold the award unless its invalidity is clear.' John Reiner & Co. v.

---

1. Those regulations specify the standards for determining whether a bid should be rejected because of substantial deviation from the terms of the invitation for bids. Section 1—2.404—2(a), set forth in 41 C.F.R., provides that '(a)ny bid which fails to conform to the essential requirements of the invitation for bids, such as specifications, delivery schedule, or permissible alternates thereto, shall be rejected as nonresponsive.' It states that '(o)rdinarily, a bid shall be rejected where the bidder imposes conditions which would modify requirements of the invitation for bids or limit his liability to the Government so as to give him an advantage over other bidders.' It also states that a low bidder may be requested to delete from its bid objectionable conditions that 'do not go to the substance, as distinguished from the form of the bid,' and that a condition goes to the substance of the bid 'where it affects price, quantity, quality, or delivery of the items offered. § 41 C.F.R. 1—2.404— 2(b) (1975). Section 1—2.405 permits the disregarding of 'minor informalities or irregularities,' which are those the 'significance (of which) as to price, quantity, quality, or delivery is trivial or negligence when contrasted with the total cost or scope of the supplies or services being procured.' It gives as examples of such defects the bidder's failure to return the appropriate number of copies of his bid, or his failure to furnish required information concerning the number of his employees. 41 C.F.R. s 1—2.405 (1975).

United States, 325 F.2d 438, 440, 163 Ct.Cl. 381, 386, 387 (1963), cert. denied 377 U.S. 931, 84 S.Ct. 1332, 12 L.Ed.2d 295 (1964) (footnote omitted). On the other hand, the government

> may disclaim a contract on the ground of voidness ab initio because of the nonresponsiveness of the bid. Where a public contract is to be let pursuant to formal advertising, the strictures upon defendant's contracting agent are such 'that the contract awarded must be the contract advertised and * * * if it is not, the Government is not bound, since defendant's contracting agent could not bind the Government beyond his actual authority.§ Prestex Inc. v. United States, 320 F.2d 367, 371, 162 Ct.Cl. 620, 625 (1963).

Albano Cleaners, Inc. v. United States, supra, 455 F.2d at 559, 197 Ct.Cl. at 455. In these circumstances 'the Government is not estopped to deny the limitations on (the contracting officer's) authority, even though the private contractor may have relied on the contracting officer's apparent authority to his detriment, for the contractor is charged with notice of all statutory and regulatory limitations.§ Prestex Inc. v. United States, supra, 320 F.2d at 371, 162 Ct.Cl. at 625 (footnotes omitted).

These principles rest upon and effectuate important public policies. 'Rejection of irresponsive bids is necessary if the purposes of formal advertising are to be attained, that is, to give everyone an equal right to compete for Government business, to secure fair prices, and to prevent fraud.' Prestex Inc. v. United States, supra, 320 F.2d at 372, 162 Ct.Cl. at 626 (footnote omitted). The requirement that a bid be responsive is designed to avoid unfairness to other contractors who submitted a sealed bid on the understanding that they must comply with all of the specifications and conditions in the invitation for bids, and who could have made a better proposal if they imposed conditions upon or variances from the contractual terms the government had specified. The rule also avoids placing the contracting officer in the difficult position of having to balance the more favorable offer of the deviating bidder against the disadvantages to the government from the qualifications and conditions the bidder has added.

* * *

Responsiveness is determined by reference to the bids when they are opened and not by reference to subsequent changes in a bid. Id. at 261. Allowing a bidder to modify a nonresponsive bid when, upon opening the bids, it appears that the variations will preclude an award, would permit the very kind of bid manipulation and negotiation that the rule is designed to prevent. Otherwise bidders would be encouraged to submit nonresponsive bids on terms favorable to the government but subject to certain conditions, in the hope that if their bids were the top ones, they could then negotiate about and retain some of their proposed changes. In this way they could obtain a contract that they could not have received had they complied with the specification in the invitation for bids.

We therefore conclude that if Toyo's original bid deviated so substantially from the invitation with respect to price, quantity or quality that it materially changed the terms of the government's offer, the contracting officer had no authority to award the contract to Toyo but should immediately have rejected it as nonresponsive. As we now show, Toyo's bid contained these fatal flaws.

b. The conditions Toyo attached to its bid made such significant changes in price, quantity and quality, to the prejudice of the other bidders, that the bid was nonresponsive, and the ensuing contract therefore was void.

1. Price.

(a) Although the invitation stated that the purchaser was responsible for removing, loading and transporting the rice, Toyo's bid provided that it would pay no more than $5 per ton for fobbing charges if the rice were loaded from the naval pier, and no more than $20.94 in loading charges if the rice were loaded from a commercial pier. The district court found that the cost of loading rice at the commercial pier would be $34.41 per ton. The effect to Toyo's condition was that if the rice were loaded from a commercial pier, Toyo's expenses would have been about $28,300 less than those of the completing bidders.

* * *

(b) Toyo required the government to pay all export taxes and duties on the rice at Guam. The invitation, however, stated that the purchaser, not the government, would pay 'all customs, duties, taxes, and similar charges....'

2. Quality and Quantity.

We consider these two factors together since the requirements Toyo imposed with respect to quality also affected the quantity of rice the contract would cover.

The invitation provided that the rice would be sold 'as is' and that the government made no warranty concerning 'its fitness for any use or purpose.' Toyo's bid, however, required the government to guarantee that the rice was fit for human consumption and to assume the risks that the rice might be rejected by Hong Kong authorities. Moreover, the bid covered only 'clean and sound bagged rice.' * * *

C. As noted (supra p. 9), the responsiveness of a bid is determined when the bids are opened and not on the basis of subsequent changes made in the bid before the contract is signed. In the present case, however, even if responsiveness were judged in the light of the changes made in the contract as executed, the bid as thus amended still would be unresponsive. We have pointed out (supra pp. 5—6) that the contract signed on October 16 contained five material variations from the invitation. These deviations largely followed the conditions Toyo originally had imposed.

D. The government's own actions in this case confirm that Toyo's bid was not responsive. The contracting officer's first message to Washington merely stated that Toyo had qualified its bid and requested authority to accept the next highest bid if these qualifications could not be negotiated. Washington agreed to such negotiations, provided that any sale to Toyo would be 'consistent with' the 'as is' provision and other terms of the invitation. * * *

The day after the bids were opened, the contracting officer furnished the details of Toyo's conditions to Washington. A week later, Washington responded that because Toyo's bid contained 'qualifications contrary to tender terms,' the contracting officer could award the contract to the next highest bidder. Although this latter response was received by the contracting officer only after he had signed a contract (but on the same day), it reflects the government's own recognition that the conditions Toyo had imposed constituted sufficiently substantial deviations from the invitation to make Toyo's bid nonresponsive.

IV.

A. Alternatively, Toyo contends that if the contract was invalid, it may recover for breach of a contract implied-in-fact. It argues that it is entitled to damages measured by the additional amount the government received when the rice was resold or, at least, the amount Toyo expended in anticipation of performing the original contract.

The problem with Toyo's argument on this branch of the case is that because the contracting officer had no authority to enter into the contract on the terms Toyo demanded, there was no implied-in-fact contract. None of the expenses that Toyo incurred after it signed the first contract on October 16 in anticipation of performing it were for goods or service that inured to the benefit of the government. The government gained nothing as a result of Toyo's arranging for a ship to transport the rice to Hong Kong, its signing of a contract to sell the rice there, or any incidental expenses Toyo may have incurred in making those arrangements.

Nor was Toyo responsible for the additional amount the government received upon the second sale of the rice. The second sale resulted not from anything Toyo did but from the successful lawsuit Ambyth brought to enjoin performance of the original contract. Although the end result of that suit was an increase of $129,400 in the amount the government obtained upon sale of the rice, Toyo did nothing that would entitle it rather than the government to that amount.

B. Finally, Toyo contends that the cancellation of the original contract by the district court constituted a taking of its property by the government for which it is entitled to just compensation. Since the property that Toyo asserts was taken was its interest in the contract, our holding that the contract was invalid eliminates the basis for that claim.

Plaintiff's motion for summary judgment is denied, the defendant's motion to dismiss is granted, and the petition is dismissed.

Notes and Questions

1. The concept of responsiveness directly relates to trying to eliminate any prejudice against any particular bidder. The FAR speaks to bids complying in all "material respects" (FAR 14.301(a)) and "essential requirements" (FAR 14.404-2) of invitations for bids. Substantial deviations in proposed contract terms relating to price, quantity, or quality are considered to be the most likely to result in prejudice to other bidders. Is the variation of *any* contract term always going to result in prejudice to other bidders? For example, if one bidder proposes a different delivery date than the one called for in the solicitation, does that result in prejudice? Does it matter whether the delivery date is sooner or later than the solicitation proposed date?

2. Is the government willing to pay a premium in support of its policy of a level playing field? Is there ever an instance where a particular deal is so good that the government would be foolish to pass it up notwithstanding the fact that it violates procurement policies and requirements? Conversely, does fairness dictate that the government must always award a contract to the responsible bidder offering the lowest price? What should be the result if the lowest offered price is unreasonably high? Who is responsible for making such a determination?

3. What would have been the result if Toyo had been allowed to amend its bid after opening in order to delete the differing provisions? Would such action encourage bidders to vary the terms of sealed bids in order to be able to decide, after public opening, whether to accept the government contract or not?

4. Toyo's claim for quantum meruit damages goes to the heart of companies seeking to be made whole when caught in the net of basic government contracting principles

that deny them the benefit of what should have been the bargain. Should the government compensate bidders that act in good faith on the promises made by government contracting officials, even when those promises are later determined to be improper? Can bidders ever protect themselves?

5. Notice the government remedy in this instance. It was not to recognize the mistake and then award to the properly responsive bidder who had gone to the expense of filing and litigating a bid protest. Rather, the government gave all parties the opportunity to rebid including Toyo, the party that had engaged in improper action to begin with, and thereby reaped the benefit of its mistake in the form of higher prices for the rice it was selling. Should government contracting officials have unbridled discretion in the remedy they select to fix improper action? What about the bidder that properly brings to light the improper government action—what benefit does it reap? Is the integrity of the overall procurement system more important than fairness to a single bidder in a particular instance? Can both goals be served?

6. How could this dispute have been avoided all together? Should there be an opportunity for prospective bidders to ask questions and seek clarifications of solicitation terms prior to submitting bids? Should answers to such questions and clarifications be made available to all bidders?

7. Unbalanced bids. An unbalanced bid consists, in essence, of a bid that seems deceptively low because its structure might let the bidder benefit from high charges on some items without the government ultimately benefitting from low charges on other items. Scrutiny of a possibly unbalanced bid may particularly occur for proposals involving high start-up costs for the government. While some of these may legitimately be line item expenses in the base term of the contract, others may simply be front-loading the profits of a multi-year contract, anticipating that subsequent years will not occur quite as predicted. The crux of the analysis in evaluating bids which include below-cost items is whether other line items are overpriced in relation to cost. If there are no such items, the bid cannot be deemed mathematically unbalanced.

In the event that a line item is found to be overpriced, the second step of the analysis is to determine whether "...there is a reasonable doubt that the bid will result in the lowest overall cost to the Government even though it may be the low evaluated bid, or if it is so unbalanced as to be tantamount to allowing an advance payment." (FAR§52.214-(10)(e)(1990)). For a more detailed discussion of this subject, see Daniel I. Gordon, *Unbalanced Bids*, 24 Pub. Con. L.J. 1 (1994); *Matter of General Atronics Corp.*, B-272685, 1996 WL 625079 (C.G.); *Wizards-Movers Elite, Inc.*, B-255753.2 (1994); *Matter of Atlantic Research Corp.*, B-247650 (1992)(protester must indicate overstated prices as basis for conclusion of mathematical unbalancing); *Matter of Earth Engineering and Sciences, Inc.*, B-248219 (1992) (protester must show reasonable doubt that mathematically unbalanced bid will result in lowest overall cost to Government).

2. Responsibility

Unlike commercial counterparts who are free to do business at their own risk and risking their own money with whomever they please, including scoundrels and the like, government contracting officers can do business only with contractors that are deemed to be responsible. Whereas responsiveness concerns *what* gets offered, responsibility concerns *who* offers it. The contracting officer must decide as to a potential awardee whether to make an affirmative determination of responsibility, or, a negative determinations of responsibility. In such a case, the party affected by such a determination clearly has standing and a direct economic interest in maintaining its capability to do business with the government. As a result, such negative determinations are likely to result in disputes and possible litigation. In contrast, it has sometimes been suggested that competitors cannot challenge an affirmative determination of responsibility. The following case shows otherwise.

IMPRESA CONSTRUZIONI GEOM. DOMENICO GARUFI, Plaintiff-Appellant, v. UNITED STATES, Defendant-Appellee.

United States Court of Appeals,
Federal Circuit 238 F.3d 1324 Jan. 3, 2001.

Before NEWMAN, LINN, and DYK, Circuit Judges.

DYK, Circuit Judge.

* * * * [W]e find that a substantial question has been raised concerning the rationality of the contracting officer's responsibility determination. We therefore reverse and remand the case to the Court of Federal Claims to allow a limited deposition of the contracting officer concerning the basis for the responsibility determination so that the Court of Federal Claims can properly review the responsibility determination * * * *

I

This case involves a contract for maintenance, groundskeeping, janitorial, and other services, to be performed at the United States Naval Air Station in Sigonella, Italy. The appellant, Impresa Construzioni Geom. Domenico Garufi ("Garufi"), an unsuccessful bidder, challenged the award of the contract to Joint Venture Conserv ("JVC"). The background of this controversy is as follows:

On August 28, 1998, the Navy issued a Request for Proposals ("RFP") for the services contract at the Sigonella base. Four offerors responded to the solicitation, including Garufi and JVC. JVC is a joint venture composed of three companies: Lara Srl ("Lara"), Impredil Construzioni Srl ("Impredil"), and Coop. Bosco Etneo arl ("Bosco"). It appears that Lara and Impredil had previously performed similar contracts at the Sigonella base. Also, these two companies (Lara and Impredil), at least previously, were controlled by Carmelo La Mastra, while Bosco was controlled by Carmelo La Mastra's brother-in-law, Alfio Bosco.

In a 1997 proceeding, an Italian court, the Court of Catania Third Penal Division, found that Carmelo La Mastra had engaged in bid rigging and was involved in a Mafia organization in connection with previous contracts at the Sigonella base, apparently in the early 1990's. The Italian court found that Carmelo had been involved in intimidating a competitor into withdrawing from a bid for a contract at the Sigonella base, and that "probably in connection with that [same] bid the owner of another firm...was killed." The Italian proceeding was also directed against Salvatore La Mastra and Alfio Bosco, the son and brother-in-law of Carmelo La Mastra. The court found that the seizure of property levied against Carmelo "La Mastra's children" and Bosco "appears to be legitimate" in light of "the free availability of immovable properties and societies registered fictitiously under the name of people close to him" and that such past and future transfers of property "may facilitate the consummation of other similar crimes or may make worse the consequences of the crimes already consummated." As a result of these findings the Court of Catania, in December 1997, placed Lara, Impredil, and Bosco under a receivership run by a legal administrator. The receivership papers gave the legal administrator authority to perform "all the necessary or opportune lawful acts for the management and administration" of the companies.

Shortly thereafter, also in December 1997, Lara and Impredil, with the approval of the legal administrator, conferred signatory power on Salvatore La Mastra, Carmelo La Mastra's son, to negotiate contract changes and sign modifications for various contracts at the Sigonella base.

Furthermore, in May 1998, also after the receivership had been established, Impredil filed registration papers at the Chamber of Commerce, Industry, Handicraft and Agriculture of Catania specifically listing Carmelo La Mastra as a "Company Officer" with the title of "Technical Manager appointed on 25 Jan. 1998" and as a "company signatory" of Impredil. The term "Technical Manager" is not defined in the document nor does the document disclose the job description or amount of control that a technical manager has over the company.

In June 1998, Carmelo La Mastra was indicted by the Anti Mafia District Office in Catania for his involvement in a "Mafia-type association" and for involvement in bid-rigging at the Sigonella base. The record does not disclose the outcome of that proceeding.

All of the events described in the preceding four paragraphs occurred before the 1998 RFP involved here. The RFP for the Sigonella contract, issued on August 28, 1998, stated that the contract would be awarded to the offeror who submitted the proposal that represented the best value to the government. On September 15, 1998, Lara, Impredil, and Bosco formed JVC as a temporary joint venture for the purpose of making a joint bid in response to the RFP. * * * *

Garufi and JVC submitted proposals, along with two other offerors. * * * *

Upon initial evaluation by a technical board and a price board, one of the competitors was eliminated from the competitive range by the contracting officer, leaving appellant Garufi, JVC, and one other bidder. * * * *

Under the Federal Acquisition Regulation ("FAR") the contract could not be awarded to JVC unless JVC was found to be "responsible," including a finding of "a satisfactory record of integrity and business ethics." 48 C.F.R. §9.104-1(d). On March 5, 1999, the contracting officer signed a responsibility determination, noting that JVC had "a satisfactory record of performance, integrity, and business ethics" and is "otherwise qualified and eligible to receive an award under applicable laws and regulations." The contracting officer therefore awarded the contract to JVC on March 5, 1999.

Garufi filed several protests with the General Accounting Office ("GAO"), challenging the Navy's elimination of Garufi from the competitive range and the grant of the contract to JVC. The GAO issued a final decision on June 17, 1999, denying Garufi's protests.

On June 28, 1999, Garufi filed a bid protest suit in the United States Court of Federal Claims pursuant to 28 U.S.C. §1491(b)(1), which grants the Court of Federal Claims jurisdiction over bid protest actions against the government.* * *

Garufi and the government then filed cross-motions for summary judgment. On July 30, 1999, the Court of Federal Claims denied Garufi's motion for summary judgment and granted the government's cross-motion. *Impresa Construzioni Geom. Domenico Garufi v. United States*, 44 Fed. Cl. 540 (1999). * * * *

III

The history of the judicial review of government contracting procurement decisions is both long and complicated. In *Perkins v. Lukens Steel Co.,* 310 U.S. 113, 60 S.Ct. 869, 84 L.Ed. 1108 (1940), the Supreme Court held that private parties lacked standing to challenge a government contract award for violation of procurement law, concluding that Congress enacted procurement laws for the protection of the government, rather than for those contracting with the government. * * * *

However, following the 1946 enactment of the Administrative Procedure Act ("APA"), 5 U.S.C. §§ 551–559, 701–706, the District of Columbia Circuit in 1970 in *Scanwell Laboratories, Inc. v. Shaffer,* 424 F.2d 859 (D. C. Cir.1970), held that in the APA Congress had statutorily changed the rule of *Lukens Steel* and that APA review of the procurement decisions of government agencies and officials was available in district courts. * * * *

Bid protest cases were also brought in the Court of Federal Claims and its predecessor courts, but on a very different theory—that the government made an implied contract with prospective bidders to fairly assess their bids, and that the Court of Federal Claims had jurisdiction under the Tucker Act * * * *

IV

In 1996, Congress passed the ADRA, thereby clarifying the Court of Federal Claims' bid protest jurisdiction. *See* Administrative Dispute Resolution Act of 1996, Pub. L. No. 104-320, § 12, 110 Stat. 3870, 3874-76. The ADRA provides that the Court of Federal Claims and district courts shall have concurrent jurisdiction over bid protest actions, and that the courts "shall review the agency's decision pursuant to the standards set forth in section 706 of title 5" of the APA. 28 U.S.C. § 1491(b)(1), (4). Pursuant to the ADRA, the district courts' jurisdiction over bid protests was to terminate on January 1, 2001, unless extended by Congress, and the Court of Federal Claims was to have exclusive jurisdiction over bid protest actions. *See* ADRA § 12(d).

The legislative history of the ADRA confirms what is obvious on the face of the statute—that the new legislation "applies the Administrative Procedure Act standard of review previously applied by the district courts (5 U.S.C. § 706) to all procurement protest cases in the Court of Federal Claims." H.R. Conf. Rep. No. 104-841, at 10 (1996). Under the ADRA, all bid protest actions under the APA are now reviewed under the standards applied in the *Scanwell* line of cases. * * * *

Under the APA standards that are applied in *Scanwell* line of cases, a bid award may be set aside if either: (1) the procurement official's decision lacked a rational basis; or (2) the procurement procedure involved a violation of regulation or procedure. * * * *

What we have said so far is sufficient to dispose of the government's first argument, i.e., that "absent allegations of fraud or bad faith" by the contracting officer, the responsibility determination of the contracting officer is immune from judicial review. In this connection, the government relies primarily on our predecessor court's decisions in *Keco Indus., Inc. v. United States,* 203 Ct.Cl. 566, 492 F.2d 1200 (Ct.Cl.1974) and *Trilon Educational Corp. v. United States,* 217 Ct.Cl. 266, 578 F.2d 1356, 1358 (Ct.Cl.1978). The government has seriously misread these cases, which impose no such limits. * * * *

VI

We turn now to Garufi's claim that the contracting officer's responsibility determination concerning JVC's "record of integrity and business ethics" violated the APA. Under the Federal Acquisition Regulation, "[n]o purchase or award shall be made unless the contracting officer makes an affirmative determination of responsibility." 48 C.F.R. §9.103(b). In making the responsibility determination, the contracting officer must determine that the contractor has "a satisfactory record of integrity and business ethics." 48 C.F.R. §9.104-1(d). Furthermore, "[i]n the absence of information clearly indicating that the prospective contractor is responsible, the contracting officer shall make a determination of nonresponsibility." 48 C.F.R. §9.103(b). FAR 9.105-2(b) requires that "[d]ocuments and reports supporting a determination of responsibility or nonresponsibility...must be included in the contract file." However, the contracting officer is not required to explain the basis for his responsibility determination, and he has not done so here. Rather, the contracting officer signed the contract thereby making the required determination according to FAR 9.105-2(a) and in conclusory fashion determined that JVC had "a satisfactory record of performance, integrity, and business ethics."

Contracting officers are "generally given wide discretion" in making responsibility determinations and in determining the amount of information that is required to make a responsibility determination. *John C. Grimberg Co. v. United States*, 185 F.3d 1297, 1303 (Fed. Cir.1999). But this discretion is not absolute.

Unfortunately, the regulations concerning responsibility determinations are cryptic, but this court in *Trilon*, 578 F.2d at 1360, and the Comptroller General have recognized that we may look to the more extensive debarment regulations for guidance, at least on questions related to the "integrity and business ethics" requirement. *See, e.g., Steptoe & Johnson*, Comp. Gen. Dec. B-166118, 1969 WL 4287, at *5 (Mar. 28, 1969); *Secretary of the Army*, 39 Comp. Gen. 868, 872, 1960 WL 1741 (1960).

In this case, Garufi alleges that the contracting officer's responsibility determination is arbitrary because JVC does not fulfill the "satisfactory record of integrity and business ethics" requirement of FAR 9.104-1(d). This is said to be so because of the alleged involvement of Carmelo La Mastra and his relatives in JVC, and the findings of the Italian court in 1997 that Carmelo La Mastra engaged in criminal activities with respect to earlier contracts at the Sigonella base.

Two relevant propositions are established by earlier cases and supported by the debarment regulations. First, past criminal activities by a corporate officer do not automatically establish that the bidder fails the responsibility requirement. * * * * The regulations make clear that "the existence of a cause for debarment, however, does not necessarily require that the contractor be debarred," and directs the agency official to balance the seriousness of the contractor's actions against the "remedial measures or mitigating factors" before making any debarment decision. 48 C.F.R. §9.406-1(a).

The government urges that similarly, past improper actions by the former principal owner and head of two of JVC's components does not mandate a finding of non-responsibility of JVC. In view of the seriousness of the offenses found by the Italian court to have been committed by Carmelo La Mastra and his relatives, his and his relatives' central past role in the companies comprising JVC, and the direct relationship between these offenses and the predecessor government contracts at the Sigonella base, the government would be hard pressed to support a responsibility finding with respect to JVC save for the court-appointed Italian receivership. However, the debarment regulations specifically recognize that a "bona fide change in ownership or management" may result in a reduction in the scope or period of debarment, 48 C.F.R. §9.406-4(c)(3), and the District of Columbia Circuit has similarly recognized that an effective receivership may make debarment inappropriate. *Robinson v. Cheney*, 876 F.2d 152, 160 (D. C.

Cir.1989). The government here urges that the Italian receivership eliminated the control of Carmelo La Mastra and his relatives over JVC, making it appropriate to find JVC responsible.

This leads, however, to a second proposition: the creation of a receivership does not necessarily achieve a change in control or require a finding that the contractor in receivership is responsible.

Here the government points out that the administrator is empowered to "represent and run the joint venture without any limitations or exceptions." The government urges that Carmelo La Mastra and his relatives accordingly no longer control JVC, and therefore any misconduct by them should not be imputed to the company.

The appellant denies that the appointment of the legal administrator divested Carmelo La Mastra and his relatives of control over the company. Appellant notes that the record before the contracting officer showed that, after the appointment of the administrator, Carmelo's son Salvatore was given signatory power over the contracts previously held by Lara and Impredil at Sigonella, as well as the power to negotiate contract changes and modifications. The debarment regulations themselves recognize the relevance of family connections. 48 C.F.R. §9.403. Furthermore, Carmelo himself was appointed technical manager of Impredil, one of the component companies of JVC, and was listed as a company signatory of Impredil.

The appellant relies on *Robinson*, 876 F.2d at 160–61, for the proposition that the appointment of a receivership, by itself, is not necessarily sufficient to establish a company's present responsibility and cleanse the company of the consequences of past improper conduct. In *Robinson*, the owner of a military clothing supply company, fearing debarment for bribing government officials, transferred his company to a trust (naming himself as beneficiary) in order to avoid his company being debarred by the government for his past actions, which allegedly included bid rigging. Despite the trust arrangement, the government initiated debarment proceedings against the supply company "based upon 'information…indicating that [the supply company] lacks the business integrity and present responsibility to be a Government contractor.'" *Id.* at 155. The government then debarred the company, finding that the existence of the trust agreement failed to adequately screen the company from the former owner's (and now beneficiary's) acts of bid rigging, and that his actions therefore affected the company's responsibility. *See id.* at 157. The trustee challenged the debarment proceedings and the findings of non-responsibility in light of the trust agreement.

The court in *Robinson* sustained the debarment. The court acknowledged that the "ultimate inquiry as to 'present responsibility' relates directly to the contractor itself, not to the agent or former agent personally responsible for its past misdeeds. Thus, the contractor can meet the test of present responsibility by demonstrating that it has taken steps to ensure that the wrongful acts will not recur." *Id.* at 160. Although the trust agreement in *Robinson* gave ultimate decision-making authority to someone other than the wrongdoer, who was accused of bid rigging, the court nevertheless held that the trust agreement on its face was not sufficient to assure that the wrongdoer would "not continue to act improperly in [the company's] interest." *See id.* at 161. Particularly important was the absence in the trust agreement of specific terms barring the wrongdoer from acting on behalf of the company or participating in its management. *See id.* at 160. Furthermore, "nothing in either the trust agreement or in any other submission by the company gave the Government any assurance that [the wrongdoer] would not conduct illicit dealing on behalf of [the company] entirely outside company channels." *Id.*

This case is similar to *Robinson* in that the receivership agreement does not specifically bar Carmelo La Mastra from acting on behalf of or participating in the management of JVC. Indeed, as previously discussed, official papers filed by Impredil specifically list Carmelo La Mastra as a "technical manager" with signatory authority. It is noticeably unclear from the record what type of control or influence a "technical manager" has over a company. Furthermore, the record shows that prior to the award Carmelo La Mastra's son Salvatore La Mastra was given signatory authority to act on behalf of Impredil and Lara.

If this were a debarment proceeding involving government debarment of JVC, where the burden rests on the debarred company to show that it has taken steps to ensure that the wrongful acts will not recur, *see id.* at 160, we would follow *Robinson* and hold that the record does not establish the effectiveness of the receivership to insulate Carmelo La Mastra from control of JVC. But this is not a debarment proceeding, and the burden of establishing arbitrary and capricious action rests on the disappointed bidder. *See* 5 U.S.C. § 706. * * * *

This conundrum leads us into a most difficult and confusing area of administrative law, namely the circumstances under which an administrative agency will be compelled to provide an explanation for its decision. * * * *

Contracting officers are not obligated by the APA to provide written explanations for their actions. Decisions by contracting officers are not adjudicatory decisions to be made on the record after a hearing. *See John C. Grimberg Co. v. United States,* 185 F.3d at 1303. Nor are they formal rulemakings. As the government correctly points out, where the contracting officer makes a determination of responsibility, as opposed to the situation in which he makes a determination of non-responsibility, the regulations do not require the contracting officer to "make, sign and place in the contract file a determination of" responsibility which states the basis for the determination. 48 C.F.R. § 9.105-2(a).

However, under the APA even where an explanation or reason is not required, a reviewing court has power to require an explanation. * * *

Based on the evidence of the Italian court proceedings, the Impredil filing at the Chamber of Commerce listing Carmelo La Mastra as a technical manager and company signatory, and the letters granting Salvatore La Mastra signatory authority of Lara and Impredil, which the parties agreed were all before the contracting officer, we conclude that this is one of those rare cases in which an explanation is required. * * *

In ordering the deposition of the contracting officer, we wish to make clear that we are not ordering a deposition into the contracting officer's mental process, that is, the thought process by which he made his decision. Such inquiries are inappropriate. *See, e.g., United States v. Morgan,* 313 U.S. 409, 422, 61 S.Ct. 999, 85 L.Ed. 1429 (1941). The deposition is to be confined strictly to placing on the record the basis for the contracting officer's responsibility determination, that is, his grounds for concluding that JVC had a "satisfactory record of performance, integrity, and business ethics," including most particularly his assessment of the control issue. In order to answer the question of whether there was a lack of rational basis for the contracting officer's decision, we must know: (1) whether the contracting officer, as required by 48 C.F.R. § 9.105-1(a), possessed or obtained information sufficient to decide the integrity and business ethics issue, including the issue of control, before making a determination of responsibility; and (2) on what basis he made the responsibility determination. * * * *

This is a most unusual case. Upon remand, the scope of discovery and the review of the contracting decision are to be appropriately limited in scope.

CONCLUSION

For the reasons stated above, we affirm the Court of Federal Claims' decision in part, and reverse and remand in part.

AFFIRMED-IN-PART, REVERSED-IN-PART, AND REMANDED.

Notes and Questions

1. In *Garufi*, the responsibility issue arises in the unusual way that a competing offeror challenges the responsibility of the awardee. Why does the government object to judicial review of responsibility determinations, particularly in the context of competitor protests? What would make a contracting officer's responsibility determination differ from her other determinations such as regarding the responsiveness of a contractor's bid, or evaluating a proposal?

2. How is a finding of lack of responsibility for a single procurement different from a total debarment from doing business with the government in all instances? Note how the *Garufi* opinion distinguishes nonresponsibility from debarment in terms of the government's burden and the appropriate levels of requisite contracting officer explanation. Why? See Steven W. Feldman, The *Impresa* Decision: Providing the Correct Standard of Review for Affirmative Responsibility Determinations, The Procurement Lawyer, Winter 2001, at 5.

3. In *Garufi*, the offeror whose responsibility is in question is an enterprises in which an individual plays a role who personally has an unsatisfactory record. Much of the issue is whether the enterprise is run in a way that should relieve it from that individual's record. Consider this in forward business planning terms, as well as how it is presented in these cases, of subsequent litigation defense. How much can counsel for an enterprise that will seek government contracts deal with past bad records by purely formal steps, and how much must an enterprise actually and substantively purge itself of links to such past records?

4. The regulations on responsibility are found at FAR 9.104. These cover a diverse range of issues. For example, in recent years, the criterion of satisfactory past performance of previous government contracts has increased in importance as a component of determination of responsibility. Current regulations mandate a negative presumption regarding would-be awardees who have recently defaulted on other contracts, and direct contract officers to examine "[p]ast failure to apply sufficient tenacity and perseverance," which is specified as "strong evidence of nonresponsibility." See FAR 9.104(3)(b); *Matter of Information Resources Incorporated*, B-271767 (1996); *Matter of North American Construction Corp.*, B-270085 (1996)(contractor characterized as "change order artist" by one of its references.); *Matter of Shepard Printing*, B-260362 (1995).

5. Bankrupt offerors. The Government can find that a contractor lacks responsibility because of lack of financial ability to perform the contract (FAR 9.104-1(a)). However, ironically, the bankruptcy statutes preclude the use of this fact as the *sole* basis of a nonresponsibility determination. See, e.g., *Matter of: Harvard Interiors Manufacturing Co.*, B-247400 (1992).

2. Process

CAROTHERS CONSTRUCTION INC., Plaintiff,
v. The UNITED STATES, Defendant,
Barron Construction Company, Intervenor.

United States Claims Court. Nov. 29, 1989 18 Cl. Ct. 745

FUTEY, Judge.

This pre-award contract action is before the court on defendant's motion for summary judgment and plaintiff's cross-motion for injunctive and declaratory relief. This action originally came before the court on plaintiff's motion filed on October 18, 1989, requesting that the Department of the Navy be enjoined from awarding a contract to Barron Construction Company to construct an Aviation Support Equipment Training Facility at the Naval Air Station in Millington, Tennessee. Before the contracting officer decided whether Barron's bid was responsive, plaintiff filed a protest with the General Accounting Office which alleged that Barron's bid was untimely submitted and therefore non-responsive. The General Accounting Office issued a recommendation which concluded that the bid was responsive and the Navy announced that it will adopt the General Accounting Office's recommendation. Plaintiff asserts, inter alia, that Barron's bid was not timely submitted and a determination to the contrary violates Federal procurement practices and the government's obligation to consider Carothers Construction Inc.'s bid fairly and honestly. For the reasons stated hereinafter, defendant's motion for summary judgment, which requests denial of plaintiff's claim for a permanent injunction of the award of the subject contract to Barron, is granted and plaintiff's cross-motion for injunctive and declaratory relief is denied and its complaint is dismissed.

Factual Background

On February 27, 1989, the Southern Division of the Naval Facilities Engineering Command (Navy) issued a solicitation, No. N62467-84-B-0153 (solicitation) for submission of sealed bids on the construction of an Aviation Support Equipment Training Facility at the Naval Air Station Memphis in Millington, Tennessee. Subsequently, several amendments to the solicitation changed the date and place of the bid opening, which was finally set for 2:00 p.m. on June 1, 1989, in Building S-236, room 116, Naval Air Station, Memphis, Tennessee.

The events at issue occurred in room 116 and principally involve three individuals: Dolores Quinton (Quinton), the bid opening officer for the solicitation, Luke Thoele (Thoele), a contracts specialist, and Allen Townsend (Townsend), a representative of Barron Construction Company (Barron), a contractor which bid on the solicitation. Sometime before 2:00 p.m. on June 1, 1989, Townsend submitted a bid on behalf of Barron (Barron's bid) then several minutes later he retrieved it from Quinton and left the room. Later, he resubmitted Barron's bid with a notation on the outside of the envelope which stated, "DEDUCT $40ooo AL TOWNSEND 1:54 P.M." Quinton took Barron's bid to her immediate supervisor, Richard Johnson, who told her that the attempted modification was ineffective. After being told of this, Townsend again retrieved Barron's bid and immediately left the room. At approximately three minutes before 2:00 p.m., Townsend contacted O.P. Barron, president of Barron, and asked for instruction. O.P. Barron told Townsend to open Barron's bid envelope and deduct $40,000.00. With approximately two minutes to go before bid opening, Townsend removed documents from Barron's bid envelope and wrote on them. At five seconds before 2:00 p.m., Quinton instructed Townsend to "hand me something." Townsend handed Quinton a set of documents with a copy of Barron's bid on top. At 2:00 p.m., Quinton began announcing that the time for receipt of bids had passed. What happened next is contested by the parties. Defendant contends that simultaneously with Quinton's announcement, Townsend threw the rest of the Barron bid documents on the table in front of Quinton. After Quinton finished, Thoele took the documents from Quinton and collected the rest of Barron's bid documents from the table. In contrast, plaintiff avers that up to fifteen seconds after the commencement of Quinton's announcement, Townsend continued to place the remainder of Barron's bid documents in the possession of the government and did not relinquish control of all Barron's bid documents before the 2:00 p.m. bid deadline. The parties agree that nine bids were received and Barron's was found to have submitted the lowest bid, with a bid price of $9,680,000.00 while the second lowest bidder, Carothers Construction Inc. (Carothers) submitted a bid price of $9,822,045.00.

Plaintiff filed a pre-award protest by letter with the Navy contracting officer (CO) on June 5, 1989 * * * After contacting the CO on June 19, 1989, and learning that a decision had not yet been rendered,[1] plaintiff filed on that same day a protest by letter with the General Accounting Office (GAO) which realleged the contentions in the CO protest.

The Navy agency issued a report on July 26, 1989, which addressed plaintiff's arguments, as expressed in its letters to the CO and the GAO, and denied its protest.[3] In response, on August 9, 1989, plaintiff submitted comments on the agency report to the GAO and requested that its protest be sustained because Barron's bid "(i) was not submitted prior to the scheduled time of submission of bids, and/or (ii) failed to include the required bid bond."

The GAO issued a recommendation dated October 11, 1989, which determined that Barron's bid was not submitted late. Relying on the declarations of Quinton, Thoele and Dana Brignole (Brignole), an agency procurement clerk present at the bid opening, the GAO held that "while the manner of the submission of the bid...was irregular, the evidence clearly shows that the Barron representative relinquished control of its bid (including all bid documents) simultaneously with...[Quinton's]...declaration that the time for receipt of bids had passed. Accordingly, we find that Barron's bid was not submitted late."

Plaintiff filed a "Complaint for Declaratory And Injunctive Relief" in this court on October 18, 1989, requesting that the Navy be enjoined from awarding the contract to Barron. The government represented to this court in a telephone conference held on October 19, 1989, that the Navy decided to abide by the recommendation of the GAO, but would not award the contract until November 9, 1989. In addition, on this

---

1. There is no indication in the pleadings that there was a decision by the Contracting Officer (CO); however the parties stated during oral argument that there was a decision which, in essence, ratified Quinton's acceptance of Barron's bid.

3. The report noted that Barron's bid failure to enclose a bid in a sealed envelope as provided by the terms of the invitation is a technicality which can be waived by the CO. Matter of R. Bruce Hoffe, B-153288 (Mar. 19, 1964); see Central Mechanical Construction Inc., B-220594, 85-2 CPD 730 (Dec. 31, 1985); see also FAR § 14.405.

date, Barron gave notice to the court that it would appear in this action and assert its interest.

On October 25, 1989, defendant filed a motion for summary judgment. On October 31, 1989, plaintiff filed a response to defendant's motion for summary judgment and a cross-motion for injunctive and declaratory relief. On November 6, 1989, Barron filed a motion to intervene. Oral argument was held on November 7, 1989.

In the present action, plaintiff asserts that Barron's bid was untimely submitted. Therefore, such an award would violate Federal procurement law, regulations and policies, and constitute a breach of the Navy's contractual obligation to consider plaintiff's bid fairly and honestly.

Discussion

Jurisdiction to review pre-award contract decisions of a government agency is conferred on this court pursuant to 28 U.S.C. § 1491(a)(3) (1982), of the Federal Courts Improvement Act of 1982. United States v. John C. Grimberg Co., 702 F.2d 1362, 1366–72 (Fed. Cir.1983). Section 1491(a)(3) provides:

> To afford complete relief on any contract claim brought before the contract is awarded, the court shall have exclusive jurisdiction to grant declaratory judgments and such equitable and extraordinary relief as it deems proper, including but not limited to injunctive relief. In exercising this jurisdiction, the court shall give due regard to the interests of national defense and national security.

Pre-award contract claims under this statute are founded upon an implied-in-fact contract which arises by virtue of the bid solicitation process which obligates the government to consider offers fairly and honestly. Keco Indus., Inc. v. United States, 192 Ct.Cl. 773, 784, 428 F.2d 1233, 1237 (1970); Heyer Pro. Co. v. United States, 135 Ct.Cl. 63, 69, 140 F. Supp. 409, 413 (1956); Paxson Elec. Co. v. United States, 14 Cl. Ct. 634, 638 (1988). Accordingly, plaintiff's suit is properly before this court.

* * *

The issue before the Claims Court is whether the Navy can justifiably follow the GAO's recommendation that Barron's bid was submitted timely and, therefore, was responsive to solicitation. The dispositive inquiry in deciding that question was a rational one. Honeywell v. United States, 870 F.2d 644, 647 (1989); Hayes Int'l Corp. V. United States, 7 Cl.Ct. 681, 684–85 (1985) (citations omitted); Caddell Const. Co. v. United States, 7 Cl.Ct. 236, 241 (1985) (citations omitted). As subsequently discussed, a rational basis existed.

Recommendations of the GAO are accorded "due weight and deference by this court given the GAO's long experience and special expertise in...bid protest matters." Baird Corp. v. United States, 1 Cl.Ct. 662, 668 (1983) (citations omitted). Because the GAO has such an important role in resolving contested procurement matters, normally the agencies will follow its decisions. Honeywell, 870 F.2d at 647, 648. In addition, Congress intended that procurement agencies would follow the Comptroller General's recommendation, because an agency's failure to follow requires notice to the Comptroller General and an eventual report to Congress. Id. at 648.

* * *

Plaintiff also alleges that the GAO violated procurement statutes and regulations by concluding that Barron's bid was timely. Specifically, the GAO violated FAR § 14.304-1 which provides that bids "received in the office designated in the invitation for bids after the exact time set for opening are 'late bids.'" Plaintiff reads this in conjunction with the solicitation which states that "[a]ny bids submitted by hand after the time set for receipt will not be accepted" and argues that the GAO must reject Barron's bid because there is no evidence that it was submitted at 2:00 p.m., the exact time specified in the solicitation. In addition, plaintiff asserts that the evidence shows that Quinton's announcement was not commenced until after 2:00 p.m. and for that reason the bid was untimely, whether or not it was submitted simultaneously with the announcement.

This court notes that plaintiff's interpretation of FAR § 14.304-1 is unsupported by FAR § 14.402-1 and the GAO decisions which have interpreted both provisions. FAR § 14.402-1(a) provides that "[t]he bid opening officer shall decide when the time set for opening bids has arrived and shall inform those present of that decision." See K. L. Conwell, B-220561, 86-1 CPD § 79 (Jan. 23, 1986). Consistent with that provision is the rule of law applied in the GAO's decision "[t]he bid opening officer's declaration of bid opening time is determinative of lateness unless it is shown to be unreasonable under the circumstances." Chattanooga Office Supply Co., B-228062, 87-2 CPD § 221 (Sept. 3, 1987).

The record before the GAO shows that Quinton made several announcements of the bid opening time prior to the final announcement at 2:00 p.m. Therefore, the GAO concluded, the record shows that Quinton's announcement was reasonable and determinative of lateness. "The time when a bid is submitted is determined by the time that the bidder relinquishes control of the bid." Chestnut Hill Constr., Inc., B-216891, 85-1 CPD § 443 (Apr. 18, 1985). The GAO interpreted this to mean that a bid is late if submitted after the time the contracting or bid opening officer announces that the time set for bid opening has arrived, citing Amfel Constr., Inc., B-233493.2, 89-1 CPD § 477 (May 18, 1989). It was upon this basis that the Comptroller General framed the critical inquiry of when Barron relinquished control of its bid documents in relation to the bid opening officer's declaration that the time for receipt of bids had passed. In finding that the bid was relinquished simultaneously with Quinton's 2:00 p.m. announcement, the GAO also found that the bid was timely under Amfel, because the bid was not submitted after the time of the announcement. In light of the precedent cited and applied by the GAO, this court cannot hold that the GAO's decision was irrational.

The GAO's finding that Townsend relinquished control of Barron's bid (including all bid documents) simultaneously with Quinton's announcement that the time for receipt of bids had passed had ample support in the record. The GAO based its finding on the unsworn declarations of Quinton, Brignole and Thoele. The Comptroller General focused on the following: Quinton declared that she was watching the clock, and "when the second hand reached the 12 she began to announce that the time for receipt of bids had passed. At that time . . . [Townsend] threw the other copies of the bid (and other bid documents) on the table in front of her." Supporting this was the statement of Brignole that Townsend placed the other bid documents simultaneously with Quinton's announcement. Finally, the Comptroller General noted Thoele's declaration that he picked up the documents on the table. Based on these unsworn declarations, the court finds that a rational basis existed for the GAO's decision.

* * *

Conclusion

For all the above reasons, the court finds that the Comptroller General's decision that Barron's bid was not submitted late had a rational basis and, therefore, the decision to follow the recommendation by the CO was not arbitrary and capricious, and not contrary to the law.

Notes and Questions

1. Take this opinion as a vivid description of the bid opening, that formal peak of the bidding process. This seems to have been a particularly colorful opening. Throw in a few clerical errors and borderline nonresponsive specifications, and this could be a whole exam question. Does the highly structured and formal nature of this process derive from the formality in classic private offer and acceptance, e.g., the well-known formalities at auctions and the "mirror image" rule for acceptances? Or, does it derive from formality in public policy, such as the limits on authority of officials and the imperative to curb favoritism and corruption?

2. Fundamental to the sealed bidding and public opening of bids is the requirement that all bids be received by a date and time certain. Mountains of litigation have ensued from trying to decide acceptable reasons for considering a late bid. For example, is a bid sent by facsimile late when the first page is received prior to the time stated for receipt of bids but the last page is received just minutes afterwards? Or is a bid late when the courier delivering acts as a good Samaritan in an auto accident thereby saving a life but delaying the delivery of the bid beyond the stated time?

3. Why should the government deny itself the benefit of a late bid, especially where the late bid is the most advantageous bid for the government? FAR 14.304-1 provides for very limited circumstances whereby late bids can be considered—all relating to government (including U.S. Postal Service) mishandling of the bid. (See *Matter of C.R. Hipp Construction Co., Inc.*, B-274328, 1996 Wl 669947 (C.G.)(bid received from agency mailroom staff by opening officer after announcement that no more hand-carried bids would be accepted but prior to bid opening was timely); *Matter of Family Stress Clinics of America*, B-270993 (1996)(contract officer's oral amendment extending submission date over duration of government shutdown not communicated to one firm on RFP distribution list); FAR §§14.304-1(a)(1)-(4); 52.214-7). With respect to bid modifications, FAR §52.214-7(2)(f) allows but does not compel consideration of "…a late modification of an otherwise successful bid that makes its terms more favorable to the Government…"

4. For a discussion, see Brian P. Waagner & Elizabeth D. Evans, Agency Discretion in Bid Timeliness Protests: The Case for Consistency, 29 Pub. Cont. L. J. 713 (2000).

McCLURE ELECTRICAL CONSTRUCTORS, INC., Appellant, v. John H. DALTON, Secretary of the Navy, Appellee.

United States Court of Appeals, Federal Circuit.
Dec. 17, 1997 132 F.3d 709

Before NEWMAN, PLAGER, and RADER, Circuit Judges.

RADER, Circuit Judge.

McClure Electrical Constructors, Inc. (McClure Electrical) challenges denial of its claim for contract reformation. McClure Electrical sought contract reformation to correct its unilateral bid mistake. On September 26, 1996, the Armed Services Board of

Contract Appeals (Board) affirmed the contracting officer's final decision not to reform the contract. See McClure Elec. Constructors, Inc., ASBCA No. 49,711, 96-2 BCA § 28,593 (1996). Because the Board did not err in so deciding, this court affirms the Board's decision.

I.

McClure Electrical entered into a contract to build an electrical substation at a naval center in Louisville, Kentucky. Mr. McClure, the company's president, prepared three bid worksheets to determine the bid amount for this project. However, in preparing a recapitulation sheet, Mr. McClure did not transfer the amount from the third bid worksheet and instead twice transferred the amount from the first bid worksheet. Due to this error, McClure Electrical's bid was $16,530 lower than intended.

Due to this error, McClure Electrical's bid was the lowest of the eight entered bids by $28,000. When the contracting officer at the Department of the Navy reviewed the bids, she noticed the disparity between McClure Electrical's $145,000 bid and the Government estimate of $282,869. Suspecting a possible error and wishing to confirm the apparent low bid, the contracting officer sent a bid verification request to McClure Electrical. The letter did not state explicitly the contracting officer's suspicion of a possible error. In the relevant portion of that letter, the contracting officer wrote: "[a]s evidenced by the enclosed Abstract of Offers, you are the apparent low bidder. Please review your bid worksheets for possible errors or omissions." The contracting officer enclosed abstracts showing the amount of each bid and the amount of the Government estimate for the project. These amounts were appreciably higher than McClure Electrical's bid.

With the contracting officer's bid verification request and the amounts of each bid in his possession, Mr. McClure reviewed his company's bid and confirmed its accuracy in a letter to the contracting officer. After completion of the project, Mr. McClure's son, vice-president of McClure Electrical, reviewed the project to determine why McClure Electrical had lost money on the contract and discovered the error. McClure Electrical then sought reformation of the contract to increase its price by $19,000—the mistakenly omitted materials costs of $16,530, plus sales tax, overhead, profit, and bond costs. McClure Electrical argued that the Navy's bid verification request was inadequate because the contracting officer did not expressly state her suspicion that McClure Electrical had submitted an erroneous bid. The contracting officer denied relief, and the Board affirmed. McClure Electrical now appeals to this court.

II.

* * * The FAR set forth a process for handling suspected mistakes in bids. 48 C.F.R. §§ 14.406-1, 14.406-3(g) (1992). To determine adequacy of a bid verification request, this court examines de novo the Board's interpretation of the controlling FAR. "Notwithstanding this lack of deference on questions of law, [this court] accord[s] respect to the board's interpretation of regulations that are within its field of expertise: federal procurement law." Ingalls Shipbuilding, Inc. v. Dalton, 119 F.3d 972, 975 (Fed.Cir.1997); see also Erickson Air Crane Co. v. United States, 731 F.2d 810, 814 (Fed.Cir.1984) ("[L]egal interpretations by tribunals having expertise are helpful to us, even if not compelling.").

III.

In Solar Foam Insulation, ASBCA No. 46,921, 94-2 BCA § 26,901 (1994), the Board set out its rules for allowing reformation of a contract due to a contractor's unilateral bid mistake. The contractor must show by clear and convincing evidence that:

(1) a mistake in fact occurred prior to contract award; (2) the mistake was a clear-cut, clerical or mathematical error or a misreading of the specifications and not a judgmental error; (3) prior to award the Government knew, or should have known, that a mistake had been made and, therefore, should have requested bid verification; (4) the Government did not request bid verification or its request for bid verification was inadequate; and (5) proof of the intended bid is established.

Id.

In this appeal, the parties do not dispute that the contractor has shown sufficient evidence to satisfy elements (1)—(3) and (5). Only element (4), the adequacy of the Government's request for bid verification, is at issue. In reviewing this appeal, this court examines the request for verification of a bid for adequacy.

The controlling regulations, 48 C.F.R. §§ 14.406-1 and 14.406-3(g) (1992), set forth a process for handling suspected bid mistakes:

After the opening of bids, contracting officers shall examine all bids for mistakes. In cases of apparent mistakes and in cases where the contracting officer has reason to believe that a mistake may have been made, the contracting officer shall request from the bidder a verification of the bid, calling attention to the suspected mistake.

48 C.F.R. § 14.406-1 (1992). The regulations further provide that:

[s]uspected or alleged mistakes in bids shall be processed as follows.... (1) The contracting officer shall immediately request the bidder to verify the bid. Action taken to verify bids must be sufficient to reasonably assure the contracting officer that the bid as confirmed is without error, or to elicit the allegation of a mistake by the bidder. To assure that the bidder will be put on notice of a mistake suspected by the contracting officer, the bidder should be advised as appropriate—(i) That its bid is so much lower than the other bids or the Government's estimate as to indicate a possibility of error...or (iv) Of any other information, proper for disclosure, that leads the contracting officer to believe that there is a mistake in [the] bid.

48 C.F.R.§ 14.406-3(g)(1) (1992).

Although the contracting officer did not expressly state that she suspected an error, she did reveal the amounts of all bids. With this information in hand, McClure Electrical could see that the next lowest bid was almost 20% higher than its bid. In other words, the next lowest bid was equal to McClure Electrical's bid plus 20% of McClure Electrical's bid. The disparity between McClure Electrical's bid and the Government estimate was even greater. The Government estimate was $282,869, or almost twice McClure Electrical's bid.

In a similar case, Klinger Constructors, Inc., ASBCA No. 41,006, 91-3 BCA § 24,218 (1991), the contracting officer sent the low bidder a letter stating that its bid was "substantially lower than the Government estimate." Id. The bid verification request also disclosed the difference between the contractor's bid and the Government estimate. This discrepancy was the only information that could have formed a basis for the contracting officer's opinion that an error in the bid may have been made. In Klinger, the Board correctly determined that "the contracting officer's notification adequately alerted the contractor to the possibility of a mistake and the basis for the suspicion." Id.

McClure Electrical asserts that the record suggests that the Navy sends a bid verification request to low bidders as a matter of standard operating procedure. Thus, McClure Electrical argues, its receipt of such a letter did not give adequate notice of a suspected error because a "bid verification" letter comes to every low bidder regardless of the presence of a suspected error. To the contrary, the contracting officer in this case testified the Navy sends these letters only if the contracting officer has a concern that there may be a bid error.

In requesting bid verification, the contracting officer, although not expressly so stating, informed McClure Electrical that its bid was considerably lower both than any other bid and the Government's estimate by providing the Abstract of Offers. With that information (i.e., the bid abstracts) in hand, McClure Electrical should have been able to infer that a possible error occurred in its bid calculations and thus, was on notice of the possibility of such an error.

The contracting officer did not, of course, have access to McClure Electrical's bid worksheets, which contained the error. The contracting officer only suspected an error due to the discrepancy between McClure Electrical's bid and other bids. Thus, by disclosing the other bids and the Government's estimate, the contracting officer called attention to all information on which she had based her suspicion of a mistake. Under the circumstances, this disclosure was fully adequate. The contracting officer had no way of knowing McClure Electrical had made an error on its worksheets. Because the bid verification request sent out by the contracting officer was adequate to put McClure Electrical on notice of a suspected bid mistake, this court affirms the decision of the Board.

IV.

The Navy's contracting officer provided McClure Electrical with an adequate request for bid verification. McClure Electrical had in its possession all of the information known to the contracting officer, information from which it was just as able as the contracting officer to infer the possibility of a mistake. Therefore, the bid verification request placed McClure Electrical on notice of a suspected error. The Board properly affirmed the contracting officer's denial of contract reformation.

AFFIRMED.

Notes and Questions

1. FAR 14.407-2 permits correction only after the bidder submits verification of the bid intended for clerical mistakes that are facially obvious, such as misplaced decimal points, obviously incorrect discounts, obvious mistakes in designation of unit, or similar typographical errors. See, e.g., *Matter of H. A. Sack Co., Inc.*, B-278359 (1998)(Awardee permitted to correct spreadsheet error after bid submission.); *Matter of Brazos Roofing, Inc.*, B-275319.2, 1997 WL 49033 (C.G.); William P. Rudland, *Rationalizing the Bid Mistake Rules*, 16 Pub. Cont. L.J. 446 (1987). What type of verification could be used to support the correction of such mistakes? Does allowing such correction serve the policy of promoting a level playing field?

2. Consider that the contractor satisfied four of the five elements for reformation of a contract due to a unilateral bid mistake" mistake in fact, of a clerical nature, which the government should have known, and regarding which the contractor can prove its intended bid. Looking at the matter from the contractor's perspective, should not its right to reformation turn on the factors bearing on the nature of its mistake, which are the

same regardless of what kind of bid verification form the Navy sends? Why make reformation turn on the adequacy of the government's request for bid verification?

3. Two-Step Sealed Bidding. Without going deeply into the topic of the chapter regarding negotiated proposals, brief mention may occur of a hybrid between sealed bids and negotiated proposals, namely, the hybrid method of Two-Step Sealed Bidding. This is the preferred procurement method for acquisition of rapidly evolving technical items or services. The first step is the issuance of a Request for Technical Proposals (RFTP), which must include a description of the items or services sought, evaluative criteria to be employed, and due date, among other features (FAR 14.503-1). In response to proposals that are considered at least "reasonably susceptible of being made acceptable," the government may conduct discussions with offerors. (FAR 14-503-1(a)(8)(iii)).Step two is the usual sealed bidding process, except that participation is limited (via invitations for bids, or IFBs) to those firms which were determined to have submitted technically acceptable proposals in the first phase (FAR 14.503-2).

B. Competitive Negotiation

The method of requesting competitive proposals, principally known by the initials "RFP" for "Request for Proposals" and formally known as "negotiated procurement," is by far the most common method by which the government purchases products and services with a value in excess of the simplified acquisition threshold of $100,000. It is the second principal leg of a triangle of procurement methods that includes sealed bids and sole source contracting. Whereas the prospective contractors in sealed bidding are generally known as "bidders" that submit "bids," with competitive proposals, prospective contractors are generally known as "offerors" that submit "offers" or "proposals." The very broad discretion given government contracting officials, based upon a mandatory impartial and comprehensive evaluation process, to select the offer representing the "best value" to the government makes the use of competitive proposals the favorite competitive procurement methodology for large dollar items and services.

An RFP contains, at a minimum, the: (1) government's requirements which include restrictive specifications only to the extent necessary to satisfy the needs of the agency; (2) anticipated terms and conditions of the contract; (3) information required to be in the offeror's proposal; and (4) factors and significant subfactors along with their relative importance to be used to evaluate the proposals received. After issuance of an RFP, there is a well-developed process in the government by which potential offerors can submit written questions and receive written answers to those questions, distributed to all interested offerors in the form of an amendment to the solicitation.

The RFP process differs from the sealed bids or IFBs in two critical ways. First, in comparison to sealed bids where price and price-related factors are the only evaluation factors, in competitive proposals, price or cost is not the only factor. Indeed, price or cost is often not even a principal factor (although by statute price or cost is always at least one of the factors.) An agency has broad discretion to include evaluation factors that represent the key areas of importance and emphasis to be considered in the contract award decision. The evaluation factors are to allow for a meaningful comparison and discrimination among proposals. There is no statutory or regulatory limit on the type or scope of non-price related evaluation factors that may be considered by an agency when reviewing proposals. Such factors most often include items such as: technical expertise; technical capability and management capability; personnel qualifications; offeror past performance; method of compliance with specific specifications; and delivery times. The only limit that exists, and it is one that is strictly enforced, is that all factors to be evaluated must be listed in the solicitation. A sure way for an agency to have a bid protest sustained against it is to make an award decision based on undisclosed evaluation factors.

In addition, the solicitation must disclose whether all evaluation factors other than cost or price, when combined, are significantly more important, equal to, or significantly less important than to the cost or price evaluation factor. Cost or price generally is a more important evaluation factor when the government requirement is clearly definable and risk of unsuccessful contract performance is slight. This is often the case for widely available commercial items and services being purchased by the government. Where the government requirement is less definitive, more development work is required, or the performance risk is higher, technical or past performance considerations may be more important than cost or price. Such is often the case for new weapon system development or complete government system overhauls.

The second critical way in which competitive proposals differ from the sealed bid process is the process that follows. In the typical sequence, a federal agency, after establishing a competitive range of the most initially highly ranked proposals, will hold discussions with the offerors in the competitive range prior to making an award decision. Thereby, offerors are given a chance to improve their proposals to be more consistent with the government requirements so that the government may make a best-value determination and contract award. During these discussions, the government identifies significant weaknesses, deficiencies, and other aspects of the offeror's proposal, e.g., cost, price, technical approach, past performance, and proposed contractual terms and conditions, for each offeror. The purpose of the discussions is to allow each offeror to revise its proposal based upon information discussed during the negotiations. Then, each offeror makes its "best and final offer" or "BAFOs," now known as "final proposal revisions."

While award may be made only to a "responsible" offeror, just as award may be made only to a responsible bidder under sealed bids, the concept of "responsiveness" critical in the sealed bid environment is not applicable in the competitive proposal environment. Offerors are free to propose alternative approaches to meeting the government needs — with the single caveat that an offer must meet the material requirements of the solicitation.

For further discussion of these subjects, see: Shereen M. Marcus, Note, *Efficiency in Exchange: An Economic Analysis of Acquisition by* Negotiation, Note, 32 Pub. Cont. L.J. 659 (2003); David A. Whiteford, *Negotiated Procurements: Squandering the Benefit of the Bargain*, 32 Pub. Cont. L.J. 509 (2003); David T. Douthwaite, *Why Procure Construction by Negotiation?* 25 Pub. Cont. L.J. 423 (1996); Richard J. Webber, *'Best Value' Procurement: a Primer on Selling Computers to the Government*, 7 J. Proprietary Rts. 8 (July 1994); Carl J. Peckinpaugh & Joseph M. Goldstein, *Best Value Source Selection: Contracting for Value, or Unfettered Agency Discretion?*, 22 Pub. Cont. L.J. 275 (1993); Steven W. Feldman, *Agency Evaluators in Negotiated Acquisitions*, 21 Pub. Cont. L.J. 279 (1992); Jamie S. Gorelick and Paul F. Enzinna, *Restrictions on the Release of Government Information*, 20 Pub. Con. L.J. 427 (1991); Christopher A. Barnes, *New and Improved Awards Without Discussions or Foreign Competition*, 20 Pub. Cont. L.J. 532 (1991); Michael A. Mark, *Contract Award on Initial Source Selection Proposals*, 19 Pub. Cont. L.J. 252 (1990).

1. Negotiation Process

The competitive proposal process is often considered superior to sealed bids by those directly involved with actual procurements because it allows the government and prospective contractors to discuss the solicitation requirements and the offeror's response to those requirements, prior to the government making an award decision. This early exchange of information and concerns can eliminate post-award confusion and problems that can result in costly and time-consuming litigation and delayed delivery. At the same time, however, in an environment that seeks to create a level playing field among all competitors, discussions offer a greater opportunity for one competitor to receive "extra" help or consideration by government officials not offered to others.

As previously noted, the competitive proposal process has an idealized sequence — RFP, proposals, competitive range, discussions, BAFO, award. However, it can have a number of variants. The contracting officer might decide, looking at the proposals, to pick the best and make an award without discussions, either on the initial proposals, or after some clarifications or other steps. As a result, the decision to hold discussions and the content thereof is a serious one. Before 1997, FAR part 15 imposed very rigid requirements on the duty to conduct discussions with all offerors once discussions were opened. While the concept existed of providing to some offerors mere clarifications without across-the-board discussions, it gave little room for meaningful exchange. Then, a signal "FAR Part 15 rewrite" occurred. One of the purposes of the FAR part 15 rewrite, in loosening the definitions triggering discussions with all offerors, was to lighten the burden on contracting officers faced with many offerors. *See, e.g.,* Computer Literacy World v. Department of the Air Force, GSBCA 134238-P (1995)(granting protest in which the Air Force received fifty-three proposals and disqualified forty-seven on minor grounds, including the six lowest-price ones, without any discussions). The next opinion reflects what the rewrite produced.

A few other terms deserve brief introduction before seeing them in action in the cases. The "evaluation factors" in the RFP play a key role in this process, providing the basis for deciding which proposals get into the competitive range, and later serving as the basis for discussions and for evaluating the BAFO for award. And, when proposals get eliminated, the rejected offeror can request and receive a "debriefing" as to the reason. The debriefing assists the offeror in deciding whether to protest.

INFORMATION TECHNOLOGY & APPLICATIONS CORPORATION, Plaintiff-Appellant, v. UNITED STATES, Defendant-Appellee,

United States Court of Appeals, Federal Circuit.
316 F.3d 1312 Jan. 10, 2003.

Before NEWMAN, DYK and PROST, Circuit Judges.

DYK, Circuit Judge.

This case involves the distinction between "clarifications" and "discussions" under the 1997 revision to Subpart 15.3 of the Federal Acquisition Regulations. 48 C.F.R. §§ 15.300-08 (2002). Information Technology and Applications Corporation ("ITAC") appeals the decision of the United States Court of Federal Claims denying its bid protest and granting the United States motion for summary judgment on the administrative record. *Info. Tech. & Applications Corp. v. United States,* 51 Fed.Cl. 340 (Fed.Cl.2001). * * * [W]e affirm.

BACKGROUND

On March 19, 2001, the Air Force issued Solicitation and Request for Proposals No. FA2550-01-R-0001 ("RFP") to obtain a contract for professional services in support of its Space Warfare Center. The winning contractor was to examine, assess and develop means of integrating national intelligence assets with the Department of Defense space systems, in order to enhance combat and research and development capabilities at the Space Warfare Center. The Air Force intended to make an award to one lead contractor, which would perform overall program management and integration, operations support, systems engineering and analysis, and other work related to the Space Warfare Center. The term of performance was to be twelve months, beginning on October 1, 2001, with seven one-year options.

Under the RFP, the contract was to be awarded "to an offeror who gives the Government the greatest confidence that it will best meet [the] requirements affordably." RFP at 81. In accordance with 10 U.S.C. § 2305(a)(2)(A) and 41 U.S.C. § 253a(b)(1), the RFP also disclosed "all the significant factors and significant subfactors" that the agency "reasonably expect[ed] to consider," and their relative importance. 10 U.S.C. § 2305(a)(2)(A) (2000); 41 U.S.C. § 253a(b)(1) (2000); RFP at 81–85.

ITAC, [RS Information Systems, Inc. ("RSIS")] and a third offeror submitted timely proposals in response to the RFP. All three proposals anticipated that some of the work would be performed by subcontractors. RSIS's proposal relied heavily on the role of its subcontractors, which were to perform at least 75% of the work on the contract.

The Air Force sent various "evaluation notices" ("ENs") to all three offerors. These evaluation notices were brief letters to the offerors requesting additional information regarding their proposals. The Air Force sent three ENs to ITAC, five ENs to RSIS, and three ENs to the third offeror. At issue in this case are ENs Nos. 0001, 0002 and 0002a, which the Air Force sent to RSIS after the offerors had submitted "past performance" information, but before the due date for the other parts of the proposals. The ENs at issue sought "additional information...to verify relevant past performance for [the] lead and support roles" of at least ten subcontractors that RSIS listed in its proposal. EN No. 0002. The Air Force sent ENs to the other bidders requesting additional information on their subcontractors as well. The disputed ENs were labeled "FAR 15.306(a) Clarification [s]" and included the notice, "Please note that this clarification does not constitute oral discussions with the offeror." EN 0002, referring to 48 C.F.R. § 15.306(a).

RSIS responded to the ENs on May 1, 2001, explaining which parts of the project each subcontractor would support and detailing the subcontractors' relevant experience with regard to those tasks. For example, in response to EN 0002, RSIS responded, "[subcontractor] Aerojet has developed and integrated the CTPP/ALERT and the JTAGS IR missile warning processing systems into the tactical missile warning C2 operational architecture, (Similarities to [contract] Requirements, V-57, and V-59)." (RSIS Response to Evaluation Notice.)

The Air Force gave both ITAC and RSIS an "overall exceptional rating" for their "past performance" experience. (Proposal Analysis Report for RFP # FA2550-01-R-0001, July 11, 2001). The Air Force determined that prior contracts of RSIS and its subcontractors were relevant to their ability to perform the Space Warfare Center contract.

The Air Force performed an independent "Most Probable Cost analysis" on the proposals submitted by RSIS and the third bidder. The "Most Probable Cost analysis" was an independent analysis of the bidder's estimated cost for "reasonableness" and "realism." RFP at 85. The Air Force "assess[ed] the compatibility of the overall proposed costs with the scope of effort to be performed." *Id.* The Air Force did not perform a "Most Probable Cost analysis" on ITAC's proposal, because its evaluation team found that ITAC's proposed hours were so minimal and unrealistic that it was infeasible to perform an adequate analysis. (Source Selection Decision Document at 4.) As a result of this independent analysis performed with respect to RSIS and the third bidder, the Air Force increased the estimated labor hours for RSIS and the third bidder, after determining "that additional hours were required in each labor category to successfully perform the effort." *Info. Tech. & Applications Corp. v. United States*, No. 01-637 C, slip op. at 9 n. 15 (Fed.Cl. Dec. 7, 2001). There is no suggestion that these adjustments resulted from RSIS's responses to the disputed ENs.

On July 23, 2001, the Air Force announced its decision to award the contract to RSIS. In its Source Selection Decision Document, the Air Force explained that all three proposals were rated equally for "Program Management and Integration" and for "Past Performance" (which was the subject of the disputed ENs), and that these were not, therefore, "discriminating factors." (Source Selection Decision Document at 2.) The Air Force determined that although "[a]ll Offerors provided proposals which met minimum contract requirements," and "all proposals were fundamentally sound," "key discriminators were made in Mission Capability…, Proposal Risk, and Cost/Price." *Id.* at 1. RSIS performed higher than ITAC in the categories of "Mission Capability" and "Proposal Risk." *Id.* at 2–4. In the area of "Cost/Price," the Air Force found, "RSIS provided the lowest overall price for the written Task Order and provided the best overall price to the Government." *Id.* at 5. The Air Force concluded:

> In summary, RSIS offered an excellent proposal with lower risk and several innovative approaches to improve efficiency of SWC operations that were deemed to be beneficial to the Government. As a result, the RSIS proposal provided the overall best value to the Government. Based on my integrated assessment that the RSIS proposal provided a better technical and lower risk offer, I direct the award to RS Information Systems.

Id. Because "Cost/Price" was one of the categories in which RSIS scored higher than ITAC, the refusal of the Air Force to conduct a "Most Probable Cost analysis" of ITAC's proposal or make a similar adjustment to its labor hours to make them more realistic is alleged to have been a significant factor in ITAC's not winning the contract.

On August 6, 2001, ITAC filed a bid protest with the General Accounting Office ("GAO"). The GAO denied the bid protest and the Air Force awarded the contract to RSIS on November 7, 2001.

On November 13, 2001, ITAC filed this post-award bid protest in the Court of Federal Claims. * * * The theory was that if discussions had been opened, ITAC would have had the opportunity to cure the weaknesses in its proposal.

The ability of the contracting officer to conduct "discussions" is governed by both statute and regulation. Under 41 U.S.C. § 253b(d) and 10 U.S.C. § 2305(b)(4)(A), an agency may award a contract "after discussions with the offerors" or "based on proposals received and without discussions with the offerors." 41 U.S.C. § 253b(d) (2000); 10 U.S.C. § 2305(b)(4)(A) (2000). If the agency decides to hold discussions, however, it first must establish a "competitive range comprised of all the most highly rated proposals." 48 C.F.R. § 15.306(c)(1) (2002). In order to determine the competitive range, the agency may engage in "communications" with the offerors, which are defined as "exchanges, between the Government and offerors, after receipt of proposals, leading to establishment of the competitive range." 48 C.F.R. § 15.306(b) (2002).

If the agency decides to award the contract after holding discussions, it must hold discussions "with all responsible offerors who submit proposals within the competitive range." 41 U.S.C. § 253b(d)(1)(A) (2000); 10 U.S.C. § 2305(b)(4)(A)(i) (2000). However, the agency may hold "discussions conducted for the purpose of minor clarification" with one or more offerors. 41 U.S.C. § 253b(d)(1)(B) (2000); 10 U.S.C. § 2305(b)(4)(A)(ii) (2000). The procurement regulations define "clarifications" as "limited exchanges, between the Government and offerors, that may occur when award without discussions is contemplated." 48 C.F.R. § 15.306(a)(1) (2002).

On December 7, 2001, the Court of Federal Claims denied the bid protest, granting the government's motion for summary judgment on the administrative record. * * * *

DISCUSSION

* * *

The appellant's primary argument, and the only argument worthy of extended treatment, is that the Air Force violated the statute and regulations by holding "discussions" with RSIS and not with the appellant.

The statute provides, in part:

(1) An executive agency shall evaluate competitive proposals in accordance with subsection (a) of this section and may award a contract—

(A) after discussions with the offerors, provided that written or oral discussions have been conducted with all responsible offerors who submit proposals within the competitive range; or

(B) based on the proposals received and without discussions with the offerors (other than discussions conducted for the purpose of minor clarification)....

41 U.S.C. § 253b(d)(1) (2000). Substantively identical language appears in 10 U.S.C. § 2305(b)(4)(A). The purpose of the rule that the government may not hold discussions with only one bidder is "to prevent a bidder from gaining an unfair advantage over its competitors by making its bid more favorable to the government in a context where the other bidders have no opportunity to do so." *Data Gen. Corp. v. Johnson,* 78 F.3d 1556, 1561 (Fed.Cir.1996). The government contends that the ENs in question did not constitute discussions, but rather were "clarifications."

In order to construe the meaning of the terms "discussion" and "minor clarification" in the statute, we begin with an analysis of the language of the statute itself. * * *

The relevant dictionary definitions are as follows:

"Discussion" is defined as, "consideration of a question in open usu. informal debate: argument for the sake of arriving at truth or clearing up difficulties." *Webster's 3d International Dictionary* 648 (1968) ("Webster's"). Webster's defines "to clarify" in the relevant sense alternatively as, "to free (the mind or understanding) of confusion, doubt, or uncertainty"; "to explain clearly: make understandable"; and "to make less complex or less ambiguous: put in order." *Id.* at 415. Webster's defines "minor" in the relevant sense alternatively as, "1 a: inferior in importance: comparatively unimportant: lower in standing or reputation than others of the same kind. . . . b: being the less important of two things." *Id.* at 1439.

Although these definitions make clear that "discussions" are more substantial communications than "minor clarifications," none of these various definitions serves to illuminate with any precision which specific exchanges of information constitute "discussions," and which exchanges constitute "minor clarifications." * * *

We first note that the regulations were altered significantly in 1997. *Compare* 48 C.F.R. §§ 15.601, 15.607, 15.610 (1991), *with* 48 C.F.R. § 15.306 (2002). The preexisting regulations strictly limited the definition and purpose of clarifications. * * *

Under the new regulation, 48 C.F.R. § 15.306, "clarifications" are defined as "limited exchanges, between the Government and offerors, that may occur when award without discussions is contemplated." 48 C.F.R. § 15.306(a) (2002). The regulation further provides examples of clarifications:

> If award will be made without conducting discussions, offerors may be given the opportunity to clarify certain aspects of proposals (*e.g., the relevance of an offeror's past performance information and adverse past performance information to which the offeror has not previously had an opportunity to respond*) or to resolve minor or clerical errors.

48 C.F.R. § 15.306(a)(2) (2002) (emphasis added).

In contrast, under the regulation, "discussions" involve "negotiations": "When negotiations are conducted in a competitive acquisition, they take place after establishment of the competitive range and are called discussions." 48 C.F.R. § 15.306(d) (2002). Because discussions involve negotiations, they may include "bargaining," which "includes persuasion, alteration of assumptions and positions, give-and-take, and may apply to price, schedule, technical requirements, type of contract, or other terms of a proposed contract." *Id.* And unlike clarifications, discussions "are undertaken with the intent of allowing the offeror to revise its proposal." *Id.* Also unlike clarifications, discussions take place after the government has established a "competitive range" of the most highly rated proposals. 48 C.F.R. § 15.306(c) (2002). Discussions need only be held with each offeror within the competitive range. 48 C.F.R. § 15.306(d)(1) (2002).

The stated purpose of the 1997 amendments to section 15 of the regulations was to "provide for empowerment and flexibility" and "shift from rigid rules to guiding principles." 62 Fed. Reg. 51,225 (Sept. 30, 1997). Specifically, the new regulations were intended to "[s]upport[ ] more open exchanges between the Government and industry, allowing industry to better understand the requirement [sic] and the Government to better understand industry proposals." *Id.* at 51,224. The order adopting the new regulations stated that:

> We drafted the rule to allow as much free exchange of information between offerors and the Government as possible, while still permitting award without discussions and complying with applicable statutes. . . . This policy is expected to help offerors, especially small entities that may not be familiar with proposal preparation, by permitting easy clarification of limited aspects of their proposals.

Id. at 51,228–29. Thus, the definition of "clarifications" was significantly broadened. Rather than being "for the sole purpose of eliminating minor irregularities, informalities, or apparent clerical mistakes," clarifications now provide offerors "the opportunity to clarify certain aspects of proposals (e.g., the relevance of an offeror's past performance information and adverse past performance information to which the offeror has not previously had an opportunity to respond)...." *Compare* 48 C.F.R. § 15.601 (1991), *with* 48 C.F.R. § 15.306(a)(2) (2002).

* * * * Because the regulation's definitions represent a reasonable interpretation of the statutory terms, we defer to them and turn to the question of whether this regulation was properly applied to the facts of this case.

IV

The communications in question in this case, ENs 0001, 0002 and 0002a, were for the purpose of obtaining additional information about the subcontractors that RSIS had listed in its proposal. Specifically, the ENs asked RSIS to provide "additional relevant past performance information, to further describe the lead role for [the subcontractors]." EN 0002. In its response, RSIS explained which parts of the project each subcontractor would support and detailed their relevant experience with regard to those tasks. The government argues that these communications constituted clarifications, and not discussions. We agree for two reasons.

First, these communications were not discussions. As explained above, the new regulation contemplates discussions as occurring in the context of negotiations. 48 C.F.R. § 15.306(d) (2002). As such, when discussions are opened, bidders have the opportunity to revise their proposals, in order "to maximize the Government's ability to obtain the best value." *Id.* at § 15.306(d)(2). In this case, the government did not give RSIS the opportunity to revise its proposal, and RSIS did not change the terms of its proposal to make it more appealing to the government. Under these circumstances, it is clear that ENs 0001, 0002 and 0002a, and RSIS's response to them, did not constitute discussions.

Second, the Air Force's request was merely a request for clarification of the relevant experience of RSIS's subcontractors, as permitted by the regulation. The regulation provides that "offerors may be given the opportunity to clarify certain aspects of proposals." 48 C.F.R. § 15.306(a)(2) (2002). One example that the regulation provides of such a clarification is "the relevance of an offeror's past performance information...." *Id.* We can discern no distinction between this clear example in the regulation and the Air Force's request for clarification of the subcontractors' relevant experience in this case. We therefore conclude that the challenged communications, ENs 0001, 0002 and 0002a, were merely requests for clarification.

We reject appellant's argument that the ENs could not be clarifications because they "requested additional information." Any meaningful clarification would require the provision of information, and the example of a clarification given in the regulation, "the relevance of an offeror's past performance information," requires the provision of information. *Id.* The appellant also contends that a clarification cannot call for new information if the information is "necessary to evaluate the proposal." There is no requirement in the regulation that a clarification not be essential for evaluation of the proposal. * * * Appellant's cramped conception of "clarification" is, moreover, not in harmony with the stated purpose of the 1997 amendments, which was to "[s]upport[ ] more open exchanges between the Government and industry, allowing industry to better understand the requirement [sic] and the Government to better understand industry proposals." 62 Fed. Reg. at 51,224.

* * * * For the foregoing reasons, the decision of the United States Court of Federal Claims is

AFFIRMED.

PAULINE NEWMAN, Circuit Judge, dissenting.

I agree with the panel majority that the 1997 amendment to section 15 of the Federal Acquisition Regulations was intended to liberalize the protocol governing exchanges between federal acquirers and bidders during the procurement process. Section 15 was designed to enhance convenience, but without diminution in fairness. The amended regulation does not exonerate the agency's unusual procedure in this case, however generously it may be construed. Whatever the distinction between "clarifications" and "discussions" in 48 C.F.R. § 15.306, the procedure by which the Air Force implemented its "independent cost evaluation" without informing ITAC of the agency's action when advised that the labor hours of all bids were too low, does not meet any reasonable definition of "clarification."

"Clarifications" are defined as "limited exchanges, between the Government and offerors, that may occur when award without discussions is contemplated." 48 C.F.R. § 15.306(a)(1) (2001). The agency's unilateral increase of the labor hours of two of the three offerors, without disclosure to the third of the agency's concern, cannot be rationalized as mere "clarification." It is surely not the type of individual interchange that was intended to be authorized by the amendment to section 15.

ITAC states that had it been told that its labor hours were too low, it would have explained the economies that it expected to achieve through certain new cost-saving technologies. ITAC was no stranger to this contract; it was the incumbent contractor and it must be assumed to have known, as well as anyone, the labor needed to perform the contract. ITAC was not offered the same opportunity of a revised proposal as were the other bidders. Instead, the Air Force simply refused to perform a "most probable cost analysis" on the ITAC proposal, thereby precluding the award to ITAC. While the labor hours of the other offerors were unilaterally increased by the evaluation team, by ten percent for one offeror and thirty percent for the other, ITAC was simply disqualified.

The purpose of the section 15 amendment was to "support[ ] more open exchanges between the government and industry, allowing industry to better understand the requirements and the government to better understand industry proposals." 62 Fed. Reg. at 51,224. It was not intended to authorize agencies to act without regard to fundamentals of fair procurement. From my colleagues' blanket ratification of a procurement that was seriously flawed, I respectfully dissent.

Notes and Questions

1. The court majority obviously gives the rewritten FAR Part 15 an expansive reading. Do you understand the dissent, particularly its observation that the protesting party is the incumbent contractor? Is it striking that the Air Force could, in effect, kick out the existing contractor and move in a new one without discussions that would give a warning as to what it was doing?

2. Was the Air Force avoiding burdensome discussions in this instance? Ordinarily, observers find it more suspicious when an agency pushes the rules to keep an incumbent contractor than when it displaces one. In this case, did the elimination of the safeguard of discussions mean that the incumbent could have been the favourite of the pre-2001 decisionmakers and the new contractor the favourite of the post-2001 ones?

3. As with other acquisition reform, the FAR Part 15 rewrite has received some critical scrutiny about whether it fosters competition or just works to the advantage of whatever contractors obtain awards. An Air Force contract attorney found in a scholarly study that the government has not gotten the benefit of the new bargaining flexibility. Among other reasons, the unchecked discretion of the contracting officers, coupled with the downsizing of the acquisition personnel workforce, has led contracting officers to use their freedom as they feel they must, merely to process acquisitions in the most minimal way to meet the larger per-person burdens, not to flexibly deploy resources in order to bargain hard when the government would benefit David A. Whiteford, *Negotiated Procurements: Squandering the Benefit of the Bargain*, 32 Pub. Cont. L. J. 509 (2003). For background, see Paul E. Van Maldeghem, *The FAR Part 15 Rewrite: Road to the Final Rule*, 33 Procurement Law., Summer 1998, at 3.

4. FAR provisions for award without discussion. By statute, defense agencies may invite proposals for award without discussions, provided that the solicitation states that proposals are intended to be evaluated and an award made without discussions unless they are determined to be necessary. 10 U.S.C. §2305(b)(4)(A)(ii). The Defense FAR Supplement (DFARS) provides for an award without discussions for a solicitation for commercial items based on price and price-related factors, and specifically states that the government may accept other than the lowest offer. 48 C.F.R. §252.211-7014 (1991). Conversely, another FAR provision permits an award on initial proposals without discussion only when full and open competition exits, or there is prior cost experience such that award without discussion would result in the lowest overall cost to the government. 48 C.F.R. §15.610 (a)(3) (1997).

5. Protests of awards without discussions. Protests of awards without discussion are common and yield a variety of results. In the *University of South Carolina (USC)*, the Comptroller General found that review and approval of personnel substitutions in a proposal prior to award constituted discussions, and, hence, required that discussions be conducted with other offerors in the competitive range. B-240208, 90-2 CPD ¶249 (1990). Awards to other than the lowest offer are commonly protested but found appropriate when the low offeror's proposal is non-conforming. *Sterling Machine Co.*, B-236585, 89-2 CPD ¶409 (1989). Protests are also not sustained where an urgency in procurement is demonstrated and justifies an award to other than the lowest offer. *Raytheon Co.*, B-240333, 90-2 CPD ¶384 (1990). For more information on the issue of awards without discussions, see Christopher A. Barnes, *New and Improved Awards Without Discussions or Foreign Competition*, 20 Pub. Cont. L.J. 532 (1991), and Michael A. Mark, *Contract Award on Initial Source Selection Proposal*, 19 Pub. Cont. L.J. 252 (1990).

6. One way agencies have of ensuring a fair procurement process while still taking advantage of discussions, if need be, is to issue a solicitation whereby award will be made to the lowest priced, technically acceptable offer. Using this procedure, the solicitation contains the evaluation factors and significant subfactors that will be used to establish whether a proposal is technically acceptable or not, with offers not being ranked, but merely evaluated as technically acceptable or unacceptable. Award is then made to the lowest priced, technically acceptable offeror. FAR 15.101-2. Discussions, if any, are only needed to assist certain offerors to cross the technically acceptable threshold, rather than improving their offer in comparison to others received. The competition is essentially based upon price, with the government reserving the ability to discuss potential problem areas with offerors prior to award.

W & D Ships Deck Works, Inc., Plaintiff, v. United States, Defendant

United States Court of Federal Claims
No. 97-308C. 39 Fed. Cl. 638 (1997)

WEINSTEIN, Judge.

On April 30, 1997, plaintiff filed a complaint seeking to enjoin award of a federal government contract until plaintiff's proposal was reinstated in the negotiation process, together with a motion for a temporary restraining order (TRO). The government indicated it would take no further action on the contract until a hearing was held on May 5, 1997. At the hearing, after a full argument on the merits of plaintiff's complaint, the court denied the TRO motion and, sua sponte, granted judgment to the government on the pleadings, and dismissed the complaint. This opinion constitutes the court's written findings of fact and conclusions of law.

Facts

* * *

On December 11, 1996, the United States government, acting through the Military Sealift Command, Atlantic (MSCLANT), of the United States Navy, issued Solicitation No. N62381-97-R-0300 (the solicitation), requesting proposals on a negotiated fixed-price contract to: (1) paint the topsides of ships; (2) repaint the topsides of ships; (3) paint the decks of ships; (4) apply non-skid surfaces to the decks of ships; (5) paint interiors of ships; and (6) clean the exterior painted surfaces of ships. Solicitation at 1, 8, 12, 16, 19, 23, 26. All the ships subject to the contract were located either in Norfolk, Virginia, or in Baltimore, Maryland. Id. at 28. The government designated the contract as a 100% set-aside for small businesses. Id. at 1. Plaintiff, W & D Ships Deck Works, Inc. (W & D), a small company located in Atlantic Beach, Florida, submitted a timely proposal. Compl. ¶¶1, 6.

Around March 21, 1997, the contracting officer ("CO") for the solicitation notified plaintiff that its proposal was determined to be outside the competitive range for negotiations due to unacceptable deficiencies in the technical proposal. Id. ¶7. Plaintiff's protest of this decision with MSCLANT was filed on March 28, 1997, and rejected by the CO, with a detailed explanation of the reasons, on April 22, 1997. Id. ¶¶8, 9; MSCLANT letter at 1 (Ex. D to Compl.)

Plaintiff's complaint seeking injunctive relief in this court, filed on April 30, 1997, alleges that there was "no major deviation in Plaintiff's proposal from any of the Solicitation's requirements," Compl. ¶11, and that any deviations were "minor irregularities," Id. ¶13, involving "post-bid responsibility matters or post-award contract administrative matters." Id. ¶11.

Discussion

At the hearing, the court denied plaintiff's motion for a TRO as unlikely to succeed on the merits and dismissed the complaint, sua sponte, pursuant to Rules of the United States Court of Federal Claims (RCFC) 12(b)(4), because there were no material facts in question and the government was clearly entitled to judgment.

* * *

III. Merits of Plaintiff's Complaint

In the case currently before the court, plaintiff does not object to the solicitation, nor to any award (since none has been made). Therefore, it may obtain review under §1491(b)(1) based only on an objection to the proposed award or violation of a statute or regulation. Plaintiff's complaint does not identify any specific statute or regulation that MSCLANT officials allegedly violated to plaintiff's prejudice in reviewing the proposal. Rather, the complaint merely alleges generally that plaintiff's proposal is satisfactory and complete in respects MSCLANT found unsatisfactory and incomplete and implicitly contends that the CO abused his discretion in making the competitive range determination. Plaintiff's sole basis for objecting to the proposed award—to another—is that its own bid was not considered although it was within the competitive range.[1]

The competitive range is the group of proposals submitted in response to a government solicitation "that could be made competitive through negotiation." CACI, 719 F.2d at 1571. Under the federal regulation controlling evaluation for inclusion in the competitive range of negotiated bid proposals, a CO, after receiving all the proposals, must determine which proposals are in the competitive range for the purpose of conducting further negotiations. 48 C.F.R. §15.609(a) (FAR §15.609(a)). All proposals not in the competitive range are excluded from further negotiations and consideration.

The Federal Circuit has determined that COs have broad discretion in evaluating proposals and determining which, if any, fall into the competitive range. Birch & Davis Int'l, Inc. v. Christopher, 4 F.3d 970, 973 (Fed.Cir.1993). Contracting officers' statutory discretion even permits them to limit the competitive range to exclude some proposals that otherwise would be included if this will promote efficient competition by narrowing the field. See 10 U.S.C. §2305(b)(4)(B); 41 U.S.C. §253b(d)(2).

Proposals need not be included within the competitive range if they are "so technically inferior or out of line as to price, as to render discussions meaningless." Birch & Davis, 4 F.3d at 974 (quoting M.W. Kellogg Co./ Siciliana Appalti Constr., S.p.A. v. United States, 10 Cl.Ct. 17, 23 (1986)). By regulation, the CO is instructed to include only those proposals that have "a reasonable chance of being selected," excluding all others. FAR §15.609(a). However, the FAR requires that the benefit of the doubt be given to those proposals that are on the borderline for inclusion. Id.

Courts may not overrule agency competitive range decisions except where the CO's actions are clearly unreasonable. Birch & Davis, 4 F.3d at 973. "Close scrutiny" is given only to decisions that result in a competitive range of only one bidder.[2] Id. at 974. GAO decisions uniformly hold that agency decisions establishing the competitive range are "primarily a matter of administrative discretion which will not be disturbed...absent a clear showing that the determination lacked a reasonable basis." PRC Computer Center, Inc., 55 Comp. Gen. 60, 68 (1975); see also Talco, Inc., 89-2 CPD 171 (1989); Interaction Research Institute, Inc., 89-2 CPD 15 (1989). Although not binding, see e.g., National Forge Co. v. United States, 779 F.2d 665, 668 (Fed.Cir.1985) (citing Burroughs Corp. v. United States, 223 Ct.Cl. 53, 617 F.2d 590, 597 (1980)), GAO decisions on this topic are more numerous and detailed than decisions by this court or the Federal Cir-

---

1. At the hearing, defendant disclosed that plaintiff's bid was the lowest.

2. While the plaintiff did not seek "close scrutiny" review, the court determined at the hearing that the CO's competitive range included three of the seven proposals submitted. Therefore, the heightened level of review would not apply to this protest.

cuit. Because the decisions are well reasoned, this court adopts the GAO's approach in these competitive range decisions.

The CO, by statute, is limited to evaluating proposals based on the factors identified in the solicitation. 10 U.S.C. §2305(b)(1). The FAR too states that the competitive range determination is based on price and "other factors that were stated in the solicitation." FAR §15.609(a). The CO informed plaintiff that it had been rejected because its technical proposal did not contain a substantial amount of information required by the solicitation. Plaintiff received unsatisfactory ratings on items within each of the four sections in the evaluation factor sequence.

Section L-16 of the solicitation ("Requirements for submission of Proposals") states that the "offeror's technical proposal must contain, but not necessarily be limited to, data set forth for the [enumerated] evaluation factors.... Failure to respond to any one of the evaluation factors may result in disqualification of the proposal." Id. at 82 (emphasis in original). It also states that "[d]ata previously submitted, or presumed to be known,... cannot be considered unless they are physically incorporated in the proposal," and that "[a]ll information must be presented in sufficient depth to allow for the Government to make a fair and comprehensive evaluation of the offeror's understanding of the specification." Id. at 81. These statements make it clear that MSCLANT may disqualify an offeror if its technical proposal is deemed incomplete and that the technical proposals had to contain all of the information specifically requested.

Section M of the solicitation ("Evaluation Factors for Award"), notes that for proposals to be technically acceptable, "all categories [listed in section L] must be evaluated as technically acceptable." Id. at 85. Gaps in the following information led the CO to find plaintiff's proposal to be technically unacceptable and, as a result, outside of the competitive range.

First, in section 16.1.0, the solicitation required offerors to include in their technical proposals "a narrative which demonstrates an understanding of the overall scope of work." Id. at 82. The narrative also had to describe in detail how the contractor intended to perform the work. Id. There are six work items involved in the contract: (1) topside initial coating, id. at 8; (2) topside maintenance recoating, id. at 12; (3) exterior decks initial coating, id. at 16; (4) exterior deck non-skid coating, id. at 19; (5) interior painting, id. at 23; and (6) cleaning of exterior painted surfaces, id. at 26. Each item is described separately and in detail in section C of the solicitation.

Plaintiff's proposal discussed items three and four, regarding deck work only and thus, as the CO reasonably found, did not "demonstrate a satisfactory understanding of the overall scope of work required," which merited an unsatisfactory rating. MSCLANT letter at 1 (emphasis in original). Plaintiff failed even to mention any aspect of the contract not related to the deck work. Plaintiff's narrative provides only a cursory discussion, in fewer than twenty lines of text, of only one item — item four, the application of non-skid surface material. Proposal at 1.

Second, the solicitation in section 16.1.3 required offerors to provide information concerning five specific areas of material control. The CO reasonably found that the plaintiff's answers were "vague and brief," essentially failing to address any of the five areas in sufficient depth. MSCLANT letter at 1. Plaintiff's proposal mentions all five items, but in such cursory fashion as to be practically useless to evaluators. For example, with respect to item five, ripout material to be reinstalled, the proposal states: "Material which has been removed from the ship for reinstallation at a later dateis [sic] also kept segregated and inventoried separately." Proposal at 3. That is a conclusory statement, not a description of how it is done, including pertinent data, as is required. Similarly, in response to item three, environment protection for material stored (covered stowage and/or weather proofing) and size, location and type of material storage, the proposal states: "When received, the products are stored in an environmentally controlled warehouse." Id. The answer again contains less information than the question. The point of these questions is to provide the government evaluators with sufficient information to determine which offerors have the ability to perform the contract. Plaintiff's answers simply do not meet that need and it was reasonable for the agency to find them deficient.

Third, in section 16.2.0, the solicitation required offerors to submit a list of the capital equipment available to perform the contract and to provide a description of the facility. Plaintiff's proposal merely states that it "has all the necessary tools," "such as grinders, needle guns, descobraders, air tools, and air compressors." Proposal at 4 (emphasis added). Thus, it does not specify any, never mind all, the equipment it has. (A simple affirmation that plaintiff has the tools, accompanied by an illustrative listing premised with "such as" may be read to mean that plaintiff does not actually have any of those particular items). The proposal also states that plaintiff has a tentative agreement to lease 10,000 square feet from its subcontractor to use as its facility for this contract but does not further describe this facility. Clearly these disclosures do not permit the agency to make an informed selection among offerors and warrant the CO's rating of the solicitation as unsatisfactory on these points. MSCLANT letter at 2.

Fourth, in section 16.3.1, the solicitation required offerors to identify subcontractors and "explain the procedures to be utilized to control materials, quality assurance and inspections." Solicitation at 83. The CO reasonably rated plaintiff's response to this item to be unsatisfactory, MSCLANT letter at 2, because in response to this item, plaintiff merely identified the subcontractor (Surface Technologies) that would be used on the contract. Proposal at 5. Plaintiff did not even hint at the procedures that it intended to use to control materials used by the subcontractor and to perform quality assurance and inspections of the subcontractor's work, as specifically required by the solicitation. The proposal simply concludes that the subcontractor is "fully cognizant of the contract requirements and specifications for the performance of those requirements," id., but does not explain how the conclusion was reached, or how the contractor will ensure subcontractor compliance, as is specifically required by the solicitation.[3]

Fifth, in section 16.3.2, the solicitation required a detailed description of the quality control plan the contractor intended to implement, including providing the identity of the "individuals" who would perform quality control functions and discussing their other duties, as well as listing all NACE Certified Coating Inspectors who would be involved. Solicitation at 83. The CO reasonably rated plaintiffs reply to this section as unsatisfactory because plaintiff did not identify any specific individuals who would perform quality control functions and, perforce, did not list the other duties of those individuals. MSCLANT letter at 2. According to the agency, the plan also cited a calibration system standard that had been canceled several years earlier. Id. It is obvious to the court that information like the identity of the quality control officers and the extent of

---

3. This complete nonresponsiveness on the part of plaintiff was deemed sufficient by plaintiff's counsel at the hearing because the agency knew the subcontractor. However, the proposal specifically states: "Data previously submitted, or presumed to be known...cannot be considered unless they are physically incorporated in the proposal." Solicitation at 81. Confronted with this discrepancy, plaintiff's counsel had no further explanation.

their other duties is essential to the government's analysis of a bid such as this. Without this information, the adequacy of plaintiff's proposal is purely speculative.

Sixth, in section 16.4.0, the solicitation required the offerors to discuss relevant past experience. The section listed seven specific items that the offerors "shall" address with respect to prior experience. Solicitation at 83–84. The CO reasonably rated plaintiff's response to this section as unacceptable because plaintiff cited only its previous experience with non-skid deck surface application (only one part of the contract) and because plaintiff failed to answer at least five of the seven specific requests for information concerning previous contract experience. MSCLANT letter at 2–3. (Plaintiff did not provide types of availability, man-days expended, required and actual completion dates, original and final contract prices, and percentages of growth. Id.) In response to this request, which obviously would provide exceptionally valuable information to government officials deciding to whom to award the contract, plaintiff's proposal lists several previous jobs, but provides only the ship name, the job location, and a contact name and phone number, and does not even identify the type of work done on these jobs. Again, for no reason apparent from the proposal, plaintiff withheld specifically requested information that appears to be essential to MSCLANT's decision-making process.

The GAO has soundly upheld agency exclusions of proposals from the competitive range for technical unacceptability when the proposal would require "major revisions" to become acceptable. See, e.g., Interaction Research, 89-2 CPD 15 (1989); PRC, 55 Comp. Gen. at 69 (citing other decisions). That would be the case in this instance. For plaintiff to make its proposal technically acceptable, it would have to revise, and substantially amplify, all but one section. Most of those revisions would entail significant changes or extensive additions, thus requiring a "major revision" of the original proposal.

The GAO has also properly concluded that if a proposal fails to provide information sufficient to determine if the offeror is technically acceptable, it is reasonable for the agency to exclude it from the competitive range, Talco, 89-2 CPD 171 (1989); that if an offeror fails to demonstrate in its proposal how it will perform the work required by the contract, as required by the solicitation, it is within the agency's discretion to exclude the proposal from the competitive range, Federal Services, Inc., 89-2 CPD 182 (1989); and that it is within an agency's discretion to exclude a technically unacceptable proposal from the competitive range even if it is from the low price bidder. Id. This court agrees with these standards, and each supports upholding the CO's decision in this case.

The GAO has outlined five factors that it considers in reviewing an agency decision to exclude a proposal from the competitive range. PRC, 55 Comp. Gen. at 69; see also Electrospace Systems, Inc., 58 Comp. Gen. 415 (1979). This court finds those factors well reasoned (and even self-evident) and adopts them for use in this case. Those factors are: (1) did the solicitation specifically call for the information that the agency found lacking; (2) do the informational deficiencies tend to show the offeror did not understand the contract's requirements; (3) does the offeror essentially have to rewrite the proposal to correct the deficiencies; (4) was only one offeror left in the competitive range; and (5) whether the proposal, if reasonably correctable, would provide a cost savings. Id.

Considering these five factors in turn, it is clear, first, that the solicitation specifically called for the information that the agency found lacking. Indeed, items 16.1.3 and 16.4.0 broke the specific information required down into enumerated subparts that plaintiff did not even attempt to address. This court finds that every item found lacking in plaintiff's proposal was specifically requested by the government in the solicitation.

Plaintiff did not provide any reasons why its proposal was deficient in so many respects. Except for an unconvincing explanation (in court) of why it was unable to provide the costs or man-days expended on earlier contracts in response to a specific request in the relevant experience section, Tr. 38–42, plaintiff contends that its proposal is as complete as it needs to be. The court disagrees. The proposal fails to demonstrate how plaintiff will perform the work required under the contract and is thus, as the CO found, grossly deficient.

Second, the informational deficiencies in the proposal tend to show that plaintiff did not understand the scope of the contract. Even at the outset, in the statement of work, plaintiff never mentioned at least four of the six major work components of the contract. Plaintiff provided a quality control plan that the agency determined did not apply to this contract. And finally, in the list of experience required by 16.4.0, plaintiff discussed only non-skid application experience, ignoring the other large components of the project.

At the hearing, plaintiff argued that there was no need for it to address the aspects of the contract it ignored because any firm that had the technical ability to apply the non-skid surface could also do all the other work. Even if it were true that plaintiff had the technical ability to perform the painting and cleaning aspects of the contract, and that all others capable of doing one type work could do it all, plaintiff nonetheless was required to demonstrate to MSCLANT that plaintiff had this ability and that it understood the scope of the contract, and it was required to do this in the proposal.

Third, plaintiff would have to rewrite most of its proposal in order to provide the missing information. The solicitation required that offerors' technical proposals provide information basically in nine areas. MSCLANT reasonably found plaintiff's proposal deficient in all but one of those areas. In order to correct these deficiencies, plaintiff would have to add so much additional information in most of the sections that the final product would be tantamount to a complete rewriting of the proposal. For example, in the statement of the work section, plaintiff would have to add information about at least four of the six work components of the contract. Or, in the experience section, plaintiff would have to add information concerning five of the seven specific requested items for every job listed. After such changes, the new proposal would necessarily be drastically different than the one submitted.

Fourth, plaintiff has not alleged that the CO approved only one offeror for the competitive range, so this factor does not apply in this case. See footnote 6, supra (discussing this point).

Fifth, because this court agrees with the agency's determination that plaintiff's proposal was not reasonably correctable, the cost savings factor does not apply in this case.

Each of the applicable factors weighs heavily in favor of upholding the agency's decision in this case. In light of the broad discretion accorded contract officers in making competitive range determinations by the Federal Circuit, Birch & Davis, 4 F.3d at 973, MSCLANT's evaluation of plaintiff's proposal was not "clearly unreasonable," id., but rather, manifestly reasonable.

* * *

Conclusion

If the government were required to give further consideration to proposals like that submitted by plaintiff, or allow further response, bidders would have no incentive to make their best (or even responsive) proposals early in the process. This would make the bidding process completely chaotic; bids and requests for proposals would become moving targets, never to be halted or hit. This court will not accept plaintiff's invitation to establish a contracting scheme that would be so contrary to the established rules governing bid proposals and their evaluation, particularly when the solicitation warned that it would not permit supplementation, or the cross-referencing envisioned by plaintiff.

For the reasons stated herein, plaintiff's motion for a TRO is denied and its complaint is dismissed, without prejudice. The Clerk is directed to enter judgment for defendant.

Notes and Questions

1. The court's decision not to require discussions with the offeror may legitimately defer to the contracting officer. However, is there any reason to fault the contracting officer for eliminating this offer. Without forgiving the errors and faults of the offeror, study the clues in this opinion as though you were a contracting officer with the time and energy, as well as the zeal, to foster competition and save the government money. The offeror is a low-budget, out-of-town (Florida) operation which threw in a sketchily documented but potentially promising bit of competition. By eliminating it, does the contracting officer signal to the local (Baltimore, Norfolk) contractors that they need not cut their prices to meet that kind of competition?

2. Note how the multi-stage operation of the competitive proposals system produces much more room for strategizing—and, hence, the need by the government to structure the situation so as not to be gamed—than with sealed bids. A bidder on an IFB dare not hold back her best offer for later because there will not be a "later"—the award goes to the lowest responsive and responsible bid. In contrast, an offeror on an RFP might hold back her best offer initially, figuring to make a better offer at the final stage, after using discussions and other clues provided later on to try to gauge the competition. If an offeror puts in too inferior an initial offer, what does this case show will happen? However, is that what happened in this case?

Key to the process of competitive proposals is the statutory requirement that the solicitation include all significant evaluation factors and subfactors and the relative importance of each. This requirement promotes the fundamental policy of establishing a level playing field so that each competitor will know what is expected rather than having to rely on best guesses or even worse, improperly obtained agency information. Such a policy also promotes the elimination of the unstated personal bias of government selection officials. This next case demonstrates how the courts enforce this requirement.

Isratex, Inc. v. United States

United States Claims Court. 25 Cl. Ct. 223 Feb. 6, 1992.

NETTESHEIM, Judge.

On cross-motions for summary judgment after argument, this pre-award bid protest action questions whether the Government lawfully can exclude an offeror from participation in a negotiated procurement. The offeror's product demonstration model failed a mandatory test. The request for proposals, however, did not indicate the relative importance of the characteristics involved, nor did it advise offerors that automatic exclusion would follow from the test failure.

FACTS

The following facts are undisputed. On March 25, 1991, the Department of Defense, Defense Logistics Agency ("DLA"), Defense Personnel Support Center ("DPSC"), issued Solicitation DLA100-91-R-0120. DPSC is a supply center located in Philadelphia, Pennsylvania, that is maintained by DLA. The solicitation requested proposals for the manufacture of "792,408 EA Parka, Extended Cold Weather Clothing System (ECWS) Woodland Camouflage." Half of the quantity was set aside for small businesses. The solicitation requested that proposals be submitted by April 19, 1991.

On April 17, 1991, Amendment 0002 modified the solicitation; this amendment, inter alia, extended the closing date for proposals to May 21, 1991, and added a requirement that offerors submit a Product Demonstration Model (the "PDM"). Section L of the solicitation, entitled "INSTRUCTIONS, CONDITIONS AND NOTICE TO OFFERORS," stated, after modifications by Amendment 0002, that the proposal was to be submitted in three parts: PDM, Past Performance, Accelerated Delivery. Section L also stated that "[a] properly executed solicitation constitutes an acceptable pricing proposal." Section L required that each offeror submit two PDMs. With respect to the submission of the PDMs, Section L provided, in pertinent part, the following:

SUBMISSION OF PRODUCT DEMONSTRATION MODEL:

a. Models, as specified below, must be furnished as part of the offer and must be received by the time set forth for closing of offers. Models will be evaluated to determine compliance with all characteristics listed in the end item specification.

b. Failure of the models to conform to all such characteristics may result in rejection of the offer.

. . . .

d. The PDM's shall be tested as follows:

1. One (1) complete garment shall be tested for hydrostatic resistance of the seams in accordance with para. 4.5.1 of MIL-P-44188B ["The parka shall be tested at four different locations. . . . Evidence of leakage in one or more seam locations shall be considered a test failure."].

2. The other complete garment shall be subjected to visual and dimensional examination in accordance with paras. 4.4.2 and 4.4.3 of MIL-P-44188B. [Paragraph 4.4.2 provides an extensive list of possible defects for which end items are to be examined. Defects include cuts, tears, holes, omitted items, incorrectly placed or attached items, and improper stitching. Paragraph 4.4.3 specifies dimensions to which the end items must conform.]

Section M, entitled "EVALUATION CRITERIA AND BASIS FOR AWARD," as modified by Amendment 0002, stated, in part, the following:

b. The technical quality of proposals shall be determined by assessment of the following technical evaluation factors. They are listed in descending order of importance:

1. Product Demonstration Model

2. Past Performance

3. Accelerated [D]elivery[.]

With respect to the requirement that offerors provide two PDMs, Section M provided the following:

EVALUATION OF THE PRODUCT DEMONSTRATION MODELS:

Product Demonstration Models must be submitted as part of the offer at no expense to the Government. Characteristics for which the models will be tested or evaluated are:

1. Quality of construction (including seam sealing)

2. Workmanship

3. Conformance to the dimensional and visual requirements of the end item specification.

4. Test requirements: One (1) complete garment shall be tested for hydrostatic resistance of the seams in accordance with para. 4.5.1 of MIL-P-44188B. The other complete garment shall be subjected to visual and dimensional examination in accordance with paras. 4.4.2 and 4.4.3 of MIL-P-44188B....

Jacqueline Pelullo, the contracting officer who drafted Amendment 0002, was tasked with buying the items required under the solicitation. She testified on deposition that the manner of listing these subfactors was not intended to show their order of importance. Specifically, she stated:

When I wrote this [the subfactors] up, I just listed them. They're—in my mind there was no separate weight for any of the items....

....

In my mind, they are not all even. I just wanted to say, the way they're listed here was not meant to show an order of importance. I don't believe that we indicated that.

In addition, Contracting Officer Pelullo stated that she knew the hydrostatic resistance test was "very important." Section M also provided an "ADJECTIVAL RATING SYMBOLOGY" that set forth three possible ratings: "Acceptable," "Marginally Acceptable," and "Unacceptable." The definition given for "Unacceptable" read, as follows:

Unacceptable: Proposal fails to meet solicitation requirements. Offeror's record of past performance demonstrates a lack of commitment to customer satisfaction and timely delivery of quality goods. A rating of this magnitude indicates a product of unacceptable quality with no probability of successful performance. The technical proposal is unacceptable without substantial correction which would constitute a new proposal.

Amendment 0006 to the solicitation, issued on June 27, 1991, established the final quantity of parkas required by the solicitation and the final closing date for offers. The number of parkas was 672,888, 336,432 of which were set aside for small businesses. The closing date for offers was extended to July 15, 1991. DPSC received 20 offers by the closing date. Isratex, Inc. ("plaintiff"), was one of the offerors that submitted a timely proposal to DPSC. Two of DPSC's employees, along with two employees of the United States Army Natick Research, Development and Engineering Center ("Natick"), conducted the evaluations of plaintiff's and the other offerors' PDMs. Plaintiff's PDM failed the hydrostatic resistance test due to three leaks in the back neck hood seam. Three other offerors' PDMs also failed the hydrostatic resistance test. PDMs that failed the hydrostatic resistance test received automatically, i.e., regardless of any other factor, a rating of "Unacceptable." DPSC eliminated from further consideration proposals that received a rating of "Unacceptable" on the PDM. PDMs that passed the hydrostatic resistance test, but exhibited other specification deficiencies—either workmanship or dimensional deficiencies—received ratings of "Marginally Acceptable." DPSC directed some of the offerors that received a "Marginally Acceptable" rating on their PDMs to submit new PDMs.

On November 12, 1991, DPSC sent a letter to plaintiff and the other three offerors whose PDMs failed the hydrostatic resistance test, notifying them that their proposals would not receive further consideration. The letter to plaintiff stated, in part:

> [Y]ou are advised that your proposal submitted in response to subject solicitation was determined not to be within the competitive range determined for negotiation purposes. This determination was made after an integrated assessment of all evaluated factors, such as Production Demonstration Models, technical proposal, acceleration of delivery and price. Therefore, your proposal, as well as any further revisions, will not be considered.

Attached to the letter was an evaluation of plaintiff's PDM, rating the PDM as "Unacceptable" and noting the deficiencies with the PDM. With respect to the other factors that the solicitation stated would be evaluated, Ms. Pelullo testified in her deposition that plaintiff's past performance was rated "Marginally Acceptable," that plaintiff's accelerated delivery was rated as "Acceptable," and that plaintiff's price appeared to be in the competitive range.

On November 12, 1991, in addition to notifying those offerors that failed the hydrostatic resistance test that their proposals had been eliminated from further consideration, DPSC issued Amendment 0007 to the solicitation. Amendment 0007, in relevant part, modified the definition of "Unacceptable" to read:

> Unacceptable: The Production Demonstration Model fails to meet the stated technical features of the specification/solicitation requirements. Offeror's record of past performance demonstrates a lack of commitment to customer satisfaction and timely delivery of quality goods. A rating of this magnitude indicates a product of unacceptable quality with no probability of successful performance. The Model is unacceptable as submitted and cannot be made acceptable without substantial correction which would constitute a new proposal.

Contracting Officer Pelullo explained that this modification was intended to expand the symbology in Amendment 0002, which originally had added the PDM requirement. Plaintiff's proposal was evaluated under the definition of "Unacceptable" as it was formulated in Amendment 0002, not as it appeared in Amendment 0007.

Subsequent to receiving notification that its proposal was no longer under consideration, plaintiff submitted two new PDMs to DPSC. DPSC advised plaintiff that these PDMs would not be evaluated. No offeror whose PDMs failed the hydrostatic resistance test was permitted to submit new PDMs.

Plaintiff filed a complaint and motion for a temporary restraining order pursuant to 28 U.S.C. §1491(a)(3) (1988), seeking to enjoin DPSC from awarding the contract unless and until DPSC evaluates plaintiff's resubmitted PDMs. During briefing defendant reported that contract award was deferred until at least February 7, 1992. Plaintiff's request for permanent injunctive relief consequently proceeded to the merits without an interim order. At argument defendant advised the court that the earliest date for contract award had been extended to February 21, 1992. The parties agreed that disposition by summary judgment was appropriate.

DISCUSSION

1. Standards for injunctive relief

Pursuant to 28 U.S.C. §1491(a)(3), the Claims Court may grant injunctive relief in a pre-award bid protest case where the Government has breached its implied duty to consider a bid honestly and fairly.

2. Evaluation of plaintiff's proposal

Plaintiff contends that DPSC's evaluation of plaintiff's proposal for Solicitation DLA100-91-R-0120 was not in accordance with the evaluation scheme set forth in the solicitation. Plaintiff relies, in part, on 10 U.S.C. §2305 (1988 & Supp. II 1990), to support its position. 10 U.S.C. §2305 provides, in pertinent part:

§2305. Contracts: planning, solicitation, evaluation, and award procedures

(a)(1)(A) In preparing for the procurement of property or services, the head of an agency shall—

(i) specify the agency's needs and solicit bids or proposals in a manner designed to achieve full and open competition for the procurement;

. . . .

(2) In addition to the specifications described in paragraph (1), a solicitation for sealed bids or competitive proposals...shall at a minimum include—

(A) a statement of—

(i) all significant factors (and significant subfactors) which the head of the agency reasonably expects to consider in evaluating sealed bids (including price) or competitive proposals...

(ii) the relative importance assigned to each of those factors (and subfactors)....

Plaintiff's contention with respect to section 2305(a)(2) is that DPSC's solicitation did not state the relative importance of the subfactors relating to the PDM.

The solicitation listed four subfactors that would be evaluated with respect to the PDM. The solicitation numbered these subfactors, but did not state the relative importance of each of them. Contracting Officer Pelullo acknowledged that the order in which the subfactors were listed was not intended to represent their relative importance and that the solicitation did not state the relative importance of the subfactors. Nevertheless, the contracting officer stated that in her evaluation of the proposals she considered subfactor 4, the hydrostatic resistance test, as "very important;" that failure of the hydrostatic resistance test resulted in rejection of the PDM, regardless of any other factor; and that rejection of an offeror's PDM resulted in automatic rejection of the offeror's proposal.

Consequently, the issue for decision is whether there was a clear and prejudicial violation of an applicable procurement statute. Section 2305(a)(2) requires that a solicitation set forth the relative importance of subfactors. Solicitation DLA100-91-R-0120 did not state the relative importance of the four subfactors listed for the PDM. When no indication of relative importance is given, an offeror can assume that the subfactors will be equally weighted. Informatics, Inc., No. B-194734, 79-2 C.P.D. (Fed.Pub.) P 144, aff'd sub nom. Information Processing Servs. Div., Info. Servs. Group of Informatics, Inc. v. Harris, 26 C.C.F. (CCH) ¶83,698 (D.D.C.1979); Dikewood Servs. Co., No. B-186001, 76-2 C.P.D. (Fed.Pub.) ¶520. If the relative importance of all subfactors was not given because a solicitation contemplated that all subfactors were of equal importance, the solicitation would comport with section 2305. In that circumstance no relative importance would exist among the subfactors. That situation is not present in the case at bar.

In this case the contracting officer considered the hydrostatic resistance test as a "very important" subfactor, so important, in fact, that failure of the test caused offerors' proposals to be rejected. Deficiencies relating to workmanship or dimensional requirements of the PDM did not result in rejection of other offerors' proposals; indeed, DPSC directed those offerors to submit new corrected PDMs. Thus, the hydrostatic resistance test was accorded far greater weight than the other subfactors in evaluation of an offeror's PDM and proposal. Section 2305(a)(2) required that DPSC weigh equally the subfactors, in the absence of a statement of their relative importance. DPSC neither stated the relative importance of the subfactors nor equally weighed the subfactors. DPSC therefore violated 28 U.S.C. §2305(a)(2) when it gave predominant weight to the hydrostatic resistance test subfactor.

Having established the clear violation of an applicable procurement statute, the next question to be addressed is whether the violation was prejudicial. If defendant's contention were accepted—that the solicitation alerted offerors that a PDM's passing the hydrostatic resistance test was a sine qua non for staying in the competition—DPSC's violation of the statute would not have prejudiced plaintiff. In other words, if the solicitation put offerors on notice that passing the hydrostatic resistance test was a mandatory requirement of the solicitation, DPSC's violation of section 2305 would not be deemed prejudicial.

Amendment 0002 to the solicitation put plaintiff and the other offerors on notice that failure of the PDM "to conform to all such characteristics [all characteristics listed in the end-item specification] may result in rejection of the offer." This language, however, does not effect notice that passing the hydrostatic resistance test was a mandatory requirement. The language applies to all end-item specifications relating to the PDM. If the court were to construe the language as putting an offeror on notice that passing the hydrostatic resistance test was mandatory, the court effectively would be holding that satisfying all end-item specifications relating to the PDM was required or a PDM would be rejected. Such a construction would transmute the permissive "may" to a mandatory "shall." To the contrary, Contracting Officer Pelullo did not view the satisfaction of all end-item specifications as mandatory; acting pursuant to this standard, she decided not to reject some proposals with PDMs that exhibited deficiencies. If DPSC intended that passing the hydrostatic resistance test was a mandatory requirement, DPSC should have stated so in language typically used for such purposes. See Hughes Advanced Sys. Co., GSBCA No. 9601-P, 88-3 B.C.A. (CCH) ¶21,115, at 106,602 (citing International Business Machs. Corp., GSBCA No. 9293-P, 88-1 B.C.A. (CCH) ¶20,512, at 103,697 (RFP stated: "Proposals...shall meet all the [G]overnment's requirements in Section C in order to be eligible for evaluation...."); Spectragraphics Corp., GSBCA No. 9194-P, 88-1 B.C.A. (CCH) ¶20,333, at 102,786 (RFP stated: "The Government shall not consider for award proposals that do not meet the mandatory requirements."); CPT Corp., GSBCA No. 8134-P-R, 86-1 B.C.A. (CCH) ¶18,727, at 94,206 (RFP stated: "In order to have an acceptable proposal, the offeror must meet all of the mandatory requirements set forth in Section C.2 of the Solicitation Document....")).

Had the solicitation given notice that the hydrostatic resistance test would be the deciding factor in an evaluation of an offeror's proposal, DPSC's violation of 28 U.S.C. §2305(a)(2) would not have prejudiced plaintiff. Defendant argues unpersuasively that the solicitation gave such notice. Defendant contends that because a separate garment was required for the hydrostatic resistance test, because leakage in a seam caused failure of that test, and because the defining characteristic of the garment to be manufactured was its waterproof nature, an offeror was on notice that the hydrostatic resistance test was of predominant importance. The law does not support defendant's argument.

"[W]here one factor is to have predominant consideration over the other factors, this should be disclosed to the offerors." Sperry Rand Corp., Univac Div., No. B-179875, 74-2 C.P.D. (Fed.Pub.) ¶158, at 11. "As a matter of sound procurement policy, the fullest possible disclosure of all of the evaluation factors and their relative importance is to be preferred to reliance on the reasonableness of the offerors' judgment as to the relative significance of the various evaluation factors." BDM Servs. Co., No. B-180245, 74-1 C.P.D. (Fed.Pub.) ¶237, at 8. In the case at bar, offerors were not given notice that the hydrostatic resistance test would be a predominant factor in the evaluation of proposals. The solicitation stated that one garment was required for the hydrostatic resistance test and one garment was required for visual and dimensional examination. The solicitation listed the hydrostatic resistance test and the visual and dimensional examination together as one of the four subfactors relating to the PDM that would be evaluated. The solicitation did not specify that the hydrostatic resistance test would be of predominant importance.

The inference that defendant asks this court to draw is not unreasonable: An offeror could have been expected to discern that a waterproof PDM was an absolute requirement for award. See supra note 10. However, an offeror also could have been expected to discern that a PDM must be void of visual and dimensional defects, such as cuts, tears, holes, incorrectly attached components or improperly sized components. The offeror would have to have been clairvoyant to anticipate that failing the hydrostatic resistance test alone would automatically disqualify its proposal, while exhibiting other deficiencies would allow the offeror to be given a second chance at contract award.

Defendant's contentions that the solicitation gave notice that passing the hydrostatic resistance test would be a mandatory requirement or a predominant factor in evaluation of proposals do not provide a credible basis for holding that DPSC's violation of the statute was nonprejudicial to plaintiff. Because the solicitation did not state the relative importance of the subfactors, plaintiff could assume that the subfactors would be equally weighed. When DPSC accorded predominant weight to the hydrostatic resistance test — in effect making it a mandatory requirement—DPSC violated section 2305(a)(2).

Plaintiff was prejudiced thereby, since DPSC rejected its proposal while at the same time not rejecting other proposals that exhibited deficiencies with respect to subfactors that should have been accorded weight equal to that of the hydrostatic resistance test. The evidence supports a finding that DPSC's violation of section 2305(a)(2) was both clear and prejudicial.

Notes and Questions

1. The solicitation stated in this instance "[f]ailure of [the bid sample] to conform to all such characteristics [specifications] *may* result in rejection of the offer." Emphasis

added. How does such language distinguish competitive proposals/RFPs from sealed bids/IFBs? Had the agency used the IFB process with passing the waterproofing test a mandatory specification requirement, would the protester still have been able file a successful protest?

2. The court made a finding not only of a violation of procurement law, but in order to sustain the protest, also made a finding that the violation prejudiced the protestor. How was prejudice established in this case? Do all violations of procurement law result in prejudice to the protester? What must a finding of prejudice include generally?

John H. DALTON, Secretary of the Navy, Appellant, v. CESSNA AIRCRAFT COMPANY, Appellee.
United States Court of Appeals, Federal Circuit.
98 F.3d 1298 Oct. 22, 1996.

Before NEWMAN, LOURIE, and SCHALL, Circuit Judges.

Opinion for the court filed by Circuit Judge SCHALL. Dissenting opinion filed by Circuit Judge NEWMAN.

SCHALL, Circuit Judge.

This action arises under the Contract Disputes Act of 1978, as amended ("CDA"), 41 U.S.C. § 601–613 (1994). The United States Navy ("Navy") appeals from part of the decision of the Armed Services Board of Contract Appeals ("Board") in CESSNA Aircraft Co., ASBCA No. 48118, 95-1 BCA (CCH) § 27,560, 1995 WL 113915 (March 6, 1995). In its decision, the Board sustained the appeal of CESSNA Aircraft Company ("Cessna") seeking an equitable adjustment under its contract with the Navy for flight training services. We reverse.

BACKGROUND

I.

Cessna was awarded Contract No. N00019-83-C-0090 ("the contract") by the Navy on May 10, 1983. Cessna, 95-1 BCA at 137,344. The contract was a firm fixed-price services contract titled "Undergraduate Naval Flight Officer/Training System Upgrade (UNFO/TSO)." Id. Under the contract, Cessna was to provide services to assist in radar and navigation training for undergraduate naval flight officers ("UNFOs"). Id. The procurement grew out of the fact that the T-39 aircraft the Navy had been using in its UNFO training program were becoming obsolete. Id. at 137,345. In 1981, the Navy decided to enter into a multi-year contract for training services under 10 U.S.C. § 2306(g) (1994),[1] rather than purchase its own equipment. Id.

The Navy issued a Request for Information ("RFI") on May 14, 1982, setting forth what it was contemplating in its procurement and inviting potential bidders to attend a presolicitation conference to be held on May 27, 1982. Cessna, 95-1 BCA at 137,345. In

---

1. 10 U.S.C. § 2306(g) allows an agency to "enter into contracts for periods of not more than five years" for certain types of services, "for which funds would otherwise be available for obligation only within the fiscal year for which appropriated."

its RFI, the Navy stated: "Annual flight training systems will be designed to support a tactical [Naval Flight Officer] training rate of from 300–350 students per year. For planning purposes the estimated flying hours needed to conduct this training will range from 12,000–17,000 hours per year." The RFI did not specify any contemplated number of hours per graduated student. Id. at 137,346. The Navy also stated that the RFI "represents a reliable statement of the Navy requirement and possible procurement approaches for satisfying this requirement."

At the pre-solicitation conference, potential bidders asked questions about the procurement and had them answered. Cessna, 95-1 BCA at 137,345. On June 29, 1982, the Navy distributed to potential bidders, in written form, the questions and answers from the pre-solicitation conference. Id.

A number of questions at the conference addressed the issue of the rate of flight training services that the contractor would be required to provide. In response to all such questions, the Navy consistently referred potential bidders to the then-forthcoming Request for Quotations ("RFQ"). One question asked, "If [Navy] is going to modify the [training] syllabus where will they get their info and training?" The distributed answer read: "The Navy does not intend to modify the syllabus."

Cessna representatives met with the Navy's Wing Commander, Captain Thaubald, on September 9, 1982, and questioned him about the 17,000 hour provision. Cessna, 95-1 BCA at 137,346. Captain Thaubald testified before the Board that, at that meeting, he indicated to Cessna that "current usage projected 12,000 flying hours annually, but that if Congress approved a battle group increase the [Navy] would use 17,000 hours." Id.

On October 1, 1982, the Navy issued its RFQ. Cessna, 95-1 BCA at 137,345. The services that the contractor was to provide were described in Section C, titled "Description or Specifications." It stated that the contractor was to

> provide services to assist in Radar and Navigation training of Undergraduate Naval Flight Officers. These services shall consist of an annual rate of 17,000 airborne training service hours (approximately 58 airborne training hours per graduated student) on Contractor-furnished radar equipped aircraft of common configuration.

Id. at 137,344. Because of a gradual phase-in of services, the contractor was to begin providing a total of 17,000 airborne training service hours in the third year of the contract (FY 1986). Id. The "Program Description and Objectives" section of the RFQ reiterated the language of Section C, stating that "[h]ands-on training on the radar within the aircraft, as well as the training instructor pilot services, will consist of airborne training services of 17,000 hours per year (approximately 58 hours per student)." Other parts of the contract recited the 17,000 airborne training service hours ("ATSH") provision unaccompanied by the 58-hour parenthetical. These clauses called for 17,000 hours of flight services to be provided in the third, fourth, and fifth program years and in the option years.

Attached to the RFQ were a Statement of Work ("SOW") and the training syllabus then used by the Navy in the UNFO program. Paragraph 3.1.2 of the SOW defined the scope of contractor support services:

> The Contractor shall furnish all equipment and services required to ensure the UNFO Training System is available for Navy use in accordance with the provisions of this SOW.... The Contractor shall provide sufficient aircraft to accomplish the annual UNFO training rate requirement and meet a 95% mission

completion rate. The Government may or may not order flights on any given day, depending on the necessity of the work and suitability of flying conditions. The schedule of operations will be planned by the Government with the cooperation of the Contractor's Representative. Most flight operations will be conducted during daylight hours, however some night and overnight operations will be required. The current training syllabus requires three (3) overnight flights per week of one (1) or two (2) night's duration.

Attached to the SOW was the training syllabus or "curricula" then in use by the Navy. Paragraph 3.1.1 of the SOW stated, "For Contractor planning purposes, copies of the existing curricula currently used by the Chief of Naval Air Training for training student Naval Flight Officers are attached." There was no indication in the SOW as to whether or not the syllabus would be altered by the Navy. According to the syllabus appended to the SOW, the UNFO training program was to be conducted in five curricula grouped into three phases: basic (one curriculum), intermediate (one curriculum), and advanced (three curricula).

The basic flight training was conducted on Navy aircraft, not on Cessna's T-47 aircraft, and thus was not part of the 17,000 hour requirement. The intermediate curriculum required 12 hours of training for all UNFOs. After completing the intermediate phase, an UNFO would take one of the three curricula in the advanced phase. Each curriculum in the advanced phase had its own hourly training requirement. For example, UNFOs in the "Tactical Navigation" segment would receive 37.2 training flight hours; UNFOs in the "Overwater Jet Navigation" segment would receive 37.2 training flight hours; and UNFOs in the "Radar Intercept Officer" segment would receive 46.3 training flight hours. Therefore, UNFOs in the Radar Intercept Officer program would receive the most training flight hours. By adding the 12 flight hours in the intermediate curriculum to the 46.3 flight hours in the Radar Intercept Officer curriculum, a bidder could deduce that an UNFO would receive up to 58.3 hours of training.

After the RFQ was issued, a post-solicitation conference was held on October 18–19, 1982. Cessna, 95-1 BCA at 137,346. At the conference, potential bidders had a chance to ask questions and have them answered. On October 29, 1982, the Navy distributed the questions asked at the conference, along with answers to the questions. Id. Among the questions asked and answered were the following:

> Question: Would the annual rates for services remain constant over the life of the contract? If not, what factors could cause it to change? If an option to extend the contract is exercised, how would the rate change?

> Answer: The annual rate ... for services needed should be proposed by the contractor based on RFQ requirements.

> Question: What factors will be used to determine the annual rate for services?

> Answer: The contractor should propose the annual rate for services based on the RFQ.

On November 8, 1982, the Navy released the answers to additional questions that had been received. One question and its answer were as follows:

> Question: To enable each offeror to propose the most cost effective solution, will the government specify the following:

> 1) Fuel cost per gallon.

> 2) Escalation factor.

3) Expected flight hours (We understand that the 17,000 may be the maximum[)].

Answer: As previously stated, we cannot reveal the price of fuel to be used, nor can we reveal the other factors used to estimate fuel costs.

In its proposal, submitted in response to the RFQ on December 1, 1982, Cessna stated: "Personnel and aircraft requirements have been derived based on required training service levels and are based on current experience as modified to meet the levels established in the RFQ." Before the Board, James Lyle, Program Manager for Cessna, testified that Cessna relied upon the training syllabus attached to the SOW in preparing its bid.

In its April 4, 1983 best and final offer, which incorporated by reference its December 1, 1982 proposal and which was revised on April 25, 1983, Cessna offered fifteen radar equipped T-47 aircraft to replace the Navy's T-39 aircraft, rather than the twenty it had originally thought necessary. Cessna, 95-1 BCA at 137,347. Cessna also offered a lower price in its best and final offer than it had previously bid. Id. Cessna based its best and final offer upon the training syllabus that was attached to the RFQ, and upon the clause stating that approximately 58 flight hours per student would be required. Id. at 137,346–47. According to Cessna, it calculated that the Navy would use the full contingent of 17,000 hours contemplated in the specification only if the Navy increased the number of students it trained under the program. Id. at 137,347. The Board found that both Cessna and the Navy projected that if the Navy were to keep training students at the same rate as it had under the training syllabus, a maximum of only 12,000 flight hours would be utilized. Id. at 137,346.

In its December 1, 1982 proposal, however, Cessna referred to the 17,000 ATSH provision without qualification. In describing radar and navigation training, Cessna stated that "[u]nder the prospective contract, Cessna is to provide services to assist in radar and navigation training of UNFOs consisting of an annual rate of 17,000 airborne training service hours in Cessna-furnished radar-equipped aircraft of common configuration." Referring to the "Full-Up Operational UNFO/TSU Services Phase" of the contract, Cessna stated: "During this phase, flying hour availability will be 17,000 hours per year."

II.

After entering into the contract and reaching the later years, the Navy realized that it was not utilizing 17,000 ATSH per year. Cessna, 95-1 BCA at 137,348. In order to use all of the ATSH for which it believed it had contracted, the Navy updated its training syllabus to increase the number of flight hours per UNFO to 78 hours. Id. at 137,349. The Navy also made operational changes to the scope of the services it was utilizing under the contract. Id. at 137,349–51. In terms of operational changes, the Navy began requiring Cessna to transport non-student passengers, such as Navy VIPs and Navy officers who needed to log flight hours in order to receive flight pay. Id. at 137,349–50. The Navy also required Cessna to perform rescue flights, and to make overnight flights above and beyond those specified in the contract. Id. at 137,350. In addition, the Navy used Cessna's aircraft to conduct target flights. Id. at 137,359–51.

Objecting to the use of the updated syllabus and to the operational changes, Cessna filed a certified claim for an equitable adjustment with the contracting officer on June 1, 1987. Cessna stated that it was seeking an equitable adjustment because the Navy had made constructive changes to the contract, such as (i) using Cessna's "services to fly nontraining missions as well as to fly missions outside the contract's training parameters," and (ii) changing "the UNFO training syllabus to increase the flight training requirements from those provided by the Navy for bidding purposes." Cessna and the Navy negotiated until October 4, 1988. On October 11, 1988, pursuant to the CDA, Cessna filed an appeal with the Board on the ground that the contracting officer had not issued a final decision within a reasonable time.

On February 2, 1989, the contracting officer issued his decision denying Cessna's request for an equitable adjustment. With respect to the issue of whether the updated syllabus constituted a change requiring an equitable adjustment under the changes clause of the contract, the contracting officer stated, "I find that the syllabus is irrelevant to the annual 17,000 hour requirement. I find that the contract clearly entitles the Navy to 17,000 hours of airborne training services each year." With respect to the operational changes, the contracting officer found that Cessna was not entitled to an equitable adjustment.

The Board rendered a 3-2 split decision in the appeal. * * * *

DISCUSSION

I.

* * *

What the government does challenge on appeal is the Board's holding that Cessna is entitled to an equitable adjustment as a result of the syllabus change increasing the number of flight hours per UNFO to 78 hours. The government contends that the Board's holding is incorrect as a matter of law in two respects. First, the government argues, the Board erred in construing the phrase "annual rate of 17,000 airborne training service hours (approximately 58 airborne training hours per graduated student)" as calling for 17,000 ATSH, qualified by the provision of approximately 58 training hours per UNFO. As seen above, the Board determined that the 17,000 hour requirement set forth in Section C was merely a contingency that would depend upon an increased number of students, rather than a flat requirement of 17,000 hours of service annually. The government's interpretation is that the Navy contracted for an unqualified 17,000 ATSH and that the reference to 58 hours per student was merely an estimate. Under the government's interpretation, a change in the syllabus to increase the number of training hours per student could not give rise to a claim for an equitable adjustment so long as the Navy did not use more than 17,000 ATSH. Second, the government asserts that Cessna's interpretation of the contract necessarily gave rise to an ambiguity of which Cessna was aware. Under these circumstances, Cessna was under a duty to seek clarification before submitting its proposal, which it did not do. Accordingly, Cessna is barred from recovery. For its part, Cessna responds that the Board correctly interpreted the contract. Addressing the government's second argument, Cessna contends that any ambiguity in the contract was latent and that, accordingly, under the doctrine of contra proferentem, it was not required to seek clarification. For the reasons set forth below, we hold that Cessna is barred from seeking an equitable adjustment for the syllabus change because, in view of its interpretation of the contract, it was under a duty to seek clarification before submitting its proposal.

II.

It is undisputed that the contract was a firm fixed-price services contract. Such a contract

> provides for a price that is not subject to any adjustment on the basis of the contractor's cost experience in performing the contract. This contract type places upon the contractor maximum risk and full responsibility for all costs

and resulting profit or loss. It provides maximum incentive for the contractor to control costs and perform effectively and imposes a minimum administrative burden upon the contracting parties.

48 C.F.R. § 16.202-1 (1995).

According to the Federal Acquisition Regulations ("FAR"), fixed-price contracts are "suitable for acquiring commercial items...or for acquiring other supplies or services on the basis of reasonably definite functional or detailed specifications." Id. at § 16.202-2. The regulations suggest situations where this type of contract may be appropriate, such as when performance uncertainties can be identified and reasonably quantified. Id. at § 16.202-2(d). Because fixed-price contracts do not contain a method for varying the price of the contract in the event of unforeseen circumstances, they assign the risk to the contractor that the actual cost of performance will be higher than the price of the contract.

Contract interpretation is an issue of law. Interstate Gen. Gov't Contractors v. Stone, 980 F.2d 1433, 1434 (Fed.Cir.1992). Reading the 58-hour statement in the context of the entire contract, we conclude that it was reasonable for the Navy to interpret the statement as an estimate. First, given that this was a firm fixed-price contract that assured Cessna would be paid regardless of the number of airborne flight hours the Navy consumed,[6] it was reasonable for the Navy to take the position that the contract should not be interpreted as containing a provision potentially qualifying the manner in which the Navy used the full amount of the services procured. Put another way, in the setting of this contract, in the absence of language clearly and unambiguously placing a qualification on the manner in which the Navy could consume the services it was procuring, it was reasonable for the Navy to interpret the reference to 58 hours per graduated student as an estimate. This was especially so, we believe, in view of the fact that the 58-hour statement appeared in parentheses and was qualified by the word "approximately." In short, it can hardly be said that the statement was clothed in the garb of a binding contractual provision.

In addition, settled principles of contract interpretation lead us to the conclusion that it was reasonable for the Navy, when viewing the contract as a whole, to construe the 58-hour parenthetical as an estimate, rather than a binding provision. We read the language of a particular contractual provision in the context of the entire agreement, United States v. Johnson Controls, Inc., 713 F.2d 1541, 1555 (Fed.Cir.1983), and construe the contract so as not to render portions of it meaningless, Fortec Constructors v. United States, 760 F.2d 1288, 1292 (Fed.Cir.1985). Also, we apply the interpretation that accords a reasonable meaning to each of the provisions. Hol-Gar Mfg. Corp. v. United States, 169 Ct.Cl. 384, 351 F.2d 972, 979 (1965). Finally, where an agreement contains general and specific provisions which are in any respect inconsistent, "the provision directed to a particular matter controls over the provision which is general in its terms." Hills Materials Co. v. Rice, 982 F.2d 514, 517 (Fed.Cir.1992). Here, we are faced with separate provisions of a single contract, one set of provisions specific and one general. The specific provisions of the contract are the portions of the syllabus noted above that

---

6. Before the Board, the contracting officer testified that the Navy intended to "pay for 17,000 [hours] whether [they] flew it or not."

called for 17,000 hours of flight services for various work items for the third, fourth, and fifth program years and for the option years, without qualification as to the number of hours per student. The general provisions, of course, are the sections of the contract containing the "58 airborne training hours per graduated student" parenthetical. The Navy could reasonably take the position that the contract as a whole, including the more specific provisions, compelled the conclusion that the 58-hour parenthetical merely represented an estimate and therefore did not place a qualification on the extent of the services to which the Navy was entitled under the contract.

The foregoing notwithstanding, we will assume for the purpose of deciding this appeal that it was reasonable for Cessna to construe the "annual rate of 17,000 airborne training service hours" provision as qualified by the "approximately 58 airborne training service hours" parenthetical. We hold as a matter of law, however, that, in view of the nature of the contract and the principles of contract interpretation noted above, this construction of the contract gave rise to a patent ambiguity. See Newsom v. United States, 230 Ct.Cl. 301, 676 F.2d 647, 649 (Cl.Ct.1982) ("The existence of a patent ambiguity is a question of contractual interpretation which must be decided de novo by the court."). We presume both Cessna and the government "to be endowed with at least a modicum of business acumen," Firestone Tire & Rubber Co. v. United States, 195 Ct.Cl. 21, 444 F.2d 547, 551 (1971), and we view Cessna as a knowledgeable bidder. Cessna should have recognized that its construction of the contract—based as it was upon a qualified parenthetical statement—was squarely in conflict with the construction of the contract that reasonably flowed from the basic nature of the contract (firm fixed-price) and its provisions. This patent ambiguity created an obligation on Cessna's part to seek clarification before submitting its proposal. Fortec Constructors, 760 F.2d at 1291 ("The existence of a patent ambiguity in the contract raises the duty of inquiry, regardless of the reasonableness of the contractor's interpretation."); S.O.G. of Arkansas v. United States, 212 Ct.Cl. 125, 546 F.2d 367, 369 (1976) ("The case presents another example of a contractor who, faced with a patent ambiguity in Government bid documents, did not meet his responsibility to have the ambiguity resolved before bidding.").

Faced with what it should have recognized as a patent ambiguity—in light of its interpretation of the firm fixed-price contract—Cessna did not meet its obligation of inquiry. It has never been asserted that Cessna sought clarification from the Navy with regard to its interpretation of the RFQ before submitting its proposal. At the same time, none of the questions and answers provided to prospective bidders by the Navy clarified the point. We have quoted above the questions and answers that are pertinent to this issue. These questions and answers either do not address the issue or are ambiguous. In any event, contrary to what the Board determined, it cannot be said that they provide a basis for concluding that the Navy shared Cessna's construction of the contract. Under these circumstances, Cessna did not meet its obligation of seeking clarification. See Community Heating & Plumbing Co., Inc. v. Kelso, 987 F.2d 1575, 1580 (Fed.Cir.1993) ("The Navy's response to the...letter expressly failed to address the issue of the conduit sleeves and thus provided a strong indication to Community that confusion still existed between the parties. Community was therefore obligated to request further clarification regarding the proper installation of the conduit sleeves."); Aviation Contractor Employees, Inc. v. United States, 945 F.2d 1568, 1571 (Fed.Cir.1991) (holding that a "somewhat evasive" response by the government to bidders' pre-bid questioning was sufficient to "clearly put bidders on notice" that the government intended to restrict option pricing). Having failed to seek clarification, Cessna was not entitled to rely upon its interpretation of the contract. Grumman Data Sys. Corp. v. Dalton, 88 F.3d 990, 998

(Fed.Cir.1996) ("If a solicitation contains contract language that is patently ambiguous, a protestor cannot argue, before the Board or before this court, that its interpretation is proper unless the protestor sought clarification of the language from the agency before the end of the procurement process.") The Board therefore erred in holding that Cessna was entitled to an equitable adjustment by reason of the syllabus change.

CONCLUSION

For the foregoing reasons, the part of the Board's decision that relates to the syllabus change is reversed.

COSTS

Each party shall bear its own costs.

REVERSED.

PAULINE NEWMAN, Circuit Judge, dissenting.

The Armed Services Board of Contract Appeals, resolving the several disputes arising from this contract, found that the Navy did not have unrestricted use of Cessna's aircraft and flight services up to 17,000 hours of flight time. The Board held that it was an incorrect interpretation of the contract to require Cessna to provide services beyond those explicitly set forth in the contract, up to the maximum of 17,000 hours. This is the ruling that the Navy appeals.

* * *

There was no unresolved, patent ambiguity at the time the contract was entered into.

The contract explicitly provided for "approximately 58 hours" of flight training per student. In evidence was the statement of the contracting officer that the Navy "does not intend to modify the syllabus." Section 3.1.1 of the Statement of Work provided that the curriculum for student training (the Syllabus) was attached for "Contractor planning purposes" and that its purpose was to "define the contractor effort necessary to support the training requirement of Undergraduate Naval Flight Officers." Although the panel majority chooses to find that there was a patent ambiguity concerning the obligation to provide 58 hours per student, in view of the ceiling of 17,000 hours, the Board, viewing the mutual understandings embodied in the contract, did not find such ambiguity. Indeed, the Navy did not state that it was entitled to 78, not 58, hours per student until three years into contract performance.

The Navy does not dispute, as indeed it can not, that the contract is explicit as to the "approximately 58 hours" of flight time per student. The Navy does not argue that 78 is approximately 58. The Board rejected the Navy's litigation-created position that it had unlimited call on the Cessna planes and personnel, and held that the Navy was bound by the provisions of the contract, including the provision of approximately 58 hours per student. Indeed, the Navy has taken the strange position of arguing that its own contract requirement is of no significance.

Evidence as to the representations during the bid process were before the Board. There was an inquiry as to the 17,000 figure, and witnesses for both sides testified that their understanding was that this figure was a maximum, "if Congress approved a battle group increase," in the words of the Navy wing Commander. The Navy represented explicitly that its training schedule was 58 hours per student, and included this figure in the contract. The contract states:

SECTION C—DESCRIPTION OR SPECIFICATIONS...These services shall consist of an annual rate of 17,000 airborne training service hours (approximately 58 airborne training service hours per graduated student)....

Cessna structured its low bid in accordance with these representations and requirements. See Sylvania Elec. Prods., Inc. v. United States, 198 Ct.Cl. 106, 458 F.2d 994, 1008 (1972) (if contractors can not rely on government representations "the amounts of the bids received would soon show the results").

The Board held that the Navy was bound by the representations in the Training Syllabus, the pre-bid explanations, and the contract itself. The panel majority, overruling the Board, holds that Cessna was properly required to provide 78 airborne training hours when the Navy so chose, three years into contract performance. The Board found that was not the agreement. Although Cessna took the risk of whether "Congress approved a battle group increase," the stated purpose of the 17,000 hour limit, that did not include a change of the 58 hour figure to 78 hours, any more than it included the Navy's other excursions beyond the contract provisions. * * * *

Notes and Questions

1. Using the opinion, reconstruct the process of negotiation, and specifically the back and forth over the contractor's obligations as to the quantity of airborne training hours. What did each of these stages signify, and what took place at that stage: the RFI; the pre-solicitation conference with its Q&A; Cessna's meeting with the "customer" (the Wing Commander); the various contents of the RFQ; the post-solicitation conference with its Q&A and the additional answers; Cessna's proposal; Cessna's BAFO; and, the awarded contract

2. Imagine that you were a lawyer either in the role of counsel to Cessna's team seeking the contract, or in the role of counsel to the Navy team going through the negotiation process. Can you articulate the tension on each team: on Cessna's side, wanting to win the contract without an overgenerous proposal (and therefore craving clarity); on the Navy's side, wanting meaningful negotiations within the limits of what internal bureaucratic agreement could be obtained in advance (and therefore maintaining flexibility and ambiguity)?

3. As this opinion discuses, the courts impose a duty of inquiry and clarification where there is a patent ambiguity. *Sturm v. United States,* 421 F.2d 723 (Cl. Ct. 1970), *Community Heating & Plumbing Co. v. Kelso,* 987 F.2d 1575 (Fed. Cir. 1993). A term is patently ambiguous where it is "so glaring as to raise a duty to inquire." *Hills Materials Co. v. Rice,* 982 F.2d 514, 516 (Fed. Cir. 1992). Conversely, latent ambiguity is "not glaring, substantial, or patently obvious." *Grumman Data Sys. Corp. v. Dalton,* 88 F.3d 990, 997 (Fed. Cir. 1996).

4. Consider the opposite of the ambiguous provisions of this case's solicitation— the unduly restrictive provisions that, by excessively narrow constraints on what the government will take from offerors—for example, specifications that only allow a specific brand name of some product or component—inhibits full and open competition. The Competition in Contracting Act only speaks of allowing restrictive provisions in meeting the contracting agency's minimum needs. 10 U.S.C. §2305(a)(1)(B). FAR 10.004(b) provides for the use of brand name specifications or its equivalent only in the absence of any other available specification. However, such specifications determined to further a federal policy have been held not to be unduly restrictive. *Marlen C.*

Robb & Son Boatyard & Marina, Inc., B-256316 (1994); *Accord Trilectron Indus*, B-248475 (1992).

2. Evaluation

Lockheed Missiles & Space Co., Inc., Appellant, v. Lloyd Bentsen, Secretary of the Treasury, Appellee, et al.

United States Court of Appeals, Federal Circuit. 4 F.3d 995 (1993)

Before NIES, Chief Judge, BENNETT, Senior Circuit Judge, and NEWMAN, Circuit Judge.

BENNETT, Senior Circuit Judge.

DECISION

Appellant, Lockheed Missiles & Space Co., Inc. (Lockheed), appeals from the decision of the General Services Administration Board of Contract Appeals (board) denying Lockheed's bid protest in connection with the Treasury Multi-User Acquisition Contract (TMAC) awarded by appellee Department of the Treasury to intervenor AT & T Federal Systems (AT & T). We affirm the decision of the board.

BACKGROUND

On January 4, 1989, a Request for Proposals (RFP), Solicitation No. IRS-88-079, was issued in connection with TMAC, a contract for the procurement of office automation systems, software, and maintenance/support services for use by the IRS. The goods and services supplied by TMAC would directly affect approximately 130,000 IRS employees. Section M of the RFP stated that award would be made to the vendor whose proposal offers "the best overall value to the Government" as determined by "comparing differences in the value of technical features with difference in overall cost to the Government." Section M stressed technical factors over price but also indicated that the IRS would not award the contract at a significantly higher cost to achieve slightly superior technical features.

Section M.3 of the RFP divided the technical factor into two major features each worth 100 points. The features were in turn divided into subfactors of equal "point value" within their respective feature groups. Cost/price was assigned a value of zero points. Section M.4 of the RFP explained the technical evaluation methodology. To select the winning proposal, the IRS created a formal source selection structure. The structure contained the following entities: (1) a Source Selection Official (SSO) to make the source selection decision; (2) a Source Evaluation Board (SEB) to make recommendations to the SSO; (3) a Technical Evaluation Panel (TEP) to perform the technical evaluations of proposals; and (4) a Business Management Evaluation Panel (BMEP) to evaluate the price proposals.

In response to the IRS solicitation, proposals were submitted in confidence by various vendors including AT & T, Lockheed and International Business Machines Corporation (IBM). Each submitted proposal contained a recommended system/software/services package and its estimated cost to the government. The cost of the IBM proposal was approximately $700 million while the cost of the Lockheed proposal was about $900 million. In comparison, AT & T's proposal would cost the government approximately $1.4 billion. Nevertheless, AT & T was awarded the contract.

Thereafter, IBM and Lockheed protested the nonselection of their proposals. In a hearing before the board (TMAC I), both protestors asserted that the IRS: (1) conducted an improper price evaluation; (2) failed to follow the evaluation scheme stated in the RFP; and (3) misevaluated the protestors' proposals. In a decision dated September 25, 1991, the board granted the bid protests. In its opinion, the board stated that although the RFP placed technical factors above price, the IRS evaluation scheme had improperly "discount[ed] price as a factor almost entirely." Slip op. at 28. In support of its conclusion, the board noted that there was no analysis explaining why the government would receive benefits commensurate with the excessive price charged by AT & T.

The board's TMAC I decision was also critical of the RFP. "[N]othing in the RFP justified the overwhelming priority that the IRS accorded technical factors over price. The mere statement that technical was more important than cost in no way communicated the degree to which the IRS emphasized the former." Slip op. at 29. Accordingly, the board instructed the IRS as follows:

> If the agency believes a suitable price/technical tradeoff analysis can be prepared that would comply with the RFP, it may proceed to make one and either confirm the previous award or make a new selection determination as appropriate. Alternatively, based on the award decision that the agency made, if it appears possible that the RFP, as written, will not permit an award in conformance with the Government's needs, respondent retains discretion to amend the RFP to provide a clear statement of its intention to emphasize technical over cost to the degree it believes necessary, and reopen negotiations or take other appropriate actions in accordance with statute and regulation.

Slip op. at 30.

After the board's decision in TMAC I, the IRS formed a "working group" to advise the SEB and the SSO on how best to proceed. The working group produced a report which concluded that: (1) a price/technical tradeoff could be performed in accordance with the RFP and (2) the tradeoff supported the award to AT & T. The working group report served as the basis for the decision to award AT & T the contract a second time. Once again, Lockheed and IBM protested, and the action was ultimately brought before the board.

In TMAC II, the board found that the selection of AT & T was consistent with the RFP solicitation and was the most advantageous choice for the government, price and other factors considered. The board noted that because no vendor had timely protested the RFP's evaluation provisions, the IRS was left with considerable discretion in conducting its analysis. Accordingly, the board denied the bid protests stating that the IRS decision was reasonable and not an abuse of discretion. Lockheed now appeals.

OPINION

The parties do not dispute the board's findings of fact. The decision of the board on any question of law is neither final nor conclusive and is reviewed de novo by this court. 41 U.S.C. §609(b) (1988); Planning Research Corp. v. United States, 971 F.2d 736, 740 (Fed.Cir.1992)

As an initial matter, we note that in its arguments before this court, Lockheed did not protest alleged improprieties in the RFP. Moreover, because Lockheed failed to timely file a protest with the board based upon alleged improprieties in the RFP's proposal evaluation provisions, see GSBCA Rules of Practice 5(b)(3)(i), the board did not address that issue and it cannot be raised now on appeal. Broughton Lumber Co. v. Yeutter, 939 F.2d 1547, 1555 (Fed.Cir.1991); Finch v. Hughes Aircraft Co., 926 F.2d 1574, 1576 (Fed.Cir.1991).

Effective contracting demands broad discretion. * * *

Lockheed argues that the IRS violated applicable statute and regulation by reducing price as a factor in its decision to award the TMAC contract to such an extent that price was effectively eliminated as a consideration. Price (or cost) must always be a "factor" in an agency's decision to award a contract. 10 U.S.C. §2305(b)(4)(B); 41 U.S.C. §253a(b)(1)(A) (1988); FAR §15.605(b). Moreover, the importance of price in a price/technical tradeoff must not be discounted to such a degree that it effectively renders the price factor meaningless. See Grumman Data Sys. Corp., GSBCA No. 11635-P, 92-1 BCA CCH ¶24,700 at 123,721.

At first glance, Lockheed's argument appears persuasive. For example, Lockheed points out that the AT & T proposal costs 100% more than the IBM proposal and one-half billion dollars more than Lockheed's. Lockheed further notes that, despite the huge difference in price, the board found only two quantified technical subfactors representing less than 15% of all available technical points in which the higher priced AT & T proposal was technologically superior to the Lockheed proposal. Finally, Lockheed asserts that under the IRS's method of evaluation, Lockheed would not have been awarded the contract even if elements of its proposal were given away for free. Accordingly, Lockheed argues that the IRS would have paid almost any amount to acquire the most technically advantageous package.

In TMAC I, the board properly found that the price/technical tradeoff analysis presented by the IRS was deficient because it failed to indicate whether the government would receive benefits commensurate with the price premium it proposed to pay. Without that missing information, the board could not confirm that price had been a factor in the award decision. Similarly, we cannot determine whether the IRS effectively discounted price as a factor without first ascertaining whether the technical advantages of the AT & T proposal were worth their additional cost.

The board in TMAC II found, based upon the IRS's price/technical tradeoff analysis, that the AT & T technical advantages were worth the extra cost. For example, the board found that the Lockheed software would not increase productivity as much as the AT & T software because Lockheed's software required users to memorize various operating system commands. While such a small software advantage may have only resulted in a few extra points for the AT & T proposal in the overall evaluation, the board found that the actual dollar value of the software advantage to the IRS was significant. The total productivity value of the AT & T software solution was calculated to be $467 million as compared to $80 million for Lockheed.

In addition, the board found that AT & T's models 2 and 3 multi-user systems (MUSs) significantly outperformed their Lockheed counterparts during the "Functional Workload Demonstrations." The IRS quantified this advantage and calculated productivity values of $500,720,221 for the AT & T MUS models and $35,295,084 for the Lockheed devices. Finally, the board considered the impact of the nonquantified discriminators and found that the AT & T proposal offered substantially more value to the government than the other proposals.

Accordingly, the findings of the board indicate that the IRS, through its price/technical tradeoff analysis, neither disregarded price nor discounted it to such a degree that it was effectively rendered meaningless. * * *

Lockheed raises a second argument in its brief when it asserts that the IRS abused its discretion by skewing the importance of the two aforementioned technical subfactors, software and MUS productivity, beyond the limits established by the RFP. Lockheed argues that although the two subfactors represented less than 15% of all available technical points, those subfactors provided the IRS's main justification for spending millions of additional dollars for the AT & T proposal.

Section M.3 of the RFP identifies and assigns point values to the technical subfactors considered important by the IRS. The IRS used the assigned point values to evaluate and compare the technical strengths of the different proposals. Cost/price considerations did not enter into this part of the analysis since cost was assigned a value of zero points. After the AT & T proposal's technical strengths were determined, the IRS then went on to decide whether the value of those technical strengths was worth the higher price.

Neither the FAR nor the broad language of the RFP requires that evaluation points be proportional to cost. Accordingly, a proposal which is one point better than another but costs millions of dollars more may be selected if the agency can demonstrate within a reasonable certainty that the added value of the proposal is worth the higher price. Here, as we have already noted, the IRS tradeoff analysis revealed that the dollar value of the two technical subfactors together with the value of the nonquantified discriminators justified the additional price of the AT & T proposal. Thus, use of the IRS's evaluation method did not constitute an abuse of discretion because the method did not skew the importance of the two technical subfactors.

CONCLUSION

Government agencies are accorded a good deal of deference in awarding contracts. FAR §15.605(b) (1992). Here, the IRS has sufficiently demonstrated that price was a factor in the final decision to award the TMAC contract. The decision of the board is therefore

AFFIRMED.

Notes and Questions

1. The court concluded that even a single point difference in technical scores can allow an agency to spend millions of additional tax dollars on the slightly higher rated proposal. What review standard will the courts employ to determine whether the correct decision was made? When is the court justified in overturning a procurement decision?

2. The court noted that the protestor's failure to timely protest the solicitation evaluation factors and procedures resulted in the agency having broad discretion as to their use. Such protests of asserted deficiencies in the solicitation must be filed prior to the date for receipt of initial proposals, i.e., a prospective offeror must sue its prospective customer while everyone is still in the starting gate, something that many companies are unwilling to do. However, the failure to resolve ambiguities or potentially unfair evaluation factors on a timely basis ensures broad discretion in the use of those evaluation procedures after proposals are received.

3. Note that the protestors alleged the agency: (1) failed to evaluate proposals in accordance with the solicitation criteria, i.e,. used factors not listed in the solicitation; and (2) failed to evaluate the protestor's proposal in accordance with the factors listed, i.e., the protestor's offer did not receive as high a rating as the protestor believed it should. These two protest grounds form the basis of many if not most protests involving competitive proposals.

Sheila Widnall, Secretary of the Air Force, Appellant, et al. v. B3H Corporation, Intervenor et al.

United States Court of Appeals, Federal Circuit.
75 F.3d 1577. Feb. 8, 1996.

Before NEWMAN, LOURIE, and CLEVENGER, Circuit Judges.

CLEVENGER, Circuit Judge.

The Secretary of the Air Force (Air Force) and Logistics Techniques, Inc. (LOGTEC) appeal the July 8, 1994 decision of the General Services Administration Board of Contract Appeals (GSBCA or Board), B3H Corp. v. Department of Air Force, GSBCA No. 12813-P, 94-3 B.C.A. (CCH) P 27,068, 1994 WL 372020 (1994), granting the protest of B3H Corporation (B3H) in a best value procurement. B3H cross-appeals the GSBCA's dismissal of B3H's protest based on alleged improprieties involving Air Force personnel and LOGTEC. We reverse the Board's granting of B3H's protest on the best value issue and affirm the Board's denial of B3H's protest on the procurement impropriety issue.

I

On June 8, 1992 the Air Force solicited a contract on an indefinite delivery/indefinite quantity basis to provide technical support for the Air Force Material Command at Wright-Patterson Air Force Base. The solicitation stated that evaluation of the offerors would be based on technical, managerial, and cost factors in descending order of importance. At issue in this case are the portions of that solicitation reserved for small businesses. Section M-991 of the solicitation provided, in pertinent part, that "[t]he Government will award a contract resulting from this solicitation to the responsible offeror whose offer, conforming to the solicitation, will provide the best value to the Government.... The Government reserves the right to award to other than the lowest offeror."

The Source Selection Evaluation Board (SSEB) evaluated, among other companies, the proposals of LOGTEC, Aries Systems International, Inc. (Aries), and B3H. The SSEB determined that while the estimated cost of the LOGTEC offer was higher than B3H and Aries, LOGTEC and Aries were higher rated in the technical area. LOGTEC was also higher rated than Aries and B3H in the management area. After a working group performed a price/technical tradeoff analysis, on February 18, 1994 the Source Selection Authority (SSA) awarded the contracts at issue to LOGTEC and Aries determining that these offerors provided the best value to the Government.

B3H filed a protest in response to the SSA's findings on April 15, 1994. * * * [T]he GSBCA granted B3H's protest on the best value issue. The GSBCA held that the SSA did not adequately justify the higher cost of LOGTEC and Aries, even after the price/technical tradeoff analysis had been considered. Nor, in the Board's opinion, did the record as a whole demonstrate that the added value of the LOGTEC and Aries proposals were worth their higher price. Having granted B3H's best value protest, the GSBCA allowed the Air Force to continue its contracts with LOGTEC and Aries, but prohibited the Air Force from renewing the options on the contracts unless the awards were affirmed in a new source selection.

* * *

III

At issue in this case is a best value procurement authorized by 48 C.F.R. §15.605(c) (1994) ("[I]n certain acquisitions the Government may select the source whose proposal offers the greatest value to the Government in terms of performance and other factors."). * * *

In an early post-CICA decision, DALFI, Inc., GSBCA No. 8755-P, 87-1 B.C.A. (CCH) ¶19,552, 1986 WL 20777 (1986) (DALFI I), the Board upheld a protest of DALFI for a contract selection by the Naval Aviation Logistics Center (NALC). The NALC had chosen the lower rated $17 million proposal of SDI over the higher rated $20 million DALFI proposal. The GSBCA held that the NALC erred in part by taking SDI's assertion of a lower cost to the Government at face value and not conducting a price realism analysis that would assess the proposal's true cost. The Board stated that the procurement had been "converted...from one for the highest technically rated proposal representing the best buy to the Government into one for the lowest price for a technically acceptable proposal." DALFI I, at 98,809. Nevertheless, the Board later accepted the agency's choice after the agency quantified the proposal's technical differences and determined that the technical superiority of DALFI was not worth its higher cost. DALFI, Inc., GSBCA No. 8975-P-R, 87-3 B.C.A. (CCH) ¶20,070, at 101,628, 1987 WL 41150 (1987) (DALFI II); cf. Pyramid Technology Corp., GSBCA No. 8743-P, 87-1 B.C.A. (CCH) ¶19,580, at 99,022-23, 1987 WL 46607 (1987) (contracting officer properly relied on lower price when the technical merits of the offerors were similar).

Once an agency has independently rated each proposal to determine its fulfillment of the requirements of the contract's solicitation, the agency typically performs a tradeoff analysis singling out and evaluating the differences between each of the qualifying proposals. These differences, often termed discriminators, may be either quantified or non-quantified for the Board does not require that each difference in a proposal be assigned an exact dollar value representing its worth to the Government. See TRW Inc., GSBCA No. 11309-P, 92-1 B.C.A. (CCH) ¶24,389, at 121,789, 1991 WL 175673 (1991).

* * *

Recently, this court has reviewed * * * cases in which the Board initially refused to accept an agency's procurement decision based on the lack of a reasoned explanation for the selection. * * * [T]he Board and this court later upheld the agency selection after the agency reevaluated its decision and proffered reasonable explanations as to why its initial choice was correct. In International Business Machs. Corp. & Lockheed Missiles & Space Co., GSBCA Nos. 11359-P, 11362-P, 94-2 B.C.A. (CCH) ¶26,782, 1991 WL 542336 (1991) (Lockheed I), the Board granted IBM's and Lockheed's protests, rejecting the IRS' acceptance of AT & T's proposal to build its automation system. The IRS could not justify the increased cost of $500–700 million for the project simply by stating that AT & T's winning proposal was technically superior to the lower offers. Furthermore, AT & T's offer was only 15% more technically superior than the other proposals. The Board directed the IRS to justify its award to AT & T or initiate a new procurement for the contract. Lockheed I, at 133,201-03.

The IRS formed a working group to re-analyze the procurement, which performed a price/technical tradeoff analysis by identifying quantifiable and non-quantifiable discriminators between the various proposals. The group assigned dollar values to four quantifiable discriminators (price risk, software integration, system performance and training) in an attempt to determine the true cost to the Government of each proposal. The group also designated negative, positive or neutral ratings for ten non-quantifiable discriminators. Based on this analysis, the IRS concluded that the technical superiority of the AT & T proposal made it the best value to the Government despite its higher price. Lockheed Missiles & Space Co. v. Department of Treasury, GSBCA Nos. 11776-P, 11777-P, 93-1 B.C.A. (CCH) ¶25,401, at 126,499-501, 1992 WL 512122 (1992) (Lockheed II), aff'd, 4 F.3d 955 (Fed.Cir.1993). * * *

IV

This case involves a solicitation which stated that technical, managerial and cost factors would be evaluated in that order of precedence. The offers of LOGTEC and Aries were judged to be superior in the technical area. While LOGTEC was rated higher than Aries and B3H in the management area, total cost evaluations revealed that LOGTEC and Aries were respectively 15% and 8.8% more expensive than B3H's offer. The Air Force created a price/technical tradeoff working group (P/TTO Group) to further analyze the proposals. The P/TTO Group identified one quantified discriminator quantifying the estimated risk that an offeror would need to expend additional funds to provide trained personnel than the offeror originally calculated. This dollar value was added to the total evaluated cost of each offer to obtain a value adjusted cost. Although B3H's price risk was approximately four times higher than LOGTEC's and Aries', the value adjusted costs of LOGTEC and Aries were still respectively 16% and 4% higher than B3H.

The P/TTO Group also identified six non-quantified discriminators: (1) experience with the relevant Air Force software; (2) hardware maintenance experience; (3) hardware sizing experience; (4) data management experience; (5) whether the offeror already had offices near the Air Logistics Centers (ALC co-location); and (6) the offeror's subcontractor control plan. Each offeror was assigned a positive, neutral or negative evaluation for all six discriminators. The P/TTO Group gave LOGTEC a positive rating for the subcontractor control plan discriminator and assigned Aries and B3H neutral ratings for that category. While LOGTEC and Aries received a negative rating and B3H a neutral one for the hardware maintenance experience discriminator, the ratings of LOGTEC and Aries were superior to B3H's for all other non-quantified discriminators. With respect to those superior ratings, the P/TTO Group predicted that the proposal of B3H would result in completing the task order in a longer period of time and with a lower level of quality.

Relying upon the analysis of the P/TTO Group, the SSA in his written determination that LOGTEC's superior proposal was worth its extra cost stated: "I assess that the relative superiority of the [LOGTEC] proposal as indicated in the [excellent] rating in the Management Area will result in improved quality and cost control that represents value to the Government which mitigates the...difference in cost." As to the award to Aries, the SSA similarly wrote: "B3H had more negative and fewer positive non-quantified discriminators than [Aries].... The technical superiority of [Aries] represents the Best Value to the Government considering the [small] difference in cost...."

At the B3H protest hearing, the SSA elaborated at length on the rationale for choosing LOGTEC and Aries. When B3H asked the SSA to explain in specific detail the basis for his decision, the SSA's response took up forty-three pages of testimony and covered all seven discriminators explaining how he considered them, evaluated their import, and why he did what he did. He had earlier given twenty-two pages of testimony on the same subject. In general, the SSA's testimony was that prior experience in the areas of the various non-quantifiable discriminators resulted in shorter start up times, quicker execution, a better quality product, shorter learning curves, and less staffing time, all of which would produce economic benefits to the Air Force. With respect to the issue of what justifies the higher estimated costs of the awards, the SSA testified:

> If specifically you mean what do we expect would occur through the execution of the contract with Aries and Logtec that would justify the increased price...we can go back through the discriminators if you like and we can go back through the superior technical management proposal for characteristics. But in summary, what we would expect is that we would get a...substantially higher quality product. We would expect that we would be in a better position to control and understand the cost that would be expended in the conduct of the individual task. That is that the costs that are identified in the initial response to the statement of work, would in fact be much closer to the cost that would be expected to be incurred through the conduct of that cost.

In essence, the SSA determined that the inferior management and lower non-quantified discriminator ratings of B3H meant that there was a likelihood that B3H's offer would produce unnecessary cost overruns and actually cost more than an estimated value adjusted cost, which was designed to factor in that risk. Thus, the SSA concluded the superior management and technical evaluations of LOGTEC and Aries justified incurring the increased value adjusted cost.

V

* * * Fulfilling its statutory duty under 41 U.S.C. §607(e) (1988), the Board in this case reviewed the Air Force's procurement decision. The Board found that one non-quantified discriminator, the ALC co-location, did not have a rational basis. Except for this finding, the Board found no fault with the methodology of the SSA's decision. Just as in Computer Sciences Corp., the Board here did not reject the procurement on the basis of one suspect discriminator, but continued its analysis with the offending discriminator factored out of its inquiry.

Although the SSA gave a reasoned explanation as to why he chose LOGTEC and Aries, the GSBCA did not defer to his reasonable decision. For example, the Board found fault with the SSA's emphasis on LOGTEC's and Aries' superiority over B3H in the software experience and data management experience non-quantified discriminators. The Board held that the record does not support the SSA's decision to emphasize these two discriminators over the others. Yet, weighing which non-quantified discriminator to emphasize in an analysis is exactly the type of decision the SSA is entrusted to make. As the Board does not require that every discriminator be assigned an exact dollar value, TRW, it necessarily must rely on an agency's judgment in giving disparate weight to the various non-quantified discriminators in a best value determination.

The Board should have followed its clear line of precedent and deferred to the reasonable decision of the SSA in this case. The Air Force's P/TTO Group developed seven discriminators and assessed how each of the offeror's proposals fared under those chosen criteria. Using his independent judgment and consistent with the solicitation's stipulation that cost was the least important factor for this contract, the SSA relied on this analysis and reasonably determined that the technical and managerial superiority of LOGTEC's and Aries' proposals were worth the 15% and 8.8% higher cost. This case is no different from the many previous cases in which the GSBCA deferred to reasonable best value decisions made using substantially similar forms of analysis. Indeed, the SSA's concern that B3H's proposal might lead to excessive cost overruns seems no different from such recent explanations accepted by the Board in ATLIS (fear of cost overruns due to new technology) and Titan (fear of cost overruns due to subcontractor problems.) In reversing the GSBCA's grant of B3H's protest on the best value issue, we emphasize that the settled law remains settled.

Notes and Questions

1. Numerical weights. Under the FAR any RFP must clearly state all factors which are to be the major considerations in evaluation, and their relative importance and weight in comparison to the other criteria set forth in the proposal. FAR 15.304(d). The FAR further provides that any changes made to these evaluation factors for one offeror requires that the RFP be amended and re-submitted to all offerors. FAR 15.304(d). The GAO and the General Service Board of Contract Appeals hold consistently, however, that these FAR provisions do not require a government agency to disclose in an RFP the specific numerical weights being applied to each evaluation factor. See, e.g., *Network Solutions Incorporated (NSI)*, Comp. Gen. 89-1 CPD ¶459 (1989), *citing* 48 C.F.R. §15.605 (e).

2. Construing silence about factor importance. Where a proposal fails to expressly state the relative importance of technical and price factors to each other, they are considered to be of equal importance. The Comptroller General found this to be applicable in the *Johns Hopkins University*, when the University protested the award by the Agency for International Development to another offeror for the provision of a maternal and neonatal health and nutrition project in developing countries. Comp. Gen. 89-1 CPD ¶240 (1989). The protest was denied when no prejudice was found to have resulted from the solicitation's failure to indicate that the technical and price factors would be weighted equally in evaluation. *Id.*

Matter of: Environmental Tectonics Corporation

General Accounting Office B-280573.2 December 1, 1998

Environmental Tectonics Corporation (ETC) protests the issuance of a purchase order to USA Models, Inc. under request for quotations (RFQ) No. N61339-98-Q-2010, issued by the Naval Air Warfare Center Training Systems Division (NAWCTSD), Department of the Navy, for acrylic replacement windows for hypobaric low pressure chambers.[1] ETC challenges the agency's evaluation of its past performance and the agency's decision to issue a purchase order to a higher-priced vendor.

We deny the protest.

The RFQ, issued in April 1998 as a combined synopsis/solicitation for commercial items, provided that the agency intended to issue a purchase order to the responsible vendor whose quotation was most advantageous to the government, price and other factors considered. The RFQ provided that the best value award factors, in descending order of importance, were pricing, delivery schedule, risk, and past performance. Combined synopsis/solicitation, Apr. 8, 1998; CO Statement at 1. The RFQ stated that simplified acquisition procedures applied to this procurement. See Federal Acquisition Regulation (FAR) Part 13.

---

1. The acrylic windows, which represent a safety upgrade, will replace existing glass windows which may implode into the chambers when internal pressures are lowered, causing injury or death to government personnel. The window replacement has been ranked a top priority modification for aviation physiology trainers. Contracting Officer's (CO) Statement at 1; Source Selection Decision (SSD), Sept. 4, 1998, at 1.

Three firms, including ETC and USA Models, submitted quotations which were rated as follows:[2]

	ETC	USA Models
Delivery Schedule	Acceptable	Acceptable
Risk	Acceptable	Acceptable
Past Performance	High Risk	Low Risk

ETC's quotation was approximately 46 percent lower than the quotation from USA Models. SSD at 2.

With respect to past performance, for ETC, the agency checked the firm's performance under eight contracts for various training equipment. Three contracts were with the British government. The British references (a contracting director and a technical person) reported that ETC's performance under a contract for a fire service trainer had deficiencies which took the firm a long time to correct; ETC's performance under a contract for a maintenance trainer had delivery delays; and ETC's performance under a contract for a critical design review for a human-carrying centrifuge had delivery delays and, over the objections of the British government, ETC ordered long lead-time items prior to design approval. The British references further reported that [deleted]. Past Performance Questionnaire (PPQ), July 20, 1998. In addition, the British references reported [deleted]; the British references reported that they [deleted]. Id.; see also Memo to the File, July 20, 1998. Another contract (the one listed by ETC in its quotation as a past performance reference) was for two unique high altitude chambers for the Federal Aviation Administration (FAA). The FAA reference (the contracting officer), noting that "ETC had very good people and a very good product," reported that ETC had delayed delivery of the product and was "slow in delivering," but eventually had resolved technical and software problems. Memo to the File, Oct. 1, 1998; PPQ, July 21, 1998. Finally, NAWCTSD had a contract with ETC to provide a centrifuge-based flight environment trainer (CFET). The agency reported late, unacceptable delivery by ETC; agency acceptance of the trainer as nonconforming; and difficulty in engaging in discussions with ETC to settle a substantial monetary claim filed by the firm under the CFET contract. PPQ, Aug. 13, 1998.[3]

For USA Models, the agency checked the firm's performance under four contracts. The reference for a contract for a prototype of a smoke control model to be used as a teaching tool reported that USA Models was ahead of schedule and was an outstanding performer, delivering the highest quality product. PPQ, Aug. 5, 1998. The reference for an acrylic windows contract reported timely and very good performance by USA Models. PPQ, Aug. 5, 1998. The reference for a contract for plastic acrylic models of rockets and mines reported early delivery by USA Models, with the firm doing extra work under the contract. PPQ, Aug. 3, 1998. Finally, the reference for a contract for various trainers, including a cockpit simulator, reported on-schedule delivery and correction of a deficiency by USA Models. PPQ, Aug. 3, 1998.

---

2. These ratings reflect the agency's assessment after taking corrective action in response to an earlier protest filed by ETC challenging, among other things, the agency's evaluation of the firm's past performance.

3. The agency also checked references for an Air Force contract for centrifuge maintenance, PPQ, July 28, 1998, and two Navy contracts for environmental chambers at China Lake. PPQ, July 21, 1998. These references, which reported satisfactory performance by ETC, were also considered by the agency.

The contracting officer, who served as the source selection authority, selected USA Models as the most advantageous vendor. In this regard, the contracting officer determined that ETC's low-priced quotation did not offset the unacceptably high risk of ETC not meeting the critical terms and conditions of the contract, based on ETC's past performance history showing that its corporate management had not committed to timely delivery of quality products, to correcting deficiencies, and to settling disputes. The contracting officer concluded that the performance risk associated with ETC outweighed the value to the agency of the firm's low-priced quotation. Therefore, given USA Models' record of superior past performance history and its minimal performance risk, the contracting officer determined that it was worth paying a price premium to that firm. Accordingly, the agency issued a purchase order to USA Models as the most advantageous vendor. SSD at 3-5.

ETC challenges the agency's evaluation of its past performance, objecting to the agency's consideration of its performance under the CFET contract and the British contracts, which were not listed in ETC's quotation for past performance references. ETC maintains that its performance under these contracts is not relevant because the deliverables were for sophisticated design/build, as opposed to commercial, items. ETC believes only the FAA contract (listed in its quotation for a past performance reference) and the China Lake contracts should have been considered by the agency in evaluating the firm's past performance.

When using simplified acquisition procedures, an agency must conduct the procurement consistent with a concern for fair and equitable competition, and must evaluate quotations in accordance with the terms of the solicitation. M3 Corp., B-278906, Apr. 1, 1998, 98-1 CPD p 95 at 3. In reviewing protests against an allegedly improper evaluation, we will examine the record to determine whether the agency met this standard and reasonably exercised its discretion. Id.

Contrary to ETC's assertion, in evaluating quotations, an agency may properly consider evidence of a vendor's past performance from sources that are not listed in the vendor's quotation. See, e.g., TEAM Support Servs., Inc., B-279379.2, June 22, 1998, 98-1 CPD p 167 at 6. Here, the agency had direct knowledge of ETC's performance and associated problems under the Navy's CFET contract, and the agency sought specific information addressing ETC's performance under the British contracts. In response to ETC's primary contention, while the design/build technology for the deliverables under the Navy CFET and British contracts may have been distinguishable from the commercial item technology for the acrylic windows being procured under this RFQ, the record shows that for the most part, the negative past performance information conveyed to the agency by the various references related not so much to the technical aspects of ETC's performance, but to broader aspects of ETC's performance—ETC's corporate management's effectiveness in ensuring timely delivery of products and timely correction of deficiencies, and its receptiveness to engaging in claims settlement discussions. In fact, consistent with what was reported by the Navy and the British references, the FAA contracting officer also reported that ETC was slow to deliver. Because timeliness of delivery, timeliness of resolving deficiencies, and corporate attitude and responsiveness are considerations which are common to all contracts regardless of the technology involved, we believe the information reported concerning ETC's corporate management's working relationship with its customers is clearly relevant to the agency's evaluation of ETC's past performance. Id.; see also SDA Inc., B-256075, B-256206, May 2, 1994, 94-2 CPD p 71 at 6–7. Accordingly, based on reports of ETC's past performance and the agency's own experience with ETC, we believe the agency could reasonably conclude that ETC presented a high performance risk.

ETC also argues that the agency was required to conduct discussions with the firm regarding the referenced negative past performance information. However, ETC confuses the requirements applicable to negotiated procurements with those applicable to procurements using simplified acquisition procedures. Specifically, the provisions of FAR Part 15, see FAR s 15.306 (FAC 97-02), governing exchanges with offerors in a negotiated procurement about their past performance are not applicable in a procurement, like this one, conducted using simplified acquisition procedures. See M3 Corp., supra, at 4–5. While FAR Part 13, see FAR s 13.106-2(b)(1), affords an agency the discretion to use the provisions of FAR Part 15 in conducting a simplified acquisition procurement, the agency, here, exercised its discretion and chose not to conduct exchanges concerning vendors' past performance during the reevaluation of quotations.[5] We have no basis to object to the agency's action in this regard.

Finally, ETC, the low-priced vendor, challenges the agency's best value determination resulting in the issuance of a purchase order to USA Models, a higher-priced vendor.

In a best value procurement, price is not necessarily controlling in determining the quotation that represents the best value to the government. Rather, that determination is made on the basis of whatever evaluation factors are set forth in the solicitation, with the source selection official often required to make a price/technical trade-off to determine if one quotation's technical superiority is worth the higher price that may be associated with that quotation. In this regard, price/past performance trade-offs are permitted when such tradeoffs are consistent with the solicitation's evaluation scheme. See Rotair Indus., Inc., B-276435.2, July 15, 1997, 97-2 CPD p 17 at 3. In this case, where the RFQ does not expressly specify that price will be the determinative factor for award, the agency retains the discretion to select a vendor with a higher-priced quotation and higher past performance rating, if doing so is in the government's best interest and is consistent with the solicitation's stated evaluation and source selection scheme. See University of Kansas Med. Ctr., B-278400, Jan. 26, 1998, 98-1 CPD p 120 at 6.

While ETC's quotation was approximately 46 percent lower than the quotation of USA Models, we conclude that the contracting officer reasonably determined that the performance risk associated with ETC, based on past performance information, outweighed the value to the agency of the firm's low price. More specifically, five of the eight past performance references for ETC reported poor timeliness and quality of performance and provided an overall negative past performance assessment. SSD at 3. The contracting officer noted that at the time of his selection decision, only the Navy CFET trainer and the British fire trainer had been delivered, inspected, and accepted; both of these contracts were delivered late and with major deficiencies. Id. The contracting officer noted that meeting the schedule under this RFQ is a critical factor, and based on ETC's past performance history, concluded that ETC's inability to timely deliver quality products made ETC an unacceptably high performance risk. Id. at 4. In addition, the contracting officer expressed a concern with ETC's lack of willingness to resolve disputes in a cooperative and businesslike manner, as evidenced by the Navy's experience with ETC in attempting to resolve the claim under the CFET contract. Id.

---

5. Although the agency held discussions with vendors, including ETC, prior to taking corrective action, during the reevaluation process, the agency did not conduct discussions. Since the reevaluation process superseded and mooted the initial evaluation process, consistent with the terms of the RFQ, the agency could properly issue the purchase order to USA Models on the basis of initial quotations without conducting discussions. See Combined synopsis/solicitation, supra.

Therefore, based on this record, the contracting officer concluded there was an unacceptably high risk of ETC not performing in accordance with the terms of the RFQ because its corporate management failed to demonstrate on other contracts a firm commitment to timely delivery of acceptable products, to correcting deficiencies, and to settling disputes. Id. The contracting officer believed the performance risk associated with ETC outweighed any price savings associated with its low-priced quotation. Id.

In contrast, USA Models had a superior past performance history, delivering products on time or ahead of schedule, performing in a highly satisfactory manner, doing extra work, and correcting deficiencies. The contracting officer believed USA Models would satisfy the RFQ requirements in a timely manner, and that the firm's superior past performance history justified the payment of a price premium and outweighed the price differential between ETC and USA Models. Id. at 5.

Under these circumstances, we have no basis to question the reasonableness of the agency's price/past performance tradeoff and its decision to issue a purchase order to USA Models as the most advantageous vendor.

The protest is denied.[7]

Comptroller General of the United States

Notes and Questions

1. This GAO opinion reflects the greatly increased importance of past performance. Look at the case, first from the perspective of ETC, then from the perspective of the contracting officer. ETC must consider a price 46 percent lower than its competition as highly deserving of success. On the other hand, the contracting officer looked at ETC's poor past performance record as foreshadowing trouble both for the Navy "customer" and for the contracting officer herself.

2. The 1990s witnessed the rise of past performance as a criterion of proposal evaluation. This began in 1993 with Office of Federal Procurement Policy (OFPP) Policy Letter No. 92-5 encouraging that "past performance be utilized as an evaluation factor for award in solicitations... expected to exceed $100,000." Section 1091 of the Federal Acquisition Act of 1994 (FASA) requires the OFPP to "establish policies and procedures concerning past performance." In 1995, the FAR Council promulgated Federal Acquisition Circular 90-26 on past performance information. In 1995, the OFPP issued an interim edition of "A Guide to Best Practices for Past Performance," intended as a nonmandatory guide for recording and using contractor past performance in the award selection process.

In 1997, the rewritten Part 15 of the FAR mandated that past performance be included as an evaluation factor in each competitively negotiated acquisition expected to exceed the $100,000 mark. FAR § 15.304. Other FAR Part 15 provisions afford the contractor the opportunity to identify all types of prior contracts that might have a bearing on their past performance record, while prohibiting agencies from making findings about a contractor's past performance where there is no available past

---

7. Since we conclude that the agency's evaluation of ETC's past performance was reasonable, there is no credible basis to find that the agency acted in bad faith in performing this evaluation. Moreover, contrary to ETC's assertion, the agency chose not to issue the purchase order to the firm as a result of the price/past performance tradeoff based on the underlying evaluation, not because the agency had de facto debarred the firm.

performance information. Additionally, FAR § 42.15 addresses the rule and timetables for compiling past performance, while § 2.206 states that past performance is a relevant evaluation factor in all commercial item contract awards. In 1999, the Department of Defense issued its own guide on past performance information. For a fuller treatment, see Nathanael Causey, Past Performance Information, *De facto* Debarments, and Due Process: Debunking the Myth of Pandora's Box, 29 Pub. Cont. L. J. 638 (2000).

3. The GAO has held in favor of bidders protesting noncompliance by agencies with the FASA and FAR requirements of past performance as an evaluation criterion. *Nav-Com Defense Electronics, Inc.,* B-276163 (1997); *In the Matter of: Holiday Inn-Laurel-Protest and Request for Costs,* B-270860.3 (1993). Appellate courts have also held in favor of the protestor where an agency ignored the past performance evaluation factor altogether. *Latecoere International Inc. v. United States Department of the Navy,* 19 F.3d 1342 (11th Cir. 1994).

4. On the other hand, the GAO sustains protests by offerors claiming misevaluation of past performance where the record fails to support the agency conclusion. *The Real Estate Center-Cost,* B-274081 (1998); *Mechanical Contractors, S.A.,* B-277916 (1997); *Ogden Support Services, Inc.,* B-270012.3 (1996); and others. Such protests may be sustained by the GAO even when the agency decision is not unreasonable on its face.

5. For a comprehensive discussion and potential concerns on the use of contractor past performance as an evaluation factor, see W.W. Goodrich, *Past Performance as an Evaluation Factor in Public Contract Source Selection,* 47 Am. U. L. Rev. 1539 (1998).

3. Contracting-Out: Public-Private Competition

All previous discussion in the chapters on sealed bids and competitive negotiation have concerned procurements in which the government had decided to buy from the private sector and the competition occurred between private offerors. In contrast, the government sometimes decides whether to provide something internally, that is, by the work of government employees, or to contract the work out. In order to make this decision, the government may use the formal process of a public-private competition, in which it makes the decision about whether to buy from the private sector by a competition between an internal government mode of performance, on the one hand, and one or more potential private contractors, on the other.

In the federal government, an elaborate mechanism has evolved to govern such public-private competitions. This is known as the "A-76" process, because its principal and most detailed guidance comes from Circular No. A-76 of the Office of Management and Budget and its Revised Supplemental Handbook promulgated in 1996. Since the A-76 process can end in protests by disappointed private offerors, the GAO and the courts have written opinions about the A-76 process.

The *Space Mark* judicial opinion, which describes the process of a public-private competition and the subsequent reviews and protest, is provided. Subsequently, in 2003, OMB substantially revised A-76 directive. The revised A-76 sought to merge the previously very separate processes of public-private competition, and private-private competition, into one "standard" competition. As before, an MEO would be designed, and its cost determined. However, many of the previous steps and safeguards were eliminated. Also, for limited-scale work, a "streamlined" form of the competition could occur. See Charles Tiefer, "OMB's New A-76: Tilting the Contracting-out Process," Federal Bar Association Government Contracts Section Newsletter, Spring 2003, at 6.

In contemporary government contracting, the A-76 process has special importance. This is an era in which, due to political and economic developments, much argument is being made in other countries and in the United States to privatize activity which had previously been performed by the government. In other countries, this takes the more dramatic form of proposals to privatize whole sectors of production that had been nationalized, such as utility systems like telephone services. By contrast, for the federal government, the proposals are usually more modest in their individual scope, often being proposals to contract out services of a particular kind at a particular facility, such as clerical or information technology services at a particular civilian or defense center.

Even so, the aggregate of all such proposals amounts to a substantial potential change in public operations. An Administration may set goals, and seek to adjust procedures, to extensively contract out. A-76 competitions may simply seem a nuts-and-bolts variant on other competitive processes, with disputes that concern discrete, concrete, and specific accounting details. However, A-76 competitions reflect major philosophical issues about where the boundaries ought to be in society between public and private activity. It is a measure of the sophistication of government contract law that it can and does deal with such issues.

For further discussion, see: Janna J. Hansen, Note, Limits of Competition: Accountability in Government Contracting, 112 Yale L.J. 2465 (2003); Charles Tiefer & Jennifer Ferragut, Letting Federal Unions Protest Improper Contracting Out, 10 CORNELL J.L. & PUB. POL. 581 (2001); Robert H. Shriver, No Seat at the Table: Flawed Contracting Out Process Unfairly Limits Front-Line Federal Employee Participation, 30 Pub. Cont. L. J. 613 (2001); Mary E. Harney, *The Quiet Revolution: Downsizing, Outsourcing, and Best Value*, 158 MIL. L. REV. 48 (1998). Gregory E. Lang, *Best Value Source Selection in the A-76 Process*, 43 A.F.L. REV. 239 (1997).

SPACE MARK, INC., Plaintiff,
v. The UNITED STATES, Defendant.

United States Court of Federal Claims
45 Fed. Cl. 267 Nov. 9, 1999.

FIRESTONE, Judge.

This case arises from a solicitation issued by the Air Force for a Communications and Information Management contract at Los Angeles Air Force Base. The solicitation was part of a two step process aimed at determining whether the services described in the solicitation could be performed more economically by a private contractor when compared to the costs of the Air Force's in-house personnel performing the same work.[1]

---

1. A variety of statutes and regulations govern how the Department of Defense is to compare the cost of private contractors providing supplies and services with the cost of the government providing those same goods or services. *See* 10 U.S.C. § 2462(b) (1994); Office of Management and Budget ("OMB") Circular A-76 and its Supplement. This action centers on the Air Force's compliance with those statutes and regulations.

In this action brought pursuant to 28 U.S.C. § 1491(b)(1) (1994 & Supp. III 1997), plaintiff, Space Mark, Inc. ("SMI"), the contractor that won the private competition challenges the Air Force's final cost comparison, which concluded that the Air Force's in-house organization could perform the work more economically than SMI. SMI contends that the Air Force's cost comparison was flawed procedurally and contains mistakes in violation of the relevant sections of OMB Circular A-76 and its Supplements, as well as 10 U.S.C. §§ 2304, 2462, 2468 and 32 C.F.R. Parts 169 and 169a.

FACTUAL BACKGROUND

The facts are set forth in the Administrative Record filed with the court on September 27, 1999. On November 25, 1998, the United States Air Force, acting through the Los Angeles Air Force Base Space and Missile Systems Center ("Air Force"), issued Solicitation No. F04693-98-R-0006 ("Solicitation") seeking proposals for the performance of communications and information management services at the base for a five-year term. The performance requirements were set forth in a Performance Work Statement ("PWS") accompanying the Solicitation.

The Air Force issued the Solicitation in support of a cost comparison study it was conducting under OMB Circular No. A-76, which states that it is the general policy of the federal government to rely upon commercial sources to provide the products and services the government needs. *See* 48 Fed. Reg. 37,110, 37,114 (1983). OMB Circular No. A-76 also provides that in-house performance of a commercial activity is authorized if a "cost comparison" demonstrates that the federal agency is operating *or* can operate the activity at a lower estimated cost than a qualified commercial source. *See id.* at 37.115.

The Air Force designed the subject cost comparison study to determine whether the services described in the PWS could be performed more economically by the Air Force's "most efficient, cost effective organization" or "MEO"[2] capable of performing the services, or if a commercial source could perform the services more economically. The Solicitation indicated that the competition would be divided into two stages. First, there would be a competition among commercial sources to select the lowest-priced, technically acceptable proposal. Second, the prevailing commercial source's proposal would be evaluated against the MEO's proposal. The Solicitation, as amended, set February 25, 1999, as the due date for proposals from both the private contractors and the MEO.

On December 9, 1998, the Air Force conducted a pre-proposal conference with potential contractors, including SMI. At the conference the Air Force gave the attendees information about the competition and the cost comparison procedures set forth in OMB Circular No. A-76; the Circular No. A-76 Revised Supplemental Handbook (March 1996) ("A-76 Supplemental Handbook"); Department of Defense Instruction ("DODI") 4100.33; Air Force Pamphlet ("AFP") 26-12; Supplemental Guidance to AFP 26-12 issued September 6, 1996; and Air Force Manual ("AFM") 64–108.

In accordance with the above-noted requirements, SMI submitted a timely proposal prior to the February 25, 1999 deadline. The Air Force also submitted their MEO pro-

---

2. The MEO is not the existing in-house organization, but the organization the agency would establish if it were competing for the work. In other words, the existing organization is allowed to make itself more efficient in order to compete. The A-76 Supplemental Handbook provides that "[a]gencies may consider existing management reinvention, consolidation, re-engineering, personnel classification, market and other analyses in the identification and development of the MEO." OFFICE OF MANAGEMENT AND BUDGET, CIRCULAR NO. A-76, REVISED SUPPLEMENTAL HANDBOOK 11 (1996) [hereinafter A-76 SUPPLEMENTAL HANDBOOK].

posal by February 25, 1999. The Air Force, however, revised the MEO proposal on April 22, 1999. It was the April 22, 1999 revised MEO proposal that the Air Force used to compare costs.

During March 1999, the Air Force's Source Selection Team performed an evaluation of proposals submitted by commercial sources in response to the solicitation. Following its evaluation, the Source Selection team determined that SMI's proposal was the only technically acceptable proposal. The Source Selection Team asked SMI to submit a final proposal for a cost comparison with the MEO's in-house cost proposal, which was to take place on April 23, 1999. On or about April 21, 1999, SMI submitted its final revised proposal.

On April 23, 1999, the Air Force's Contracting Officer ("CO") conducted the cost comparison and in accordance with the regulations publicly announced the results. SMI attended the public announcement. The CO first opened SMI's final revised proposal, which reflected a total price of $15,324,374. The CO then opened the Air Force's revised MEO cost comparison worksheet, which indicated that the MEO's final in-house cost estimate was $18,208,353. Because adjustments must be made to do a final comparison, the CO entered SMI's price information on the requisite OMB cost comparison worksheet. The data on the cost comparison worksheet was then entered into OMB's "COMPARE" computer program. The program generated a new worksheet indicating that in-house performance was more economical than contractor performance by $274,232. Based on these results, the CO announced the Air Force's tentative cost comparison decision in favor of the MEO. The decision would not become final, however, until SMI exhausted its administrative appeals.

In accordance with the Air Force's rules governing the cost comparison process, SMI received a copy of the tentative cost decision on May 3, 1999. The Air Force contends that it also sent SMI a copy of all of its supporting documentation, including a copy of the February 1999 initial proposal and the explanation of the changes to the April 1999 proposal. Under the Air Force's regulations, the February 1999 proposals and the change sheet should have been disclosed at the April 23 public announcement. It is not disputed that the Air Force did not publicly disclose that it had amended the February 1999 MEO proposal at the April public announcement, as required by the Air Force's procurement regulations. In addition, SMI contends that it never received a copy of these documents in the May package.

On May 12, 1999, SMI submitted a timely appeal of the Air Force's tentative cost comparison decision to the CO, based on the limited information it claims it had received. In its appeal SMI challenged the tentative cost comparison decision on two grounds. First, SMI asserted that the Air Force had violated OMB Circular No. A-76 and the A-76 Supplemental Handbook by adding the cost of three quality assurance evaluators ("QAE"), at a pay grade of GS-12, to SMI's proposed contract administration costs. Second, SMI challenged the Air Force's decision to add the relocation costs of 13 employees to SMI's proposed costs.

In accordance with AFP 26-12, the Los Angeles Air Force Base Cost Comparison Review Team heard SMI's appeal. The Review Team was made up of independent evaluators who did not participate in the cost comparison or evaluation of the April proposals. The Review Team denied SMI's appeal on May 30, 1999.

Thereafter, on June 2, 1999, SMI filed a protest with the General Accounting Office ("GAO") contesting the Air Force's cost comparison decision. After the protest was filed, the Air Force and SMI entered into a settlement agreement in which SMI agreed to withdraw its GAO protest and pursue its final administrative appeal to the major command under Section 15-2 of AFP 26-12. *See* AFP 26-12, *supra,* at 74. Pursuant to the terms of the settlement agreement, SMI submitted a major command-level appeal of the Air Force's cost competition decision to the Air Force Materiel Command ("AFMC"), on June 7, 1999.

* * *

By memorandum dated September 3, 1999, AFMC notified SMI that the final decision of the Air Force was to uphold the CO's cost comparison decision and to proceed with implementation of the MEO. By memorandum dated September 8, 1999, the AFMC instructed SMC to cancel the Solicitation and take appropriate action to implement the MEO.

On September 17, 1999, SMI filed its complaint and motion for a temporary restraining order in this court, challenging the September 3, 1999 AFMC decision and seeking to enjoin the Air Force from implementing the MEO. On September 21, 1999, the Air Force agreed to wait 60 days before taking any action adverse to SMI. The matter was briefed, and the court heard oral argument on November 3, 1999.

DISCUSSION

* * *

II. The Inclusion of Quality Assurance in Contract Administration Costs

SMI challenges as arbitrary and unreasonable the Air Force's decision to include in its cost comparison the costs of three quality assurance evaluators at the GS-12 and GS-11 level to oversee the private contractor's performance. In SMI's view, quality assurance costs are common to both the government and a private contractor and should not have been considered as an added cost to SMI's proposal. SMI further states that, in any event, the inclusion of three QAEs at such high GS levels is unsupportable when examined against the contract administration requirements of the solicitation.

The AFMC determined that these three positions were created for the purpose of assuring contractor compliance with contract terms and conditions and were therefore properly included as contract administration costs under the OMB Circular A-76 Revised Supplemental Handbook, which states that contract administration costs "includes the cost of reviewing compliance with the terms of the contract...." *See* A-76 SUPPLEMENTAL HANDBOOK, *supra,* at 25. Additionally, the AFMC determined that the QAE duties are not common to both contract and Government performance, as required by the OMB Handbook. *See RTS Travel Services,* B-283055, 1999 WL 754536, at *3 (September 23, 1999). The AFMC determined that Air Force regulations support a ratio of 3 contract administrators for a 51-person commercial operation. In addition, the AFMC noted that a review of the QAE Core Personnel Documents ("CPD") reveals that these three positions are intended to provide contract administration for each of three areas of performance; namely, Visual Information Services, Communications and Computer Systems, and Records Management. The AFMC concluded that these positions would not be needed if the work were not contracted out.

The court finds that the inclusion of three QAEs was rational and consistent with the applicable regulations. As a review of the CPDs reveals, the QAEs are required to perform contract administration functions including: certifying invoices, verifying claims, approving contract payments, and interfacing with the CO on negotiating contract changes. These tasks are clearly identified as contract administration functions in the A-76 Supplemental Handbook and AFP 26-12.[12]

The fact that these same employees also are tasked to perform certain quality assurance functions does not disqualify them as contract administrators. *See RTS Travel Services*, 1999 WL 754536 at *3. Where quality assurance functions are performed in the context of other contract administration functions, they properly may be included as contract administration costs. *See id.* Accordingly, the Air Force's decision to include these positions as contract administration costs is not arbitrary, capricious, or otherwise not in accordance with law. [FN13]

III. The Inclusion of Relocation Costs for 12 Employees

SMI argues that the administrative record does not support the AFMC's conclusion that privatizing the PWS would result in 12 relocations. SMI contends that data on the existing work force shows that only 5 existing employees would need to be relocated and that after applying the Air Force Command's general 10.11% "right of first refusal" statistic to the 5 employees, SMI should be responsible for only 4 relocations. SMI suggests that the data it relies upon is more realistic.

As discussed above, the AFMC addressed this argument in its decision, explaining that SMI was wrong to rely on data about the existing organization when SMI argued previously that only 5 existing employees would need to be relocated. As the AFMC stated: "The only position data relevant to the placement of employees is position data from the MEO, and not the original organization."

* * *

V. CONCLUSION

For all of the above-noted reasons, the court concludes that the Air Force's procurement decision was not arbitrary, capricious, or otherwise not in accordance with law. Accordingly, judgment for plaintiff on the administrative record and request for a permanent injunction is DENIED and judgment for defendant is GRANTED. The clerk is directed to enter judgment accordingly. Each party shall bear their own costs.

Notes and Questions

1. Space Mark presents a chronology of the procedural steps packed into less than a year from the issuance of the solicitation to the judicial decision on the protest. Can you identify each one and its significance? How do they match, or differ from, the steps in a regular, non-A-76, "private-private" competition? As noted earlier, in 2003 OMB issued a revised A-76, which changed the process significantly from that described in this

---

12. Under A-76 guidelines, "contract administration" includes "the cost of reviewing compliance with the terms of the contract, processing payments, negotiating change orders, and monitoring the closeout of contract operations [but] does not include inspection and other administrative requirements that would be common to contract and Government performance to assure acceptable performance." A-76 SUPPLEMENTAL HANDBOOK, *supra*, at 25. Similarly, Air Force guidance provides that contract administration costs include "the cost of reviewing contractor performance for compliance with the terms of the contract (quality assurance surveillance), processing contract payments, negotiating contract changes, and monitoring the closeout of contract operations." AFP 26-12, *supra*, at 55.

opinion. See Charles Tiefer, "OMB's New A-76: Tilting the Contracting-out Process," Federal Bar Association Government Contracts Section Newsletter, Spring 2003, at 6.

2. The two substantive issues are quality assurance costs and employee relocation costs. Are these mundane accounting disputes? How might they reflect the deeper questions of whether to transform public into private activity?

3. Note the interesting concept of what is the public side of the competition, the "Most Efficient Organization." It "is not the costs of the existing in-house organization, but the organization the agency would establish...to make itself more efficient in order to compete." Fn. 2. Opponents of the concept may complain that it presents potential private offerors with a "moving target" that is difficult to beat and that they may consider unfairly advantaged. Supporters of the concept may respond that the MEO is no less concrete than a private organization's projected plan for how it will perform, and that the MEO means that even if the work is not contracted out, the A-76 process forces the government to figure out how to be more efficient.

4. Procedurally, current government employees, particularly those organized in a public employees union, often provide their own input in the development of an MEO, and take advantage of their A-76 rights to participate in the internal reviews of the A-76 competition. Most courts, and the GAO, have not let public employee unions file protests if the private offeror wins and the MEO loses, while the private offeror can file a protest if it loses and the MEO wins. For a discussion of the controversy regarding this denial of standing to unions, see Charles Tiefer & Jennifer Ferragut, *Letting Federal Unions Protest Improper Contracting Out*, CORNELL J.L. & PUB. POL. (2001). Does it seem to you unfair that only one side can protest the outcome? Or do you draw a sharp distinction between contractors' rights and those of government employees and their unions?

Chapter 3

Contracting Methods

The 1990s and 2000s brought rapid evolutions in contracting methods generally described as "acquisition reform." Broadly speaking, the classic methods of sealed bids and competitive proposals involved fostering of competition along formalized processes. Acquisition reform involved reducing the formalized aspects, and following the less formal procurement methods of the commercial market.

Given the pace of developments in this context, the cases and materials in this section cannot be taken as describing enduring guides to the process that will be followed in coming years. Change happens too fast for that. Rather, these are intended as examples which would assist in understanding up-to-the-minute procedures.

For further discussion of the subjects in this chapter, see: Karen DaPonte Thornton, *Fine-Tuning Acquisition Reform's Favorite Procurement Vehicle, the Indefinite Delivery Contract*, 31 Pub. Cont. L.J. 383 (2002); Stephen M. Daniels, *An Assessment of Today's Federal Procurement System*, 38 Procurement Lawyer, Fall 2002, at 1; Robert Mahealani M. Seto, *Basic Ordering Agreements: The Catch-22 Chameleon of Government Contract Law*, 55 SMU L. Rev. 427 (2002); Steven L. Schooner, *Fear of Oversight: The Fundamental Failure of Businesslike Government*, 50 Am. U. L. Rev. 627 (2001); Neil S. Whiteman, *Charging Ahead: Has the Government Purchase Card Exceeded Its Limit?*, 30 Pub. Cont. L.J. 403 (2001); Carl J. Vacketta & Susan H. Pope, *Commercial Item Contracts: When Is a Government Contract Term or Condition Consistent with "Standard" or "Customary" Commercial Practice?*, 27 Pub. Cont. L.J. 291 (1998); Charles Tiefer & Ron Stroman, *Congressional Intent and Commercial Products*, Procurement Lawyer, Spring 1997, at 22

A. Commercial Item Contracting

Generally speaking, commercial contracting involves foregoing government-specific procurement formalities and following instead the analogy of commercial (private marketplace) methods. It also includes more government openness to purchasing items with characteristics, contract terms, and vendors, like those purchased by commercial (private) buyers. FAR Part 12 plays an important part.

To sketch polar opposites, before commercial contracting, a Defense Department purchase of a consignment of spare parts might, in theory, have occurred by soliciting sealed bids, using highly formal and rigid specifications, an elaborate government-specified set of terms, and a set of prospective vendors who sold only to the government because only these could and would deal with the government's procedures and requirements. In contrast, with commercial contracting, the same spare parts would get purchased from commercial vendors, on commercial terms, without formal or rigid specifications or processes, just by seeking a few price quotes and deciding among them. The following case shows some of the contrasts in methods.

Matter of: Access Logic, Inc.
January 3, 1997
B-274748.2

Access Logic, Inc. protests the award of a contract to EISI, Inc, under request for offers (RFO) No. 2-36632(CDT), issued by the National Aeronautics and Space Administration (NASA), for a 360-degree rear projection display system which will be used to simulate the outside view from an air traffic control tower.

We sustain the protest.

NASA conducted this procurement under the procedures set forth in Part 12 of the Federal Acquisition Regulation (FAR), "Acquisition of Commercial Items." Pursuant to FAR § 12.202 (Federal Acquisition Circular (FAC) 90-39), the agency conducted market research to determine which products would best meet its needs. After evaluating various projectors and screens during demonstrations held at vendor and customer sites and an industry convention, pursuant to the streamlined procedures set forth in FAR Subpart 12.6, and in particular FAR § 12.603, the agency issued the RFO as a combined synopsis/solicitation. The RFO incorporated FAR § 52.212-1 (FAC 90-39), "Instructions to Offerors—Commercial Items," which stated that offers must show, among other things, "[a] technical description of the items being offered in sufficient detail to evaluate compliance with the requirements of the solicitation. This may include product literature, or other documents, if necessary." The RFO also stated that award would be made to the responsible offeror which submitted the lowest-priced, technically acceptable offer responsive to the solicitation.

Among other items, the RFO specified the Electrohome Marquee 9501LC ACON brand name projection systems, or equal, and Optawave projection screens, or equal.[1] Although the RFO specified brand name or equal items, it did not include the standard "brand name or equal" clause which alerts offerors to include information in their offers sufficient to establish the equality of the products they are offering to the listed brand name. The RFO included a "Projection Display System Requirements Document," which apparently constituted the agency's salient characteristics, and included required specifications for the projectors and screens. That document also stated that the contractor is to provide all necessary design, engineering, installation labor, projector adjustments, project management, documentation, screens, equipment and materials, to furnish a complete and operational projection display system.

Six proposals were submitted. Instead of the brand name projection system, Access Logic proposed as an equal a BarcoGraphics 1209 rear projection display system; the firm also proposed Dia-Nippon ProScreen 180 degree viewing cone screens as equal to the brand name screens. Access Logic's proposal, which was priced at $665,901, was re-

---

1. The RFO in fact only stated that "or equal" offers would be considered for the projectors, and not the screens. Nonetheless, the solicitation included detailed technical requirements for the screens—suggesting that a brand name or equal method also was intended for the screens. More importantly, in its evaluation of proposals and its defense of this protest, NASA has treated the solicitation as a brand name or equal solicitation for both the projectors and the screens. Under these circumstances, we have reviewed the evaluation as if the RFO permitted offers of equal products for both items.

jected as technically unacceptable for reasons which we will address in detail below. Award was made to EISI at a price of $773,168, as the lowest-priced, technically acceptable offeror.

Based on our review of the record, we conclude that NASA improperly found Access Logic's offer unacceptable for failing to meet requirements not set forth in the RFO. Once offerors are informed of the criteria against which proposals will be evaluated, the agency must adhere to them. Grey Advertising, Inc., 55 Comp. Gen. 1111 (1976), 76-1 CPD p 325. In a brand name or equal acquisition, the contracting agency has an obligation to inform offerors of the characteristics that are essential to the government's needs and a product offered as an "equal" one need not meet unstated features of the brand name product. Tri Tool, Inc., B-265649.2, Jan. 22, 1996, 96-1 CPD p 14. Similarly, in an acquisition of commercial items, the description of the agency's needs "must contain sufficient detail for potential offerors of commercial items to know which commercial products or services to offer." FAR § 12.202(b); Metfab Eng'g, Inc.; Mart Corp., B-265934; B-265934.2, Jan. 19, 1996, 96-1 CPD p 93.

Among the reasons for rejecting Access Logic's offer, NASA concluded that Access Logic's offer did not meet RFO requirements concerning the "gain" and "half gain" angle for the projection screens and took exception to an RFO requirement concerning vertical mullions between the screens. Concerning these requirements, the RFO stated that:

"The [c]ontractor shall provide a 360 degree rear projection screen system, with minimum vertical mullions,...Use only products which comply with the following requirements:

1. Custom fresnel/lenticular acrylic optical screens with 4.0 gain,...

* * *

3. Physical separation between the screens to be as small as possible so as to make it difficult to see the screen edge lines."

The only reference in Access Logic's proposal concerning the mullions was a statement that "[t]he screens will be installed as-close together as-possible, with minimal vertical mullions." NASA reports that Access Logic's proposal "did not provide any actual designs or other supporting information indicating an acceptable construction method. Thus, [Access Logic's] proposal was considered unclear and in need of clarification." NASA orally requested Access Logic to clarify the reference in its proposal to mullions. According to Access Logic, it responded to this inquiry by stating that, based on a post-award review of the site, including a seismic review, in the best case, it would fuse the screens together so there would be no mullions and, in the worst case, 3/4-inch wide mullions would be used to connect the screens.[2] According to NASA, Access Logic's response to the agency's questions indicated the firm was uncertain as to how to satisfy the installation requirements and, absent more specific information about the fusing alternative, the agency was obligated to evaluate the 3/4-inch mullion alternative. NASA found the proposal's reference to mullions and Access Logic's explanation to be

---

2. Access Logic explains that it informed the agency that it intended to perform an on-site engineering review, including a seismic review (given that the facility will be located in an earthquake zone) to determine the most effective installation to meet technical requirements and building codes, including seismic considerations. The firm also states that it explained that it expected the mullions to be barely visible with the screens fused together and that "at worst case we expected the mullions would be 3/4 of an inch, which would provide sufficient support from a seismic perspective."

unacceptable because 3/4-inch mullions "would create a thick defined edge line between screens and significantly distract from images of aircraft and ground equipment
moving across the screens." Also, according to NASA, Access Logic's apparent need for
post-award input "cast doubt on whether [Access Logic] was capable of designing and
installing the screens in a manner that would satisfy the Government's requirements."
NASA also states that Access Logic's experience—which appears to involve mostly two-
screen, co-planar installations rather than curved, seamless installations like that required by the solicitation—did not alleviate this concern.

The RFO did not require mullions of any specific width. The only requirements were
for "minimum vertical mullions" and for "[p]hysical separation between the screens…
as small as possible so as to make it difficult to see the screen edge lines." Nothing in Access Logic's proposal indicated that it would not meet these requirements in installing
the system. On the contrary, the proposal statement that "[t]he screens will be installed
as-close together as-possible, with minimal vertical mullions," is entirely consistent with
the RFO requirements. Moreover, nothing in the market research submitted by NASA
indicates there is a consensus in the industry that 3/4-inch mullions would not be "as
small as possible" or that the screens could be attached with no visible line between
them. In fact, NASA's market research report states the expectation that in NASA's
planned facility "the screens will have a small but discernible line between them." In addition, NASA makes no effort to rebut Access Logic's belief that the 3/4-inch mullion
size would be "as small as possible" depending upon the seismic protection need. Thus,
it appears that NASA simply has its own view, one that would not be readily apparent to
the commercial sector, as to the width of the mullions that it would be willing to accept.
To the extent that NASA had such a specific requirement, it should have specified it in
the RFO. Since it did not, a vendor's failure to meet the requirement cannot provide a
basis for rejecting the vendor's proposal.[3] Industrial Storage Equip.-Pac., B-228123,
Dec. 4, 1987, 87-2 CPD p 551. Under the circumstances, we conclude that NASA's determination that Access Logic's proposal took exception to an RFO requirement concerning the mullions was unreasonable.

* * *

In other words, while NASA's concern about the brightness consistency of the projection screens and its desire for projection screens with a high half gain angle are reasonable, these concerns were not reasonably conveyed to vendors. In this respect, the
record does not show that the specification of a gain of 4.0—the only information in
the RFO concerning brightness of the screens—should have conveyed to vendors in the
commercial marketplace that high half gain angles were mandatory.

NASA also concluded that the projectors proposed by Access Logic failed to meet a
requirement of the RFO for automatic convergence. * * * Automatic convergence is a
function that automatically converges or focuses a picture on a screen for maximum
clarity and avoids the need for manual focusing.

On its face, Access Logic's proposal stated that the proposed projectors have an automatic convergence feature and NASA does not question whether that feature would be
provided. Rather, the agency explains that it considered Access Logic's proposal unacceptable because it did not include documentation demonstrating that the automatic

---

3. Although the agency also argues the proposal should have included design or other supporting information to show compliance with this requirement, the RFO had no such requirement. The
RFO only required design information during performance of the contract.

convergence system proposed by the firm would work in the rear projection system required by the agency. In our view, however, since the proposal otherwise recognized the system would use rear projection and did not take exception to the requirement for automatic convergence in the rear projection format, the absence of a specific statement that the automatic convergence feature of the proposed equipment would work in the rear projection system provided no basis for concluding that the proposal was unacceptable.[4] See Inframetrics, Inc., B-257400, Sept. 30, 1994, 94-2 CPD p 138.

Finally, NASA found Access Logic's proposal unacceptable because it did not list the firm's key personnel or design and engineering staff that would install the projection system. As Access Logic points out, however, the RFO did not require the submission of information about key personnel or staff. Although the contractor is to provide all necessary design, engineering, installation labor, projector adjustments, project management, etc., to provide a complete and operational projection display system, there was no requirement for offerors to submit any information concerning staff. Under the circumstances, the absence of such information in Access Logic's proposal provided no basis for finding that proposal unacceptable. Grey Advertising, Inc., supra.[5]

Although the record indicates that EISI delivered the projectors and screens and related equipment to NASA before the contract was suspended as a result of this protest, the equipment has not yet been installed. Accordingly, we recommend that NASA terminate the contract and resolicit with an appropriate statement of the agency's needs.
* * * *

The protest is sustained.[6]

Notes and Questions

1. The drive toward commercial acquisition encompasses many aspects, and this opinion reflects perhaps the most key one - having the contracting agency open itself to, and make a genuine choice among, commercially available items, rather than imposing overelaborate specifications (especially insufficiently articulated ones) and making con-

---

4. Agency officials assert they orally asked Access Logic's president about the automatic convergence capability of the projectors proposed by the firm and the firm failed to provide information responsive to that question. While the record concerning the communications between NASA and Access Logic is unclear, Access Logic's president states that, when asked, he orally informed the agency that the firm's proposed projectors do provide automatic convergence for a rear screen projection format and that, had NASA asked, the firm would have submitted commercial literature specifically stating that it does. We note that Access Logic has submitted to this Office commercial literature that shows that its proposed automatic convergence unit will work in a rear projection screen system. * * *

5. NASA also concluded that Access Logic's proposal was unacceptable because it did not include information concerning service personnel. As a matter of contract performance, the RFO required that "the Contractor shall have an office with full time service personnel located within 100 miles of the [NASA] site." Since the RFO did not require the submission of information about personnel or staff and NASA has referred to nothing in Access Logic's offer that suggests the firm would not meet this requirement, we conclude it was unreasonable to find the proposal unacceptable on this basis.

6. Access Logic filed a supplemental protest in which it argues (1) NASA illegally conducted this procurement as a "brand name only" procurement under the guise of a "brand name or equal" procurement without properly documenting the "brand name only" procurement, and (2) NASA was biased against Access Logic because agency officials were predisposed to award only to an offeror proposing the brand name products. Since we have sustained the protest and since it is not practicable for us to make a recommendation for corrective action, no useful purpose would be served by addressing these issues.

tractors thus provide, at higher-than-market price, what specifications demand. See the entire Winter 1998 issue of the Public Contract Law Journal, notably, Carl J. Vacketta & Susan H. Pope, *Commercial Item Contracts: When Is a Government Contract Term or Condition Consistent with "Standard" or "Customary" Commercial Practice?*, 27 Pub. Cont. L.J. 291 (1998). For a critical perspective on the uses being made of commercial contracting procedures, see Stephen M. Daniels, *An Assessment of Today's Federal Procurement System*, 38 Procurement Lawyer, Fall 2002, at 1.

2. Notice that the RFO stated that award would be made to the lowest-priced, technically acceptable responsive offer. In other words, the agency did not say that it would trade off technical merit for price. To deny Access Logic the award, the agency had to find its offer not merely technically inferior, but technically unacceptable. Hence the piling-on of NASA criticisms of Access Logic, and the apparent conviction of the GAO that underneath all those NASA criticisms was a simple unwillingness by NASA to recognize that, by the RFO's stated criteria, Access Logic's offer was technically acceptable - whether imperfect or even inferior.

3. Did NASA try to use commercial item acquisition methods just to buy from a preferred vendor? Or did GAO decide the protest in a way that put the rigidity of classic contracting methods back into the commercial item acquisition process?

Consider the following discussion regarding simplified acquisitions. It is useful to understand how the process looks from "inside" government procurement, that is, from the perspective of the contracting officer and her counsel. While the specifics regarding the role played by FACNET, the federal government's first major effort at electronic commerce, become increasingly dated, they serve as a reminder of the link between commercial contracting and electronic contracting, discussed later in this chapter.

Simplified Acquisitions
From the Judge Advocate General's School
Source: Government Contract Law: The Deskbook for Procurement
Professionals (Excerpt from Chapter 9, "Simplified and
Commercial Acquisitions")

(Provided on diskette by the Judge Advocate General's School (1998); edition of
Major M. Warner Meadows, 141st Contract Attorneys Course, August 1998;
prior version published by the Section on Public Contract Law of the American
Bar Association (1995))

CHAPTER 9, SIMPLIFIED AND COMMERCIAL ACQUISITIONS
* * *

III. BACKGROUND.

When FAR part 13 was amended in accordance with the federal acquisition streamlining act (FASA), the federal acquisition computer network (FACNET) became the required method for acquiring supplies and services for contract actions exceeding the micro-purchase threshold but not exceeding the simplified acquisition threshold, when practical and cost effective FAR 13.103(g).

A logical consequence of using FACNET to conduct acquisitions under the simplified acquisition threshold was that the traditional select vendor community that previously was the primary source for small dollar transactions would be replaced by a nationwide vendor community made up of many unknown suppliers offering unfamiliar products.

This greatly increased supplier base, offering many unfamiliar products would have to be evaluated by substantially reduced agency procurement workforces that had not been exempted from the downsizing experienced by federal agencies over the last several years.

Private industry, on the other hand, was concerned that the push for increased streamlining with the emphasis on "efficiency" would result in a system that gave individual contracting officers too much discretion. The new rules attempt to allay those concerns by language that indicates "all" offers will be evaluated... Somehow.

IV. PUBLICATION.

A.   Contracting officers shall promote competition to the maximum extent practicable to obtain supplies and services from the source whose offer is the most advantageous to the Government, based, as appropriate, on either price alone or price and other factors (e.g., past performance and quality) including the administrative cost of the purchase. Solicitations shall notify suppliers of the basis upon which award is to be made FAR 13.106-2(a)(1).

B.   Commerce Business Daily (CBD).

1.   Thresholds. As required by the Small Business Act (15 U.S.C. 607(e)) and the Office of Federal Procurement Policy Act (41 U.S.C. 416) contracting officers shall disseminate information for proposed contract actions expected to exceed $25,000 by synopsizing in the Commerce Business Daily (CBD). FAR 5.201(b)(1).

2.   Exceptions. The contracting officer need not submit the notice required by FAR 5.201 when the contracting officer determines that:

a.   The contract action is for an amount expected to exceed $25,000 but not expected to exceed the simplified acquisition threshold and is made by a contracting activity that has been certified as having implemented a system with interim (until December 31, 1999) or full (after December 31, 1999) FACNET and the contract action will be made through FACNET. FAR 5.202(a)(13).

b.   The contract is for an amount at or below $250,000 and is made through FACNET * * *

3.   Response Times. Whenever agencies are required to publish notice of contract actions under FAR 5.201, they shall proceed as follows:

a.   A notice of contract action shall be published in the CBD at least 15 days before issuance of a solicitation except when the combined CBD synopsis/solicitation procedure for acquisition of commercial items is used. See FAR 12.603.

b.   The contracting officer shall establish a solicitation response time which will afford potential offerors a reasonable opportunity to respond to-

(1)   each contract action including actions via FACNET, in an amount estimated to be greater than $25,000 but not greater than the simplified acquisition threshold; or

(2)   each contract action for the acquisition of commercial items in an amount estimated to be greater than $25,000.

c.   The contracting officer shall consider the circumstances of the individual acquisition, such as the complexity, commerciality, availability, and urgency, when establishing the solicitation response time.

d.   Except for the acquisition of commercial items, agencies shall allow at least a 30-day response time for receipt of bids or proposals from the date of issuance of a solicitation, if the contract action is expected to exceed the simplified acquisition threshold.

4.   Soliciting Competition. * * *

V. EVALUATION.

A.   When evaluating quotes or offers the evaluation must be made on the basis established in the solicitation. FAR 13.106-2(b)(1).

1.   All quotations or offers must be considered.

2.   The contracting officer has "broad discretion" in fashioning suitable evaluation procedures.

3.   Use of FAR Part 14 or 15 procedures is not required.

B.   The contracting officer shall use the procedures that will ensure that the evaluation of quotations can be performed in an efficient and minimally burdensome fashion. FAR Part 13.302(b).

C.   The following are not required of simplified acquisitions:

1.   Formal evaluation plans,

2.   The conduct of discussions,

3.   The scoring of quotes or offers

D.   Evaluation of past performance does not require the creation or existence of a formal database, but may be based on such information as the contracting officer's knowledge of and previous experience with the item or service being purchased, or

1.   Customer surveys, or

2.   other reasonable basis.

E.   For purchases conducted using FACNET, the contracting officer may-

1.   After preliminary consideration of all offers, identify from all quotes received one that is suitable to the user, such as the lowest-priced brand name product and quickly screen all lower priced quotes based on readily discernible value indicators, such as past performance warranty conditions, and maintenance availability; or

2.   Where an evaluation is based only on price and past performance, make an award based on whether the lowest priced offer having the highest past performance rating possible represents the best value when compared to any lower priced quotes. FAR Part 13.302(b)(2).

F.   Contracting officers shall not limit solicitations to suppliers of well-known and widely distributed makes or brands, or solicit quotations on a personal preference. (FAR 13.106-2(a)(7)). * * *

G.   Pre-award "clarifications." If the acquisition was conducted through FACNET, agencies need not respond to inquiries that are made telephonically or by facsimile unless they are unable to receive inquiries through FACNET. In addition, an agency is not required to receive questions through any medium (including FACNET) if doing so would interfere with its ability to conduct the procurement in an efficient manner. FAR 13.302(a)(7).

VI. AWARD

A.   Notice. FAR 13.106-2(c).

1.   For acquisitions not exceeding the simplified acquisition threshold, except for awards conducted through FACNET, notification to unsuccessful suppliers shall be given only if requested.

2.   If a supplier requests information on an award which was based on factors other than price, a brief explanation of the basis for the contract award decision shall be provided.

3.   Reasonableness 13.106-2(d). The determination that a proposed price is reasonable should be based on competitive quotations/offers. If only one response is received, a statement shall be included in the contract file giving the basis of the determination of fair and reasonable price. * * *

B.   Documentation should be kept to a minimum. * * *

Notes and Questions

1. Note how much of the discussion consists of the procedures that do not have to be followed, the broad discretion, and the reduced documentation. And, note again the attempt to link up with electronic contracting (at the time, FACNET). How far does this procedure go from classic government contracting methods?

2. Another subject consists of the procedures for "micro-purchases," including the use of government purchasing cards, very much related to use of credit cards by private buyers. See Neil S. Whiteman, *Charging Ahead: Has the Government Purchase Card Exceeded Its Limit?*, 30 Pub. Cont. L.J. 403 (2001).

B. Multiple Award Schedule Contracting

This section introduces the important Federal Supply Schedule (FSS). The General Services Administration (GSA) has administered the FSS for decades. Under the FSS, GSA enters into government-wide contracts with commercial firms to provide commercial products and services, at stated prices, for given periods of time. What the GSA has done is to enter into indefinite quantity contracts with these firms, and then list them in what become, for agency buyers, publications akin to governmentwide shopping catalogs. The government buyers then buy products and services on the FSS by placing "delivery orders" or "task orders" directly with the contractor and receiving the deliveries directly, without having to engage in elaborate bidding procedures.

GSA not only has a "Single Award Schedule" for the government buyer to buy from a particular (unique) source but, more important, GSA has a Multiple Award Schedule (MAS), in which GSA awards these indefinite quantity contracts to all of the companies supplying comparable commercial services and products at varying prices, provided these prices are "fair and reasonable." When Congress enacted the Competition in Contracting Act in 1984, it accepted that the FSS, including the MAS, might be a form of "full and open competition."

Acquisition reform statutes of the 1990s expanded upon the flexible use of government-wide contracts. In particular, FASA intended to advance the use by agencies of the FSS. This included exempting task or delivery orders under the FSS from protest.

ATA DEFENSE INDUSTRIES, INC., Plaintiff,
v. The UNITED STATES, Defendant.

United States Court of Federal Claims.
June 27, 1997. 38 Fed. Cl. 489

ANDEWELT, Judge.

In this post-award bid protest action, brought pursuant to 28 U.S.C. § 1491(b), plaintiff, ATA Defense Industries, Inc. (ATA), seeks an injunction ordering the Department of the Army to suspend performance of and to terminate a purchase order contract awarded to Caswell International, Inc. (Caswell), on May 13, 1997. Pursuant to the requests of the parties, this case was handled on an expedited basis. Plaintiff filed its complaint on May 30, 1997, and on June 24, 1997, after the parties conducted discovery, this court held a trial on the merits. For the reasons set forth below, plaintiff's request for a permanent injunction is granted.

I.

The purchase order contract in issue covers the upgrading of two target ranges at Fort Stewart, Georgia, used for training and qualification of tanks and infantry fighting vehicles. The contract lists separately the prices for the different products and services required for the upgrade. The total dollar value of the contract is $673,376. Certain products included on the purchase order, amounting to approximately 65 percent of the total contract value, were covered in an existing General Services Administration (GSA) Federal Supply Schedule (FSS) agreement between Caswell and the GSA. The products and services covering the remaining 35 percent of the contract value were not covered in the FSS agreement.

The contracting officer ultimately limited his search for potential suppliers to those with FSS agreements and concluded that Caswell was the only firm with an FSS agreement that met the Army's minimum requirements for the upgrade. The contracting officer selected Caswell to supply these FSS-covered products as well as the remaining required products and services not covered in the FSS agreement. Prior to awarding the contract, the contracting officer issued a "Justification and Approval for Other than Full and Open Competition" in which he explained his rationale for choosing Caswell as follows:

> Caswell International was the only contractor on the [FSS] which met the minimum requirements of the Government. Since the [FSS-covered] hardware being purchased is unique and proprietary to Caswell International, the associated installation hardware and rail kits [not listed on the FSS] must [also] be acquired from Caswell International.

Plaintiff is a competitor of Caswell in the sale of products and services used in upgrading target ranges for the Army. At the time of the purchase order agreement, plaintiff did not have an FSS contract covering its target-related products. The essence of plaintiff's complaint is that plaintiff was in a position to compete with Caswell for the products and services required to upgrade the target ranges at Fort Stewart but that the Army, in violation of 10 U.S.C. § 2304, denied plaintiff the opportunity to compete.

Indeed, plaintiff had made the Army aware of its intent to compete for the upgrade work. In response to a March 5, 1997, Commerce Business Daily notice of the Army's requirement for a target system upgrade at Fort Stewart, ATA submitted a letter to the Army stating that ATA was a "manufacturer of range and target systems" and requesting that it be added to the bidders' mailing list. When the Army later announced in the Commerce Business Daily its intent not to purchase the upgrade products and services through a solicitation requesting bids or proposals but rather to order the products and services against the GSA's FSS, ATA submitted a letter arguing that only a fraction of the contract work was covered in the FSS and requesting that instead of using the FSS, the Army adopt "a proper competitive procurement strategy." The Army, however, did not solicit a proposal from ATA. Instead, the Army issued a 15- page, highly detailed statement of work (SOW) setting forth the technical and performance specifications for the Fort Stewart upgrade. Caswell submitted a technical proposal in response to the SOW and the Army issued Caswell the disputed purchase order contract.

II.

Pursuant to 10 U.S.C. § 2304, when procuring products or services, the head of an agency is obliged to use competitive procedures and obtain full and open competition unless one of the exceptions listed therein applies. Section 2304 provides:

Contracts: competition requirements

(a)(1) Except as provided in subsections (b), (c), and (g) and except in the case of procurement procedures otherwise expressly authorized by statute, the head of an agency in conducting a procurement for property or services—

(A) shall obtain full and open competition through the use of competitive procedures in accordance with the requirements of this chapter and the Federal Acquisition Regulation; and

(B) shall use the competitive procedure or combination of competitive procedures that is best suited under the circumstances of the procurement.

Defendant contends that it complied fully with the requirements of Section 2304. To support this contention, defendant in effect divides the purchase order contract into two distinct parts: the products covered in the FSS agreement (approximately 65 percent of the total contract value) and the products and services not covered in the FSS (approximately 35 percent of the contract value). With respect to the products that constitute the 65 percent, defendant takes the position that purchasing these products against the FSS qualifies as a competitive procedure that brings the benefits of full and open competition. With respect to the products and services that make up the remaining 35 percent, defendant does not dispute that the Army purchased these products and services without the benefit of full and open competition. Defendant contends, however, that the procurement of these products and services falls within the following exceptions contained in Sections 2304(c)(1) and (c)(2):

(c) The head of an agency may use procedures other than competitive procedures only when—

(1) the property or services needed by the agency are available from only one responsible source or only from a limited number of responsible sources and no other type of property or services will satisfy the needs of the agency; [or]

(2) the agency's need for the property or services is of such an unusual and compelling urgency that the United States would be seriously injured unless the agency is permitted to limit the number of sources from which it solicits bids or proposals....

The Administrative Record, as filed by defendant, contains two written justifications issued by the contracting officer respectively covering the exceptions contained in subsections (c)(1) and (c)(2). The contracting officer based the first justification, referenced above and issued prior to award of the disputed contract, on Federal Acquisition Regulation (FAR) 6.302-1, which implements the exception contained in subsection (c)(1). FAR 6.302-1 allows government agencies to purchase products and services on a noncompetitive basis where there is "[o]nly one responsible source and no other supplies or services will satisfy agency requirements." As quoted above, this first justification rests on the conclusion that, as a result of the nature of the products and services involved in the upgrade, because the Army had determined to purchase 65 percent of the items from Caswell under the FSS, the remaining 35 percent of the items were unique and proprietary to Caswell and hence Caswell became the only possible source for these products and services.

The second justification, issued subsequent to the filing of the instant complaint and subsequent to this court's initial hearing on plaintiff's request for a temporary restraining order, covers most of the products and services included in the 35 percent of the purchase order contract that were not covered in the FSS. The contracting officer apparently offered this new justification in part because he had determined that he had erred in his first justification in that contrary to the position taken therein, the products and services not covered in the FSS were available competitively in the marketplace and hence did not qualify for sole source procurement under FAR 6.302-1. The contracting officer based this second justification on FAR 6.302-2 which implements the exception contained in subsection (c)(2) and allows the use of other than competitive procedures where there is an "[u]nusual and compelling urgency."

In the second justification, the contracting officer explained for the first time the apparent basis for his decision not to solicit offers for the contract work from sources that did not have FSS contracts. The contracting officer explained that "[i]n accordance with FAR 8.001, [the] statutory preference is to fulfill agency requirements against the GSA Federal Supply Schedule." With respect to the products and services not covered in Caswell's FSS contract, the contracting officer concluded that a competitive award for these items would result in a minimum delay of 210 days (90 days up through contract award and the remainder for delivery and installation) and that in view of the urgent need for the target range upgrade, such a delay would adversely affect the Army's "COMBAT READINESS" and in addition would cost the government approximately $6.5 million.

* * *

V.

The court will address first the justification issued subsequent to the commencement of this action based upon FAR 6.302-2. Prior to the issuance of the purchase order contract with Caswell, certain Army employees had expressed concern that any delay in completing the procurement would have an adverse impact on the Army's training of its troops. The Administrative Record and the contracting officer's testimony, however, demonstrate that the contracting officer made no determination as to whether FAR 6.302-2 could be used and that the contracting officer did not intend to rely upon FAR 6.302-2 as the justification for the sole source portion of the contract. Instead, the contracting officer approved the procurement based exclusively on his determination to purchase a portion of the needed products against the FSS and that FAR 6.302-1 allowed a sole source procurement of the remaining products and services required under the contract.[3] Indeed, had the contracting officer concluded that FAR 6.302-2 also applied, he could not have properly issued the first justification under FAR 6.302-1 because FAR 6.302-1(b) provides that "[t]his authority...shall not be used when any of the other circumstances is applicable." It was not until after plaintiff filed the instant suit and this court first conversed with counsel concerning plaintiff's request for a temporary restraining order that the contracting officer determined to rely upon FAR 6.302-2 to justify the purchase order contract. This is too late. The controlling statutes and regulations require the agency to evaluate its options and to make any determination to use other than full and open competition in procurement prior to entering the contract.

In this regard, 10 U.S.C. § 2304(f)(1) provides:

> Except as provided in paragraph (2), the head of an agency may not award a contract using procedures other than competitive procedures unless—
>
> (A) the contracting officer for the contract justifies the use of such procedures in writing and certifies the accuracy and completeness of the justification....

By providing that an agency "may not award a contract" (emphasis added) without justifying in writing the use of noncompetitive procedures, Section 2304(f)(1) necessarily contemplates that the determination that an exception applies will precede the award. Section 2304(f)(1) references subsection (f)(2) which concerns procurements under the urgency exception contained in Section 2304(c)(2) and FAR 6.302-2. Subsection (f)(2) allows the contracting officer when issuing a contract based on "unusual and compelling urgency" to delay the justification and approval until after the contract award. But that delay pertains only to the drafting of the written justification, not the making of the actual determination that the exception applies. Indeed, FAR 6.301(b) requires the agency not only to determine prior to contract award which exception applies, but also to specify in the contract the statutory basis for that exception. FAR 6.301(b) provides: "Each contract awarded without providing for full and open competition shall contain a reference to the specific authority under which it was so awarded. Contracting officers shall use the U. S. Code citation applicable to their agency. (See 6.302.)"

This requirement that an agency determine prior to contract award the precise exception upon which it will rely is not happenstance, but rather is part of a comprehensive plan by Congress to improve the efficiency with which federal agencies procure products and services. As explained in detail below, the Competition in Contracting Act of 1984 (CICA), Pub. L. No. 98- 369, 98 Stat. 1175 (1984), which

---

3. In the approval portion of the first justification, the contracting officer stated: "Based on the foregoing justification, I hereby approve the procurement of installation hardware and railbeds [not listed on the FSS] associated with the order of M31A1 targetry upgrades against the GSA, [FSS] on an other than full and open competition basis based on the authority of 10 U.S.C. 2304(c)(1)...."

amended 10 U.S.C. § 2304, seeks to make government contracting more efficient and rests on a commitment, where practicable, to bring the benefits of competition to government procurement. Application of the CICA anticipates that prior to entering a contract, an agency will make a reasoned determination as to which procedures, competitive or otherwise, would best serve the needs of the agency. If an agency attempts such a reasoned determination and acts consistent with that determination, then the agency is granted extensive deference. An agency's actions are overturned only if they are "arbitrary, capricious, an abuse of discretion, or otherwise not in accordance with the law." 5 U.S.C. § 706(2)(A). But such deference is not granted where the agency changes its rationale for taking an action after a suit is instituted attacking the original rationale. * * *

The court must stress, however, that to conclude that the contracting officer herein could not legally invoke FAR 6.302-2 retroactively is not to say that the facts that led the contracting officer to issue the second justification are irrelevant to this litigation. In a post-award bid protest action, if the court concludes that the agency's award of the contract was unlawful, the court must next address the appropriateness of granting an injunction. To the extent it were apparent to the court that if the court granted an injunction the agency would simply proceed, within the agency's discretion, to make a new award to the same contractor, then the grant of an injunction would tend to raise form over substance and ordinarily not be warranted. In addition, as described below, one of the factors courts must consider in determining whether to grant an injunction is the harm that would result from such a grant. Hence, to the extent defendant has an urgent and compelling need for target upgrades, the court must consider that need before granting an injunction.

VI.

Turning to the first justification issued prior to contract award under FAR 6.302-1, to understand the deficiencies therein it is necessary to understand the statutory and regulatory framework in which the contracting officer issued the justification. The CICA was enacted in part because of congressional concern that federal agencies were paying too high a price in their procurement of products and services. Congress was concerned that these agencies too often resorted to sole source procurements and did not take advantage of the lower prices that may result when a procurement is subject to full and open competition. The Court of Appeals for the Federal Circuit explained the purpose of the CICA, as follows:

> The [CICA] was "designed to increase the use of competition in Government contracting and to impose more stringent restrictions on the awarding of non-competitive—sole-source—contracts." H.R. Conf Rep. No. 861, 98th Cong., 2d Sess. 1421, reprinted in 1984 U. S. Code Cong. & Ad. News 697, 1445, 2109. The Conference agreement on CICA rejected "effective" competition as too low a standard for government procurements, and instead substituted "full and open" competition as the standard, "to emphasize that all responsible sources are permitted to submit bids or proposals for a proposed procurement." H.R. Conf. Rep. No. 861 at 1422, 1984 U. S. Code Cong. & Ad. News 2110. Indeed, "full and open competition" "means that all responsible sources are permitted to submit sealed bids or competitive proposals on the procurement."

10 U.S.C. § 2302(3); 41 U.S.C. § 403(7) (Supp. III 1985).

SMS Data Prod. Group, Inc. v. United States, 853 F.2d 1547, 1554 (Fed.Cir.1988).

The CICA embodies a strong commitment to achieving the benefits of competition in government procurement by providing, in 10 U.S.C. § 2304(a)(1), as follows:

Except as provided in subsections (b), (c), and (g) and except in the case of procurement procedures otherwise expressly authorized by statute, the head of an agency in conducting a procurement for property or services—

   (A) shall obtain full and open competition through the use of competitive procedures in accordance with the requirements of this chapter and the Federal Acquisition Regulation; and

   (B) shall use the competitive procedure or combination of competitive procedures that is best suited under the circumstances of the procurement.

The premise that underlies this strong preference for "full and open competition" is the economic premise that has long been recognized as the basis for a free market economic system—that full and open competition brings consumers the widest variety of choices and the lowest possible prices. See Adam Smith, Wealth of Nations 112 (1776).

Congress' strong commitment to competition is apparent from the narrow breadth of the exceptions to the general mandate to secure full and open competition, such as those contained in 10 U.S.C. § 2304(c)(1) and (c)(2). For example, 10 U.S.C. § 2304(c)(2) authorizes the purchase of products and services without the benefit of full and open competition only in those situations where "the agency's need for the property or services is of such an unusual and compelling urgency that the United States would be seriously injured unless the agency is permitted to limit the number of sources from which it solicits bids or proposals." Hence, Congress expresses a willingness to yield the benefits of full and open competition, but only when the alternative is "serious[] injur[y]" to the United States. In addition, even if full and open competition would result in serious injury to the United States, Congress demonstrates its paramount concern for competition by mandating in 10 U.S.C. § 2304(e) that the agency "request offers from as many potential sources as is practicable under the circumstances." Hence, faced with such emergency, an agency still must maintain competition to the extent practicable.

Similarly, 10 U.S.C. § 2304(c)(1) allows a departure from full and open competition only in narrowly defined circumstances. Subsection (c)(1) allows an agency to resort to other than full and open competition for a procurement where:

   (1) the property or services needed by the agency are available from only one responsible source or only from a limited number of responsible sources and no other type of property or services will satisfy the needs of the agency....

Where in fact "the property or services needed...are available from only one responsible source," and the selling party knows that it is the only source, then this exception is hardly a significant departure from full and open competition. In such a case, if the agency used competitive procedures and solicited offers or bids from other sources, that act would be futile because the supplier would be aware, in setting its price, that it was not bidding against any competition.[5] As to the use of sole source procurement where there is more than one but only a limited number of responsible sources, FAR 6.301 still

---

5. Full and open competition in such a case could bring benefits to the government when the contracting officer is not absolutely certain that only one responsible source is available in that soliciting bids could produce a bid from an unexpected source.

requires that "the contracting officer...solicit offers from as many potential sources as is practicable under the circumstances."

Next, the CICA recognizes that there are a variety of different procedures that can be classified as "competitive procedures" because they can produce the competitive prices that result from full and open competition. Pursuant to 10 U.S.C. § 2304(a)(2), the head of an agency is authorized to achieve full and open competition through the use of sealed bids or through the solicitation of competitive proposals. Section 2302(2) further provides:

> The term "competitive procedures" means procedures under which the head of an agency enters into a contract pursuant to full and open competition. Such term also includes—
>
> * * *
>
> (C) the procedures established by the Administrator of General Services for the multiple award schedule program of the General Services Administration if—
>
> (i) participation in the program has been open to all responsible sources; and
>
> (ii) orders and contracts under such program result in the lowest overall cost alternative to meet the needs of the United States....

The FSS, which the contracting officer used herein, qualifies as a "multiple award schedule program of [GSA]." FAR 8.401 explains the purpose and operation of the FSS as follows:

> (a) The [FSS], directed and managed by the [GSA], provides Federal agencies with a simplified process for obtaining commonly used supplies and services at prices associated with volume buying. Indefinite delivery contracts (including requirements contracts) are established with commercial firms to provide supplies and services at stated prices for given periods of time. The schedule contracting office issues publications, titled Federal Supply Schedules, containing the information necessary for placing delivery orders with the contractors. Ordering offices issue delivery orders directly to the schedule contractors for the required supplies or services.

Thus, the FSS is directed at the purchase of "commonly used supplies and services" and potentially benefits the federal government, inter alia, by allowing GSA to aggregate potential future demands for certain products and services among the various federal agencies and, by using that leverage, to negotiate a price based on volume discounts. The FSS thereby permits individual agencies to purchase a relatively small number of products at prices that ordinarily would be reserved for high volume buyers. The FSS also is beneficial to the government in that it can lower the administrative costs involved in procurement by potentially avoiding the necessity of conducting a new competitive procurement each time a new need for a certain product or service arises.

Although there are different competitive procedures available to federal agencies, it is important to stress that the CICA does not leave these agencies with unlimited discretion to select among them. Rather, Section 2304(c)(1) mandates that the head of an agency "use the competitive procedure or combination that is best suited under the circumstances of the procurement."

VII.

A.

With this understanding of the statutory and regulatory background of FAR 6.302-1, the legal inadequacy of the contracting officer's first justification becomes apparent. The total contract value is $673,376 and the first justification covers $228,985 worth of products and services that are covered in the contract but not listed in Caswell's FSS agreement. The contracting officer's rationale in the first justification for not subjecting this $228,985 worth of products and services to full and open competition is that "[s]ince the [FSS-covered] hardware being purchased is unique and proprietary to Caswell International, the associated installation hardware and rail kits [not listed on the FSS] must [also] be acquired from Caswell International." As described above, in the second justification, issued pursuant to FAR 6.302-2 and subsequent to the filing of the instant complaint, the contracting officer acknowledged that this conclusion was erroneous and in fact that $193,060 of the $228,985 of products and services "could...be solicited in a competitive environment, if urgency did not exist."

Defendant contends that even though the contracting officer erred in his first justification, the court nevertheless should uphold that justification because the contracting officer reasonably relied on the advice of a subordinate in reaching his conclusion that a sole source purchase was warranted. But that reliance was not reasonable. The purchase order itself belies the conclusion expressed in the first justification because the purchase order includes products and services, such as computer monitors, laser printers, and the burying of cables, which should be recognized as readily available from sources other than Caswell. * * *

B.

Defendant contends that assuming the grounds stated in the first justification do not support the purchase of the $193,060 worth of products and services that presumably could have been purchased using full and open competition, the court nevertheless should uphold this purchase because these goods and services are "incidental" to the goods that were purchased against Caswell's FSS contract. Defendant cites a series of GAO decisions which defendant contends allow a contracting officer, when purchasing goods from a party with an FSS contract, to include in a single purchase order both those products that are covered in the FSS and those products that are not but are "incidental" thereto. In re Vion Corp., B-275063.2, 97-1 CPD 53; 1997 WL 42513; In re Raymond Corp., B-246410; 1992 WL 52427; In re Amray, Inc., 69 Comp. Gen. 456; 1990 WL 269572; In re Rack and Stanley, 61 Comp. Gen. 414; 1982 WL 26627. In Raymond, the GAO approved the award of a purchase order contract where the "incidental" items amounted to 17 percent of the total value of the contract. Relying on Raymond, defendant argues that because the purchase of incidental products amounting to 17 percent of the total contract price was allowed in Raymond, the contracting officer herein could not be deemed to have abused his discretion in purchasing approximately 35 percent of the value of the contract on a noncompetitive basis because these items also were properly classifiable as "incidental" to the products purchased against the FSS.

The first problem with defendant's argument is that it involves a post hoc rationalization by government counsel and does not represent any decision actually made by the contracting officer. * * * *

Second, there is an even more basic problem with defendant relying on the Raymond approach to "incidentals." It is fundamentally inconsistent with Congress' unambiguous statutory mandate in the CICA to allow a contracting officer, when purchasing products against the FSS, to include in the purchase order "incidental" products that are competitively available, unless the prices charged for these "incidental" products are the product of full and open competition. As noted above, Congress unequivocally states in 10 U.S.C. § 2304(a)(1)(A) that in conducting a procurement, unless an exception applies, an agency "shall obtain full and open competition through the use of competitive procedures." As summarized above, these exceptions are specific and narrow in scope. There is no exception that even arguably covers "incidentals."

The authority of an agency to purchase products against the FSS does not extend to incidentals. That authority is based in 10 U.S.C. § 2302(2) which potentially includes, within the definition of the term "competitive procedures," certain procedures established by the Administrator of General Services for the multiple award schedule program. Section 2302(2), however, is in no sense a departure from Congress' strong reliance on competition in government procurements. Rather, Section 2302(2) simply provides contracting officers with an alternative "competitive procedure" by which to achieve the benefits of full and open competition as required in Section 2304(a)(1)(A).

The legislative history of the CICA indicates that the view had been expressed to Congress that GSA's multiple award schedule program should be abolished because it did not result in competitive prices for government agencies. H.R.Rep. No. 861, 98th Cong. (1984), U.S. Code Cong. & Admin. News at 697. Congress, however, decided not to invoke a blanket ban. Instead, Congress classified the procedures established by the Administrator of General Services for the multiple award schedule program as "competitive procedures," and thereby authorized agencies to purchase thereunder without the benefit of competition, but only if:

(i) participation in the program has been open to all responsible sources; and

(ii) orders and contracts under such program result in the lowest overall cost alternative to meet the needs of the United States. . . .

10 U.S.C. § 2302(2)(C). When GSA procedures satisfy these conditions, the argument proceeds, purchases against the FSS bring the benefits of full and open competition and result in competitive prices.[8]

* * *

But a conclusion that the FSS prices are competitive is necessarily based on price negotiations and evaluations that preceded the inclusion of the specified products and prices in the FSS contract. GSA apparently does not make any effort to negotiate or evaluate prices for products and services that are not listed on the FSS but could be classified as "incidental" to those listed products. This being the case, there is no basis for concluding that the prices negotiated between the contracting officer and the FSS contractor for "incidentals" is the product of full and open competition. In this regard, defendant has not pointed to any procedures adopted by the Administrator of General Services that are directed at assuring that the prices of such "incidental" products would be established by competitive procedures and would be "the lowest overall cost alternative."

---

8. The Administrative Record raises an issue as to whether current GSA procedures are adequate to meet the goal upon which Congress conditioned the status of the multiple award schedule program as a "competitive procedure." In an April 1, 1997, E-mail, an Army employee explained that "[p]ast experience is that competitive cont[r]act costs are usually 20% lower than GSA [schedules]."

Hence, unless a product or service falls within an exception contained in Section 2304 or can be classified as de minimis, Section 2304 mandates that the product be purchased on a competitive basis using a competitive procedure as defined in Section 2302. There is no exception covering "incidentals."

* * *

C.

Next, defendant argues that the FSS-covered portion of the disputed contract was clearly within the contracting officer's discretion and hence, that any injunction should address only the approximate 35 percent of the contract that was not covered in the FSS. Defendant bases this argument in part on FAR 8.001, which provides:

(a) Except as required by 8.002, or as otherwise provided by law, agencies shall satisfy requirements for supplies and services from or through the sources and publications listed below in descending order of priority—

(1) Supplies.

* * *

(vii) Optional use Federal Supply Schedules (see subpart 8.4); and

(viii) Commercial sources (including educational and nonprofit institutions).

Defendant contends that because purchasing against the FSS is a higher priority than purchasing from a commercial source, the contracting officer's decision to fill the agency's needs first from the FSS is necessarily correct and not subject to review. This contention is incorrect.

FAR 8.001 applies "[e]xcept…as otherwise provided by law." To the extent FAR 8.001 is interpreted to oblige the Army to purchase all products and services necessary for the target range upgrade against the FSS and then to proceed to competitive sources for the remaining needed products and services not covered in the FSS, the regulation would conflict with Section 2304(a)(1)(B), which mandates that the head of the agency "use the competitive procedure or combination of competitive procedures that is best suited under the circumstances of the procurement."

* * *

The Army has recognized the need to modernize the RC-H and RC-G ranges since at least January 1995 and similar modernizations are scheduled for a variety of target ranges throughout the United States over the next few years. Initially, the upgrades to the RC-H and RC-G ranges were scheduled to be completed at a date later than that specified in the contract. By February 1997, the two upgrades had been rescheduled to their present dates.

To date, the need to upgrade the RC-H and RC-G ranges has not resulted in any troops failing to meet Army requirements. The Army evaluators have developed subjective methods of evaluating performance on these ranges and the troops eventually qualify on the MPRC range. In the past, ranges have occasionally been closed and troops that would have trained on those ranges were sent to other ranges that are later in progression than the closed ranges. The MPRC range, which is fully modernized and available at Fort Stewart for qualifying troops, is later in progression than both the RC-H and RC-G ranges.

Conclusion

For the reasons set forth above, plaintiff's motion for a permanent injunction is granted. Defendant shall suspend performance under and take the necessary steps to terminate Purchase Order DAAE20-97-F-0048. No costs.

Notes and Questions

1. In this case, Caswell had an MAS contract, but ATA did not. The Army ordered its target range upgrade as a MAS purchase even though thirty-five percent of the products were not carried on Caswell's MAS contract and hence not within the FSS's satisfaction of CICA. The Army cited GAO decisions that had accepted the rationale that a purchase could satisfy CICA if, along with what was bought from the FSS, some non-FSS "incidental" items were purchased. This rationale was disdained by the court. Stripped of this justification and others, the Army's decision stood revealed as the kind of sole-source purchase heavily disfavored by CICA.

2. In the 1990s and 2000s, the MAS program got pushed ahead in a number of complex ways by FASA and FARA. See Carl L. Vacketta, *Comprehensive Portrait of Multiple Award Schedule Now Available*, 32 Pub. Cont. L.J. 607 (2003)(reviewing John W. Chierichella & Jonathan S. Aronie, et al., Multiple Award Schedule Contracting (2002); Cheryl Lee Sandner & Mary Ita Snyder, *Multiple Award Task and Delivery Order Contracting: A Contracting Primer*, 30 Pub. Cont. L J. 461 (2001); Robert J. Sherry, Thomas F. Burkey & Kimberly C. Welch, *The Present and Future of MAS Contracting*, 27 Pub. Cont. L.J. 369 (1998).

LABAT-ANDERSON INC., Plaintiff,
v. THE UNITED STATES, Defendant,
and JHM Research and Development Inc., Intervenor.

United States Court of Federal Claims,
2001. 50 Fed.Cl. 99

WILSON, Judge.

This matter is before the Court on Labat-Anderson, Inc.'s (LABAT's) motion for a preliminary injunction, pursuant to RCFC 65, following the issuance of a ten-day temporary restraining order, which was extended for five days to June 30, 2001. Also before the court is intervenor JHM Research and Development's (JHM's) motion to dismiss for lack of subject matter jurisdiction, pursuant to RCFC 12(b)(1), or in the alternative, for failure to state a claim upon which relief can be granted pursuant to RCFC 12(b)(4). For the reasons discussed below, both intervenor's motion to dismiss and plaintiff's motion for a preliminary injunction are denied.

FINDINGS OF FACT

The Immigration and Naturalization Service of the U.S. Department of Justice (INS) operates four Service Centers in California, Nebraska, Texas, and Vermont to process the applications and petitions of aliens seeking benefits under federal immigration and nationality laws. Under the Direct Mail Program initiated in 1986, personnel at these Service Centers process approximately five million applications and petitions each year. (Administrative Record (AR) at 6211; Def.'s Answer at 2.) For the past five and a half years, LABAT has performed records management and other operations support services at these Service Centers on a "time and materials" basis. LABAT employs approximately 1,500 employees on the contract, which is the primary contract around which its business is built (TRO Hearing Transcript (Tr.) at 8). The Service Centers' task areas include: mailroom operations, file assembly, data collection, document preparation, fee collection and processing, fileroom operation, quality control, word processing, project management, and business processing reengineering. (AR at 6211-12.)

This post-award bid protest challenges the award of Blanket Purchase Agreement No. COW-1-A-1027 (BPA) to provide records management and forms processing services at the four INS Service Centers. On June 26, 2000, the INS announced in Request for Quotations No. HQ-0-Q-0044 (RFQ) that it planned to award the fixed-price BPA to a single contractor holding a Federal Supply Schedule (FSS) contract under the General Service Administration's Document Management Services and Products Schedule, Special Item Number (SIN) 51-504, "Records Management Services," and other applicable SINs. (AR at 265.) The RFQ estimated that the volume of purchases under the BPA would be $344 million over 60 months. The RFQ further indicated that the BPA would be awarded to the proposal presenting the best value to the government, which would be evaluated in terms of technical approach, past performance, and discounted prices. (AR at 265, 266.)

Although the FSS program enables agencies to adopt a simplified and more flexible approach to the procurement of services on a recurring basis, the source selection process and criteria described in the RFQ contained several procedures and structures more typical of a negotiated procurement. For example, the RFQ provided that price proposals would be analyzed in accordance with techniques referenced in 48 C.F.R. § 15.404 (AR at 287), technical proposals would be rated in accordance with criteria defined by 48 C.F.R. § 15.301 (AR at 837), and debriefing would be conducted pursuant to 48 C.F.R. §§ 15.505-15.506 (AR at 836).

For purposes of this case, the most significant requirement of the RFQ was that each offeror submit two "estimating models" that formed the bases of its price and technical proposals. In addition to serving as tools to assess an offeror's ability to provide the required services with an appropriately sized work force, the INS planned to use the estimating models as management aids in the administration of the BPA's performance. * * * * The INS established a technical evaluation committee (TEC) to evaluate the technical proposals and a business evaluation committee (BEC) to evaluate the price proposals. (AR at 6209-10.)

In rating the proposals, the technical approach and past performance factors combined were to be more heavily weighted than the proposal's price factor. As the Source Selection Award Council's (SSAC) Report stated, "the Government is more concerned with obtaining superior technical performance than lowest overall price." (AR at 6210-11.)

Four offerors submitted "final" proposals to the INS by the original closing date of August 7, 2000: LABAT, JHM, and two other offerors eventually eliminated from the competition. (AR at 1346.) LABAT's initial final proposal scored higher than JHM for technical approach, management, and past performance. (AR at 1509.)

On October 19, 2001, the SSAC determined that it needed additional information from LABAT and JHM prior to the final award decision. (AR at 6216.) Consequently, the INS revised its procurement and issued Amendment No. 6 on October 26, 2001. Amendment No. 6 added language to the RFQ requiring the electronic versions of the estimating models to contain all formulae and links between spreadsheets and tables contained in the offerors' proposals. (AR at 803.)

* * *

In the last round of evaluations, the BEC found LABAT's final proposal revision to be noncompliant with Amendment No. 6. (AR at 1357.) * * * The BEC recommended that the INS eliminate LABAT from further consideration for award * * *

* * *

The SSAC determined that the BEC and TEC evaluations fairly represented the merits of each proposal and unanimously accepted the committees' evaluation results. (AR at 6220.) Despite the BEC recommendation that LABAT be eliminated from consideration for award, the SSAC continued with the evaluation process and conducted a best-value analysis for the limited purpose of determining whether JHM's proposal offered value. (AR at 6221-22.) In the best-value analysis, the technical and past performance ratings were combined, yielding an overall rating of "good" for JHM and "marginal" for LABAT. (AR at 6219.) * * *

The INS awarded the BPA to JHM on January 3, 2001. Following a post-award debriefing, LABAT filed a protest before the General Accounting Office (GAO) on January 12, 2001, which was subsequently denied on April 16, 2001. See Labat-Anderson, Inc., B-287081, 2001 WL 410356 (Comp.Gen. April 16, 2001). * * * LABAT filed a post-award bid protest action in this Court on June 11, 2001. Following a hearing on the application for a temporary restraining order, the Court entered a temporary restraining order for ten days, which was extended during the pendency of the preliminary injunction hearing for an additional five days. * * *

CONCLUSIONS OF LAW

Subject Matter Jurisdiction

* * *

In 1996 Congress amended the Tucker Act to grant the U.S. Court of Federal Claims jurisdiction to entertain post-award bid protest actions. See 28 U.S.C. § 1491(b) (Supp. II 1996). Specifically, § 1491(b)(1) provides that the U.S. Court of Federal Claims:

> shall have jurisdiction to render judgment on an action by an interested party objecting to a solicitation by a Federal agency for bids or proposals for a proposed contract or to a proposed award or the award of a contract or any alleged violation of statute or regulation in connection with a procurement or a proposed procurement.

The amendment also incorporates the standard of review applicable to Administrative Procedure Act cases. 28 U.S.C. § 1491(b)(4) ("In any action under this subsection, the courts shall review the agency's decision pursuant to the standards set forth in section 706 of title 5."). Pursuant to this standard, the Court can hold unlawful, and set aside, an agency action which is "found to be arbitrary, capricious, an abuse of discretion, or otherwise not in accordance with law." 5 U.S.C. § 706(A) (1994).

Intervenor JHM's jurisdictional challenge is two-pronged. First, JHM contends that LABAT's protest of the BPA award at issue falls outside the scope of the Tucker Act, because it is neither related to "a proposed contract or to a proposed award of a contract" nor related to any "alleged violation of statute or regulation in connection with a procurement." Second, JHM claims that the Federal Acquisition Streamlining Act of 1994 (FASA), 41 U.S.C. § 253j(d), which prohibits protests "in connection with the issuance or proposed issuance of a task or delivery order" except under circumstances not relevant here, bars the protest of the BPA award at issue in this case. The Court rejects both of these arguments.

The Request for Quotations issued by the INS on June 23, 2000 states that the INS intended to award a Blanket Purchase Agreement against the awardee's GSA FSS contract. (AR at 252, 265.) Federal Acquisition Regulation (FAR) 8.404(b)(4) authorizes the government to use Blanket Purchase Agreements to establish accounts with contractors holding Federal Supply Schedule contracts to fulfill recurring requirements. 48 C.F.R. § 8.404(b)(4) (2000). The FSS program "provides Federal agencies with a simplified process for obtaining commonly used commercial supplies and services at prices associated with volume buying." 48 C.F.R. § 8.401(a). Under the program, an agency may select products and services from a list of eligible contractors whose pricing schemes have been pre-approved by GSA. An agency procuring goods or services pursuant to an FSS contract need not comply with the more formal and rigorous procedures for negotiated procurements set forth in FAR Part 15. Because the "GSA has already determined the prices of items under [the FSS program] to be fair and reasonable," agencies "need not seek further competition, synopsize the requirement, make a separate determination of fair and reasonable pricing, or consider small business programs." 48 C.F.R. § 8.404(a).

For the purpose of awarding this BPA, the INS chose to conduct a competitive source selection process aimed at selecting a single offeror already holding a GSA FSS contract. The INS adopted many of the procedures specified in FAR Part 15 for negotiated procurements, including: 1) price analysis techniques prescribed by FAR § 15.404; 2) post-award debriefing prescribed by FAR § 15.506; and 3) technical evaluation definitions prescribed by FAR § 15.001 (formerly codified at 48 C.F.R. § 15.301 (1999)). While this Court has held that FSS acquisitions are not transformed into negotiated procurements simply because an agency chooses to utilize in its evaluation process more formal elements typically used in a negotiated procurement, where an agency engages in a more comprehensive selection process than contemplated by the FSS scheme, a frustrated bidder may still challenge the agency award under the arbitrary and capricious standard articulated in 5 U.S.C. § 706(2)(A). Ellsworth Assocs., Inc. v. United States, 45 Fed.Cl. 388, 395-96 (1999).

JHM's argument that LABAT's complaint does not allege a violation of a statute or regulation in connection with a procurement is unpersuasive. The Tucker Act's grant of jurisdiction over an alleged "violation of a statute or regulation in connection with a procurement or a proposed procurement is sweeping in scope." RAMCOR Servs. Group, Inc. v. United States, 185 F.3d 1286, 1289 (Fed.Cir.1999). That FAR Part 8 does not contain procedural or substantive standards equivalent to those provided by the FAR for more structured negotiated procurements is inconsequential. As the Federal Circuit explained in RAMCOR, the Administrative Dispute Resolution Act (ADRA), 28 U.S.C. § 1491(b)(1), explicitly imports the Administrative Procedure Act (APA) standards of review into the Court of Federal Claims' review of agency decisions. RAMCOR, 185 F.3d at 1290. Section 1491(b)(4) thus provides the substantive requirements that a statute or regulation connected to procurement-such as the authorization in FAR Part 8 to enter into Blanket Purchase Agreements-may lack. Just as an agency may "violate" the agency override provision at issue in RAMCOR "by issuing a written finding that does not meet the substantive review criteria of 1491(b)(4)," an agency may "violate" FAR 8.404(b)(4) by acting arbitrarily and capriciously when entering into a BPA.

The Court also rejects JHM's argument that the alleged violation was not "in connection with a procurement," because a BPA is not a contract. Although the Tucker Act does not define "procurement," as used in 28 U.S.C. § 1491(b), Congress has defined the term broadly in 41 U.S.C. § 403(2) (1994) and 41 U.S.C. § 2302(3)(A) (1994): "The term 'procurement' includes all stages of the process of acquiring property or services, beginning with the process for determining a need for property or services and ending with contract completion and closeout." The award of the BPA to JHM is one of the "stages" in the process of acquiring records management and forms processing services that occurred after the INS "determined a need for . . . services," the point at which the procurement process begins under the statutory definition. Thus, LABAT's objection to the reasonableness of the INS's award of a BPA against an FSS contract pursuant to FAR Subpart 8 falls squarely within the jurisdictional ambit of § 1491(b)(1).

The Court is similarly not convinced that the Federal Acquisition Streamlining Act of 1994's (FASA's) prohibition against protests in connection with the issuance or proposed issuance of a task or delivery order applies to the BPA awarded by the INS to JHM. Section 253j(d) of the FASA states:

> A protest is not authorized in connection with the issuance or proposed issuance of a task or delivery order except for a protest on the ground that the order increases the scope, period, or maximum value of the contract under which the order is issued.

While the plain language of the statutory provision clearly bars task order protests, the critical point here is that the award at issue in this case constitutes far more than the mere issuance of a task order against an already- existing GSA FSS or multiple-award contract. Because LABAT is challenging the award of a FAR Part 8 BPA and not the issuance of a task order under FAR Part 16, JHM's argument that the FASA task order protest exemption, 41 U.S.C. § 253j(d), strips the Court of jurisdiction in this case is rejected.

JHM analogizes the award of the Blanket Purchase Agreement to the establishment of a charge account. The award at issue can be more accurately characterized as an agency decision about which one of several charge accounts to select. As the RFQ explains, the INS intended to acquire Service Center operations support services "by awarding a competitive Blanket Purchase Agreement to a single offeror-who has a current [FSS] contract with the GSA. . . ." (AR at 265) (emphasis in original). While it is undisputed that the issuance of task orders against the account and not the establishment of the account itself obligates funds, the decision being challenged is the selection of JHM instead of LABAT as the single "account" against which orders for INS Service Center Operations Support will be issued in the future. The language of the RFQ makes clear that the BPA is not a task order itself, but rather a vehicle against which task orders will be placed. (AR at 260) ("each task order placed under this BPA will include. . . ."), 874 ("That offeror affording INS the best value as determined by the source selection criteria in the solicitation will be awarded a Blanket Purchase Agreement under which orders may be issued.") Therefore, § 253j(d), by its terms, does not apply here.

In LABAT's first protest of the INS award, the GAO primarily relied on the FASA's legislative history, as explicated in Severn Cos., Inc., B-275717, 97-1 CPD ¶ 181, at 2 n. 1, 1997 WL 270342 (Comp. Gen. Apr. 28, 1997), to refute JHM's argument that the FASA's task order protest bar applies to this procurement challenge. As the GAO noted in Severn, there is "no evidence that [253j(d)] is intended to preclude protests with respect to the placement of orders against GSA FSS contracts." Id. Relying on the suggestion in the FASA's legislative history that the FASA was intended to encourage the use of multiple-award contracts, rather than single-award order contracts, the GAO in Severn reasoned that no such incentive was required with respect to the FSS, since it already afforded users a choice of multiple contractors. Id. at 2 n. 1 (citing H.R. Conf. Rep. No. 103-712, at 178 (1994), reprinted in 1994 U.S.C.C.A.N. 2607, 2608; S.Rep. No. 103-258, at 15-16 (1994), reprinted in 1994 U.S.C.C.A.N. 2561, 2575-76).

In establishing jurisdiction, the Court does not rely on the FASA's legislative history because it does not shed meaningful light on the scope of the task order protest bar. However, the language and regulatory history of FAR Part 16 support the interpretation that the task order restriction was not intended to apply to FSS procurements. Tracking in part the language of the FASA, section 16.500(c) of the FAR states:

> Nothing in this subpart restricts the authority of the General Service Administration (GSA) to enter into schedule, multiple award, or task or delivery order contracts under any other provision of law. Therefore, GSA regulations and the coverage for the Federal Supply Schedule program in Subpart 8.4 and Part 38 take precedence over this Subpart [16.5].

The regulatory comments accompanying the Final Rule codified at 48 C.F.R. § 16 further explain that "[c]ontracts subject to Part 38 were exempted from coverage because [FASA] specifically exempted GSA's Federal Supply Schedule Program." 61 Fed. Reg. 39,201, 39,202 (July 26, 1996).

In sum, the procurement at issue in this case is not exempt from protest under the FASA, 41 U.S.C. § 253j(d), and may be reviewed for reasonableness pursuant to the Tucker Act. 28 U.S.C. § 1491(b)(1).

Preliminary Injunction

* * *

Based on the administrative record, and oral arguments on the motion for a preliminary injunction, the Court concludes that plaintiff has not demonstrated a likelihood of success on the merits of its claim that the INS award to JHM was unreasonable. Central to the Court's review is the agency's elimination of LABAT's proposal based on its finding that LABAT did not comply with the RFQ by failing to provide a clear rationale for hard-coded entries in its priced estimating model. Amendment No. 6 explicitly states that "[i]f an Offeror…provides an estimating model that contains hard coded entries without any rationale for or explanation of the hard coded entries, the BEC will determine the Offeror's proposal to be non-compliant with the RFP instructions and recommend to the Contracting Officer that the Offeror's proposal be eliminated from further consideration in the evaluation." (AR at 803.)

The purpose of the amendment was to enable the INS to evaluate the realism and reasonableness of an offeror's price proposal and its reliability as a pricing tool. As the GAO noted in Labat, while the realism of offerors' proposed prices is not ordinarily considered in the context of a fixed-price BPA because the contractor bears the risk of unreasonable cost estimates under such a vehicle, 48 C.F.R. § 15.404-1(d)(3) (authorizing use of cost realism analyses in fixed-price contracts in exceptional cases), the nature and extent of an agency's price realism analysis are matters within the agency's discretion. Hydraulics Int'l Inc., B-284684, 2000 WL 1371001, at *11 (Comp.Gen. May 24, 2000). LABAT did not challenge Amendment No. 6 at the time it was issued; it argues in this bid protest only that the agency's application of the amendment and the other requirements of the solicitation were unreasonable. The Court is not empowered to reevaluate the utility of the estimating model criteria imposed by the agency; its duty is to ensure that the RFQ requirements were rationally applied. See Citizens to Preserve Overton Park, 401 U.S. 402, 91 S.Ct. 814, 28 L.Ed.2d 136 (1971); Technical & Admin. Servs. Corp., B-279828, 1998 WL 681275, at *2 (Comp.Gen. July 24, 1998) ("[T]he determination of the relative desirability and technical adequacy of proposals is primarily a matter of agency discretion, which we will not disturb unless it is shown to be without a reasonable basis or inconsistent with the stated evaluation criteria."), cited with approval in Cube Corp. v. United States, 46 Fed.Cl. 368, 386 (2000).

* * *

Technical Evaluation

LABAT's technical approach received a "marginal" rating on the basis of the agency's assessment that its proposal had one deficiency and two weaknesses. All three of these problems arose in the final proposal stage, and all three implicated the validity of LABAT's estimating model. Although LABAT has highlighted some computational errors made by the INS and argues persuasively that some of the omissions in its proposal were insignificant, its arguments fall short of demonstrating a likelihood of success on its claim that the agency's technical evaluation overall was unreasonable.

The INS assessed a deficiency based on LABAT's failure "to provide a model that describes the discrete labor in each major process…for each form type and task area." (AR at 1564.) The RFQ incorporates the FAR's definition of a deficiency as "a material failure of a proposal to meet a Government requirement or a combination of significant weaknesses in a proposal that increases the risk of unsuccessful contract performance to an acceptable level." 48 C.F.R. § 15.001. (AR at 837, 991.) The two major aspects of the deficiency relate to LABAT's failure to adequately explain the bases for adjustments made to the INS-supplied workload data to derive components of its technical estimating model. First, the INS found that LABAT understated the quantity of mail processed in the mailroom task area at every Service Center by more than seven million pieces of mail [FN1] in the base year, thereby significantly underestimating the required mailroom staffing (AR at 1567).

* * *

LABAT's technical proposal was based on a 28-month sample of workload data rather than the 1999 data supplied by the INS. In addition, in order to maximize efficiency, LABAT's model transferred certain mailroom transactions to the fileroom.

* * *

Finally, the record reveals that the INS fulfilled its obligation under the RFQ (AR at 833) to conduct discussions in accordance with FAR procedures. FAR 15.306(d) requires contracting agencies to indicate to, or discuss with, any offeror remaining in the competitive range any significant weaknesses, deficiencies, and other aspects of its proposal that could be altered or explained to enhance materially the proposal's potential for award. 48 C.F.R. § 15.306(d). Here, the INS informed LABAT on numerous occasions that it had problems with LABAT's estimating model. * * * By engaging in these and other communications, the INS satisfied its obligation under the RFQ to engage in meaningful discussions with LABAT about its proposal's weaknesses and deficiencies. To the extent that the INS discovered additional faults in LABAT's final proposal, it was under no obligation to reopen discussions post-award. Labat-Anderson, Inc. v. United

States, 42 Fed.Cl. 806, 848 (1999) (holding that contracting agency had no obligation to discuss deficiencies first identified in Best and Final Offers).

* * *

CONCLUSION

For the reasons discussed above, the intervenor's motion to dismiss for lack of subject matter jurisdiction or, in the alternative, for failure to state a claim, is DENIED. Plaintiff's motion for a preliminary injunction is also DENIED.

Notes and Questions

1. The Court explores FASA's intent in its exemption of task or delivery orders under the FSS from protest, and concludes that the INS's award of this Blanket Purchasing Agreement went far beyond that exemption. How can a would-be protester distinguish between what does , and does not, fall under the FASA exemption?

2. How many different hallmarks of the flexible "acquisition reform" approach do the actions of the INS display? Note in particular that this is a contract to perform support services for a large government center. Hence, the INS acting flexibly, in contracting out something not at all as simple as old-fashioned goods, in its arrangements for obtaining the "amount" of what it wants, and in the procedures for obtaining what it wants in the way it wants. After this case, what is the extent, and what (if any) are the limits, of agency flexibility in these matters? See an extensive study by a distinguished judge, Robert Mahealani M. Seto, *Basic Ordering Agreements: The Catch-22 Chameleon of Government Contract Law*, 55 SMU L. Rev. 427 (2002).

Matter of: REEP, Inc.

General Accounting Office, 2002

B-290,665

REEP, Inc. protests the Department of the Army's issuance of delivery order Nos. DAKF23-02-F-5215 and DAKF23-02-F-5315 to Worldwide Language Resources, Inc. under that firm's Federal Supply Schedule (FSS) contract in connection with its acquisition of language training services for the 5th Special Forces Group (SFG). The protester maintains that the agency improperly issued these delivery orders on a sole-source basis to Worldwide, even though REEP could have provided the same services under its FSS contract at a lower price.

We sustain the protest.

The 5th SFG has an ongoing requirement for language training services and has been meeting its need through the award of delivery orders under the FSS. Worldwide had been performing these services under a prior 1-year delivery order awarded in March 2001 and due to expire on March 15, 2002. On March 4, 2002, the agency issued request for quotations (RFQ) No. DAKF-23-02-Q-0040 (RFQ 0040) in an effort to meet its requirement for language training services. REEP filed a protest in our Office in which it asserted that the RFQ's terms were unduly restrictive and that Worldwide had a conflict of interest that should preclude the firm from competing to provide language training services. In response to that protest, the agency advised our Office that it intended to cancel the RFQ, redraft the solicitation and evaluate REEP's conflict of interest allegation with a view to avoiding, neutralizing or mitigating any possible conflict on the part of Worldwide. Based on this proposed corrective action, we dismissed REEP's protest (B-290155, April 29, 2002). On May 24, the agency issued a new solicitation (RFQ No. DAKF23-02-Q-0059) for its language training services requirement. REEP has filed a protest in our Office challenging the terms of that RFQ, which we intend to address in a separate decision.

In order to meet its ongoing requirement for language training services during this same period, the agency issued two FSS delivery orders to Worldwide, the first on March 15 and the second on June 3. These delivery orders were executed without issuance of solicitations or receipt of competitive quotations. The delivery orders were awarded against Worldwide's contract under FSS No. 69; Worldwide is the only vendor with a language training contract under that schedule. In contrast, REEP, Worldwide and numerous other vendors hold language training contracts under FSS No. 738-II.

REEP maintains that it was improper for the agency to award the delivery orders to Worldwide without also considering vendors' prices under FSS No. 738- II. REEP states, and the agency does not dispute, that its prices under its FSS contract are lower than Worldwide's.

We agree with REEP. Agencies are not required to conduct competitive acquisitions when making purchases under the FSS; by statutory definition, the award of a delivery order under the FSS satisfies the requirement for full and open competition—so long as award is made to the vendor providing the best value to the government at "the lowest overall cost." 10 U.S.C. § 2302(2)(c) (2000); Federal Acquisition Regulation (FAR) § 8.404(a). Provided that agencies satisfy this statutory condition, they are not required to seek further competition, synopsize the requirement or make a separate determination of fair and reasonable pricing before awarding an FSS delivery order. *FAR § 8.404*. To ensure that it is meeting the statutory obligation to obtain the best value at the lowest overall cost to the government when placing orders under the FSS, an agency is required to consider reasonably available information, typically by reviewing the prices of at least three schedule vendors. *FAR § 8.404(b)(2)*; *Commercial Drapery Contractors, Inc., B-271222, B-271222.2, June 27, 1996, 96-1 CPD 290 at 3.*

Here, the agency's only explanation for its actions is that it placed the delivery orders with Worldwide because it was the only vendor with a contract under FSS No. 69. However, the record shows that the agency had actual knowledge of numerous other vendors that offered the same language training services under FSS No. 738-II. The agency has not asserted that there is anything unique about the training offered by Worldwide under its FSS contract—for example, that it includes features not available from other vendors—that would provide a basis for paying a price premium for the services. Accordingly, we find that the agency failed to meet its obligation to consider reasonably available information, namely, the prices offered by other vendors under FSS No. 738-II, before placing its delivery orders with Worldwide. Had it done so, it would apparently have discovered that the same requirement could be met at a lower overall cost to the government. Under these circumstances, we sustain REEP's protest.

Since the agency continued (and has completed) performance under the delivery orders awarded to Worldwide, corrective action is not practicable. Accordingly, we recommend that REEP be reimbursed the costs of filing and pursuing its protest, including reasonable attorneys' fees. 4 C.F.R. § 21.8(d)(1) (2002). REEP's certified claim, detailing the time spent and the costs incurred, should be submitted to the agency within 60 days of receiving this decision. 4 C.F.R. § 21.8(f)(1).

The protest is sustained.

Notes and Questions

1. This opinion suggests the situation that the Special Forces Group strongly desires to continue purchasing its language training from Worldwide; REEP doggedly insists on some kind of competition; the Special Forces Group is trying to use the tools of commercial contracting to buy from its preferred vendor; and the GAO does not think too highly of that use of those tools. Is purchasing from a preferred vendor an improper goal for such tools?

2. See Michael J. Benjamin, *Multiple Award Task and Delivery Order Contracts: Expanding Protest Grounds and Other Heresies*, 31 Pub. Cont. L.J. 429 (2002).

C. Electronic Contracting

The government's movement toward electronic commerce has occurred much more by announcement and regulation than by case law. Describing the details of such contracting in the 1990s and the early 2000s has the flavor of describing contracting methods in the 1800s and early 1900s; historically of interest, and faintly foreshadowing contemporary practice, but, of course, hardly a guide to what is done at the moment. This section uses a 1995 case simply as a transition from pre-electronic to electronic issues. Notes after the case - and periodic supplements - are the only way to bring the issues up to date.

Matter of: Arcy Mfg. Company, Inc.; Beard Services, Inc.; Keys Wholesale, Inc.; Craftmaster Hardware Company, Inc.
August 14, 1995 B-261538

Arcy Mfg. Company, Inc., Beard Services, Inc., Keys Wholesale, Inc., and Craftmaster Hardware Company, Inc. protest the requirement that firms respond by electronic transmission to certain requests for quotations (RFQ) issued for small purchases by the Defense Industrial Supply Center (DISC), Defense Logistics Agency. The protesters argue that this requirement is overly restrictive of competition.

We deny the protests.

The RFQs challenged by the protesters have been issued by DISC under "automated" procedures initiated by the agency for purchases up to $25,000. Under these procedures, RFQs are transmitted directly to an electronic bulletin board (EBB) maintained by the agency and, with certain exceptions not relevant here, remain on the EBB for 15 days. Firms desiring access to the EBB to review the RFQs and submit quotes are required to first register with the agency by completing a small purchase agreement.[3] Once registered,[4] vendors can access the EBB by contacting an Electronic Data Interchange (EDI) service

---

3. These agreements set forth certain terms, conditions, provisions and clauses which are incorporated into any purchase orders subsequently issued to the registered vendors who have submitted quotes through the EBB.

4. The agency represents that as of June 20, 1995 (the day before the agency filed its administrative report in response to these protests), there were 1,489 vendors registered for the EBB

provider,[5] or through the vendors' own personal computers by dialing a telephone number or logging on to the Internet. As stated in a notice to DISC suppliers dated March 3, 1995, the agency began requiring on May 15 that all quotes in response to RFQs issued by DISC under its automated procedures be submitted electronically through DISC's EBB.

The protesters argue that the requirement that all quotes be submitted electronically is inconsistent with the mandate that the agency "promote competition to the maximum extent practicable." The protesters explain that the requirement effectively precludes them from submitting quotes because they do not own computers.

As a general rule, the Competition in Contracting Act of 1984 (CICA) requires contracting agencies to obtain full and open competition through the use of competitive procedures when conducting procurements for property or services. 10 U.S.C. § 2304(a)(1) (1994). However, CICA authorizes the use of less competitive, simplified procedures that "promote competition to the maximum extent practicable" for small purchases of property and services, that is, for purchases not expected to exceed $25,000. 10 U.S.C. § 2304(g) (1988). An agency is to promote efficiency and economy in small purchase procurements by using simplified procedures in soliciting quotations, and is generally considered to have complied with the mandate that it "promote competition to the maximum extent practicable" when it solicits quotations from three or more qualified sources.[7] Federal Acquisition Regulation (FAR) § 13.106(b)(1); Alpha Executive Servs., Inc., B-246173, Feb. 18, 1992, 92-1 CPD p 197.

As an initial matter, we note that many of the protested RFQs do not exceed $2,500 in estimated value. Under the Federal Acquisition Streamlining Act of 1994 (FASA), s 4301, 41 U.S.C.A. s 428(d) (West Supp. 1995), "[a] purchase not greater than $2,500 may be made without obtaining competitive quotations if the contracting officer determines that the price for the purchase is reasonable."[8] Because there is no allegation that the quotations received will be unreasonable as to price, there is no basis to object to the requirement that quotations in response to these "micro-purchase" RFQs be submitted electronically.

The question presented for the remaining small purchases protested here—those in excess of $2,500—is whether the agency's requirement that quotes be submitted in a certain format, that is, electronically, constitutes a violation of the statutory requirement that competition be promoted to the maximum extent practicable. As set forth in detail below, we conclude, after evaluating the needs of the agency and the burdens imposed on the protesters by this requirement, that it does not.

The agency explains that its receipt of electronic quotations, as opposed to "paper" quotations, allows DISC to be more efficient, thereby reducing the administrative cost attendant with these small purchases. In this regard, the agency points out that, in contrast to the paper system which required manual receipt, processing, recording, and filing of the paper quotes, electronic quotes are automatically received, recorded, and distributed to the cognizant DISC buyer through DISC's computer system. The agency

---

5. The agency maintains and makes available to interested vendors a list of EDI service providers that have been certified by the Department of Defense.

7. In contrast, full and open competition is defined as meaning that all responsible sources are permitted to submit bids or proposals on the procurement. 10 U.S.C. § 2302(3) (1994); 41 U.S.C. § 403(6) (1988).

8. This provision was effective upon the October 13, 1994, enactment of FASA and has been implemented by FAR s 13.603(a)(FAC 90-24). FASA s 4301(c), 41 U.S.C.A. §10a note (West Supp. 1995). In addition, FAR § 13.601(c) encourages agencies to use electronic purchasing techniques to the maximum extent practicable for purchases up to $2,500.

provides summary data which supports its claim that under the electronic method of purchasing its contracting personnel "are able to process more acquisitions in less time." For example, the agency points out that the purchasing units within DISC that rely on DISC's electronic method of purchasing accomplish small purchases on the average within 20 days (measured from the date of the purchase request to the date of award), as opposed to an average of 100 days for the purchasing units which continue to use the paper method of purchasing. The agency explains that approximately 3 labor hours are expended per purchase under the electronic method of purchasing, in comparison to an average of 7 hours where the paper method is used.

The agency also asserts that its use of the EBB to fulfill its small purchase requirements, rather than "paper" procedures, increases the contracting opportunities available to prospective vendors, and is thus consistent with the mandate that it promote competition to the maximum extent practicable. The agency explains here that through the EBB it solicits all vendors who have access to the EBB through an EDI service provider or through the use of their own personal computers, as opposed to the three vendors which ordinarily would be solicited under the agency's "paper" procedures.

With regard to the burden imposed on the protesters by the requirement that quotes be electronically transmitted, the essential difference between the electronic method of responding to RFQs and the paper method is that under the electronic method the protester is required to have access to a personal computer, certain telecommunications software, and a modem. These items are readily available for purchase on the commercial marketplace, or, as the record demonstrates, should a vendor not desire to purchase such equipment, access to the EBB can be obtained by contacting an EDI service provider. As such, we fail to see how requiring access to the EBB can be considered overly burdensome to a prospective DISC supplier.

In our view, the record establishes that the agency has a reasonable basis for requiring that quotes be submitted electronically and that this requirement is not overly burdensome on the vendor community. In this regard, we note that no potential vendor is precluded from submitting quotes; only the format of quotes is being restricted. [10] See Essex Electro Eng'rs, Inc., B-252288.2, July 23, 1993, 93-2 CPD p 47 (protest that proposal format instructions were overly burdensome because they required an unnecessary amount of desktop publishing capabilities was denied where the formatting requirements were determined reasonable and could easily be met using a personal computer). In sum, under the circumstances here, DISC's requirement that quotes be submitted electronically is reasonable and consistent with the mandate that it promote competition to the maximum extent practicable for small purchase acquisitions.

The protests are denied.

Notes and Questions

1. The government's movement toward electronic commerce has occurred much more by announcement and regulation than by case law. *Arcy Mfg. Co.* is a rare example

---

10. Although the protested procurements were not conducted through the Federal Acquisition Computer Network (FACNET) authorized by FASA § 9001, 41 U.S.C.A. s 426 (West Supp. 1995), DISC's requirement that all quotes in response to RFQs posted on the EBB be submitted electronically is consistent with the requirement set forth in the regulations implementing FASA "that all responses to solicitations issued ... through FACNET ... be submitted through FACNET." FAR § 4.505 - 1(b)(FAC 90-29).

of an opinion discussing electronic commerce. For the government contracting counsel, the challenge in this context is much more giving advice in view of the relatively rapid pace of developments, than in handling litigation over disputes. For example, in an article on this subject, Michael Hordel & Lara L. Hoffman, *Federal E-Commerce: Where We've Been, Where We're Going*, 35 Procurement Lawyer, Spring 2000, at 1, most of the 40 footnotes have citations to websites to find the relevant document or information.

2. For further discussion of electronic commerce, see Jennifer E. McCarthy, *Commerce Business Daily is Dead: Long Live FedBizOpps*, 31 Pub. Cont. L. J. 523 (2002); Tiffany A. Mendez, Note, *Adopting the Digital Signature Guidelines in Implementing Public Key Infrastructure for Federal Procurement of Electronic Commerce*, 29 Pub. Cont. L. J. 285 (2000); Mathew C. Blum & Julie Basile, *Managing the Government's Quest to Use EC in Procurement*, 34 Procurement Lawyer, Summer 1999, at 18; the articles collected in *Electronic Commerce for the Procurement Practitioner: 6th Annual Federal Procurement Institute* (March 2000)(published by the Public Contract Law Section of the American Bar Association); Scott N. Godes, *Government Contracting on the Internet: Abandoning Facnet as the Government's Network for Electronic Commerce*, 26 Pub. Cont. L.J. 663 (1997).

3. For the current single point of entry for electronic contracting see www.fedbizopps.gov.

Chapter 4

Contract Types, Costs, and Budgets

The previous chapters regarding sealed bidding and negotiated procurement start from a process familiar in basic (private) contract law, namely, offer and acceptance. In contrast, this chapter addresses topics with few analogies in private contract law, having to do with a group of unique constraints in government contracting arising from how the government pays for what it buys. These topics range from how the government funds its contracts and the variety of types of contracts including their variety as to the methods of contractor charging of the government, to the various controls devised by the government to constrain special charging methods.

Starting with the government's elaborate funding system, briefly touched upon in the first chapter, the principal interest is the government's unique constraints. These flow from appropriations and, particularly, the doctrines that limit how appropriations can be spent, including time and object limitations.

Then, the following section addresses the different types of contracts. Of course, the government, like private commercial buyers, may pay a fixed price for a well-determined amount of goods or services. However, the government's special needs induce it to purchase in other ways far different than a fixed price for a fixed quantity. Of particular importance for the rest of the chapter, the government frequently purchases on a "cost" basis, as when it funds development of a new high-technology fighter plane not by paying a fixed price, but by reimbursing the contractor for all the costs of research and includes a profit. Cost-based purchasing is invaluable when the risks and uncertainties are too great to sensibly shift from the government to the contractor, but the open-ended nature of cost-based purchasing requires the government to constrain the contractor's charges.

The same is true of many fixed-price purchases where insulation of the government-supply market from the open competition of the commercial sector might also allow unreasonable overcharging. Accordingly, one Congressional act, the Truth in Negotiating Act ("TINA"), requires certain kinds of government contractors to provide "cost or pricing data," so that the government's contracting officers can ascertain that the government is paying a reasonable price. Failure to provide required data can constitute "defective pricing" warranting government recovery of overpayments when audits subsequently uncover these. As would be expected from this combination of mandatory-disclosure, audits, and price-control systems, TINA requires much attention from lawyers.

Finally, cost-based contracting requires constraints on just what categories of expenses the government will reimburse in the way of costs, i.e., what costs are "allowable." The FAR establishes categories of allowable and unallowable costs. Additionally, broad principles apply, referred to as reasonableness and allocability. And, an entire set of accounting standards, the Cost Accounting Standards, lets the government pay the costs of different contractors without too-wide differences in their internal accounting systems leading either to chaos or to playing games with the Treasury.

For further discussion of the subjects in this chapter, see: Brett W. King, *Federal Acquisition Law in an Era of Declining Defense Spending: Defining the Government's Interest in Defense Contractor Property,* 42 Naval L. Rev. 35 (1995); C. Stanley Dees, *The Tenth Annual Gilbert A. Cuneo Lecture: The Role of Procurement Lawyers in the Era of Reduced Defense Spending,* 41 Mil. L. Rev. 199 (1993); Dennis L. Phillips & Raymond M. Saunders, *Multiyear Contracts for Major Systems,* 22 Pub. Cont. L.J. 161 (1993)

A. Funding

Judge Advocate General's School, Funding and Funding Limitations

From: Government Contract Law: The Deskbook for
Procurement Professionals (published by the Section on
Public Contract Law of the American Bar Association (1995))

FUNDING AND FUND LIMITATIONS

I. INTRODUCTION.

The Appropriations Process.

U.S. Constitution, art. I, §8, grants to Congress the power to "... lay and collect Taxes, Duties, Imports, and Excises, to pay the Debts and provide for the common Defense and general Welfare of the United States.

U.S. Constitution, art. I, §9, provides that "...No Money shall be drawn from the Treasury but in Consequence of an Appropriation made by Law...."

Congress has limited the ability of executive departments to obligate and expend funds by passage of the "Antideficiency Act". The Act consists of several statutes that authorize administrative and criminal sanctions for the unlawful obligation and expenditure of appropriated funds. *See* 31 U.S.C. §§1341, 1342, 1511–19.

Congress has directed agency heads to prescribe regulations that restrict obligations and expenditures to the amounts of apportionments and reapportionments, and to fix responsibility for overobligations and overexpenditures. 31 U.S.C. §1514.

Historical Perspective.

1. Reference: Hopkins and Nutt, *The Anti-Deficiency Act (Revised Statutes 3679) and Funding Federal Contracts: An Analysis,* 80 Mil L. Rev. 51 (1978).

For many years after the adoption of the Constitution, executive departments exerted little fiscal control over the monies appropriated to them. During these years, departments commonly:

Obligated funds in advance of appropriations.

Commingled funds and used funds for purposes other than those for which they were appropriated.

Obligated or expended funds early in the fiscal year and then sought deficiency appropriations to continue operations.

Congress passed the so-called **Antideficiency Act (ADA)**, 31 U.S.C. §§1301, 1341, 1342, 1350, 1351 and 1511–1519 to curb the abuses of the executive departments in creating coercive deficiencies that required supplemental appropriations.

Initially the statute only prohibited contracts if adequate appropriations were unavailable.

Later, Congress amended the Act to prohibit all obligations unless adequate appropriations were available, to forbid the acceptance of voluntary services, to require apportionment by monthly payments (unless waived), and to impose criminal penalties for violations of the Act.

II. TERMINOLOGY.

A. Fiscal Year.

The federal government's Fiscal Year begins on 1 October and ends on 30 September.

B. Period of Availability.

Most appropriations are available for obligation for a limited period of time, e.g., one fiscal year for operation and maintenance appropriations. If activities do not obligate the funds during the period of availability, the funds expire and are generally unavailable for obligation thereafter.

C. Obligation.

An obligation is any act that legally binds the government to make payment. Obligations represent the amounts of orders placed, contracts awarded, services received, and similar transactions during an accounting period that will require payment during the same or a future period. AR 37-1, para. 9-1; AFR 177-16; AFR 170-8, para. 2; sec. 22.1; OMB Cir. A-34; DOD Manual 7220.9-M, ch. 24, para. B-3.a.(l).

D. Budget Authority.

1. Congress finances federal programs and activities by granting budget authority. Budget authority is also called obligational authority.

2. Agencies do not receive cash from appropriated funds to pay for services or supplies. Instead they receive the authority to obligate a specified amount.

3. Budget authority means "...authority provided by law to enter into obligations which will result in immediate or future outlay involving government funds ....." 2 U.S.C. §622(2).

4. Budget authority should be distinguished from contract authority, which is a sub-category of budget authority. Contract authority is statutory authority specifically permitting obligations to be incurred in advance of appropriations. See 2 U.S.C. §651(a); 31 U.S.C. §1301(d).

E. Authorization Act.

1. An authorization act is a statute, passed annually by Congress, that authorizes programs and the maximum amounts that can be appropriated for programs.

2. An authorization does not provide budget authority.

F. Appropriation Act.

1. An appropriation act is the most common form of budget authority.

2. An appropriation is "an authorization by an Act of Congress to incur obligations for specified purposes and to make disbursements for them from the U.S. Treasury. It may include authorizations to create obligations in advance of appropriations or other fund authority." AR 37-1, Glossary, sec. H, Terms; AFR 177-16, sec. A.

G. Apportionment.

1. An apportionment is a distribution of budget authority within the Executive Branch by the Office of Management & Budget (OMB). It limits the amount of obligations allowed during a given period. 31 U.S.C. §1512; AR 37-1, Glossary, sec. 11, Terms; AFR 177-16, sec. A.

2. An appropriation may be apportioned by: months, calendar quarters, operating seasons, or other time periods; activities, functions, projects, or objects; or by a combination of the methods mentioned above. 31 U.S.C. §1512.

H. Allocation.

1. An allocation is a distribution of budget authority by the agency to an operating agency for suballocation or allotment to its subordinate activities. AR 37-1, Glossary, sec. II, Terms; AFR 177-16, sec. A.

2. An ADA violation occurs if obligations or expenditures exceed the amount of an allocation. AR 37-1, Glossary, sec. H, Terms.

3. Allocations are formal subdivisions of funds.

I. Allotment.

1. An allotment is an administrative distribution of budget authority by an operating agency to its subordinate activities. AR 37-1, Glossary, sec. H, Terms; AFR 177-16, sec. A.

2. An ADA violation occurs if obligations or expenditures exceed the amount of an allotment. AR 37-1, Glossary, sec. II, Terms.

3. An allotment is a formal subdivision of funds.

J. Allowance/Target.

1. An allowance/target is an administrative distribution of budget authority by an operating agency to its subordinate activities. AR 37-1, Glossary, sec. II, Terms; AFR 177-16, para. 24.

2. An allowance is an informal subdivision of funds.

K. Rate of Obligation.

Appropriations made to the Department of Defense (DOD) or to a military department are available for obligation and expenditure only under scheduled rates of obligation, or changes thereto, that have been approved by the Secretary of Defense. 10 U.S.C. §2204.

* * *

V. LIMITATIONS ON THE USE OF APPROPRIATED FUNDS.

A. General Limitations on Authority.

The authority of executive agencies to spend appropriated funds is limited. The principal limitations are:

a. Purpose.

b. Time.

c. Amount.

An agency may expend an appropriation only for the purposes for which Congress appropriated it. 31 U.S.C. §1301(a) ("purpose" statute).

A government officer or employee may not make or authorize expenditures or incur obligations exceeding amounts available in an appropriation.

A government officer or employee may not make or authorize expenditures or incur obligations in advance of an appropriation.

A government officer or employee may not make or authorize expenditures or incur obligations in excess of apportionments or in excess of amounts permitted by regulations.

B. Limitations Based Upon Purpose.

1. Major military appropriations accounts characterized by purpose.

Military personnel: used for pay and benefits of officers and enlisted personnel.

Operations and Maintenance (O&M): used for day-to-day operational costs.

Procurement: used for purchase of high-dollar value, mission-essential, tactical items.

Research, Development, Test, and Evaluation (RDTE): used for basic research; development of new equipment; test of new, civilian, or foreign equipment; and evaluation of the performance of equipment in use.

Military Construction: used for specific construction projects in excess of $1,500,000. Projects less than $1,500,000 are funded with Unspecified Minor Military Construction funds or O&M funds.

2. The purpose rule.

31 U.S.C. S 1301(a), the "purpose statute" provides that appropriations shall be applied only to the objects for which the appropriations were made, except as otherwise provided by law. AR 37-1, para. 7-9; AFR 177-16, para. 40.

The DOD has nearly one hundred separate appropriations available to it. These appropriations are used for specific and different purposes.

The "purpose statute" does not require that every item of expenditure be specified in an appropriation act. DOD has reasonable discretion to determine how to accomplish the purpose of an appropriation. *Internal Revenue Serv. Fed. Credit Union - Provision of Automatic Teller Mach.*, B-226065, 66 Comp. Gen. 356, 359 (1987). The standard for measuring the propriety of a particular expenditure, not specified in the statute, is whether:

(1) The expenditure is reasonably necessary to carry out an authorized function, or

(2) The expenditure contributes materially to the effective accomplishment of an authorized function.

C. Limitations Based Upon Time.

The Time Rule: An appropriation is available for obligation for a definite period of time, and it must be obligated during this period of availability. If it is not, the authority to obligate expires. 31 U.S.C. §1552.

Moreover, an appropriation is available only for payment of bona fide needs of the time period during which it is available for obligation. 31 U.S.C. §1502(a).

Agencies may not obligate funds until the President signs the Appropriation Act. 31 U.S.C. §1341 (a)(1)(B). *See Cessna Aircraft Co.* ASBCA No.43196, 93-2 BCA ¶ 25,912 (allowing obligation after signature of appropriation act even though agency had not received apportionment from OMB).

Types of appropriations characterized by duration.

Annual Appropriation: an appropriation account available for obligations only during the fiscal year specified in the appropriation act. AR 37-1, Glossary, sec. II, Terms; AFR 177-16, para. 4(e)(1). Examples include Operations and Maintenance appropriations and Military Personnel account appropriations.

Multi-year Appropriation: an appropriation account that is available for incurring obligations for a definite period in excess of one fiscal year. AR 37-1, Glossary, sec. II, Terms; AFR 177-16, para. 4(e)(2). Examples include Research and Development appropriations (2 years), Procurement appropriations (3 years), and Military Construction appropriations (5 years).

No-year Appropriation: an appropriation account that is available for incurring obligations for an indefinite period of time (until exhausted or accomplishment of its stated purpose). AR 37-1, Glossary, sec. II, Terms; AFR 177-16, para. 4(e)(3). Examples include Industrial Funds and Stock Funds.

Practical Applications: There are four important exceptions to the general prohibition against obligating funds after the period of availability.

Protests: "[Funds available to an agency for obligation for a contract at the time a protest is filed in connection with…award of such a contract shall remain available for obligation for 90 working days after the date on which the final ruling is made on the protest." 31 U.S.C. §1558. This statutory provision is incorporated at FAR 33.102(b). 55 Fed. Reg. 55,782 (1990), (Federal Acquisition Circular 90-3).

Terminations for default: If a contract or order is terminated for default, and a *bona fide* need still exists for the supplies or services, the original funds remain available for obligation for a reprocurement, even if they otherwise would have expired. The agency must award the reprocurement contract without undue delay, and the contract must be for substantially the same item or service. AR 371, para. 12-2(e), *citing Lawrence W. Rosine Co.,* B-185405, 55 Comp. Gen. 1351 (1976).

Terminations for convenience, pursuant to court order. If a court or other competent authority determines that the original award of the contract was improper, the agency may use the originally cited funds on the replacement contract. This exception is limited to contracts originally awarded in good faith, for which the agency has a continuing *bona _fide* need, which will replaced promptly with a contract of the same size and scope as the original contract. *Replacement Contracts,* B- 232616, 68 Comp. Gen. 158 (1988).

The GAO has expanded the principle articulated in *Replacement Contracts, supra.* An agency may use funds obligated on a contract that is terminated for the convenience of the government, if the government terminates the contract because the government determines the award was improper. The GAO determined that the same rule should apply if the government decides to terminate the contract as the result of an impropriety in the award process or if a court orders the termination. The requirements discussed in para. c, *supra* also apply in this situation. *Navy, Replacement Contract,* B-238548, 91-1 CPD ¶117.

Limitations Based Upon the *Bona Fide* Need Rule.

The statutory basis: "[t]he balance of an appropriation or fund limited for obligation to a definite period is available only for payment of expenses properly incurred during the period of availability, or to complete contracts properly made within that period of availability and obligated consistent with section 1501 of this title. However, the appropriation or fund is not available for expenditure for a period beyond the period otherwise authorized by law." 31 U.S.C. §1502(a).

The government may only obligate appropriated funds for properly incurred expenses. That is, the requirement must be a *bona fide* need of the requiring activity arising during the period of availability of the funds proposed to be used for the acquisition. *See Magnavox—Use of Contract Underrun Funds,* B-207453, Sept. 16, 1983, 83-2 CPD ¶401; *To the Secretary of the Army,* B-115736, 33 Comp. Gen. 57 (1953).

The *bona fide* need rule applies only to appropriations with limited periods of availability for obligation.

The Anti-deficiency Act prohibits creating a contract or obligation before an appropriation is made. 31 U.S.C. §1341(a)(1)(B). The intent of Congress is to avoid situations that require 'coercive deficiency' appropriations. *See Project Stormfury—Australia—Indemnification of*

Damages, B- 198206, 59 Comp. Gen. 369 (1980); AR 37-1, paras. 3-1, 8- 1(d)(1); AFR 177-16, sec. D.

Supply Contracts: Generally, supplies are the *bona fide* need of the fiscal year in which the agency uses the supplies. *To Chairman, United States Atomic Energy Comm'n,* B-130815, 37 Comp. Gen. 155 (1957); *To Betty F. Leatherman, Dep't of Commerce,* B-156161, 44 Comp. Gen. 695 (1965); *To Adm'r, Small Business Admin.,* B-155876, 44 Comp. Gen. 399 (1965).

Lead-Time Exception: It is appropriate to consider the normal production lead-time in determining the *bona fide* need for an acquisition.

For example, if the normal lead-time between order and delivery of an item is 45 days, an obligation of FY 1994 funds is appropriate for a delivery on or before 15 November 1994. (Remember: 1 October 1994 is the beginning of FY 1995.) This is *a bona fide* need of FY 1994. If the government permits delivery after 15 November 1994, a question as to whether there *is a bona fide* need for the item in FY 1994 arises.

If the government establishes a delivery date for an item and that delivery date is beyond the normal lead time and in the next fiscal year, it must use funds available for that later fiscal year. In the example 1 above, if the government permits delivery after 15 November 1994, it must use FY 1995 funds. *See Farmers Home Administration,* B-251706, Aug. 17, 1994, 73 Comp. Gen. _____ (agency must correct bona fide need violation by adjusting accounts to charge correct fiscal year funds).

Service Contracts: Generally a *bona fide* need does not arise until the services are rendered. *Theodor Arndt GmbH & Co.,*B-237180, 90-1 CPD ¶64; *EPA Level of Effort Contracts,* B-214597, 65 Comp. Gen. 154 (1985). Thus, severable service contracts generally cannot cross fiscal years. The government must fund such contracts with dollars available for obligation on the date the contractor performs the services.

Exception: If the services produce a single or unified outcome, product, or report, the services are nonseverable. If so, the government must fund the entire effort with dollars available for obligation at the time the contract is executed, and the contract may cross fiscal years. *Incremental Funding of U.S. Fish and Wildlife Serv. Research Work Orders,* B-240264, Feb. 7, 1994 (unpub.); *Proper Appropriation to Charge Expenses Relating to Nonseverable Training Course,* B-238940 70 Comp. Gen. 296 (1991*); Acumenics Research and Technology, Inc. - Contract Extension,* B-224702, Aug. 5, 1987, 87-2 CPD ¶128; *Proper Fiscal Year Appropriation to Charge for Contract and Contract Increases,* B-219829, 65 Comp. Gen. 741 (1986).

Construction: The government may obligate current funds for construction, to include maintenance and repair contracts involving traditional construction trade skills, near the end of the fiscal year, even if performance may not begin until the next fiscal -year. AR 37-1, tbl. 9-2, fn. 5; AFR 170-8, para. 7(c)(1).

This authority is limited to the following situations:

The requirement must represent a *bona fide* need of the current or a prior fiscal year;

Work must start on or before January 1 of the following calendar year, except in contracts with a foreign government, or contracts entered into pursuant to a binding international agreement. Commencement of work is evidenced by:

(1) Physical on-site evidence based upon a visual inspection; or

(2) Documentary evidence of costs incurred or materials ordered.

A project that cannot reasonably be expected to commence before the onset of winter weather probably is not the *bona fide* need of the prior fiscal year. For example, a contract for paving 37 miles of roads in Alaska probably should not be awarded on 30 September 1994 and funded with FY 1994 dollars.

If mission requirements prevent commencement of the work until 1 January, the requirement may not be the *bona fide* need of the prior fiscal year. AR 37-1, para. 9-5. AFR 170-8, para 7.c.(1)

D. Limitations Based upon the Amount of Funds.

"An officer or employee of the United States government...may not make or authorize an expenditure or obligation exceeding an amount available in an appropriation..." 31 U.S.C. §1341(a)(l)(A). There must be an available appropriation to support every obligation or expenditure. 31 U.S.C. §§1341, 1342, 1511–1519.

Executive agencies must establish administrative systems to ensure that obligations and expenditures of appropriated funds do not exceed the amount appropriated, apportioned, or reapportioned. 31 U.S.C. §1514(a)(1).

The rules governing the commitment and obligation of funds are a part of the fund control system used to ensure that appropriation limits are not exceeded. *See, e.g.,* AFR 170-13, para. 7.

Notes and Questions

1. Alexander Hamilton set up the federal funding system as the masterful first Secretary of the Treasury in the 1790s. If he came back, he would compare this section to the system he developed when the only office copiers were clerks with quill pens, when the only office calculators were those same clerks' ten fingers, and when rapid communication consisted of horseback riders carrying letters back and forth on bad roads over quite great distances. Would the system described in this section that is in use two centuries later, implemented by computers and electronic communications, strike him as new? Or does that system follow in large measure from the Anglo-American concept of legislatively- and legally-directed spending shaped by the struggles of medieval Parliaments and colonial legislatures in the centuries before the 1790s with kings and governors? In short, is the federal funding system part of modern sophisticated accounting, or part of classic democratic governance?

2. Why is it that a government contracting practitioner can function quite adequately knowing only what this section describes (and perhaps less), while his opposite number, a government official with a major function in contracting, would probably want to know much more than this section, particularly as regards the funding of her particular sphere of contracting?

3. A large part of pertinent funding law can be found in the General Accounting Office's (GAO's) opinions and other pronouncements. Most notably, GAO has a multivolume reference work, *Principles of Federal Appropriation Law*, that is not considered light reading but can answer many questions in this subject.

4.For further discussion of the subjects of this section, see: Major Timothy D. Matheny, *Go On, Take the Money and Run: Understanding the Miscellaneous Receipts Statute and its Exception*, 1997-SEP. Army Law. 31 (1997); Steven N. Tomanelli, *Fiscal Implications of Contract Disputes*, 31 Procurement Law., Summer 1996, at 1; Karen L. Manos, *The Antideficiency Act: Constitutional Control Gone Astray*, 11 Pub. Cont. L.J. 155 (1979).

Charles Tiefer, Controlling Federal Agencies by Claims on Their Appropriations? The Takings Bill and the Power of the Purse
13 Yale Journal on Regulation 501 (1995)

Principle of Lump-Sum Discretion: Executive Branch Authority Over Allotment of Lump-Sum Appropriations

When the Appropriations Clause declares that no money shall come from the Treasury except pursuant to "Appropriations made by Law," it leaves open the question of who will exercise, and how, the power to decide the specific objects of spending. As Professor Stith has observed, "[t]he Constitution does not require any particular degree of specificity in appropriations language." During the government's formative years, Jeffersonian philosophy, in contrast to Hamilton's views, limited the Executive role. Until well into the twentieth century, Congress followed the Jeffersonian lead in implementing the Appropriations Clause by drafting spending bills with numerous expressly detailed line items specifying the particular objects for which funds were available. In response, agencies would overspend their detailed line items, "coercing" Congress to appropriate more money to cover the "deficiency" in their funds, thereby engendering the passage of bills understandably known as "coercive deficiency appropriations."

Those maneuvers shaped today's system. With the expansion of the federal government in the early and mid-twentieth century, passage of a series of "framework" statutes for the fiscal constitution, notably, the Budget and Accounting Control Act of 1921 and the Anti-Deficiency Act, overhauled the old machinery and ended both detailed line itemization and coercive deficiency appropriations. These framework statutes created the Executive's "allotment" power for breaking the lump sum down into the specific objects for which funds are available. The principle of lump-sum discretion became the dominant organizing principle for Appropriations Clause implementation. Congress shifted to enacting far more general line items in the appropriation bills, each of which would "fund each broadly defined federal program or activity in one lump sum, termed a budget 'account.'" The President's annual proposed budget now includes a massive description of the various accounts, with Treasury identification numbers and object classifications. Once Congress enacts the lump-sum appropriation for an agency's operations, the agency head formally allots the lump sum. Each allotment is exclusively available for a particular object. As discussed below, during the fiscal year, an agency can change its allotments by another power known as "reprogramming."

It has become increasingly important that the Anti-Deficiency Act precludes not only obligations in excess of appropriations, but also obligations in excess of allotments. To avoid a situation in which an agency can either coerce a deficiency appropriation to cover the excess outflow or be required to curtail operations, agencies have the power and the duty to allot funds so as to limit how much of an appropriation can be drained for any object.

In 1993, the Supreme Court reinforced and elaborated the "lump-sum discretion" principle at the heart of this twentieth century system. In *Lincoln v. Vigil*, the Court rejected a suit challenging the Indian Health Service's decision to end the allotment from its lump-sum appropriation of funds for one particular object, a specific Indian health program. Despite numerous indications that Congress intended that the agency should continue to spend the appropriation on that program, the Court held that

> [t]he allocation of funds from a lump-sum appropriation is another administrative decision traditionally regarded as committed to agency discretion. After all, the very point of a lump-sum appropriation is to give an agency the capacity to adapt to changing circumstances and meet its statutory responsibilities in what it sees as the most effective or desirable way.

The Court quoted with approval the fuller discussion in a classic 1984 D.C. Circuit opinion by then-Judge Scalia, *UAW v. Donovan*, that "[a] lump-sum appropriation leaves it to the recipient agency (as a matter of law, at least) to distribute the funds among some or all of the permissible objects as it sees fit."

Limitation of Cost Clause

The government has a mechanism, even with cost-reimbursement contracts, of putting a limit on what it will pay. The Limitation of Cost Clause (LOCC) as provided in the FAR § 52.232-20, provides for contractors to notify the government as costs of contract performance exceed those estimated costs specified in the Schedule. The FAR sets forth the procedure by which contractors must notify the C.O. of any anticipated increase in costs for the performance of the contract. *See* John D. Schminky, *Proper Funding of Contract Modifications Under the Antecedent Liability Rule*, 26 Pub. Cont. L. J. 221 (1997). There will be no reimbursement for cost overruns in cost-reimbursement contracts where the contractor "knew or should have known" that costs would be excessive but did not notify the government. *Titan Corp. v. West*, 129 F.3d 1479 (Fed. Cir. 1997). It is a contractor's duty to monitor costs and to inform the government of probable overruns prior to their occurrence. *Advanced Materials, Inc. v. Perry*, 108 F.3d 307 (Fed. Cir. 1997).

B. Contract Types

Government contract types fall into two categories based on how the government pays: fixed price and cost-reimbursement. To illustrate, the government may want to buy ten more units of a type of computer it has bought before. It would likely issue an invitation for bids on a fixed-price contract, and award a contract to pay a fixed sum ($1,000, or $10,000, or $100,000) per computer. In contrast, the government might want to hire a research and development firm to develop some new type of instrument specially adapted to its meteorological needs at unheated Arctic facilities. It would likely issue a request for proposals on a cost-reimbursement contract, and award a contract to pay the costs of a research and development firm to attempt to develop that instrument. The government would pay the firm's costs for the project—salaries and other personnel costs, materials, overhead—plus profit.

Fixed-price contracts shift the risks of production to the contractor. The contractor who must supply computers for $10,000, makes the most profit if the costs of production turn out the same or less than expected. However, if the costs of production go up, the contractor makes less profit or may even have to fulfill the contract at a loss. This encourages efficiency among contractors since they bear the risks, but it would also force the government, if the risks and unknowns are great, to pay a premium price, as contractors build a risk-premium into their bids.

In contrast, cost-reimbursement contracts shift the risks of production to the government. The research and development firm that takes on a cost-reimbursement contract to attempt to develop a new instrument will have its costs paid whether the project turns out doable in six months, nine months, or twelve months, or even if twelve months of effort turn out not enough to surmount the technical challenges involved. This reduces the profit figure the government must pay because it does not have a large risk-premium built in, but is less efficient since the contractor lacks the motivation that every dollar of costs saved goes into its pocket.

The government has an array of variations on these two basic categories, as elaborated in the following discussion. Also, note the brief discussion at the end about other contract types such as "indefinite delivery contracts" and "basic ordering agreements," seen in the previous chapters on contract awarding. The government makes increasing use of such flexible arrangements that are open-ended about quantities and times.

COYLE'S PEST CONTROL, INC., Appellant, v. Andrew CUOMO, Secretary of Housing and Urban Development, Appellee.

United States Court of Appeals, Federal Circuit.
154 F.3d 1302 Aug. 24, 1998.

Before NEWMAN, PLAGER, and RADER, Circuit Judges.

RADER, Circuit Judge.

On summary judgment, the Department of Housing and Urban Development's Board of Contract Appeals (the Board) denied Coyle's Pest Control, Inc.'s (Coyle's) breach of contract claim for $1,525,170.74. See Coyle's Pest Control, Inc., HUD BCA No. 96-A-121-C10, 97-1 BCA ¶ 28,717 (Jan. 6, 1997). Because the Board correctly determined that the contract was invalid and unenforceable when interpreted as either a requirements or an indefinite quantity contract, this court affirms.

I

The Department of Housing and Urban Development (HUD), through the Small Business Administration, awarded Contract No. H06C94050400000 to Coyle for termite inspection and subterranean treatment of HUD-owned properties in thirty-four Texas counties. Section B.1 of the contract required Coyle "to furnish all labor, service, equipment, transportation, materials and supplies to provide subterranean termite control and related services on assigned properties owned by [HUD]." Clause C.2.D stated that properties would be "assigned on an as-needed basis." (emphasis added).

The contract, effective December 20, 1993, provided for a one-year term (the base year) as well as two one-year options. Section B.2 established a fixed price for inspection services and a two-tier, fixed price scheme for treatment services. This section set treatment prices at one of two levels depending on whether the range of properties assigned monthly was 0-170 or 171-240; the option years included modest increases for each of the two levels. The estimated value of the contract, including the base year and the two option years, was $1,930,000.

Section L.14 labeled the contract a "fixed unit rate-indefinite quantity contract." Nonetheless, the contract did not include two provisions typically present in indefinite quantity contracts: (1) a specified minimum number of properties to be assigned to Coyle; and (2) the indefinite quantity clause found in Federal Acquisition Regulation (FAR) 52.216-22 and then required by FAR 16.505(e). See 48 C.F.R §§ 52.216-22, 16.505(e) (1993). Also absent were two provisions generally associated with require-ments contracts: (1) a clause requiring HUD to order all of its subterranean termite in-spections and treatments from Coyle; and (2) the requirements clause found in FAR 52.216-21 (a mandatory feature of requirements contracts then under FAR 16.505(d)). See id §§ 52.216-21, 16.505(d).

In June 1995, during the first option year, HUD proposed Modification No. 4 to the contract. The proposed modification prevented Coyle from treating properties that HUD had already inspected and found free of termite infestation. Coyle rejected the modification. Thereafter, HUD informed Coyle that it would receive a "substantially lesser amount of properties" for termite services. At about the same time, in July 1995, HUD also altered its national policy for termite services and began to permit buyers of HUD properties to order their own termite inspections. Due to changes in the parties' relationship, ultimately, on September 25, 1995, they agreed to a revised version of Modification No. 4. As adopted, Modification No. 4 increased prices for both inspec-tion and treatment services beyond that originally contemplated for the option years. More specifically, the parties changed the two-tiered pricing system for treatment ser-vices to a higher, single-rate system.

In sum, HUD assigned properties to Coyle from the beginning of the base year to slightly beyond the contract's first option year and paid to Coyle $694,228.04 for ser-vices during this period. On December 7, 1995, however, Coyle submitted a certified claim for $1,525,170.74—an amount equal to the difference between the estimated value of the contract ($1,930,000) and the amount HUD actually paid during the base year ($404,829.26). Coyle asserted that the contract was a firm fixed price agreement that entitled it to the estimated value of the contract. The contracting officer rejected Coyle's characterization of the contract and denied its claim. On appeal to the Board, Coyle asserted an alternative theory for recovery, that the contract was susceptible to in-terpretation as a valid and enforceable requirements contract. The Board rejected this characterization and denied Coyle's claim on January 6, 1997. Coyle appeals.

* * *

III

The Board, in a concise, well-reasoned opinion, held:

> The contract at issue in this appeal…does not contain the necessary elements of an enforceable indefinite quantity contract, nor an enforceable requirements contract. The enforcement of such a contract would fail for lack of considera-tion in the absence of a clause stating a minimum quantity or a clause requir-ing [HUD] to purchase all of its requirements from [Coyle]. Because the con-tract is not enforceable for lack of consideration, [Coyle] is entitled to payment only for services ordered by [HUD] and performed by [Coyle]. It is undisputed that [Coyle] has been paid for all services performed. Consequently, we must

conclude that [Coyle's] claim for an additional payment of $1,525,170.74 fails as a matter of law.

Coyle's Pest Control, 97-1 BCA ¶ 28,717 at 143,345. This court discerns no error in the Board's reasoning or conclusion.

In approving the Board's judgment, this court rejects the notion that Torncello v. United States, 231 Ct.Cl. 20, 681 F.2d 756 (1982) (en banc), requires it to save an otherwise unenforceable indefinite quantity contract by interpreting it as an "implied" requirements contract. See id. 681 F.2d at 761-62. Coyle extracts out of context from Torncello two inflexible rules for contract interpretation. First, "contract terms...must fit into one of the three possible types of supply contracts: those for a definite quantity, those for an indefinite quantity and those for requirements." Id. at 761 (citing Mason v. United States, 222 Ct.Cl. 436, 615 F.2d 1343, 1347 (1980)). Second, a court must "assume that the parties intended that a binding contract be formed. Thus, any choice of alternative interpretations, with one interpretation saving the contract and the other voiding it, should be resolved in favor of the interpretation that saves the contract." Id. Applying its reading of Torncello to this case, Coyle argues that its contract with HUD qualifies as either an indefinite quantity contract or a requirements contract. Because it lacks a minimum quantity term, Coyle continues, the contract should be interpreted as a requirements contract.

* * *

This case, however, does not fit into any of the three neat categories Coyle extracts from Torncello. The record does not support the conclusion that the agreement was a requirements contract. Indeed the contract called itself an indefinite quantities contract (albeit without a minimum quantity clause) and lacked the terms of a requirement contract. Finally, Coyle does not maintain that the contract fits into the third category of definite quantities contracts.

IV.

Setting aside Coyle's overreaching interpretation of Torncello renders analysis of this contract relatively straightforward. At the outset, neither party disputes the existence of a valid, binding agreement; the dispute here centers on the scope and nature of the agreement. Next, this court assesses the merits of interpreting this agreement as a requirements contract, as Coyle has asserted

> A requirements contract is formed when the seller has the exclusive right and legal obligation to fill all of the buyer's needs for the goods or services described in the contract.... [A]n essential element of a requirements contract is the promise by the buyer to purchase the subject matter of the contract exclusively from the seller.

Modern Sys. Tech. Corp. v. United States, 979 F.2d 200, 205 (Fed.Cir.1992) (citations omitted). As this passage suggests, a requirements contract necessarily obligates the Government to purchase exclusively from a single source. Because this agreement does not include the FAR requirements clause, it is more difficult to find the required exclusivity.

The contract does include terms that suggest exclusivity. For instance, the contract obligates Coyle "to furnish all labor, service, equipment, transportation, materials and supplies to provide subterranean termite control and related services on assigned properties by [HUD]." (emphasis added). While the contract states that Coyle will provide all labor and services for a given property, the clause does not require HUD to assign

Coyle all properties in the region. Thus, this contract language falls short of the exclusivity language necessary for a requirements contract.

This court finds no reason to interpret this agreement as a requirements contract based on Coyle's affidavit evidence. Even assuming that these affidavits accurately reflect Coyle's beliefs, they cannot override or contradict the plain language of the contract, which does not require sufficient exclusivity for a requirements contract. See Gould, Inc. v. United States, 935 F.2d 1271, 1274 (Fed.Cir.1991). Moreover Coyle's affidavits do not reconcile Coyle's intent with the contrary intent of HUD. Cf. Crown Laundry & Dry Cleaners, Inc. v. United States, 29 Fed. Cl. 506, 518 (1993) (finding an implied requirements contract when testimony from both parties evinces a clear intent to form a requirements contract). This court therefore affirms the Board's determination that this agreement is not a requirements contract.

This court next analyzes the merits of interpreting this agreement as an indefinite quantity contract. While many factors are relevant, including the absence of the FAR-mandated "indefinite quantity" clause, this court cannot read this agreement as an indefinite quantity contract because it lacks a minimum quantity term. Regardless of whether the contract is susceptible to interpretation as an indefinite quantity contract, a contract lacking this term cannot be construed as a valid indefinite quantity contract. See Willard, Sutherland & Co. v. United States, 262 U.S. 489, 493, 43 S.Ct. 592, 67 L.Ed. 1086 (1923) ("[If t]here is nothing in the writing which required the Government to take…any ascertainable quantity[, i]t must be held that, for lack of consideration and mutuality, the contract was not enforceable [as an indefinite quantity contract]."). Thus, this court affirms the Board's determination that the contract cannot be an enforceable indefinite quantity contract.

This contract neither required HUD to order from Coyle termite services for all its properties nor contained a minimum quantity term. Thus, the contract is not enforceable as either a requirements contract or as an indefinite quantity contract. As such, Coyle is entitled to payment only for services actually ordered by HUD and provided by Coyle. See Willard, 262 U.S. at 494, 43 S.Ct. 592 ("By the conduct and performance of the parties, the contract was made definite and binding as to the [quantity] ordered and delivered according to its terms."). In other words, this court has reached the same conclusion as and affirms the Board's decision.

AFFIRMED.

Notes and Questions

1. Various trends in recent years have led to increased use of contracting flexibility in matters such as quantity. The government contracting lawyer should understand how a proposed, or awarded, contract works in these regards because it affects judgments about other legal actions and issues from protesting to termination. This court looks through the contract for use of FAR clauses for indefinite quantity and requirements contracts (particularly the minimum quantity term). What does the court find, in looking for those clauses, and how does it reason from this? The following notes delve into the significant content of those FAR clauses.

2. ID/IQ Contracts

Under FAR 16.504, Indefinite-Quantity/Indefinite-Delivery contracts are described as those in which the government contracts for a quantity within a limited range of a defined minimum up to a defined maximum quantity, over a fixed period. The contracting agency schedules deliveries or performance through the issuance of task orders based on needs. Binding contracts require more than a nominal quantity be contracted for, and maximum quantity estimates should be based on records of prior requirements and consumption or the most current information available. Additionally, the FAR sets forth solicitation and contract requirements for indefinite-quantity contracts, and describes a multiple award preference in § 16.504(c). Where government agencies fail to order the minimum quantity estimated, the courts nevertheless have favored the agencies, finding that the termination for convenience clause provides adequate consideration to the contractor. *Appeal of Montana Refining Co.*, ASBCA No. 50515 (1999) *(distinguishing Maxima Corp. v. United States*, 847 F.2d 1549 (Fed. Cir. 1988)), and *PHP Healthcare Corp.*, ASBCA No. 39207 (termination for convenience cannot occur after the end of the contract term).

FAR 52.211-16 sets forth the Variation in Estimated Quantity clause, providing for estimated quantities of unit-priced items in fixed-price contracts. This clause provides for equitable adjustment of the contract when the actual quantity of the items varies more than 15 percent above or below the estimated quantity. Re-pricing requests by the contractors, of items outside the 15 percent variation range are at the discretion of the Contracting Officer, and are not required. *Foley Co. v. United States*, 11 F.3d 1032 (Fed. Cir. 1993). When adjustments are made, they must be based on cost variations created by quantity variations. *Clement-Mtarri Cos.*, 92-3 BCA ¶ 25,192 (1992).

3. Requirement Contracts

Requirement contracts, as stated in the FAR § 16.503, provide that all actual purchase requirements by the contracting agency for supplies or services over a specified period be filled by the contractor. The agency schedules deliveries or performance with the contractor. The estimation of requirements is performed by the contracting officer and is based on records of previous requirements and consumption, and is *not* a representation that the quantity will be actually required or ordered. Such contracts are useful where the agency anticipates recurring requirements but can not state precise quantity needs during the defined period of the contract.

Challenges of breach of contract are upheld where the government purchases the same goods or services elsewhere. *Cleek Aviation v. United States,* 19 Cl. Ct. (1990). Where there is an issue of quantity miscalculation attributable to negligent estimates or mathematical error, the courts have likewise favored the contractor in recouping costs. *See Celeron Gathering Corp. v. United States,* 34 Fed. Cl. 745 (1996), and *Chemical Technology, Inc. v. United States,* 645 F.2d 934 (Ct Cl. 1981).

Types of Contracts Authorized

From: Fundamentals of Federal Contract Law (1990) Eugene W. Massengale
Copyright (c) (1991) by Greenwood Press Reproduced with permission of
Greenwood Publishing Group, Inc., Westport, CT

The Contracting officer has authority to award any type, or combination of types, of contract that will promote the government's interest in negotiation except the cost-plus- percentage-of-cost contract, which is prohibited by law. 10 U.S.C. §2306(a); 41 U.S.C. §254(a). The contract type ultimately selected for award by the Contracting Officer determines the performance risk to be borne by the parties. The fixed-price group of contracts places cost and performance risk on the contractor, whereas the cost reimbursement group places cost risk on the government.

Selecting the type of contract to be awarded is a matter of negotiation between the parties and requires the exercise of sound judgment on the part of the Contracting Officer. The objective is to negotiate a contract type that will result in reasonable contractor risk and provide the greatest incentive for efficient and economical performance.

A firm-fixed-price contract, which best utilizes the profit motive of business enterprise, is required for use when the risk involved is minimal or can be predicted with an acceptable degree of certainty. When a reasonable basis for firm pricing does not exist, other contract types should be considered, and negotiations should be directed toward selecting a contract type, or combination of types, that ties profit to contractor risk and performance.

Fixed-Price Contracts

In addition to the contract types discussed in Chapter 4, the Contracting Officer may use any of the contracts discussed here in the negotiated method of procurement. The firm-fixed-price incentive contract provides for adjusting profit and establishing the final negotiated total cost to total target cost. Under this form of contract, both cost and performance characteristics can be incentivized. It is appropriate for use when the nature of the acquisition is such that the contractor's assumption of a degree of cost responsibility will provide a profit incentive for effective cost control or performance.

The fixed-price prospective-price-redeterminable contract is suitable for use for long-range quantity production or service contracts , when it is impossible to negotiate for the entire period of performance. A fair and reasonable price is negotiated for the initial period of the contract and redetermined upward or downward at a specific point in time established during negotiations.

The fixed-ceiling-price contract with retroactive price determination features is generally appropriate for research and development contracts of $100,000, or less, when it is established at the time of contract award that a fair and reasonable contract cannot be negotiated for the entire period of performance. A ceiling price is negotiated at levels that reflect a reasonable sharing of risk by the contractor.

The firm-fixed-price term type of contract requires that the contractor deliver for a fixed price a specified level of effort over a stated period on work that can be stated in general terms. While it is suitable for investigations or research and development efforts, and the contractor may furnish a report at the end of contract performance, payment is based on actual hours delivered. Under this form of contract, the contractor assumes negligible risk.

Cost Reimbursement Contracts

Cost reimbursement contracts provide that the Government will reimburse the contractor for all incurred costs, given that they are reasonable, allowable, and allocable to the contract. A ceiling is established at the outset for the purpose of fixing a ceiling on the contract and obligating funds; such ceiling cannot be exceeded by the contractor except at his own risk. Limitation of Cost or Limitation of Funds articles apply to these contracts, requiring that the contractor place the government on notice if the contract ceiling is to be either exceeded or underrun. A cost reimbursement contract may be used only when the contractor has an adequate accounting system, appropriate government surveillance is available to assure that effective cost controls and efficient performance methods are employed by the contractor, and a determination and findings have been prepared by the Contracting Officer. The contractor assumes little, if any, risk under these types of contracts, and there is little incentive to control costs.

The cost contract is suitable for research and development efforts with nonprofit organizations. Under this form of contract, the contractor receives no fee, but all incurred costs are reimbursed by the government.

The cost-sharing contract is suitable for use where the contractor agrees to absorb some portion of the costs in return for some compensating benefit, such as the right to commercially market the item. The contractor receives no fee and absorbs some mutually agreed-on portion of costs incurred under this contract arrangement

Under the cost-plus-incentive fee contract, a target cost, target fee, minimum and maximum fees, and a fee adjustment formula are negotiated at the time of contract award. This form of contract is suitable for development and test programs, under which a cost reimbursement contract is necessary and a target cost and a fee adjustment formula can be negotiated that are likely to incentivize the contractor to manage effectively. While cost control will always be incentivized under this contract, it is also possible to incentivize performance characteristics. The amount of fee payable is determined at the completion of contract performance, based on the formula agreed to at contract award.

The cost-plus-award fee contract provides for a base fee, which may be zero, fixed at contract award, and an award amount judged by the government to be sufficient to motivate excellence in contract performance. Cost controls and performance characteristics may be incentivized. This form of contract requires the development of evaluation criteria at the outset of performance, against which the contractor's performance will be measured in accordance with agency regulations. The single most important disadvantage to this form of contract lies in the administrative burden placed on the acquiring agency in administering the contract.

The cost-plus-fixed-fee contract is a cost reimbursement contract that provides for payment of a fixed fee that is negotiated at the time of contract award and that does not vary with actual costs insured. The fixed fee may be adjusted as a result of changes in the work to be performed. This form of contract presents the contractor with little incentive to control costs.

All cost reimbursement contracts are subject to statutory limitations as to the amount of fee that may be awarded. Research and development contracts shall not exceed 15 percent of the contractor's estimated cost, whereas all other cost reimbursement contracts are subject to a ceiling of 10 percent. A deviation to the maximum-fee limitation on cost-plus-award fee and cost-plus-incentive fee contracts-may be obtainable in accordance with subpart 1.4 of the FAR. The ceiling on architect and engineering contracts has been fixed at 6 percent of the estimated cost and engineering of construction of the public work. *See* 10 U.S.C. §2306(d); 41 U.S.C. §254(d).

Other Contract Types

Indefinite delivery contracts permit the government to maintain stocks at minimum levels and direct shipment to users when appropriate. The definite quantity contract provides for delivery of specific supplies or services within a fixed period, with deliveries to be scheduled at designated locations upon order. The requirements contract provides for filling all actual purchase requirements for specific supplies or services within a fixed period, with deliveries being scheduled by placing orders under the contract. This form of contract contains a total estimated quantity, whereas the indefinite quantity contract provides for stated minimum and maximum levels of supplies and services.

The time-and-materials contract provides for the contractor to supply direct labor hours at fixed hourly rates, which include overhead, general and administrative expenses, and profit. Materials are furnished to the government at cost and may include a materials-handling charge. The labor hour contract is a variation, which differs only in that the government furnishes materials.

The letter contract is a written preliminary instrument that permits the contractor to commence performance immediately, pending definitization of the agreed-to contract. It should be as complete as possible, to include a price ceiling where appropriate. The letter contract should be definitized within 180 days or before completion of 40 percent of the work.

The basic ordering agreement is not a contract as such. Rather, it is a written instrument of understanding that sets forth appropriate terms and conditions, a description of the supplies and services that may be furnished thereunder, and the methods of pricing, issuing delivery orders, and making deliveries under the agreement.

C. TINA and Defective Pricing

The Truth in Negotiating Act ("TINA") requires certain kinds of government contractors to provide "cost or pricing data," so that the government's contracting officers can ascertain that the government is paying a reasonable price. This statutory requirement dates back to the Congressional reaction in the early 1960s to overcharging scandals of the 1950s relating to the sudden explosion of cost-based purchasing, particularly in the then-new aerospace realm. A sharper break between the government contracting realm and the realm of private commercial contracting could hardly be imagined. In commercial contracting, it is the norm for the seller to keep to itself its costs, what it charges others, and other cost-pricing data. "Overcharging" in the sense of charging more than a "reasonable" price is not an abuse in commercial contracting. However, since TINA requires disclosures, failure to make its required disclosures renders a government contractor vulnerable to serious accusations that can prove expensive to defend and, if the accusations have merit, very expensive to resolve.

One whole set of issues concerns TINA duties: which contracting requires the providing of "cost or pricing data," what data is provided, and how the penalties (for "defective pricing") work. These are the subject of the first reading.

In some ways, the most interesting TINA questions in recent years have concerned the exemptions from the duty to provide "cost or pricing data." There have always been exemptions from TINA for suppliers who could prove that they were so fully a part of a highly competitive commercial market that this market itself so thoroughly disciplined their prices that the government could readily forego disclosure. Over time, those exemptions have expanded, relieving categories of government contractors of burdensome disclosure, but posing problems for government officers charged with securing reasonable prices and government auditors charged with determining whether the contractor failed to make required disclosures.

For further discussion of the subject of this section, see: Carl L. Vacketta & Susan H. Pope, *Commercial Item Contracts: When Is a Government Contract Term or Condition Consistent with "Standard" or "Customary" Commercial Practice?*, 27 Pub. Cont. L.J. 291 (1998); Richard J. Wall & Christopher B. Pockney *Revisiting Commercial Pricing Reform*, 27 Pub. Cont. L.J. 315 (1998); Steven A. Kaufman & Clayton S. Marsh, *The Law of De-*

fective Pricing: Its Shape and Fit with Commercial Law, 19 Pub. Cont. L.J. 559 (1990); Jeffrey A. Lovitky, *Applying the Exemptions to Cost or Pricing Data*, 19 Pub. Cont. L.J. 156 (1989).

Truth in Negotiations Act
From: Government Contract Guidebook Donald P.Arnavas &
William J. Ruberry (Federal Publications Inc. 2d ed. (1994))

In 1962, Congress passed a law known as the Truth in Negotiations Act (TINA). The purpose of the Act was to put the Government on an equal footing with contractors in contract negotiations by requiring contractors to provide the Government with cost or pricing information relevant to the expected costs of contract performance. TINA, as amended, and the implementing procurement regulations require prime contractors and subcontractors to submit cost or pricing data to the Government and to *certify* that, to the best of their knowledge and belief, the data submitted are accurate, complete, and current. These rules have had a tremendous impact on the Government contractor: the slightest defect or omission in cost or pricing data submitted to the Government-even if unintentional-may lead to a reduction in the contract price128 or even to a fraud investigation of the contractor.

1. Applicability

Although TINA originally applied only to DOD, the National Aeronautics and Space Administration, and the Coast Guard, Congress extended the coverage of the Act in 1985 to civilian agencies. The Act now applies to any negotiated contract expected to exceed $500,000, a modification of a negotiated or sealed bid contract involving a price adjustment exceeding $500,000, the award of a subcontract exceeding $500,000 if the prime contractor and each higher-tier subcontractor are required to submit cost or pricing data, or the modification of a subcontract involving a price adjustment exceeding $500,000. The dollar threshold for TINA applicability may be adjusted every five years to account for inflation.

When determining the threshold for application of the Act to a contract or subcontract modification, the price adjustment amount includes both increases and decreases totaling more than $500,000. For example, a $150,000 modification resulting from a reduction of $350,000 and an increase of $200,000 is a price adjustment exceeding $500,000.

The head of the procuring activity may require cost or pricing data from a contractor where the price of the contract (or modification) is less than the established threshold amount only if the head determines in writing that the data are necessary for the evaluation by the agency of the reasonableness of the price of the contract. The agency may not require certified cost or pricing data to be submitted, however, for any contract, modification, or subcontract covered by a statutory exemption (discussed below). When certified cost or pricing data are not -required, the head of the activity may nevertheless require the submission of the minimum of data necessary to determine price reasonableness.

2. Exemptions & Waiver

TINA exempts prime contracts, subcontracts, and contract modifications from the requirements of the Act where (1) the price negotiated is based on (a) adequate price competition, (b) established catalog or market prices of commercial items sold in substantial quantities to the general public, or (c) prices set by law or regulation, or (2) in the procurement of a commercial item, the procurement is conducted on a competitive basis and based upon adequate price competition. In addition, in exceptional cases, the head of the agency may waive TINA requirements.

a. Adequate Price Competition. The first basis for exemption-"adequate price competition"-has spawned confusion over the years. Under the current FAR, price competition exists if (1) the Government solicits offers, (2) two or more responsible offerors that can satisfy the Government's requirements submit priced offers responsive to the solicitation, and (3) these offerors compete independently for a contract to be awarded to the responsible offeror submitting the lowest evaluated price. Price competition is presumed to be adequate price competition except under narrowly defined circumstances delineated in the FAR. Thus, assuming that at least two responsible offerors submit responsive offers, the key to finding price competition is whether the contract is to be awarded to the offeror submitting the "lowest evaluated price". This does not mean the "lowest price.". According to the Comptroller General, adequate price competition exists…where…price is a substantial, though not necessarily determinative factor in the prescribed evaluation criteria.".

Contracting Officers have been reluctant to implement the adequate price competition exemption over the years, often requiring the submission and certification of cost or pricing data where circumstances warranted an exemption. As a result, the DOD FAR Supplement currently instructs that the Contracting Officer "rarely should need to require the submission or certification of cost or pricing data on acquisitions where adequate price competition is expected (regardless of the type of contract anticipated)," as long as price is a substantial factor in the source selection criteria.

b. Established Catalog Or Market Price. The "established catalog or market price" exemption pertains to commercial items that are sold regularly to other than Government customers. These items must be sold in "substantial quantities" to the "general public," without regard to the quantity of items that may be sold to the Federal Government.

c. Price Set By Law Or Regulation. A price is "set by law or regulation," and hence exempt from the cost or pricing data submission requirement, if the price is set by "a governmental body." This exemption applies chiefly to public utilities and has limited application to other contractors.

d. Commercial Item Procurements. In 1994, Congress added special exceptions to TINA for commercial item acquisitions. For commercial item procurements based on adequate price competition, cost or pricing data shall not be required. For commercial item procurements not based on adequate price competition (and not covered under another TINA exemption), the Contracting Officer initially should seek information on prices at which the same or similar items have been sold in the commercial market that is adequate for analyzing price reasonableness. If the Contracting Officer is unable to obtain such price reasonableness information, however, he may require the submission of cost or pricing data.

e. Waiver. In exceptional cases, the head of an agency may waive cost or pricing data requirements for a particular procurement. The waiver must be in writing, and the authority to grant waivers cannot be delegated by the agency head.

3. "Cost Or Pricing Data" Defined"

TINA defines "cost or pricing data" as follows:

> [T]he term "'cost or pricing data" means all facts that, as of the date of agreement on the price of a contract or the price of a contract modification), a

prudent buyer or seller would reasonably expect to affect price negotiations significantly. Such term does not include information that is judgmental, but does include the factual information from which a judgment was derived.

The definition thus has three elements: (1) all *facts* (but not judgments), (2) existing at the *date of agreement,* on price, (3) that are *significant* to price negotiations.

Under the above definition of cost or pricing data, the contractor must disclose as "facts" the data forming the basis for any judgment, projection, or estimate that is made. The nondisclosure of this data will render the submission incomplete or inaccurate.

The "date of price agreement" means the "handshake" date of price agreement between the parties, even though no legal contract may actually exist at that time. Data are required to be current as of the time of price agreement. Some "lag time" is inherent, however, between the time when data are submitted and the time of price agreement. The contractor's failure to update the data at the negotiations has been held to be a violation of the Act. However, new or changed .facts occurring *after* the "handshake" date need not be disclosed.

Information on which a contractor cannot reasonably have been expected to rely in formulating its price, is not cost or pricing data because "prudent buyers and sellers" could not be expected to consider it "significant." For example failure to disclose a vendor quote that was not seriously considered at the proposal stage would not constitute failure to disclose significant data. The question in specific cases is whether "prudent buyers and sellers" would regard the quote as significant.

The concept of a "significant effect" on the price negotiations has been interpreted very broadly. For example, in one case it was held that $20,000 out of a target price of $15 million was "significant". Moreover, it has been held that in determining whether defective data have had a significant effect on the contract price, all defective pricing data must be considered cumulatively."' Thus, a defect that, standing alone, could not be considered sufficiently grave to warrant further action may be added to other defects (whether related or not) to cumulatively arrive at a significant defect. In addition, significance has been determined in absolute dollar terms rather than as a percentage of the total contract price.

4. Submission Of Data

a. Form. Cost or pricing data must be submitted on Standard Form 1411, "Contract Pricing Proposal Cover Sheet," along with supporting attachments. The Form 1411 is set forth in the FAR, and a reduced reproduction appears in Figure 5-1.

There are few definite rules regarding precisely what constitutes a proper submission of cost or pricing data. Obviously, the contractor must do more than-merely make records available for Government inspection. Data disclosed to an auditor but contradicted or not accurately represented in negotiations have also been held not to have been properly disclosed. Moreover, the duty to furnish accurate and complete data-since it is imposed by statute-cannot be waived or modified by the Contracting Officer. And, as a general rule, the contractor cannot escape liability by proving merely that the Government should have been aware that the data were defective.

b. When Submitted. TINA requires that data be submitted *before the award* of a contract, subcontract, or contract modification expected to exceed the statutory price thresholds, but the FAR requires that data be submitted or identified in writing by the time of *agreement on price.* There will likely be more than one submission of data needed to comply with TINA and the regulations, including a submission with the initial proposal and the updating of the data during negotiations. Many contractors-out of an abundance of caution-will perform a "sweep" (an updating of all cost or pricing data after the conclusion of negotiations but prior to executing the "Certificate of Current Cost or Pricing Data") to ensure that all relevant data in the contractor's possession when negotiations were concluded have, in fact, been submitted to the Government. Contractors customarily furnish any additional data discovered as a result of the sweep with their executed "Certificate." (Prudent prime contractors require their subcontractors to engage in. similar sweeps and include any additional subcontractor data in their supplemental data submissions.)

c. Subcontractor Data. Prime contractors must obtain certified cost or pricing data before the award of any subcontract when (1) the subcontract is expected to exceed the applicable dollar threshold for TINA coverage and (2) the prime and each higher-tier sub have been required to submit data. A subcontractor is *not* required to submit its cost or pricing data if any party in the chain above was not required to submit such data or if the subcontract price is based on one of the exemptions discussed in Section C.2 above. For modifications to subcontracts, the dollar threshold is the same as for modifications to prime contracts, and is based on the aggregate price adjustment, considering both increases and decreases (see Section C. 1 above). Under TINA, a subcontractor must certify that the cost or pricing data it submits-are accurate, complete, and current. A prime contractor is liable to the extent defective subcontractor data cause an increase in price, costs, or fee to the Government.

d. Failure To Submit Data. The FAR provides guidance for the situation where required cost or pricing data are not submitted to a Contracting Officer. If this occurs, the Contracting Officer "shall again attempt to secure the data." If the contractor persists in its refusal, the Contracting Officer must then withhold making the contract award or contract adjustment. If this happens, the Contracting Officer is required to forward the contract action to higher authority, together with details of the attempts made to resolve the matter, and a statement of the practicability of obtaining the supplies or services sought under the contract from another source.

5. Certification Of Data

TINA requires not only that contractors and subcontractors submit all cost or pricing data significant to price negotiations at the time of agreement on price, it also requires that they certify that, to the best of their knowledge and belief, the data submitted to the Government are *accurate, complete,* and *current.* The FAR requires that the contractor do so in a prescribed "Certificate of Current Cost or Pricing Data." The form of the Certificate, as set forth in the FAR, appears in Figure 5-2.

The FAR provision containing the Certificate states that only one Certificate must be submitted, and that it must be submitted "as soon as practicable after pride agreement is reached". Thus, a Certificate should not be requested by the Government in the solicitation or furnished by the contractor with the proposal. The Certificate covers all cost or pricing data that are "reasonably available" at the "handshake" date.

6. Liability For Defective Data

The "Price Reduction for Defective Cost or Pricing Data" contract clause implementing TINA states that if "any price, including profit or fee ....was increased by any significant amount" because the contractor or subcontractor submitted data "that were not complete, accurate, and current as certified," the contract's "price or cost shall be reduced accordingly." The contractor's liability is usually measured as the difference between the actual contract price based on the defective data and the price that would have been negotiated had accurate, complete, and current data been disclosed. Generally, the Government will receive this dollar-for-dollar reduction in the contract price as a matter of course unless the contractor presents evidence that the defective data did not have such an impact on the negotiated price. In addition, if the contractor or subcontractor knowingly or intentionally submitted defective data, it may be liable for a wide variety of civil and criminal penalties, including fines, imprisonment, and suspension and debarment from contracting with the Government (see Chapter 7) To recover under any of these theories, however , the Government must prove that it *relied* on the defective data .

Appeal of University of California, San Francisco

1996 WL 681971 (V.A.B.C.A.), 97-1 BCA 28,642,
VABCA No. 4661 November 25, 1996

OPINION BY ADMINISTRATIVE JUDGE McMICHAEL

On Cross Motions for Summary Judgment

The University of California, San Francisco (UCSF or Contractor) appeals a claim by the Department of Veterans Affairs (VA or Government) seeking to recover certain sums paid to the Contractor under a series of six extensions to a negotiated firm fixed price contract for anesthesiology services. Alleging that the Contractor failed to supply certified cost and pricing data to support its 27% price increase in contract extensions, the VA final decision sought to recover $169,400, the difference between "what was paid to UCSF and the amount reflected [in] UCSF's payroll records."

UCSF has filed a MOTION FOR SUMMARY JUDGMENT asserting that the Government may not recover moneys paid because the contract did not contain a "Price Reduction for Defective Cost or Pricing Data" clause. * * *

FINDINGS OF FACT

For approximately nine years the Government had been negotiating annual contracts with UCSF for the "Scarce Medical Specialist Services" of anesthesiologists which were furnished to the VA Medical Center, San Francisco (VAMC). * * * In a technical review of the proposed 1990 Contract, as required by VA Acquisition Regulation (VAAR) 801.602-70, officials at VA Central Office in Washington, DC approved the contract with UCSF subject to a number of revisions, including insertion of FAR Clause 52.215-22. (R4, tab 4) Notwithstanding this conditioned approval, the 1990 Contract as executed did not include FAR Clause 52.215-22, PRICE REDUCTION FOR DEFECTIVE COST OR PRICING DATA, as required by FAR 15.804-8(a). * * *

During this same period, UCSF transmitted to the VA on April 8, 1991, "cost and pricing documentation" in connection with RFP 662-20-91 (the proposed 1991 Contract). (R4, tab 16) The information, in the form of a letter from Dr. Ronald Miller, Chairman of UCSF's Department of Anesthesia, was directed to Jerry Prescott, a contract specialist at the San Francisco VAMC who was acting as contracting office liaison for negotiation of the new scarce medical services contract. (Prescott Aff. at 1) * * * Dr. Miller concluded by stating that there was "no indirect cost associated with this contract" and that he hoped that he had answered any "questions regarding the basis for the $726,997 annual contract price." * * *

By letter dated July 23, 1991, the Western Regional Director of the Veterans Health Services and Research Administration (VHA) informed the Medical Center that the proposed scarce medical specialist contract with UCSF had been disapproved based on a June 7th memorandum from Dr. McDonald, the Chairman of the Sharing Contract Committee in Washington. Questions were raised about why the anesthesiologists who would be performing the work could not be identified, and about the composition of fringe benefits for which a "breakdown...with respect to each professorial level" was needed. As for the requested administrative costs, Dr. McDonald said that he interpreted this as an "indirect cost," adding:

> The total of $77,196.66 as administrative or indirect cost is far more than any possible cost for performing the activity specified by Dr. Miller in his letter. As a matter of policy, VA cannot pay for administrative, overhead, or indirect cost for these personal contracts...Indirect costs and overhead only can be included if they are a part of the operation. In this instance, schedules are made out by VA and all operation factors conducted in VA by VA personnel. Hence, personal contracts, such as this contract, incurs no indirect or administrative costs.

* * *

The continued funding of the anesthesiology scarce medical services contract by a series of 90 day extensions for over a year had attracted the attention of the VA's Office of Inspector General. * * * On August 28, 1992, David Sumarl, Regional Manager of the VA OIG Regional Office of Audit in Seattle, Washington transmitted a final "Report of Audit, Anesthesiology Services Contract VA Medical Center San Francisco." (R4, tab 45) The report concluded that the 1990 Contract extensions were "not managed in accordance with VA policy" and that the VAMC staff "did not properly use cost or pricing data to set the contract price" with the result that it "paid excessive charges on the contract." The report noted that, during calendar year 1991, the VA paid UCSF $715,000 through the four separate extensions to the 1990 Contract. This represented a 27% increase to the 1990 Contract price, although the "contracted level of services remained the same." (R4, tab 45 at 6) The report states that it could not "determine with certainty" why the price increase was agreed to on the extensions, observing that the "file did not contain any documentation to support" the new price.

The OIG report said that the "most important aspect" of its audit methodology was a comparison of what "VA paid for contract anesthesiology services to the cost UCSF incurred in providing the services" because:

> VA can pay only for direct medical services. SMS [Scarce Medical Services] contracts cannot be used to pay for administrative support, research, supplies, or any other expense not directly related to patient care. The applicable law (38 U.S.C. 7409) does not give VA medical centers authority to use SMS contractors to purchase any types of services other than medical services.

* * *

The OIG report recommended that action be taken to recover the excessive charges * * * , and on March 17, 1995, VA Contracting Officer Judy Infusino issued a final decision demanding recovery of $169,400 in "overpayments" under Contract V662P-4744 which "occurred on a series of...contract extensions between January 1, 1991 and June 30 [sic, July 31], 1992." (R4, tab 46)

In her final decision the CO said the overpayments were identified during an OIG audit which found the 27% increase in contract price for the interim extensions "was not supported with certified cost or pricing data" and further, that the "audit also determined that UCSF funded unallowable administrative costs with the 27% increase." "[I]n support of the Contracting Officer's final decision," CO Infusino stated that UCSF "did not provide certified cost or price data to support the proposed price" of the contract extension and that the "IG determined that from January 1, 1991, to July 31, 1992, there was a difference of $169,400 between what was paid to UCSF and the amount reflected [in] UCSF's payroll records."

These funds were used for "administrative support for research in academic activities of the contracted anesthesiologists and were not authorized by the contract." CO Infusino concluded that:

> The VAMC Contracting Officer acted outside the scope of his authority by granting UCSF's 27% price increase without requesting certified cost or pricing data or granting an exemption to the requirement. The Contracting Officer's failure to request certified cost or pricing data, or to grant an exemption does not relieve UCSF of responsibility... UCSF knew or should have known that in accordance with FAR 15.804-2(a)(1)(ii), cost or pricing data is required on all contract actions and modifications exceeding $100,000....

* * *

DISCUSSION

I.

In its MOTION FOR SUMMARY JUDGMENT, Appellant initially observes that the Government is seeking a defective pricing adjustment in the pending appeal even though neither the 1990 Contract nor any of the 6 extensions thereto, totaling 16 months, contained the Price Reduction for Defective Cost of Pricing Data clause as outlined in 48 CFR s 52.215-22. Although the Contract did require the Contractor to submit certified cost or pricing information, UCSF argues that the Government's entitlement to a cost reduction is "not automatic or granted by the [Truth in Negotiations Act (TINA)] itself," but rather is "based solely upon having included the proper [price reduction] clause in the contract." (App. Mot. at 9) As for the possible incorporation of that clause into the contract as a matter of law pursuant to G.L. Christian & Associates v. United States, 312 F.2d 418 (Ct.Cl.), reh'g denied 320 F.2d 345, cert. denied 375 U.S. 954 (1963), Appellant notes the "judicious" application of the Christian doctrine by Courts and Boards which have limited it "to clauses which advance particularly significant public policies." Such significant public policies do not, in its view, apparently include defective pricing clauses.

In any event, Appellant argues that the Christian doctrine is "inapplicable" where, "as here, the CO has discretion as to whether or not the clause must be included," citing IBI Sec. Serv. v. United States, 19 Cl. Ct. 106 (1989), aff'd without op. 918 F.2d 188 (Fed Cir. 1990). In the case before us, the Contracting Officer "appears to have determined that UCSF was exempt from application of TINA." That is, in a contract for anesthesiologist services, it is "reasonable to assume that the CO determined UCSF was exempt from the requirement to submit certified cost or pricing data because the Contract price was based on established market prices of commercial items sold in substantial quantities to the general public." (App. Mot. at 10-11)

The Government in its OPPOSITION TO MOTION FOR SUMMARY JUDGMENT, argues that the Truth in Negotiations Act is "mandatory" with respect to noncompetitively negotiated contracts such as Scarce Medical Services contracts, and that the defective pricing clause required by TINA reflects a "significantly ingrained strand of public procurement policy." Thus, Christian doctrine principles would clearly incorporate such an omitted clause into the contract, a position which is also supported by existing case authority. Moreover, the Contracting Officer "could not waive the requirements of TINA by omission or inaction." The record is clear that the "CO did not apply any exemptions of TINA nor did the agency head grant a wavier of the Act." (Gov't Opp. at 42)

In Christian, the Government terminated a housing contract and the Appellant sought to recover anticipated but unearned profits under a breach theory, noting that the contract did not include a standard "termination for convenience" clause limiting its recovery for profits to work actually completed. The Government argued that the contract should be read as if it did contain a termination for convenience clause noting that procurement regulations "issued under statutory authority" required such a clause be inserted into the contract. In reviewing the history of the termination for convenience clause the court found the profit limitation contained therein to be "a deeply ingrained strand of procurement policy" and concluded that "the Defense Department and the Congress would be loath to sanction a large contract which did not provide the power to terminate and at the same time proscribe anticipated profits if termination did occur." G.L. Christian, 312 F.2d at 426. It also found that Appellant was an "experienced contractor" who "could not have been wholly unaware" of the prospects of a termination for convenience of the Government. Unearned profits have not been paid for such terminations "[f]or many years" and it was "probable too that [the Contractor] knew of that general policy." Accordingly, the court found it "fitting and legally proper for the clause to be "incorporated into [the contract] by operation of law" Id. at 427

On a motion for rehearing and reargument, the Court stated that it was important that "procurement policies set by higher authority not be avoided or evaded (deliberately or negligently) by lesser officials, or by a concert of contractor and contracting officer." It added:

> To accept plaintiff's pleas that a regulation is powerless to incorporate a provision into a new contract would be to hobble the very policies which the appointed rule makers considered significant enough to call for mandatory regulation. Obligatory Congressional enactments are held to govern federal contracts because there is a need to guard the dominant legislative policy against ad hoc encroachment or dispensation by the executive. There is a comparable need to protect the significant policies of superior administrators from sapping by subordinates. Like other individuals who deal with the Federal Government, potential contractors can validly be bound to discover the published directives telling them the limits and scope of the agreements the Government can make. (citations omitted)

320 F.2d at 351

The Christian doctrine was recently considered in two Federal Circuit cases. In General Engineering & Machine Works v. O'Keefe, 991 F.2d 775, 779 (Fed. Cir. 1993), the court reaffirmed that "the Christian doctrine applies to mandatory contract clauses which express a significant or deeply ingrained strand of public procurement policy." It affirmed a decision incorporating a requirement for separate cost pools into a contract. The regulation requiring separate cost pools was determined to be "sufficiently ingrained" in public procurement policy because it deterred double payments and "thus discouraged the unnecessary and wasteful spending of government money." Id. at 780

In S.J. Amoroso Construction Co., Inc., 12 F.3d 1072 (Fed.Cir.1993), the Court affirmed the incorporation into a contract of Buy American Act requirements which the parties had stricken. Initially observing that "[a]pplication of the Christian doctrine turns not on whether the clause was intentionally or inadvertently omitted," the court emphasized that that Buy American Act itself required that "[e]very contract for construction...shall contain a provision" with respect to materials, supplies and articles manufactured in the United States. Thus:

> The statute alone, therefor, evidences a significant and deeply ingrained strand of public procurement policy sufficient to require incorporation of the clause prescribed...as a matter of law.

> In addition, the procurement regulations themselves have reflected this significant statutory policy for over 25 years.

Id. at 1076.

In considering the applicability of the Christian doctrine to the case at hand, it should be recognized that the Truth in Negotiations Act, first enacted almost 35 years ago, requires certified disclosure of cost or pricing data for certain negotiated contracts and mandates, in pertinent part, that:

> A prime contract (or change or modification to a prime contract) under which a certificate...is required, shall contain a provision that the price of the contract to the United States...shall be adjusted to exclude any significant amount by which...such price was increased because the contractor...submitted defective cost or pricing data.

41 U.S.C. §254d (emphasis added).

We are thus presented with not only a long standing policy but one that has as its basis, an explicit statutory mandate requiring that such contracts contain a price reduction provision which is to operate in the event defective cost or pricing data is submitted. As the court stated in M-R-S Manufacturing Company v. United States, 492 F.2d 835, 842 (Ct.Cl.1974):

> [T]he purpose of then Truth in Negotiations Act was to avoid excessive costs that result from a contractor having in his possession accurate, complete, and current information when the Government does not possess the same data.

Incorporation of the defective pricing clause into negotiated contracts in order to protect the taxpayer's dollar from "excessive costs" and "unnecessary and wasteful spending" is, in our view, a "deeply ingrained strand of procurement policy." Moreover, failure to incorporate this clause into the contract by operation of law would be a failure to "guard the dominant legislative policy against ad hoc encroachment or dispensation by the executive." Appellant's citation of IBI Sec. Serv. v. United States, 19 Cl. Ct. 106 (1989), aff'd without op. 918 F.2d 188 (Fed. Cir. 1990) does not support its position. As that court stated, "[t]he Christian doctrine is available only when relevant statutory or regulatory provisions are required to be included in an agency's contracts." Id. at 109. But as we have previously observed, the price reduction provisions in issue here have been required to be included in the contract by both statute and regulation for over 35 years. See also Palmetto Enterprises, ASBCA No. 22839, 79-1 BCA p. 13,736 (TINA provisions incorporated by operation of law under the Christian doctrine).

It should also be pointed out that here, as in the G.L. Christian case, it is "probable" that the contractor "knew of the general policy" concerning the requirement for a defective pricing clause. UCSF had a nine year history of negotiated contracts with the VA which contained the price reduction clause for defective pricing. Even the 1990 contract from which the clause was omitted, required the submission of certified cost and pricing data which should have alerted this "experienced contractor" that consequences were intended to flow from the submission of defective cost or pricing data.

* * *

Notes and Questions

1. Just what did UCSF not disclose to the government? UCSF stands accused of slipping through 27% price increases that turned out to be for "administrative support for research in academic activities of the contracted anesthesiologists." Described one way, that is a sinister overcharging of the government for something it would never knowingly pay. Described another way, anesthesiologists who engage in research and teaching charged the payer for medical service, that is, the government, an added price to cover the costs of their research; that is exactly what everyone (except government auditors, perhaps) expects of such university hospital physicians. To put it differently, the physicians were not caught siphoning off government money for a corrupt reason. If you were the research anesthesiologists caught up in years of government auditing cases, what would you think of government contract law?

2. At first glance, nothing could differ more from the original circumstances that brought forth TINA than this UCSF case. TINA arose from scandals involving defense procurement, particularly of high-cost, high-technology aerospace items. UCSF concerns procuring the services of a few medical professionals. What do the original reasons for TINA have in common with the facts of UCSF? To put it differently, why does the government believe it needs disclosure of kinds of "cost or pricing data" that private-sector buyers do not typically obtain from sellers? Does it have to do with unique vulnerabilities of the government (regardless of what the government buys)? Or with a breakdown of market discipline in certain categories of purchases (regardless of who, public or private, makes such purchases)?

3. How would you argue as a matter of justice on UCSF's behalf? The Veteran's Administration sought competent service of a highly expensive medical specialty, anaesthesiology, in the high-cost location of San Francisco, at $73/hour, which may be described as a very low price. UCSF found a billing method that met the government's need, at the government's price, with what presumably was an acceptable quality. Was UCSF bad not to explain fully to the government how it did that? Could UCSF argue that at least some of the government officials involved must have known and acquiesced? Is the "defective pricing" case a method by which auditors, acting afterwards, penalize government contractors simply for sensible "don't ask, don't tell" billing arrangements with quite willing contracting officers? On the other hand, much of government contract law aims to limit the ability of contracting officers to enter into cozy arrangements, regardless of how sensible they seem to those who enter into them.

4. How would you argue as a matter of classic economic policy on UCSF's behalf? Critics charge that TINA, by requiring special disclosures to the government, tends to create a separate and higher-cost sector of government suppliers. Those willing to supply the government's special paperwork needs, the argument goes, make up for their

costs or take advantage of the lack of competitors in this isolated sector either by charging more or by providing less, but not by providing more at a lower price. What would these critics anticipate that the Veteran's Administration will get in the future: more honest anaesthesiological services, or just more heavily papered and expensive and lower-quality services?

Appeal of Honeywell Federal Systems, Inc.

Under Basic Ordering Agreement No. DAAB07-81-G-6156 March 26, 1992

OPINION BY ADMINISTRATIVE JUDGE STEMPLER

This is a timely appeal from a contracting officer's decision asserting a Government claim for defective pricing against appellant in the amount of $10,500,000. The Contract Disputes Act is applicable. The Government has moved for summary judgment on three legal entitlement issues. They are:

1. Did the Government's contracting officers act outside the scope of their authority when they permitted Appellant to withhold cost or pricing data when prices were determined for future use for orders placed against the subject Basic Ordering agreement?

STIPULATED UNDISPUTED FACTS

1. In April 1979, the Army competitively awarded contract No. DAHC26-79-C-0011 to Management & Technical Services Co. 'GE/MATSCO,' a subsidiary of General Electric Co., to provide a decentralized automated service support system ('DAS-3'). The DAS-3, a van-mounted (mobile) data processing unit, would be fielded world-wide to provide inventory and stock control capability to Army field commanders. The DAS-3 program was predicated on the use of commercial, off-the-shelf computers. Because of the mobility of the systems, the Army adopted a 'self-maintenance' philosophy for the DAS-3 program and, therefore, spare parts kits were included as line items in the competitive contract awarded to GE/MATSCO.

2. By firm-fixed price subcontract No. 167-H0029, GE/MATSCO procured 'Level 6 ' commercial computers and associated spare parts to be used for the DAS-3 program from appellant's predecessor in interest, Honeywell Information Systems, Inc. ('Honeywell'). The term of the subcontract was June 1979 to May 1991.

3. In or about late 1980 or early 1981, the Army began negotiations with appellant for a direct Basic Ordering Agreement ('BOA,') excluding GE/MATSCO, for DAS-3 spare parts. The Army sought such an agreement with Honeywell and fifteen other DAS-3 original equipment manufacturers, intending to gain the price benefits generally realized by 'breaking out' the procurement of spare parts in this manner.

4. At or prior to the time of the negotiations, the Army was aware that Honeywell did not sell the spare parts at issue separately, since most commercial customers chose to obtain spare parts as part of maintenance agreements which encompassed the provision of spare parts as necessary. Generally, the spare parts used during maintenance were not priced separately but rather Honeywell charged an established lump sum rate for the work. Honeywell did maintain a price list, known as the 'Master Parts Price List, ' for parts in its inventory. This list was 'published' in the sense that, upon request, a commercial customer would be allowed to view it at Honeywell's location. Relevant portions of this list could also be sent to customers on request.

5. Honeywell did not sell spare parts separately to commercial customers in substantial quantities.

6. Honeywell spare parts were also available for purchase by Government agencies under Honeywell's then-current General Service Administration ('GSA ') Automated Data Processing Equipment 'ADPE' Multiple Award Schedule ('MAS ') contract. In that regard, Honeywell's GSA ADPE MAS contract incorporated by reference Honeywell's published Master Parts Price List for commercial customers. The spare parts sought by the Army under the BOA remained available for purchase by Government agencies under Honeywell's GSA ADPE MAS contracts throughout the period of the BOA at prices based on Honeywell's published Master Parts Price List for commercial customers.

7. The Army prepared a draft BOA in early 1981. The designated contracting officer ('CO') for the BOA at this time was Captain Carol L. Anstey. By a memorandum dated 28 January 1981, CO Anstey recommended pre-award approval of the BOA to the U.S. Army Communications-Electronic Command (hereinafter referred to as 'CECOM') Awards Committee. On 31 March 1981, the Awards Committee of CECOM recommended award of the BOA to Honeywell.

21. Honeywell responded to CO Satterfield's request for support of its claim for exemption under TINA by letter dated 15 March 1982, stating, essentially, that:

a. Proof of commerciality for DAS-3 spares being ordered under the BOA was unnecessary, since those spares were used in Basic Level 6 end-item computer equipment and the Level 6 end-item equipment was available on Honeywell's GSA DPE MAS contract.

b. The spare parts were found in Honeywell's published Master Parts Price List for commercial customers, hence further proof of commerciality was not required.

22. Under cover of its 15 March 1982 letter, Honeywell also submitted a DD Form 633-7, entitled 'Claim for Exemption from Submission of Cost or Pricing, ' which listed data relative to previous sales of DAS-3 spares as 'NOT AVAILABLE.' The DD Form 633-7 did provide, however, sales data for Honeywell's Level 6 'Mini Computer Equipment,' which showed sales of the equipment for the period 1 January 1980 to 31 December 1980 as 89.5% to the general public and 10.5% to the Government.

23. In response to CO Satterfield's request, DCAA issued Audit Report No. 6151-2F2100412-0594, dated 4 May 1982, which stated in pertinent part:

2. Circumstances Affecting the Examination. The contractor could not provide us with supporting data which would enable us to perform a proper evaluation of its claim for exemption from submission of certified cost or pricing data covering the various parts proposed under the subject basic ordering agreement. The results of our audit are therefore qualified to the extent that the lack of supporting data may have an adverse effect on the results of our audit.

3. Conclusion

...The contractor stated that the proposed parts were not normally sold by themselves (separately) to commercial customers but instead the contractor supplied these parts as a part of maintenance services (a package) for a predetermined contract price. As stated in Paragraph 2, "Circumstances Affecting the Examination,' we were unable to evaluate the contractor's claim for an exemption of cost or pricing data. The contractor could not provide us with adequate sales data in order to determine whether contractor's proposed prices are, or are based on, established catalog or market prices of commercial items sold in substantial quantities to the general public or are prices set by law or regulation as required by DAR 3-807.3(e). Therefore, we do not consider the proposal to be acceptable as a basis for negotiation of a price.

In view of the contractor's statement that the proposed spare parts are not normally sold to commercial customers, we believe it appropriate to request the contractor to submit cost or pricing data for the proposed spare parts...

26. On 28 June 1982, CO Satterfield executed a 'Determination as to Reasonableness of Price,' stating:

Prices determined by the use of an established Pricelist which was generated by Honeywell Information Systems, Inc. was subject to audit by DCAA (audit Report 6141- 2F210041-S1-2-0687 [sic] attached). The results of this audit have determined that the prices offered to the Government are the same as those offered to Honeywell's most preferred customers. The parts purchased with this delivery order are a part of the Level 6 end item equipment which is on the GSA contract.

27. CO Satterfield's Determination reflected his conclusion that Honeywell was entitled to a commerciality exception under TINA, see 10 U.S.C. sec. 2306a(b)(1)(B), and his decision to dispense with the submission by Honeywell of cost or pricing data in connection with BOA DOs.

42. During February 1985, Captain Carl Tegen replaced CO Walsh as the CECOM CO responsible for negotiating the successor BOA.

43. During negotiations of the successor BOA, Honeywell did not submit certified cost or pricing data. This was consistent with its actions since March 1982 when dealing with CO Satterfield on DO No. 0007.

44. CO Tegen elevated appellant's failure to provide cost and pricing data for the new BOA to higher Government levels. This culminated in its elevation to the attention of the Department of Defense ('DOD') Inspector General ('IG') on or about 5 July 1985.

45. During 1985 Honeywell began making efforts to, and subsequently did, alter its accounting system to permit future compliance with Cost Accounting Standards ('CAS') and the submission and certification of cost or pricing data. As a result of these changes and further discussions with CECOM, Honeywell furnished cost or pricing data for DAS-3 spares for the new BOA.

46. Acting in response to a CECOM request, the DOD IG conducted a review of the prices the Government had paid to Honeywell under the subject BOA. The DOD IG found: 'CECOM granted an improper exemption because Honeywell's claimed commercial catalog spare parts were not supportable as commercial items and the prices set for the spare parts had no direct relationship to Honeywell's costs to produce or purchase the items.' Based on this finding and its review of certain Honeywell cost data, the DOD IG concluded that: 'Honeywell overpriced spare parts sold to CECOM under contract DAAB07-81-C-6156 by a net of $10.5 million.'

47. By letter dated March 22, 1988, the Army forwarded to Honeywell a draft of the DOD IG's Audit Report. On the basis of the draft report's conclusion that CECOM had improperly exempted Honeywell from the submission of cost or pricing data, and consistent with the approach recommended by the draft report (and the final DOD IG Audit Report) the Army requested a 'voluntary refund' of $10,500,000 from Honeywell for alleged overpricing on the BOA.

49. Upon Honeywell's refusal to comply with the Army's request for a voluntary refund, the final decision which is the subject of the instant appeal was issued by then BOA CO Gregory Coben on September 18, 1989. In his final decision, CO Coben (a) alleged that the determinations by prior BOA COs to exempt Honeywell from submis-

sion of cost or pricing data were improper and (b) claimed that the lack of Honeywell cost or pricing data had increased prices under the BOA by $10,500,000.

50. HFS initiated the instant appeal of the final decision by its Notice of Appeal filed December 6, 1989.

DECISION

The first issue presented by the parties for decision in their motions is whether the BOA COs acted outside the scope of their authority when they granted Honeywell's (HFS) commerciality exemptions from the requirement to submit cost or pricing data to support its proposals for the delivery orders under the BOA. The Government contends that the relevant statute (10 U.S.C. sec. 2306 (f)(1)) and the relevant regulations (DAR sec. 3-807) mandated that Honeywell submit cost or pricing data and that the BOA COs exceeded their authority by granting the exemptions.

* * *

Further, the Government argues that the COs, in effect, waived the statute and regulatory requirements and that they had no authority to do that and therefore the COs' actions were an abuse of discretion.

* * *

The statute provides in relevant part:

* * *

Provided, that the requirements of this subsection need not be applied to contracts or subcontracts where the price negotiated is based on adequate price competition, established catalog or market prices of commercial items sold in substantial quantities to the general public, prices set by law or regulation or, in exceptional cases, where the head of the agency determines that the requirement of this subsection may be waived and states in writing his reasons for such determination.

(10 U.S.C. sec. 2306(f)(2))

The regulations governing this issue are lengthy and are set forth in relevant part in the appendix to this opinion.

The Government is correct that contractors dealing with COs assume the risk that the COs' actions are within the scope of their authority. Federal Crop Insurance v. Merrill, 332 U.S. 380 (1947); The American Aerospace Technology Corp., ASBCA No. 36049, 89-3 BCA par. 22,100. Further, the Government is correct that COs have no authority to waive mandatory statutory or regulatory requirements. Paul E. Lehman, Inc. v. U.S., 673 F.2d 352 (Ct. Cl. 1982); Singer Company, Librascope Division v. U.S., 576 F.2d 905 (Ct. Cl. 1978); M-R-S Manufacturing Company v. U.S., 492 F.2d 835 (Ct. Cl. 1974); Numax Electronics, Inc., ASBCA No. 29186, 85-3 BCA par. 18,396; Beech Aircraft Corporation, ASBCA No. 25388, 83-1 BCA par. 16,532. The statute and regulations, however, in this instance, specifically provide for the exemption at issue and it is undisputed that the BOA COs had the authority to exercise their discretion and judgment in granting or denying the exemptions. The relevant statute is quoted above. The regulatory instructions that accompany the DAR 7-104.29 provide in relevant part:

The following clause [DAR 7-104.29 Price Reduction for Defective Cost or Pricing Data] shall be inserted in negotiated contracts which when entered into exceed [the statutory amount], except where the price is based on adequate price competition, established catalog or market prices of commercial items sold in substantial quantities to the general public, or prices set by law or regulation.

* * *

Whether or not to grant a commerciality exemption is clearly within the discretion of a CO, and is part of his duty to secure a fair and reasonable price on a case-by-case basis. Sperry Flight Systems - Division of Sperry Rand Corporation, ASBCA No. 17375, 74-1 BCA par. 10,648; aff'd, 548 F.2d 915 (Ct. Cl. 1977); cf., Resource Consultants, Inc., GSBCA No. 8342-P, 86-2 BCA par. 18,942 (discretionary with CO to determine if cost or pricing data is needed in protest situation); cf., Digital Equipment Corporation, B-219435, 85-2 CPD par. 456 (within CO discretion to grant commerciality exemption in protest situation). What the Government really complains of is that it now believes that the BOA COs exercised their judgment and discretion poorly and the Government would like to substitute the current CO's discretion and decisions on the exemption question for those determinations made by the BOA COs years ago. Clearly, in arguing that the BOA COs had no authority, the Government is confusing authority with judgment. There is no hint of fraud, bad faith or collusion in the BOA COs' determinations to grant the exemptions. The BOA COs clearly made reasoned independent decisions to grant the exemptions and there is sufficient evidence in the record to establish that these decisions had support. The BOA COs' decision process included: (1) the COs' examination of HFS' Master Parts Price List, (2) consideration of HFS' GSA ADPE BOA, (3) seeking legal advice, (4) requesting information from HFS, (5) requesting DCAA audits and (6) making written commerciality exemption decisions. If the BOA COs had the authority to made 'correct' determinations on the exemption issue, they had authority to make 'incorrect' ones. We will not, as the Government requests, measure authority by the results obtained rather than the scope of actual authority granted. Broad Avenue Laundry and Tailoring v. U.S., 681 F.2d 746 (Ct. Cl. 1982); Liberty Coat Company, ASBCA Nos. 4119, 4138, 4139, 57-2 BCA par. 1576. The BOA COs made determinations to grant the exemptions and such determinations were squarely within their authority and are binding on successor COs. Bell Helicopter Company, ASBCA No. 17776, 74-1 BCA par. 10,411.

We hold that the BOA COs did not act outside the scope of their authority in granting the exemptions and refuse to re-examine the specifics of the decisions to determine, in hindsight, if they were correct or incorrect. Accordingly, the Government is bound by the COs' determinations.

In view of our answer to the first issue, we do not reach the second or third issues.

CONCLUSION

The Government's motion for summary judgment is denied. The appellant's cross-motion for summary judgment is granted. The appeal is sustained.

Notes and Questions

1. The case concerns one simple question: Did Honeywell get to retain the benefit of a Contracting Officer's exempting it from TINA? However, consider the great variety and diversity of arguments on that question. How many different arguments can you find in each of these subcategories:

what is a commercial market for purposes of government supply;

whether Honeywell was truly in a commercial market as to spare parts;

how much authority a CO should have, vis-a-vis (1) the DCAA, and (2) later COs ; and how much repose - that is, protection against later review of earlier actions - should government contractors have.

2. Do you understand what the DCAA thought about giving Honeywell an exemption in 1982? The CO did not explain why he decided to give the exemption despite the DCAA's thoughts. Later, the DCAA seemed to get its revenge, though not in the end. Can you picture the changing Defense Department background of this case? Honeywell received its exemption during the heyday of defense suppliers in the early 1980s, during the major increase in defense spending that started with the American reaction to the U.S.S.R.'s invasion of Afghanistan in 1979 and reached peak levels during the Reagan Administration. Contracting officers had large budgets that they were under pressure to convert into defense supplies. Then, as years passed, scandals began breaking about overcharging of the government, including on such matters as spare or extra parts. New laws, regulations, and policies went into place to address those scandals. As more years went by, cases like this one gradually worked their way through the slow sequence of auditing, disputes, and litigation in an entirely different defense spending climate than the one at the time of the original spending spree.

3. Since the Honeywell decision, statuory and regulatory changes have expanded the commercial exemption from TINA. Regulations now provide the following:

48 C.F.R. 15.403-1 Prohibition on obtaining cost or pricing data (10 U.S.C. 2306a and 41 U.S.C. 254b).

(b) Exceptions to cost or pricing data requirements. The contracting officer shall not require submission of cost or pricing data to support any action (contracts, subcontracts, or modifications) (but may require information other than cost or pricing data to support a determination of price reasonableness or cost realism) —

(3) When a commercial item is being acquired (see standards in paragraph (c)(3) of this subsection);

* * *

(c) Standards for exceptions from cost or pricing data requirements —

(3) Commercial items. Any acquisition for an item that meets the commercial item definition in 2.101, or any modification, as defined in paragraph (c)(1) or (2) of that definition, that does not change the item from a commercial item to a noncommercial item, is exempt from the requirement for cost or pricing data.

* * *

The regulation's definitional section, 48 C.F.R. 2.101, specifies that commercial items include those which are sold or offered for sale, lease, or license to the general public, including those with minor modifications, and meet the exception if they are publicly available at or before the delivery date of a government solicitation.

4. Something else changed during the course of this case Honeywell. Paragraph 45 says: "45. During 1985 Honeywell began making efforts to, and subsequently did, alter its accounting system to permit future compliance with Cost Accounting Standards ('CAS') and the submission and certification of cost or pricing data. As a result of these changes and further discussions with CECOM, Honeywell furnished cost or pricing

data for DAS-3 spares for the new BOA." Do you understand Honeywell's changeover, not just on this contract, but on a large-scale basis? What would you have had to do, if you were the lawyer at Honeywell in charge of that changeover?

Charles Tiefer & Ron Stroman,
Congressional Intent and Commercial Products
The Procurement Lawyer, Spring 1997, at 22

In enacting the Federal Acquisition Reform Act (FARA) of 1996, Congress carefully balanced its intent- to continue partially "deregulating" commercial acquisition with the need for requiring competitive purchasing, directing contractor disclosure, and maintaining government remedies for overpayments. The enactment process for FARA presents a challenge in understanding congressional intent. Procurement reform laws typically have emerged from Congress after a relatively open process. FARA was passed in the 104th Congress, however, fairly suddenly on the heels of the Federal Acquisition Streamlining Act (FASA) enacted a year earlier. During a three-month conference committee in late 1995, Congress worked out .a number of FARA's complex aspects in internal discussions from which few details emerged. FARA became law through a compromise process involving both the legislative and executive branches that is not easy to follow without careful study.

What Was the Congressional Intent?

This article attempts to identify clearly the congressional intent in passing FARA by focusing on the provisions in FARA connected with commercial product acquisition, particularly with vendors' duties to provide information on pricing. This article begins with House passage and Senate preparation for conference and further reviews the process of the all-important three-month conference (September to December 1995) before the bill eventually became law as Division D of the 1996 Defense Authorization Act. Also addressed are several sections of FARA concerning "full and open competition," simplified commercial product acquisitions below a dollar threshold, and section 4201 concerning price reasonableness disclosures—even after government contractors have been exempted from the requirements of the Truth in Negotiation Act (TINA).

The enactment of FASA, signed into law on October 13, 1994, was the culmination of several initiatives.

FASA was the most comprehensive procurement reform in a decade. In the late 1980s and early 1990s, the House Committee on Government Operations under Chairman John Conyers conducted extensive oversight on procurement problems. The Clinton administration undertook an effort to implement reform as part of Vice President Gore's National Performance Review—popularly known as "Reinventing Government". Another initiative resulted from activities of the Defense Department and the Armed Services Committees, symbolized by the well-known Section 800 Advisory Panel and its extensive report.

In the emerging area of procurement of commercial products, FASA expanded the exceptions requiring cost and pricing data under the Truth in Negotiations Act (TINA). FASA relaxed the previous requirements qualify for the "catalog or market pricing" exception to TINA by creating a new category of commercial product exception requiring only a "substantial quantity" of an item's sales be to the general public. Throughout 1995 and 1996 federal agencies worked to implement FASA's provisions by promulgating regulations on commercial product acquisition.

A month after FASA's enactment, the November 1994 election brought in the 104th Congress and a new majority party in each chamber. The incoming House Chair, Representative Clinger, and the incoming Democratic Member, Representative Collins, of the renamed House Committee on Government Reform and Oversight, had established themselves as effective legislators, interested in successful enactments rather than failed crusades. Thus, where the 104th Congress had difficulty in enacting a number of pieces of legislation, it was able to enact FARA due to an existing bipartisan philosophy. This philosophy emphasized competition and market effectiveness—with deregulation of commercial acquisition on one side and continuation of necessary pricing, product, and procurement integrity safeguards on the other.

* * *

FARA Section 4201-Commercial Product Exception

This section will address section 4201 of FARA, the commercial item exception to TINA's requirement for cost or pricing data, and, specifically, the exception in that exception, namely, the surviving requirements for vendors of commercial products to submit "other information." The exception to the exception arose because contracting officers must ensure that the government obtains a "reasonable" price.

When Congress defines the commercial product exception narrowly, as under TINA and even under FASA, it applies only to products in which the market is comparatively closer to being "perfect"—that is, the existence of competition forces prices to be reasonable even without disclosures to contracting officers. Conversely, when Congress defines the commercial product exception more broadly, as the House did in H.R. 1670, it applies to products in which the market is further from perfection and competition, by itself, is not safeguarding the market.

Reliance on Deregulation

In the House-passed bill, the expansion of the commercial exception from TINA's certified cost and pricing data disclosure included a very limited commitment to requiring compensating submission of other price reasonableness information. The limited commitment appeared in the bill's section 201(d) nonmandatory allowance of FAR provisions covering information that "contracting officers *may* consider on price reasonableness."

The House's view in section 201(d) was consistent with other provisions expressing great confidence in commercial product deregulation to replace traditional government protections. The House bill included a very broad provision for deregulated or -simplified- acquisition of commercial products. Section 202 extended "simplified" acquisition to commercial items without any dollar ceiling, even when this involved sole source acquisition. The committee report noted that "the Committee is aware that some have expressed a concern that there is no dollar threshold," but "[t]he purchase of a commercial item logically lends itself to simplified procedures because there exists a yardstick in the commercial marketplace against which to measure price and product quality and to serve as a surrogate for government-unique procedures."

Conference Committee Begins Work

The conference began its work in late September and early October through the exchange of Senate and House proposals. The first step was the Senate's formulation of proposals in areas covered by the House bill but not addressed by any Senate-passed bill. In many respects, the Senate position, as one would expect from the Senate's reliance upon Senators Cohen and Levin, leaned toward the reliance on "full and open competition" and toward balanced changes in current government protections. Regarding commercial items, the Senate's proposals centered on a narrow concept of "commercially available off-the-shelf products, "sold in substantial quantities in the commercial marketplace," and "offered to the Government, without modification, in the same form in which it is sold in the commercial marketplace." The FASA regulatory relaxations would be applied only for these "off-the-shelf" commercial items.

Mid-October 1995 was a dramatic time in the Congress. As the major budget proposals left committee and headed for the floor, the head-on clash between Congress and the president drew nearer, and the feeling in some quarters that the president and his party could be ignored in the legislative process subsided to a certain degree. The House definitely wanted to achieve a procurement law, not just an unproductive fight over an unenacted bill. Accordingly, at the end of mid-October, the House came back with an omnibus package proposal that sought to bridge the gap between the House-passed bill and the Senate's initial conference proposals. This began with the revision of the definition of competition, in which the House dropped the wording that had been the target of the Collins amendment with the intent of preserving the "full and open competition" language.

For the specific area of what became section 4201, the House proposal kept to its comparatively broad definition of commercial products, rather than adopting the Senate's narrow "off-the-shelf" view. The House provided that even where commercial products fit this new TINA exception, however, the agency head might nevertheless require submission of certified cost or pricing data where necessary for evaluating price reasonableness as long as the head of the procuring activity offered written justification. Moreover, even when the vendor did not have to submit certified cost or pricing data, the contracting officer might require submission of other data to the extent necessary to determine price reasonableness.

The Senate was required to make the final counterproposal at the end of October that became—in large measure—the conference report. The statement of the managers accompanying the conference report showed the influence of Senator Cohen in the following words: "This provision makes no change to the requirement for full and open competition or to the definition of full and open competition."

Senate Maintains "Off-the-Shelf" Provisions

The compromise involved a limited adherence to the Senate's early position of limiting the "commercial" relaxation to "off-the-shelf" products. The Senate still tried, in what became section 4202, to maintain the "off-the-shelf" position. However, it gave that up in what became section 4201. Specifically, the Senate counterproposal, like the final provision as enacted, stated that the contracting officer "shall require submission of data than certified cost or pricing data to the extent necessary to determine the reasonableness of the price" and that for the new commercial product exception, "the data submitted *shall* include, at a minimum, appropriate information on the prices at which the same item or similar items have previous been sold...."

With that, the House and Senate almost had a deal. The back-and-forth over simplified procedures for competitive acquisitions had still not been resolved with the House attempting to avoid a dollar ceiling and the Senate adhering to the narrow category of "off-the-shelf" products. The final compromise is codified in section 4202 that put a ceiling of $5 million and sunset the provision to expire after three years. The conference report was filed on December 13, 1995. 'The bill went through some uncertainties from being tied to a defense bill that was vetoed on unrelated grounds. Nevertheless, the conference version was placed aboard a new vehicle and it became law when the Congress passed, and the president signed on February 10, 1996, the Defense Department appropriation for FY 1996. At that point, public interest turned to how FARA would be implemented.

After the enactment of FASA, Senator Bingaman's article on the law's origins and development concluded with some 'lessons for the future—ideas matter—details matter—analysis matters—bipartisanship matters—administration support matters." Nothing has happened in the last two years to question the significance of ideas, details, and analysis. This article confirms the Senator's comments about the significance of bipartisanship and administration support. The concept of producing bills acceptable to only one party does not apply to procurement reform, a highly technical and, to the public, arcane area. There, as Senator Bingaman wrote, "[w]hen you undertake to change a large number of existing statutes, you are likely to face opposition from those who have supported those laws. In this circumstance, bipartisan support is crucial to overcome opposition...."

Analysis

Congress's intent in FARA to retain mandatory information-submission requirements for price reasonableness while easing TINA's burdens is symbolic of the debate over the direction of procurement reform. There was always an exception for commercial products in TINA. When Congress first enacted TINA in 1962, however, the exception was simply a pragmatic one. In later years a major thrust developed toward relaxing statutory and regulatory requirements for commercial procurement. The leading articulations of this thrust are too well known to require extended recitation. At its strongest, the commercial products "movement" served well in showing how TINA's requirements might simply amount to an undesirable entry barrier for commercial product vendors, actually lessening competition, raising costs, and impeding efficient procurement.

Pressure to Reduce Regulations

As the relaxation of regulatory requirements for "commercial" products expands beyond the area of true markets, the thrust to relax the requirements becomes less arguable as a policy matter. It then begins to appear as a thinly disguised effort to lower the protections of the Treasury against unreasonable vendor prices. Even at the peak of procurement reform sentiment, Congress would not do that.

As the procurement regulation enters and contracting officers implement FASA and FARA in years to come, they will often face pressures, either industrywide or from particular vendors, to relax various regulatory protections in the name of commercial product acquisition. An example is the continuing dispute between contracting agencies and industry over protections against overpricing. The largest scale dispute concerns the elaborate law surrounding the various remedies, both civil and criminal, for defective or fraudulent pricing. Knowing submission of fraudulent cost or pricing information will be treated as such by Inspectors General. Of course, the government has a difficult burden in making a fraud case out of complex aspects of disputed pricing questions.

Congress showed only measured and limited willingness in FARA to allow the undermining of price reasonableness by rolling back informational requirements. Accordingly, it raises serious questions of congressional intent to expect agencies to roll back other protections against overpricing based on generalized "commercial products" notions. For example, there has been a debate within the Public Contract Law Section about GSA's price reduction clause for its multiple award schedule. GSA supports that clause based on a 1995 Inspector General study and a 1993 GAO report. Without getting into the details of the debate, this review of the congressional intent in FARA shows the measured manner with which Congress approaches such issues. Provisions on such subjects had to obtain strong bicameral and bipartisan support and made little progress without extensive consultation with the administration. For all the desire to relax the entry barriers for commercial products, there was a strong competing awareness that there was a need to protect the government from the possibility of overpricing.

Conclusion

FARA stands out as a notable accomplishment for the 104th Congress. It must not be read, however, as a statement going further than congressional intent. The bill emerged from an elaborate conference consideration in which the thrust toward relaxing regulatory requirements in the initial version of the House bill was tempered by the need to build bicameral and bipartisan rapport and to consult with the administration. Where the commercial market was imperfect, that tempering took the form of the changes worked out with the Senate and placed in the final version.

FARA considerably relaxed the requirements of TINA for submission of certified price and cost data in carefully measured fashion. The proposal to relax all mandatory requirements for submission of price reasonableness information were considered and rejected.

D. Cost Accounting and Auditing

When the government contracts to pay a contractor for its costs on some project like the research for a new aircraft, both sides then have recourse to a body of law regarding what counts as "costs." That body of law may sometimes apply even to fixed-price contracts, such as when the government changes the required work and must pay the contractor for this modification. FAR Subpart 31.2 summarizes that body of law.

In terms of practical interactions, the initial discussions about costs may occur between the contracting officer's representatives and the contractor. However, further stages may involve the government's audit personnel, who can review the costs submitted by the contractor to decide whether to accept them, to investigate further, or to reject them. In this section, the *Newport News* case involves a dispute between government auditors wanting broad access to contractor documents as part of an investigation of costs, and the contractor personnel. It provides a general review of costs and of disputes over costs, before moving into the particular subject of what auditors can subpoena.

As *Newport News* alludes to, and as the next subsection addresses, much of the body of law regarding "costs" concerns the criterion called "allowability." To take obvious extreme examples, contractors who speeded up their progress by assassinating anyone getting in their way would not recover from the government the costs of those assassinations. The government has taken a great distance the notion that it will define the kinds of costs it will reimburse. The other subsection of this section picks up several types of issues in the body of law about costs: allocability, reasonableness, and the Cost Accounting Standards. "Allocability" is the process of assigning costs to cost objectives. A contractor may build an electric generating plant to service some government contract and also some unrelated nongovernment contracts. That would make some of the plant's costs allocable to the government contract, and some not. The Cost Accounting Standards comprise a special area of law concerning costs, establishing some uniformity and consistency as the government resolves cost issues on different contracts. For example, a government contractor will have a pension plan for its employees. It takes an elaborate Cost Accounting Standard to decide what the government should pay into that pension plan as part of "costs," and all the related issues, such as what happens if the contractor tried to liquidate the pension plan.

That pension plan example shows that this subject can matter a great deal. Like issues of tax law bound up with tax accounting, lawyers take a larger interest in the disputed issues of government contract cost accounting when the sometimes-enormous scale of what is at stake gets noted. Defense contractor pension plans can contain $100 billion of assets, with the Cost Accounting Standards controlling what can be done with that money.

For further discussions of this section's subject, see R. David Carlton & Karen L. Manos, *Voluntary Accounting Changes Under CAS: A Windfall for the Government?*, 25 Pub. Cont. L.J. 457 (1996); Gerard E. Wimberly, Jr. *Business Reorganization ("No Matter How Large") and No Change In Accounting Practice*, 5 Fed. Circuit B.J. 233 (1995); Ron R. Hutchinson, *The Government's Audit and Investigative Powers Over Commercial Item Contracts and Subcontracts*, 27 Pub. Cont. L.J. 263 (1998); Evan R. Farber, *The Allowability of Costs Incurred in the Preparation of REAs After* Reflectone, 25 Pub. Cont. L.J. 781 (1996); Michael W. Clancy, *1995 Year in Review: The Federal Circuit's Government Contracts Decisions*, 25 Pub. Cont. L.J. 537, 582-87 (1996)(discussing the *Bill Strong Enterprises* case); William H. Murphy, *Applying G & A Costs to Termination Settlement Expenses and Subcontract Settlements*, 33-SPG Procurement Law 13 (Spring, 1998); John W. Chierichellan & Louis D. Victorino, *Commercial Item Exemptions to the Truth in Negotiations Act And Cost Accounting Standards under FASA and the Clinger-Cohen Act Part II*, 4/3/97 Andrews Gov't Cont. Litig. Rep. 3.

Eugene W. Massengale, "Audits by the Defense Contract Audit Agency"
From: Fundamentals of Federal Contract Law (1990) Copyright (c) (1991) by Greenwood Press Reproduced with permission of Greenwood Publishing Group, Inc., Westport, CT

Of all the controls exercised over a defense contractor's business affairs, the Defense Contract Audit Agency (DCAA) is the one that most challenges the contractor's entrepreneurial management. The purpose of contract auditing as performed by the DCAA, is to assist in achieving the objective of prudent contracting by providing those responsible for procurement and contract administration with financial information and advice on proposed or existing contracts and contractors. Under the provisions of the directive establishing the audit agency, DoD acquisition and contract administration agencies are required to utilize the audit services of the DCAA to the extent appropriate in connection with the negotiation, administration, and settlement of contract prices or payments that are based on costs (incurred or estimated) or on cost analysis.

Section 15.805-5 of the FAR requires that, when cost or pricing data are required, Contracting Officers request a field pricing report (which may include an audit review by the cognizant audit activity) before negotiating any contract or contract modification resulting from a proposal in excess of $500,000, unless information available to the Contracting Officer is considered adequate to determine the reasonableness of the proposed cost or price.

The DCAA's responsibilities include performing necessary audits for DoD and its procuring agencies, and for other government agencies, and for other government agencies as appropriate, as well as providing accounting and financial advisory services regarding contracts and subcontracts to all DoD components responsible for acquisition and contract administration. The DCAA's principal functions provide for it to

1.   Audit, examine, and/or review contractors' and subcontractors' accounts, records, documents, and other evidence, systems of internal control; and accounting, costing, and general business practices and procedures; and

2.   Examine reimbursement vouchers received directly from contractors and subcontractors, under cost-type contracts, transmitting those vouchers for payment to the cognizant issuing office or, alternatively, issuing DCAA Form 1, "Notice of Costs Suspended and/or Disapproved," with a copy to the cognizant Contracting Officer, with respect to costs claimed, but not considered allowable.

The DCAA's access rights to a contractor's books and records are set forth in standard FAR clauses. Section 52.214-26 applies to the pricing of modifications to sealed-bid contracts when the contract amount is expected to exceed $100,000. By its terms, if the contractor has submitted cost or pricing data in connection with the pricing of any modification to the contract—unless the pricing was based on adequate competition or on established catalog or market prices of commercial items sold in substantial quantities to the general public or was set by law or regulation—the Contracting Officer or a representative who is an an employee of the government shall have the right to examine and audit all books, records, documents and other data of the contractor (including computations and projections) related to negotiation, pricing, or performing the modification in order to evaluate the accuracy, completeness, and currency of the cost or pricing data.

Section 52.215-2 of the FAR applies to negotiated cost reimbursement, incentive labor hour, time and materials, and price redeterminable contracts, or any combination of these, and provides that the contractor shall maintain—and the Contracting Officer or representative of the Contracting Officer shall have the right to examine and audit books, documents, records, and other evidence and accounting procedures and practices sufficient to reflect properly all costs claimed to have been incurred in performing the contract. Both clauses require the retention of records, papers, documents, and associated material for a period of three years following final payment under the contract.

With the establishment of the DoD Inspector General, the DCAA has been assigned new responsibilities, with corresponding authority, with respect to fraud, waste, and abuse cases in federal contracting. At the minimum, it is required to report irregularities to the Inspector General. As a practical matter, the DCAA has become deeply involved in the fraud, waste, and abuse campaign. Indeed, it is responsible for detecting many of the irregulatories that have been uncovered in recent years. On February 12, 1983, in a speech in New Orleans, before the Public Contract Law Section of the American Bar Association, Charles 0. Starrett, Jr., Director, Defense Contract Audit Agency, indicated that his agency had reported 150 irregularity cases to the Inspector General. Of these reports, 75 percent were "audit-detected," and 40 percent were related to time-keeping problems.

During the past several years, the DCAA has aggressively sought to perform "floor audits" in the facilities of many government contractors. During such audits, the DCAA auditors interview individual employees of the contractor to determine the work being performed by the employee, the work order being charged, any instructions concerning time charging given by supervisors, and the employee's view of the accuracy of the time card. In view of the new role of the DCAA, prudent contractors should establish an access management program for DCAA floor audits. As a minimum, the program should provide for (1) obtaining advance notification of the DCAA's intention to conduct a floor audit, (2) designating a company official to escort the DCAA auditor, (3) reviewing and approving the DCAA questionnaires, and (4) restricting the questions to be asked by the DCAA to specific subject areas that relate to the contract(s) that the DCAA is in fact auditing.

As was the case with the GAO, and in spite of its broad authority, the DCAA's powers are not without limitation. If the government agrees to pay a contractor's cost of performance, it also reserves the right to satisfy itself with reasonable certainty what those costs truly are. When a contractor's obligation is to deliver to the government something for a competitively arrived at fixed price, he retains the right to keep his own counsel and strict privacy as to his costs of delivering that item. On the other hand, if a contractor enters into a contract which the government agrees essentially to pay him what it costs him to perform, that contractor has also invited the government into his office to determine what those costs are. Thereafter, a government auditor looks over his shoulder.

The marriage of government auditor and contractor is not easily dissolved. That auditor certainly has no right to roam without restriction through all the contractor's business documents that have no connection with the government contract. But he has a right to satisfy himself as to items claimed to be part of the costs of performing the government contract. When the claim is as to an overhead or indirect cost, there may be some necessity to look at entries other than those for labor, material, and equipment used directly in the performance of the government contract. The courts and Boards conceive of the audit function, when ft applies, as a broad rather than a narrow one. *Grumman Aircraft Engineering Corp.*, ASBCA No. 10309, 66-2 BCA 5846. *Accord American Business Systems,* GSBCA Nos. 5140 & 5141, 80-1 BCA 14,461; *Hayes International Corp.,* ASBCA No. 18447, 75-1 BCA 11,076.

The fundamental purpose of a government audit of a contractor's books and records is to assure that claimed costs were in fact incurred, or are to be incurred, and that they were reasonable. However, the government is not entitled to assume the role of management or to review records and books not associated with or directly related to the public contracts performed, or to be performed, by the contractor. The audit clauses contain broad authority for the government, but they also contain limitations. While the government's auditors have ready access to directly pertinent books, documents, papers, and records that reflect incurred costs on specific public contracts, they have no authority to review purely commercial transactions of the contractor.

United States of America, Plaintiff-Appellant, v. Newport News Shipbuilding and Dry Dock Company, Defendant-Appellee,

No. 88-3520. United States Court of Appeals,
Fourth Circuit. 862 F.2d 464. Decided Dec. 5, 1988.

Before MURNAGHAN, WILKINSON and WILKINS, Circuit Judges.

WILKINSON, Circuit Judge:

This case concerns the scope of the subpoena power of the Defense Contract Audit Agency. DCAA seeks to subpoena the federal income tax returns, financial statements, and supporting schedules of Newport News Shipbuilding and Dry Dock Company, a large defense contractor. Because the order of the district court denying enforcement of the subpoena unduly restricts DCAA's statutory subpoena power, we reverse the order and remand for further proceedings consistent with this opinion.

I.

Newport News Shipbuilding and Dry Dock Company (NNS) is a major defense contractor. A large percentage of NNS's work is performed for the United States government; its business includes the design, construction, repair, and overhaul of vessels for the United States Navy. Much of its work for the Navy is performed under "cost" or "cost-plus" contracts, in which the contract price is based on NNS's cost or its cost plus a fixed fee.

DCAA was established in 1965 as a separate agency in the Department of Defense. DCAA's function is to assist DOD with audits during the negotiation, administration, and settlement of defense contracts. DCAA also provides accounting and financial advisory services to DOD entities responsible for procurement and government contract administration.

DCAA audits defense contractors' books and records in order to establish what constitutes an allowable cost under a particular government contract and federal procurement regulations. See Federal Acquisition Regulation §§31.201- 2, 31.201-3 & 31.201-4, 48 C.F.R. §§31.201-2, 31.201-3 & 31.201-4 (1987). A contractor's total reimbursable cost is the sum of its allowable "direct" and "indirect" costs. A direct cost is one that can be identified with a particular contract. Indirect costs, such as general and administrative overhead, are those that are identified with two or more contracts. The allocation of indirect costs to particular contracts is often a complex process involving sophisticated cost accounting techniques. DCAA performs detailed analyses of a contractor's claimed costs in order to verify their accuracy and to identify unallowable costs. To assist in its responsibilities, DCAA is authorized by statute to inspect the plant and subpoena the books and records of a defense contractor. It is the scope of DCAA's subpoena power that is at issue here.

On February 11, 1987, DCAA issued a subpoena duces tecum to NNS pursuant to 10 U.S.C. §2313(d) demanding:

Trial balance, adjusting entries, segment financial workpapers, consolidating entries, formal consolidated balance sheet and income statement, Federal income tax return, Virginia income tax return and any other supporting schedules, documentation or correspondence related to preparation and issuance of financial statements or preparation or payments of any tax liabilities on a Federal, state or local level for the period 1 January 1983 to the present [.]

NNS furnished the requested state tax returns to DCAA but refused to provide the remainder of the subpoenaed materials. NNS instead filed a declaratory judgment action to have the subpoena declared unlawful and unenforceable. The government moved to dismiss NNS's suit and subsequently petitioned for summary enforcement of the DCAA subpoena. On December 23, 1987, the district court denied enforcement of the subpoena, holding that the subpoenaed materials were not related to cost or pricing data connected to a particular contract, and did not form the basis for costs claimed, or anticipated, in connection with particular contracts. According to the district court, DCAA did not need the subpoenaed materials in order to properly perform its auditing function. The government appeals from this ruling.

Subsequent to the district court's refusal to enforce DCAA's subpoena, this court announced its decision in United States v. Newport News Shipbuilding & Dry Dock Co., 837 F.2d 162 (4th Cir.1988) ("Newport News I "), another subpoena enforcement dispute involving these parties. In that case, DCAA subpoenaed audits conducted by NNS's internal audit department. We affirmed the district court's refusal to enforce the subpoena and held that DCAA's statutory subpoena power extends to objective cost information related to government contracts, but not to all corporate materials such as the internal, subjective evaluations at issue there.

II.

DCAA's statutory subpoena power is set forth in 10 U.S.C. §2313(d)(1), which reads:

The Director of the Defense Contract Audit Agency (or any successor agency) may require by subpoena the production of books, documents, papers, or records of a contractor, access to which is provided to the Secretary of Defense by [§2313(a)] or by section 2306a of this title.

By its terms, §2313(d)(1) authorizes DCAA to subpoena only materials to which it has access under 10 U.S.C. §2313(a) or 10 U.S.C. §2306a. Resolution of this case therefore depends on the construction of these two statutory provisions. See Newport News I, 837 F.2d at 166 n. 2.

Sections 2313(a) and 2306a provide in pertinent part:

§2313.

(a) An agency named in section 2303 of this title is entitled, through an authorized representative, to inspect the plant and audit the books and records of—

(1) a contractor performing a cost or cost-plus-a-fixed-fee contract made by that agency under this chapter; and

(2) a subcontractor performing any subcontract under a cost or cost-plus-a-fixed-fee contract made by that agency under this chapter.

§2306a(f).

(1) For the purpose of evaluating the accuracy, completeness, and currency of cost or pricing data required to be submitted by this section with respect to a contract or subcontract, the head of the agency...shall have the right to examine all records of the contractor or subcontractor related to—

(A) the proposal for the contract or subcontract;

(B) the discussions conducted on the proposal;

(C) pricing of the contract or subcontract; or

(D) performance of the contract or subcontract.

* * *

(3) In this subsection, the term "records" includes books, documents, and other data.

It is pursuant to these statutes that DCAA issued the subpoena giving rise to this dispute.[1]

III.

NNS asserts that DCAA may subpoena materials only if they are used as a basis for determining contract costs or are relied upon in the process of allocating costs to a specific contract. This argument suggests that only cost or pricing data used to calculate costs charged to the government are reviewable by DCAA. Based on our review of the relevant statutes, we reject such a narrow construction of DCAA's auditing function and subpoena authority. We hold that 10 U.S.C. §2313(a) and 10 U.S.C. §2306a(f) provide DCAA access to objective factual materials useful in verifying the actual costs, including general and administrative overhead costs, charged by companies performing cost-type contracts for the government.

The language of 10 U.S.C. §2313(a) and 10 U.S.C. §2306a(f) supports this construction of DCAA's statutory subpoena authority. Section 2313(a), for example, permits DCAA auditors to "inspect the plant and audit the books and records" of a company performing a cost-type contract for the government. A plain reading of the statute suggests that DCAA may review a contractor's financial and cost data. Similarly, §2306a(f)(1) provides DCAA access to all "records" related to the negotiation, administration, or settlement of cost-type contracts where such records are necessary "[f]or the purpose of evaluating the accuracy, completeness, and currency of cost or pricing data" submitted to the government by a defense contractor. The term "records" is defined to include "books, documents, and other data," 10 U.S.C. §2306a(f)(3), and it is plain from the face of the statute that DCAA enjoys access to objective factual information concerning contract costs. No language in the statute limits DCAA's subpoena authority to data actually submitted to the agency or actually relied upon by the contractor in determining contract costs. In fact, DCAA's statutory task of "evaluating the accuracy, completeness, and currency" of submitted data suggests that DCAA is not confined solely to that data in performing its auditing function.

The statutory language, however, is not so conclusive that we can forego an analysis of "the policies underlying the statutory provision to determine its proper scope." Bowsher v. Merck & Co., 460 U.S. 824, 831 n. 7, 103 S.Ct. 1587, 1592 n. 7, 75 L.Ed.2d 580 (1983). The legislative histories of §§2313(a) and 2306a(f) reveal Congress' intent to provide DCAA access to objective financial data to verify the actual costs incurred in the performance of cost-type contracts. Section 2313(a) was enacted as part of the Armed Services Procurement Act of 1947, which was a comprehensive revision and restatement of military procurement law. * * *

The legislative history of §2306a(f) reveals a similar congressional intent. What is now §2306a(f) originally was enacted in 1968 as part of the Truth in Negotiations Act,

---

1. 10 U.S.C. §2306(f)(5) was the predecessor statute to 10 U.S.C. §2306a(f). Congress recodified §2306(f)(5) in 1986, but the statute's content remains unchanged.

Pub.L. No. 90-512, 82 Stat. 863 (September 25, 1968), reprinted in 1968 U.S. Code Cong. Serv. & Admin. News 1003. The Act gave the government the right to examine a defense contractor's records, documents, and other data in order to verify cost and pricing information submitted during the contracting process. See S.Rep. No. 1506, 90th Cong., 2d Sess. (1968), reprinted in 1968 U.S. Code Cong. & Admin. News 3589. Sponsors and supporters of the legislation believed that a "post-award" audit, based on actual contract performance, was the best means of verifying whether cost charges submitted by defense contractors were accurate, current, and complete. Senator Proxmire of Wisconsin, the Senate sponsor of the bill, stated that congressional action on this access-to-records provision made it "unmistakably clear that the Government has full authority to conduct postaudit investigations of a contractor's cost data" in order to verify costs charged to the government. 114 Cong.Rec. 26333 (1968). * * *

DOD regulations implementing §§2313(a) and 2306a(f) reinforce our construction of DCAA's statutory subpoena power. Federal Acquisition Regulation §15.106-2, 48 C.F.R. §15.106-2 (1987), which specifically implements 10 U.S.C. §2313(a), requires that defense contracts contain a clause guaranteeing DCAA access to certain documents. This standard contract clause provides in relevant part that:

> representatives of the Contracting Officer shall have the right to examine and audit — books, records, documents, and other evidence and accounting procedures and practices, sufficient to reflect properly all costs claimed to have been incurred or anticipated to be incurred in performing this contract.

Federal Acquisition Regulation §52.215-2(a), 48 C.F.R. §52.215- 2(a) (1987). Objective data "sufficient to reflect properly all costs claimed" are reviewable by the government, id., and are therefore within the scope of DCAA's statutory subpoena authority. In addition, if a defense contractor is required to submit cost or pricing data to the government, DCAA has the right:

> to examine and audit all books, records, documents, and other data of the Contractor (including computations and projections) related to negotiating, pricing, or performing the contract..., in order to evaluate the accuracy, completeness, and currency of the cost or pricing data.

Federal Acquisition Regulation §52.215-2(b), 48 C.F.R. §52.215- 2(b) (1987). DCAA's right of examination is not limited to cost or pricing data alone; it extends "to all documents necessary to permit adequate evaluation" of cost or pricing data submitted to the government. Id. See also Federal Acquisition Regulation §15.106-2, 48 C.F.R. §15.106-2 (1987) (DOD regulation specifically implementing 10 U.S.C. §2306a(f)).

In sum, the scope of DCAA's statutory subpoena authority is not limited in the manner NNS suggests. Nowhere in §2313(a) or §2306a is DCAA's access to corporate records and documents restricted to those materials actually submitted or relied upon by contractors in calculating their claimed costs. The singular purpose of both statutory grants of subpoena authority was to enable DCAA to evaluate and verify the costs claimed by defense contractors. That purpose is not served, in our judgment, by the most cramped and restrictive reading possible of the statutory text. DCAA may thus subpoena objective factual information for the purpose of verifying costs, including general and administrative overhead costs, associated with being audited by DCAA. The agency performs an important function in the defense procurement system: cost auditing for the purpose of assisting in the negotiation and administration of defense contracts. 32 C.F.R. §357.2 (1987). Cost verification data therefore is the proper subject of a DCAA subpoena. Sections 2313(a) and 2306a(f)(1) are intended to provide DCAA access to objective financial and cost information, contained in a defense contractor's books, records, and other documents, that reflects upon the accuracy of cost charges submitted to the government.

IV.

The scope of DCAA's statutory subpoena authority also must be read against a practical understanding of the defense procurement process and sound auditing practice. Reviewed in this light, we disagree with the district court's conclusion that NNS's federal income tax returns, financial statements, and supporting schedules must fall outside the scope of DCAA's subpoena power.

We have noted that DCAA enjoys access to materials needed for factual verification of general and administrative overhead costs. Newport News I, 837 F.2d at 166. These costs are "indirect" costs and, by definition, cannot be identified with a specific contract. Indirect costs are, however, an allowable component of a contractor's total cost, Federal Acquisition Regulation §§31.201-1 & 31.203, 48 C.F.R. §§31.201-1 & 31.203 (1987), and as such, a defense contractor may allocate them to particular contracts and claim reimbursement for them from the government. DCAA therefore may subpoena objective factual records that reflect upon the accuracy of overhead cost charges submitted to the government.

Federal procurement regulations, for example, allow reimbursement for the reasonable cost of renting or leasing real or personal property required for the performance of a government contract, such as a warehouse for storing contract materials. Federal Acquisition Regulation §31.205-36, 48 C.F.R. §31.205-36 (1987). A defense contractor, however, is entitled to reimbursement only for that part of the warehouse dedicated to the performance of that particular contract. If the defense contractor were to sublease a portion of its warehouse space to an entity unrelated to that particular contract, the overhead cost for the warehouse charged to the government must be offset by any rental income received by the contractor. By reviewing the contractor's financial statements, which should include entries for such rental income, DCAA is better able to verify whether the contractor has properly computed and allocated its overhead costs as required by the contract and federal procurement regulations. The contractor's financial statements afford DCAA a useful method of corroborating overhead cost information submitted to the government.

More generally, a defense contractor's federal tax returns, financial statements, and supporting schedules may be subpoenaed to the extent that they assist DCAA in verifying costs charged under cost-type contracts. It is an essential element of sound auditing practice to obtain sufficient corroborative information to satisfy the auditor that other information upon which he relies is accurate and complete. This principle is, as we have noted, recognized in 10 U.S.C. §2306a(f)(1) which authorizes DCAA to subpoena books, documents, and other objective factual materials that can be used to evaluate the "accuracy, completeness, and currency of cost or pricing data" submitted by a defense contractor.

A defense contractor, for example, must identify and exclude from any claim for government reimbursement all unallowable costs, such as certain bad debt, interest, lobbying, entertainment, public relations, and advertising expenses. Federal Acquisition Regulation §31.201-6, 48 C.F.R. §31.201-6 (1987). See also Federal Acquisition Regulation §31.205, 48 C.F.R. §31.205 (1987) ("Selected Costs"). Federal procurement regulations provide DCAA access to corporate materials in order to verify whether defense contractors have complied with this obligation. Federal Acquisition Regulation §52.230-3, 48 C.F.R. §52.230-3 (1987). A contractor's corporate tax return, for example, would include an entry for advertising expenses because they may be deductible for federal tax purposes. The tax return therefore may be helpful in verifying whether the contractor has identified and excluded its unallowable advertising expenses.

Similarly, the profit realized from a contractor's purchase of materials from a division or subsidiary cannot ordinarily be included in the allowable costs charged the government. Federal Acquisition Regulation §31.205-26(e), 48 C.F.R. §31.205-26(e) (1987). The government contends that cost entries submitted to it may not reveal the amount of profit hidden in the purchase price or the relationship between the companies involved in the transaction. A contractor's tax return, on the other hand, may well disclose the relevant corporate affiliations.

In short, we disagree with the district court's conclusion that the subpoenaed materials are not necessary for DCAA to properly perform its statutory function. First, many of these financial statements are in a readily usable form. Second, some of these statements have a high degree of reliability because they are independently reviewed and the contractor is subject to serious sanctions for supplying incorrect information. See, e.g., 26 U.S.C. §§7201-07 (criminal and civil penalties for supplying incorrect or incomplete federal tax information). Third, a contractor's tax returns and financial statements bear upon the consistency of its costing methods and the reconcilability of costs claimed for tax purposes and costs claimed in contract billings to the government. Fourth, access to these materials may allow DCAA to verify the accuracy of cost information submitted by NNS; it may allow DCAA to corroborate NNS's computation and allocation of direct and indirect costs to particular government contracts. All of these factors are relevant to DCAA's auditing mission. * * *

V.

NNS contends, finally, that the materials subpoenaed by DCAA contain proprietary and business-sensitive information which should remain confidential. To some extent, of course, every auditor seeks information which the subject of the audit regards as confidential, and the audits here are no exception. DCAA's statutory subpoena authority, however, does not confer a privilege of confidentiality with respect to objective financial and cost information. Like other private firms, defense contractors have an interest in maintaining the confidentiality of their corporate materials. Newport News I, 837 F.2d at 170. But a contractor's interest in maintaining the confidentiality of these materials cannot outweigh, in all instances, DCAA's interest in reviewing them. By claiming reimbursement for its contract costs, a defense contractor represents that the costs are reasonable and allocable to a particular contract. DCAA is granted access to defense contractors' books and records; it does not, however, disclose these materials publicly or to the defense contractors' competitors. See, e.g., 32 C.F.R. §§290.20-290.29 (1987) ("Availability of DCAA records"); 32 C.F.R. §286.13(a)(4) (1987) (DOD Freedom of Information Act exemptions).

NNS's claim of confidentiality was more persuasive on the facts of our earlier decision. There we held that the scope of DCAA's statutory subpoena authority did not extend to the subjective assessments of NNS's internal audit staff. Newport News I, 837 F.2d at 170. We recognized that internal audits may "rely for their effectiveness on the candor that confidentiality allows." Id. In contrast, the subpoena at issue here requests production of objective financial and cost data and summaries, not the subjective work product of NNS's internal auditors. To the extent that the materials subpoenaed here would assist DCAA in verifying and evaluating the cost claims of the contractor, they are within the contemplation of DCAA's statutory subpoena authority.

VI.

The district court took too restrictive a view of DCAA's access to defense contractor records. Its blanket refusal to enforce the subpoena impaired DCAA's statutory subpoena power. We are unable to examine each requested document in light of the relevant statutory purposes. We therefore reverse the judgment of the district court and remand for review of DCAA's individual requests in light of the general standards of agency subpoena power and the particular principles set forth herein.

The order of the district court denying enforcement of the subpoena is hereby

REVERSED AND REMANDED.

Notes and Questions

1. The court uses many potential cost accounting disputes to illustrate the need for broad subpoena power. How many disputes did you spot?

2. For a case that proceeds with a much different spirit, see *Bowsher v. Merck*, 460 U.S. 824 (1983). There, a subpoena for government contractor records was rejected. The contractor, a drug company, had a fixed-price negotiated contract with the government, and the auditing authority, the Comptroller General, had statutory authority to inspect records only "directly pertinent" to the contracts in question. How would you distinguish the two cases?

3. This case brings the DCAA into center focus. The DCAA has a large role in government contracting so little understood by outsiders that it has a full-length manual, the DCAA Manual (or "DCAAM") which provides informal guidance in many areas of how government contract law operates in practice - much as an IRS audit manual would provide much informal guidance about tax law in practice. Can you explain the difference between "routine" auditing and investigation?

4. Is it hopelessly wasteful and needlessly adversarial to have government auditors and investigators tasked with thorough scrutiny of the details of cost reimbursement requests? On the other hand, is it an invitation to waste, fraud, and abuse not to give them that task?

5. Potential purveyors of commercial items continue to contend that the burdens associated with audit and investigative mechanisms deter them from selling to the government, while government auditors warn of the dangerous effects of depriving the government of its audit rights. Provisions of FASA merged and consolidated government audit powers, and FARA §4201 abolished executive agency audit powers over contracts for commercial items. However, the General Services Administration Multiple Awards Schedule Program requires an audit clause in all its contracts. For a detailed discussion of the complex collision of commercial sales streamlining, and auditing, see Ron R. Hutchinson, *The Government's Audit and Investigative Powers Over Commercial Item Contracts and Subcontracts*, 27 Pub. Con. L.J. 263 (1998); Richard J. Wall & Christopher B. Pockney, *Revisiting Commercial Pricing Reform*, 27 Pub. Con L.J. 315 (1998).

1. Allowability

The FAR sets forth a number of detailed cost principles for specific contexts: the *Bill Strong Enterprises* case itself describes that there is a list in FAR Subpart 31.2 of 51 such cost principles. They deal with a number of particular issues, from alcoholic beverages (unallowable) to rental costs (allowable, except for sale-and-leaseback charges beyond the costs if the contractor retained title). These detailed cost principles generate a considerable need for legal advice, both for planning and in the event of investigation or disputes.

Bill Strong Enterprises illustrates the diverse historic sources of the cost principles. The opinion's discussion works its way from the regulations before World War II, through a number of successor regulations, to the FAR. Similarly, it works its way through case law and contract board decisions on these issues. Finally, it considers the statutory law, particularly in 1985. In other words, the FAR summarizes the law of allowability, but the law itself is far more complex than the few words in the FAR convey.

The particular cost principle at issue in the *Bill Strong Enterprises* case has its own intrinsic interest. This cost principle concerns disputes with the government, and which costs incurred in connection with them the government should pay. Since lawyers have large roles in the managing of disputes, they have reason to learn just what costs during disputes might ultimately be paid by the government to help them give sound advice about what to spend on a dispute.

Bill Strong Enterprises, Inc., Appellant, v. John Shannon, Acting Secretary of the Army, Appellee

No. 94-1013. United States Court of Appeals, Federal Circuit.
49 F.3d 1541. March 2, 1995.

Before RICH, CLEVENGER, and SCHALL, Circuit Judges.

CLEVENGER, Circuit Judge.

Bill Strong Enterprises, Inc. (BSE) appeals from a decision of the Armed Services Board of Contract Appeals (ASBCA or Board) denying BSE's claim for recovery of consulting costs. Bill Strong Enters., Inc., ASBCA Nos. 42946, 43896, 93-3 BCA ¶ 25,961 (1993). Because the Board misconstrued the applicable regulation, we reverse and remand for further proceedings.

I

On June 18, 1987, the Department of the Army (Government) awarded BSE a fixed-price contract (Contract No. DACA27-87-C-0073) for the renovation of family housing units at Selfridge Air National Guard Base, Mt. Clemens, Michigan. By a letter dated May 26, 1988, BSE notified the Government that houses were being released to it out of sequence, resulting in increased costs of approximately "$300,000 to date" and an estimated $1,500,000 for the entire contract. In a letter to the contracting officer (CO), dated June 9, 1988, BSE requested a final decision regarding the out-of-sequence availability of houses, but the letter did not request monetary relief, nor was it certified. Subsequent letters from the CO to BSE requested itemization of BSE's increased costs and informed BSE that an audit would be necessary.

On May 24, 1989, BSE sent the Government a letter, entitled "Claim against Government." In this letter, BSE alleged that the Government's delay in making the housing units available to BSE increased BSE's cost of performance by $520,001. BSE also alleged that, by consistently releasing the housing units out of sequence, the Government increased BSE's cost of performing the contract by an additional $52,000. In a letter dated

June 6, 1989, the Government requested BSE to submit cost and pricing data with a Standard Form 1141, in accordance with Clause 71 of the contract. On June 14, 1989, BSE supplied the Government with a completed Standard Form 1141. On June 16, 1989, the Government requested the Defense Contract Audit Agency (DCAA) to audit BSE's claims, specifically, the significant discrepancy between the Government's records of the number of houses made available to BSE and the number alleged by BSE. DCAA was also asked to examine BSE's basis for determining its costs due to the out-of-sequence availability of housing units.

Renovation of all housing was completed and accepted by the Government on July 31, 1989.

On September 14, 1989, in response to DCAA's requests for specific cost data and additional information, BSE hired Excell, Inc., a consulting firm, to revise its data for resubmission to the CO.

According to the contract between Excell and BSE, Excell's responsibilities were to review, analyze, and determine the technical and overall merit of issues, develop a specific proposal, and prepare a Request for an Equitable Adjustment (REA) for BSE. The contract further stated that the REA preparation effort was "undertaken with no view toward litigation.... [but was limited] to the pursuit of an administrative remedy." In a letter dated September 28, 1989, BSE notified the Government that BSE's claim needed modification and requested an "immediate abeyance" of its previously submitted May 24 claim, stating that BSE would revise its claim documents.

On November 30, 1989, BSE submitted a revised certified claim, entitled "Request for Equitable Adjustment," for a total amount of $995,568, which included the costs for delay, and included $122,336 (eventually amended to $190,248) in costs for Excell's work in preparing the submittal. * * *

On December 14, 1989, the Government ordered DCAA to audit BSE's November 30, 1989 claim. The DCAA audit report noted that BSE had submitted the revised claim because of DCAA's questions in its preliminary review of the May 24, 1989 claim. DCAA found that, unlike BSE's initial calculation, the calculation by Excell was based upon actual costs and employee time card records. DCAA questioned $529,572 of BSE's alleged substantive cost increase, but did not question the claimed amount for Excell's costs.

On October 26, 1990, the parties reached a settlement in which the Government agreed to pay BSE $290,000 for the delay and out-of-sequence availability costs. The settlement agreement, memorialized in Modification P00019, explicitly excluded the preparation costs BSE paid to Excell. In a memorandum of understanding, the parties agreed that the CO would issue a final decision regarding the recoverability of Excell's fees. The administrative aspects of the contract thus concluded with Modification P00019, executed one year and a half after field work under the contract was completed.

In a March 1, 1991 decision, the CO denied the recovery of Excell's costs incurred in preparing the November 30, 1989 submission. The CO found that the Government had acknowledged the shortage of unit availability and had discussed with BSE "that it recognized partial merit for the issues of lack of available units and the issuance of houses out of the specified sequence." The CO emphasized, however, that the Excell claim preparation was performed after the completion of the contract work and was consequently "not incurred in connection with the actual performance of the work." BSE appealed this final decision to the Board.

II

* * *

In a 3-2 split decision, the Board affirmed the CO's decision. The majority of the Board found that, at the time of BSE's November 30, 1989 submission, the Government did dispute the amount claimed by BSE. The Board held that, under FAR 31.205-33(d), BSE's consultant costs were "unallowable" because they were "incurred in the 'prosecution of claims…against the Government.'" * * * * [1]

* * * On October 10, 1993, BSE appealed the Board's decision to this court.

IV

* * *

A

The 1987 regulation at issue in this case resides in Part 31 of the FAR (48 C.F.R. §§31.000-.703 (1987)), which is entitled, "Contract Cost Principles and Procedures." FAR 31.204(a) states that "[c]osts shall be allowed to the extent they are reasonable, allocable, and determined to be allowable under 31.201, 31.202, 31.203, and 31.205." Section 31.205 is entitled "Selected costs" and contains fifty-one provisions governing the allowability of fifty-one different categories of costs. Section 31.205-33, entitled "Professional and consultant service costs," is the relevant regulation in this case. Section 31.205-33(a) states that costs of professional and consultant services are allowable, in general, subject to the exceptions in paragraphs (b), (c), (d), and (e). Section 31.205-33(d) provides that "[c]osts of legal, accounting, and consultant services…incurred in connection with…the prosecution of claims or appeals against the Government (see 33.201) are unallowable." The cross-referenced section 33.201 is in the "Disputes and Appeals" part of the FAR and defines a "claim" to mean

> [a] written demand or written assertion by one of the contracting parties seeking, as a matter of right, the payment of money in a sum certain, the adjustment or interpretation of contract terms, or other relief arising under or relating to the contract. A claim arising under a contract, unlike a claim relating to that contract, is a claim that can be resolved under a contract clause that provides for the relief sought by the claimant. However, a written demand or written assertion by the contractor seeking the payment of money exceeding $50,000 is not a claim under the Contract Disputes Act of 1978 until certified as required by the Act and 33.207. A voucher, invoice, or other routine request for payment that is not in dispute when submitted is not a claim. The submission may be converted to a claim, by written notice to the contracting officer… if it is disputed either as to liability or amount or is not acted upon in a reasonable time.

In order to advance the interpretation of these regulations, we pause to examine their historical roots. Prior to World War II, the Treasury, War, and Navy Departments

---

1. FAR 31.205-33(d) states in full: Costs of legal, accounting, and consultant services and directly associated costs incurred in connection with organization and reorganization (see also 31.205-27), defense of antitrust suits, defense against Government claims or appeals, or the prosecution of claims or appeals against the Government (see 33.201) are unallowable (but see 31.205-47).

promulgated regulations classifying expenses incident to and necessary for the performance of a government contract. One of those regulations stated:

> Among the items which shall not be included as a part of the cost of performing a contract or subcontract or considered in determining such cost, are the following:... legal and accounting fees in connection with... the prosecution of claims against the United States (including income tax matters);....

T.D. 5000, 1940-2 C.B. 397, 407; see Robert Braucher & Covington Hardee, Cost-Reimbursement Contracts With the United States, 5 Stan.L.Rev. 4, 14–15 (1952). This regulation suggests an expansive scope of the phrase "claims against the United States." Then, in 1949, the Armed Services Procurement Regulations were promulgated and provided that legal, accounting, and consulting services were allowable costs except when "incurred in connection with... the prosecution of claims against the United States." See 14 Fed.Reg. 683, 684 (Feb. 16, 1949). From 1949 until 1983, the language of this regulation remained virtually unchanged. See 32 C.F.R. §15.205-31 (1960); 32 C.F.R. §15.205-31 (1983). In 1983, the Federal Acquisition Regulations were established, and these regulations adopted the same language concerning the allowability of costs of legal, accounting, and consulting services. See 48 Fed.Reg. 42,102, 42,322 (Sept. 19, 1983); 48 C.F.R. §31.205-33 (1984). Also, the newly-established FAR defined, for the first time, the term "claim" as it is set out above. See 48 Fed.Reg. at 42,349; 48 C.F.R. §33.001 (1984). The language in both of these regulations remained unchanged until new language was promulgated in 1986, and that language appeared in the 1987 version of the Code of Federal Regulations as FAR 31.205- 33(d).

In applying the regulations of this period between 1949 and 1986, the ASBCA inconsistently interpreted the language concerning the allowability of legal, accounting, and consulting costs. On the one hand, several Board decisions denied recovery of such costs. * * * On the other hand, a number of Board decisions permitted recovery of legal or consulting costs. * * *

The Court of Claims also addressed the allowability of legal and consulting costs. In Singer Co. v. United States, 215 Ct.Cl. 281, 568 F.2d 695 (1977), the contractor sought recovery of attorney and technical consultant fees incurred in connection with the preparation and documentation of its claims for equitable adjustment that it presented to the CO. Id. 568 F.2d at 720. The court distinguished the Allied Materials decision by noting that, in Allied Materials, Government liability was not disputed and the REA occurred in the midstream of contract performance. Id. at 721. In denying recovery of the costs, the Singer court stated:

> [T]he claims for equitable adjustment were not presented to the contracting officer until all work had been completed, they addressed no situation in which Government liability was clear or apparent and, in content, they offered nothing that could reasonably be considered as benefiting the contract purpose. Judged both from the standpoint of the time of their submission and the purpose of their submission, [the contractor's] requests for equitable adjustment were not performance-related; they bore no beneficial nexus either to contract production or to contract administration.

Id. * * *[2]

---

2. . See Melvin Rishe, Government Contract Costs 20-16 (1st ed. 1983); 2 Nash & Cibinic Report ¶24, at 63 (Apr.1988); Richard J. Bednar, et al., Construction Contracting 781 (1991); John Cibinic, Jr. & Ralph C. Nash, Jr., Cost-Reimbursement Contracting 828 (2d ed. 1993).

It was within this context that Congress passed the Defense Procurement Improvement Act of 1985, Pub.L. No. 99-145, §911, 99 Stat. 583, 682 (codified at 10 U.S.C. §2324 (1988 & Supp. V 1993)). The Act specified that penalties would be assessed against a Government defense contractor that claimed an unallowable cost in a submitted proposal for settlement of indirect costs. 10 U.S.C. 2324(a)-(d). The Act also directed the Secretary of Defense to promulgate regulations prescribing specific categories of unallowable costs. Id. §2324(e). Finally, the Act ordered the Secretary of Defense to clarify the FARs concerning the allowability and unallowability of a different set of categories of costs:

> The Secretary shall prescribe proposed regulations to amend those provisions of the Department of Defense Supplement to the Federal Acquisition Regulation dealing with the allowability of contractor costs. The amendments shall define in detail and in specific terms those costs which are unallowable, in whole or in part, under covered contracts. These regulations shall, at a minimum, clarify the costs principles applicable to contractor costs of the following:

> * * *

> (H) Professional and consulting services, including legal services.

Id. §2324(f)(1) (emphasis added).

Although the Conference Report accompanying the Act does not elaborate on the requirement to clarify the cost principles of allowable and unallowable costs, see S.Rep. No. 118, 99th Cong., 1st Sess. 447-50 (1985), reprinted in 1985 U.S.C.C.A.N. 472, 601-04, a House Report accompanying an earlier version of the bill casts significant light on the subject. See H.R.Rep. No. 169, 99th Cong., 1st Sess. 11–13 (1985). That Report states:

> Although the committee expects the department to review and revise all cost principles as appropriate, 14 specific cost principles which have been the subject of numerous disputes in the past must be clarified.

> ...In order to eliminate ambiguity and doubt, the revised regulations are to define unallowable costs in detail and in specific terms.

Id. at 11-12. Congress thus instructed the Department of Defense to clarify the unsettled and confused cost principles concerning the allowability of certain costs, including legal and consulting costs, and to define the specific categories of costs that are unallowable.

In response to this congressional mandate, the Department of Defense and the General Services Administration amended the FAR. See 50 Fed.Reg. 51,778, 51,778 (Dec. 19, 1985) (notice of proposed rule-making). The relevant portion of FAR 31.205-33 was changed to make unallowable the costs incurred in defense against Government claims or appeals and the costs incurred in the prosecution of appeals against the Government. See 51 Fed.Reg. 12,296, 12,298 (Apr. 9, 1986) (final rule). According to the agencies, this change would assure consistent treatment of the costs in FAR 31.205-33. 51 Fed.Reg. at 12,298. Also, the amendment to FAR 31.205-33 added, without comment, the cross- reference "(see 33.201)" after the phrase, "the prosecution of claims or appeals against the Government." See 51 Fed.Reg. at 12,301.

We hold that, by referring specifically to FAR 33.201, the amended cost principle of FAR 31.205-33 recognized the word "claim" as a term of art, the meaning of which is set forth in FAR 33.201. See, e.g., Bos'n Towing & Salvage Co., ASBCA No. 41357, 92-2 BCA ¶ 24,864, at 124,034 (1992). Thus, the revised regulation, in response to the congressional directive, provides for a specific, clear, bright-line test for unallowability: a legal, accounting, or consulting cost incurred in connection with the prosecution of a CDA claim or an appeal against the Government is per se unallowable.[3]

Our interpretation of the term "claim" in FAR 31.205-33 thus promotes uniformity and clarity in the FAR. Our conclusion is further supported by the fact that the revisions to FAR 31.205-33 included, for the first time, costs incurred in connection with appeals against the Government, which can only be brought after a contractor has made a 33.201 "claim" against the Government. Accordingly, the alternative holding in the Board's majority decision, stating that the requirements for a "claim against the Government" under FAR 31.205-33 are different from the CDA requirements for a "claim" for jurisdictional purposes, is an incorrect interpretation of the regulations.

B

Our next step in analyzing FAR 31.201-33 is to interpret what is meant by "incurred in connection with the prosecution of a [CDA] claim against the Government." We note that there are at least three distinct categories of legal, accounting, and consultant costs in the contract cost principles: (1) costs incurred in connection with the work performance of a contract; (2) costs incurred in connection with the administration of a contract; and (3) costs incurred in connection with the prosecution of a CDA claim. Since Congress demanded that the regulations state specifically what costs are unallowable and since the regulations only make the third category of costs unallowable, costs that fall within the first and second categories are presumptively allowable if they are also reasonable and allocable. See 48 C.F.R. §31.204(a) (1987). Moreover, costs incurred in connection with contract performance or contract administration should ordinarily be recoverable because they normally "benefit[ ] the contract purpose," see Singer, 568 F.2d at 721, and "reimbursement of [these costs is] in the best interest of the United States." See H.R.Rep. No. 169, supra, at 12. Benefit to the contract purpose, whether in its work performance or administration, is therefore a prerequisite for allowability.

To assess allowability of a cost, the particular cost must be classified into a particular category. Costs that are incidental to contract performance are easily discernable and usually pose no problem. However, the line between costs that are incidental to contract administration and costs that are incidental to prosecution of contract claims is rather indistinct, see 2 Nash & Cibinic Report, supra, ¶24, at 63, and in need of clarification.

In the practical environment of government contracts, the contractor and the CO usually enter a negotiation stage after the parties recognize a problem regarding the contract. The contractor and the CO labor to settle the problem and avoid litigation. Although there is sometimes an air of adversity in the relationship between the CO and the contractor, their efforts to resolve their differences amicably reflect a mutual desire to achieve a result acceptable to both. This negotiation process often involves requests for information by the CO or Government auditors or both, and, inevitably, this exchange of information involves costs for the contractor. These costs are contract administration costs, which should be allowable since this negotiation process benefits the Government, regardless of whether a settlement is finally reached or whether litigation

---

3. . We note that this holding does not pertain to consulting costs incurred in settlement of claims made when a contract is terminated for the convenience of the Government. Such situations are governed by a separate regulation and separate case law, under which such costs are generally allowable. See 48 C.F.R. §31.205-42(g) (1987); Acme Process Equip. Co. v. United States, 171 Ct.Cl. 251, 347 F.2d 538, 544–45 (1965); Baifield Indus., ASBCA No. 20006, 76-2 BCA ¶ 12,096, at 58,102-04 (1976); see also Rishe, supra note 5, at 6-57, 20-10, 20-15.

eventually occurs because the availability of the process increases the likelihood of settlement without litigation. See 48 C.F.R. §33.204 (1987) ("It is the Government's policy to try to resolve all contractual issues by mutual agreement at the contracting officer's level, without litigation.") Additionally, contractors would have a greater incentive to negotiate rather than litigate if these costs of contract administration were recoverable. See 7 Nash & Cibinic Report, supra, ¶ 48, at 134–35.

In classifying a particular cost as either a contract administration cost or a cost incidental to the prosecution of a claim, contracting officers, the Board, and courts should examine the objective reason why the contractor incurred the cost. See Singer, 568 F.2d at 721 (judging the "purpose" of the contractor's submission). If a contractor incurred the cost for the genuine purpose of materially furthering the negotiation process, such cost should normally be a contract administration cost allowable under FAR 31.205-33, even if negotiation eventually fails and a CDA claim is later submitted. See Armada, 84-3 BCA ¶ 17,694, at 88,242-43. On the other hand, if a contractor's underlying purpose for incurring a cost is to promote the prosecution of a CDA claim against the Government, then such cost is unallowable under FAR 31.205-33.

C

Applying the foregoing discussion to the issues in the present case, we find that the majority opinion of the Board is flawed. First, as discussed above, the Board erred by holding that the cost principle in FAR 31.205-33 does not involve the same requirements for a claim under the CDA as set forth in this court's decisions in Dawco and Transamerica. As we held above, the definition of a "claim" under FAR 31.205-33 is the same as the definition of a claim for purposes of establishing jurisdiction under the CDA.

Second, the Board majority also erred in concluding that BSE submitted a CDA claim. As the majority correctly states, the May 24, 1989 submission was not a formal CDA claim because the Government did not at that time dispute BSE's assertion of a right to increased compensation. Nor did the situation ever ripen into a dispute. The Government never challenged BSE's assertion of its right, and the Government had even recognized that there was "partial merit" to BSE's contention that the houses were being issued out of the specified sequence. In the time period between the May 24, 1989 submission and the November 30, 1989 submission, the parties were in a negotiation posture. The Government was conducting an audit and requested more information from BSE to help analyze BSE's request. This exchange of information is exactly what is encompassed in the concept of contract administration. * * *

Third, the Board majority also erred by classifying BSE's consultant costs as costs incurred in connection with the prosecution of a CDA claim under FAR 31.205-33. Since a CDA claim did not arise before BSE incurred Excell's costs, there is a strong legal presumption that the costs incurred were not incurred in connection with the prosecution of such a claim against the Government. Since BSE and the Government were consistently in a negotiation posture and since the consultant costs were incurred as part of the exchange of information, the facts demonstrate that BSE hired Excell for the purpose of promoting contract administration and that BSE incurred Excell's costs in order to further a negotiation process that benefitted the Government. Thus, as discussed above, these costs are not unallowable under FAR 31.205-33.

Finally, under the factual circumstances of this case, the Board majority erred in holding that the consulting costs were unallowable because they were incurred after the contract work performance was completed. First, in delay cases such as this, the contractor cannot calculate the additional expenses caused by the Government's delay until completion of the contract work. Thus, BSE's calculations prepared with Excell's assistance understandably awaited completion of the contract work. In addition, contract administration may continue, as it did in this case, after completion of contract work.

We are not, however, able simply to reverse with instructions to award BSE the contested sum. Neither the CO nor the Board made a determination regarding the reasonableness and allocability of these costs. Consequently, we remand this case with instructions to find the consultant costs allowable to the extent those costs were reasonable and allocable.[4]

V

For these reasons, the decision of the Board is reversed and the case is remanded with instructions.

REVERSED AND REMANDED.

Notes and Questions

1. If you were counsel to Bill Strong Enterprises all the way through this case, which of your legal bills would the government pay?

2. Note how the legal issue of the allowability of these costs took a turn when Congress passed the Defense Procurement Improvement Act of 1985 requiring clarification of the allowability of many categories of costs, including these. During the military buildup of the 1980s, massive spending was followed by charges of significant abuse. Audits provided such examples as charges to government contracts for babysitting, kennel fees, jewelry, country club fees, and even a case in which expenditures for bribery of procurement officials were submitted for reimbursement as part of the cost of securing the contract. Some criticized high costs assigned to particular contract items (e.g. a $44 light bulb; $7,622 for a coffee maker; and perhaps most memorably, $640 for a toilet seat cover). Among the legislative responses was the Defense Procurement Improvement Act of 1985, Title IX of the Defense Authorization Act for 1986, Pub. L. 99-145, 99 Stat 699 (1985). See generally *Sundstrand Corp. v. Commissioner*, 98 T.C. 518 (1992); *United States v. Sperry Corporation and UNISYS Corporation*, No. 91 Cr. 00355 (E.D. Va. 1991); Michael S. McGarry, *Winning the War on Procurement Fraud: Victory at What Price?*, 26 CLMJLSP 249 (1993); Richard R. Kaesar, *Major Defense Acquisition Programs: A Study of Congressional Control Over DoD Acquisitions*, 34 Fed. Bar. N.J. 430 (1987); Dennis L. Phillips and Raymond M. Saunders, *Multiyear Contracts for Major Systems*, 22 Pub. Con. L.J. 161 (1993); Remarks of Rep. Gonzalez, 133 Cong. Rec. H6152-04 (daily ed. July 9, 1987).

3. Note that costs incurred in resolving a termination for convenience are allowable, while costs incurred in resolving other types of claim are not. The opinion plays down the element that the government would not want to fund the costs of pumping up the expenditures on consultants and lawyers to fight it. Why would that be a significant interest?

4. The opinion says the line between costs for negotiation and costs for prosecuting a claim is "rather indistinct." Suppose a contractor uses alternative dispute resolution

---

4. We note that at the time of the appeal to this court, BSE and Excell were engaged in litigation in state court concerning the reasonableness of Excell's fees.

with his contracting officer: preparing for mediation, for example, to make the negotiation more effective, or hiring an independent-minded "special counsel" to sort out internally some of its own dubious contractor practices. Allowable?

5. For a discussion, see Stephanie M. Himel-Nelson, *Recovery of Legal Expenses as Costs of Government Contract Administration*, The Procurement Lawyer, Fall 2001, at 13.

2. Allocability and Reasonableness

Cost Principles: Reasonableness and Allocability

From: Government Contract Guidebook Donald P. Arnavas & William J. Ruberry (Federal Publications Inc. 2d ed. (1994))

* * *

Reasonableness

The criteria set forth to determine whether a cost is "reasonable" for purposes of allowability are somewhat vague and subjective. The FAR provides that a "cost is reasonable if, in its nature and amount, it does not exceed that which would be incurred by a prudent person in the conduct of competitive business."

A contractor's incurred costs are not presumed to be reasonable but must be proved reasonable by the contractor. The presumption of reasonableness previously established by case law was abolished by regulation in 1987. This rule applies also to estimates of future costs (or unidentifiable costs), where the contractor also has the legal burden of establishing the reasonableness of its estimate. Neither the Government's nor the contractor's estimate is entitled to a presumption in its favor.

A second key concept in determining reasonableness is that the Government will not be allowed to engage in "second guessing" the contractor's judgment. It is the contractor's judgment that is considered, not that of the Government or of some hypothetical (and extremely efficient) contractor. Therefore, it is not enough for the Government to say that the costs should have or could have been expended in a different (or more advantageous) manner. As long as the contractor's decision involves the use of reasonable judgment, that judgment will not be overruled.

As a practical matter, the Government has had relatively little success in disallowing costs solely on the basis of unreasonableness. Where it has been successful, the Government has established that the contractor abused its discretion, such as where a contractor retained a large, unproductive work force for longer than was prudent under the circumstances, and where a contractor incurred excessive promotional costs with regard to the preparation of an unsolicited proposal. Most frequently, however, the Government will not be able to have a cost deemed unreasonable on the basis of the contractor's judgmental decision. The concept of reasonableness (as it applies to cost-reimbursement contracts) was summed up by the Armed Services Board of Contract Appeals as follows:

The contracting officer's function is not that of a boss over the contractor, telling him what he can and cannot buy, whom he shall employ and how much he is allowed to pay employees. True, the contract bestows upon the contracting officer the authority to disapprove for reimbursement the costs involved in the contractor's performance, but unless he is able to demonstrate that the contractor's acts, or the costs he incurs, violate the terms of the contract or the guides found in (the cost principles), it is the contracting officer's duty to approve the contractor's acts and to approve the costs thereof for reimbursement.

A Contracting Officer may attempt to eliminate the need for reasonableness determinations by including a requirement in the contract that his approval be obtained before a cost is incurred by the contractor. However, unless specifically called for by the contract, such prior approval is not required. Moreover, Government attempts to control costs through this device have not been successful because the Government must specify and justify the basis for refusing approval.

Allocability

As indicated above, "allocability" is a factor listed in FAR Subpart 31.2 for determining allowability. In its simplest terms, allocation of costs is the process of assigning costs to cost objectives. The FAR cost principles contain the following definition of allocability:

A cost is allocable if it is assignable or chargeable to one or more cost objectives on the basis of relative benefits received or other equitable relationship. Subject to the foregoing, a cost is allocable to a Government contract if it—

Is incurred specifically for the contract;

Benefits both the contract and other work, and can be distributed to them in reasonable proportion to the benefits received; or

(c)   Is necessary to the overall operation of the business, although a direct relationship to any particular cost objective cannot be shown.

In determining questions of allocability, it is always necessary to assess whether an allowable cost should be charged as a direct cost or as an indirect cost. The FAR defines a *direct cost* as "any cost that can be identified specifically with a particular final cost objective. The provision goes on to say that costs "identified specifically with the contract are direct costs of the contract and are to be charged directly to the contract," and that "[a]ll costs specifically identified with other final cost objectives of the contractor are direct costs of those cost objectives and are not to be charged to the contract directly or indirectly."

In accordance with this definition, costs that are incurred for materials, labor, or other purposes that are clearly necessary for performance of a particular contract are direct costs of the contract. Even if a cost expenditure should eventually be determined to have been unnecessary for contract performance, it will nonetheless be allocable as a direct charge if the contractor reasonably believed it was necessary when it made the decision to incur the cost. The legal test is sometimes referred to as the "but for" test (i.e., would the cost have been incurred but for the existence of the contract).

The FAR also defines an *indirect cost* as "one not directly identified with a single, final cost objective, but identified with two or more final cost objectives or an intermediate cost objective." The provision requires that "[i]ndirect costs shall be accumulated by logical cost groupings with due consideration of the reasons for incurring such costs," and advises that "[c]ommonly, manufacturing overhead, selling expenses, and general and administrative (G&A) expenses are separately grouped."

Cost allocations are essentially a function of the contractor's own accounting system. In this regard, it is clear that selection of an accounting system is the prerogative of the contractor's management, as long as the system follows generally accepted accounting principles and the Cost Accounting Standards (if they apply). The Government, accordingly, may not disturb a contractor's otherwise proper method of keeping its books solely in order to obtain a financial advantage. For the Government to require a change in a contractor's accounting system, it must either direct the change prospectively, pursuant to a statute or regulation, or show that the contractor's system is clearly inequitable.

3. Cost Accounting Standards

Cost Accounting Standards

From: Government Contract Guidebook Donald P. Arnavas & William J. Ruberry (Federal Publications Inc. 2d ed. (1994))

In 1970, Congress passed a statute that provided for the establishment of the Cost Accounting Standards Board (CAS Board). The statute directed the Board to devise cost accounting standards that would achieve uniformity and consistency in the cost accounting practices followed by prime contractors and subcontractors in estimating, accumulating, and reporting costs under certain negotiated prime and subcontract procurements. In addition, the CAS Board was directed to prepare regulations requiring contractors—as a condition of contracting with the Government—to (1) disclose in writing their cost accounting practices and (2) agree to a contract price adjustment in the event of noncompliance with applicable Cost Accounting Standards or inconsistent adherence to disclosed cost accounting practices.

The CAS Board carried out its mission with vigor, promulgating regulations establishing a number of individual Standards (which are collectively referred to as the Cost Accounting Standards) and requirements for contractor disclosure statements and contract price adjustments. The Board also promulgated regulations covering its own administration.

As the result of legislation enacted late in 1988, a new, independent CAS Board was created. This legislation provides that all Standards, interpretations, modifications, rules, regulations, waivers, and exemptions promulgated by the first CAS Board "remain in effect unless and until amended, superseded or rescinded by the new Board," and gives the new Board exclusive authority to promulgate, amend, interpret, and rescind Cost Accounting Standards. The new Board is composed of the Administrator of the Office of Federal Procurement Policy, one representative each from the DOD and the General Services Administration, and two private sector members.

The CAS Board has promulgated a recodified set of rules and Cost Accounting Standards. Where the CAS and FAR cost allocability provisions conflict, the CAS have been held to govern.

1. Applicability

The CAS Board's Cost Accounting Standards and regulations apply to both defense and nondefense negotiated prime and subcontracts over $500,000.

Implementation of the CAS and contractor disclosure requirements are accomplished by including a notice in solicitations and a "Cost Accounting Standards" clause in contracts. Thus a prospective offeror will be advised in the solicitation as to whether or not the particular contract is subject to the CAS Board's requirements.

a. **Exemptions & Waiver.** The following categories of contracts and subcontracts are generally *exempt* from all CAS requirements sealed bid contracts; negotiated contracts not exceeding $500,000; contracts with small businesses, foreign governments, or their agents; contracts where the price is set by law or regulation or is based on established catalog or market prices of commercial items sold in substantial quantities to the general public; fixed-price contracts or subcontracts (without cost incentives) for commercial items; contracts with educational institutions other than those to be performed by Federally Funded Research and Development Centers; contracts awarded to labor surplus area set-asides; certain contracts to be executed and performed outside the U.S.; and firm-fixed-price contracts and subcontracts awarded without submission of any cost data.

In some instances, all or part of the CAS Board's Standards and requirements may be *waived* for a particular contractor or subcontractor. Generally, to obtain a waiver, the Contracting Officer (not the contractor) must demonstrate that the proposed contractor or subcontractor refused to accept a contract containing all or part of the CAS and that it is impractical to obtain the materials, supplies, or services from. Any other source.

b. **Types Of Coverage.** There are two types of CAS coverage, — "full" and "modified." *Full* coverage applies to any contractor business unit that (a) receives a single CAS-covered contract or subcontract of $25 million or more or (b) received $25 million or more in net CAS-covered awards during its preceding cost accounting period, of which at least one award exceeded $1 million. A contractor subject to full coverage must follow all of the Cost Accounting Standards.

A business unit that receives a covered contract of less than $25 million may elect modified CAS coverage if (1) the-covered contracts that it was awarded in the immediately preceding cost accounting period totaled less than $25 million, or (2) it did not receive at least one CAS-covered contract that exceeded $1 million. Modified coverage requires that the business unit comply with CAS 401, CAS 402, CAS 405, and CAS 406 (see Section B.4 below).

2. Contractor Obligations

The "Cost Accounting Standards" clause must be inserted in contracts subject to full coverage of the Cost Accounting Standards. The clause requires contractors to do all of the following:

(1) Disclose in writing their cost accounting practices through completion of a "Disclosure Statement."

(2) Follow their disclosed practices consistently in estimating, accumulating, and reporting costs.

(3) Comply with all of the individual Cost Accounting Standards in effect on the contract award date.

(4) Agree to an adjustment of the contract price when the contractor fails to comply with existing Standards or its own disclosed practices.

Besides implementing the substantive content of the law, the "Cost Accounting Standards" clause also establishes the *price adjustment* procedure to be followed for adjusting a contract whenever a contractor departs from basic CAS policy by making an accounting change. The clause identifies several types of adjustments in various provisions. One provision permits an upward adjustment in contract price only when a new Standard is issued that has the effect of increasing the cost of a previously-awarded covered contract. Another requires downward adjustment, if appropriate, pursuant to a "voluntary" accounting change by the contractor, but does not permit upward adjustment. A third provision entitles the contractor to an adjustment for a "voluntary" accounting change, without regard to increased costs to the Government, if the Contracting Officer finds the change to be "desirable" and "not detrimental to the interests of the Government." Finally, a fourth provision deals with the consequences of a failure to comply with the Standards or disclosed accounting practices, whether intentional or inadvertent. This liability is equal to the amount of the increased costs paid by the Government as a result of noncompliance.

3. Disclosure Statements

a. **Requirements.** Unless exempted from filing requirements, a contractor covered by the Cost Accounting Standards is obligated to file a "Disclosure Statement"—a written description of the contractor's cost accounting practices and procedures. As indicated above, the "Cost Accounting Standards" clause for full-coverage contracts covers this requirement. Specifically, the contractor shall:

> By submission of a Disclosure Statement, disclose in writing the Contractor's cost accounting practices...including methods of distinguishing direct costs from indirect costs and the basis used for allocating indirect costs. The practices disclosed for this contract shall be the same as the practices currently disclosed and applied on all other contracts and subcontracts being performed by the Contractor and which contain a Cost Accounting Standards (CAS) clause. If the Contractor has notified the Contracting Officer that the Disclosure Statement contains trade secrets and commercial or financial information which is privileged and confidential, the Disclosure Statement shall be protected and shall not be released outside of the Government.

There are certain Government responsibilities regarding Disclosure Statements. After including an appropriate notice in the solicitation for a proposed contract to indicate that the contract is subject to CAS Board requirements, the Contracting Officer must ensure that offerors submit required Disclosure Statements. The appropriate Government auditor is designated to conduct an initial review of Disclosure Statements. Thereafter, the cognizant Administrative Contracting Officer determines whether a Statement is adequate and notifies the contractor in case of any deficiency.

Notes and Questions

1. Note the comprehensive, integrated system by which the government applies cost accounting standards. By statute, Congress created the cost accounting system. Regulations provide for CAS coverage and exemptions. Contractors must submit a CAS Disclosure Statement form describing the practices. Contracting Officers include CAS clauses in the contracts. What can a commercial contractor, which may make only a small fraction of its sales to the government on CAS-covered contracts, do to comply with CAS and yet not have to redo the whole company's accounting system?

2. Contractor desire to be rid of interference with their accounting has called the continuing existence of the Cost Accounting Standards Board into question from time to time. For an account of one such debate, see Charles Tiefer & Danielle Brian, "Grab-

bing for the Purse Strings: Defense Contractors Take Aim At a Critical Accounting Watchdog," *Legal Times of Washington*, August 10, 1998, at 19.

Chapter 5

Contract Administration

In the specialized field of government contracting, much public attention is, by necessity and design, focused on the solicitation and contract award process. The actual administration of the contract receives much less public attention. Nevertheless, one must not lose sight of the fact that the government spends all those billions of federal dollars annually on government contracts to produce tangible benefit to the government, which thus makes the administration of those contracts of considerable importance and value.

This chapter begins with a section on the government contracting officer's discretion and the related issue of interpretation of the contracts. The role of the government contracting officer in the contract administration process cannot be overestimated. At the same time, contractors can, and do, interpret contracts differently than contracting officers. Contract interpretation issues involve a number of considerations such as the application of *contra proferentum*, a canon of interpretation with particular applicability in government contracts because most of their language is drafted by the government.

Next, the chapter addresses the related topics of specifications, inspections and warranty. Typically, contract specifications describe the work that the contractor undertakes to do, thus having critical importance in the administration of the contract. Conversely, the contractor relies, and legitimately so, on some of what the government tells the contractor in the specifications, such as the implied feasibility of prescribed work procedures. As the contract goes forward and the contractor completes work, the government will inspect that work, and the duties and rights bound up with such government inspection have a major role in contract administration. So, too, do the warranties that the contractor provides the government regarding the work.

Another section of the chapter addresses the specialized topic of technical data and other intellectual property rights. Some contractor work involves patents, copyrights, technical data, and other intellectual property. In fact, the main point of some contracts, such as contracts to perform research, may involve the development of new intellectual property. The government has certain policies worth study regarding such matters as what rights the government and the contractor have regarding such property.

A last section deals with the complexly interrelated subjects of progress payments, prompt payment, and other government assistance. The government might wish to pay contractors only when work has been done, and indeed, some time later when bureaucratic procedures have been completed. Yet, contractors may need progress payments during the course of their work, and even when they only get payment when the work is done, they have a statutorily-protected interest in prompt payment as soon as they submit a proper invoice. The government also provides other assistance, such as types of property contractors may need for their work.

A. Contracting Officer Discretion and Interpretation

As noted, the role of the government contracting officer in the contract administration process cannot be overestimated. Of course, the government contracting officer can receive assistance, comments, and recommendations from numerous other government officials interested in contract performance, such as program managers and technical representatives, auditors, budgeters, and attorneys. Nevertheless, it is the government contracting officer alone who is the focal point with the appropriate authority for addressing and resolving contract administration issues.

The first case in this section, *Ensign-Bickford*, illustrates the scope of contracting officer discretion in a unique way. In that case's peculiar facts, quite identical contracts got awarded to two contractors (one of them being the Ensign-Bickford Company), each supervised by a different contracting officer unaware of how the identical other contract was being handled. As each contract got accelerated and thereby elicited contractor claims for higher payment, administration of the two identical contracts took radically different tacks. One contract was audited, and the government ultimately provided only a relatively small adjustment ($16,500); the other contracting officer's representative negotiated a generous settlement with the contractor, and when the government later sought only to pay a low adjustment, it had to pay a high one ($41,651). The case illustrates the wide discretionary range by which different contracting officers administer identical contracts.

As is the case with contracts between private entities, there are numerous areas that are subject to possible dispute between the contractor performing the work and the entity intended to receive the benefit, in this instance, the government. As a result, interpreting the intent of the contracting parties is of critical importance in resolving any such disputes.

Of considerable aid in such conflict resolution is the fact that government contracts are most often reduced to writing with numerous and detailed contract clauses that govern many aspects of performance. Both standard government clauses found in the Federal Acquisition Regulation and its supplements as well as clauses drafted by individual agencies and buying offices responsible for particular specialized areas, (e.g., information technology acquisition or real property construction), create a focused body of law on the responsibility of each party during contract performance. However, given the very wide variety of goods, property, and services purchased by the government as well as the often unique needs of government customers, the courts must rely on many of the same contract interpretation rules used at common law for discerning the intent of the parties when a dispute arises.

Although the occasional clear and unambiguous breach by one party or the other will arise in government contracting, it is far more common for a dispute about contract performance to be centered on an ambiguous provision with each side espousing an interpretation favorable to its position. Where both interpretations are considered reasonable, the courts, relying on the rule of *contra proforentum*, will often interpret the provision against the drafter if the other party can demonstrate reliance on its reasonable interpretation. This rule most often works to the benefit of contractors due to the simple fact that the government is most often the source of contract specifications and clauses.

As a counter to the *contra proforentum* rule, the courts can also examine whether the ambiguity was the result of an obvious and patent defect in the wording thereby requiring the other party (most often the contractor) to seek clarification. The failure to seek timely clarification can shift the burden back to the contractor to perform in accordance with the government's interpretation. In support of this process, contractors are often given a specific time period during the solicitation process to submit written questions about contract requirements and receive written responses. Such an exchange of correspondence is often useful in examining whether a defect was so obvious that a reasonable person would consider it as such.

In addition to determining responsibility for a particular contract provision, the courts will attempt to harmonize all provisions of the contract together. In a sealed bid situation where the bidder's offer is a mirror image of the solicitation document, this process of harmonization is straightforward. However, the much more common use of competitive proposals whereby an offeror is free—and often required—to submit a considerable amount of verbiage in response to the government's solicitation presents greater difficulties in attempting to harmonize all contract provisions. This process is further complicated by the fact that contractors often take exception, although often not clearly, to one or more requirements or provisions listed in the government solicitation as well as the government's fondness for incorporating by reference or including as attachments numerous other documents that may only generally have applicability to the specific contract at hand.

As an aid to such contract interpretation problems, the government solicitation will often include an "Order of Precedence" clause that sets forth the order by which the different parts of a contract are to be given precedence should a dispute arise. For example, FAR 52.215-8 provides that inconsistencies in the contract are to be resolved by giving precedence to the following sections of the contract in the following order: First, the Schedule, including contract forms, the description of supplies or services and the prices, packaging and marking requirements, inspection and acceptance terms, delivery or performance requirements, contract administration data, and special contract requirements; Second, Representations and other instructions listed in the solicitation; Third, Contract clauses (most often written by the government); Fourth, other documents, exhibits and attachments; and Fifth, the specifications. Note that the probable source of most disputes, the actual contract specifications, are last in line for determining the intent of the parties.

Finally, trade usage, the parties' acts during actual contract performance, and prior experience are also factors that a decisionmaker will use to determine the intent of the parties when resolving a contract dispute.

Appeal of The Ensign-Bickford Company

ASBCA No. 6214, 60-2 BCA ¶ 2817
October 31, 1960

OPINION BY MR. WINTER

After this contract was awarded changes were ordered. The changes include a requested acceleration. The parties agree that appellant is entitled to an upward equitable adjustment for the changes. They disagree upon the amount. Appellant requests $41,651.63. The Government would allow $22,018.67. Thus the amount in dispute is $19,632.96. The dispute arises out of the fact that two identical contracts were awarded and thereafter were subject to the same changes. The contractor not before us settled for $16,500. This has occasioned the Government to seek a substantially similar settlement with appellant.

In May of 1958 the Government had a requirement for 2,016 demolition kits. The responsibility for contracting for this requirement was assigned to the Picatinny Arsenal. Half of the quantity (1,008) was set aside for negotiation with firms located in labor surplus areas. The balance (1,008) became the subject of an invitation for Bids issued on 14 May 1958.

* * *

Appellant submitted a bid dated 29 May 1958. This bid was accepted on 10 June 1958 thus resulting in the contract before us. The contract is for 1,008 demolition kits at $396.00 each for a total of $399,168.00. It is a formally advertised fixed price contract not subject to price redetermination.

On 27 June 1958 the Arsenal awarded a negotiated contract for the set aside portion to Industrial Metal Fabricating Co., Inc. This contract was likewise for 1,008 demolition kits at $396.00 each for a total of $399,168.00.

After the two contracts had been awarded the one with appellant was transferred to the Boston Ordnance District and the one with Industrial Metal Fabricating Co., Inc., was transferred to the New York Ordnance District.

* * *

At about this time Industrial Metal Fabricating Company requested from appellant a quotation on detonating cord. This led appellant to seek a quotation from Industrial Metal Fabricating Company on the parts which appellant needed. A quotation of $64.53 was submitted on 18 June 1958. After an investigation this quotation was accepted on 25 June 1958.

As a subcontractor, appellant did the final assembly and packaging operations for Industrial Metal Fabricating Company and also furnished detonating fuze.

The persons administering the Industrial Metal Fabricating Company contract at the New York Ordnance District were unaware of the contract being administered by the Boston District, and vice versa.

On or about 17 July 1958 appellant was asked to give a cost estimate as to what a proposed acceleration of deliveries would cost. After an informal discussion with Industrial Metal Fabricating Company, and computations of its own, appellant estimated such costs at about $42,000.

Whether or not the Government made a similar inquiry of Industrial Metal Fabricating Company is not disclosed by the record. However, by Modification 4 dated 29 August 1958 the New York District did order Industrial Metal Fabricating to accelerate but with the proviso that acceleration costs would not exceed $42,500.

* * *

By letter dated 10 September 1958 the Government advised appellant of various changes that would apply to the contract. This letter provided for the required acceleration.

On 15 September 1958 appellant contacted Industrial Metal Fabricating Company to secure its price for changes and acceleration. Initially the price had been $64.53. Industrial Metal Fabricating Company requested an additional $7.18 for changes and an additional $23.26 for acceleration for a new price of $94.97. Appellant accepted this new price. Appellant did not attempt to secure quotations from other sources. Nor did appellant make, or attempt to make, the new price of $94.97 redeterminable. Appellant paid this new price to Industrial Metal Fabricating Company.

By letter dated 10 November 1958 appellant requested an upward equitable adjustment of $57,781.66. This consists of changes and acceleration on the original 1,008 kits ($55,056.96), plus the price of 10 additional kits that had been added to the contract ($3,960.00), plus changes and acceleration on the 10 additional kits ($546.20), minus $1,781.50 for a change in delivery point from destination to origin. (The New York District had also added 10 kits to the Industrial Metal Fabricating Company contract.)

By letter dated 18 November 1958 the Government forwarded to appellant copies of Cost and Price Analysis Form DD 633 and requested a breakdown of appellant's 10 November 1958 requested adjustment.

Deliveries under appellant's contract and under the Industrial Metal Fabricating Company contract were completed in November or December of 1958 and prior to 10 December 1958.

On 10 December 1958 the New York District asked the Army Audit Agency to audit the change and acceleration costs of Industrial Metal Fabricating Company under its contract. The contracting personnel of the Boston District did not know of this request or of the existence of the Industrial Metal Fabricating Company. The contracting personnel of the New York District did not know of appellant's contract.

By letter dated 30 December 1958 appellant submitted the cost and price analysis requested by the Government's 18 November 1958 letter. An increase of $51,165.87 was requested. This included an increase of $30,905.28 for subcontracted items. Other increases (supervision, overtime, shift bonus) brought increased costs to $31,321.27. On these costs a profit of $20,880.73 was requested for a total adjustment of $52,202. An addition of $727.87 for special tooling and a deletion of $1.764 for the change in delivery point gave a final balance of $51,165.87.

On 5 March 1959 the New York District received the Army Audit Agency's report on the Industrial Metal Fabricating Company contract. At or about this time the New York District contracting personnel learned of appellant's contract.

* * *

On 10 April 1959 Mr. Lynch, a contract specialist at the Boston District, called appellant and spoke to appellant's director of marketing. Mr. Lynch outlined a proposed settlement for the changes and acceleration. Mr. Lynch proposed a settlement of $41,651.63. This proposal included appellant's requested costs of $31,321.27, added $7,485.78 for G&A, added $727.87 for special tooling, added $3,880.71 for profit, deducted $1,764 for the delivery point change, for the balance of $41,651.63. ****

By letter dated 14 April 1959 appellant advised the Boston District that the $41,651.63 proposal appeared to be an equitable one, that it would like to proceed on that basis, and requested a contract modification so it could submit a final billing.

Appellant argues that by the telephone conversation on 10 April 1959 and letter of 14 April 1959 the parties reached an enforceable agreement upon a $41,651.63 adjustment and that this agreement should now be confirmed and honored. The Government contends that Mr. Lynch had no authority to make an agreement binding upon the Government and that Mr. Lynch made no offer that could be accepted by appellant.

On 17 April 1959 the New York District advised the Boston District as to the existence of the Industrial Metal Fabricating Company contract and the subcontract arrangements with appellant. The New York District advised the Boston District to hold up any settlement with appellant as it appeared from the audit made for the New York District that the Industrial Metal Fabricating Company had been overcharging appellant for the changes and acceleration.

Appellant had already paid Industrial Metal Fabricating Company. The last payment had been made on 9 January 1959.

On 28 April 1959 the New York District held a negotiation conference with Industrial Metal Fabricating Company. That contractor was requesting an adjustment of $49,500. The New York District which had ordered the changes and acceleration but which had made no price adjustment therefor was negotiating upon the basis of audited historical costs. The conferees finally reached an agreement, after concessions by both sides, upon 16,500 as the equitable adjustment. This agreement was reduced to writing as Modification 13, Supplemental Agreement, to the contract.

On 27 May 1959 appellant invoiced the Boston District for $41,651.63.

By letter dated 26 June 1959 the Government returned the $41,651.63 invoice stating that payment of that amount was not due. The letter further stated that the New York District had reached an agreement with Industrial Metal Fabricating Company for an adjustment of $16,500 and that it was the position of the Boston District that the provision in the 'Changes' article for an equitable adjustment imposed a responsibility on appellant to protect appellant's position with its subcontractors so that appellant would not find appellant's position prejudiced. The letter went on to say that quotations appellant had made to Industrial Metal Fabricating Company had to be considered in adjusting appellant's price. The letter proposed an adjustment of $15,089. This proposal allowed no G&A costs and no profit. It used $16,500 for increased subcontract costs.

Appellant rejected the $15,089 proposal by letter dated 2 July 1959. Appellant pointed out that it had paid Industrial Metal Fabricating Company. Appellant did indicate that if the Government could negotiate with Industrial Metal Fabricating Company and secure a refund to appellant then appellant could adjust its claimed adjustment. Appellant requested that the matter be reviewed and appellant advised.

* * *

By letter dated 4 January 1960, headed 'Final Decision of Contracting Officer' and inviting attention to the right of appeal, the contracting officer found that the adjustment was $22,018.67. Referring to and relying upon the adjustment that the New York District had reached with Industrial Metal Fabricating Company, the contracting officer included $16,500 for subcontracting in his $22,018.67 allowance. The balance ($22,018.67 - $16,500 =) of $5,518.67 is not explained in the decision. [The parties agree, however, that the only dispute is as to the amount to be allowed as subcontract costs; viz.: $30,905.28 per appellant as opposed to $16,500 per the Government.]

A timely appeal was taken by letter dated 15 January 1960. In its complaint filed on 2 March 1960 appellant contends for the adjustment of $41,651.63. The position of the parties, insofar as amount is concerned, remains the same in their post-hearing briefs.

DECISION

This appeal presents the question as to the amount of the equitable adjustment to which the appellant is entitled for changes ordered by the Government. As both parties to this appeal have recognized, the request for acceleration was in this case a change which increased appellant's costs and for which appellant is entitled to an equitable adjustment.

* * *

The Board believes from the wording of the 'Changes' article itself that it is contemplated by that article that equitable adjustments for changes will be arrived at by negotiations upon the basis of estimates and before the changed work is done, but the Board realizes that equitable adjustments for changes are not exclusively to be so arrived at and that on occasion they are arrived at after the changed work is done. We know that on occasion the Government uses the former system (forward pricing) and on occasion uses the latter system (retroactive pricing). See Bruce Construction Corp., ASBCA No. 5932, 30 August 1960, 60-2 BCA p ___. And we would expect that contractors in their dealings with their subcontractors would likewise from time to time use both systems.

We believe that it was reasonable and appropriate in the instant case for the appellant, upon receipt of the changes, to use the forward pricing system in making its price adjustment with its subcontractor. This decision, we believe, rested within the sound discretion of the appellant. Nor are we persuaded that appellant, to protect itself, should have made the price increase redeterminable.

Since appellant did use the forward pricing system in this case and since it was reasonable and appropriate to do so we believe that the question to be decided in this case is whether or not the adjustment appellant made with its subcontractor was reasonable when viewed from the standpoint of 10 to 15 September 1958 (the period when the change was ordered and the adjustment made) rather than from the standpoint of December 1958 and thereafter (the period when the subcontractor's costs had become historical).

* * *

We note in this connection that when in July of 1958 appellant was asked to give an estimate of acceleration costs it gave an estimate of about $42,000. This apparently did not shock the Government at that time. The record discloses no protest that $42,000 seemed unreasonably high, no indication that Government estimates were considerably lower, no request for a justification of the estimate, and no request that it be refigured. And we note that when on 29 August 1958 the Government ordered acceleration of the Industrial Metal Fabricating Company it did so with a proviso that costs would not exceed $42,500. * * *

When on 10 September 1958 appellant was ordered to accelerate it seems reasonable that appellant would go to its existing subcontractor to arrange for acceleration. Alternate sources of supply might have been found but we believe that the ordered acceleration would most reasonably be expected to be achieved by accelerating the existing subcontractor rather than by trying to put a new subcontractor into production. In going to the subcontractor to arrange for acceleration it seems reasonable that appellant would ask for a price on the acceleration so that the subcontract could be adjusted as to delivery and price. Appellant did ask for and did receive a price. This brings us to what we think is the crucial question in this case. Was the price received such that reasonably prudent contractors would have demanded breakdowns and justifications of the increase or would have rejected it as unreasonably high and have undertaken to secure a better price or a redeterminable price? On the record before us we think not. We think that reasonably prudent contractors would have considered it a fair price for the acceleration and other changes.

* * *

Having found that the changes ordered by the Government increased appellant's subcontract costs by $30,905.28 and that the increase was reasonable, we do not consider an adjustment that includes but $16,500 of the $30,905.28 equitable. We believe that equity requires that the entire $30,905.28 be included.

Thus we find the equitable adjustment to be $41,651.63.

Under the circumstances we find it unnecessary to rule upon appellant's contention that the parties, by their conversation on 10 April 1959 and the letter of 14 April 1959, disposed of the dispute by agreeing on an adjustment of $41,651.63.

* * *

The appeal is sustained.

Notes and Questions

1. What impact did the August 29, 1958 modification with a "not-to-exceed" price issued by the government contracting officer have on the outcome of this case?

2. The Board of Contract Appeals notes in the decision that the "Changes" clause anticipates that equitable adjustments (e.g., price increases or decreases) for changes mandated by the government are to be negotiated in advance of the work actually being performed. What is the policy basis for such a requirement? Which party has the advantage in negotiating an equitable adjustment prior to the work being performed? At the same time, the Board of Contract Appeals recognizes the "practice" of equitable adjustments occurring after the changed work has been completed. Why is the Board willing to accept this practice even though it contravenes specific contract language? Which party has the advantage during negotiations after the work is performed?

3. Note the limited effect of Mr. Lynch, a government official assisting the contracting officer, whose actions did not bind the government as would the actions of a contracting officer.

Recall the discussion in the first chapter of the limited authority of government officers, particularly those below the level of contracting officer. To negotiate a government contract on behalf of the government, a contracting officer must be appointed. See FAR 1.602-1; FAR 1-603-2 (stating the criteria government uses in selecting a qualified contracting officer). As an agent of the government, the contracting officer must operate within the limits set forth by the government. If a contracting officer exceeds the scope of his authority, then the government may not be bound by the actions of the contracting officer. See FAR 1-603-3 (discussing appointment procedure). Once the government appoints a contracting officer, the officer is responsible for contract compliance, enforcing contract provisions, timely performance, payment approvals, and contract modifications.

4. Also note the significance of the subcontract, and the contracting officer's interest in the subcontract despite the lack of privity. For example, what would the effect have been if the contract between Ensign-Bickford, as prime, and IMF as subcontractor, had included clauses to make price increases redeterminable?

METRIC CONSTRUCTORS, INC., Appellant, v. NATIONAL AERONAUTICS AND SPACE ADMINISTRATION, Appellee.

United States Court of Appeals, Federal Circuit.
169 F.3d 747, March 3, 1999

Before RICH, PLAGER, and RADER, Circuit Judges.

RADER, Circuit Judge.

The National Aeronautics and Space Administration (NASA) awarded a $56,215,000 contract to Metric Constructors, Inc. (Metric) for construction of the Space Station Processing Facility (SSPF) at the Kennedy Space Center in Florida. On December 10,

1993, NASA issued a contract modification deleting a contract requirement to install new light bulbs before project completion. NASA deducted $132,570 from the contract for the deleted work. When Metric appealed, the Armed Services Board of Contract Appeals (Board) upheld this deduction. See ASBCA No. 48852 (Nov. 21, 1997). Because the Board erred in construing the contract to require replacement of all lamps before project completion rather than replacement of only burned out, broken, or defective lamps, this court reverses.

I.

NASA awarded the contract to construct the SSPF on February 15, 1991. The SSPF, completed in June 1994, consists of approximately 500,000 square feet and contains offices, computer and communications facilities, clean rooms, bays for processing space station payloads, and a parking lot. Approximately 13,000 light bulbs (referred to as "lamps" in the industry) light these areas. In March 1991, Metric entered into a subcontract with Meisner Electric, Inc. (Meisner) to perform the electrical work described in the specifications of the contract. At issue are three sections of those specifications relating to the installation of lamps.

Section 16511, entitled "Fluorescent Fixtures," required:

3.1 Installation

. . . . .

A fixture shall be installed at each outlet indicated on the drawings, and lamps of the proper type and wattage shall be installed in each fixture.

New lamps shall be installed immediately prior to completion of the project, unless directed by the designated NASA representative.

Section 16517, entitled "High Intensity Discharge Lighting," required:

3.1 Installation

. . . . .

A fixture shall be installed at each outlet indicated, and lamps of the proper type, voltage, and wattage shall be installed in each fixture.

New lamps shall be installed immediately prior to completion of the project, or earlier if construction conditions dictate.

Section 16531, entitled "Parking Lot and Roadway Lighting," required:

3.2 Installation

. . . . .

New lamps shall be installed immediately prior to completion of the project unless construction conditions indicate otherwise.

Metric and Meisner interpret these sections to require replacement of only defective, burned out, or broken lamps immediately before project completion. NASA contends that they require replacement of all lamps, known as "relamping" in the industry, before project completion.

The parties discovered their divergent views when NASA performed a "walkdown" of the project on September 20, 1993. Under the terms of the contract, NASA planned to take possession of several rooms in the facility in October 1993, known as early completion date (CD) rooms. NASA conducted the walkdown to identify items requiring completion before delivery of the CD rooms. The resulting NASA punchlist identified re-lamping as a requirement. The relamping requirement appeared on subsequent punch-lists of September 27 and October 4, 1993.

In response to the punchlists, Meisner sent a letter to NASA on October 19 noting NASA's request for relamping, but maintaining that "[r]emoval and replacement of flo-rescent [sic] lamps in fixtures that have been installed for CD is wasteful and not re-quired. The fixtures have just recently been installed and the lamps are fine." In response to Meisner's letter, the contracting officer issued Modification 1345 on December 10, uni-laterally deleting "the contract requirement to install new lamps prior to completion of the project…as set forth in specification Sections 16511,3.1, 16517,3.1, and 16531,3.1."

After several months of unsuccessful negotiations about the amount of credit due NASA for deleting the relamping requirement, Metric and Meisner informed NASA that they did not interpret the original contract to require relamping. Accordingly they suggested that Modification 1345 cost nothing. After more negotiation, the contracting officer, on October 4, 1994, issued Modification 1476 unilaterally reducing the contract price by $132,570 for the work deleted by Modification 1345.

Metric then submitted a claim to the contracting officer seeking recovery of the credit taken by NASA. When the contracting officer issued no decision, Metric appealed to the Board asserting its competing interpretation of the contract and, in the alterna-tive, alleging numerous deficiencies in NASA's calculation of the $132,570 credit. In particular, Metric produced evidence showing that trade practice and custom, as well as the conduct of both parties, supported its interpretation. The Board accorded this evi-dence no weight "in light of the clear words" of the contract. According to the Board, the contract unambiguously required relamping the facility.

Aside from the purportedly clear language of the contract, the Board relied on two other grounds in support of its decision. First, it concluded that Metric's interpretation of the specifications to require replacement of only defective, burned out, or broken lamps would render those specifications meaningless in light of the warranty provision in the contract. The warranty provision (Section 16003,2.7) required Metric to "[l]eave entire electrical system in proper working order." The Board reasoned that this provision would already require the replacement of broken lamps before project completion. Second, the Board placed "great weight" on the six-month period from October 1993 to April 1994 during which the parties negotiated the amount of the credit due NASA for the work deleted by Modification 1345. The Board found it significant that Meisner did not assert that NASA was due no money until the negotiations between the parties failed.

Metric appeals the Board's decision. Metric relies, as it did before the Board, on evi-dence that trade practice and custom in the industry show that it was only to replace broken or defective lamps prior to project completion, not relamp the facility, and that the conduct of the parties shows that both parties acted in conformity with this inter-pretation of the contract.

As to trade usage and custom, Metric points out, and the Board found, that the term "relamping" is commonly used in the electrical industry to mean the total replacement of lamps at a particular facility. The Board also found that it is uncommon for specifica-tions for new construction to require relamping. Evidence showing that neither Meis-ner's project manager nor its president had ever seen a requirement to relamp a newly constructed facility in forty-five years of combined experience underlies that finding. The Board further found that, during construction of the SSPF, Meisner received an unrelated subcontract to perform electrical work on the Kennedy Space Center Transportation Canister Facility. That contract contained a specification identical to Section 16511 of the SSPF contract, but NASA did not require Meisner to relamp the facility, nor did it issue a contract modification deleting a relamping requirement from that contract. Instead, Meisner replaced only broken or burned out lamps before project completion.

Metric also points this court to other findings of the Board supporting the reasonableness of its interpretation. Metric notes, for example, that Meisner's bid for the electrical work included labor to install only one set of lamps. Moreover, when Meisner presented the specifications to four prospective lamp suppliers for competitive bids, none submitted bids for a second set of lamps.

Metric contends that NASA's conduct, too, supports its interpretation of the contract. NASA selected Jacobs Engineering Group, Inc. to prepare the contract specifications and an estimate of the costs of constructing the SSPF. Jacobs' estimate did not include relamping the facility. In addition, NASA issued numerous unilateral change orders during the project affecting the number of lamps, but at no time sought a credit for a second set of lamps or required Metric to price a second set of lamps. Finally, the contract required Metric to prepare and maintain a detailed schedule of performance activities based on the critical path method (CPM). The CPM schedule did not include relamping as an activity. NASA reviewed and approved Metric's CPM schedule. NASA responds that these were "mere oversights."

Finally, Metric points out that the vast majority of lamps for this project (nearly 12,000 of about 13,000) had a life of six years and eight months. The Board found that most of the lamp installation occurred during the summer of 1993. Metric delivered more than half of the facility in June and October 1993, and ultimately completed the project the following summer. Based on this sequence of events, Metric points to the absurdity and waste of relamping recently installed, long-lived lamps.

For its part, NASA relies primarily on the language of the contract itself, which it contends unambiguously requires relamping. NASA also relies on the additional grounds identified by the Board, namely, that Metric's interpretation of the specifications would render them meaningless in view of the warranty provision, and that Metric participated in negotiations with NASA for six months before definitively taking the position that the original contract did not require relamping.

II.

This court reviews contract interpretation without deference. See Grumman Data Sys. Corp. v. Dalton, 88 F.3d 990, 997 (Fed.Cir.1996). This court will accept any underlying findings of the Board, however, unless they are "fraudulent, or arbitrary, or capricious, or so grossly erroneous as to necessarily imply bad faith, or…not supported by substantial evidence." 41 U.S.C. § 609(b) (1994).

III.

When a contract is susceptible to more than one reasonable interpretation, it contains an ambiguity. See Hills Materials Co. v. Rice, 982 F.2d 514, 516 (Fed.Cir.1992). To show an ambiguity it is not enough that the parties differ in their respective interpretations of a contract term. See Community Heating & Plumbing Co. v. Kelso, 987 F.2d 1575, 1578 (Fed.Cir.1993). Rather, both interpretations must fall within a "zone of reasonableness." See WPC Enters., Inc. v. United States, 163 Ct.Cl. 1, 323 F.2d 874, 876 (1963). If this court interprets the contract and detects an ambiguity, it next determines whether that ambiguity is patent. See Newsom v. United States, 230 Ct.Cl. 301, 676 F.2d 647, 649-50 (1982). The doctrine of patent ambiguity is an exception to the general rule of contra proferentem which construes an ambiguity against the drafter, here, NASA. See id.; Sturm v. United States, 190 Ct.Cl. 691, 421 F.2d 723 (1970). An ambiguity is patent if "so glaring as to raise a duty to inquire[.]" Newsom, 676 F.2d at 650. If an ambiguity is not patent but latent, this court enforces the general rule. See Fort Vancouver Plywood Co. v. United States, 860 F.2d 409, 414 (Fed.Cir.1988).

This case squarely presents the recurring issue of the role of evidence of trade practice and custom in contract interpretation. The case law identifies two seemingly divergent roles for such evidence. One line of cases holds that this court may consult evidence of trade practice and custom to discern the meaning of an ambiguous contract provision, but not to contradict or override an unambiguous contract provision. In R.B. Wright Construction Co. v. United States, 919 F.2d 1569 (Fed.Cir.1990), for example, the contract required the contractor to apply three coats of paint to specified surfaces. The contractor applied three coats of paint to previously unpainted surfaces and, in accordance with industry practice, applied only two coats of paint to previously painted surfaces. This court interpreted the contract to unambiguously require three coats of paint on all surfaces, regardless of industry practice: "Neither a contractor's belief nor contrary customary practice…can make an unambiguous contract provision ambiguous, or justify a departure from its terms." Id. at 1572; see also WRB Corp. v. United States, 183 Ct.Cl. 409 (1968) (finding that a trade practice of using masonite doors on paint-grade cabinets does not overcome an unambiguous contract provision requiring wood doors on paint-grade cabinets); George Hyman Constr. Co. v. United States, 215 Ct.Cl. 70, 564 F.2d 939, 945 (1977) ("A trade practice cannot prevail over unambiguous provisions of a contract….").

The second line of cases holds that this court may consult evidence of trade practice and custom to show that "language which appears on its face to be perfectly clear and unambiguous has, in fact, a meaning different from its ordinary meaning." Gholson, Byars, and Holmes Constr. Co. v. United States, 173 Ct.Cl. 374, 351 F.2d 987, 999 (1965). In Gholson, this court's predecessor considered the meaning of a contract term requiring "painting of all previously painted or varnished surfaces." The contractor contended that a baked enamel surface, although admittedly a "previously painted surface," was not regarded as such in the industry. The Board declined to consider the evidence of trade practice because the contract language was clear on its face. On appeal, the United States Court of Claims reversed: "[T]he principle is now established in this court (and almost every other court) that in order that the intention of the parties may prevail, the language of a contract is to be given effect according to its trade meaning notwithstanding that in its ordinary meaning it is unambiguous." Id.; see also W.G. Cornell Co. v. United States, 179 Ct.Cl. 651, 376 F.2d 299, 311 (1967) (finding legal error where the Board failed to consider trade practice and custom because of its holding that the contract was unambiguous).

These two lines of cases, however, only seem to diverge. In practice, they are both consistent with contract interpretation doctrines and practices. The United States Court of Federal Claims recognized those unifying principles in Western States Construction Co. v. United States, 26 Cl.Ct. 818 (1992). In that case, the trial court considered the meaning of a contract term requiring wrapping of underground "metallic pipe" with protective tape. The contractor introduced evidence showing that, in the industry, "cast iron soil pipe," although technically "metallic pipe," was not wrapped with protective tape. The Court of Federal Claims, aptly reconciling the two seemingly conflicting lines of cases of this court and its predecessor, consulted trade practice and custom to determine whether wrapping of cast iron soil pipe was consistent with the contract and thus whether an ambiguity arose at all. See id. at 826. This Western States analysis correctly applies the law of contract interpretation.

This court adheres to the principle that "the language of a contract must be given that meaning that would be derived from the contract by a reasonably intelligent person acquainted with the contemporaneous circumstances." Hol-Gar Mfg. Corp. v. United States, 169 Ct.Cl. 384, 351 F.2d 972, 975 (1965). Thus, to interpret disputed contract terms, "the context and intention [of the contracting parties] are more meaningful than the dictionary definition." Rice v. United States, 192 Ct.Cl. 903, 428 F.2d 1311, 1314 (1970); see also Western States, 26 Cl.Ct. at 825; Corman v. United States, 26 Cl.Ct. 1011, 1015 (1992). Trade practice and custom illuminate the context for the parties' contract negotiations and agreements. Before an interpreting court can conclusively declare a contract ambiguous or unambiguous, it must consult the context in which the parties exchanged promises. Excluding evidence of trade practice and custom because the contract terms are "unambiguous" on their face ignores the reality of the context in which the parties contracted. That context may well reveal that the terms of the contract are not, and never were, clear on their face. On the other hand, that context may well reveal that contract terms are, and have consistently been, unambiguous.

Thus, evidence of trade practice and custom plays an important role in contract interpretation. Before arriving at a legal reading of a contract provision, a court must consider the context and intentions of the parties. That context may or may not disclose ambiguities. In any event, evidence of trade practice and custom is part of the initial assessment of contract meaning. It illuminates the contemporaneous circumstances of the time of contracting, giving life to the intentions of the parties. It helps pinpoint the bargain the parties struck and the reasonableness of their subsequent interpretations of that bargain.

This role for evidence of trade usage, however, does not mean that a court should always accept evidence of trade practice and custom in interpreting the terms of a contract. A contracting party cannot, for example, invoke trade practice and custom to create an ambiguity where a contract was not reasonably susceptible of differing interpretations at the time of contracting. Trade practice evidence is not an avenue for a party to avoid its contractual obligations by later invoking a conflicting trade practice. R.B. Wright and similarly decided cases stand for this important proposition of contract interpretation law.

Instead, a court should accept evidence of trade practice only where a party makes a showing that it relied reasonably on a competing interpretation of the words when it entered into the contract. Without such a showing, evidence that some practitioners customarily accomplish tasks differently from the manner called for by the contract will not overcome the clear language of the contract. This requirement helps ensure that the evidence of trade practice and custom truly reflects the intent of the contracting party, and avoids according undue weight to that party's purely post hoc explanations of its conduct.

The Gholson rule and these principles of contract interpretation find general support in authoritative legal commentaries. The commentaries agree that courts should use evidence of trade practice and custom not only to determine the meaning of an ambiguous provision, but to determine whether a contract provision is ambiguous in the first instance. See, e.g., Restatement (Second) of Contracts § 220 cmt. d (1981) ("[U]sage relevant to interpretation is treated as part of the context of an agreement in determining whether there is ambiguity or contradiction...."); 3 Arthur L. Corbin, Corbin on Contracts § 555 at 232-39 (1960) ("Seldom should the court hold that the written words exclude evidence of the custom, since even what are often called 'plain' meanings are shown to be incorrect when all the circumstances of the transaction are known; and usages and customs are a part of those circumstances by which the meaning of words is to be judged."); 5 Samuel Williston, Williston on Contracts § 648 at 6-7 (3d ed. 1961) ("Usage is an ordinary means of proving the local or technical meaning of language, and even language which is normally clear and unambiguous may be shown by usage to bear, under the circumstances of the case, a meaning different from its normal sense.").

Of course, even when accepted, evidence of trade practice and custom does not trump other canons of contract interpretation, but rather cooperates with them. Courts prefer, for example, an interpretation of a contract that gives effect to all its terms and leaves no provision meaningless. See United States v. Johnson Controls, Inc., 713 F.2d 1541, 1555 (Fed.Cir.1983). Thus, a court should consider whether adopting the interpretation advanced by the party relying on trade practice and custom would deprive the specification at issue of all meaning, or if there is a more limited sense in which the requirement still applies. Where canons of contract interpretation point to different interpretations, resolution of the conflict is necessarily left to the facts of the particular case.

Armed with these principles, this court examines anew whether the contract specifications at issue here are ambiguous, and finds that they are. Metric introduced sufficient evidence of trade practice and custom, and reasonable reliance on that trade practice and custom, to show that the specifications are susceptible to two different reasonable interpretations. The evidence shows that the electrical industry commonly uses the term "relamping" to mean the total replacement of lamps at a particular facility. Not only does that term not appear in the contract, relamping is rarely performed in connection with a newly constructed facility. This evidence is buttressed by NASA's interpretation of the Canister facility contract which contained identical language to Section 16511 of the SSPF contract, but which neither party interpreted as requiring relamping. Metric's reliance on its interpretation is reflected in its bid, which included labor to install only one set of lamps and the cost of only one set of lamps.

In contrast to the Board and NASA, this court does not believe that adopting Metric's construction of the contract to require replacement of only broken and defective lamps before project completion deprives those specifications of all meaning in view of the contract's warranty provision. The warranty provision only required Metric to leave the "electrical system" in proper working order. It did not hold Metric accountable for everything plugged into the electrical system, such as lamps, in addition to the electrical system itself. In other words, properly interpreted, the warranty provision only required Metric to leave the electrical infrastructure in proper working order. Thus, that provision did not render Metric's interpretation of the specifications at issue meaningless, but rather left them with a more limited sense in which they still applied. That is, the contract required replacement of defective, burned out, or broken lamps immediately before project completion.

This court also does not consider the Board's alternative ground—the six- month period of negotiations between the parties—to show that Metric's claim interpretation is unreasonable. Many factors influence negotiations, not the least of which is the desire to avoid costly litigation. In light of this fact and the substantial other evidence discussed above, this single factor cannot support the conclusion that the meaning NASA and the Board ascribe to the contract is the only reasonable one. Therefore, this court detects an ambiguity in the contract.

Finally, this court does not perceive the ambiguity as "so glaring as to raise a duty to inquire[.]" Newsom, 676 F.2d at 650. Because this contract contains a latent ambiguity, this court construes that ambiguity against the drafter, NASA. Accordingly, this court reverses the decision of the Board on contract interpretation, rendering moot the issue of the quantum of NASA's equitable adjustment.

REVERSED.

Notes and Questions

1. Pull back from the specific issue of interpretation in the case, and look broadly at the general role of interpretation in government contract law. Procedurally, the issue starts with the provisions of the initial contract—often, as in this instance, the initial contract's specifications which describe the work to be performed. Later, a dispute occurs over what the contractor must do, with the contracting officer taking one interpretation, and the contractor another. The dispute becomes a claim, resolved through the government contract machinery for such claims. Suppose a similar disagreement occurred about whether the contract required relamping between a private developer and its general contractor: what would be the same, and what would be different, in the private contracting context?

2. In some respects, this case seems to present a classic issue about contract interpretation familiar in private contracting, with the court citing the Restatement (Second) of Contracts and the treatises of Corbin and Williston. Its verbal formulation about admitting trade practice and custom only where the contract was "reasonably susceptible of differing interpretations" echoes the familiar formulation of first-year private contract law. The view that the court rejected seems, at first, quite unreasonable—namely, it seems absurd to refuse to admit trade practice and custom just because a contract provision seems clear without them.

Note, however, several aspects in which this court's openness to trade practice and custom clashes somewhat with doctrines specific to government contract law and reflected in the several cited prior Federal Circuit and Court of Claims precedents on the following of clear contract language. Metric cited NASA's conduct, such as its approving Metric's critical path method schedule. There is some tension here with the usual rule that the government is not estopped by its own conduct. And, the language of the contract specifications presumably passed through all manner of formal procedures, from agency review prior to issuance, to availability to all competitors for the contract. Industry custom does not pass through such formal procedures.

B. Specifications, Inspection and Acceptance

By statute, federal agencies are required to specify needs for goods and services that will promote full and open competition and include restrictive provisions only to the extent necessary to satisfy the needs of the agency. 10 U.S.C. § 2305(a)(1); 41 U.S.C. § 253a(a). In addition, to the maximum extent practicable, specifications are to be stated in terms of functions to be performed, performance required, or essential physical characteristics. When functional and performance specifications are not possible, the government relies on design specifications that mandate how the contractor is to perform the required work.

Inspection constitutes the process by which the government ensures contract performance in compliance with contract specifications. The government can choose to either

(1) rely on a contractor's own internal quality controls and inspect the final product or service when delivered to the government or (2) mandate, as part of the contract requirements, the maintenance of a quality control program that meets specific government requirements and allows for government inspections during performance. Either way, the ultimate goal is a product that the government can accept. Inspection is thus the bridge between specifications and acceptance.

The determination as to whether a proffered good or service meets contract requirements rests with the government contracting officer and is generally evidenced by the execution of a formal acceptance certificate. The responsibility for acceptance can be transferred from the contracting officer to a cognizant contract administration office or to another agency. Acceptance can occur before delivery, at the time of delivery, or after delivery depending upon contract terms.

For more on this topic, refer to: Frank Baltz, *The* Spearin *Doctrine: How Far Does It Go?*, 33 Procure. Law., Summer 1998, at 11; Kacey Reed, *The Supreme Court's Rejection of Government Indemnification to Agent Orange from Manufacturers in Hercules, Inc. v. United States: Distinguishing the Forest from the Trees?* 31 U. Rich. L. Rev. 287 (1997); Kevin C. Golden & James W. Thomas, *The* Spearin *Doctrine: The False Dichotomy Between Design and Performance Specifications*, 25 Pub. Cont. L.J. 47 (1995); Paul A. D'Aloisio, *The Design Responsibility and Liability of Government Contractors*, 25 Pub. Cont. L.J. 47 (1995); William R. Medsger, *Weapon System Warranties: Unleashing the Genius in American Industry?* 127 Mil. L. Rev. 63 (1990); Saul Perloff & Hal Perloff, *Latent Defects in Government Contracts Law*, 27 Pub. Cont. L.J. 87 (1997); Thomas E. Shea, *The Magic Keys: Finality of Acceptance Under Government Contracts*, 86 Mil. L. Rev. 111 (1979); Neil G. Wolf, *Boyle v. United Technologies Corp.: A Reasonably Precise Immunity-Specifying the Defense Contractor's Shield*, 39 DePaul L. Rev. 825 (1990); Mark S. Jaeger, *Contractor Liability for Design Defects Under the Inspection Clause: Latent Design Defects—A Sleeping Giant?*, 21 Pub. Cont. L.J. 331 (1992); Commander George E. Hurley, Jr., *Government Contractor Liability in Military Design Defect Cases: The Need for Judicial Intervention*, 117 Mil. L. Rev. 219 (1987).

1. Specifications

Specifications describing the work undertaken by the contractor have two implications, represented by the very different cases in this section. On the one hand, the specifications impose a duty on the contractor who must provide what the specifications require, even though the contractor finds this onerous in the course of performing the contract. The contractor may then dispute whether the contract really imposes what the specifications apparently require; the government may respond by insisting on literal compliance.

On the other hand, the contractor may rely upon the specifications, expecting that anything they require, particularly in terms of methods of performance, will prove feasible. Then, if the requirements prove impossible or impractical, the contractor may insist that the government "impliedly warranted" the feasibility of the specifications; the government may respond by pointing to clauses intended to shift responsibility to the contractor, such as "site inspection" clauses.

The contractor's reliance upon the government's contract takes on particular urgency when the contractor gets sued for impacts upon third parties. While the government has power to shield contractors from, or to indemnify them regarding, liability to third parties, the government also has considerable reluctance to be so generous. Determining the extent of such immunity or indemnification raises again the issues recurring throughout government contracts, concerning the extent to which the rigid requirements such as affirmative statutory authorization surround the providing of public powers, resources, or assistance to private parties, even those awarded government contracts.

J.L. Malone & Associates, Inc., Appellant, v. The United States, Appellee.

United States Court of Appeals, Federal Circuit.,
No. 89-1056., 879 F.2d 841 July 13, 1989.

Before FRIEDMAN, NIES, and MAYER, Circuit Judges.

FRIEDMAN, Circuit Judge.

This is an appeal from a decision of the Veterans Administration Board of Contract Appeals rejecting a contractor's appeal from the contracting officer's decision denying the contractor an equitable adjustment under a contract. The contractor sought compensation for (1) the additional cost it incurred for expanding the capability of an existing computer, as the contract required, rather than substituting a different computer, as the contractor proposed, and (2) the delay damages it incurred because of the government's alleged unreasonable delay in considering the proposed substitute. The Board denied both of these claims. Appeal of J.L. Malone & Assoc., 88-3 B.C.A. ¶ 20,894 (VABCA 1988). We affirm.

I

The Veterans Administration (VA) planned to replace the outdated fire alarm system at its Medical Center in Lexington, Kentucky. The VA's design called for integrating the new fire alarm system with the Center's recently installed heating ventilation and air conditioning (HVAC) system, which was operated by a JC-80 computer manufactured by Johnson Controls. Integration was to be accomplished by expanding the memory of the existing JC-80 computer so as to allow it also to operate the new fire alarm system.

The VA's Invitation for Bids described the work as follows:

> Services of contractor to furnish all labor and materials…to remove existing fire alarm system including transmitter, signaling devices and control panels and replace with a frequency multiplexed system utilizing and expanding existing transmitters, panels and Johnson [Controls] JC-80 computer at the Veterans Administration Medical Center,…per specifications and Drawings. [Emphasis added.]

The specification stated at section 808-1(E) that:

> E. The contractor shall furnish, install and place in operating condition a fire safety system as herein described. The fire safety system shall operate as an integral part of the existing computerized building automation system.…[Emphasis added.]

The specification further provided that the new central processing unit (C.P.U.) was to be provided with 64,000 words of memory and that "[t]he existing C.P.U. shall be provided with an additional 32 thousand words of memory."

The contract contained two so-called "or equal" clauses that permitted the contractor to use substitutes of equal quality for products the contract specified.

General Provision 9 provided in pertinent part:

(a)...Unless otherwise specifically provided in this contract, reference to any equipment,...by trade name, make, or catalog number, shall be regarded as establishing a standard of quality and shall not be construed as limiting competition, and the Contractor may, at his option, use any equipment,...which in the judgment of the Contracting Officer, is equal to that named.

The second "or equal" clause appears in section 8 of the specifications describing the fire alarm system:

800-5. Equipment Ratings And Approval Of "Equal Equipment

B. Prior to construction, written approval shall be obtained by the Contractor from the Contracting Officer for any equipment which differs from the requirements of the drawings and specifications.

....

3. Any other items required for the satisfactory installation of the equal equipment shall be furnished and installed at no additional cost to the Government. This includes but shall not be limited to changes to branch circuits, circuit protective devices, conduits, wire, feeders, controls, panels,....

800-10. Drawings and Specifications: The drawings and specifications indicate the requirements for the systems, equipment, materials, operation, quality, etc. They shall not be construed to mean limitation of competition to the products of specific manufacturers.

There were four bids on the contract. The appellant's bid of $1,456,502 was more than $120,000 lower than the second lowest bid.

In preparing its bid the appellant obtained price quotations for fire alarm systems from two subcontractors, Johnson Controls and Honeywell. The Honeywell system was $152,000 lower than the Johnson Controls system.

The appellant was awarded the contract on December 7, 1981.

On April 19, 1982, the appellant made its first fire alarm submittal, which proposed a Honeywell fire alarm system separate and independent from the Johnson Controls HVAC system. The agency rejected this system as not complying with the contract specifications.

The appellant's second submittal, dated May 7, 1982, again proposed a separate Honeywell system. The proposal stated that the Honeywell system "meets and or exceeds every requirement" of the specifications "with the single exception of operating as an integral part of the existing computerized building automation system." The submittal further stated that "[t]he specification requirements for utilizing and expanding the existing Johnson Control[s] JC-80 computer and supplying a new identical 64K memory computer that will function as a back-up to the existing JC-80 computer cannot be provided due to the obsolescence of the existing computer." The agency rejected the second proposal on June 1, 1982.

The appellant's third submittal, dated July 28, 1982, the submittal here at issue, proposed to remove the existing JC-80 computer and furnish a Honeywell computer that would be capable of operating both the new fire alarm system and the existing HVAC system.

The submittal was reviewed for the VA by the engineering firm of Watkins & Associates. It informed the VA that the "proposed Honeywell system is not an integral part of the existing [computerized building automation] system," as required by paragraph 808-1(E) of the specifications, "but a replacement of it," and, therefore, in Watkins' opinion, the proposal "is an exception to the specifications and should not be honored at this time because this option was not given to the other bidders." The memorandum noted that although the VA "would be getting all new equipment and wiring for both the fire alarm as well as the HVAC control," there were at least eight disadvantages of accepting the Honeywell system in lieu of expanding the existing JC-80 system, the foremost of which would be the involvement of the VA in "legal problems with the other bidders."

At a September 28, 1982 meeting between the appellant and the VA, the appellant pointed out that the third submittal work would be done at no additional cost to the government. The contracting officer requested that the appellant provide, among other things, a statement "address[ing] the company's interpretation of the legalities of accepting this proposal and avoiding potential litigation." The appellant's response was that other bidders were "on notice that [the] 'or equal' provision was included in the referenced contract...and were free to let that fact [a]ffect their bid in any way they so chose."

At a meeting the contracting officer held on October 14, 1982 with officials of Johnson Controls, at their request, a Johnson Controls representative "implied that if the Honeywell submittal were approved and the Johnson [Controls] equipment removed, a protest would be lodged through one or all of the other bidders."

In response to a request from the contracting officer that the VA's Office of General Counsel provide a legal opinion concerning the acceptability of the appellant's third submittal, the Assistant Deputy Administrator for Procurement and Supply informed the Center's Director on November 19, 1982, that:

> Our recommendation, with the concurrence of General Counsel, is to enforce the requirements of the contract. The contractor must install a fire alarm system which will operate as an integral part of the existing computerized building automation system. If the contractor fails to provide a submittal which meets specifications, default action should be initiated.

The contracting officer so notified the appellant by letter on November 19, 1982:

> The specifications state that "the fire safety system shall operate as an integral part of the existing computerized building automation system." The system is interpreted as meaning the JC80 computer which must, therefore, remain in place. Since your submittal would require replacing the JC80, it is considered not in conformance with the specifications.

The appellant performed the contract using the Johnson Controls equipment. It then filed a claim of $292,459.07, covering (1) the $152,000 difference between the price for the Johnson Controls equipment and the Honeywell equipment, (2) increased installation costs, (3) project delay costs for overhead of $76,839.27, and (4) markups for overhead and profit.

The contracting officer denied the claim for a price adjustment, and the appellant appealed that decision to the Veterans Administration Board of Contract Appeals (Board). The Board denied the appeal. It held that "the 'or equal' provisions of the contract do not permit a contractor to remove and replace existing items of equipment which have been specified to remain." The Board explained:

> Those cases [holding that a contractor is permitted under an "or equal" provision of a contract to substitute items from another source if they are equal to

the items from the source designated in the contract] do not discuss a situation, such as here, where a contract requires that a new system to be installed must be integrated with an existing system, and that certain specific items of equipment which are part of that existing system are to remain, be utilized and expanded.

The Board further stated that "[although] the evidence indicates that [the Honeywell system] was more advanced than the older existing computer" and the government "would have received a more state-of-the art computer with no additional cost," the issue "is not whether the Government exercised good judgment in drawing up its contract, or whether it would have benefitted by allowing [the appellant] to replace its existing equipment"; rather "[t]he integrity of the Government's competitive procurement system is involved." The Board explained:

> What [the appellant] proposed was a major change in the contract, which no reasonable bidder, in our opinion, would have anticipated as permissible when preparing its bid. The requirement for integrating the new system with the existing system and retaining the JC-80 computer was clear. It would have been unfair to the other bidders to have permitted such a basic change in the contract after award....
>
> If [the appellant], or any other bidder, felt that the proposed contract was unduly restrictive of competition by requiring that the existing Johnson Controls computer be utilized and expanded, and that the new fire alarm system be integrated with the existing system, rather than permitting replacement of the existing system, it should have protested prior to award.

The Board also rejected the appellant's delay claim, ruling that the contracting officer had not unreasonably delayed her decision on the third submittal.

* * *

II

A. The appellant's principal contention is that under the "or equal" clauses of the contract, it had the right to substitute the Honeywell computer for the existing Johnson Controls computer because the former was equal in quality to the latter. This argument rests upon a misconstruction of the contract.

The contractual reference to the Johnson Controls computer was not intended to define quality or type of product to be used. Its purpose was to describe the work the contractor was to perform. As the contractual specification stated, that work was to "replace" the "existing fire alarm system" by utilizing and expanding the existing "Johnson JC-80 computer," so that the new fire alarm system would "operate as an integral part of the existing computerized building automation system." In other words, the new fire alarm system was to be integrated with the existing computerized building automation system by "utilizing and expanding" existing equipment, including the Johnson Controls computer.

As the contract specifically pointed out, an essential element of the new fire alarm system was its utilization and expansion of the existing computer. The specifications explained how that computer was to be utilized and expanded to make it an "integral part" of the "existing computerized building automation system." They required that "[t]he new [central processing unit] shall be provided with 64 thousand words of memory. The existing C.P.U. [central processing unit, which included the Johnson Controls computer] shall be provided with an additional 32 thousand words of memory."

There is nothing in the contract that authorized, or even suggested, that Malone could remove the existing Johnson Controls computer and substitute a Honeywell computer. As the Board correctly noted:

> What Malone proposed was a major change in the contract, which no reasonable bidder, in our opinion, would have anticipated as permissible when preparing its bid. The requirement for integrating the new system with the existing system and retaining the JC-80 computer was clear. It would have been unfair to the other bidders to have permitted such a basic change in the contract after award.

In at least its second submittal to the contracting officer, the appellant recognized that the existing Johnson Controls computer was to be utilized and expanded and that any other design was at variance with the contractual requirement. The appellant there acknowledged that although the existing JC-80 computer was to be utilized and expanded, that "cannot be provided due to the obsolescence of the existing computer." The submittal further recognized that the fire alarm system was to operate as an integral part of the existing building automation system but maintained that that requirement was "impossible."

There was a similar recognition of the requirement in the statement that "[t]he requirement for the existing C.P.U. to be provided with an additional 32 thousand words of memory could be accomplished by installing a 32K memory plane of the same type as the existing memory plane if one could be found."

"It is settled that the Government is entitled to obtain precisely what it contracts for as long as it does not mislead the contractor." American Elec. Contracting Corp. v. United States, 579 F.2d 602, 608, 217 Ct.Cl. 338 (1978). The VA made a design decision that the existing JC-80 computer would be utilized and expanded. The Board found that the VA's primary reason for doing so was that "the existing equipment had been in use for about a year and a half, had been debugged and would presumably be 'cost effective.' " We cannot say that that design decision was impermissible or that there was any reason why the government was not entitled to obtain exactly what its contract specified.

The Board found that the Honeywell computer that the appellant proposed to install in its third submittal was more advanced than the existing JC-80 computer that the contract specified was to be utilized and expanded. The government, however, was not required to alter the basic design requirements of the contract. The government carefully considered the appellant's third submittal and justifiably concluded that the major change the appellant proposed would be inappropriate for various reasons, including the likelihood of protests by unsuccessful bidders.

B. The appellant relies heavily on Jack Stone Co. v. United States, 344 F.2d 370, 170 Ct.Cl. 281 (1965). In that case, a contract for the renovation of an electric power and a fire alarm system provided that:

> The Contractor shall furnish all labor and materials necessary to install complete all additions and revisions to the existing Fire Alarm System as herein specified and as shown on Drawings.... The existing system is of Sperti Faraday manufacture. All new equipment and parts furnished shall be of the same manufacturer to insure full and satisfactory performance of the completed system.

344 F.2d at 372. The specifications contained sixteen separate references to Sperti Faraday items. The contract also contained the following "or equal" provision:

> Reference in the specifications to any article, device, product, materials, fixture, form or type of construction by name, make, or catalog number, shall be

interpreted as establishing a standard of quality, and not as limiting competition. The Contractor may make substitutions equal to the items specified if approved in advance in writing by the Contracting Officer.

The Court of Claims, reversing the Board, held that the contract authorized the contractor to use components manufactured by another company that were the equal of the Sperti Faraday components. The court stated that the effect of the "or equal" provision of the contract was that "under this contract plaintiff was not required to furnish Sperti Faraday equipment alone, but could supply articles from another source if they were equal to Sperti Faraday and if the consent of the contracting officer was sought in advance." 344 F.2d at 376.

Jack Stone did not address the situation here of a contractor who proposes to remove an existing item of equipment, which the contract expressly required was to be "utilized and expanded," and replace that item with one manufactured by a different source. In Jack Stone, the contractor proposed merely to use a "different manufacturer's components in conjunction with the existing fire alarm [system]." 344 F.2d at 372. In Jack Stone, the reference to Sperti Faraday products, in light of the "or equal" clause, was a designation of the kind and quality of product to be used.

In the present case, on the other hand, the reference to the Johnson Controls computer was a description of the work the contractor was to perform, namely, the replacement of the existing fire alarm system with a new system that would utilize and expand the Johnson Controls computer. Unlike the contract in Jack Stone, here the "or equal" clause did not authorize the contractor to substitute another product, even if it was of equal quality, for the Johnson Controls computer that the contract required the contractor to utilize and expand. Indeed, the general "or equal" clause of this contract applied "[u]nless otherwise specifically provided in this contract." The "utilizing and expanding" and the "integral part" provisions of the contract "otherwise specifically provided."

C. The appellant further contends that if the contract is construed to require it to utilize the existing Johnson Controls computer, the contract would be a "sole source" procurement that would require compliance with the provisions governing such procurement, and would be inconsistent with the "or equal" provisions of the contract. Our conclusion that the contractual requirement to utilize the existing Johnson Controls computer described the work to be performed and not the product to be used in performing the contract undermines the basis for this argument. A contractual requirement that in performing the work the contractor must utilize an existing item of equipment, which is identified by its manufacturer, does not make the contract a sole source procurement.

* * *

CONCLUSION

The decision of the Veterans Administration Board of Contract Appeals denying the appellant an equitable adjustment is

AFFIRMED

Notes and Questions

1. Does the fact that the Veterans Administration issued the solicitation as an IFB rather than an RFP have an impact on the outcome of this case? What could the con-

tractor have done prior to submission of bids that would have altered this case? Why would a prospective contractor not take action prior to submission of bids?

2. Of critical importance to the outcome of this case is the conclusion of the courts that "the Government is entitled to obtain precisely what it contracts for as long as it does not mislead the contractor." *American Elec. Contracting Corp. v. United States*, 579 F.2d 602, 608, 217 Ct.Cl. 338 (1978). What policies support such a conclusion? What responsibility does a contractor have to inform the government that a proposed solution may not be the most desirable or least expensive?

3. FAR 11.105 provides:

> Agency requirements shall not be written so as to require a particular brand-name product, or a feature of a product, peculiar to one manufacturer, thereby precluding consideration of a product manufactured by another company, unless—

> (a) The particular brand-name, product, or feature is essential to the Government's requirements, and market research indicates other companies' similar products, or products lacking the particular feature, do not meet, or cannot be modified to meet, the agency's minimum needs;

> (b) The authority to contract without providing for full and open competition is supported by the required justifications and approvals ....

What was the justification for specifying a particular brand in this instance?

United States v. Spearin

Supreme Court of the United States

248 U.S. 132 Argued Nov. 14 and 15, 1918, Decided Dec. 9, 1918.

Mr. Justice BRANDEIS delivered the opinion of the Court.

Spearin brought this suit in the Court of Claims demanding a balance alleged to be due for work done under a contract to construct a dry dock and also damages for its annulment. Judgment was entered for him in the sum of $141,180.86 (51 Ct. Cl. 155), and both parties appealed to this court. The government contends that Spearin is entitled to recover only $7,907.98. Spearin claims the additional sum of $63,658.70.

First. The decision to be made on the government's appeal depends upon whether or not it was entitled to annul the contract. The facts essential to a determination of the question are these:

Spearin contracted to build for $757,800 a dry dock at the Brooklyn Navy Yard in accordance with plans and specifications which had been prepared by the government. The site selected by it was intersected by a 6-foot brick sewer; and it was necessary to divert and relocate a section thereof before the work of constructing the dry dock could begin. The plans and specifications provided that the contractor should do the work and prescribed the dimensions, material and location of the section to be substituted. All the prescribed requirements were fully complied with by Spearin; and the substituted section was accepted by the government as satisfactory. It was located about 37 to 50 feet from the proposed excavation for the dry dock; but a large part of the new section was within the area set aside as space within which the contractor's operations were to be carried on. Both before and after the diversion of the 6-foot sewer, it connected, within the Navy Yard but outside the space reserved for work on the dry dock, with a 7-foot sewer which emptied into Wallabout Basin.

About a year after this relocation of the 6-foot sewer there occurred a sudden and heavy downpour of rain coincident with a high tide. This forced the water up the sewer for a considerable distance to a depth of 2 feet or more. Internal pressure broke the 6-foot sewer as so relocated, at several places; and the excavation of the dry dock was flooded. Upon investigation, it was discovered that there was a dam from 5 to 5 1/2 feet high in the 7-foot sewer; and that dam, by diverting to the 6-foot sewer the greater part of the water, had caused the internal pressure which broke it. Both sewers were a part of the city sewerage system; but the dam was not shown either on the city's plan, nor on the government's plans and blueprints, which were submitted to Spearin. On them the 7-foot sewer appeared as unobstructed. The government officials concerned with the letting of the contract and construction of the dry dock did not know of the existence of the dam. The site selected for the dry dock was low ground; and during some years prior to making the contract sued on, the sewers had, from time to time, overflowed to the knowledge of these government officials and others. But the fact had not been communicated to Spearin by any one. He had, before entering into the contract, made a superficial examination of the premises and sought from the civil engineer's office at the Navy Yard information concerning the conditions and probable cost of the work; but he had made no special examination of the sewers nor special inquiry into the possibility to the work being flooded thereby, and had no information on the subject.

Promptly after the breaking of the sewer Spearin notified the government that he considered the sewers under existing plans a menace to the work and that he would not resume operations unless the government either made good or assumed responsibility for the damage that had already occurred and either made such changes in the sewer system as would remove the danger or assumed responsibility for the damage which might thereafter be occasioned by the insufficient capacity and the location and design of the existing sewers. The estimated cost of restoring the sewer was $3,875. But it was unsafe to both Spearin and the government's property to proceed with the work with the 6-foot sewer in its then condition. The government insisted that the responsibility for remedying existing conditions rested with the contractor. After 15 months spent in investigation and fruitless correspondence, the Secretary of the Navy annulled the contract and took possession of the plant and materials on the site. Later the dry dock, under radically changed and enlarged plans, was completed by other contractors, the government having first discontinued the use of the 6-foot intersecting sewer and then reconstructed it by modifying size, shape and material so as to remove all danger of its breaking from internal pressure. Up to that time $210,939.18 had been expended by Spearin on the work; and he had received from the government on account thereof $129,758.32. The court found that if he had been allowed to complete the contract he would have earned a profit of $60,000 and its judgment included that sum.

The general rules of law applicable to these facts are well settled. Where one agrees to do, for a fixed sum, a thing possible to be performed, he will not be excused or become entitled to additional compensation, because unforeseen difficulties are encountered. **** Thus one who undertakes to erect a structure upon a particular site, assumes ordinarily the risk of subsidence of the soil. **** But if the contractor is bound to build according to plans and specifications prepared by the owner, the contractor will not be responsible for the consequences of defects in the plans and specifications. **** This responsibility of the owner is not overcome by the usual clauses requiring builders to visit the site, to check the plans, and to inform themselves of the requirements of the work, as is shown by Christie v. United States, 237 U. S. 234, 35 Sup. Ct. 565, 59 L. Ed. 933; Hollerbach v. United States, 233 U. S. 165, 34 Sup. Ct. 553, 58 L. Ed. 898, and United States v. Stage Co., 199 U. S. 414, 424, 26 Sup. Ct. 69, 50 L. Ed. 251, where it was held that the contractor should be relieved, if he was misled by erroneous statements in the specifications.

In the case at bar, the sewer, as well as the other structures, was to be built in accordance with the plans and specifications furnished by the government. The construction of the sewer constituted as much an integral part of any part of the dry dock proper. It was as necessary as any other work in the preparation for the foundation. It involved no separate contract and no separate consideration. The contention of the government that the present case is to be distinguished **** on the ground that the contract with reference to the sewer is purely collateral is clearly without merit. The risk of the existing system proving adequate might have rested upon Spearin, if the contract for the dry dock had not contained the provision for relocation of the 6-foot sewer. But the insertion of the articles prescribing the character, dimensions and location of the sewer imported a warranty that if the specifications were complied with, the sewer would be adequate. This implied warranty is not overcome by the general clauses requiring the contractor to examine the site,[1] to check up the plans,[2] and to assume responsibility for the work until completion and acceptance[3]. The obligation to examine the site did not impose upon him the duty of making a diligent inquiry into the history of the locality with a view to determining, at his peril, whether the sewer specifically prescribed by the government would prove adequate. The duty to check plans did not impose the obligation to pass upon their adequacy to accomplish the purpose in view. And the provision concerning contractor's responsibility cannot be construed as abridging rights arising under specific provisions of the contract.

Neither section 3744 of the Revised Statutes (Comp. St. 1916, §6895) which provides that contracts of the Navy Department shall be reduced to writing, nor the parol evidence rule, precludes reliance upon a warranty implied by law. See Kellogg Bridge Co. v. Hamilton, 110 U. S. 108, 3 Sup. Ct. 537, 28 L. Ed. 86. The breach of warranty, followed by the government's repudiation of all responsibility for the past and for making working conditions safe in the future, justified Spearin in refusing to resume the work. He was not obliged to restore the sewer and to proceed, at his peril, with the construction of the dry dock. When the government refused to assume the responsibility, he might have terminated the contract himself, Anvil Mining Co. v. Humble, 153 U. S. 540, 551, 552, 14 Sup. Ct. 876, 38 L. Ed. 814; but he did not. When the government annulled the contract without justification, it became liable for all damages resulting from its breach.

---

1. "27. Examination of Site.—Intending bidders are expected to examine the site of the proposed dry dock and inform themselves thoroughly of the actual conditions and requirements before submitting proposals."

2. "25. Checking Plans and Dimensions; Lines and Levels.—The contractor shall check all plans furnished him immediately upon their receipt and promptly notify the civil engineer in charge of any discrepancies discovered therein. *** The contractor will be held responsible for the lines and levels of his work, and he must combine all materials properly, so that the completed structure shall conform to the true intent and meaning of the plans and specifications."

3. "21. Contractor's Responsibility.—The contractor shall be responsible for the entire work and every part thereof, until completion and final acceptance by the Chief of Bureau of Yards and Docks, and for all tools, appliances, and property of every description used in connection therewith. ***"

Second. Both the main and the cross appeal raise questions as to the amount recoverable.

The government contends that Spearin should, as requested, have repaired the sewer and proceeded with the work; and that having declined to do so, he should be denied all recovery except $7,907.98, which represents the proceeds of that part of the plant which the government sold plus the value of that retained by it. But Spearin was under no obligation to repair the sewer and proceed with the work, while the government denied responsibility for providing and refused to provide sewer conditions safe for the work. When it wrongfully annulled the contract, Spearin became entitled to compensation for all losses resulting from its breach.

Spearin insists that he should be allowed the additional sum of $63,658.70, because, as he alleges, the lower court awarded him (in addition to $60,000 for profits) not the difference between his proper expenditures and his receipts from the government, but the difference between such receipts and the value of the work, materials, and plant (as reported by a naval board appointed by the defendant). Language in the findings of fact concerning damages lends possibly some warrant for that contention; but the discussion of the subject in the opinion makes it clear that the rule enunciated in United States v. Behan, 110 U. S. 338, 4 Sup. Ct. 81, 28 L. Ed. 168, which claimant invokes, was adopted and correctly applied by the court.

The judgment of the Court of Claims is, therefore, affirmed.

Mr. Justice McREYNOLDS took no part in the consideration and decision of these cases.

Notes and Questions

1. Key to this case is the determination of which party had responsibility to disclose superior knowledge. The government attempted to avoid this responsibility by formal and broad contract clauses placing the burden of discovery of defects and potential problems directly and unambiguously on the contractor. Why did this attempt fail notwithstanding the contract language to the contrary?

2. Would the government have overcome the implied warranty associated with the government specifications if it had used functional and performance specifications rather than detailed design specifications?

3. Due to the government's breach of the contract, the contractor received full compensation for money expended during performance plus the estimated profit he would have received if allowed to complete the work. In addition, the contractor sought but was denied compensation for the actual value of the work performed rather than for money actually spent. Which remedy was the contractor seeking in that instance?

4. Contracting officers, aware of the Spearin doctrine, may want to word their IFBs or RFPs to prevent government liability by clearly worded disclaimers of warranty, or exculpatory clauses. A classic discussion of this is in *Rixon Electronics, Inc. v. United States*, 536 F. 2d 1345, at 1351–52 (Ct. Cl.1976)

(T)he question boils down to this: is the disclaimer clear enough, alone or as aided by the warning to check the bid? You can engage a contractor to make snowmen in August, if you spell it out clearly, you are not warranting there will be any subfreezing weather in that month. But if you say...that the bid will generate a loss, and the bidder doesn't, apparently, believe you, what more can you say, legitimately, that will be more persuasive? Will you, with reason, conclude that the bidder wants to lose money, or at least, wants to break into this market so badly that loss of money is accepted as a minor consideration?

Mere general exculpatory clauses disclaiming any liability for accuracy of data that contractors may use in proposal preparation do not invariably defeat implied warranties of specifications. Exculpatory clauses are narrowly construed, particularly where the government attempts to avoid a remedy under a contract relief clause by means of a disclaimer. See *Teledyne Lewisburg v. United States*, 699 F. 2d 1336 (Fed. Cir. 1983). Furthermore, where the government has knowledge that information it provided contains incorrect, misleading or dangerous components, it has a duty to disclose this to the contractor. *Black v. Fairchild Industries*, No. 84-C-29223 (E.D. N.Y. 1986). That duty cannot be defeated by inclusion of an exculpatory clause. *Appeal of V & Z Heating Corporation*, 1998 WL 331671, DOTCAB No. 2953; *Christy Corporation v. United States*, 198 Ct. Cl. 986 (1972).

5. On the other hand, to find an implied warranty of specifications, it does not suffice merely that the government has detailed some characteristics, but requires that the specifications tell the contractor "just how to do the job". See *Appeal of Reflectone, Inc.* ASBCA No. 42,363, 1998 WL 354206. Moreover, the contractor must demonstrate it could not reasonably discover the actual facts, and the flawed specifications were material in nature. Whether it would have been reasonable for the prospective bidder to conduct further testing or investigation depends on the particular facts of each procurement, such as the cost of tests relative to the size of the job and the time available to prepare the bid or proposal. See *Robert E. McKee, Inc. v. City of Atlanta*, 414 F. Supp. 957 (N.D. Ga 1976).

Delbert BOYLE, Personal Representative of the Heirs et al. Petitioner, v. UNITED TECHNOLOGIES CORPORATION.

Supreme Court of the United States 487 U.S. 500
Argued Oct. 13, 1987. Reargued April 27, 1988.
Decided June 27, 1988.

Justice SCALIA delivered the opinion of the Court.

This case requires us to decide when a contractor providing military equipment to the Federal Government can be held liable under state tort law for injury caused by a design defect.

I

On April 27, 1983, David A. Boyle, a United States Marine helicopter copilot, was killed when the CH-53D helicopter in which he was flying crashed off the coast of Virginia Beach, Virginia, during a training exercise. Although Boyle survived the impact of the crash, he was unable to escape from the helicopter and drowned. Boyle's father, petitioner here, brought this diversity action in Federal District Court against the Sikorsky Division of United Technologies Corporation (Sikorsky), which built the helicopter for the United States.

At trial, petitioner presented two theories of liability under Virginia tort law that were submitted to the jury. First, petitioner alleged that Sikorsky had defectively repaired a device called the servo in the helicopter's automatic flight control system, which allegedly malfunctioned and caused the crash. Second, petitioner alleged that Sikorsky had defectively designed the copilot's emergency escape system: the escape hatch opened out instead of in (and was therefore ineffective in a submerged craft because of water pressure), and access to the escape hatch handle was obstructed by other equipment. The jury returned a general verdict in favor of petitioner and awarded him $725,000. The District Court denied Sikorsky's motion for judgment notwithstanding the verdict.

The Court of Appeals reversed and remanded with directions that judgment be entered for Sikorsky. 792 F.2d 413 (CA4 1986). * * * * It also found, as a matter of federal law, that Sikorsky could not be held liable for the allegedly defective design of the escape hatch because, on the evidence presented, it satisfied the requirements of the "military contractor defense," which the court had recognized the same day * * * *

II

Petitioner's broadest contention is that, in the absence of legislation specifically immunizing Government contractors from liability for design defects, there is no basis for judicial recognition of such a defense. We disagree.* * * * [W]e have held that a few areas, involving "uniquely federal interests," *Texas Industries, Inc. v. Radcliff Materials, Inc.*, 451 U.S. 630, 640, 101 S.Ct. 2061, 2067, 68 L.Ed.2d 500 (1981), are so committed by the Constitution and laws of the United States to federal control that state law is pre-empted and replaced, where necessary, by federal law of a content prescribed (absent explicit statutory directive) by the courts—so-called "federal common law." See, *e.g., United States v. Kimbell Foods, Inc.*, 440 U.S. 715, 726–729, 99 S.Ct. 1448, 1457–1459, 59 L.Ed.2d 711 (1979); *Banco Nacional v. Sabbatino*, 376 U.S. 398, 426–427, 84 S.Ct. 923, 939–940, 11 L.Ed.2d 804 (1964); *Howard v. Lyons*, 360 U.S. 593, 597, 79 S.Ct. 1331, 1333, 3 L.Ed.2d 1454 (1959); *Clearfield Trust Co. v. United States*, 318 U.S. 363, 366–367, 63 S.Ct. 573, 574–575, 87 L.Ed. 838 (1943); *D'Oench, Duhme & Co. v. FDIC*, 315 U.S. 447, 457–458, 62 S.Ct. 676, 679–680, 86 L.Ed. 956 (1942).

The dispute in the present case borders upon two areas that we have found to involve such "uniquely federal interests." We have held that obligations to and rights of the United States under its contracts are governed exclusively by federal law. See, *e.g., United States v. Little Lake Misere Land Co.*, 412 U.S. 580, 592–594, 93 S.Ct. 2389, 2396–2397, 37 L.Ed.2d 187 (1973); *Priebe & Sons, Inc. v. United States*, 332 U.S. 407, 411, 68 S.Ct. 123, 125, 92 L.Ed. 32 (1947); *National Metropolitan Bank v. United States*, 323 U.S. 454, 456, 65 S.Ct. 354, 355, 89 L.Ed. 383 (1945); *Clearfield Trust, supra*. The present case does not involve an obligation to the United States under its contract, but rather liability to third persons. That liability may be styled one in tort, but it arises out of performance of the contract—and traditionally has been regarded as sufficiently related to the contract that until 1962 Virginia would generally allow design defect suits only by the purchaser and those in privity with the seller. See *General Bronze Corp. v. Kostopulos*, 203 Va. 66, 69–70, 122 S.E.2d 548, 551 (1961); see also Va. Code § 8.2-318 (1965) (eliminating privity requirement).

Another area that we have found to be of peculiarly federal concern, warranting the displacement of state law, is the civil liability of federal officials for actions taken in the course of their duty. We have held in many contexts that the scope of that liability is controlled by federal law. * * * * The present case involves an independent contractor performing its obligation under a procurement contract, rather than an official performing his duty as a federal employee, but there is obviously implicated the same interest in getting the Government's work done.[1]

We think the reasons for considering these closely related areas to be of "uniquely federal" interest apply as well to the civil liabilities arising out of the performance of federal procurement contracts. We have come close to holding as much. * * * *

The imposition of liability on Government contractors will directly affect the terms of Government contracts: either the contractor will decline to manufacture the design specified by the Government, or it will raise its price. Either way, the interests of the United States will be directly affected.

That the procurement of equipment by the United States is an area of uniquely federal interest does not, however, end the inquiry. That merely establishes a necessary, not a sufficient, condition for the displacement of state law. Displacement will occur only where, as we have variously described, a "significant conflict" exists between an identifiable "federal policy or interest and the [operation] of state law," *Wallis, supra,* at 68, 86 S.Ct., at 1304, or the application of state law would "frustrate specific objectives" of federal legislation, *Kimbell Foods,* 440 U.S., at 728, 99 S.Ct., at 1458. * * * *

Here the state-imposed duty of care that is the asserted basis of the contractor's liability (specifically, the duty to equip helicopters with the sort of escape-hatch mechanism petitioner claims was necessary) is precisely contrary to the duty imposed by the Government contract (the duty to manufacture and deliver helicopters with the sort of escape-hatch mechanism shown by the specifications). Even in this sort of situation, it would be unreasonable to say that there is always a "significant conflict" between the state law and a federal policy or interest. If, for example, a federal procurement officer orders, by model number, a quantity of stock helicopters that happen to be equipped with escape hatches opening outward, it is impossible to say that the Government has a significant interest in that particular feature. That would be scarcely more reasonable than saying that a private individual who orders such a craft by model number cannot sue for the manufacturer's negligence because he got precisely what he ordered. * * * *

There is, however, a statutory provision that demonstrates the potential for, and suggests the outlines of, "significant conflict" between federal interests and state law in the context of Government procurement. In the FTCA, Congress authorized damages to be recovered against the United States for harm caused by the negligent or wrongful conduct of Government employees, to the extent that a private person would be liable under the law of the place where the conduct occurred. 28 U.S.C. § 1346(b). It excepted from this consent to suit, however,

> "[a]ny claim...based upon the exercise or performance or the failure to exercise or perform a discretionary function or duty on the part of a federal agency or an employee of the Government, whether or not the discretion involved be abused." 28 U.S.C. § 2680(a).

---

1. Justice Brennan's dissent misreads our discussion here to "intimat[e] that the immunity [of federal officials]...might extend...[to] nongovernment employees" such as a Government contractor. *Post,* at 2524. But we do not address this issue, as it is not before us. We cite these cases merely to demonstrate that the liability of independent contractors performing work for the Federal Government, like the liability of federal officials, is an area of uniquely federal interest.

We think that the selection of the appropriate design for military equipment to be used by our Armed Forces is assuredly a discretionary function within the meaning of this provision. It often involves not merely engineering analysis but judgment as to the balancing of many technical, military, and even social considerations, including specifically the trade-off between greater safety and greater combat effectiveness. And we are further of the view that permitting "second-guessing" of these judgments, see *United States v. Varig Airlines,* 467 U.S. 797, 814, 104 S.Ct. 2755, 2765, 81 L.Ed.2d 660 (1984), through state tort suits against contractors would produce the same effect sought to be avoided by the FTCA exemption. The financial burden of judgments against the contractors would ultimately be passed through, substantially if not totally, to the United States itself, since defense contractors will predictably raise their prices to cover, or to insure against, contingent liability for the Government-ordered designs. To put the point differently: It makes little sense to insulate the Government against financial liability for the judgment that a particular feature of military equipment is necessary when the Government produces the equipment itself, but not when it contracts for the production. In sum, we are of the view that state law which holds Government contractors liable for design defects in military equipment does in some circumstances present a "significant conflict" with federal policy and must be displaced.

We agree with the scope of displacement adopted by the Fourth Circuit here, which is also that adopted by the Ninth Circuit, see *McKay v. Rockwell Int'l Corp., supra,* at 451. Liability for design defects in military equipment cannot be imposed, pursuant to state law, when (1) the United States approved reasonably precise specifications; (2) the equipment conformed to those specifications; and (3) the supplier warned the United States about the dangers in the use of the equipment that were known to the supplier but not to the United States. The first two of these conditions assure that the suit is within the area where the policy of the "discretionary function" would be frustrated— *i.e.,* they assure that the design feature in question was considered by a Government officer, and not merely by the contractor itself. The third condition is necessary because, in its absence, the displacement of state tort law would create some incentive for the manufacturer to withhold knowledge of risks, since conveying that knowledge might disrupt the contract but withholding it would produce no liability. We adopt this provision lest our effort to protect discretionary functions perversely impede them by cutting off information highly relevant to the discretionary decision.

We have considered the alternative formulation of the Government contractor defense, urged upon us by petitioner, which was adopted by the Eleventh Circuit in *Shaw v. Grumman Aerospace Corp.,* 778 F.2d 736, 746 (1985), cert. pending, No. 85-1529. That would preclude suit only if (1) the contractor did not participate, or participated only minimally, in the design of the defective equipment; *or* (2) the contractor timely warned the Government of the risks of the design and notified it of alternative designs reasonably known by it, *and* the Government, although forewarned, clearly authorized the contractor to proceed with the dangerous design. While this formulation may represent a perfectly reasonable tort rule, it is not a rule designed to protect the federal interest embodied in the "discretionary function" exemption. The design ultimately selected may well reflect a significant policy judgment by Government officials whether or not the contractor rather than those officials developed the design. In addition, it does not seem to us sound policy to penalize, and thus deter, active contractor participation in the design process, placing the contractor at risk unless it identifies all design defects.

* * *

Accordingly, the judgment is vacated and the case is remanded.

So ordered.

Justice BRENNAN, with whom Justice MARSHALL and Justice BLACKMUN join, dissenting.

* * *

Our "uniquely federal interest" in the tort liability of affiliates of the Federal Government is equally narrow. The immunity we have recognized has extended no further than a subset of "officials of the Federal Government" and has covered only "discretionary" functions within the scope of their legal authority. * * * * Never before have we so much as intimated that the immunity (or the "uniquely federal interest" that justifies it) might extend beyond that narrow class to cover also nongovernment employees whose authority to act is independent of any source of federal law and that are as far removed from the "functioning of the Federal Government" as is a Government contractor, *Howard, supra,* 360 U.S., at 597, 79 S.Ct., at 1334.

The historical narrowness of the federal interest and the immunity is hardly accidental. A federal officer exercises statutory authority, which not only provides the necessary basis for the immunity in positive law, but also permits us confidently to presume that interference with the exercise of discretion undermines congressional will. In contrast, a Government contractor acts independently of any congressional enactment. Thus, immunity for a contractor lacks both the positive law basis and the presumption that it furthers congressional will.

Moreover, even within the category of congressionally authorized tasks, we have deliberately restricted the scope of immunity to circumstances in which "the contributions of immunity to effective government in particular contexts outweigh the perhaps recurring harm to individual citizens," *Doe v. McMillan,* 412 U.S. 306, 320, 93 S.Ct. 2018, 2028, 36 L.Ed.2d 912 (1973); see *Barr, supra,* 360 U.S., at 572–573, 79 S.Ct., at 1340, because immunity "contravenes the basic tenet that individuals be held accountable for their wrongful conduct," *Westfall, supra,* 484 U.S., at 295, 108 S.Ct., at 583. The extension of immunity to Government contractors skews the balance we have historically struck. On the one hand, whatever marginal effect contractor immunity might have on the "effective administration of policies of government," its "harm to individual citizens" is more severe than in the Government-employee context. Our observation that "there are...other sanctions than civil tort suits available to deter the executive official who may be prone to exercise his functions in an unworthy and irresponsible manner," *Barr,* 360 U.S., at 576, 79 S.Ct., at 1342; see also *id.,* at 571, 79 S.Ct., at 1339, offers little deterrence to the Government contractor. On the other hand, a grant of immunity to Government contractors could not advance "the fearless, vigorous, and effective administration of policies of government" nearly as much as does the current immunity for Government employees. *Ibid.* In the first place, the threat of a tort suit is less likely to influence the conduct of an industrial giant than that of a lone civil servant, particularly since the work of a civil servant is significantly less profitable, and significantly more likely to be the subject of a vindictive lawsuit. In fact, were we to take seriously the Court's assertion that contractors pass their costs—including presumably litigation costs—through, "substantially if not totally, to the United States," *ante,* at 2518, the threat of a tort suit should have only marginal impact on the conduct of Government contractors. More importantly, inhibition of the Government official who actually sets Government policy presents a greater threat to the "administration of policies of government," than does inhibition of a private contractor, whose role is devoted largely to assessing the technological feasibility and cost of satisfying the Government's predetermined needs. Similarly, unlike tort suits against Government officials, tort suits against Government contractors would rarely "consume time and energies" that "would otherwise be devoted to governmental service." 360 U.S., at 571, 79 S.Ct., at 1339.

In short, because the essential justifications for official immunity do not support an extension to the Government contractor, it is no surprise that we have never extended it that far.

I respectfully dissent.

Notes and Questions

1. The opinion begins with the interesting federal-vs.-state choice of law question that turns up most prominently in first-year law school in the line of cases applying the *Erie* decision in civil procedure. Note the somewhat offbeat positioning: Justice Scalia, who ordinarily opposes creation of federal common law, supports it here; his dissenting colleagues to the left, who ordinarily support creation of federal common law, oppose it here. Why? This choice of law issue returns in the chapter on subcontracting.

2. What are the premises of the decision to provide tort immunity to this contractor?

3. Justice Scalia and the dissent make a centerpiece of their discussion the law-and-economics debate over whether the cost of tort suits against a defense contractor will be passed along to the government. You are aware of the distinction between alternative pricing methods—fixed-price or cost-reimbursement—and how much they matter to government contract lawyers. Is Justice Scalia saying that this distinction does not matter to economists—and hence, to policy decisions about law?

4. How does this decision apply if the contractor produces under performance rather than design specifications? If the contractor produces for the commercial market rather than just for defense? If the contractor produces services—or construction, as in *Spearin*—rather than goods?

5. Reconcile this decision with the following one—*Hercules*. See Charles E. Cantu & Randy W. Young, The Government Contractor Defense: Breaking the Boyle Barrier, 62 Alb. L. Rev. 403 (1998); Ronald A. Cass & Clayton P. Gillette, The Government Contractor Defense: Contractual Allocation of Public Risk, 77 Va. L. Rev. 257 (1991).

Hercules Incorporated, et al., Petitioners, v. United States

Supreme Court of the United States, 516 U.S. 417
Argued Oct. 30, 1995, Decided March 4, 1996.

On Writ of Certiorari to the United States Court of Appeals for the Federal Circuit.

Chief Justice REHNQUIST delivered the opinion of the Court.

Petitioners in this case incurred substantial costs defending and then settling third-party tort claims arising out of their performance of Government contracts. In this action under the Tucker Act, they sought to recover these costs from the Government on alternate theories of contractual indemnification or warranty of specifications provided by the Government. We hold that they may not do so.

When the United States had armed forces stationed in Southeast Asia in the 1960's, it asked several chemical manufacturers, including petitioners Hercules Incorporated (Hercules) and Wm. T. Thompson Company (Thompson), to manufacture and sell it a specific phenoxy herbicide, code-named Agent Orange. The Department of Defense wanted to spray the defoliant in high concentrations on tree and plant life in order to both eliminate the enemy's hiding places and destroy its food supplies. From 1964 to 1968, the Government, pursuant to the Defense Production Act of 1950 (DPA), 64 Stat. 798, as amended, 50 U.S.C.App. § 2061 et seq. (1988 ed. and Supp. V), entered into a series of fixed-price production contracts with petitioners. The military prescribed the formula and detailed specifications for manufacture. The contracts also instructed the suppliers to mark the drums containing the herbicide with a 3-inch orange band with "[n]o further identification as to content." Lodging 30. Petitioners fully complied.

In the late 1970's, Vietnam veterans and their families began filing lawsuits against nine manufacturers of Agent Orange, including petitioners. The plaintiffs alleged that the veterans' exposure to dioxin, a toxic by-product found in Agent Orange and believed by many to be hazardous, had caused various health problems. The lawsuits were consolidated in the Eastern District of New York and a class action was certified. In re "Agent Orange" Product Liability Litigation, 506 F.Supp. 762, 787–792 (1980).

* * *

In May 1984, hours before the start of trial, the parties settled. The defendants agreed to create a $180 million settlement fund with each manufacturer contributing on a market-share basis. Hercules' share was $18,772,568, Thompson's was $3,096,597. Petitioners also incurred costs defending these suits exceeding $9 million combined.

Petitioners want the United States to reimburse them for the costs of defending and settling this litigation. They attempted to recover first in District Court under tort theories of contribution and noncontractual indemnification. Having failed there, they each sued the Government in the United States Claims Court, invoking jurisdiction under 28 U.S.C. § 1491, and raising various claims sounding in contract. On the Government's motions, the Claims Court granted summary judgment against petitioners and dismissed both complaints. Hercules, Inc. v. United States, 25 Cl.Ct. 616 (1992); Wm. T. Thompson Co. v. United States, 26 Cl.Ct. 17 (1992).

The two cases were consolidated for appeal and a divided panel of the Court of Appeals for the Federal Circuit affirmed. 24 F.3d 188 (1994). *** We granted certiorari, 514 U.S. — —, 115 S.Ct. 1425, 131 L.Ed.2d 308 (1995), and now affirm the judgment below but on different grounds.

We begin by noting the limits of federal jurisdiction. "[T]he United States, as sovereign, 'is immune from suit save as it consents to be sued … and the terms of its consent to be sued in any court define that court's jurisdiction to entertain the suit.' " United States v. Testan, 424 U.S. 392, 399, 96 S.Ct. 948, 953, 47 L.Ed.2d 114 (1976), quoting United States v. Sherwood, 312 U.S. 584, 586, 61 S.Ct. 767, 769–770, 85 L.Ed. 1058 (1941). Congress created the Claims Court to permit "a special and limited class of cases" to proceed against the United States, Tennessee v. Sneed, 96 U.S. 69, 75, 24 L.Ed. 610 (1878), and the court "can take cognizance only of those [claims] which by the terms of some act of Congress are committed to it," see Thurston v. United States, 232 U.S. 469, 476, 34 S.Ct. 394, 395, 58 L.Ed. 688 (1914); United States v. Sherwood, supra, at 586–589, 61 S.Ct., at 769–771. The Tucker Act confers upon the court jurisdiction to hear and determine, inter alia, claims against the United States founded upon any "express or implied" contract with the United States. 28 U.S.C. § 1491(a).

We have repeatedly held that this jurisdiction extends only to contracts either express or implied-in-fact, and not to claims on contracts implied in law. * * * Each material term or contractual obligation, as well as the contract as a whole, is subject to this juris-dictional limitation. See, e.g., Sutton, supra, at 580–581, 41 S.Ct., at 565–566 (refusing to recognize an implied agreement to pay the fair value of work performed because the term was not "express or implied in fact" in the Government contract for dredging ser-vices); Lopez v. A.C. & S., Inc., 858 F.2d 712, 714–715, 716 (C.A.Fed.1988) (a Spearin warranty within an asbestos contract must be implied in fact).

The distinction between "implied in fact" and "implied in law," and the consequent limitation, is well established in our cases. An agreement implied in fact is "founded upon a meeting of minds, which, although not embodied in an express contract, is in-ferred, as a fact, from conduct of the parties showing, in the light of the surrounding circumstances, their tacit understanding." Baltimore & Ohio R. Co. v. United States, 261 U.S. 592, 597, 43 S.Ct. 425, 426–427, 67 L.Ed. 816 (1923). See also Russell v. United States, 182 U.S. 516, 530, 21 S.Ct. 899, 904, 45 L.Ed. 1210 (1901) ("[T]o give the Court of Claims jurisdiction the demand sued on must be founded on a convention between the parties — 'a coming together of minds' "). By contrast, an agreement implied in law is a "fiction of law" where "a promise is imputed to perform a legal duty, as to repay money obtained by fraud or duress." Baltimore & Ohio R. Co., supra, at 597, 43 S.Ct., at 426.

Petitioners do not contend that their contracts contain express warranty or indemni-fication provisions. Therefore, for them to prevail, they must establish that, based on the circumstances at the time of contracting, there was an implied agreement between the parties to provide the undertakings that petitioners allege. We consider petitioners' warranty-of-specifications and contractual-indemnification claims in turn.

The seminal case recognizing a cause of action for breach of contractual warranty of specifications is United States v. Spearin, 248 U.S. 132, 39 S.Ct. 59, 63 L.Ed. 166 (1918). In that case, Spearin had contracted to build a dry dock in accordance with the Govern-ment's plans which called for the relocation of a storm sewer. After Spearin had moved the sewer, but before he had completed the dry dock, the sewer broke and caused the site to flood. The United States refused to pay for the damages and annulled the con-tract. Spearin filed suit to recover the balance due on his work and lost profits. This Court held that "if the contractor is bound to build according to plans and specifica-tions prepared by [the Government], the contractor will not be responsible for the con-sequences of defects in the plans and specifications." Id., at 136, 39 S.Ct., at 61. From this, petitioners contend the United States is responsible for costs incurred in defending and settling the third-party tort claims. Neither the warranty nor Spearin extends that far. When the Government provides specifications directing how a contract is to be per-formed, the Government warrants that the contractor will be able to perform the con-tract satisfactorily if it follows the specifications. The specifications will not frustrate performance or make it impossible. It is quite logical to infer from the circumstance of one party providing specifications for performance that that party warrants the capabil-ity of performance. But this circumstance alone does not support a further inference that would extend the warranty beyond performance to third-party claims against the contractor. In this case, for example, it would be strange to conclude that the United States, understanding the herbicide's military use, actually contemplated a warranty that would extend to sums a manufacturer paid to a third party to settle claims such as are involved in the present action. It seems more likely that the Government would avoid such an obligation, because reimbursement through contract would provide a contractor with what is denied to it through tort law. See Stencel Aero Engineering Co. v. United States, 431 U.S. 666, 97 S.Ct. 2054, 52 L.Ed.2d 665 (1977).

* * *

[The dissenting opinion of Justice Breyer is omitted.]

Notes and Questions

1. Would it have been improper for the contractor in this instance to purchase liability insurance and include the cost of such insurance as part of the fixed price contract for Agent Orange? Why would a contractor choose not to do so?

2. What is the impact of Congress' refusal to grant the Court of Federal Claims (formerly the Claims Court) jurisdiction over implied-in-law contracts? What is the policy basis for not doing so?

3. The Court discusses the *Spearin* decision, reaffirming it and distinguishing it in interesting ways. When the government awards a contract, it wants the contractor to fulfill the contract's specifications. This decision holds, to oversimplify the matter, that the government stands behind those specifications for contract law purposes but not for tort law purposes. Why? And, why would the statutory and administrative authorizations that suffice for the government to have to pay when its specifications result in contractual burdens on the contractor, not suffice to say that the government should pay tort liability burdens?

L.W. Foster Sportswear Co., Inc. v. The United States

No. 77-65, United States Court of Claims
405 F.2d 1285, Jan. 24, 1969

DAVIS, Judge.

This controversy arises out of two contracts entered into in 1958, under which plaintiff agreed to manufacture and deliver approximately 54,000 goatskin flying jackets for use of the Department of the Navy. Plaintiff requested the contracting officer to make an equitable adjustment in contract price under the Changes article to reimburse it for additional costs allegedly resulting from defective specifications and improper inspections. From a denial by the contracting officer of an equitable adjustment under the contracts, plaintiff appealed to the Armed Services Board of Contract Appeals which denied the appeal. In this court, plaintiff challenges the ASBCA decision as being arbitrary and capricious, not supported by substantial evidence, and as being erroneous as a matter of law in designated particulars. Plaintiff also asserts alternatively that it is entitled to recover on the same facts on a theory of breach of contract. Since its claims were entirely redressable under the contract, however, plaintiff is limited to that relief. It cannot maintain a separate breach of contract action which seeks no further or different relief. Fort Sill Associates v. United States, 355 F.2d 636, 183 Ct.Cl. 301, 304 (1968); Morrison-Knudsen Co., Inc. v. United States, 345 F.2d 833, 170 Ct.Cl. 757 (1965).

From 1949 to 1956, plaintiff successfully manufactured approximately 200,000 flying jackets for the Bureau of Aeronautics of the Department of the Navy under a series of contracts which contained specifications the same as or very similar to those in the contracts in suit. In the performance of these prior contracts, plaintiff was permitted by the Navy to make certain deviations from the specifications, and plaintiff was thoroughly familiar with the practices and procedures used by Navy inspectors in inspecting the jackets. In 1956 the Military Clothing and Textile Supply

Agency (MCTSA), an agency created under the Department of the Army, assumed responsibility for procurement of flying jackets of this type, but until entering into the instant contracts the MCTSA had never contracted for any such flying jackets. Prior to letting the instant bids, the MCTSA prepared Interim Quality Assurance Provisions (IQAP) relating to inspections of the flying jackets. These were then approved by the Navy and incorporated in the contracts. The provisions of the IQAP were substantially the same as those which governed the inspections under the prior contracts.

At the time it entered into these contracts, plaintiff did not discuss with MCTSA the problems which it encountered under the prior contracts, but 'took it for granted' that any such problems would be resolved in the same manner in its performance under the new contracts, and that it would be permitted to make deviations from the specifications in order to produce an acceptable garment. Plaintiff's agent testified before the ASBCA that plaintiff 'envisioned no difference' as to what would constitute an acceptable garment under the present contracts, because, although the procurement agency was different, plaintiff was contracting to make the same jackets which it had previously made for the Navy.

**** Because the deliveries under both contracts were later than the delivery schedule as extended, the contracting officer terminated both contracts, with the result that certain questions, not here at issue, were presented to and decided by the ASBCA.

From the commencement of its production, plaintiff complained to defendant regarding the specifications, the IQAP and the inspections, which plaintiff felt were too stringent and based in part upon a misinterpretation of the specifications and the IQAP.

* * *

In denying plaintiff's appeal, the ASBCA stated that plaintiff was 'aware that it could not or did not intend to manufacture in strict compliance with the specifications'; that the evidence failed to establish that the difficulties encountered because of the specification requirements 'were not the normal, minor, and relatively insignificant specification requirements which often necessitate slight adjustment in mass production and for which additional compensation is neither sought nor expected'; that the 'delay, if any, in reaching satisfactory solutions *** must be charged to (plaintiff) because of its failure to timely alert the contracting officer of the problems known to it before the contract award'; and that while 'some evidence indicates error in certain matters on the part of an inspector', '(t)he record will not support a finding that the defects scored in the inspections were not in fact defects as defined by the specifications nor that lot rejections were not made as dictated by the contract provisions.'

We hold that the ASBCA's characterization of the specification defects as minor is not supported by substantial evidence and that its ruling that the delay was attributable primarily to the plaintiff was erroneous. Therefore we reverse the Board, hold that the plaintiff is entitled to an equitable adjustment in the contract price, and suspend our proceedings in order for the parties to return to the Board for a determination of the amount of the adjustment.

There is no doubt, in the first place, that the specifications were defective. The record clearly reflects instances in which defendant's agents admitted as much. The Government later amended the specifications in question, incorporating many of the changes found necessary in the performance of this contract. The ASBCA actually assumed that they were defective, finding that the plaintiff had been granted deviations under its earlier contracts, and that the design requirements 'could not be strictly complied with'; the Board's ruling rested on its characterization of the defects as minor and its allocation of fault to the plaintiff.

The Government argues that, even though there were defects in the specifications, they did not make performance impossible. Plaintiff's officers admitted that single garments could be produced under these limitations—they became unworkable only when applied to the production of flying jackets in mass quantities. This court has adopted an approach to impossibility based on 'commercial impracticability' which fully embraces the concept that 'commercial practicability ceases where the demands of mass procurement can no longer be satisfied through the means of mass production.' Natus Corp. v. United States, 371 F.2d 450, 456, 178 Ct.Cl. 1, 10 (1967). In Natus, supra, and Clark Grave Vault Co. v. United States, 371 F.2d 459, 178 Ct.Cl. 52 (1967), we held that the Government did not guarantee that a contractor could successfully and profitably produce an item by a means chosen entirely by him from several alternatives available. Here the plaintiff was forced to make the jackets by particular procedures and according to detailed standards spelled out in the specifications, which were not compatible with mass production—an entirely different situation. See also Centre Mfg. Co., Inc. v. United States, 392 F.2d 229, 233, 241, 183 Ct.Cl. 115, 121—122, 136 (1968).

These defects were not the 'normal, minor, and relatively insignificant specification requirements which often necessitate slight adjustments in mass production and for which additional compensation is neither sought nor expected.' They related to the methods of (1) combining the leather, rayon and knit elements of the jacket, (2) sewing on the pocket flap, (3) sewing all the leather seams (number of stitches per inch), (4) completing each seam (backstitching), (5) attaching the wristbands and waistband to the jacket (the size of the margin), and (6) to the types of repairs which would be tolerated (inspection of mended knits). Almost the only parts of the job which would not be affected by these functions are the size of the jackets and the construction and sewing on of zippers. While we give great deference to the expertise and hence to the findings of the Board on these matters (cf. Red Circle Corp. v. United States, 398 F.2d 836, 842, 185 Ct.Cl. 1 (July 1968)), here the record does not at all support the Board's conclusion that these defects were so minor as to be de minimis or expectable in ordinary course. The only inference the record will properly sustain is that the defects were material and significant.

It is now familiar law that a contractor is entitled to an equitable adjustment under the Changes article for increased costs of performance due to defective specifications. Bell v. United States, 404 F.2d 975, 186 Ct.Cl.—(Dec.1968); Red Circle Corp. v. United States, 398 F.2d 836, 841—842, 185 Ct.Cl. 1 (July 1968); Centre Mfg. Co., Inc. v. United States, supra, 392 F.2d 229, 232—233, 241, 183 Ct.Cl. 115, 121, 136 (1968); Maxwell Dynamometer Co. v. United States, 386 F.2d 855, 872, 181 Ct.Cl. 607, 634 (1967); Hol-Gar Mfg. Corp. v. United States, 360 F.2d 634, 638, 175 Ct.Cl. 518, 524 (1966); J. D. Hedin Constr. Co., Inc. v. United States, 347 F.2d 235, 246, 171 Ct.Cl. 70, 85—86 (1965). However, we have consistently held that 'an experienced contractor cannot rely on government-prepared specifications where, on the basis of the government furnished data, he knows or should have known that the prepared specifications could not produce the desired result for '*** he has no right to make a useless thing and charge the customer for it.' R. M. Hollingshead Corp. v. United States, 111 F.Supp. 285, 286, 124 Ct.Cl. 681, 683 (1953).' J. D. Hedin Constr. Co. Inc. v. United States, supra, 347 F.2d at 241, 171 Ct.Cl. at 77; See also, Allied Contractors, Inc. v. United States, 381

F.2d 995, 1000, 180 Ct.Cl. 1057, 1064—1065 (1967); Beacon Constr. Co. of Mass. v. United States, 314 F.2d 501, 504, 161 Ct.Cl. 1, 7 (1963); Ring Constr. Corp. v. United States, 162 F.Supp. 190, 191—192, 142 Ct.Cl. 731, 734 (1958); Anthony M. Meyerstein, Inc. v. United States, 137 F.Supp. 427, 431, 133 Ct.Cl. 694, 700 (1956); DuBois Constr. Corp. v. United States, 98 F.Supp. 590, 594, 120 Ct.Cl. 139, 169 (1951); cf. Leal v. United States, 276 F.2d 378, 383, 149 Ct.Cl. 451, 460 (1960); Ragonese v. United States, 120 F.Supp. 768, 770—771, 128 Ct.Cl. 156, 162 (1954).

The rationale of these two lines of cases is that the contractor can rely upon the Government's representations as to how a desired product should and can be made, unless he ought to know better. In the latter situation, he cannot argue that he has been misled or that he had any right to make his bid on the basis of the specifications which he knew (or should have realized) were not correct. The rule is parallel to the ordinary defense to a suit for misrepresentation that the plaintiff did not, or had no right to, rely upon the challenged statement.

Plaintiff admittedly knew that it could not produce an acceptable flying jacket under the contract specifications, as written, at the time that it submitted its bid. But it had had five or six previous contracts with the Navy for the same type of jacket, with the same or very similar specifications, and in every case deviations were made and allowed as a matter of course—and had to be made for production to go on. Both the plaintiff and the Navy were aware of this past history, and necessarily relied upon it in entering into new contracts of the same type. We have no doubt that plaintiff would have a sound claim if the Navy had abruptly changed its practices under the same contract specifications. We likewise have no doubt that plaintiff would not have to indicate at the time it bid on the successor Navy contracts that it expected to obtain the same deviations. See Franklin Co. v. United States, 381 F.2d 416, 420, 180 Ct.Cl. 666, 673—674 (1967). Does it make any difference that plaintiff was dealing in this instance with the MCTSA and not the Navy?

There is no finding and little evidence that the MCTSA actually knew of the defects in the specifications or the prior practice with regard to deviations from the flying jacket contract requirements, or that it had consulted with the Navy prior to the award concerning the problems involved in this sort of procurement. But the actual knowledge of the MCTSA is not controlling. In considering the sufficiency of the Government's defense to plaintiff's claim for relief arising out of defective specifications, the Board is not confined to the subjective knowledge of the procuring agency but must look to the reasonableness of the contractor's actions and beliefs. The issue is whether or not the contractor reasonably believed that the MCTSA knew of the defects and could be expected to continue the pattern of deviations established in prior procurements of the same jackets. If that was a reasonable assumption, plaintiff cannot be said to know, or have reason to know, that the specifications and standards which would actually be used in performance would be faulty.

Recently, in J. A. Jones Construction Co. v. United States, 390 F.2d 886, 182 Ct.Cl. 615 (1968), we considered a somewhat comparable problem relating to inter-agency relationships. That plaintiff contracted with the Army Corps of Engineers, acting as construction agency for the Air Force, to build certain facilities at Cape Kennedy. At the time the contract was let, the Air Force, but not the Corps of Engineers, knew that a large, high priority ICBM construction program, based on the payment of premium wages, was to be undertaken in the same area. The resulting drain on the labor force caused the plaintiff to incur greatly increased labor costs. We held that, in those circumstances, the Air Force had a duty to disclose the information to persons contracting with the Corps of Engineers on its behalf (or to warn them), since there was a 'meaningful connection' between the two agencies with respect to the procurement which cast an affirmative responsibility upon the Air Force as the using agency.

In this case the relationship between the Navy and MCTSA, with respect to this procurement, was such that the contractor could reasonably anticipate that they would consult, that the latter would learn from the former of the deviations which had been permitted, and that the new agency would follow the same policies. Foster was to produce jackets with a perforation reading 'U.S. Navy' and to deliver them directly to various Navy depots. The procurement was therefore on behalf of the service with which the plaintiff had previously worked directly in supplying these same jackets. As already indicated, the specifications were identical or very closely similar to those used in the Navy contracts. Furthermore, the MCTSA was not a separate and independent government unit but was within the Defense Department, and in particular was the successor purchasing agency to the Navy procurement office for textile products like these jackets. In these circumstances we hold that the only acceptable conclusion is that plaintiff acted reasonably in relying upon the likelihood that the knowledge of the former agency would be carried over into the latter, that the contractor would be treated as before in its jacket procurement contracts, and that it could act as if the Navy were still the procuring unit. In short, plaintiff acted reasonably in assuming that the formal change in procurement offices did not rupture the relationship which had already been established between the contractor and the Government with respect to the manufacture of these particular garments. From this it follows that the Board was in error in holding that Foster was to blame for the damages resulting from the faulty specifications. The burden of the defective plans and contract requirements, including any delay in remedying the defects, remains upon the Government.

* * *

We hold, in sum, that plaintiff is entitled to an equitable adjustment in the amount of its increased costs as a result of the defective specifications (including inspection standards), and suspend proceedings for 90 days in this court in order for the parties to return to the Armed Services Board of Contract Appeals for a determination of the proper amount of such an adjustment, in accordance with this opinion, either on the present record or after further evidence is produced, as the Board may decide. To that extent plaintiff's motion for summary judgment is granted and defendant's is denied. Plaintiff will comply with Rule 100 and the General Order of April 1, 1968.

Notes and Questions

1. At what point in time can the government change its pattern of practice in dealing with a contractor that is performing pursuant to government specifications? If the government had notified the contractor and other prospective bidders prior to submission of bids that specifications would be strictly enforced, would the result have been different?

2. The court found that it was reasonable for the contractor to conclude in this instance that the procurement practices of the Navy—in particular, the willingness to accept deviations from the specifications—would be carried over to the Army. What is the Army's argument in this case? Is there a tension between the result in this case and the principle that estoppel does not run against the government? If Navy personnel had regularly overpaid the contractor, and the Army ceased doing so, would the Army have been liable?

3. Before the contractor prevailed, the contractor spent almost ten years litigating this issue. What action could the contractor have taken in order to avoid such a result?

4. Note the interaction between specifications, inspection, and acceptance. In theory, the Army inspectors have to inspect by comparison with a standard; they use the specifications as the standard. Work that passes inspection receives acceptance. How much does the case undermine the bona fides of this legal structure, suggesting that contracting officers and contractors engage in informal practical arrangements for the agency client to get what it wants from the contractor, with the formal aspects being seen as often merely an inconvenience and sometimes a completely impractical obstacle?

2. Inspection and Acceptance

Inspection is how the government determines whether the contractor has followed the specifications. As noted, the government may inspect for itself, direct the contractor to maintain a quality control system that does the inspection, or both. The decision as to which system to rely on often depends upon the type of product or service being acquired. Commercial items are generally purchased with no government inspections prior to delivery and reliance on the contractor's quality assurance program, if any. FAR 52.212-4(a). In contrast, contracts for government-unique, non-commercial items will almost always permit government, in-process inspection and may mandate a quality assurance program that meets specific government requirements. FAR 52.246-2. Under reasonable circumstances, the degree and amount of government inspection and mandating of quality assurance requirements will vary with the nature of the item or service being acquired. The more critical the item, the more detailed the requirements. Of note, the government inspection when conducted at the contractor's facility is performed at the contractor's expense.

Where a formal acceptance certificate is lacking, the exercise of control and possession of an item can lead to an implied acceptance by the government. Whether by formal document or implication, final acceptance, in the context of government contracting, means that the contractor has performed in compliance with contract specifications and requirements. In order to recover damages suffered as a result of an inappropriate acceptance, the government must prove the existence of a latent defect, fraud, or gross mistake amounting to fraud that could not have reasonably been discovered at time of acceptance. Without such latent defects or fraud, the government is estopped from later rejecting non-conforming supplies or services that it properly accepted.

When a contractor tenders non-conforming goods, the government can select from various options based upon the provisions of standard contract clauses. The government can simply reject the non-conforming goods or services and demand performance consistent with contract requirements and within the timeframe provided for in the contract. Failure to comply can result in a default termination with excess costs of reprocurement being assessed to the contractor. As an alternative, the government can require repair of non-conforming products or reperformance of non-conforming services at no additional cost to the government. In circumstances where the repair or reperformance cannot be accomplished within the time specified for performance, the government can insist upon additional consideration being received from the contractor, generally in the form of reduced prices.

In certain circumstances, the government can and will accept non-conforming goods and services. Such a discretionary determination is based upon such factors as urgency or financial considerations and the conclusion that the supplies or services will perform their intended services in a safe manner. In such situations the government can and will demand consideration for accepting non-conforming goods.

One particularly important type of contract is the "first-article contract." The government may want to see the contractor produce an example of the product—a prototype—and decide whether to approve it before exercising its purchase options. Thus, a critical phase of examination and testing of the prototype occurs before full-scale performance. Only after approval of the first article does the contractor produce and deliver substantial numbers of units.

First-article contracts suit situations where the contractor has to design and build a new or substantially modified product. In effect, the contractor sets off with just the government contract's "Statement of Work" to explore some terra incognita of production. A contractor faces a substantial risk of default termination if the government comes down hard on its deficiencies.

INSPECTION OF SUPPLIES CLAUSE—Fixed-Price
(Aug 1996)

(a) Definition. "Supplies," as used in this clause, includes but is not limited to raw materials, components, intermediate assemblies, end products, and lots of supplies.

(b) The Contractor shall provide and maintain an inspection system acceptable to the Government covering supplies under this contract and shall tender to the Government for acceptance only supplies that have been inspected in accordance with the inspection system and have been found by the Contractor to be in conformity with contract requirements. As part of the system, the Contractor shall prepare records evidencing all inspections made under the system and the outcome. These records shall be kept complete and made available to the Government during contract performance and for as long afterwards as the contract requires. The Government may perform reviews and evaluations as reasonably necessary to ascertain compliance with this paragraph. These reviews and evaluations shall be conducted in a manner that will not unduly delay the contract work. The right of review, whether exercised or not, does not relieve the Contractor of the obligations under the contract.

(c) The Government has the right to inspect and test all supplies called for by the contract, to the extent practicable, at all places and times, including the period of manufacture, and in any event before acceptance. The Government shall perform inspections and tests in a manner that will not unduly delay the work. The Government assumes no contractual obligation to perform any inspection and test for the benefit of the Contractor unless specifically set forth elsewhere in this contract.

(d) If the Government performs inspection or test on the premises of the Contractor or a subcontractor, the Contractor shall furnish, and shall require subcontractors to furnish, at no increase in contract price, all reasonable facilities and assistance for the safe and convenient performance of these duties. Except as otherwise provided in the contract, the Government shall bear the expense of Government inspections or tests made at other than the Contractor's or subcontractor's premises; provided, that in case of rejection, the Government shall not be liable for any reduction in the value of inspection or test samples.

(e) (1) When supplies are not ready at the time specified by the Contractor for inspection or test, the Contracting Officer may charge to the Contractor the additional cost of inspection or test.

(2) The Contracting Officer may also charge the Contractor for any additional cost of inspection or test when prior rejection makes reinspection or retest necessary.

(f) The Government has the right either to reject or to require correction of nonconforming supplies. Supplies are nonconforming when they are defective in material or workmanship or are otherwise not in conformity with contract requirements. The Government may reject nonconforming supplies with or without disposition instructions.

(g) The Contractor shall remove supplies rejected or required to be corrected. * * *

(h) If the Contractor fails to promptly remove, replace, or correct rejected supplies that are required to be removed or to be replaced or corrected, the Government may either

(1) by contract or otherwise, remove, replace, or correct the supplies and charge the cost to the Contractor or

(2) terminate the contract for default. Unless the Contractor corrects or replaces the supplies within the delivery schedule, the Contracting Officer may require their delivery and make an equitable price reduction. Failure to agree to a price reduction shall be a dispute.

(I) (1) If this contract provides for the performance of Government quality assurance at source, and if requested by the Government, the Contractor shall furnish advance notification of the time

(i) when Contractor inspection or tests will be performed in accordance with the terms and conditions of the contract and

(ii) when the supplies will be ready for Government inspection.

(2) The Government's request shall specify the period and method of the advance notification and the Government representative to whom it shall be furnished. Requests shall not require more than 2 workdays of advance notification if the Government representative is in residence in the Contractor's plant, nor more than 7 workdays in other instances.

(j) The Government shall accept or reject supplies as promptly as practicable after delivery, unless otherwise provided in the contract. Government failure to inspect and accept or reject the supplies shall not relieve the Contractor from responsibility, nor impose liability on the Government, for nonconforming supplies.

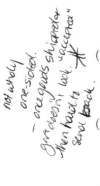

(k) Inspections and tests by the Government do not relieve the Contractor of responsibility for defects or other failures to meet contract requirements discovered before acceptance. Acceptance shall be conclusive, except for latent defects, fraud, gross mistakes amounting to fraud, or as otherwise provided in the contract.

(l) If acceptance is not conclusive for any of the reasons in paragraph (k) hereof, the Government, in addition to any other rights and remedies provided by law, or under other provisions of this contract, shall have the right to require the Contractor

(1) at no increase in contract price, to correct or replace the defective or nonconforming supplies at the original point of delivery or at the Contractor's plant at

the Contracting Officer's election, and in accordance with a reasonable delivery schedule as may be agreed upon between the Contractor and the Contracting Officer; provided, that the Contracting Officer may require a reduction in contract price if the Contractor fails to meet such delivery schedule, or

(2) within a reasonable time after receipt by the Contractor of notice of defects or nonconformance, to repay such portion of the contract as is equitable under the circumstances if the Contracting Officer elects not to require correction or replacement. When supplies are returned to the Contractor, the Contractor shall bear the transportation cost from the original point of delivery to the Contractor's plant and return to the original point when that point is not the Contractor's plant. If the Contractor fails to perform or act as required in (1) or (2) above and does not cure such failure within a period of 10 days (or such longer period as the Contracting Officer may authorize in writing) after receipt of notice from the Contracting Officer specifying such failure, the Government shall have the right by contract or otherwise to replace or correct such supplies and charge to the Contractor the cost occasioned the Government thereby.

Appeal of Technical Ordnance, Inc.
1989 WL 48024 (A.S.B.C.A.), 89-2 BCA 21,818,
ASBCA No. 34,748 April 4, 1989

OPINION BY ADMINISTRATIVE JUDGE LIPMAN

The Government terminated the contract for default due to appellant's failure to satisfy the contract's first article testing requirements. Appellant seeks conversion of the default termination to a termination for the convenience of the Government.

FINDINGS OF FACT

The Department of the Navy, Navy Ships Parts Control Center (the Government) awarded contract No. N00104-84-C-A079 to Technical Ordnance, Inc. (appellant) on 25 April 1984. The contract required appellant to provide 6247 explosive bolts for the MK46 torpedo exercise head at $62.50 each, or a fixed price of $390,437.50.

The explosive bolts fasten onto the exercise head of the MK46 missile. During fleet training, at a certain point in the missile's run the exercise head gives a signal to the bolt to explode. The bolt's explosion drops two lead weights. The release of the weights results in the missile achieving a positive buoyancy so that the Navy can recover the missile after the exercise run. If the explosive bolt fails to operate, the weapon may sink (and the Navy may lose an expensive weapon) or the weapon may float at an unknown level under the water (which could result in its recovery by someone other than the United States).

The contract contained the FIRST ARTICLE APPROVAL-GOVERNMENT TESTING, ASPR 1- 1906(b) (1969 SEP) clause. This clause indicated that "if the Contracting Officer disapproves any first article, the Contractor shall be deemed to have failed to make delivery within the meaning of the 'Default' clause of this contract, and this contract shall be subject to termination for default...." The delivery schedule required appellant to provide 50 first article samples by 24 July 1984.

The contract incorporated by reference MILITARY SPECIFICATION CARTRIDGES, EXPLOSIVE BOLT (For Torpedoes MK 46 All Mods) MIL-C-81093A. MIL-C-81093A stated, in pertinent part:

4.3.1 First article sample....Acceptance of the first article sample shall be based on no defects in the sample. Further production of the cartridge by the supplier prior to approval of the first article sample, shall be at the supplier's risk....

* * *

4.5.6.2 Firing Test. Each cartridge to be tested shall be mounted in the fracturable bolt accepted to Dwg 2132278 and tested under the test circuit of FIGURE 3 and the test configuration of FIGURE 4. The firing signal shall be 0.5 plus or minus 0.02 ampere, applied alternately to the AB and CD bridgewire circuits in any group of functional samples. The firing signal shall be monitored and the magnitude and the duration of the signal recorded....Acceptance criteria for the firing test shall be as follows:

(a) A 15 millisecond maximum firing delay, as shown by the duration of the electrical signal.

(b) Detonation after ignition.

(c) Complete fracture of the bolt.

Appellant incorporated MIL-C-81093A paragraphs 4.5.1 and 4.5.6.2 into its inspection plan and used the inspection plan in administration of the contract.

Appellant's first two first article test submissions failed to gain the Government's acceptance. The first failure resulted from firing deficiencies. The second first article test failure resulted from leakage problems.

In a 14 January 1987 report, the Government summarized test results from appellant's third first article test—a preproduction test sample of 50 explosive bolts submitted by appellant on 6 November 1986. The report stated:

2. TEST RESULTS

* * *

b. Test U—Firing Test 0 degrees F

Two bolts failed to meet the 15 millisecond bolt separation requirement. ***

3. CONCLUSION

It is concluded that the explosive bolts...manufactured by Technical Ordnance, Incorporated...failed to meet the requirements of [MIL-C-81093A].

The report also noted that: (1) although certain serial numbers were illegible, this was a discrepancy, not a defect, and (2) although 10 of 44 bolts leaked, none failed the post fire leak test requirements.

A 15 December 1986 memorandum from the Naval Undersea Warfare Engineering Station to the Navy Ships Parts Control Center recommended termination of the contract due to (1) the 15.98 and 16.13 millisecond firing times and (2) the illegible serial numbers.

The Government's test engineer tested the explosive bolts, and he used the specifications and the unpublished Naval Undersea Warfare Engineering Station STANDARD EVALUATION PROCEDURE FOR PREPRODUCTION EVALUATION OF THE EXPLOSIVE BOLT, DWG 2539131, PROCEDURE NO. WCB-T-056. ***

The manner in which the Government tested the explosive bolts differed from the specifications in both equipment and procedure. ***

By letter of 23 February 1987, the contracting officer terminated the contract for default. The only test failure cited for the third first article submission was the failure of the two bolts to meet the 15 millisecond maximum bolt separation time.

Appellant filed a timely appeal. ***

DECISION

The contract for the production and supply of explosive bolts was terminated for default due to the alleged failure of two of 50 bolts in the first article submittal to meet specification requirements for bolt separation. Appellant seeks a conversion of the default termination into one for the convenience of the Government based upon the Government's testing procedures.

Appellant cites Bula Forge, Inc., PSBCA No. 1490, 87-3 BCA p 20,159, for the proposition that the Government bears the burden of proving that the Government properly rejected the first article submission. In Bula Forge, the Postal Board explained:

To support the default termination or rejection of a product because of failure to meet contract requirements, Respondent has the burden of proving the contractor's default. Roosevelt Components, Inc., ASBCA No. 17970, 74-2 BCA p 10,661. If it makes a prima facie case, the burden of going forward with evidence then shifts to the Appellant. Rohr-Plessy Corp., PSBCA No. 36, 76-2 BCA p 11,995. However, the ultimate burden of persuasion to prove by a preponderance of evidence that the rejection or termination was proper remains with the Government. Cf. Harco Manufacturing Co., ASBCA No. 27567, 85-1 BCA p 17,926.

(87-3 BCA at 102,034) We focus, therefore, on whether the Government has met its burden of proving, by a preponderance of the evidence, that the failure of the first article submission and resulting termination for default were proper.

The Government concedes that its testing practices deviated from MIL-C- 81093A. The Government added a Government designed and built pulse generator to the constant power source. The Government added a counter to test apparatus and read the test results from the counter in lieu of the specified oscilloscope. Finally, the Government failed to record the testing with a camera.

The Government cites Solar Laboratories, ASBCA No. 19269, 74-2 BCA p 10,897, for the proposition that a deviation from contractual test procedures does not invalidate the test results as a matter of law. In Solar Laboratories, where the Government substituted thermocouples for mercury thermometers, the Board found that testing not prescribed in the contract could be used as a basis for rejection of contract items, provided that the tests did not impose a more stringent standard than the contract or the testing method prescribed. The Board explained:

If the contractor shows that the testing was not in accordance with the contract, the burden shifts back to the Government to show comparability of the testing with the contractually prescribed method....

In this case, it is undisputed that the Government's testing found that appellant's first articles failed to meet contractual heating requirements. It is likewise undisputed that the Government's testing procedures departed from the contract in three respects. Hence, the threshold question for us is whether the Government has established the comparability of its testing with contractually required testing.

(74-2 BCA at 51,859-60) To the extent that the Board there found comparability between the thermometers and the thermocouples, we distinguish the holding in Solar Laboratories.

In Solar Laboratories, all thermocouples were calibrated against a National Bureau of Standards thermometer before and after the testing and between the third and fourth test cycles, 74-2 BCA at 51,858, the Government brought forth extensive expert testimony including comparability experimentation establishing that there was no material difference in the results, 74-2 BCA at 51,861, the Government curtailed the tests due to the contractor's excessive failures, 74-2 BCA at 51,862, and the Government choice to use thermocouples derived from the thermocouples' automatic recording device which resulted in considerable personnel time savings, 74-2 BCA at 51,861.

In the present appeal, the Government used a self-constructed pulse generator which lacked instruction or calibration manuals. In addition, although the Government's witnesses asserted a preference for counters over oscilloscopes, the Government presented no evidence of their comparability. Further, unlike the excessive temperature failures in Solar Laboratories, the present appeal presents deviations of less than 2 milliseconds on two out of fifty bolts. Finally, the Government here presented no evidence that savings in time or effort would result from (1) its failure to use the camera, (2) its addition of the pulse generator, or (3) the substitution of the counter for the oscilloscope.

The Government deviated from the contractually specified test procedures. Moreover, the Government failed to show that the results achieved are comparable to those under the contractually designed procedures. The contract required that the Government record, in a specific manner, the results, as obtained by specific equipment, of these destructive tests. We cannot find the Government's rejection of the first articles to be proper. See Mega Construction, Inc., ASBCA No. 32127, 88-1 BCA p 20,427; Solar Laboratories, supra.

We sustain appellant's appeal, and the default termination is converted to a termination for the convenience of the Government.

Notes and Questions

1. First article testing as a form of inspection and acceptance is appropriate in four circumstances. First, it is appropriate when a contractor has not previously furnished the product to the Government. Second, it is appropriate when the contractor has previously furnished the item, but there have been subsequent changes in processes or specifications, production has been discontinued for an extended period of time, or problems surfaced with products previously submitted and accepted. Third, it is appropriate where the product is described by a performance specification. Finally, it is appropriate where it is essential to have an approved first article to serve as a manufacturing standard. FAR 9.303. Which of the above cited reasons could have been used to justify the use of first article testing in *Technical Ordnance, Inc.*?

2. First article testing is generally not used for research and development contracts, products already on a qualified products list wherein the products have previously been tested, commercial products, and products built to detailed technical specifications. FAR 9.304.

3. When the government imposes first article testing on contractors, the FAR mandates that the contractor must be apprised of the performance or other characteristics that the first article must meet for approval and the tests to which the first article will be subjected for approval. FAR 9.306. The failure by the government to abide by the stated tests can release the contractor from the consequences of a default termination. However, note the remedy sought in *Technical Ordnance, Inc.* — a conversion of a default termination to one for the convenience of the government. The failure of a contractor to provide the desired government product, even when the failure is due to unclear gov-

ernment direction, will most often result not in the contractor receiving the benefit of its bargain (i.e., its profit), but merely avoiding excess costs of reprocurement associated with a default termination.

4. Under certain circumstances a contractor may be able to use the standard of "reasonable" government inspections as a defense to government claims. For example, if the government interferes with the performance of a contract through excessive supervision, by making it difficult for the contractor's employees to complete their work, or conducting multiple inspections, the contractor may be able to recover the costs of delay as well and receive an extension of time for completing the contract schedule. In addition, a contractor may recover costs if the government changes the location of the inspection or the contractor could not have reasonably anticipated the inspection at the time of contracting. An equitable adjustment may be proper if the government imposes an inspection standard stricter than the industry custom.

Mann Chemical Laboratories, Inc., Plaintiff v. United States of America, Defendant

Civ. A. No. 57-300 United States District Court for the District of Massachusetts 182 F.Supp. 40, March 2, 1960

SWEENEY, Chief Judge.

This is an action brought under the authority of 28 U.S.C. § 1346(a)(2), and is alleged to arise out of an express contract between the parties. The contract was for the furnishing of certain bottles of water purification tablets on specified dates. These tablets were intended for the use of the Armed Forces.

The case comes before this Court after decision by the Armed Services Board of Contract Appeals, hereinafter referred to as the 'Board', and in accordance with the Court's Order of December 29, 1958, D.C. 174 F.Supp. 563, was tried on the record and not 'de novo'. The plaintiff was allowed to testify at length on the facts surrounding the rejection of the tablets because of their spotted appearance.

Findings of Fact

The plaintiff contracted to furnish the defendant on specified dates with a large number of bottles of water purification tablets. The delivery dates in question were May 5th, May 20th, and June 5th, all in the year 1951. The plaintiff's claim is divisible into two parts: (1) Damages for wrongful termination of the contract with relation to the plaintiff's inability to secure acceptable bottles, and (2) Damages caused to the plaintiff by reason of the government's failure to accept the tablets themselves when proffered.

Both claims were processed before the Contracting Officer and the Board, and were decided against the plaintiff. The Board specifically found on reconsideration of its prior decision that the bottle delay was not excusable in that 'the condition necessary for holding the default to have been excusable was not shown'. The record amply supports this finding, and in fact at the hearing before this Court the plaintiff limited its evidence and argument to the second phase of this case.

Next we are met with the question whether the government unreasonably delayed the acceptance of the proffered tablets to the damage of the plaintiff, thereby breaching the contract. This Court is limited in its adjudication to the question whether the administrative decision by the Board was supported by the evidence and was not capricious or arbitrary. A review of the record taken in conjunction with the evidence presented at the trial convinces the Court that the plaintiff is not entitled to be compensated for its expenses attendant upon the defendant's delay in immediately accepting the tablets delivered on the three dates in question.

Late in June or in early July the plaintiff anticipated that certain brown spots would appear on what should be white tablets, and communicated this fact to the defendant, advising it that the spots were the result of excess moisture due to high humidity, and that they were not impurities. The government, in spite of the representations by the plaintiff, refused to accept the tablets until after an independent analysis of the tablets had been made. As a result of this analysis, the government, in December of 1951, issued shipping instructions to the plaintiff, and accepted the tablets in question. Thereafter the plaintiff submitted claims against the government for the wrongful termination of and for breach of the contract by reason of its failure to accept the deliveries as and when proffered.

The tablets were for the purification of what might otherwise be contaminated water, and it could be reasonably assumed that they were to be used under extreme conditions attendant upon the military invasion of new territory, and were for the safety and well being of the invading troops. While the contract did not call for white tablets, nevertheless the appearance of brown spots was not common, and suggested the probable presence of a foreign material.

Actually, if the quality of the tablets was impaired by the brown spots, they were worthless for the purpose intended, and this Court feels that the government was quite right in the careful steps that it took to be sure that the tablets were in strict conformance with the specifications. They could hardly do less, having in mind the purpose for which the tablets were intended. I find that the failure to accept the tablets when first offered because of their appearance was reasonable. The methods of sampling and testing by the governments were normal under the circumstances, and fully supported the Board's decision.

Conclusions of Law

From the foregoing I find and rule that judgment should be entered for the defendant.

Acceptance

From: Fundamentals of Federal Contract Law (1990) by Eugene W. Massengale Copyright (c) (1991) by Greenwood Press. Reproduced with permission of Greenwood Publishing Group, Inc., Westport, CT

Acceptance is defined as an act of an authorized representative of the government by which the government, for itself or as an agent of another, assumes ownership of existing identified supplies tendered or approves specific services rendered as partial or complete performance of the contract. FAR §46.101. The act of assuming ownership constitutes acknowledgment that the supplies or services conform with applicable quality and quantity requirements and with other turn and conditions of the contract. Acceptance may take place before delivery, at the time of delivery, or after delivery, depending on specific provisions of the contract. Supplies or services ordinarily will not be accepted before completion of government quality assurance actions, unless a certificate of conformance is utilized. Moreover, acceptance is normally evidenced by execution of an acceptance certificate, an inspection or receiving report, or a commercial shipping document. FAR §46.501.

Final acceptance can mean only one thing within the context of a government contract: conclusive and decisive action by which the government determines through its authorized agents that, on the basis of all the facts within its knowledge, the contractor has satisfactorily performed his obligations under the contract. *C.G. McQuagge v. United States,* 197 F. Supp. 460 (D.C.La. 1961). Further, inspection and acceptance of projects by phases or parts of the work comprise a recognized way of conducting construction projects. *L.A. Barton & Co.,* ASBCA No. 17547, 73-2 BCA 10,249. Supply contracts provide for acceptance either at the origin or at the destination. Normally, supplies accepted at a place other than the destination will not be reinspected at the destination for acceptance purposes, but are examined only for quantity, damage in transit, or possible product substitution or fraud.

Under ordinary circumstances, contractors tendering nonconforming goods or services are given the opportunity to replace or correct such goods or services and thus permit government acceptance, when this can be accomplished within the required delivery schedule. Unless the contract specifies otherwise, is may be the case with cost reimbursement contracts, replacement or correction is to be made without additional cost to the government. Otherwise, the Contracting Officer is ordinarily required to reject supplies or services when the nonconformance affects safety, health, reliability, durability, performance, interchangeability of parts or assemblies, weight, or appearance. See FAR § 46.407.

The government may, and often does, accept nonconforming supplies or services. There may be circumstances (i.e., reasons of economy or urgency) when acceptance of such supplies or services is determined to be in the government's best interest The Contracting Officer's determination will normally take into consideration such factors as (1) the advice of technical specialists that the material is safe to use and will perform its intended purpose, (2) information regarding the nature and extent of the nonconformance, and (3) the contract price adjustment considered appropriate under the circumstances. As a matter of policy, Contracting Officers are required to discourage the repeated tender of nonconforming supplies or services, including those with only minor discrepancies, by appropriate action, such as rejecting the tender and documenting the contractors performance record. See FAR § 46.607.

Where the work is accepted with knowledge that it has not been done according to the contract, or under such circumstances that knowledge of its imperfect performance may be imputed, the acceptance will generally be deemed a waiver of the defective performance. But this rule does not apply to latent defects. The acceptance of work that has been defectively done, the defects being unknown and not discoverable by inspection, does not amount to a waiver of the imperfect performance. This rule respecting final acceptance with knowledge of defects is the same in federal courts as in the *City of Seaside v. Randles,* 92 Or. 650, 180 P. 319 (1919). *C.H. McQuagge v. United States, supra.*

Acceptance of an initial delivery of nonconforming supplies or services does not prevent rejection of later deliveries for failure to meet the contract's specifications. The government will not be shipped to refuse to grant waivers, unless it has a consistent practice of granting waivers in every case. *Doyle Shirt Mfg. Corp. v. United States,* 199 Ct. Cl. 150, 462 F.2d 1150 (1972). But in some cases, government conduct could result in a waiver of nonconformity. If there exists a valid agreement between the contractor and a duly authorized government representative to omit certain production tests and to accomplish the same function by increased visual and mechanical inspections, the courts have held that a waiver of nonconformity has been granted. *Northbridge Electronics v. United States,* 175 Ct. Cl. 426 (1966).

Thus, the government may alter the original terms of a contract by subsequent action or conduct imputing acceptance of irregular performance. It is a familiar principle of equity that long-continued acquiescence in a course of conduct by one interested in it, especially when the rights of others are affected thereby, will induce the court to refuse him relief upon his subsequent complaint of it. It would be contrary to equity and good conscience to enforce such rights when a contractor has been led to suppose by the word, silence, or conduct of government representatives that there was no objection to his operations. *See Ucello v. Golden Foods,* 325 Mass. 319,90 N.E. 250 (1950).

Under the Uniform Commercial Code, an acceptance of goods occurs when the buyer does any act inconsistent with the seller's ownership. U.C.C. § 2-606. Thus, government promptness in giving notice of rejection of goods or services tendered by a contractor is essential because if timely notice of rejection is not furnished, acceptance may in certain cases be implied as a matter of law. See FAR § 46.407.

The most common act resulting in a finding of implied acceptance is the retention and use of the seller's goods by the buyer. Thus, a construction contractor was entitled to recover the cost of repairing a boiler it had installed that exploded prior to acceptance, while being operated by government employees, because it had been under control of the government for three months at the time of the explosion. This was so even though the government had not formally inspected and accepted the boiler. The acts of taking possession of and operating the boiler constituted an implied acceptance. No provision of the contract authorized the government either to take possession of or to operate the boiler prior to the written notification from the contractor that the boiler was ready for final inspection and acceptance. To the extent that notice was a condition precedent to acceptance of the boiler, it was equally a condition precedent to the government's possession and operating it. Yet the government did take possession and did operate the boiler for an extended period. By placing the boiler in operation, it rendered unnecessary a written notice from the contractor that work on the boiler was complete and that the boiler was ready for inspection.

No useful purpose would have been served by the contractor's advising the government of what it was already well aware. In short, the failure of the government to await a written notice from the contractor before taking possession of the boiler constituted a waiver of the notice provision of the contract. Nor having waived the notice requirement could the government revive it and assert it as an impediment to acceptance. The final inspection was the government's responsibility, and since it did take possession of the boiler and place it in operation, it was in no position to complain that it did not make a final inspection. The government was deemed to have accepted the boiler because during the period in which its representatives operated it, the contractor had no control over the boiler or the employees operating it. *John C. Kohler Co .v. United States,* 204 Ct.Cl. 777,498 F.2d l360 (1974).

Where the government, or a prime contractor, installs equipment or a component, it must pay the contract rate for any such goods deemed to have been accepted. *Fram Corp. v. Crawford,* 443 F.2d 611 (5th Cir. 1971). If the government accepts supplies and subsequently pays for them, with knowledge that the contract had been terminated for default, it has been estopped to rescind the acceptance..Controlling were the facts that the government, with full knowledge of the default and questionable acceptance, paid the contractor in full 13 days after acceptance and that it then waited another 23 days before initiating rescission action. Because of its delay, the government lost the right to rescind its acceptance. *Norwood Precision Products,* ASBCA No. 24083, 80-1 BCA 14,405.

In *Makoor Products Manufacturing Co.,* GSBCA No. 5779, 81-1 BCA 15,135, the government was found to have improperly terminated contracts for the supply of hand cleaner for default based on leakage found after a reinspection because the containers for the cleaner had previously been inspected and accepted by the government. Absent latent defects, fraud, or gross mistake amounting to fraud, there was no basis for revoking the acceptance to restore the status quo ante. The government attempted to revoke its prior acceptance of supplies, which, at the time of the attempted revocation, consisted in a significant, but undetermined, part of quite acceptable units notwithstanding that the contract did not contain any methodology for rejection on a lot basis for failures of the product to meet the shelf life requirements of the contract after acceptance. There was no postacceptance right on the part of the government to reject the supplies.

Acceptance is conclusive on the government, except for latent defects, fraud, or gross mistake amounting to fraud. See FAR § 52.246-2(k). The effect of a latent defect is to remove the finality of the final acceptance, thereby entitling the government to the same remedies it would have had if acceptance had not occurred (e.g., correction of defects, the cost of which would be borne by the contractor, or rejection). *United States v. Franklin Steel Products*, 482 F.2d 400 (9th Cir. 1973).

As to fraud, the government must prove that the contractor, with an intent to deceive the government has knowingly or in reckless and wanton disregard of the truth, misrepresented or concealed a material fact on which the government relied in making acceptance. Fraudulent practices could include the submission of false certifications or false inspection or laboratory reports, or the substitution of products not in conformance with the government's specifications after inspection.

With respect to a gross mistake amounting to fraud, the government has the burden of proving (1) that its acceptance was induced by its reliance on (2) a misrepresentation of fact, actual or implied, or the concealment of a material fact, (3).made with knowledge of its falsity or in reckless and wanton disregard of the facts, (4) with intent to mislead the government into relying on the misrepresentation, (5) as a consequence of which the government has suffered injury. Gross mistake connotes a mistake so serious or uncalled for as not to be reasonably expected, or justifiable, in the case of a responsible contractor for the items concerned. It must also be so palpable or flagrant, or so irreconcilable with good faith, as to constitute a gross mistake amounting to fraud. It is essential to demonstrate that the gross mistake complained of actually induced the final acceptance that was sought to be set aside. *Stewart Avionics*, ASBCA No. 15512, 75-1 BCA 11,253.

Notes and Questions

1. Testing methods and inspection standards are subject to a reasonableness standard. The actual intended use of the product or service and the usual quality of such products or services under similar conditions form the basis of a reasonableness test. How did the court apply the reasonableness test in *Mann Chemical Laboratories, Inc.*?

2. As noted, the government cannot reject what it has previously accepted absent certain matters, notably the existence of latent defects. A latent defect is one that existed at time of acceptance and could not be discovered by ordinary and reasonable care or by a reasonable inspection. It is the duty of the government to prove that the defect is latent. *See e.g.*, FAR 52.246-12 (Inspection of Construction clause); FAR 52.246-21 (Warranty of Construction clause); *Windsor Mount Joy Mutual Ins. Co., v. Giragosian*, 57 F.3d 50 (1st Cir. 1995) (holding that the district court's finding that a latent defect caused the boat to sink was not inconsistent with the insured being "on notice of the boat's unsea-

worthy condition before setting sail," when the insured was not aware of the defect.); Mark S. Jaeger, *Contractor Liability for Design Defects under the Inspection Clause: Latent Design Defects—a Sleeping Giant?* 21 Pub. L. J. 331 (1992); *Kaminer Constr. Corp. v. United States,* 203 Ct.Cl. 182 (1973) (while inspection would have revealed defect, requiring an inspection to locate sixteen bolts out of 12,000 bolts was unreasonable).

3. When can and will the government rely upon contractor inspection? Generally, the government relies on the contractor to complete all necessary inspections to determine if supplies and services conform to quality requirements. *See* FAR 46.202-2. However, subsection "b" of the same FAR provision allows the government to consider the nature of supplies and services, the potential for economic loss due to defect, the likelihood of contractor correction of any defects, and the cost of a government inspection when determining if the government is not to rely on a contractor inspection. *See* FAR 46.202-3 (standard inspection requirements for contractors); FAR 46.202-4 (quality requirements for inspections for complex contracts).

4. The contract should specify the terms of acceptance of contractor supplies. *See* FAR 46.503 (discussing the place of acceptance). When the contracting officer accepts supplies either formally or impliedly from the contractor, the government is effectively acknowledging that the supplies comply with the terms of the contract. *See* FAR 46.501 (denoting usual method of acceptance is by a written certificate or report).

In the Matter of INSTRUMENTS FOR INDUSTRY, INC., Debtor-Appellee, v. UNITED STATES of America, Appellant.

United States Court of Appeals, Second Circuit. 496 F.2d 1157
Argued March 12, 1974., Decided May 28, 1974.

Before HAYS and MANSFIELD, Circuit Judges, and DAVIS, Judge.

DAVIS, Judge:

Instruments for Industry, Inc. ('IFI'), the appellee, entered into a contract in 1960 with the Bureau of Naval Weapons of the Navy Department for twenty units of electronic countermeasure equipment. The agreement contained a standard form 'Disputes' clause requiring initial administrative determination of disputes arising under the contract. The equipment was delivered and accepted by the Government. Under the contract terms inspection was made, and acceptance finalized, at the contractor's plant. In 1965, within one year of delivery, the contracting officer notified IFI that the equipment had allegedly been defective upon delivery and acceptance, and that IFI owed more than three hundred ninety thousand dollars under the 'Guaranty' clause of the contract. However, no final contracting officer's decision to this effect was issued until July 1972.

* * *

In 1966 IFI filed for a Chapter XI arrangement under the Bankruptcy Act in the United States District Court for the Eastern District of New York. A few months later, the United States filed proof of claim in these proceedings for the amount said to be due because of the faulty equipment, as well as for an uncontested balance owing under another contract. IFI moved to delete the Navy's claim for the defects, arguing that final acceptance under the 'Inspection' clause prevented recovery, but the Bankruptcy Judge denied the motion and designated the Armed Services Board of Contract Appeals as a fact- finding body to liquidate the Navy's claim. On review, the District Court reversed this order. The court decided that the Navy's rights were cut short by the 'Inspection' clause, and expunged the claim. This appeal tests the correctness of that legal ruling.

This is another instance of the frequent tension in federal procurement between two form clauses, both bearing on the same general subject and both inserted into the same government contract without explicit reconciliation. The 'Guaranty' clause, under which the Navy makes its claim, provides in relevant part:

The Contractor guaranties that at the time of delivery thereof, the supplies provided for under this contract will be free from any defects in material or workmanship and will conform to the requirements of the contract. Notice of any such defect or nonconformance shall be given by the Government to the Contractor within one year of the delivery of the defective or nonconforming supplies. If required by the Government within a reasonable time after such notice, the Contractor shall with all possible speed correct or replace the defective or nonconforming supplies or part thereof. * * * If the Government does not require correction or replacement of defective or nonconforming supplies, the Contractor, if required by the Contracting Officer within a reasonable time after the notice of defect or nonconformance, shall repay such portion of the contract price of the supplies as is equitable in the circumstances.

This clause shall not limit any rights of the Government under the clause of this contract entitled 'Inspection.'

The section of the 'Inspection' clause relied upon by the contractor is:

(d) * * * Except as otherwise provided in this contract, acceptance shall be conclusive except as regards latent defects, fraud, or such gross mistakes as amount to fraud.

At no time has the Government contended that the defects it claims to have discovered were latent, or that any fraud or gross mistakes amounting to fraud were in any way involved. Nor is it asserted that the defects surfaced or came into being after delivery. The only issue is whether the Navy's rights under the 'Guaranty' clause, with respect to pre-existing non-latent defects, survive acceptance under the 'Inspection' provision.

It is very difficult to harmonize the face of the two clauses which do not in words or by clear inference refer to each other. On the one hand, if the 'Guaranty' article preserves the Government's rights to order correction of or payment for non-latent defects for one year after delivery—as it seems to say—then the earlier acceptance is clearly not 'conclusive' as the 'Inspection' clause explicitly declares for non-latent deficiencies. On the other, if the 'Guaranty' clause in this contract is limited in application—because of the presence of the 'Inspection' provision—to latent defects, then its actual scope would be less than its literal terms. The 'Guaranty' article, thus restrictively read, would give the Government a flat right to correction of, or price adjustment for, latent defects for one full year after delivery, but with a co-existing further right, if the circumstances prove it reasonable, thereafter to revoke acceptance under the 'Inspection' clause with respect to latent defects.

It has been suggested (see Federal Pacific Electric Co., IBCA 334, 1964 BCA P4494) that full reconciliation of the literal terms of the two clauses can be attained through the prefatory phrase of the 'Inspection' article—'Except as otherwise provided in this contract.' This language, it is said, refers to the 'Guaranty' clause, and on the assumption the latter article 'provides otherwise' the 'Inspection' provision becomes wholly inoperative for non-latent defects.[7] The obvious vice of this suggested adjustment is that it

---

7. Taken by itself, the 'Guaranty' provision seems to cover all types of defects, latent and non-latent, in its twin references to 'defects in materials and workmanship' and 'conform(ity) to the requirements of the contract.'

subverts the clear import of the most important aspect of subpart (d) of the 'Inspection' article— 'acceptance shall be conclusive except as regards latent defects, fraud or such gross mistakes as amount to fraud'— which affirmatively gives significant rights to the contractor in the absence of the stated exceptions.

* * *

The upshot is that the combination of the two mismatched clauses in this one agreement, without adequate textual harmonization, makes them both ambiguous and evokes the familiar principle of contra proferentem— 'the general maxim that a contract should be construed most strongly against the drafter, which in this case was the United States.' United States v. Seckinger, 397 U.S. 203, 210, 90 S.Ct. 880, 884, 25 L.Ed.2d 224 (1970). * * * 'This oft-repeated and much-applied rule serves important purposes. It puts the risk of ambiguity, lack of clarity, and absence of proper warning on the drafting party which could have forestalled the controversy; it pushes the drafters toward improving contractual forms; and it saves contractors from hidden traps not of their own making.' Sturm v. United States, 421 F.2d 723, 727, 190 Ct.Cl. 691, 697 (1970).

There can be no doubt that the interpretation favoring the contractor is 'reasonable and practical.' See United States v. Seckinger, supra, 397 U.S. at 210–211. The express terms of the 'Inspection' clause are given full effect as to non-latent defects, and, absent an acceptance expressly and reasonably conditioned upon the Government's later inspection of the supplies and equipment, the one-year-after-delivery portion of the 'Guaranty' article is confined to latent defects. See notes 5 and 6, supra, and the pertinent text. That is not an unreasonable or unacceptable rationalization, in the absence of more precise guidelines. It is preferable to the opposite reading which would give full scope to the literal terms of the 'Guaranty' article, at the cost of obliterating the 'acceptance' portion of the 'Inspection' clause. There is a less drastic intrusion upon both the contract language and the reasonable expectations of the parties.

* * *

It follows that the Government has no proper claim and that the District Court was correct in expunging it.

Affirmed.

Notes and Questions

Instruments for Industry underlines the Inspection Clause's powerful policy of finality in government acceptance. It is a particularly striking policy because, in contrast to so many government contracting policies, it is a policy for protecting the contractor against the government, not vice versa. Is the source of the policy just a notion of fairness toward contractors in the form of repose? Or, does the policy work, in the long run, for the government's benefit as well, by such means as reducing the contractor's need to price into its bid a risk premium to cover post-acceptance government claims?

C. Technical Data, Patents, and Copyrights

There probably is no more contentious area of government contract law than the protection of, and right to use, intellectual property rights regarding the utilization of data.

The reasons for such contentiousness are straightforward. Government agencies must promote full and open competition, which can lead to lower prices and lower expenditures of tax dollars. In order to accomplish those goals, the government agencies must be able to supply all potential contractors with the data necessary to produce the desired product or service. Contractors, on the other hand, view data as the crown jewels of their corporation, the exclusive use of which leads to higher profits and fewer corporate dollars spent competing for business. The entity that controls the data necessary for the manufacture of a product or the provision of a service can often control the price and the terms under which it is sold. Congressional focus on the high prices paid by the government for spare parts for weapon systems and other government-needed items has generated considerable interest in this area. Careful attention to the potential for conflict prior to entering into a contract will serve both the government purchaser and the government contractor well. The issue of rights in data is generally divided into three areas: patents, copyrights, and technical data. *See* FAR Part 27. Those first and second areas are not particularly controversial with standard, well-developed FAR clauses clearly delineating the rights of both the government and contractor. The area of technical data, however, has been the subject of intense scrutiny, debate, and statutory enactment. However, with the promulgation in 1995 of regulations for Department of Defense acquisitions, some semi-permanent order was brought to this area. Still, civilian agencies and the Department of Defense have separate and specific regulations.

1. Patents

Government policy with regard to patents encourages the maximum practical commercial use of inventions made during the course of a contractor performing a federally funded research and development contract. Furthermore, the government encourages the use of inventions in performing contracts and will even, by appropriate contract clause, authorize and consent to such use while indemnifying the contractor against possible infringement claims. However, when purchasing commercial items, the government generally seeks indemnification from patent infringement claims by the contractor in the production of the necessary items.

In addition, since 1983 by Presidential Memoranda all contractors have been extended the right to retain title in inventions made while performing government contracts. This patent policy is based on the assumption that the best incentive for a contractor to further develop inventions made while performing a government contract is to allow the contractor to retain the patent rights. As a result, with very limited exceptions, contractors may elect by following specifically prescribed procedures that includes disclosure to the government to retain title to any invention made in the performance of a contract. In exchange for obtaining patent rights, the contractor grants to the government a nonexclusive, nontransferable, irrevocable, paid-up license to practice, or have practiced on its behalf, any subject invention throughout the world. The government also retains the right to "march in" and require the contractor to grant to the government a license for the use of the invention if the contractor has not taken effective steps to achieve its practical application, or if it is necessary for public health or safety needs.

Restrictions to patent rights are placed on contractors when: (1) the contractor is not located or does not have a place of business in the United States or if the contractor is subject to the control of a foreign government; (2) the government determines in exceptional circumstances that it would be in the public interest for the government to re-tain title; (3) the government determines that the patent is necessary to protect the se-curity of foreign intelligence or counterintelligence activities; and (4) the contract in-volves a Department of Energy government-owned, contractor-operated facility dedicated to naval nuclear propulsion or weapons-related programs.

Central to the patent policy in government contracting are the definitions of the terms "invention" and "subject invention." The term *invention* means "any invention or discovery which is or may be patentable or otherwise protectable under title 35 of the United States Code...." FAR 52.227-11(a)(1). The term *subject invention* means "any in-vention of the contractor conceived or first actually reduced to practice in the perfor-mance of work..." under a contract. FAR 52.227-11(a)(6). The use of the word *or* in the definition of "subject invention" ensures that inventions "conceived" of prior to a con-tract but reduced to practice during the performance of a contract are covered by the government's patent policies. Similarly, if an invention is "conceived" of during contract performance, but reduced to practice after the contract is ended, the invention is still covered by the policy and most importantly, by the requirements for notification and filing for patent protection and the granting to the government of license rights.

2. Copyrights

With the written permission of a government contracting officer, a contractor may copyright data first produced in the performance of a contract. When such a claim is made, the contractor must affix the applicable copyright notice and acknowledgment of government sponsorship and contract number. The latter requirements help ensure that the government and others acting on its behalf can take advantage of the paid-up, nonexclusive, irrevocable worldwide license that the contractor must grant to the gov-ernment to reproduce, prepare derivative works, distribute copies to the public, and perform publicly and display publicly the copyrighted data.

When copyrighted data not first produced in the performance of a contract is incor-porated into data delivered under a contract, the contractor must first obtain approval of the contracting officer to do so and must grant the government the same type of paid-up, nonexclusive, irrevocable worldwide license to use the data. In exchange, the government agrees not to remove any copyright notices and to include such notices on all reproductions of the data.

3. Technical Data

The term *data* is simply defined as "recorded information, regardless of form or the media on which it may be recorded." FAR 27.401. The term *technical data* is defined as "data other than computer software, which are of a scientific or technical nature." *Id*. As stated above, the allocation of rights in and use of technical data generate considerable controversy in government contracting. On the one hand, the government seeks to ac-quire or obtain access to technical data in order to: (1) obtain competition among con-tractors; (2) fulfill governmental responsibilities for disseminating the results of tax dol-lar sponsored activities; (3) ensure the appropriate utilization of research and development so that additional technological development is encouraged; (4) meet the specialized needs of military activities; and (5) ensure the capability of supplying the needs of military activities. On the other hand, contractors seek to protect their proprietary and economic interests in technical data in order to avoid jeopardizing their commercial position in the marketplace and the economic investment spent on developing the data into a useful property interest.

As a result of these conflicting policy demands, federal statute and regulation have developed an approach to the rights in technical data that attempts to serve the interest of both parties to a contract. Although actual ownership of data is generally vested in the contractor, the allocation of the actual rights to use that data is set forth in a stair step approach for levels of use.

The first step and goal of any government agency is to obtain "unlimited rights" in technical data. Such rights allow the government to use, disclose, reproduce, prepare derivative works, distribute copies to the public, and perform publicly and display publicly, in any manner and for any purpose, and to have or permit others to do so. In essence, with unlimited rights in technical data, the government can achieve each of the policy purposes cited above including allowing all interested contractors to use the data in order to compete for government contracts.

A contractor grants civilian agencies of the government "unlimited rights" in: (1) data first produced in the performance of a contract; (2) form, fit, and function data delivered pursuant to a contract; (3) data delivered under the contract in the form of manuals or instructional and training material for installation, operation, or routine maintenance and repair of items, components, or processes delivered or furnished for use under the contract; and (4) all other data delivered under a contract unless otherwise protected by the contractor. Similarly, a contractor grants an agency of the Department of Defense "unlimited rights" in: (1) data which has been or will be developed exclusively with government funds; (2) studies, analyses, or test data required as an element of performance under the contract; (3) data created exclusively with government funds; (4) form, fit, and function data; (5) data necessary for installation, operation, maintenance, or training purposes; (6) corrections or changes to technical data furnished to the contractor by the government; (7) data that is publicly available without restrictions; (8) data in which the government obtained unlimited rights pursuant to another contract or pursuant to negotiations; or (9) data previously furnished with "government purpose rights" and those rights have expired.

A second level or step toward data rights is "government purpose rights" wherein the government has the rights to: (1) use, modify, reproduce, release, perform, display, or disclose technical data within the government without restriction; and (2) release or disclose technical data outside the government and authorize persons to whom release or disclosure has been made to use, modify, reproduce, release, perform, display, or disclose that data for US government purposes that includes any activity in which the government is a party including competitive procurements. An agency obtains "government purpose rights" in data that was developed with mixed funding, i.e., both the contractor and the government contributed funds toward the development of the data. Although the term *government purpose rights* is only found in the regulations applicable to the Department of Defense, a similar concept is used with civilian agencies where the development of the data is funded by both parties and the agency and the contractor are permitted to agree to limiting the use of the data by the government to governmental purposes.

The third level or step is actually divided into two terms: (1) "limited rights" for data other than software; and (2) "restricted rights" for software. With limited rights, the government may not disclose the data outside the government nor use the data for purposes of manufacturing. The government may, however, identify specific purposes for which the limited rights data may be used including: (1) use by support service contractors; (2) evaluation by nongovernmental evaluators; (3) use by other contractors in the same program; (4) emergency or repair work; or (5) release to a foreign government for information or evaluation or emergency repair or overhaul work. A contractor can grant the government "limited rights" in data that was developed exclusively with private funds. In order to protect such data, a contractor is required to mark the data with a "limited rights" notice. Failure to mark the data will result in the government receiving unlimited rights in that data.

For software, the regulations speak in terms of "restricted rights" which mean that the software may only be: (1) used or copied for use on the computer for which it was acquired; (2) used or copied for a backup computer if the original computer is inoperative; (3) reproduced for safekeeping or backup purposes; (4) modified or adapted for use with other restricted rights software; (5) disclosed to service contractors for any of the first four uses; and (6) used on a replacement computer. Software receives the protection of "restricted rights" when it is: (1) developed at private expense and is a trade secret; (2) commercial or financial and is confidential or privileged; or (3) is published copyrighted computer software. As is the case with limited rights data, the contractor must mark the software with a "restricted rights" notice in order to protect it. Failure by the contractor to do so will give the government unlimited rights in that software.

For both civilian and defense agencies, the key factor is whether the data were developed with government funds or private funds—a determination that is not as easy at it may seem, especially for contractors that regularly do business with the government. For data relating to noncommercial items, the government may challenge the "limited rights" or "restricted rights" notice placed on data by a contractor. If the markings are challenged, the contractor must present evidence so as to justify the marking, i.e., the source of funding for development of the data.

It is very important to note that since December 1, 1995, the acquisition of rights in technical data for commercial items and commercial computer software has been substantially simplified. In essence, unless otherwise negotiated with the contractor, for commercial items the government gets the very same rights in technical data that a commercial customer would receive and the government receives the very same license rights for commercial computer software that a commercial customer receives. Furthermore, the burden of proof as to the source of funding for the technical data is shifted from the contractor to the government. In other words, if the government wants to challenge the status of the technical data, it must prove that the data were developed at government expense rather than having the contractor prove the data were developed at private expense.

Ultimately, because of the complexity of the statutes and regulations involving data rights, it is to the benefit of the contractor and government alike to determine with certainty the rights in the data that will be delivered under a contract prior to the contract being executed. The failure to delineate those rights ahead of time can only lead to disputes as the government seeks to use the data for reprocurement or other purposes and the contractor seeks to protect its crown jewels.

For further discussion of the subjects in this section, see David A. Vogel, *Does the FAR Violate the Copyright Law?*, 33 Procurement Law., Summer 1998, at 12; Jeff E. Schwartz, *The Acquisition of Technical Data Rights by the Government*, 23 Pub. Cont. L.J.

513 (1994); Matthew S. Simchak, David A. Vogel, *A Few Words of Advice: Protecting Intellectual Property When Contracting with the Department of Defense According to the October 1988 Regulations,* 23 Pub. Cont. L.J. 141 (Winter, 1994) ; William L. Geary, Jr., *Protecting the Patent Rights of Small Businesses: Does the Bayh-Dole Act Live Up to Its Promise?,* 22 Pub. Cont. L.J. 101 (1992); Jerome S. Gabig, Jr., *Federal Research Grants: Who Owns the Intellectual Property?,* 16 Pub. Cont. L.J. 187 (1986); Barton Bolling Davis, *Acquisition of Rights in Computer Software by the Department of Defense,* 17 Pub. Cont. L.J. 77 (1987).

Dowty Decoto, Inc., Plaintiff-Appellee,
v. Department of the Navy et al. Defendants-Appellants.

No. 88-3732. United States Court of Appeals, Ninth Circuit.
Argued and Submitted June 6, 1989, 883 F.2d 774 Decided Aug. 23, 1989.

Before SCHROEDER, BEEZER and BRUNETTI, Circuit Judges.

SCHROEDER, Circuit Judge:

The Navy appeals from a district court's permanent injunction prohibiting disclosure of a subcontractor's technical data. We affirm the injunction, holding that under any applicable regulations, the subcontractor never surrendered disclosure rights to the Navy.

The challenged injunction was obtained by the appellee Dowty Decoto, a manufacturer of aeronautical equipment. Since 1971 Dowty Decoto has supplied the Navy with "repeatable holdback bars" used in launching F-14 Tomcat fighter planes from aircraft carrier decks. Decoto has supplied the bars pursuant to a subcontract with Grumman Aerospace Corp., the prime contractor supplying the Navy with F-14s. Decoto also sells the bars directly to the Navy on a purchase order basis for use as spares. In addition to the F-14, Decoto also supplies holdback bars for the F-18 Hornet and T-45A trainer aircraft.

On all drawings and data Decoto supplied pursuant to the subcontract, Decoto placed a restrictive legend stating that the data was proprietary and subject only to limited disclosure rights under the contract. It is not disputed that the form of the legend was appropriate for reserving limited disclosure rights in Decoto.

In 1983 the Navy wrote to Decoto asking Decoto voluntarily to remove the restrictive legends from data it had furnished the Navy. Decoto refused, stating that the Navy had never obtained disclosure rights from Decoto. Three years later, the Navy requested Decoto to substantiate its position that the government had acquired only limited rights in the data. After an informal administrative review of Decoto's submissions, and some informal discussions, the Navy handed down an administrative decision in a letter dated April 27, 1987, advising that Decoto had failed to substantiate its use of restrictive rights legends. It advised that it would obliterate or ignore the legends on the data, and would disclose the data to third parties for the purpose of obtaining competitive bids. Decoto then filed this suit for a permanent injunction in district court, pursuant to the Administrative Procedure Act ("APA"), 5 U.S.C. §706 (1982), to prohibit the Navy from disclosing the data. The district court granted the injunction.

There is no dispute that unless the Navy has a right to Decoto's data and drawings, they otherwise represent trade secrets of Decoto. The Trade Secrets Act forbids government agents from disclosing confidential information "in any manner or to any extent not authorized by law." 18 U.S.C. § 1905 (1982). If the Navy has no authority to disclose the holdback bar data, its disclosure of Decoto's trade secret would violate section 1905, and "any disclosure that violates § 1905 is 'not in accordance with law' within the meaning of 5 U.S.C. § 706(2)(A)." Chrysler Corp. v. Brown, 441 U.S. 281, 318, 99 S.Ct. 1705, 1726, 60 L.Ed.2d 208 (1979). Thus, the APA authorizes this injunction preventing the Navy from disclosing Decoto's data, provided that such disclosure violates the Trade Secrets Act. Id. at 316–17, 99 S.Ct. at 1724–25; Conax Florida Corp. v. United States, 824 F.2d 1124, 1128 (D.C.Cir.1987).

Our determination of whether the Navy's action was properly enjoined as a violation of the Trade Secrets Act is in turn guided by regulations governing the Navy's authority to disclose the data in the absence of Decoto's acquiescence. The contentions of the parties center on a particular provision of the Armed Services Procurement Regulations (ASPR), regulations promulgated by the Department of Defense governing the acquisition of items for military use, which were in effect when the contract between Decoto and Grumman was signed.[1]

The provision at issue is contained in ASPR §§ 9-202 & 9-203, 32 C.F.R. §§ 9-202 & 9-203 (1965),[2] which deal with rights in technical data. Section 9-202.2 declares the governmental policy of granting to the government unlimited rights to disclose data concerning any item developed at government expense. The policy restricts governmental disclosure of data only where an item was developed at private expense, and where the contractor takes care to mark all data and drawings with a legend prescribed by the regulations setting forth the proprietary nature of the data and the contract under which the data was furnished. Section 9-203(a) implements the policy by requiring that the text of section 9-203(b), which takes the form of a contract clause, be inserted into all government contracts. The language of section 9-203(b) carries out the apportionment of data rights anticipated by the ASPR.[3]

---

1. The ASPR have since been integrated into the new Federal Acquisition Regulations System. See 48 Fed.Reg. 42,103 (1983). The old regulations were amended as necessary and recodified into C.F.R. Title 48.

2. Congress later enacted a specific statute regarding rights in technical data, 10 U.S.C. § 2320 (Supp. V 1987), directing the Secretary of Defense to prescribe regulations defining the interests and rights of the government, contractors, and subcontractors in technical data. The statute to a great degree merely codifies the then-existing ASPR regulations. H.R.Rep. No. 690, 98th Cong. 2d Sess. 15, reprinted in 1984 U.S.Code Cong. and Admin.News 4237, 4246. Section 2320 and the regulations promulgated under it, 48 C.F.R. Ch. 2, Sbpt. 227.4, carry forward generally unchanged the provisions of ASPR §§ 9-202 & 9-203.

3. Section 9-203(b) provides in pertinent part:
(b) Basic Data Clause.
RIGHTS IN TECHNICAL DATA (FEB.1965)
(a) Definitions.

* * *

(b) Government Rights.
(1) The Governmental shall have unlimited rights in:
(i) technical data resulting directly from performance of experimental, developmental or research work which was specified as an element of performance in this or any other Government contract or subcontract;

* * *

(2) The Government shall have limited rights in:

* * *

(ii) technical data pertaining to items, components or processes developed at private expense, other than such data as may be included in the data referred to in (b)(1)(i), (iii), (iv), (v), and (vi);

Throughout the administrative and district court proceedings, as well as in this appeal, the dispute between Decoto and the Navy has centered on two issues, one legal and one factual. The legal issue concerns whether ASPR § 9-203 applies at all between Decoto and the Navy, since the form clause language anticipated by the regulations was never inserted into the Decoto-Grumman subcontract and the Navy was not a party to that contract. The factual issue concerns whether, assuming that the regulations do apply, the holdback bar was "developed" at private expense within the meaning of the regulations.

* * *

While we recognize the significance of the legal issues presented in this regard, we find it unnecessary in this case to resolve them, for the decision of the district court must be affirmed on its alternative, factual grounding. Even if the ASPR regulations were read into the subcontract and superseded its express terms, Decoto nevertheless retained its rights to the technical data because the holdback bar was developed at private expense. See ASPR §§ 9.202.2(c) & 9-203(b) clause (b)(2)(ii).

Under the APA, we may overturn the contracting officer's decision that the Navy was authorized to disclose Decoto's data only if the decision was arbitrary, capricious, an abuse of discretion, or otherwise not in accordance with law. See 5 U.S.C. § 706(2)(A). After reviewing the record, we conclude that it compelled the district court's holding that the bar was developed at private and not government expense. The Navy contracting officer's decision was arbitrary, and its implementation was therefore properly enjoined by the district court.

The contracting officer's decision relied in part upon language of the Decoto-Grumman subcontract, which the Navy contends created unlimited data rights in the government under the ASPR. The subcontract language relied upon recited that design and development were within the subcontract's scope. The subcontract language calls for Decoto to "design, develop, manufacture, test and deliver all items as required."

The Navy, however, is mistaken in its belief that the recitals of a contract alone can determine whether an item was actually developed at private expense. ASPR § 9-203(b) clause (b)(1)(i) purports to grant unlimited rights in the government to "technical data resulting directly from performance of experimental, developmental, or research work which was specified as an element of performance in this or any other Government contract or subcontract" (emphasis added). The regulation requires actual development and work, not merely contract recitals. Procurement authorities use a test based on physical and economic reality, not language, to determine which party actually "develops" an item within the meaning of the statutes and regulations. This test has now been codified within the new Federal Acquisition Regulations System (FARS). See 48 C.F.R. § 227.471 (1987).

The leading administrative decision in this area, from which the current regulation is derived, is In re Bell Helicopter Textron, 85-3 B.C.A. (CCH) ¶ 18,415 (A.S.B.C.A.1985). It concerned a defense research project that had gone through vari-

---

provided that each piece of data to which limited rights are to be asserted pursuant to (2)(i) and (ii) above is marked with the [proper] legend in which is inserted the number of the prime contract under which the technical data is to be delivered and the name of the Contractor or subcontractor by whom the technical data was generated.

ous phases of funding alternately provided by the government and the private contractor. The Armed Services Board of Contract Appeals there recognized that the crucial factor in determining who "developed" an item concerned who took the risk of investing money to transform the item from a speculative idea into a workable item that would probably succeed in its intended use. The Board defined the term "developed" accordingly:

> In order to be "developed," an item or component must be in being, that is, at least a prototype must have been fabricated...; and practicability, workability, and functionality (largely synonymous concepts) must be shown through sufficient analysis and/or test to demonstrate to reasonable persons skilled in the applicable art that there is a high probability the item or component will work as intended. All "development" of the item or component need not be 100 percent complete, and the item or component need not be brought to the point where it could be sold or offered for sale. An invention which has been "actually reduced to practice" under patent law has been "developed," but the converse is not necessarily true in every case.

85-3 B.C.A. (CCH) at 92,434.

The Department of Defense adopted this "workability" definition in a regulation it implemented in 1987 for defining the term "developed" in this context:

> "Developed", as used in this subpart, means that the item, component or process exists and is workable. Thus, the item or component must have been constructed or the process practiced. Workability is generally established when the item, component, or process has been analyzed or tested sufficiently to demonstrate to reasonable people skilled in the applicable art that there is a high probability that it will operate as intended....To be considered "developed," the item, component or process need not be at the stage where it could be offered for sale or sold on the commercial market, nor must [it] be actually reduced to practice within the meaning of [the patent law].

48 C.F.R. § 227.471. The Navy points to no authority adopting a different definition for the term "developed," nor does it argue that the definition has changed since the time when the holdback bars were developed.

Under this standard, our review of the record must focus on the realities of who invested the money that transformed the holdback bar from an uncertain idea into a workable device for its intended application. The record overwhelmingly shows that Decoto's money, and not the Navy's, played this role.

The record reflects that Decoto clearly had the technology in place and had developed the bar to the point of workability even before Decoto entered into the contract with Grumman. By the time Decoto originally approached the Navy with the design for the bar, Decoto already had two patents in place on the "high energy release locking actuator ring," which forms the heart of the bar's design. The Navy apparently believed in the feasibility of Decoto's existing design, inasmuch as the Navy itself referred Decoto to Grumman for further funding. In negotiating the contract with Grumman, Decoto never quoted or asked for any funds for design effort or production tooling. The contract calls for the production of first units of the bar within a very short time; four preproduction units were to be delivered within three and a half months, and six production models were to follow within approximately three more months. Decoto's technology was sufficiently developed to allow Decoto successfully to meet these commitments.

The entire framework of the Decoto-Grumman subcontract operates as a straight parts procurement agreement rather than one for research and development. The contract calls for Decoto to supply holdback bars to the Navy as finished products. It contains no expenditure category for research and development work. The total price paid to Decoto under the contract represents simply the aggregate of individual payments for manufactured bars and supporting documentation. The contract is of the "fixed-price" type, promising payment of a specific price for each unit delivered, rather than a "cost-type" contract, which would reimburse the contractor for whatever expenses it incurred plus adding percentage for the contractor's profit. Fixed-price contracts like Decoto's have not normally been used for projects requiring research and development. See Bell Helicopter Textron, 85-3 B.C.A. (CCH) at 92,401.

The contracting officer's decision pointed to changes occurring in the bar's design during the course of performance of the subcontract to support the conclusion that the Navy indirectly financed design and development of the bar through payments by Grumman. The only evidence in the record that supports the position that the Navy actually financed any of the bar's development is a "Subcontractor Change Proposal" (SCP) that Decoto sent to Grumman during the term of the contract. The original preproduction contract, dated December 1970, carried a price of $72,344.88. Roughly two years later, in November 1972, Decoto sent six SCPs to Grumman in response to Grumman's request that the bars withstand 2,000 successful launch cycles rather than the 700 cycles demonstrated by the preproduction units. The proposals sought increases in the contract price, all of which were to be passed through to the Navy, requesting a total of $141,875.20 in additional payments to Decoto. Five of the six SCPs concerned small specific changes in the bar's design, and were approved by Grumman for the full amounts requested. The sixth request, upon which the Navy here relies, was characterized by Grumman as a "change in scope." It was the largest and most general in nature, and requested $106,724.22, of which Grumman approved only $53,000. As a result, the SCPs added only $88,158.98, bringing the total government expenditures for the bars from $151,721.94 to $239,880.92 as of that time.

The justification provided by Decoto in the sixth SCP for seeking reimbursement of nearly $107,000 refers to a "completely new design" that had been developed by Decoto in response to Grumman's demands that the bars last longer.[7] The contracting officer's

---

7. The justification provided by Decoto in the sixth SCP reads in full:
Following receipt of a purchase order from Grumman to design and produce Repeatable Release Holdback Bars, Decoto began a program determined to provide Grumman and the Navy with a completely successful unit. Following design and fabrication of two different configurations, both approved by Grumman, it became clear to Decoto that the goal was not attainable with these designs.
A completely new design was developed and Grumman Engineering agreed that the concept had merit. Decoto management after reviewing the program status showing that all areas had large cost overruns from the previous designs, made the decision to go ahead. All previous hardware was scrapped and machining began again on the new design.
Now, after some additional minor set backs the goal is in sight. The Navy will receive a successful Repeatable Release Holdback Bar, something for which large sums have been spent earlier without success.
The redesign and rebuilding stages have been expensive, far in excess of the dollar value of the original purchase order. Decoto committed this money without hesitation in the belief that should the effort produce a unique Holdback Bar, all or most of these funds could be recovered due to the exceptional value of the product to the Navy.
Through this change, Decoto is submitting a recap of the additional Decoto money that was spent. It is requested that Grumman review these statements and acknowledge the

decision held, and the Navy argues on appeal, that this demonstrates that the Navy paid for development of the bar, the payment flowing through Grumman during the term of the contract.

Despite Decoto's assertions at the time that $107,000 was necessary, there exists no evidence in the record to show that the money actually paid by the Navy through the SCP "developed" the bar to workability within the definition established by Bell Helicopter Textron and 48 C.F.R. § 227.471. The record contains nothing to suggest that prior to this SCP the holdback bar had a low probability of success in its intended application, or that the bar obtained a high probability of success only as a result of the funding provided by the SCP. Indeed, since the government provided less than half of the development costs requested in 1972, and in effect provided only partial reimbursement for development that had already taken place, the SCP does not support the government's position that the Navy financed the crucial research and development.

Other evidence in the record suggests that the bars had achieved workability before any government money was paid to Decoto, and that the changes that the government helped finance during the course of the contract were aimed at increasing performance rather than achieving workability. When the original Decoto-Grumman contract was amended to reflect the increase in contract price, the additional payment was not placed under a research and development category, but was accounted for under a new heading of "qualification test."

The Navy itself recognized that the bars manufactured without the design changes covered by the SCP were workable. This is most clearly evidenced by the fact that, although the Navy was aware of the changes wrought by the SCPs, it nevertheless approved the ordering and use of forty-two pre-change design bars for use in launching F-14s from aircraft carriers. The Navy merely assigned a different part number to these pre-change units to keep track of their shorter life span. There is nothing in the record to suggest that any of these pre-change bars ever failed to operate properly. The record does contain evidence that in over 250,000 deck launches using the bar only one possible operational failure has ever been noted.

The government directs us to language in Bell Helicopter Textron, 85-3 B.C.A. (CCH) at 92,423, suggesting that if a contractor receives even partial reimbursement for development costs previously voluntarily expended, the government may receive unlimited data rights. We do not believe such a rule, even if appropriate in some cases, should apply in a situation like this where the contractor could not reasonably have been aware that an application for reimbursement could later lead to total forfeiture of data rights which the contractor had in good faith sought to retain by appropriate legends. Here the government did not give Decoto any notice of its intent to claim data rights until ten years after the SCP was submitted.

The Navy contracting officer's findings that the key research and development, as defined under the standard of Bell Helicopter Textron and 48 C.F.R. § 227.471, occurred after the contract had begun and was financed by the government were arbitrary and unsupported by the record, and are therefore insufficient under the APA to support a holding that the holdback bars were developed other than at private expense. Because Decoto's holdback bar was privately developed and its technical data contained the proper restrictive legend, ASPR §§ 9-202 & 9-203 granted only restricted data rights in

---

diligence and determination of Decoto by increasing Purchase Order 7-04384 by this amount.

the bar to the Navy. These regulations do not authorize the Navy to disclose Decoto's technical data. Such disclosure would violate the Trade Secrets Act, and is therefore properly enjoinable under the APA.

The district court's entry of injunction against the Navy was proper and is AFFIRMED.

Notes and Questions

1. Government-funded research and development ("R&D") leads to many patents, with the perennial issue being whether the government should receive full title to the patents or just a license for their use. The government has made policy on this by the 1980 "Bayh-Dole" Act, Patent and Trademark Amendments of 1980, P.L. 96-517, 94 Stat. 3019, 35 USC § 200 et seq., and by a 1983 executive branch memorandum, President's Memorandum to the Heads of Executive Departments and Agencies, "Government Patent Policy" (Feb. 18, 1983). These are reflected in the FAR and the various FAR "Patent Rights" clauses. FAR patent rights clauses mandate contractors to disclose to the government any "subject invention" which is "any invention of the contractor conceived or first actually reduced to practice in the performance of work under this contract." FAR 52.227-12(a). Once disclosed, a contractor has the option to retain title to the invention. FAR 27.302(b).

However, the FAR also allows agencies to provide otherwise if: "(1)...the contractor is not located in the United States or is subject to control of foreign government, (2) when the contract is for operation of certain government-owned contractor-operated Department of Energy facilities, (3) in 'exceptional circumstances' when a restriction on contractor title rights will better serve FAR policy objectives, and (4) when granting title in an invention would endanger national security." If a contractor retains title to the patent, the government receives a license which permits other contractors to sell products to the government even if they are in direct competition. See FAR 52.227-11(b); FAR 52.227-12(b). For a general discussion, see William L. Geary, Jr., *Protecting the Patent Rights of Small Businesses: Does the Bayh-Dole Act Live Up to Its Promise?*, 22 Pub. Cont. L.J. 101 (1992).

For discussions of developments regarding what the government and the contractor receive in terms of rights in discoveries, see Jack E. Kerrigan & Christopher J. Brasco, *The Technology Transfer Revolution: Legislative History and Future Proposals*, 31 Pub. Cont. L. J. 277 (2002); Diane M. Sidebottom, *Updating the Bayh-Dole Act: Keeping the Federal Government on the Cutting Edge*, 30 Pub. Cont. L. J. 225 (2001); Richard N. Kuyath, *Barriers to Federal Procurement: Patent Rights*, The Procurement Lawyer, Fall 2000, at 1.

2. Technical Data. FAR 27.403 provides that: "all contracts that require data to be produced, furnished, acquired or specifically used in meeting contract performance requirements, must contain terms that delineate the respective rights and obligations of the government and the contractor regarding the use, duplication, and disclosure of such data..."

The government can acquire unlimited rights for "data first produced in the performance of a contract...; form, fit and function data...; data that constitutes manuals or instructional and training material..." and data that is not limited rights data or restricted data for computer software. FAR 27.404(a). Limited rights data concerns trade secrets, commercial, financial, confidential or privileged information, or items developed by private funding. See FAR 27.404(b); see also FAR 52.227-14(definitions of terms); Jeff E. Schwartz, *The Acquisition of Technical Data Rights by the Government*, 23 Pub. Con. L. J. 513 (1994).

FN MANUFACTURING, INC., Plaintiff,
v. The UNITED STATES, Defendant,
and Colt's Manufacturing Company, Inc., Intervenor.

United States Court of Federal Claims.
No. 98-447 C., 42 Fed.Cl. 87 Oct. 28, 1998.
REDACTED

WIESE, Judge.

RULING ON LAW

This is a suit for declaratory and injunctive relief. Plaintiff, FN Manufacturing, Inc. (FNMI), the domestic subsidiary of a European arms manufacturer, is asking the court to declare illegal, and to enjoin the Government from continuing with performance under, a sole-source contract awarded to Colt's Manufacturing Company, Inc. (Colt's), the intervenor here, on May 5, 1998. The challenged award involves the manufacture of a quantity of M4/M4A1 carbines—the successor weapon to the M16 rifle currently in use by the United States Army and North Atlantic Treaty Organization ground forces. FNMI is one of the Government's principal manufacturing supply sources for the M16 rifle.

This is the third time this case has come before the court. * * * *

We turn now to the issue of current concern. In the interest of seeking an expeditious resolution of this controversy, the parties have asked the court to rule on the following question: whether the Government, in the settlement of a contract dispute, is free to relinquish rights in technical data, if by doing so, it disables itself from competitively conducting future procurements involving the use and application of the relinquished data. Put another way, does a contracting agency have the authority to agree to a contract settlement that establishes a contractor's exclusive ownership of technical data, thereby restricting all future procurements involving the data to sole-source purchases?

Facts

On June 30, 1967, Colt's entered into a technical data and patent license agreement with the Government, affording the Army limited rights to the M16 rifle and the XM177 submachine gun. Under the terms of this license, the Army was permitted to release the technical data package (TDP) for use in competitive procurements involving the acquisition of the M16 and its component parts, subject to the limitation that the manufacture be carried out in the United States.

Subsequent to the signing of the M16 licensing agreement, Colt's developed the M4 and M4A1 carbines, weapons derived from, and sharing a majority of their parts with, the M16 rifle. While the parties do not agree to what extent—if at all—the Government contributed financially to the development of the M4 and M4A1, it is clear that Colt's committed its own funds to the project. In a letter dated March 5, 1985, Colt's informed the Army that, based on the fact that the M4 and M4A1 were derived from the M16, Colt's considered the M4 and M4A1 to be covered by the 1967 Licensing Agreement. The Government did not challenge that assertion.

In January 1996, an Army engineer authorized the release of the M4A1 TDP to the Navy. The Navy, unaware of the terms of the 1967 Licensing Agreement, used the TDP in conjunction with an advertised solicitation for M4A1 adapters,[1] thereby improperly disclosing the TDP to some 21 contractors, including FNMI. This disclosure was improper for several reasons, including the fact that it did not relate to an authorized use (the solicitation at issue did not involve the procurement of a weapon or a weapon component) and the information was disseminated without obtaining required non-disclosure statements from the participating contractors. Upon learning of the solicitation, Colt's notified the Government on December 26, 1996, that it had violated the 1967 Licensing Agreement by failing adequately to protect Colt's proprietary data. And, because it believed the breach to be material, Colt's further advised the Government that the licensing agreement was terminated and that the Government would no longer be permitted to use the data in the procurement or manufacture of the M16, M16A1, XM177, XM177E2, M4 or M4A1.

The Government responded to Colt's letter on February 14, 1997. In its reply, the Government acknowledged that Colt's might in fact be entitled to damages because of the unauthorized release, but disputed that the licensing agreement had been materially breached. Relying on Article XX of the licensing agreement, the Government asserted that a breach would arise—and termination would be appropriate—only in the event that the Government failed to use its best efforts to remedy the violation. Because it had presumably corrected its error by recovering all copies of the TDP from the Navy and by securing non-disclosure statements from 19 of the 20 contractors (with FNMI, the lone hold-out, providing a letter attesting that it had not improperly used the data), the Government maintained that it had met its obligation under the licensing agreement, and that the 1967 Licensing Agreement therefore remained intact.

An investigation of the incident by the Inspector General—prompted by congressional inquiry—concluded that both the release of the data to the Navy, and the Navy's distribution to contractors, were improper. In its June 17, 1997, audit report, the Inspector General recommended that procedures be implemented to better safeguard Colt's proprietary data.

In a July 29, 1997, letter to the Army, Colt's estimated the damages arising from the improper release of Colt's technical data at between 43.5 and 70 million dollars. At Colt's request, a series of meetings were held during the late summer and early fall of 1997 to discuss the M16 licensing issue and also—at Colt's insistence—ownership of the technical data rights relating to the M4 carbine. Although Colt's had previously characterized the M4 as subject to the 1967 Licensing Agreement, the company now sought the Army's confirmation that the M4 Carbine was not covered by the licensing agreement. In support of that contention, Colt's offered evidence that * * of the M4's parts had been developed, tested and refined solely at Colt's expense.

Colt's and the Army conducted settlement discussions in September 1997. Despite the Army's earlier representation to Colt's that the disclosure did not constitute a breach of the licensing agreement, the Army nonetheless possessed, in the words of an Army attorney involved in the settlement negotiations, a "great concern" that a resort to litigation in the absence of a settlement might jeopardize the Army's right to use Colt's proprietary technical data in the manufacture of the M16.

---

1. M4A1 adapter kits permit modification of the M4A1 to allow the weapon to allow the weapon to fire during training exercises.

A final agreement, referred to as the "M4 Addendum," was reached on December 24, 1997. Described by the participants as a "global settlement," the addendum and an earlier-executed Memorandum of Understanding were designed to address the entire range of issues then existing between Colt's and the Government, including clarification of a military use restriction in the 1967 Licensing Agreement, that, according to Colt's, barred the Government from selling surplus weapons to state and local police authorities. The M4 Addendum itself was comprised of two parts: first, a characterization of the Army's rights in the M4 technical data; second, a clarification of the status of the M16 licensing agreement.

With regard to the M16 rights, the Addendum reaffirmed the status quo set forth in the 1967 Licensing Agreement, thus constituting, by its terms, the complete satisfaction of all claims arising from the improper disclosure (meaning that the terms of the 1967 license essentially would remain in place with Colt's neither pursuing its multi-million dollar damage claim nor maintaining its position that the license was terminated in light of the alleged breach). As to the M4 data rights, the Addendum granted the Government a non-exclusive, non-transferable limited rights license in M4 data that precluded the Government from using the M4's technical data package in competitive procurements until the year 2011. Edward L. Stolarun, a patent attorney employed by the U.S. Army Material Command Headquarters and a participant in the negotiations, later characterized the Addendum's resolution of the M4 data issue as an acknowledgment by the Government, reached after careful review of Colt's documentation, that Colt's indeed possessed proprietary rights in the M4 technical data.

On May 5, 1998, the Army awarded a sole-source contract for M4 carbines to Colt's, citing as its justification for the sole-source award the Army's lack of technical data rights in certain components of the M4. In response, FNMI filed a protest in this court, challenging the justification on the ground that the Army had improperly relinquished data rights in the M4 that it already possessed, and in doing so had impermissibly created the very circumstance—the absence of data rights—on which it then relied to support its sole-source decision. While the question of whether the Government *relinquished* data rights already in its possession or merely *acknowledged* data rights belonging to Colt's is central to the resolution of this case, we need not reach that issue in order to present the following Ruling on Law.

Analysis

FNMI's argument against the legitimacy of the Government's actions is twofold. It contends, first, that the Government, in relinquishing technical data rights in the M4, violated the terms of 10 U.S.C. § 2320 (1994) by failing to retain rights sufficient to allow for competitive procurement, and, second, that the M4 addendum to the M16 licensing agreement impermissibly inhibited competition in contravention of the Competition in Contracting Act (CICA), 10 U.S.C. § 2304 (1994). We address these arguments in turn.

The Addendum as a Violation of 10 U.S.C. § 2320

Plaintiff's first challenge to the sole-source award arises from its assertion that the Government unlawfully relinquished rights in technical data to which it was otherwise entitled. Leaving aside the issue of whether the Government in fact possessed any such rights—an assertion we accept as true only for purposes of this Ruling on Law—we turn to the question of what limits, if any, 10 U.S.C. § 2320 imposes on the Government's authority to relinquish technical data rights.

The subsection of the statute on which plaintiff relies, 10 U.S.C. § 2320(a)(2)(G)(ii), reads as follows:

(G) The Secretary of Defense may—

…

(ii) agree to restrict rights in technical data otherwise accorded to the United States under this section if the United States receives a royalty-free license to use, release, or disclose the data for purposes of the United States (including purposes of competitive procurement).

* * * * We cannot accept the argument that the Government, in relinquishing a right to use the M4 technical data for proposes of competitive procurement, thereby violated 10 U.S.C. § 2320(a)(2)(G)(ii) because the limitations imposed by that subsection have no application where—as here—the data at issue was developed either wholly or partially at private expense. That conclusion derives both from the specific language of the referenced subsection—it applies only to those rights "specifically *accorded* to the United States" (italics supplied) under the provisions of 10 U.S.C. § 2320—and from the remainder of the statutory framework, in particular § 2320(a)(2)(E), which authorizes the Government, in situations where a developmental effort involves both federal and private funding, to negotiate the particular rights it will receive. We explain further.

Under 10 U.S.C. § 2320, the United States is "accorded" rights in technical data in one instance only, *i.e.,* where Government money represents the *exclusive* funding source in the development of the item or process in question. In that circumstance alone, the statute gives to the United States a right, described as an "unlimited" right. * * * *

Conversely, in the situation where an item or process is developed by a contractor or subcontractor exclusively at private expense, the contractor or subcontractor "may restrict the right of the United States to release or disclose technical data pertaining to the item or process to persons outside the Government, or permit the use of the technical data by such persons." 10 U.S.C. § 2320(a)(2)(B).

In contrast to the exclusive funding situations identified above, the statute does not specify any minimum rights that the Government or the contractor must receive where the development of an item has been achieved through the use of *both* Government funds and private funds. Rather, in such instances, the statute specifies that "the respective rights of the United States and of the contractor…in technical data pertaining to such item or process shall be established as early in the acquisition process as practicable…and shall be based upon negotiations between the United States and the contractor taking into account:

* * *

(ii) The interest of the United States in increasing competition and lowering costs by developing and locating alternative sources of supply and manufacture.

(iii) The interest of the United States in encouraging contractors to develop at private expense items for use by the Government.

(iv) Such other factors as the Secretary of Defense may prescribe.

10 U.S.C. § 2320(a)(2)(E).

Two conclusions are evident from the statutory framework set forth in 10 U.S.C. § 2320. First, rights which result from negotiations between contractor and Government cannot be said—in contrast to the unlimited rights specifically conferred by section 2320(a)(1)(A) in the case of exclusive Government funding—to have been *ac-*

corded under the statute. Rather, they are rights sanctioned by the statute. Hence, in mixed funding situations, the limitations of section 2320(a)(2)(G)(ii) do not, by their terms, apply.

Second, the negotiation process prescribed for the mixed funding situation imposes no minimum requirement as to the level of rights in technical data that the Government must obtain. Rather, what is called for is an evaluative process in which the Government's interests in securing broad rights in technical data are weighed against the economic incentive to the private sector that the acceptance of more limited Government rights might help secure. Were we to interpret the limitations set forth in § 2320(a)(1)(G)(ii) as applying to a mixed funding situation, the Government would be required to *retain* a higher level of rights in technical data in subsequent negotiations (meaning, the settlement negotiations) than it would have been required to *obtain* during initial negotiations. Since 10 U.S.C. § 2320 imposes no minimum requirement on rights the Government must negotiate in the mixed funding context, we see no reason to preclude it from relinquishing rights it had no obligation to obtain in the first instance. Contrary to plaintiff's argument, we see nothing within the statutory language of 10 U.S.C. § 2320 to change that result.

To the extent, then, that it is correct to view this case as one in which the development of the M4 was achieved through both public and private sources, the Government clearly had the right to relinquish any rights it may otherwise have negotiated.

The Addendum as a Violation of the Competition in Contracting Act (CICA)

Our holding that the Government has the right to relinquish its interest in technical data does not, however, immunize the Addendum from challenge on the grounds that it violated the Competition in Contracting Act's mandate for full and open competition in Government procurements. 10 U.S.C. § 2304. Plaintiff argues that the practical effect of the M4 Addendum—the limiting of competition until 2011—runs afoul of CICA, and must, as a consequence, be struck down as contrary to law. While we agree that certain relinquishments of technical data rights could in fact represent impermissible violations of CICA, we refuse to go so far as to conclude that *any* relinquishment of data rights which serves to limit or eliminate competition must necessarily be found unlawful.

If the Government relinquishes data rights as a bargaining tool to satisfy or extinguish an unrelated claim, it comes into conflict with the Competition in Contracting Act and its actions must be voided. *Executive Business Media v. United States Department of Defense*, 3 F.3d 759 (4th Cir.1993) and *Earth Property Servs., Inc.*, B-237742, March 13, 1990, 90-1 CPD ¶ 273, the primary cases on which plaintiff relies, illustrate that principle. The Government may not simply "give away" data rights which are not at stake if, in doing so, it subverts the goals of CICA.

If instead, however, the Government relinquishes data rights that are themselves in dispute, its actions cannot be said impermissibly to contravene CICA. This is so because the range of settlement possibilities available to the Government as a litigant seeking to establish its data rights cannot be narrower than the range of possible outcomes litigation of the matter could produce. Put differently, we do not read CICA as preventing the Government from achieving, through settlement, a result with regard to data rights that a court, faced with the identical dispute, could itself reach as an adjudicated outcome.

Applying that rationale to the case before us, we conclude that the Government's relinquishment of its rights in the M4 technical data would run afoul of CICA if the Government's rights could not, under any reasonable assessment of the litigation risks, have been construed as being in jeopardy. More specifically, if neither the alleged breach of the M16 Licensing Agreement nor Colt's independent claim that the M4 had been developed at private expense reasonably held out the possibility that the Government's rights in the M4 would be compromised or lost through litigation of those issues, then the terms of the settlement must be deemed illegal. The Government's relinquishment of rights that were not legitimately in dispute would amount to an impermissible give-away—an action prompted not by a bonafide assessment of the risks facing it in litigation nor by the factors enumerated in §2320(a)(2)(E), but rather by an interest in ridding itself of the burden of a lawsuit at the price of granting the contractor exclusive control over important technical data, thereby subverting the aims of the Competition in Contracting Act. That, as discussed above, is something the Government may not do.

Conclusion

To the extent that the M4 was not developed solely at public expense, the Government was free, under 10 U.S.C. §2320, to relinquish rights in technical data without retaining the authority competitively to procure the items dependent on that data. The relinquishment may nonetheless represent an impermissible violation of CICA, however, if the settlement reached with respect to the technical data rights at issue adopted a position not realistically within the outcome risks posed either by the threatened breach of contract action or by Colt's separate claim of ownership of the M4. We leave open for further inquiry the factual issues this Ruling poses: specifically, whether the M4 rights belonged to the Government in the first instance, and if so, whether the loss of those rights could reasonably be interpreted as within the litigation risks the Government faced.

Notes and Questions

1. There are relatively few recent judicial opinions illuminating the interface of government contracting and intellectual property rights, because most issues are resolved in negotiations, not by litigation. The *FN* opinion itself includes a thirty-year chronology of such issues resolved between Colt and the government. What was worked out at each stage? What kinds of documentation do lawyers—for Colt and for the government—create at each stage?

2. Both *Dowty Decoto* and *FN* make the rights in technical data a function of where the money came from for development. What is a short statement of the rules that emerge from this opinion?

3. Does the government's position reflect weakness vis-a-vis Colt? How? Why?

D. Government Assistance, Including Progress Payments and Prompt Payment, and Sureties

The government's system of payment, bonding, and other assistance such as furnishing property is a major, complex topic. The system seeks to resolve several competing tensions. On the one side, contractors for the government, like private contractors, need a system of payment, financing, and assistance that sustains them. On the other hand, the government has both its public fiscal constraints and its policy reasons, for caution about going too far in such sustaining of contractors. These tensions have produced a variety of mixed and compromised arrangements, some effectively combining legal strictness and practicality, some not.

As to payments, the first question concerns what comes first, contractor performance or government payment. This question arises in basic (private) contract law, as the issue of the order of performance, also known as "constructive conditions of performance." In each situation of exchanging performance for payment, either the exchange occurs simultaneously, or one precedes the other; at common law, usually performance precedes payment, but by contract, interim or advance payments may be arranged by explicit provision. For government contracting, the various possibilities get arranged by explicit choice of applicable FAR provisions and contract clauses.

In general, the government starts out with a strong preference for completion of the work before payment. That serves the public fiscal constraint that public funds be spent for Congressionally and administratively decided public purposes, namely, the work, which is most simply and directly assured if the work is completed before payment. That also avoids the practical risks, which the government prefers not to carry, of payments before completion. But for many kinds of contracts the government does provide partial or "progress" payments, paying as the work is done, before completion. Under limited circumstances, the government even makes "advance" payments, paying before the work is done, effectively loaning the contractor funding.

The second question regarding payments concerns the government making payments promptly once due. Given the government's elaborate fiscal controls and bureaucratic complexities, government agencies readily fall into the practice of paying contractors late. However, contractors need payments on time to meet their own responsibilities without undue burdens of financing. So, Congress passed the Prompt Payment Act, providing limited but definite rights to contractors to obtain their payments on time.

For the government's assurance of protection if contractors do not meet their obligations, the government requires the posting of various kinds of security. Most significantly, the government may require contractors to post performance bonds, especially contractors on construction-type projects who receive progress payments. Such performance bonds create a three-sided relationship involving the government, the contractor, and the surety that stands behind the performance bond. When the contractor may falter, the government contracting officer must balance between making payments to and expecting performance from the contractor, or, turning to the surety, expecting performance from the surety but also therefore giving notice and handling payments as the surety would want.

Another large area concerns other non-funding assistance the government provides to contractors, in terms of government-furnished property. The government can provide help to contractors ranging from limited special tools or equipment, all the way to entire facilities that the contractor merely operates. While common themes and tensions run through all these areas, in each distinct statutes, FAR provisions, clauses, and doctrines have produced whole separate bodies of law.

For further discussions of the issues in this section, see: Ronald A. May, Russell I. Marmor, R. Earl Welbaum & David D. Crane, *Annual Survey of Fidelity and Surety Law,* 62 Def. Couns. J. 434 (1995)(re: remedies for sureties); Keith Witten, *Current Develop-*

ments in Bad Faith Litigation Involving the Performance and Payment Bond Surety, 28 Tort & Ins. L.J. 611 (1993); Steven N. Tomanelli, *Rights and Obligations Concerning Government-Furnished Property*, 24 Pub. Cont. L.J. 413 (1995); Steven N. Tomanelli, *Competitive Advantage Arising from Contractor Possession of Government-Furnished Property*, 23 Pub. Cont. L.J. 243 (1994); Bank of Washington, N.A , *Bank's Claim to Defaulting Contractor's Money Slightly Better*, 11 No. 9 Andrews Gov't Cont. Litig. Rep. 7 (May 20, 1998).

1. Government-Furnished Property

The government may furnish property to help contractors. FAR 45.101 defines Government Furnished Property ("GFP") as "property in the possession of or directly acquired by the government and made available to the contractor." Such property may be real, personal, tangible, or intangible. The government may provide "material" (that gets incorporated into or expended in performance like supplies), motor vehicles (under quite restricted circumstances), "special tooling" and "special test equipment" (bearing on the particular supplies or services), and an umbrella term called "production and research property."

Among the subjects covered by the law regarding GFP, the government limits the advantage of bidders already in possession of GFP vis-a-vis others without it. Accordingly, under the FAR, the government has a duty to provide GFP under the terms of the contract, including related data and information, in a timely fashion and in a suitable manner for the intended use. *See* FAR 52.245(a). If the government does not provide GFP by the required time and this causes a delay, the contractor may receive an equitable adjustment. *See* FAR 52-245-2(a)(4). However, the government can furnish property "as is" or with disclaimers.

The FAR and standard clauses provide elaborate rules for the protection of the government's interest in all such government-furnished property. The government wants clear record-keeping, amounting to a written property control system. Also, the government wants allocation of responsibility for damage. For loss or damage to the GFP while it is in the contractor's possession, a contractor with a competitive fixed price contract will be held liable regardless of fault. In contrast, for a negotiated fixed price contract not based on competition or market prices, the contractor only bears a limited risk. When the contractor no longer needs the GFP, it must prepare a contractor inventory schedule.

Additionally, the government has provisions as to title that protect the government's interest against risks from contractor insolvency. Title to government-furnished property remains in the government.

For further discussion, see Steven N. Tomanelli, *Rights and Obligations Concerning Government-Furnished Property*, 24 Pub. Cont. L.J. 413 (1995); Steven N. Tomanelli, *Competitive Advantage Arising from Contractor Possession of Government-Furnished Property*, 23 Pub. Cont. L.J. 243 (1994).

FRANKLIN PAVKOV CONSTRUCTION CO.,
Appellant, v. James G. ROCHE, Secretary of the Air Force, Appellee.

United States Court of Appeals, Federal Circuit.
279 F.3d 989, No. 01-1010, Decided: Jan. 28, 2002.

Before CLEVENGER, GAJARSA and DYK, Circuit Judges.

GAJARSA, Circuit Judge.

This is an appeal from the Armed Services Board of Contract Appeals (the "Board"). On appeal, Franklin Pavkov Construction Company ("FPC") seeks an equitable adjustment for claims arising from a fixed-price contract to install four sets of three-story stairs on two dormitory buildings at Shaw Air Force Base, South Carolina (the "Project"). FPC argued that it received defective specifications and defective government-furnished material, and that it was entitled to other adjustments. The Board denied all but one of FPC's claims. We affirm the Board's decision.

I. BACKGROUND

On October 26, 1995, the Twentieth Contracting Squadron at Shaw Air Force Base, South Carolina (the "Government") awarded the Project to FPC. The Project had been previously bid and contracted to a different contractor in 1991. The previous attempt to implement the project was unsuccessful.

* * *

On October 26, 1995, the Government awarded the Project to FPC as a fixed-price contract for $158,100. The completion date was scheduled for November 26, 1996.

* * *

The contract for the Project also included a short-form Government Furnished Property ("GFP") clause. This clause required the Government to supply GFP identified in the list. Federal Acquisition Regulations ("FAR") Government-Furnished Property (Short Form) § 52.245-4(a); 48 C.F.R. § 52.245-4(a) (2000). However, the contract did not explicitly obligate the government to provide shop drawings as part of the GFP.

Just before FPC started construction, the Government moved the purportedly listed GFP to a fence-enclosed but unlocked location 100 to 200 yards from the job site. The Government made two attempts to meet with Vince Pavkov in November 1995 to take an inventory of the GFP. Vince Pavkov cancelled the first planned meeting. At the second meeting in late November 1995, the parties met at the fenced location and began to take the inventory. However, before completing the inventory, Vince Pavkov had to leave. One of the items that the parties did not inventory were the "stair nosings," devices that prevent slipping on the steps. The GFP list indicated that the Government was to supply eighty-seven stair nosings, but when Vince Pavkov later went to retrieve them he found only ten in the fence-enclosed area. FPC advised the Government of the missing nosings on May 14, 1996, approximately six months after the GFP was delivered. Fabricating and procuring the missing stair nosings had a long lead-time. In order to avoid delaying the Project, FPC obtained permission from the Government to use a substitute aluminum channel.

FPC recognized another problem with the GFP. The configuration of some of the parts caused FPC to question whether all of the stairs were "typical" as shown on the

1995 drawings. After it discovered the D & H drawings, FPC determined that some stair directions were not typical as indicated. The direction of a set of stairs is the direction in which they rise or fall when viewing the side of the building. A note on the D & H drawings indicated that the stair parts may be matched to stairs running in specific directions. This knowledge made the work go more smoothly for FPC. However, for one of the buildings, FPC had to unexpectedly construct new concrete forms for stairs running in the opposite direction in order to use the GFP because some of the stair railings would only fit stairs running in the reverse direction. FPC did not bring the stair direction problem to the attention of the Government until the claim was filed. On March 21, 1997, the Government deemed all the work acceptable and formally accepted it as of that date.

On March 28, 1997, FPC submitted a certified claim to the contracting officer for additional costs and other adjustments, totaling $117,129, and resulting from, among other items, the allegedly defective specifications and the missing GFP. On June 17, 1997, the contracting officer denied FPC's claim. FPC appealed the contracting officer's decision to the Board.

The Board ruled against FPC for all but one count of its claim. *See Franklin Pavkov Constr. Co.,* 2000 ASBCA LEXIS 136, 00-2 B.C.A. (CCH) ¶ 31,100, 153,597, ASBCA No. 50828, 2000 WL 1279909 (Aug. 29, 2000).

* * *

With respect to the GFP, the Board held that delivery occurred when the Government and Vince Pavkov met in the fence-enclosed location near the job site to inventory the material in late November 1995, before commencement of the work. *Id.* at 153,609. The GFP clause in the contract required FPC to give written notice if the GFP is not suitable for its intended use. The Board reasoned that the notice must be timely and therefore that the contract implicitly required FPC to inventory the GFP even though the contract did not explicitly have a clause requiring the parties to conduct a joint inventory. FPC gave the Government notice of unsuitable GFP in May 1996, six months after the Government and Vince Pavkov first met in the fence-enclosed area. The Board found that this notice was not timely. *Id.* The Board denied FPC's requested relief except as to one count.

On appeal, FPC asserts that it is entitled to equitable adjustment for three reasons: * * * (2) the GFP was inadequate and incomplete because it did not comply with the 1995 drawings and this caused FPC additional cost to build additional concrete forms; and (3) the Government never properly discharged its duty to deliver the GFP and is therefore responsible for the costs to replace the missing material. We have jurisdiction under 41 U.S.C. § 607. *See* 41 U.S.C. § 607(g)(1)(A) (1994).

* * *

III. DISCUSSION

* * *

FPC next argues that the Government never completed delivery of the GFP. Its logic is as follows. The contract did not state a time or location for delivery. Thus, a reasonable delivery is required. Only after delivery is accepted does the risk of loss shift to FPC. The GFP remained in the care, custody and control of the Government until FPC came to the fence-enclosed area and retrieved it piece by piece. Thus, FPC alleges error by the Board in its holding that delivery occurred when the Government and FPC met in the fence-enclosed area to inventory the GFP in November 1995, which was only a partial inventory due to Vince Pavkov leaving during the inventory process.

The Board decided the GFP issue against FPC on two bases. First, it found that the parties completed delivery and that the risk of loss shifted to FPC. Second, it found that FPC did not timely notify the Government that there were problems with the GFP.

Both bases go to the question of each parties' respective obligations for delivery of GFP. Although the Government is obligated to supply the GFP, delivery is not a one-sided affair. Delivery is the voluntary transfer of possession. *See* U.C.C. §1-201(14). [3] transfer requires each party to fulfill its role in conveying the physical possession or control of the GFP. The time, place and manner of delivery, if not specified in the contract or by subsequent agreement of the parties, should be a reasonable time, place and manner that enables the contractor to perform under the contract. *See Blaine Co. v. United States,* 157 Ct.Cl. 53, 57 (1962); U.C.C. §2-503(1)(a). In other words, absent agreement otherwise, the Government must "put and hold [the GFP] at the [contractor's] disposition and give the [contractor] any notification reasonably necessary to enable the [contractor] to take delivery." U.C.C. §2-503(1)(a).

Concomitantly, absent agreement otherwise, the contractor has a duty to reasonably respond to such notification. It must promptly and properly receive the GFP to complete delivery. This includes inspecting and taking an inventory of the GFP within a reasonable time. *See* U.C.C. §2-606(1)(a); *see also* FAR §52.245-4(b) ("The Contractor shall maintain adequate property control records in accordance with sound industrial practice."). If the contractor does not so inspect and inventory the GFP and promptly notify the Government of any shortcomings, or reject the GFP, acceptance of delivery is deemed to occur. *See* FAR §52.245-4(a)(1) (requiring a contractor to submit timely written notice to obtain equitable adjustment for ineffective delivery of GFP); *see also* U.C.C. §2-606(1)(a). Rejection of the GFP is ineffective unless the contractor notifies the Government within a reasonable time. *See* FAR §52.245-4(a)(1); *see also* U.C.C. §2-602(2)(a). Timely notification of any deficiencies with the GFP provides the Government an opportunity to cure.

In *Blaine,* the contract obligated the government to supply cloth for the contractor to manufacture jackets for the Army under a delivery schedule spanning seven months in 1951. *Blaine,* 157 Ct.Cl. at 54. So that the contractor could complete another jacket-manufacturing contract, the parties agreed to delayed deliveries of cloth and jackets during the first few months of the schedule, with the entire contract to be completed by the final delivery. *Id.* at 55. The government made the cloth available at a government facility, but the contractor delayed in picking up the cloth because the contractor was unable to secure storage space. *Id.* The contractor was five days late for final delivery and sought to recover labor and overhead costs for these five days, alleging that the delay resulted from the government's failure to deliver sufficient quantities of cloth in time for the contractor to manufacture the jackets by the deadline. Our predecessor court, the Court of Claims, held that once the parties deviated from the original schedule, the government's duty was to "make sufficient cloth available at proper times to enable [the contractor] to perform under the contract—that is, to make reasonable shipments under the circumstances." *Id.* at 57.

---

3. Although the Federal Acquisition Regulations are extensive and usually specify the meaning of terms in government contracts, in the past we have relied on the Uniform Commercial Code ("U.C.C.") in cases such as this where a gap needs to be filled or the meaning of a term requires supplementation. *See Texas Instruments Inc. v. United States,* 922 F.2d 810, 814 (Fed.Cir.1990) (citing U.C.C. §2-209(2) to support the proposition that an integrated executory contract requires a signed writing for modification). Thus, the U.C.C. can inform the analysis of issues raised in government contracts.

As in *Blaine*, the Government here tendered delivery of the GFP in a time, place and manner that enabled FPC to perform the contract. Therefore, the Board had substantial evidence to conclude that any issues of delivery, or resulting problems with the GFP, are not a basis of recovery due to: (i) the risk of loss shifting to FPC because it did not inspect and inventory the GFP within a reasonable time; and (ii) FPC's failure to timely notify the Government of problems with the GFP.

The Board found that the GFP was available for use by FPC from the day the work began. *Pavkov*, at 153,608. The contract did not specify a time for delivery, thus the Government is "obligated to deliver the [GFP] in sufficient time for it to be installed in the ordinary and economical course of performance." *Pavkov*, at 153,608 (citing *Peter Kiewit Sons' Co. v. United States*, 138 Ct. Cl. 668, 674–75, 151 F. Supp. 726 (1957); *Oxwell, Inc.*, 86-2 B.C.A. (CCH) ¶ 18,967, 95,776, ASBCA No. 27523 (June 2, 1990)). FPC claims that the Government never completed delivery. However, FPC ignores its own duty in the delivery process. FPC was willing to meet the Government at the fence-enclosed location to undertake an inventory of the GFP. This indicates that the fence-enclosed location was of a time, place and manner for delivery acceptable to both parties. Given that the contract did not specify formalities of delivery, this meeting constituted a reasonable tender of delivery and notice to FPC that the Government had put the GFP at FPC's disposition for it to construct the Project. FPC should have promptly and properly "received" the GFP at that time by inspection and inventory. FPC removed material from the fence-enclosed location without complaint as to delivery by that method. FPC had the opportunity to inspect and inventory the GFP on the day of the meeting and every day thereafter. That it never did so is due to no fault of the Government. Because FPC failed to fully inspect and inventory the GFP within a reasonable time, the Board was justified in deeming delivery to occur at the initial meeting in the fence-enclosed location. With delivery deemed to have occurred at that time, it was not error for the Board to apply the contract's risk of loss provision against FPC.

The contract's GFP clause requires FPC to submit a timely written request to obtain an equitable adjustment for flawed or missing GFP. The Board reasoned that implicit in this written request provision is the requirement that FPC inspect and inventory the GFP upon receipt. *Pavkov* at 153,609 (citing *Logicon, Inc.*, 90-2 BCA ¶ 22,786, ASBCA No. 39683, 1990 WL 42074 (Apr. 3, 1990)). FPC never fully inspected or inventoried the GFP. As a result, FPC delivered notice of missing GFP to the Government on May 14, 1996, six months after the Government and FPC partially inventoried the GFP. This delay is almost half of the estimated contract length of one year. FPC did not provide timely notice to the Government of any problems arising with the GFP as delivered. This untimely notice did not give the Government an opportunity to cure any deficiency. The Board correctly concluded that FPC's notice was not timely and proper notification of defective or missing GFP was not issued within a reasonable time after the meeting at the fence-enclosed location.

In sum, in a case where the contract does not specify the formalities of delivery, the Government reasonably met its delivery obligations by making the GFP available to FPC in a reasonable time, place and manner. However, FPC failed to discharge its obligations in the delivery process, neglecting to inspect and inventory the GFP, thereby also failing in its duty to notify the Government of any deficiencies in the inventory, which would allow the Government the opportunity to cure any such deficiencies. Therefore, the Board's legal determinations concerning delivery are correct.

C. Suitability of the GFP

FPC also argues that the Government violated its contractual requirement that the GFP be suitable for its intended use. FPC contends that the GFP was not suitable because it did not conform to the 1995 drawings, resulting in additional cost for FPC. FPC complains that the Board never addressed this element of FPC's equitable adjustment claim and it argues that if the Government had provided it with a complete drawing set the problems would have been less costly. FPC's arguments are not persuasive. We have concluded that the Government had no obligation to supply the drawings. FPC therefore cannot recover alleged damages resulting from its unawareness of those drawings.

CONCLUSION

Because we hold that the Board's findings are supported by substantial evidence, and its legal conclusions are correct that FPC does not have a claim for recovery arising from the specifications and drawings, and did not timely notify the Government of the missing items of GFP, we affirm the Board's decision.

AFFIRMED.

Notes and Questions

1. It is said that the government has two obligations in providing GFP—timeliness and suitability. This case touches on both, although with greater emphasis on timeliness. Note how the court's reasoning resembles what would be applied in a U.C.C. case regarding private sellers and buyers of goods. That is, the court sorts out which party carries the risk, and how the risk transfers from one party to another, by having this turn on obligations of notification and response to notification. Does it matter that this is a case of a contractor who filed a claim, belatedly and affirmatively, to be paid more? Would the contractor get a more sympathetic hearing if this were a case of the government seeking, belatedly, to impose penalties for late performance, and the contractor were merely raising, defensively, the ground of that the requisite government-furnished property had not been timely furnished?

2. This case emphasizes aspects of GFP not particularly government-unique, what might be called the "contract," as distinct from the "property," side of GFP. Consider how differently the reasoning in the case would proceed if the issues involved the difference in the legal nature of ownership of property between a private and a government owner. For example, the government may shift risks involving GFP to a contractor, but it never relinquishes title. This matters considerably if, say, the contractor goes bankrupt. As to property that the contractor itself acquires after entering into the contract with an expectation that this will become government property, the point at which title vests in the government can turn on the type of contract. In a fixed-price contract, title does not shift to the government until delivery; in a cost-reimbursement type of contract, title vests earlier.

2. Progress Payments and Sureties

As noted, the government prefers to pay after the competion of work, but often contractors require payment during the period of performance. Partly this avoids the difficulties of contractors who would not be able to raise the capital needed during the period until completion, and thus would have difficulty paying their own employees, subcontractors, and other obligations. This is particularly so because the government imposes rules, such as barriers to financial institutions placing liens on government work-in-progress and to contractors assigning their right to payment, which interfere with normal methods of securing business loans. Partly the providing of progress payments shifts the cost of financing from contractors to the government, a cost-shift which should then allow the contractor to perform at a lower price.

Progress and advance payments require their own special statutory, FAR, contract clause, and administrative arrangements, to reconcile them with the government's other interests. Progress payments are based either on costs or completion of work. Cost progress payments normally only occur in contracts over one million dollars in worth that are to be completed over a long period of time. In addition, cost progress payments factor in payments already made. Generally, progress payments determined by the percentage of completion are limited to construction, shipbuilding and conversion, alteration and repair.

The Progressive Payment Clause, FAR § 52.232-16, requires that progress payments be made at a contractor's request as work progresses. It further provides the means by which the contracting officer shall compute these payments, which can not occur more frequently than monthly under the provision. Contractors may receive no more than 80 percent of the total contract price as progress payments and can only bill the agency for supplies and services it has already actually paid for in performing the contract. Under FAR § 52.232-16(d), title to property defined by the clause vests in the government at the onset of the contract. In order to acquire for use or dispose of property with government title investiture, a contractor must obtain approval from the Contracting Officer regarding the terms. The contractor's failure to comply with material provisions, performance endangering the contract, or unsatisfactory financial condition are only a few of the defined conditions for which a Contracting Officer may reduce or suspend progress payments without excusing the contractor from further performance.

A point of particular interest concerns the coordination between release of progress payments to contractors who have sureties that have posted performance bonds. Sureties serve an invaluable purpose in government contracting, and much complex law concerns the legally protected interests of sureties. Case law has established some government obligation to take care in releasing progress payments, not to do so in a way that will leave a surety unprotected if the contractor fails to complete performance and the surety must take over. Payment bonds are required under the FAR § 28.103-3 for contracts in which performance bonds are required, generally construction contracts exceeding $100,000. Payment bonds assure that required payments be made to suppliers and subcontractors of work contracted for by the principal contractor. FAR § 28.001(e). FAR § 28.106-7 distinguishes between "during contract performance" and "after contract performance" when an agency considers withholding payments to contractors defaulting on supplier and subcontractor payments.

The key doctrines as to claims against the government by sureties got their launch in Balboa Ins. Co. v. United States, 775 F.2d 1158 (Fed. Cir. 1985). A surety told the government not to release progress payments to a contractor, and, when the government did so anyway, sued on the ground the payments should have gone to it, not the contractor. The court agreed with the surety that the government became a stakeholder about unexpended amounts when notified of default. Helpfully, the Court listed eight factors - the Balboa factors - for whether the government has exercised reasonable discretion in distributing funds These factors, on 775 F.2d at 1164-65, are (with citations omitted):

"(1) Attempts by the Government after notification by the surety, to determine that the contractor had the capacity and intent to complete the job..

(2) Percentage of contract performance completed at the time of notification by the surety.(3) Efforts of the Government to determine the progress made on the contract after notice by the surety.

(4) Whether the contract was subsequently completed by the contractor * * *

(5) Whether the payments to the contractor subsequently reached the subcontractors and materialmen * * *

(6) Whether the Government contracting agency had notice of problems with the contractor's performance previous to the surety's notification of default to the Government.

(7) Whether the Government's action violates one of its own statutes or regulations.

(8) Evidence that the contract could or could not be completed as quickly or cheaply by a successor contractor."

NATIONAL SURETY CORPORATION, Plaintiff-Appellee, v. The UNITED STATES, Defendant-Appellant.

United States Court of Appeals, Federal Circuit.
118 F.3d 1542, July 3, 1997.

Before ARCHER, Chief Judge, NEWMAN and PLAGER, Circuit Judges.

Opinion for the Court filed by Circuit Judge PAULINE NEWMAN. Dissenting opinion filed by Chief Judge ARCHER.

PAULINE NEWMAN, Circuit Judge.

The government appeals the decision of the United States Court of Federal Claims holding the government liable to the surety for the improper release of retainage for a construction contract upon which National Surety Corporation served as guarantor. The decision of liability is affirmed, albeit on a different ground than that selected by the Court of Federal Claims. We remand for redetermination of the amount of damages.

BACKGROUND

National Surety furnished performance and payment bonds in connection with a contract between Dugdale Construction Company and the Department of Veterans Affairs, for construction of a water distribution system at Fort Harrison, Montana. The construction contract provided that the government would retain ten percent of all progress payments until Dugdale submitted, and the contracting officer approved, a "complete project arrow diagram," which is a detailed schedule of the critical path for performing the contract. The retainage provision was as follows:

> Clause G-7(A). Payment to Contractor Clause 7 of the General Provisions (Contractor Contract) is supplemented to include the following:

> Retainage: This contract shall have 10 percent retainage withheld on each progress voucher until the complete project arrow diagram has been approved. Once the schedule has been approved and the Contracting Officer has determined that the Contractor's progress is satisfactory, the Contracting Officer may elect not to withhold any additional retainage. Previous retainage will not be re-

duced and future payments will be made in full. If during subsequent project updates the Contracting Officer determines that the Contractor's progress is unsatisfactory, he may withhold 10 percent retainage on the current payment request and subsequent payments to protect the interests of the Government and until he again determines that the Contractor's progress is satisfactory.

Dugdale did not provide the requisite project arrow diagram. Nonetheless, the government did not withhold the ten percent retainage from the progress payments, as the contract required.

Dugdale abandoned the project before its completion, and the government then terminated the contract for default. National Surety completed the construction in accordance with its performance bond, and was paid the difference between the contract price and the payments that had been made to Dugdale, i.e., $126,333, less liquidated damages for late completion. National Surety then filed a claim for the funds that were required to have been retained by the government from the progress payments to Dugdale. The contracting officer did not act on the claim within the statutory period, and National Surety brought suit in the Court of Federal Claims.

On cross motions for summary judgment, the Court of Federal Claims held that National Surety was a third party beneficiary of the contract between Dugdale and the government and that the government breached this obligation when it improperly paid the retainage to Dugdale, thereby incurring liability to National Surety. The court awarded as damages the amount that should have been retained ($97,742) plus statutory interest. This appeal followed.

DISCUSSION

In the Court of Federal Claims the parties offered alternative theories of their legal relationships and ensuing liabilities. Although we affirm the court's conclusion as to liability, we do so on application of suretyship principles.

A

The view that the surety is a third party beneficiary of the contract whose performance it assures is not the usual premise of surety claims against an obligee, although, to be sure, the surety's obligations are affected by that performance. See Arthur Adelbert Stearns, The Law of Suretyship § 1.1 (1951) ("Suretyship may be defined as a contractual relation whereby one person engages to be answerable for the debt or default of another"); Balboa Ins. Co. v. United States, 775 F.2d 1158, 1160 (Fed.Cir.1985) ("suretyship is the result of a three-party agreement").

Suretyship law derives from a different legal premise than whether the bonded contract, or any provision thereof, was made for the surety's direct benefit. The surety bond embodies the principle that any material change in the bonded contract, that increases the surety's risk or obligation without the surety's consent, affects the surety relationship. The principles are set forth in, e.g., Gritz Harvestore, Inc. v. A.O. Smith Harvestore Prods., Inc., 769 F.2d 1225, 1230 n. 7 (7th Cir.1985):

> Where, without the surety's consent, the principal and the creditor modify their contract otherwise than by extension of time for payment

* * *

(b) the compensated surety is

(i) discharged if the modification materially increases his risk, and

(ii) not discharged if the risk is not materially increased, but his obligation is reduced to the extent of loss due to the modification.

(citing Restatement, Security § 128 at 340-41 (1941)). These principles have been elaborated upon in the Third Restatement, including a synthesis of the circumstances under which the surety is entitled to relief against the obligee based on impairment of suretyship status. See Restatement (Third) of Suretyship & Guaranty § 37 (1996). Extensive precedent illustrates the discharge or pro tanto reduction of the surety's obligation, varying in implementation based on the particular facts. The general rule with respect to retainage in construction contracts is the subject of the following example in the Third Restatement:

> 1. S has issued a performance bond with respect to P's contract to construct a house for O for $100,000. Pursuant to the contract between O and P, O is to pay P monthly for the portion of the work completed that month minus a 15 percent "retainage." After completing 60 percent of the project and receiving $51,000 ($60,000 minus the $9,000 retainage) from O, P defaults. S completes the project at a cost to S of $40,000. After S completes the project, O pays the $9,000 retainage to P, who, despite this payment, is insolvent. Had O paid the retainage to P before S completed the project, S would have been discharged to the extent of $9,000 by application of § 38 (impairment of collateral). S has a claim against O for $9,000 because the payment to P would have discharged S from the secondary obligation to that extent.

Id. § 37, illus. 1. See, e.g., Home Indem. Co. v. United States, 180 Ct.Cl. 173, 376 F.2d 890, 895 (1967) (United States liable to surety despite the fact that the government had disbursed the retainages); Hochevar v. Maryland Cas. Co., 114 F.2d 948 (6th Cir.1940) (improper release of 15% retainage in construction contract released the surety pro tanto); Maryland Cas. Co. v. Board of Water Commissioners, 66 F.2d 730 (2d Cir.1933) (same).

The surety's rights and obligations are not based on third-party beneficiary concepts, but on principles of suretyship law. Applying these principles we conclude, as did the Court of Federal Claims, that the government has incurred liability to the surety. However, on the facts of this case we conclude that damages are fairly measured not by the calculated amount of the required retention, but by the injury, loss, or prejudice to the surety due to the government's failure to implement the required retention.

B

National Surety argued at trial that, based on principles of suretyship and the doctrine of subrogation, it was entitled to the retainage security that was required to have been withheld from the contractor. We agree that this is the appropriate theory of liability. The Supreme Court explained the subrogation right in an early case concerning retainage in a construction contract with the government:

> [The surety's] right of subrogation, when it became capable of enforcement, was a right to resort to the securities and remedies which the creditor (the United States) was capable of asserting against its debtor, had the security not satisfied the obligation of the contractors; and one of such remedies was the right, based upon the original contract, to appropriate the 10 per cent. retained in its hands. If the United States had been compelled to complete the work, its right to forfeit the 10 per cent., and apply the accumulations in reduction of the damage sustained, remained. The right of [the surety] to subrogation,

therefore, would clearly entitle him, when, as surety, he fulfilled the obligation of [the contractor] to the government, to be substituted to the rights which the United States might have asserted against the fund.

Prairie State Nat'l Bank v. United States, 164 U.S. 227, 232–33, 17 S.Ct. 142, 144, 41 L.Ed. 412 (1896). See also Balboa Insurance, 775 F.2d at 1161 (discussing the equitable doctrine of subrogation as applied to a bonded government contract).

The retainage provision in a bonded construction contract serves to protect the surety as well as the government, and is an interest of the surety that can not be disregarded or diminished by a party to the contract:

> That a stipulation in a building contract for the retention, until the completion of the work, of a certain portion of the consideration, is as much for the indemnity of him who may be guarantor of the performance of the work, as for him for whom the work is to be performed, that it raises an equity in the surety in the fund to be created, and that a disregard of such stipulation by the voluntary act of the creditor operates to release the sureties, is amply sustained by authority.

Prairie State, 164 U.S. at 233, 17 S.Ct. at 145 (citations omitted). In Pearlman v. Reliance Ins. Co., 371 U.S. 132, 83 S.Ct. 232, 9 L.Ed.2d 190 (1962) the Court reaffirmed the surety's right to subrogation in such a retention fund:

> These two cases [Prairie State and Henningsen v. U.S. Fidelity & Guar. Co., 208 U.S. 404, 28 S.Ct. 389, 52 L.Ed. 547 (1908)] therefore, together with other cases that have followed them, establish the surety's right to subrogation in such a fund whether its bond be for performance or payment.

Pearlman, 371 U.S. at 139, 83 S.Ct. at 236 (footnote omitted). Indeed, in Pearlman the Court confirmed that the surety's right to subrogation is superior to that of the contractor's bankrupt estate to which the government had paid the retainage.

* * *

The duty devolves upon the government to administer the contract, during the course of its performance, in a way that does not materially increase the risk that was assumed by the surety when the contract was bonded. U.S. Fidelity & Guar. Co. v. United States, 201 Ct.Cl. 1, 475 F.2d 1377, 1384 (1973):

> During the performance of the contract, the Government has a duty to exercise its discretion responsibly and to consider the surety's interest in conjunction with other problems encountered in the administration of the contract.

The ten percent retainage provision was in the contract between Dugdale and the government when National Surety set the price for and executed its surety bonds. The retainage requirement served as security for performance of the bonded contract, and this requirement contributed to the surety's assessment of the risk involved. The surety was entitled to rely on the government's obligation to retain this percentage in accordance with the terms of the bonded contract, and on its right of subrogation to this security. National Surety's right was fixed upon execution of the surety bonds, and was not dissolved or altered when the government failed to implement the retainage required by the contract. See Balboa Insurance, 775 F.2d at 1161 (subrogation rights encompass funds wrongfully disbursed). The government, with knowledge that Dugdale had not met the contractual condition predicate to release of the retainage, did not defeat National Surety's subrogation right. Home Indemnity, 376 F.2d at 895 (government held liable to surety despite having disbursed the retainages).

The government argued at trial that the contract was "implicitly" modified by its release of the retainage, and that the surety was bound thereby. The Court of Federal Claims discussed this theory, and found that the parties "did not even attempt to properly modify the contract." Although the contract requires that modifications be made by written change order (clause 3(a)), that oral modifications are ineffective unless confirmed in writing (clause 3(b)), and that under no other circumstances would the contracting officer's conduct be treated as modifying the contract (clause 3(c)), the government presented no evidence, either to the Court of Federal Claims or to this court, of the requisite procedures. See Mil-Spec Contractors, Inc. v. United States, 835 F.2d 865, 869 (Fed.Cir.1987) ("[A]n oral modification of a written contract, which may be modified only by bilateral written agreement, is ineffective.") (citing SCM Corp. v. United States, 219 Ct.Cl. 459, 595 F.2d 595, 598 (1979)). It is apparent that the government simply departed from the contractually required retainage. See Gritz Harvestore, 769 F.2d at 1230-32 (material alteration in the terms of the principal's obligation, to the detriment of the surety, discharges the surety when the modification materially increases the assumed risk); United States v. Reliance Ins. Co., 799 F.2d 1382, 1385 (9th Cir.1986):

> As a general rule a surety will be discharged where the bonded contract is materially altered or changed without the surety's knowledge or consent. In addition, where, as here, a compensated surety seeks exoneration, it must show that the alteration caused prejudice or damage. [Citations omitted.]

Trinity Universal Ins. Co. v. Gould, 258 F.2d 883, 885 (10th Cir.1958):

> It is of course almost axiomatic that any change or modification of the construction contract which materially increases a compensated surety's risk discharges the obligation.

Surety bonds are integral to the government contracting process, for through the surety system the government enters into arrangements with reduced risk, by drawing on the responsibility and resources of the surety. Contract terms that provide security for the bonded performance can not be ignored, waived, or modified without consideration of the surety's interests. Great American Ins. Co. v. United States, 203 Ct.Cl. 592, 492 F.2d 821 (1974); U.S. Fidelity, 475 F.2d at 1384. The government's failure to retain the required sums during performance of the Dugdale contract was a change in the terms from those on which the surety provided its bonds. When National Surety completed the contract in accordance with its performance bond, it was entitled to the benefit of the contractually-required retainage. The government's improper release of this security does not avoid liability to the surety for losses thereby sustained.

C

The Court of Federal Claims rejected National Surety's subrogation theory, based on the Federal Circuit's statement in Fireman's Fund Ins. Co. v. United States, 909 F.2d 495, 498 (Fed.Cir.1990) that "the government as obligee owes no equitable duty to a surety like Fireman's Fund unless the surety notifies the government that the principal has defaulted under the bond." The Court of Federal Claims found that National Surety did not notify the government that Dugdale had defaulted, and that in accordance with Fireman's Fund it was required to do so.

In Fireman's Fund the surety was held to have been required to notify the government that it wished the retainage to be preserved or payments withheld, for absent such notice the government could, in its discretion, "authorize such payment to be made in full without retention of a percentage." 909 F.2d at 497. In Fireman's Fund the government had initially retained ten percent of the progress payments despite satisfactory performance by the contractor. Then, when performance faltered, the government released this past discretionary retainage in order to provide sustenance to the contractor. The surety had been notified of the contractor's faltering performance, yet took no position concerning the retainage or other payments to the contractor until after the contractor had defaulted. On these facts the Federal Circuit held that specific notice from the surety was required, stating that "for the rule [of pro tanto discharge] to operate to Fireman's Fund's benefit, the government must have departed from the terms of the bonded contract." 909 F.2d at 497. The court observed that there had been no such departure. Id.

In contrast, Dugdale's bonded contract gave no discretion to the government to depart from the requirement of the ten percent retainage until after the complete project arrow diagram was submitted and approved. That condition was never met. When the contractor abandoned performance before completion, as did Dugdale, and the government had knowledge of the default, as here, and so informed the surety, as here, Fireman's Fund does not impose a further requirement that the surety notify the government that "the principal has defaulted." The holding in Fireman's Fund did not change the rules of subrogation, but simply dealt with the rights and obligations of the parties on the conditions of that case.

We conclude that National Surety's right of subrogation was not defeated by the government's release of the retainage in contravention of the terms of the bonded contract. On this ground, we affirm the decision of the Court of Federal Claims on the issue of liability.

D

The Court of Federal Claims awarded, as damages, the full amount of the contractually required retainage. We conclude that National Surety is not automatically entitled to this measure of damages, but that the surety's recovery should be measured by its actual damages attributable to the release of the retainage.

AFFIRMED IN PART, VACATED IN PART, AND REMANDED.

ARCHER, Chief Judge, dissenting.

Although I agree with the majority that National Surety cannot recover under a third-party beneficiary claim, I respectfully dissent because I believe the majority has confused two distinct areas of surety law, equitable subrogation and discharge, neither of which is applicable in this case. * * * *

II

As recognized by the majority, "the traditional means of asserting a surety's claim is under the equitable doctrine of subrogation." Balboa, 775 F.2d at 1161. The majority's analysis, however, confuses equitable subrogation and discharge, two principles of surety law that are distinct. Under equitable subrogation, "a surety who pays the debt of another is entitled to all the rights of the person he paid to enforce his right to be reimbursed." Pearlman v. Reliance Ins. Co., 371 U.S. 132, 137, 83 S.Ct. 232, 235, 9 L.Ed.2d 190 (1962). Under this theory, a surety "stands in the place of one whose claim he has paid" and "cannot acquire by subrogation what another whose rights he claims did not have." United States v. Munsey Trust Co., 332 U.S. 234, 242, 67 S.Ct. 1599, 1603, 91 L.Ed. 2022 (1947).

In contrast, the discharge doctrine excuses, to the extent of the prejudice to the surety, the obligation of the surety to perform under the bond when there has been an

312 GOVERNMENT CONTRACT LAW

impairment of the surety's rights under the contract through, for example, modification of the bonded contract or impairment of collateral. See National Union Indem. Co. v. G.E. Bass and Co., 369 F.2d 75, 77 (5th Cir.1966); Restatement (Third) of Suretyship and Guaranty §§ 41(b), 42 (1996). This right belongs to the surety and is not derivative of either the government or the contractor; hence, it is distinct from equitable subrogation. The majority opinion confuses these two principles and improperly treats pro tanto discharge as merely a measure of recovery under equitable subrogation. I consider both in turn and conclude that neither applies in this case.

A. Equitable Subrogation

Under equitable subrogation, a surety is entitled to a retainage held by the government because "[i]f the United States had been compelled to complete the work, its right to forfeit [the retainage], and apply the accumulations in reduction of the damage sustained, remained. The right of [the surety] to subrogation, therefore, would clearly entitle him, when, as surety, he fulfilled the obligation of [the contractor] to the government, to be substituted to the rights which the United States might have asserted against that fund." Prairie State, 164 U.S. at 232-33, 17 S.Ct. at 144; see Restatement (Third) of Suretyship and Guaranty § 31 (1996) (noting secondary obligor's right to return performance of duty still owed by obligee); cf. Balboa, 775 F.2d at 1161.

Because the surety stands in the place of the government, however, its recovery under equitable subrogation is limited to funds presently in the possession of the government. * * * *

It is undisputed both that no funds remained in the government's possession and that National Surety failed to provide the government with notice of Dugdale's default. Thus, National Surety cannot recover under a claim of equitable subrogation.

B. Discharge

The facts in this case seem to fit more appropriately a claim for pro tanto discharge. Under the rule of pro tanto discharge, "[w]here there has been a material departure from contractual provisions relating to payments and the security of retained funds, a compensated surety is discharged from its obligations on the performance bond to the extent that such unauthorized payments result in prejudice or injury." National Union Indem., 369 F.2d at 77; see United States v. Reliance Ins. Co., 799 F.2d 1382, 1385 (9th Cir.1986) (noting that alteration of the bonded contract must be material and prejudice the surety); United States v. Continental Casualty Co., 512 F.2d 475, 478 (5th Cir.1975) ("[A] surety is entitled to be subrogated to the benefit of all securities and means of payment under the creditor's control, and any act by the creditor depriving the surety of this right discharges it pro tanto.").

The first problem with affording National Surety recovery under a pro tanto discharge claim, however, is that it never made this claim in the Court of Federal Claims. * * *

Moreover, the record does not support such a claim. * * * *

It is not improper, however, for the government to fail to enforce a provision in a contract which is for its own benefit and to accept lesser performance. See Restatement (Second) of Contracts § 84 (1981). * * * *

Admittedly, under suretyship law, a surety can recover under the pro tanto discharge rule if the underlying contract is materially modified, resulting in prejudice to the surety. See National Union Indem., 369 F.2d at 77; M. Michael Egan, Discharge of the Performance Bond Surety, in The Law of Suretyship at 12-8 to 12-11 (Edward G. Gallagher ed., 1993). The appropriate measure of damages is "the extent of loss due to the modification." St. Petersburg Bank & Trust Co. v. Boutin, 445 F.2d 1028, 1031 (5th Cir.1971); see Restatement (Third) of Suretyship and Guaranty § 37 (1996). * * * *

Accordingly, I respectfully dissent from the majority opinion and would reverse the judgment of the Court of Federal Claims.

Notes and Questions

1. Government contract law requires some contractors to obtain bonds from sureties to carry certain risks. Then, the sureties seek through litigation to put some risks back on the government. This opinion contains a mix of references to the law of suretyship generally, and to the prior authorities as to the law of suretyship for government contracts specifically. Should the rules for sureties on government contracts be the same or different as on private contracts?

2. The opinion points out the issue of the extent to which the surety can put risks back on the government based on a contracting officer's actions, inactions, waivers, or asserted violations of statutes, regulations, or contract provisions in administering the contract. On the one hand, the surety will contend that in undertaking its responsibility it appropriately anticipates that contracting officers will do their part, particularly to the extent of following the law. On the other hand, part of what the government seeks, in requiring a surety, is to put risks on the surety even if those risks could have been reduced by different activity of a contracting officer. Suretyship law has traditionally provided the balance as to what is within, and not within, the surety's undertaking. How much is this balance affected by the difference between the government's system for directing the activity of contracting officers, and what a private sector enterprise would do to direct the activity of the equivalent private supervisors of construction contracts?

3. The dissent argues that the law of discharge, not of equitable subrogation, applies, since the surety seeks something other than suing to obtain the (nonexistent) retainage. On the other hand, the majority thinks the law of equitable subrogation has relevance insofar as it shows how important that retainage was and thus how injured was the surety by the release of that retainage. Who is more persuasive?

3. Prompt Payment

The Prompt Payment Act aims to reduce the practice by government agencies of making late payments. It has broad, government-wide applicability. It applies if the government does not promptly pay undisputed invoices, if deliveries of supplies or performance are partial or periodic, or if a construction contract provides for progress payments. 31 USC 3903(a)(5)-(6). However, it applies only to payments for supplies or services accepted by the government, that is "invoice payments" rather than those made prior to acceptance of supplies or services. Its requirements for the government are triggered by invoices in proper form. Under the Prompt Payment Act, a payment is prompt upon receipt thirty days after the government receives a proper invoice for amount due. 31 U.S.C. § 3901; see also FAR 32.905(e)(list of what constitutes a proper invoice).

For late payments, the government incurs an interest penalty. Interest begins to accrue the day after the payment due date and ends when payment is made calculated by the date of the check. If the invoice is not proper, the government must notify the contractor within seven days. FAR 32.905(b). While Congress intended the act to expedite invoice payments, Congress did not intend to speed up the array of other kinds of payments. It only applies to government delay in paying undisputed invoices, not to disputed or questioned ones, to change orders or requests for equitable adjustments.

NORTHROP WORLDWIDE AIRCRAFT SERVICES INC., Appellant v. DEPARTMENT OF THE TREASURY, Respondent

January 30, 1992, GSBCA No. 1162-TD

Before Board Judges SUCHANEK (Chief Judge), LaBELLA, and HYATT.

Board Judge LaBELLA.

This appeal concerns a dispute over the application of the Prompt Payment Act ("PPA" or "The Act"), 31 U.S.C. §3901 et. seq., to payments made under cost reimbursement contracts between the Department of the Treasury ("Treasury") and Northrop Worldwide Aircraft Services, Inc. ("Northrop"). Treasury contends that payments it rendered to Northrop for services performed pursuant to these contracts are exempted from PPA interest penalties under the proper interpretation of that Act. Northrop insists that the charges it invoiced and the payments it received were payments for services already rendered in partial fulfillment of its contracts, and, as such, were subject to PPA interest penalty provisions. We * * * grant the appeals. * * * *

Findings of Fact

The contracts at issue, Tc-85-37, Tc-87-38 and Tc-90-059, obligated Northrop to provide transportation, maintenance, storage and auction functions for items seized by Treasury's Customs Service under the direction and supervision of Custom's employees. Joint Stipulations 79, 81, 82, 84, 85, 87, 89–94, 98–103, 105, 107, 112, 113, 114, 117. These services were either performed by Northrop directly or through subcontractors which Northrop paid directly. Joint Stipulation 121. Only after Northrop had performed or provided an individual service, be it flying a seized aircraft to storage, or auctioning seized property and depositing the proceeds in a Government account, did it invoice the items of expense and present those invoices to Treasury for payment. Joint Stipulations 60, 82, 91, 94.

All three contracts are explicitly made subject to the PPA in clauses that are incorporated by reference. At the same time, none of the three prohibit partial payments being made to recognize progress. Appeal File, Exhibits 5, 6, 9; Appellant's Supplement to Appeal File, Exhibits 10, 12, 14; Joint Stipulations 9, 27, 44. The payment terms of the contracts further provide for payment to be divided into cost reimbursement, base, and award fees. Joint Stipulations 14, 32. To initiate payment of these costs and fees, Northrop was required to submit vouchers detailing its expenditures. Joint Stipulations 13, 31, 43. Contracts Tc-85-37 and Tc-87-38 each contain a provision that authorizes the payment of base and award fees before the completion of the contract. Joint Stipulations 15, 16, 19, 33–37. Although this provision is not incorporated in contract Tc-90-059, this contract provides that:

payment for goods and services is made after charges invoiced against the procurement authorization are validated by an Accounts Payable Clerk. In order to verify an invoice, the following criteria must be met:

- Goods or services were properly authorized.

- Goods or services have been received.

- Invoiced amounts match those authorized by the purchase order or property services subcontract.

Only invoiced amounts meeting these criteria will be approved for payment.

Joint Stipulation 45. All of the services performed by Northrop or its subcontractors were provided in response to a request by Customs. Although no formal procedure for acceptance of services was instituted, performance was monitored and evaluated by Customs personnel, who were generally pleased with Northrop's performance. Joint Stipulations 79–81, 83–122.

Northrop never requested contract financing on these contracts, nor did the contracting officer make the legally required determinations to extend contract financing to Northrop. Joint Stipulations 3, 24, 41, 51–53.

None of the payments made under these contracts were progress payments, advance payments or prepayments, nor were they made before the receipt of property or services by the Government. Joint Stipulations 60–63. However, all payments under these contracts were subject to later audit, and possible correction, until final payment had occurred. Joint Stipulations 20, 21, 38, 46.

During fiscal years 1988, 1989, and 1990, the Customs Service paid interest penalties on late payments to Northrop under contracts Tc-85-37 and Tc-87-38. Joint Stipulation 77. Customs has since determined that these interest penalties were not required by the PPA. Consequently, Customs has recouped prior interest payments and denied appellant's claims for PPA interest under the three contracts. The amounts claimed are $100,708.81 on contracts Tc-85-37 and Tc-87-38, and $8,221.81 on contract Tc-90-059. Joint stipulations 68, 72. These claims were properly submitted to the contracting officer, who denied them in their entirety, and are the subject of these timely appeals. Joint Stipulations 68–70, 72–74, 76.

Discussion

Treasury points to the 1989 revision of OMB circular 125-A, the OMB circular promulgated to assist in the appropriate implementation of the PPA, as a final clarification of the Act as it applies to all three contracts. This latest circular, which specifically includes interim payments under cost type contracts as contract financing exempt from the PPA, is merely a clarification of the law as it has always existed, and Treasury contends that even the two contracts entered into before its issuance should be construed pursuant to its definition of contract financing. Under Treasury's reading, the PPA exempts all payments made on a cost reimbursement contract, except the final payment, from interest penalties.

The payments made to Northrop under the contracts in question are unquestionably for services either performed by Northrop or performed by subcontractors and paid for by Northrop prior to the submission of invoices to Treasury for payment. Respondent has also stipulated that it monitored appellant Northrop's performance to ensure compliance with the contract requirements. Such monitoring included both announced and unannounced inspections, the submission by Northrop of monthly progress reports, quarterly evaluations, Customs' field organizations reports, and Northrop's submission of activity reports. Although Treasury emphasizes the fact that nothing in the contracts in issue sets out exact prices to be paid, or "establishes a unit price to cover one month's services," Respondent's Appeal Brief at 25, we are not persuaded that this precludes acceptance of work performed by Northrop on a monthly basis. Acceptance is defined in the 1989 final revision of OMB circular 125-A as "acknowledgement by the Government that property and services conform with the requirements of the contract." 54 Fed.Reg. 4700 (1989). It is clear from the stipulations that Treasury closely monitored the performance of Northrop to ensure that the services provided did conform to the contract. This kind of close scrutiny warrants a finding of acceptance of work not timely rejected as non-compliant.

The PPA was intended to "provide incentives for the Federal Government to pay its bills on time." H.R.Rep. No. 461, 97th Cong., 2nd Sess. 1, reprinted in 1982 U.S.Code Cong. & Admin.News 111. The incentive took the form of an interest penalty, to be borne by an agency which failed to pay duly submitted invoices within a commercially reasonable time. Prior to the passage of the Act, suppliers of goods and services to the Government had no choice but to bear the cost of any agency delay in payment. Consequently, some companies ceased competing for Government contracts, and others built estimated interest into their bids. Id. The PPA was passed to alleviate the inequity caused by allowing the Government to pay its bills late with impunity, and to give the contractors and companies doing business with the Government a method of redress.

The payment of interest on late payments is not always required under the PPA, however. In particular, it would be beyond the scope of the Act to require an interest penalty on advance payments or other contract financing provided by the Government. The Office of Management and Budget (OMB), the executive agency charged with implementing the PPA through the issuance of clarifying rules and regulations, recognized this fact, and so explicitly excluded payments made "solely for financing purposes" from incurring interest penalties in its regulations governing implementation of the PPA. OMB Circular A-125, 47 Fed.Reg. 37,321, at 37,322 (1982). This circular, which has been revised several times, remains the best expression of OMB's position regarding the implementation of the PPA. The circular recognizes that in some circumstances the Government may make payments in advance of receipt of goods and services, and that "these payments, or contract financing, are referred to as progress payments, advances, or prepayments." OMB Circular 125-A, 49 Fed.Reg. 28,140 (1984). This type of payment arrangement must be requested by the contractor and approved by the agency following established guidelines. Id.

Contract financing is defined as:

> a Government disbursement of monies to a contractor under a contract clause or other authorization prior to acceptance of supplies or services by the Government. Contract financing payments include advance payments, progress payments based on cost under the clause at 52.232-16, Progress Payments, progress payments based on a percentage or stage of completion (see 32.102(e)(1)) other than those made under the clause at 52.232-5, Payments Under Fixed-Price Construction Contracts or the clause at 52.232-10, Payments Under Fixed-Price Architect-Engineer Contracts, and interim payments on cost-type contracts. Contract financing payments do not include invoice payments or payments for partial deliveries.

48 CFR 32.902 (1990) (FAR 32.902). Contract financing is only provided at the request of a contractor with approval of the Government, and it is not the favored

method of conducting Government procurements. OMB Circular 125-A, 52 Fed.Reg. 21,926, at 21,928 (1987).

The dispute in this case largely hinges on the factual determination of whether the payments made to Northrop by Treasury constitute contract financing. If they do, they are largely exempt from the PPA interest penalty provisions. The Department of the Treasury acknowledges that the payments in question are not true contract financing, but nonetheless contends that they should be considered financing for the purposes of PPA interest penalties. Respondent's Appeal Brief, at 21-22. Treasury readily concedes that no traditional contract financing was requested or received by Northrop. Instead Treasury argues that contracts awarded not on a fixed price, but rather on a cost reimbursement, basis carry no obligation to comply with PPA provisions, and incur no interest penalties on any late payments other than on the final contract payment. Id. Respondent bases this conclusion on its reading of the 1989 final version of OMB Circular 125-A and the inclusion of the phrase "interim payments on cost-type contracts," the circular's definition of contract financing which is republished in FAR 32.902. Treasury's reliance on this one phrase of the definition is misplaced because the phrase is merely one component of the definition of contract financing, not the only component. Treasury's reading of FAR 32.902 completely ignores the first and last sentences of the definition, which state: "Contract financing payments" are those made in "advance of acceptance of supplies or services," and "do not include invoice payments or payments for partial deliveries." FAR 32.902 (emphasis added).

OMB itself emphasized the distinction between cost reimbursements and contract financing in an Attachment to OMB Circular 125-A:

1. This Attachment establishes standards for assuring that appropriate payment terms are included in all Government contracts. It supplements the guidance provided in paragraph g, "Payment Standards," of the basic Circular.

2. Generally, payments for goods and services acquired by the Federal Government are made after receipt, inspection, and acceptance of the goods and services, or through reimbursements on cost type contracts.

3. In other cases, payment may be made before receipt of goods or services. These payments, or contract financing, are referred to as progress payments, advances, or prepayments.

49 Fed.Reg. 21,140, at 21,141 (1984). OMB's segregation of contract financing from cost reimbursement establishes its belief that the two methods of payment are not part of the same category. The use of the term cost type contract in the definition of contract financing cannot, therefore, be read to mean all cost type contracts, but only those that fit the remainder of the definition. Where invoices have been submitted for payment after actual performance and receipt of services it would be illogical to call the payments for those rendered services contract financing merely because the service was not rendered under a set price contract.

The June 1987 revision to Circular 125-A was intended to "close loopholes in the circular that allow agencies to pay their bills late without including the required interest penalty." 52 Fed.Reg. 21,926 (1987). Respondent would have us open a new loophole, exempting from the PPA all cost type contracts, based on one phrase in the 1989 revision to OMB circular 125-A. To do so would be inconsistent with the PPA, and our reading of the intent of the 1989 revised circular. The commentary preceding the final revision of OMB Circular 125-A states:

> The proposed circular prohibited payment of late payment interest penalties on periodic payments under cost reimbursement contracts unless the contracts defined these payments as partial payments for property or services furnished. Three industry associations recommended that interest be paid on such late payments. The intent of the proposed restriction was to prohibit payment of interest on contract financing payments.

54 Fed.Reg. 52,700, at 52,701 (1989). This prohibition does not appear in the revised circular. From its omission we can only conclude that the OMB either never intended to prohibit interest on cost reimbursements, or changed its mind after objection by the industry groups.

The commentary goes on to state:

> The 1988 amendments require that interest penalties be paid on late payments when a contractor makes a partial delivery of supplies or periodic performance of service, performance has been accepted, and a proper invoice submitted under a contract where periodic payments are not prohibited.

Id. The revised circular itself provides: "an agency shall pay for partial delivery of supplies or partial performance of services unless specifically prohibited by the contract." OMB Circular 125-A; 54 Fed.Reg. 52,709 (1989). When taken together these statements and revisions contradict respondent's assertion that OMB was trying to carve out an exception to PPA interest penalties for payments under cost reimbursement contracts. This Board would be remiss in presuming from the mere use of one undefined phrase that OMB intended to contradict its prior position and promulgate regulations which are very likely in conflict with the purposes of the PPA. This is especially the case when, as here, the evidence so overwhelmingly points to a contrary conclusion.

In conclusion, appellant performed services for and at the request of Customs and, under Customs' supervision, incurred and paid expenses on behalf of the Government. Appellant then submitted invoices to the proper authorities which were not timely paid. The nature of these services precluded a fixed price contract because Customs did not know from month to month what service it would require. Instead, it requested service as needed, and confirmed that service was provided prior to issuing payments on submitted vouchers. Respondent has not alleged that the tardy payments in question were late because of a dispute over the propriety of the invoiced expense or dissatisfaction with appellant's performance. In fact, the Joint Stipulations indicate that the work was satisfactory; the tardiness of the payments is simply unexplained.

Payments made after performance and acceptance of goods or services do not fit the definition of contract financing. As we conclude that the payments made to Northrop were made after the performance and acceptance of the corresponding services, these payments were not contract financing. Therefore, any payments not timely made were subject to PPA interest penalty provisions.

Decision: The appeals are GRANTED. Appellant is entitled to receive interest penalties on payments not timely made under the cost reimbursement contracts in issue, plus interest on its claim as provided by law.

Notes and Questions

1. Why did the government oppose applying the prompt payment act to payments under cost reimbursement contracts?

2. What might "periodic performance of service" mean in the diverse circumstances of cost reimbursement contracts? Suppose a research and development contractor provides quarterly progress reports, with invoices, even if no particular milestones in the research should be expected to be achieved in that kind of short-term intervals. Can its lawyer draft into the terms of the contract some language that would classify the reports, and the research they describe, as a "periodic performance of service"?

3. Regulations were promulgated at 5 C.F.R. part 1315 - not in the Federal Acquisition Regulation. Note the reference in the opinion to OMB Circular 125-A. What kinds of payment might the OMB Circular, or the Prompt Payment Act, cover, beyond those for contracting under the FAR?

4. Assignment as Security for Credit

INDUSTRIAL BANK OF WASHINGTON, Appellant, v. UNITED STATES of America et al.

United States Court of Appeals, District of Columbia Circuit
424 F.2d 932 No. 22790, Argued Jan. 22, 1970.
Decided March 9, 1970.

Before FAHY, Senior Circuit Judge, and LEVENTHAL and MacKINNON, Circuit Judges.

PER CURIAM:

Appellant Industrial Bank of Washington (Bank), on March 1, 1966, loaned money to Art's Decorating and Cleaning Company (Contractor), on the security of the Contractor's assignment to the Bank of all moneys due or to become due from the Government under contract executed October 29, 1965, for rendering by Contractor of cleaning services at a General Services Administration (GSA) building. The Bank gave notice of its assignment to the GSA, and to appellee Reliance Insurance Company (Surety) which had, under date of November 3, 1965, executed a performance bond to protect the Government against loss occasioned by the failure of the Contractor to perform the contract. On May 14, 1966, the Contractor defaulted. GSA terminated the contract and entered into a replacement contract that resulted in a contract loss to the Government.

Payments due the Contractor under the contract for services performed amounted to $4685. The Bank claimed the money due it from the Contractor on the loan, some $3896, plus interest. The Government declined to pay this on the ground that the unpaid balance will be set off against the Contractor's indebtedness to the United States resulting from the termination and reprocurement from another source.

The Bank brought an action against the United States, joining the Surety as a defendant, basing jurisdiction on the Tucker Act, 28 U.S.C. § 1346. The Government contested jurisdiction, and in the alternative sought summary judgment. The Surety also sought summary judgment. So did plaintiff Bank. The District Court, assuming jurisdiction for purposes of decision, granted the motion of each defendant for summary judgment, and denied the Bank's motion. We affirm the dismissal of the Bank's action with prejudice.

1. The District Court had jurisdiction of the action under the Tucker Act, which gives the District Courts concurrent jurisdiction with the Court of Claims of any civil

action against the United States, not exceeding $10,000 in amount, founded upon any contract with the United States. 28 U.S.C. § 1346 (1964). Plaintiff sues on its rights pursuant to an assignment, expressly authorized by the Assignment of Claims Act of 1940 as amended, from one who had a right founded on a contract with the United States.

* * *

2. Proceeding to the merits, the Surety rightly points out that it is established doctrine that the surety on a performance or payment bond has a right of subrogation, derived from the right to resort to the remedy the United States was capable of asserting against the contractor, resulting in priority of undisbursed contract funds.

The Bank relies on the wording of the Assignment of Claims Act of 1940, as amended, as establishing a higher right in the assignee bank. The 1940 statute removes a disability on the bank to enforce its assignment of a claim against the Government. The words of the act are not properly applied if, following a termination for default, they are construed to give the bank as assignee of the contractor a right to funds in the hands of the Government which are needed for completion of the contract. The surety, upon completion of the contract, or payment of the funds needed for completion of the contract becomes entitled to those funds as the subrogee of the Government; its equitable right of subrogation relates back to the time of the giving of the bond; and it has priority over the subsequent right obtained by the bank by virtue of the assignment which was taken with knowledge of and subject to the equity of the surety. This is the view of the Court of Claims, the leading case being Royal Indemnity v. United States, 93 F.Supp. 891, 117 Ct.Cl. 736 (1950), which was cited with approval in Pearlman v. Reliance Insurance Company, 371 U.S. 132, 141, 83 S.Ct. 232, 9 L.Ed.2d 190 (1962).

* * *

When a surety on a Government contractor's performance bond makes a payment thereunder to or for the United States, he is subrogated to the rights of the Government as to any funds due or to become due under the contract. This subrogation, sometimes called an 'equitable lien,' relates back to the date of the bond, and is therefore superior to any conflicting claim thereafter asserted by another. * * * This right is potential only until the contractor's default causes the surety to pay. It is a shadowy thing until it is given substance by the occurrence of a loss to the surety; theretofore a mere right to subrogation, it then becomes an actuality. And the law gives the surety the added advantage of having subrogation effective as of the date of his original undertaking.

This court, analyzing the provision of the 1940 law, held the Government precluded from recovering amounts already paid to the assignee bank even after default, in the absence of fraud, and that hence the surety's right of subrogation gave it no rights against the bank for such funds. But its reasoning establishes that a contrary result is applicable as to funds still in the hands of the Government, that the bank is not entitled to these funds if needed by the Government to complete the contract or pay for the work needed to complete the contract, and that the surety making such payments has a right of subrogation as to those funds. Our 1950 decision was accomplished by a careful review of the authorities, the pre-1940 pronouncements of the Supreme Court, the post-1940 decisions of the Court of Claims and other courts. The Fifth Circuit's analysis, which our 1950 case cited for another point, was not persuasive on this issue. We adhere to the reasoning already stated by our court.

We have no occasion to consider any questions that may arise concerning funds in the hands of the Government in excess of those required to complete the contract. The judgment dismissing the Bank's claim with prejudice will be

Affirmed

Notes and Questions

1. Historically, units of government not only resisted delegation of a performing party's duties under the government contract, but also resisted assignment of the performing party's right to receive payment. Local governments which attempt to do so today, discover that U.C.C. section 9-318(4) changed the law to bar them from doing so (absent special provision of state law). This section declares: "A term in any contract between an account debtor and an assignor which prohibits assignment of an account or contract right to which they are parties is ineffective." See, e.g., *American Bank of Commerce v. City of McAlester*, 555 P.2d 581 (Okl. 1976). But, did the U.C.C. similarly change federal government contract law?

2. At the federal level, Congress enacted the Assignment of Claims Act in 1862, which ostensibly prohibited all assignments of performance of government contracts. It had the narrower goal to deal with Civil War problems with noncontractor middlemen securing government contracts (by favoritism or worse) and then turning the contract over to others who gave sub-par performance. The courts created limits on the act, notably in *Thompson v. Commissioner*, 205 F.2d 73 (3d Cir. 1953). Ultimately, an important practical aspect consists of the FAR novation process, by which the government formally recognizes a contractor's assignee. For a fuller look, see David R. White, *To Dance with the One You Came with: Federal Government Regulation of Assignments of Contractual Performance* , 29 Pub. Cont. L. J. 601 (2000).

3. As this case indicates, Congress made room by a 1940 statute, not for assignments of contract rights in general, but just for assignments to financing institutions as security for contract financing. This is governed by the Assignment of Claims clause in the FAR, 32.805 and 52.232-23 (clause itself). In this case, the bank loses. Why is the surety's right superior to the bank's?

Chapter 6

Changes

Government contracting law arranges an important compromise differing from basic (private) contract law in the common situation that the contracting officer, or simply the work itself, calls for something more or different than the contract specifies. The law, particularly that key standard clause the Changes Clause, strikes a compromise between the government's need for operational flexibility to make more or different demands without contractor resistance, and the contractor's need, without the weapon of resistance, to secure fair payment.

Historically, the government always wanted the ability to impose new demands on contractors. Because public purposes, rather than profitmaking, drive government contracting, the expense of changes during contracting does not deter the government from requiring them. At the same time, the government cannot put itself in a situation where the only way to obtain changes is to pay whatever the contractor demands. So, the government must insist on changes, but without letting contractors resist.

Contractors, meanwhile, generally welcome changes. They enjoy additional work for additional compensation. Changes occur without the open competition of contract formation, so that the contractor, who had to keep its proposals low to get the contract, makes much more profit on the changes. However, the contractor finds that the government uses the concept of the "equitable adjustment," with a set of formulae and procedures, to put some limits on wide-open demands.

In basic contract law, recent scholarship has suggested the general concept of the "relational" contract. At common law, the model contract consisted of a one-time exchange, like a single purchase of a single lot of goods. However, in recent times, a large category of contract law consists of complex relationships, such as between long-term buyers and suppliers, or between businesses and employee unions. In the relational contract, the initial offer and acceptance merely start a long-term process in which what is to be provided changes over time. Many aspects of the government contract, and particularly the "Changes" aspect, fit this relational model.

In particular, a relational contract not only anticipates changes, it calls for processes to resolve issues on an ongoing basis without jeopardizing the contract by such blunt tactics as cancellation or refusal to perform. Commercial arbitration, or management-labor grievance procedures, provide such processes. The Changes Clause and the equitable adjustment provide that process for government contracts. What gives it such interest is that this process has a large role for law and lawyers, rather than market bargaining, to determine the payment for changes.

For further discussions of this chapter's overall subject, see the sources cited in each section, plus: John D. Schminky, *Proper Funding of Contract Modifications Under the Antecedent Liability Rule*, 26 Pub. Cont. L. J. 221 (1997); William D. Lyman, ILL-

CLE, *Construction Law in Illinois: Contract Changes, Extras, and Additions*, 7-1 (MAIN HANDBOOK) (1997); Evan R. Farber, *The Allowability of Costs Incurred in the Preparation of Requests for Equitable Adjustments After Reflectone*. 25 Cont. L.J. 781 (1996); Richard C. Johnson, *Price Adjustment Clauses for State and Local Taxes in Federal Government Contracts: Aerospace and Taxes Charged to Contracts Through Overhead*, 26 Pub. Cont. L.J. 599 (1997); George E. Powell, Jr., *The Cardinal Change Doctrine and Its Application to Government Construction Contracts*, 24 Pub. Cont. L.J. 377 (1995); Hal J. Perloff, Comment, *The Economic-Waste Doctrine in Government Contract Litigation*, 43 DePaul L. Rev. 185 (1993); F. Trowbridge vom Baur, *The Origin of the Changes Clause in Naval Procurement*, 8 Pub. Cont. L.J. 175 (1976).

A. The Changes Clause, Cardinal Changes, and Formal Changes

The text of the Changes Clause well repays a close reading. First, section (a) provides that the "Contracting Officer may at any time, by written order . . . make changes within the general scope of the contract." This distinguishes between changes "within" the contract's scope, and something else, which would be changes outside the contract's scope. The latter are called "cardinal changes." A contracting officer has the right pursuant to the contract to order changes, but not cardinal changes. If the contracting officer orders cardinal changes, the government has breached the contract and the contractor is entitled to cancel the contract and obtain a generous measure of damages. This, however, is rare. The case below, *Boston Shipyards*, shows why.

Second, the section (a) confines formal changes to those by the "Contracting Officer . . . by written order." Extensive case law over the years has concerned the authority and methods for such formal changes. A contractor frequently receives instructions from one of the many representatives, project officers, inspectors, technical assistants, and other working for, or with, the contracting officer, and the contractor often obeys these. They may or may not have the authority to make formal changes. Even if not, they may or may not be making a "constructive change."

If contractors obey their lawyers, then when someone other than the Contracting Officer ordered a change, the contractor would promptly inform the Contracting Officer before performing the work, or, if such notice were impractical, write the Contracting Officer describing the change, and advising that a formal claim will be filed. Often, however, contractors do not do so but contact their counsel only much later.

Third, section (e) of the clause provides that "Failure to agree to any adjustment shall be a dispute under the Disputes clause." Hence, the Changes and Disputes clauses together create an orderly mechanism for resolving the issue of how much to pay. Section (e) further states "However, nothing in this clause shall excuse the Contractor from proceeding with the contract as changed."

As discussed in the chapter on termination, government contract law does not embrace the doctrine in basic (private) contracting of "efficient breach"; it penalizes, often severely, the government contractor who does not proceed with the contract.

What this clause indicates is how government contract law penalizes the contractor who fails to proceed even when the government has changed the contract by imposing new and different demands, and even when the contract is in dispute. A change might well seem to a contractor not efficient. For example, it might double the contractor's government workload at a time when the contractor could make more profit by increasing its non-government workload. In a basic (private) contract situation, the contractor might refuse to perform the change, pay the damages caused by the need for the buyer to find another contractor, and emerge with a net profit. That is not the choice government contracting law anticipates for contractors to make. Rather, an array of penalties await the contractor who does so, and while abandonment of government contracts certainly occurs, it is hard to view it as "efficient" for all involved.

For further discussions of this section's overall subject, see T. Scott Leo, B. Scott Douglass & Cathleen M. Jareczek, *The Obligee's Duties to Provide Plans and Specifications, Make Payment, and Process Change Orders*, 32 Tort & Ins. L.J. 961, 1997.

CHANGES CLAUSE —
Fixed-Price
(Aug 1987)

(a)   The Contracting Officer may at any time, by written order, and without notice to the sureties, if any, make changes within the general scope of this contract in any one or more of the following:

(1)   Drawings, designs, or specifications when the supplies to be furnished are to be specially manufactured for the Government in accordance with the drawings, designs, or specifications.

(2)   Method of shipment or packing.

(3)   Place of delivery.

(b)   If any such change causes an increase or decrease in the cost of, or the time required for, performance of any part of the work under this contract, whether or not changed by the order, the Contracting Officer shall make an equitable adjustment in the contract price, the delivery schedule, or both, and shall modify the contract.

(c)   The Contractor must assert its right to an adjustment under this clause within 30 days from the date of receipt of the written order. However, if the Contracting Officer decides that the facts justify it, the Contracting Officer may receive and act upon a proposal submitted before final payment of the contract.

(d)   If the Contractor's proposal includes the cost of property made obsolete or excess by the change, the Contracting Officer shall have the right to prescribe the manner of the disposition of the property.

(e)   Failure to agree to any adjustment shall be a dispute under the Disputes clause. However, nothing in this clause shall excuse the Contractor from proceeding with the contract as changed.

In re Boston Shipyard Corp., Debtor.
Appeal of Boston Shipyard Corp.

No. 89-1144. United States Court of Appeals, First Circuit. 886 F.2d 451.
Heard June 7, 1989. Decided Sept. 27, 1989.

Before CAMPBELL, Chief Judge, REINHARDT[1] and TORRUELLA, Circuit Judges.

TORRUELLA, Circuit Judge.

Boston Shipyard Corporation ("BSC") appeals from the decision of the district court, which affirmed the bankruptcy court's grant of summary judgment in favor of appellee, the United States Military Sealift Command ("MSC").

I. Background

BSC entered into a contract with MSC to overhaul the USNS Mississinewa. This contract was awarded even though BSC was in the midst of a Chapter 11 reorganization in the bankruptcy court. The original contract called for a 100 day performance period and for BSC to be paid $4,997,925.

As often happens, the contract proved to require much more time and expense than was originally anticipated. Each point that BSC realized a change in the contract specifications would be required, it filed a condition report or change order requesting authorization for the necessary changes so that the work could be done. Hundreds of these change orders were submitted and BSC claims that the delay in their resolution led to increased financial burdens on BSC, as well as to greatly hindered progress, causing the work to fall far behind schedule.

By the end of August 1985, BSC's financial condition had worsened and MSC payments were necessary for the company's continued ability to perform on the contract. * * *

BSC curtailed its operations on the contract effective October 17, due, it claims, to the "effect of MSC's delays, disruption and failure to compensate BSC." Brief of Appellant at 24. A press release issued on that day stated that "[t]oday Boston Shipyard Corp. is forced to cease operations." On November 15, MSC terminated the contract because of this default by BSC.

The government filed a Proof of Claim in the United States Bankruptcy Court on February 25, 1986 seeking $9.2 million in reprocurement costs. BSC objected to the Proof of Claim and filed a counterclaim seeking to convert the default termination into a termination for the convenience of the government.

* * * Six months later, after full briefing and a hearing on the issues, the bankruptcy court entered summary judgment in favor of the government on the remainder of the case, based on its conclusion that BSC had inexcusably abandoned the contract. Upon appeal, the district court affirmed both summary judgment orders and BSC now appeals this decision.

* * *

IV. The Summary Judgment

BSC also challenges the district court's decision affirming the grant of summary judgment to MSC on the remainder of the claims. This decision is dependent upon

---

1. Of the Ninth Circuit, sitting by designation.

whether BSC's termination of services constituted abandonment and breach of contract, thereby warranting the government's termination of the contract, or whether BSC's cessation of work could be justified by MSC's actions.

In granting MSC's motion, the bankruptcy court relied upon the Master Agreement for Repair and Alteration of Vessels (the "Master Agreement") as the controlling contract between the parties. Clause 13 of the Master Agreement consists of Federal Acquisition Regulation ("FAR") §52.233-1, which states

> (h) The Contractor shall proceed diligently with performance of this contract, pending final resolution of any request for relief, claim, appeal, or action arising under the contract, and comply with any decision of the Contracting Officer.

The bankruptcy court held that under this provision BSC was obligated to continue work until its dispute with MSC was resolved and that therefore its cessation constituted wrongful abandonment of the contract. The court carefully examined the actions of MSC and concluded that BSC's breach was not justified by these actions. This decision was affirmed without significant discussion by the district court.

* * *

BSC bases the second part of this argument on MSC's alleged failure to make progress payments and other acts which led to BSC's weakened financial condition, which, it argues, justified abandonment of the contract. We agree with the decisions of the courts below.

Although Clause 13 is admittedly controlling, BSC argues that its work cessation was justified because MSC's actions had caused a cardinal change to the agreed-upon contract. See Air-A-Plane Corp. v. United States, 187 Ct.Cl. 269, 408 F.2d 1030 (1969). A cardinal change is considered a breach of the contract and therefore further work, even when a disputes clause exists, is not required. General Dynamics Corp. v. United States, 218 Ct.Cl. 40, 585 F.2d 457, 462 (1978); Allied Materials & Equipment Co. v. United States, 215 Ct.Cl. 406, 569 F.2d 562, 563 (1978). Change orders or other changes are considered to be cardinal changes if they greatly increase the burden of the contract, in effect changes that are outside the scope of the contract itself. General Dynamics, 585 F.2d at 462. A cardinal change is said to occur

> when the government effects an alteration in the work so drastic that it effectively requires the contractor to perform duties materially different from those originally bargained for. By definition, then, a cardinal change is so profound that it is not redressable under the contract, and thus renders the government in breach.

Allied Materials, 569 F.2d at 563-64 (emphasis added). In making this determination, the court is to look at all relevant circumstances, including, but certainly not limited to, the increase in cost of completing the contract and the number of changes made. See Air-A-Plane, 408 F.2d at 1033.

There were 86 post-August change orders, most of which were initiated by BSC through condition reports. The contract between the parties contained a change clause, providing for an effective and efficient procedure for dealing with changes that would arise in the course of the contract's performance. Thus, the parties clearly anticipated that changes would need to be made.

Moreover, the contract was an "open and inspect" contract calling for reconditioning work throughout the ship. In this type of contract the full amount of the work that will be necessary can not be known until the ship is opened up in dry dock and only then can the full extent of the contract be established. Moreover, the contract provided for a large number of so-called "B" items, which were not required by the contract, but which the government could, at its discretion, require BSC to perform. These factors also indicate that the need for change orders must have been anticipated by the parties from the contract's inception.

We cannot conclude that these change orders amounted to a cardinal change, putting the government in breach and justifying BSC's abandonment of the contract. Some delay and disruption must be expected in the performance of any contract. See Magoba Construction Co. v. United States, 99 Ct.Cl. 662, 690 (1943). Accepting all of BSC's allegations as true, the change orders that arose were predictable, due to the type of contract at issue in this case. Moreover, they were not of the magnitude or extent that would signify a cardinal change.

BSC also argues that its failure to perform due to its financial incapacity must be excused because its money problems had been caused by MSC's actions. Unfortunately, it concentrates this part of its argument on cases which hold that the government must make financial remuneration for change orders issued, a premise not disputed, it seems, by either party. Nevertheless, we will use what guidance the cases do give to properly focus this inquiry.

We start with the general premise that a contractor's default may be excused if the causes of the default were beyond the contractor's control. Southeastern Airways Corp. v. United States, 230 Ct.Cl. 47, 673 F.2d 368, 377–78 (1982). Financial incapacity, however, is generally not considered beyond the contractor's control. Id. 673 F.2d at 378. This rule is understandable, as a contractor who makes and then accepts a bid should have the financial ability to perform. But, as with most rules, there are always exceptions. Thus, if the financial problems are caused by factors beyond the contractor's control, or by the government's actions themselves, then the contractor's default may be justified. Id.; see also National Eastern Corp. v. United States, 201 Ct.Cl. 776, 477 F.2d 1347, 1356 (1973) (stating that a contractor's incapacity is "a fortiori " beyond the control of the contractor if caused by acts of the Government).

The period in question ranged from September 1 to October 15, when BSC stopped its operations. BSC argues that government delays resulted in non- payment of $218,907, plus $30,608 for contract modifications which went uncollected. Thus, BSC argues that a total of $249,515, delayed in payment over short periods of time, prevented it from working on a contract worth, by the termination date, over $6.5 million. We cannot agree. The evidence in the record indicates that BSC's "thin capitalization made it impossible for it to absorb even routine and foreseeable problems." Southeastern Airways, 673 F.2d at 378. It is clear that in this case BSC's financial problems were not caused by any delay or disruption by MSC. Rather, BSC's "[f]inancial incapacity predated commencement of performance." Id.

A different decision would make government contracts truly unworkable, allowing contractors to demand immediate reimbursement for cost overruns, even if the government disagrees with the claim. There would then be no meaning to default or dispute clauses that define procedures in case of disputes.

Affirmed.

Notes and Questions

1. In a basic (private) contract, what kinds of argument would a contractor like Boston Shipyards make that the buyer of its shipyard services ultimately sought from it more than it had bound itself to? How did the common law regard contracts like this

"open and inspect" contract, that is, contracts that left key aspects for future determination? Would Boston Shipyards have a better chance than it had in this case? What is the difference?

2. The court says that the "change clause" provides "an effective and efficient procedure for dealing with changes." How so? Is that a happy coincidence, or if not, what is the tie between the change clause and the government getting what it wants in this case?

3. The court rejects the argument that a contractor's financial vulnerability can justify its demanding "immediate reimbursement for cost overruns." And, the court seeks to assure that there is "meaning to default or dispute clauses that define procedures in case of disputes." Surely the government knew who it was contracting with: the shipyard was in bankruptcy at the time of award, and the government presumably did a preaward survey to determine the contractor's responsibility. Is the government truly without a role in the contractor's inability to perform? The doctrine of "efficient breach" might have suggested that when the government contracts with so vulnerable a contractor, the government should divert some of what it saved by taking the contractor's offer to buying insurance for itself (e.g., by a backup deal with another shipyard). That is not the route the government or the court take here. What in the nature of the public purposes behind government contracting necessitates the government's toughness, backed up by the court, in dealing with a contractor when the government might well have been the least cost avoider in this situation?

4. The opinion refers to a large number of formal change orders. Changes may be initiated by the government or proposed by the contractor. Often the process is something of a hybrid, where the contractor is encouraged to formulate a detailed proposal. In such cases, the contractor is generally deemed to be a volunteer, and therefore not eligible for compensation for the costs of preparing the proposal. See, e.g. *Appeal of BMT Services*, IBCA No. 3794A-97, 1998 WL 422560.

The following is a typical procurement regulation (this one for the Department of Agriculture) regarding how adjustments for change orders are to be priced:

7 C.F.R. §3016.36 (f)(1):

> Grantees and subgrantees must perform a cost or price analysis in connection with every procurement action including contract modifications. The method and degree of analysis is dependent on the facts surrounding the particular procurement situation, but as a starting point, grantees must make independent estimates before receiving bids or proposals. A cost analysis must be performed when the offeror is required to submit the elements of his estimated cost, e.g., under professional, consulting, and architectural engineering services contracts. A cost analysis will be necessary when adequate price competition is lacking, and for sole source procurements, including contract modifications or change orders, unless price reasonableness can be established on the basis of a catalog or market price or a commercial product sold in substantial quantities to the general public or based on prices set by law or regulation. A price analysis will be used in all other instances to determine the reasonableness of the proposed contract price.

5. Both the changes clause and the disputes clause require the contractor to perform the work, that is, the contractor has a duty to proceed. If the contractor asserts wrongly that the government breached the contract by ordering a cardinal change which the contractor refused to follow, then the contractor can get terminated for default. But, if

the contractor asserts rightly that the government breached the contract by ordering a cardinal change, then the contractor receives damages.

For examples of cases of contractors held to have breached their duty to proceed pending outcome of dispute resolution processes, see *Appeals of Benju Corporation*, ASBCA No. 43,648, ASBCA No. 43,841, ASBCA No. 43,954, ASBCA No. 46,220, 1997 WL 593961; *Judiciary Square Ltd. Partnership v. S.E.C.*, GSBCA No. 12920-SEC, 1996 WL 559866; *William A. Hulett*, AGBCA No. 92-196-3 1992 WL 228400 (Ag. B.C.A.).

6. As to the complex issue of how to handle a government contractor's bankruptcy, see Samuel R. Maizel & Tracy J. Whitaker, *The Government's Contractual Rights and Bankruptcy's Automatic Stay* 752 PLI/Comm 603 (Practising Law Institute Commercial Law and Practice Course Handbook Series) PLI Order No. A4-4519 (April, 1997); David M. Pronchik, "What Do You Mean...You Can't Terminate This Contract for Default?," Procurement Law., Winter 1995, at 11.

B. Equitable Adjustments and Constructive Changes

Equitable adjustments have an important history which has helped shape the contemporary rules of computation and proof. Tracking some of that history provides a useful introduction.

The equitable adjustment as its hallmark includes payment for increased costs and for profits on work performed, but not profits on work unperformed, so-called "unearned" profits. A classic image behind this doctrine consists of the hasty change, such as the end of World War I or World War II, which necessitates immediate ending of what had been an all-out production drive. To pay off what would have been the full measure of wartime profits to contractors who had done nothing yet to earn them would have seemed scandalous.

An elaborate line of legal evolution thereafter concerned "impact costs." When the government adds work, what about paying the contractor not just for the added work, but for the "impact" of the added work on the duration or cost of the work not changed? In *United States v. Rice*, 317 U.S. 61 (1942), the Supreme Court held that the contract made no provision for any increase in the cost of the work not changed. Subsequently, the government developed the Suspension of Work Clause to give a mechanism for government-imposed increase in the duration of work. As for government-imposed increase in costs, in the 1960s the changes clauses were amended for payment of impact costs. *Merritt-Chapman & Scott Corp. v. United States*, 192 Ct. Cl. 848, 429 F.2d 431 (1970).

What that history shows is the complex balance involved in the contemporary rules, both the rules about when the contractor can obtain an equitable adjustment and the rules of computation and proof. The equitable adjustment diverged long ago from the measure of damages in basic (private) contract law. At common law, there is no hesitation as a measure of contract damages to pay "unearned" profits; that is what the expectation interest is all about. Just why government contract law diverges so much merits consideration after some case reading. In any event, the story of the overruling of the

Rice doctrine shows that the government has not simply redrafted its clause to squeeze contractors as tightly as possible. Government contracting law must strike a balance between the government's need for flexibility without paying scandalous unearned profits and the reasonable rewarding of contractors for compliance with changes.

1. Constructive Changes

The success of the disputes process and the equitable adjustment has caused their utilization in many government contracting situations besides formal changes. Hence, the concept of the "constructive change" has ballooned. It includes contract interpretations, government interferences with work, defective specifications, nondisclosure of vital information, and speeding up the work ("acceleration"). Several of these receive discussion in other chapters. In this chapter, the goal is not to expound rules for all the different types, but to illustrate some common elements.

Two cases here illustrate equitable adjustments in situations other than formal change orders. The *General Builders* case illustrates the connection between termination for convenience and the equitable adjustment formula. In *General Builders*, the contractor succeeded in showing that its termination for default was wrongful and it should receive treatment as though terminated for convenience. However, that just starts the process, which then turns to what the contractor should receive as an equitable adjustment.

In *Blinderman*, the contractor seeks an equitable adjustment under the "Suspension of Work" clause. It contends that the government did not cooperate enough, in effect delaying the work. Obviously, this differs from a formal change order, as the government got nothing more, and sought nothing more. Still, the flexible concepts of constructive change and equitable adjustment get stretched to apply.

General Builders Supply Co., Inc., on Behalf of Itself and for the Benefit of Hupp, Inc. v. The United States

No. 188—68. United States Court of Claims.
409 F.2d 246., April 11, 1969.

DAVIS, Judge.

General Builders Supply Co., Inc., the plaintiff, made a contract in 1964 with the General Services Administration to furnish 7,859 refrigerators, for use in Germany, at $119 each. General Builders then subcontracted to purchase these articles from the Gibson Refrigerator Division of the Hupp Corporation, at $116. Hupp built pre-production models and submitted them for inspection to the Government, which rejected them three times. The contract was then terminated for default on the ground that the pre-production models failed to meet the specifications. No production refrigerators were made or delivered.

On appeal, the Board of Contract Appeals of the General Services Administration determined that the work had been improperly terminated for default. The case was returned to the contracting officer for calculation of the recovery for the erroneous termination. General Builders made claim, not only for the costs actually incurred before termination, but also for the anticipated profits said to have been lost by plaintiff and by

Hupp. These amounted, plaintiff said, to more than $23,500 for itself and slightly over $102,400 for the subcontractor. The contracting officer allowed recovery of $6,491.77, for the costs, but denied the demand for unearned but anticipated profits. Plaintiff was satisfied with the cost computation but appealed the rejection of the profit. The Board of Contract Appeals affirmed, holding that the default clause in the contract did not permit the award of anticipatory gain. The suit in this court attacks that conclusion. Both parties have moved for summary judgment and there is no factual controversy bearing on the legal question of the Government's liability for such profits.

The concept of an 'equitable adjustment' has had a long history in federal procurement, going back for about fifty years. See United States v. Callahan Walker Constr. Co., 317 U.S. 56, 63 S.Ct. 113, 87 L.Ed. 49 (1942); United States v. Rice, 317 U.S. 61, 63 S.Ct. 120, 87 L.Ed. 53 (1942); Ribakoff, Equitable Adjustments Under Government Contracts, in Government Contracts Program, The George Washington University, Changes and Changed Conditions 26, 27 (Gov't Contracts Monograph No. 3, 1962). First used in the standard 'changes' and 'changed conditions' articles, the term has been taken over for other clauses, such as the 'suspension of work' and 'government-furnished property' provisions. See J. Paul, United States Government Contracts and Subcontracts 430 (1964). The consistent practice appears to have been that an 'equitable adjustment', as that phrase is used in these articles, can cover an allowance for a profit on work actually done, but does not encompass unearned but anticipated profits. See United States v. Callahan Walker Constr. Co., supra, 317 U.S. at 61, 63 S.Ct. 113; Bennett v. United States, 371 F.2d 859, 864, 178 Ct.Cl. 61, 69—70 (1967); cf. Bruce Constr. Corp. v. United States, 324 F.2d 516, 163 Ct.Cl. 97 (1963). This is far from an unnatural interpretation since, in these clauses, the 'equitable adjustment' is usually tied by express words to an increase or decrease in the contractor's costs.

The plaintiff, which impliedly concedes that this has been the practice under the other clauses, maintains that a different reading for 'equitably adjusted' is proper in the newer 'default' article. The contention is that the 'changes', 'changed conditions', and similar clauses dealt with a different problem, and the interpretation which was appropriate in that context does not fit as well into the present situation. There are, we think, two related answers to that argument. One is that 'equitable adjustment' has become a term of art (in federal contracts) with a commonly understood meaning in the aspect involved in this case (compare Ambrose-Augusterfer Corp. v. United States, 394 F.2d 536, 545, 184 Ct.Cl. 18, 33 (1968)), and that accepted content should be followed unless there are very strong counterbalancing reasons. Such a counterweight might be a marked alteration in context, but if the change is not significant and drastic it should not be sufficient to alter the established meaning of this specialized term. Here, the change in context—even if one accepts plaintiff's point that the context does in fact differ—is moderate, rather than severe. A concept hitherto applied to an ongoing agreement is now to be applied to one which is at its end, without any future. That change in context does not seem any greater than the transfer of the concept of an 'equitable adjustment' from the 'changes' article to the clause controlling 'government-furnished property' or allowing an award for 'suspension of work'.

The more basic reason for rejecting plaintiff's argument is that, at bottom, the context is not at all different in kind. With regard to amounts, a termination is essentially the same as a change under the 'changes' clause reducing the number of items to be furnished. In fact, a 'change' of that kind can often be characterized as a partial termination, and vice versa. Cf. Williamsburg Drapery Co. v. United States, 369 F.2d 729, 177 Ct.Cl. 776 (1966); Nesbitt v. United States, 345 F.2d 583, 170 Ct.Cl. 666 (1965), cert.

denied, 383 U.S. 926, 86 S.Ct. 931, 15 L.Ed.2d 846 (1966); National Presto Indus., Inc. v. United States, 338 F.2d 99, 102, 167 Ct.Cl. 749, 753 (1964), cert. denied, 380 U.S. 962, 85 S.Ct. 1105, 14 L.Ed.2d 153 (1965). Whether the decrease be total or partial, and whether it be called a change or a termination, the focus will still be on the amount of money with which the contractor should be left as a result of the transaction. In that calculation, reasonable costs and a reasonable profit on work actually done will normally be important, regardless of whether one proceeds by subtracting from the original fixed-price or by adding from zero. In other words, the problem of the 'equitable adjustment' is entirely comparable whether the contractor is faced with a termination or with a change in quantity of work. There is therefore no reason for discarding the historical meaning that term has acquired under the 'changes' and like clauses.

It is possible that this particular plaintiff did not comprehend the impact of the meaningful words 'equitably adjusted' in the 'default' article of the contract, but nevertheless there was much to put it on notice. FPR Circular No. 25, supra, which spelled out the aim of the new clause, was available to government contractors and to the public. The Federal Procurement Regulations provided that, on termination of a fixed price contract, '(a)nticipatory profits and consequential damages shall not be allowed' (41 C.F.R. s 1—8.303 (a) (1968)), and said expressly that directives like the one just quoted could be used (in addition to computing the award on a convenience-termination) 'for guidance in negotiating a settlement agreement, or in making an equitable adjustment' (41 C.F.R. §1—8.000(b) (1968) (emphasis added)). Moreover, the meaning of 'equitable adjustment' had become, so to speak, a 'trade usage' for those engaged in contracting with the Federal Government. The knowledgeable federal contractor would understand it, and plaintiff, if it was not so knowledgeable, was charged with making itself aware of that usage. Cf. Uniform Commercial Code §1—205. Since it was dealing with the Government, as to which a whole body of special contract provisions has developed, plaintiff could hardly take the naive stance that it had the right to read its contract as an unsophisticated layman might, without bothering to inquire into the established meaning and coverage of phrases and provisions which appear to be unusual or special to federal procurement. Cf. Beacon Constr. Co. of Mass. v. United States, 314 F.2d 501, 161 Ct.Cl. 1 (1963). In this instance, slight inquiry would have brought forth the information that 'equitably adjusted' was a term of art, and anticipatory profits would not be allowed.

Although plaintiff urges us, in effect, to strain to read the contract as permitting the recovery of such unearned gain—on the ground that the policy of the law has been to avoid allowing the defendant to escape payment of such profits where it has acted improperly—the fact is that the development of federal procurement has been to the contrary. It has long been held that, on cancellation of a contract under the power of eminent domain, just compensation does not include anticipatory profits. Russell Motor Car Co. v. United States, 261 U.S. 514, 523—24, 43 S.Ct. 428, 67 L.Ed. 778 (1923). A major reason for the initiation and increasing use of convenience-termination articles has been to allow the Government to avoid paying unearned profits. G. L. Christian & Assoc. v. United States, 312 F.2d 418, 426—427, 160 Ct.Cl. 1, 15—16, rehearing denied, 320 F.2d 345, 160 Ct.Cl. 58, cert. denied, 375 U.S. 954, 84 S.Ct. 444, 11 L.Ed.2d 314 (1963); Nolan Bros., Inc. v. United States, supra note 3, 405 F.2d, at 1256, 186 Ct.Cl at 607. As for default terminations, the clauses first recognized a breach if the invocation of the article was shown to be wrong or the default excusable (see J. D. Hedin Constr. Co. v. United States, supra, 408 F.2d 424, 187 Ct.Cl. —). They were then modified to reject such profits if the default for which the contractor was terminated turned out to be excusable, leaving untouched the situation where there was in fact no default (and the Government invoked the default article). After Klein v. United States, supra, 285 F.2d 778, 152 Ct.Cl. 8 (1961), granting unearned profits in such a case, the default articles were further amended, in general, to bar anticipated profits even in the instance in which it was found that there had been no default at all, and the contracting officer had acted erroneously. See Schlesinger v. United States, 390 F.2d 702, 710 n. 11, 182 Ct.Cl. 571, 585 n. 11 (1968). In 1967, GSA required convenience-termination clauses in contracts like the present one, so that from that time on the problem now before us is unlikely to arise. All in all, there appear today to be very few government contracts in which unearned gain can be granted if there is a termination (either for default or for convenience). The trend has been steadily adverse to the allowance of that component of common-law damages, and the policy of federal procurement law is no longer what plaintiff insists. See Nolan Bros., Inc. v. United States, supra, and cases cited.

The result is that plaintiff cannot recover on its claim for anticipatory profits, the demand it makes here. * * *

Notes and Questions

1. The case makes clear that the equitable adjustment draws the line against paying "unearned" profits. That phrase has a kind of populist ring, like refusing to pay those who have not labored and sweated for their reward, but that has, of course, nothing to do with it. At common law, contractors receive their expectation interest in the event of breach. In the realm of private contracts, the argument might well be made that if a merchant put into a contract of adhesion with a non-merchant a clause denying the latter the ordinary measure of direct damages ("unearned" profits), the clause was unconscionable. Why can the government do this?

One argument in basic (private) contract law for paying the measure of expectation damages has been that there are reliance damages that would be hard to prove and would go uncompensated, thereby discouraging reliance in the future absent payment of expectation damages. Do government contractors, knowing that the public needs the freedom to cancel contracts in response to shifts in policy, have forewarning enough to make a judgment about reliance? Or is it that, just like the government cannot lets its authority be curtailed by estoppel, the government cannot let its budget be mortgaged by reliance? Is it the ample measure of profit in government contracting when performed that allows the government to withhold profits when changes eliminate performance?

Blinderman Construction Co., Inc., Appellant, v. The United States, Appellee

Appeal No. 53-82. United States Court of Appeals, Federal Circuit. 695 F.2d 552. Dec. 10, 1982.

COWEN, Senior Circuit Judge.

Pursuant to the Contract Disputes Act of 1978, 41 U.S.C. §§601, et seq., the appellant (contractor) appeals from a decision of the Armed Services Board of Contract Appeals (Board) which denied, in part, the contractor's claim in the amount of $45,312, and its request for a time extension of 13 days for the completion of the contract. The case is before us on cross-motions for summary judgment filed in the United States Court of Claims prior to October 1, 1982, and thereafter transferred to this court.

The claim grows out of a contract entered into between the contractor and the Department of the Navy (Navy) for installation of permanent improvements in multifamily housing at the Great Lakes, Illinois Naval Base (Base).

The claim of $45,312, includes three separate items.

* * *

The third and largest item is for damages sought for what the Board refers to as a claim for "access delays," and a time extension of 13 days. The contractor contends that the additional expense and delay were incurred by reason of the Navy's failure to discharge its contractual obligation to provide access to apartments occupied by Naval personnel. A summary of the claim of $45,312 shows that it includes an item of $11,579 for "delay costs," and $33,733 claimed on the ground that the impact of the delays was to extend the completion of the project by 9 working days.

The claim for access delays involves an interpretation of the provisions of the contract, and for the reasons to be set forth, we disagree with the Board's interpretation and reverse its decision on this question of law. However, in view of its holding, the Board did not decide whether or to what extent the Navy's delay was unreasonable. Also, at oral argument, Government counsel stated that if we disagreed with the Board, the case should be remanded because of concurrent delays attributable to the contractor and its subcontractor. We agree, and therefore we deny both motions for summary judgment, except as stated above, and remand the case to the Board for further proceedings in accordance with this opinion.

I. Factual Background and Prior Proceedings.

By contract dated March 31, 1978, the contractor was required to furnish and install electrical meters, gas meters, hot water meters, hot water heating meters and condensate meters in the apartments housing Naval personnel at the Base. The contract was to have been completed by September 12, 1978, but the completion date was extended by a change order to October 3, 1978. The contract was let in conformity with the national policy to conserve energy by metering energy usage in military housing. About 139 buildings and 656 individual apartments were involved in the work to be performed.

The contractor was required to provide a quality control inspection system to insure compliance with the contract plans and specifications. The contract contained the standard clauses for construction contracts including "Changes," "Suspension of Work," and "Liquidated Damages". Since the work was not completed until October 20, 1978, the contractor was charged by the Navy with liquidated damages of $2,975 for 17 days of inexcusable delays. On other claims not in issue, the Board found that the contractor was entitled to a time extension of 6 days and remission of liquidated damages in the amount of $1,050; thus the contractor was charged with net liquidated damages of $1,925 for 11 days of inexcusable delays.

Following the adverse decision of the contracting officer, the contractor elected to proceed under the Contract Disputes Act of 1978 and appealed the decision to the Board. The Board denied the claim before us in an initial opinion of November 14, 1980, and then, in an opinion on motion for reconsideration, on February 25, 1981. The cross-motions for summary judgment on the contractor's appeal from the Board's decision were thereafter filed in the United States Court of Claims.

* * *

III. The Claim for Delays in Obtaining Access to the Apartments.

This claim presents the only difficult issue in this appeal, because its resolution involves an interpretation of the following provisions of the contract:

SCHEDULING OF WORK: Work shall be scheduled to issue [sic] minimum description [sic] of service to the housing units. The contractor shall notify the occupants of the housing unit [1] at least 3 days prior to commencing any work in a housing unit. Thecontractor shall perform his work between the hours of 8:00 A.M. and 5:00 P.M. and having once started work in a housing unit shall work to completion in consecutive work days. * * *

In no case shall a unit be left overnight without a completed meter installation, including testing and resumption of gas service.

PROGRESS CHARTS: The Contractor shall, within 15 days after receipt of notice of award, prepare and submit to the Contracting Officer for approval, a practicable construction schedule in accordance with Clause entitled 'Progress Charts and Requirements for Overtime Work' of the General Provisions except as modified herein. Progress chart shall clearly indicate when the contractor will require access to individual buildings and shall further indicate the anticipated durations of all utility outages.

METHODS AND SCHEDULES OF PROCEDURES: The work shall be executed in a manner and at such times that will cause the least practicable disturbance to the occupants of the buildings and normal activities of the station. Before starting any work, the sequence of operations and the methods of conducting the work shall have been approved by the Contracting Officer.

The facts as found by the Board or which are otherwise established by undisputed evidence, show that the contractor experienced considerable difficulty and delays in gaining access to approximately 60 apartments. After the contractor had prepared and delivered to the Navy a progress chart showing when the contractor required access to the buildings, the contractor's quality control manager (CQC) had the responsibility for notifying the occupants of the time when the work in their apartments was to be performed. The specifications required that this notice be given 3 days before work was to be commenced, and the CQC attempted to notify them personally at least 3 but usually 7 days before the work was to begin.

Notices to the occupants were given in the morning, during the noon-hour, or in the afternoon. If CQC could not reach the occupants during the day, he tried to see them in the evening. If all of these efforts failed, the CQC would, in accordance with a suggestion made by the Navy's project manager, leave a yellow card on the door-knob of the apartment, indicating when the work in that unit would begin. The Navy had, at the site of the work, a project manager who represented the contracting officer in the administration of the contract, and most of the contractor's dealings were with this project manager. In some instances, the occupants refused to permit the contractor's workmen to enter their apartments, even after notice was received by them. At times, the contractor was unable to serve personal notice because the occupants were on military leave for periods for as long as 2 weeks. In other instances, the occupants would go out during the lunch hour while the work was being performed, leaving their doors locked with the tools of the workmen inside. On most of the occa-

---

1. An amendment to the IFB changed 'contracting officer' to 'occupants of the housing unit.'

sions complained of by the contractor, the occupants were not at home when the work was scheduled despite notice given to them in person or by a card left on the doorknob.

Whenever the contractor or the subcontractors were unable to gain access to an apartment for any of the reasons mentioned above, they would call on the project manager to provide the access they needed. If the occupants could be contacted by telephone, the project manager would ask them to return home and permit entry into their apartments. If the occupants were absent from the apartment on vacation, the project manager first telephoned them to get permission to enter their apartments. Then he would obtain keys from the Housing Section at the Base to admit the workmen. Thus on occasion, access by the workmen could not be obtained until several days after the scheduled date for commencing work. The workmen were carpenters, plumbers, pipefitters, electricians, and laborers, and their work had to be coordinated and performed in a planned sequence. Because of the delays, they would have to leave buildings with work unfinished in several apartments and work in another building. To complete the contract, they would have to backtrack to those apartments which they were unable to enter during the time previously scheduled for the work.

Shortly after experiencing delays for lack of access to the apartments, the contractor notified the project manager that the contractor's responsibilities ended after it had notified the occupants in the manner described above; that a record would be kept of the delays, and that a claim would be submitted later for the increased costs incurred as a result of such delays.

As previously stated, the contractor gave the project manager notice that claims would be submitted for the increased costs due to the delays in getting access to the apartments. On December 1, 1978, after the contract had been completed, the contractor submitted to the project manager the claim in issue. Attached thereto was an itemized breakdown of the dates and extent of the delays. * * *

At the contractor's request, the claim was submitted to the contracting officer, who agreed with the project manager and denied the claim by written "final decision."

* * *

On appeal, the contractor argued before the Board that the 150-day completion schedule, the provision for liquidated damages, the specification limiting work hours, and the requirement for the contracting officer's approval of the construction schedule and sequence of the work, implied a duty on the part of the Navy to make the apartments in the buildings available in accordance with the schedule and sequence of work which had been approved by the project manager.

In its opinion, the Board noted that the invitation for bids had originally provided that the contractor would notify the contracting officer at least 3 days prior to commencing work in any unit, but that this requirement was amended to state that the notification was required to be given by the contractor to the occupants of the housing units. The Board concluded that the necessary implication of this change was that "the contractor, and not the Navy, was obliged to make arrangements with each tenant as to the specific time work would start and any necessary preparations by the tenants in each apartment." Thus, the Board essentially adopted the project manager's view that the specifications required the contractor, not only to give notice to the occupants, but also to obtain in each case, an agreement permitting entry into the individual apartments, specifying the time for the work, and covering necessary preparations by the occupants.

The Board's holding on this crucial issue is a decision on a question of law, which is not final or conclusive on judicial review. 41 U.S.C. §609(b). It is with this conclusion of law that we disagree.

The Government has correctly observed that this is not a case in which the Government expressly contracted to provide access to the premises to perform the contract work, as in Delta Equipment & Constr. Co. v. United States, 104 F.Supp. 549, 122 Ct.Cl. 340 (1952). Nor is it a case like Broome Constr., Inc. v. United States, 492 F.2d 829 (Ct.Cl.1974), and similar cases where the courts have held that the contractor is not entitled to an adjustment under the "Suspension of Work" clause where the claimed delays were due to the acts of another contractor or to bad weather.

The answer to the question is not free of doubt. However, after considering the language of the specifications and other pertinent facts and circumstances, we conclude that there should be applied here the rule enunciated in Worthington Pump & Machinery Corp. v. United States, 66 Ct.Cl. 230, 240 (1928) and Edward E. Gillen Co. v. United States, 88 Ct.Cl. 347, 368 (1939). Therefore, we hold that the contractor complied with the "Scheduling of Work" provision by giving as much notice as was reasonably required by that provision. After the contractor notified the project manager that the contractor's reasonable efforts had not resulted in gaining entry to certain apartments, the Navy was under an implied obligation to provide such access so that the contractor could complete the contract within the time required by its terms. Consequently, if any part of the contractor's work was thereafter delayed for an unreasonable period of time because of the Navy's failure to provide access to the apartments, the contractor is, under the "Suspension of Work" clause,[2] entitled to an increase in the cost of performing the contract. Chaney and James Constr. Co. v. United States, 421 F.2d 728, 190 Ct.Cl. 699 (1970). We have reached this conclusion on several grounds.

We find that if their ordinary meaning is attributed to the words used in the "Scheduling of Work" provision, there is simply nothing in that specification or elsewhere which states that the contractor is required to make an arrangement with or obtain an agreement from each apartment occupant as the Board decided.

It was reasonable for the contractor to interpret this provision of the specifications to relieve it of further responsibility to notify the occupants after reasonable efforts to give the notice had been exhausted. If the Government had intended the specifications to convey an intent to require the contractor to make an agreement covering the matters found by the Board with each of the 656 occupants, the drafters of the specifications wholly failed to convey this meaning. Therefore, the provision must be construed against the Government. Troup Bros., Inc. v. United States, 643 F.2d 719, 224 Ct.Cl. 594 (1980); Singer-General Precision, Inc. v. United States, 427 F.2d 1187, 192 Ct.Cl. 435 (1970); Jefferson Constr. Co. v. United States, 151 Ct.Cl. 75 (1960).

---

2. SUSPENSION OF WORK (1968 FEB)

(b) If the performance of all or any part of the work is, for an unreasonable period of time, suspended, delayed, or interrupted by an act of the Contracting Officer in the administration of this contract, or by his failure to act within the time specified in this contract (or if no time is specified, within a reasonable time) an adjustment shall be made for any increase in the cost of performance of this contract (excluding profit) necessarily caused by such unreasonable suspension, delay, or interruption and the contract modified in writing accordingly. However, no adjustment shall be made under this clause for any suspension, delay, or interruption to the extent (1) that performance would have been so suspended, delayed, or interrupted by any other cause, including the fault or negligence of the Contractor or (2) for which an equitable adjustment is provided for or excluded under any other provision of this contract.

The conduct of both parties during construction and before the contractor's claim was submitted to the project manager provides persuasive evidence that the contract should be construed as urged by the contractor. * * * *

We do not hold that the contractor was justified in believing that it would encounter no difficulty in notifying the occupants when the work would begin. However, the evidence shows that in view of the contractor's previous experience on the same base, it believed the Navy would provide access to the apartments when such difficulties arose.

IV. The Contractor's Right to Recover Damages.

Our holding with respect to the Government's liability should not be construed as a decision that the contractor is entitled to recover the increased costs it claims were incurred because of lack of access to the apartments. In view of its interpretation of the contract, the Board made no finding on the extent of the Government's unreasonable delay or on the issue of damages. As previously stated, Government counsel at oral argument contended that if we disagreed with the Board on the access claim, the case should be remanded because of concurrent delays attributable to the contractor and its subcontractor.

The Board found that:

> The mechanical subcontractor needed 20 workers to do the mechanical work required in the time allowed. It was never able to hire that many workers. That labor shortage, in part, caused the subcontractor to fall behind schedule and required it to hire Hans Jensen to do some of the mechanical work.

This finding is supported by substantial evidence.

Where both parties contribute to the delay "neither can recover damage, unless there is in the proof a clear apportionment of the delay and the expense attributable to each party." Coath & Goss, Inc. v. United States, 101 Ct.Cl. 702, 714–15 (1944); Commerce International Co. v. United States, 338 F.2d 81, 90, 167 Ct.Cl. 529 (1964).

* * *

V. Conclusion.

For the reasons stated, the Board's decision involving the power outage of August 18, 1978, is affirmed, but its decision on the access claim is reversed. With these exceptions, both motions for summary judgment are denied and the case is remanded to the Board to make such findings of fact and conclusions of law as will enable it to determine: (1) whether and to what extent any part of the contractor's work was unreasonably delayed by the Navy's failure to provide access to the apartments; (2) whether any unreasonable delays caused by the Navy were concurrent with or separate from delays due to the subcontractor's shortage of labor or other delays chargeable to the contractor, and (3) whether the contractor is entitled to a time extension and/or a recovery of damages and if so, how much.

AFFIRMED IN PART, REVERSED IN PART, AND REMANDED.

Notes and Questions

1. One way into this case is to recognize how strong the government's argument is. Did the CO grant the contractor's claim? No. Did the ASBCA? No. And did the Court of

Claims come close to not granting it? It said, "The answer to the question is not free of doubt." Why? Consider this short formulation of the argument against the contractor: This contractor bid on an IFB. If the contractor was not willing to deal with the problems, it should have put in a higher bid, and let the next highest bidder, if willing, take the contract. What interpretive question did the board of contract appeals resolve to find against the contractor?

2. On the other hand, can you describe the delicate situation faced by the contractor? How do you suppose those in the military housing greeted contractor employees showing up to install energy charging meters? One hopes the heavy armament had not been brought home back to the military housing when the meter-installers rang the doorbell. It seems as though the military housing occupants viewed this as an exercise for practicing a cross between nonviolent protest and guerrilla warfare. What interpretive rule did this court apply to find for the contractor?

3. Is the Suspension of Work clause a general "excusable delay" clause? A prior version of it was called the "Stop Work Order" clause, signifying how extreme the government interference had to be to justify relief for the contractor. What happens if the delay is the result of the "acts of another contractor or bad weather," to quote the case? Did the government itself affirmatively act in this case to delay the contractor?

SUSPENSION OF WORK CLAUSE
(Apr 1984)

(a) The Contracting Officer may order the Contractor, in writing, to suspend, delay, or interrupt all or any part of the work of this contract for the period of time that the Contracting Officer determines appropriate for the convenience of the Government.

(b) If the performance of all or any part of the work is, for an unreasonable period of time, suspended, delayed, or interrupted

(1) by an act of the Contracting Officer in the administration of this contract, or

(2) by the Contracting Officer's failure to act within the time specified in this contract (or within a reasonable time if not specified), an adjustment shall be made for any increase in the cost of performance of this contract (excluding profit) necessarily caused by the unreasonable suspension, delay, or interruption, and the contract modified in writing accordingly. However, no adjustment shall be made under this clause for any suspension, delay, or interruption to the extent that performance would have been so suspended, delayed, or interrupted by any other cause, including the fault or negligence of the Contractor, or for which an equitable adjustment is provided for or excluded under any other term or condition of this contract.

(c) A claim under this clause shall not be allowed

(1) for any costs incurred more than 20 days before the Contractor shall have notified the Contracting Officer in writing of the act or failure to act involved * * *

(2) unless the claim, in an amount stated, is asserted in writing as soon as practicable after the termination of the suspension, delay, or interruption, but not later than the date of final payment under the contract.

Excusable Delays

From: Fundamentals of Federal Contract Law (1990) by Eugene W. Massengale
Copyright (c) (1991) by Greenwood Press Reproduced with permission of
Greenwood Publishing Group, Inc., Westport, CT

INTRODUCTION

Delays in contract performance can be caused by a wide variety of factors, both excusable and unexcusable, resulting in either late completion or increased costs, or both. The Excusable Delays clause provides relief for the contractor for a performance failure if the failure arose from well-defined causes beyond the control and without the fault or negligence of the contractor. Similar provisions are contained in the Default articles. The Default clause for fixed-price construction contracts contains the additional proviso that the contractor's right to proceed shall not be terminated, nor shall the contractor be charged with damages if the delay in completing the work arises from *unforeseeable causes* beyond the control and without the fault or negligence of the contractor.

THE EXCUSABLE DELAYS CLAUSE

The Excusable Delays clause provides that, except for defaults of subcontractors at any tier, the contractor shall not be in default for any failure to perform the contract if the failure arises from causes beyond the control and without the fault or negligence of the contractor. Examples of such causes include acts of God or of the public enemy, acts of the government in either its sovereign or its contractual capacity, fires, floods, epidemics, quarantine restrictions, stakes, freight embargoes, and unusually severe weather. See FAR §52.249-14.

As to performance failures of subcontractors at any tier, the contractor shall not be in default if the cause of the failure was beyond the control and without the fault or negligence of either the prime contractor or the subcontractors. The delay is not excusable as to the prime contractor if the contracted supplies or services were obtainable from another source, or if the Contracting Officer ordered the contractor to obtain the supplies or services from another source and the contractor failed to comply reasonably with that order.

If the completion date was delayed by the inability of the contractor or his subcontractor to procure necessary materials, through a failure either to obtain timely commitments or to ascertain the availability of such materials prior to the submission of the bid, that is a matter for which relief cannot be granted even in equit3r. A prime contractor is excused from nonperformance or delays, to the extent that they render performance impossible, caused by defaults of subcontractors or suppliers if such defaults cannot be charged to the fault or negligence of the prime contractor, and it is immaterial whether or not the default of the subcontractor can be placed under one of the enumerated causes of excusability because such causes are illustrative and not exclusive. 39 Comp. Gen. 343 (1959).

In order to avail himself of the article, the contractor is required to request a time extension of the Contracting Officer, setting forth the facts and extent of the failure. If the Contracting Officer determines that the delay is in fact excusable, the delivery schedule is to be revised.

PURPOSE OF THE ARTICLE

The purpose of the article is to remove uncertainty and needless litigation by defining with more particularity the otherwise hazy area of unforeseeable events that might excuse nonperformance within the contract period and to protect the contractor from the unforeseeable. Contractors thus know they are not to be penalized for unexpected impediments to prompt performance, and since their bids can be based on the foreseeable and probable, rather than possible, hindrances, the government secures the benefit of lower bids and an enlarged selection of bidders.

In its grammatical sense, the provision militates against holding that the listed events are always to be regarded as unforeseeable, no matter what the attendant circumstances are. Rather, the adjective "unforeseeable" must modify each event in the "including" phrase. *United States v. Brooks Callaway Co.,* 318 U.S. 120 (1943). Moreover, a contractor cannot benefit from delay, for it is unlikely that the government would accede to a contract provision providing for a price escalation for deliveries that were inexcusably late. *United States v. DeLoro Smelting & Refining Co.,* 161 Ct. Cl. 489, 317 F.2d 382 (1963).

UNUSUALLY SEVERE WEATHER

A prudent contractor, in preparing bids for the commencement of work within a specified period and for the completion of the same within certain stipulated days thereafter, normally considers the weather conditions that ordinarily prevail during such season of the year at the site of the work. Inasmuch as weather conditions could adversely impact on the ability of a contractor, particularly a construction contractor, to perform, contractors are expected to include time in their bids or offers for foreseeable weather delays. *Carney General Contractor,* NASA BCA No. 375-4, 80-1 BCA 14,243; *Larsen-Meyer Constr..Co.,* IBCA No. 85, 58-2 BCA 1987. However, notice of lost time due to adverse weather conditions is not the same as notice of an excusable delay due to unusually severe weather because the Contracting Officer has no information as to what was foreseeable by the contractor. Carney *General Contractors, supra.*

The term "unusually severe weather" does not include any and all weather that prevents work under the contract, but only means weather surpassing in severity the weather usually encountered or reasonably to be expected in the particular locality and during the same time of year involved in the contract. 14 Comp. Gen. 431 (1934). It must be weather that could not have been reasonably anticipated and that impeded performance over and above the amount that work would been impeded in a normal year. *John E Faucett,* AGBCA No. 396, 76-2 BCA 11,946. But the mere fact that the weather was cold enough to make performance of the work substantially more expensive than at other seasons of the year is not sufficient to substantiate an excusable delay, unless the contractor demonstrates that the weather was unusual. *T.C. Bateson Constr Co.,* GSBCA No. 2656, 68-2 BCA 7263.

ACTS OF GOD

Though rarely invoked as an excusable cause of delay, an act of God may occasion performance failures. Thus, a termination for default was held to be improper where the contractor was entitled to a time extension as a result of an act of God. The contract required tree planting within a certain period of time, but the eruption of Mt. St. Helens delayed performance, and it was determined to be an act of God sufficient to constitute an excusable delay even though the contractor was behind schedule before the eruption occurred. *Nogier Tree Farin,* AGBCA No. 81-104-1, 81-2 BCA 15,315.

STRIKES

A contractor will not be automatically excused from performance merely because he establishes the existence of a strike. It must also be shown that the delay caused by the strike was beyond the control and without the fault or negligence of the contractor, *Sun Constr Co.*, IBCA No. 208, 61-1 BCA 2926. He will not be excused where the strike resulted from his own unfair labor practices. *Transit Warehouse Corp.*, ASBCA No. 16761, 72-2 BCA 9696. Even if a contractor bears no initial fault for a particular cause of excusable delay, he must mitigate the effect of that delay. He cannot allow a possible cause of delay to develop, but must take such action as is reasonably available to him to prevent the delay. *Harris & Covington Hosiery Mills Co.*, 4 CCF 60,906 (1949). Therefore, if the strike involved a subcontractor or supplier, and if the contractor could have obtained the required supplies or materials from another source, but elected not to do so because of higher prices, he will normally not be excused. *Southern Steel Corp.*, ASBCA No. 6579, 61-1 BCA 2965. Similarly, the contractor will not be excused if he could not obtain the supplies delayed by the strike because he failed to place the order in a timely manner. *Bogue Electric Mfg. Co.*, ASBCA No. 16957, 73-1 BCA 9885.

LACK OF ADEQUATE FINANCING

It is well settled that the contractor has the responsibility of either having adequate capital or having a reasonably established arrangement for obtaining the necessary capital required for contract performance at the time of contract execution. This is not intended to imply that the contractor must have on hand the cash reserves to finance the entire cost of performance. Rather, the contractor must have available reasonable financial resources in the light of business customs and practices to finance the expected cost of production or performance. *Security Signals*, ASBCA No. 4634, 58-2 BCA 2045.

Where the cause of the contractor's inability to perform lies solely in a conspicuous undercapitalization of the corporation with relation to the obligation it undertakes under the contract, rather than deriving from a contingency beyond its control, such undercapitalization is not a circumstance beyond the contractor's control as to be within the purview of any *force majeure* clause. *Williams Industries v. United States*, 155 Ct. Cl. 360 (1961).

If the contractor's financial condition was such that attempted performance of the contract would have rendered him hopelessly insolvent, or even an adjudicated bankrupt, he is not excused from the default in contract performance as a matter of law. Actual bankruptcy, a fortiori the mere possibility or threat of the same, is no excuse for nonperformance under the Default article and does not relieve the contractor from liability for excess costs of reprocurement. Bankruptcy, insolvency, or undercapitalization cannot be considered as a cause for nonperformance beyond the control and without the fault of the contractor. *Consolidated Airborne Systems v. United States*, 172 Ct. Cl. 588, 348 F.2d 941 (1965).

Notes and Questions

1. Closely akin to the contractor's rights when the government causes "unreasonable delays" are the contractor's rights when the government violates its implied duty to cooperate and to prevent interference with the contractor's performance. Interference claims arise when the government's inexcusable conduct precludes or increases

the cost of performance by the contractor. This includes the government's excessive inspection, incompetence, and physical interference attributable to the government. See *WRB Corp. v. United States*, 183 Cl.Ct. 409 (1968)(government must act reasonably in inspection of contractor's work); *Harvey C. Jones, Inc.*, IBCA No. 2070, 90-2 BCA ¶ 22, 762 (incompetence by government is interference); *C.M. Lowther, Jr.*, ASBCA No. 38407, 91-3 BCA ¶ 24,296 (water seepage from the government's malfunctioning sump pump is interference)). Additionally, the case of *R.B. Bewachungsgessellschaft mbH*, ASBCA No. 42213, 91-3 BCA ¶ 24,310 held that it was interference when the government conducted disruptive criminal investigations in its contractual capacity.

2. When the contractor invokes its right to cooperation, the government may raise the interesting defense that interference is the result of a sovereign act, for it is well established that the government cannot be held liable for costs of interference resulting form sovereign acts. *Hills Materials Co.*, ASBCA No. 42410, 92-1 BCA ¶ 24.636 (*citing Deming v. United States*, 1 Ct.Cl. 190 (1865)). The doctrine may apply to an act by Congress that is out of the control of the contracting agency, while not applying where an agency retains discretion in allocating and distributing funds under an existing contract. *Appeal of Contract Management*, ASBCA No. 44885, 95-2 BCA ¶ 27,886. The sovereign acts doctrine is an affirmative defense for which the government bears the burden of proof. *Appeal of Dyncorp*, ASBCA No. 49714, 97-2 BCA ¶ 29,233.

3. Another related ground upon which contractors may seek an equitable adjustment consists of additional effort or cost as a result of the government's failure to disclose vital information. There are several circumstances that all must exist in order for the government's duty to arise. First, the procuring agency must possess important, relevant information that was available at the time of procurement activity. *Bethlehem Corp. v. United States*, 462 F.2d 1400 (Ct.Cl. 1972) (knowledge by non-procuring agency having no connection to procuring agency does not make government liable for nondisclosure). Next, the information must not be that which the contractor could reasonably be expected and able to seek elsewhere. *H. N. Bailey & Assocs. v. United States*, 499 F.2d 376 (Ct.Cl. 1971) (information that is general industry knowledge is not required to be disclosed by the government); *Maitland Bros. Co.*, ENG BCA No. 5782, 94-1 BCA ¶ 26,473). Finally, the government must know that the contractor lacks the information. *Hardeman-Monier-Hutcherson v. United States*, 458 F.2d 1364 (Ct.Cl. 1972); *Max Jordan Bauunternehmung v. United States*, 820 F.2d 1208 (Fed. Cir. 1987). The issue of superior government knowledge can arise in cases regarding surprises on construction sites; see *Covco Hawaii* and its notes in this chapter's section on differing site conditions.

4. Yet another related issue regarding equitable adjustments consists of constructive acceleration, which occurs when a contractor, faced with an excusable delay, is ordered to complete performance in accordance with the original contract schedule. One type of action leading to a finding of constructive acceleration occurs when the contractor encounters threats of @noindent:termination in the presence of an excusable delay. *Intersea Research Corp.*, IBCA No. 1675, 85-2 BCA ¶ 18.058. In *Norair Engineering Corp. v. United States*, the court found the government's refusal to grant a delay for an excusable delay, and subsequent threats of liquidated damages constituted a constructive acceleration (666 F.2d 546 (Ct.Cl. 1981)). Delay in governmental approval for a requested time extension by the contractor has also been found to be constructive acceleration by the agency (*Fishbach & Moore Int'l Corp.*, ASBCA No. 18146, 77-1 BCA ¶ 12,300, *aff'd*, 617 F.2d 223 (Ct.Cl. 1980).

2. Computation and Proof of Equitable Adjustments

Computation and proof of equitable adjustment follow from the previously discussed considerations. The components of computation should keep the contractor whole, preserving the government's position as to what the change did not affect.

Looking at components, the adjustment process can be broken down into three component parts: work added, work deleted, and overhead and profit. When the contracting officer (or, on appeal, a tribunal) sets the adjustment, she prices the new work as the reasonable cost to the contractor. Ideally, pricing occurs before the costs are actually incurred, by estimating them from actual or historical costs. The adjustment thus relates to the contractor's costs, not the value to the government. When the change deletes work, the government gets a downward adjustment equal to the amount of cost the contractor would have incurred had the work been performed.

Figuring overhead and profit pose particular problems. Normally, direct costs can bear a standard amount of overhead. However, the parties may demonstrate that the change produces extra high overhead. Similarly, the CO can apply a standard profit percentage, but the changed work could warrant different profit by being more or less demanding or risky. The FAR provides direction for considering factors called the "weighted guidelines" method. FAR 15.902, 15.905.

As for proof, the tribunals prefer actual cost data; if the contractor offers estimates, they should be prepared with detailed substantiating data by experts who are knowledgeable, competent, and familiar with the facts. Of four methods, the "actual cost" method uses the actual costs relating to the change. The "total cost" method compares the total cost of the work performed, minus the original estimate of the work. A "modified total cost method" excludes from the total cost comparison amounts attributable to underbidding, contractor inefficiency, and unrelated contractor costs. Finally, the "jury verdict" method simply takes conflicting evidence and lets an approximation be made.

The *Dawco* case provides an impressive example of the kind of range spurned by calculations using differing computations. See as you read it whether you maintain your faith in the splendid concept of the flexible equitable adjustment, or yearn instead either for some rigid but reliable rule, or for a market-based solution.

Dawco Construction, Inc., Plaintiff-Appellee, v. The United States, Defendant-Appellant

No. 90-5074. United States Court of Appeals, Federal Circuit.
930 F.2d 872. Decided April 3, 1991

Before MARKEY, ARCHER, and MICHEL, Circuit Judges.

MICHEL, Circuit Judge.

The United States appeals the judgment of the United States Claims Court awarding Dawco Construction, Inc. ("Dawco") $529,935, plus interest, as an equitable adjustment for differing site conditions encountered in performance of the landscape portion of a housing refurbishment contract. Dawco Construction, Inc. v. United States, No. 450-86C (Cl.Ct. Nov. 17 & 22, 1989, 18 Cl.Ct. 682 and Feb. 5, 1990). * * *

Although the Claims Court correctly ruled that it could hear Dawco's claim, it erroneously adopted the "jury verdict method" to measure the quantum of damages due the contractor. Accordingly, we affirm-in-part, upholding its ruling on jurisdiction, reverse-in-part, overturning the judgment awarding damages, and remand for a proper determination of damages.

BACKGROUND

A. The Contract Dispute

Dawco was awarded a contract to refurbish the Cabrillo-Larksdale Naval housing project near San Diego, California, in August 1983. As part of the contract, Dawco was also required to landscape the grounds around six individual housing areas, a total of 903,000 square feet. Dawco, in turn, subcontracted this portion of the work to J.C. Landscape ("JCL") for $460,000.

After the contract award, the Navy determined that the grading required by the contract specifications would not produce acceptable drainage and in a September 26, 1983 letter, directed Dawco to suspend all landscaping work until further notice and to continue only refurbishing the buildings. The Navy then developed a new drainage plan calling for installation of an underground drainage system in four of the six areas. The drainage system redesign was detailed in a Change Order Request, and was accompanied by a request for a cost proposal. The Navy, however, rejected Dawco's proposed costs, presented in a May 21, 1984 letter from JCL to the Navy, and decided instead to landscape only the two of the six areas that did not need underground drainage lines.

On May 29, 1984, the Navy formally issued a change to the contract, designated "PCO 20," "[d]elet[ing] entirely" all landscaping work on four areas and directing Dawco to complete, in accord with the original contract specifications, the landscaping site work on the other two areas. In addition, the two areas were enlarged by 35,900 square feet. The change resulted in a net reduction of 397,540 square feet, or at least 44 percent, of the original 903,000 square foot area to be landscaped.

After resuming the landscaping work over the two areas, JCL encountered the differing site conditions that are the subject of this appeal. JCL contended that the areas were not maintained during the eight-month suspension in work, causing the site to "deteriorat[e] significantly." Dawco Construction, Inc. v. United States, 18 Cl.Ct. 682, 685 (1989). The resulting new conditions consisted primarily of overgrowth and other obstructions on or within the topsoil, characterized by the Claims Court as "unexpected massive rambling dispersed subsurface running tree roots, rock, boulders, cobble, abandoned water lines not shown on the drawings, weed root masses, demolition debris, galvanized copper piping, asphalt, [and] concrete." Id. at 695-96.

On October 9, 1985, Dawco's counsel sent a letter to Richard G. Thurman, the Navy "contracts manager" and the representative of the Resident Officer In Charge of Construction ("Resident Officer"), explaining that Dawco "would like to start settlement discussions as soon as possible" concerning additional costs arising from the differing site conditions. Jt.App. at 110. Although there may have been an earlier undated proposal in the same amount, on November 22, 1985, the Navy received a proposal from Dawco seeking $325,063 as an equitable adjustment.

* * *

On July 21, 1986, well after the 60-day period for decision had expired, Dawco filed suit in the Claims Court seeking an additional $591,678 for the landscape portion of the contract.

B. Claims Court Proceedings

In a series of orders ultimately awarding Dawco an equitable adjustment of $529,935, the Claims Court began by acknowledging the "natural assumption" that a contract change reducing the amount of work to be performed "would, on its face, entitle [the Navy] to a corresponding reduction in the price of the [sub]contract." Dawco, 18 Cl.Ct. at 685. However, the court explained, Dawco, and its subcontractor, JCL, both formulated their bids on the "existing conditions" at the time of bidding. By the time JCL resumed its landscaping work, those conditions had changed significantly, nullifying the "natural assumption" that a corresponding decrease in costs should follow an at least 44 percent decrease in the area to be landscaped.

At trial, the court relied heavily on the testimony of Lance Edmunson, the owner/operator of a tractor service, to whom JCL subcontracted the excavation work needed to overcome the differing site conditions. It was Edmunson, the court said, who "bore the main brunt of the extra efforts; his task was to remove the thatch and roots and grade the surface. In so doing, he directly encountered, more than any other person or firm, the material that constituted the differing site condition." Id. at 700. The court found that Edmunson's records, unlike Dawco's or JCL's, "were kept in such a manner that he could show to the satisfaction of the court that it cost him an additional $8,100 to perform the extra work caused by the differing site condition, an increase of twenty-seven percent." Id.

To determine the equitable adjustment, the Claims Court adopted the "jury verdict method," in part due to the "wildly divergent" estimates of costs presented by Dawco and the government. Id. at 699. It concluded that Dawco was unable, despite Edmunson's testimony, to "prove actual damages," although the court was nevertheless able "to arrive at a fair approximation of the damages." Id. at 698.

Initially, the court calculated the effect of the change order, decreasing the area to be landscaped by at least 44 percent on the subcontract as a whole, and reduced the original price from $460,000 to $303,155. That price included a 17.6 percent surcharge, assessed by the court to cover additional expenses attributed to a "loss of economy of scale," because the contract had originally been bid on a substantially larger area. Id. at 700. To that amount, the court added $81,852 for "damages suffered by JCL by virtue of the differing site condition." Id. These additional "damages" were derived by extrapolating from the 27 percent figure provided by Edmunson's testimony to estimate the costs of all of JCL's extra work. Id. This first "adjustment" was added to the revised subcontract price and together they totalled $385,007.

To that amount the Claims Court then added $15,000 for claim preparation costs, $15,000 to cover the premium on the additional subcontractor's bond insurance, and $1,608 for ancillary repairs. From this subtotal, now standing at $416,615, the court calculated Dawco's field and home office overhead and the "prime on subcontractor rate" (the contractor's premium) at $113,320 and added that to the subtotal, bringing the quantum of the equitable adjustment to $529,935. This amount constituted, the court said, the damages suffered by plaintiff and JCL due to "extra work found to be caused by the differing site condition." Id. at 704. From this amount, the court subtracted the original subcontract price, $460,000, and found that the total equitable adjustment due Dawco was $69,935 with interest accruing from May 21, 1984, the date of JCL's cost proposal, forwarded by Dawco, in response to the change order request.

On November 22, 1989, the Claims Court amended, apparently sua sponte, its November 17, 1989 order by deleting its final paragraph in which an equitable adjustment of $69,935 was awarded and, instead, ruled that Dawco was entitled to $529,935. Dawco Construction, Inc. v. United States, 18 Cl.Ct. 682 (1989).

* * *

DISCUSSION

* * *

III

To establish the amount of the equitable adjustment due Dawco, the Claims Court resorted to the "jury verdict method." Dawco, 18 Cl.Ct. at 696-700. This approach, most often employed when damages cannot be ascertained by any reasonable computation from actual figures, however, is not favored and may be used only when other, more exact, methods cannot be applied. Specialty Assembling & Packing Co. v. United States, 355 F.2d 554, 572, 174 Ct.Cl. 153 (1966). Before adopting the "jury verdict method," the court must first determine three things: (1) that clear proof of injury exists; (2) that there is no more reliable method for computing damages; and (3) that the evidence is sufficient for a court to make a fair and reasonable approximation of the damages. WRB Corporation v. United States, 183 Ct.Cl. 409, 425 (1968). In this case, the court's determinations that Dawco had met the first and second of these requirements were erroneous.

The selection of the proper method for determining damages is a legal decision which we review non-deferentially on the basis of reasonableness. Cf. Electronic and Missile Facilities, Inc. v. United States, 416 F.2d 1345, 1354, 189 Ct.Cl. 237 (1969) (review goes to the reasonableness of what the agency did on the basis of the evidence before it). Although the Claims Court agreed that Dawco had submitted what amounted to a "total cost" claim,[1] it nevertheless resorted to the "jury verdict method," rather than require a detailed and documented cost breakdown from Dawco. The court's conclusion that the "jury verdict method" was appropriate was based on a determination that it was "not possible for [Dawco] to prove actual damages, [although] sufficient information exist[ed] to enable the court to arrive at a fair approximation of the damages." Dawco, 18 Cl.Ct. at 698. However, "it is equally well-settled that the amount of the recovery can only be approximated in the format of a 'jury verdict' where the claimant can demonstrate a justifiable inability to substantiate the amount of his resultant injury by direct and specific proof." Joseph Pickard's Sons Co. v. United States, 532 F.2d 739, 742, 209 Ct.Cl. 643 (1976).

Contrary to Dawco's assertion, the contractor bears the burden of establishing that no more reliable method is available than the "guesstimate" of the "jury verdict method," i.e., a method that would more precisely calculate the cost for the extra work.

---

1. The government contended that Dawco, in effect, presented the court with a "total cost claim," i.e., a summary of expenses attributable to the execution of the contract as a whole. What the court should have required, the government asserts, is an "actual cost claim," detailing only the expenses arising from the differing site conditions. "Total cost claims," like the "jury verdict method," are not favored and should only be resorted to when "actual costs" cannot be determined. Wunderlich Contracting Co. v. United States, 351 F.2d 956, 965, 173 Ct.Cl. 180 (1965); G.M. Shupe, Inc. v. United States, 5 Cl.Ct. 662, 676 (1984). Here, however, since we conclude that Dawco has not shown it could not have presented the court with an "actual cost claim," there is no reason for us to reach the issue of whether a "total cost claim" submission was required rather than a "jury verdict method" approximation.

Id.; see also Boyajian v. United States, 423 F.2d 1231, 1235–36, 191 Ct.Cl. 233 (1970). This burden is especially relevant here. From the record, as well as testimony cited by the court, Dawco did not establish that it could not have identified to an acceptable degree of certainty its and JCL's costs attributable to the differing site conditions. Its failure to do so should have precluded the Claims Court from adopting the "jury verdict method." Boyajian, 423 F.2d at 1236. Here, the Claims Court found that Edmunson, the tractor operator hired by JCL, who, the court said, "[f]ortuitously...bore the main brunt of the extra effort," was able to keep his "records, unlike [Dawco's] and JCL's,...in such a manner...[to] show to the satisfaction of the court that it cost him an additional $8,100 to perform the extra work." Dawco, 18 Cl.Ct. at 700. However, the record is barren of other evidence that, under the WRB test's first prong, Dawco suffered any injuries beyond Edmunson's costs and any related JCL and Dawco overhead. Without such proof, the "jury verdict method" cannot properly be used to estimate what would be nothing more than speculative damages. See Assurance Co. v. United States, 813 F.2d 1202, 1205 (Fed.Cir.1987).

Nor has Dawco demonstrated any "justifiable inability to substantiate" its damages, Joseph Pickard's Sons, 532 F.2d at 742, beyond Edmunson's documented additional expenses. Clearly, Dawco was in an ideal position to detail all its costs. Or, at least, it could have, and should have, been. The issuance of a change order request should signal to the prudent contractor that it must maintain records detailing any additional work, just as should the encountering of differing site conditions. The Claims Court has not identified, nor has Dawco presented us with, any justification why such precision, or something sufficiently close, could not have been accomplished as to Dawco's other costs, including any additional overhead. Therefore, Dawco's inability to substantiate the existence, to any degree of certainty, of costs beyond those incurred by Edmunson, precludes resort to the "jury verdict method." See Electronic and Missile Facilities, 416 F.2d at 1358.

If anything, the twisted road the Claims Court traveled from Edmunson's $8,100 documented additional expense to the court's final determination that Dawco was entitled to $529,935 as an equitable adjustment for the differing site conditions underscores the dangers of using the "jury verdict method." Its primary peril, as evidenced in this case, is the risk that unrealistic assumptions will be adopted and extrapolated, greatly multiplying an award beyond reason, and rewarding preparers of imprecise claims based on undocumented costs with unjustified windfalls. Here, the Claims Court was presented with a well documented actual additional expense of $8,100 by Edmunson. That additional expense by the independent subcontractor who "bore the brunt of the extra work" ballooned, under the "jury verdict method," by a factor of 10 to $81,852 as an estimate of JCL's cost. Then, as described above, that figure increased to an equitable adjustment due Dawco of $529,935, for the landscape work compared to the original price of $460,000. That result is roughly twice as much money for about half the landscaping work despite little proof of causation by the differing site conditions.

Clearly, the "actual cost method" is preferred because it provides the court, or contracting officer, with documented underlying expenses, ensuring that the final amount of the equitable adjustment will be just that— equitable—and not a windfall for either the government or the contractor.

Because the record does not show that Dawco justifiably could not have submitted an "actual cost claim," we remand to the Claims Court for a redetermination of the equitable adjustment due Dawco by the "actual cost method."

* * *

CONCLUSION

* * * On remand the Claims Court is to consider only costs Dawco proves arise merely from the differing site conditions and from specific documented figures on derivative expenses, such as overhead, from which the equitable adjustment can be calculated ("actual costs"), and the court may not estimate damages by the "jury verdict method." Damages are to be determined accordingly.

Notes and Questions

1. How did the Claims Court get from firm proof of $8000 in increased costs, to an equitable adjustment of $559,000? Why is the "jury verdict" method disfavored? Parenthetically, on an unrelated procedural point regarding the point at which a claim is presented in the form that triggers the Disputes Clause, a part of the Federal Circuit opinion in *Dawco* not reprinted here was subsequently overruled in the *Reflectone* case reprinted in another chapter.

2. The court chides the contractor for not responding to the formal change order by arranging to carefully record costs. What about the corollary that in a situation without a formal change order, namely, one of the common constructive change situations, a court cannot have the same expectation that a contractor, caught by surprise, will have well-recorded costs?

3. Dawco claimed, among other items, its claim preparation costs. In the Costs chapter, the *Bill Strong Enterprises* case focuses on the allowability of that item. In that case, the contractor hired a firm professionally specializing in organizing and presenting claims, and once it did so, its claim went much more smoothly. From *Dawco*, can you see why that would be?

4. Another element of importance in such cases consists of interest, or to describe it more elaborately, an adjustment for the cost of financing. Contractors may seek interest on the claim from submission to payment. If the CO agrees to part of the claimed amount and the contractor appeals only the disputed portion, the ASBCA has held that the contractor was entitled of interest on both the disputed and undisputed portions. *Oxwell, Inc.*, ASBCA 25703 81-2 BCA para. 15392.

C. Differing Site Conditions

A lot of litigation occurs over the issue of differing site conditions, which is what makes so narrow an issue matter so much. In other changes cases, the government changes its mind about what it wants; in differing site conditions, the government changes nothing, but the construction contractor discovers something different than it expected. If government contracting law put all the risk of such discoveries on the contractor, there would be little need for all that litigation.

However, government contracting law instead lifts a good deal of risk off of contractors and puts it on the government. The reason is simple. Between the government and the contractors the government can carry the risk better. If the government put the risk on the contractors, they would have to inflate their bids to match the risk, plus a premium for their difficulty in self-insuring against the risk. So, instead, the government effectively sets up a system by which it insures the contractors against two types of bad conditions. As the Court of Claims has stated, this means that contractors "will have no windfalls and no disasters." *Foster Constr. Co. v. United States*, 435 F.2d 873 (Ct. Cl. 1970). Considering the amount of litigation lawyers who handle these matters, though, may have no disasters and quite a few windfalls.

The FAR's standard "Differing Site Conditions" clause names the type of conditions that will justify an equitable adjustment. A contractor who encounters these "shall promptly, and before the conditions are disturbed, give a written notice of the Contracting Officer." Thereupon, "The Contracting Officer shall investigate...." If the claim checks out and the conditions "cause an increase or decrease in the Contractor's cost of, or the time required for, performing any part of the work..." then "an equitable adjustment shall be made under this clause..."

Two types of "Differing Site Conditions," naturally called Type I and Type II, get mentioned in the clause and stay quite separate as theories or litigation. They have in common a material difference between what the contractor reasonably expected and what it actually encountered; what differentiates them is the nature of that difference. In Type I conditions, the conditions differ from those represented in the contract. So, the focus concerns contractual representations. In Type II conditions, the conditions differ from the conditions that would usually be encountered.

In each of the two cases in this section, there is a preliminary jurisdictional issue. In *COVCO*, a federal case, it concerns the nonappropriated funds status of the project. In *Harmans*, a state case, it concerns whether a complex sale-and-leaseback counts as construction. Because the states do so much construction contracting, many differing site condition cases occurs at the state level and often closely follow the federal law.

The issue of differing site conditions tends to involve other important standard, and nonstandard government contract clause language besides the differing site conditions clause itself. As to standard language, contracts usually contain a standard "site inspection" clause, and the ability of a contractor to assert reimbursable surprise often depends upon what a site inspection would have found. As to nonstandard language, the government shapes future differing site condition cases by what it says in the contract about what the contractor must handle, and government's language in the contract can foreshadow that a project will be either a cakewalk or a hard struggle.

For further discussions of this section's overall subject, see Hazel Glenn Beh, *Allocating the Risk of the Unforeseen, Subsurface and Latent Conditions in Construction Contracts: Is There Room for the Common Law?* 46 U. Kan. L. Rev. 115 (1997); Frank Baltz, *Does the Government Really Accept the Risk for Differing Site Conditions?*, 31 Procurement Law., Spring 1996, at 9; Leslie A. Sherman, *Recent Decision: Sovereign Immunity-Government Contractor Defense-Implied Warranty of Specifications...*, 35 Duq. L. Rev. 1045 (1997); Steven C. Sanders, Unanticipated Environmental Costs in Construction Contracts: The Differing Site Conditions Clause as a Risk Allocation Tool, 10 J. Nat. Resources & Envtl. L. 53 (1995).

DIFFERING SITE CONDITIONS
(Apr 1984)

(a)   The Contractor shall promptly, and before the conditions are disturbed, give a written notice to the Contracting Officer of

(1) subsurface or latent physical conditions at the site which differ materially from those indicated in this contract, or

(2) unknown physical conditions at the site, of an unusual nature, which differ materially from those ordinarily encountered and generally recognized as inhering in work of the character provided for in the contract.

(b)   The Contracting Officer shall investigate the site conditions promptly after receiving the notice. If the conditions do materially so differ and cause an increase or decrease in the Contractor's cost of, or the time required for, performing any part of the work under this contract, whether or not changed as a result of the conditions, an equitable adjustment shall be made under this clause and the contract modified in writing accordingly.

(c) No request by the Contractor for an equitable adjustment to the contract under this clause shall be allowed, unless the Contractor has given the written notice required; provided, that the time prescribed in paragraph (a) of this clause for giving written notice may be extended by the Contracting Officer.

(d)   No request by the Contractor for an equitable adjustment to the contract for differing site conditions shall be allowed if made after final payment under this contract.

Appeal of — Covco Hawaii Corporation
83-2 BCA ¶ 16,554. May 13, 1983
OPINION BY ADMINISTRATIVE JUDGE TING

* * *

We first consider whether the Contract Disputes Act of 1978 (CDA), 41 U.S.C. 601 et seq., is applicable to this appeal. Section 3 of the CDA provides that it 'applies to any express or implied contract (including those of the nonappropriated fund activities described in sections 1346 and 1491 of Title 28, United States Code) entered into by an executive agency....' Since sections 1346 and 1491 of Title 28 describe only the exchange activities of the various military services, we conclude that the Act does not apply to the United States Army Support Command, Hawaii Installation Club System, a nonappropriated fund instrumentality of the Department of the Army (finding 1). See, e.g., Commercial Offset Printers, Inc., 81-1 BCA p14,900; Potomac Company, Inc., ASBCA No. 25371, 81-1 BCA p14,950. There are precedents for Board jurisdiction over disputes involving nonappropriated fund contracts of the United States however, where such contracts contain a 'Disputes' clause. Rainbow Valley Corporation, ASBCA No. 11691, 68-1 BCA p6840, 68-2 BCA p7195; Beigh and Peck, ASBCA No. 7711, 1963 BCA p3740. Here, the 'Disputes' clause prescribed by Army Regulation 230-1 was included in appellant's contract (finding 23). We therefore have jurisdiction over the dispute.

Appellant seeks an equitable adjustment under the 'Differing Site Condition' clause. It contends that the profiles on the 'Profiles & Details' drawing (Drawing No. 31-02-01, Sheet No. 4, Ring No. 5) misled it into believing that 'earth' rather than 'rock' would be encountered (finding 28). Appellant's president says in an affidavit that during this site visit, large trees and thick vegetation were noted around the general area of Fort Ruger but he 'saw nothing which indicated that this area contained a ledge of solid lava rock.' (Finding 13) Appellant also alleges that since the Government had previously excavated the area and built a swimming pool, it must have known about the presence of rock (Finding 30). It alleges that the Government concealed this vital information (App. br.

at 5). Finally, appellant says that although the Hawaiian Islands were formed by 'volcanic processes...solid lava rock ledges of the kind encountered...are not normally found when excavating to this depth....' (Finding 13).

The 'Differing Site Conditions' clause provides for two different types of conditions. Type I involves the discovery of subsurface or latent physical conditions at the site differing materially from those indicated in the contract. Type II provides for unknown physical conditions at the site of an unusual nature, differing materially from those ordinarily encountered.

As to what the contract documents indicate, we do not accept appellant's position that the term 'EXST. GROUND' on the Profiles & Details drawing (Drawing No. 31-02-01, Sheet No. 4, Ring No. 5) could be taken to mean that 'earth' or 'soil' would be encountered upon excavation. The broken lines designated as 'EXST. GROUND' merely show the elevation of then existing ground levels for grading purposes. The profiles make no representations as to the nature of the substance that a contractor would be expected to encounter. Indeed, appellant's interpretation would be in direct conflict with other provisions of the contract. For example, Note 6 of the Site & Utility Plan (Drawing No. 31-02-01, Sheet No. 1, Ring No. 2) cautioned appellant that 'no foundation investigation was performed...rock excavation for installation and construction of access path ramp including retaining wall will be on an unclassified basis.' (Finding 6) Section 2A, Division 2, paragraph 6 of the Technical Provisions of the contract required '[t]he contractor [to] perform excavation of every type of material encountered including rock....' (Finding 25) The interpretation appellant urged upon us would violate the well-settled principle that an interpretation which gives a reasonable meaning to all parts of an instrument will be preferred to one which leaves a portion of it meaningless, and that a provision should not be construed as being in conflict with another unless no other reasonable interpretation is possible. Hol-Gar Mfg. Corp. v. United States, 169 Ct. Cl. 384, 351 F.d 972 (1965). Furthermore, the contract drawings clearly warned appellant that rock excavation would be on an 'unclassified basis.' (Finding 6) In Lang-Miller Development Co., AGBCA No. 81-129-3, 81-2 BCA p15,433, the Board there held that the Government's use of the term 'unclassified' in the contract documents does not imply a particular material or the absence of rock. The Government's case is far stronger here—appellant was told to expect rock; only the type of rock was not specified. Based upon the foregoing, we conclude that the contract documents did not misrepresent the subsurface physical conditions at the site. And since we have also found that the presence of lava rock could be ascertained by a reasonable pre-bid site investigation (findings 14-17), we conclude that no latent physical conditions existed. Hence, appellant is not entitled to recover under Type I conditions of the 'Differing Site Conditions' clause.

We now turn to appellant's Type II 'Differing Site Conditions' claim. In proving such a claim, a contractor must carry 'a relatively heavy burden of proof' in demonstrating that it has encountered a condition 'materially different from the 'known' and the 'usual.'' Charles T. Parker Construction Co. v. United States, 193 Ct. Cl. 320, 333, 433 F.2d 771, 778 (1970). In order to prevail, a contractor must also show that the condition could not have been reasonably anticipated or discovered prior to its bid. Perini Corporation v. United States, 180 Ct. Cl. 768, 381 F.2d 403 (1967); James E. McFadden, Inc., ASBCA No. 19921, 76-2 BCA p11,983; Kasmet Electrical, Inc., ASBCA Nos. 23473, 23474, 80-1 BCA p14,310. In connection with its Type II claim, appellant does not appear to be saying that the lava rock found at the site differed materially from the 'known' and 'usual' conditions prevalent in the Hawaiian Islands. Goolsby and Slavens' affidavits both state 'the Hawaiian Islands were formed in their entirety by volcanic processes, yet solid lava rock ledges of the kind encountered in this excavation are not normally found when excavating to this depth in Hawaiian soil.' (Aff. Warren H. Goolsby, III, p6; Aff. Donald M. Slavens, p11) The record evidence does not show the nature of the 'solid lava rock ledges' appellant allegedly encountered. Nor does the record evidence show the depth to which appellant excavated when it allegedly encountered the solid lava rock ledges. Without such evidence, we are unable to conclude that appellant encountered an unknown physical condition of an unusual nature. As we have already noted, the presence of lava rock could have been discovered by appellant prior to its bid (findings 14-16). Furthermore, appellant was required by paragraph 6, Section 2A, Division 2 of the Technical Provisions of the contract to '[excavate]...every type of material...including rock...to the lines, grades and elevations indicated and as specified....' (Finding 25)

Nor has appellant made out a case of Government superior knowledge. The evidence show that the swimming pool was built by military personnel with Army and Navy materials in 1943 (finding 8). The Government has researched its records; no records describing the surface or subsurface conditions of the site before or during excavation for the pool have been found (finding 9). To make out a case of superior knowledge, a contractor must show that the Government possesses knowledge which is vital to the successful completion of the contract, and that it is unreasonable to expect the contractor to obtain that vital information from any other accessible source. H.N. Bailey & Associates v. United States, 196 Ct. Cl. 156, 499 F.2d 376 (1971). Here, appellant has alleged but has failed to prove that the Government possessed any vital information which it had not already made known to appellant in the pre-bid and contract documents. Accordingly we find no merit to this allegation.

As the Government correctly points out in its partial motion to dismiss filed on 25 April 1983, the Court of Appeals for the Federal Circuit has held in Fidelity Construction Company v. United States, USCC (18 February 1983), 1 FPD p68, Petition for rehearing en banc denied, 17 March 1983, that the Equal Access To Justice Act, Pub. L. No. 96-481, 94 Stat 2325, 28 U.S.C. s 2412 (Supp. V 1981), does not authorize boards of contract appeals to award attorney fees and expenses against the United States. In any event the matter is moot in view of the disposition of the appeal on the merits.

This appeal is denied.

Notes and Questions

1. The case begins with a discussion of how a club although not operating with appropriated funds follows government contracting law. This points off into the great diversity and variety of systems operating in the grey zone surrounding the federal government, from the United States Postal Service to Medicaid.

2. The contractor's first theory is Type I. This turns on what the contract actually specified. What was that? Many other items besides the written specifications can count as the contract, from test borings to soil reports to government representations. In addition, the contractor's Type I theory turns on whether the subsurface problem was "latent." Why was this not latent? Interestingly, "subsurface" has not been considered to require that the problem be underground. For example, the clause applies to the situation of inability to obtain expected access to a work site because of who owns the trail. *E.R. McKee Const. Co. v. United States*, 500 F.2d 525 (Ct. Cl. 1974).

Observe the close relation of this issue to the issue of defective specifications, from the *Spearin* case in the chapter on contract administration.

3. The contractor's Type II theory turns, as the opinion states, on whether what the contractor encounters differs "materially different from the known and the usual." A contractor faces a heavy burden in proving this, which is less frequently alleged and more difficult to prove than the Type I conditions. Why did this theory fail? The contractor did have expert affidavits to support it. Perhaps experts are easier to line up when their duty involves an expenses-paid sojourn to the Hawaiian Islands.

4. The contractor's other theory concerns superior government knowledge. If Type II differing site conditions bear a resemblance to the basic (private) contract law issue of impracticability, this issue bears a resemblance to theories of fraud or misrepresentation; the government owes the contractor because of the wrong it did in withholding knowledge. Look at the sleuthing job done by the contractor's attorneys in this case trying to find such withheld knowledge.

Department of General Services
v. Harmans Associates Limited Partnership
No. 491, Sept. Term, 1993. Court of Special Appeals
of Maryland. 633 A.2d 939. Dec. 8, 1993.

Argued before WILNER, C.J., and BISHOP and FISCHER, JJ.

WILNER, Chief Judge.

The State Department of General Services (DGS) appeals from a judgment of the Circuit Court for Baltimore City affirming, with one modification, a decision of the Board of Contract Appeals (BCA) awarding $163,719 in extra compensation to appellee, Harmans Associates Limited Partnership. * * * We shall deny the motion to dismiss, affirm the judgment in part, and reverse it in part.

Underlying Facts

The State owned a tract of unimproved land in Anne Arundel County on which it desired to have constructed a headquarters facility for the State Highway Administration. The facility was to consist of three buildings and related storage and parking areas. Normally, the State would have proceeded to procure the services of an architect/engineer to design the facility and then, through competitive bidding, select a contractor to build it in accordance with the plans and specifications prepared by the architect/engineer. It would have financed the construction through the sale of State general obligation bonds. See, in general, Md.Code, State Fin. & Proc. art., §§13-102, 8-114.

In this instance, the State chose a different method of achieving the result, one that involved a form of "creative financing." The principal objective, we are informed, was to avoid the creation of a State "debt"—i.e., a pledge of the full faith and credit of the State—to finance the construction and yet have the interest paid on the private financing remain tax-exempt.

Through a number of agreements entered into in March and April, 1988, including a ground lease, a conditional purchase agreement, and a facility agreement, the deal was structured in the following manner. Subject to certain contingencies, the State leased the unimproved land to Harmans for a 16-year period at a rental of $1/year. Harmans designed and constructed a facility "substantially in accordance with the Conceptual

Plans and Technical Specifications" that were included with the State's request for proposals. When the facility was completed, Harmans subleased the ground to the State for
the remaining term of the ground lease and sold the improvements to the State in accordance with the conditional purchase agreement. At the end of the 16-year period,
the ground lease (and the sublease) will end, and the State will own both the land and
the improvements free of any encumbrances.

The $10.9 million cost of construction was financed through a private sale of certifi-
cates of participation. The proceeds were deposited with a trustee and were used to pay
Harmans as construction proceeded. To secure the certificates, Harmans mortgaged to
the trustee its interest in the land and in the contracts with the State. The State, as "purchaser" of the facility, is required to make semi-annual payments to the trustee in
amounts sufficient to pay the principal and interest on the certificates over the term of
the ground lease. The State retains the right, however, to terminate its obligation to
make these payments at any time, in which event the trustee has the right to take possession of the land and improvements and either to sell or operate them in order to discharge its obligations to Harmans and the certificate holders.

In November, 1989, Harmans filed with DGS two formal claims for an equitable adjustment in the contract price, each claim having several sub-parts. One claim sought
$186,860 for unexpected site conditions, including excessive amounts of topsoil * * *.
When, on May 24, 1990, the procurement officer denied those claims, Harmans appealed to BCA. In November, 1990, BCA, in a Memorandum Decision, concluded that
it had no jurisdiction and, for that reason, dismissed the appeals. BCA viewed the
transaction from which the claims arose as a lease of real property rather than as a construction contract, and Md.Code, State Fin. & Proc. art., §15-211(a)(2) excepts from
BCA's jurisdiction contract claims relating to a lease of real property. Harmans sought
judicial review of that decision, and, in an order entered in April, 1991, the Circuit
Court for Baltimore County concluded, as a matter of law, that the claims were not
contract claims relating to a lease of real property. It therefore reversed the dismissals by
BCA and remanded the case to that Board for further proceedings.

Upon the remand, BCA heard evidence bearing on what remained of the two claims.
In a decision filed on May 7, 1992, BCA directed a total equitable adjustment of
$163,719, consisting principally of $113,329 for the soil conditions * * *.

* * *

Jurisdiction Of BCA

The issue here, as we indicated, is whether the arrangement between DGS and Harmans, from which Harmans' claims arose, constitutes a lease or sale of real property.
Through a combination of the definition of "procurement" in SFP, §11-101(l), the definition of "contract claim" in §15-215(b) of that article, and the stated jurisdiction of
BCA in §15-211, it is clear that BCA has jurisdiction to decide a claim that relates to a
procurement contract, including a contract for construction, but that it does not have
jurisdiction to decide claims arising from the sale or leasing of real property.

DGS's position, as stated in its brief, is that "[t]he essence of the transaction was the
creation and transfer of interests in real property, not the mere construction of a building." This position is based principally on the ground lease and sublease used to implement the arrangement. A fair consideration of the overall transaction, especially in light
of the State's own request for proposals, establishes exactly the contrary, however. The
"essence of the transaction" was not the creation and transfer of interests in real prop-

erty but the construction of the State Highway Aministration facility. The State's request for proposals (RFP) stated explicitly:

"The solicitation is based on the following concept:

(1) The offeror shall design, construct and finance the facilities on property owned by the State.

(2) The entire improved property shall be leased to the State Highway Administration under a lease/purchase agreement, or other creative financing mechanism as may be proposed by the offeror."

The acquisition by the State of a completed facility was the sole objective of the transaction. Neither the State nor Harmans had any business interest in leasing and subleasing unimproved land. The State needed a building and Harmans, as a developer, was willing to build it; that was the heart and soul of the agreements between them. The fact that this complex arrangement, designed to avoid the creation of a State "debt," utilized a lease and sublease cannot and does not change the true nature of the arrangement.

Even if we were to give some higher regard to the property instruments, the fact would remain that at least part of the transaction involved the construction of the facility. That is what the State was paying $10.9 million for, and, more important, that is the source of Harmans' claims. The claims for unexpected site conditions and smoke vents did not arise from any lease or sublease but solely from the construction work.

For these reasons, we find that the disputes were within the statutory jurisdiction of BCA.

Site Conditions

Harmans' claim for an equitable adjustment based on differing site conditions is based on a clause that should have been in the contract; DGS's defense is based on clauses that were in the contract. The simple question is which prevails.

As we indicated earlier, the traditional process for construction projects is for the State to select an architect/engineer to prepare detailed plans and specifications and then to select a contractor to build the facility in accordance with those plans and specifications. In requesting proposals from contractors, the State will normally provide information, taken from test borings, regarding soil conditions. In that regard, SFP, §13-218(b) requires that "a procurement contract for construction shall include a clause providing for contract modification if the condition of a site differs from the condition described in the specifications." The particular clause that is mandated is set forth in the procurement regulations adopted by the Board of Public Works, COMAR 21.07.02.05. It requires (1) the contractor to notify the procurement officer promptly of subsurface conditions "differing materially from those indicated in this contract," (2) the procurement officer to investigate the conditions, and (3) if the procurement officer finds that such conditions do materially so differ and cause an increase or decrease in the contractor's cost of performance, "an equitable adjustment shall be made and the contract modified in writing accordingly."

The very next regulation, COMAR 21.07.02.06, requires construction contracts also to contain a clause in which the contractor acknowledges that he has "satisfied himself as to the character, quality and quantity of surface and subsurface materials or obstacles to be encountered insofar as this information is reasonably ascertainable from an inspection of the site, including all exploratory work done by the State, as well as from information presented by the drawings and specifications made a part of this contract."

Notwithstanding that both of these clauses are required by State procurement regulations to be included in every State construction contract, only the second one was included; the first was not.

Before soliciting proposals for this project, the State employed Greiner Engineering Services, Inc. to develop Conceptual Plans and Specifications, which were included with the RFP. Indeed, the Special Conditions, also made part of the RFP, required the contractor to construct the facilities "substantially in accordance with the Conceptual Plans and Technical Specifications enclosed as Exhibits I and II." Included in the drawings prepared by Greiner were 48 foundation boring logs. The bidders were informed that actual copies of the test boring logs and information regarding tests conducted on soil samples were available for examination.

Having provided this information and having required that construction be in substantial accord with the Conceptual Design and Specifications, the RFP then backed away from making any warranties as to subsurface soil conditions. In the Special Conditions attached as Schedule C to the RFP, the State said that the inclusion of the Conceptual Design and Specifications was for "informational purposes only," and that they were not to be taken as "construction documents and specifications" or as a representation as to the "technical sufficiency, or adequacy or safety of...the subsoil conditions involved in the project." In the section of the Special Provisions attached to Greiner's drawings dealing with subsurface exploration, reference was made to the 48 test borings, but that reference was immediately followed by the disclaimer:

> "While the Owner believes the results of the test borings accurately indicate the existing soil conditions below the surface at points and planes indicated, the Owner assumes no responsibility for the actual conditions which may be encountered in the execution of the Contract. Offerors are advised to make their own subsurface investigations."

This, in turn, was followed by other statements to the effect that, if the offeror relies on the accuracy or completeness of the test borings, he does so "at his own risk," and that the information available as to underlying earth strata "must be used by the offeror at his discretion, and is not guaranteed as factual."

DGS's position is that the arrangement is not a construction contract, that, as a result, SFP, §13-218(b) and COMAR 21.07.02.05 are irrelevant, that the provisions just noted make clear that no representations were made as to soil conditions, and that, accordingly, there is no basis for an equitable adjustment. We have, of course, rejected the major premise of that argument by concluding that the arrangement was a procurement contract for construction. Still, DGS contends, even if that is the case, the specific disclaimers, which were approved by the Board of Public Works as part of its approval of the lease, conditional purchase agreement, and facilities agreement, override the differing site clause required by the statute and the regulation. That is the issue upon which we need to focus.

It is not uncommon for procurement statutes or regulations to require a site condition clause similar to that at issue here, for the perception is that such a clause serves the interest of both the government and the contractor. As noted in Foster Const. C.A. & Williams Bros. Co. v. United States, 435 F.2d 873, 887, 193 Ct.Cl. 587 (1970), the clause is designed to ameliorate the risk to contractors from unknowable subsurface conditions. When dependable information on such conditions is unavailable, bidders will either have to make their own test borings or include in their bids a contingency element to cover the risk, either of which inflates the cost to the government. By providing test

Christian
Doctrine
applies to MD.

borings and an equitable adjustment clause, the government can avoid that inflation. 435 F.2d at 887, the Court explained:

"The purpose of the changed conditions clause is thus to take at least some of the gamble on subsurface conditions out of bidding. Bidders need not weigh the cost and ease of making their own borings against the risk of encountering an adverse subsurface, and they need not consider how large a contingency should be added to the bid to cover the risk. They will have no windfalls and no disasters. The Government benefits from more accurate bidding, without inflation for risks which may not eventuate. It pays for difficult subsurface work only when it is encountered and was not indicated in the logs."

See also Stock & Grove, Inc. v. United States, 493 F.2d 629, 204 Ct.Cl. 103 (1974); Spirit Leveling Contractors v. U.S., 19 Cl.Ct. 84 (1989). BCA has adopted that same line of reasoning with respect to the Maryland requirement. See Appeal of Hardaway Constructors, Inc., MSBCA 1249, 3 MSBCA ¶227, p. 42 (MICPEL, 1989).

Maryland has adopted the general rule that contracts are made with reference to existing law and that laws affecting particular contracts are incorporated by implication in them. Denice v. Spotswood I. Quinby, Inc., 248 Md. 428, 237 A.2d 4 (1968). See also 17A Am.Jur.2d Contracts §381. In a series of cases beginning with G.L. Christian & Assoc. v. United States, 312 F.2d 418, 160 Ct.Cl. 1 (1963), the Federal courts have adopted the more specific rule that, where procurement regulations adopted pursuant to statutory authority require that a contract contain a particular clause, the contract must be read as though it contained that clause, whether or not the clause was actually written in the contract. See S.J. Amoroso Const. Co., Inc. v. U.S., 26 Cl.Ct. 759 (1992); SCM Corp. v. United States, 645 F.2d 893, 227 Ct.Cl. 12 (1981); DeMatteo Const. Co. v. United States, 600 F.2d 1384, 220 Ct.Cl. 579 (1979).

This approach is not only consistent with Denice, supra, but is necessary for a proper implementation of the State procurement laws. The General Assembly has, by law, required a site condition clause to be included in every State construction contract, presumably for the reasons noted in the Foster Const. case. Although the Board of Public Works has the authority, through its regulations, to draft the specific language of the clause, which it has done, neither the Board nor DGS is empowered to dispense with the clause altogether where the contract in question is a construction contract. To hold otherwise would be to permit Executive agencies to ignore the clear legislative mandate. Because we have concluded that this arrangement was a construction contract, we conclude further that the site condition clause set forth in COMAR 21.07.02.05 is effectively a part of the Harmans contract.

Normally, when examining a claim for equitable adjustment due to differing site conditions, two questions need to be addressed: (1) whether the site conditions were, in fact, different from what the contractor was led to expect; and (2) whether it was reasonable for the contractor to rely on the information supplied by the government. There is no real dispute here as to the first question. BCA found that the 48 soil boring logs indicated approximately 3-6 inches of topsoil when, in fact, Harmans encountered 1.5 to 2 feet, resulting in an excess of 12,000 cubic yards of topsoil that had to be moved. That was nearly double the 13,000 cubic yards estimated in the drawings. BCA found that this "unexpected condition was dramatically different from what any of the parties expected, requiring the removal of the unsuitable material and importation of borrow to complete construction." DGS does not contest BCA's finding that this was a material difference; its argument is that, in light of the various disclaimers, Harmans was not justified in relying on the Greiner conceptual plans and specifications.

BCA found that reliance by Harmans was reasonable. It quoted with approval statements by the U.S. Court of Claims and the Armed Services Board of Contract Appeals that soil borings "are the most specific and usually the most reliable indications of subsurface conditions," that, while those borings show the conditions only in the bored hole, it is simply not practical "to drill every square inch of a proposed construction site to determine subsurface conditions," and that "[t]his fact of life has to be taken into consideration in determining what use prospective bidders can make of the boring log information furnished to them."

On this basis, BCA observed:

> "The [Greiner] plans included soil boring samples which clearly indicated topsoil a contractor would reasonably expect to encounter. Based upon these borings bids resulted. The small percentage of work done to the plans by the contractor's architect in no way affected the representations by the State in providing the boring samples. Harmans had nothing to do with the preparation of the boring samples. The State offered this information in the RFP and bidders reasonably relied upon them in making their bids."

The reasonableness of Harmans' reliance on the test borings is a question of fact, to be determined from all of the circumstances, including, but not limited to, the provisions in the RFP and the various agreements. Applying normal rules of administrative law, BCA's findings of fact are entitled to deference if they are supported by substantial evidence. Here, they are.

The State's reliance, almost exclusively, on the various disclaimers noted misses two important points. The first is, if DGS really had no intention of allowing bidders to rely on those borings, why did it bother to have them made and to include them in the RFP? If prospective bidders were not permitted to rely on them in preparing their bids, what conceivable purpose did they serve? The State has informed us of no other purpose for including the boring logs in the RFP, and so we cannot conclude that BCA was clearly erroneous in finding that they amounted to representations upon which bidders reasonably could rely. Indeed, the inclusion of the clause required by COMAR 21.07.02.06 confirms the importance of the information supplied by the State. Supporting this as well is the illogic of the converse. As we indicated, the Legislature has required every State construction contract to contain a differing site condition clause. Representations with respect to site conditions are necessary to give that clause meaning. If, through its RFP, the State can disavow such representations, it can, in effect, thwart the legislative mandate.

In summary, it is apparent to us that, in using this scheme of "creative financing" to avoid the creation of a State debt, DGS has wittingly or unwittingly trampled upon some basic procurement requirements. BCA did not err in redressing that situation.

* * *

Notes and Questions

1. This is a state case illustrating the common occurrence of differing site conditions cases at state as well as federal levels. Would the opinion be any different if composed wholly from federal law? How does the court decide the jurisdictional question? Of

course, ordinarily real estate acquisition differs from competitive bidding, with the government deciding what land it wants and then acquiring that by negotiated purchase or condemnation. If the government acquired land by competitive bidding, where would roads go? Exactly in the opposite direction than they should. The land offered for the lowest price would be in the direction away from people and business, and so roads would head straight for where roads are not needed.

2. This is a Type I case, concerning the asserted inclusion in the RFP of the information from soil borings and how the site differed from expectations. Someone has to bear the risk that soil borings will not forecast fully the subsurface conditions. Should the government recover from the Greiner firm?

3. The case turns partly on the important issue of the contractor's duty to investigate the site. The RFP included a standard "site investigation" clause, like FAR 52.236-3. As quoted here, the contractor must have "satisfied himself as to the character…of surface and subsurface materials…insofar as this information is reasonably ascertainable from an inspection of the site…." The clause limits the contractor to knowing what is "reasonably" ascertainable. A contractor who fails to inspect the site may be assuming the risk of what the investigation would have discovered.

4. The case also turns partly on the important issue of the nature of the government's disclaimers in the RFP. In this RFP, the government did not effectively disclaim responsibility for the inadequacy of the soil borings. By contrast, in the *COVCO* case the government escaped liability in part from having warned that the contractor might have to deal with rock. Contrast ineffective general disclaimers, such as in this case, *Fehlhaber Corp. v. United States*, 138 Ct. Cl. 571, *cert. denied*, 355 U.S. 877 (1957), with effective specific warnings, such as in the *COVCO* case, *Jefferson Construction v. United States*, 364 F.2d 420 (Ct. Cl.), *cert. denied*, 386 U.S. 914 (1966).

Chapter 7

Specialized Issues

Government contracting law constantly moves in the seemingly contradictory directions of unity and specialization. As to unity, the government contracting system has powerfully steered since World War II toward a unified set of procurement regulations, the FAR, applicable equally, as much as possible, to all procurement. In turn, the FAR prescribes a unified set of clauses, so that the diverse array of government contracts bear many resemblances. Procedurally, the unified systems for administrative and judicial resolution of acquisition protests and contract disputes also unify the law of government contracting.

At the same time, government contracting law seems to move in the opposite direction of specialization. The trends toward specialization have historical origins although they reflect the felt necessities of widely different contracting circumstances. Historically, military and civilian procurement law differ because each arose entirely distinctly, and their differences have been preserved by the existence of specialized regulations operating alongside the FAR, namely the departmental regulations such as the Department of Defense procurement regulations ("DFARS"). The procurement law of goods or "supply" of construction and of services also had distinct historical origins, preserved by the existence of special statutes and their administrative implementations for construction and for services procurement. These areas of law preserve their differences within the FAR by such adaptations as different FAR clauses for supply contracts and for construction contracts.

A different path brings health care procurement law together with what will be called, by contrast, "regular" government procurement of goods and services. For pertinent purposes, federal health care contracting law starts with the enactment in 1964 of Medicare, to pay for health care for seniors, and Medicaid, to pay for health care for the poor. Congress did not model these on the systems for regular government procurement, but rather on a combination of the income security entitlement systems in the Social Security Act of 1935 and the private-sector mechanisms for health care insurance. Accordingly, the discussion of Medicare and Medicaid below must begin with some fundamental descriptions of these quite different payment systems.

To this day, much of Medicare and Medicaid practice remains a part of health care law without connection to government contracting law generally. However, certain similarities and trends have brought these areas together. Essentially, health care providers contract primarily with individual beneficiaries themselves, provide their services directly to the beneficiaries, and then submit claims for payment to the government, in contrast to regular government contractors who contract with, and provide goods and services for, the government, before then submitting claims for payment to the government. The key point in common is that both health care providers and regular government contractors submit to the government their claims for payment for what they sell. The dynamic development of False Claims Act law since the 1986 Amendments, by making that Act an important part of both health care contracting law and regular government contracting law, has brought together the law of the two types of "claims" on the government. Since the False Claims Act applies equivalently to fraud by health care providers and regular government contractors, it spawns a uniform law of federal procurement fraud applicable to both.

Second, Medicare and Medicaid originally began as systems for reimbursement of privately set fees. However, as health care costs soared from 1965 to the 1990s, health care contracting law developed mechanisms for government administrators to restrict prices. This meant more intense administrative review of provider claims. In this way, the health care claims-processing system developed limited, but important, resemblances to classic government contract administration.

A. Health Care

1. Medicare: Physician

To describe in a highly simplified way, Congress established the Medicare program by Title XVIII of the Social Security Act, enacted in 1965 and codified at 42 U.S.C. sec. 1395 et seq. Medicare pays for health care for seniors by its two distinct parts: Part A for inpatient hospital care and Part B for physician care. For this book's purposes, we may disregard the eligibility, coverage, benefits, financing, and numerous other aspects of Medicare, and focus on its payment of provider claims. For fuller treatment of Medicare subjects generally, see Barry R. Furrow, Thomas L. Greaney, Sandra H. Johnson, Timothy Jost, & Robert L. Schwartz, Health Law (1995); Rand E. Rosenblatt, Sylvia S. Law, Sara Rosenbaum, Law and the American Health System (1997); Charles Tiefer, *Treatment for Medicare's Budget: Quick Operation or Long-Term Care?*, 16 St. Louis U. Pub. L. Rev. 27 (1996).

The Health Care Finance Administration ("HCFA") of the Department of Health and Human Services administers the Medicare program. HCFA promulgates extensive regulations, codified at 42 C.F.R. Parts 405-424, and 482-498, and also issues key manuals and instructions. The most important of the manuals are the Provider Reimbursement Manual, the Intermediary Manual, and the Carriers Manual. As the Supreme Court's *Guernsey* opinion below makes clear, when Medicare claims issues reach the courts, the courts analyze these regulations and manuals much as, in regular government contract claims cases, they analyze the regulations and manuals of the contracting departments.

Given the enormous scale of the program, HCFA could not process the claims itself. Rather, it delegates the processing and paying of claims to Medicare Part A "fiscal intermediaries" and Medicare Part B "carriers." These are private entities, often Blue Cross or Blue Shield associations, under contract with the Secretary of HHS. For Part A providers to receive payment, they must meet conditions of participation and enter into a contract called a provider agreement. Part B providers must meet conditions of coverage. As with regular government contracting law, a large part of the legally significant contract interaction between claimants and the government consists of submissions of the basis for the claim on government-prescribed forms. The forms serve as the government-directed embodiment of the government contracting law in statutes and regulations and, for Medicare, of the conditions of participation or coverage.

Physicians commonly submit their claims on HCFA form, "HCFA 1500." The *Krizek* case brings together some of the essentials linking and differentiating claims payment under government contract law, and under health care contracting law: the unifying law of the False Claims Act; the centrality of legal analysis of the fundamental unit, the "claim"; and the respective roles assigned by Medicare's mechanism for claims payment to HCFA, the carrier, and the provider.

For further discussions of health care contracting, particularly the recent emerging law of health care fraud, see:

Joan H. Krause, *"Promises to Keep": Health Care Providers and the Civil False Claims Act,"* 23 Cardozo L. Rev. 1363 (2002);

Joan H. Krause, *Health Care Providers and the Public Fisc: Paradigms of Government Harm Under the Civil False Claims Act*, 36 Ga. L. Rev. 121 (2001);

Charles Tiefer & Heather Akehurst-Krause, *Risky Business: Medicare's Vulnerability to Selection Games of Managed Care Providers*, 28 U. Balt. L. Rev. 319 (1999);

Aaron M. Altschuler, Sarah Henley Kanwit, Theodore L. Radway, *Health Care Fraud*, 35 Am. Crim. L. Rev. 841 (1998).

Jeffrey A. Lovitky, *Medicare/Medicaid Fraud: A Growing Area of Concern for Health Care Providers*, 76 Mich. B.J. 308 (1997).

Kaz Kikkawa, Note, *Medicare Fraud and Abuse and Qui Tam: The Dynamic Duo or the Odd Couple?* 8 Health Matrix 83 (1998).

Leon Aussprung, *Fraud and Abuse: Federal Civil Health Care Litigation and Settlement*, 19 J. Legal Med. 1 (1998).

John R. Munich, *The Medicaid Anti-Fraud Amendments of 1994: Attorney General's Newest Weapon in the Fight Against White Collar Crime*, 52 J. Mo. B. 26 (1996).

Pamela H. Bucy, *Crimes by Health Care Providers,* 1996 U. Ill. L. Rev. 589 (1996).

Cathy L. Naugle, *How to Recognize a Health Care Fraud Case Before They Serve the Search Warrant!* 40-FEB Advocate (Idaho) 15 (1997).

United States of America, Appellant/Cross-Appellee v. George O. Krizek, M.D., et al., Appellees/Cross-Appellants

Nos. 96-5045, 96-5046. United States Court of Appeals,
District of Columbia Circuit. 111 F.2d 934.
Decided May 2, 1997.

Before: SILBERMAN, GINSBURG and SENTELLE, Circuit Judges. Opinion for the court filed by Circuit Judge SENTELLE.

SENTELLE, Circuit Judge.

This appeal arises from a civil suit brought by the government against a psychiatrist and his wife under the civil False Claims Act ("FCA"), 31 U.S.C. §§3729-3731, and under the common law. The District Court found defendants liable for knowingly submitting false claims and entered judgment against defendants for $168,105.39. The government appealed, and the defendants filed a cross-appeal. We hold that the District Court erred and remand for further proceedings.

I.

The government filed suit against George and Blanka Krizek for, inter alia, violations of the civil FCA, 31 U.S.C. §§3729-3731. Dr. George Krizek is a psychiatrist who practiced medicine in the District of Columbia. His wife, Blanka Krizek, worked in Dr. Krizek's practice and maintained his billing records. At issue are reimbursement forms submitted by the Krizeks to Pennsylvania Blue Shield ("PBS") in connection with Dr. Krizek's treatment of Medicare and Medicaid patients. The government's complaint alleged that between January 1986 and March 1992 Dr. Krizek submitted 8,002 false or unlawful requests for reimbursement in an amount exceeding $245,392. The complaint alleged two different types of false claims: first, some of the services provided by Dr. Krizek were medically unnecessary; and second, the Krizeks "upcoded" the reimbursement requests, that is billed the government for more extensive treatments than were, in fact, rendered.

A doctor providing services to a Medicare or Medicaid recipient submits a claim for reimbursement to a Medicare carrier, in this case PBS, on a form known as the "HCFA 1500." The HCFA 1500 requires the doctor to provide his identification number, the patient's information, and a five-digit code identifying the services for which reimbursement is sought. A list of the five-digit codes is contained in the American Medical Association's Current

Procedures Terminology Manual ("CPT"). For instance, the Manual notes that the CPT code "90844" is used to request reimbursement for an individual medical psychotherapy session lasting approximately 45 to 50 minutes. The CPT code "90843" indicates individual medical psychotherapy for 20 to 30 minutes. An HCFA 1500 lists those services provided to a single patient, and may include a number of CPT codes when the patient has been treated over several days or weeks.

Before the District Court, the government argued that the amount of time specified by the CPT for each reimbursement code indicates the amount of time spent "face-to-face" with the patient. The government focused on the Krizeks' extensive use of the 90844 code. According to the government, this code should be used only when the doctor spends 45 to 50 minutes with the patient, not including time spent on the phone in consultation with other doctors or time spent discussing the patient with a nurse. The government argued that the Krizeks had used the 90844 code when they should have been billing for shorter, less-involved treatments.

Based on its claims of unnecessary treatment and up-coding the government sought an extraordinary $81 million in damages. This amount included $245,392 in actual damages and civil penalties of $10,000 for each of 8,002 separate CPT codes. During a three-week bench trial, the District Court determined that the case would initially be tried on the basis of seven patients which the government described as representative of the Krizeks' improper coding and treatment practices. United States v. Krizek, No. 93-0054 (D.D.C. March 9, 1994) (Protective Order). The determination of liability would then "be equally applicable to all other claims." Id. On July 19, 1994, the District Court issued a Memorandum Opinion, United States v. Krizek, 859 F.Supp. 5, 8 (D.D.C.1994) [hereinafter Krizek I], holding that the government had not established that the Krizeks submitted claims for unnecessary services. The Court noted that the government's witness failed to interview the patients or any doctors or nurses. Id. The District Court also rejected the government's theory that the Krizeks were liable for requesting reimbursement when some of the billed time was spent out of the presence of the patient. Id. at 10. The Court found that it was common and proper practice among psychiatrists to bill for time spent reviewing files, speaking with consulting physicians, etc. Id.

Despite having rejected the government's arguments on these claims, the Court determined that the Krizeks knowingly made false claims in violation of the FCA. Id. at 13. The Court found that because of a "seriously deficient" system of recordkeeping the Krizeks "submitted bills for 45–50 minute psychotherapy sessions...when Dr. Krizek could not have spent the requisite time providing services, face-to-face, or otherwise." Id. at 11, 12. For instance, on some occasions within the seven-patient sample, Dr. Krizek submitted claims for over 21 hours of patient treatment within a 24-hour period. Id. at 12. The Court stated, "While Dr. Krizek may have been a tireless worker, it is difficult for the Court to comprehend how he could have spent more than even ten hours in a single day serving patients." Id. The Court stated that these false statements were not "mistakes" nor merely negligent conduct. Under the statutory definition of "knowing" conduct the Court is compelled to conclude that the defendants acted with reckless disregard as to the truth or falsity of the submissions. As such, they will be deemed to have violated the False Claims Act. Id. at 13-14.

Having found the Krizeks liable within the seven-patient sample, the Court attempted to craft a device for applying the determination of liability to the entire universe of claims. Here, the District Court relied on the testimony of a defense witness that he could not recall submitting more than twelve 90844 codes—nine hours worth of patient treatment—for a single day. Id. at 12. Based on this testimony, the District Court stated that nine hours per day was "a fair and reasonably accurate assessment of the time Dr. Krizek actually spent providing patient services." Id. The Court, accordingly, determined that the Krizeks would be liable under the FCA on every day in which claims were submitted in excess of the equivalent of twelve (12) 90844 claims (nine patient-treatment hours) in a single day and where the defendants cannot establish that Dr. Krizek legitimately devoted the claimed amount of time to patient care on the day in question. Id. at 14. On April 6, 1995, the District Court, with the consent of the parties, referred the matter to a Special Master with instructions to investigate the 8,002 challenged CPT codes and, applying the nine-hour presumption, to determine 1) the single damages owed by the Krizeks; 2) the amount of the single damages trebled; 3) the number of false claims submitted by defendants; and 4) the number of false claims multiplied by $5000. United States v. Krizek, No. 93-0054 (D.D.C. April 6, 1995) (Order of Reference). After considering evidence submitted by the parties, the Special Master determined that the defendants requested reimbursement for more than nine hours per day of patient treatment on 264 days. United States v. Krizek, No. 93-0054, at 15 (D.D.C. June 6, 1995) (Special Master Report). The Special Master found single damages of $47,105.39, which when trebled totaled $141,316.17. He then determined to treat each of the 1,149 false code entries as a separate claim, even where several codes were entered on the same HCFA 1500. Multiplied by $5000 per false claim, this approach produced civil penalties of $5,745,000. After considering motions by the parties, the District Court issued a second opinion, United States v. Krizek, 909 F.Supp. 32 (D.D.C.1995) [hereinafter Krizek II], which modified its earlier decision. The Court stated that it accepted the Special Master's factual findings, id. at 33, but was applying a different approach in calculating damages. First, the Court awarded damages of $47,105.38 to the government for unjust enrichment based on the nine-hour presumption. Id. at 33. The Court then stated:

While the Court set a nine hour benchmark to determine which claims were improper, the Court will now set an even higher benchmark for classifying claims that fall under the False Claims Act so that there can be no question as to the falsity of the claims. The Court has determined that the False Claims Act has been violated where claims have been made totaling in excess of twenty-four hours within a single twenty-four hour period and where defendants have provided no explanation for justifying claims made for services rendered virtually around the clock. Id. at 34. Claims in excess of twenty-four hours of patient treatment per day had been made eleven times in the six-year period. Id. The Court assessed fines of $10,000 for each of the eleven false claims, which, combined with single damages of $47,105.39, totaled $157,105.39. Id. The Court also assessed Special Master's fees against the Krizeks in the amount of $11,000. Id. The government appealed, and the Krizeks cross-appealed. We first turn to the government's appeal.

* * *

III.

The Krizeks cross-appeal on the grounds that the District Court erroneously treated each CPT code as a separate "claim" for purposes of computing civil penalties. The Krizeks assert that the claim, in this context, is the HCFA 1500 even when the form contains a number of CPT codes.

The FCA defines "claim" to

> include any request or demand, whether under a contract or otherwise, for money or property which is made to a contractor, grantee, or other recipient if the United States Government provides any portion of the money or property which is requested or demanded, or if the Government will reimburse such contractor, grantee, or other recipient for any portion of the money or property which is requested or demanded.

31 U.S.C. §3729(c). Whether a defendant has made one false claim or many is a fact-bound inquiry that focuses on the specific conduct of the defendant. In United States v. Bornstein, 423 U.S. 303, 307, 96 S.Ct. 523, 527, 46 L.Ed.2d 514 (1976), for instance, the Supreme Court considered the liability of a subcontractor who delivered 21 boxes of falsely labeled electron tubes to the prime contractor in three separate shipments. The prime contractor, in turn, delivered 397 of these tubes to the government and billed the government using 35 invoices. The trial court awarded 35 statutory forfeitures against the subcontractor, one for each invoice. The Court of Appeals reversed, holding that there was only one forfeiture because there had been only one contract. The Supreme Court disagreed with both positions and held that there had been three false claims by the subcontractor, one for each shipment of falsely labeled tubes. Id. at 313, 96 S.Ct. at 529–30. The Court stated, "[T]he focus in each case [must] be upon the specific conduct of the person from whom the Government seeks to collect the statutory forfeitures." Id. Because the subcontractor committed three separate causative acts—dispatching each shipment of the falsely marked tubes—it would be liable for three separate forfeitures. Id.; see also United States ex rel. Marcus v. Hess, 317 U.S. 537, 552, 63 S.Ct. 379, 388, 87 L.Ed. 443 (1943) (holding that the government was entitled to a forfeiture for each project for which a collusive bid was entered even though the bids included additional false forms); United States v. Grannis, 172 F.2d 507, 515 (4th Cir.) (assessing ten forfeitures against defendant for each of ten fraudulent vouchers even though the vouchers listed 130 items), cert. denied, 337 U.S. 918, 69 S.Ct. 1160, 93 L.Ed. 1727 (1949).

* * *

The gravamen of these cases is that the focus is on the conduct of the defendant. The Courts asks, "With what act did the defendant submit his demand or request and how many such acts were there?" In this case, the Special Master adopted a position that is inconsistent with this approach. He stated, The CPT code, not the HCFA 1500 form, is the source used to permit federal authorities to verify and account for discrete units of medical service provided, billed and paid for. In sum, the government has demanded a specific accounting unit to identify and verify the services provided, payments requested and amounts paid under the Medicare/Medicaid program. The CPT code, not the HCFA 1500 form, is that basic accounting unit. United States v. Krizek, No. 93-0054, at 21 (D.D.C. June 6, 1995) (Special Master Report). The Special Master concluded that because the government used the CPT code in processing the claims, the CPT code, and not the HCFA 1500 in its entirety, must be the claim. This conclusion, which was later adopted by the District Court, misses the point. The question turns, not on how the government chooses to process the claim, but on how many times the defendants made a "request or demand." 31 U.S.C. s 3729(c). In this case, the Krizeks made a request or demand every time they submitted an HCFA 1500. Our conclusion that the claim in this context is the HCFA 1500 form is supported by the structure of the form itself. The medical provider is asked to supply, along with the CPT codes, the date and place of service, a description of the procedures, a diagnosis code, and the charges. The charges are then totaled to produce one request or demand—line 27 asks for total charges, line 28 for amount paid, and line 29 for balance due. The CPT codes function in this context as a type of invoice used to explain how the defendant computed his request or demand. The government contends that fairness or uniformity concerns support treating each CPT code as a separate claim, arguing that "[t]o count woodenly the number of HCFA 1500 forms submitted by the Krizeks would cede to medical practitioners full authority to control exposure to [FCA] simply by structuring their billings in a particular manner." Precisely so. It is conduct of the medical practitioner, not the disposition of the claims by the government, that creates FCA liability. See Alsco-Harvard Fraud Litigation, 523 F.Supp. 790, 811 (D.D.C.1981) (remanding for determination whether invoices were presented for payment at one time or individually submitted as separate demands for payment). Moreover, even if we considered fairness to be a relevant consideration in statutory construction, we would note that the government's definition of claim permitted it to seek an astronomical $81 million worth of damages for alleged actual damages of $245,392. We therefore remand for recalculation of the civil penalty.

* * *

Having determined that liability was properly determined by the seven-patient sample, we turn now to the question whether, in considering the sample, the District Court applied the appropriate level of scienter. The FCA imposes liability on an individual who "knowingly presents" a "false or fraudulent claim." 31 U.S.C. §3729(a). A person acts "knowingly" if he: (1) has actual knowledge of the information; (2) acts in deliberate ignorance of the truth or falsity of the information; or (3) acts in reckless disregard of the truth or falsity of the information, and no proof of specific intent to defraud is required. 31 U.S.C. §3729(b). The Krizeks assert that the District Court impermissibly applied the FCA by permitting an aggravated form of gross negligence, "gross negligence-plus," to satisfy the Act's scienter requirement. In Saba v. Compagnie Nationale Air France, 78 F.3d 664 (D.C.Cir.1996), we considered whether reckless disregard was the equivalent of willful misconduct for purposes of the Warsaw Convention. We noted that reckless disregard lies on a continuum between gross negligence and intentional harm. Id. at 668. In some cases, recklessness serves as a proxy for forbidden intent. Id. (citing SEC v. Steadman, 967 F.2d 636, 641 (D.C.Cir.1992)). Such cases require a showing that the defendant engaged in an act known to cause or likely to cause the injury. Id. at 669. Use of reckless disregard as a substitute for the forbidden intent prevents the defendant from "deliberately blind[ing] himself to the consequences of his tortious action." Id. at 668. In another category of cases, we noted, reckless disregard is "simply a linear extension of gross negligence, a palpable failure to meet the appropriate standard of care." Id. In Saba, we determined that in the context of the Warsaw Convention, a showing of willful misconduct might be made by establishing reckless disregard such that the subjective intent of the defendant could be inferred. Id. at 669.

The question, therefore, is whether "reckless disregard" in this context is properly equated with willful misconduct or with aggravated gross negligence. In determining that gross negligence-plus was sufficient, the District Court cited legislative history equating reckless disregard with gross negligence. A sponsor of the 1986 amendments to the FCA stated,

> Subsection 3 of Section 3729(c) uses the term "reckless disregard of the truth or falsity of the information" which is no different than and has the same meaning as a gross negligence standard that has been applied in other cases. While the Act was not intended to apply to mere negligence, it is intended to apply in situations that could be considered gross negligence where the submitted claims to the Government are prepared in such a sloppy or unsupervised fashion that resulted in overcharges to the Government. The Act is also intended not to permit artful defense counsel to require some form of intent as an essential ingredient of proof. This section is intended to reach the "ostrich-with-his-head-in-the-sand" problem where government contractors hide behind the fact they were not personally aware that such overcharges may have occurred. This is not a new standard but clarifies what has always been the standard of knowledge required.

132 Cong. Rec. H9382-03 (daily ed. Oct. 7, 1986) (statement of Rep. Berman). While we are not inclined to view isolated statements in the legislative history as dispositive, we agree with the thrust of this statement that the best reading of the Act defines reckless disregard as an extension of gross negligence. Section 3729(b)(2) of the Act provides liability for false statements made with deliberate ignorance. If the reckless disregard standard of section 3729(b)(3) served merely as a substitute for willful misconduct— to prevent the defendant from "deliberately blind[ing] himself to the consequences of his tortious action"—section (b)(3) would be redundant since section (b)(2) already covers such struthious conduct. See Kungys v. United States, 485 U.S. 759, 778, 108 S.Ct. 1537, 1550, 99 L.Ed.2d 839 (1988) (citing the "cardinal rule of statutory interpretation that no provision should be construed to be entirely redundant"). Moreover, as the statute explicitly states that specific intent is not required, it is logical to conclude that reckless disregard in this context is not a "lesser form of intent," see Steadman, 967 F.2d at 641–42, but an extreme version of ordinary negligence.

* * *

We are also unpersuaded by the Krizeks' argument that their conduct did not rise to the level of reckless disregard. The District Court cited a number of factors supporting its conclusion: Mrs. Krizek completed the submissions with little or no factual basis; she made no effort to establish how much time Dr. Krizek spent with any particular patient; and Dr. Krizek "failed utterly" to review bills submitted on his behalf. Krizek I, 859 F.Supp. at 13. Most tellingly, there were a number of days within the seven-patient sample when even the shoddiest recordkeeping would have revealed that false submissions were being made—those days on which the Krizeks' billing approached twenty-four hours in a single day. On August 31, 1985, for instance, the Krizeks requested reimbursement for patient treatment using the 90844 code thirty times and the 90843 code once, indicating patient treatment of over 22 hours. Id. at 12. Outside the seven-patient sample the Krizeks billed for more than twenty-four hours in a single day on three separate occasions. Krizek II, 909 F.Supp. at 34. These factors amply support the District Court's determination that the Krizeks acted with reckless disregard. Finally, we note that Dr. Krizek is no less liable than his wife for these false submissions. As noted, an FCA violation may be established without reference to the subjective intent of the defendant. Dr. Krizek delegated to his wife authority to submit claims on his behalf. In failing "utterly" to review the false submissions, he acted with reckless disregard.

Notes and Questions

1. The reader may find some of Krizek a challenge when reading it apart from the chapter on the False Claims Act. When reading the case just for its place in this chapter (rather than as another False Claims Act case), simply note the common applicability of the False Claims Act to (1) the health care services rendered by Dr. Krizek to Medicare and Medicaid patients, and to (2) regular government contracting. This serves to create a unifying bond between those two systems of government payment of "claims" for contractually-provided services. Of course, the text of the False Claims Act applies to both types of "claims." Note, in addition, that the case law for each type of "claim" applies to the other. For example, the Krizek opinion relies upon such classic Supreme Court opinions applying the False Claims Act to regular government contracting as United States ex rel. Marcus v. Hess, 317 U.S. 537 (1943), and United States v. Bornstein, 423 U.S. 303 (1976).

What does this unifying bond of the nature of the "claim" and the protections of the Treasury against fraud tell about the deep structure of government contract law? If you were to describe to a interested layperson (assuming there were such a person) the fundamentals of government contracting, would you start with how "claims" are submitted and paid, or would you start elsewhere: with how the contracting officer supervises the systems for competitive acquisition, contract administration, disputes and termination? There is a law of the federal fisc even more fundamental than the law of what contracting officers do. Think back to where Chapter 1 of this casebook started: with the essential doctrines unique to (public) government contract law and differentiating it from basic (private) contract law, such as the lack of estoppel against the government and the limited authority of government agents. Those fundamental doctrines arise from the limitations under the Constitution and its implementing statutory system on payments out of the Treasury with no meaningful parallel in basic (private) contracting. The law of "claims" and fraud similarly arises from that fundamental law of the federal fisc. It is that special public law regarding controls on payments out of the public Treasury that unifies regular government contracting law and health care contracting law.

2. What do you think of the defenses argued by Dr. Krizek, who readers of this opinion have nicknamed the "24 hour doctor"? Does his talk of leaving the billing to someone else (in this case, his wife) seem to you fanciful? Defense arguments look one way when viewed with a focus on the extreme case of the physician who bills for more than 24 hours in a day. However, the law established in this case applies to the non-extreme cases, namely, the countless health care providers who would vastly prefer to devote their time, skill, and attention to health care rather than to government contracting law. Do we really expect to obtain maximum compliance with the rules of health care contracting by the brute-force method of threatening them with $10,000 statutory penalties for miscoding?

In regular government contracting, most of control on the contractor comes not from fraud law, but from contracting officer supervision as the contractors do their work and make their deliveries. However, the government does not come into the health care picture until after the work is done and "delivered," at the late stage of claims payment. Can fraud case law substitute as a control for the entire regular government contracting apparatus of contracting officer supervision?

3. How many different arguments on each side regarding the "$81 million question," whether the claim is the item of coded medical service, or the entire HCFA 1500 form can you tease apart? Try this chart:

Gov't: claim is each billed service HCFA 1500 form	Dr. Krizek: claim is each whole
CPT Code is what gov't uses as basic accounting unit	precedents Bornstein: 397 false tubes, 35 invoices, 3 shipments = 3 forfeitures Miller: 5 monthly bilings, 11 invoices, = 5 false claims
don't want doctor to reduce liability by writing a long form	it's doctor's conduct that creates FCA liability; $81 million is unfair

4. How many different argument on each side can you tease apart about the issue of the scienter level for which the statute says the standard is "reckless disregard?" Try this chart:

Gov't: expansion of gross negligence	Dr. Krizek: needs intent
e.g., Dr. Krizek not paying attention to what his wife's billing	e.g., no proof of any bad intent by Dr. Krizek; just wife's sloppiness
legislative history: sloppy or unsupervised ostrich-in-the-sand, deliberately blinding self	FCA is almost penal ($10,000 forfeitures per wrong)
billed more than 24 hours/day	(the upcoding defense): "90843" vs. "90844" — doctors have better things to do than check billing coding

Kailash C. PANI, M.D. et al., Plaintiffs-Appellants,
v. EMPIRE BLUE CROSS BLUE SHIELD,
Defendant-Appellee.

Docket No. 97-7086, United States Court of Appeals, Second Circuit.
152 F.3d 67, Decided July 24, 1998.

Before: VAN GRAAFEILAND and WALKER, Circuit Judges, and KOELTL, District Judge.

JOHN M. WALKER, JR., Circuit Judge:

This appeal raises the issue of whether a private insurance company is entitled to official immunity when acting as a fiscal intermediary or a carrier on behalf of the United

States in the administration of a Medicare program. We hold that a fiscal intermediary or carrier is immune from suit for torts that arise out of the performance of its duty to investigate and report possible Medicare fraud.

BACKGROUND

Plaintiff-appellant Kailash C. Pani, M.D., a neurosurgeon and sole principal in plaintiff-appellant Kailash C. Pani, M.D., P.C. (collectively "Pani"), maintained a medical practice in Tarrytown, New York. Defendant-appellee Empire Blue Cross Blue Shield ("Empire") was the Medicare carrier for Westchester County under contract to the Department of Health and Human Services ("HHS"). Under the Medicare Act, 42 U.S.C. § 1395 et seq., a "carrier" is a private insurance company that contracts with HHS to administer claims submitted under the Medicare "Part B" program, a voluntary supplemental medical insurance program, while a "fiscal intermediary" is a private insurance company that contracts with HHS to administer major medical claims under the Medicare "Part A" program. See 42 U.S.C. §§ 1395h(a), 1395u(a). As a carrier, Empire was responsible for processing Medicare claims submitted by health-care providers, including assigning authorization codes, making payments, and reviewing claims for possible fraud. Id.

Between September 1981 and February 1983, Pani submitted Medicare claims to Empire for a procedure Pani called a "facet rhizotomy." At first Pani submitted claims that did not contain a procedure code. After Empire's claims department assigned the code "5211," a code for rhizotomy, to these claims based on the procedure described by Pani, Pani submitted several more claims using that code number.

Sometime in 1983, Empire reported to HHS that it suspected Pani had submitted claims for procedures he had not performed or for procedures that were not "facet rhizotomies." Following an investigation by the United States Attorney's Office, Pani was indicted on nine counts of mail fraud, in violation of 18 U.S.C. §§ 1341-42; 63 counts of filing false claims against the government, in violation of 18 U.S.C. § 287; and 50 counts of conversion of government funds, in violation of 18 U.S.C. § 641. See United States v. Pani, 717 F.Supp. 1013, 1014 (S.D.N.Y. 1989). Pani was ultimately convicted, following a bench trial, on four counts of mail fraud, three counts of making false claims, and three counts of conversion. See id. The district judge acquitted Pani on the remaining counts finding that Empire "certainly had an obligation to find out more about what they were approving, and they were...on warning that these were not rhizotomies, surgical rhizotomies, performed in a hospital." United States v. Pani, 83 CR. 0735, Hearing tr. at 10-11 (S.D.N.Y. May 14, 1984). In subsequent proceedings, Pani was found liable to the federal government for civil damages under the False Claims Act, 31 U.S.C. §§ 3729–31, and convicted in a state prosecution for Medicaid fraud. See United States v. Pani, No. 86 Civ. 4970, slip op. at 5-6 (S.D.N.Y. Oct. 15, 1991); United States v. Pani, 717 F.Supp. 1013, 1019 (S.D.N.Y. 1989); People v. Pani, 138 A.D.2d 532, 525 N.Y.S.2d 912 (N.Y.App.Div. 1988).

In October of 1993, Pani filed suit in New York state court against Empire. Pani's complaint sought $10 million based on claims for (1) negligence; (2) tortious interference with contractual relations; and (3) breach of contract arising out of Empire's report to the United States government of possible fraud by Pani. Empire removed the action to federal district court pursuant to 28 U.S.C. §§ 1441(b) and 1442(a)(1), which permits removal by "[t]he United States or any agency thereof or any officer (or any person acting under that officer) of the United States or of any agency thereof, sued in an official or individual capacity for any act under color of such office."

Empire's initial answer asserted that Pani had failed to state a claim and that Pani's claims were barred by the statute of limitations. On April 18, 1995, the United States moved to be substituted as the proper party defendant, or, alternatively, to be allowed to intervene pursuant to Fed. R. Civ. P. 24. The United States also moved to dismiss Pani's complaint under Fed. R. Civ. P. 12(b)(1) and (6) for lack of subject matter jurisdiction, for failure to state a claim, and because Pani's claims were barred by the statute of limitations, or, in the alternative, for summary judgment. On the same day, Empire sought leave to file an amended answer in order to assert official immunity as an additional defense and moved to dismiss the complaint for the reasons submitted in the government's brief.

The United States District Court for the Southern District of New York (Sidney H. Stein, Judge) granted Empire's motion to dismiss and denied the government's motion as moot. Pani v. Empire Blue Cross Blue Shield, No. 93 Civ. 8215, 1996 WL 734889 (S.D.N.Y. Dec. 23, 1996). Pani's breach of contract claim was dismissed for lack of subject matter jurisdiction, pursuant to Fed R. Civ. P. 12(b)(1) and 42 U.S.C. §1395u(b)(3)(c). Id., 1996 WL 734889 at *3. The claim for tortious interference with contractual relations was dismissed because Pani had failed to establish the prima facie elements of the tort. Id., 1996 WL 734889 at *2. Finally, the district court dismissed Pani's claim for negligence on the ground of official immunity, and added that immunity provided an alternative basis for dismissing Pani's other claims. Id., 1996 WL 734889 at *3-*5.

DISCUSSION

* * *

Several circuits have held that a fiscal intermediary or carrier is entitled to sovereign immunity on the rationale that the suit at issue is really one against the United States because the fiscal intermediary or carrier is a government agent that "act[s] on behalf of the [Medicare] Administrator in carrying out certain administrative responsibilities that the law imposes" and is entitled to indemnification from the United States, which, therefore, is "the real party of interest." 42 C.F.R. 421.5(b) * * * *

Fewer circuit courts have decided the issue of whether fiscal intermediaries and carriers are entitled to official immunity for discretionary acts taken within the scope of their authority under the Medicare Act. See, e.g., Bushman v. Seiler, 755 F.2d 653, 655–56 (8th Cir.1985) (official immunity granted to consultant of Medicare carrier for reporting fraud to carrier); Peterson v. Blue Cross/Blue Shield, 508 F.2d 55, 58 (5th Cir.1975) (holding by implication that employee of both fiscal intermediary and carrier was entitled to official immunity in connection with suspension of payments for fraud). Several district courts, however, have held that fiscal intermediaries and carriers are entitled to official immunity. See, e.g., Midland Psychiatric Assocs. v. United States, 969 F.Supp. 543, 551-52 (W. D. Mo.1997) (carrier entitled to official immunity for alleged wrongful denial of benefits); C. Jack Friedman, Ph.D. & Assocs., P.C. v. Pennsylvania Blue Shield, 836 F.Supp. 263, 268 (E.D. Pa.1993) (carrier entitled to official immunity for claims based on its report of fraud); Livingston v. Blue Cross and Blue Shield, 788 F.Supp. 545, 549–50 (S.D. Ala.1992) (fiscal intermediary entitled to official immunity for claims arising from intermediary's instigation of fraud prosecution); Group Health Inc. v. Blue Cross Ass'n, 739 F.Supp. 921, 932–33 (S.D.N.Y. 1990) (fiscal intermediary entitled to official immunity for claims based on negligent misrepresentations).

In Westfall v. Erwin, 484 U.S. 292, 295–97, 108 S.Ct. 580, 98 L.Ed.2d 619 (1988), the Supreme Court held that a federal official is shielded from state-law tort liability for acts that are discretionary in nature and fall within the outer perimeter of the official's duties. As Westfall made clear, the determination of whether immunity should apply requires a functional inquiry: "immunity attaches to particular official functions, not to particular offices." Id. at 296 n. 3, 108 S.Ct. 580. The rationale behind such immunity is a concern that "the threat of liability will make federal officials unduly timid in carrying out their official duties, and that effective government will be promoted if officials are freed of the costs of vexatious and often frivolous damages suits." Id. at 295, 108 S.Ct. 580.

The application of the Westfall test to federal officials was superseded by Congress's passage in 1988 of the Federal Employees Liability Reform and Tort Compensation Act, also known as the Westfall Act, which eliminated the requirement that the acts be discretionary. See 28 U.S.C. §2679(d). However, the Westfall test remains the framework for determining when nongovernmental persons or entities are entitled to the same immunity. See Mangold v. Analytic Servs., Inc., 77 F.3d 1442, 1446–50 (4th Cir.1996); Slotten v. Hoffman, 999 F.2d 333, 336 (8th Cir.1993); Midland Psychiatric, 969 F.Supp. at 551–52.

If Empire had been an actual federal official, it unquestionably would have been entitled to official immunity for investigating and reporting possible fraud. See Peterson v. Weinberger, 508 F.2d at 50-51 (finding government integrity specialist officially immune because it was his responsibility to investigate claims of fraud and abuse and there was no evidence that he had acted beyond his scope of employment); Mangold, 77 F.3d at 1447 (recognizing as a general matter that official immunity would protect official decisions to investigate suspected fraud in the administration of government contracts).

The policy considerations underlying the extension of official immunity to a federal official's duty to investigate and report suspected fraud apply with equal force to a fiscal intermediary or carrier. "The complexities and magnitude of governmental activity have become so great that there must of necessity be a delegation and redelegation of authority as to many functions, and we cannot say that these functions become less important simply because they are exercised by officers of lower rank in the executive hierarchy" or by private contractors. Barr v. Matteo, 360 U.S. 564, 572–73, 79 S.Ct. 1335, 3 L.Ed.2d 1434 (1959); see also Mangold, 77 F.3d at 1447–48 (concluding that official immunity attaches to discretionary governmental functions even when they have been delegated to the private sector); cf. Boyle v. United Techs. Corp., 487 U.S. 500, 512, 108 S.Ct. 2510, 101 L.Ed.2d 442 (1988) (finding that "[i]t makes little sense to" hold government contractor liable for design defects in military equipment when government would have been shielded from liability had it produced the defective equipment itself). "Even though private persons under contract with the government act only partly in the public sphere, the public interest may demand that immunity protect them to the same extent that it protects government employees." Mangold, 77 F.3d at 1447.

The investigation and reporting of possible Medicare fraud is precisely the type of delegated discretionary function that the public interest requires to be protected by immunity. Medicare fraud exacts an enormous toll on the public fisc—estimated losses from fraud and other improper Medicare payments exceed $20 billion a year. See Department of Health and Human Services, CFO Audit Action, 1998 WL 213154 (Apr. 24, 1998). The carriers and fiscal intermediaries that administer the millions of Medicare claims filed annually are indispensable components of the governmental program and are in a unique position to combat the drain on public resources caused by fraudulent claims. See Group Health Inc., 739 F.Supp. at 933 ("HHS and the Secretary rely heavily on the participation of fiscal intermediaries, who possess accounting and health care expertise, in order to efficiently administer the [Medicare] program."); see generally

United States v. Erika, Inc., 456 U.S. 201, 203, 208 n. 11, 102 S.Ct. 1650, 72 L.Ed.2d 12 (1982) (discussing efficiency of having private insurance companies pay Medicare claims and volume of Medicare claims). The public interest in having Medicare fraud detected and prevented would be thwarted if these non-government entities, who have no personal financial interest in detecting or preventing Medicare fraud, were to find themselves facing damages suits for their efforts in doing so. See 42 U.S.C. § 1395t; cf. Friedman, 836 F.Supp. at 265 n. 2 (noting that carriers have "no financial stake in whether a claim is denied or approved because any payment for claims is made from the [Federal Supplementary Medical Insurance Trust Fund]").

* * *

CONCLUSION

We hold that a private insurance company acting as a fiscal intermediary or carrier on behalf of the United States in the administration of a Medicare program is entitled to official immunity for claims that arise out of the performance of its duty to investigate and report possible fraud. Accordingly, the judgment of the district court dismissing claims brought against Empire for investigating and reporting Pani for fraud is AFFIRMED.

Notes and Questions

1. This opinion reflects the large role in Medicare law of the fiscal intermediary or carrier such as Empire Blue Cross Blue Shield in this case. Note that it is no accident that a "Blue Cross Blue Shield" entity fills this role; the original Medicare statute in 1964 envisioned such preexisting carriers as the model for what would handle the new federal program's needs, and to an amazing degree that has continued even as the Medicare program has grown enormously in scale. In some respects, the medical provider may well look on the carrier in the way that some government contractors may look at their administrative contracting officer, namely, as the decision-maker on what they will be paid to do.

2. Note how close the carrier comes to the status of a governmental entity itself - much closer than the typical government contractor. As the opinion states, the carrier acts as an "adjunct" to the government and carries out a "traditional government function," protected by government indemnification agreements and, pursuant to this opinion, by official immunity. What are the other consequences for the carrier's having so large a public role? If the carrier has some of the functions and protections of contracting officers or at least of the auditors and other personnel assisting contracting officers, to what extent should the carrier have the legal restrictions surrounding contracting officers?

3. For a discussion of Medicare contracting with another set of contractors to ferret out fraud and abuse, see Richard J. Webber, *Medicare Integrity Program: Health Care Financing Administration Readies Its First Competitive Solicitation*, 33 Procurement Lawyer, Spring 1998, at 3.

2. Medicare: Hospital

The evolution of Medicare pricing has brought Medicare hospital payment to sophistication of a kind resembling regular government procurement. In brief, Medicare

Part A requires providers like hospitals to enter into a contract with Medicare called a provider agreement. Provider agreements impose elaborate conditions of participation. 42 U.S.C. §1395cc. Providers receive payment under a complex system derived from the 1960s and 1970s when pricing was simple—Medicare virtually paid what the hospitals charged— that has adapted only somewhat to the new pricing system after the 1980s, when HCFA controls pricing.

To understand Medicare hospital payment, start with the evolution in the pricing systems, as summarized in the following segment:

Payment and Delivery Systems

From: Charles Tiefer, "Budgetized" Health Entitlements
and the Fiscal Constitution,
33 Harv. J. Legis. 411, 449-451 (1996)

The current provider payment system, which constitutes the core of modern federal health insurance finance, arose and developed almost wholly through provisions in budget reconciliation bills. Medicare and Medicaid initially employed retrospective payment systems, uder which the government reimbursed providers retrospectively for their actual costs. This funding system contributed to the explosion of health care costs since it gave providers incentives to charge more, to control costs little, and to increase their incomes and profits * * *

During the 1980s and early 1990s, Congress authorized the change from retrospective to prospective payment systems for several programs. Under the Boren Amendment to reconciliation bills in 1980 and 1981, Congress allowed states to operate their Medicaid programs under prospective payment systems, in which states could decide prospectively what rates to pay providers for particular kinds of services. Pursuant to the 1983 Social Security legislation, Medicare hospital reimbursement switched to a prospective payment system, known generally as Diagnosis Related Groups ("DRGs"). Through reconciliation bills during the late 1980s, Medicare doctror reimbursement switched to a prospective payment system known as the Medicare Fee System, or MFS.

Prospective payment has been considered a successful health care cost control policy. It discourages providers from running up consts by reimbursing at prospectively set rates. The existing prospective rate-setting system allows Congress to make savings simply by legislating rate reductions.

Claims Payment

Although the pricing system changed greatly after the 1980s, the system for payment of claims, which is the focus of legal practice interest, has adapted only somewhat. Hospitals' claims get submitted, processed, and paid in what could be summarized as three stages: claims for DRG services, annual cost reports, and audits. Take, for example, a brief inpatient hospitalization of a Medicare beneficiary for an operation. The prospective payment system (PPS) for DRGs allows hospitals to submit claims soon after they render the services. Thus, a hospital would submit the bill for the operation, priced according to the DRG system, to its fiscal intermediary soon after the operation and the fiscal intermediary would process and pay it.

At the end of a year, the hospital submits an enormous form, its annual "cost report." This summarizes the services for which it has already billed under the DRG system. It also provides information on various costs which HCFA still reimburses apart from the DRG pricing system. The Supreme Court's *Guernsey* opinion below treats one of these types of costs, namely, certain kinds of capital costs. Other elements paid on this annual basis include hospital units excluded from PPS, like psychiatric and rehabilitation units, and other types of costs not handled through DRGs, such as the costs of graduate medical education which Medicare agrees to pay. Again, the fiscal intermediary processes and pays the net balance owed by the Medicare system to the hospital.

Ultimately, an audit occurs of the cost report. That audit may disallow some of the claims submitted by the hospital. The *Consumer Health Services* case illustrates one of the kinds of legal conundrums that arise during this multi-stage claims process: what is the status of the amounts already paid by the fiscal intermediary to the hospital if hospital bankruptcy intervenes?

Another kind of legal conundrum arises from the system of hospital claims payment, illuminated by the *Columbia Health Care* case. Health care law imposes many conditions and duties on providers, much as government contract law imposes many conditions and duties on contractors. Does the provider lose the right to payment by failing to meet some of those conditions and duties? The conditions at issue in that case have particular interest for lawyers for they do not concern some esoteric medical standard, but the "Stark laws," a set of conflict-of-interest rules imposed by Congress on health care providers. Government contract lawyers will recognize the *Columbia* case as part of questions that have often arisen with regular government contracting, namely, what is the impact upon the right to payment of transgressions of ethics rules regarding conflicts-of-interest, self-dealing, kickbacks, and the like.

Donna E. Shalala, Secretary of Health and Human Services v. Guernsey Memorial Hospital

No. 93-1251. Supreme Court of the United States 514 U.S. 87.
Decided March 6, 1995.

Justice KENNEDY delivered the opinion of the Court.

In this case a health care provider challenges a Medicare reimbursement determination by the Secretary of Health and Human Services. What begins as a rather conventional accounting problem raises significant questions respecting the interpretation of the Secretary's regulations and her authority to resolve certain reimbursement issues by adjudication and interpretive rules, rather than by regulations that address all accounting questions in precise detail.

The particular dispute concerns whether the Medicare regulations require reimbursement according to generally accepted accounting principles (GAAP) * * *

I

Respondent Guernsey Memorial Hospital issued bonds in 1972 and 1982 to fund capital improvements. In 1985, the Hospital refinanced its bonded debt by issuing new bonds. Although the refinancing will result in an estimated $12 million saving in debt service costs, the transaction did result in an accounting loss, sometimes referred to as an advance refunding or defeasance loss, of $672,581. The Hospital determined that it was entitled to Medicare reimbursement for about $314,000 of the loss. The total allowable amount of the loss is not in issue, but its timing is. The Hospital contends it is entitled to full reimbursement in one year, the year of the refinancing; the Secretary contends the loss must be amortized over the life of the old bonds.

The Secretary's position is in accord with an informal Medicare reimbursement guideline. See U.S.Dept. of Health and Human Services, Medicare Provider Reimbursement Manual §233 (Mar. 1993) (PRM). PRM §233 does not purport to be a regulation and has not been adopted pursuant to the notice-and-comment procedures of the Administrative Procedure Act. The fiscal intermediary relied on §233 and determined that the loss had to be amortized. The Provider Reimbursement Review Board disagreed, see App. to Pet. for Cert. 54a, but the Administrator of the Health Care Financing Administration reversed the Board's decision, see id., at 40a. In the District Court the Secretary's position was sustained, see Guernsey Memorial Hospital v. Sullivan, 796 F.Supp. 283 (SD Ohio 1992), but the Court of Appeals reversed, see Guernsey Memorial Hospital v. Secretary of HHS, 996 F.2d 830 (CA6 1993). * * *

We granted certiorari, 511 U.S. 1016, 114 S.Ct. 1395, 128 L.Ed.2d 69 (1994), and now reverse.

II

Under the Medicare reimbursement scheme at issue here, participating hospitals furnish services to program beneficiaries and are reimbursed by the Secretary through fiscal intermediaries. See 42 U.S.C. §§1395g and 1395h (1988 and Supp. V). Hospitals are reimbursed for "reasonable costs," defined by the statute as "the cost actually incurred, excluding therefrom any part of incurred cost found to be unnecessary in the efficient delivery of needed health services." §1395x(v)(1)(A). The Medicare statute authorizes the Secretary to promulgate regulations "establishing the method or methods to be used" for determining reasonable costs, directing her in the process to "consider, among other things, the principles generally applied by national organizations or established prepayment organizations (which have developed such principles) in computing" reimbursement amounts. Ibid.

The Secretary has promulgated, and updated on an annual basis, regulations establishing the methods for determining reasonable cost reimbursement. See Good Samaritan Hospital v. Shalala, 508 U.S. 402, —— , 113 S.Ct. 2151, 2155, 124 L.Ed.2d 368 (1993). The relevant provisions can be found within 42 CFR pt. 413 (1993). Respondent contends that two of these regulations, §§413.20(a) and 413.24, mandate reimbursement according to GAAP, and the Secretary counters that neither does.

A

Section 413.20(a) provides as follows:

"The principles of cost reimbursement require that providers maintain sufficient financial records and statistical data for proper determination of costs payable under the program. Standardized definitions, accounting, statistics, and reporting practices that are widely accepted in the hospital and related fields are followed. Changes in these practices and systems will not be required in order to determine costs payable under the principles of reimbursement. Essentially the methods of determining costs payable under Medicare involve making use of data available from the institution's basis accounts, as usually maintained, to arrive at equitable and proper payment for services to beneficiaries."

Assuming, arguendo, that the "[s]tandardized definitions, accounting, statistics, and reporting practices" referred to by the regulation refer to GAAP, that nevertheless is just the beginning, not the end, of the inquiry. The decisive question still remains: Who is it that "follow[s]" GAAP, and for what purposes? The Secretary's view is that §413.20(a) ensures the existence of adequate provider records but does not dictate her own reimbursement determinations. We are persuaded that the Secretary's reading is correct.

Section 413.20(a) sets forth its directives in an ordered progression. The first sentence directs that providers must maintain records that are sufficient for proper determination of costs. It does not say the records are conclusive of the entire reimbursement process. The second sentence makes it clear to providers that standardized accounting practices are followed. The third sentence reassures providers that changes in their recordkeeping practices and systems are not required in order to determine what costs the provider can recover when principles of reimbursement are applied to the provider's raw cost data. That sentence makes a distinction between recordkeeping practices and systems on one hand and principles of reimbursement on the other. The last sentence confirms the distinction, for it contemplates that a provider's basic financial information is organized according to GAAP as a beginning point from which the Secretary "arrive[s] at equitable and proper payment for services." This is far different from saying that GAAP is by definition an equitable and proper measure of reimbursement.

* * *

The regulations' description of the fiscal intermediary's role underscores this interpretation. The regulations direct the intermediary to consult and assist providers in interpreting and applying the principles of Medicare reimbursement to generate claims for reimbursable costs, §413.20(b), suggesting that a provider's own determination of its claims involves more than handing over its existing cost reports. The regulations permit initial acceptance of reimbursable cost claims, unless there are obvious errors or inconsistencies, in order to expedite payment. §413.64(f)(2). When a subsequent, more thorough audit follows, it may establish that adjustments are necessary. Ibid.; see also §§421.100(a), (c). This sequence as well is consistent with the Secretary's view that a provider's cost accounting systems are only the first step in the ultimate determination of reimbursable costs.

* * *

B

The Secretary's reading of her regulations is consistent with the Medicare statute. Rather than requiring adherence to GAAP, the statute merely instructs the Secretary, in establishing the methods for determining reimbursable costs, to "consider, among other things, the principles generally applied by national organizations or established prepayment organizations (which have developed such principles) in computing the amount of payment... to providers of services." 42 U.S.C. §1395x(v)(1)(A).

* * * The regulations are comprehensive and intricate in detail, addressing matters such as limits on cost reimbursement, apportioning costs to Medicare services, and the specific treatment of numerous particular costs. As of 1993, these regulations consumed some 620 pages of the Code of Federal Regulations.

As to particular reimbursement details not addressed by her regulations, the Secretary relies upon an elaborate adjudicative structure which includes the right to review by the Provider Reimbursement Review Board, and, in some instances, the Secretary, as well as judicial review in federal district court of final agency action. 42 U.S.C.

§1395oo(f)(1); see Bethesda Hospital Assn. v. Bowen, 485 U.S. 399, 400–401, 108 S.Ct. 1255, 1256–1257, 99 L.Ed.2d 460 (1988). * * *

III

We also believe it was proper for the Secretary to issue a guideline or interpretive rule in determining that defeasance losses should be amortized. * * *

Although one-time recognition in the initial year might be the better approach where the question is how best to portray a loss so that investors can appreciate in full a company's financial position, see APB Opinion 26, ¶¶4-5, reprinted at App. 64, the Secretary has determined in PRM §233 that amortization is appropriate to ensure that Medicare only reimburse its fair share. The Secretary must calculate how much of a provider's total allowable costs are attributable to Medicare services, see 42 CFR §§413.5(a), 413.9(a) and (c)(3) (1993), which entails calculating what proportion of the provider's services were delivered to Medicare patients, §§413.50 and 413.53. This ratio is referred to as the provider's "Medicare utilization." App. to Pet. for Cert. 49a. In allocating a provider's total allowable costs to Medicare, the Secretary must guard against various contingencies. The percentage of a hospital's patients covered by Medicare may change from year to year; or the provider may drop from the Medicare program altogether. Either will cause the hospital's Medicare utilization to fluctuate.

Given the undoubted fact that Medicare utilization will not be an annual constant, the Secretary must strive to assure that costs associated with patient services provided over time be spread, to avoid distortions in reimbursement. As the provider's yearly Medicare utilization becomes ascertainable, the Secretary is able to allocate costs with accuracy and the program can bear its proportionate share. Proper reimbursement requires proper timing. Should the Secretary reimburse in one year costs in fact attributable to a span of years, the reimbursement will be determined by the provider's Medicare utilization for that one year, not for later years. This leads to distortion. If the provider's utilization rate changes or if the provider drops from the program altogether the Secretary will have reimbursed up front an amount other than that attributable to Medicare services. The result would be cross-subsidization, id., at 50a, which the Act forbids. 42 U.S.C. §1395x(v)(1)(A)(I).

* * *

[The dissenting opinion is omitted.]

Notes and Questions

1. Note the general structure of policy implementation and dispute resolution for Medicare hospital payment issues indicated in the opinion. HCFA issues both regulations-which, the opinion casually notes, fill up 620 pages in the Code of Federal Regulations, suggesting an impressive quantity of material for lawyers to work on-and other forms of guidance, namely, the HCFA Manuals. Hospitals submit their claims to their fiscal intermediary. If disputes arise, in certain circumstances the hospitals can take them to the Prover Reimbursement Review Board, and, ultimately, to the courts. The PRRB had far more work under the pre-DRG system in which all payments to hospitals consisted of cost reimbursements, than under the DRG system in which most (but not all) issues of pricing get resolved by uniform national rate-setting mechanisms.

2. Also note how much the *Guernsey* case turns on accounting issues. Recall the chapter on cost issues and its criteria of allowability, reasonableness, allocability, and Cost Accounting Standards (CAS). The issue raised in this case is the sufficiency of GAAP (generally accepted accounting principles), as argued by claimants, versus the necessity of accounting methods more focused on assuring that payments from the Treasury only go for what Congress has agreed, as argued by the government. This same issue arises in regular government contracting, as to the sufficiency of GAAP, as argued by contractors, versus the necessity of CAS. Four justices dissented in this case. Can you imagine their reasoning?

3. What is the division of labor on such issues between lawyers and accountants? Should accountants brief and argue Supreme Court cases? Should lawyers pore over hospital cost reports deciding how to allocate administrative costs between different hospital units?

4. Also note the importance in the opinion of recordkeeping requirements, reminiscent of the discussion in the chapter on cost issues of the importance there of government investigator access to a broad range of contractor records. Cost-reimbursement systems, whether in regular government contracting or in health care contracting, call for massive recordkeeping and massive government (or fiscal intermediary) review of those records. The "form" for a hospital's annual cost report today covers several reams of papers when printed out, and it must be distributed, filled out, and returned in electronically-readable format for the system to cope.

Would doing away totally with massive recordkeeping and record-review produce the improved efficiencies that resulted from the successful deregulations of the 1980s such as those of transportation and energy rate regulation? Or, would doing away with such mechanisms of supervision of claims drawn out of the Treasury produce the scandalous waste, abuse, and fraud that resulted from the unsuccessful deregulation of the 1980s, namely, the effective deregulation of the savings and loan industry? One answer is that the shift to date, away from retroactive reimbursement of "reasonable" hospital charges and toward forward and fixed-pricing through DRGs, has been a great success story, taming what loomed as a monster of paperwork, disputation, and zooming charges.

United States ex rel. James M. Thompson, Plaintiff-Appellant, v. Columbia/HCA Healthcare Corporation, et al., Defendants-Appellees

No. 96-40868. United States Court of Appeals,
Fifth Circuit. 125 F.3d 899. Oct. 23, 1997.

Before REYNALDO G. GARZA, HIGGINBOTHAM and DAVIS, Circuit Judges.

W. EUGENE DAVIS, Circuit Judge:

Relator, James M. Thompson, M.D., a physician in private practice in Corpus Christi, Texas, brought this qui tam action pursuant to the federal False Claims Act ("FCA"), 31 U.S.C. §§3729 et seq., against defendants Columbia/HCA Healthcare Corporation and certain affiliated entities (collectively, "Columbia/HCA") and Corpus Christi Bay Area Surgery, Ltd. The district court dismissed Thompson's complaint for failure to state a claim under Rule 12(b)(6) of the Federal Rules of Civil Procedure. For the reasons set out below, we affirm in part, vacate in part, and remand for further proceedings.

I.

In his second amended complaint, at issue in this appeal, Thompson alleged that defendants submitted false or fraudulent claims under the FCA by submitting Medicare claims for services rendered in violation of the Medicare anti-kickback statute,[1] 42 U.S.C. §1320a-7b, and two versions of a self-referral statute, 42 U.S.C. §1395nn, commonly known as the "Stark" laws after the statute's congressional sponsor, United States Representative Fortney H. "Pete" Stark. He further alleged that defendants made false statements to obtain payment of false or fraudulent claims in violation of the FCA by falsely certifying in annual cost reports that the Medicare services identified therein were provided in compliance with the laws and regulations regarding the provision of healthcare services. Finally, Thompson alleged that defendants violated the FCA by submitting Medicare claims for medically unnecessary services.

The district court granted defendants' motions to dismiss Thompson's second amended complaint for failure to state a claim. The court held that Thompson's allegations that defendants submitted Medicare claims for services rendered in violation of the anti-kickback statute and the Stark laws were insufficient, by themselves, to state a claim for relief under the FCA. The court also held that Thompson's allegations that defendants falsely certified in annual cost reports that the Medicare services identified therein were provided in compliance with the laws and regulations regarding the provision of healthcare services were insufficient to state a claim for release under the FCA. The court concluded that these allegations were insufficient because Thompson had not alleged that defendants submitted false certifications to obtain payment of false or fraudulent claims, i.e., claims or claim amounts that the government would not have paid but for the alleged fraud. Finally, the court held that Thompson's allegations that defendants submitted claims for medically unnecessary services were insufficient to state a claim because he failed to plead his allegations with particularity as required by Rule 9(b) of the Federal Rules of Civil Procedure.

II.

* * *

The FCA provides, in relevant part:

(a) Liability for certain acts. — Any person who —

---

1. Thompson alleged that defendants violated the Medicare anti-kickback statute by inducing physicians to refer Medicare patients to Columbia/HCA hospitals in the following ways:

(cont'd from page before) (1) Offering physicians preferential opportunities not available to the general public to obtain equity interests in Columbia/HCA healthcare operations through partnership or corporate structure arrangements;

(2) Offering loans or assistance in obtaining loans to physicians to finance capital investments in equity interests in Columbia/HCA entities;

(3) Making payments disguised as "consultation fees" to physicians in order to guarantee on a risk-free basis their capital investments in equity interests in Columbia/HCA entities;

(4) Paying physicians "consultation fees," "rent" or other monies;

(5) Providing physicians with free or reduced rent for office space near Columbia/HCA hospitals in facilities owned or operated by Columbia/HCA;

(6) Offering physicians free or reduced-rate vacations and other recreational opportunities;

(7) Offering physicians free or reduced-cost medical training;

(8) Providing physicians with income guarantees; and

(9) Granting physicians superior or exclusive rights to perform procedures in particular fields of practice.

(1) knowingly presents, or causes to be presented, to an officer or employee of the United States Government...a false or fraudulent claim for payment or approval...; [or]

(2) knowingly makes, uses, or causes to be made or used, a false record or statement to get a false or fraudulent claim paid or approved by the Government...

* * *

is liable to the United States Government for a civil penalty of not less than $5,000 and not more than $10,000, plus 3 times the amount of damages which the Government sustains because of the act of that person....

31 U.S.C. §3729(a)(1), (2).

A. Thompson's Claims Predicated on Statutory Violations

Thompson alleged that defendants violated the FCA by submitting Medicare claims for services rendered in violation of the Medicare anti-kickback statute and the Stark laws. The Medicare anti-kickback statute prohibits (1) the solicitation or receipt of remuneration in return for referrals of Medicare patients, and (2) the offer or payment of remuneration to induce such referrals. 42 U.S.C. §1320a-7b(b).

The first Stark law, commonly known as "Stark I," was in effect between January 1, 1992 and December 31, 1994. Stark I prohibited physicians from referring Medicare patients to an entity for clinical laboratory services if the referring physician had a nonexempt "financial relationship" with such entity. 42 U.S.C.A. §1395nn(a)(1)(A) (West 1992). Stark I also prohibited the entity from presenting or causing to be presented a Medicare claim for services furnished pursuant to a prohibited referral. 42 U.S.C.A. §1395nn(a)(1)(B) (West 1992). With certain exceptions, "financial relationship" was defined as (1) an ownership or investment interest in the entity, or (2) a compensation arrangement with the entity. 42 U.S.C.A. §1395nn(a)(2) (West 1992). Stark I expressly prohibited payment of Medicare claims for services rendered in violation of its provisions. 42 U.S.C.A. §1395nn(g)(1) (West 1992).

Stark II became effective January 1, 1995, and prohibits physicians from referring Medicare patients to an entity for certain "designated health services," including inpatient and outpatient hospital services, if the referring physician has a nonexempt "financial relationship" with such entity. 42 U.S.C. §1395nn(a)(1), (h)(6). Like its predecessor, Stark II provides that the entity may not present or cause to be presented a Medicare claim for services furnished pursuant to a prohibited referral, and expressly prohibits payment of Medicare claims for services rendered in violation of its provisions. 42 U.S.C. §1395nn(a)(1), (g)(1).

We agree with the district court that claims for services rendered in violation of a statute do not necessarily constitute false or fraudulent claims under the FCA. In United States ex rel. Weinberger v. Equifax, Inc., 557 F.2d 456, 460-61 (5th Cir.1977), we held that claims submitted by a government contractor who allegedly violated the Anti-Pinkerton Act did not necessarily constitute false or fraudulent claims under the FCA. In so holding, we observed that the FCA is not an enforcement device for the Anti-Pinkerton Act. We recognized, however, that the FCA "interdicts material misrepresentations made to qualify for government privileges or services." Id. at 461.

The Ninth Circuit has taken a similar approach concerning the scope of the FCA. In United States ex rel. Hopper v. Anton, 91 F.3d 1261, 1266 (9th Cir.1996), the court held that "[v]iolations of laws, rules, or regulations alone do not create a cause of action under the FCA." The court concluded, however, that false certifications of compliance create liability under the FCA when certification is a prerequisite to obtaining a government benefit.

Thus, where the government has conditioned payment of a claim upon a claimant's certification of compliance with, for example, a statute or regulation, a claimant submits a false or fraudulent claim when he or she falsely certifies compliance with that statute or regulation.

Thompson alleged that, as a condition of their participation in the Medicare program, defendants were required to certify in annual cost reports that the services identified therein were provided in compliance with the laws and regulations regarding the provision of healthcare services. He further alleged that defendants falsely certified that the services identified in their annual cost reports were provided in compliance with such laws and regulations. Thus, Thompson fairly alleged that the government's payment of Medicare claims is conditioned upon certification of compliance with the laws and regulations regarding the provision of healthcare services, including the anti-kickback statute and the Stark laws, and that defendants submitted false claims by falsely certifying that the services identified in their annual cost reports were rendered in compliance with such laws and regulations.

Columbia/HCA argues that the certifications of compliance contained in annual cost reports are not a prerequisite to payment of Medicare claims because Medicare claims are submitted for payment shortly after services have been rendered and well before annual cost reports are filed. Thompson contends that such certifications are indeed a prerequisite to payment because the retention of any payment received prior to the submission of an annual cost report is conditioned on the certification of compliance contained therein. We are unable to determine from the record before us whether, or to what extent, payment for services identified in defendants' annual cost reports was conditioned on defendants' certifications of compliance. We therefore deny defendants' 12(b)(6) motions as they relate to this issue and remand to the district court for further factual development.

Thompson also contends that, in any event, claims for services rendered in violation of the Stark laws are, in and of themselves, false or fraudulent claims under the FCA. Thompson bases his contention on provisions in the Stark laws expressly prohibiting payment for services rendered in violation of their terms. In holding that Thompson failed to allege a violation of the FCA, the district court did not specifically consider this contention. Because the district court must determine whether the government's payment of defendants' Medicare claims was conditioned on defendants' certifications of compliance in their annual cost reports, we will give the district court the opportunity to consider this argument on remand as well.

* * *

Notes and Questions

1. What do the Stark laws prohibit? What did Columbia allegedly do to violate them? The opinion describes the violations, if you will excuse the word, clinically. Why did the public get outraged at the practices prohibited by the Stark laws? Studies suggested that physicians prescribed more laboratory tests, and probably more of everything, when the physicians had a financial interest in the entity that would do the work. Yet, physicians clearly had other things to do when telling patients to get some frightening labora-

tory tests than to explain the complexities of such financial interests, and even if they had tried, the patients, too, have their attention on other matters. So, patients end up submitting to medical procedures that statistically might have been skipped if not for some undisclosed financial benefits flowing to the physicians involved. On the other hand, the hospital does perform the medical procedure and no proof was being offered, in a case based purely on a Stark law theory, of anything wrong with the particular prescriptions for the particular medical procedures. In any event, Congress enacted the explicit Stark laws and made obedience to them a condition of payment. Should the Stark-violating hospital be paid? Should fraud enforcement apply?

2. Can you tease apart the variety of arguments on each side? Try these:

"Government" (in this case, key tam relator)	Columbia
Columbia (allegedly) violated the anti-kickback statute, Stark I, and Stark II	not every statutory violation is fraud
Columbia must certify compliance with these statutes on its annual cost reports ["2552's"]	Medicare pays when billed [by "UB-92"] after each service, not on the annual cost report
Stark I and II expressly prohibit payments in violation	full, satisfactory services were rendered. Unfair to pay multiple damages, or fines.
(Qui tam remedy exists so "whistleblowers" can sue)	(Leave it to the United States government to enforce the Stark laws)

3. Does the need for conditions on payment like those in the Stark laws against conflicts of interest arise from the special nature of health care? Or from the fact that payment comes from the federal government?

United States of America, Appellant, v. Consumer Health Services of America, Inc. et al., Appellees

No. 96-5148. United States Court of Appeals,
District of Columbia Circuit. 108 F.3d 390 Decided March 18, 1997.

Before: SILBERMAN, SENTELLE, and RANDOLPH, Circuit Judges. Opinion for the Court filed by Circuit Judge SILBERMAN. Concurring opinion filed by Circuit Judge SENTELLE.

SILBERMAN, Circuit Judge:

The United States appeals the district court's affirmance of the bankruptcy court's denial of its motion to deduct prior Medicare overpayments from reimbursement otherwise due the appellees. We reverse.

Consumer Health Services of America was a provider of home health care services. In 1976, it signed a Medicare provider agreement that qualified it to participate in Medicare Part A, which compensates providers of certain health care services for the elderly in accordance with regulations promulgated by the Secretary of Health and Human Services. To ensure that Medicare service providers such as Consumer are paid promptly, the Medicare statute provides for periodic payments for services on an estimated basis prior to a determination of the exact amount of reimbursement due for those services. These interim payments, to be made not less often than monthly, are calculated and made by a "fiscal intermediary" designated by the Secretary. At the end of each "reporting period" (the length of which is currently set at one year), the intermediary audits the provider to determine whether the provider has been over or underpaid, and by how much. While the provider is obliged to submit its "cost report" to the intermediary within five months of the close of a cost period, the intermediary must only complete the audit within a reasonable time.

When the audit is completed, the service provider is subject to a "retroactive adjustment." If the provider has been underpaid, it receives a "final adjustment" amounting to the difference between "the reimbursement due" and "the payments made." If the provider has been overpaid, it need not necessarily remit the balance of the overpayment immediately. Although the intermediary may suspend a provider's authorization to participate in Medicare if the provider's account is out of balance, the regulations also provide for an arrangement by which the intermediary and the provider may "enter[ ] into an agreement...for liquidation of the overpayment." The agreement envisaged by this regulation is quite simple: the provider will keep performing Medicare services, and the intermediary will deduct from its periodic payments amounts to be applied to liquidation of the prior overpayment. In determining how much to deduct, the intermediary balances two objectives: it wants to liquidate the debt, but it also wants to ensure that the provider has sufficient incentive to continue performing needed services.

In 1984, Consumer's fiscal intermediary concluded its audit for 1981-82 and determined that it had overpaid Consumer by approximately $81,000. Pursuant to an "agreement...for liquidation of the overpayment," the intermediary began deducting from Consumer's periodic payments amounts necessary to recover the excess. In 1987, Consumer petitioned to reorganize its business under Chapter 11 of the Bankruptcy Code. At that time, Consumer still owed over $32,000 on the 1981-82 overpayments. Operating under Chapter 11, Consumer continued to provide Medicare services and to receive periodic payments. Its intermediary did not, however, continue to deduct the amounts attributable to the 1981–82 overpayment, because it was uncertain concerning the legal issue in this case—whether such deductions would violate the Bankruptcy Code's automatic stay of actions to recover pre-petition debts. After a little more than a year of operation under Chapter 11, Consumer converted its bankruptcy case into a liquidation proceeding under Chapter 7, and it submitted claims for reimbursement for Medicare services performed during the period it was operating under Chapter 11. Assuming no deduction for the 1981–82 overpayments, the intermediary estimated that these claims amounted to about $15,000. The government then brought a motion in the bankruptcy court requesting "that the court affirm [its] right to reduce payments due to account for prior overpayments."

For reasons not apparent from the record, the matter was pending before the bankruptcy court for six years, and then, after the Third Circuit decided a virtually identical case, see In re University Medical Center, 973 F.2d 1065 (3d Cir.1992), the bankruptcy court denied the government's motion. The court assumed the Bankruptcy Code's automatic stay applied to the government's claim for the pre-petition overpayments, and so it saw the issue as whether the government was entitled "to make recoupment" on the provider agreement between Consumer and the Secretary. The court characterized the agreement as an "executory contract," i.e., a contract on which performance is due from both parties, and it recognized that if Consumer could be said to have "assumed" the contract, "the contract would be enforceable... and the Secretary's withholding of payments would merely be the exercise of a contractual right." The court rejected, however, the argument that Consumer's post-petition provision of Medicare services constituted assumption of the contract. It relied on the prevailing view that a debtor operating under Chapter 11 cannot "assume" an executory contract without formal approval by the bankruptcy court, which the parties agreed had been neither sought nor received. The court also rejected the government's claim for "equitable recoupment," under which a creditor may deduct a pre-petition debt from payments for post-petition services, if (and only if) the debt and the services are part of a single "transaction." According to the court, under the Medicare statute and regulations, "the amount due the provider for one year [i.e., the pre-petition debt] stems from services completely unrelated to those provided in later years [i.e., the post-petition services]." It thus concluded that the government's claim for overpayments made in 1981-82 and calculated in 1984 was not part of the same transaction as Consumer's claim for compensation for services performed in 1987–88. Finally, relying on NLRB v. Bildisco & Bildisco, 465 U.S. 513, 104 S.Ct. 1188, 79 L.Ed.2d 482 (1984), the bankruptcy court determined that even though performance under the provider agreement did not amount to assumption of it, Consumer was still entitled to the "reasonable value" of the Medicare services it provided while operating under Chapter 11.

The government appealed to the district court, which affirmed in a one-sentence order embracing the reasoning of the bankruptcy court. This appeal followed.

II.

The government's primary contention is that the bankruptcy court failed to recognize that the amount of Medicare's substantive liability for any services rendered (including those rendered by a debtor operating under Chapter 11) must by statute take into account prior overpayments. In the alternative, the government argues that it should be able to deduct the overpayments under the doctrine of equitable recoupment, since those overpayments and the post-petition services were part of a single transaction. We see these two arguments not as true "alternatives" but rather as closely related.

The Medicare statute provides that the amount due for Medicare services be calculated as follows:

> The Secretary shall periodically determine the amount which should be paid under this part to each provider of services with respect to the services furnished by it, and the provider of services shall be paid, at such time or times as the Secretary believes appropriate (but not less often than monthly) and prior to audit or settlement... the amounts so determined, with necessary adjustments on account of previously made overpayments or underpayments. 42 U.S.C. §1395g(a) (emphases added).

The statute quite clearly says that the government is liable for particular Medicare services only in the amount that "shall be paid," and that amount consists of what the Secretary has determined "should be paid" for those services, less adjustments for prior overpayments. The bankruptcy court's decision, which did not focus on the statute's actual language, had the effect of eliminating from the statute the words "with necessary adjustments on account of previously made overpayments" when a provider seeks the protection of the bankruptcy law.

* * *

We think the Third Circuit, and the bankruptcy court below, overlooked the importance of the language of the substantive Medicare statute. Those courts assumed that the amount due on post-petition services was to be determined by the regulations detailing how much a provider normally gets for the services rendered. Only then, after that determination, did the courts inquire into whether the prior overpayments could be deducted from the amount due. And in completing that inquiry, the courts looked to principles governing pre-assumption performance of executory contracts by debtors operating under Chapter 11. As we have explained, we disagree with the premise that the "amount due" should be calculated with reference to the fee schedule set out in the regulations. That fee schedule only determines what "should be paid"; the amount actually due under the statute is the amount which "shall be paid"— which includes "necessary adjustments for prior overpayments." In this case, then, the amount due is the approximately $15,000 Consumer "should be paid" for post-petition services rendered, less the "necessary" adjustment for the as-yet-unremitted overpayments. To conclude otherwise, we think, would allow the Bankruptcy Code to modify an explicit statutory scheme defining liability for particular services. Neither the trustee, the bankruptcy court, nor the Third Circuit in In re University Medical Center has offered authority for the proposition that the Bankruptcy Code can act to override an explicit statutory limitation on what the government owes for a particular service. That the limitation in question is defined by the amount the government has previously (over)paid to the provider does not, in our view, alter the analysis.

Nor does our analysis differ significantly under the doctrine of equitable recoupment, which exempts a debt from the automatic stay when the debt is inextricably tied up in the post-petition claim. See generally In re B&L Oil, 782 F.2d 155, 156 (10th Cir.1986); Howard C. Bushman III, Benefits and Burdens: Post-Petition Performance of Unassumed Executory Contracts, 5 BANKR.DEV. J. 341, 352–53 (1988).

Whether the recoupment exception applies in a particular case turns on whether the creditor's and debtor's respective claims arise out of the same "transaction," and what exactly constitutes a "transaction" is not readily apparent from the caselaw. In In re University Medical Center, the court rejected an "open-ended" definition of "transaction" in favor of a "stricter" requirement that "both debts...arise out of a single integrated transaction so that it would be inequitable for the debtor to enjoy the benefits of that transaction without also meeting its obligations." 973 F.2d at 1080–81. The court concluded that the annual account reconciliation process described above defined the scope of any single transaction under Medicare Part A. The Third Circuit thought that since the provider's account was reconciled each year, any particular pre-petition monthly payment should be thought to apply to the services rendered that month and any prior overpayment that had given rise to a "retroactive adjustment." The payment could not be construed as an "advance payment[ ]" for future services. Thus, the provider's "post-petition services were the beginning of transactions that would stretch into the future, but they were not part of the [pre-petition] transactions." 973 F.2d at 1081-82.

Even under the Third Circuit's stricter standard, we believe that Consumer's claim for post-petition services and the pre-petition overpayments qualify. Unlike the Third Circuit, we do not think the frequency of the audit appropriately defines the "transaction." The audit is simply the mechanism by which the intermediary determines whether and by how much it ought to adjust subsequent periodic payments to a particular provider. Its frequency is determined by the Secretary, presumably in the interests of an efficient reimbursement scheme; it would seem to have little to do with how one conceptualizes the relation between past overpayments and current compensation due.

It is the statute and regulations which dictate the effect of the audit on the provider's participation in Medicare. An audit is nothing more than a snapshot in time—whether it is monthly, annual, or decennial is, in our view, irrelevant.

In determining whether the pre-petition and post-petition services should be thought of as one transaction, the key to us is the Medicare statute. Since it requires the Secretary to take into account pre-petition overpayments in order to calculate a post-petition claim—as we have described above—Congress rather clearly indicated that it wanted a provider's stream of services to be considered one transaction for purposes of any claim the government would have against the provider. The Third Circuit said that "[t]he [pre-petition] overpayments...cannot be deemed advance payments for [the provider's subsequent] services." Id. at 1081. That observation, in our view, is contrary to manifest congressional intent. In sum, it does not matter whether we consider the government's claim in terms of its statutory substantive liability or in terms of the equitable recoupment doctrine. Under either analysis, the automatic stay is of no consequence. Accord In re Harmon, 188 B.R. 421, 425 (9th Cir. BAP 1995).

* * *

III.

As is apparent, our analysis is driven by the explicit statutory directive that, in compensation for its services rendered post-petition, Consumer "shall be paid" the amount the Secretary has determined it "should be paid," "with necessary adjustments on account of previously made overpayments." 42 U.S.C. §1395g(a). The amount Consumer "should be paid" is approximately $15,000. What it "shall be paid," then, turns on what adjustments are "necessary."

The government would have us decide that the "necessary" adjustment in this case is the entire outstanding balance on the 1981–82 overpayments, $32,000. Such a deduction would leave the trustee owing approximately $17,000, a debt which would presumably be treated as a run-of-the-mill pre-petition claim. The statute itself does not really mandate the government's reading, however. It is not entirely clear what Congress meant by "necessary," or, to put it another way, what is necessary in any given case may involve drawing a balance between what would be the quickest repayment to the government, and what would give the provider sufficient incentive to continue providing services. As Congress has not "spoken unambiguously to the precise issue at hand," we turn to "the agency's action under 'Step Two' of Chevron, and defer to the agency's interpretation if it represents a 'permissible construction' of the statute." Consumer Fed'n of America and Public Citizen v. U.S. Dep't of Health and Human Servs., 83 F.3d 1497, 1503 (D.C.Cir.1996) (quoting Chevron U.S.A. Inc. v. Natural Resources Defense Council, Inc., 467 U.S. 837, 842–43, 104 S.Ct. 2778, 2781–82, 81 L.Ed.2d 694 (1984)).

The Secretary's regulation permits the intermediary, in an overpayment situation, either to seek to recover the full extent of prior overpayments— threatening to suspend a provider's participation in Medicare if it does not pay—or to enter into an agreement with the provider (which is what occurred here) whereby the provider continues its services with appropriate deductions for the past overpayments. See 42 C.F.R. §405.373(a)(2). To be sure, the latter alternative forms an executory contract, but it is not to be treated as would the post-petition performance of an ordinary executory contract under bankruptcy law; it is the statute which sets forth the extent of the government's obligation—the contract only implements the timing and pace of the payment of that obligation. If we were to conclude otherwise, the Secretary might be forced to insist on a provider's immediate repayment of the full amount once the intermediary determined the government overpaid—which could jeopardize the operation of the program. We do not think that comports with the statute, which sought to protect the taxpayer's interest yet provide the Secretary with the flexibility necessary to operate the program.

On the record before us, we cannot say what the "necessary" deduction is, for the parties have not included in the record documentation explaining exactly how much the intermediary was deducting from Consumer's periodic payments to account for the 1981–82 overpayments at the time Consumer petitioned for Chapter 11. On remand, the bankruptcy court will be able to calculate the amount Consumer "shall be paid," since the intermediary can clarify what it has determined "should be paid," and the parties can supplement the record to allow the court to determine what deductions are "necessary."

* * *

The district court decision is reversed, and the case is remanded to the bankruptcy court for proceedings consistent with this opinion.

So ordered.

SENTELLE, Circuit Judge, concurring:

I concur with the majority's result and join in much of its reasoning. However, I would base the result solely on the majority's statutory rationale. That is, although I do not think the question free from doubt, I agree that the bankruptcy court in this case and the Third Circuit in In re University Medical Center, 973 F.2d 1065 (3rd Cir.1992), concluded without adequate authority that the bankruptcy code modifies the Medicare statute's explicit scheme for defining the government's liability to service providers. While any act of the bankruptcy court under the code is in a sense in breach of the source of law that gives rise to the obligation that the bankruptcy court reduces or extinguishes, this does not imply that the bankruptcy court is empowered by the code to depart from the statutory definition of the obligation in the first instance. To that extent, I think the bankruptcy court has overreached, and I concur in the reversal.

As I think the first rationale is sufficient, I do not join the majority in deciding the second question as to what constitutes a single "transaction." While I am not convinced that the majority is incorrect, neither am I convinced that it is necessary to create a precedent on that question which might arise in some other context. With that one reservation, I join the majority's opinion and result.

Notes and Questions

1. This is a 1997 remand, anticipating more proceedings to come, of a case regarding 1981–82 overpayments. How does that strike you?

2. The case alludes to "periodic estimated payments," a system of less significance in recent years as Medicare pricing and payment has evolved. Apart from that, this case illustrates the special workings of the Medicare claims payment system that continues: early submission to, and processing and payment of claims by, a fiscal intermediary; years later, audit and "necessary adjustment." How does this compare with the system in regular government contracting, for certain types of work, of early submission of requests for progress payments for processing and payment; years later, upon final delivery or completion of the work, acceptance and final payment?

3. There are two issues: (1) whether the government can deduct as an "adjustment" from later (post-petition) payments its prior overpayments; and, (2) what counts as a "necessary" adjustment. On that first issue, the court finds a great deal of guidance in the wording of the Medicare statute, 42 U.S.C. §1395g(a). What would the counter-argument be? Do the words of this provision, or anything else for that matter, suggest that Congress wrote the section to give guidance about bankruptcy? On that second issue, the court does not find so much guidance in the statute's wording and so it defers to HCFA's flexible approach. Who gets power under the court's approach to decide the division of losses between the government and the bankrupt's creditors? Did Congress, which was not specifically talking about bankruptcy, make that power allocation, or does the court decide for itself on policy grounds?

4. The case is a foray into the sub-specialty of government contracting law, namely, dealing with bankruptcy. To some extent, Congress and the procuring agencies can, and do, take precautions to safeguard the government's special interests against the vicissitudes of contractor bankruptcy. To some extent, the government has to cope with contractor bankruptcy much like private contractual parties do. What does the court identify as the government's special interest regarding bankrupt, but still-functioning health care providers? Like the sub-specialty of government contracting law dealing with intellectual property, this sub-specialty can hardly be appreciated without grounding in the other area of law at issue.

3. Medicaid and Military

Besides Medicare, the federal government funds two large systems of payment for health care. It funds Medicaid which pays for health care for the poor. Medicaid is a joint federal-state program, operating through individual programs managed by each of the fifty states. To some extent, like Medicare, it is a system by which Treasury payments flow to provider-claimants; to some extent it is, like numerous other programs of grants by the federal government to the states, a system run by states belonging to the realm of state rather than federal law. The *Krizek* opinion above deals with a health care provider for both the Medicare and Medicaid programs. For discussion of Medicaid law, see Furrow, Greaney, et al., HEALTH LAW, *supra*, chapter 14; Rosenblatt, Law & Rosenbaum, LAW AND THE AMERICAN HEALTH CARE SYSTEM, *supra*, chapter 2, section H.

The Department of Defense has two systems for procuring health care: TRICARE, a medical program for active duty personnel; and CHAMPUS, for eligible retirees and their families. To some extent, the Department of Defense buys, through TRICARE and CHAMPUS, health care the way it buys goods and services from regular government contractors; to some extent, just as Medicare and Medicaid operate as claim payment systems mimicking private insurance systems, so too does CHAMPUS. The *Total Medical Management v. U.S.* case, in the chapter on "Introduction," discusses the CHAMPUS system and illustrates its dual nature; the case concerns resistance by a Defense Department health care contractor to the introduction of pricing systems developed for Medicare.

For further discusion of Department of Defense health care procurement, see: Stephanie P. Gilson & Frank Rapoport, *What's New in Federal Health Care Contracting?*, 33 Procurement Law., Spring 1998, at 1.

THE FEDERAL GOVERNMENT AND HEALTHCARE CONTRACTORS: MAXIMIZING YOUR RESULTS WHEN PARTICIPATING IN THE FEDERAL MARKETPLACE

Frank M. Rapoport and Samantha L. Southall
Practicing Law Institute, Corporate Law and Practice Course Handbook
Series 118 PLI/Corp 267, May, 1999

I. INTRODUCTION

The Departments of Veterans Affairs ("VA") and Defense ("DoD") comprise the largest healthcare system today in the United States. In Fiscal Year 1997, the DoD spent $15.5 billion on the Defense Health Program and the VA spent $17.7 billion on medical care expenditures. These systems offer tremendous opportunities to suppliers and manufacturers of medical, surgical, pharmaceutical, and other health care supplies and equipment. Moreover, although these systems offer financially rewarding opportunities, they are also difficult to navigate and require an understanding of the law as well as careful planning. This article highlights some of the opportunities and pitfalls awaiting healthcare contractors.

II. THE DEPARTMENT OF VETERANS AFFAIRS

A. Federal Supply Schedules

The VA, by a delegation of authority from the General Services Administration, purchases the majority of its healthcare supplies through the use of the Federal Supply Schedule ("FSS"). This program permits the VA to purchase health care supplies from multiple contractors. Each contract is individually negotiated between the VA National Acquisition Center and the contractor. Moreover, the VA has begun to develop an "open season" which permits the VA to enter into contracts on an ongoing basis rather than during a specific time period.

The VA administers the following schedules:

- Medical Supplies
- Dental Equipment and Supplies
- Pharmaceuticals
- Invitro Diagnostics and Reagents
- Medical Equipment
- Pacemakers
- Antibacterial Soap
- Wheelchairs
- Cost-per-test Laboratory
- Subsistence
- New Item Introductory Schedule
- X-ray Equipment and Supplies (Including Medical/Dental X-ray Film)

Entities in addition to the VA can purchase off of a FSS contract. These entities include: DoD, the Public Health System ("PHS"), the Bureau of Prisons, State Veterans Homes with sharing agreements with a VA facility, and the Coast Guard.

B. Blanket Purchase Agreements

Contractors who enter into a FSS contract with the VA may also enter into a Blanket Purchase Agreement ("BPA"). A BPA is "a simplified method of filling anticipated repetitive needs for supplies or services by establishing 'charge accounts' with qualified sources of supply."[1] The government may use a BPA when there is a need for a wide variety of items, but the exact items, quantities, and delivery requirements are not known in advance; when there is a need for commercial source of supply for offices that do not have purchase authority; or to reduce the administrative burden of writing numerous purchase orders. In a BPAs, the contractors may offer additional volume-based discounts. Moreover, the contractor can enter into a BPA with a VA hospital, one of the Veterans Integrated Service Networks ("VISNs")[3], or the entire system.

C. The National Formulary

During the past few years, the VA has begun to standardize the procurement of pharmaceutical and medical/surgical items in order to achieve concentrated buying power. Because the VA expends nearly $1 billion in the procurement of pharmaceuticals each year, "the VA seeks to accomplish its 'greater goals of quality care, access, customer service, and cost efficiency' by creating 'national formularies' for various drugs." [FN5] The National Formulary program offers contractors the opportunity to be the sole supplier of one product to be used nationally. The VA contends that this standardization will reduce the costs of procurement.

The VA has awarded several national contracts, including contracts for H2 Antagonists, LHRH Antagonists, Proton Pump Inhibitors, HMG CoA Reductase Inhibitors, ACE Inhibitors, Alpha Blockers, Nifedipine, and Diltiazem. A national contract is typically for one-year with four one-year options.

A recent development may have lasting effects upon contractors. In May 1998, the DoD announced its Basic Core Formulary ("BCF"). The DoD stated its version of the National Formulary would involve collaborating with the VA. Indeed, the recent procurements for Diltiazem and Albuteron were a joint effort of the DoD and VA. It remains to be seem whether this is a continuing trend in government procurement.

D. Prime Vendor Program

Both the VA and DoD maintain Prime Vendor programs. A prime vendor is a contractor who acts as a distributor on behalf of the government, taking orders from and delivering products to customers within its region. There are different prime vendors for pharmaceuticals and medical/surgical items. Contractors who hold a FSS contract or DAPA agree to permit the prime vendor to distribute their product and charge the prime vendor the agreed-upon price.

---

1. FAR 13.303-1(a).

3. As a part of its procurement efforts, the VA has created the VISN. The VA has divided the country into twenty two geographical areas, each of which has a VISN formulary. Each VISN is run by a director, CFO, and a clinical director. Moreover, each VISN has the authority to enter into a BPA with contractors based upon their FSS contract. If the VA awards a national contract, however, the national contract normally overrides any contract entered into by the individual VISN.

II. THE DEPARTMENT OF DEFENSE

A. Distribution and Pricing Agreements

Although the DoD can purchase equipment off of the FSS schedules administered by the VA, it also maintains its own procurement system through the Distribution and Pricing Agreement ("DAPA"). The Directorate of Medical Material ("Medical Directorate") located at the Defense Supply Center-Philadelphia ("DSCP") administers DAPAs. Contractors can submit a DAPA for approval on an ongoing basis and the Medical Directorate negotiates prices with the potential contractor like the VA does. The Medical Directorate examines proposed DAPAs for price reasonableness and seeks the most favored customer price under similar terms and conditions. Often, negotiations result in setting the DAPA price at the FSS contract price. The length of a DAPA is five years.

DAPAs offer more flexibility for contractors than FSS contracts. First, DAPAs does not contain a price reduction clause and does not require the maintenance of a price or discount relationship during the contract. Under DAPAs, however, the government may request additional pricing information at any time to support the negotiations and reserves the right to terminate the agreement at any time. Second, DAPAs do not contain a price adjustment clause, which entitles the government to reduce a contract price for failure to provide accurate information. Last, DAPAs may be canceled by either party for any reason with thirty days notice.

III. POTENTIAL AREAS OF VULNERABILITY

Although contracting with the government yields numerous financial benefits, it is also fraught with potential difficulties. Indeed, a complex series of regulations govern the creation and administration of government contracts. Some of the most common issues targeted by the VA and DoD Offices of Inspector General are discussed below.

A. Failure to Disclose Current, Accurate, and Complete Discount Information at the Time of Contracting

When a potential VA FSS contractor submits an offer to the government, it is required to submit a Commercial Sales Practice ("CSP") sheet. This sheet requires, inter alia, that the potential contractor disclose any discounts which are equal to or better than the discount offered to the government. It is important to note that disclosing a discount does not mean the potential contractor must offer that discount to the government. Instead, the contractor negotiates a price with the government, with the government's negotiation objective being "most favored customer" status.

The regulations state that the information provided on the CSP sheet to the VA must be current, accurate, and complete. If the government learns during the course of the contract (usually through an audit by the Inspector General) that the negotiated price was significantly increased because the contractor failed to provide required information, failed to submit accurate, current, and complete information, or failed to disclose changes which occurred after the original submission and before the completion of negotiations, the government may reduce the negotiated price. The contractor is therefore charged with "defective pricing" and must repay the VA the amount of the overpayment and simple interest. For purposes of this clause, information provided by the contractor is satisfactory so long as it is current, accurate, and complete fourteen days before the conclusion of negotiations. The contractor must therefore periodically update the information provided on the CSP sheet during the course of negotiations.

B. Failure to Offer Discounts to the Government During the Contract

The VA FSS contracts include the price reduction clause which obligates the contractor to ensure that, throughout the duration of the contract, the government continues to receive the price/discount advantage that it originally negotiated relative to the Customer(s) of Comparability[15] ("CoC") upon which the award was predicated.[16] If a contractor reduces its price to the CoC at any time during the contract, the government must be notified of the reduction and the contractor must offer the same reduction to the government. The contractor must notify the government within fifteen days of the reduction's effective date.

Several different types of events can trigger the price reduction clause. Generally, any program that may result in a discount to the CoC should be offered to the government even if it is unclear that the government is eligible or the CoC will earn the discount. More specific examples include:

• Reduction of the prices contained in the commercial catalog, price list, or schedule used to establish contract prices;

• Granting a price reduction to the CoC which disturbs the price/discount relationship;

• Granting the CoC more favorable terms and conditions;

• A FSS price increase approved by the Contracting Officer under the Economic Price Adjustment Clause if the price/discount relationship is disturbed; and

• Granting temporary promotional discounts to the CoC which disturbs the price/discount relationship.

Failure to disclose a price reduction can result in the government taking the price reduction, even if the government would not be entitled to receive the price reduction otherwise. It may also result in termination of the contract for default and a potential civil or criminal action under the False Claims Act. Failure to report in a timely manner is unlikely to result in these penalties unless the VA has reason to believe fraud has been committed.

C. Failure to Comply with the Veterans Health Care Act

The Veterans Health Care Act[20] ("VHCA") requires pharmaceutical companies to list their covered drugs[21] on the FSS, as a condition of continued participation in the Medicaid program. Moreover, the VHCA requires that the contractor enter into a Master Agreement with the VA. This agreement requires companies to list covered drugs on the FSS at or below a calculated Federal Ceiling Price ("FCP"). Further, for each covered drug listed on the FSS, the manufacturer must enter into a Pharmaceutical Pricing Agreement ("PPA") with the VA that restricts prices to the calculated FCP for the VA, DoD, PHS, Indian Health Service, and Coast Guard.

---

15. The CoC is a negotiated item and is stated in the contract. During negotiations, it is important to narrowly define a CoC. This reduces the contractor's administrative burden and decreases the likelihood that the customer will run afoul of the price reduction clause. If a contractor is unhappy with its CoC, the VA will entertain proposals for a new CoC..

16. GSAR 552.238-76.

20. Pub. L. No. 102-585, Title VI,§ 603, 106 Stat. 4971 (1992)

21. Covered drugs include single source drugs produced or distributed under an original new drug application approved by the FDA; multiple innovator source drugs originally marketed under an original NDA approved by the FDA; biological products approved under 21 C.F.R. § 600.3; and insulin certified under section 506 of the Federal Food, Drug & Cosmetic Act.

Contractors are most likely to run afoul of the VHCA by miscalculating the FCP. The FCP is equal to seventy-six percent of the Non-Federal Average Manufacturers Price ("Non-FAMP") minus an additional discount. The Non-FAMP is the weighted average price paid by wholesalers, taking into account any cash discounts or similar price reductions, but not taking into account prices paid by the government, nominal prices, and returned goods. It is essential that the contractor be able to calculate the Non-FAMP and FCP accurately. A failure to calculate the FCP correctly can result in a government claim for any increased costs.

Some of the issues that can pose difficulties for contractors include:

• Nominal prices may be excluded from the Non-FAMP calculation. Nominal prices are no more than ten percent of the previous quarter's Non-FAMP and are usually below cost, designed to benefit the public by financially aiding disadvantaged, not-for-profit covered drug dispensaries, or researchers using a drug for an experimental purpose.

• Sales to Section 602 entities do not have to be included in Non-FAMP calculations.

• The VA may permit companies use smoothing or accrual processes that eliminate sales fluctuations from quarter to quarter.

• The prompt payment discount is applied to gross wholesale sales.

• Rebates paid to wholesalers must be included in the Non-FAMP calculations.

• Returns can be excluded from the Non-FAMP calculation if records are available for verification.

• Drug samples allowed by 21 U.S.C. 353 do not need to be included in Non-FAMP calculations.

• Free goods contingent upon any written or verbal commercial agreement are not considered exempt from inclusion in the Non-FAMP calculations.

D. The Government's Audit Authority

The VA FSS contract also contains a clause which permits the VA to examine any books, documents, papers, computer tapes, and any other directly pertinent records related to the contract for over billings, billing errors, compliance with the price reduction clause, and compliance with the Industrial Funding Fee. The VA may conduct post-award audits for these reasons until three years after final payment.

The VA may also modify the examination of records clause in certain situations to include two year post-award audit rights to investigate suspected price adjustment clause violations. After modifying the clause, the VA can verify whether the pre-award/modification pricing that formed the basis of the award was accurate, complete, and current at the time of award.

IV. DEVELOPING A COMPLIANCE PROGRAM

Many of the potential problems discussed above can be averted by developing a corporate compliance program. Moreover, government auditors, routinely review compliance programs in place during an audit. Indeed, if a contractor runs afoul of the law, a compliance program is often a mitigating factor when the government determines what type of punishment is appropriate.

A compliance program should include both a statement of policies and procedures. The statement of policies should set forth the principles to which the contractor adheres when it enters into a contract with the government. Appropriate sections
for this section include: a statement banning gifts to the government, the importance
of providing accurate data to the government, and training provided to applicable
personnel. The statement of procedures, by contrast, should contain a detailed, step-
by-step analysis of how to complete a CSP sheet, calculate the FCP, and other reports
that the government requires. A well-developed compliance program will help avert
many of the potential liabilities a contractor faces when it does business with the
government.

Notes and Questions

1. This piece shows the health care programs of the Departments of Defense and Veterans Affairs, as they buy health care supplies and equipment, do not follow the insurance model of the Medicare and Medicare programs. Rather, their use of the Federal
Supply Schedule, Blanket Purchase Agreements, and Distribution and Pricing Agreements, recalls the chapter on contracting types.

2. Also, the piece warns contractors of the perils of not disclosing or offering to the
government the discounts offered to other customers. This recalls the chapter on the
Truth in Negotiations Act ("TINA"). And, the piece warns of audit and compliance issues. Can those on each side, contractors and government alike, get enough guidance
from the statutes, regulations, clauses, and informal instructions on this subject? Or,
must they draw on the longer experience, but different context, reflected in the past
decades of TINA?

3. For a discussion of related issues, see Richard J. Wall & Christopher B. Pockney,
*Pricing Pharmaceuticals for the Government (Where Policy Quirks and Economic Realities
Collide)*, 29 Pub. Cont. L. J. 91 (1999).

B. Construction

The distinctions between construction contracts and "supply" (goods) in government contracting law arise partly from considerations present in basic (private) contract
law as well. A student of basic (private) contract law will recall some of those different
considerations: that construction work once performed cannot be resold, unlike goods.
This leads to the criterion for fulfillment of the constructive condition of performance
of "substantial performance" for construction, instead of the perfect tender rule for
goods, and to the availability of restitution for valuably if partially completed construction (that is, for benefits received and accepted). Moreover, since in the absence of any
clauses completion of all performance would be a constructive condition prior to any
payment, the result is that construction contracts must often contain explicit clauses regarding progress payments and/or other financing. Lastly, the uncertainty of measure-
ment of damages for breach leads to much use in construction contracts of liquidated
damages. For quite similar reasons to these, a separate body of specialized government
contract law applies to construction as distinguished from supply.

However, atop these considerations, a whole additional layer of government contract
law especially for construction contracts gets added, that is, a large accumulation for

construction contracts of additional statutes, regulations, clauses, and doctrines. Since the government will not tolerate mechanics liens on its buildings, Congress passed a bond-mandating statute, the Miller Act, to provide a substitute. The government's inability to abide delay has elicited an elaborate evolution of clauses meant to balance penalties for the construction contractor with relief when the government itself causes the delay, referred to as the "suspension of work" clauses. Because the government considers an important secondary goal of its public works projects as providing decent jobs, it has elaborate labor standards.

Two special, often-invoked construction contract aspects deserve additional mention. One, discussed in the chapter on changes, consists of the "differing site conditions" clauses. By these, government contracting establishes an entire system for dealing with the common complaint that construction contractors find conditions on the site during construction that come as a nasty surprise. The other, for which this section contains a case, consists of a doctrine for discussing how much the government owes contractors, when it keeps them waiting, for the cost of overhead. For lawyers, this doctrine, the *Eichleay* doctrine, represents a very complex evolution of consequential damages accounting; for construction firms, it represents a simple, straightforward response to the major question of paying for overhead.

The first reading in this section starts with a survey of the many special aspects of government construction contracting. The *DeKonty* case which follows gives a pithy account of the rules of progress payments and project abandonment. Finally, the *Wickham* case lays out the *Eichleay* doctrine for factoring overhead into delay damages.

For further discussions of the general subject of government construction contracting, see: Adrian L. Bastianelli III, et al., Federal Government Construction Contracts (ABA Forum on the Construction Industry 2003); David T. Douthwaite, *Why Procure Construction by Negotiation?* 25 Pub. Cont. L.J. 423 (1996); Gene Ming Lee, Note, *A Case for Fairness in Public Works Contracting,* 65 Fordham L. Rev. 1075 (1996); Kenneth M Roberts, Nancy C. Smith, *Design-Build Contracts Under State and Local Procurement Laws,* 25 Pub. Cont. L.J. 423 (1996); Carl J. Circo, *Small Construction Contracts: Big Issues,* 11-DEC Prob. & Prop. 32 (1997); Bernard B. Kolodner, *The Construction Manager Who Would Be Contractor,* 10-DEC Prob. & Prop. 40 (1996); Peter M. Kutil, Andrew D. Ness, *Concurrent Delay: The Challenge to Unravel Competing Causes of Delay,* 17-OCT Construction Law. 18 (1997); John S. Pachter & Carl T. Hahn, *Jumping On (of Off) the* Eichleay *Bandwagon: Do We Have a Sticky* Wickham?, 31 Procurement Law., Summer 1996, at 3; Linda L. Shapiro & Margaret M. Worthington, *Use of the Eichleay Formula to Calculate Unabsorbed Overhead for Government-Caused Delay Under Manufacturing Contracts,* 25 Pub. Cont. L.J. 513 (1996); Michael W. Kauffman & Craig A. Holman, *The* Eichleay *Formula: A Resilient Means for Recovering Unabsorbed Overhead,* 24 Pub. Cont. L.J. 319 (1995)

Construction Contracts vs. Supply Contracts
From: Fundamentals of Federal Contract Law (1990)
Eugene W. Massengale

1.   Similarities

The basic principles of Government contracting are the same whether a contract is for supplies or construction (although supply contracts involve more varied procedures and contract types than construction contracts). Thus, the policy of obtaining the widest competition possible, small business and minority business preferences, the rules limiting the authority of Government agents, the Government's duty of fairness and noninterference with contractors, policies regarding patents and data, and the other fundamental policies and procedures explored in earlier chapters in this book with regard to supply contracts apply with equal force to construction contracts.

For example, if a contract is awarded through sealed bidding, the rules governing that method of contracting (see Chapter 3) are generally the same whether the contract is for supplies or construction. Similarly, the rules of fixed-price contracting are the same for supply and construction contracts. In addition, although there are differences between supply and construction contract clauses and circumstances, similar rights and obligations attach in connection with terminations for default or terminations for convenience furnishing of Government property, contract changes, equitable adjustments, payment, inspections and warranties and disputes.

2.   Differences

Not surprisingly, the differences between supply and construction contracts are primarily traceable to the different physical environments in which they are performed and to the differences in the nature of the contract work. Some of the most significant differences between supply and construction contracting are briefly reviewed below.

a.   **Government Control.** Whereas supply contracts are typically performed in a production facility owned or leased by the contractor and generally under its control, a construction contract is performed at a location owned or controlled by the Government. The construction contractor—even when it is responsible for quality control— is subject to a great deal more surveillance and control by Government inspectors and other Government representatives than the supply contractor.

A burdensome feature of construction contracts is the number of reports the contractor is required to file with the Government. Daily reports of work accomplished are often required, as well as reports involving (a) quality control activities, (b) safety procedures, (c) labor disputes, (d) construction or completion schedules, and (e) descriptions—even samples—of materials the contractor proposes to use.

b.   **Work Site.** The fact that the contract is performed on a Government-owned site or in a Government-controlled facility also poses problems of *access* to the work site by the contractor's workers, subcontractors, and material suppliers. Other difficulties faced by the construction contractor are interference from Government activities conducted while work is being performed and from the activities of other Government contractors, as well as the possible damage or loss of equipment and materials after work hours. The contractor is also responsible for maintaining a safe and clean site. Moreover, even though the work is done on federal property, the construction contractor is responsible for properly disposing of hazardous substances.

c.   **Contract Clauses.** Construction contractors also must comply with the standard clauses used only in construction contracts. For example, the standard "Permits and Responsibilities" clause makes the contractor "responsible for all damages to persons or property that occur as a result of [its] fault or negligence." That clause also makes the contractor responsible for all materials delivered and work performed "until completion and acceptance of the entire work, except for any completed unit of work which may have been accepted under the contract." Thus, under this clause, a contractor could be required to bear the cost of construction material stolen or otherwise removed from the contract site or damaged by the weather. The "Permits and Responsibilities" clause also requires the contractor to obtain necessary permits and comply with federal, state, and local safety standards.

Another important standard clause in construction contracts is the "Material and Workmanship" clause. This clause requires the work to be performed in "a skillful and workmanlike manner" and also states that "[a]ll equipment, material, and articles incorporated into the work covered by [the] contract shall be new and of the most suitable grade for the purpose intended."

When the contract is over $1 million (as is not unusual), the "Performance of Work by the Contractor" clause requires that the general contractor perform a stipulated percentages the work with its own forces. For purposes of this clause, "work" includes both labor and materials.

Examples of other standard clauses typically found in Government construction contracts (besides the "Specifications and Drawings" clause mentioned above in Section A) include (1) the "Accident Prevention" clause, (2) the "Differing Site Conditions" clause, (3) the "Other Contracts" clause requiring the contractor to cooperate with other contractors and Government employees working at or near the work site, (4) the "Use and Possession Prior to Completion" clause permitting the Government to take possession of or use any completed or partially completed part of the project without legally "accepting" the contract work, and (5) the "Cleaning Up" clause.

d.   **Bonds.** Construction contractors must also comply with many pervasive statutory requirements. For example, the Miller Act requires construction contractors in the United States to furnish payment and performance bonds. Failure to furnish Miller Act bonds or furnishing forged bonds is a basis for termination of a contract for default.

e.   **Labor Standards.** Construction contractors are subject to stringent statutory requirements regarding the treatment and payment of laborers.

f.   **Contract Changes.** One of the most notable features of construction contracts is the number of contract modifications that may be necessary in performing the contract. Although modifications of supply contracts are not uncommon, it is rare when a construction contract is not changed during performance as to some aspect of the work. In fact, most construction projects usually undergo numerous modifications. These modifications take the form of ordered changes under the "Changes" clause or constructive changes, such as acceleration of the contract schedule or defective specifications. Such changes to the contract work invariably disrupt the project's schedule and increase its costs.

g.   **Default Termination.** Terminations for default are much less frequent in construction than in supply contracts. In construction contracts, the imposition of liquidated damages for delayed completion of work is more common. A major advantage for construction contractors is that they are entitled to payment for the value of work they have performed at the time of a termination for default, whereas supply contractors may get nothing for the work they have completed but not delivered.

Even when termination of a construction contract does occur, disputes concerning repurchase actions and excess costs of completion are relatively rare. This is because defaulted construction contracts are usually completed by the surety company that has guaranteed performance by issuing a performance bond. However, if the surety company is unwilling or unable to complete performance, a performance bond has not been furnished (as is the case, for example, in most contracts performed outside the United States), or there is an urgent need to complete the work, the Government may finish the job with its own forces and charge the defaulted contractor its costs of completing performance or may award a contract to another construction firm to finish the project and assess the defaulted contractor any excess costs.

The United States, Appellant, v.
Dekonty Corporation, Appellee

No. 90-1356. United States Court of Appeals,
Federal Circuit. 922 F.2d 826., Jan. 4, 1991.

Before RICH, MAYER, and RADER, Circuit Judges.

RADER, Circuit Judge.

The United States (Government) appeals from the judgment of the Armed Services Board of Contract Appeals (Board). DeKonty Corp., 90-2 BCA (CCH) ¶ 22,645, at 113,584 (ASBCA 1990). The Board found that the Government breached its contract with the DeKonty Corporation (DeKonty) by expressing an intent to withhold a scheduled progress payment. The Government appeals. This court reverses.

BACKGROUND

The United States Navy (Navy) contracted with DeKonty for the construction of a child care facility at the Los Angeles Air Force Station. On several occasions during DeKonty's performance, the Resident Officer in Charge of Construction (ROICC) warned DeKonty that the Navy might terminate the contract for default. On July 5, 1985, the ROICC finally recommended a default termination. When informing DeKonty of the recommendation, the ROICC noted that "only a fraction of Termination for Default recommendations are ultimately approved and issued."

DeKonty stopped working at the site on July 16, 1985. On July 19, 1985, the Assistant ROICC wrote a memorandum to the Commanding Officer of the Western Division Naval Facilities Engineering Command (NAVFACENGCOM):

1. The Contractor, DeKonty Corporation, is currently being processed for default. WESTDIV has recommended default: the default package has been forwarded to NAVFACENGCOM for the final decision of the Contracting Officer.

2. Please process partial payment # 5.

3. Prior to issuing partial payment # 5, please check with Bobette Hill [the Termination Contracting Officer], Code 022, X7253, to determine 1) status of contract and 2) whether funds should be released at the time.

Six days later, Mr. DeKonty called the payment office to inquire about the status of progress payment # 5, due on August 8, 1985. He spoke with an unidentified individual who stated that the payment was on hold. Mr. DeKonty made notes of the conversation:

10:00 a.m. Called San Bruno about our June pay request, they informed us that of the $87,590.20 we applied for, approximately $9,000 was approved and they have this on hold until advised by Contracting Div. The Government/U.S. Navy has refused to comply with its contractual obligations.

On July 22, 1985, the ROICC told DeKonty to keep working. Nonetheless, on August 1, 1985, DeKonty formally abandoned performance. DeKonty alleged that the Navy had breached the contract by refusing to make the scheduled progress payment. The Navy later terminated the contract for default. DeKonty appealed to the Board which determined that the Navy committed an anticipatory breach before DeKonty abandoned performance. The Board stated that the Navy breached by expressing a clear intent not to make the August 8, 1985 progress payment. The Board awarded common law breach of contract damages.

DISCUSSION

Under 41 U.S.C. §609(b) (1987), this court reviews de novo the Board's conclusions of law and defers to its findings of fact unless unsupported by substantial evidence. This court determines that the Board erred.

The Supreme Court set forth the standard for anticipatory breaches:

> When one party to [a]...contract absolutely refuses to perform his contract, and before the time arrives for performance distinctly and unqualifiedly communicates that refusal to the other party, that other party can, if he choose, treat that refusal as a breach and commence an action at once therefor.

Dingley v. Oler, 117 U.S. 490, 499–500, 6 S.Ct. 850, 853, 29 L.Ed. 984 (1886). Dingley further adopted the language of an earlier case which stated:

> [A] mere assertion that the party will be unable, or will refuse to perform his contract, is not sufficient; it must be a distinct and unequivocal absolute refusal to perform the promise, and must be treated and acted upon as such by the party to whom the promise was made....

Id. at 503, 6 S.Ct. at 854 (quoting In re Smoot, 82 U.S. 36, 21 L.Ed. 107 (1872)). This court followed that standard in Cascade Pacific Int'l v. United States, 773 F.2d 287 (Fed.Cir.1985). Cascade held that a contracting officer may terminate a contract for anticipatory breach in the event of a

> positive, definite, unconditional, and unequivocal manifestation of intent... on the part of the contractor...not to render the promised performance when the time fixed...by the contract shall arrive....

Cascade, 773 F.2d at 293.

The Board relied on two events to support its anticipatory breach determination. The Board found positive and unequivocal intent to breach in the July 19 memorandum. The Board also found an intent to breach in the July 25 statement by the unidentified individual at the payment office. These two events, however, considered individually or collectively, do not show a "positive, definite, unconditional and unequivocal" intent to refuse timely performance of a contract obligation. Rather the record contains substantial evidence showing that the Navy did not express any intent to breach.

The July 19, 1985 Memorandum

The only portion of the July 19, 1985 memorandum which might be germane to DeKonty's allegation of breach is paragraph 3. In that paragraph, the Assistant ROICC asks the contracting officer to check the contract status before releasing payment. This paragraph is not an express refusal to pay DeKonty before the August 8 payment deadline. Rather the Assistant ROICC simply advised NAVFACENGCOM to check to see if the contract was still in effect before payment.

The circumstances justified the caution exhibited in the July 19 memorandum. DeKonty stopped performance at the job site on July 16. Default seemed imminent. Therefore, the Assistant ROICC correctly recommended that the Commanding Officer check the status of the contract before releasing funds. The July 19 memo is not "positive, definite, unconditional and unequivocal [evidence] of intent" to breach, but merely appropriate contract administration.

The July 25, 1985 Conversation

Even assuming that the unidentified person who answered the telephone at the payment office had authority to speak for the Navy, the July 25 conversation did not supply evidence of an anticipatory breach. DeKonty contends that this conversation confirmed suspicions raised by the July 19 memorandum. As stated earlier, the July 19 memorandum did not express an intent to refuse contract performance. Similarly, putting a payment "on hold" does not mean that it is not going to be paid on time. The payment was not due until August 8, 1985.

Moreover, after the July 19 memorandum, the Navy encouraged continued performance on the contract. On July 22, 1985, the ROICC, Commander Niece, and the Assistant ROICC, Lt. Com. Dampier, recommended that DeKonty "proceed with diligence in the execution of construction on this project." At that time, DeKonty remained under an obligation to perform. The Navy's efforts to encourage DeKonty's performance show that the Navy had not earlier expressed an unequivocal intent to breach.

The Navy also processed and approved DeKonty's sixth payment request. As the ROICC explained at a hearing before the Board, this action showed that the Navy considered the contract active. The Navy approved the sixth payment— dated July 31, 1985—on August 9, 1985. This evidence shows that the Navy intended to make timely payments.

In sum, the Navy's actions as a whole fall far short of communicating an intent not to perform in a "positive, definite, unconditional and unequivocal" manner. The July 19 memorandum and the July 25 telephone conversation do not satisfy the Cascade standard for an anticipatory breach.

CONCLUSION

The Board's decision was erroneous. In the absence of an anticipatory breach on this record, we need not reach the issue of damages.

REVERSED.

Notes and Questions

1. What are the multiple roles of progress payments? What does the ability to obtain them mean for a contractor? What does the ability to defer their payment mean for a contracting officer? This is a case that has two sides. What are the best arguments for each side? Can you tell the "story" of the case, at it seemed to the ASBCA? And the "story" as it seems to the Federal Circuit? Note how the Federal Circuit deems irrelevant most of the background, namely, that the government was processing a termination for default of the contractor. Shall we take a postmodern view and respect each story-narrative as true on its own terms? Or, does the opinion analyze the combination of the July 19th memorandum

and the July 25th conversation to the point that, like a completed exam answer, it lays out a determinate series of criteria for the law of progress payments and project abandonment?

2. Generally speaking, under the Federal Acquisition Regulations (FAR), firm-fixed-price contracts in construction may be priced on a lump-sum or unit-price basis or by a combination of these. 48 C.F.R. §36.207 (1998). Lump-sum pricing is when a lump sum is paid for defined parts of or the total work; unit pricing is payment for a specified quantity of work units. Id. Lump-sum pricing is preferable under specific circumstances set forth in FAR 36.207, and an economic price adjustment provision may be included in defined instances as well. Id.

"Repricing" of a unit-priced contract may occur. Under the Variation in Estimated Quantity (VEQ) clause, when a variation exists between the estimated and the actual quantity of the unit-priced item of more than 15 percent above or below the esti-mated quantity, an equitable adjustment in the contract price may be made. 48 C.F.R. §52.212-11 (1992). In *Foley Co. v. United States*, 11 F.3d 1032 (Fed. Cir. 1993), the Court of Appeals held that the government was not entitled to equitable adjustment under the VEQ clause when the contractor actually removed greater than 115% of the estimated volume of sludge; the government failed to prove that Foley experienced a cost savings due solely to the increased volume removed. (The government unsuc-cessfully attempted to distinguish that case from the 1975 controlling case in which the Court of Claims found no basis for replacing a negotiated unit price with a repricing based on actual costs plus a reasonable profit. *Victory Construction Co. v. United States*, 510 F.2d 1379, 206 Ct. Cl. 274 (1975).) For more information on the evolution of the judicial treatment of this issue, see *Government Contracts Cases Before the United States Court of Appeals for the Federal Circuit*, 43 Am. U. L. Rev. 1417, 1475 (1994).

Wickham Contracting Co., Inc., Appellant, v. Dennis J. Fischer, Acting Administrator, General Services Administration, Appellee

No. 93-1146. United States Court of Appeals,
Federal Circuit. 12 F.3d 1574., Jan. 6, 1994.

Before RICH, MICHEL and CLEVENGER, Circuit Judges.

MICHEL, Circuit Judge.

Wickham Contracting Company appeals from a decision of the General Services Ad-ministration Board of Contract Appeals (Board), denying Wickham's claim for an equi-table adjustment for overhead expenses incurred under a contract with the General Ser-vices Administration (GSA) as a result of GSA-imposed delays. * * * Regarding the Eichleay formula, we hold it is the only proper method of calculating unabsorbed home office overhead. No other formula may be used.

I. BACKGROUND

On July 28, 1977, Wickham entered into a contract with GSA to renovate the Fed-eral Post Office and Courthouse in Albany, New York, for the sum of $2,968,000. The contract allowed 365 days from the notice to proceed to perform the work which was due to be completed on August 15, 1978. Early in the renovation process, GSA be-came concerned about structural problems with the building and ordered many delays in the work. The parties agree that, due to GSA-imposed delays, the work was not substantially complete until April 10, 1981, 969 days after the contracted date. Many of Wickham's claims against the government for additional costs due to such delays have been settled. However, certain costs associated with home office overhead have not.

Wickham's home office staff during the renovation work consisted of the president, a construction engineer, the project manager, and three secretaries. In addition to the Albany project, Wickham performed only two other major contracts during the same time frame—the West Point project and the Foley Square project. Both of these projects were managed mainly on site while the Albany project was managed mainly from the home office.

In June 1986, the contracting officer awarded Wickham an additional $333,084 on its claim for unabsorbed home office overhead due to the delay, based on the Eichleay formula.[1] Before the Board, Wickham argued that, for three reasons, it was due a larger amount for the unabsorbed home office overhead. Wickham complained that the percentage of the home office overhead pool allocated to the Albany contract based on the Eichleay formula, approximately 34%, was too low and did not fairly compensate Wickham for its overhead expenses. The contractor argued that it was entitled to be reimbursed for 80% of its overhead expenses incurred during the delay period because 80% of its home office activity and, therefore, 80% of its home office overhead expense was devoted to the Albany contract during that time frame. Wickham made the argument first to the contracting officer, then to the Board.

On appeal to us, Wickham repeatedly states that the 80% figure is undisputed. However, the government points out that Wickham did not keep current books or records which could document the 80% figure and that Wickham did not develop that figure until January 1985. The record supports the government's assertions. Therefore, we conclude the figure is disputed.

The Board did not make a clear finding as to whether Wickham actually proved that 80% of its home office activity was devoted to the Albany contract. Instead, the Board rejected Wickham's theory of recovery on the basis that unabsorbed overhead is always calculated according to the Eichleay formula when a contractor meets the Eichleay requirements after government-imposed delay. The Board applied the Eichleay formula based on the notion that it is a theoretical construct of the amount of unabsorbed overhead caused by the contract delay and, therefore, the actual amount of overhead allegedly caused by the contract was not relevant.

The parties agree on many of the components of the overhead pool. The components of the overhead pool to which the Board applied the Eichleay formula are general and administrative salaries, rent, insurance, depreciation, hospitalization and medical costs, dues and subscriptions, office expenses, auto and truck maintenance, utilities, plans and specifications, cleaning, protection, taxes and licenses, and officer's salaries. 92-3 BCA ¶ 25,040 at 124,818-19.

Before the Board, however, Wickham also argued that the contracting officer wrongly excluded several specific field costs from the overhead pool. The field costs are for travel and business meetings, telephones, professional fees, union welfare benefits,

---

1. Wickham had already been partially compensated for overhead costs because the original contract price included a markup for overhead. In addition, when GSA issued change orders to pay Wickham for additional work, almost all of the orders included a markup of 10% for overhead.

payroll taxes and equipment rental. Their inclusion would increase the amount paid to Wickham under either the Eichleay formula or Wickham's allocation figure of 80%. The Board, however, found that as direct, not overhead costs, they may not be included in the overhead pool.

* * *

Wickham appealed to this court pursuant to the Contract Disputes Act of 1978 (CDA), 41 U.S.C. §607(g)(1) (1988). Our jurisdiction rests on that Act and 28 U.S.C. §1295(a)(10) (1988).

* * *

III. ANALYSIS

A. The Eichleay Formula is Exclusive

1. Federal Circuit Law on Eichleay

The Board used the Eichleay formula [2] to calculate the amount of home office overhead costs for which Wickham would be reimbursed due to the GSA-imposed delay. Application of the Eichleay formula requires "that compensable delay occurred, and that the contractor could not have taken on any other jobs during the contract period." [3] C.B.C. Enters., Inc. v. United States, 978 F.2d 669, 673–74 (Fed.Cir.1992). Government contractors may use the Eichleay formula to calculate unabsorbed home office overhead when disruption, delay or suspension caused by the government has made uncertain the length of the performance period of the contract. Id. 978 F.2d at 672. The uncertainty often precludes additional jobs.

Suspension or delay of contract performance results in interruption or reduction of the contractor's stream of income from payments for direct costs incurred. This in turn causes an interruption or reduction in payments for overhead, derived as a percentage of direct costs, which is set by the contract. Home office overhead costs continue to accrue during such periods, however, regardless of direct contract activity. Consequently, this decrease in payments for direct costs creates unabsorbed overhead, unless home office workers are laid off or given additional work during such suspension or delay periods. When the period of delay is uncertain and the contractor is required by the government to remain ready to resume performance on short notice (referred to as "standby"), the contractor is effectively prohibited from making reductions in home office staff or facilities or by taking on additional work. See Capital Elec. Co. v. United States, 729 F.2d 743, 748 (Fed.Cir.1984) (Friedman, J., concurring) ("[I]t is, ordinarily, not practicable to lay off main office employees during a short and indefinite period of delay."). Other reasons such as exhaustion of bonding

---

2. The Eichleay formula requires three steps: 1) to find allocable contract overhead, multiply the total overhead cost incurred during the contract period times the ratio of billings from the delayed contract to total billings of the firm during the contract period; 2) to get the daily contract overhead rate, divide allocable contract overhead by days of contract performance; and 3) to get the amount recoverable, multiply the daily contract overhead rate times days of government-caused delay. Capital Elec. Co. v. United States, 729 F.2d 743, 747 (Fed.Cir.1984).

3. The parties stipulated that the government caused delay and disruption in Wickham's performance of the GSA contract such that Wickham satisfies the requirements for application of the Eichleay formula. GSA admitted to the Board that GSA had caused compensable delay of 969 days. Wickham's witness testified that because of the disruption, it was unable to commit to any additional contract work during the delay and GSA did not dispute this testimony.

capacity may also preclude additional contracts. Interstate Gen. Gov't Contractors, Inc., 12 F.3d 1053 (Fed.Cir.1993).

For the purpose of compensating Wickham for the effects of a project delay on home office overhead, the Board properly defined overhead as "those costs which are expended for the benefit of the business as a whole and which usually accrue over time." 92-3 BCA ¶ 25,040 at 124,818. The pool to which the Eichleay formula is applied must contain only such indirect costs. Home office costs, by their nature, cannot be traced to any particular contract. Thus, they are properly categorized as overhead costs and, assuming their allowability, included in the Eichleay pool. Were it possible to trace a cost to a particular contract, it would be a direct cost of the contract. C.B.C. Enters., 978 F.2d at 672.

The Armed Services Board of Contract Appeals devised the Eichleay formula to provide a fair method for allocating home office overhead costs, otherwise inallocable, to specific contracts. Eichleay Corp., ASBCA No. 5183, 60-2 BCA ¶ 2688, 1960 WL 538 (July 29, 1960), aff'd on reconsid., 61-1 BCA ¶ 2894, 1960 WL 684 (1960). The Eichleay board found it necessary to allocate overhead costs pro-rata because they "cannot ordinarily be charged to a particular contract. They represent the cost of general facilities and administration necessary to the performance of all contracts." 60-2 BCA ¶ 2688 at 13,574, 1960 WL 538. Thus, the Eichleay formula seeks to equitably determine allocation of unabsorbed overhead to allow fair compensation of a contractor for government delay. Id. at 13,573, 1960 WL 538. Allocation based on a pro-rata share is necessary because overhead cannot be traced to any particular contract since overhead consists of expenses which benefit and are necessary to every contract. Id.

2. Wickham's Arguments

In this case the ratio of billings from the delayed contract to total billings is about 34%. Thus, under the Eichleay formula, 34% of Wickham's overhead expense, incurred during the contract period, is allocable to the contract. However, Wickham claims that approximately 80% of its home office activity and, therefore, 80% of its home office overhead expense was devoted to the Albany contract during the delay period.[4] Thus, Wickham seeks compensation for 80% of the home office overhead costs actually incurred during the delay because, according to Wickham, they are directly attributable to the Albany contract. Wickham argues the Eichleay calculation is unfair because it is less than the actual percentage of overhead devoted to the delayed project. Therefore, per Wickham, the Eichleay formula should be used only when overhead costs cannot otherwise be accurately determined. In short, Wickham seeks to completely avoid the Eichleay formula.

Wickham's argument fails for a fundamental reason—Wickham confuses direct and overhead costs. As the Board noted, overhead costs benefit and are caused by the business as a whole, not any one project. Thus, overhead costs are never attributable to or caused by any one contract. Wickham's claim to "directly attributable" home office overhead is a non sequitur. If a cost is directly attributable to a contract, then it is a direct cost, not an overhead cost.

Wickham attempts to blur the distinction between overhead and direct costs simply to avoid the clear rule that the Eichleay formula governs the calculation of unabsorbed over-

---

4. This is because Wickham's other two contracts were managed mainly on site while the Albany project was managed from the home office.

head. A contractor who wishes reimbursement for a cost directly attributable to a contract must submit it as a direct cost. In a case such as this, where a contractor and the government have already consistently treated a cost as overhead, we will not upset their agreement by ourselves treating that cost as a direct cost and ordering reimbursement as such. In any event, we would lack jurisdiction under the CDA to do so because there were no contracting officer and board decisions denying such costs as direct costs. Therefore, there is no fact finding or ruling for us to review; and, of course, as an appellate court we may not make fact findings or initial rulings, generally or in the circumstances of this case.

Responding to Wickham's argument, the Board said, "[i]t makes no difference what the actual overhead effort was. We are here dealing with theoretics which produce approximations because more precise results cannot be obtained." 92-3 BCA ¶ 25,040 at 124, 818, 1992 WL 88326. In this statement the Board refers to the concept that the Eichleay formula calculates the unabsorbed overhead by a pro-rata share out of necessity. The Eichleay pool contains only overhead costs, those which cannot be attributed to a particular contract and which benefit and are caused by the business as a whole. To accurately determine how much unabsorbed overhead was caused by any one contract is impossible, even though Wickham claims to have done so.

Unlike direct costs which are incurred only because of a particular contract, overhead costs are incurred even if the contractor had not undertaken a particular project. Ordinarily, all home office expenses fall into the overhead category because the contractor must operate a home office in order to seek work and administer contracts whether or not he is performing a particular contract. For instance, a contractor must provide for the home office space, pay for utilities pertaining to that space, pay licensing fees and officer's salaries even when the contractor has no current contracts and is merely seeking work.

Given this established definition of overhead costs, the very premise of Wickham's argument is incorrect. Wickham contends that because 80% of its home office activity related to the Albany contract, 80% of its home office costs is directly attributable to that contract. Wickham fails to recognize that a cost is directly attributable to a contract only when the cost is caused by the contract. The Albany project did not cause 80% of Wickham's home office costs because Wickham would have incurred the individual cost components of the home office overhead whether or not it ever undertook the Albany project. For instance, the Albany project did not cause 80% of Wickham's home office rent even if 80% of the activity in that office related to the Albany project. Because Wickham would have incurred the same or similar rental expense in any event, no portion of the rent is directly attributable to the Albany project.

* * *

The Board's decision is therefore, in all respects,

AFFIRMED.

Notes and Questions

1. The opinion provides a mini-course in cost accounting. Can you explain and illustrate each of these concepts: cost "pools"; direct vs. overhead expenses; allocability? Note that these cost accounting concepts apply even though the underlying contract may be firm-fixed-price because cost accounting governs the figuring of equitable adjustments. What do you suppose happens if a commecial contractor, which does not keep its books in a way that makes cost accounting easy, runs into a situation like this

case where it has to make an *Eichleay* claim based on elaborate cost figures? What's the sense of the requirement that the contractor be idle during the delay period? See *Satellite Electric Co. v. John H. Dalton*, 105 F.2d 1418 (Fed. Cir. 1997).

2. How does this way of figuring damages relate to basic (private) contract damages? Could you imagine similar arrangements to these between a private developer and its construction company?

3. Liquidated damages are estimated when actual damages are difficult to calculate or estimate. ACC Alderman Construction Co., ASBCA 43958, 96-1 BCA ¶ 28046 (1995). Before a reasonable estimate of damages can be determined, the government first must clearly defined what the agency need is and which commercial products or services are suitable to meet the need. Federal Acquisition Regulation (FAR) 12.202 addresses this market research and description of need, and contains a description of the type of product or service, how the agency intends its use, and any performance requirement or essential physical characteristics. 48 C.F.R. §12.202 (1997). FAR 36.206 designates the determination of the need for liquidated damages in a construction contract to the contracting officer. 48 C.F.R. §36.202 (1995) .

In J.H. Strain and Sons, Inc., ASBCA 34432, 90-2 BCA ¶ 22770 (1990), the Administrative Judge held that the formula used in determining liquidated damages was appropriate and the assessment of them justified, stating "whether actual damages did or did not occur or was not proved to have occurred does not prevent recovery" (Martin J. Simko Construction, Inc v. United States, 11 Cl. Ct. 257, 271 (1986), quoting United States v. J. D. Street & Co., 151 F. Supp. 469, 472 (E. D. Mo. 1957)). This, however, is not the case when there has been substantial performance, as in *Sauer Incorporated*, ASBCA 39605 (1998), in which liquidated damages were reduced to 80% of the contract amount based on the Navy's acceptance and use as substantially complete of 20% of a facility contracted for.

C. Information Technology

Information technology has become a big part of what government purchases, from weapons control systems for the military, to accounting systems for the civilian agencies, to hardware and software for students at the state and local government level. To some extent, the federal government has sought to make special provision for information technology procurement, hoping perhaps that some higher-level coordination and direction would keep the government's information systems compatible, or at least prevent such nightmares as widespread government obsolescence or total inability for different government agencies to communicate. In particular, Congress enacted the Information Technology Management Reform Act (ITMRA) of 1996. *See, e.g.*, John A. Howell, *Governmentwide Agency Contracts: Vehicle Overcrowding on the Procurement Highway*, 27 Pub. Cont. L.J. 395 (1998).

However, in many respects, information technology procurement draws upon provisions available in government contracting generally, just adapting them to the particular context. Given the very rapid pace of private sector innovation as to hardware and software, the government may try more to keep up with that pace by procurement from the commercial sector, rather than trying to sponsor government-unique efforts. For example, in the *L.A. Systems* case, the contracting officer resorted to simplified acquisition procedures, available for information technology and other procurement alike, to speed along a computer purchase.

L.A. SYSTEMS, Protester, v. DEPARTMENT OF THE ARMY, and DEFENSE INFORMATION SYSTEMS AGENCY, Respondents.

GRANTED: February 12, 1996

GSBCA No. 13472-P

Before Board Judges PARKER, WILLIAMS, and GOODMAN.

GOODMAN, Board Judge.

On November 9, 1995, protester, L.A. Systems, filed the instant protest challenging an alleged improper sole-source acquisition of central processing units (CPUs) from Amdahl Corporation (Amdahl). The procurement was by the Rock Island Arsenal defense megacenter (Rock Island DMC) through the delegated procurement authority of the Defense Information Systems Agency (DISA). The protest alleges that respondents have impermissibly evaded full and open competition as required by the Competition in Contracting Act (CICA), 10 U.S.C. s 2304(a)(1) (1994), by dividing a requirement for the CPUs into a number of smaller acquisitions in order to use the simplified acquisition procedures of Federal Acquisition Regulation (FAR) Part 13 and thereby avoid the requirements for full and open competition in FAR Part 6. * * * * We grant the protest.

Findings of Fact

Amdahl proposal

1. In July 1995, Amdahl presented a proposal (Amdahl proposal) to the DISA WEST-HEM Configuration Control Board (CCB) to upgrade, through leasing, approximately twenty Amdahl 5890-600E (600E) CPUs in use at six defense megacenters with either 1100A or 1400A CPUs. Protester's Exhibit 2.

2. On August 1, 1995, the CCB reviewed the Amdahl proposal. The minutes of the CCB meeting of that date read, in relevant part:

> Amdahl has made an offer to DISA WESTHEM to replace all 5890-600E's with 5995-1100s for $49.9K each. * * *

> Since the capital funding is below $50,000, the DMC may exercise this option using their own funds without prior CCB approval. * * * *

Rock Island DMC decides to upgrade

3. The Director of Rock Island DMC (the Director) made a decision to upgrade the DMC's 600E CPUs. This decision was confirmed in an e-mail message dated August 11, 1995, to staff members, which read, in relevant part:

> [The Amdahl] offer was approved in concept by the CCB on 1 Aug 95. It is open to any DISA WESTHEM megacenter with 600E machines. The megacenter must provide $49.9K and can make the decision to exercise this option on a case by case basis. Upgrading the 1100A to a 1400A requires approximately $300,000 in additional capital, and CCB and CRC approval for the additional capital funding.

* * *

Procurement of CPUs

4. In mid and late August 1995, Rock Island DMC prepared requirements packages supporting the two CPU upgrades which are the subject of this protest. The require-

ments package which accompanied each. purchase request included a mission needs statement, a statement of urgency, and an AMC Form 2110, Purchase Request and Commitment. Transcript at 92-93.

5. On August 21, 1995, the Director signed the mission needs statement for the first CPU upgrade and obtained concurrence.

* * *

6. The mission needs statement listed the "Amdahl 59995[sic]-1400A" as the item which needed to be acquired. Protester's Exhibit 25.

7. A statement of urgency was prepared to support the procurement. The statement read as follows:

> Defense Megacenter Rock Island is currently utilizing an Amdahl 5890-600E in support of a large Army Material [sic] Command workload. it is installed as two 300Es to provide more domain capacity than a single 600E permits. It is fully utilized and incapable of providing additional support for growing customer requirements or new workload.

> The CPU has a MVS/XA operating systems [sic] installed. IBM has announced it will discontinue support for this operating level soon. * * * *

> Amdahl has announced that it will shortly discontinue support of the 600E series hardware.

> In order to continue servicing current customer base at an acceptable level during fiscal year end, to have resources to service their growth requirements and to support any new requirements, this machine must be upgraded.

* * *

8. The contracting officer received the documentation supporting the procurement of the first CPU in early September 1995. Protester's Exhibit 27.

9. The contracting officer decided not to synopsize the procurement of the first Amdahl CPU in the Commerce Business Daily (CBD) based on her evaluation of the urgency statement. She confirmed this decision in a memorandum dated September 11, 1995. Protester's Exhibit 22. The contracting officer testified that she used the urgency statement solely for the purpose of avoiding synopsizing the requirements in the CBD. Transcript at 40, 98. * * * *

11. On September 13, 1995, the contracting officer conducted what she characterized as "an informal market survey" with regard to an Amdahl 1400A. She solicited an oral quote from Amdahl and reviewed commercial literature from another potential supplier and the General Services Administration (GSA) schedule contract of at least one other firm for additional quotes. This process took less than one hour. The contracting officer determined that Amdahl offered the lowest price. Transcript at 53-56; Protester's Exhibit 23.

12. On September 13, 1995, the contracting officer telephoned a representative of Amdahl and placed an oral order for an Amdahl 1400A with 512 mb of main memory, 0 mb of expanded storage, and 128 parallel channels. Transcript at 28, 416. The contracting officer issued purchase order number DAAA08-95-M-4632 on September 13, 1995, to confirm her oral order. Transcript at 29; Protester's Exhibit 9.

13. On September 14, 1995, the contracting officer received a purchase request from Rock island DMC to procure a second CPU upgrade. When she received this request,

the contracting officer had already awarded the first CPU upgrade. The contracting officer testified:

> A: The first CPU, [purchase order DAAA08-95-M-] 4632, was complete and off my desk the time I did the second one.

> Q: Any reason why you didn't do the two of them together?

> A: One was already done. I didn't get the other requirement until afterwards.

Transcript at 77-78.

14. The requirements packages for both CPU upgrades were identical except for the dates documents were prepared and approved. * * * *

15. The contracting officer handled this procurement in the same manner as she had the earlier one. She decided not to synopsize the procurement in the CBD based upon the statement of urgency, and she used the market information she had already gathered. * * * *

Procurement of expanded memory * * * *

[Two purchase orders were issued for expanded memory, without synopsizing, based on the statement of urgency.]

Alleged justification for urgency and four separate purchase orders

32. According to the Director, the requirement for additional computing power (and therefore to upgrade the CPUs) and for additional expanded memory had existed in January 1995. The fact that the acquisition had not been made by August 1995 now made the requirement urgent as "[t]he longer the requirement goes, the more urgent it becomes." Transcript at 294. * * * *

34. The Director said there were four separate purchase orders for the two CPUs and the two expanded memory units because he did not have the funds all at once. Transcript at 319. As the funds became available for each purchase order, the requirements packages were issued. Id. at 321. The Director did not want to let the total amount of funds accumulate before issuing the purchase orders, as he was afraid that the CCB would "get [the] money." Id. at 320.

35. When the Director executed the mission needs statements for the CPUs and the expanded memory units, he knew the funds to acquire these items were available. Transcript at 314. Based on the signatures on the mission needs statements, funds were available for the CPUs on August 21 and 29, 1995, and for the expanded memory units on August 30 and September 13, 1995. Id. at 319.

36. The Director testified that a factor contributing to the perceived urgency was the desire "to spend...year-end '95 dollars to reduce...costs in '96." Transcript at 307. * * * *

Discussion

The Competition in Contracting Act (CICA) requires that contracting officers shall promote and provide for full and open competition in soliciting offers and awarding government contracts. Federal Acquisition Regulation (FAR) Part 6 contains policies and procedures designed to promote full and open competition.

The requirements for full and open competition set forth in FAR Part 6 need not be utilized for "contracts awarded using the simplified acquisition procedures of [FAR] Part 13." 48 CFR 6.001 (1995) (FAR 6.001). According to FAR Part 13, "Simplified acquisition procedures shall be used to the maximum extent practicable for all purchases of supplies or services not exceeding the simplified acquisition threshold...." FAR 13.103(a).[8]

The threshold for determining when the simplified acquisition procedures are applicable to a given procurement requires that the aggregate purchase fall under $100,000. FAR 13.101. However, if the contracting officer wants to use the simplified acquisition procedures for a purchase over $50,000, he/she must use the Federal Acquisition Computer Network (FACNET), which is the preferred means for soliciting simplified acquisitions. FAR 13.103(b), 13.106-1(a)(2).

FAR 13.103(c) contains the following prohibition:

> Requirements aggregating more than the simplified acquisition threshold shall not be broken down into several purchases that are less than the threshold merely to permit use, of simplified acquisition procedures.

Additionally, FAR 6.302-2, sets forth circumstances in which full and open competition need not be provided:

> 6.302-2 Unusual and compelling urgency.
>
> (a) Authority. (1) Citations: 10 U.S.C. 2304(c)(2) or 41 U.S.C. 253(c)(2).
>
> (2) When the agency's need for the supplies or services is of such an unusual and compelling urgency that the Government would be seriously injured unless the agency is permitted to limit the number of sources from which it solicits bids or proposals, full and open competition need not be provided for.
>
> (b) Application. This authority applies in those situations where (1) an unusual and compelling urgency precludes full and open competition, and (2) delay in award of a contract would result in serious injury, financial or other, to the Government. * * * *
>
> (c) Limitations. * * * *
>
> (2) This statutory authority requires that agencies shall request offers from as many potential sources as is practicable under the circumstances.

* * *

FAR 5.201(b)(1) requires procurements to be synopsized in the Commerce Business Daily (CBD) unless one of the exceptions in FAR 5.202 apply. FAR 5.201(b)(1) reads as follows:

> (b) For acquisitions of supplies and services other than those covered by the exceptions in 5.202, and special situations in 5.205, the contracting officer shall transmit a notice to the CBD (synopsis)(see 5.207) for each proposed—
>
> (1) contract actions meeting the thresholds in 5.101(a)(1);

FAR 5.101(a)(1) reads as follows:

---

8. FAR 13.101 defines "simplified acquisition procedures" as "the methods prescribed in [FAR Part 13] for making purchases of supplies or services using imprest funds, purchase orders, blanket purchase agreements, Government-wide commercial purchase cards, or any other appropriate authorized method."

(a) As required by the Small Business Act (15 U.S.C. 637(e)) and the Office of Federal Procurement Policy Act (41 U.S.C. 416), contracting officers shall disseminate information on proposed contract actions as follows:

(1) For proposed contract actions expected to exceed $25,000, by synopsizing in the Commerce Business Daily (CBD) (see 5.201);

FAR 5.202(a)(2) provides that the Government need not synopsize a proposed contract action in the CBD if the contracting officer determines, that:

(2) The contract action is made under the conditions described in 6.302-2 and the Government would be seriously injured if the agency complies with the time periods specified in 5.203;

Protester's grounds of protest allege violations of the above statutes and regulations.

* * *

Respondent's use of the simplified acquisition procedures and decision not to synopsize

In the procurements which are the subject of the instant protest, respondents used the simplified acquisition procedures, and did not synopsize the requirement in the CBD based upon the statements of urgency.

Improper fragmentation to avoid simplified acquisition procedures

The first ground of protest addressed by protester is:

The Respondents improperly fragmented the requirement for two Amdahl 5995 1400A's, each including 512 MB's of memory, to avoid the $100,000 simplified acquisition threshold in violation of FAR 13.000 and FAR 13.103(c). Each of the four purchase orders had a value of $49,900 so the aggregate of the four purchase orders equalled $199,600, which exceeded the $100,000 simplified acquisition threshold. Accordingly, pursuant to FAR 6.001, the Respondents had to comply with the competition requirements of FAR Part 6. The Respondents failed to comply with FAR Part 6. The Respondents did not obtain full and open competition as required by FAR 6.101.

Protester's Post-Hearing Brief at 45-46

Respondents respond to this ground by arguing that:

Protester has introduced no evidence indicating that Rock Island deliberately manipulated its requirements in order to use the Simplified Acquisition procedures. After the CCB approved the CPU upgrades, [the Director] established an internal priority list for his office identifying the acquisition of two CPU upgrades and two segments of expanded memory as the megacenter's top priority. When Rock Island collected sufficient year-end funds from its customers, the megacenter initiated the purchase of these items. Documentary evidence introduced at the hearing reveals that funding became available on August 21 and 29, 1995, for the two CPU upgrades, and on August 30 and September 13, 1995, for the expanded memory segments. Although Protester may argue that the Contracting Officer intentionally divided these requirements in order to avoid the simplified acquisition threshold the record does not support such a conclusion. The contracting officer processed and completed these procurements on an individual basis because that is how she received them from the megacenter. There is no evidence that the had any advance knowledge of the megacenter's total requirements, i.e, 2 CPUs and 2 purchases of expanded memory, before receiving them.

Clearly, if circumstances permitted, Respondent would have preferred to conduct these acquisitions in a consolidated fashion that allowed for separate awards for the CPUs and the expanded memory. In fact, this conclusion is supported by [the Director] who indicated, but for an insufficient quantity of funds, these procurements would have been combined.

Respondent's Post-Hearing Brief at 13-14 (citations omitted).

That the contracting officer had no "advance knowledge of the megacenter's total requirements" is not dispositive of the issue. The prohibition in FAR 13.103(c) against breaking down requirements into several purchases that are less than the simplified acquisition threshold does not excuse fragmentation merely because the contracting officer is unaware that a series of orders is actually one requirement. To read the regulation as respondent suggests would allow a contracting officer to receive orders for a fragmented requirement and circumvent the regulation as long as the contracting officer is not told of the true nature of the requirement by individuals who had such knowledge.

In this instance, the Director did have knowledge that the two CPUs and the two expanded memory units were to be purchased, and the determination that these items were required was made at the same time. Findings 33-34. When the CPUs were purchased, the expanded memory was configured on the two upgraded CPUs. Finding 28. Respondent alleges that these purchases could not have been made in a consolidated fashion because of a lack of available funding. The Director testified as to his belief that to allow funds to accumulate in sufficient quantity to purchase the two CPUs and two expanded memory units would result in a loss of funds. Finding 34. However, sufficient funds were approved for all four purchase orders before the first of the four purchase orders was issued. Finding 35. All of these circumstances demonstrate that the acquisition of the two CPUs and two expanded memory units were not four separate events, but in fact: were components of one requirement. Fragmentation of the requirement was a violation of FAR 13.103(c). See, e.g., Digital Services Group, GSBCA 8735-P, 87-1 BCA p 19,555, 1987 BPD p 6.

Failure to comply with FAR 6.302-2 and to synopsize the procurement in the CBD

Protester's second ground of protest is as follows:

FAR 5.201(b)(1) required the Respondents to synopsize because each $49,900 purchase order exceeded the $25,000 threshold in FAR 5.101(a)(1). The Respondents improperly claimed an urgency exception under FAR 5.202(a)(2), which authorizes the Contracting Officer not to synopsize [the contract action in the CBD] only if (1) the contract actions were made under the conditions described in FAR 6.302-2, and (2) the Respondents would have been "seriously injured" if synopsis occurred. According to the Contracting Officer, the purchase orders were not issued subject to FAR 6.302-2. The Urgency Statements and the memoranda of record justifying the avoidance of synopsizing the requirements did not establish urgency or the possibility of the Respondents being "seriously injured" if synopsis occurred.

Protester's Post-Hearing Brief at 47.

Respondents have alleged that the procurements were in accordance with FAR 6.302-2, which permits less than full and open competition under certain circumstances, including situations of urgent need. Finding 10. However, the record does not support respondents, alleged compliance with this regulation. * * * * The only alleged urgency factor which was time related was the attempt to spend funds before the CCB took the funds away from the megacenter and to spend year-end funds in 1995 to reduce costs in 1996. Findings 34, 36. Such a circumstance is not considered urgent to justify less than full and open competition. Computer Literacy World v. Department of the Air Force, GSBCA 13438-P, 1995 BPD p 231 (Dec. 11, 1995).

Additionally, even though respondents contend that the procurements were meant to comply with FAR 6.302-2, the justifications and approvals for awarding a contract without full and open competition as required by FAR 6.303-1, 6.303-2, and 6.304 were not provided. Finding 37.

Since the procurements were not in compliance with FAR 6.302-2, they are not encompassed by the exception in FAR 5.202(a)(2) to avoid synopsizing in the CBD. The failure to synopsize was a violation of FAR 5.101(a)(1).

Alleged failure to solicit a reasonable number of sources

Protester's third ground of protest is as follows:

> 10 U.S.C. § 2304 provides that except in certain situations, "the head of an agency in conducting a procurement for property or services shall obtain full and open competition through the use of competitive procedures in accordance with the requirements of this chapter and the Federal Acquisition Regulation." 10 U.S.C. § 2304(a)(1). Full and open competition means that "all responsible sources are permitted to submit sealed bids or competitive proposals on the procurement." 10 U.S.C. § 2302(3)(D) and 41 U.S.C. § 403(6).

* * *

> Respondent asserts that the two "informal market surveys" conducted by the contracting officer for the CPUs and expanded memory units, which took less than an hour, Findings 11, 21, were sufficient. Additionally, respondent argues, "Agencies may use informal market surveys in lieu of formal solicitation mailing lists when conducting small purchase acquisitions."

Respondent's Post-Hearing Brief at 19.

As we have found that the simplified acquisition procedures were not applicable this procurement should not have been conducted as a small purchase acquisition. There were other suppliers of comparable and compatible equipment who were not provided an opportunity to compete. Finding 38. Respondent's "informal market surveys" combined with its failure to synopsize the contract action in the CBD were insufficient to provide full and open competition.

Relief

The Amdahl 600Es that were replaced with Amdahl 1100As remain at Rock Island DMC and are kept in storage. Finding 27. The upgraded CPUs and expanded memory are currently being used by Rock Island DMC, but acceptance has been suspended pending the resolution of this protest. Finding 39. It would be wasteful and inconvenient to have respondent revert to using the previously dismantled 600Es * * *. Accordingly, respondent should conduct a competitive procurement in accordance with law and regulation, and replace the upgraded CPUs and expanded memory if another offeror is successful in that procurement.

Decision

The protest is GRANTED. The suspension order remains in effect until the procurement is concluded.

ALLAN H. GOODMAN
Board Judge

Notes and Questions

1. The case depicts a tension for the contracting officer between conducting "full and open competition," which involves procedures that take time and effort, and instead resorting to alternatives that bring faster results. Does information technology procurement present this tension no differently than in any other context? Note that although some aspects of the urgency here are both dubious and nonspecific to information technology, both IBM and Amdahl were relentlessly phasing out old products. Does the pace at which new products emerge from the high technology sector to replace old ones in information technology, and the need to move more promptly through the procurement process than with mere commodities or with items procured for a stockpile, create a greater need for the faster, simpler, more commercial procurement methods?

2. Use the time-labeled events of August and September 1995 in this case as a revealing roadmap of information technology procurement. In sum, Amdahl made a proposal in 1995. An information technology control board analyzed and approved the offer, the director of the agency customer decided to upgrade, staff prepared a documentation "package," the Director approved the package, and it went to the contracting officer; then, the contracting officer decided how to procure, conducted an informal market survey, telephoned a purchase order, and issued a written purchase order, then went through a second cycle for the next purchase request.

How much does the seller in Amdahl's position likely understand of all this? Note that it would not at all be astonishing for some of the documentation for a government contracting purchase to be drafted by the potential seller, though that is not suggested in this case. If you were Amdahl's counsel, could you assist government contracting personnel to prepare the documentation needed for an agency to make a rapid purchase, either the (unsuccessful) way in this case, or the (more complete) way that the Board requires? Could you at least discuss knowledgeably with them what they were doing? If you were counsel for the protester, could you have picked apart the procurement so well?

Chapter 8

Small Business and Subcontractors

While government contract law focuses principally on government dealings with prime contractors, subcontractors do play a vital role in the government contracting process. And although the very largest of federal contracts with amounts in the hundreds of millions of dollars or more, and the headlines to match, go to large companies, the fact of the matter is that the vast majority of federal contracts, by sheer number, are small dollar purchases including a large portion from small businesses. Even the contractors on the very largest of prime contracts generally perform through a series of subcontracts with suppliers, manufacturers, and service providers of various sizes, and with varying sophistication about the complex set of applicable legal rules. Add to that mix the political importance of supporting "small businesses" by those elected to Congress and the White House, with the resulting orientation toward small business in legislation and regulations, and it becomes apparent why a whole separate area of law concerns subcontractors and small businesses.

A. Privity and Subcontractors

Privity of contract and the lack thereof is one legal phrase that every subcontractor on a federal contract learns at some point, particularly when a dispute or claim arises as a result of government action or inaction. Due to lack of privity of contract between the government and a subcontractor, the courts have consistently barred subcontractors from direct access to the various Boards of Contract Appeals and the federal courts in actions against the government. Only a very limited exception occurs when the prime contractor acts as a purchasing agent for the government. Any uncertainty about the longstanding law in this regard ended with the enactment of the Contract Dispute Act of 1978, Pub. Law 95-563, by which only contractors, not subcontractors, may pursue claims against the government, and the term "contractor" is clearly defined as "a party to a Government contract other than the Government." 41 U.S.C. §601(4). To make the matter even clearer, the FAR prohibits a government contracting officer from consenting to a subcontract that obligates the contracting officer to deal directly with a subcontractor or that makes the results of arbitration, judicial determination, or voluntary settlement between the prime contractor and subcontractor binding on the government. FAR 44.203(b).

Lack of privity and the resulting barrier to direct claims does not, however, mean that no way whatsoever exists for a subcontractor's claim to be heard. The regulations permit, and the astute government subcontractor will ensure, that its subcontract with the federal prime contractor will provide for "sponsorship" of a subcontractor's claim. Sponsorship is the practice whereby the prime contractor nominally prosecutes what in fact is the subcontractor's claim against the government. The appeal of the claim is brought in the name of prime contractor even though the subcontractor is the real party in interest. FAR 44.203(c) states:

> Contracting officers should not refuse consent to a subcontract merely because it contains a clause giving the subcontractor the right of indirect appeal to an agency board of contract appeals if the subcontractor is affected by a dispute between the Government and the prime contractor. Indirect appeal means assertion by the subcontractor of the prime contractor's right to appeal or the prosecution of an appeal by the prime contractor on the subcontractor's behalf. The clause may also provide that the prime contractor and subcontractor shall be equally bound by the contracting officer's or board's decision. The clause may not attempt to obligate the contracting officer or the appeals board to decide questions that do not arise between the Government and the prime contractor or that are not cognizable under the clause at 52.233-1, Disputes.

Payment for such indirect appeal is generally the responsibility of the subcontractor.

Cases in this section illustrate the application of the classic barrier of privity. The *Merritt* case provides one of those rare but blessed occasions of a relevant Supreme Court opinion by Justice Brandeis which describes what is still good government contracting law, regarding the essential impact of the privity barrier. Then, the *Navcom* case shows the interaction of the privity barrier between government and subcontractor, and, what forum resolves issues between subcontactor and prime contractor. The *Erickson* case reflects how sponsorship works.

For further discussion of the subject of this section, see: Robert T. Ebert, Joseph W.C. Warren, & Kris D. Meade, The Impact of Procurement Reform Legislation on Subcontracting for Commercial Items: Easing But Not Eliminating the Burdens, 27 Pub. Cont. L.J. 343 (1998); John J. Thrasher, Subcontractor Dispute Remedies: Asserting Subcontractor Claims against the Federal Government, 23 Pub. Cont. L.J. 39 (1993); Robert G. Bugge, A User's Guide to the ABA's Model Fixed-Price Supply Subcontract, 15 Pub. Cont. L.J. 502 (1985).

Merritt v. United States

Supreme Court of the United States 267 U.S. 338. Decided March 2, 1925

Mr. Justice BRANDEIS delivered the opinion of the Court.

In July, 1918, or earlier, the United States contracted with the Panama Knitting Mills for a quantity of khaki at $3.20 a yard. In June, 1919, this contract was canceled by a new agreement between the government and the mills, made pursuant to the Dent Act, March 2, 1919, c. 94, 40 Stat. 1272 (Comp. St. Ann. Supp. 1919, §§3115 14/15 a-3115 14/15 e). Under the cancellation agreement the government adjusted its liability by accepting delivery of half of the khaki originally contracted for, paying the contract rate together with the carrying charges. The mills had a subcontract with the plaintiff for the supply of the khaki. By falsely representing that the government compelled settlement on the basis of $2.50 a yard plus the carrying charges, the mills induced the plaintiff to release it, on that basis, from the subcontract. When the government learned of the fraud thus perpetrated, it exacted from the mills a repayment of $5,210.02 — the difference between the amount actually paid by the government and what would have been paid if settlement had been made on the basis of $2.50 a yard. This suit was brought in March, 1923, to recover from the United States the sum so repaid. The Court of Claims dismissed the petition on demurrer for failure to state a cause of action. The case is here on appeal under section 242 of the Judicial Code (Comp. St. §1219).

Plaintiff cannot recover under the Dent Act. There are three obstacles. It does not appear, as required by section 1 (Comp. St. §3115 14/15 a), that, prior to November 12, 1918, an agreement with the plaintiff, express or implied, was entered into by the Secretary of War, or 'by any officer or agent acting under his authority, direction, or instruction, or that of the President.' Baltimore & Ohio R. R. Co. v. United States, 261 U. S. 385, 43 S. Ct. 384, 67 L. Ed. 711; Baltimore & Ohio R. R. Co. v. United States, 261 U. S. 592, 43 S. Ct. 425, 67 L. Ed. 816. It does not appear, as required by section 1, that any such agreement had been 'performed, * * * or expenditures * * * made or obligations incurred upon the faith of the same * * * prior to' November 12, 1918. Price Fire & Water Proofing Co. v. United States, 261 U. S. 179, 183, 43 S. Ct. 299, 67 L. Ed. 602. It does not appear, as required by section 1, that the claim sued on was presented before June 30, 1919. The Dent Act affords relief, although there is no agreement 'executed in the manner prescribed by law,' but only under the conditions stated. The plaintiff is not helped by section 4 (Comp. St. §3115 14/15 d), which deals with subcontracts; among other reasons, because it does not appear, as therein prescribed, that, before the payment made by the government to the prime contractor, the plaintiff had 'made expenditures, incurred obligations, rendered service, or furnished material, equipment, or supplies to such prime contractor, with the knowledge and approval of any agent of the Secretary of War duly authorized thereunto.'

Plaintiff cannot recover under the Tucker Act (Judicial Code, §145, 24 Stat. 505 [Comp. St. §1136]). The petition does not allege any contract, express or implied in fact, by the government with the plaintiff to pay the latter for the khaki on any basis. Nor does it set forth facts from which such a contract will be implied. The pleader may have intended to sue for money had and received. But no facts are alleged which afford any basis for a claim that the repayment made by the mills was exacted by the government for the benefit of the plaintiff. The Tucker Act does not give a right of action against the United States in those cases where, if the transaction were between private parties, recovery could be had upon a contract implied in law. Tempel v. United States, 248 U. S. 121, 39 S. Ct. 56, 63 L. Ed. 162; Sutton v. United States, 256 U. S. 575, 581, 41 S. Ct. 563, 65 L. Ed. 1099, 19 A. L. R. 403. For aught that appears repayment was compelled solely for the benefit of the government, under the proviso in section 1 of the Dent Act, which authorizes recovery of money paid under a settlement, if it has been defrauded.

The practice of the Court of Claims, while liberal, does not allow a general statement of claim in analogy to the common counts. It requires a plain, concise statement of the facts relied upon. See rule 15, Court of Claims. The petition may not be so general as to leave the defendant in doubt as to what must be met. Schierling v. United States, 23 Ct. Cl. 361; The Atlantic Works v. United States, 46 Ct. Cl. 57, 61; New Jersey Foundry & Machine Co. v. United States, 49 Ct. Cl. 235; United States v. Stratton, 88 F. 54, 59, 31 C. C. A. 384.

Affirmed.

Notes and Questions

1. The Court in *Merritt* distinguishes between the authority of the Court of Claims to hear cases involving contracts "implied in fact" and the lack of such authority to take

jurisdiction over claims of contracts "implied in law." What is the difference and why would Congress want to limit jurisdiction to just those implied in fact contracts?

2. In *Merritt*, the prime contractor was, under current terminology, terminated for the convenience of the government. The prime contractor had not, however, protected itself against such an occurrence in its contract with its subcontractor Merritt. This failure was the apparent basis for the fraud allegedly perpetrated against Merritt. How can a prime contractor protect itself against such terminations without having to resort to fraudulent activity?

3. Note the choice-of-law and procedural implications of *Merritt*. It sharply distinguishes between claims by the prime contractor which occur against the United States under federal statutes and other federal law in a federal forum, and the claims of the subcontractor which cannot occur directly against the United States. The subcontractor may or may not have a claim against the prime contractor, but if it does, what body of law governs that claim, federal law or basic contract law (today, the Uniform Commercial Code or the common law of contracts, both matters of state rather than federal law)? What forum does such a claim get litigated in, federal court or state court?

NAVCOM DEFENSE ELECTRONICS, INC., Plaintiff-Appellee, v. BALL CORPORATION, Defendant-Appellant.

No. 94-56396. United States Court of Appeals, Ninth Circuit.
92 F.3d 877 Decided Aug. 8, 1996.

Before BROWNING, WALLACE, and Farris, Circuit Judges.

PER CURIAM:

This is an appeal from the district court's order granting summary judgment for NavCom and enjoining Ball from submitting its contract dispute with NavCom to arbitration. For the reasons set out below, we affirm the district court's denial of Ball's motion to dismiss, reverse the court's grant of summary judgment, vacate the order prohibiting arbitration, and remand for entry of an order consistent with this opinion.

I.

The Air Force awarded NavCom a contract to produce a radar altimeter system. NavCom subcontracted with Ball to design and manufacture antennas to be used as part of the system. The Air Force required that the antennas meet certain pass/fail criteria, including the "MIL-STD-810" salt fog test. NavCom developed the NavCom Salt Fog Test Procedure to ensure that its antennas met Air Force specifications, and the Air Force approved the test. The subcontract required Ball's antennas to pass the NavCom Salt Fog Test.

Ball asserted that NavCom's test procedures were more rigorous than those required by the Air Force, but eventually performed the test according to NavCom's procedure. NavCom claimed that the antennas failed, while Ball insisted that the antennas passed the Air Force's criteria. NavCom directed Ball to redesign the antennas.

Ball asked NavCom to pay an equitable adjustment for redesign costs in the amount of $1,467,949. Ball claimed its prototype antenna could meet Air Force pass/fail criteria and failed only because of the more stringent NavCom testing procedure. Ball also claimed NavCom required a redesign option that was more costly than other options.

The central question is whether the dispute between NavCom and Ball should have been submitted to an Air Force contracting officer or to arbitration. The Ball/NavCom contract required that the decision of a contracting officer about the prime contract would be binding on the two parties in disputes about the subcontract.[2] In the same paragraph the contract provided that any dispute not settled by agreement of the parties would be submitted to arbitration.[3]

NavCom informed Ball that it planned to submit a claim to the contracting officer as specified in the contract. The claim submitted by NavCom described the dispute between NavCom and Ball and then argued, ostensibly on behalf of Ball, that the Air Force should be liable for increased costs because the Air Force's pass/fail criteria were ambiguous..Although Ball cooperated to at least some degree in drafting the claim (as required under the contract), Ball objected throughout the process to submission of the claim to the contracting officer. For instance, in a letter commenting on a draft version of the claim NavCom planned to submit, Ball wrote:

> Ball wishes to be on record that it has no claim against the Air Force and therefore does not endorse NavCom's statements in the draft letter that Nav-Com is "sponsoring" a claim "on behalf of Ball" pursuant to a "contractual obligation".... [I]f Ball was being sponsored, the effort was noticeably lacking in fervor; two, NavCom seems more intent on sidestepping or evading its liability to Ball by attempting to divert Ball's claims to the Air Force.

The Contracting Officer eventually denied the claim, finding that "Ball's argument that the MIL-STD-810 failure criteria are ambiguous is unfounded" and that the antennas had failed the test.

Just prior to the Contracting Officer's decision, Ball filed a demand for arbitration under the contract's arbitration provision. After initially participating, objecting to locale and choosing acceptable arbitrators, NavCom filed this suit in state court seeking to enjoin the arbitration. Ball removed the suit to federal court.

NavCom moved for a preliminary injunction prohibiting arbitration, and for partial summary judgment prohibiting arbitration and determining the subcontract required the disputed claim be resolved in the Court of Federal Claims where appeal of the contracting officer's decision was pending. Ball moved to dismiss for failure to state a claim.The district court summarily granted NavCom's motion for a preliminary injunction and partial summary judgment and denied Ball's motion to dismiss. * * *

Ball appeals * * * arguing that its claim against NavCom was not and could not be resolved by the contracting officer and that its dispute with NavCom was arbitrable under the contract.

---

2. "All Disputes between [NavCom] and [Ball] under this Purchase Order shall be resolved in the courts of competent jurisdiction provided, however, that if the face of this Purchase Order refers to a contract with the United States Government, then and in that event, any decision of the Contracting Officer under a Government prime contract, which relates to this Purchase Order shall be conclusive and binding upon [NavCom] and [Ball]."

3. "Any dispute arising under this Purchase Order which is not settled by agreement of the parties shall be subjected to arbitration in accordance with the rules of the American Arbitration Association, and judgment of the award rendered by the arbitrator(s) may be entered into any court having jurisdiction thereof."

II.

The Contract Disputes Act of 1978, 41 U.S.C. §§ 601-613 ("CDA"), provides the statutory framework for resolving disputes between government contractors and the government. Section 605(a) provides that "[a]ll claims by a contractor against the government relating to a contract...shall be submitted to the contracting officer for a decision," and § 601(a)(4) defines a "contractor" as "a party to a Government contract other than the Government." Under the CDA, contracting officers have jurisdiction only over claims by *contractors* against the government, not over claims brought directly by subcontractors. *Erickson Air Crane Co. v. United States,* 731 F.2d 810, 813 (Fed.Cir.1984)("hornbook rule" that subcontractors have no standing to enforce claims under CDA); *United States v. Johnson Controls, Inc.,* 713 F.2d 1541, 1548–49 (Fed.Cir.1983); *Clean Giant, Inc. v. United States,* 19 Cl.Ct. 390, 392 (1990); *see also* Senate Report No. 1118, 95th Cong., 2d Sess. 16–17, *reprinted in* 1978 U.S.Code Cong. & Ad.News 5235, 5250–51 (discussing exclusion of claims brought by subcontractors).

A subcontractor may assert a claim against the government only by having the prime contractor "sponsor" and certify the subcontractor's claim. *Erickson Air Crane,* 731 F.2d at 813; *See* Federal Acquisition Regulation 44.203(c); Major John J. Thrasher, "Subcontractor Dispute Remedies: Asserting Subcontractor Disputes against the Federal Government," 23 Pub. Cont. L.J. 39, 82-99 (1993). The contracting officer has no jurisdiction to resolve disputes between a subcontractor and the prime contractor. *U.S. West Communications Servs. v. United States,* 940 F.2d 622, 627 (Fed.Cir.1991)("A government contractor's dispute with its subcontractor was by definition specifically excluded from CDA coverage.").

III.

Whether Ball's claims could be submitted to the contracting officer depends upon whether they are claims against NavCom or against the Air Force. Ball has consistently alleged that NavCom, and not the Air Force, was responsible for the increased costs: Ball has contended that the NavCom Salt Fog Test procedure was too rigorous and the results were therefore invalid, and that the redesign of the antennas directed by NavCom was more expensive than other alternatives. These claims do not challenge Air Force conduct or suggest the Air Force was responsible for increased costs. They are claims by a subcontractor against a contractor, and the contracting officer therefore had no jurisdiction to resolve the dispute under the CDA.

NavCom's arguments to the contrary are unpersuasive. NavCom asserts that it did, in fact, submit Ball's claims to the contracting officer. However, Ball's allegations were neither presented to nor decided by the contracting officer. NavCom's claim did note that "[t]he language of MIL-STD-810 is overly restrictive," but Ball did not challenge the government's MIL-STD-810 pass/fail criteria but NavCom's test procedure. NavCom argued only that Ball and NavCom had arrived at different and reasonable interpretations of the Air Force's test criteria, and that because the redesign costs stemmed from ambiguity in the criteria which was attributable to the Air Force, the Air Force should pay the equitable adjustment. NavCom's claim that the pass/fail criteria were ambiguous simply did not address or include Ball's claims that NavCom's testing procedures were too rigorous or that NavCom demanded that Ball redesign the antenna in too costly a fashion. Nor did the contracting officer rule on Ball's claims; he found only that the "argument that the MIL-STD-810 failure criteria are ambiguous"—the theory advanced by NavCom, not Ball—was "unfounded."

Citing no authority, NavCom contends Ball's claims were claims against the government which NavCom could properly bring before the contracting officer if the claims could "be flowed up to the government so that ultimate financial responsibility will rest with that entity." This formulation begs the question it purports to answer—whether the claims allege government liability. In essence, NavCom contends that if it can transform Ball's claims into a claim against the government, no matter how distorted or unrelated to Ball's original claims, review by the contracting officer is Ball's sole avenue for relief and Ball is precluded from asserting its claims in any other forum. Neither the statute nor the contract contemplates that result.

NavCom points out that the subcontract provides that "if the face of this Purchase Order refers to a contract with the United States Government then...any decision of the Contracting Officer under a Government prime contract, which relates to this Purchase Order shall be conclusive and binding," and argues that because the subcontract does refer to a government contract and the contracting officer's decision relates to the subcontract, Ball is bound by that decision and barred from arbitrating its claims.

This argument fails. The parties cannot by contract expand the contracting officer's jurisdiction beyond that granted by the CDA. As we have said, contracting officers have no jurisdiction over claims on disputes between the contractor and subcontractor. Moreover, the contracting officer decided only whether the Air Force was liable; that determination cannot bind the parties on the question of whether NavCom is liable to Ball. The extent to which Ball may be bound by the contracting officer's holdings on the issues he did decide—that the MIL-STD-810 was not ambiguous and that the antennas failed the MIL-STD-810 requirements—and the impact the contracting officer's findings may have on Ball's claims, can be determined in arbitration.

NavCom argues that the Court can supply missing words in the contract to carry out the intent of the parties, *Heidlebaugh v. Miller,* 126 Cal.App.2d 35, 38, 271 P.2d 557 (1954), and submitted evidence that but for a drafting error, the arbitration clause would have provided that "[a]ny dispute arising under this Purchase Order *which is not covered by [the Contracting Officer provision],* and which is not settled by agreement of the parties shall be decided by arbitration." This added language cuts against NavCom's position rather than supporting it—since the dispute between NavCom and Ball cannot be submitted to a contracting officer under the CDA, it is arbitrable under the contract.

NavCom goes on to argue that the Court should give effect to the mutual intent of the parties, Cal. Civ. Code §§ 1636, and that the "main purpose" of the contract was to safeguard NavCom from inconsistent judgments. Even if NavCom had presented some evidence to support this theory, Ball could still arbitrate its claims against NavCom; were the arbitrator to find NavCom liable, there would be no inconsistency between findings that the Air Force is not liable but NavCom is because NavCom alone caused the additional costs.

We conclude that Ball's claims against NavCom are arbitrable under the contract.

Notes and Questions

1. The Navcom opinion weaves together two analytically distinct questions: the boundary limits of the system for disputes between the government and prime, and the a contest over the forum for disputes between prime and subcontractor. Even recognizing

that most disputes involving the subcontractor do not overlap with the limited jurisdiction of the system under the CDA for resolving disputes between the government and the prime contactor, still, sometimes there can be some overlap. Suppose the contracting officer had decided, in the course of reviewing NavCom's claim, that (1) that the Air Force had indeed changed (i.e., tightened) the contractual requirements in relation to NavCom's test procedures; (2) that NavCom's redesign option was what the Air Force wanted and indeed insisted upon; and (3) that the government owed a $500,000 equitable adjustment to NavCom which NavCom then tendered to Ball. (Assume that the ambivalence described in the opinion had not existed - that NavCom had fought tooth-and-nail to obtain this nice set of rulings for Ball.) Should those determinations now allow NavCom to bar an arbitration by Ball? If not, should they at least be treated by the arbitrator as binding? Who is making the relevant distinctions here between arbitrable and non-arbitrable issues: Congress, the courts, the contracting officer, or the private parties?

2. Note the discussion of how the Contract Disputes Act of 1978, by confining the uses of the disputes system rather narrowly, shaped this case. The CDA, and the privity doctrine discussed in *Merritt*, function similarly. In the wake of the privity doctrine and the CDA, case law developed which defines the limited number of exceptions to the general rule that a subcontractor cannot bring a direct dispute or appeal against the government. One of them, discussed in *United States v. Johnson Controls, Inc.*, 713 F.2d 1541 (Fed. Cir. 1983), concerns when the government has used a contractor as a mere agent to place contracts for performance, in which case these contracts are then directly between the government and the performing businesses even though these businesses may get the label "subcontractor" stuck to them.

For example, in the construction context, the government might hire one contractor to find and to contract with various specialized ones, contemplating that the government itself will deal directly with those specialized ones. (Note, as a side-problem, that the Federal Acquisition Regulation, 48 C.F.R. 44.203(b)(3), precludes contracting officers from consenting to direct disputes by subcontractors.) Conversely, when the government puts in an "ABC" clause, both in its prime contract and in the agreements between the prime and the subcontractors, unequivocally stating that no contractual relationship shall exist between the government ("A") and the "subcontractors" ("C"), but only between each of them and the prime ("B" - hence, "ABC clause"), that is an important factor suggesting no direct relationship does, in fact, exist between government and subcontractor.

Erickson Air Crane Company of Washington, Inc., Appellant, v. The United States, Appellee

Appeal No. 83-891 United States Court of Appeals, Federal Circuit.
731 F.2d 810., March 26, 1984

Before MARKEY, Chief Judge, FRIEDMAN, Circuit Judge, and NICHOLS, Senior Circuit Judge.

NICHOLS, Senior Circuit Judge.

This is an appeal from a United States Department of Energy Board of Contract Appeals (EBCA or board) decision, 83-1 BCA ¶ 16,145 (1982), denying recovery to appellant of amounts allegedly due it under certain clauses and due to breaches of other clauses of United States Contract No. 6/07/DC/71720. We affirm.

I.

Background

On January 12, 1976, the United States Department of the Interior's Bureau of Reclamation (government) entered into Contract No. 6/07/DC/71720 with Erickson Air Crane Company of Washington, Inc. (Erickson) to construct approximately 136 miles of 345 kilovolt transmission line from a point near Steamboat Springs, Colorado to Ault, Colorado. The contract required Erickson to have the transmission line in service by November 30, 1977, or suffer liquidated damages of $5,250 per additional day.

Since much of the transmission line's route lay over mountainous and heavily timbered terrain, Erickson intended to assemble and erect the steel transmission towers with a Sikorsky S-64 Sky Crane helicopter. Erickson subcontracted for the other "more routine" parts of the project with Pacific States Clearing (PSC) to build access roads and to clear the structure sites and the right-of-way; with a joint venture of Professional Hole Drilling, Inc. and Caissons, Inc. (PHD/C) to construct foundations for the transmission towers; with Tri-O, Inc. to string the conductor and overhead ground wire on the towers; and with New Growth, Inc. to landscape and revegetate the tower sites and temporary roads.

Erickson developed a comprehensive schedule for it and its subcontractors to follow: in rapid succession, PSC would clear a site, PHD/C would lay a foundation, Erickson would erect a transmission tower, Tri-O would begin wire stringing, and New Growth would begin revegetation. Due to Erickson's tight scheduling, however, single problems during construction often multiplied into several problems affecting other subcontractors down the line. Subcontractors' schedules became unsynchronized; costs rose for most of those involved in the project.

Erickson subsequently filed several dozen claims on its and its subcontractors' (claimants) behalf with the government's contracting officer, then in the Department of Energy (DOE). (DOE assumed responsibility for the project pursuant to the Department of Energy Organization Act, Pub.L. No. 95-91, 91 Stat. 565 (1977). DOE assigned the project's administration to the Western Area Power Administration.) The contracting officer made his final decision on July 18, 1979, holding for the government on some claims, and against it on others.

Erickson, on behalf of all the claimants, appealed thirty-five of these adverse decisions to the EBCA pursuant to section 7 of the Contract Disputes Act of 1978, 41 U.S.C. §606 (1982). The EBCA consolidated claimants' appeals for the purpose of a hearing. Counsel represented each of the claimants, with Erickson's counsel designated as "lead" counsel and called upon mostly for procedural matters.

Claimants' claims fell into three general categories. The first category consisted of claims alleging that during construction, the government delayed the work and disrupted the work sequence, and thus breached its contractual obligations or constructively changed the terms of the contract. Claimants argued that these government actions caused them to incur additional time, labor, and equipment costs for which the government is liable. The government responded that it merely enforced the terms of the contract and that any damages claimants suffered were due to their own failure to observe, acknowledge, or reasonably interpret various contract provisions.

The second general category consisted of claims alleging that the government's bid documents misrepresented the physical conditions under which claimants would work, and that this misrepresentation affected the required method and manner of performance. The government responded that the specifications clearly spelled out the required performance and the working conditions associated therewith.

The third category contained one claim for costs under the value engineering (VE) provisions of the contract. Erickson based this claim on the government's acceptance of a proposal Erickson presented to it on behalf of PHD/C to allow the modification of a specified type of tower footing under certain conditions. The government denied that Erickson's proposal for use of the particular footing was a VE proposal. The government also asserted that Erickson's proposal did not meet the technical requirements of a VE change proposal but was merely a contract change proposed and approved under the contract's "Changes" clause.

The EBCA issued its decision on September 30, 1982. Erickson, PHD/C, and Tri-O each filed a notice of appeal of the board's decision adverse to them. Over the objection of the United States, we allowed PHD/C's and Tri-O's motions to attack through their own briefs the EBCA decisions adverse to them.

II.

Standing of Subcontractors

It is a hornbook rule that, under ordinary government prime contracts, subcontractors do not have standing to sue the government under the Tucker Act, 28 U.S.C. §1491, in the event of an alleged government breach or to enforce a claim for equitable adjustment under the Contract Disputes Act of 1978. United States v. Johnson Controls, Inc., 713 F.2d 1541 (Fed.Cir.1983); Putnam Mills Corp. v. United States, 479 F.2d 1334, 202 Ct.Cl. 1 (1973). The government consents to be sued only by those with whom it has privity of contract, which it does not have with subcontractors. Johnson Controls, Inc., 713 F.2d at 1550–52. Aggrieved subcontractors have the option of enforcing their subcontract rights against the prime contractor in appropriate proceedings, or of prosecuting a claim against the government through and in right of the prime contractor's contract, and with the prime contractor's consent and cooperation.

As a practical matter, prime contractors often do allow subcontractors to prosecute claims in the prime's name when they perceive that the subcontractors really have more at stake in a claim and are therefore willing to work harder on its enforcement. Subcontractors may also be the only ones in full possession of the facts. In the former Court of Claims, in contract cases, it was quite usual for prime contractors to step aside and allow counsel retained by subcontractors to prosecute claims, though always in the name and right of the prime. It is to be noted, too, that bonding requirements are often for protection of subcontractors and give them better assurance of being paid, in compensation for their inability to enforce liens against work which has become property of the government. Johnson Controls, Inc., 713 F.2d at 1553–54; United States Fidelity & Guaranty Co. v. United States, 475 F.2d 1377, 1381, 201 Ct.Cl. 1 (1973). In this case the board stated that Erickson took all the appeals before it, but elsewhere used language implying that subcontractors were appellants. Counsel entered appearances for them and the board made awards to them.

We directed the clerk in this case to accept briefs on behalf of subcontractors in their own names. This was done because of the role played by them below, because of recollection of the Court of Claims practice, and because the prime contractor sponsored their claims.

By hindsight, this was probably a mistake. It allowed avoidance of the rule of this court respecting length of briefs, Rule 13(b). In view of the number of appeal issues, it is possible, perhaps probable, the court would have allowed additional pages, but the procedure adopted denied the court any opportunity to keep down the briefing to the length most helpful to it. The object of briefs is, after all, to aid the court, not to enhance the earnings of counsel.

A more serious unfortunate consequence of our decision was that the brief writers, giving lip service to the rule that the subcontractors had no privity of contract with the government, in practice seemed to assume that the contrary was the law. They argued, ostensibly against the government, grievances that if valid were valid only against the prime. They tended to disregard negotiations between the prime and the government, or else agreements or transactions, in which they did not participate, that would have a strong bearing on whether the government was liable to pay an equitable adjustment to the prime. For this reason, the briefs were confusing and difficult for the court to follow. It appeared from statements by counsel that some suit or suits by the subcontractors against the prime are pending in other courts, but are stayed pending the outcome of this case. It seems almost as if there may be a feeling that the subcontractors must exhaust their remedies against the government before their claims against the prime can be adjudicated.

It is but fair to say that despite the confusion incident to allowing subcontractors to participate as if parties, the appeal board in its able decision before us always kept clearly in mind who was the party against whom the claims were made, and who was the party properly prosecuting those claims. This is probably easier for a body specializing in contract cases than it is for a court with a more generalist jurisdiction.

Notice is hereby given that in future contract cases in this court, only the prime contractor may be the appellant, absent, of course, special contract or regulatory provisions not here involved which, in some other cases, might confer standing on subcontractors or persons who normally would be deemed only subcontractors. The procedure followed in this case will not be regarded as a precedent in future cases. A party in interest whose relationship to the case is that of the ordinary subcontractor may prosecute its claims only through, and with the consent and cooperation of, the prime, and in the prime's name. Prime contractors may turn over part of their briefing space, and part of their argument time, to representatives of subcontractors, but this, when it occurs, is a private arrangement among interested parties which may not add to the jurisdiction of the court, or the burdens upon it. Specifically, for purposes of briefing space and argument time, a prime contractor and its subcontractors are, whatever their private understandings, one party for purposes of Rule 13(b).

Notes and Questions

1. What is the policy basis for allowing a prime contractor to sponsor a subcontractor's claim, as discussed in the *Erickson* case? Shouldn't the subcontractor be required first to litigate its claims against the prime contractor, with the prime contractor filing suit against the government only after the prime contractor's liability has been determined by a court of competent jurisdiction? Or would this only disadvantage the contractor and subcontractor forced to multi-stage litigation?

2. Generally, in pursuing claims against the government, subcontractors are required to either secure consent to proceed in the name of the prime or to have their appeals prosecuted by the prime (FAR §44.203(c)). Under a sponsorship arrangement, the words and concerns of the subcontractor are mouthed by the prime, which must certify

the good-faith basis for claims over $100,000. (FAR §52.233-1; Contract Disputes Act of 1978, 41 U.S.C.§601 et seq.).

Where they do not enjoy such a cooperative relationship, subcontractors, lacking privity with the government necessary to make claims in their own right, have been seeking a serviceable substitute for decades. Three theories of subcontractor standing are agency (as was unsuccessfully alleged in *Johnson Controls*); contract implied-in-fact (as claimed to no avail in *National Micrographics v. United States*, 38 Fed. Cl. 46 (1997)); and third-party beneficiary status, which found the court's favor in *D & H Distributing Co. v. United States*, 102 F.3d 542 (Fed. Cir. 1996). For a more detailed examination of this topic, see Major David A. Wallace et al., *Contract Law Developments of 1997-The Year in Review,*1998-JAN ARMLAW 3; Stephen G. Lee, *Hiring the Cheapest Piper: Arbitration of Subcontractor Disputes by Boards of Contract Appeals*, 23 Pub Con. L.J. 105 (1993).

3. Traditionally, notwithstanding the privity barrier, many requirements have been placed on subcontracts, from disclosure of cost and pricing data to compliance with labor standards. In 1994, Congress enacted the Federal Acquisition Streamlining Act allowing prime contractors greater freedom to subcontract commercially. Specifically, FASA's pertinent provision, codified at 41 U.S.C. §427, removed most barriers between prime contractors seeking commercial items or components, and prospective subcontractors, who were previously deterred by cost and pricing documentation requirements. Additionally, FAR §12.50 ends the applicability of 18 varied restrictions on subcontractors, including the Walsh-Healey Act (41 U.S.C. §43), the Service Contract Act (41 U.S.C. §351), the Tariff Act of 1930 (19 U.S.C. §1202), and the Drug-Free Workplace Act of 1988 (41 U.S.C.§701, et seq.), and modifies the applicability of CAS (41 U.S.C.§422) and TINA (41 U.S.C.§254(d) and 10 U.S.C.§2306(a)) requirements. FAR 13.006 makes numerous part 52 provisions inapplicable to contracts and subcontracts at or below the simplified acquisition threshold. For an examination of this subject, see Robert T. Ebert, Joseph W.C. Warren and Kris D. Meade, *The Impact of Procurement Reform Legislation on Subcontracting for Commercial Items: Easing But Not Eliminating the Burdens*, 27 Pub. Cont. L.J. 343 (1998).

4. Perhaps the legally most interesting requirement placed on subcontracts consists of "flow-down" clauses. "Flow-down" clauses are prime contract provisions that become part of a subcontract by one of four mechanisms. First, a prime contract clause may be expressly written as mandatory flow-down clause. Second, a prime contract may require that the substance of a clause "flow-down" to any subcontract. Third, as a matter of an operation of law, e.g., a provision in the FAR, a clause may be required to flow from the prime to the subcontract. Finally, absent a required "flow-down, a clause may still do so if the duties imposed on the prime contractor by the clause make the contract incapable of being effectively fulfilled unless that duty also flows to a subcontractor.

5. Examples of "flow-down" clauses are numerous. "Inspection" clauses, "Termination" clauses, and "Disputes" clauses are all clauses that, while not mandatory as "flow-down" clauses to a subcontract, are recommended for inclusion by the prime contractor where there is reliance on subcontractor performance and cooperation. "Changes" clauses, "Limitation of Liability", "Cost and Pricing Data", and "Warranty" clauses are examples of provisions that require "flow-down" by their substance, to subcontracts when they are present in the prime contract. Some examples of mandatory clauses include "Subcontracts (Fixed-Price Contract)" clauses, "Examination of Records by the Comptroller General" clause, and "Insurance" clauses (where the subcontractor is working on a government installation). Additionally, there are clauses that may have a substance requirement for flow-down in some instances, but are expressly mandatory to particular subcontract types.

6. There is a detailed "ABA Model for Fixed-Price Supply Subcontract Terms and Condition". This form sets forth the terms and conditions of the subcontract inclusive of applicable clauses. See Robert G. Bugge, *A User's Guide to the ABA's Model Fixed-Price Supply Subcontract*, 15 Pub. Cont. L.J. 502 (1985). A 1996 revision of this model introduced significant changes in the form, most significantly removing the "optional clauses" previously supplied in the prior form, but including specific "flow-down" clauses for defense contracts, both short and full versions of the applicable clauses, and a user's guide.

WOODWARD GOVERNOR CO., Plaintiff-Appellant, v. CURTISS-WRIGHT FLIGHT SYSTEMS, INC., Defendant-Appellee.

Docket No. 98-7910, United States Court of Appeals, Second Circuit. 164 F.3d 123, Decided Jan. 8, 1999.

Before: WALKER and McLAUGHLIN, Circuit Judges, and PRESKA, District Judge.

McLAUGHLIN, Circuit Judge:

BACKGROUND

In 1990, the United States contracted with the Lockheed Corporation ("Lockheed"), for the design and manufacture of a new fighter plane, the F-22 "Raptor." As is typical in such cases, a series of subcontracts ensued. Lockheed subcontracted the weapons bay doors to Curtiss-Wright Flight Systems, Inc. ("Curtiss-Wright"). Curtiss-Wright, in turn, chose the plaintiff, Woodward Governor Co. ("Woodward"), to produce "test stands" that would allow the bay doors to be tested before they were actually installed in the F-22. It is this latter subcontract that generated this litigation.

The subcontract between Curtiss-Wright and Woodward set a price of $1.5 million for the test stands. It provided that the subcontract was governed by New Jersey law unless New Jersey law was "not dispositive," in which case the "federal common law of government contracts" governed. The subcontract also contained provisions relating to the rights and responsibilities of the parties vis a vis the federal government.

In January 1994, Woodward began work on the test stands. The work quickly fell behind schedule, however, because Curtiss-Wright had not yet finished designing the weapons bay doors. In late 1995, Curtiss-Wright ordered Woodward to bring the unfinished test stands to Curtiss-Wright's facility in New Jersey, even though under the subcontract delivery of the test stands by Woodward to Curtiss-Wright was not yet due. To meet this demand, Woodward was forced to transport its materials and employees to New Jersey to continue work on the test stands at Curtiss-Wright's facility. This, of course, caused further delay and added expense.

Throughout 1995, Curtiss-Wright remained unable to provide Woodward with prototypes of the weapons bay doors. In exasperation, Woodward demanded that Curtiss-Wright provide the weapons bay doors by January 1996, at the latest. Curtiss-Wright responded that it could not provide the bay doors until May 1996. In the end, Curtiss-Wright never provided Woodward with a prototype.

By August 2, 1996, Curtiss-Wright had paid Woodward all the progress payments called for by the subcontract, with only the last $317,000 progress payment still due. However, as a result of the substantial delays and the need to work on the test stands at

Curtiss-Wright's facility, Woodward concluded that construction of the test stands would cost substantially more than the $1.5 million originally agreed upon. Woodward thus sought to re-negotiate the terms of the subcontract. After a flurry of correspondence about who would pay for the cost over-runs, Curtiss-Wright broke off the negotiations by informing Woodward that it considered Woodward to have defaulted on the subcontract. Curtiss-Wright then engaged another company to complete construction of the test stands.

In December 1997, Woodward filed suit in the United States District Court for the District of Connecticut (Covello, Judge), seeking damages and declaratory relief for Curtiss-Wright's alleged breach of the subcontract. Subject matter jurisdiction was premised on a federal question under 28 U.S.C. § 1331. It is undisputed that there is no diversity under 28 U.S.C. § 1332.

Curtiss-Wright moved to dismiss the complaint, arguing that there is no federal question because none of Woodward's claims is governed by federal law. Woodward countered that federal common law governs because its claims arise out of the breach of a subcontract relating to defense procurement. Judge Covello concluded that federal common law does not apply and dismissed the complaint under Fed. R. Civ. P. 12(b)(1) for lack of subject matter jurisdiction.

Woodward now appeals, advancing three main arguments for its position: (1) the nature of the subcontract requires that this case be governed by federal common law; (2) the parties elected to be governed by federal common law; and (3) Woodward's claim for equitable relief under federal law requires the application of federal common law.

DISCUSSION

The sole issue is whether the district court had subject matter jurisdiction. We review the factual findings of the district court on a motion to dismiss for lack of subject matter jurisdiction for clear error, while we review the district court's legal conclusions de novo. See Wake v. United States, 89 F.3d 53, 57 (2d Cir.1996). We conclude that Curtiss-Wright is correct, and federal common law does not apply in this breach of contract suit. Because there is no other basis for federal subject matter jurisdiction, we affirm Judge Covello's dismissal of the complaint.

It is beyond dispute that if federal common law governs a case, that case presents a federal question within the subject matter jurisdiction of the federal courts, just as if the case were governed by a federal statute. See 28 U.S.C. § 1331; Illinois v. City of Milwaukee, 406 U.S. 91, 100, 92 S.Ct. 1385, 31 L.Ed.2d 712 (1972).

In recent years, the Supreme Court has sought to clarify when federal common law enters the picture. See Atherton v. FDIC, 519 U.S. 213, 117 S.Ct. 666, 670, 136 L.Ed.2d 656 (1997); Boyle v. United Technologies Corp., 487 U.S. 500, 504–07, 108 S.Ct. 2510, 101 L.Ed.2d 442 (1988); but see 19 Charles Allan Wright, et al., Federal Practice and Procedure § 4514, at 458–59 (1996) (Court's attitude produces "an anomaly," and there are no bright-line rules). The Court has explained that, as a threshold matter, a case must implicate "uniquely federal interests" for federal common law to apply. Boyle, 487 U.S. at 504, 108 S.Ct. 2510 (internal quotation marks omitted). As Justice Scalia explained in Boyle, such interests arise only in a few areas, such as: (1) the obligations to, and rights of, the United States under its contracts; (2) the liability of federal officers for official acts; and (3) civil liabilities arising out of federal procurement contracts relating to national defense. See id. at 504–06; Erwin Chemerinsky, Federal Jurisdiction §§ 6.2 at 337-52 (2d ed.1994).

Even when "uniquely federal interests" are implicated, federal common law applies only where there is a "significant conflict between some federal policy or interest and the use of state law." O'Melveny, 512 U.S. at 87, 114 S.Ct. 2048; see Boyle, 487 U.S. at 504, 108 S.Ct. 2510 * * * *

Woodward accepts these principles in the abstract, but argues that federal common law applies here because: (1) the subcontract between Woodward and Curtiss-Wright relates to national defense, which Woodward asserts is an issue of "uniquely federal interest"; and (2) application of New Jersey law would conflict with the federal interest in having a uniform legal standard apply to all its defense procurement contracts.

A. Issue of Uniquely Federal Interest

Woodward's position—that this case involves an issue of uniquely federal interest—is not without some merit. Several cases do indeed suggest that federal procurement contracts relating to national security implicate uniquely federal interests. See, e.g., Boyle, 487 U.S. at 507, 108 S.Ct. 2510; United States v. Allegheny County, 322 U.S. 174, 182, 64 S.Ct. 908, 88 L.Ed. 1209 (1944). The subcontract here bears a connection to a government contract for the design and manufacture of a fighter plane; it would seem to meet the first requirement for application of federal common law. See Pescatore, 97 F.3d at 10; see also Boyle, 487 U.S. at 507, 108 S.Ct. 2510. Upon closer scrutiny, however, it becomes apparent that this subcontract is too far removed from issues of uniquely federal concern to call for the application of federal common law.

Woodward interprets our decision in United States v. Pappas, 94 F.3d 795, 801 (2d Cir.1996), as holding that any contract that bears any relation to national security is governed by federal common law. Pappas, however, cannot bear the weight of so sweeping a proposition. Pappas involved an attempt by the United States to enforce a provision in Pappas' employment contract prohibiting him from disclosing secrets that he learned while working for the government. We held that such a contract, which directly affected national security because it related to the disclosure of state secrets, was governed by federal common law. See id. at 801-02.

Pappas is inapposite because: (1) the United States itself was trying to enforce the contract in Pappas; and (2) the contract in Pappas related directly to national security. In this case, the United States has no immediate interest in Woodward's dispute with Curtiss-Wright, and there is no allegation that the United States could incur liability. Indeed, Curtiss-Wright has admitted that it is estopped from attempting to recover any damages in this suit from the government. Moreover, Woodward has not alleged that national security would be imperiled if it is not paid for its work on the test stands. Thus, the sort of direct federal interest that permeated Pappas is absent here.

Woodward also relies on a smattering of cases suggesting that all subcontracts relating to defense procurement contracts are governed by federal common law. Woodward relies heavily upon New SD, Inc. v. Rockwell Int'l Corp., 79 F.3d 953 (9th Cir.1996), where the Ninth Circuit so held.

We find New SD unpersuasive for several reasons. First, the New SD court itself conceded that its holding was contrary to "a number of forceful arguments" and authority from other circuits, but felt bound by its earlier decision in American Pipe & Steel Corp. v. Firestone Tire & Rubber Co., 292 F.2d 640 (9th Cir.1961). See New SD, 79 F.3d at 954–55. Moreover, the reasoning behind New SD is, in our opinion, flawed. While there is no question that contracts relating directly to government liability for procurement decisions are governed by federal common law, the issue gets muddier as the contract gets further removed from the government. A subcontract for the provision of a toilet seat for a bomber, probably three or four subcontracts removed from privity with the federal government, would not seem to concern an issue of uniquely federal interest. However, the New SD analysis provides no touchstone to distinguish between the contract for the bomber itself and the subcontract for the toilet seat. In this case, where the test stands do not become a part of the F-22, but are only a tool to help Curtiss-Wright perfect the bay doors, the New SD analysis is especially unhelpful.* * * *

Boyle held that federal common law should apply to prevent government liability arising out of procurement activities. See Boyle, 487 U.S. at 507, 108 S.Ct. 2510; Northrop, 959 F.2d at 1427. Moreover, the Supreme Court's decision in O'Melveny (which expressed a distinct distaste for displacing state law) confirms that the Seventh Circuit's reluctance in Northrop to apply federal common law is the better approach. Because the Woodward—Curtiss-Wright "'litigation is among private parties and no substantial rights or duties of the United States hinge on its outcome,'" application of federal common law is particularly inappropriate. Northrop, 959 F.2d at 1428 (quoting Miree v. DeKalb County, 433 U.S. 25, 31, 97 S.Ct. 2490, 53 L.Ed.2d 557 (1977)); see Boyle, 487 U.S. at 507, 108 S.Ct. 2510.

B. Conflict Between Federal Interest and State Law

Even if Woodward were correct that its dispute with Curtiss-Wright implicates an issue of uniquely federal interest, federal common law still would not apply here because Woodward cannot show that state law conflicts with a significant federal policy or interest.

The only federal interest that Woodward claims conflicts with the application of New Jersey law is the purported need for a uniform rule of decision in government procurement cases. However, in numerous cases, courts have rejected similar attempts to rely on vague assertions about the need for uniformity. See, e.g., Atherton, 117 S.Ct. at 671; O'Melveny, 512 U.S. at 88, 114 S.Ct. 2048; Pescatore, 97 F.3d at 11. Indeed, the Supreme Court has specifically held that "generalized pleas for uniformity" do not sufficiently allege an actual conflict between state law and a federal interest. Kimbell Foods, 440 U.S. at 730, 99 S.Ct. 1448. We have followed the same rule. See B.F. Goodrich, 112 F.3d at 91 (reliance on federal interest in uniformity insufficient absent actual, substantial conflict with state law).

* * *

C. Choice of Law Clause in the Subcontract

Woodward also contends that the choice of law provision in the subcontract calls for the application of federal common law. We disagree.

The subcontract contains two provisions relating to choice of law. Article 34 states that "[t]his Purchase Order shall be governed by and construed in accordance with the law (exclusive of the law with respect to the conflict of laws) of the State of New Jersey." Later, in the standard terms and conditions that the parties incorporated in the subcontract, it provides that "[t]his Order shall be construed and interpreted according to the law of the State of New Jersey..., [and if] the law of the State of New Jersey is not dispositive, the federal common law of government contracts shall govern."

Woodward maintains that New Jersey law is not dispositive in this case, and, accordingly, the subcontract calls for the application of federal common law. However, Woodward fails to explain why New Jersey law is not dispositive in this garden variety breach of contract case. As explained above, the U.C.C. governs this dispute, and Woodward fails to make clear how the U.C.C. is not dispositive.

* * *

D. Claim for Equitable Adjustment under Federal Common Law

Woodward's complaint also asserted a cause of action for an "equitable adjustment"— essentially, restitution for unjust enrichment—under federal common law. Woodward maintains that this claim was sufficient to support federal question jurisdiction.

We note also that Woodward delivered the test stands to, and worked on them in, Curtiss-Wright's New Jersey facility. New Jersey law provides an equitable remedy for unjust enrichment. See St. Paul Fire & Marine Ins. Co. v. Indemnity Ins. Co. of N. Am., 32 N.J. 17, 22, 158 A.2d 825 (1960). Therefore, to the extent that federal common law would provide Woodward with an equitable remedy, New Jersey would provide the same remedy. Thus, no conflict between state law and a federal interest in providing restitution is present in this case, and application of federal common law is inappropriate. See O'Melveny, 512 U.S. at 87–88, 114 S.Ct. 2048; Pescatore, 97 F.3d at 10.

CONCLUSION

Federal common law does not apply to Woodward's claims, and there is no other basis for federal subject matter jurisdiction in this case. Accordingly, Judge Covello properly dismissed Woodward's complaint under Fed. R. Civ. P. 12(b)(1), and the judgment of the district court is hereby AFFIRMED.

Notes and Questions

1.   Students will recall, from their course in Civil Procedure, the so-called *Erie* questions about when federal courts establish federal law to follow, and when they follow state law. In recent decades, the Supreme Court has tended to reduce the occasions for federal courts to establish federal common law. An exception is the Supreme Court's opinion in *Boyle,* found elsewhere in these materials, and much cited in *Woodward,* which did create federal common law regarding the tort immunity of government contractors. The *Woodward* opinion follows the Court's tendency in declining to find this subcontracting case an occasion for federal common law. As the opinion itself points out, the appellate courts have divided somewhat on this issue, although each case tends to be somewhat idiosyncratic, with the opinion of *New SD. Inc. v. Rockwell Int'l Corp.,* 79 F.3d 953 (9th Cir. 1996), creating federal common law for a subcontracting case.

2.   Does this opinion establish a universal rule against applying federal common law to subcontracting cases? Note the consequences each way. On the one hand, a universal rule puts subcontracting disputes, even when they might involve important points as to contacting for national defense, to state lawmaking. In this case, the Uniform Commercial Code provides uniformity and avoids idiosyncratic or government-hostile state lawmaking, but the UCC only covers part of contract law. On the other hand, an uncertain rule produces the problem as here, that it takes several years of litigation from district to appellate federal courts, just to resolve the choice-of-law question, not a resolution of the case on its merits.

3.   Can, or should, contracting officers anticipate or resolve questions of subcontracting case forum and choice-of-law? The opinion notes that the subcontract contained provisions as to the parties' rights and responsibilities vis-a-vis the federal gov-

ernment, presumably including "flowdown" provisions, the inclusion of which in sub-contracts occurs under the supervision of the contracting officer. Does the inclusion in the subcontract of a clause saying New Jersey law governs, answer this question? Could the FAR provide a flowdown clause that did not itself provide substantive rules for sub-contracting cases but that expected federal courts to do so as a matter of federal com-mon law?

    4.   For a discussion of the issue of mandatory flowdown into subcontracts, see Frank J. Baltz & J. Russell Morrissey, *Do You Know If You Are a Government Contractor: FAR Clauses Incorporated Into Subcontracts Without Reference*, 34 Procurement Lawyer, Summer 1999, at 36.

Arthur S. LUJAN, Labor Commissioner of California, et al., v. G & G FIRE SPRINKLERS, INC.

Supreme Court of the United States, 532 U.S. 189 No. 00-152.
Argued Feb. 26, 2001., Decided April 17, 2001.

Chief Justice REHNQUIST delivered the opinion of the Court.

    The California Labor Code (Code or Labor Code) authorizes the State to order with-holding of payments due a contractor on a public works project if a subcontractor on the project fails to comply with certain Code requirements. The Code permits the con-tractor, in turn, to withhold similar sums from the subcontractor. The Court of Appeals for the Ninth Circuit held that the relevant Code provisions violate the Due Process Clause of the Fourteenth Amendment because the statutory scheme does not afford the subcontractor a hearing before or after such action is taken. We granted certiorari, 531 U.S. 924, 121 S.Ct. 297, 148 L.Ed.2d 239 (2000), and we reverse.

    Petitioners are the California Division of Labor Standards Enforcement (DLSE), the California Department of Industrial Relations, and several state officials in their official capacities. Respondent G & G Fire Sprinklers, Inc. (G & G) is a fire-protection company that installs fire sprinkler systems. G & G served as a subcontractor on several California public works projects. "Public works" include construction work done under contract and paid for in whole or part by public funds. Cal. Lab. Code Ann. § 1720 (West Supp.2001). The department, board, authority, officer, or agent awarding a contract for public work is called the "awarding body." § 1722 (West 1989). The California Labor Code requires that contractors and subcontractors on such projects pay their workers a prevailing wage that is determined by the State. §§ 1771, 1772, 1773 (West 1989 and Supp.2001). At the time relevant here, if workers were not paid the prevailing wage, the contractor was required to pay each worker the difference between the prevailing wage and the wages paid, in addition to forfeiting a penalty to the State. § 1775(West Supp. 2001). The awarding body was required to include a clause in the contract so stipulat-ing. *Ibid.*

    The Labor Code provides that "[b]efore making payments to the contractor of money due under a contract for public work, the awarding body shall withhold and re-tain therefrom all wages and penalties which have been forfeited pursuant to any stipu-lation in a contract for public work, and the terms of this chapter." § 1727 (West Supp.2001). If money is withheld from a contractor because of a subcontractor's failure to comply with the Code's provisions, "[i]t shall be lawful for [the] contractor to with-hold from [the] subcontractor under him sufficient sums to cover any penalties with-held." § 1729 (West 1989).

The Labor Code permits the contractor, or his assignee, to bring suit against the awarding body "on the contract for alleged breach thereof in not making…payment" to recover the wages or penalties withheld. §§ 1731, 1732 (West Supp.2001). The suit must be brought within 90 days of completion of the contract and acceptance of the job. § 1730. Such a suit "is the exclusive remedy of the contractor or his or her assignees." § 1732. The awarding body retains the wages and penalties "pending the outcome of the suit." § 1731.

In 1995, DLSE determined that G & G, as a subcontractor on three public works projects, had violated the Labor Code by failing to pay the prevailing wage and failing to keep and/or furnish payroll records upon request. DLSE issued notices to the awarding bodies on those projects, directing them to withhold from the contractors an amount equal to the wages and penalties forfeited due to G & G's violations. The awarding bodies withheld payment from the contractors, who in turn withheld payment from G & G. The total withheld, according to respondent, exceeded $135,000. App. 68.

G & G sued petitioners in the District Court for the Central District of California. G & G sought declaratory and injunctive relief pursuant to Rev. Stat. § 1979, 42 U.S.C. § 1983, claiming that the issuance of withholding notices without a hearing constituted a deprivation of property without due process of law in violation of the Fourteenth Amendment. The District Court granted respondent's motion for summary judgment, declared §§ 1727, 1730–1733, 1775, 1776(g), and 1813 of the Labor Code unconstitutional, and enjoined the State from enforcing these provisions against respondent. App. to Pet. for Cert. A85-A87. Petitioners appealed.

A divided panel of the Court of Appeals for the Ninth Circuit affirmed. *G & G Fire Sprinklers, Inc. v. Bradshaw,* 156 F.3d 893, 898 (C.A.9 1998) *(Bradshaw I).* The court concluded that G & G "has a property interest in being paid in full for the construction work it has completed," *id.,* at 901, and found that G & G was deprived of that interest "as a result of the state's action," *id.,* at 903. It decided that because subcontractors were "afforded neither a pre-nor post-deprivation hearing when payments [were] withheld," the statutory scheme violated the Due Process Clause of the Fourteenth Amendment. *Id.,* at 904.

* * *

Where a state law such as this is challenged on due process grounds, we inquire whether the State has deprived the claimant of a protected property interest, and whether the State's procedures comport with due process. *Sullivan, supra,* at 59, 119 S.Ct. 977. We assume, without deciding, that the withholding of money due respondent under its contracts occurred under color of state law, and that, as the Court of Appeals concluded, respondent has a property interest of the kind we considered in *Logan v. Zimmerman Brush Co.,* 455 U.S. 422, 102 S.Ct. 1148, 71 L.Ed.2d 265 (1982), in its claim for payment under its contracts. 204 F.3d, at 943–944. Because we believe that California law affords respondent sufficient opportunity to pursue that claim in state court, we conclude that the California statutory scheme does not deprive G & G of its claim for payment without due process of law. See *Logan, supra,* at 433, 102 S.Ct. 1148 ("[T]he Due Process Clause grants the aggrieved party the opportunity to present his case and have its merits fairly judged").

* * *

In *Cafeteria & Restaurant Workers v. McElroy,* 367 U.S. 886, 895, 81 S.Ct. 1743, 6 L.Ed.2d 1230 (1961) (citations omitted), we said:

"The very nature of due process negates any concept of inflexible procedures universally applicable to every imaginable situation. "'[D]ue process,' unlike some legal rules, is not a technical conception with a fixed content unrelated to time, place and circumstances.' It is 'compounded of history, reason, the past course of decisions....'"

We hold that if California makes ordinary judicial process available to respondent for resolving its contractual dispute, that process is due process.

The California Labor Code provides that "the contractor or his or her assignee" may sue the awarding body "on the contract for alleged breach thereof" for "the recovery of wages or penalties." §§ 1731, 1732 (West Supp.2001). There is no basis here to conclude that the contractor would refuse to assign the right of suit to its subcontractor. In fact, respondent stated at oral argument that it has sued awarding bodies in state superior court pursuant to §§ 1731-1733 of the Labor Code to recover payments withheld on previous projects where it served as a subcontractor. See Tr. of Oral Arg. 27, 40-41, 49-50. Presumably, respondent brought suit as an assignee of the contractors on those projects, as the Code requires. § 1732 (West Supp.2001). Thus, the Labor Code, by allowing assignment, provides a means by which a subcontractor may bring a claim for breach of contract to recover wages and penalties withheld.

Respondent complains that a suit under the Labor Code is inadequate because the awarding body retains the wages and penalties "pending the outcome of the suit," § 1731, which may last several years. Tr. of Oral Arg. 51. A lawsuit of that duration, while undoubtedly something of a hardship, cannot be said to deprive respondent of its claim for payment under the contract. Lawsuits are not known for expeditiously resolving claims, and the standard practice in breach-of-contract suits is to award damages, if appropriate, only at the conclusion of the case.

Even if respondent could not obtain assignment of the right to sue the awarding body under the contract, it appears that a suit for breach of contract against the contractor remains available under California common law. See 1 B. Witkin, Summary of California Law §§ 791, 797 (9th ed.1987) (defining breach as the "unjustified or unexcused failure to perform a contract" and describing the remedies available under state law). To be sure, § 1732 of the Labor Code provides that suit on the contract against the awarding body is the "exclusive remedy of the contractor or his or her assignees" with respect to recovery of withheld wages and penalties. § 1732 (West Supp.2001). But the remedy is exclusive only with respect to the contractor and his assignees, and thus by its terms not the exclusive remedy for a subcontractor who does not receive assignment. See, e.g., *J & K Painting Co., Inc. v. Bradshaw*, 45 Cal.App.4th 1394, 1402, 53 Cal.Rptr.2d 496, 501 (1996) (allowing subcontractor to challenge Labor Commissioner's action by petition for a writ of the mandate).

In *J & K Painting*, the California Court of Appeal rejected the argument that § 1732 requires a subcontractor to obtain an assignment and that failure to do so is "fatal to any other attempt to secure relief." *Id.*, at 1401, n. 7, 53 Cal.Rptr.2d, at 501, n. 7. The Labor Code does not expressly impose such a requirement, and that court declined to infer an intent to "create remedial exclusivity" in this context. *Ibid.* It thus appears that subcontractors like respondent may pursue their claims for payment by bringing a standard breach-of-contract suit against the contractor under California law. * * * We therefore conclude that the relevant provisions of the California Labor Code do not deprive respondent of property without due process of law. Accordingly, the judgment of the Court of Appeals is reversed.

Notes and Questions

1. This Supreme Court case makes a point about privity, but several other government contract issues make cameo appearances: labor rules, subcontractor rights, and constitutional due process.

2. Note how the privity barrier creates the issue in this case. The due process problem is much less acute when the government mulcts its direct general contractor for violation of a labor standard, without any subcontractor being in the picture. In that situation, the direct contractor has any normal remedy it wishes to pursue. Here, however, the privity barrier puts the subcontractor in some doubt where it can find its forum to contest the government's determination.

Why would a subcontractor like G & G consider its general contractor insufficiently interested in proceeding? Review the chapter on labor standards. Note that the main effect of an adverse public decision may be to brand violators as outlaws and, hence, to deny them future contracts. A general contractor might well be indifferent to the subcontractor receiving that branding, and, indeed, might consider passing on to the subcontractor, or even absorbing itself, some relatively limited monetary penalties as a small price to pay for showing the government that it had neither any role in, nor tolerance of, the subcontractor's alleged transgressions. Chief Justice Rehnquist goes through all the ways privity allows the subcontractor to proceed in the face of the privity barrier and the general contractor's indifference. If you were G & G and you feared potentially disastrous future exclusion from subcontracts, would you be reassured? Observe that G & G fought this from the case's start in 1995 until the decision in 2001.

B. Miller Act

The lack of privity prevents subcontractors from seeking compensation directly from the government when the prime contractor has failed to pay the subcontractor for goods or services delivered to the government. Moreover, subcontractors cannot file mechanics liens against federal building projects or otherwise encumber federal work in order to secure payment. However, Congress has not forgotten subcontractors entirely. Performance and payment bonds are an available tool to be mandated by the government for the protection of itself and of subcontractors. This is particularly true for subcontractors, laborers, and materialmen on federal construction projects where the Miller Act, 40 U.S.C. §270, requires the prime contractor to obtain performance and payment bonds on all contracts for the construction, alteration, or repair of any public building or public work of the United States exceeding $100,000. The Miller Act still does not give a right of action by a subcontractor against the government. But, it does offer the subcontractor protection in the form of providing security that subcontractors with valid claims under their subcontracts for materials delivered and services performed can obtain payment of those claims regardless of a prime contractor's insolvency or similar problems.

A performance bond is a written instrument executed by the prime contractor (the "principal") and a second party (the "surety" or "sureties"), to assure fulfillment of the contractor's obligations to a third party identified in the bond, generally the government. A performance bond secures performance and fulfillment of the contractor's obligations under the contract. A payment bond assures payments as required by law to all persons supplying labor or material in the prosecution of the work provided for in the contract. Each bond has a penal sum or penal amount which is the amount of money specified in a bond as the maximum payment for which the surety is obligated.

The penal amount on a Miller Act performance bond is 100% of the original contract price, unless the contracting officer determines that a lesser amount would protect the government's interests. When amendments to the contract increase the contract price, the amount of the performance bond can be increased. The penal amount on a Miller Act payment bond equals: (1) 50% of the contract price on contracts under $1 million; (2) 40% of the contract price on contracts under $5 million; or (3) $2 million if the contract price is more than $5 million. Payment bond amounts are also adjusted as the contract price is adjusted by amendment.

A contractor's failure to obtain the required performance and payments bonds is considered a breach of contract and grounds for a default termination of the prime contractor by the government. In addition to the statutory rights granted to subcontractors to proceed against sureties on Miller Act payment bonds, the subcontractor has the right to file a breach of contract action against the prime contractor when payment for goods or labor is not made.

It is of much importance, as the *MacEvoy* opinion discusses, which contractors can seek payment from Miller Act bonds. Although the Miller Act is considered remedial in nature and therefore has been construed liberally by the courts, the right to seek payment from the surety is still limited to persons who have furnished labor or material under a contractual relationship with the prime contractor or a subcontractor. The courts have taken great pain to ensure that a "subcontract" relationship exists before permitting invocation of the Miller Act. A "substantiality of the relationship" test is used to determine which party is an actual subcontractor on the theory that a prime contractor (and its surety) can protect itself by requiring performance and payment bonds from the few subcontractors with which the prime contractor has a substantial relationship in performing the prime contract.

The distinctions in this regard refer to subcontractors by "tiers," in the sense that a subcontractor who deals directly with a contractor is "1st tier," a subcontractor to a subcontractor is "2nd tier," and so on. A subcontractor to a subcontractor (2nd tier subcontractor) can be protected by the Miller Act if it provides notice of the claim to the prime contractor, but the employees or laborers of the 2nd tier subcontractor are not protected because they lack privity of contract with a subcontractor (that is, with a 1st tier subcontractor). Furthermore, where a "subcontractor" is considered to be merely a supplier with no substantial relationship to the prime, 2nd tier subcontractors to that supplier are similarly not protected by the Miller Act.

Recovery under the Miller Act is limited to payment for labor and materials used in the performance of a federal public building construction project. The labor and materials need not actually be used in the construction itself, but only need be used in the performance of the contract. This includes payment for rented equipment used during construction and equipment repairs.

In order to obtain protection under the Miller Act, the subcontractor must provide the prime contractor written notice of the claim after the last of the labor or material has been provided for which payment has not been received. Notice need not be given for each separate item furnished, thus allowing for timely notice to be made within 90 days after the final shipment of materials or items. There is no particular form required of the written notice of the claim, but it must sufficiently inform the prime contractor that a claim is being made. A letter advising the prime contractor of an outstanding balance due is generally considered insufficient notice.

Once written notice has been provided to the prime contractor, the claimant must file a claim within one year of the last delivery of supplies or performance of labor, in the name of the United States, in the federal district court in which the contract is being performed and executed regardless of the amount in controversy or diversity of jurisdiction. The Federal Rules of Civil Procedure will generally apply to issues relating to third party intervenors, counterclaims, setoffs, and the like.

Many states have enacted state statutes for state contracts similar to the Miller Act for federal contracts, sometimes called "little Miller Acts." These state statutes have particular importance because the Miller Act has its chief application for public works construction contracts, and a large percentage of state contracts are for public works construction. Accordingly, the opinion below which illustrates much of the practical workings of the Miller Act, the *Allied Building* opinion, arises under a state equivalent of the Miller Act.

For further discussion of the subject of this section, and sureties generally, see: David C. Farmer, *Hawaii's Amended Little Miller Act: A Catch 22 for Gap Claimants?* 1996-Nov. Haw. B.J. 37 (1996); Ronald A. May, Randall I. Marmor, *Annual Survey of Fidelity and Surety Law, 1995-Part II*, 63 Def. Couns. J. 407 (1996); Michael J. Weber, Audrey A. Berish and Cathleen M. Jareczek, *Surety Bonds*, CLaw IL-CLE 10-1 (Main Handbook) (1997).

Clifford F. MacEvoy Co. et al. v. United States, for Use and Benefit of Calvin Tomkins Co.

Supreme Court of the United States, 322 U.S. 102. No. 483.
Argued March 7, 1944. Decided April 24, 1944

The United States entered into a contract with the petitioner Clifford F. MacEvoy Company whereby the latter agreed to furnish the materials and to perform the work necessary for the construction of dwelling units of a Defense Housing Project near Linden, New Jersey, on a cost-plus-fixed-fee basis. Pursuant to the Miller Act, MacEvoy as principal and the petitioner Aetna Casualty and Surety Company as surety executed a payment bond in the amount of $1,000,000, conditioned on the prompt payment by MacEvoy 'to all persons supplying labor and material in the prosecution of the work provided for in said contract.' The bond was duly accepted by the United States.

MacEvoy thereupon purchased from James H. Miller & Company certain building materials for use in the prosecution of the work provided for in MacEvoy's contract with the Government. Miller in turn purchased these materials from the respondent, Calvin Tomkins Company. Miller failed to pay Tomkins a balance of $12,033.49. There is no allegation that Miller agreed to perform or did perform any part of the work on the construction project. Nor is it disputed that MacEvoy paid Miller in full for the materials.

Within ninety days from the date on which Tomkins furnished the last of the materials to Miller, Tomkins gave written notice to MacEvoy and the surety of the existence and amount of Tomkins' claim for materials furnished to Miller. Tomkins as use-plaintiff then instituted this action against MacEvoy and the surety on the payment bond. The District Court granted petitioners' motion to dismiss the complaint for failure to state a claim against them. 49 F.Supp. 81. The Circuit Court of Appeals reversed the judgment. 137 F.2d 565. We granted certiorari because of a novel and important question presented under the Miller Act. 320 U.S. 733, 64 S.Ct. 267.

Specifically the issue is whether under the Miller Act a person supplying materials to a materialman of a Government contractor and to whom an unpaid balance is due from the materialman can recover on the payment bond executed by the contractor. We hold that he cannot.

The Heard Act, which was the predecessor of the Miller Act, required Government contractors to execute penal bonds for the benefit of 'all persons supplying him or them with labor and materials in the prosecution of the work provided for in such contract.' We consistently applied a liberal construction to that statute, noting that it was remedial in nature and that it clearly evidenced 'the intention of Congress to protect those whose labor or material has contributed to the prosecution of the work.' United States, for Use of Hill, v. American Surety Co., 200 U.S. 197, 204, 26 S.Ct. 168, 170, 50 L.Ed. 437. See also Mankin v. United States to Use of Ludowici-Celadon Co., 215 U.S. 533, 30 S.Ct. 174, 54 L.Ed. 315; United States Fidelity & Guaranty Co. v. United States for Benefit of Bartlett, 231 U.S. 237, 34 S.Ct. 88, 58 L.Ed. 200; Brogan v. National Surety Co., 246 U.S. 257, 38 S.Ct. 250, 62 L.Ed. 703, L.R.A.1918D, 776; Fleishmann Construction Co. v. United States to Use of Forsberg, 270 U.S. 349, 46 S.Ct. 284, 70 L.Ed. 624; Standard Accident Insurance Co. v. United States for Use and Benefit of Powell, 302 U.S. 442, 58 S.Ct. 314, 82 L.Ed. 350. We accordingly held that the phrase 'all persons supplying (the contractor) * * * with labor and materials' included not only those furnishing labor and materials directly to the prime contractor but also covered those who contributed labor and materials to subcontractors. United States, for Use of Hill, v. American Surety Co., supra, 200 U.S. 204, 26 S.Ct. 170, 50 L.Ed. 437; Mankin v. United States for Use of Ludowici-Celadon Co., supra, 215 U.S. 539, 30 S.Ct. 176, 54 L.Ed. 315; Illinois Surety Co. v. John Davis Co., 244 U.S. 376, 380, 37 S.Ct. 614, 616, 61 L.Ed. 1206. We had no occasion, however, to determine under that Act whether those who merely sold materials to materialmen, who in turn sold them to the prime contractors, were included within the phrase and hence entitled to recover on the penal bond.

The Miller Act, while it repealed the Heard Act, reinstated its basic provisions and was designed primarily to eliminate certain procedural limitations on its beneficiaries. There was no expressed purpose in the legislative history to restrict in any way the coverage of the Heard Act; the intent rather was to remove the procedural difficulties found to exist under the earlier measure and thereby make it easier for unpaid creditors to realize the benefits of the bond. Section 1(a)(2) of the Miller Act requires every Government contractor, where the amount of the contract exceeds $2,000, to furnish to the United States a payment bond with a surety 'for the protection of all persons supplying labor and material in the prosecution of the work provided for in said contract for the use of each such person.' Section 2(a) further provides that 'every person who has furnished labor or material in the prosecution of the work provided for in such contract' and who has not been paid in full therefor within ninety days after the last labor was performed or material supplied may bring suit on the payment bond for the unpaid balance. A proviso then states:

'Provided, however, That any person having direct contractual relationship with a subcontractor but no contractual relationship express or implied with the contractor furnishing said payment bond shall have a right of action upon the said payment bond upon giving written notice to said contractor within ninety days from the date on which such person did or performed the last of the labor or furnished or supplied the last of the material for which such claim is made * * *.'

The Miller Act, like the Heard Act, is highly remedial in nature. It is entitled to a liberal construction and application in order properly to effectuate the Congressional intent to protect those whose labor and materials go into public projects. Fleisher Engineering & Construction Co. v. United States, for Use and Benefit of Hallenbeck, 311 U.S. 15, 17, 18, 61 S.Ct. 81, 82, 83, 85 L.Ed. 12; cf. United States to Use of Noland Co., Inc., v. Irwin, 316 U.S. 23, 29, 30, 62 S.Ct. 899, 902, 86 L.Ed. 1241. But such a salutary policy does not justify ignoring plain words of limitation and imposing wholesale liability on payment bonds. Ostensibly the payment bond is for the protection of 'all persons supplying labor and material in the prosecution of the work' and 'every person who has furnished labor or material in the prosecution of the work' is given the right to sue on such payment bond. Whether this statutory language is broad enough to include persons supplying material to materialmen as well as those in more remote relationships we need not decide. Even if it did include such persons we cannot disregard the limitations on liability which Congress intended to impose and did impose in the proviso of Section 2(a). However inclusive may be the general language of a statute, it 'will not be held to apply to a matter specifically dealt with in another part of the same enactment. * * * Specific terms prevail over the general in the same or another statute which otherwise might be controlling.' Ginsberg & Sons v. Popkin, 285 U.S. 204, 208, 52 S.Ct. 322, 323, 76 L.Ed. 704.

The proviso of Section 2(a), which had no counterpart in the Heard Act, makes clear that the right to bring suit on a payment bond is limited to (1) those materialmen, laborers and subcontractors who deal directly with the prime contractor and (2) those materialmen, laborers and sub-contractors who, lacking express or implied contractual relationship with the prime contractor, have direct contractual relationship with a subcontractor and who give the statutory notice of their claims to the prime contractor. To allow those in more remote relationships to recover on the bond would be contrary to the clear language of the proviso and to the expressed will of the framers of the Act.[1] Moreover, it would lead to the absurd result of requiring notice from persons in direct contractual relationship with a subcontractor but not from more remote claimants.

The ultimate question in this case, therefore, is whether Miller, the materialman to whom Tomkins sold the goods and who in turn supplied them to MacEvoy, was a subcontractor within the meaning of the proviso. If he was, Tomkins' direct contractual relationship with him enables Tomkins to recover on MacEvoy's payment bond. If Miller was not a subcontractor, Tomkins stands in too remote a relationship to secure the benefits of the bond.

The Miller Act itself makes no attempt to define the word 'subcontractor.'[2] We are thus forced to utilize ordinary judicial tools of definition. Whether the word includes laborers and materialmen is not subject to easy solution, for the word has no single, exact meaning. In abroad, generic sense a subcontractor includes anyone who has a contract to furnish labor or material to the prime contractor. In that sense Miller was a

---

1. 'A sub-subcontractor may avail himself of the protection of the bond by giving written notice to the contractor, but that is as far as the bill goes. It is not felt that more remote relationships ought to come within the purview of the bond.' H. Rep. No. 1263 (74th Cong., 1st Sess.), p. 3.

2. In analogous situations, state and lower federal courts have expressed divergent opinions as to whether the word 'subcontractor' includes laborers and materialmen. See annotation in 141 A.L.R. 321 for a summary of the conflicting cases. We have not heretofore had occasion to define the word in this connection. Any loose, interchangeable use of 'subcontractor' and 'materialman' in any prior decision of ours is without significance.

subcontractor. But under the more technical meaning, as established by usage in the building trades, a subcontractor is one who performs for and takes from the prime contractor a specific part of the labor or material requirements of the original contract, thus excluding ordinary laborers and materialmen. To determine which meaning Congress attached to the word in the Miller Act, we must look to the Congressional history of the statute as well as to the practical considerations underlying the Act.

It is apparent from the hearings before the subcommittee of the House Committee on the Judiciary leading to the adoption of the Miller Act that the participants had in mind a clear distinction between subcontractors and materialmen. In opening the hearings, Representative Miller, the sponsor of the bill that became the Miller Act, stated in connection with the various proposed bills that 'we would like to have the reaction and opinion of members in reference to those bills that deal with the general subject of requiring a bond for the benefit of laborers and materialmen who deal with subcontractors on public works.' And the authoritative committee report made numerous references to and distinguished among 'laborers, materialmen and subcontractors.' Similar uncontradicted statements were made in both houses of Congress when the Act was pending before them. The fact that subcontractors were so consistently distinguished from materialmen and laborers in the course of the formation of the Act is persuasive evidence that the word 'subcontractor' was used in the proviso of Section 2(a) in its technical sense so as to exclude materialmen and laborers.

Practical considerations underlying the Act likewise support this conclusion. Congress cannot be presumed, in the absence of express statutory language, to have intended to impose liability on the payment bond in situations where it is difficult or impossible for the prime contractor to protect himself. The relatively few subcontractors who perform part of the original contract represent in a sense the prime contractor and are well known to him. It is easy for the prime contractor to secure himself against loss by requiring the subcontractors to give security by bond, or otherwise, for the payment of those who contract directly with the subcontractors. United States, for Use of Hill, v. American Surety Co., supra, 200 U.S. 204, 26 S.Ct. 168, 50 L.Ed. 437; Mankin v. United States for Use of Ludowici-Celadon Co., supra, 215 U.S. 540, 30 S.Ct. 177, 54 L.Ed. 315. But this method of protection is generally inadequate to cope with remote and undeterminable liabilities incurred by an ordinary materialman, who may be a manufacturer, a wholesaler or a retailer. Many such materialmen are usually involved in large projects; they deal in turn with innumerable sub-materialmen and laborers. To impose unlimited liability under the payment bond to those sub-materialmen and laborers is to create a precarious and perilous risk on the prime contractor and his surety. To sanction such a risk requires clear language in the statute and in the bond so as to leave no alternative. Here the proviso of Section 2(a) of the Act forbids the imposition of such a risk, thereby foreclosing Tomkins' right to use on the payment bond.

The judgment of the court below is reversed.

Allied Building Products Corporation
v. United Pacific Insurance Company

No. 279, Sept. Term, 1988. Court of Special Appeals of Maryland.
Nov. 10, 1988.

Argued Before GILBERT, C.J., and ROSALYN B. BELL and FISCHER, JJ.

ROSALYN B. BELL, Judge.

Allied Building Products Corporation (Allied) appeals from a decision of the Circuit Court for Baltimore City granting cross-summary judgment for United Pacific Insurance Company (United Pacific). Allied is a large supplier of roofing and other building materials. United Pacific was the surety of a payment bond posted by Triangle General Contractors, Inc. (Triangle), guaranteeing payment for labor and materials on a State building project. Allied filed suit against United Pacific on August 20, 1987, alleging that it was entitled to relief from United Pacific due to the nonpayment of a subcontractor, Sain & Son Contractors, Inc. (S & S).

We are presented with two issues in this appeal:

Did a joint check agreement operate to extinguish Allied's right to recover under Maryland's Little Miller Act?

Was Triangle's affidavit, alleging that Allied had billed it for more roofing materials than actually delivered, sufficient to withstand Allied's summary judgment motion?

We reverse and remand.

The relevant facts are as follows. Triangle was the general contractor on a State project to construct the Francis Scott Key Elementary-Middle School in Baltimore City. United Pacific, appellee, was the surety for Triangle in accordance with Triangle's obligations to provide a payment bond pursuant to §13-501(a)(2) of the Little Miller Act, Md. State Fin. & Proc. Code Ann. (1985). Briefly stated, this section requires a general contractor to post a payment bond in any construction contract awarded by the State which exceeds $50,000 in order to make certain that persons providing building materials are paid. By providing the payment bond, United Pacific guaranteed payment to all persons supplying materials for the school building project undertaken by Triangle. S & S, a construction subcontractor for Triangle, used roofing and other building materials supplied by Allied, which Allied delivered to the job site.

After the project was underway, Allied became concerned about receiving its payments on an open account it had provided to S & S. Consequently, Allied, S & S, and Triangle entered into a joint check agreement in November of 1985, pursuant to which Triangle agreed to pay S & S with joint checks made payable to S & S and Allied, thus ensuring that Allied would be paid for the building materials it had supplied to S & S. The agreement provided that Triangle assumed no liability for any materials purchased in excess of $100,000. Nevertheless, Triangle paid out a total of $123,846.74 to Allied under the joint check agreement.[1] When S & S did not meet its obligations, Allied gave notice and filed suit on the payment bond underwritten by United Pacific, claiming an unpaid balance of $75,889.18 for building materials delivered to the job site.

---

1. Although the record extract does not specify, we assume Allied did furnish at least $100,000 in materials and was paid for them out of the $123,846.74 as no issue is raised in this regard.

The trial court granted Allied's summary judgment motion on November 10, 1987, and United Pacific filed a motion to vacate the judgment, a motion in opposition of the summary judgment, and a cross-motion for summary judgment on November 20, 1987. These motions were heard in an unrecorded hearing in chambers on January 5, 1988. Judgment was entered in favor of United Pacific on both motions. Because the hearing was unrecorded, we can only assume that the trial court entered judgment for United Pacific based on its pleadings, which asserted, in essence, that the joint check agreement limiting Triangle's liability to $100,000 operated as a waiver of Allied's rights under the Little Miller Act.

The effect of the joint check agreement is thus the primary issue in this case. We hold that the lack of a specific waiver was fatal to United Pacific's cross-motion. The second question involves Allied's own motion, and for that answer we revisit the problem of the adequacy of an affidavit opposing summary judgment. We hold that United Pacific's affidavit was sufficient to raise a material factual issue regarding delivery, and as a result, Allied was not entitled to summary judgment. We begin our explanation with a brief history of the Little Miller Act and what it was intended to accomplish.

HISTORY

Construction projects such as office buildings and factories have increased dramatically. These projects typically involve large amounts of money; hence, if the contractor's business failed, suppliers who had extended credit could suffer substantial losses. Since suppliers had no recourse at common law, statutes providing for mechanics' liens were enacted to address this problem. See Cahn, Contractors' Payment Bonds in Maryland, 32 Md.L.Rev. 226 (1972).

Public projects such as schools, highways and public hospitals were typically exempt from mechanics' liens, however, and suppliers on State public projects in Maryland had no remedy until 1918, when Maryland adopted its version of a federal law known as the Heard Act, which required contractors to post bonds for State projects. 1918 Md.Laws ch. 127. In 1959, Maryland replaced this law with a new statute requiring contractors to post payment bonds on State construction projects. This new statute was patterned on a federal act known as the Miller Act.

Although nothing in the legislative history of the Maryland Act explicitly states that it was based on the federal Miller Act, the legislative history does show parallel development and, except for minor variations, the language of the two statutes is essentially the same.

* * *

The purpose of the Little Miller Act is remedial. The Act is intended to protect suppliers on State and other public projects where they would otherwise have no lien as a result of sovereign immunity. Hamilton & Spiegel, Inc. v. Board of Educ. of Montgomery County, 233 Md. 196, 200, 195 A.2d 710 (1963). The Act is to be liberally construed to effectuate this public purpose. Montgomery County Bd. of Educ. v. Glassman Constr. Co., 245 Md. 192, 201, 225 A.2d 448 (1967).

Under the Miller Act,

> "[t]he liability of the surety is measured by that of the prime contractor for the bond. The liability of the prime contractor to a project supplier of a subcontractor is governed by the subcontractor's obligation."

D & L Constr. Co. v. Triangle Elec. Supply Co., 332 F.2d 1009, 1013 (8th Cir.1964). The obligation is one, not of contract, but of statute, and therefore privity is not required.

The liabilities of lower tier subcontractors to their suppliers are passed up the ladder to the surety. For example, in the instant case, it is S & S's liability to Allied that becomes the benchmark in determining Allied's damages as against Triangle, and ultimately United Pacific.

What is significant about both the federal and the state acts is that, although there have been amendments to both statutes, the basic coverage, purpose and procedures remain substantially the same. Generally, this Court will look to federal decisions construing the Miller Act to provide guidance in interpreting the Little Miller Act.

EFFECT OF THE JOINT CHECK AGREEMENT

On appeal, Allied contends that the trial court erred in granting judgment for United Pacific, asserting that at no time did it waive its right to the protection of the Little Miller Act. On the other hand, United Pacific asserts that it had no obligation to Allied because Triangle fulfilled its obligations under the joint check agreement. Since Triangle had no further liability to Allied, United Pacific claims it follows that it had no liability as Triangle's surety. We disagree with United Pacific's position, and explain.

Whether the cross motion for summary judgment was properly granted to appellee rests on the claim that Triangle's liability to appellant under the Little Miller Act was limited to $100,000. The joint check agreement was in the form of a letter from Triangle to S & S dated November 25, 1985. The letter stated in pertinent part:

> "You have asked us to make checks in payment for your work, under the above referenced contract, payable jointly to you and to Allied Roofers Supply Corporation. We are willing to do this, and will do so, subject to the following conditions:

> * * *

> "2 We assume no liability for any materials purchased in excess of the total purchase of One Hundred Thousand Dollars and no/cents. Tax Included, ($100,000.00). Also we assume no liability for any materials not delivered to the job site and signed for by Triangle General Contractor's job superintendent for verification."

> "3. We will require a partial Release of Liens, and a Release of rights against our Payment Bond, from both you and your supplier as a condition of each payment to you.

> "4. Also it is agreed, that all joint check payments will be applied by the Supplier to only S & S Drywall Contractor's account for the Francis Scott Key Middle School and no other accounts."

The letter was accepted by Triangle, S & S and Allied.

The Court of Appeals held in N.S. Stavrou, Inc. and Reliance Insurance Co. v. Beacon Supply Co., 249 Md. 451, 458–59, 240 A.2d 278 (1968), that the joint check agreement was not intended to guarantee payment in lieu of the contractor's bond obligation. The joint check agreement in Stavrou imposed a duty on the contractor to pay the supplier for materials not to exceed $20,000. The Court held that the contractor's conduct had the effect of exceeding this obligation. Stavrou, 249 Md. at 451, 240 A.2d 278. The Court pointed out that the contractor could have protected himself by requiring (in addition to the joint check agreement) the supplier to execute a bond waiver, but this was not done. The Court noted that in order to prevail the contractor "would had to have shown by a fair preponderance of the evidence an express or implied waiver on the part of [the supplier]...." Stavrou, 249 Md. at 458, 240 A.2d 278. Thus, the Court implicitly would have required language additional to or more specific than that of the joint check agreement in Stavrou in order to find a bond right waiver. The Stavrou Court, however, did not elaborate on what sort of language could constitute an express or implied waiver.

* * *

In United States ex rel. Koppers Co. v. Five Boro Construction Corp., 310 F.2d 701, 703 (4th Cir.1962), the Court held that a supplier had not waived its Miller Act rights by entering into a joint check agreement with the contractor and subcontractor. The agreement, reached by letter, was entered into after the supplier became apprehensive concerning the subcontractor's ability to pay for railroad materials delivered for a Navy building project. The Court found nothing in the joint check agreement which indicated that the supplier intended to waive its rights, observing that the supplier had three options when the subcontractor's ability to pay became questionable. The supplier could have (1) continued supplying materials until the job was completed and then file against the payment bond pursuant to the Miller Act, (2) refused to deliver any more materials, or (3), as happened in Koppers, agreed to deliver supplies pursuant to a joint check agreement. The Court stated:

"This insured payment to [the supplier] as the work progressed instead of delay in payment until completion of the job, but a request for and the acceptance of additional security does not indicate an intention to waive the right to that already in hand."

Koppers, 310 F.2d at 703.

United States ex rel. Clark-Fontana Paint Co. v. Glassman Construction Co., 397 F.2d 8 (4th Cir. 1968), involved a factual situation similar to that in the instant case. In Clark-Fontana, a paint supplier agreed to supply materials to a subcontractor, but requested the general contractor to make its checks jointly payable to the paint supplier and the subcontractor. Each check contained a notation that the subcontractor and supplier "waived and released to the extent of the full face value hereof any right any of them may have" to assert a claim under "any bond" given by the contractor. Clark-Fontana, 397 F.2d at 9. The supplier then allowed the subcontractor to keep most of the proceeds of these checks because the subcontractor was having trouble meeting his payroll. This subcontractor eventually went bankrupt, and the supplier filed suit under the Miller Act to recover the unpaid balance. The defendants (contractor, insurance company and subcontractor) claimed that the language on the checks constituted a waiver of the supplier's right to recover under the Miller Act. Clark-Fontana, 397 F.2d at 10.

The Court held that the notation was not a waiver because its language did not explicitly "say that the materialman [supplier] was obligated to deduct his current due from each check at the peril of losing his statutory rights." Clark-Fontana, 397 F.2d at 10. The Court stated:

"[W]e do not hold that protection of laborers and materialmen may never be accomplished by other means so as to avoid the general contractor's statutory obligation. But where that result is attempted by means of express waiver, we think that congressional purpose requires that waiver be clear and explicit.... Absent the clear language of an express waiver, we think that none is to be implied; as we have held in the past, requesting and accepting additional security does not indicate an intention to waive the right to that already in hand."

Clark-Fontana, 397 F.2d at 10-11 (citation omitted).

Clark-Fontana illustrates the approach taken by the federal courts—while it is possible for a supplier to waive his rights under the Act, see, e.g., United States ex rel. B's Co. v. Cleveland Electric Co., 373 F.2d 585, 588 (4th Cir.1967), "the federal courts have been uniform in their insistence that a waiver be clear and explicit." United States ex rel. Youngstown Welding & Eng'g Co. v. Traveler's Indem. Co., 802 F.2d 1164, 1166 (1986). We adopt the federal position, holding that only a clear and express waiver will terminate a supplier's rights under a Little Miller Act payment bond, and that the taking of additional security by itself does not constitute a waiver of a bond claim. In the instant case, the joint check agreement did not waive Allied's rights under the Little Miller Act.

The joint check agreement itself, and the circumstances prompting its creation, indicates that it was intended to create additional security for Allied—not to narrow the security Allied already possessed under the Little Miller Act. The agreement came into being because Allied was concerned that S & S was a poor credit risk.[1] It was obviously Allied's reluctance to give S & S materials on credit which induced S & S to ask for this arrangement, as evidenced by the letter creating the joint check agreement, sent by Triangle to S & S, which began: "You have asked us to make checks in payment for your work... payable jointly to you and to Allied...." Simply put, Allied would not have given S & S roofing materials unless it had some additional assurance of payment. Since paragraph 2 of the Joint Check Agreement limits the liability that Triangle would "assume," it is expressly indicative of the parties' intention that they were creating rights in Allied as against Triangle, not limiting ones that already existed, so that Allied would continue to supply the project.

As in Koppers, Allied as a supplier could have continued supplying materials to the job site and then filed (after proper notice) under the payment bond or it could have simply refused to supply any more materials on credit. It opted instead to work matters out via an agreement which was nothing more than a joint check agreement.

Joint check agreements are a commonly used payment method in the construction industry.

> "In order to induce a supplier to deal with a subcontractor whose credit is questionable, the general contractor may agree to pay the subcontractor with checks payable to the joint order of the subcontractor and the supplier."

Cahn, Contractors' Payment Bonds in Maryland at 259. The subcontractor endorses the checks and turns them over to the supplier. The supplier then deducts the amount owed for materials, and returns the balance. Id., at 259. Triangle and United Pacific could have had Allied execute a waiver of its bond rights, but did not. The situation in the instant case is thus similar to Stavrou, where the Court declined to find a waiver in the joint check agreement. As held in Koppers, a joint check agreement, standing alone, will not constitute a waiver.

Moreover, the language in this agreement is far less specific than that contained in Clark-Fontana, which the Court held not specific enough to constitute a waiver. Additionally, paragraph 3 of the joint check agreement specified that Triangle "will re-

---

1. Allied's concern about S & S's credit is evidenced by the fact that it used S & S's credit application as an exhibit in its bond action. The credit application showed that S & S had been in existence for just two-and-one-half years, was a father-son operation, and had never done business with Allied before.

quire...a [r]elease of rights against our [p]ayment [b]ond from both you and your supplier as a condition of each payment to you." "Will require" clearly indicates future action, and by drafting this provision Triangle clearly contemplated obtaining separate signed releases for each payment at some future date. This provision would have no meaning if the paragraph immediately before it, paragraph 2, was intended by the parties to be a complete waiver.

Finally, United Pacific argues that, by paying Allied in excess of the stated $100,000.00 contract limit, Triangle fully satisfied its contractual obligation and hence no waiver is involved. We think that any distinction to be made here between a liability cap and a waiver is academic at best. Following Union Pacific's line of reasoning to its logical end, prior to the execution of the joint check agreement Allied possessed the right to sue under the Little Miller Act without limitation as to amount. Yet, Union Pacific contents that, immediately after the joint check agreement was executed, Allied's right to sue under the Miller Act for sums in excess of $100,000 suddenly disappeared. How would this be possible except by virtue of waiver? Since the joint check agreement did not constitute a waiver, we hold the trial court erred in granting the cross-summary judgment to United Pacific.

JUDGMENT VACATED AND CASE REMANDED FOR FURTHER PROCEEDINGS CONSISTENT WITH THIS OPINION.

Notes and Questions

1. In *Clifford F. MacEvoy Co.*, the court limited coverage of the Miller Act to subcontractors which perform part of the original contract on the theory that the prime contractor cannot be asked to be responsible for "unlimited liability" from the myriad number of materialmen and suppliers that might supply product or laborers during the course of a construction project. Yet, on fixed-price construction contracts, the total "liability" for materials and labor should be relatively well-known and not an "unlimited liability." What is another reason for the courts to limit the coverage of the Miller Act and the amount of bonds required?

2. Why have the courts gone to the great lengths reflected in the *Allied Building* case to protect subcontractors from contentions that they have waived their protections regarding Miller Act bonds? Are those protections creatures of the statute or of the subcontract?

3. Pursuant to Section 4104(b)(2) of the Federal Acquisition Streamlining Act of 1994 (Public Law 103-355), for construction contracts greater than $25,000 (the prior Miller Act applicability amount) and less than $100,000 (the new Miller Act applicability amount), a contracting officer is to select two or more of the following payment protections as a means of protecting the interests of the government: (1) A payment bond; (2) An irrevocable letter of credit; (3) A tripartite escrow agreement; (4) Certificates of deposit; or (5) U.S. Bonds, certified or cashier's check, bank draft, Post Office money order, or currency. The contractor is permitted to select one of the various forms of payment protection. FAR 28.102-1(b). What is the policy basis behind allowing for different forms of payment protection on smaller dollar construction contracts?

4. The one year statute of limitations for filing a claim under the Miller Act is not a jurisdictional requirement, so that a contractor's assurances that a bill would be paid can act as an estoppel against the contractor asserting the statute of limitations.

C. Small Business Programs and Affirmative Action Issues

For the political reason that elected leaders like being viewed as assisting the small entrepreneur, as well as for the policy reason of creating a broad base of actual and potential suppliers to enhance competition and to handle national emergencies, the government has procurement preferences for small businesses. This particularly extends to preferences for small, disadvantaged businesses, with their own additional policy and political rationales. These preferences can take the form of set-asides, either of limiting competition to the exclusive participation of small businesses—the small business set-aside program—or limiting competition to the exclusive participation of certain minority owned and economically disadvantaged businesses—the 8(a) Business Development Program (formerly known as the Minority Small Business and Capital Ownership Development Program or simply the "8(a)" Program).

For further discussion of the issues in this section, see: Gilbert J. Ginsburg and Janine S. Benton, *One Year Later: Affirmative Action in Federal Government Contracting After Adarand* 45 Am. U. L. Rev. 1903, (1996); Steven K. DiLiberto, Comment: *Setting Aside Set Asides: The New Standard for Affirmative Action Programs in the Construction Industry*, 42 Vill. L. Rev. 2039 (1997); Laura M. Padilla, *Intersectionality and Positionality: Situating Women of Color in the Affirmative Action Dialogue* 66 Ford. L. Rev. 843 (1997); Mary K. O'Melveny, *Playing the "Gender" Card : Affirmative Action and Working Women*, 84 Ky. L.J. 863 (1995–1996).

1. The Small Business Set-Aside Program

In fulfillment of the policies set forth in the Small Business Act, 15 U.S.C. §§631-647, the FAR directs federal contracting officers to set aside an individual acquisition or class of acquisitions for exclusive participation by small business concerns when it is determined to be in the interest of: maintaining or mobilizing the nation's full productive capacity for war or national defense programs; or, assuring that a fair proportion of government contracts in each industry category is placed with small business concerns. *See* FAR 19.5. In order to "assist" contracting officers in making such determinations, the FAR requires *all* procurements under the Simplified Acquisition Threshold (in the 1990s, at $100,000) be set aside for small business concerns unless the contracting officer determines that he or she will not receive offers from two or more responsible small business concerns offering competitive terms.

Acquisitions over $100,000 in value are to be set aside for exclusive small business concern participation if the contracting officer has a reasonable expectation that: (1) offers will be obtained from at least two responsible small business concerns offering the products of small business concerns (with certain limited exceptions); and (2) award will be made at fair market prices. This is known as the "Rule of Two." The determination of what constitutes a "fair market price" is left to the contracting officer who can exercise very broad authority in making such a determination. Small business "fair market prices" can be considerably higher than what a large business would charge the government for a similar product or service and still be considered "reasonable." In essence, contracting officers are permitted to pay premium prices for products and services offered by small business concerns in support of congressional policy of assisting and en-suring the continued viability of small business concerns through the procurement process.

Because of the distinct advantages a small business concern can have in many federal acquisitions, the determination of what constitutes a small business concern is of criti-cal importance. The Small Business Administration ("SBA") has been delegated the au-thority for making such determinations and has issued regulations that contain the rel-evant criteria and size standards. *See* 13 CFR Part 121. Industry categories follow the four digit code set forth in the Standard Industrial Classification ("SIC") Manual pre-pared by the Office of Management and Budget. The size standards are generally based on number of employees with most industry categories limited to 500 employees to be considered as a small business concern although there are a few that have a 100 em-ployee limit and others that go as high as 1,500 employees. For a number of industry categories, the SBA relies upon a three year average of gross revenues for the concern with most categories limited to annual receipts of $5 million, although a few go as low as $500,000 and some go as high as $20 million. Because a single company can operate under various SIC codes, a concern may be an eligible small business concern for some federal acquisitions and ineligible for others, depending upon the SIC code assigned to the procurement by the contracting officer.

In addition to looking at either the number of employees or annual revenues, SBA has fairly strict regulations concerning permissible and non-permissible business "affili-ates" of a small business concern. Such regulations are intended, in part, to eliminate business that act as "fronts" for large business concerns in order to take advantage of the procurement opportunities reserved for small business concerns. The SBA will examine factors such as stock ownership, common management, common facilities, key em-ployees, and contractual relationships in making a determination as to the affiliation between two businesses. Should two businesses be "affiliated," they must count either the total number of employees of both or the total annual receipts of both to determine their eligibility as a small business concern. The actual determination as to whether a particular business qualifies as a small business concern is one of self-certification, al-though either a government contracting officer or a business competitor can challenge the size status of a concern through an administrative size protest process established and maintained by the SBA.

2. Minority Small Businesses

As part of the Small Business Act, 15 U.S.C.§637, Congress established the policy of assisting socially and economically disadvantaged persons by providing them the maxi-mum practicable opportunity to participate in government contracts. Similar pro-nouncements have been issued in the form of executive orders. The March 5, 1969 Ex-ecutive Order 11458 provided that it was in the national interest to utilize minority business enterprises in the national defense. Executive Order 11625, issued on October 14, 1971, created a national program for minority business enterprises based on the premise that full participation in the free enterprise system by socially and economically disadvantaged persons is essential in order to obtain social and economic justice and improve the functioning of the national economy. Executive Order 12928, issued on September 16, 1994, seeks "vigorous" enforcement of the statutory and regulatory goals of assisting small business owned and controlled by socially and economically disadvantaged individuals, historically black colleges and universities, and minority institutions. Much of these efforts have been focused on what is now called the "8(a) Business Development Program."

To date, the definition of socially and economically disadvantaged individuals has focused on the race or ethnic status of individuals seeking to take advantage of federal contracting opportunities reserved for minority firms, although late 1990s regulations provide that women-owned firms may be able to qualify as well. 13 C.F.R. §124.103(c). Current racial and ethnic categories that qualify include Black Americans, Hispanic Americans, Native Americans, Asian-Pacific Americans, Subcontinent Asian Americans and other minorities as well as Indian Tribes and Native Hawaiian Organizations. In order to be considered "economically disadvantaged" an individual must first be considered "socially disadvantaged" and then have a net worth at time of qualification of less than $250,000 (excluding the individual's primary personal residence).

There are fairly strict regulatory requirements as to the business concerns that qualify for procurement assistance from the 8(a) Business Development Program. *See* 13 C.F.R. Part 124. The concern must be a small business and unconditionally owned (51%) by one or more qualified socially and economically disadvantaged individuals. Also, the concern cannot be controlled by non-qualified companies and must have a detailed business plan and have a potential for success in order to be admitted to the program. Once in the program, contracting opportunities, with the assistance of the SBA, are set aside for the exclusive participation of qualified 8(a) firms, either on a sole source basis or a limited competition basis where more than one such qualified firm is able to compete for and provide the required products or perform the necessary services. The selected contract is awarded to the SBA which in turn awards a subcontract to the qualified small disadvantaged concern.

The decision to set aside such procurements can dramatically effect the fortunes of small and large businesses alike and is a decision that can generate a fair amount of controversy as the next case demonstrates.

RAY BAILLIE TRASH HAULING, INC., et al., v. Thomas S. KLEPPE, Administrator, Small Business Administration, et al.,

United States Court of Appeals,
Fifth Circuit. 477 F.2d 696 No. 72-1163.
April 18, 1973.

Before WISDOM, THORNBERRY and GODBOLD, Circuit Judges.

WISDOM, Circuit Judge:

* * *

In this case the plaintiffs attack the Small Business Administration's program for awarding government procurement contracts to small business concerns owned by "socially or economically disadvantaged persons." 13 C.F.R. § 124.8-1(c). The district court held that the section 8(a) program is not authorized by statute. We reverse. * * *

I.

The plaintiffs * * * are engaged in the business of collecting and hauling refuse to disposal sites. They qualify as small business concerns under both the Small Business Act,

15 U.S.C. § 631 et seq., and the applicable regulations of the Small Business Administration. All American Waste, Inc., named as a defendant, is a black-owned firm that competes with the plaintiffs in the business of collecting and hauling refuse and also qualifies as a small business concern. The dispute in the present case relates to a contract for the collection and removal of refuse from Homestead Air Force Base in Homestead, Florida. In 1968 and 1969, the Small Business Administration and the Department of the Air Force, pursuant to a joint program, set aside the contracts for placement with small business concerns. The Air Force awarded the contracts after formal advertising and competitive bidding restricted to small business concerns. Jones and Santo successfully bid for the contract in 1968 and 1969 respectively.

In 1970, the Small Business Administration promulgated new regulations establishing a "section 8(a) program" providing for assistance to small business concerns owned by disadvantaged persons. 13 C.F.R. § 124.8-1. As part of the program, the SBA secured a prime contract from the Air Force for the collection and removal of refuse from the Homestead base for a two year period commencing July 1, 1970. The SBA then negotiated a similar subcontract with All American for the performance of the services in the prime contract between the SBA and the Air Force for a one year period commencing July 1, 1970 at $65,000.

Upon being advised that the SBA intended to enter into a second subcontract with All American for the performance of the prime contract services at Homestead for the fiscal year 1971, the plaintiffs demanded an opportunity to compete for the contract. They did not apply for participation in the program and they did not contend that they were eligible. The SBA rejected the demand and later executed the second subcontract with All American. On June 29, 1971, the plaintiffs commenced the present action for injunctive and declaratory relief in the District Court for the Southern District of Florida. The defendants were the Administrator of the Small Business Administration, the Secretary of the Department of the Air Force, the Contracting Officer assigned to Homestead Air Force Base, and All American Waste, Inc. In the complaint, the plaintiffs sought a permanent injunction enjoining the SBA from letting the Homestead contract under the section 8(a) program without competitive bidding * * *

On October 29, 1971, the district court entered its judgment. 334 F. Supp. 194. The court found that the SBA's section 8(a) program, providing for assistance to small business concerns owned by disadvantaged persons, was not authorized by the Small Business Act and violated the federal statutes requiring competitive bidding in government procurement. * * * The defendants appealed.

* * *

III.

As stated in the regulations promulgated by the SBA, the purpose of the section 8(a) program is "to assist small business concerns owned by disadvantaged persons to become self-sufficient, viable businesses capable of competing effectively in the market place." 13 C. F.R. § 124.8-1(b). Authority for the program is derived from section 8(a) of the Small Business Act, 15 U.S.C. § 637(a), empowering the SBA to enter into all types of contracts (including contracts for supplies, services, construction, research, and development) with other departments and agencies of the federal government and to arrange for the performance of such contracts by negotiating or otherwise letting subcontracts to small business concerns. In awarding subcontracts under the section 8(a) program, the SBA limits eligibility to small businesses "owned or destined to be owned by socially or economically disadvantaged persons." 13 C.F.R. §124.8-1(c). As the regulations recognize, this "often includes, but is not restricted to, Black Americans, Americans, American Indians, Spanish Americans, Oriental Americans, Eskimos and Aleuts." *Id.*

The district court held that the SBA's section 8(a) program was statutorily unauthorized, that the SBA's powers under section 8(a) of the Small Business Act are limited to periods of emergency, and that the SBA was bound by other statutes requiring government procurement contracts to be awarded competitively. We disagree.

A. The declared policy of the Small Business Act is to "aid, counsel, assist, and protect...the interests of small-business concerns in order to preserve free competitive enterprise [and] to insure that a fair proportion of the total purchases and contracts or subcontracts for property and services for the Government...be placed with small-businesses enterprises." The Act is premised on the idea that "the essence of the American economic system of private enterprise is free competition," "[that] the preservation and expansion of such competition is basic not only to the economic well-being but to the security of this Nation," and that "[s]uch security and well-being cannot be realized unless the actual and potential capacity of small business is encouraged and developed." 15 U.S.C. §631.

To accomplish this goal, Congress vested the Small Business Administration with broad powers and responsibility over the economic life of small business concerns. The SBA is authorized to make loans to small business concerns, to provide technical and managerial aids, and to assist small business concerns in obtaining government contracts. 15 U.S.C. §§636, 638, 644. Most importantly, in section 8(a) of the Act the SBA is authorized to enter into procurement contracts with other federal agencies and to arrange for the performance of those contracts by subcontracting with small business concerns. 15 U.S.C. §637(a). This section unequivocally states that the SBA is empowered to let subcontracts to "small business concerns or others." 15 U.S.C. §637(a) (2). In accordance with this statutory mandate, the SBA adopted its section 8(a) program through which government procurement contracts are awarded to small business concerns owned by disadvantaged persons.

The plaintiff contends, however, that the section 8(a) program is unauthorized because it is not specifically mentioned in the statute. This argument is without merit. * * *

* * *. Congress has declared that the actual and potential capacity of small business concerns must be developed and that a fair proportion of total purchases and contracts of the federal government must be placed with such firms. 15 U. S.C. §631. It has given the SBA the statutory authority and necessary discretion in awarding subcontracts to accomplish that goal. The discretion as to which firms shall receive subcontracts and the decision as to what regulations shall govern procurement is left to the SBA. 15 U.S.C. §637. It must select the programs that will insure the economic development of small business concerns and provide for their participation in government procurement contracts. * * *

The SBA's program is also supported by congressional and presidential mandates issued after the passage of the Act. The first of these mandates is contained in the 1967 Amendment to the Economic Opportunity Act, 42 U.S.C. §2701 et seq. This amendment directs the SBA to "assist in the establishment, preservation, and strengthening of small business concerns...with special attention to small business concerns (1) located in urban or rural areas with high proportions of unemployed or low-income individuals, or (2) owned by low-income individuals." 42 U.S.C. §2901. In addition, the Administrator of the SBA is specifically instructed to "take such steps as may be necessary

and appropriate, in coordination and cooperation with the heads of other Federal departments and agencies, *so that contracts, subcontracts, and deposits made by the Federal
Government or in connection with programs aided with Federal funds are placed in such a
way as to further the purposes of this subchapter.*" 42 U.S.C. §2906c(a). (emphasis
added.)

* * *

The presidential mandates for the SBA's section 8(a) program are found in Executive
Orders 11458, 11518, 11625. In the first order, issued March 5, 1969, the President instructed the appropriate federal departments and agencies to establish programs to
strengthen minority business enterprise. Exec.Order No. 11458, 34 Fed.Reg. 4937
(1969). In the second order, issued March 21, 1970, the President called for increased
representation of the interests of small business concerns, particularly minority-owned
business concerns, within federal departments and agencies. Exec.Order No. 11518, 35
Fed.Reg. 4939 (1970). In the third order, issued October 13, 1971, the President directed all federal departments and agencies to "continue all current efforts to foster and
promote minority business enterprises." Exec.Order No. 11625, 36 Fed. Reg. 19967
(1971). In terms substantially identical to the SBA's section 8(a) program, the order defines "minority business enterprise" as "a business enterprise that is owned or controlled by one or more socially or economically disadvantaged persons." *Id.*

The SBA's section 8(a) program clearly promotes the goals articulated in both the
1967 Amendment to the Economic Opportunity Act and the executive orders. We conclude that there is ample support for the section 8(a) program.

* * *

C. As an additional ground for its decision, the district court held that section 8(a)
prohibits the SBA's action awarding the Homestead contract to All American without
formal advertising or competitive bidding. Again, we disagree.

Section 8(a) empowers the SBA to arrange for the performance of prime contracts by
"negotiating or otherwise letting subcontracts." 15 U.S.C. §637(a) (2). The statute does
not require the SBA to engage in competitive bidding. The plaintiffs contend, however,
that to construe the phrase "or otherwise letting" as permitting the SBA to dispense
with competition would be inconsistent with the congressional intent expressed in
other statutes requiring competition in government procurement. These statutes recognize, however, that competition may be dispensed with when other statutes so provide,
41 U.S.C. §252(c) (15), or when the purposes of the relevant program make it impractical to secure competition. 41 U.S.C. §252(c) (10). Both exceptions are applicable here.

First, section 8(a) of the Small Business Act clearly constitutes specific statutory authority to dispense with competition. 15 U.S.C. §637(a). It provides that the SBA may
let subcontracts by negotiation or any other method.

Second, competition is impractical in the present case. The purpose of the Act is to
assist small business concerns. The Act is based on the premise that such firms are unable to compete effectively in the marketplace and therefore cannot secure government
procurement contracts awarded through competitive bidding. By increasing their participation in government procurement, however, these firms can eventually become
self-sufficient, viable businesses capable of competing effectively in the marketplace.
Private negotiation of subcontracts is the best means of accomplishing this goal. To require competitive bidding would be contrary to the basic rationale of the Act. Even if
competition were limited to small business concerns, there would still be many small

business concerns that would never receive government procurement contracts. This result would clearly frustrate the congressional intent to assist small businesses. * * * *

We conclude, therefore, that subcontracts under the section 8(a) program may be awarded on a noncompetitive basis. * * * *

The decision of the district court must be

Reversed.

San Antonio General Maintenance, Inc., et al., Plaintiffs, v. James Abnor, et al., Defendants

Civ. A. No. 87-1861. United States District Court,
District of Columbia 691 F. Supp. 1462. Nov 16, 1987

JOYCE HENS GREEN, District Judge.

Most litigation involving federal programs produces predictable arguments on both sides: the government attempts to withdraw benefits and the individual asserts continued eligibility and entitlement. This case, however, presents an interesting twist on that familiar scenario. Plaintiffs San Antonio General Maintenance, Inc. (SAGM) and Pedro G. Molina, Jr., brought this action for declaratory and injunctive relief against defendants James Abdnor, Administrator of the Small Business Administration (SBA), and Edward C. Aldridge, Jr., Secretary of the Air Force. SAGM, which currently holds a contract to provide custodial services at Kelly Air Force Base in San Antonio, Texas, seeks to require defendants to permit competitive bidding on their next awarding of the contract; the SBA and the Air Force, however, have determined to retain the contract under a special program for socially and economically disadvantaged small business concerns. Simultaneously with the filing of its complaint, SAGM moved for a temporary restraining order and for a preliminary injunction, and defendants responded with a motion to dismiss or, in the alternative, for summary judgment. These matters were considered at a final hearing held in September 1987. For the reasons set forth below, plaintiffs' requests for injunctive and declaratory relief will be denied and defendants' motion for summary judgment will be granted.

I. Background

Section 2[8](a) of the Small Business Act of 1958, 15 U.S.C. §637(a), established a special program designed to benefit "socially and economically disadvantaged" small business concerns.[1] In order to "foster business ownership" and "promote the competitive viability" of these firms, 15 U.S.C. §631(e)(2), the Act authorizes the SBA to enter into procurement and construction contracts with any federal agency. The SBA then subcontracts with qualifying small businesses, which actually provide the services directly to the federal agency. See 15 U.S.C. §637(a)(1). Contracts designated for the 2[8](a) program are therefore effectively withdrawn from the customary competitive bidding procedures generally applicable to federal procurements.

Id. §§631(e)(1)(C) and 637(a)(5) & (6).

Participation in the 2[8](a) program is not eternal, however. Mindful that "these contracts be a means to fostering competitive viability...and not an end in themselves,"

---

1. The Act defines these concerns by means of a numerical formula, see 15 U.S.C. §637(a)(4), and specifically identifies certain minorities—such as blacks, Hispanics and Indians—that qualify for the program.

S.Rep. No. 974, 96th Cong., 2d Sess. 3 (1980), U.S.Code Cong. & Admin.News 1980, pp. 4953, 4954, Congress amended the Act in 1980 and directed the SBA to establish a fixed period of time within which each 2[8](a) participant could remain within the program. See 15 U.S.C. §636(j)(10)(A)(i). After reaching the end of its fixed term the disadvantaged concern is "graduated" from the 2[8](a) program and expected to compete for government contracts on an equal footing with other non-disadvantaged firms. Plaintiff SAGM, a Texas corporation, and its president, plaintiff Pedro Molina, Jr., were accepted into the 2[8](a) program in 1976 and 1972, respectively, and were graduated in June 1985. In 1984, however, SBA awarded SAGM a one-year 2[8](a) contract, with two one-year extensions, to provide custodial services at the Kelly Air Force Base in San Antonio, Texas. Having graduated from the 2[8](a) program and with its contract due to expire on September 30, 1987, SAGM initiated discussions with SBA representatives in early 1987 in order to assure that SAGM would be permitted to bid on the Kelly contract when it was released into the competitive procurement process. In June 1987, however, the SBA and the Air Force decided that the Kelly contract would remain within the 2[8](a) program and be awarded to another disadvantaged small business, Rite-Way Services, Inc.

SAGM filed this action on July 9, 1987. In its complaint, it contends that the SBA maintained a general policy and practice allowing a graduating 2[8](a) firm to competitively bid on the next contract awarded for the same services after the 2[8](a) participant's fixed term had expired. Plaintiffs claim that the SBA's actions (1) violated the Administrative Procedure Act, 5 U.S.C. §§701 et seq., because the agency arbitrarily departed from its established practices without prior notice or an adequate explanation; and (2) contravened several SBA regulations governing the 2[8](a) procurement program.

* * *

IV. The Merits

A. SBA Decision

Before considering whether the SBA's decision to award the Kelly contract to Rite-Way was an arbitrary and capricious departure from existing agency policy regulations, the Court must resolve issues strenuously disputed by the parties: exactly what was the existing agency policy and what are the regulations that govern this action? Plaintiffs contend that SBA's decision to retain the Kelly contract within the 2[8](a) program violated three agency regulations applicable to this case. The complaint first alleges that the SBA's actions contravened 13 C.F.R. §124.301(b)(8)(iii) and (b)(8)(iv)(B), which required the SBA to make a number of findings with respect to the adverse impact upon SAGM before retaining the contract within the 2[8](a) program. The plain language of these regulations, however, demonstrates the futility of plaintiffs' reliance upon them. Section 124.301(b)(8) states: "SBA will not accept for 8(a) award proposed procurements not previously in the section 8(a) program if any of the following circumstances exist..." (emphasis added). The highlighted language clearly indicates that these regulations are designed to serve as guidance to SBA officials considering the addition of new contracts to the 2[8](a) program; the regulation nowhere mentions graduation from the program or the fixed program participation term. These regulations do not, therefore, apply to this case.

SAGM also vigorously asserts that the SBA's "past policy and practice" permitted graduating 2[8](a) firms to bid competitively on the next contract to be awarded for the same services once the 2[8](a) participant's eligibility for the program had expired, Complaint P 11, and, to support its view, offers two pieces of evidence: (1) plaintiff Molina's assertion that, at a February 26, 1987, meeting in San Antonio, he was informed by two local SBA officials that SBA policy "had always been" to allow graduating firms to bid competitively on the 2[8](a) contracts that they had just relinquished, see Molina Affidavit at 4-5; and (2) the fact that six former 2[8](a) contractors have indicated that their contracts were competitively bid after completion of their program eligibility. Fiorino Affidavit, Exh. P-3 to Plaintiffs' Supplemental Filing at 4-6.

Defendants steadfastly oppose this view. First, they assert that the SBA prefers to keep contracts within the 2[8](a) program whenever possible, thus preventing a graduating 2[8](a) firm from "taking his contract" with him after graduation. Memorandum in Support of Motion to Dismiss at 14; Luna Dep. at 30-31. In certain selected instances, however, the SBA does allow 2[8](a) contracts to be released for competitive bids on a case-by-case basis in accordance with the factors set forth in paragraph 46(e) of SOP 80-05. Thus, defendants contend that paragraph 46(e) constitutes the agency policy governing graduating firms. Second, defendants contest plaintiffs' factual claims regarding the former 2[8](a) firms that were allowed to bid after expiration of their program eligibility. See Luna Declaration, Exh. G to Memorandum in Support of Motion to Dismiss.

* * *

The SBA's decision to retain the Kelly contract within the 2[8](a) program was made by Joseph Luna, the Assistant Regional Administrator in SBA's Dallas office, and is memorialized in a June 26, 1987, memorandum. See Exh. B to Motion to Dismiss. * * *

Although far from a model of clarity, the Luna memorandum establishes that SBA did not act in an arbitrary or capricious manner in deciding to forego competitive bidding on the Kelly contract. The memorandum discloses that the agency considered the relevant factors and articulated its reasons for reaching the decision that it did. Only one of these factors supported SAGM's desire to engage in competitive bidding, and the other factors all militated in favor of retaining the Kelly contract in the 2[8](a) program. Given that the SBA's general policy was to retain 2[8](a) contracts within the program whenever possible and to release these contracts only in the limited circumstances specified in paragraph 46(e), given that Mr. Luna addressed these factors and concluded that the Kelly contract should remain as an 2[8](a) procurement, and given the deferential review accorded to federal agencies in procurement matters, the Court concludes that plaintiffs have failed to carry their burden of demonstrating that the SBA's actions were arbitrary and capricious.

B. The Air Force Decision

Section 1207(a) of the National Defense Authorization Act of 1987, Pub.L. No. 99-661, 100 Stat. 3816, 3973, establishes "a goal of 5 percent" of all Defense Department contracts be awarded to small, disadvantaged businesses (SDBs), black colleges, and other minority institutions. Plaintiffs claim that the Air Force's decision to retain the Kelly contract as an 2[8](a) contract, rather than as an SDB set-aside, violates section 1207 and two of its implementing regulations.[2] The rather unusual chain of events leading up to the Air Force's conclusion that the Kelly contract should be kept within the 2[8](a) program is recounted in the Declaration of Stephanie Apple, the Kelly con-

---

2. There is no dispute that SAGM would qualify as an SDB if the Air Force had chosen to go that route.

tracting officer at the time. See Exh. C to Motion to Dismiss. In February 1987, Apple approved the award of the Kelly contract to the SBA under the 2[8](a) program. In April 1987, however, Apple learned that the procuring unit at Kelly was dissatisfied with the qualifications of Rite-Way (which had been chosen by the SBA under the 2[8](a) program); she therefore decided to utilize the SDB set-aside route in filling the contract. After the SBA appealed this decision to the Secretary of the Air Force, after a congressional inquiry into the matter, and after SBA assured the Air Force that Rite-Way would receive the technical assistance it needed to perform the contract,[3] Apple reconsidered her position and decided, in June 1987, to keep the contract within the 2[8](a) framework.

Plaintiffs do not attack the Air Force's decisional process as arbitrary and capricious under section 706(2)(A), see Complaint PP 22-24, nor do they seriously dispute Apple's version of these facts. Rather, the complaint first asserts (P 22) that the Air Force failed to comply with section 1207 when it made the determination to maintain the contract in 2[8](a) status. This claim is completely without merit and must be rejected as a matter of law. First, the very language of section 1207(a) states that the 5% contract figure is merely a "goal" that the Defense Department should seek to attain. But—above and be-yond that—section 1207(e)(3) plainly authorizes the use of 2[8](a) awards to reach the 5% contracting goal ("the Secretary of Defense may enter into contracts using less than full and open competitive procedures (including awards under section 8(a) of the Small Business Act)"). Plaintiffs' contention based on the language of section 1207 must fail.

On May 7, 1987, the Department of Defense issued interim regulations interpreting section 1207. See 52 Fed. Reg. 16,263-67. Plaintiffs assert that the Air Force's actions vi-olated two provisions of these interim regulations that require it to publish a synopsis of the Kelly contract and to make certain findings when setting-aside a contract for SDB treatment. See 48 C.F.R. §205.207(d) and 219.502-72(a) (52 Fed. Reg. at 16,264, 16,266). Plaintiffs' argument puts the cart before the horse, however. In accordance with the language of section 1207, the interim regulations make clear that Department of Defense agencies have discretion in determining whether to proceed by way of an SDB set-aside or through the 2[8](a) program. See 48 C.F.R. §219.201(a) (52 Fed. Reg. at 16,265). Moreover, the regulations stress that the 2[8](a) program, rather than the set-aside procedure, is the preferred path. See 48 C.F.R. §219.801 ("The Department of Defense, to the greatest extent possible, will award contracts to the SBA under the au-thority of section 8(a) of the Small Business Act and will actually identify requirements to support the business plans of 8(a) concerns") (emphasis added) (52 Fed. Reg. at 16,267). Because they do not challenge the Air Force's exercise of its discretionary au-thority to award the contract by means of an 2[8](a) award, plaintiffs cannot be heard to complain that the agency failed to apply proper set-aside procedures.

V. Conclusion

The defendants' motion for summary judgment will be granted. The applicability of SBA and Air Force regulations and the interpretation of relevant statutory provisions are questions of law appropriate for resolution on a motion for summary judgment. And the only issue that is not a pure question of law—whether the SBA acted in an ar-bitrary and capricious fashion under paragraph 46(e) of SOP 80-05—presents no gen-uine issues of material fact that would preclude summary judgment. Because the defen-

---

3. Ironically, one of the consultants being considered by the SBA to provide technical assistance to Rite-Way is plaintiff Molina. See Tr. 26-29.

dants did not violate applicable laws, rules or regulations, plaintiffs' request for declaratory and injunctive relief will accordingly be denied.

Notes and Questions

1. Initially, the 8(a) program did not require qualified firms to leave the program, i.e., "graduate." This "eternal" preference led to abuses whereby certain firms carefully remained qualified in order to focus solely on federal contracts with little or no effort being expended to be successful in the commercial marketplace. Congress finally amended the Small Business Act by requiring a set term for graduation. The current term for participation in the program is nine years. 13 CFR §124.2.

2. The requirement of possessing the "potential for success" is intended to ensure that only truly capable firms receive benefits from the 8(a) program. Currently, a firm must be in business in its primary industry classification for at least two full years immediately prior to the date of its 8(a) application unless a waiver is obtained. 13 CFR §124.107 The two year requirement helps weed out those firms established for the sole reason of taking advantage of the program by individuals that would normally not qualify.

3. As is the case with small business set asides, the award to an 8(a) qualified firm must be made at a "fair market price." FAR 19.806. In estimating the fair market price for an acquisition, the contracting officer is to use cost or price analysis and consider commercial prices for similar products and services, available in-house cost estimates, data obtained from the SBA or the proposed contractor, or data obtained from other government agencies. The contracting officer is granted broad authority in making the determination of what is a fair market price and such decisions can be successfully challenged only if proven to be arbitrary and capricious.

4. A less often used procurement preference statute is the Buy Indian Act, 25 U.S.C. §47. The Act requires the government to contract for the use of American Indian labor to the extent practicable and authorizes discretionary purchases of the products of Indian industry in the open market. Contracts can be but are not required to be set aside for exclusive participation by Indian firms. As a result, the number of such set asides is limited.

3. Affirmative Action Challenges

The federal government's efforts to aid minorities connect this chapter of government contracting law with one of the most controversial issues of our time. To the practically-minded, this controversy simply makes this a fast-changing and uncertain subject. To those interested in larger issues, this controversy makes what would otherwise seem the relatively humdrum subject of small business contracting a matter of special interest and excitement.

ADARAND CONSTRUCTORS, INC., Petitioner v. Federico PENA, Secretary of Transportation, et al.

Supreme Court 515 U.S. 200, Decided June 12, 1995.

Justice O'CONNOR announced the judgment of the Court * * *

Petitioner Adarand Constructors, Inc., claims that the Federal Government's practice of giving general contractors on Government projects a financial incentive to hire subcontractors controlled by "socially and economically disadvantaged individuals," and in particular, the Government's use of race-based presumptions in identifying such individuals, violates the equal protection component of the Fifth Amendment's Due Process Clause. * * *

I

In 1989, the Central Federal Lands Highway Division (CFLHD), which is part of the United States Department of Transportation (DOT), awarded the prime contract for a highway construction project in Colorado to Mountain Gravel & Construction Company. Mountain Gravel then solicited bids from subcontractors for the guardrail portion of the contract. Adarand, a Colorado-based highway construction company specializing in guardrail work, submitted the low bid. Gonzales Construction Company also submitted a bid.

The prime contract's terms provide that Mountain Gravel would receive additional compensation if it hired subcontractors certified as small businesses controlled by "socially and economically disadvantaged individuals," App. 24. Gonzales is certified as such a business; Adarand is not. Mountain Gravel awarded the subcontract to Gonzales, despite Adarand's low bid, and Mountain Gravel's Chief Estimator has submitted an affidavit stating that Mountain Gravel would have accepted Adarand's bid, had it not been for the additional payment it received by hiring Gonzales instead. *Id.*, at 28–31. Federal law requires that a subcontracting clause similar to the one used here must appear in most federal agency contracts * * *

These fairly straightforward facts implicate a complex scheme of federal statutes and regulations, to which we now turn. The Small Business Act (Act), 72 Stat. 384, as amended, 15 U.S.C. §631 *et seq.*, declares it to be "the policy of the United States that small business concerns, [and] small business concerns owned and controlled by socially and economically disadvantaged individuals,...shall have the maximum practicable opportunity to participate in the performance of contracts let by any Federal agency." §8(d)(1), 15 U.S.C. §637(d)(1). * * *.

In furtherance of the policy stated in §8(d)(1), the Act establishes "[t]he Government-wide goal for participation by small business concerns owned and controlled by socially and economically disadvantaged individuals" at "not less than 5 percent of the total value of all prime contract and subcontract awards for each fiscal year." 15 U.S.C. §644(g)(1). It also requires the head of each federal agency to set agency-specific goals for participation by businesses controlled by socially and economically disadvantaged individuals. *Ibid.*

The Small Business Administration (SBA) has implemented these statutory directives in a variety of ways, two of which are relevant here. One is the "8(a) program," which is available to small businesses controlled by socially and economically disadvantaged individuals as the SBA has defined those terms. The 8(a) program confers a wide range of benefits on participating businesses, see, *e.g.*, 13 CFR §§124.303-124.311, 124.403 (1994); 48 CFR subpt. 19.8 (1994), one of which is automatic eligibility for subcontractor compensation provisions of the kind at issue in this case, 15 U.S.C. §637(d)(3)(C) (conferring presumptive eligibility on anyone "found to be disadvantaged...pursuant to section 8(a) of the Small Business Act"). To participate in the 8(a) program, a business must be "small," as defined in 13 CFR §124.102 (1994); and it must be 51% owned by individuals who qualify as "socially and economically disadvantaged," §124.103. * * *

The other SBA program relevant to this case is the "8(d) subcontracting program," which unlike the 8(a) program is limited to eligibility for subcontracting provisions like the one at issue here. * * *

The contract giving rise to the dispute in this case came about as a result of the Surface Transportation and Uniform Relocation Assistance Act of 1987, Pub.L. 100-17, 101 Stat. 132 (STURAA), a DOT appropriations measure. Section 106(c)(1) of STURAA provides that "not less than 10 percent" of the appropriated funds "shall be expended with small business concerns owned and controlled by socially and economically disadvantaged individuals." 101 Stat. 145. STURAA adopts the Small Business Act's definition of "socially and economically disadvantaged individual," including the applicable race-based presumptions, and adds that "women shall be presumed to be socially and economically disadvantaged individuals for purposes of this subsection." § 106(c)(2)(B), 101 Stat. 146. * * *

The operative clause in the contract in this case reads as follows:

> "*Subcontracting.* This subsection is supplemented to include a Disadvantaged Business Enterprise (DBE) Development and Subcontracting Provision as follows:

> "Monetary compensation is offered for awarding subcontracts to small business concerns owned and controlled by socially and economically disadvantaged individuals....

> "A small business concern will be considered a DBE after it has been certified as such by the U.S. Small Business Administration or any State Highway Agency. * * *

* * *

> "The Contractor will be paid an amount computed as follows:

> "1. If a subcontract is awarded to one DBE, 10 percent of the final amount of the approved DBE subcontract, not to exceed 1.5 percent of the original contract amount.

> "2. If subcontracts are awarded to two or more DBEs, 10 percent of the final amount of the approved DBE subcontracts, not to exceed 2 percent of the original contract amount." App. 24–26.

To benefit from this clause, Mountain Gravel had to hire a subcontractor who had been certified as a small disadvantaged business * * * The record does not reveal how Gonzales obtained its certification as a small disadvantaged business.

After losing the guardrail subcontract to Gonzales, Adarand filed suit * * * The District Court granted the Government's motion for summary judgment. *Adarand Constructors, Inc. v. Skinner*, 790 F.Supp. 240 (1992). The Court of Appeals for the Tenth Circuit affirmed. 16 F.3d 1537 (1994). * * *

* * *

III

* * * Respondents concede * * * that "the race-based rebuttable presumption used in some certification determinations under the Subcontracting Compensation Clause" is subject to some heightened level of scrutiny. *Id.*, at 27. The parties disagree as to what that level should be. * * *,

The Court resolved the issue, at least in part, in 1989..*Richmond v. J.A. Croson Co.*, 588 U.S. 469 (1989), concerned a city's determination that 30% of its contracting work should go to minority-owned businesses. A majority of the Court in *Croson* held that "the standard of review under the Equal Protection Clause is not dependent on the race of those burdened or benefited by a particular classification," and that the single standard of review for racial classifications should be "strict scrutiny."

* * * *

A year later, however, the Court took a surprising turn. *Metro Broadcasting, Inc. v. FCC,* involved a Fifth Amendment challenge to two race-based policies of the Federal Communications Commission (FCC). * * * [It held] that "benign" federal racial classifications need only satisfy intermediate scrutiny, even though *Croson* had recently concluded that such classifications enacted by a State must satisfy strict scrutiny. "[B]enign" federal racial classifications, the Court said, "—even if those measures are not 'remedial' in the sense of being designed to compensate victims of past governmental or societal discrimination—are constitutionally permissible to the extent that they serve *important* governmental objectives within the power of Congress and are *substantially related* to achievement of those objectives." * * *

[W]e hold today that all racial classifications, imposed by whatever federal, state, or local governmental actor, must be analyzed by a reviewing court under strict scrutiny. In other words, such classifications are constitutional only if they are narrowly tailored measures that further compelling governmental interests. To the extent that *Metro Broadcasting* is inconsistent with that holding, it is overruled.

* * *

IV

Because our decision today alters the playing field in some important respects, we think it best to remand the case to the lower courts for further consideration in light of the principles we have announced. The Court of Appeals, following *Metro Broadcasting* * * * the case in terms of intermediate scrutiny. It upheld the challenged statutes and regulations because it found them to be "narrowly tailored to achieve [their] *significant governmental purpose* of providing subcontracting opportunities for small disadvantaged business enterprises." 16 F.3d, at 1547 (emphasis added). The Court of Appeals did not decide the question whether the interests served by the use of subcontractor compensation clauses are properly described as "compelling." It also did not address the question of narrow tailoring in terms of our strict scrutiny cases, by asking, for example, whether there was "any consideration of the use of race-neutral means to increase minority business participation" in government contracting, *Croson, supra,* at 507, 109 S.Ct., at 729, or whether the program was appropriately limited such that it "will not last longer than the discriminatory effects it is designed to eliminate[.]" * * *.

Moreover, unresolved questions remain concerning the details of the complex regulatory regimes implicated by the use of subcontractor compensation clauses. * * * The question whether any of the ways in which the Government uses subcontractor compensation clauses can survive strict scrutiny, and any relevance distinctions such as these may have to that question, should be addressed in the first instance by the lower courts.

Accordingly, the judgment of the Court of Appeals is vacated, and the case is remanded for further proceedings consistent with this opinion.

It is so ordered.

[Concurring and dissenting opinions omitted]

Notes and Questions

1. Ray Bailee, decided in 1973, came relatively soon after the Nixon Administration first strongly boosted the strategy of using the existing small business program to help minority businesses. At the time this seemed a relatively mild and non-controversial measure compared to the raging controversies over issues such as school integration by metropolitan-area busing. Adarand, decided in 1995, came after decades of controversy about affirmative action. Indeed, the 8(a) program obviously seemed much more controversial in 1995 for Justice O'Connor than it appeared in the early case for Judge Wisdom, one of the renowned Fifth Circuit judges in the cases ending formal segregation in the South. For all that has changed, some aspects of what the two opinions discuss does remain constant. The SBA still has its 8(a) program, it still is being used to help minority businesses, and although it remains controversial, the program seems to survive despite all, as do the other major such programs. See Danielle Conway-Jones & Christopher Leon Jones, Jr., *Department of Defense Procurement Practices After* Adarand: *What Lies Ahead for the Largest Purchaser of Goods and Services and its Base of Small Disadvantaged Business Contractors*, 1 How. L.J. 391 (1995).

2. Even the Supreme Court decision in Adarand did not have the immediate terminating effect on federal government contracting affirmative action programs that some anticipated. The Justice Department continued to justify and to defend such programs. On remand, the Eleventh Circuit sustained the program, citing new Congressional actions as well as that Justice Department defense. The Supreme Court again granted certiorari, which surely must have made observers wonder whether the program had finally used up all its nine lives, but after oral argument, the Court decided to dismiss the case on procedural grounds, apparently taking its cue from the suggestions of the Justice Department.

3. The facts of these cases reflect the two strategies for affirmative action in government contracting. In Ray Baillee, the SBA directly contracts with the minority business, a hands-on approach of the public agency relating directly, hands-on, to the minority business. The SBA serves as an incubator. In Adarand, the government contracts with Mountain Gravel, and Mountain Gravel, in turn, subcontracts with the minority business. This subcontracting strategy is an indirect one, depending more on the private sector, as statutorily steered via the Subcontractor Compensation Clause, to forward the policy goal by relating to the minority business. Rather than serve as an incubator, the government leaves the private sector to do its own incubation.

Chapter 9

Policies

Generally, government contract law aims for the government to obtain what it needs focusing on the price and utility of the product. However, government contract law also implements other government goals. In this chapter, these are typified by the labor standard and Buy American policies: the government insists that contractor employees have certain minimum forms of fair labor treatment, and that preferences be accorded to domestic rather than foreign products, over and above its mechanisms for obtaining desired product characteristics and prices.

As a policy and conceptual matter, the very notion of implementing such policies through procurement raises a set of interesting questions. First, the purists in government contract law contend that promoting such policies, however laudable they may be, undermines the government's primary goal of efficient procurement. They argue that the government could better achieve these policies' goals either by spending, by regulation, or by some other mechanism primarily directed toward the policies, without burdening the activity of procurement with extraneous and inefficient-to-handle considerations. The purists press this argument with particular force as the government attempts greater "commercial" procurement, that is, procurement from an open competitive market. They suggest that the government raises ever-higher barriers against efficient market suppliers every time it requires on policy ground its contractors to: meet additional criteria, jump additional hurdles to obtain contracts, perform additional duties, comply with additional contract clauses, submit to additional supervision, go through additional waiver or appeal procedures, and face additional uncertainties in getting payment and avoiding sanctions.

Second, policy goals pose challenges in terms of effective implementation through the normal mechanisms of the procurement system. Does the procurement system task its regular contracting officers to implement the policy goal, or does it make them coordinate with specialized agencies or personnel? The section on labor standards shows the complex interaction between procuring agencies and the Department of Labor. Does the procurement system impose commands through proposal and bid requirements, clauses, certifications, and enforcement, or does it factor in the achievement of the policy goal like a percentage change in price or cost? The section on Buy American shows a policy goal sought by such price-like factoring-in.

This is the aspect that most frequently preoccupies the lawyers practicing procurement law. Whether their client is a contractor or an agency, it often experiences these policy requirements as an additional, specialized problem in the midst of handling all the regular procurement issues. A lawyer advising a highway construction contractor may thus face in the midst of ordinary issues about bid protests and satisfying of contract specifications the sudden intrusion of unfamiliar issues, from labor standards to environmental clauses. While, substantively, the issues are unfamiliar, they arise in the ordinary course of procurement, and employ the usual government contract law skills

467

of fathoming the regulations and contract clauses, negotiating with contracting officer representatives, and defending contract compliance.

Third, how do the Congress, the President, the agencies, and the courts divide up the authority involved in implementing such policies? Some major separation of powers issues arise at this point. The commitment of the Congress and the President to the regular goals of procurement, in terms of low price and high product utility, do not change radically from election to election. By contrast, the commitment of the political branches to these other policies may well change a great deal, and the Congress and the President very often do not change in perfect synchronization. Congress may impose policy goals, like Buy American, that have popular support but strike the procuring agencies as unwanted impositions. Conversely, Presidents may impose policy goals in the absence of any Congressional enactment, raising questions of the extent of Presidential authority. The section on other goals highlights these issues by focusing on a case, *Chamber of Commerce v. Reich*, in which President Clinton imposed a new policy goal—that of opposing employer replacement of striking employees—without any particular Congressional support, only to have his Executive Order invalidated by the court.

A. Labor Standards

Starting in the 1930s, Congress established an elaborate system to require government contractors not to afford substandard wage rates or working conditions to their employees. Two of these statutes, the Davis-Bacon Act and the Contract Work Hours and Safety Standards Act ("CWHSSA"), tightly control government construction work. The Services Contract Act applies, naturally enough, to services contracts. After regulatory elaboration in the decades after enactment, they have largely withstood efforts in the 1980s and 1990s by contractors to obtain deregulation, although some limited changes were made by the Federal Acquisition Reform Act ("FARA") of 1994. In effect, these statutes represent organized labor's effort to cement labor protections through government rules against efforts at release by government contractors.

Thus, the labor standards represent a stronghold that has withstood the trends toward globalization, deregulation, outsourcing, downsizing, and other techniques by which employers in the 1980s and 1990s freed themselves from bargained-for labor protections in non-government contexts. On the one hand, opponents may deride them as imposing expenses on the government that these trends have reduced elsewhere, and as creating "entry barriers" against efficient competition. On the other hand, supporters may defend them as necessary for a fair division of taxpayer expenditures on contracting between labor and management. In their absence, the competitive bidding system might become an engine for shifting government work away from employers of organized or otherwise decently-treated labor.

Strikingly, the Department of Labor, not contracting agencies, administers these labor standards. The case in this section, *Janik Paving*, demonstrates this in action, with a proceeding involving Department of Labor investigators, hearings, administrative law judges, and appeal boards. The book excerpt in this section, on "Selected Labor Standards," shows this more extensively; while it concerns Department of Defense contracts, it discusses the array of determinations, waivers, appeals, and so forth made by the Department of Labor. Presumably, the labor supporters of these standards doubt that they would be administered with equivalent understanding of their goals by departments other than the Department of Labor.

The *Janik Paving* case deals with a contractor violating a key portion of the CWHSSA, regarding required overtime payment. It reflects the "tough" side of labor standard enforcement. On one side, the contractor allegedly not only failed to pay its employees the mandated rates for their overtime on a government-funded project, but falsified records to cover this up. On the other side, the Department of Labor hits back, not only by requiring the contractor to make compensatory payments, but by debarring it for two years. While the standards operate in a government contracts context, they also bring the harshness of management-labor clashes.

Then, the book excerpt on "Selected Labor Standards" covers more broadly how the CWHSSA and other labor standards operate. The Department of Labor and the contracting agencies have a complex division of their efforts. Not only does the Department of Labor handle the enforcement and adjudications discussed in *Janik Paving*, it also does such decisions as "wage determinations," setting the prevailing wage rates throughout the country to which some labor standards are pegged. Hence, government contractors may well find themselves dealing with the Department of Labor. On the other hand, contracting officers still have a large role, as they supervise and pay the contractor

Janik Paving & Construction, Inc., et al., Plaintiffs-Appellants, v. William E. Brock, III, as Secretary of the United States Department of Labor, et al., Defendants-Appellees

No. 1322. Docket 87-6113. United States Court of Appeals, Second Circuit. 828 F.2d 84. Decided Sept. 9, 1987.

Before FEINBERG, Chief Judge, and LUMBARD and MINER, Circuit Judges.

LUMBARD, Circuit Judge:

On this appeal, we are primarily asked to decide whether the Secretary of Labor has the statutory authority to "debar" a contractor which has violated overtime hours and pay provisions of the Contract Work Hours and Safety Standards Act ("CWHSSA"), 40 U.S.C. ss 327-333, from working on any contract or subcontract receiving federal funding under numerous specified statutes, for a period of up to three years. Appellants, Janik Paving and Construction, Inc. and William J. Janik, its president, appeal from an order of the district court for the Western District (Elfvin, J.), which dismissed their action. They challenge the Secretary's authority to debar them from such work, as well as the sufficiency of the evidence which the Department of Labor amassed in support of the debarment order. We affirm.

Janik Paving has been primarily engaged in the highway paving and construction business since 1979. Most of its business, according to appellants, involves work on highway paving and construction projects which receive federal funding. This appeal arises from Janik's performance on two such contracts.

In 1980, Janik was awarded the prime contract by the Town of West Seneca, New York for the construction of certain sidewalks, curbs, and drains ("the Edson Street contract"); the work was to be financed under the Housing and Community Development Act of 1974. That same year, Janik was also awarded the prime contract by the New York State Department of Transportation for the installation of concrete and asphalt pavement in Holland, New York ("the Route 16 contract"), with financing to be provided under the Federal-Aid Highway Act of 1956.

Both of these federal financing statutes contained "Davis-Bacon" provisions, which obligated Janik, as contractor, to pay the laborers and mechanics it employed on these contracts the wages prevailing for similar construction in the same localities. See Davis-Bacon Act, 40 U.S.C. ss 276a-276a-5 (1931); Federal-Aid Highway Act of 1956, as amended, 23 U.S.C. s 113(a); Housing and Community Development Act of 1974, 42 U.S.C. ss 5310, 1440(g). Because both contracts involved federal assistance under statutes prescribing wage standards, Janik also was required to comply with the provisions of CWHSSA, which, in pertinent part, required contractors on federally-funded construction projects to pay their laborers and mechanics "time and one-half" for hours worked in excess of eight hours in one day or forty hours in one week. 40 U.S.C. ss 328, 329.[1] Under the statute then and now, a contractor found in violation of overtime pay and hour requirements may be held liable to its affected employees for failure to pay the required amounts and to the government for liquidated damages in the sum of $10 for each calendar day on which these employees were underpaid. 40 U.S.C. s 328. A contracting governmental agency may withhold and pay directly to the affected workers any amounts in contract monies necessary to satisfy the contractor's overtime obligations. Id. at s 330(a). Criminal penalties may also be assessed. 40 U.S.C. s 332.

Enforcement of the CWHSSA is also subject to a regulatory regime which applies to sixty statutes prescribing labor standards for federal or federally-assisted contracts. See 29 C.F.R. s 5.1 (1983) (listing the statutes, collectively referred to as "Davis-Bacon Related Acts"). As pertains here, the regulations provide that, Whenever any contractor or subcontractor is found by the Secretary of Labor to be in aggravated or willful violation of [overtime hours and pay requirements of the CWHSSA or] the labor standards of any of the [other Davis-Bacon Related Acts], such contractor or subcontractor or any firm, corporation, partnership, or association in which such contractor or subcontractor has a substantial interest shall be ineligible for a period not to exceed 3 years... to receive any contracts or subcontracts subject to any of the statutes listed in s 5.1. 29 C.F.R. s 5.12(a)(1) (the "debarment regulations").

Between February and June, 1981, the Department of Labor, through the Wage and Hour Division of its Employment Standards Administration, investigated Janik's performance of the Edson Street and Route 16 contracts. A Division investigator, Patrick Rafter, inspected payroll records and employee time cards which Janik kept for the two contracts. Rafter also interviewed, directly or through questionnaires, approximately 35 past and present Janik employees, 12 or 13 of whom complained about the insufficient overtime wages they had received on the Route 16 and Edson jobs. Based on Rafter's findings, the Division concluded that certain of Janik's employees had not been paid at overtime rates for all such hours worked and that certain of Janik's payroll records had been falsified. On May 9, 1983, the Wage and Hour Division notified Janik Paving and William Janik of its finding and advised them that they would be debarred from future federally-sponsored work. On May 25, 1983, appellants challenged these findings and requested an administrative hearing. See 29 C.F.R. ss 5.11(b), 5.12(b).

---

1. In Kahn, we concluded that since the Executive Order did not "subvert the integrity of [the collective bargaining] process" the NLRA was not implicated. 618 F.2d at 796.

More than two years later, on June 12 and 13, 1985, an evidentiary hearing was held before Administrative Law Judge ("ALJ") Edward J. Murty, Jr. The Division's case consisted of the testimony of six of Janik's former employees who had worked on the Edson Street project during the period in question, 1980, as well as the testimony of Rafter, the Division's investigator.[2]

The former employees testified that they had consistently noticed that the hours which they recorded on the employee timecards submitted to the company were greater than those reflected on their pay stubs. All were aided in testifying by contemporaneous personal records which they kept of the hours they reported. Only two of the employees produced their records for the hearing, however, and only the records of one, Timothy Hart, were received in evidence.

Four of the employees further testified that they had consistently logged their hours on Janik's employee timecards in one-half hour increments. Janik's certified payroll records, however, showed that payments for overtime hours were made to the nearest quarter-hour. * * *

Rafter testified he had concluded, from interviews with Janik's employees, that in 1980 Janik had a practice "of falsifying its payroll and reducing the hours and overtime situations so that when overtime was paid on reduced hours, straight time pay would result." He explained that many of the 20 to 22 workers who indicated no problems with their overtime pay had not worked for Janik during the period in question or had worked in capacities not subjecting their wages to the CWHSSA. He further testified the difference in time increments used by Janik and its employees in recording hours worked indicated improper recordkeeping. In his experience, Rafter stated, the use of quarter-hour increments could indicate that reported overtime hours were being manipulated to achieve straight time pay rates.

Janik presented three rebuttal witnesses. William Janik denied that his company had a policy of reducing overtime hours but avoided categorically denying that Janik had not reduced overtime hours. * * *

By decision dated May 1, 1986, ALJ Murty found that the evidence conclusively established that Janik had "willfully paid employees straight time for overtime hours worked and willfully falsified their certified payrolls to conceal this practice," agreeing with the Division's charge that Janik had manipulated overtime pay rates by reducing overtime hours by one-third. The ALJ credited the testimony of the Division's six employee witnesses. He compared Timothy Hart's personal records with his pay stubs and found a pattern of reduction of overtime hours which corroborated the others' testimony. The ALJ found that Janik's witnesses "unconvincingly answered" the questions raised.

ALJ Murty ordered Janik to pay a total of $1,123.72 in back wages to nine specified employees. Finding Janik's violations to be willful, he also ordered that the company and its president be debarred. Since there was no evidence that Janik or William Janik had previously violated wage and hour laws, and since Janik had cooperated in settling the Route 16 charges, however, ALJ Murty prescribed a two year debarment period, instead of the maximum three years permitted by regulation.

---

2. The Wage and Hour Division's allegations with respect to the Route 16 contract were settled prior to the hearing. Janik agreed to pay the affected workers $13,000 in back overtime pay. The Division agreed that Janik's settlement of these charges would not constitute evidence or admission of wrongdoing. Evidence pertaining to Janik's performance on the Route 16 contract was nonetheless received, as it pertained to the debarment issue.

Dept. Labor wage appeals board dismissed action. (margin note)

Following unsuccessful appeals to the Department of Labor's Wage Appeals Board, appellants, on February 5, 1987, commenced this action to enjoin preliminarily the Secretary of Labor, other Department of Labor officials, and the Comptroller General from implementing the debarment order and to annul the debarment on the grounds that it was unsupported by substantial evidence. Judge Elfvin merged the motion for preliminary injunction with an expedited consideration of the merits of appellants' action. Appellees, in turn, withheld appellants' names from the Comptroller General's list of ineligible contractors pending the district court's determination.

On April 16, 1987, Judge Elfvin dismissed the action. * * * This appeal followed.

don't have power to debar (margin note)

In assessing appellants' challenge to the Secretary of Labor's authority to debar violators of the CWHSSA's overtime provisions, we begin with the language of the statute. While expressly setting forth certain civil and criminal consequences attending a violation of overtime pay requirements, described above, the statute nowhere mentions debarment. The CWHSSA does, however, contain two provisions delegating rulemaking authority to the Secretary, only one of which is germane.

Section 330(d) of the CWHSSA states:

> Reorganization Plan Numbered 14 of 1950...shall be applicable with respect to the provisions of this subchapter, and section 276c of this title, shall be applicable with respect to those contracts and subcontractors referred to therein who are engaged in the performance of contracts subject to the provisions of this subchapter.

Section 276c, adopted as part of the Copeland Anti-Kickback Act, 18 U.S.C. s 876 empowers the Secretary to "make reasonable regulations for contractors and subcontractors" engaged in federally-financed public work projects, 40 U.S.C.§276c (1964). Reorganization Plan No. 14 of 1950, 5 U.S.C. Appendix IX, p. 242, in pertinent part states:

> In order to assure coordination of administration and consistency of enforcement of the labor standards of each of the following Acts by the Federal agencies responsible for the administration thereof, the Secretary of Labor shall prescribe appropriate standards, regulations, and procedures, which shall be observed by these agencies, and cause to be made by the Department of Labor such investigations, with respect to compliance with and enforcement of such labor standards, as he deems desirable...

One of the statutes which the plan initially covered was the Eight Hours Laws, 37 Stat. 137 (1912), as amended, 40 U.S.C. §§324-26 (1958), the CWHSSA's predecessor. Like the CWHSSA, this act specifically provided civil and criminal sanctions for violations of overtime work requirements but failed to mention debarment.

* * *

Based on the failure of the statute and legislative history to refer to debarment, appellants conclude that Congress did not mean to allow the Secretary of Labor such power. They argue that debarment constitutes a penalty, which, under well-established law, can be authorized only by specific statutory language. We disagree.

Circuit Ct (margin note)

The debarment regulation at issue has been in effect since 1951 and has been relied upon since then by the Secretary in enforcing, not only the provisions of the CWHSSA, but also scores of other Davis-Bacon related acts which do not include their own enforcement mechanisms. While "the mere fact that the [regulation] is of long standing does not relieve us of our responsibility to determine its validity, see SEC v. Sloan, 436

U.S. 103, 98 S.Ct. 1702, 56 L.Ed.2d 148 (1978), it is noteworthy that no court has ever held that the [regulation] is invalid." Touche, Ross & Co. v. S.E.C., 609 F.2d 570, 578 (2d Cir.1979). Indeed, prior to the appellants' challenge to the validity of the Secretary's debarment regulation, the only such reported challenge was in Copper Plumbing & Heating Co. v. Campbell, 290 F.2d 368 (D.C.Cir.1961), where it was rejected.

In Copper Plumbing, the court had before it a challenge to the Secretary of Labor's debarment authority under the Eight Hours Laws. Relying on the Supreme Court's reasoning in Steuart & Bro. v. Bowles, 322 U.S. 398, 64 S.Ct. 1097, 88 L.Ed. 1350 (1944), the Court first determined that debarment was not a penal sanction.

* * *

We agree with the reasoning of Copper Plumbing and believe that it applies with equal force to the Secretary's authority under the current statute, the CWHSSA.

The effective enforcement of a statute often requires the use of coercive means. That a measure, such as debarment, may incidentally punish while it deters a statutory violation does not transform it into a purely punitive sanction. Consequently, we are not persuaded by the appellants' contention that debarment is a penalty and therefore is available as a sanction only when the statute specifically authorizes it.

We understand Steuart & Bro. to teach that if the sanction serves to compel compliance with the statute's substantive goals, then it should not be deemed a "penalty". That test is clearly satisfied here. Debarment of contractors found in willful violation of overtime requirements is as essential to the enforcement of labor standards in federal contracting as suspension was to wartime rationing; both serve to protect the integrity of their respective statutory schemes. Indeed, debarment may be the only realistic means of deterring contractors from engaging in willful overtime pay violations based on a cold weighing of the costs and benefits of noncompliance.

Moreover, the debarment prescribed by regulation is subject to modification. After six months, a debarred contractor may petition the Department of Labor to be removed from the Comptroller General's list of ineligible contractors. In deciding whether to remove the debarred contractor, the Department considers whether there has been a showing of "current responsibility to comply with the [the relevant] labor standards provisions." 29 C.F.R. §5.12(c). These aspects of the debarment regulation make clear that it was promulgated primarily to enforce the statute, not to administer punishment.

* * *

Appellants further contend that the district court erred in applying an "arbitrary and capricious" rather than the "substantial evidence" standard to review the Secretary's debarment order. They alternatively argue that the order is not supported by substantial evidence. As it is clear to us that there was substantial evidence justifying appellants' debarment, we find it unnecessary to discuss the appropriate scope of judicial review.

"Substantial evidence", according to well-worn definition, is "such relevant evidence as a reasonable mind might accept as adequate to support a conclusion." See, e.g., Local One, Amalgamated Lithographers v. N.L.R.B., 729 F.2d 172, 175 (2d Cir.1984) (quoting Consolidated Edison Co. v. N.L.R.B., 305 U.S. 197, 229, 59 S.Ct. 206, 217, 83 L.Ed. 126 (1938)).

Here, the employee testimony—together with the personal time records of one of them, Timothy Hart, and the expert opinion of investigator Rafter—adequately supported ALJ Murty's conclusion that the Department of Labor had presented a prima facie case that not all of Janik's employees had been properly paid for overtime hours on the contracts in question.

All of the employee-witnesses testified that the overtime hours for which they were paid were consistently lower than those they actually reported. They came to this conclusion, their testimony makes clear, not as the result of an amorphous feeling, but based on contemporaneous records. ALJ Murty expressly found their testimony credible. We see no reason to differ with the ALJ's credibility determinations. The ALJ's credibility determinations were not so "hopelessly incredible" or "flatly contradicted" either by the "law of nature" or "undisputed documentary testimony" as to require being overturned. N.L.R.B. v. American Geri-Care, Inc., 697 F.2d 56, 60 (2d Cir.1982), cert. denied, 461 U.S. 906, 103 S.Ct. 1876, 76 L.Ed.2d 807 (1983).

It is not unusual, given the five year hiatus between appellants' alleged wage violations and the administrative hearing, that the employees' testimony lacked sharpness concerning the specific circumstances under which they worked undercompensated overtime hours or that some of the employees had made prior inconsistent statements concerning whether, or when, they had complained to the company about their pay. Nor, for similar reasons, is it surprising to find that many of the employees could no longer find or produce the original wage and hour records they kept of five year old jobs. Indeed, the Supreme Court, in articulating the burden of proof to which the Department and employees were generally subject in wage-standard violations noted that "[e]mployees seldom keep records themselves" and "even [when] they do, the records may be and frequently are untrustworthy." Anderson v. Mt. Clemens Pottery Co., 328 U.S. 680, 687, 66 S.Ct. 1187, 1192, 90 L.Ed. 1515 (1946).

* * *

In sum, we find no basis for disturbing ALJ Murty's decision to credit the testimony of the Department's witnesses. The former employees' testimony, which is corroborated by personal time records, sufficiently demonstrated the fact of underpayment for overtime hours. Janik's unjustified use of quarter-hour increments in recording overtime sufficed to give rise to a presumption of concealment, adequate, under the Department's regulations, to show a willful violation of overtime requirements necessary for debarment.

Affirmed.

Notes and Questions

1. A skeptic might ask just what this opinion has to do with government contracting. Procedurally, it involved the investigators of the Labor Department's Wages and Hours Division, a Labor Department Administrative Law Judge, the Labor Department Wage Appeals Board, and an appeal to the district court and to the 2d Circuit. That sounds like procedures for employment law. Moreover, the contracts were awarded by state and local authorities. How much does it signify that (1) the Davis-Bacon Acts, including CWHSSA, get implemented through government contract clauses; (2) Janik Paving mainly works on federal construction projects; (3) the contracts are financed federally; and, (4) the remedy is debarment from government contracting?

2. It is often argued that the labor standards statutes impose not only substantive burdens (higher labor costs) on federal contractors but also, unnecessary procedural burdens such as interference in payroll arrangements and added paperwork. What do the facts of this case suggest regarding such arguments?

3. How must Janik Paving's counsel have analyzed the situation in deciding upon settling the Route 16 contract allegations by paying the workers $13,000 in back overtime

pay, asking for a hearing on the Edson Street allegations that ended with an order to pay the employees $1,123 in back wages, and litigating the case, including the debarment decision, up to the 2d Circuit? How did the procedural and legal expenditures on both sides compare with the wage remedy? What do contractors think of the sanction of debarment for labor standards violations? In the next reading, the many occasions for contractors to seek waivers, determinations, modifications, and other anticipatory, proper rulings on disputed matters will be indicated. How does a decision like Janik Paving affect contractors' willingness to employ counsel to help go through such procedures?

Selected Labor Standards

From: Government Contract Law: The Deskbook for Procurement Professionals
(Excerpt from Chapter 20, "Selected Labor Standards")

(Provided on diskette by the Judge Advocate General's School; edition of MAJ Dave Freeman, 140th Contract Attorneys Course, March 1998; prior version published by the Section on Public Contract Law of the American Bar Association (1995))

CHAPTER 20

SELECTED LABOR STANDARDS

* * *

III. CONTRACT WORK HOURS AND SAFETY STANDARDS ACT (CWHSSA). 40 U.S.C. §§327-333; FAR Subpart 22.3; FAR 22.403-3; DFARS Subpart 222.3.

A. Application.

1. Types of employees covered-laborers and mechanics.

2. The CWHSSA applies to construction and service contracts exceeding $100,000 in value.

3. The CWHSSA usually does not apply to supply contracts. FAR 22.305(c).

B. Purposes.

1. CWHSSA establishes a forty-hour work week and requires the payment of overtime wages for public works and other covered contracts. See Maitland Bros. Inc., ENG BCA No. 5782, 94-1 BCA ¶26,473.

2. CWHSSA specifies health and safety requirements.

C. Government Policy. It is government policy that contractors perform without using overtime. FAR 22.103-2. The government will not reimburse the contractor for overtime payments unless the contracting officer determines that overtime is in the government's interest. FAR 52.222-2.

IV. COPELAND (ANTI-KICKBACK) ACT. 18 U.S.C. §874; 40 U.S.C. §276c; 29 C.F.R. Part 3; FAR 22.403-2.

A. Application.

1. The Anti-Kickback Act protects the wages of any person engaged in the construction or repair of a public building or public work (including projects that are financed at least in part by federal loans or grants).

2. The Act requires prime contractors and subcontractors to submit a weekly statement of compliance pertaining to the wages paid to each employee during the preceding week. FAR 22.403-2; FAR 52.222-10.

B. Purpose. The Act prohibits employers from exacting "kickbacks" from employees as a condition of employment.

C. Recordkeeping Requirements. The Anti-Kickback Act requires contractors and subcontractors to submit weekly payroll reports and statements of compliance. Both the contractors and the agency must keep these records for three years after completion of the contract. FAR 22.406-6.

V. DAVIS-BACON ACT (DBA). 40 U.S.C. §§276a to 276a-7; 29 C.F.R. Part 5; FAR Subpart 22.4; DFARS Subpart 222.4.

A. Statutory Requirements. 40 U.S.C. §276a; FAR 22.403-1.

1. Contractors must pay mechanics and laborers a "prevailing wage rate" on federal construction projects performed in the United States that exceed $2,000.

2. The prevailing wage rate is the key to the Davis-Bacon labor standards. The Department of Labor determines the minimum wage which normally is based on the wage paid to the majority of a class of employees in an area. 29 C.F.R. §1.2 (1995).

a. A wage rate determination is not subject to review by the General Accounting Office or boards of contract appeals. American Fed'n of Labor-Congress of Indus. Org., Bldg., and Constr. Trades Dep't, B-211189, Apr. 12, 1983, 83-1 CPD ¶386; Woodington Corp., ASBCA No. 34053, 87-3 BCA ¶19,957. But see Inter-Con Security Sys., Inc., ASBCA No. 46251, 95-1 BCA _ 27,424 (board does have jurisdiction to consider the effect of a wage rate determination on the contractual rights of the party).

b. "Wages" under the terms of the DBA include the basic hourly rates of pay plus fringe benefits.

B. Application. FAR 22.402.

1. The DBA applies to federal contracts primarily involving the construction of public buildings.

a. The DBA only applies to construction activity performed on "the site of the work." Generally, construction activity does not encompass manufacturing, supplying materials, or performing service/maintenance work.

b. Construction does not include transportation of materials to and from the project site. See Building & Constr. Trades Dep't, AFL-CIO v. Department of Labor Wage Appeals Board, 932 F.2d 985 (D.C. Cir. 1991), rev'g 747 F. Supp. 26 (D.D.C. 1990). Cf. 29 C.F.R. §3.2(b) (1995); 29 C.F.R. §5.2(j) (1995).

c. The "site of the work" is limited to the geographical confines of the construction jobsite. Ball, Ball, and Brossamer, Inc. v. Reich, 24 F.3d 1447 (D.C. Cir 1994), rev'g Ball, Ball, and Brossamer, Inc. v. Martin, Sec'y of Labor, 800 F. Supp. 967 (D.D.C. 1992); L.P. Cavett Co. v. United States Dep't. of Labor, 101 F.3d 1111 (6th Cir. 1996). But see Bechtel Constructors Corp., DOL ARB No. 95-045A, July 15, 1996.

d. "Public building" or "public work" means a construction or repair project which is carried on by the authority, or with the funds, of a federal agency to serve the interests of the general public.

2. Dual Coverage. See DFARS 222.402-70.

a. The DBA also may apply to construction work performed under a non-construction contract, e.g., installation support contracts. Apply DBA standards if the contract requires a substantial and segregable amount of construction, repair, painting, alteration, or renovation.

b. The DBA applies to repairs but not to maintenance. The DFARS provides a bright line test to determine whether work is maintenance (Service Contract Act work) or repair (Davis-Bacon Act work). If a service order requires 32 or more work hours, the work is "repair." Otherwise, consider the work to be "maintenance." For painting, the work is subject to the DBA if the service order requires painting of 200 square feet or more, regardless of work hours.

3. Non-Dual Coverage. The DBA does not apply to construction work to be performed as part of non-construction contracts, if:

a. The construction work is incidental to other contract requirements; or

b. The construction work is so merged with nonconstruction work, or so fragmented in terms of the locations or time spans in which it is to be performed, that it cannot be segregated as a separate contractual requirement.

C. Employees Covered and Exempted. 29 C.F.R. §5.2(m) (1995); FAR 22.401.

1. "Laborers or mechanics" are covered, including:

a. Manual laborers employed by a contractor or subcontractor at any tier. But see Ken's Carpets Unlimited v. Interstate Landscaping, Inc., No. 92-6571, 1995 U.S. App. LEXIS 24419 (6th Cir. Sept. 6, 1994) (non-precedential) (subcontractor not bound to pay Davis-Bacon wages when prime fails to include proper clauses in subcontract).

b. Working foremen who devote more than 20 percent of their time during a workweek to performing duties as a laborer or mechanic.

2. Office workers, superintendents, technical engineers, scientific workers, and other professionals, executives, and administrative personnel are exempt. 29 C.F.R. Part 541.

D. Types of Wage Determinations. 29 C.F.R. §1.6 (1995); FAR 22.404-1.

1. General Wage Determinations. 29 C.F.R. §§1.5(b) and 1.6(a)(2) (1995); FAR 22.404-1(a). A general wage rate determination contains prevailing wage rates for the types of construction specified in the determination, and is used in contracts performed within a specified geographical area. General wage determinations remain valid until modified or cancelled by the Department of Labor.

2. Project Wage Determinations. 29 C.F.R. §1.6(a)(1); FAR 22.404-1(b).

a. The contracting officer uses a project wage determination when no general wage determination applies to the work. The determination is effective for 180 calendar days from the date of its issuance. * * *

E. Procedures for Obtaining Wage Determinations. FAR 22.404-3.

* * *

G. Modifications of Wage Determinations. FAR 22.404-6.

* * *

H. Contract Administration-Compliance Checks and Investigations.

* * *

I. Withholding and Suspending Contract Payments. FAR 22.406-9.

* * *

J. Disputes Relating to DBA Enforcement. FAR 22.406-10; FAR 52.222-14.

1. The DOL settles labor disputes that are not resolved at the local level. Labor disputes are not reviewable under the Disputes clause. Emerald Maint., Inc. v. United States, 925

F.2d 1425 (Fed. Cir. 1991); Page Constr. Co., ASBCA No. 39685, 90-3 BCA ¶23,012; M.E. McGeary Co., supra.

2. Boards of contract appeals and courts review claims relating to labor disputes if the dispute is based on the contractual rights and obligations of the parties. See, e.g., Central Paving, Inc., ASBCA No. 38658, 90-1 BCA _ 22,305 (board had jurisdiction to review claim that the original wage rate information in the contract was incorrect); Commissary Svcs. Corp., ASBCA No. 48613, 97-1 BCA _ 28,749 (board has jurisdiction over dispute regarding DBA offset when ultimate issue was whether the same prime contractor was involved in both contracts). Cf. Page Constr. Co., ASBCA No. 39685, 90-3 BCA ¶23,012 (no jurisdiction over claim that government breached a statutory obligation); American Maint. Co., ASBCA No. 42011, 92-2 BCA _ 24,806 (BCA has jurisdiction over contractor's claim for reimbursement of fringe benefits).

3. Federal district courts have jurisdiction to review DOL's implementation of the DBA, i.e., district courts entertain appeals from DOL decisions. See, e.g., Building and Constr. Trades Dep't, AFL-CIO v. Secretary of Labor, 747 F. Supp. 26 (D.D.C. 1990).

VI. MCNAMARA-O'HARA SERVICE CONTRACT ACT OF 1965 (SCA). 41 U.S.C. §§351-358; 29 C.F.R. Part 4; FAR Subpart 22.10; DFARS Subpart 222.10.

A. Statutory Requirements.

1. Contractors performing any service contract shall pay their employees not less than the FLSA minimum wage.

2. Service contracts over $2,500 shall contain mandatory provisions regarding minimum wages and fringe benefits, safe and sanitary working conditions, notification to employees of the minimum allowable compensation, and equivalent federal employee classifications and wage rates. However, even if omitted from the solicitation, the SCA and applicable wage determinations are binding on contractors. Kleenco, Inc., ASBCA No. 44348, 93-2 BCA ¶25,619; Miller's Moving Co., ASBCA No. 43114, 92-1 BCA ¶24,707.

3. For contracts over $2,500, the minimum wage and fringe benefits are based on either:

a. Wage and fringe benefit determinations issued by DOL (FAR 22.1002-2), or

b. Wages and fringe benefits established by a predecessor contractor's collective bargaining agreement (CBA). 29 C.F.R. §§4.5 and 4.152 (1995); FAR 22.1002-3.

B. Application. FAR 22.1002; FAR 22.1003. The SCA applies to:

1. Service contracts.

a. "Service contract" means any federal contract, except as exempted by the SCA, the principal purpose of which is to furnish services in the United States through the use of service employees. 29 C.F.R. §4.111 (1995); FAR 22.1001.

b. The SCA does not apply if the principal purpose of a contract is to provide something other than services of the character contemplated by the SCA. Further, the SCA is not applicable to services performed incidental to a non-service contract. J.L. Assocs., B-236698.2, Jan. 17, 1990, 90-1 CPD ¶60. See Westbrook Indus., Inc., B-248854, Sept. 28, 1992, 92-2 CPD ¶213 (agency reasonably determined that rental of washers and dryers was not subject to SCA).

c. The SCA applies to service contracts performed in the United States. 29 C.F.R. §4.112(a) (1995); FAR 22.1003-2. "United States" includes any state, the District of Columbia, Puerto Rico, and certain specified possessions and territories.

2. Performed by service employees.

a. The SCA applies only to service employees. "Service employee" means any person engaged in the performance of a service contract or subcontract, other than persons employed in bona fide executive, administrative, or professional capacities. 29 C.F.R. §4.113 (1995); FAR 22.1001. See 29 C.F.R. Part 541 (defines executives, professionals, and others).

b. The term "service employee" includes all nonexempt persons engaged in the performance of a service contract regardless of any contractual relationship alleged to exist between a contractor or subcontractor and such persons. 29 C.F.R. §§4.113 and 4.155 (1995); FAR 22.1001.

C. Statutory Exemptions and Dual Coverage Under the Service Contract Act.

* * *

E. Compensation Standards Under the SCA.

1. Regardless of the amount of a contract or subcontract, a contractor or subcontractor on a contract covered by the SCA must pay service employees at least the minimum wage specified by the FLSA. 29 C.F.R. §§4.159 and 4.160 (1995); FAR 22.1002-4.

2. DOL has removed from its regulations the requirement that contracts under $2,500 contain a provision notifying contractors of the requirement to pay at least FLSA minimum wages. See 60 Fed. Reg. 51275 (1995) (removing and reserving 29 C.F.R. §4.7). See also FAR 22.1005.

3. Service contracts over $2,500. 29 C.F.R. §§4.161 through 4.163 (1995); FAR 22.1002.

a. A contractor must pay service employees not less than the wage rate issued by DOL for the contract. DOL's wage determination is based either on a prevailing wage plus fringe benefit rate, or a collective bargaining agreement (CBA).

b. If there is no wage determination or effective CBA, the FLSA minimum wage applies.

F. Obtaining Wage Rate Determinations (WD).

FAR 22.1007 and 22.1008; DFARS 222.1008; 29 C.F.R. §4.143 (1995).

* * *

H. Price Adjustments for Wage Rate Increases.

* * *

VII. WALSH-HEALEY PUBLIC CONTRACTS ACT OF 1936 (WHA). 41 U.S.C. §§35-45; 41 C.F.R. Parts 50-201 to 50-210; FAR Subpart 22.6; DFARS Subpart 222.6.

A. 1994 Amendments. Section 7201 of the Federal Acquisition Streamlining Act of 1994, Pub. L. No. 103-355, 108 Stat. 3243 (1994), eliminated the requirement that contractors must be a regular dealer or manufacturer of the items to be furnished under a contract.

* * *

VIII. REMEDIES FOR LABOR STANDARDS VIOLATIONS.

A. Termination for Default.

1. WHA—41 U.S.C. §36.

2. DBA—40 U.S.C. §276a-1. See Kelso v. Kirk Bros. Mech. Contractors, Inc., 16 F.3d 1173 (Fed. Cir. 1994); Quality Granite Constr. Co., ASBCA No. 43846, 93-3 BCA

¶26,073, aff'd sub nom Quality Granite Constr. Co. v. Aspin, No. 93-1547, 1994 U.S. App. LEXIS 7755 (Fed. Cir. Apr. 14, 1994) (non-precedential).

3. SCA—41 U.S.C. §352(c).

4. CWHSSA—40 U.S.C. §333(b) (after DOL makes a determination of noncompliance).

B. Debarment.

1. WHA—41 U.S.C. §37; 41 C.F.R. §50-203.1 (violation of stipulations or representations of the Act).

2. DBA—40 U.S.C. §276a-2(a); 29 C.F.R. §5.12 (for disregard of its obligations to employees or subcontractors under the Act).

3. SCA—41 U.S.C. §354(a).

4. CWHSSA—40 U.S.C. §333; 29 C.F.R. §5.12 (for aggravated or willful violation).

C. Withholding Contract Funds.

1. WHA—41 U.S.C. §36 (held in account and paid directly to employees on order of DOL).

2. DBA—40 U.S.C. §276a-2 (turned over to GAO, which may pay employees directly).

3. SCA—41 U.S.C. §352(a); 29 C.F.R. 4.187 (turned over to DOL on order); Castle Bldg. Maint., Inc., GSBCA No. 10003, 90-3 BCA ¶23,271; National Sec. Serv. Co., DOT CAB NO. 1033, 80-1 BCA ¶14,268. But see Jeanneate M. Bailey v. Dep't of Labor, 810 F. Supp. 261 (Alaska D.C., 1993) (contracting officer's withholding of underpaid SCA wages arising under another contract was an unconstitutional denial of the contractor's due process.

4. CWHSSA—40 U.S.C. §328(b)(2) (held in account and paid directly to employees).

D. Liquidated Damages ($10.00 a day for each employee improperly paid).

1. WHA—41 U.S.C. §36.

2. DBA/SCA (per CWHSSA)—40 U.S.C. §328(b)(2); United States v. Munsey Trust Co., 332 U.S. 234 (1947); To the Secretary of the Air Force, B-123227, 48 Comp. Gen. 387 (1968).

UNITED STATES of America, ex rel. PLUMBERS AND STEAMFITTERS LOCAL UNION NO. 38 et al., v. C. W. ROEN CONSTRUCTION CO., et al..

No. 97-17204. United States Court of Appeals, Ninth Circuit.
183 F.3d 1088, Filed July 13, 1999.

Before: SCHROEDER, REINHARDT, and SILVERMAN, Circuit Judges.

Opinion by Judge REINHARDT; Dissent by Judge SILVERMAN.

REINHARDT, Circuit Judge:

In this qui tam action, Plumbers and Steamfitters Local No. 38 alleges that C. W. Roen Construction Company and its president and office manager violated the False Claims Act (FCA), 31 U.S.C. §§3729-33, by certifying falsely that the Company had paid the applicable prevailing wage as required by the Davis-Bacon Act and related federal laws, when in fact it had paid its employees at a lower rate. The district court found that because the Department of Labor had not conducted an area practice survey for the area in question, and because the Department's other efforts to establish the prevailing wage were "uncertain," no reasonable juror could find that the defendants acted with the scienter necessary to violate the FCA. The court then granted summary judgment for the defendants. We conclude, however, that an area practice survey is not necessary in all cases to establish the prevailing wage, and that the status of the Department of Labor's determinations did not compel the conclusion that the plaintiffs could under no circumstances prove that the defendants acted with the requisite scienter. Given these determinations, and the presence of complex legal and factual issues that are not resolvable on the current state of the record, we hold that the district court erred in granting summary judgment to the defendants. We therefore reverse and remand for further proceedings.

Background

On September 1, 1994, C.W. Roen Construction Company entered into a construction contract with the City of Santa Rosa, California, to make improvements to the Laguna Wastewater Treatment Plant. (ER 158). The Laguna Plant was a federally funded project, and hence subject to the prevailing wage and reporting requirements set forth in the Davis-Bacon Act, 40 U.S.C. §§ 276a, et seq., and the Copeland Anti-Kickback Act, 40 U.S.C. § 276c. These statutes required Roen to pay its workers prevailing wages, and to submit weekly statements reflecting the wages it paid. See 40 U.S.C. § 276a & 276c. Under federal law, Roen was also required to certify its payments of the applicable wage rates. Under the relevant regulations:

> Each payroll submitted [to the Department of Labor] shall be accompanied by a "Statement of Compliance," signed by the contractor or subcontractor or his or her agent who pays or supervises the payment of persons employed under the contract and shall certify the following:
>
> . . .
>
> (3) That each laborer or mechanic has been paid not less than the applicable wage rates....

29 CFR § 5.5(a)(3)(ii)(B). The regulations also dictate that:

> (D) The falsification of any of the above certifications may subject the contractor or subcontractor to civil or criminal prosecution under... section 231 of title 31 of the United States Code [The False Claims Act].

29 C.F.R. § 5.5(a)(3)(ii)(D). It is undisputed that Roen did submit the certifications as required by federal law. The plaintiffs allege, however, that Roen's certifications amounted to false statements because the Company paid employees performing certain types of work less than the prevailing wage rate.

At issue in this case is the classification and payment of workers who performed certain types of piping work on the Laguna project (namely "mechanical, pressure, process, soil, waste, vent, potable, and non-potable water piping" (Complaint ¶ 14, ER 4)) between August 15, 1994 and February 1997. Roen classified workers who performed this piping work as Laborers, and paid them at the Laborer wage rate. It then certified that it was paying these workers the appropriate wage rates under Davis-Bacon. The plaintiffs claim that Roen thereby misclassified these workers; according to the plaintiffs, all workers who perform this type of piping work on wastewater treatment plants in Northern California must, under Davis-Bacon, be classified as Plumbers & Steamfitters and paid at the higher Plumbers & Steamfitters wage rate. The plaintiffs argue that as a result of misclassifying and underpaying the workers, Roen violated the FCA.

The plaintiffs point out that in May 1992, the United Association of Journeymen and Apprentices of the Plumbing and Pipe Fitting Industry, AFL-CIO, Pipe Trades District Council No. 51(UA) and the Northern California District Council of Laborers signed a jurisdictional agreement (1992 Agreement) that resolved the classification of piping workers on Northern California water treatment plant projects. According to the 1992 Agreement:

[i]n the construction of water treatment plants, wastewater (i.e., sewage) treatment plants, water reclamation plants, and all pumping facilities related to such plants, for work performed both inside and outside of buildings, the prevailing rate of per diem wages established for Plumber-Steamfitter-Pipefitter is paid to those employees who perform all piping work of every description and material (except as noted in paragraph 2), including but not limited to...all process piping, soil, waste, vent,...domestic and process water piping,...all mechanical process equipment.

(ER 4). Paragraph 2 of the 1992 Agreement states that "[t]he prevailing rate of per diem wages established for Laborers is paid to those employees who, on the facilities described above, perform the installation of non-pressurized surface and storm drain piping...." (ER 40). That is, according to the 1992 Agreement, the workers who performed the piping work at issue in this case (again, "mechanical, pressure, process, soil, waste, vent, potable, and non-potable water piping" (Complaint ¶ 14, ER 4)) were classified as Plumber-Steamfitter-Pipefitters.

In January 1994, the District Director of the U.S. Department of Labor's Wage and Hour Division, Frank Conte, determined that the 1992 Agreement between the Plumbers and the Laborers established the appropriate classifications and wages for work done on water treatment plants in Northern California. In a letter to John Davis, counsel for the Plumbers and Steamfitters Local 38, the District Director wrote that:

As of September, 1992, the agreement [between Northern California District Council of Laborers and Pipe Trades District Council No. 51] establishes the prevailing practice in Northern California for the construction of water treatment plants, wastewater treatment plants, water reclamation plants and all pumping facilities related to such plants in Northern California. For contracts for the construction of such plants awarded after September, 1992 and subject to Davis-Bacon and Related Acts the Wage and Hour Division will require the payment of prevailing wages in accordance with the agreement. (ER 39). In July 1994, plaintiff sent a copy of the District Director's 1994 letter to Roen Construction, putting Roen on notice of the Wage and Hour Division's determination that the relevant wage rate and job classifications would be derived from the 1992 Agreement. (ER 36–40).

In June 1994, the business manager of the Laborers District Council sent a letter to the UA purporting to terminate the 1992 Agreement that formed the basis of the original Conte letter. (ER 43). The UA, however, refused to accept the termination of the Agreement, and as far as the rather sparse record before us reflects, the Laborers took no further action to validate its position. In any event, in March 1996, nearly two years after the purported termination of the Agreement, Conte, along with Richard Cheung, a Labor Department Regional Wage Specialist, again wrote to Mr. Davis and reconfirmed the Department's earlier conclusion that the relevant wage classifications were those set forth in the Agreement. In this letter, the District Director stated:

The Wage and Hour Division has determined that the Agreement between Northern California District Council of Laborers and Pipe Trades District Council No. 51...reflects a longstanding prevailing practice. The Department of Labor will therefore accept this Agreement as reflecting the prevailing practice.

Accordingly, for contracts for the construction of such plants awarded after September, 1992 and subject to the Davis-Bacon and Related Acts, the Wage and Hour Division will require the payment of prevailing wages in accordance with the Agreement.

(ER 24). It does not appear that the Labor Department's 1996 letter was ever sent to Roen.

In March 1997, following the time period charged in the plaintiffs' False Claims Act complaint, the Labor Department sent Davis another letter. In this letter, signed by John Fraser, the Acting Administrator of the Wage and Hour Division, the Department stated that it had "reexamined [its] position regarding Wage and Hour Division's ability to enforce the 1992 jurisdictional agreement." (ER 27). The letter concluded that the Department was unable to enforce that agreement because "there are indications that the written agreement was not followed." (ER 27). In such circumstances, the letter stated, an area practice survey is required to determine the actual practice before classifications may be enforced. It is undisputed that no such area practice survey has been completed, and the record suggests that the Department of Labor has now decided not to conduct such a survey.

Analysis

We first address a threshold question. In granting the defendants' motion for summary judgment, the district court relied on the sole ground that "no reasonable juror could find that defendants' scienter rose to the level required by the False Claims Act." (ER 229). The court appears to have assumed, without deciding, that the FCA extends to false claims that an employer has paid the prevailing wage required by the Davis-Bacon Act. The district judge did comment, however, that "[o]ther courts have been hesitant to hear FCA claims based on the alleged misclassification of workers because of the Davis-Bacon Act's regulatory scheme," suggesting that the FCA might, in fact, not cover claims such as the one before us today. (ER 229; citing United States ex rel. I.B.E.W., AFL-CIO, Local 217 v. G.E. Chen Construction, Inc., 954 F.Supp. 195 (N.D. Cal.1997); United States ex rel. Plumbers and Steamfitters Local Union 342 v. Dan Caputo Co., 1996 WL 400967 (N.D.Cal.1996); United States ex rel. Windsor v. DynCorp. Inc., 895 F.Supp. 844 (E.D. Va.1995)). Contrary to such suggestion, the FCA does indeed extend to false statements regarding the payment of prevailing wages.

As we noted in United States ex rel. Hopper v. Anton, 91 F.3d 1261, 1266 (9th Cir.1996), "the archetypal qui tam FCA action is filed by an insider at a private company who discovers his employer has overcharged under a government contract." It is also true, however, that FCA actions may be sustained under different theories of liability, including "false certification." See id. (citing United States v. Gibbs, 568 F.2d 347 (3d Cir.1977)). As we held in Anton, "[i]t is the false certification of compliance which creates liability when certification is a prerequisite to obtaining a government benefit." Id. (emphasis in original).

As shown above, in order to qualify for federal construction projects subject to Davis-Bacon and related Acts, contractors must "certify" that "each laborer or mechanic has been paid not less than the applicable wage rates." 29 CFR § 5.5(a)(3)(B)(3). Under Anton, therefore, if a contractor submits a false certification pursuant to this requirement he may be liable under the FCA. Moreover, the regulations governing federal construction contracts make this perfectly clear. Those regulations state explicitly that "[t]he falsification of any [such] certification[ ] may subject the contractor to civil... prosecution under...section 231 of title 31 of the United States Code [The False Claims

Act]." 29 CFR § 5.5(a)(3)(D). We have no doubt, therefore, that a false certification that workers have been paid at the legally required wage rate may give rise to liability under the FCA. If, as the Plumbers allege, Roen and its president and office manager submitted such false certifications, it may be liable under the False Claims Act. See Anton, 91 F.3d at 1266.

We turn now to the question of scienter. The False Claims Act imposes liability only on those who "knowingly" present a "false or fraudulent claim" to the government. See 31 U.S.C. § 3729(a)(1). Mere negligence and "innocent mistakes]" are not sufficient to establish liability under the FCA. United States ex rel. Hochman v. Nackman, 145 F.3d 1069, 1073 (9th Cir.1998). While some of our cases may contain extraneous comments that might be read out of context to suggest that the FCA requires an intentional lie to trigger liability, those cases almost invariably reiterate the controlling statutory language that is determinative of their outcome. As the FCA provides, to rise to the level of "knowing" presentation, all that is required is that the party:

   (1) has actual knowledge of the information;

   (2) acts in deliberate ignorance of the truth or falsity of the information; or

   (3) acts in reckless disregard of the truth or falsity of the information, and no proof of specific intent to defraud is required.

31 U.S.C. § 3729(b). We have repeatedly emphasized this statutory language when describing the scienter requirement under the FCA. See, e.g., Hagood v. Sonoma County Water Agency, 81 F.3d 1465, 1478 (9th Cir.1996); Wang v. FMC Corp., 975 F.2d 1412, 1420 (9th Cir.1992); United States ex rel. Hagood v. Sonoma County Water Agency, 929 F.2d 1416, 1421 (9th Cir.1991). Thus, in order to be liable for an FCA violation, Roen's conduct need only qualify under one of the alternative statutory standards, such as "deliberate ignorance" or "reckless disregard".

The district court granted summary judgment to the defendants for two reasons. As the district court held:

   [The plaintiffs' claim] fails due to the FCA's scienter requirement: plaintiffs are unable to show that defendants knew of an intentional misclassification in their payroll records. This failure is inevitable given the uncertainty surrounding the Department of Labor's efforts to establish the classification relevant to this case and the undisputed fact that the Wage and Hour Division of the Department of Labor has not yet performed an area practice survey in Sonoma County to determine the actual classification practices there.

(ER 228). That is, the district court found summary judgment to be appropriate because (1) the Department of Labor had not conducted an area practice survey, and (2) the Department's other efforts to establish the prevailing wage were "uncertain." We disagree as to both reasons.

Under Davis-Bacon, employers are required to pay prevailing wages to all employees on covered federal construction projects. The wage rate an employer must pay is determined in two steps: first, the employer must ascertain an employee's proper job classification; second, the employer must ascertain the prevailing wage rate for that job classification. By matching the rate to the classification, the appropriate wage is derived. Although area practice surveys are one way in which wage classifications may be established, they are not the only way. Over twenty years ago, the Labor Department's Wage Appeals Board decided Matter of Fry Bros. Corp., 123 WAB No. 76-6, 1977 CCH Wages-Hours Administrative Rulings ¶ 31,113 at 42,757 (June 14, 1977). In Fry Brothers, the Department of Labor withheld funds from the contractor for underpayment of prevailing wages based on the misclassification of carpenters as laborers. Id. at 42,758. The Assistant Secretary of the Employment Standards Administration upheld the withholding of funds. Because the prevailing wage determinations that had been issued by the Department of Labor reflected union negotiated rates, the Secretary concluded that job classifications for the disputed project would be based correspondingly on the union negotiated agreements. The contractor objected to this method of establishing prevailing job classifications, and thus the wage rate applicable to its employees. The Wage Appeals Board, however, affirmed the Secretary's decision. The Board held that where the Department determines that the prevailing wage rate for an area derives from a collectively bargaining agreement, then the job classifications for that area must also be derived from that agreement. As the Board wrote:

> When the Department of Labor determines that the prevailing wage for a particular craft derives from experience under negotiated agreements, the Labor Department has to see to it that the wage determinations carry along with them as fairly and fully as may be practicable, the classifications of work according to job content upon which the wage rates are based.

Id. at 42,762.

There are two elements of the Fry Brothers decision relevant to the case before us. First, the Wage Appeals Board made clear that prevailing wage rates may be derived from collective bargaining agreements, not just from an area practice survey conducted by the Labor Department. Second, where the Department determines that prevailing wages are established by a collectively bargained agreement, the job classifications for the project or area at issue are also established by that agreement. We find both elements of two-decades old rule of Fry Brothers to be eminently reasonable. As the Wage Appeals Board explained:

> If a construction contractor who is not bound by classifications of work at which the majority of employees in the area are working is free to classify or reclassify, grade or subgrade traditional craft work as he wishes, such a contractor can, with respect to wage rates, take almost any job away from the group of contractors and the employees who work for them who have established the locality wage standard. There will be little left to the Davis-Bacon Act.

Fry Brothers at 42,762. In order to ensure that this evisceration of Davis-Bacon does not occur whenever the Department of Labor decides not to conduct an area practice survey, we adopt the rule of Fry Brothers here. Accordingly, we hold that an area practice survey is not a prerequisite to the determination of prevailing wage rates or job classifications.

Second, contrary to the district court's conclusion, there was nothing uncertain about the Department's efforts to establish the relevant wage classifications, at least during the period of time that Roen was making its wage certifications. The District Director of the Labor Department's Wage and Hour Division, in both his 1994 and 1996 letters to Plumber's counsel, made explicit that the 1992 Agreement established the prevailing practices for water treatment plants in Northern California. (ER 39). The letters could not have been clearer. The 1994 letter, for example, stated that "As of September, 1992, the agreement establishes the prevailing practice for Northern California for the construction of water treatment plants.... For contracts for the construction of such plants awarded after September 1992 and subject to Davis-Bacon and Related Acts the Wage and Hour Division will require the payment of prevailing wages in accordance with the [1992] agreement." (ER 39). The 1996 letter simply reconfirmed the 1994 letter. Moreover, although the letters were clear enough in themselves, the

District Director also attached to his letters copies of the paragraphs of the 1992 Agreement that specified the relevant job classifications for piping work on water treatment facilities. The inclusion of these attachments enunciated the point that, according to the Wage and Hour Division, the relevant job classifications were established by the 1992 Agreement.

* * *

If Roen believed that the Laborers' attempted recission of the Agreement affected the Department's classifications during the period covered by the complaint, it could have sought clarification. Yet Roen, without making any effort to obtain such clarification, certified that the Laborer's rate was the prevailing wage and that it had paid that wage. Roen does not explain the theory under which it certified that the Laborer's rate constituted the prevailing wage rate—even Roen acknowledges that the Department of Labor is the sole authority responsible for determining prevailing wages, (Appellee's Brief at 25), and the DOL's letter had adopted a different and higher rate. This suggests that Roen's certification may well have risen at least to the level of "deliberate ignorance" or "reckless disregard".

We express no view on any other ground on which summary judgment might be based, or rejected. We may reverse an order granting summary judgment where the district court record " 'has not been sufficiently developed to allow the court to make a fully informed decision on particularly difficult and far reaching issues.' " Anderson v. Hodel, 899 F.2d 766, 770 (9th Cir.1990) (quoting William Schwarzer, Summary Judgment Under the Federal Rules: Defining Genuine Issues of Material Fact, 99 F.R.D. 465, 475 (1984)). We have held, moreover, that in certain cases "summary judgment may be inapposite because the legal issue is so complex, difficult, or insufficiently highlighted that further factual elucidation is essential for its prudently considered resolution." Eby v. Reb Realty, Inc., 495 F.2d 646, 649 (9th Cir.1974); see also Tovar v. United States Postal Serv., 3 F.3d 1271, 1278–79 (9th Cir.1993). The case before us fits this bill. Questions regarding the precise manner in which the Department may or must determine prevailing wage rates and job classifications, the effect of the Department's post-hoc repudiation of earlier wage-rate determinations on the question of the falsity of previously submitted wage-rate certifications, the extent to which contractors may be deemed to have knowledge of the Department's actions, the type of certification that is appropriate if the contractor contends that no prevailing wage exists or that the classification issue remains unresolved, and the various other questions the resolution of which may be required before this case can be finally resolved are both difficult and insufficiently developed on the current record to allow for summary judgment. To this point, neither the district court nor the parties have devoted sufficient attention to the elucidation and resolution of these issues to permit us to deem a grant of summary judgment appropriate.

The district court erred in concluding that because no area survey had been conducted and because the Department's other efforts to establish the relevant classifications were uncertain, summary judgment was proper. (ER 229). Further, development of numerous legal and factual issues is necessary before this case may be decided. We therefore reverse the district court's grant of summary judgment and remand for further proceedings not inconsistent with this opinion.

REVERSED AND REMANDED.

SILVERMAN, Circuit Judge, dissenting:

The majority's discourse on labor law is interesting, scholarly, probably correct, but largely beside the point. This is a False Claims Act case. The point is not whether an area practice survey is the only way to establish prevailing wages. The point is that the undisputed facts did not show that Roen's certifications, even if incorrect, were made with an intent to deceive as required by the FCA.

"For a qui tam action to survive summary judgment, the relator must produce sufficient evidence to support an inference of knowing fraud." United States ex rel. Hopper v. Anton, 91 F.3d 1261, 1267 (emphasis added) (quoting United States ex rel. Anderson v. Northern Telecom, Inc., 52 F.3d 810, 815 (9th Cir.1995)). As we said in Wang v. FMC Corp., 975 F.2d 1412, 1421 (9th Cir.1992):

> The weakest account of the act's "requisite intent" is the "knowing presentation of what is known to be false." Citing Hagood, supra, 929 F.2d at 1421. The phrase "known to be false" in that sentence does not mean "scientifically untrue"; it means "a lie."

This is especially true in a False Claims Act case premised on a false certification. In Hopper, we specifically held, "For a certified statement to be 'false' under the Act, it must be an intentional, palpable lie." Hopper, 91 F.3d at 1267. The majority argues that these principles are "extraneous comments" that have been "read out of context to suggest that the FCA requires an intentional lie to trigger liability,..." With all due respect, if anything is out of context, it is the attempt to apply the False Claims Act to the resolution of a jurisdictional dispute between two unions, especially when one of the unions is not even a party to the lawsuit.

It is undisputed that at the time Roen submitted its first certification, both the Laborers and the Plumbers claimed jurisdiction over the piping work at the Laguna project. Two years earlier, prior to the commencement of the job, the Plumbers and the Laborers had a jurisdictional agreement regarding the type of work in issue. The two unions had agreed that it was Plumbers' work. It is undisputed that before Roen ever filed its first allegedly fraudulent certification, the Laborers rescinded the agreement and claimed the work as their own. The majority makes much of the 1994 letter from the Department of Labor. The problem with the letter is that it is specifically premised on the existence of the Plumbers-Laborers agreement, the very agreement that the Laborers rescinded before the Laguna job began.

Perhaps the Laborers' attempted recission of the agreement was ineffective. Perhaps Roen could have sought a clarification. Perhaps Roen was governed by the Department of Labor's letter regardless of the status of the jurisdictional dispute between the Plumbers and the Laborers. Perhaps an area practice survey is not a prerequisite to the determination of prevailing wages. Perhaps, in other words, Roen's certifications were mistaken. All that may be true, but in a False Claims Act case, that's not enough. To survive Roen's summary judgment motion, the Plumbers also had to show that Roen acted with an intent to deceive. In my view, Judge Illston got it exactly right when she held that in light of the then-existing jurisdictional war between the two unions, "[The Plumbers] are unable to show that [Roen] knew of an intentional misclassification in their payroll records." I would affirm.

Notes and Questions

1. Under the Davis-Bacon Act, laborers under a domestic construction contract receive no less than the minimum wage determined by the Secretary of Labor to be the prevailing wage rate for their particular category. 29 C.F.R. § 1.3 provides that the Secretary may base these rates on information submitted voluntarily, field surveys, or formal hearings. Prevailing wages are based on the type of construction and the specific geo-

graphical area where performed. (FAR 22.404-1(a)). The wage determination also includes classification of laborers by the work they perform.

An aid to this process is the concept of "area practice". Wage rates for workers performing the same type of work on a similar project within a close geographic region are considered the "area practice" rates, and are to be used in determining wages in a contract. Where a geographic region surrounding the site of a government construction contract lacks a similar project for comparison, then "area practice" is absent and should not be substituted by extending the geographic area to include such a project. Comp. Gen. B-153051, 1964 CPD ¶ 8, 43 Comp. Gen. 623 (Contracting Officer erred in using a distant project in determining wage rates for ironworkers for a bridge construction contract).

Cases and contract appeals have generally found the Secretary's determination to be non-reviewable. *U. S. v. Binghamton Const.* Co., 347 U.S. 171 (1954); *Jack Picoult*, GSBCA 2923, 69-2 BCA ¶ 7845; *American Fed'n. of Labor-Congress of Indus. Org., Bldg., and Const. Trades Dept.*, B-211189, Apr. 12, 1983, 83-1 CPD § 386; *Woodington Corp.*, ASBCA No. 34053, 87-3 BCA ¶ 19,957. However, there is jurisdiction by the contract appeals boards to review a wage rate determination where it may have an effect on the contractual rights of the party. *Inter-Con Security Sys., Inc.*, ASBCA No. 46251, 95-1 BCA ¶ 27,424). Further information on these issues can be found in the casebook excerpt from the Judge Advocate General's deskbook section on Selected Labor Standards.

2. Does applying the False Claims Act increase or decrease the significance of the Department of Labor's regulatory system? It does make the tribunal a federal court, rather than an administrative adjudicator within the Department. On the other hand, ratcheting up the penalties makes it that much more important for contractors to have the defense handy that they have made efforts to stay in compliance—such as by working with the Department of Labor's regulatory system.

3. The Janik Paving case used the contractor's falsification of records as a reason for debarment. This case uses the contractor's false certification as a reason for False Claims Act liability. Such intensification of penalties by targeting not just the contractor's (arguably good faith) noncompliance but the contractor's falsifications is controversial. On the one hand, market pressures might well lead to a crumbling of the whole labor standard system in the absence of intensified penalties for falsification, since the worst contractor practices, by allowing the lowest bids, would drive out any better ones. On the other hand, contractors argue that labor standards are collateral (if not opposed) to the primary goal of government contracting anyway, the obtaining by the government of goods and services of adequate quality at low price, so contractors should not be penalized so heavily when they accomplish the primary goal and fall short only on collateral ones.

4. Why have labor standard statutes and regulations largely endured since the 1930s despite contractor criticism, which from the 1980s on has taken the form of intense lobbying in Congress to create exceptions to the Davis-Bacon Act for defense contracting? Keep in mind the delicate regional balance involved in the original enactment of labor standards in the 1930s and not so obsolete. Regions and even local areas differ, in how unionized they are, and in their wage levels. Labor standard defenders argue that these statutes keep the federal government from becoming an anti-union force (for immobile work, locally; for movable work, nationally) by transferring work from unionized, high-wage workforces to non-unionized low-wage ones. Does the debate on this issue basically follow the debate on such issues as whether to raise national minimum wages, or are there special aspects having to do with government contracting?

B. International

Broadly speaking, the term "international" government contracting covers two very different sectors: when potential contractors or subcontractors in other nations play a role in government contracting in the United States, and when potential contractors or subcontractors in the United States play a role in government contracting in other nations. Each sector has a large policy component because of the historic sensitivity of nations, the United States as well as others, regarding giving "away" "their" contracts.

As for federal government contracting, the central aspect is the "Buy American Act," discussed below both by a book except and a case decision. The "Buy American Act" signifies an array of statutory and regulatory rules that give limited preferences to domestic products. In practice, these often involve determinations and calculations of various kinds that may be disputed legally about the application and scale of the preference. If parts from Country A are assembled in Country B and then used as materials in a proposal by a United States construction firm, how much of a preference should be given to a competing proposal by another United States construction firm with other parts from Country D assembled in Country E? Detailed answers may be found to some extent in the FAR and in agency-specific regulations, but in approaching these regulations it helps to have a general understanding.

The application of these preferences has been considerably affected by the network of international trade agreements joined by the United States. Obviously, for example, by joining the North American Free Trade Agreement ("NAFTA") with Canada and Mexico, the United States committed itself to opening its markets, including its government contracting market, to contractors in those countries. More broadly, by joining the GATT Agreement on Government Procurement which now operates through the World Trade Organization ("WTO"), the United States committed itself to opening its government contracting market to contractors in countries around the world. In fact, the GATT Agreement on Government Procurement involved a further commitment not only for the federal government contracting market, but also the state and local contracting markets to open—somewhat.

Accordingly, the first discussion in this subchapter is a brief general introduction to the Buy American Act. The second piece is the *John C. Grimberg* case, which illustrates how the statutes and regulations actually get applied in a dispute. That case includes a vigorous dissent which reflects the disagreements lurking here amidst the technical rules. Another discussion is an analysis of what the GATT Agreement on Government Procurement means for state and local government procurement, again reflecting the debated perspectives. Then comes the Supreme Court's opinion in *Crosby v. National Foreign Trade Council*, about pre-emption of state procurement-conditioning international policies, with background about the applicable international trade law.

Viewed one way, the Buy American Act and related preferences are a barrier to world free trade and an uneconomical means by which the costs of goods and services bought by the taxpayers gets inflated for the benefit of inefficient domestic producers and labor. Viewed another way, the trade agreements and the efforts of sharp lawyers to get government contracts for foreign products are a method by which the American industrial base and American jobs are exported abroad to countries that find ways to subsidize and protect their own home market. With rising globalization of production trade, these issues become increasingly important.

Finally, some consideration should go to the flip side: legal issues regarding selling to governments abroad. An issue of particular legal interest is selling to the foreign equivalent of the Department of Defense, that is, arms sales abroad. While a detailed treatment of this topic belongs to courses in international business transactions, government contracting law appropriately discusses a topic which, after all, involves "government" in contracting at both ends, because not only is the buyer a foreign country, but the United States government regulates such transactions on the seller's side too.

Foreign governments obtain U.S. military items and services in two major ways: government-to-government sales under the foreign military sales (FMS) program, and direct commercial sales to the foreign governments.

An example of the intricacies of this subject is discussed in *U.S. Defense Exports: Update on Offsets*, the Procurement Lawyer, Summer 1998, at 23, by William H. Carroll, an adjunct professor at American University Law School. As discussed there, foreign governments often demand "offset" transactions, in which the U.S. contractor selling military items and services offsets the sales price by foreign participation through co-production, licensed assembly, subcontractors, or other direct or indirect means. United States law imposes reporting requirements as part of high level concerns that offsets may adversely affect national security, supplier base, and jobs. But, offsets often seem necessary to meet the competition from other supplier nations. The government contract lawyer may be asked how to structure them.

Another example of the intricacies of this subject is discussed in Robert A. Borich Jr., *Globalization of the U.S. Defense Industrial Base: Developing Procurement Sources Abroad Through Exporting Advanced Military Technology*, 31 Pub. Cont. L.J. 623 (2002). This traces the impact on procurement of export control laws applicable to transfers of military technology.

For further discussion of the subject of this section, see: Miguel Rocha de Gouveia, *The Price Factor in EC Public Tenders*, 31 Pub. Cont. L.J. 679 (2002); Paul Carrier, *Domestic Price Preferences in Public Purchasing: An Overview and Proposal of the Amendment to the Agreement on Government Procurement*, 10 N.Y. Int'l. L. R. 59 (1997).

The Buy American Act

From: Fundamentals of Federal Contract Law (1990) Eugene W. Massengale
Copyright (c) (1991) by Greenwood Press Reproduced with permission of
Greenwood Publishing Group, Inc., Westport, CT

The Buy American Act, Pub. L No. 428,41 U.S.C. §10, was enacted during the Great Depression in 1933 to give preferential treatment to U.S. producers and manufacturers in the case of purchases of materials and supplies by federal agencies and establishments, as well as to construction contractors. The Act provides that, notwithstanding any other provision of law, and unless the head of the department or independent agency determines the requirement to be inconsistent with the public interest or the cost to be unreasonable, only such articles, materials, or supplies as have been manufactured in the United States from articles, materials, or supplies mined, produced or manufactured, as the case may be, in the United States shall be acquired for public use. The same restrictions apply to construction contracts with respect to articles, materials, or supplies used in the project. The Act does not apply to supplies, materials, or articles purchased for use outside the United States. Through Executive Order 10,582, December 17, 1954, the President has determined that materials are to be considered of foreign origin if the cost of the foreign products used constitutes 50 percent or more of all the products used in such materials or supplies.

In implementing the Act, the executive branch established the policy that bids and proposals will be evaluated so as to give preference to domestic bids, except that bids or proposals offering certain supplies mined, produced, or manufactured in certain foreign countries shall be evaluated on a parity with domestic bids and proposals. FAR §25.103. The offered price of a domestic end product is considered unreasonable when the lowest acceptable bid or offer exceeds the lowest acceptable foreign bid or offer, inclusive of duty, by more than 6 percent if the domestic bid or offer is from a large business concern that is not a labor surplus concern or by more than 12 percent if the bid or offer is from either a small business concern. or a labor surplus concern.

The broad implications. of the Act have generated considerable litigation as to what constitutes foreign products within the meaning of the Act. For example, a contractor's use of domestically processed foreign-made steel tubing in manufacturing construction material was in violation of the Act because the cost of the components of the construction material, the tubing, constituted more than 50 percent of the cost of all products used. The contractor contended that the resulting construction was domestic because the cost of the tubing was less than half the value of the finished product The Comptroller General ruled that it is the cost of the components of the construction material, rather than the final completed cost of such construction material, that must be considered in applying the 50 percent rule. Comp. Gen. B-166613 (1969). The total cost of the end product, what it would sell for minus profit, is irrelevant since it includes noncomponent costs. Labor and other overhead costs and packaging, testing, and evaluation costs incurred in manufacturing the end product are not included as part of the total costs of all the components used to make the end product, but are included in determining what the component itself cost. Comp. Gen. B-1666405 (1969).

If an end product is assembled outside the United States from domestic components, it is not a domestic product even though substantially all of the costs of the product are incurred domestically. 52 Comp. Gen. 13 (1972).

The prohibitions of the Act do not apply in those situations where the supplies or materials are not mined, produced, or manufactured in the United States in sufficient and reasonably available commercial quantities of a satisfactory quality. FAR §25.108. Accordingly, it was not a violation of the Act to purchase cork board from foreign sources since cork is not an item that is native to, or grown in, the United States. Comp. Gen. B-84306 (1949).

The Department of Defense and the National Aeronautics and Space Administration have determined that it is inconsistent with the public's interest to apply the restrictions of the Act to the acquisitions for public use of certain supplies mined, produced, or manufactured in certain foreign countries. FAR §25.103. Since Canada has long been one of those "certain" foreign countries to which the prohibitions do not apply, a domestic labor surplus area bidder did not have preference over a Canadian bidder that had submitted a lower bid. Since it was clearly the intent of the Armed Services Procurement Regulations to exclude all Canadian purchases from the application of the Buy American Act and from the restrictions of section 3(c) of Executive Order 10,582, an award to a Canadian firm was not only proper but also required under the military competitive statute (10 U.S.C. §2305). Comp. Gen. B-150183 (1963).

John C. Grimberg Company, Inc., Appellant, v. The United States, Appellee

No. 88-1378. 869 F.2d 1475 United States Court of Appeals,
Federal Circuit. March 15, 1989.

Before RICH and BISSELL, Circuit Judges, and BENNETT, Senior Circuit Judge.

BISSELL, Circuit Judge.

The decision of the Armed Services Board of Contract Appeals (ASBCA), John C. Grimberg, Co., ASBCA No. 32288, 88-1 BCA ¶20,346 (1987) [1987 WL 46574], reconsideration denied, 88-2 BCA ¶20,713 (1988) [1988 WL 44422], affirming the contracting officer's denial of the equitable price adjustment claim of John C. Grimberg Company, Inc. (Grimberg), is reversed and remanded.

BACKGROUND

On December 9, 1983, the United States Navy issued an invitation for bids on construction work at the Bethesda, Maryland Naval Center. The $3,330,000 fixed price contract included fabrication and installation of exterior precast concrete wall panels. Prior to bidding, Grimberg solicited precast panel quotations from several domestic subcontractors but received only one. Arban & Carosi (A & C) quoted a price of $245,000 — $165,500 for fabrication and $79,500 for erection, caulking and cleaning. The Navy awarded Grimberg the contract on March 15, 1984. Shortly thereafter, Grimberg unsuccessfully attempted to contact A & C to consummate the subcontract. After failing to reach A & C, Grimberg resolicited the domestic vendors previously contacted and received two quotations of $205,000 and $200,918 covering only the precast panel fabrication. Grimberg, however, subcontracted the fabrication and erection to a Canadian firm, Beer Precast Concrete, Ltd., for $237,000 — $120,000 for fabrication and delivery and $117,000 for erection and other miscellaneous work.

The Navy rejected the submittal of panel drawings because use of the Canadian fabricator violated the Buy American Act, 41 U.S.C. §§10a-10d (1982) (BAA). Grimberg requested a waiver of the BAA but the Navy refused. Faced with construction deadlines, Grimberg chose to obtain the precast panels from a domestic subcontractor and incurred costs of $200,000 for fabrication, $59,000 for erection, and approximately $23,000 for miscellaneous work.

Pursuant to the contract's disputes clause, Grimberg submitted an equitable adjustment claim for $53,847. The Navy denied the claim, determining that a post-award BAA waiver was not warranted. The ASBCA denied Grimberg's appeal, Grimberg, 88-1 BCA at 102,895, and subsequent motion for reconsideration, Grimberg, 88-2 BCA at 104,664.

ISSUE

Whether the ASBCA erred as a matter of law by failing to apply the criteria for determining unreasonable price differentials under the BAA and thereby abused its discretion by not granting an equitable adjustment.

OPINION

I.

Grimberg's claim is based on the Navy's failure to grant a post-award exception to the BAA. Without a waiver, Grimberg was prohibited from using the lower priced Canadian fabricated panels. The BAA requires that only domestic materials be used for public works contracts unless the head of an agency determines that such use is inconsistent with the public interest or the cost is unreasonable. 41 U.S.C. §10d. The BAA primarily provides a competitive preference to domestic materials in awarding government contracts. Watkins,Effects of the Buy American Act on Federal Procurement, 31 Fed.Bar J. 191, 194 (1972); see also John T. Brady & Co. v. United States, 693 F.2d 1380 (Fed.Cir.1982) (stating that the BAA "is directed primarily to the period prior to the award").

The BAA is implemented by an Executive Order that provides in pertinent part:

> [Section 2.](b) For the purposes of…this order, the bid or offered price of materials of domestic origin shall be deemed to be unreasonable…if the bid or offered price thereof exceeds the sum of the bid or offered price of like materials of foreign origin and a differential computed as provided in subsection (c) of this section.

> [Section 2.](c) The executive agency concerned shall in each instance determine the amount of the differential referred to in subsection (b) of this section on the basis of one of the following-described formulas…:

> (1) The sum determined by computing six percentum of the bid or offered price of materials of foreign origin.

> ….

> [Section 5.]…In any case in which the head of an executive agency proposing to purchase domestic materials determines that a greater differential than that provided in this order between the cost of such materials of domestic origin and materials of foreign origin is not unreasonable…this order shall not apply.

Exec. Order No. 10,582, 3 C.F.R. 230 (1954–58), reprinted in 41 U.S.C. §10d app. at 1042 (1982) (hereinafter Executive Order No. 10,582).

II.

The ASBCA's interpretation of the BAA is a conclusion of law freely reviewable by this court. See United States v. Lockheed Corp., 817 F.2d 1565, 1567 (Fed.Cir.1987). The ASBCA denied Grimberg's appeal because it determined that the cost of domestic panels was not unreasonable in light of "the flexibility afforded procuring departments and agencies by Section 5 of the Executive Order [No. 10,582], and in light of the Brady guidelines." Grimberg, 88-1 BCA at 102,895. With regard to post-award equitable adjustments, we conclude that the ASBCA erred as a matter of law in interpreting the BAA and Brady.

The ASBCA erroneously construed section 5 of Executive Order No. 10,582 and disregarded the flexibility it affords the agencies in determining BAA waivers. The fact that the head of an agency is empowered to establish greater price differentials under section 5 does not mean that one should be established. Section 5 does not dictate greater price differentials, but rather represents an available option. If the agency head chooses not to exercise that option, the price differentials of section 2 become mandatory for determining what is unreasonable under the BAA. See L.G. Lefler, Inc. v. United States, 6 Cl.Ct. 514, 519 & n. 5 (1984) (holding that a waiver must be granted when the price differential standards are met and that the same standards used pre-award should apply post-award); Keuffel & Esser Co., 42 Comp.Gen. 608, 612 (1963) (explaining that the "Executive order fixes the differentials which shall be considered in determining unreasonable cost, unless the agency head determines," under section 5, that a greater price differential is not unreasonable); see generally Watkins, 31 Fed.Bar J. 191.

The plain language of Executive Order No. 10,582 supports this conclusion. Section 2(b) provides that the price of domestic materials "shall be deemed to be unreasonable" if it exceeds the price of like foreign materials plus a section 2(c) differential. Section 2(c) requires the executive agency to determine the price differential of section 2(b) based on one of the formulas set forth in section 2(c)(1) and (2). Therefore, in evaluating unreasonableness under the BAA, the formulas of section 2 become mandatory unless the head of the agency determines that a greater price differential should be applied.

In this case the fabrication price differential between the Canadian firm and the domestic firm is more than three times the differential established by section 2(c)(1), and the agency head has never determined that an alternative differential should be applied. Therefore, the ASBCA erred in not applying the prescribed formulas.

In post-award situations, however, that does not end the inquiry. Post award, an exception to the BAA is granted under the contract's changes clause only where warranted by the circumstances. Brady, 693 F.2d at 1385–86. If all existing BAA criteria are met, the decision to grant a change is discretionary. See John T. Brady & Co., VABCA No. 1300, 84-1 BCA ¶16,925, at 84,196 (1983) [1983 WL 13698] (interpreting the Federal Circuit's instructions on remand). The ASBCA misconstrued Brady, by reading that decision as establishing a narrow range of circumstances for granting post-award exceptions. Grimberg, 88-2 BCA at 104,664. Brady merely holds that the BAA does not preclude post-award waivers and that additional factors may be considered in determining whether or not to grant an equitable adjustment.[1]

See Brady, 693 F.2d at 1385–86.

In granting an equitable adjustment in the Brady remand, the Veterans Administration Contract Appeals Board (VACAB) recognized that "the request for an exception would have resulted in no increase in cost to the Government, in fact there may have been sufficient basis for a credit to the Government." Brady, 84-1 BCA at 84,196–97. The VACAB also realized the severe consequences to the contractor that the additional cost would bring and stated: "[i]t is certainly in the public interest to grant legally permissible exceptions where there is no resulting expense to the Government, and where to grant such an exception serves to increase the public's perception of its Government as one which deals fairly with its contractors." Id., at 84,197.

Here, Grimberg originally bid the panel fabrication at $165,500. After being awarded the contract, Grimberg found that it could not obtain the panels domestically at that price. Grimberg solicited a foreign bid of $120,000 and the Navy improperly denied a BAA waiver. Grimberg, ultimately obtained the panels from a domestic source for $200,000. Had the Navy granted the waiver, no increase in cost would have been incurred and the government may have been entitled to a credit. Instead, Grimberg was saddled with an additional fabrication cost of $34,500 beyond that which it had originally quoted.[2]

---

1. The dissent's conclusion sets forth a bright line test for permitting post-award exceptions to the BAA. Such a test is unwarranted; the granting of an equitable adjustment is discretionary and should not be so limited.

2. Footnote two of the dissent misreads the function served by the calculation delineated in Allis-Chalmers Corp. v. Friedkin, 481 F.Supp. 1256, 1266-68 (M.D.Pa.), aff'd, 635 F.2d 248 (3d Cir.1980). That calculation is for ascertaining the lowest bidder after the BAA surcharges have been

The failure to grant the requested waiver was an abuse of discretion. The Navy's actions constituted a constructive change and Grimberg is entitled to an equitable adjustment as prescribed by the contract. Accordingly, we reverse and remand to the ASBCA for a determination of the quantum due Grimberg.

COSTS

Each party is to bear its own costs.

REVERSED AND REMANDED.

BENNETT, Senior Circuit Judge, dissenting.

The issue set forth in the majority opinion is correct. Stated another way, the issue before us is whether the Armed Services Board of Contract Appeals (Board) erred in its determination that Grimberg (plaintiff/appellant) was not entitled to an equitable adjustment under the Changes clause on the grounds Grimberg was not entitled to an exception to the Buy American Act (BAA). 41 U.S.C. §10a-b, 10d, and Executive Order No. 10,582 (1954), as amended by Executive Order No. 11,051 (1962). I dissent from the conclusion that the Board was in error.

OPINION

The majority opinion asserts this court's decision in John T. Brady & Co. v. United States, 693 F.2d 1380 (Fed.Cir.1982), is precedent for its position. I think not. First, with regard to the express holding of Brady, the issue decided was "whether the Board erroneously held that exceptions to the Buy American Act [could not] be granted after the contract [had] been awarded." Id. at 1384. In affirming the Claims Court's decision to remand to the Board in that case, this court reasoned that "it may be impossible for the contractor in some instances to make a pre-award request for the exemption." Id. at 1386 (emphasis added).

The fact situation in Brady was such a case. That is, a case where it was impossible for the contractor to make a pre-award request for a BAA exemption. The contractor could not enter a contract with the aluminum supplier since the Veteran's Administration (VA), the contracting agency, had not yet supplied the contractor with specific aluminum sheet sizes. A binding contract cannot be formed without sufficient specificity of the subject matter. It was on these facts that this court in Brady decided a post-award exemption to the BAA can in some instances be granted. The facts in the instant appeal, as discussed below, are very different from those in Brady and do not merit the same result as was reached in Brady.

Second, in addition to there being no express holding in Brady for the proposition that pre-and post-awards are treated equally, the rationale expressed in Brady also does not support any inferential rule that a post-award exemption should have been granted on the facts of the instant appeal. The cases discussed and relied upon by the court in Brady show that the Brady decision cannot support the granting of a post-award exemption (or an equitable adjustment in lieu thereof) except under extraordinary circumstances.

The BCA and Comptroller General (CG) decisions reviewed in the analysis section of Brady all demonstrate some of the extraordinary circumstances which would merit a post-award exemption.

---

properly added to the foreign bid, not for determining the propriety of granting a waiver to the BAA. The dissent's calculations are misleading.

* * *

Nor is there any harshness in requiring the contractor to bear the additional material costs. In Brady, harshness would have resulted since the difference in the actual cost of aluminum versus the expected cost was $50,806 which was 35.71% higher than expected.[1]

In the instant appeal the difference between the expected domestic cost and the foreign cost was only $800 which was 0.33% higher than the domestic cost.[1] It is the A & C bid of $245,000 and not the actual cost claimed by the contractor of $282,000 that should be used in considering harshness. That was the amount on which the contractor based its original bid and that was the amount for which it would have obtained the materials had the contractor done what was reasonably necessary to finalize the contract with A & C. No written communication with A & C was ever attempted by Grimberg, only telephone calls. Board opinion at 2 (finding of fact No. 5). While it might be considered harsh to require the contractor to bear a 35.71% higher actual cost, a 0.33% increase does not even approach being harsh.

The majority opinion's reference to language in the BCA's discussion of Brady on remand is inapposite. The Board applied this court's instructions and found "[i]t is the opinion of the Board that the price escalation of the domestic aluminum meets all existing criteria for granting an exception to the "Buy American' provisions." Brady, 84-1 BCA at 84,196. The fact that granting the exemption would not have resulted in a cost increase to the government is not a rationale which supports the finding that the exemption should have been granted. If obtaining the lowest cost to the government was the predominant policy consideration in issue, all foreign materials would be allowed whenever they cost any amount less than domestic materials, and Congress never would have enacted the Buy American Act. See 48 C.F.R. §14.404-1(a)(1) (1987) (requiring contracts to be awarded to lowest bidder, absent compelling contrary reasons).[2]

Instead the general policy of reducing costs to the government must be balanced with the underlying policy of the Buy American Act to give a preference to domestic materials and thereby protect American workers and industry. See Watkins, Effects of the Buy American Act on Federal Procurement, 31 Fed.Bar J. 191, 191 (1972). In regard to the policy of increasing "the public's perception of its Government as one which deals fairly

---

1. [($190,000.87 (actual cost) - $140,000 (expected cost)) / $140,000 (expected cost)] x 100% = 35.71%.

1. $120,000 (foreign materials portion) x 1.06 (the 6% differential) + $117,000 (nonmaterial costs) = $244,200 (total foreign cost when adjusted with 6% differential). Percentage difference = [($245,000 (domestic price with A & C) - $244,200) / $244,200] x 100% = 0.33%. The proper application of the differential requires it only be applied to the materials portion of the foreign item. See, e.g., Allis-Chalmers Corp. v. Friedkin, 481 F.Supp. 1256, 1266–68 (M.D.Pa.1980). Then the nonmaterial portion of the foreign item is added back before comparing the foreign goods with the domestic goods. Id.

Footnote three of the majority contends these calculations are misleading. The majority does not, however, propose a different method of applying the differential. It is true that Allis-Chalmers was a protest by a domestic bidder of a contract award to a foreign bidder. The proper application of the differential is the same, however, whether it is for the purpose of determining the lowest bidder or the propriety of granting a BAA exemption. Both the statute and the executive order speak in terms of "materials" and not of labor, thus supporting the interpretation by the district court in Allis-Chalmers that the differential is only applied to the foreign materials.

2. But cf. Watkins, Effects of the Buy American Act on Federal Procurement, 31 Fed.Bar J. 191, 204–05 (1972) (discussing hidden costs to the government inherent with the use of foreign materials, e.g., increased unemployment compensation, welfare, and loss of personal and corporate income tax revenue).

with its contractors," 84-1 BCA at 84,197, Brady is substantially distinguishable from the facts of the instant appeal. As previously discussed, it was the government's delay in providing the exact dimensions for the aluminum sheets that prevented the contractor in Brady from entering a firm contract with ALCOA. Thus, holding for the contractor in Brady merely was in accordance with the rule that the government is liable for any additional cost caused by its own delay. Chalender, 127 Ct.Cl. at 563–64, 119 F.Supp. at 190. In contrast, in the instant appeal it was not the fault of the government that caused the failure of the contractor to firm up the subcontract on which it based its bid. Therefore the government should not be liable for the additional cost. WRB, 183 Ct.Cl. at 511–12.

* * *

CONCLUSION

Post-award exemptions are only granted in very limited circumstances. They have been granted where it was impossible for the contractor to request a pre-award exemption or where the material in issue was unavailable domestically. Neither of these circumstances nor any other circumstances requiring equity exists in the present appeal. Thus, the decision of the Board denying an equitable adjustment should be affirmed.

Notes and Questions

1. Start with the mechanics. Where does the 6% differential discussed in both the Massengale excerpt, and the *Grimberg* opinion come from? What does it apply to, i.e., what are the "rules of origin" that determine what is a foreign product? How is it determined what countries the Act's restrictions apply to? (For example: would *Grimberg* be analyzed differently as a result of the subsequent free trade agreements with Canada?) How does an agency head exercise discretion as to pre-award situations, compared to post-award situations?

2. Elsewhere in government contracts are many other situations deemed "constructive changes" warranting "equitable adjustments." How does the *Grimberg* possible foreign supplier situation resemble or contrast with those?

3. Distinguish two different, though complementary, debates about introducing Buy American Act substantive and procedural complexities into government contracting.

One debate occurs on economic grounds throughout trade questions. Should trade be completely "free" or are there policy reasons for preferences? For the tension between NAFTA and the Buy American Act, see Laura Eyster, NAFTA and the Barriers to Federal Procurement Opportunities in the United States, 31 Pub. Cont. L.J. 695 (2002).

A second debate is special to government contracting. How appropriate are government contracting procedures and personnel for managing a domestic preference? The "purist" view of government contracts sees the intrusion of Buy American as sheer interference with the straightforward goals of obtaining best value for the government with the lowest transactional costs. Yet, government contracting has devised an elaborate machinery of statutes, regulations, Executive orders, agency policies, contracting officer procedures, and administrative and adjudicative appeals for Buy American considerations. Is that machinery alien to the rest of government contracting? Note that unlike labor standards, where the government contracting agencies must share jurisdiction with an external specialized agency (the Department of Labor), the government contracting agencies administer Buy American themselves, without having recourse to external specialized trade-managing agencies like the United States Trade Representative or the Departments of Commerce and State.

The GATT Agreement on Government Procurement in Theory and Practice

Charles Tiefer, 26 U. Balt. L. Rev. 31 Summer, 1997

The Uruguay Round GATT Agreement on Government Procurement (AGP), which became effective January 1, 1997, appeared at first glance to end the preference barriers against foreign suppliers in procurement by American state and local governments. Such preference barriers are widespread. The United States' main international trading partners objected to these trade barriers in the Uruguay Round of GATT trade negotiations. They refused to open up protected procurement sectors of their own, while the American state government procurement sector remained discriminatory toward them. To bring the Uruguay Round to fruition, American negotiators had to, and did, match foreign concessions with the AGP's bar against in-state procurement preferences. In implementing the AGP, Congress had to, and did, approve this.

Accordingly, as described in this Article's next section, the AGP does extend GATT's principle of "non-discrimination" against foreign enterprise to the sector of state and local procurement. However, as the section further discusses, a closer look at the compromises made in the AGP negotiation and implementation processes at least begins raising questions about just how strongly the AGP acts.

As discussed in the Article's third section, the AGP explicitly limits its own scope of coverage: it only applies to thirty-seven states, and even to those, does not reach excepted sectors; moreover, the AGP creates ambiguity in implementation because it does not render in-state preferences invalid on their face or as applied to out-of-state domestic suppliers, only purporting to except selected foreign suppliers from their application. Most important, Congress's implementation of the AGP limits the remedying of state preferential decisions in major, if unobvious, ways. Congress has precluded, in the GATT implementation act, any private federal judicial remedy under the AGP.

Thus, procedurally, the AGP offers the foreign supplier considerably less than a smooth procedural route to American state contracts. * * *

State Preferences

For obvious reasons, state and local government procurement often favors domestic suppliers, through a patchwork of formal and informal preferences that work against foreign suppliers. Congress has led the way in having a formal national "Buy America" preference in federal procurement, so, naturally, a number of the states have a similar one in their state procurement. The Congressionally enacted "Buy America" preference primarily serves a national goal to reduce domestic unemployment. It is implemented in each particular procurement by the federal contracting officer adding to each foreign proposal a "Buy America" factor, typically a six percent differential. Additionally, that central "Buy America" preference, and certain other formal "Buy America" preferences like a fifty percent differential for defense purchases, serve particular purposes in particular procurement sectors, such as the national security purpose of building up our domestic defense supply industry.

The federal "Buy America" regulations embody provisions for exceptions for foreign suppliers whose countries have joined the United States in reciprocal efforts at free trade, generally referred to as "qualified" countries. These exception regulations are implemented in each procurement by the contracting officer deciding whether a particular foreign supplier falls under an exception to the application of the differential and becomes a "BAA qualified" supplier. As a prime example, the federal government implemented GATT's AGP, negotiation of which is discussed below, at the level of federal procurement by regulatory exceptions for suppliers in the GATT nations.

Those federal exception regulations teach an important lesson: it makes a difference how Congress implements international trade arrangements. Congress did not repeal the Buy America Act in favor of free trade. It did not even create some separate procedural system for implementing the GATT AGP. Rather, Congress kept the Buy America Act in effect, with a system for accommodations to free trade agreements on a procurement-by-procurement basis. This substantive and procedural arrangement for making exception decisions in individual procurements reflects how the balance of political forces in this context does not accord completely with either the vision of the purist free trade supporter, who might prefer an outright repeal of the Buy America Act, or that of domestic preference supporters, who regret any incursion into the Buy America Act's operation. Rather, the system reflects Congress's delicate political balance between a willingness to match foreign trade concessions and a desire to continue favoring domestic employment.

A second formal state rule has no matching federal counterpart. Many of the states have formal in-state preferences, that favor the state's own suppliers over out-of-state ones, both domestic and foreign. Some particular state legislatures simply declare that the state's procurement officers should favor suppliers of that state. Alternatively, some state legislatures specify particular differentials favoring suppliers within that state over outsiders. Often the preference concerns particular sectors, like western states with in-state preferences for their own beef. Given the small fraction of commerce in America that comes from overseas, such in-state preferences presumably operate primarily against other domestic suppliers rather than foreign ones.

States may also discriminate in favor of in-state suppliers by informal means. It stands to reason that the same political factors leading to the many "Buy America" and in-state preferences enacted formally as state legislation also lead to informal preferences by state administrators. Like state legislators, the state governors and their administrations are accountable to their state's public and their state's particular interest groups. Just as the local political support for favoring local suppliers influences state legislators, it may influence state administrations.

Both formal and informal in-state preferences can have two types of goals, just like the national "Buy America" goals: general favoring of state employment, and some particular interest regarding a particular procurement sector. At the state level, the particular interest would not be national defense, of course, or relief of some special political concern regarding that particular sector, much like a subsidy program meant to draw or to retain particular business for that state.

* * *

CONCLUSION

On its surface, the AGP appears to promise as a matter of substantive principle the opening of American state procurement on an equal basis to foreign suppliers. Its substantive coverage rules and, more important, the mechanisms of its remedies actually limit considerably its effect. In particular, in those states and at those times that the population strongly desires to favor its own firms in state procurement, the state government has ways of doing so. Correspondingly, foreign suppliers will find it difficult to engage in any kind of across-the-board campaign to pry open all the American state markets.

However this seems as economics, it makes good sense as politics. When the issues concern sensitive questions of federalism, the goals of free trade should not be considered matters of ironclad principle. Evolving politics forces and processes, rather than predetermined inflexible legal rules, will determine the pace and avenue of the opening to the world of the American state procurement sector.

At times this may prove an international embarrassment or an economic loss. It may create battle-points in future trade disputes. Yet, one of the main benefits of the American dual sovereignty system is its array of political mechanisms for adjustments between an overall set of national interests and the intense resistance of particular local populations on particular points. The AGP makes wise use of that flexibility to put future conflicts into political channels.

Notes and Questions

1. As the reading indicates, governments throughout the world have moved towards opening their government procurement to foreign providers, albeit with some resistance. Many governments have had to do much more than the United States, having virtually to establish a transparent government purchasing system for the first time. For details, see James J. Myers, *The New Uncitral Model Law on Procurement*, 23 Pub. Cont. L.J. 267 (1994).

Stephen P. CROSBY, Secretary of Administration and Finance of Massachusetts, et al., Petitioners, v. NATIONAL FOREIGN TRADE COUNCIL.

No. 99-474., Supreme Court of the United States
Argued March 22, 2000., Decided June 19, 2000.

Justice SOUTER delivered the opinion of the Court.

The issue is whether the Burma law of the Commonwealth of Massachusetts, restricting the authority of its agencies to purchase goods or services from companies doing business with Burma,is invalid under the Supremacy Clause of the National Constitution owing to its threat of frustrating federal statutory objectives. We hold that it is.

I

In June 1996, Massachusetts adopted "An Act Regulating State Contracts with Companies Doing Business with or in Burma (Myanmar)," 1996 Mass. Acts 239, ch. 130 (codified at Mass. Gen. Laws §§ 7:22G-7:22M. The statute generally bars state entities from buying goods or services from any person (defined to include a business organization) identified on a "restricted purchase list" of those doing business with Burma. §§ 7:22H(a), 7:22J. * * * There are three exceptions to the ban: (1) if the procurement is essential * * * ; (2) if the procurement is of medical supplies, § 7:22I; and (3) if the procurement efforts elicit no "comparable low bid or offer" by a person not doing business with Burma, §7:22H(d), meaning an offer that is no more than 10 percent greater than the restricted bid, §7:22G. * * *

In September 1996, three months after the Massachusetts law was enacted, Congress passed a statute imposing a set of mandatory and conditional sanctions on Burma. * * *

II

Respondent National Foreign Trade Council (Council) is a nonprofit corporation representing companies engaged in foreign commerce; 34 of its members were on the Massachusetts restricted purchase list in 1998. *National Foreign Trade Council v. Natsios,* 181 F.3d 38, 48 (C.A.1 1999). Three withdrew from Burma after the passage of the state Act, and one member had its bid for a procurement contract increased by 10 percent under the provision of the state law allowing acceptance of a low bid from a listed bidder only if the next-to-lowest bid is more than 10 percent higher. *Ibid.*

In April 1998, the Council filed suit * * * After detailed stipulations, briefing, and argument, the District Court permanently enjoined enforcement of the state Act * * * The United States Court of Appeals for the First Circuit affirmed on three independent grounds. * * * The State's petition for certiorari challenged the decision on all three grounds and asserted interests said to be shared by other state and local governments with similar measures.[5] * * *

III

A fundamental principle of the Constitution is that Congress has the power to preempt state law. * * *

Applying this standard, we see the state Burma law as an obstacle to the accomplishment of Congress's full objectives under the federal Act.[7] * * *

* * *

B

Congress manifestly intended to limit economic pressure against the Burmese Government to a specific range. * * *

The State has set a different course, and its statute conflicts with federal law at a number of points by penalizing individuals and conduct that Congress has explicitly exempted or excluded from sanctions. While the state Act differs from the federal in relying entirely on indirect economic leverage through third parties with Burmese connections, it otherwise stands in clear contrast to the congressional scheme in the scope of subject

---

5. "At least nineteen municipal governments have enacted analogous laws restricting purchases from companies that do business in Burma." * * *

7. The State concedes, as it must, that in addressing the subject of the federal Act, Congress has the power to preempt the state statute. See Reply Brief for Petitioners 2; Tr. of Oral Arg. 5-6. We add that we have already rejected the argument that a State's "statutory scheme...escapes pre-emption because it is an exercise of the State's spending power rather than its regulatory power." *Wisconsin Dept. of Industry v. Gould, Inc.,* 475 U.S. 282, 287, 106 S.Ct. 1057, 89 L.Ed.2d 223 (1986). In *Gould,* we found that a Wisconsin statute debarring repeat violators of the National Labor Relations Act, 29 U.S.C. §151 *et seq.,* from contracting with the State was preempted because the state statute's additional enforcement mechanism conflicted with the federal Act. 475 U.S., at 288–289, 106 S.Ct. 1057. The fact that the State "ha[d] chosen to use its spending power rather than its police power" did not reduce the potential for conflict with the federal statute. *Ibid.*

matter addressed. It restricts all contracts between the State and companies doing business in Burma, §7:22H(a), except when purchasing medical supplies and other essentials (or when short of comparable bids), §7:22I. It is specific in targeting contracts to provide financial services, §7:22G(b), and general goods and services, §7:22G(d), to the Government of Burma, and thus prohibits contracts between the State and United States persons for goods, services, or technology, even though those transactions are explicitly exempted from the ambit of new investment prohibition when the President exercises his discretionary authority to impose sanctions under the federal Act. §570(f)(2).As with the subject of business meant to be affected, so with the class of companies doing it: the state Act's generality stands at odds with the federal discreteness. The Massachusetts law directly and indirectly imposes costs on all companies that do any business in Burma, §7:22G, save for those reporting news or providing international telecommunications goods or services, or medical supplies, §§7:22H(e), 7:22I. It sanctions companies promoting the importation of natural resources controlled by the Government of Burma, or having any operations or affiliates in Burma. §7:22G. The state Act thus penalizes companies with pre-existing affiliates or investments, all of which lie beyond the reach of the federal Act's restrictions on "new investment" in Burmese economic development. §§570(b), 570(f)(2). The state Act, moreover, imposes restrictions on foreign companies as well as domestic, whereas the federal Act limits its reach to United States persons. * * *

C

* * *

Second, the EU and Japan have gone a step further in lodging formal complaints against the United States in the World Trade Organization (WTO), claiming that the state Act violates certain provisions of the Agreement on Government Procurement,[19] H.R. Doc. No. 103-316, p. 1719 (1994), and the consequence has been to embroil the National Government for some time now in international dispute proceedings under the auspices of the WTO. In their brief before this Court, EU officials point to the WTO dispute as threatening relations with the United States, Brief for European Communities et al. as *Amici Curiae* 7, and n. 7, and note that the state Act has become the topic of "intensive discussions" with officials of the United States at the highest levels, those discussions including exchanges at the twice yearly EU-U.S. Summit.

IV

The State's remaining argument is unavailing. It contends that the failure of Congress to preempt the state Act demonstrates implicit permission. The State points out that Congress has repeatedly declined to enact express preemption provisions aimed at state and local sanctions, and it calls our attention to the large number of such measures passed

---

19. Although the WTO dispute proceedings were suspended at the request of Japan and the EU in light of the District Court's ruling below, Letter of Ole Lundby, Chairman of the Panel, to Ambassadors from the European Union, Japan, and the United States (Feb. 10, 1999), and have since automatically lapsed, Understanding on Rules and Procedures Governing the Settlement of Disputes, 33 International Legal Materials 1125, 1234 (1994), neither of those parties is barred from reinstating WTO procedures to challenge the state Act in the future. In fact, the EU, as *amicus* before us, specifically represents that it intends to begin new WTO proceedings should the current injunction on the law be lifted. Brief for European Communities et al. as *Amici Curiae* 7. We express no opinion on the merits of these proceedings.

against South Africa in the 1980's, which various authorities cited have thought were not preempted.[25]* * *

The judgment of the Court of Appeals for the First Circuit is affirmed. It is so ordered.

(Concurring opinion omitted)

Notes and Questions

The Supreme Court decided the case based on preemption, but the opinion's interest for this book concerns the special window it opens into the international dimensions of government contract law. Part of the opinion discusses the mechanics of how Massachusetts proceeded, such as the exception if a potential contractor doing business with Burma makes a bid ten percent better than all other bids. How do these mechanics compare with the mechanics of federal or state "Buy America Acts"?

The opinion discusses the contention the complaints that the state law violated the Agreement on Government Procurement (AGP), and the remedy for those who allege such a violation. The European Union and Japan did not, and could not, bring an AGP suit in federal court against the state, nor could the plaintiff in this case put an AGP count in this suit. Instead, the EU and Japan must lodge a complaint against the United States in the WTO, which then convened a WTO panel to resolve the dispute. Moreover, even if the EU and Japan won, that would not have the effect, under domestic law, of invalidating the Massachusetts statute. Rather, it would then become the federal government's problem either to do something about Massachusetts, or, to deal with the EU and Japan as they either impose some kind of sanction or seek some arrangement. The AGP's lack of a direct federal judicial remedy for violation of international government contracting law is no accident, but was part of getting the states not to appeal Congressional approval of the AGP. See Charles Tiefer, Free Trade Agreements and the New Federalism, 7 Minn. J. Glob. Trade 45 (1998). If a foreign business came to you as a client complaining about their bids being rejected in violation of the AGP, what would you advise? What might happen if they simply used the ordinary protest machinery?

C. Other

The labor standard and Buy American rules represent only a couple of examples of the many policies implemented through government contractors. Others include the small business, nondiscrimination, and affirmative action policies discussed in another chapter, and the environmental and drug-free workplace policies mentioned briefly below. Any of these other policies may pose the kinds of questions raised in previous

---

25. See, e.g., *Board of Trustees v. Mayor and City Council of Baltimore,* 317 Md. 72, 79–98, 562 A.2d 720, 744–749 (1989) (holding local divestment ordinance not preempted by Comprehensive Anti-Apartheid Act of 1986 (CAAA)), cert. denied sub nom. *Lubman v. Mayor and City Council of Baltimore,* 493 U.S. 1093, 110 S.Ct. 1167, 107 L.Ed.2d 1069 (1990); Constitutionality of South African Divestment Statutes Enacted by State and Local Governments, 10 Op. Off. Legal Counsel 49, 64–66, 1986 WL 213238 (state and local divestment and selective purchasing laws not preempted by pre-CAAA federal law); H.R. Res. Nos. 99-548, 99-549 (1986) (denying preemptive intent of CAAA); 132 Cong. Rec. 23119-23129 (1986) (House debate on resolutions); id., at 23292 (Sen. Kennedy, quoting testimony of Laurence H. Tribe). * * *

sections: as with labor standards, the policy goals bringing a specialized enforcement scheme or coordination with specialized agencies or personnel who handled that policy; as with Buy American, the complex way the policy goal gets incorporated or factored into the regular procurement decisionmaking.

These additional goals may also raise new questions because of the wide variety of ways, in terms of separation of powers, that the policy goals travel the distance between first proposal and actual imposition on the contractor. Some goals arise in explicit Congressional commands, like the statutes cited in the section on labor standards. Even these explicit Congressional commands can arise in a multitude of ways, from elaborate and detailed legislation to terse and cryptic mentions on appropriation laws. Beyond Congressionally-commanded policy goals, some policy goals arise from Presidential or agency direction, without much express Congressional guidance. Then the first question may well be that of authority.

For further discussions of the subject of this section, see:

Michael H. LeRoy, *Presidential Regulation of Private Employment: Constitutionality of Executive Order 12,954 Debarment of Contractors Who Hire Permanent Striker Replacements*, 37 B.C. L. Rev. 229 (1996).

Charles Thomas Kimmett, Note, *Permanent Replacements, Presidential Power, and Politics: Judicial Overreaching in Chamber of Commerce v. Reich*, 106 Yale L.J. 811 (1996).

Gordon M. Clay, Comment, *Executive (Ab)Use of the Procurement Power: Chamber of Commerce v. Reich*, 84 Geo. L.J. 2573 (1996).

Chamber of Commerce of the United States, et al., Appellants, v. Robert B. Reich, Secretary, United States Department of Labor, Appellee.

No. 95-5242. United States Court of Appeals, District of Columbia Circuit. 74 F.3d 1322. Decided Feb. 2, 1996.

Before: SILBERMAN, SENTELLE, and RANDOLPH, Circuit Judges. Opinion for the Court filed by Circuit Judge SILBERMAN.

SILBERMAN, Circuit Judge:

Appellants challenge President Clinton's Executive Order barring the federal government from contracting with employers who hire permanent replacements during a lawful strike. The district court determined that appellants' challenge is not judicially reviewable and, in any event, the Order is legal. We conclude that judicial review is available and that the Order conflicts with the National Labor Relations Act, and therefore we reverse.

I.

President Clinton issued Executive Order No. 12,954, 60 Fed.Reg. 13,023 (1995), on March 8, 1995, pursuant to his authority under the Federal Property and Administrative Services Act, 40 U.S.C. §471 et seq. (the Procurement Act), which declares:

> It is the policy of the executive branch in procuring goods and services that, to ensure the economical and efficient administration and completion of Federal Government contracts, contracting agencies shall not contract with employers that permanently replace lawfully striking employees.

Order at 13,023, §1. The Order applies to all government contracts over $100,000. In 1994, federal procurement exceeded $400 billion and constituted approximately 6.5% of the gross domestic product. See STATISTICAL ABSTRACT OF THE UNITED STATES 451 (115th ed. 1995). As of 1993, approximately 26 million workers, 22% of the labor force, were employed by federal contractors and subcontractors. GENERAL AC-COUNTING OFFICE, REPORT TO SENATOR PAUL SIMON, WORKER PROTEC-TION: FEDERAL CONTRACTORS AND VIOLATIONS OF LABOR LAW (Oct. 1995) (GAO REPORT).

The Order explains that the "balance" between allowing businesses to operate during a strike and preserving worker rights is disrupted when an employer hires permanent replacements during a strike. "It has been found" that the hiring of permanent replace-ments results in longer strikes, can change a "limited dispute into a broader, more con-tentious struggle," and results in the loss to the employer of the "accumulated knowl-edge, experience, skill, and expertise" of the striking workers. These consequences adversely affect federal contractors' ability to supply high quality and reliable goods and services.

The Secretary of Labor is charged with implementing and enforcing the Order. If the Secretary finds that a contractor has permanently replaced lawfully striking workers, the Secretary "may make a finding that it is appropriate to terminate the contract for conve-nience" unless the head of the contracting agency objects. The Secretary is also to debar contractors that have permanently replaced striking workers from future government contracts unless the "labor dispute precipitating the permanent replacement of lawfully striking workers has been resolved, as determined by the Secretary" or the head of the agency determines that there is a compelling reason to lift the debarment. A debarment "normally will be limited to those organizational units of a Federal contractor that the Secretary finds to have permanently replaced lawfully striking workers."

On May 25, Secretary Reich issued final implementing regulations. See Permanent Replacement of Lawfully Striking Employees by Federal Contractors, 60 Fed.Reg. 27,856 (1995). * * *

Prior to the President's Executive Order, there were numerous legislative attempts to restrict the use of permanent replacements. In 1993 the Workplace Fairness Act was in-troduced in the Senate, see S. 55, 103d Cong., 1st Sess., which would have made the use of permanent replacements an unfair labor practice. Supporters similarly argued that the use of permanent replacements upsets the "balance" between labor and manage-ment and leads to lower productivity. See S.REP. NO. 110, 103d Cong., 1st Sess. 20-25 (1993). It failed to pass.

Appellants, the Chamber of Commerce, American Trucking Associations, Inc., Labor Policy Association, National Association of Manufacturers, Bridgestone/Fire-stone, Inc., and Mosler Inc., filed suit on March 15, prior to the Secretary's promulga-tion of the regulations, seeking declaratory and injunctive relief against the Secretary of Labor's enforcement of the Executive Order. They alleged that the Order is contrary to the National Labor Relations Act, 29 U.S.C. §151 et seq. (NLRA), the Procurement Act and the Constitution. On expedited appeal we reversed the district court's determina-tion that appellants' claims were not ripe. See Chamber of Commerce v. Reich, 57 F.3d 1099 (D.C.Cir.1995). The district court, on remand, again ruled in favor of the govern-ment. It held that appellants' statutory claim that the Executive Order violated the NLRA is not judicially reviewable since the Procurement Act vests broad discretionary authority in the President just as did the statute at issue in Dalton v. Specter, 511 U.S.

462, 114 S.Ct. 1719, 128 L.Ed.2d 497 (1994), in which the Supreme Court refused to review a claim that the President had abused his statutory discretion. Appellants' constitutional claim similarly was held to be unreviewable as nothing more than an argument that the President abused his statutory powers. The district court, in the alternative, rejected appellants' statutory claim on the merits, reasoning that under the Executive Order the government was acting in a proprietary capacity and, therefore, NLRA preemption was inapplicable. The court stressed that the President's interpretation of the Procurement Act as authorizing the Order was entitled to Chevron-like deference and was reasonable because it furthered the statutory values of "economy" and "efficiency" (the government does not attempt to defend on appeal the court's deference to the President's interpretation). The court also noted that the government was merely exercising an option "available" to a private contractor.

* * *

III.

Appellants' most powerful argument on the merits, it strikes us, is their claim that the Executive Order is in conflict with the NLRA. If that is so, it is unnecessary to decide whether, in the absence of the NLRA, the President would be authorized (with or without appropriate findings) under the Procurement Act and the Constitution to issue the Executive Order. It is, in that regard, undisputed that the NLRA preserves to employers the right to permanently replace economic strikers as an offset to the employees' right to strike. Almost 60 years ago, the Supreme Court explained that an employer retained the right "to protect and continue his business by supplying places left vacant by strikers. And he is not bound to discharge those hired to fill the places of strikers, upon the election of the latter to resume their employment, in order to create places for them." NLRB v. Mackay Radio & Tel. Co., 304 U.S. 333, 345–46, 58 S.Ct. 904, 910–11, 82 L.Ed. 1381 (1938). The Court has repeatedly approved and reaffirmed Mackay Radio. * * *

The government would have us look at the case somewhat differently. Although nothing in the Procurement Act, passed in 1949 long after the original version of the NLRA, addresses labor relations—let alone the specific issue of replacement of strikers—the government, as we have noted, emphasizes the broad discretion that statute bestows on the President to set procurement policy for the entire government. Presidents have sought to affect, inter alia, the private employment practices of government contractors under that authority by issuing Executive Orders designed to ensure equal employment opportunities, see E.O. 11,246, 3 C.F.R. 339 (1964–65 Compilation) (1965); E.O. 11,141, 3 C.F.R. 179 (1964–65 Compilation), reprinted in 5 U.S.C. §3301 Note (1976); E.O. 11,114, 3 C.F.R. 774 (1959–63 Compilation) (1963); E.O. 10,925, 3 C.F.R. 448 (1959–63 Compilation) (1961); E.O. 10,557, 3 C.F.R. 203 (1954–58 Compilation) (1954); E.O. 10,479, 3 C.F.R. 961 (1949–53 Compilation) (1953), and to limit the size of wage increases, see E.O. 12,092, 43 Fed.Reg. 51,375 (1978). These Orders were sustained in courts of appeals against attacks that asserted, inter alia, that the President exceeded his authority under the Procurement Act. See Contractors Ass'n of Eastern Pennsylvania v. Secretary of Labor, 442 F.2d 159 (3d Cir.), cert. denied sub nom. Contractors Ass'n of Eastern Pennsylvania v. Hodgson, 404 U.S. 854, 92 S.Ct. 98, 30 L.Ed.2d 95 (1971); Kahn, 618 F.2d 784. The government calls our attention to two Executive Orders issued by President Bush that actually dealt with matters covered by the NLRA. One of those barred government contractors from signing pre-hire agreements expressly permitted under the construction industry proviso to §8(e) of the NLRA, see E.O. 12,818, 57 Fed.Reg. 48,713 (1992), and another required government contractors to post notices informing their employees that they could not be required to join or remain a member of a union, see E.O. 12,800, 57 Fed.Reg. 12,985 (1992). (Neither of these orders provoked litigation so no court passed on their legality.)

Accordingly, the government suggests that if the authority to issue the Executive Order can be found in the broad reaches of the Procurement Act—the later statute—that is the end of the matter. The government explains "[t]here can be no conflict between the President's legitimate exercise of authority under the Procurement Act and [the NLRA rights] relied on by appellants." The implication of this argument, if we understand it correctly, is that if there is tension, or perhaps even conflict, between the two statutes, the Procurement Act trumps the NLRA. But the government's argument runs against the canon of statutory construction: "[t]he cardinal rule...that repeals by implication are not favored." Traynor v. Turnage, 485 U.S. 535, 547, 108 S.Ct. 1372, 1381, 99 L.Ed.2d 618 (1988) (quoting Morton v. Mancari, 417 U.S. 535, 549–50, 94 S.Ct. 2474, 2482, 41 L.Ed.2d 290 (1974)). The later statute displaces the first only when the statute "expressly contradict[s] the original act" or if such a construction "is absolutely necessary...in order that [the] words [of the later statute] shall have any meaning at all." Id. at 548, 94 S.Ct. at 2481 (quoting Radzanower v. Touche Ross & Co., 426 U.S. 148, 153, 96 S.Ct. 1989, 1992, 48 L.Ed.2d 540 (1976)); see also Wood v. United States, 41 U.S. (16 Pet.) 342, 363, 10 L.Ed. 987 (1842) (there should be a "manifest and total repugnancy in the provisions, to lead to the conclusion that the [more recent laws] abrogated, and were designed to abrogate the [prior laws]."). Furthermore, the Supreme Court has emphasized that "[w]here there is no clear intention otherwise, a specific statute will not be controlled or nullified by a general one...." Crawford Fitting Co. v. J.T. Gibbons, Inc., 482 U.S. 437, 445, 107 S.Ct. 2494, 2499, 96 L.Ed.2d 385 (1987) (quoting Radzanower, 426 U.S. at 153, 96 S.Ct. at 1992) (emphasis added in Crawford Fitting); see also Green v. Bock Laundry Mach. Co., 490 U.S. 504, 524, 109 S.Ct. 1981, 1992, 104 L.Ed.2d 557 (1989). The Procurement Act was designed to address broad concerns quite different from the more focused question of the appropriate balance of power between management and labor in collective bargaining. The text of the Procurement Act and its legislative history indicate that Congress was troubled by the absence of central management that could coordinate the entire government's procurement activities in an efficient and economical manner. The legislative history is replete with references for the need to have an "efficient, businesslike system of property management." S.REP. NO. 475, 81st Cong., 1st Sess. 1 (1949); see also H.R.REP. NO. 670, 81st Cong. 1st Sess. 2 (1949).

The President's authority to pursue "efficient and economic" procurement, see 40 U.S.C. §486(a), to be sure, has been interpreted to permit such broad ranging Executive Orders as 11,246 and 12,092, respectively guaranteeing equal employment opportunities, and restricting wage increases on the part of government contractors—measures which certainly reach beyond any narrow concept of efficiency and economy in procurement. But in those cases, the Third Circuit and this court did not perceive any conflict with another federal statute.[1] Here, undeniably there is some tension between the President's Executive Order and the NLRA. To determine whether that tension constitutes unacceptable conflict we look to the extensive body of Supreme Court cases that mark out the boundaries of the field occupied by the NLRA. Since the progenitors of these cases originally arose in the context of state actions that were thought to interfere

---

1. The CWHSSA has since been amended to require contractors to pay overtime rates only for hours worked in excess of a forty-hour work week. 99 Stat. 583, 734 (1985).

with the federal statute, they are referred to collectively as establishing the NLRA "pre-emption doctrine." The principles developed, however, have been applied equally to federal governmental behavior that is thought similarly to encroach into the NLRA's regulatory territory.

The Supreme Court has crafted two different types of NLRA pre-emption. Metropolitan Life Ins. Co. v. Massachusetts, 471 U.S. 724, 748, 105 S.Ct. 2380, 2393, 85 L.Ed.2d 728 (1985). Garmon pre-emption "forbids state and local regulation of activities that are 'protected by §7 of the [NLRA], or constitute an unfair labor practice under §8.'" Building & Constr. Trades Council v. Associated Builders & Contractors of Massachusetts/Rhode Island, 507 U.S. 218, 224, 113 S.Ct. 1190, 1194, 122 L.Ed.2d 565 (1993) (Boston Harbor) * * *

Machinists pre-emption, on the other hand, prohibits regulation of areas that Congress intended to be left "unregulated and to be controlled by the free play of economic forces." Lodge 76, International Ass'n of Machinists & Aerospace Workers v. Wisconsin Employment Relations Comm'n, 427 U.S. 132, 144, 96 S.Ct. 2548, 2555, 49 L.Ed.2d 396 (1976) (holding that a Wisconsin employment relations board could not find a refusal to work overtime, an action that did not violate the NLRA, an unfair labor practice). The underlying rationale is that union and management "proceed from contrary and to an extent antagonistic viewpoints and concepts of self-interest.... The presence of economic weapons in reserve, and their actual exercise on occasion by the parties, is part and parcel of the system that the Wagner and Taft-Hartley Acts have recognized." NLRB v. Insurance Agents' Int'l Union, 361 U.S. 477, 488–89, 80 S.Ct. 419, 426–27, 4 L.Ed.2d 454 (1960). In fact, Machinists itself refers to the "hiring of permanent replacements" as an economic weapon available to an employer. 427 U.S. at 153, 96 S.Ct. at 2559.

Nor, as we have noted, is there any doubt that Machinists "pre-emption" applies to federal as well as state action.

* * *

The Court held that since the union's activities were economic weapons preserved by the NLRA, the Board (which has the "primary responsibility for developing and applying national labor policy," Curtin Matheson, 494 U.S. at 786, 110 S.Ct. at 1549) lacked the power to conclude that the activities constituted a NLRA violation. The Court has described Machinists pre-emption as creating a "free zone from which all regulation, 'whether federal or State,' is excluded." Golden State Transit Corp. v. Los Angeles, 493 U.S. 103, 111, 110 S.Ct. 444, 451, 107 L.Ed.2d 420 (1989).

* * *

When the government acts as a purchaser of goods and services NLRA pre-emption is still relevant. In Wisconsin Dep't of Indus. v. Gould Inc., 475 U.S. 282, 106 S.Ct. 1057, 89 L.Ed.2d 223 (1986), the state of Wisconsin had passed a statute debarring persons or firms that had violated the NLRA three times within a five year period from selling products to the state. The Supreme Court rejected Wisconsin's argument that its scheme escaped NLRA pre-emption because it was "an exercise of the State's spending power rather than its regulatory power." Id. at 287, 106 S.Ct. at 1061. The Court determined that, despite the form, "[t]he manifest purpose and inevitable effect of the debarment rule is to enforce the requirements of the NLRA." Id. at 291, 106 S.Ct. at 1063.

The latest Supreme Court opinion on the subject, on which the government heavily relies, is Boston Harbor. In that case, an independent agency of the Massachusetts government, The Massachusetts Water Resources Authority (MWRA), faced with a federal court order directing it to clean up Boston Harbor, selected Kaiser Engineers, Inc. as its project manager with responsibility to advise MWRA as to work site labor-relations policy. Kaiser suggested, and MWRA agreed, that Kaiser be permitted to enter into a collective bargaining agreement with the Building and Construction Trades Council (BCTC). The agreement provided that all employees hired were obliged to become union members within seven days of their employment whether they were employed by the general contractor or any subcontractor. The bid specifications required that all bidding subcontractors agree to abide by the agreement. Such a "pre-hire" agreement in the construction industry is a legal option under §8(f) of the NLRA as an exception to the general prohibition under §8(e) against "hot cargo" agreements. Non-union construction contractors sued, asserting that the actions of the MWRA were pre-empted by the NLRA because the state agency was intruding into the collective bargaining process by forcing subcontractors to exercise the §8(f) option. The First Circuit agreed over a dissent by then-Chief Judge Breyer and the Supreme Court reversed, determining that the bid specification was "not government regulation and that it is therefore subject to neither Garmon nor Machinists preemption." Boston Harbor, 507 U.S. at 232, 113 S.Ct. at 1199.

Of course, appellants argue that the case before us is controlled by Gould and distinguished from Boston Harbor; the government urges the opposite. The government points out that in Gould, Wisconsin conceded that its purpose was to deter labor law violations, see 475 U.S. at 287, 106 S.Ct. at 1061, so the Court was easily able to determine that the state sought to address conduct that was "unrelated to the employer's performance of contractual obligations to the State…" Boston Harbor, 507 U.S. at 229, 113 S.Ct. at 1197. Echoing its arguments on reviewability, the government insists that the Executive Order is premised on the President's economic judgment that a government contractor's use of permanent replacements will cause longer, more contentious strikes and the loss of the accumulated skill of the strikers with correspondingly less efficient and economical performance by that contractor. That judgment, we are told, is certainly an economically rational one, and it is not up to a court to question either the President's motivation or the quality of his reasoning here any more than was done in Contractors Ass'n, 442 F.2d 159, or Kahn, 618 F.2d 784. Appellants, without directly challenging the President's economic analysis, observe that a struck company's use of permanent replacements is a good deal more efficient than temporary replacements; the Executive Order irrationally bars the former but not the latter.

We are similarly quite reluctant to consider the President's motivation in issuing the Executive Order. Chief Judge Breyer's dissent in Boston Harbor, on which the Supreme Court heavily relied, put the issue as follows: "In the case before us, the record makes clear that the MWRA is participating in a market place as a general contractor, like a private buyer of services. Its role as buyer is not, in any sense, a sham designed to conceal an effort to regulate." Associated Builders & Contractors of Massachusetts/Rhode Island v. Massachusetts Water Resources Auth., 935 F.2d 345, 366 (1st Cir.1991) (en banc) (Breyer, C.J., dissenting) (emphasis added). We do not think we are bound to that dichotomy, however—particularly when considering the President's Executive Order. It is not necessary for us to question the President's motivation in order to determine whether the Order is a regulation that is pre-empted by Machinists.

The Supreme Court in Boston Harbor, quoting Chief Judge Breyer, explained, "when the MWRA, acting in the role of purchaser of construction services, acts just like a private contractor would act, and conditions its purchasing upon the very sort of labor agreement that Congress explicitly authorized and expected frequently to find, it does not 'regulate' the workings of the market forces that Congress expected to find; it exemplifies them." 507 U.S. at 233, 113 S.Ct. at 1199 (quoting Associated Builders, 935 F.2d at 361 (Breyer, C.J., dissenting)). * * *

We do not think it is necessary to resolve this doctrinal dispute in this case. We would be surprised if private contractors were to care whether a struck supplier hired permanent or temporary replacements, so long as the goods or services contracted for were provided in a timely fashion and met quality standards. There may well be, however, some companies who, for political or philosophic reasons—what the Supreme Court referred to as a "labor policy concern," Boston Harbor, 507 U.S. at 229, 113 S.Ct. at 1197—would not wish to do business with a struck company that hired permanent replacements. But even if that behavior were a good deal more common than we suppose, we would still regard the Executive Order as regulatory in character.

In Boston Harbor, the Court's analysis of the behavior of MWRA was based on the premise, stated after its summary of its precedent, that:

> When the State acts as regulator, it performs a role that is characteristically a governmental rather than a private role, boycotts notwithstanding. Moreover, as regulator of private conduct, the State is more powerful than private parties. These distinctions are far less significant when the State acts as a market participant with no interest in setting policy.... We left open [in Gould] the question whether a State may act without offending the pre-emption principles of the NLRA when it acts as a proprietor and its acts therefore are not "tantamount to regulation," or policy-making.

Id. at 229, 113 S.Ct. at 1197 (emphases added). The premise on which the Court's further analysis rested, then, was that the Massachusetts governmental entity, MWRA, was not seeking to set general policy in the Commonwealth; it was just trying to operate as if it were an ordinary general contractor whose actions were "specifically tailored to one particular job, the Boston Harbor clean-up project." Id. at 232, 113 S.Ct. at 1198. Surely, the result would have been entirely different, given the Court's reasoning, if Massachusetts had passed a general law or the Governor had issued an Executive Order requiring all construction contractors doing business with the state to enter into collective bargaining agreements with the BCTC or its Massachusetts-wide counterpart containing §8(e) pre-hire agreements. Accordingly, we very much doubt the legality of President Bush's Executive Order 12,818—since revoked, but upon which the government relies—that banned government contractors from entering into pre-hire agreements under §8(f).[2]

It does not seem to us possible to deny that the President's Executive Order seeks to set a broad policy governing the behavior of thousands of American companies and affecting millions of American workers. The President has, of course, acted to set procurement policy rather than labor policy. But the former is quite explicitly based—and would have to be based—on his views of the latter. For the premise of the Executive Order is the proposition that the permanent replacement of strikers unduly prolongs and widens strikes and disrupts the proper "balance" between employers and employees. Whether that proposition is correct, or whether the prospect of permanent replace-

---

2. We also are dubious that President Bush's Executive Order 12,800, which required government contractors to post notices informing their employees that they could not be required to join or remain a member of a union, was legal. It may well have run afoul of Garmon pre-emption which reserves to NLRB jurisdiction arguably protected or prohibited conduct.

ments deters strikes, and therefore an employer's right to permanently replace strikers is simply one element in the relative bargaining power of management and organized labor, is beside the point. Whatever one's views on the issue, it surely goes to the heart of United States labor relations policy. It cannot be equated to the ad hoc contracting decision made by MWRA in seeking to clean up Boston Harbor.

That is not to say that the President, in implementing the Procurement Act, may not draw upon any secondary policy views that deal with government contractors' employment practices—policy views that are directed beyond the immediate quality and price of goods and services purchased. In Kahn, we recognized that the imposition of wage and price controls as a condition of eligibility for government contractors could result in the government actually paying more for individual government contracts than might be so otherwise. 618 F.2d at 793. We thought, however, the President's judgment that the overall impact of those controls would reduce government procurement costs was entitled to deference. Id. And, in Contractors Ass'n, the Third Circuit's opinion contained only the briefest discussion of the impact on cost of the Executive Order's requirement of an affirmative action covenant in federally assisted construction contracts. The court merely noted that this requirement would increase the pool of qualified labor and thereby reduce costs. 442 F.2d at 171. But labor relations policy is different because of the NLRA and its broad field of pre-emption. No state or federal official or government entity can alter the delicate balance of bargaining and economic power that the NLRA establishes, whatever his or its purpose may be.

If the government were correct, it follows, as the government apparently conceded, that another President could not only revoke the Executive Order, but could issue a new order that actually required government contractors to permanently replace strikers, premised on a finding that this would minimize unions' bargaining power and thereby reduce procurement costs. Perhaps even more confusing, under the government's theory, the states would be permitted to adopt procurement laws or regulations that in effect choose sides on this issue, which would result in a further balkanization of federal labor policy.

* * * We do not think the scope of the President's intervention into and adjustment of labor relations policy is determinative, but despite the government's protestations, the impact of the Executive Order is quite far-reaching. It applies to all contracts over $100,000, and federal government purchases totaled $437 billion in 1994, constituting approximately 6.5% of the gross domestic product. STATISTICAL ABSTRACT OF THE UNITED STATES 451 (1995). Federal contractors and subcontractors employ 26 million workers, 22% of the labor force. GAO REPORT. The Executive Order's sanctions for hiring permanent replacements, contract debarment and termination, applies to the organizational unit of the federal contractor who has hired permanent replacements. The organizational unit includes "[a]ny other affiliate of the person that could provide the goods or services required to be provided under the contract." 60 Fed.Reg. at 27,861 (emphasis added). If a local unit of Exxon had a contract to deliver $100,001 worth of gas to a federal agency, the organizational unit would include all the other affiliates of Exxon that could have provided the gas; no doubt a significant portion of the Exxon corporation. The broad definition of "organizational unit" will have the effect of forcing corporations wishing to do business with the federal government not to hire permanent replacements even if the strikers are not the employees who provide the goods or services to the government. Indeed, corporations who even hope to obtain a government contract will think twice before hiring permanent replacements during a strike. It will be recalled that in Kahn, 618 F.2d at 792-93, the government itself asserted that controls

imposed on government contractors—given the size of that portion of the economy—would alter the behavior of non-government contractors.

* * *

We, therefore, conclude that the Executive Order is regulatory in nature and is preempted by the NLRA which guarantees the right to hire permanent replacements. The district court is hereby

Reversed.

Notes and Questions

1. In contrast to the labor standards and Buy American rules, the rule against striker replacement at issue in *Chamber of Commerce* did not derive from focused Congressional enactments directing such a rule, but from Presidential invocation of generic authority in the 1949 act. Even with that distinction, *Chamber of Commerce* breaks with a number of previous occasions, some of which it grudgingly acknowledges, when the courts had upheld procurement-implemented policies based on a President's invocation of such generic authority. In particular, *Contractors Ass'n of Eastern Pennsylvania v. Secretary of Labor*, 442 F.2d 159 (3d Cir.), *cert. denied*, 494 U.S. 854 (1971), upheld President Nixon's order imposing affirmative action on government contractors; *AFL v. Kahn*, 618 F.2d 784 (D.C. Cir.), *cert. denied*, 443 U.S. 915 (1979), upheld President Carter's order imposing wage and price standards on government contractors.

The Court of Appeals distinguished these precedents by the asserted clarity with which the National Labor Relations Act leaves the field open for employer striker replacement. What were the counterarguments? By the same logic, could it have been said that Congress's silence equally clearly left the field open for companies not to engage in affirmative action or not to keep wages and prices down? So why did the courts uphold the affirmative action and price control executive orders?

2. How much does the President's ability to promulgate policies through government contracting depend on the few broad and vague words, little discussed on the floor of Congress, of the 1949 Federal Property and Administrative Services Act (this opinion calls it the "Procurement Act")? Presidents invoking FPASA make what is a thinly disguised claim of inherent Presidential power, albeit one which does not require them to challenge Congress, merely to act without any more sign of Congressional support than a noncontroversial statute enacted fifty years earlier without the slightest anticipation of how it would be used. Is such a Presidential assertion of power at odds with the Constitution's investiture of all legislative power in the democratically-elected Congress? Or is procurement an activity that mixes Presidential and Congressional prerogatives?

3. Space does not allow much treatment of some of the other major policies implemented in recent years through government procurement. One consists of environmental protection requirements, as statutes have directed the government to conduct procurement in ways that promote environmental policies. See FAR subpart 23.1. The government promotes environmentally responsible contracting and competition; recycling; energy efficiency and conservation; prevention of hazardous material pollution; and phasing out ozone-depleting substances. Moreover, the government does a fair amount of procurement specifically of environmental cleanup services, at Department of Energy and Department of Defense sites. Executive Order 12873, 58 Fed. Reg. 54,911, makes environmental considerations a part of acquisition planning. See ABA Section of Public Contract Law, GOVERNMENT CONTRACT LAW: DESKBOOK

FOR PROCUREMENT PROFESSIONALS (1995), chapter 25 ("Environmental Contracting Issues").

For a discussion of this subject, see John A. Herrick, Federal Financing of Green Energy: Developing Green Industry in a Changing Energy Marketplace, 31 Pub. Cont. L.J. 257 (2002); Jennifer McCadney, Note, The Green Society: Leveraging the Government's Buying Powers to Create Markets for Recycled Products, 29 Pub. Cont. L .J. 135 (1999).

A second set of policies consists of statutorily-required drug-free workplace rules. See FAR subpart 23.5. The legal superstructure consists of Congressional enactments, implementing regulations, and a contract clause requiring contractors to make a "Certification Regarding a Drug-Free Workplace."

Of course, the 9/11 attack, the domestic and international efforts against terrorism, and the occupation of Iraq produced their own policies. For example, the statute chartering the Department of Homeland Security released it from many formal requirements as to procurement. For some discussions of this new era, see Joseph Summerhill, Procurement Within the Department of Homeland Security, 39 Procurement Lawyer, Winter 2003, at 11; Charles Tiefer, Buying for Uncle Sam: Practical Mind-Set Now Prevails for Government Contracting, Legal Times, Oct. 29, 2001, at 36.

Chapter 10

Termination

The chapter concerns termination—primarily termination for default, and also termination for convenience and for breach. Termination for default warrants full treatment, because of its potent impact on the contractor and the large role given to government contracting lawyers in its handling. We can usefully contrast termination for default with contract formation by bids or proposals. Contract formation warrants full treatment because all government contracts go through it, so the scale of activity is large. However, the contract formation process often has only a limited impact upon contractors, who may bid for many contracts in the course of obtaining a few. Moreover, government contract lawyers often have a limited role in contract formation, as nonlegal personnel do most of the work of formulating and processing IFBs, RFPs, bids and proposals, with lawyers getting deeply involved especially when protests occur.

In contrast, any single termination for default has an intense impact on that contractor. Partly this occurs in basic (private) contract law as well. A private buyer may cancel a contract on asserted grounds of the other party's breach (for simple comparison, let us speak only of seller/performer breach, not payor breach), or of the failure for a condition of payment to be fulfilled. Unless the seller successfully contests, this puts an end to the seller's performance and precludes the seller from profiting. The seller's breach exposes the seller to liability for damages. Similarly, when the government terminates a government contractor for default, unless the contractor successfully contests, this puts an end to its performance, precludes it from profiting, and exposes it to liability for damages.

However, basic (private) contract law avoids, for important reasons, too intense an impact on the contractor cancelled for breach. In private contracting, the concept of "efficient breach" reflects a school of contracting law analysis backed up by economic theory, that under some circumstances it may be efficient, and thus not something to be excessively discouraged, for a party (let us say, for simplicity, a seller) to breach and thereby to elicit cancellation. The "efficient breach" concept reflects that a seller may discover, after entering the contract, other better opportunities compared to fulfilling the contract.

For example, the market may be willing to pay the seller much more for taking some other deal, or the seller may have special reasons that it would experience an unexpectedly large loss in performing. Suppose it will cost the seller $1,000 to perform, but if the seller breaches someone else can perform for $1100, and, meanwhile, the seller can take another deal for $2000. Breach would be "efficient" if the seller pays the damages, namely, pays for the other performer to perform for $1100, takes the other deal for $2000, and divides up the added profit as a result of all this in some way between itself and the buyer. Basic (private) contract law keeps the measure of damages limited so as not to excessively discourage such efficient breaches; for example, almost never, in an ordinary breach without tortious or fraudulent aspects, does the recovery include punitive damages.

In contrast, government contracting law subscribes much less to the concept of "efficient breach." The implementation of public policy, including the implementation of the decisions of the elected Congress and President and the smooth functioning of the government agencies, gets set back by contractor defaults. That set back is only imperfectly compensated by damages. An extreme example consists of wartime supply, where contractor breach, in situations where the market for many reasons cannot function perfectly, sets back the national security. Even in peacetime, and even in situations where there is an operative market where the government can find alternative suppliers, the delay, disruption, and distraction of making up for the breach create a setback for the government.

An analogy from other government "contracting" activity consists of recalling what happens when government employees in responsible positions fail to appear at their posts or to perform there. The government does not simply extract damages from them, such as docking their pay, as a private employer of temporary help might in an efficient market. For military officers, the government may court-martial the absent soldier for going AWOL ("away without leave"). Even for civilian employees, the government may respond to absence or to failure to perform by conducting a suspension or termination proceeding, in which, for due process purposes, the government makes a civil determination of employee misconduct.

Termination for default thus amounts to more than a proceeding for the government to make an efficient distribution of the losses from the substitution of an alternative supplier. Rather, it amounts to a decision—an official judgment by the sovereign—of unexcused nonfeasance or misfeasance. It stamps the contractor with a civil judgment against it that it is guilty in its relations with the state of an unexcused failure to perform the duty to its country that it solemnly, voluntarily, and formally undertook.

This has both normative and practical significance. Normatively, the government declares that the contractor terminated for default is an unexcused failure. Even if no practical consequences followed, both the government and the contractor would have their lawyers pay major attention to such a declaration. While it is a civil matter, as a normative labeling it has overtones like other government-generated civil adjudications of failure to live up to norms. The government may consider it necessary to terminate for default in order to vindicate the norms of government contracting, to uphold the symbolic authority of the state, and to deter other contractors from similar unexcused failures.

On its part, the contractor may consider it necessary to contest the termination for default in order to defend its standing in its economic community, as it is viewed by the government, the public, its peer businesses, and its own stockholders and employees. Indeed, the culpable officers in the business might well contest the termination for default, if for no other reason than for their sense of personal honor, much as they might contest a charge against them by the government in any other context from their view of themselves as individuals fulfilling all their other civic obligations.

Practically, the government has the ability by a termination for default to impose penalties. These start with the ordinary measure of damages. In addition, as discussed below, the government will also sometimes impose on the contractor an added measure called "excess costs of reprocurement." Finally, the termination amounts to a negative entry on the contractor's record that could factor into either difficulty in obtaining future contract awards, or even into a formal suspension or debarment.

Accordingly, the first section of the chapter starts with the bases and defenses for a termination for default. The second section continues with the process for default, particularly the extent to which the contractor may challenge the government's exercise of its discretion to perform a termination for default. Then, the third section discusses the government's additional remedies, notably recovering excess costs of reprocurement.

The chapter then turns to the quite different, other mechanism for termination: termination for convenience. Although this mechanism terminates the contractor, it has more contrasts than similarities to termination for default. It does not have the normative overtones. An exemplary contractor, a veritable paragon of contracting virtue, may well undergo termination for convenience simply because the government no longer requires what it had engaged the contractor to do. The government deals much more generously with the contractor terminated for convenience, although it does not allow that contractor to receive unearned profits. For example, at the end of a war, the government may terminate for convenience its most honored and treasured defense contractors, simply because the government no longer needs their weapons. Termination for convenience represents a kind of government remedy not found in typical basic (private) contracts, because the government reserves for itself this extraordinary discretion to bring a contract to an end, without the other party having the ability either to contest this effectively or to recover its anticipated profits. This section explores the bases, the mechanisms, and the scope of recovery, in termination for convenience.

At the end, a section briefly addresses another way for the government to end a contract. The government can breach by an action such a new statute or program effectively frustrating completion of existing contracts. To some extent, for the government to breach resembles breach in private contracts. However, because the government wears multiple hats, both as contract-maker and as the policy-making initiator of new statutes and programs, governmental breach presents special considerations.

For further discussion of the subject of this chapter, see: Charles Tiefer, Forfeiture by Cancellation or Termination, 54 Mercer Law Review 1031 (2003); Graeme S. Henderson, *Terminations for Convenience and the Termination Costs Clause*, 53 A.F.L. Rev. 103 (2002); Deena B. Bothello, Note, *An Unequal Balance: Repudiation and Restitution in* Mobil Oil Exploration & Producing Southeast, Inc. v. United States, 80 Ore. L. Rev. 1469 (2001); Joshua I. Schwartz, *Assembling* Winstar: *Triumph of the Ideal of Congruence in Government Contracts Law?*, 26 Pub. Cont. L.J. 481 (1997); Harris J. Handrews, Jr. & Robert T. Peacock, *Terminations: An Outline of the Parties' Rights and Remedies*, 11 Pub. Cont. L.J. 269 (1980).

A. Bases and Defenses

One of the most important standard clauses in government contracts, the Default Clause, directs the bases and defenses for termination for default. The Clause's text provides an excellent introduction to termination for default. One general type of Default Clause applies to supply and service contracts, while another applies to construction contracts, but the similarities justify treating them all at once.

The Default Clause lists separate bases for termination for default. Each of these bases has gathered a considerable amount of doctrine and case law around it. First and foremost, the clause lists the ground of "failure to deliver or perform." This can involve either the fault of lateness, that is, failure to deliver or perform by the contractually required date, or the fault of flawed performance, that is, failure to meet the specifications. The fault of lateness raises the issue that the government insists in most circumstances that "time is of the essence" in its contracts. With respect to flawed performance, the great variety of government contracts comes into play. Packing boxes for government archives have to achieve a low level of match with the specifications; missiles that will carry nuclear warheads have to achieve a higher level.

Second, the clause lists the ground of "failure to make progress so as to endanger performance." This clause represents an important change from the common law, in which a buyer had to show before cancelling a contract with a seller prior to the date of performance that it was impossible for the seller to perform. The government need not show such impossibility, just a reasonable belief that the contractor cannot perform the entire contract within the time remaining for performance. Still, this ground provides something of a level battlefield for the government and the contractor to argue. After all, a contractor who is trying hard to perform can argue, if the government is simply nervous, the government should just terminate for convenience and go hire someone else. By terminating for default, the government penalizes contractors in advance of their actually failing to perform. So, the contractor can hope to enlist the tribunal's sympathies by showing that it was trying hard, in fact, with a likelihood of fulfilling its obligations.

Third, the clause lists the ground of failure to perform other provisions of the contract. Courts and boards will not sustain a default termination unless that "other provision" of the contract is a "material" or "significant" requirement. *Stone Forest Indus. v. United States*, 973 F.2d 1548 (Fed. Cir. 1992). Considering the large number of requirements in government contracts, this ground creates quite a lot of room for debate. Note also that although the default clause does not mention it explicitly, both the government and the contractor retain their common law right to terminate upon actual or anticipatory repudiation by the other party. The *DeKonty v. U.S.* opinion, in the chapter on specialized contracting's section on construction contracts, provides the classic definition of anticipatory repudiation.

For further discussion of the subject of this section, see: Brad Fagg, *Default Terminations for Failure to Make Progress*, 25 Pub. Cont. L.J. 113 (1995); Glenn T. Carberry and Phillip M. Johnstone, *Waiver of the Governments Right to Terminate for Default in Government Defense Contracts*, 17 Pub. Cont. L. J. 470 (1988).

Default Clause
(Fixed-Price Supply and Service)
(Apr 1984)

(a) (1) The Government may, subject to paragraphs (c) and (d) of this clause, by written notice of default to the Contractor, terminate this contract in whole or in part if the Contractor fails to—

(i) Deliver the supplies or to perform the services within the time specified in this contract or any extension;

(ii) Make progress, so as to endanger performance of this contract (but see subparagraph (a)(2) of this clause); or

(iii) Perform any of the other provisions of this contract (but see subparagraph (a)(2) below).

(2) The Government's right to terminate this contract under subdivisions (a)(1)(ii) and (1)(iii) of this clause, may be exercised if the Contractor does not

cure such failure within 10 days (or more if authorized in writing by the Contracting Officer) after receipt of the notice from the Contracting Officer specifying the failure.

(b) If the Government terminates this contract in whole or in part, it may acquire, under the terms and in the manner the Contracting Officer considers appropriate, supplies or services similar to those terminated, and the Contractor will be liable to the Government for any excess costs for those supplies or services. However, the Contractor shall continue the work not terminated.

(c) Except for defaults of subcontractors at any tier, the Contractor shall not be liable for any excess costs if the failure to perform the contract arises from causes beyond the control and without the fault or negligence of the Contractor. Examples of such causes include

(1) acts of God or of the public enemy, (2) acts of the Government in either its sovereign or contractual capacity, (3) fires, (4) floods, (5) epidemics, (6) quarantine restrictions, (7)strikes, (8) freight embargoes, and (9) unusually severe weather. In each instance the failure to perform must be beyond the control and without the fault or negligence of the Contractor.

(d) If the failure to perform is caused by the default of a subcontractor at any tier, and if the cause of the default is beyond the control of both the Contractor and subcontractor, and without the fault or negligence of either, the Contractor shall not be liable for any excess costs for failure to perform, unless the subcontracted supplies or services were obtainable from other sources in sufficient time for the Contractor to meet the required delivery schedule.

(e) If this contract is terminated for default, the Government may require the Contractor to transfer title and deliver to the Government, as directed by the Contracting Officer, any

(1) completed supplies, and (2) manufacturing materials * * * [T]he Contractor shall also protect and preserve property * * * in which the Government has an interest.

(f) The Government shall pay contract price for completed supplies delivered and accepted. The Contractor and Contracting Officer shall agree on the amount of payment for manufacturing materials delivered and accepted and for the protection and preservation of the property. Failure to agree will be a dispute under the Disputes clause. * * *

(g) If, after termination, it is determined that the Contractor was not in default, or that the default was excusable, the rights and obligations of the parties shall be the same as if the termination had been issued for the convenience of the Government.

(h) The rights and remedies of the Government in this clause are in addition to any other rights and remedies provided by law or under this contract.

Radiation Technology, Inc.
v. The United States
United States Court of Claims. 366 F.2d 1003.
Decided Oct. 14, 1966.

COLLINS, Judge.

The Department of Health, Education, and Welfare agreed, on February 2, 1962, to purchase from plaintiff eight scaler-timer-high voltage systems. In April 1962, the Government terminated the contract for default. This action is based upon plaintiff's charge that the termination was wrongful. Defendant has filed a counterclaim for the difference between plaintiff's contract price and the cost of procuring the equipment from another manufacturer. Both plaintiff and defendant have moved for summary judgment.

The case was referred to Chief Commissioner Marion T. Bennett, who has submitted a report recommending that plaintiff's motion for summary judgment be denied and defendant's motion for dismissal of the petition and allowance of the counterclaim be granted. We accept the commissioner's conclusions as the appropriate outcome in this case.

The facts may be summarized as follows: The contract called for delivery of the eight instruments on April 3, 1962. Four were to be shipped to Rockville, Maryland, and the other four to Winchester, Massachusetts. * * *

Plaintiff experienced management and production difficulties and, as a result, found it necessary to seek revision of the delivery schedule. Ultimately, the delivery date was extended to April 12th for Rockville and to April 13th for Winchester. The shipments by plaintiff were made in accord with the revised schedule. Upon arrival at the respective destinations, the instruments were inspected by Government personnel.

* * * Each inspector found the systems which he examined to be defective in a number of respects. On April 19, 1962, the contracting officer, P. H. Shultz, advised plaintiff by telephone of the unsatisfactory nature of the instruments. On April 20th, Mr. Shultz wrote Radiation Technology that, because of its failure 'to deliver Scaler-Timer-High Voltage Systems in accordance with the specifications * * * ,' its right to proceed was terminated. The contracting officer added that plaintiff would be charged with the excess costs of reprocurement. The contracting officer ordered replacements from Picker X-Ray Corporation, and they were shipped within 5 days.* * *

The basic dispute between the parties relates to the propriety of terminating the contract without granting plaintiff an opportunity to repair the defective systems. This controversy pertains to the default clause which provided in part as follows:

(a) The Government may, * * * by written notice of default to the Contractor, terminate the whole or any part of this contract in any one of the following circumstances:

(i) if the Contractor fails to make delivery of the supplies or to perform the services within the time specified herein or any extension thereof; or

(ii) if the Contractor fails to perform any of the other provisions of this contract, or so fails to make progress as to endanger performance of this contract in accordance with its terms, and in either of these two circumstances does not cure such failure within a period of 10 days (or such longer period as the Contracting Officer may authorize in writing) after receipt of notice from the Contracting Officer specifying such failure.

Defendant asserts that summary termination under (a)(i) was proper contending that the term 'delivery' in this subparagraph demands the delivery of conforming goods. This position, it alleges, is in accord with the definition of delivery set forth in both the Uniform Commercial Code and the Uniform Sales Act. Plaintiff concedes that under the authorities cited, delivery is equated with the tender of conforming goods, but argues that, under the contract in issue, the concept of delivery denotes a possessory concept, i.e., the physical transfer of possession. Arguing that use of the word 'delivery' should be given a consistent interpretation, plaintiff points to the inspection provision of the contract, which anticipates acceptance or rejection after delivery.[1] It urges that the possibility of a rejection occurring after delivery would be rendered moot if delivery is to be equated with the shipment of conforming goods. Therefore, argues plaintiff, delivery relates only to a physical delivery and since, in this case, such delivery was timely (though on the last day), it is entitled to the 10-day extension available under subparagraph (a)(ii).

While there is obvious merit to both positions, it must be conceded that both are positions of the extreme. Adherence to plaintiff's view would preclude the Government's right to effect a summary termination so long as a timely shipment was made. A contractor could escape an automatic termination through the simple expedient of timely shipment, notwithstanding the distinct possibility that the shipment might be substantially defective. Frustration of delivery schedules becomes the obvious end product if this view is endorsed. By the same token, defendant's view would suggest similar undesirable consequences. Where delivery is measured against a doctrine of strict conformity, it invites the possibility of a surprise rejection occurring subsequent to a timely shipment. This, coupled with a summary termination power, would place in the hands of a contracting officer an unfettered right to reject and deny a contractor the opportunity to cure a nonconformity in his delivered product. Recourse to the courts becomes the inevitable consequence—a step made necessary because of the inflexibility inhering in defendant's view.

In our judgment, the accommodation of these conflicting positions can be best effected by defining the term delivery (as used in the default provisions) as the equivalent of a shipment which is in substantial compliance with contract specifications. In striking this balance, we necessarily reject the either/or basis upon which the parties have based their positions.

We read subparagraph (a)(i) as relating only to the issue of timeliness of delivery; it clearly does not define delivery itself. Subparagraph (a)(ii), on the other hand, speaks to circumstances other than those issuing out of delivery, i.e., events occurring prior to delivery which might suggest to the Government the possibility of the contractor's eventual default. Hence, a contractor cannot under this subparagraph claim an automatic extension when the possibility of his default is premised on the nonconformity of delivered goods.[2] Under the view which we espouse, the contractor is entitled to a reasonable period in which to cure a nonconformity provided that the supplies shipped are in substantial conformity with contract specifications.

In order to meet this requirement, it is incumbent at the outset that the contractor demonstrate that he had reasonable grounds to believe that his delivery would conform to contract requirements. Shipment alone is not an adequate badge of proof. Further, the right to cure assumes that the defects complained of are minor in nature and extent and are susceptible to correction within a reasonable time. Where extensive repair or readjustment is necessary in order to produce a fully operable product, substantial per-

---

1. The inspection provision of the contract included the following relevant section:

'(c) * * * Acceptance or rejection of the supplies shall be made as promptly as practicable after delivery, except as otherwise provided in this contract; but failure to inspect and accept or reject supplies shall neither relieve the Contractor from responsibility for such supplies as are not in accordance with the contract requirements nor impose liability on the Government therefor.'

2. This point addresses itself only to delivery occurring on the scheduled delivery date. Where delivery is in advance of this date, the contractor would be automatically entitled to the balance of the contract term in order to cure any deficiencies.

formance cannot be found and summary termination would be warranted. Other relevant considerations bearing upon the question of compliance involve the usability of the items, the nature of the product involved (whether it involves complex precision instruments as opposed to a routine production item), and the urgency of the Government's demand. The greater such urgency the greater the requirement that performance approach the overall level of strict conformity.

In concluding that the Government had an absolute right to terminate for nondelivery, Commissioner Bennett stressed the fact that, under the contract in issue, time had become 'of the essence.' While we are unable to accept his view in this regard, our differences are essentially academic and spell no departure in terms of ultimate result. And while we might question how time could become of the essence where extensions are granted after an initial delivery date has passed, we recognize, as did the commissioner, that the essential inquiry is whether the character of the rendered performance can be said to be in substantial compliance with contract demands. After a comprehensive review of the record, the commissioner upheld the board's findings that there had been no substantial compliance with the contract's specifications. This conclusion, coupled with his premise that total performance on the extended delivery date was essential, accounted for the commissioner's position.

It is our view that even where time is of the essence, i.e., where performance must occur by a given date, this factor does not demand that performance be measured in terms of strict conformity. It does require that performance be timely, but assuming this, there would thereafter remain for inquiry the question as to whether performance was substantial in other respects. However, since we accept the commissioner's basic conclusions regarding plaintiff's failure to render substantial compliance, based on the record, our disagreement with the commissioner in regard to his interpretation as to the meaning of 'time being of the essence' (or even if time was, in fact, of the essence) becomes a moot point. Plaintiff could not prevail in either case.

The main issue that we have been requested to review concerned the application of the default provisions, noted supra. We have concluded that absent a shipment meeting the standard of substantial compliance, the fact that shipment was timely cannot operate to grant a contractor an automatic 10-day extension.

* * *

For the reasons stated, plaintiff's motion for summary judgment is herewith denied. Defendant's cross-motion for summary judgment is granted, plaintiff's petition is dismissed, and judgment is entered in favor of defendant on its counterclaim in the sum of five thousand five hundred fifty- three dollars and ninety-two cents ($5,553.92).

Notes and Questions

1. The *Radiation Technology* case provides a close reading of the Default Clause. In terms of the particular termination at issue, it occurs under the first prong of the clause, the "failure to deliver or perform" prong. The question concerns whether and when, rather than be terminated under that first prong, the contractor should have an opportunity to remedy a shortcoming. In deciding that question, the court compares the wording of the first prong with the second prong, the "failure to make progress," and the third prong, the "failure to perform other provisions." For these latter prongs, the Default Clause grants procedures, including a ten-day extension. By implication, the first prong, which does not mention such procedures, denies them. Hence, failures concerning "delivery," which trig-

ger the first prong, warrant summary termination. Why is the Default Clause worded that way? That is, why does the Default Clause provide for summary termination for failures concerning "delivery," and not for failure to make progress or to fulfill other provisions?

2. The court largely ducks the question of whether "time is of the essence." This question arises in basic (private) contracts as well. For that matter, it arises in many other interactions; for example, do students who hand in good term papers late suffer grade reduction for the lateness? Look at the court's criterion, the "urgency of the demand." Time might be of the essence if the professor is leaving town immediately after the deadline for handing the papers in, but not if the professor's schedule can accommodate late receipt. Although the government is not leaving town, it tends to insist that time is of the essence. More complex questions arise with severable contracts, where late delivery of one installment may, or may not, warrant summary termination as to the whole.

3. *Radiation Technology* originates the "substantial compliance" doctrine, namely, that a contractor may have a narrow window to remedy shortcomings in its product. Note that despite how similarly the doctrine sounds, it has differences from what in basic (private) contract law is called "substantial performance" in private contracts doctrine. *Radiation Technology* concerns goods, while "substantial performance" generally concerns construction. *Radiation Technology* lays down its own quite strict requirements for the contractor to avoid termination for default by "cure"; it relates to the other areas of contract law where the notion of "cure" has found support. The "substantial performance" doctrine for private construction contracts, by contrast, does not have any necessary connection to "cure"; the plumbing contractor who installs the wrong brand of pipe ("Reading Brand") receives final payment under the substantial performance doctrine, not because the contractor cures the pipe error, but precisely because cure is wasteful, impractical, and unnecessary.

D. Joseph DeVITO, Receiver for Seaview Electric Company v. The UNITED STATES.

No. 432—65 United States Court of Claims.
413 F.2d 1147. July 16, 1969.

Before COWEN, Chief Judge, and LARAMORE, DURFEE, DAVIS, COLLINS, SKELTON and NICHOLS, Judges.

PER CURIAM:

This case was referred to Trial Commissioner C. Murray Bernhardt with directions to make recommendation for conclusions of law on plaintiff's motion for summary judgment and defendant's cross-motion for partial summary judgment under the order of reference and Rule 99(c). The commissioner has done so in an opinion and report filed on November 7, 1968. Defendant filed a request for review by the court of the commissioner's opinion and the case has been submitted to the court on oral argument of counsel and the briefs of the parties. Since the court is in agreement with the opinion and recommendation of the commissioner, with modifications, it hereby adopts the same, as modified, as the basis for its judgment in this case, as hereinafter set forth. Therefore, plaintiff is entitled to recover and its motion for summary judgment is granted and defendant's cross-motion is denied.* * * Commissioner Bernhardt's opinion, as modified by the court, is as follows:

Plaintiff seeks recovery of $150,000 resulting from the default termination of a fixed-price supply contract awarded to Seaview Electric Company by the U.S. Army Signal

Corps, for Seaview's alleged failure to timely deliver certain wire-splicing kits. The Armed Services Board of Contract Appeals (hereinafter, 'ASBCA' or 'the Board') upheld the action of the contracting officer in terminating Seaview's contract for default. Plaintiff contends that the adverse ASBCA decision is not supported by substantial evidence, is arbitrary and grossly erroneous. Also, that at the time of termination Seaview was not in default because (a) termination occurred prior to the expiration of a reasonable time for performance which should have been granted after Seaview encountered excusable causes of delay, or (b) the termination action was premature because it occurred prior to the passage of a reasonable time for performance after the Government had waived the established delivery schedule. The Board erred as will be shown.

The contract was awarded to Seaview on April 30, 1959, for 11,160 wire- splicing kits at a total contract price of $213,156. Within a month, however, the contract quantity and consideration were approximately doubled, to 22,316 items for $426,292.90, by Modification No. 1 to the contract, dated May 28, 1959. * * * Preproduction samples were timely submitted on October 29, 1959 * * *. Formal Government acceptance of the samples was issued November 23, 1959.

Thereafter, and prior to the termination, Seaview encountered five alleged causes of delay. These were: (1) the impact of a nationwide steel strike * * *; (2) production tolerance difficulties attributed by plaintiff to the extensive changes to the contract drawings and specifications previously mentioned; (3) Seaview's inability to finalize production plans and tolerances claimed to be due to Government indecision * * *; (4) a fire on August 30, 1960, which destroyed most of Seaview's production space; and (5) the closing of a key subcontractor's shop at a very critical point in production, on November 4, 1960.

The contracting officer never recognized the impact upon plaintiff caused by the second and third of these causes of delay. Due to the steel strike, however, the contract delivery schedule was extended by bilateral agreement in Modification No. 5 to the contract, dated April 7, 1960. This revised schedule required Seaview to deliver 1,000 units by July 29, 1960; 1,835 units each month thereafter through October 28, 1960; and 2,000 units on the 28th of November and each month thereafter until completion on June 28, 1961. This was the official contract delivery requirement at the time of termination on January 16, 1961. There was agreement by the parties to extend to November 29, 1960, the time for the initial delivery installment as a result of the fire at Seaview's plant, but this agreement was never consummated by formal contractual agreement. The fifth-cited cause of delay remains an issue in this litigation but mooted, as we shall see.

Seaview did not meet the July 29, 1960 first incremental delivery date established by Modification No. 5. * * * As a result of the fire which occurred on August 30, the contracting officer indicated by letter dated November 1, 1960, that he would allow a three-months' delay in delivery, and subsequently forwarded a proposed supplemental agreement incorporating a new delivery schedule proposed by Seaview. This schedule called for 1,000 units to be delivered on November 29, 1960, and 2,000 units per month thereafter, until completion of deliveries on October 29, 1961. The proposed agreement was executed for Seaview and returned to the contracting officer on December 19, 1960, but was not executed by him, and consequently never became a formal part of the contract. The Board tacitly acknowledged this extension, and so do we.

Due to the previously mentioned abrupt shutdown of a key subcontractor, J. & P. Equipment Co., Inc. (hereinafter 'J & P') on November 4, 1960, Seaview did not meet the proposed delivery schedule, but thereafter made deliveries of 420 wire-splicing kits, as follows:

* * *

On November 25, 1960, the contracting officer requested authority to terminate, and on January 16, 1961, the contracting officer received authority to, and did, terminate, pursuant to the 'Default' article of the contract, Seaview's right to deliver the balance of the contract units, citing as cause therefor Seaview's failure to timely deliver on the incremental delivery dates. Appeal was timely taken from the termination action by Seaview's letter dated February 1, 1961, in accordance with the 'Disputes' article of the contract.

In the ASBCA proceedings Seaview challenged the contracting officer's decision to terminate the contract on the grounds that its failure to timely deliver was excusable under the 'Default' article of the contract, and that the Government had 'waived' the delivery schedule. The appeal was denied * * *

While both parties conceive the case to contain two principal issues, the first (excusability of Seaview's default) is subsumed and mooted by particular resolution of the second (termination after waiver of default). Thus, if in contemplation of law the conduct of the Government following plaintiff's November 29, 1960 delivery default constituted a constructive election to permit continued performance, a 'waiver' occurred which was not subsequently cut off by a 'cure' notice under the Default clause, so that the eventual termination on January 16, 1961 would be invalid. * * * Initial attention must, therefore, be focused on the waiver-after-breach problem.

As to this issue the Board ruled as follows:

> We reject as untenable appellant's argument that the delivery schedule was waived. Termination was effected in this case on 16 January 1961 for failure to deliver the 29 November and 29 December installments. No evidence indicates an intent to waive the default and to permit continued performance. The termination notice was not unreasonably delayed, certainly not as to the 1,710 shortage with respect to the December installment. We attach no import to the fact that the contracting officer sought authority to terminate before the November installment was due because the evidence clearly establishes appellant was unaware of such action and hence it could not and did not affect appellant's efforts to produce. If appellant had made the November and December deliveries prior to 16 January, we are certain the contracting officer would not have released the termination notice.

In its later opinion on the plaintiff's Petition for Relief from Decision the Board held:

> No final and irrevocable decision to terminate the contract for default had been made or could be made by the contracting officer prior to 16 January 1961, as the contracting officer was lacking in authority to terminate for default prior to 16 January. Up to that time there was the possibility that the contractor's performance would improve sufficiently to cause the contracting officer to decide that it was not in the best interest of the Government to exercise the right to terminate for default. Under these circumstances, it might have been imprudent, and possibly prejudicial to the contractor, for the contracting officer to have advised the contractor that he intended to terminate the contract for default if he succeeded in obtaining authorization from higher authority to do so. In holding that there was no waiver of the Government's right to terminate for default, we said:

>> 'If appellant had made the November and December deliveries prior to 16 January, we are certain the contracting officer would not have released the termination notice.'

The factors controlling this legal issue start with the contracting officer's letter of November 1, 1960, which postponed the first delivery requirement to November 29, 1960, due to the fire damage to plaintiff's plant on August 30 and consequent disruption, but, said the notice—

> * * * In the event of your failure to meet this delivery schedule, the contract will be subject to an immediate termination for default. * * *.

Following that, on November 4 subcontractor J & P closed its doors due to financial difficulties brought about largely by labor troubles of which plaintiff had not been informed. Immediately the plaintiff removed from J & P's plant special tooling and supplies which it purchased from J & P and within a week relet the defaulted J & P subcontract work to three other suppliers, one of whom later proved unable to do the job and caused plaintiff further delay in again reletting that portion of the work. Plaintiff also purchased a quantity of additional tooling and equipment for standby use by its new suppliers in an emergency.

On November 23, 1960, the plaintiff advised the contracting officer that it had submitted 130 completed units for inspection and was making every possible effort to accelerate its production to meet scheduled requirements. Upon receiving this advice on November 25, the contracting officer addressed a Disposition Form to the Economics Division requesting that action be taken to initiate default proceedings because as of then the contractor had produced for inspection only 130 units and it appeared to be impossible for it to meet the revised schedule calling for 1,000 units by November 29 and 2,000 each month thereafter. On November 29 the Economics Division consulted the Legal Office, and on December 1 the latter advised the Economics Division that there was no legal objection to default termination 'provided action is promptly taken'.

Thereupon the contracting officer wrote to the Deputy for Procurement, USASSA, on December 2, 1960, requesting authority to terminate for default effective immediately. The latter recommended the termination on December 7, 1960, to the Chief Signal Officer in Washington. There the request inexplicably languished until January 11, 1961, when the Deputy Chief Signal Officer advised the Chief of the Procurement and Distribution Division that termination authority was approved, effective immediately, having coordinated the termination through the Deputy Chief of Staff for Logistics. On January 19, 1961, the Chief of the Procurement Branch advised the Commanding General of the Army Signal Supply Agency that the contracting officer could proceed to terminate immediately. In the meantime the contracting officer learned of his authorization by telephone and on January 16, 1961, issued a termination notice to plaintiff, who received it the following day.

We have purposely itemized this labyrinthine voyage of the request for termination authority through its time-consuming military channels to contrast the 48-days' delay in termination (from the delivery default of November 29, 1960, to formal termination on January 16, 1961) with the mandate of ASPR 8— 602.3(c) (32 C.F.R., Chapter 1, Part 8, Rev. Jan. 1, 1961) that the contracting officer 'shall * * * issue a notice of termination at once (emphasis supplied).', which coincides with the advice given by the Army's legal officer on December 1, 1960 (see supra). The requirement that the contracting officer receive authorization to terminate may serve to stretch the concept of what is a prompt notice, but cannot explain or excuse the 48-days' delay of termination in this case, 35 days of which were consumed in the Office of the Chief of the Signal Corps without any visible action or explanation for the delay. Until receiving the termination notice on January 17, 1961, neither the plaintiff nor the Government inspector assigned to the plant had any inkling of the contracting officer's intention to terminate. During that entire period the plaintiff made every effort to compensate for its earlier misfortunes and to catch up on delivery requirements, both by augmenting its payroll, letting subcontracts expeditiously, purchasing additional tooling, and performing some of the machining itself. (Plaintiff's role in performing the contract was essentially that of assembling parts which it acquired from suppliers and having them machined by subcontractors.) From November 30 to December 30, 1960, plaintiff made four deliveries totaling 420 units, which were accepted by the Government. At the time of contract termination on January 16, 1961, the plaintiff had nearly 2,000 assemblies in various stages of completion and was on the verge of reaching full production. By the end of December 1960, according to its Certified Public Accountant, plaintiff has expended a total of $97,583.28 in contract performance. The contracting officer, through his subordinates, was actually or constructively aware of these efforts throughout the period he was waiting for authority to terminate.

The Government is habitually lenient in granting reasonable extensions of time for contract performance, for it is more interested in production than in litigation. Moreover, default terminations—as a species of forfeiture—are strictly construed. Murphy et al. v. United States, 164 Ct.Cl. 332 (1964); J. D. Hedin Construction Co. v. United States, 408 F.2d 424, 431, 187 Ct.Cl. 45, —- (March 1969).

Where the Government elects to permit a delinquent contractor to continue performance past a due date, it surrenders its alternative and inconsistent right under the Default clause to terminate, assuming the contractor has not abandoned performance and a reasonable time has expired for a termination notice to be given. This is popularly if inaccurately referred to as a 'waiver' of the right to terminate. 5 Williston, Contracts, Third Ed., §683. The election is sometimes express, but more often is to be inferred from the conduct of the non-defaulting party. McBride and Wachtel, Government Contracts, §31.170. The determination of what conduct constitutes such an election is more conjectural than to prescribe the proper method of effecting a valid termination once the election has occurred. The principles governing the election and its consequences are aptly presented in Cuneo, Waiver of the Due Date in Government Contracts, 43 Va. L. Rev. 1 (1957). He says at page 23:

> * * * Thus when the Government terminates prior to expiration of reasonable time after proper notice it takes a substantial financial risk. Such termination should not be attempted without full knowledge of all the facts and appreciation of the consequences.

The necessary elements of an election by the non-defaulting party to waive default in delivery under a contract are (1) failure to terminate within a reasonable time after the default under circumstances indicating forbearance, and (2) reliance by the contractor on the failure to terminate and continued performance by him under the contract, with the Government's knowledge and implied or express consent.

What is a reasonable time for the Government to terminate a contract after default depends on the circumstances of each case. See Lumen, Inc., ASBCA 6431, 61—2 BCA 3210; Foster Sportswear, ASBCA 5754, 1962 BCA 3364. As stated earlier, ASPR 8—602.3(c) requires the contracting officer to issue a termination notice 'at once'. The period for termination after default will naturally be greater where the contractor abandons performance or where his situation is such as to render performance impossible or unlikely, than where he continues performance in reliance on the lack of termination and proceeds to incur obligations in efforts to perform, particularly where, as here, he has no reason to know that a decision to terminate has already been privately made by the contracting officer and is subject only to higher approval. Cf. Atlantic Fish and Oyster Co. v. United States, 116 F.Supp. 574, 126 Ct.Cl. 892 (1953).

The 48-days' period intervening between the default in delivery and the termination notice in this case cannot be considered in any sense to have been prompt, even allowing for the fact that the contracting officer was awaiting required approval from higher authority to terminate, as the contract required because of APP 8—602.3 (see footnote 6). The activities of the contractor in the interim, which have also been described, were known to the contracting officer and clearly constituted substantial reliance by the contractor on an election having been made not to terminate.

Time is of the essence in any contract containing fixed dates for performance. When a due date has passed and the contract has not been terminated for default within a reasonable time, the inference is created that time is no longer of the essence so long as the constructive election not to terminate continues and the contractor proceeds with performance. The proper way thereafter for time to again become of the essence is for the Government to issue a notice under the Default clause setting a reasonable but specific time for performance on pain of default termination. The election to waive performance remains in force until the time specified in the notice, and thereupon time is reinstated as being of the essence. The notice must set a new time for performance that is both reasonable and specific from the standpoint of the performance capabilities of the contractor at the time the notice is given. (See Lumen, Inc. and Foster Sportswear, supra, and also Bailey Specialized Buildings, Inc. v. United States, 404 F.2d 355, 186 Ct.Cl. 71 (1968).)

The latter problem is of no immediate concern, for the only post-default notice given by the contracting officer to Seaview was the termination notice on January 16, 1961, whereas the contracting officer would have been well- advised to precede his termination notice with a 'cure' notice setting a reasonable time for performance, and then to terminate at the latter date if Seaview had remained in default. The so-called 'cure' notice is that which is authorized in paragraph 1(ii) of the Default clause, which provides that the Government may terminate the whole or any part of the contract by written notice—

> (ii) if the Contractor fails to perform any of the other provisions of this contract, or so fails to make progress as to endanger performance of this contract in accordance with its terms, and in either of these two circumstances does not cure such failure within a period of 10 days (or such longer period as the Contracting Officer may authorize in writing) after receipt of notice from the Contracting Officer specifying such failure.

In the circumstances here, the elapsed time cannot be counted solely from the failure to deliver at the end of December 1960 until January 16, 1961. The defendant did not terminate because of the December failure which was apparently unknown to the higher authorities, but because of the lack of delivery at the end of November. Moreover, once the November failure was waived, as it was, the defendant had either to agree with plaintiff upon a new delivery schedule or clearly set a new schedule. Bailey Specialized Buildings, Inc. v. United States, supra, 404 F.2d at 359–360, 186 Ct.Cl. at 79–82. That was never done in this case.

* * *

CONCLUSION

For the reasons set forth above and to such extent, plaintiff's motion for summary judgment is granted and defendant's cross-motion for summary judgment is denied. The case is returned to the ASBCA for appropriate proceedings to determine the costs plaintiff is to recover with proceedings in this court to be suspended for 90 days. Plaintiff shall comply with Rule 100 and the General Order of April 1, 1968.

Notes and Questions

1. The DeVito case established the waiver doctrine in this context of government contract law and remains the leading case on it. See note 4 after the DCX case. Note that the doctrine has survived the tight judicial view that government contracting officials' statements do not support estoppel against the government in such contexts as OPM v. Richmond. What is the difference between waiver and estoppel and why is it, apparently, of fundamental and even constitutional dimension?

2. How does a contracting officer reinstate deadlines after waiving them?

3. The unavailability of estoppel precludes unauthorized payments of government funds; waiver allows extensions of time. What about other situations? If a contracting officer stated that some element of the quality of goods or services that the contract specified, or some other right of the government that had tangible monetary value, could be foregone, and the contractor relied upon this, would the contractor be able to assert waiver? Or would that amount to estoppel against the government? Or does it depend on how the skill of the advocacy for the two sides in a case, and on how much the adjudicator of the matter (board, court, or other) likes their breakfast that day?

Richard J. DANZIG, Secretary of the Navy, Appellant, v. AEC CORPORATION, Appellee.

224 F.3d 1333, United States Court of Appeals, Federal Circuit
No. 99-1343., Sept. 25, 2000

Before MICHEL, BRYSON, and GAJARSA, Circuit Judges.

BRYSON, Circuit Judge.

The dispute in this case arose when the government terminated its contract with AEC Corporation for default. The Armed Services Board of Contract Appeals ruled that the default termination was improper, and the government has appealed from that ruling. We reverse and remand for further proceedings.

I

In May 1989, the Navy awarded AEC a contract to complete the construction of a Naval and Marine Corps Reserve Training Center in Miami, Florida. The contract called for AEC to finish the work by October 14, 1990. By late 1990, it was apparent that AEC was behind schedule. AEC was having financial difficulties with its surety, and those problems were delaying the progress of the work. A cure notice issued by the Navy in December 1990 led to a meeting between the Navy and AEC on January 23, 1991. At that meeting, AEC provided a schedule with a projected completion date of April 16, 1991 [later extended to April 27]. The Navy agreed not to terminate the contract for default if AEC continued to make progress according to that schedule. * * *.

In late February 1991, AEC's surety froze the project's bank account, and the number of workers doing productive work on the project began to decline. At a meeting on March 5, 1991, the Navy asked why the project was progressing so slowly. AEC advised the Navy that it was unable to make progress on the project because the surety would not release funds from the project's bank account. The Navy responded by stating that AEC was close to being terminated for default.

On March 20, 1991, the Navy sent AEC a letter containing a cure notice. In the letter, the Navy stated that its agreement at the January 23 meeting not to pursue termination for default was contingent upon AEC's diligently pursuing completion of the contract by April 27, 1991. Since the January 23 meeting, the Navy charged, "work in place continues to progress at a dangerously low pace." Based on the decreasing number of man-hours being devoted to the job, the Navy expressed concern that AEC would not be able to complete the project by April 27. The Navy therefore stated that it considered AEC's "failure to diligently pursue completion a condition that is endangering performance of the contract" and advised that unless that condition was cured within 10 days, the Navy would consider terminating the contract for default.

AEC responded to the cure notice with a letter dated April 3, 1991. In the letter AEC explained that while it had previously appeared possible to complete the project by April 27, 1991, "numerous factors have prevented [the project's] scheduled progress." First, AEC claimed that "the many changes and delays caused by the Government have made an April completion impossible." Second, AEC complained that since January 1991 the surety had interfered with AEC and hampered its progress on the job by blocking the release of funds sufficient to enable AEC to pay its subcontractors and meet other project expenses. The "financial strangulation" by the surety, AEC stated,

> has progressed to the point of not only preventing AEC from meeting its April 27, 1991 completion date, it has made it impossible for AEC to predict an ultimate completion date at this time. As a matter of fact, unless [the surety and its affiliate] restrain [sic] from their present conduct and release the funds currently in [the project's] bank account, it is doubtful that AEC will ever be able to complete the project.

The Navy responded by letter the next day, stating that it could not evaluate AEC's response because AEC's contentions that burdensome changes and government-caused delays had made an April 27 completion impossible were vague and unsubstantiated. The Navy directed AEC to provide a detailed response to substantiate its allegations. The Navy added that the March 20 cure notice required AEC to cure the dangerously slow work pace within 10 days, and it "strongly encourage[d]" AEC to address the cure issue.

On April 5, AEC answered by stating that it "cannot cure the deficiency stated in your Cure Notice due to the restrictions that [the surety and its affiliate] have imposed on the disbursement of funds from the joint escrow account. Consequently we cannot give you any assurance as to when the project will be completed." AEC added that "[t]he financial strain of this action has been aggravated by costs incurred as a result of delays and additional work caused by the government." * * * AEC advised the Navy that it had reduced its work force at the job site to two supervisory employees because of the financial restrictions imposed by the surety.

The Navy called a meeting at the site on April 9, 1991, at which it gave AEC an unsigned letter directing AEC to "show cause" why the contract should not be terminated for default. The letter directed AEC to respond within ten days. AEC received a signed copy of the letter on April 11. During the following 10 days, AEC did not respond to the Navy's "show cause" letter, and throughout that period AEC had only a handful of workers on the job site.

On April 22, 1991, the Navy terminated the contract for default. The termination notice stated that the contract was being terminated "due to failure to make progress in the work and for default in performance." AEC responded by letter the same day, expressing surprise that the Navy had terminated the contract without waiting for AEC's response to the show cause letter.

AEC appealed the termination. After the contracting officer denied the appeal, AEC appealed to the Armed Services Board of Contract Appeals, which held the termination invalid.

* * *

We agree with the government * * *. In response to the Navy's March 20, 1991, cure notice, AEC failed to give the Navy adequate assurances that it could complete the contract on a timely basis or even that it could continue to make progress toward completion. That failure, the government argues, justified the Navy's decision to terminate the contract for default. Because we agree with the government on that issue, we reverse the Board's decision and hold that the default termination was valid.

When the government has reasonable grounds to believe that the contractor may not be able to perform the contract on a timely basis, the government may issue a cure notice as a precursor to a possible termination of the contract for default. *See Discount Co. v. United States,* 213 Ct.Cl. 567, 554 F.2d 435, 438-39 (1977) (government issued a cure notice when the contractor had done no substantial work during the construction season). When the government justifiably issues a cure notice, the contractor has an obligation to take steps to demonstrate or give assurances that progress is being made toward a timely completion of the contract, or to explain that the reasons for any prospective delay in completion of the contract are not the responsibility of the contractor. *See Tubular Aircraft Prods., Inc. v. United States,* 213 Ct.Cl. 749, 750, 566 F.2d 1190 (1977) ("Plaintiff's minimal performance efforts coupled with its perilous financial situation warranted the issuance of a cure notice.

Thereafter, plaintiff's failure to advise the Government that corrective action would be taken in order to make performance at levels reasonably commensurate with contract requirements financially possible, justified the default termination."); *Composite Laminates, Inc. v. United States,* 27 Fed.Cl. 310, 323-24 (1992) ("When the government issues a cure notice, in order for a contractor to avoid default, a contractor must be able to provide adequate assurances to the government that it can complete contract requirements on time."); *International Verbatim Reporters, Inc. v. United States,* 9 Cl.Ct. 710, 723 (1986) (once the cure notice was issued to the contractor, "its failure to correct, explain or communicate with [the government] during the period what corrective action that would be taken, justified a termination for default") * * *

The law applicable to a contractor's failure to provide assurances of timely completion is a branch of the law of anticipatory repudiation. *See, e.g., Discount Co.,* 554 F.2d at 441 (when the government was not assured of timely completion, the court could properly "rely upon cases involving abandoned or repudiated contracts"). At common law, anticipatory repudiation of a contract required an unambiguous and unequivocal statement that the obligor would not or could not perform the contract. *See Dingley v. Oler,* 117 U.S. 490, 503, 6 S.Ct. 850, 29 L.Ed. 984 (1886); *Cascade Pac. Int'l v. United States,* 773 F.2d 287, 293 (Fed.Cir.1985). As the Restatement of Contracts has recognized, however, modern decisions do not limit anticipatory repudiation to cases of express and unequivocal repudiation of a contract. Instead, anticipatory repudiation includes cases in which reasonable grounds support the obligee's belief that the obligor will breach the contract. In that setting, the obligee "may demand adequate assurance of due performance" and if the obligor does not give such assurances, the obligee may treat the failure to do so as a repudiation of the contract. *Restatement (Second) of Contracts* § 251 (1981). The Uniform Commercial Code has adopted a similar rule for contracts involving the sale of goods. *See* U.C.C. § 2-609.

The law of government contracts has adopted that doctrine, expressing it as a requirement that the contractor give reasonable assurances of performance in response to a validly issued cure notice. * * * That rule, as the Restatement explains, rests "on the principle that the parties to a contract look to actual performance 'and that a continuing sense of reliance and security that the promised performance will be forthcoming when due, is an important feature of the bargain.'" *Restatement (Second) of Contracts* § 251 cmt. a (quoting U.C.C. § 2-609 cmt. 1).

* * *

Based on AEC's performance during February and March 1991, the Navy had a reasonable basis for concern that the contract would not be completed by April 27, 1991, the completion date that AEC had projected on February 5 and presented to the Navy to avoid default termination at that time. The Navy was therefore entitled to issue a cure notice demanding a correction of the slow pace of the work or a satisfactory explanation of how AEC planned to complete the work on a timely basis. The issuance of a cure notice was justified under the circumstances, even if the circumstances did not, at that point, justify a termination for default. *See National Union Fire Ins.*, 90-1 B.C.A. (CCH) at 111,855 (noting that the "right to demand assurance need not spring merely from a performance or progress failure, but may be asserted whenever reasonable grounds exist to believe a breach will be committed").

AEC's response to the cure notice did not satisfy its obligation to provide assurances to the Navy that it could timely complete the contract. AEC did not dispute the Navy's assertion in its cure notice that at its current pace it would not be able to complete the contract by April 27. In fact, AEC's April 3 letter stated that "the financial strangulation" of AEC by its surety had prevented AEC "from meeting its April 27, 1991 completion date" and had "made it impossible for AEC to predict an ultimate completion date at this time." Moreover, AEC stated that unless the surety and its affiliate released funds in the project's bank account, "it is doubtful that AEC will ever be able to complete the project." When the Navy asked for a more specific response, AEC responded on April 5 with a letter in which it reiterated that "due to the restrictions that [the surety and its affiliate] have imposed on the disbursement of funds from the joint escrow account...we cannot give you any assurances as to when the project will be completed." Clearly, the April 3 and April 5 letters offered nothing to allay the Navy's concerns about AEC's ability to complete the contract on a timely basis.

At about the time of the April 3 and April 5 letters, AEC removed the contract files and office equipment from the work site and disconnected the telephone at the work-site office. At the same time, AEC advised the Navy that it had been forced to reduce its work force at the facility to two persons and that it could not "continue to incur costs on this project given the financial restrictions being imposed on us by [the surety and its affiliate]." Finally, at the meeting between representatives of the Navy and AEC on April 9, AEC was given a notice to show cause within 10 days why the contract should not be terminated for default, and AEC failed to respond within the 10-day period.

AEC's conduct, like its responses to the cure notice, clearly failed to provide the requisite assurances that AEC would complete the project on a timely basis. Rather than providing an assurance of timely completion, AEC told the Navy, through both its words and its conduct, that the contract was not likely to be completed until AEC was able to work out its financial difficulties with its surety. AEC offered the Navy no reason to believe that those difficulties would be resolved any time in the near future. Moreover, although AEC makes some effort to suggest that its financial difficulties were the fault of the government, there is no finding by the Board to that effect and no evidence supporting that suggestion. Thus, there is no reason in this case to depart from the normal rule that the contractor's financial difficulties are not a legitimate excuse for its failure to make progress. * * *

AEC's assertions of government-caused delay similarly did not respond adequately to the Navy's request for assurances. Although AEC referred to government-caused delays in both the April 3 and April 5 letters, it was not specific as to what changes had caused delay or how much delay it considered the government to have caused, nor did it represent that it could complete the contract within the additional time to which it believed it was entitled. * * * AEC's responses to the cure notice thus did not adequately explain how its slow progress was the product of delay caused by the government or was otherwise excusable.

Under these circumstances, we conclude as a matter of law that AEC failed to respond adequately to the Navy's reasonable request for assurances of timely performance. The Navy was therefore entitled to regard AEC's failure to provide such assurances as a breach of the contract justifying termination of the contract for default. On remand, the Board shall address the remaining issues of liability based on our holding that the default termination was valid.

REVERSED and REMANDED.

Notes and Questions

1. This case reinforces the importance of the cure notice, particularly when the termination for default is going to be grounded, as here, in "endangering performance" (due later) rather than in failure to fulfill (measured by past delivery or past due dates). Note how the issues occur in two steps: the (pre-notice) reasonableness of the government's grounds for concern, and the (post-notice) adequacy of the contractor's response. Note, also, how closely this corresponds to the similar pattern in the basic general law of contracts and particularly under the Article Two of the U.C.C. The modern general law, and U.C.C. provision, have their two steps of the existence of a reasonable basis for demanding assurances, and, afterwards, whether adequate assurances are provided. How is government contract law similar to, and different from, basic general contract law in this regard?

2. The government meets its burden as to termination on the basis of endangering performance by showing various indicators of basis for concern. What were they in this case?

DCX, Inc., Appellant, v. William J. Perry, Secretary of Defense, Appellee

No. 94-1385. United States Court of Appeals,
Federal Circuit. 79 F.3d 132. March 11, 1996.

Appealed from Armed Services Board of Contract Appeals. Before MAYER, MICHEL, and BRYSON, Circuit Judges.

BRYSON, Circuit Judge.

DCX, Inc., appeals a decision of the Armed Services Board of Contract Appeals upholding the government's termination of a contract for default. We affirm.

I.

On April 1, 1988, the Defense Logistics Agency awarded a contract to DCX for light sets to be used in medical tents. The contract required DCX to perform a series of tests on the first light set that DCX manufactured under the contract and to supply the government with a First Article Test Report. The test report was due on June 30, 1988, and delivery of the light sets was required to begin by July 18, 1988. The contract provided that if DCX failed to deliver the test report on time, it "shall be deemed to have failed to make delivery within the meaning of the Default clause of this contract."

Because it did not have the facilities to perform the first article tests, DCX subcontracted the testing to Ball Brothers Aerospace Systems. Under the subcontract, the tests were to begin on May 19. Ball, however, did not begin DCX's tests until June 17. On that date, DCX advised the government that the testing process would not be completed until July 11 and that the government therefore would not receive the First Article Test Report until July 12. DCX blamed Ball's delay on the government's Defense Priorities and Allocations System (DPAS), which it asserted required Ball to postpone the DCX tests in favor of higher priority government contracts. On July 1, the day after the test report was due under the contract, the contracting officer advised DCX that it was in default, but she agreed to forbear termination until July 12, thus effectively granting DCX the additional time requested in its June 17 letter. When DCX failed to deliver the test report on the extended due date, however, the contracting officer referred the contract to the termination contracting officer who terminated the contract for default.

DCX appealed to the Armed Services Board of Contract Appeals, alleging that its failure to deliver the First Article Test Report was excusable because it was caused by the operation of the DPAS, and that the termination contracting officer had acted arbitrarily and capriciously in terminating the contract. DCX asked that the termination for default be converted into a termination for the convenience of the government.

The Board upheld the termination for default, finding that the delay was the fault of DCX and its subcontractor, Ball. The Board focused in particular on DCX's failure to guarantee timely performance by obtaining either a backup subcontractor or a binding time commitment from Ball to complete the tests by a date certain. With respect to DCX's proffered excuse for its failure to produce the test report by the extended deadline, the Board concluded that there was insufficient evidence that the operation of the DPAS caused the delay. The Board further found that the termination contracting officer adhered to the contract terms and the applicable procurement regulations, and that his termination decision was thus not arbitrary or capricious.

II.

On appeal, DCX makes [two] arguments: that the operation of the DPAS, not the negligence of DCX or its subcontractor, caused the delay in the delivery of the First Article Test Report; [and] that the contracting officer abused his discretion when he terminated the contract for default * * *

A.

The Board found that the government met its burden of proving that DCX did not perform in a timely fashion, and that DCX failed to meet its burden of proving that its nonperformance was excusable. See Lisbon Contractors, Inc. v. United States, 828 F.2d 759, 764 (Fed.Cir.1987); Switlik Parachute Co. v. United States, 216 Ct.Cl. 362, 573 F.2d 1228, 1234 (1978). DCX contends that the evidence conclusively showed that its failure to submit the First Article Test Report in a timely fashion was not attributable to any fault of DCX or Ball, but was caused by the government through the operation of the DPAS regulations, which require contractors to give precedence to higher priority government contracts. After reviewing the record, we agree with the Board that DCX failed to meet its burden of showing that the DPAS regulations excused its failure to fulfill the testing requirements of the contract.

The default clause in the contract excused any default caused by certain enumerated actions, including "acts of the Government." The default clause added, however, that "the failure to perform must be beyond the control and without the fault or negligence of the Contractor" or (in the case of a subcontract) "beyond the control of both the Contractor and subcontractor, and without the fault or negligence of either." Although the operation of the DPAS may give rise to excusable delay in an appropriate case, the DPAS regulations require performance of a lower priority contract to be deferred only if "required delivery dates [for the higher rated contract] cannot otherwise be met." 15 C.F.R. §700.14(a). As the Board pointed out, DCX's witness, who admitted having only limited acquaintance with the government contract priority system, testified that Ball deferred DCX's tests in favor of higher priority government contracts, but he did not testify that the displacement of DCX's tests was necessary in order to meet the required delivery dates of the higher priority contracts.

Moreover, as the Board noted, DCX did not take steps to protect against the possibility of delay in the testing process. DCX did not obtain its subcontract with Ball until May 11, 1988, some six weeks after the award of the contract to DCX, and the subcontract with Ball contained no firm commitment as to the date on which the testing would be completed. In addition, the Board pointed out, DCX "had no backup arrangements or commitments from any other party, that were available, to perform the tests needed in the event Ball delayed or for any reason was unable to meet DCX's time of delivery requirements." The Board was thus warranted in finding that DCX's failure to perform was attributable to its own negligence and that of its subcontractor, rather than to the operation of the DPAS.

DCX next argues that the termination contracting officer acted arbitrarily and capriciously in terminating the DCX contract for default because he failed to follow certain provisions of the Federal Acquisition Regulation before he terminated the contract. The Board found that the termination contracting officer adhered to both the terms of the contract and the requirements of the applicable procedural regulations. Once again, we uphold the Board's findings as supported by the evidence before it.

The first regulatory provision that DCX complains was not followed is 48 C.F.R. §49.402-3(a), which requires the contracting officer to obtain legal review before terminating a contract. The termination contracting officer testified that he obtained the required legal review before terminating the contract, although he was not able to state with certainty which attorney reviewed the proposed termination action. DCX argues that the termination contracting officer's testimony was incredible, but that contention is baseless. The witness was firm in asserting that a legal review was conducted, and in light of the large number of contracts he handled over a several-year period, it is hardly surprising that he could not recall all the details of the legal review.

The second regulatory provision on which DCX relies, 48 C.F.R. §49.402-3(f), requires a contracting officer to consider various factors before exercising his discretion to terminate a contract when the contractor is in default. In this case, the termination contracting officer's contemporaneous memorandum and hearing testimony demonstrate that he addressed the pertinent regulatory factors and found that they did not counsel against termination under the circumstances of this case. Moreover, the factors in section 49.402-3(f) that contracting officers are directed to consider before terminating contracts are not prerequisites to a valid termination. Although compliance or noncompliance with section 49.402-3(f) may aid a Board of Contract Appeals or a court in determining whether a contracting officer has abused his discretion in terminating a contract for default, see Darwin Constr. Co. v. United States, 811 F.2d 593, 598 (Fed.Cir.1987); Fairfield Scientific Corp. v. United States, 222 Ct.Cl. 167, 611 F.2d 854, 862 (1979), the regulation does not confer rights on a defaulting contractor. A contracting officer's failure to consider one or more of the section 49.402-3(f) factors therefore does not require that a default termination be converted into a termination for the convenience of the government. * * *

DCX argues that the termination contracting officer acted rashly by terminating the contract on July 13 without considering the reasons for the delay. As the officer testified, however, the government had already given DCX an extension of time within which to produce the First Article Test Report. The contracting officer agreed to forbear termination until July 12, as requested by DCX. When July 13 arrived, the contracting officer had not received either the report or a request for a further extension of time. Having been given no explanation for the further delay, the termination contracting officer was not required to assume that DCX had a valid excuse for the further delay or to seek out further information about the status of the DCX's efforts. We therefore find nothing in the record to persuade us that the termination contracting officer acted arbitrarily or capriciously in terminating the contract when he did.

Notes and Questions

1. How many different issues are argued, and can you describe the arguments for both sides? Try this chart:

Issue	DCX argument	Gov't/Fed Circuit response
Default Clause excuses if caused by "acts of the gov't"	Subcontractor said "gov't had higher priorities"	not definitely "necessary" no firm commitments nor backups so, subcontractor's (and DCX's) fault
FAR: TCO should get legal review	TCO can't recall what att'y reviewed it	busy TCO, needn't recall
FAR: TCO should consider factors	abuse of discretion?	Doesn't confer rights on defaulting contractor

2. Both Radiation Technology *and this case involve the government's elaborate testing and inspection requirements. Can you explain how a "First Article" system works?*

3. In this case, the contractor offers the defense of "excusable delay." Generally, excusable delays are those which the contracting firm can prove were unforeseeable, beyond its control, and not the result of the contractor's own acts or omissions (e.g. labor strikes, weather, and certain subcontractor delays). Other excusable delays in-

clude those caused by acts or omissions of the government itself, such as an agency's failure to make timely payments; failure either to accept or to reject goods within a reasonable period; defects in specifications or drawings; delayed award of the contract that deprives the awardee of sufficient start-up time; ordered or constructive suspensions of work; or, constructive changes to the scope of the contract itself . For a more complete treatment, see James P. Wiezel, Refining the Concept of Concurrent Delay, 21 Pub. Cont. L.J. 161 (1991); Michael R. Finke, The Burden of Proof in Government Contract Schedule Delay Claims, 22 Pub. Cont. L.J. 125 (1992); *Wilner v. United States*, 24 F.3d 1397 (Fed. Cir. 1994); *Tyger Construction Co. v. United States*, 31 Fed. Cl. 177 (1994).

4. In this case, the contracting officer said she would forebear for a period of time. Suppose the contracting officer did that several more times: would she waive the government's right to terminate for default? But, then, can the contracting officer reinstate the contractor's delivery duties by unilaterally imposing a reasonable new schedule? Where a due date has passed without termination for default and the contractor relies on that forebearance, there is an implied election to waive the strict deadline for performance and the courts infer that time is no longer of the essence. The courts deem this waiver to continue so long as the contractor continues to perform, until the issuance of a notice under the default clause indicating a "reasonable and specific" new time for performance, which reflects the contractor's ability to perform at the time notice is given (*Darwin Construction Co.*, GSBCA No. 10193, 1990 WL 157087). Such conduct would effectively reinstate a new performance date, as well as the "time is of the essence" element. See generally *I.T.T. Corp. v. United States*, 598 F. 2d 541 (Ct. Cl. 1975); *DeVito v. United States*, 413 F.2d 1147 (Ct.Cl. 1969); *Precision Dynamics, Inc.*, ASBCA 41360 (1997).

Lisbon Contractors, Inc., Appellee,
v. The United States, Appellant

Appeal No. 86-1461. United States Court of Appeals,
Federal Circuit. 828 F.2d 759. Decided Sept. 9, 1987.

Before NIES, BISSELL, and ARCHER, Circuit Judges.

NIES, Circuit Judge.

The United States appeals from the judgment of the United States Claims Court, No. 288-81C, awarding $95,748.15 to Lisbon Contractors, Inc. as termination for convenience costs under a construction contract. The Claims Court held that the United States wrongfully terminated Lisbon for default thereby converting the termination to one for convenience of the government. We affirm-in-part, reverse-in-part, vacate-in-part, and remand for entry of a reduced damage award.

I.

On August 8, 1979, Lisbon and the United States Soil Conservation Service (SCS) entered into Contract No. 50-3A75-9-35 for construction of a reinforced concrete flood control channel and a bridge. With extensions of time, the completion date was December 20, 1980. Work began in the fall of 1979 on the bridge portion of the contract. As is frequent in construction projects, Lisbon encountered difficulties. Lisbon's concrete subcontractor, Versatile Constructors, was a major source of Lisbon's problems. The government attributed that difficulty to poor supervision by Lisbon.

In the succeeding months the parties exchanged numerous letters discussing Lisbon's progress on the project. On several occasions the contracting officer's representative threatened to terminate Lisbon's right to proceed unless Lisbon took immediate action to correct specific problems. SCS was concerned about the following items: (1) Versatile Constructors' performance as the concrete subcontractor, (2) Anthony Rebimbas' performance as Lisbon's construction superintendent, (3) the quality of the concrete work, and (4) Lisbon's progress on the work. Typically Lisbon responded by taking some action to correct the problems, which did not fully satisfy SCS, whereupon negotiations would continue. In January, 1980, for example, the contracting officer required Lisbon to submit a revised construction schedule with information on additional work forces and equipment. Lisbon submitted a revised schedule with some details, but the contracting officer requested more.

To meet SCS's objections, Lisbon designated its vice president, Peter Campellone, as acting superintendent (with the government's approval) until it could find a replacement, and it terminated Versatile as the concrete subcontractor once the bridge was completed. It remedied specific complaints on work item deficiencies identified by SCS. SCS inspected and paid for the work. On April 7, 1980, Lisbon requested a meeting between the contracting officer and Lisbon's president, Anthony Marques, to resolve the items still at issue, namely, the construction schedule and the superintendent issues. Also Lisbon had requested a change in the specifications to allow it to remove concrete forms more quickly (the "sleeper joint" issue).

The parties met on April 30, 1980. Lisbon renewed its request for a modification of the contracting officer's interpretation of the sleeper joint issue which would enable Lisbon to perform the work more efficiently and expeditiously. Mr. Marques became incensed because SCS never made the analysis it had promised with respect to the requested change. At the meeting, SCS adamantly refused to approve the change, and tempers flared. Following the heated altercation on this issue, during which Mr. Marques had indicated he needed the change to complete the work on time, the SCS representatives reiterated their displeasure with various aspects of Lisbon's performance. The SCS representatives then left the meeting to caucus because, per the contracting officer, everybody was going in different directions. After discussing the matter among themselves for approximately twenty minutes, they returned and the contracting officer announced that, in his opinion, Lisbon could not complete the job satisfactorily within the time limitations set in the contract, and he was terminating the contract for default.

Mr. Marques promptly withdrew his "demand" for a change and offered to do everything necessary to complete the work on time, even at a loss, in accordance with the contract. The contracting officer refused to discuss Lisbon's further performance under the contract. Thus, the matter of the superintendent and the details of the revised schedule Lisbon had submitted, which did not depend on the proposed change, were never taken up. A telegram subsequently confirmed the termination. SCS rebid the contract and engaged a follow-on contractor to complete the project. The project was eventually completed on December 10, 1981.

The action of the contracting officer in terminating Lisbon for default was taken pursuant to General Provision 5 of the contract at issue here, which contains the following standard language:

> If the Contractor refuses or fails to prosecute the work, or any separable part thereof, with such diligence as will insure its completion within the time specified in this contract, or any extension thereof, or fails to complete said work

within such time, the Government may, by written notice to the Contractor, terminate his right to proceed with the work or such part of the work as to which there has been delay.

....

If, after notice of termination of the Contractor's right to proceed under the provisions of this clause, it is determined for any reason that the Contractor was not in default under the provisions of this clause, or that the delay was excusable under the provisions of this clause, the rights and obligations of the parties shall, if the contract contains a clause providing for termination for convenience of the Government, be the same as if the notice of termination had been issued pursuant to such clause.

The contract contains a standard termination for convenience clause. On December 19, 1980, Lisbon submitted a certified claim to the contracting officer, asserting that the government's termination for default was not justified and claiming a right to certain costs under the termination for convenience clause of the contract. The contracting officer responded by referring to the default termination decision, thereby rejecting the claim, and Lisbon timely filed a direct access action in the Court of Claims pursuant to the Contract Disputes Act (CDA), 41 U.S.C. §609(a) (1982).

* * *

In this case, the government bore the burden on the issue of default raised by the contractor's complaint.

B.   Standard for Default for Failure to Prosecute with Diligence

With respect to the government's challenge to the standard imposed by the Claims Court to establish the contractor's default here, we do not agree that the Claims Court ultimately required the government to prove that the contractor could not possibly complete the work before the date fixed in the contract. To make this argument, the government relies on isolated statements of the court read out of context. On this issue, the court unequivocally held:

> The standard default clause does not require a finding that completion within the contract time is impossible. Termination for default is appropriate if a demonstrated lack of diligence indicates that [the government] could not be assured of timely completion. Case law that involves abandoned or repudiated contracts, and terminations that involve a failure to make progress, applies.

Discount Co. v. United States, 554 F.2d 435, 441 [213 Ct.Cl. 567] (1977); Universal Fiberglass Corp. v. United States, 537 F.2d at 398. Slip op. at 14.

We agree that the contractual language found in General Provision 5 does not require absolute impossibility of performance by the contractor before the government may declare the contract in default. See Discount Co. v. United States, 554 F.2d 435, 441, 213 Ct.Cl. 567, cert. denied, 434 U.S. 938, 98 S.Ct. 428, 54 L.Ed.2d 298 (1977). Nor does it permit default termination merely on the ground that performance is less than absolutely certain. Rather, we construe the contract, as did the Claims Court, to require a reasonable belief on the part of the contracting officer that there was "no reasonable likelihood that the [contractor] could perform the entire contract effort within the time remaining for contract performance." RFI Shield-Rooms, ASBCA Nos. 17374, 17991, 77-2 BCA (CCH) ¶12,714, 61,735 (Aug. 11, 1977); see also Discount, 554 F.2d at 441 (justifiable insecurity about the contract's timely completion required). Although the government argues strenuously to the contrary, the Claims Court placed upon the government no greater burden of proving default than that described in Discount.

C.   The Evidence of Default

The sole basis here for termination for default was Lisbon's failure, under General Provision 5 of the contract, "to prosecute the work...with such diligence as will insure its completion within the time specified in th[e] contract." At trial, the government did not offer direct testimony or any other direct evidence on the time which it estimated it would take Lisbon to complete the contract. Indeed, the contracting officer acknowledged that the government did not undertake a study to determine whether Lisbon could complete the work within the required time, or determine how long it would take a follow-on contractor to do the work. Such a comparison is mandated by the relevant procurement regulations. 41 C.F.R. §1-18.803-5(a)(3).

The government argues that it was, nevertheless, justified in terminating for failure to make progress because Lisbon (1) did not sufficiently support its revised construction schedule to show the manner in which it would regain time to achieve the due date and (2) failed to designate an acceptable, full-time superintendent. Thus, per the government, the contracting officer had reasonable doubts concerning Lisbon's ability to complete the job in a timely fashion. Under the Discount decision, the government argues, the default for untimely progress was justified, the contractor being required in Discount to reasonably assure the contracting officer that he could complete the job on time.

The Claims Court made the following findings:

> 26.   At the start of the April 30, 1980, meeting, the matters [the government] had complained about were in the following status:
>
> (1) Versatile's subcontract had been terminated.
>
> (2) [Lisbon] had a full-time superintendent.
>
> (3) All previous complaints on various work item deficiencies had been remedied; the work had been inspected; and [Lisbon] had been paid for the work.
>
> (4) Lisbon had submitted a revised schedule which showed the work could be completed timely, using procedures that accorded with [the government's] interpretation of the specifications on the sleeper joint issue.

Slip op. at 39.

To give any viability to the government's justification argument, the government must persuade us that findings (2) and (4) above are clearly erroneous. A finding of fact is clearly erroneous when "'although there is evidence to support it, the reviewing court on the entire evidence is left with the definite and firm conviction that a mistake has been committed.'" Milmark Servs., Inc. v. United States, 731 F.2d 855, 857 (Fed.Cir.1984) (quoting United States v. United States Gypsum Co., 333 U.S. 364, 395, 68 S.Ct. 525, 542, 92 L.Ed. 746 (1948)).

The record before us indicates that the parties arranged the April 30, 1980 meeting between Lisbon's president and the contracting officer to resolve their differences so they could pursue completion of the project. The superintendent and revised construction schedule problems were matters the parties sought to resolve at the meeting.

Whether Mr. Campellone, Lisbon's vice president, was a full-time superintendent on April 30, 1980, was disputed. The government maintains his health was too poor to permit him to work full time. He had been accepted by the government in January when there was minimal construction activity and it was intended he would serve only temporarily until the superintendent dispute was resolved. There is no dispute that Lisbon was prepared to discuss superintendence at the meeting, and that the meeting broke up before that issue was reached. On the record before us, we are not persuaded that the Claims Court's finding of fact (2) above is clearly erroneous.

The government maintains that the Claims Court erred in finding that Lisbon had submitted a revised schedule of work at the time of termination. Per the government, the schedule was not acceptable because Lisbon did not supply the details of the additional work forces and equipment necessary to complete the job under the contract. The government asked, for example, for the names of specific laborers Lisbon would commit to the job and for copies of sub-contracts. Per the government, these deficiencies, viewed in the context of past poor performance, were a sufficient basis for concluding that the contractor could not finish on time. The government also urges that Lisbon's president admitted at the meeting that Lisbon could not complete the work without a change in the contract specifications.

One purpose of the meeting was to work out problems of the work schedule. There was conflicting evidence concerning what occurred at the meeting, and the trial court found the testimony of Lisbon's witnesses more persuasive, a decision to which we must defer. Also the Claims Court took into consideration the circumstances surrounding Mr. Marques' alleged admission and discounted its importance. We agree it does not outweigh the other evidence. Per the Claims Court, the submitted revised schedule did not depend on obtaining a change in specifications and would have been taken up had the government not ended the negotiations following the altercation. The Claims Court also held, and we agree, that the contractor's failure to give all the requested details on the revised schedule was not in itself evidence of failure to make progress on the work which would justify the default termination.

In sum, we hold that on the basis of the entire record, the Claims Court did not err in determining that the government improperly terminated Lisbon for default. The Claims Court properly converted the termination for default to a termination for convenience of the government as provided by General Provision 5 of the contract.

* * *

Notes and Questions

1. *Lisbon Contractors* concerns the second prong of the Default Clause, "failure to make progress." Note how this occurs prior to the date for delivery or completion. This corresponds in basic (private) contract law to implied repudiation. However, at common law, the contractor would have to bollix or delay matters so badly that it was impossible for performance to occur, to constitute implied repudiation and thereby to justify cancellation. What standard does the government set for when it can terminate for failure to perform, prior to the date of delivery? Which of the several factors that differentiate government termination from private cancellation justify the government's terminating, not because performance is impossible, but on an easier showing?

2. Even though the government has an easier showing to terminate for failure to make progress than is required at common law, it does not succeed in this case. Did the CO have much reason to doubt progress? How many different aspects of the arguments on both sides can you separate out? Try this chart:

CO's arguments	Contractor's arguments
health too poor	full time superintendant
no lists of laborers, names of subs	revised schedule of work
concrete sub had not done well	Versatile had been terminated
Lisbon had asked for change in specs	Lisbon had withdrawn that demand
("sleeper joint")	

3. For basic (private) contract law, the Uniform Commercial Code meets the need for parties to be able to check whether performance is endangered by giving those parties the ability to request assurances. UCC 2-609; Restatement (Second) of Contracts sec. 251. What is there about modern contracting that has led both government and private contracting to fill in this gap in the common law, which largely required contractors to await the day of performance to end the suspense about whether the other party would perform? Increases in the complexity of contracting parties' interdependence and organized production interconnection?

4. The third prong of the Default Clause allows termination for "failure to perform other contract provisions." In what are called "(a)(1)(iii) cases," terminations for default have been upheld on grounds unrelated to whether the product was completed as promised. For instance, in *Kirk Brothers Mechanical Contractors, Inc. v. Kelso*, 16 F. 3d 1173, 40 Cont. Cas. Fed.(CCH) 76,889 (1994), Kirk was "removed" for failure to promptly provide a refrigeration system, and upon the Navy's discovery of defective workmanship, was ultimately subjected to termination for default. Because the contract had no completion date and Kirk had no opportunity to cure the ASBCA converted the default into a termination for convenience. On appeal, however, the Navy prevailed on alternative grounds, specifically that Kirk Bros. had violated the Davis-Bacon Act (40 U.S.C. §276 et seq.) by destroying rather than retaining employee time cards. See FAR 52-249-8 (a)(1)(iii).

5. As far as appropriate bases for termination for default, an interesting question has concerned whether a contracting officer's termination can be justified on grounds of contractor fraud. Ordinarily, issues of fraud are not for a contracting officer or for a board of contract appeals, but for a federal court. 41 U.S.C. sec. 605(a); FAR 33.210. It has been argued that a contracting officer cannot justify termination for default on grounds of contractor fraud. However, the Federal Circuit has upheld a termination for default where the government raised the issue of fraud, by holding that the validity of the CO's final decision was not diminished by the assertion of fraud as an additional basis for termination. *Daff v. United States*, 78 F.3d 1566 (F.3d Cir. 1996).

B. Process

The issues of "process" in termination for default operate at different levels: what ordinarily happens when a contracting officer invokes the default clause and what may happen when a contractor challenges the contracting officer's discretion in invoking the default clause.

Ordinary Process

At one level, the process concerns what happens when a contracting officer invokes the default clause and goes through regular procedures with a contractor. Partly, this concerns notice requirements. Ordinarily, two distinct types of notice apply. The Default Clause does not require that the government notify the contractor in writing of the possibility of the termination. However, this kind of notice, referred to in the FAR (49.607) as a "show cause" notice, ordinarily is provided, and the courts and boards may sometimes require it. *Udis v. United States*, 7 Cl. Ct. 379 (1985). Moreover, a careful contracting officer, knowing what follows from termination for default, will want all the information obtainable by such a show cause notice.

As previously discussed, the "failure to make progress" and "failure to perform any other provision" prongs include explicit requirements of a ten day opportunity to cure the failure. And while the contracting officer has the power to summarily terminate for failure to deliver or perform, a contracting officer may well decide, under the power to forebear, effectively to give the contractor under this prong the same type of opportunity to cure.

Once the contracting officer renders a final decision to terminate for default, the contractor may appeal that through the disputes process. A final decision gives the contractor notice of this. The disputes process is discussed in the chapter on remedies. Among the issues that arise about termination for default is that of the proper timing for appeal, including the effect, usually not considered to be major, of deficiencies in the notification of the right to appeal. *See Decker & Co. v. West*, 76 F.3d 1573 (Fed. Cir. 1996); *State of Florida, Department of Insurance v. United States*, 81 F.3d 1093 (Fed. Cir. 1996).

Challenging the Contracting Officer's Exercise of Discretion

At the other level of the process issue, contracting officers have broad discretion over whether, if grounds to terminate are present, to do so. The issue of "process" concerns, not whether the termination for default has sufficient justification, but how the contracting officers have exercised their discretion. Contracting officers do not operate in a vacuum. They work in an agency context with several hierarchies. One involves their "clients," so to speak, namely, those in the agency needing the goods or services being procured. Another involves the budget for contracting. Yet another involves the agencies' relations with the ultimate elected officials, the President and the Congress. A contracting officer may well make the decision to terminate for default, as opposed to simply tolerating or working out the contractor's problems, in light of the attitudes of these various hierarchies.

A powerful ambivalence runs through the termination process on this element, making this the meeting-ground of major strains in the public law of government contracting. The competing considerations resemble those concerning what checks should exist on the government firing or suspending its own employees: checking arbitary power vs. clogging the effective operation of government.

On the one hand, as noted, termination for default resembles other normative civil adjudications. The government does more than simply implement its policy: it takes a step that brands the contractor for unexcused failure. Furthermore, it penalizes the contractor. To a limited extent, the statutory and regulatory assignment of authority to make the termination decision to the contracting officer vests in that officer, and that officer alone, the discretion to brand and to penalize the contractor, so that the power to visit such sanctions will not be at large in the government. Any other system, where a contractor could be penalized by unseen and unknown forces for unstated reasons, would be Kafkaesque.

On the other hand, a termination for default ordinarily must stand or fall on whether the contractor defaulted. If the contractor defaulted then the government must be able to terminate the contractor without endless procedures of second-guessing and resistance. Otherwise the effective operation of government gets clogged and paralyzed. A contractor who should be terminated instead would seek to put the government's own decisionmaking process on trial. Instead of deterring future contractors from defaults, such a procedure deters future contracting officers from using the vital tools for managing contractors.

In the overwhelming majority of terminations for default, the tribunal declines to take an interest in putting the contracting officer on trial. However, it is appropriate to look at two cases which did reverse terminations for default, based on the process that led to the termination. Partly this owes to the importance of the issue. Also, though, these cases provide a much more complete picture of how termination works than gets provided in the vast majority of cases where the inquiry is confined to whether the contractor defaulted. Lawyers who may participate on either side of terminations for defaults, or who may give advice in situations where such termination could occur, can find much to analyze in the fuller picture that these opinions paint about what precedes a termination for default.

The first case on that issue, *Darwin*, introduces the basic concepts of the tension between the government's desire to confine the issues to the contractor's performance and the contractor's desire to broaden them to the government's arbitrariness. Then, the next case, *McDonnell Douglas*, involves a billion-dollar public issue, the termination of a major airplane development contract. It reveals the interaction of the Defense Department's planning, budgeting, and decision-making system, on the one hand, with the adjudication of terminations for default on the other.

For further discussion of the subject of this section, see: Bruce W. McLaughlin, *The Evolution of Darwin: A Contracting Officer's Primer for Default Terminations*, 19 Pub. Cont. L.J. 191 (1990).

Darwin Construction Co., Inc., Appellant, v. United States, Appellee

Appeal No. 86-1370. United States Court of Appeals, Federal Circuit. 811 F.2d 593. Feb. 12, 1987.

Before NIES, Circuit Judge, COWEN, Senior Circuit Judge, and NEWMAN, Circuit Judge.

COWEN, Senior Circuit Judge.

Appellant (Darwin) appeals from a reconsidered decision of the Armed Services Board of Contract Appeals (ASBCA or Board) which had reversed its earlier holding. The Board initially converted a termination for default into a termination for the convenience of the Government. Upon Government's motion for reconsideration, the Board reversed its earlier decision and upheld the termination for default. We reverse the Board's amended decision and remand with instructions for the Board to convert the termination for default into a termination for the convenience of the Government in accordance with the Board's initial decision.

BACKGROUND

Darwin was awarded a fixed price construction contract on June 3, 1983, for certain improvements to the Propellant Machinery Facility (PMF) at the Naval Ordnance Station (NOS) in Maryland. Contract work was to be completed within 150 calendar days, by November 15, 1983.

The contract provided that the contractor would be allowed access to the construction site only during two 14 calendar day periods which were to be separated by another period of at least 14 calendar days during which time normal Naval production operations at the facility would take place. Based upon the schedule agreed upon between the parties, the last day for construction was to have been November 7, 1983. At the conclusion of this second 14-day work period, Darwin had completed approximately 65 percent of the required contract work.

In response to a "show cause" letter Darwin noted that the late delivery of necessary equipment made it impossible for the contract to be completed by November 7. Darwin, nevertheless, asserted that it was physically and financially ready to complete the remaining contract work within a two week period beginning on December 17, 1983. Nevertheless, on February 13, 1984, the Navy terminated the contract for default, claiming that Darwin had not diligently performed during the two 14-day periods when it had access to the site. The Navy alleged that a 2-week shutdown of the facility during December was not possible in order to permit Darwin to complete the contract.

On appeal to the ASBCA, the Board found that "on the record * * * no excusable cause for delay has been proven by the appellant. Therefore, as of 15 November, the date of completion for the performance of the captioned contract, Darwin was in default." Darwin Constr. Co., ASBCA No. 29340, 84-3 BCA ¶17,673 at 88,149 (1984).

Despite its finding of default, the Board held that the termination for default "must be converted to one for convenience of the Government." The decision stated that "the Board finds that this termination for default was arbitrary and capricious because it is evident to the Board that the default action was taken solely to rid the Navy of having to further deal with Darwin." (Emphasis supplied).

The Board's conclusion regarding the arbitrary action of the contracting officer was based, among others, on the following findings of fact made by the Board:

The only reason Darwin was unable to complete the work in time was that the material needed for the unfinished portion was not delivered in the second 2- week period for performing the contract. On November 15, 1983, the Navy knew that Darwin had performed 65 percent of the work in an acceptable manner, and there was no evidence to suggest that the contractor was financially unable to complete the remainder of the work.

The Navy knew that renewed performance could not begin at the very earliest until August 1984, and therefore, the Navy had no basis for concluding that Darwin's late performance in November 1983 would still be a viable cause for delay in August 1984—9 months later.

The failure of Darwin to complete the work on time did not interfere with the Navy's use of the building, which was still used for the production of explosives since Darwin had restored the building into usable condition. Darwin contemplated working from December 27 through December 31, 1983, having estimated that the remaining work could be completed in 4 days. There was no urgency associated with the contract.

When the contract was terminated on February 3, 1984, the Navy estimated the next available date when the remaining work could be completed as August 1984, but by the date of the hearing, this hoped-for completion date had regressed to January 1985.

At the time Darwin was performing work on the contract, many other construction contracts were being performed at the same ordnance station, and the Navy was content to collect liquidated damages for those contracts in which performance had been delayed.

Although needed material was delivered by October 4, 1983, Darwin did not receive Navy approval of the material until October 19, 1983. At that time, Darwin submitted a written request for a time extension on account of that delay. The Board found that there was no evidence in the record that the contracting officer had acted on that request as required by General Provision 5 of the contract, entitled "Termination for Default—Damages for Delay—Time Extension." With respect to the default termination, the Board observed that "this termination for default exudes an odor piscatorial," citing Alinco Life Insurance Co. v. United States, 373 F.2d 336, 341, 178 Ct.Cl. 813 (1967).

Accordingly, the Board converted the default termination into one for the convenience of the Government.

On the basis of the Government's motion for reconsideration, the Board reversed its initial decision and upheld the termination for default. Darwin Constr. Co., ASBCA No. 29340, 86-2 BCA ¶18,959 (1986).

In reversing its decision on reconsideration, the Board, at the Government's urging, noted that the Board should recognize and follow the decision in Kalvar Corp. v. United States, 543 F.2d 1298, 211 Ct.Cl. 192 (1976), cert. denied, 434 U.S. 830, 98 S.Ct. 112, 54 L.Ed.2d 89 (1977), in which the court held that "well-nigh irrefragable proof" is required to induce the court to abandon the presumption of good faith dealing by public officials.

* * *

DISCUSSION

I.

Darwin accepts all of the findings of fact made by the Board in its initial decision. However, Darwin contends that the Board erred as a matter of law in holding that it could not inquire into the motives or judgment of the contracting officer in electing to terminate the contract for default, once the Government determined that the contractor was in technical default. We agree that this rule of administrative restraint is legally erroneous and contrary to long-established judicial precedent as hereinafter set forth. Moreover, the Board's holding is a ruling on a question of law, which is neither final nor binding on the court. Zinger Construction Co. v. United States, 807 F.2d 979, 981 (Fed.Cir.1986), citing American Electronic Laboratories, Inc. v. United States, 774 F.2d 1110, 1112 (Fed.Cir.1985).

II.

As stated above, the Board found that the termination for default was "arbitrary and capricious because it was evident to the Board that the default action was taken solely to rid the Navy of having to deal with Darwin." On the basis of that finding we hold that the Board's decision on reconsideration is squarely in conflict with Schlesinger v. United States, 390 F.2d 702, 709, 182 Ct.Cl. 571 (1968).

The Board's finding that the contracting officer abused his discretion provides the legal predicate for converting the termination for default into one for the convenience of the Government. As the court pointed out in Schlesinger, the default article of the contract does not require the Government to terminate on a finding of default, but merely gives the procuring agency the discretion to do so, and that discretion must be reasonably exercised. Id. at 709, 182 Ct.Cl. 571. The facts of the case before us are almost identical to the salient facts in Schlesinger, where it was found that the contractor's status of technical default served only "as a useful pretext for taking the action found necessary on other grounds unrelated to the plaintiff's performance or to the propriety of the extension of time." Id. Because of the remarkable similarity in the facts, we quote the following from Schlesinger:

> As in John A. Johnson Contracting Corp. [v. United States], supra, the Navy used the termination article as a "device" and never made a "judgment as to the merits of the case". 132 F.Supp. [698] at 705, 132 Ct.Cl. [645] at 659-660 [1955]. Such abdication of responsibility we have always refused to sanction where there is administrative discretion under a contract. New York Shipbuilding Corp. v. United States, 385 F.2d 427, 435, 436-437, 180 Ct.Cl. 446, 460 (June 1967), and cases cited. This protective rule should have special application for a default-termination which has the drastic consequence of leaving the contractor without any further compensation. See Acme Process Equip. Co. v. United States, 347 F.2d 509, 527, 528, 171 Ct.Cl. 324, 355 (1965) rev'd on other grounds, 385 U.S. 138, 87 S.Ct. 350, 17 L.Ed.2d 249 (1966).

Id.

In a recent decision, Quality Environment Systems v. United States, 7 Cl.Ct. 428, 432 (1985), the Claims Court relied on the Schlesinger decision. The court held that if it was determined that a default decision represented an abuse of discretion, the contractual remedy would be to convert the termination into one for the convenience of the Government.

Accordingly, we hold as the court held in Schlesinger that the Board's decision on reconsideration must be reversed and the case remanded with instructions for the Board to reinstate its initial decision in which the default termination was converted into one for the convenience of the Government.

III.

The Government has made only one argument as the basis for affirmance of the Board's decision. The Government asserts that since Darwin failed to demonstrate with "well-nigh irrefragable proof" that the Navy's default termination of the contract was exercised in bad faith, the termination was proper. In support of its contention, the Government cites Kalvar Corp. v. United States, 543 F.2d 1298, 1301-02, 211 Ct.Cl. 192 (1976), cert. denied, 434 U.S. 830, 98 S.Ct. 112, 54 L.Ed.2d 89 (1977), and Knotts v. United States, 121 F.Supp. 630, 636, 128 Ct.Cl. 489 (1954).

In view of the Board's unequivocal finding that the contracting officer's default decision was arbitrary and capricious, we reject the Government's argument on several grounds.

* * *

Thus, these decisions of the Court of Claims and the Claims Court make it abundantly clear that when a contractor persuades a court to find that the contracting officer's default decision was arbitrary or capricious, or that it represents an abuse of his discretion, the decision will be set aside. There is nothing in these decisions to support the Government's contention that the aggrieved contractor must add another layer of proof by demonstrating that the decision was also made in bad faith.

IV.

Although neither party has referred to them, we find that the Armed Services Procurement Regulations (ASPR) in effect at the time the contract was terminated are pertinent here and lend further support to our decision. ASPR 18-618, entitled "Termination of Fixed-Price Construction Contracts for Default," 32 C.F.R., Parts 1 to 39, Volume III, revised as of July 1, 1983, provided as follows:

18-618.4 Procedure in Case of Default.

(a) The contracting officer shall consider the following factors in determining whether to terminate a contract for default:

(i) the provisions of the contract and applicable laws and regulations;

(ii) the specific failure of the contractor and excuses, if any, made by the contractor for such failure;

(iii) the period of time which would be required for the Government or another contractor to complete the work as compared to the time required for completion by the delinquent contractor;

(iv) the effect of a termination for default on the ability of the contractor to liquidate guaranteed loans, progress payments, or advance payments; and

(v) any other pertinent facts and circumstances.

It is clear from the findings made in the Board's initial decision that the contracting officer failed to comply with the provisions of 18-618.4(a)(iii), because the Board, in its initial decision, made the following findings of fact:

As for the material delay, the Board is convinced that by 19 December, the material delay had ceased; by 3 February, we are morally certain there was no shortage and by August 1984 the Board is persuaded that the Navy would concede that the contractor could have had all the material needed to complete this contract. Therefore, the Navy, knowing that renewed performance could only begin at the earliest in August 1984, had no basis for concluding that the delay causing Darwin's late performance in November would still be a viable cause of delay in August, nine months later.

84-3 BCA at 88,150.

This and other Board findings set forth in the BACKGROUND portion of this opinion show that when the contract was terminated on February 13, 1984, the Navy knew that if another contractor were selected, it could not begin work until August of 1984 at the earliest, and that if Darwin had been allowed to do so, it could have completed the work in August 1984, at least as soon as and probably much sooner than a successor contractor could have performed the unfinished work.

Notes and Questions

1. On first reading, this seems like an easy case, with the contractor completely right and the government completely wrong. After all, how many times does a court say that government action gives out an "odor piscatorial"? However, it is worth understanding the government's side. Note that the government won in the ASBCA on rehearing. The very fact that the government so forcefully sought rehearing shows the level of its interests at stake. Putting aside why the Navy did what it did, did Darwin commit a failure of performance sufficient for it to lose a trial as to termination for default? Did Darwin

have a sufficient excuse to win a trial as to termination for default? So, who does the case put on trial?

2. Look at other sanctioning cases brought by the government; for example, can criminal defendants put the police or the prosecutors on trial for their exercise of discretion in proceeding against them when they committed the offense charged and have no adequate excuse? In a civil proceeding regarding taxpayers who fail to pay their taxes without excuse, can they put the IRS on trial? For all the satisfaction it gives to see citizens vindicated, what would happen to the enforcement of the criminal and tax codes if the defendants could put the government on trial? And if the government stops functioning, does that benefit anyone, even the contractors?

3. Something else the case illustrates: how contractors see termination for default. Look at what Darwin was willing to do to avoid it: work intensely the week between Christmas and New Year's.

4. Note how the government fights tenaciously to maintain the standard that assailing the exercise of discretion requires proof of bad faith, and that such proof must be "well nigh irrefragable." How different is the standard set forth in this case? Does it matter much what the standard is? First imagine that as a contractor's attorney, you have the awesome burden of proving government bad faith. It seems hard, with the government officers who conspired to injure your client presumably being clever enough to leave no evidence around. Then imagine that as a government official, when you terminate for default you must face Freedom of Information Act document demands, subpoenas, depositions, and comparisons with other cases to get at you any way the contractor can. The contractor might have large financial resources for this fight, while your own short-staffed office expects you to get on with the rest of your work. Now who feels the awesome burden? Both sides feel much is at stake in these cases.

McDONNELL DOUGLAS CORPORATION, Plaintiff-Cross Appellant, et al., v. UNITED STATES, Defendant-Appellant.

Nos. 98-5096, 98-5122, 98-5123. United States Court of Appeals, Federal Circuit. 182 F.3d 1319., July 1, 1999.

Before MAYER, Chief Judge, MICHEL and CLEVENGER, Circuit Judges.

CLEVENGER, Circuit Judge.

This dispute arises out of the government's default termination of a contract between the United States Navy and defense contractors McDonnell Douglas Corporation and General Dynamics Corporation ("Contractors") to develop a carrier-based, low-observable "stealth" aircraft known as the A-12 Avenger. After several years of litigation, the United States Court of Federal Claims held that the government's termination of the contract for default could not be sustained because the government did not exercise the requisite discretion before entering a default termination, see McDonnell Douglas Corp. v. United States, 35 Fed. Cl. 358, 368-71 (1996) (hereinafter McDonnell Douglas IV), and converted the termination for default into a termination for convenience, awarding Contractors costs totaling $3,877,767,376. See McDonnell Douglas Corp. v. United States, 40 Fed. Cl. 529, 555-56 (1998) (hereinafter McDonnell Douglas IX). We hold that, because the termination for default was predicated on contract-related issues, it was within the discretion of the government. Accordingly, the Court of Federal

Claims' conversion of the termination for default into a termination for convenience was in error. We reverse the trial court's judgment and remand the case to the trial court for a determination of whether the government's default termination was justified, an issue upon which we express or intimate no view.

I

A

In 1984, the Department of the Navy introduced the Advanced Tactical Aircraft Program, known as the A-12 program, to develop a carrier-based stealth aircraft for the Navy. In January 1988, Contractors entered into a Full Scale Engineering Development contract (the "A-12 FSD Contract") with the government to produce eight FSD aircraft at a target price of $4,379,219,436. See McDonnell Douglas IV, 35 Fed. Cl. at 361. The contract was structured as an incrementally funded, fixed-price incentive contract with a ceiling price of $4,777,330,294, and recited a schedule of installment payments over the five- year term of the contract. The first aircraft was originally scheduled to be delivered in June 1990, and subsequent aircraft were to be delivered each month through January 1991. See id. at 361-62.

From the outset, Contractors encountered difficulties in performing the contract. Particular problems included meeting the contract schedule and keeping the aircraft weight within specifications. ***

In June 1990, Contractors informed the Navy that they could not meet the contract schedule, that the cost of completing the contract would substantially exceed the ceiling price, and that Contractors could not absorb the loss that would result from the contract. Contractors asserted that a fundamental problem with the FSD contract was its structure as a fixed-price contract and proposed that the contract be modified. Thereafter, Contractors submitted a proposal to change the contract schedule, but the Navy and Contractors failed to reach an agreement on that issue. Instead, on August 17, 1990, the Navy unilaterally issued a contract modification that changed the delivery schedule for the aircraft. Under this modification, the delivery date of the first aircraft was delayed until December 1991, and the remaining aircraft became due periodically between February 1992 and February 1993. See Contract Modification P00046 ¶ 1(b), Joint Appendix at 15,657.

In November 1990, Contractors submitted a formal request to the Navy to restructure the contract as a cost-reimbursement type contract. ***

During the Secretary's briefing to the President of the United States in early December 1990, the Secretary indicated his disappointment with the Navy's handling of the A-12 program and promised to take appropriate actions. On December 3, the Secretary directed the Deputy Secretary of Defense to review and report on the status of the A-12 program within ten days. This resulted in several meetings by the Defense Acquisition Board and Defense Procurement Review Boards. In addition, on December 12, the Secretary of the Navy responded to Secretary Cheney's December 3 request with a memorandum that expressed concern about Contractors' ability and willingness to perform under the contract, and which noted in particular Contractors' belief that the government should assume responsibility for failure to meet goals under the contract, and that the government should restructure the contract. The memorandum concluded with a statement that the Navy would examine whether the contract should be terminated for default, and would make a recommendation to the Secretary by January 5, 1991. See id.

On Friday, December 14, Secretary Cheney directed the Secretary of Navy to show cause by January 4, 1991 why the A-12 program should not be terminated. The following Monday, December 17, the Navy issued a cure notice to Contractors stating that unless they were able to meet contract specifications by January 2, 1991, the government might choose to terminate the contract for default. In particular, the cure letter stated that, inter alia, Contractors had "failed to fabricate parts sufficient to permit final assembly in time to meet the schedule for delivery," and had "fail[ed] to meet specification requirements." Joint Appendix at 16,524. The letter asserted that "[t]hese conditions are endangering performance of [the] contract." Id.

High-level meetings between the responsible government personnel, including the contracting officer and the general counsels of the Department of Defense and of the Navy, and Contractors, including the Chief Executive Officers of McDonnell Douglas and General Dynamics, occurred on December 18 and 21. During these meetings, Contractors asserted that they "[c]an't get there if we don't change contract," id. at 16,533, and "[i]t has got to get reformed to a cost type contract or we cannot do it." Id. at 16,549. When asked by the government on December 21 "can you correct deficiencies to provide an aircraft that meets the requirements," Contractors replied "[a]ll deficiencies cannot be corrected. Can we deliver a satisfactory aircraft for the Navy? Mother nature won't allow correction of all defects. We'll do the best we can and the Navy has to decide if that's good enough." Id. at 16,548-49.

Contractors responded to the cure notice on January 2 by admitting that they "[would] not meet delivery schedules or certain specifications of the original contract, or the revised FSD delivery schedule." Id. at 18,175. Contractors did not contest that they had failed to fabricate parts in time to meet the delivery schedule for the FSD aircraft. Nonetheless, Contractors asserted that they were not in default because, in their view, the delivery schedules were invalid or unenforceable. See id. at 18,175-78. As suggested cure, Contractors submitted a proposal to restructure the contract, pursuant to which Contractors would absorb a $1.5 billion fixed loss on the cost overrun from the contract, the contract would be restructured to a cost reimbursement contract, and Contractors would waive their claims for equitable adjustment. Contractors proposed to restructure the contract pursuant to Pub. L. No. 85-804, which gives the President of the United States the power to authorize departments or agencies connected with national defense to grant extraordinary relief under contracts if such an action facilitates the national defense. See 50 U.S.C. § 1431 (1994).

On Saturday, January 5, Secretary Cheney met with Undersecretary of Defense for Acquisition Yockey, the Secretary of the Navy, and the Chairman of the Joint Chiefs of Staff to discuss the budget and the A-12 program. At the meeting, Secretary Cheney noted that a scheduled payment of $553 million—one of the largest installment payments under the A-12 contract—was due on Monday, January 7. Later that day, Secretary Cheney, acting under authority pursuant to Pub. L. No. 85-804, decided not to grant relief. On Sunday, January 6, Undersecretary Yockey informed Rear Admiral William R. Morris, who at this time was acting as contracting officer over the A-12 contract, that Secretary Cheney had denied 85-804 relief and that no further funds would be obligated under the A-12 program. The next day, Admiral Morris issued the termination letter to Contractors stating that the government was terminating the A-12 contract due to Contractors' default.

B

On February 5, 1991, the Navy sent a letter to Contractors demanding the return of approximately $1.35 billion in unliquidated progress payments under the terminated contract. On June 7, Contractors filed suit in the United States Court of Federal Claims under the Contract Disputes Act, 41 U.S.C. §609(a) (1994), requesting that the court: (1) grant their equitable adjustment claims dated December 31, 1990, (2) convert the government's termination for default into a termination for convenience, (3) deny the government's demand for return of progress payments, (4) award Contractors costs and a reasonable profit under the contract, (5) award them settlement expenses, and (6) award damages for breach of contract. See McDonnell Douglas Corp. v. United States, 25 Cl.Ct. 342, 346 (1992).

After several years of litigation in the Court of Federal Claims, that court ruled, in a decision dated April 8, 1996, that the government's default termination was invalid according to Schlesinger v. United States, 182 Ct.Cl. 571, 390 F.2d 702 (Cl.Ct.1968). See McDonnell Douglas IV, 35 Fed. Cl. at 368-71. The trial court held that under Schlesinger, the government is required to exercise "reasoned discretion" before terminating a contract for default, and that the government failed to meet this requirement because the Secretary of Defense's actions effectively forced the Navy to terminate the A-12 contract for default. See id. at 369-71. Therefore, the trial court vacated the government's termination for default and converted it into a termination for convenience. See id. at 361. * * * *

II

The level of discretion that must be exercised by the government before terminating a contract for default is a question of law, which we review de novo. See Darwin Constr. Co. v. United States, 811 F.2d 593, 596 (Fed.Cir.1987); Barseback Kraft AB v. United States, 121 F.3d 1475, 1479 (Fed.Cir.1997). We will upset the trial court's factual findings, however, only if they are clearly erroneous. See, e.g., Bass Enters. Prod. Co. v. United States, 133 F.3d 893, 895 (Fed.Cir.1998).

A

The trial court held that the government's termination of the A-12 contract did not comport with the rule laid down in Schlesinger by the United States Court of Claims, our predecessor court, for a proper default termination. Schlesinger involved a cap manufacturer who won a contract to supply the Navy with 50,000 service caps for enlisted men. The contract required the manufacturer to submit pre-production samples of component materials, as well as two samples of the completed cap, to the government for approval prior to production. In addition, the contract included a delivery schedule which set forth delivery dates for five separate installments of the completed caps. See Schlesinger, 390 F.2d at 703-04. Schlesinger did not submit the two sample caps and certain thread for pre-production approval, perhaps because he had fulfilled a contract for 240,000 identical Navy caps the previous year. Schlesinger also failed to deliver the first installment of caps as specified in the delivery schedule. See id. At the time, Schlesinger was also a prime suspect in an ongoing United States Senate subcommittee investigation regarding textile procurement irregularities within the military. Indeed, Schlesinger testified before the subcommittee during the pendency of his supply contract; shortly after his testimony, the chairman of the subcommittee sent a letter to the Navy implying that Schlesinger's contract should be terminated. This information was communicated to the contracting officer, who promptly terminated Schlesinger's contract. See id. at 705-06.

The Court of Claims held that the default termination of Schlesinger's contract was illegal. In doing so, the court first found that Schlesinger was indeed technically in default under the terms of the contract. See id. at 706-07. However, the court determined that neither the contracting officer nor anyone else in the Navy exercised independent judgment in terminating the contract for default. See id. at 707-08 (citing John A. Johnson Contracting Corp. v. United States, 132 Ct.Cl. 645, 132 F.Supp. 698, 704-05 (1955)). Thus, the court found that the contractor's "bare" or "technical" default "served only as a useful pretext for the taking of action felt to be necessary on other grounds unrelated to the [contractor's] performance...." Id. at 709.

The illegality in Schlesinger stemmed from the Navy's reliance on contractor default as a pretext to terminate its relationship with the contractor, independent of the state of actual performance under the contract. The court characterized Schlesinger's performance shortcomings as merely a "technical default" or "bare default," id. at 707, 708, and emphasized the Navy's total failure to consider the level of performance once it found a means for terminating by default. See, e.g., id. at 708 ("[T]he Navy acted as if it had no option but to terminate for default...once the mere fact of non- delivery was found."). In Schlesinger, it was improper for the Navy to terminate the contractor for default due solely to pressure from a congressional oversight committee because this ground for termination was totally unrelated to contract performance.

In short, Schlesinger bars only a termination for default in which there is no considered nexus between the default termination and the contractor's performance under the contract. * * *

A third case cited to us by Contractors, Darwin Construction Co. v. United States, 811 F.2d 593 (Fed.Cir.1987), further confirms the rule identified above. In Darwin, we adopted the Armed Services Board of Contract Appeals's finding that "the default action was taken solely to rid the Navy of having to deal with Darwin." Id. at 596 (internal quotation marks omitted). Thus, we held that the government used Darwin's technical default as a mere pretext for terminating the contract on grounds unrelated to performance. See id. Furthermore, Darwin clarifies what is meant by the "reasonable discretion" test used in Schlesinger and Johnson. In Darwin, we stated that, although a contracting officer has discretion with respect to contract termination, a termination for default will be set aside if it is arbitrary or capricious, or constitutes an abuse of the contracting officer's discretion. See id. at 598. When there is no nexus between the decision to terminate for default and contract performance, as was true in Darwin, Schlesinger, and Johnson, the termination for default may be arbitrary and capricious and set aside in favor of a termination for convenience.

Properly understood, then, Schlesinger and its progeny merely stand for the proposition that a termination for default that is unrelated to contract performance is arbitrary and capricious, and thus an abuse of the contracting officer's discretion. This proposition itself is but part of the well established law governing abuse of discretion by a contracting official. See, e.g., United States Fidelity & Guaranty Co. v. United States, 230 Ct.Cl. 355, 676 F.2d 622, 630 (1982) (listing four factors to be used in determining if conduct by a government official is arbitrary and capricious: (1) evidence of subjective bad faith on the part of the government official, (2) whether there is a reasonable, contract-related basis for the official's decision, (3) the amount of discretion given to the official, and (4) whether the official violated an applicable statute or regulation).

B

The record shows that the government's default termination was not pretextual or unrelated to Contractors' alleged inability to fulfill their obligations under the contract.

Therefore, unlike the cases cited above, the government's decision to terminate the A-12 FSD Contract for default was related to contract performance, and the Court of Federal Claims erred by converting the termination into one for convenience without first addressing the question of breach.

* * *

More importantly, however, the record demonstrates that the government properly terminated the A-12 program for reasons related to contract performance. Admiral Morris, the contracting officer, testified at length about his decisional process that led to the termination for alleged default. He thought that he had three choices: to terminate for convenience, to terminate for default, or to do nothing. He rejected the latter as "irresponsible," thus focusing his attention on the other two choices. He eliminated the termination for convenience first, because he believed Contractors to be in material breach of the contract. This was so, in his words, because, as conceded in Contractors' response to the cure notice:

> They were in default because they acknowledged they would not be able to achieve the contract specifications and the contract requirements. Two, they had indicated that they would not be able to meet the delivery schedule that was currently in the contract. And three, they would not be able to perform the contract without extraordinary relief or additional funding for the contract. So they basically said they can't perform under the contract and they were in default of it.

Joint Appendix at 3,898-99. In further elaboration of his decision, again in the context of Contractors' response to the cure notice, Admiral Morris testified as to why he thought Contractors' default was material:

> They had failed to fabricate parts so as to endanger performance of the contract, and in my judgment, as would relate to the production options, failed to make progress, and it was clear to me that is where they stood on the 7th of January when I terminated the contract for default.

Id. at 3,917. As to why a termination for convenience was inappropriate, Admiral Morris stated that:

> [B]ecause I felt very strongly that as a result of the contractors' default, it would be nothing short of unconscionable for me to put the burden of the contractors' failure to make progress and the contractors' failure to fabricate parts, so as to endanger performance of the contract, put that burden on the government and the taxpayer to reimburse all costs and to pay the contractors a profit for their failures.

Id. at 3,920. Therefore, Admiral Morris terminated the contract for failure to make progress and for failure to meet contract requirements.

Failure to meet contract specifications and inability to meet the contract delivery schedule are of course relevant considerations to whether a contractor is in default. * * *

The trial court also found that Secretary Cheney denied extraordinary relief, which led to the termination, because of concerns about the A-12 program's "cost and schedule." McDonnell Douglas IV, 35 Fed. Cl. at 372. The cost to complete a contract—more particularly, the inability of a contractor to perform a contract at the specified contract price—and the ability to meet a contract schedule are both fundamental elements of government contracts and are related to contract performance; as such, they are highly relevant to the question of default.

The government had specific concerns about when—and if—the A-12 aircraft would ever be delivered and how much it would cost. Secretary Cheney stated in testimony before Congress that the A-12 program was terminated because "no one could tell me how much the program was going to cost even just through the full-scale development phase or when it would be available. Data that had been presented at one point a few months ago turned out to be invalid and inaccurate." Hearings on National Defense Authorization Act for Fiscal Years 1992 and 1993—H.R. 2100 and Oversight of Previously Authorized Programs Before the House Comm. on Armed Servs., 102nd Cong. 60 (1991) (statement of Richard Cheney, Secretary of Defense). The evidence in the record demonstrates that the Secretary of Defense denied relief under Pub. L. 85-804, and Admiral Morris chose to terminate the contract for default, for reasons related to Contractors' state of performance of the contract. The trial court emphasized that although Contractors failed to meet the aircraft weight limit, the Navy essentially waived this requirement because the overweight aircraft would still meet all operational requirements. See McDonnell Douglas IV, 35 Fed. Cl. at 363, 376. However, although that finding is relevant to the ultimate determination of whether Contractors were in breach, or whether a breach was excused, it is insufficient to show, in light of all the other evidence in the record, that the government terminated the contract for reasons wholly unrelated to contract performance.

We think it clear beyond any doubt that Admiral Morris, unlike the contracting officer in Schlesinger, or in other cases that have upset terminations for default for lack of nexus to contract performance behavior, made his choice for reasons related to contract performance. Admiral Morris certainly knew that Contractors took another view of events transpiring during contract performance: although they admitted that they could not perform the contract according to its terms, they felt that the fault for their failure should be laid at the government's feet. Admiral Morris meant not to take away the right of Contractors to assert their defenses to termination for default, he instead only meant to assert the government's right to allege material breach on the record of contract performance that had been laid before him by Contractors themselves. Given the reasons stated for the action taken by the contracting officer in this case, it was legal error for the trial court to see these facts as commanding conversion of the termination for default into one for the convenience of the government.

To summarize, the government may not use default as a pretext for terminating a contract for reasons unrelated to performance; instead, there must be a nexus between the government's decision to terminate for default and the contractor's performance. The record and the facts found by the trial court establish that the government denied additional funding for the A-12 program and terminated the contract for default because of concerns about contract specifications, contract schedule, and price—factors that are fundamental elements of contract performance. Therefore, the trial court erred by vacating the termination for default without first determining whether a default existed. On remand, if the government can establish that Contractors were in default, then the termination for default would be valid. See Lisbon Contractors, Inc. v. United States, 828 F.2d 759, 765 (Fed.Cir.1987) (holding that the government bears the burden of proof with respect to the issue of whether termination for default was justified). Conversely, if the government is not able to make this showing, then the default termination was invalid and Contractors would be entitled to a suitable recovery, presumably under a termination for convenience theory.

CONCLUSION

We reverse the trial court's ruling that the government's default termination of the A-12 FSD Contract must be converted into a termination for convenience because the government did not exercise the necessary discretion. Of course, we do not hold today that the government's default termination is justified. As Contractors correctly point out, they have never been found to be in default of the contract. Because the trial court focused on the legitimacy of the government's default termination decision, rather than on whether Contractors were in fact in default, the parties have not yet been afforded the opportunity to fully litigate default. See McDonnell Douglas Corp. and General Dynamics Corp. v. United States, No. 91-1204C, slip op. at 2 (Fed. Cl. June 17, 1993). If the government fails to establish at trial that Contractors were in default under the contract, then the government's default termination would be improper and Contractors could rightfully recover damages under the theory of a termination for convenience. ***

Notes and Questions

1. The *McDonnell Douglas* opinion reviews the key cases regarding pressure to terminate - *Schlesinger, Johnson,* and *Darwin.* It establishes as a standard that the decision to terminate for default need only have a "nexus" to or be "predicated on" contract-related issues for validity, as contrasted with being "pretextual" or "wholly unrelated" to the contract. Assume that frequently there will be considerable pressure to terminate for default for a variety of reasons, some of which, like agency budgets, or another contractor's superior connections, are not contract- or performance-related. Does this opinion establish as a standard that unless the decision to terminate is wholly the result of pressure and is completely pretextual, that decision is valid?

2. This opinion notes tersely that on Sunday, January 6, the contracting officer, Rear Admiral Morris, found out that the A-12 program would have no further funds, and the next day, he issued the termination letter. The trial court opinion, based on extensive deposition testimony by the officials, described that sequence more fully, under the heading "Monday Morning Rush." Morris told his Navy counsel on Sunday to prepare the termination memorandum the next day, which she did, editing a termination memorandum for another aircraft, but adding little regarding the A-12 because she had little information at her disposal. She did not even consult with Morris, nor with key others, about the basis for termination. This was part of why the trial court had considered the long-standing defaults, as mere excuses.

Does it shock you to hear that the role of a government contracts attorney consists of revising a model in this way? Would you look forward to being deposed about how you prepare documents?

3. For an important analysis of this issue, see Joshua I. Schwartz, *Administrative Law Lessons Regarding the Role of Politically Appointed Officials in Default Terminations,* 30 Pub. Cont. L. J. 144 (2001). Professor Schwartz extensively contrasts the different concepts applied to significant decisions (like default terminations) in administrative and procurement law. He suggests that in some cases, rather than having the agency head only informally (if potently) involved as was Secretary Cheney, the agency head should formally displace the contracting officer and unambiguously take on the responsibility for the determination. Intriguingly, he also proposes that sometimes the remedy when a reviewing tribunal sets aside a default termination, for failure to consider the proper factors, should only be a remand to the agency for reconsideration rather than outright

conversion to a (much more contractor-friendly) termination for convenience. What do you think of what Professor Schwartz himself acknowledges might seem "radical proposals" but which reflect a half-century of rich administrative law precedent? Do the differences between administrative and procurement law reflect a deep structure of different policy or merely the accidents of their separate historical paths?

4. Now that the appellate court has established that the termination is valid unless pretextual, will the government be able to fend off intrusive discovery about the procedure followed? Or do terminated contractors get to pursue their claim of pretextuality all the way up the chain of command to the level of Cabinet Secretary?

5. The opinion tiptoes around the alternative models for a contracting officer. A contracting officer exercises discretion about termination for default, which can be an extraordinarily significant and sometimes highly stigmatizing decision. Is the contracting officer like a judge, for whom it is abhorrent to imagine command pressure or political influence? Or is the contracting officer part of a system that resolves not merely administrative but also political issues, and should be left to do so? A criminal defendant, or a civil defendant in a suit brought by the government, cannot raise as a defense the politics of the decision to indict or to file suit. Must a terminated contractor be able to do so?

C. Excess Reprocurement and Other Remedies

In basic (private) contract law, one of the developments of interest in recent years has been the interaction between contract clauses regarding remedies and statutory or other constraints on such clauses. For example, extensive case law has developed concerning warranties that limit the remedy for breach to "repair or replacement," or that exclude consequential damages. In government contracting law, the questions concerning intriguing remedies for breach involve the "excess costs of reprocurement." Pursuant to the FAR clause, FAR 52.249-8(b), after termination for default contracting officers may acquire supplies or services substituting for what the defaulted contractor failed to provide. Then, in appropriate circumstances, they assess the defaulting contractor for the excess costs.

Seemingly, this is a reasonable remedy. The government does not universally invoke it, even in proper terminations for default, but only in appropriate circumstances. Moreover, the contractor can challenge the excess cost reprocurement by appealing the assessment. The appeal tests several factors that constrain the government.

In fact, the remedy can be potent. A conscientious contracting officer focuses on getting the goods or services needed by the agency, and accomplishing the "mission" for the agency. If that requires paying costs that are high, or higher, or even higher, then depending on the urgency of reprocurement, the contracting officer may have to pay them. Beyond that, the contracting officer may experience multiple temptations to pay such a high price. There is no love lost between a contracting officer and a defaulting contractor. Moreover, the agency may benefit from reprocuring higher rather than lower quality, particularly if the defaulted contractor, not the agency, pays the bill. As the saying goes, contracting officers go shopping with the defaulted contractors' charge cards in their pockets.

This may seem to resemble remedies in basic (private) contracts, namely, the remedy of "cover," or buying substitute goods. However, even under the best of circumstances, government contracting occurs in situations very far from a market. Reprocurement, occurring after delays and with many transitional distractions in difficult situations, is even further from a market. Accordingly, a separate set of issues concern the appropriate relation of the excess reprocurement costs to the original bids on the original IFB or RFP.

Appeal of Fancy Industries, Inc.

Under Contract No. DLA100-81-C-2746 83-2
BCA ¶16,659 (ASBCA). June 24, 1983

OPINION BY ADMINISTRATIVE JUDGE FREEMAN

Fancy Industries, Inc. appeals an assessment of excess costs of reprocurement on the grounds that (1) a Government agreement to test a sample product six days before the contract delivery date was a waiver of that delivery date, and (2) the reprocurement was not conducted reasonably to mitigate excess costs.

FINDINGS OF FACT

1. On 6 February 1981, the Defense Personnel Support Center (DPSC) awarded Contract No. DLA100-81-C-2746 ('Contract 2746') to Fancy for the production of 139,000 yards of grey laminated cloth. The contract was formally advertised, and the contract price was $2.115 per yard.

2. Section F of the contract required production deliveries of 35,000 yards each on or before 21 June, 21 July and 20 August 1981 respectively, and a final delivery of 34,000 yards on or before 19 September 1981.

3. The contract included the SF 32 General Provisions (April 1975 edition). Clause 11 of those provisions entitled 'Default' stated in relevant part:

* * *

(b) In the event the Government terminates this contract in whole or in part as provided in paragraph (a) of this clause, the Government may procure, upon such terms and in such manner as the Contracting Officer may deem appropriate, supplies or services similar to those so terminated, and the Contractor shall be liable to the Government for any excess costs for such similar supplies or services:....

* * *

5. After award, Fancy determined that Northern Laminating could not produce the specified cloth. By letter dated 23 April 1981, Fancy requested contracting officer approval of a change in the place of performance to the Johnston-Morehouse-Dickey Co., Bethel Park, Pennsylvania.

* * *

7. Having received no response from Fancy to his request for a copy of its agreement with Johnston, the contracting officer by letter dated 13 May 1981 told Fancy that its request for a change in place of performance was a condition endangering performance of the contract, and directed Fancy to correct the condition within 10 days or face possible termination for default.

8. By letter dated 22 May 1981, Johnston told the contracting officer that it had a subcontract with Fancy to perform the work required by Contract 2746. Johnston's letter requested approval of this subcontract, and stated: 'subcontract agreements will fol-

low'. Johnston's letter also described Johnston as 'a qualified supplier', and stated that the delivery schedule would not be affected by the change in place of performance. Johnston did not at this time, nor at any time thereafter, have a written subcontract agreement with Fancy.

* * *

10. On 12 June 1981, a Mr. Long of Johnston told Mr. Yellis that the cloth sample which Mr. Stein intended to submit would not meet the Government adhesive specification requirements. He further stated that a proper adhesive would be received by Johnston on or about 15 or 16 June, and that a specification compliant cloth sample could be produced two or three days thereafter. Following this conversation, Mr. Yellis told Mr. Stein not to bring the first cloth sample for testing.

* * *

12. On 23 June 1981, Mr. Long told Mr. Yellis that Johnston's adhesive supplier had still not been able to develop the adhesive necessary to meet the Government specification for the cloth, but that Johnston was pursuing the matter because it wanted to bid on future laminated cloth contracts as a prime contractor.

13. The only material procured by Fancy for performance of Contract 2746 was 5,000 yards of base cloth and some plastic.

14. By 26 June 1981, no laminated cloth sample had been delivered by either Fancy or Johnston to the Government, and the scheduled 21 June 1981 production delivery of 35,000 yards had not been made. By telegram dated 26 June 1981, the contracting officer terminated Contract 2746 for default.

15. After terminating Contract 2746, the contracting officer determined that there was a continuing need for the cloth and that existing stocks would run out by the end of August 1981.

16. By telegram dated 11 August 1981, the contracting officer solicited five firms to reprocure the 139,000 yards of laminated cloth on Contract 2746. The solicitation set forth the identical specifications and substantially the same other terms and conditions as Contract 2746 except that the requested delivery dates, to which offerors could propose alternatives, were shortened by 30 days.

17. Before initial offers on the reprocurement solicitation were received, the Government prepared a price analysis which concluded that a reasonable price for reprocurement would be between $2.40 and $2.52 per yard. * * * * The Government analysis did not consider the prices received by DPSC for similar cloth between January 1981 and the date the analysis was made.

18. Four firms submitted initial offers in response to the reprocurement solicitation. The lowest initial offer was by Duracote Corporation at $2.49 per yard. The other initial offers were $2.62, $2.81 and $3.02 per yard. (R4, tab 11; tr. 18-19) Following receipt of initial offers, discussions with the offerors consisted of a single telegram dated 26 August 1981 by the contracting officer stating the Government's required delivery dates, and requesting that offerors reconsider their price and delivery proposals and submit best and final offers. The Government's required delivery dates stated in the telegram were 21 October, 21 November, 21 December 1983 and 21 January 1984.

19. Best and final offers were received from all four of the initial offerors by 2 September 1981. Duracote's best and final price offer remained at its initial price offer of $2.49 per yard. The other best and final price offers were $2.59, $2.81 and $3.00 per yard. On 9 September 1981, the reprocurement contract was awarded to Duracote at $2.49 per yard.

20. Duracote's offer for the same cloth in January 1981 on the solicitation for Contract 2746 had been $2.27 per yard. Between January 1981 and award of the reprocurement contract on 9 September 1981, Duracote had been awarded three other contracts by DPSC for laminated cloth similar except for color to the cloth specified in Contract 2746. The dates of award, quantity, color, and price per yard of these contracts were as follows:

Award	Quantity	Color	Price
20 Mar 81	40,000	Green	$2.20
11 June 81	40,000	Yellow	$2.267
1 Sep 81	206,000	White	$2.438

(App. exh. 1)

21. Yellow and green laminated cloth are generally more expensive to produce than grey or white laminated cloth.

22. The 139,000 yards on the reprocurement contract were delivered by Duracote within the specified time. The Government paid Duracote $51,082.50 more than it would have paid Fancy for the same cloth under Contract 2746.

23. By final decision in unilateral Modification No. P0002 to Contract 2746, the contracting officer found Fancy liable under the Default clause for excess costs of reprocurement in the amount of $51,082.50.

DECISION

It is undisputed that Fancy did not make the first production delivery of 35,000 yards of cloth by 21 June 1981 as required by Contract 2746 (findings 3, 14). This failure to make one of the several specified production deliveries was a default on the entire contract and permitted the Government to terminate the contract pursuant to paragraph (a)(i) of the Default clause. Artisan Electronics Corp. v. United States, 205 Ct. Cl. 126, 134, 499 F.2d 606, 611 (1974).

* * *

When the Government is faced with an imminent delinquency in delivery, it is not obligated to declare instantly its intent to terminate in order to exercise that right. The Government may take a reasonable time to make up its mind whether to extend or terminate the contract, and during that reasonable time it may cooperate with the delinquent contractor, by such actions as courtesy testing of production samples, without losing the right to terminate. H. N. Bailey & Associates v. United States, 196 Ct. Cl. 166, 178-82, 449 F.2d 376, 384-85 (1971).

* * *

* * * Fancy's contract was terminated six days after the first delinquency and within 11 days of the Government's first notice of probable delinquency. There were no deliveries of any kind by Fancy, and no substantial production in that 11 day period. The time taken by the Government to make up its mind to terminate was not unreasonable. The termination for default was proper. To recover its excess costs of reprocurement, the Government must show (1) that the reprocured cloth was similar to the terminated cloth, (2) that the excess costs were in fact paid, and (3) that the Government acted reasonably to mitigate the excess costs. Environmental Tectonics Corp., ASBCA No. 21204, 78- 1 BCA p12,986. Appellant does not dispute that the first two conditions were met. The specifications for the reprocurement were identical with those for the terminated contract (finding 16). The excess costs of $51,081.50 have been paid (finding 22).

We also find that the Government acted reasonably to mitigate the excess costs of reprocurement. The shortening of the delivery dates for the reprocurement contract was not unreasonable in view of the imminent shortage of cloth in stock (see finding 15). The 75 days between the termination of appellant's contract and the award of the reprocurement contract was not unreasonably long. See Tachtronic Instruments Inc., ASBCA No. 24473, 81-2 BCA p15,253 (98 days between termination and reprocurement not unreasonable); Marine Engine Specialties Corp., ASBCA No. 20807, 76-2 BCA p11,975 (75 days between termination and reprocurement not unreasonable).

The Government also acted reasonably to mitigate excess costs by securing competition for the reprocurement, awarding the reprocurement contract to the lowest offeror and confirming the reasonableness of the reprocurement price by price analysis. Appellant, however, contends that the Government should have done more. Specifically, appellant states that the contracting officer should have conducted oral price discussions to get a lower price, or at least should have required an explanation from Duracote for the 9.69% increase in its reprocurement price over its bid on the defaulted contract. We disagree.

The cases cited by appellant for the proposition that in a negotiated reprocurement there must be oral price discussions or explanations by the reprocurement contractor of any increase in its reprocurement price over its bid on the defaulted contract, involved either substantially larger increases than the 9.69% in appellant's case, or a lack of competition in the reprocurement, or a lack of cost or price analysis confirming the reasonableness of the reprocurement price. Reliance Maintenance Service, ASBCA No. 11010, 68-1 BCA p6853 (only one offer received; offer was 24% higher than price offered by same contractor on defaulted contract); Agni Engineering Co., ASBCA No. 11535, 67-1 BCA p6250 (sole source reprocurement; unit price was 40% higher than the same offeror's bid on defaulted contract); Consolidated Airborne Systems Inc. v. United States, 172 Ct. Cl. 588, 348 F.1d 941 (1965) (sole source reprocurement); The Lutz Company, GSBCA No. 2173, 68-1 BCA p6762 (competitive reprocurement and low offer was only 10% greater than same offeror's bid on defaulted contract, but no cost or price analysis explaining increase). See also Marine Engine Specialties Corp., ASBCA No. 20521, 76-1 BCA p11,891 at 56998 aff'd on recon. 76-2 BCA p12,180 (sole source reprocurement price was 25% greater than same offeror's bid on defaulted contract); T.M. Industries, ASBCA No. 21016, 77-1 BCA p12,451 (two bids on reprocurement; low bid was 34% higher than same offeror's bid on defaulted contract; no price analysis by Government); Fitzgerald Laboratories, Inc., ASBCA Nos 15205, 15594, 71-2 BCA p9029 (reprocurement price was 40% more than same offeror's bid on defaulted contract); Solar Laboratories, Inc. ASBCA No. 19957, 76-2 BCA p12,115 at 58197 (reprocurement 'essentially non-competitive'; no cost or price analysis; reprocurement prices were 24.8 to 27.1% higher than same offeror's bids on defaulted contract).

In appellant's case, five sources were solicited for the reprocurement, and four submitted offers. The second lowest offer was only 5% more than the lowest offer on the initial round and only 4% more on the best and final round. There is no evidence of any known source not being solicited. Cf. Republic Electronic Industries Corp., ASBCA Nos. 3788, 4478, 59-1 CA p2139. Award of the reprocurement contract was made to the lowest of the four offerors, and the reasonableness of the price was confirmed by price analysis. The price analysis took into account the three most recent purchases of the identical item, which had been made respectively 8 months, 12 months and 18 months before the reprocurement purchase. The analysis also took into account the relevant producer price index increases since the most recent purchase. Since recent prices of the same item were available, it was not unreasonable for the Government to omit from its analysis recent prices of similar items.

The Default clause gave the Government the right to reprocure 'in such manner as the Contracting Officer may deem appropriate'. This language did not obligate the contracting officer to reprocure in the manner most advantageous to appellant, or to do everything that might result in a lower price. It required only that he act within the broad limits of reasonableness and prudence. See H & H Manufacturing Co., v. United States, 168 Ct. Cl. 873, 883- 85 (1964). The contracting officer in appellant's case did not exceed those limits. Cf. T. M. Industries, ASBCA 21025, 77-1 BCA p12,400 (reprocurement upheld where only bid, 24.8% higher than the same contractor's bid on defaulted contract, was supported by price analysis).

The appeal is denied.

Notes and Questions

1. Imagine the contractor and the contracting officer here engage in contracting and termination as an intimate business game. Is the contractor a sleazy bluffer bent on dodging penalties for losing gambles, and the contracting officer a vigilant guardian of the taxpayers' money? Or is the contractor an enterprising market-oriented entrepreneur, and the contracting officer a hidebound bureaucratic disciplinarian relentlessly applying pain?

2. What is the relevance of the "price analysis"? Recall that in *Arrowhead Starr* case, the board of contract appeals cut back the excess costs of reprocurement for lack of competition in the reprocurement award. This opinion includes a string-cite of cases like that one. How can the government show reasonableness in an instance where it reprocures by contacting a sole source? Are you impressed by the procedures followed by the contracting officer to reprocure here?

3. Whether the contracting officer must entertain offers from the defaulted contractor on a repurchase contract has been much litigated. Hiring the defaulted contractor often does not appeal to the contracting officer, who has already been put through procedural paces to rid the procuring agency of the former awardee and now must accomplish the original contract task. While sometimes defaulted contractors cannot perform the job or lose interest in it altogether, often they consider themselves, perhaps rightly, all set to do the job, and would vastly prefer to do it than have the government pay someone else and charge that competitor's excess costs to them. Also, the defaulted contractor has tactical familiarity in bidding, from knowledge of the contract in general, and cost and pricing information in particular.

The government's duty to mitigate by limiting costs of reprocurement somewhat constrains the contracting officer's ability to exclude the defaulted contractor from a reprocurement process. A defaulting contractor's strong incentive and ability to come in with a low proposal means its participation may well limit the reprocurement's costs. So, the decisions have struck the balance that while automatic exclusion of a defaulting contractor would be an improperly automatic determination of non-responsibility, neither are such firms automatically entitled to resolicitation. (See ATA Defense Industries, Inc., B-275303 (1997), Montage, Inc., B-0277923 (1997), A.R.E. Manufacturing, B- 246161 (1992), Shelf-Stable Foods, B-218067 (1985), Jim Challinor B-218809 (1985), Introl Corp., B-210321 (1983), Ikard Manufacturing Co., B-192316 (1978), Ikard Manufacuring Co.58 Comp. Gen. 54 (1978), PRB Uniforms, Inc., 56 Comp. Gen 976 (1977)).

Cascade Pacific International, Appellant,
v. The United States, Appellee

Appeal No. 85-618. United States Court of Appeals, 773 F.2d 287.
Federal Circuit. Sept. 16, 1985.

Before BALDWIN and KASHIWA, Circuit Judges, and MILLER, Senior Circuit Judge.

JACK R. MILLER, Senior Circuit Judge.

This is an appeal by Cascade Pacific International ("CPI"), from a decision of the General Services Administration Board of Contract Appeals under the Contract Disputes Act of 1978, 41 U.S.C. ss 601-613 (1982) ("CDA"), upholding the Contracting Officer's decisions to default terminate the subject contract and to grant in part the Government's claim for breach of contract damages. We affirm.

* * *

BACKGROUND

CPI entered into a one-year fixed-price supply requirements contract with the General Services Administration ("GSA") for builders' hardware (GS-04S-23598) ("'598"), including full surface and half surface spring hinges, on July 1, 1980. The contract prices per pair of full surface spring hinges ranged from $2.125 to $2.585, and those for half surface spring hinges ranged from $2.485 to $2.545. The specification indicated that the spring hinges were required to conform to Federal Specification FF-H-116E, which mandated, inter alia, that the spring hinges be plated and have a US10 finish, that the thickness of the metal be 0.082 +/- 0.005 inches, and that the spring hinges have button tips.

II. Assessment of Damages

Under provision 11.(b) of the General Provisions of the contract (pursuant to 41 C.F.R. §1-8.707), when a contractor defaults, the Government "may procure, upon such terms and in such manner as the Contracting Officer may deem appropriate, supplies... [the same or] similar to those so terminated, and the Contractor shall be liable to the Government for any excess costs for such similar supplies." See also 41 C.F.R. §1-8.602-6, FPR 1-8.602-6, to the same effect. Section 11.(f) can reasonably be read to permit the Government to proceed against a Contractor under other than specific contractual remedies, including the common law cause of action for breach of contract damages (hereafter "damages"). Rumley, 285 F.2d at 777; see supra note 5. This is not contested by CPI.

CPI contends, however, that excess reprocurement costs were improperly assessed by GSA and that the sua sponte imposition of damages rather than excess costs requested by the Government violates CPI's procedural due process right to sufficient notice of the charges, under either the CDA or the Federal Claims Collection Act of 1966 ("FCCA").

To uphold the board's decision to impose a monetary assessment against CPI, we must conclude that CPI received adequate notice of the possibility of the imposition of damages from the proceedings before the board and that the board correctly imposed damages; or, alternatively, that even though the board erroneously imposed damages, the Government adequately demonstrated its entitlement to excess reprocurement costs.

A. Excess Costs or Damages

The measure of damages is the reasonable reprocurement price less the original contract price. Marley v. United States, 423 F.2d 324, 333 (Ct.Cl.1970); Rumley, 285 F.2d at 777; J. Calimari and J. Perillo, Contracts 547 (2d ed. 1977). In contrast, excess reprocurement costs may be imposed only when the Government meets its burden of persuasion that the following conditions (factual determinations) are met: (1) the reprocured supplies are the same as or similar to those involved in the termination; (2) the Government actually incurred excess costs; and (3) the Government acted reasonably to minimize the excess costs resulting from the default. 41 C.F.R. s 1-8.602-6(a), FPR 1-8.602-6(a); Astro-Space Laboratories, Inc. v. United States, 470 F.2d 1003, 1018 (Ct.Cl.1972); Environmental Tectonics Corp. v. United States, 78-1 BCA P 12,986 (ASBCA 1978); Solar Laboratories, Inc. v. United States, 76-2 BCA P 12,115 (ASBCA 1976). The first condition is demonstrated by comparing the item reprocured with the item specified in the original contract. Environmental Tectonics Corp., 78-1 BCA at 63,308. The second condition requires the Government to show what it spent in reprocurement. Fairfield Scientific Corp. v. United States, 611 F.2d 854, 863-66 (Ct.Cl.1979). The third condition requires that the Government act within a reasonable time of the default, use the most efficient method of reprocurement, obtain a reasonable price, and mitigate its losses. Astro-Space Laboratories, Inc., 470 F.2d at 1018; Environmental Tectonics Corp., 78-1 BCA at 63,308, 63,309-10; Solar Laboratories, Inc., 76-2 BCA at 58,195-96.

The board concluded that condition (2) was not met by GSA because it failed to introduce the reprocurement contract with Mallin, and states that there was inadequate information on condition (3). Also, CPI argues that the Mallin spring hinges failed to satisfy condition (1). It asserts that since the Mallin spring hinges did not perform under testing equal to or better than its spring hinges, reprocurement of Mallin spring hinges would not fulfill the condition that the reprocured spring hinges meet the requirements of the contract. We considered this argument earlier and deem it meritless because Mallin spring hinges offered to GSA were plated and otherwise met the requirements of the specifications.

We disagree with the board that GSA failed to meet condition (2), but we agree that without introduction of the follow-on contract, the board did not have sufficient evidence to make a finding on condition (3). Therefore, the board was correct in declining to assess excess costs of reprocurement against CPI.

With respect to the assessment of damages, we are persuaded that the board's conclusion that "[t]here is ample evidence in this record from which we may conclude that the price of the substituted performance, as measured by the prices the Government would have paid under Mallin's successor requirements contract, was reasonable." 84-2 BCA at 86,483. The evidence includes a Lawrence Brothers catalogue cut showing a spring hinge (not necessarily possessing a US10 finish), six competitors' bids, including that of Mallin for its plated spring hinges, and CPI's own bid prices, which were more than its original bid by an average of about $1.25 per pair. The board correctly reduced the Government's claim to reflect the true number of pairs of spring hinges reprocured.

Notes and Questions

1. What are the specific standards for excess reprocurement costs? What is the reason for each? Why would the government not introduce the follow-on contract? As in *Darwin* and *McDonnell Douglas*, so, too, in the excess reprocurement cases, the defaulted

contractor would much rather be critiquing the government that having to defend its own conduct.

2. What is the difference between excess reprocurement costs and assessment of damages? Recall the difference in the basic (private) contract law between the general measure of damages for breach by seller (market price minus contract price), and the "cover" measure of damages (cover price paid by buyer minus contract price).

D. Termination for Convenience

Termination for default can occur only if the contractor sufficiently fails to do its job. However, contracting officers may have other reasons for wishing to cancel, quite without any contractor default. They may no longer want or need what they previously thought: the classic example is the munitions contract no longer needed because of the war's end. The funding expected from the budget process may not be there. Something better may have come along. Or, the agency may be dissatisfied with the contractor, but for reasons insufficient to terminate for default. In each government contract, the government includes a clause to let it cancel in such situations: the termination for convenience clause.

The materials here treat termination for convenience in two stages. First, its ordinary operation deserves examination. The clause itself explains with unusual lucidity how the termination process works, and one case, the *Rhen* case, illustrates how issues get resolved over the scale of what the government owes the terminated contractor: From the government's perspective, the process involves an orderly wind-up of the contract, dealing with such matters as the announcement of the termination, handling work in progress and government property, and settling with subcontractors. From the contractor's perspective, the process's best part consists of the level of payment to which the government agrees, which is much more generous than in termination for default.

In a termination for default, the government merely pays for the value of what it got, which may be very little. In a termination for convenience, the government agrees to make the contractor whole. That may give the contractor's lawyer an opportunity to do well by her client, for there is considerable room for discussion and for the exercise of discretion in settling such a termination. Moreover, the termination clause itself anticipates that the contractor will play a large role in settlement.

Second, the grounds for contesting a termination for convenience, encapsulated in the *Krygoski* opinion, deserve some notice. The issue of the grounds for contesting a termination for convenience is not nearly of the practical value of the issue of the grounds for contesting a termination for default. Contractors contest few terminations for convenience, and succeed in even fewer such contests. Rather, this examination gets at what termination for convenience illuminates about some of the fundamentals of government contracting. Convenience termination represents a major difference between basic (private) contracting, where the parties would generally have no such unilateral power to cancel and to resolve the damage issues in such a way, and government contracting. Does convenience termination exist as a demonstration of absolute sovereign will by which the government has simply decided to make sure that it always holds a trump card over the contractor, regardless of whether this makes either economic sense or accords with fairness? Or does convenience termination have more limited purposes and, if so, accompanying checks? As in many other contexts of government power in government contracting, a tradeoff has to be made between the desirability of encouraging government officers to make contracting decisions to effectuate government policy without undue hindrance, and the drive, by private parties, to interest courts and boards in establishing checks on economic inefficiency or on alleged misuse of official power.

For further discussion of the subjects of this section, see: Graeme S. Henderson, *Terminations for Convenience and the Termination Costs Clause*, 53 A.F.L. Rev. 103 (2002); Joseph D. West, *Practical Advice Concerning the Federal Government's Termination for Convenience Clause*, 17-OCT Construction Law. 26 (1997); Frederick W. Claybrook, Jr., *Good Faith in the Termination and Formation of Federal Contracts*, 56 Md. L. Rev. 555 (1997); Michael D. Garson, Krygoski *and the Termination for Convenience: Have Circumstances Really Changed?*, 27 Pub. Cont. L.J. 117 (1997); William H. Murphy, *Applying G&A Costs to Termination Settlement Expenses and Subcontract Settlements*, 33 Procurement Law., Spring 1998, at 13.

1. Operation

Given the unusual clarity of the Termination for Convenience Clause, one way to describe the termination process is simply to go through the clause, provision by provision. Accordingly, it is suggested that this discussion be read simultaneously with looking at the text of the clause, which follows it. First, this discussion goes through the whole process, from notice (provision (a)) to records retention (provision (n)). Then, the discussion zeroes in on the part of greatest interest, the formula for what the government pays the terminated contractor (provisions (f) and (g)).

Termination begins with the Contracting Officer "delivering to the Contractor a Notice of Termination specifying the extent of termination and the effective date" (provision (a)). This contrasts starkly with Termination for Default: there is no ten day "show cause" period, and no required explanation of "why." The procedures that follow do not exist for explaining or disputing reasons, only for giving the directions for an orderly wind-up. That might seem Kafkaesque in its unexplained nature, and, no doubt, contractors may often have strong reactions of baffled dismay. However, the government's lack of necessity to explain, or to provide procedural due process, springs from the normatively colorless nature of the action. The government is simply exercising its reserved rights. It makes no judgment about the contractor, and what it does should not affect a contractor's record and good standing. When the Notice specifies "the extent of termination," it alludes to the distinction between total and partial terminations. The government may terminate less than a whole contract, while at the same time reducing the work more than by a mere "change." A reduction that would not warrant treatment as a partial termination is called a "deductive change."

Upon receiving the notice, the terminated contractor has a series of winding up obligations laid out in numbered subparts of provision (b). The wind-up obligation list must deal with the range of very different scenarios for termination for convenience. Imagine three different scenarios, each of which makes different aspects of winding-up matter more. Start with a scenario in which (1) the government simply no longer needs the work, like the prime contract to develop a new aircraft, still at the initial stages of hiring subcontractors for research on component systems, for which the funds did not materialize as expected. That requires a quick, hopefully inexpensive wind-up. Then, imagine (2) a general contractor deep in working on a government project when rumors of its insolvency come in. The government decides to terminate the contract partially, shifting what it can to a definitely solvent contractor and having the potentially bankrupt one stay with the part that is hard to shift. Finally, imagine (3) a contractor that is doing something vital, like supplying a key component for an important new missile, and the military service just decides to switch the work to another, bigger contractor. The Contracting Officer's chief concern is full speed continuation, just at another company, and all other considerations do not matter.

Provision (b) tells the terminated-for-convenience contractor to "stop work" ((b)(1)) and "Place no further subcontracts or orders" ((b)(2)). The contractor must wind-up with subcontractors, including "Terminate all subcontracts" ((b)(3)), "Assign to the Government…all right…under the subcontracts terminated" ((b)(4)), and "settle" what will be "arising from the termination of subcontracts" ((b))(5)). Recalling the imaginary scenarios just listed, the steps in these provisions ((b)(1) to (5)) might be most of what the terminated aircraft prime contract scenario principally involves: an orderly shutting down of what the prime contractor had done in terms of starting subcontracts.

The terminated contractor has to "transfer…and deliver to the Government" the work in progress and completed work ((b)(6)). If the Contracting Officer so directs, the contractor may "Sell…any property of the types referred to in subparagraph (6) above" ((b)(7)). In the third scenario, the urgent missile component, the government may care the most about the step of getting the work in progress transferred to the new contractor.

If the termination is only partial, the contractor must "Complete performance of the work not terminated" ((b)(7)). The contractor must also protect the government as to "the property related to this contract…in which the Government has or may acquire an interest" ((b)(8)). The scenario of the partial termination of the near-insolvent contractor may turn on these provisions. Not only must the contractor complete the work not terminated, the contractor must not prejudice the government's property interests. If the contractor is responding to other creditors' pressures to give up property interests, as when a near-insolvent contractor pledges its remaining assets in some of which the government has an interest, as security for credit from suppliers, this clause can lead to serious jockeying between the government and the private creditors.

While the terminated contractor juggles these various generalized governmental interests, the termination clause gives it a series of concrete steps to follow. It may "submit to the Contracting Officer a list, certified as to quantity and quality, of termination inventory" (provisions (c) and (d)), with various steps to follow regarding such inventory. This accords with the caution inherent generally regarding property in which the government has an interest.

As for how much the government will pay the contractor, the following provisions discuss two methods of deciding this: settlement (provisions (e) and (f)) by dint of a contractor settlement proposal, or a figure determined by the Contracting Officer (provision (g)). The task that may well engage much of terminated contractors' lawyers' attention consists here of developing and processing a settlement proposal. The contractor may have a year to develop a proposal, or more, or less (e). Then, the contractor and the Contracting Officer try to reach agreement on the settlement proposal (f). If they fail, the Contracting Officer determines a figure based on specified factors (g). That figure excludes "property that is destroyed, lost, stolen or damaged" (h) and follows the "cost principles and procedures" (i), much like an equitable adjustment. The figuring deducts payments to the contractor or government claims against the contractor (k). In a partial termination, the contractor can also propose equitable adjustments of the prices "of the continued portion of the contract." Figuring the termination payment will be further discussed shortly, and the *Rhen* opinion illustrates concretely what contractors seek to include in their settlement proposals.

The determinations by these clauses of what the terminated contractor gets is subject to the Disputes Clause (j). The government may make partial payments to the contractor (m). Finally, the contractor "shall maintain all records and documents relating to the terminated protion of this contractor for three years after final settlement," for governmental review (n).

On occasion, the parties may execute what is called a "no-cost settlement agreement." Effectively, the parties stipulate the contractor has no costs for which the government owes it and no credits owing to the government, so they might as well just walk away from the contract. This may occur either because there are, in fact, no costs or credits, or as the very simplest way to walk away from a dispute when both sides want out. It is a handy tool for government contract lawyers.

Termination for Convenience Clause (Fixed-Price)
(Sep 1996)

(a)   The Government may terminate performance of work under this contract in whole or, from time to time, in part if the Contracting Officer determines that a termination is in the Government's interest. The Contracting Officer shall terminate by delivering to the Contractor a Notice of Termination specifying the extent of termination and the effective date.

(b)   After receipt of a Notice of Termination, and except as directed by the Contracting Officer, the Contractor shall immediately proceed with the following obligations, regardless of any delay in determining or adjusting any amounts due under this clause:

(1) Stop work as specified in the notice.

(2) Place no further subcontracts or orders * * *

(3) Terminate all subcontracts to the extent they relate to the work terminated.

(4) Assign to the Government, as directed by the Contracting Officer, all right, title, and interest of the Contractor under the subcontracts terminated, in which case the Government shall have the right to settle or to pay any termination settlement proposal arising out of those terminations.

(5) With approval or ratification to the extent required by the Contracting Officer, settle all outstanding liabilities and termination settlement proposals arising from the termination of subcontracts * * *

(6) As directed by the Contracting Officer, transfer title and deliver to the Government

(i) the fabricated or unfabricated parts, work in process, completed work, supplies, and other material produced or acquired for the work terminated, and

(ii) the completed or partially completed plans, drawings, information, and other property that, if the contract had been completed, would be required to be furnished to the Government.

(7) Complete performance of the work not terminated.

(8) Take any action that may be necessary, or that the Contracting Officer may direct, for the protection and preservation of the property related to this contract that is in the possession of the Contractor and in which the Government has or may acquire an interest.

(9) Use its best efforts to sell, as directed or authorized by the Contracting Officer, any property of the types referred to in subparagraph (b)(6) of this clause * * *

(c) The Contractor shall submit complete termination inventory schedules * * *

(d)   After expiration of the plant clearance period as defined in Subpart 45.6 of the Federal Acquisition Regulation, the Contractor may submit to the Contracting Officer a list, certified as to quantity and quality, of termination inventory * * *

(e)   After termination, the Contractor shall submit a final termination settlement proposal to the Contracting Officer in the form and with the certification prescribed by the Contracting Officer. The Contractor shall submit the proposal promptly, but no later than 1 year from the effective date of termination, unless extended in writing by the Contracting Officer upon written request of the Contractor within this 1-year period. However, if the Contracting Officer determines that the facts justify it, a termination settlement proposal may be received and acted on after 1 year or any extension. If the Contractor fails to submit the proposal within the time allowed, the Contracting Officer may determine, on the basis of information available, the amount, if any, due the Contractor because of the termination and shall pay the amount determined.

(f) Subject to paragraph (e) of this clause, the Contractor and the Contracting Officer may agree upon the whole or any part of the amount to be paid or remaining to be paid because of the termination. The amount may include a reasonable allowance for profit on work done. However, the agreed amount, whether under this paragraph (f) or paragraph (g) of this clause, exclusive of costs shown in subparagraph (g)(3) of this clause, may not exceed the total contract price as reduced by

(1) the amount of payments previously made and

(2) the contract price of work not terminated. The contract shall be modified, and the Contractor paid the agreed amount. Paragraph (g) of this clause shall not limit, restrict, or affect the amount that may be agreed upon to be paid under this paragraph.

(g)   If the Contractor and the Contracting Officer fail to agree on the whole amount to be paid because of the termination of work, the Contracting Officer shall pay the Contractor the amounts determined by the Contracting Officer as follows, but without duplication of any amounts agreed on under paragraph (f) of this clause:

(1) The contract price for completed supplies or services accepted by the Government (or sold or acquired under subparagraph (b)(9) of this clause) not previously paid for, adjusted for any saving of freight and other charges.

(2) The total of—

(i) The costs incurred in the performance of the work terminated, including initial costs and preparatory expense allocable thereto, but excluding any costs attributable to supplies or services paid or to be paid under subparagraph (g)(1) of this clause;

(ii) The cost of settling and paying termination settlement proposals under terminated subcontracts that are properly chargeable to the terminated portion of the contract if not included in subdivision (g)(2)(i) of this clause; and

(iii) A sum, as profit on subdivision (g)(2)(i) of this clause, determined by the Contracting Officer under 49.202 of the Federal Acquisition Regulation, in effect on the date of this contract, to be fair and reasonable; however, if it appears that the Contractor would have sustained a loss on the entire contract had it been completed, the Contracting Officer shall allow no profit under this subdivision (iii) and shall reduce the settlement to reflect the indicated rate of loss.

(3) The reasonable costs of settlement of the work terminated, including—

(i) Accounting, legal, clerical, and other expenses reasonably necessary for the preparation of termination settlement proposals and supporting data;

(ii) The termination and settlement of subcontracts (excluding the amounts of such settlements); and

(iii) Storage, transportation, and other costs incurred, reasonably necessary for the preservation, protection, or disposition of the termination inventory.

(h)   * * * [T]he Contracting Officer shall exclude from the amounts payable to the Contractor under paragraph (g) of this clause, the fair value, as determined by the Contracting Officer, of property that is destroyed, lost, stolen, or damaged * * *

(i) The cost principles and procedures of Part 31 of the Federal Acquisition Regulation * * * shall govern all costs claimed, agreed to, or determined under this clause.

(j) The Contractor shall have the right of appeal, under the Disputes clause, from any determination made by the Contracting Officer under paragraph (e), (g), or (l) of this clause, except that if the Contractor failed to submit the termination settlement proposal or request for equitable adjustment within the time provided in paragraph (e) or (l), respectively, and failed to request a time extension, there is no right of appeal.

(k)   In arriving at the amount due the Contractor under this clause, there shall be deducted—

(1) All unliquidated advance or other payments to the Contractor under the terminated portion of this contract;

(2) Any claim which the Government has against the Contractor under this contract; and

(3) The agreed price for, or the proceeds of sale of, materials, supplies, or other things acquired by the Contractor or sold under the provisions of this clause and not recovered by or credited to the Government.

(l) If the termination is partial, the Contractor may file a proposal with the Contracting Officer for an equitable adjustment of the price(s) of the continued portion of the contract. The Contracting Officer shall make any equitable adjustment agreed upon. Any proposal by the Contractor for an equitable adjustment under this clause shall be requested within 90 days from the effective date of termination unless extended in writing by the Contracting Officer.

(m) (1)   The Government may, under the terms and conditions it prescribes, make partial payments and payments against costs incurred by the Contractor for the terminated portion of the contract, if the Contracting Officer believes the total of these payments will not exceed the amount to which the Contractor will be entitled.

(2) If the total payments exceed the amount finally determined to be due, the Contractor shall repay the excess to the Government upon demand * * *

(n)   Unless otherwise provided in this contract or by statute, the Contractor shall maintain all records and documents relating to the terminated portion of this contract for 3 years after final settlement. * * * The Contractor shall make these records and documents available to the Government, at the Contractor's office, at all reasonable times, without any direct charge. * * *

Before turning to the *Rhen* case, the issues regarding what the government owes the terminated contractor deserve attention. Note how the termination clause's provision (h) makes cost principles apply. These have been discussed in another chapter. Normally, government contracts are either fixed price—no cost principles—or cost reimbursement. What the termination clause does is make cost principles apply universally, regardless of whether the contract originally involved them in pricing. The saying is that Termination for Convenience converts a fixed price contract into a cost reimbursement contract for the work performed.

Termination clause section (f) creates wide-open flexibility for the terminated contractor and the contracting officer to agree upon a settlement figure, in contrast to the greater precision and restriction of section (g) when the contracting officer determines a figure. Still, section (e) gives some guidance. The settlement "may include a reasonable allowance for profit on work done." However, "the agreed amount, whether under this paragraph (f) or paragraph (g) below...may not exceed the total contract price" with two reductions: "payments previously made," and "the contract price of work not done." Leaving aside payments made, an agreed figure between the contracting officer and the contractor can follow a basic formula: Contract Price (total) minus Contract Price (for work not done).

Moreover, the termination clause indicates several ways of raising that figure. It exempts a category of costs in subsection (g)(3), namely, the settlement costs of the termination. These include "Accounting, legal, clerical, and other expenses reasonably necessary for the preparation of termination settlement proposals and supporting data" ((g)(3)(i)). In other words, the government contracts lawyer billing for work reasonably necessary for preparing settlement proposals can get the contractor reimbursed by the government for her bills, a factor helping the lawyer to persuade the contractor to place some of the burdens of working on the settlement proposal onto the lawyer. Also, in a partial termination, the contractor can seek an equitable adjustment for the price of the "continued portion of the contract" (provision (l)).

Both sides must consider what happens without an agreement, namely, the contracting officer reaching a determination pursuant to provision (g). This is the part that gets fought about. In contrast with the previously noted ceiling, which starts with the total contract price and subtracts from it, the calculations pursuant to provision (g) start with the "contract price for completed supplies or services accepted by the Government" ((g)(1)), and adds to that. Usually, this formula will come well below the ceiling that starts with the total contract price, unless the unusual situation is present that the government terminates a contract in which a comparatively large portion of what there was to purchase has been produced and accepted.

To the price for completed supplies or services, the determination process adds, on the termination portion, the costs already incurred, such as start-up costs on the contract or the costs of materials ordered and not returnable without some expenditure ((g)(2)(i)). It also includes the cost of terminated subcontractor settlements ((g)(2)(ii)), and a figure for profit on the costs incurred. The clause takes special note to warn that if the "contractor would have sustained a loss on the entire contract had it been completed," then no profit gets allowed and the contracting officer "shall reduce the settlement to reflect the indicated rate of loss (g)(2)(iii). This may not be all that common, but it can happen, when contractors bid low seeking the work for various reasons, and some of those reasons may vanish as a result of termination by convenience (for example, the expectation of profiting by follow-on contracts like spare parts).

Although the *Rhen* case starts as a termination for default, it falls at this stage into the category of opinions regarding what a contractor can, and cannot, receive for termination for convenience. By dint of the range of requests by this particular contractor, it is particularly illuminating.

Ronald J. Rhen, Plaintiff, v. The United States, Defendant

No. 308-88C. United States Claims Court.
17 Cl. Ct. 140. June 2, 1989.

MEMORANDUM OPINION

LYDON, Senior Judge:

Plaintiff, proceeding pro se, challenges the default termination of a contract he had with the Bureau of Land Management, Department of the Interior (BLM). In his complaint, plaintiff sets forth five separate claims for damages he seeks to recover emanating from this default termination. Defendant, after answer, has responded to the complaint by filing a motion for partial summary judgment as to three of the five claims, contending that, as to these three claims, there is no genuine issue as to any material fact and, accordingly, defendant is entitled to judgment in its favor as a matter of law. Plaintiff has filed an opposition to defendant's motion.

Upon consideration of the submissions of the parties, oral argument being considered unnecessary, the court concludes that defendant's partial motion for summary judgment should be granted.

I.

On March 5, 1985, the BLM, Portland Oregon District, issued an Invitation for Bids (IFB) for "One Time Through Precommercial Thinning." The contract work involved the cutting and thinning of surplus trees and the cutting of bushes so as to provide additional growing space for existing trees. The IFB called for work to be performed on two different sites in the North Umpqua Recourse Area in the Roseburg District, Oregon. One work site, known as "Lone Rock" contained 307 acres; the other site, known as "Above The River", contained 216 acres. Roadways through the two areas of the project were clearly delineated on contract documents. Under the IFB, an unqualified bid on both work sites required the contractor to complete the contract work in sixty days. The bid opening day was April 4, 1985.

Plaintiff was the successful low bidder at $42,846.50. His bid covered both work sites and was unqualified. Accordingly, he was required to complete the contract within sixty days. Plaintiff was awarded the contract on April 18, 1985, and the Notice To Proceed with the work became effective April 30, 1985. Plaintiff began work on April 30, 1985.

Plaintiff's progress on the contract work was slow and BLM personnel became concerned about the matter. On May 14, 1985, an "Instruction," and on May 22, 1985, a letter were sent to plaintiff by BLM warning him of BLM concern that with his present work force he would not be able to complete all of the contract work within the remaining contract period. Plaintiff was requested to submit a revised work schedule to BLM. On June 28, 1985, the contract time expired and only forty-two percent of the work had been completed.

On June 28, 1985, BLM issued a Show Cause Notice to plaintiff advising that the Government was considering terminating his contract under the default provisions of the contract. Plaintiff was given ten days to respond to this Notice.

Plaintiff responded to the Notice of July 5, 1985. He contended the contract work had not been completed on time because he had trouble locating qualified employees and also had problems with his subcontractors. He also contended that some of his workers were having problems with the BLM project inspector in that the inspector was too strict in requiring adherence to contract requirements.

On July 16, 1985, BLM terminated plaintiff's contract for default pursuant to the Default Clause of the contract and so notified plaintiff. In support of this default termination, the contracting officer issued Findings and a Decision on September 27, 1985. The contracting officer found that plaintiff had failed to complete the contract work within the time required by the contract and that his failure in this regard was not the result of any excusable delays.

On September 22, 1986, plaintiff filed suit in this court contesting the default termination and presenting a number of monetary claims. The suit was dismissed without prejudice by the court, in an unpublished Memorandum Opinion dated February 27, 1987, because plaintiff had never filed monetary claims with the contracting officer. On March 24, 1987, plaintiff filed money claims with the contracting officer. Plaintiff sought to recover approximately $520,446.63, plus interest as damages flowing from termination of his $42,846.50 contract. In his claim to the contracting officer, plaintiff alleged numerous instances of delay on the part of the Government which he claims were responsible for his failure to complete the contract work in a timely manner. No decision having been rendered on these claims by the contracting officer within sixty days, plaintiff, on March 23, 1988, filed the instant action in this court. See in this regard, Vemo v. United States, 9 Cl.Ct. 217, 221-22 (1985).

In his complaint, plaintiff seeks to recover for the alleged improper termination of his contract the following damages:

    1)   Plaintiff seeks to recover $7,005.84 which he paid the Amwest Surety Insurance Company for completing the terminated contract. This claim had been presented to the contracting officer;

    2)   plaintiff seeks to recover $11,511.52 representing income he would have earned in performing the contract had it not been terminated. This claim had been presented to the contracting officer;

    3)   plaintiff seeks to recover $1,100.00 for the value of road acreage deleted from the contract. This claim had been presented to the contracting officer;

4)   plaintiff seeks to recover $850,000 on the ground he lost his ability to get bonding as a result of the default termination of his contract by BLB. This claim had been presented to the contracting officer but only for $500,000;

5)   plaintiff also seeks interest on the above claims, attorney fees and costs of litigation.

II.

Defendant has moved for partial summary judgment, with supporting documentation, on claims (2), (3) and (4), supra.

A. The $11,511.52 Claim (# 2 supra)

As indicated above, plaintiff seeks to recover $11,511.52 on the ground he would have earned this amount had his contract not been terminated. As stated by plaintiff, this claim is one for income he would have made had he been able to complete the contract. Thus, his claim is one for anticipated but unearned profit. Defendant contends that, under the circumstances of this case, plaintiff is not entitled to recover on this claim as a matter of law. Defendant's position is well taken.

The Default Clause in plaintiff's contract provides, in substance, that if a default termination is subsequently found to be improper, "the right and obligations of the parties shall be the same as if the termination had been issued for the convenience of the Government." See Nolan Brothers Inc. v. United States, 405 F.2d 1250, 1254-55, 186 Ct.Cl. 602 (1969). Accordingly, assuming arguendo that plaintiff's contract was improperly terminated, he would not, as a matter of law, be entitled to recover anticipated profit. This is so because under the contract's Termination For Convenience Clause, anticipated, but unearned profits are not recoverable. Dairy Sales Corp. v. United States, 593 F.2d 1002, 1005, 219 Ct.Cl. 431 (1979). Plaintiff's opposition brief refuses to come to grips with this state of the law. Plaintiff's contention that he is not seeking "profits" but only "income" or "gross earnings" is most unpersuasive reasoning on the undisputed facts of this case.

In the case at bar, assuming the default termination to be improper, the measure of damages available to plaintiff under the Termination For Convenience Clause of the contract would be limited to the costs actually incurred up to the date of termination, plus a reasonable profit on work actually performed prior to termination. William Green Constr. Co. v. United States, 477 F.2d 930, 934, 201 Ct.Cl. 616 (1973).

B. The $850,000 Claim (# 4, supra):

Plaintiff seeks to recover $850,000 as lost income he suffered because of his inability to obtain bonding resulting from the default termination of his contract. Again, plaintiff seeks to recover anticipated, but unearned, profit. As discussed previously, plaintiff is not, as a matter of law, entitled to recover unearned, but anticipated profits under the circumstances of this case.

Plaintiff claims that the lack of ability to obtain bonding prevented him from obtaining other contracts which would have enabled him to obtain profits in the amount of the $850,000 claimed. In substance, plaintiff's claim is one for general loss of business as a result of the default termination. Such a damage claim is too remote or consequential in nature to allow for a recovery thereon. Since the damages claimed are too remote, consequential and speculative, they are, as a matter of law, not recoverable in any event.

William, Id. 477 F.2d at 936; Ramsey v. United States, 101 F.Supp. 353, 357, 121 Ct.Cl. 426 (1951); CCM Corp. v. United States, 15 Cl.Ct. 670, 671-72 (1988). The $850,000 claim must be, and is, denied.

C. The $1,100 Claim (# 3, supra)

Under the contract, plaintiff was to provide pre-commercial thinning services on two sites in the Umpqua Resource Area. These sites were identified as Lone Rock, a 307 acre tract, and Above The River, a 216 acre tract. The contract documents contained project area maps which clearly delineated the area to be worked on by means of cross-hatching with diagonal lines on the project area maps. The roads throughout the work site areas were also delineated on the project area maps. The roads were not cross-hatched with diagonal lines. A legend on the project area maps identified the cross-hatched with diagonal lines, area as the "Project Area", and the roads were identified as two parallel lines with no cross-hatching with diagonal lines between the parallel lines. Under the contract, plaintiff was to thin trees and cut brush on the project area maps. The cross-hatched areas of the Lone Rock tract consisted of 307 acres, whereas the cross-hatched areas of the Above The River tract consisted of 216 acres. These same acreages were also set forth in the contract Schedule of [work] Items. The acreages stated in the Schedule of Items, on which the bids were submitted, did not include the acreage occupied by roads traversing the project areas.

Plaintiff seeks to recover $1,100 for the value of road acreage deleted from the contract. As stated above, the roadways were excluded from the project area scope of work because no thinning was done on the roadways. A reasonable reading of the contract documents supports this fact. While plaintiff claims the road acreage was deleted from the contract, the fact is, according to the unrefuted affidavit of the successor contracting officer on the contract in question, that the road acreage was not included in the work project area acreages because no thinning was done on roads. The contract work acreage areas of 307 acres, Lone Rock, and 216 acres, Above The River, did not include road acreage when the contract was advertised, awarded, or at any time thereafter.

Further, the contract contained a provision that permitted plaintiff, "at anytime during the course of the contract" to request remeasurement of any work unit if he felt that the acreage stated on the project area map was incorrect. At no time during contract performance did plaintiff make a request for remeasurement of the work project acreage.

As a matter of contract interpretation, which is a question of law, George Hyman Constr. Co. v. United States, 832 F.2d 574, 579 (Fed.Cir.1987), the roadways were not designated as project work areas and were not included in the scope of the contract for pay purposes. The contract project maps clearly delineated the project work areas and this delineation clearly excluded the roadways. Since the purpose of the contract was to provide precommercial thinning, it would be unreasonable to read the contract as requiring the thinning of roadways which did not require any thinning.

* * *

Notes and Questions

1. The facts of *Rhen* allow a comparison of damage calculations in government contracting and in basic (private) contracting. Take this as a contract in which Rhen is hired for $42,000, his costs are going to be $30,000 for doing the whole thing, and

$12,000 for doing 42%. Then look at the damages if Rhen does all the work, 42% of the work, or none of the work, before buyer cancels without cause, under either of two circumstances: the buyer is a private buyer who cancels without cause (i.e., wrongfully), or, the buyer is the government exercising its power to terminate for convenience.

Rhen does	Rhen gets as damages if private contract	Rhen gets as damages by T for C
all $30,000 of work	$42K as promised	$42K—costs and "earned" profit
42% of work—$12,000 costs	$24K ($42K-$18K costs saved); or ($12K costs expended plus $12K profit on the whole contract)	$12K costs and "earned" profit, say, $4K
no work, and has no costs	$12K calculated two ways: ($42K-$30K costs saved) or, (No costs plus $12K profit on the whole contract)	nothing

2. Rhen does not get very far with the item about $850,000 for loss of bonding ability. Assuming a wrongful cancellation by buyer, would Rhen do any better on this claim in a basic (private) contract situation?

3. The opinion turns for its final item on issues of contract interpretation as to the statement of work. The statement of work is not, of course, one of the standard clauses from the FAR or other standard sources, but was drafted for this particular contract. Ordinary tools of interpretation come into play, tools which the government contracts lawyer uses like other lawyers.

4. This case started as a default termination, but the opinion considers the case, at this stage, as if the default termination were improper and it were converted to a convenience termination. This is a prime example of a category called "constructive terminations for convenience," namely, matters not initially or formally handled as terminations for convenience that get treated like them. Other examples include when the government cancels a contract or prevents the contractor from continuing performance without use of the "Termination for Convenience" Clause, e.g., the government awards a contract but cancels the award wrongfully on the belief the bidding was flawed, and then has to compensate the bidder for the cancellation. A constructive partial termination may occur in contracts without definite quantities where the government does not use due care in estimating the quantities it will order, and the quantities actually ordered prove markedly less than estimated. Then, the shortfall in orders may be treated as a constructive partial termination.

5. Partial terminations. The FAR provides the government with mechanisms by which to delete work from a fixed-price contract when the contracting officer determines it to be in the government's best interest. Under the "termination for convenience" clause the contracting officer may partially terminate the contract and the con-

tractor maintains specific obligations in such instances. 48 C.F.R. §52.249-2. The FAR also authorizes the contracting officer to enter into a settlement agreement with the contractor when termination occurs. 48 C.F.R. §49.101.

Partial terminations compensate the contractor for additional costs incurred for work not terminated resulting from the work terminated, while placing some limits: contractors still do not obtain profits beyond what would have occurred with contract completion, nor do they reverse losses occuring had the contract been completed. 48 C.F.R. §52.249-2. In the *Appeal of Power Generators, Inc.* the ASBCA held that the contractor providing a generator that became defective was entitled to costs incurred from attempts to repair it prior to subsequent partial termination, but proportionate to losses that would have been incurred had the contract been unchanged. ASBCA No. 7607, 1962 BCA ¶3358.

The other means by which work can be deleted is under the "Changes" clause, and equitable adjustment follows a different rule. 48 C.F.R. §52.243-1.

JAMES M. ELLETT CONSTRUCTION COMPANY, INC., Plaintiff-Appellant, v. The UNITED STATES, Defendant-Appellee.

No. 94-5161. United States Court of Appeals,
Federal Circuit 93 F.3d 1537., Aug. 26, 1996.

Before MAYER, MICHEL and BRYSON, Circuit Judges.

MAYER, Circuit Judge.

James M. Ellett Construction Company, Inc. appeals the judgment of the United States Court of Federal Claims, No. 90-641 C (July 29, 1994), dismissing its suit challenging a contracting officer's final decision for want of subject matter jurisdiction because Ellett had not submitted a "claim" that complied with the requirements of the Contract Disputes Act. Subsequent to the court's dismissal, this court clarified the definition of a claim, overruling the cases upon which the trial court had relied in dismissing Ellett's complaint. Reflectone, Inc. v. Dalton, 60 F.3d 1572 (Fed.Cir.1995) (in banc). Because Ellett submitted both a "claim" as that term is explained in Reflectone, and a termination settlement proposal that ripened into a claim which the contracting officer settled by determination, there was jurisdiction. Therefore, we reverse and remand for further proceedings.

Background

In July 1988, the Forest Service of the United States Department of Agriculture (agency) awarded Ellett a contract to construct a 2.7 mile logging road in the Siskiyou National Forest, Oregon. The contract contained the April 1984 version of the Federal Acquisition Regulation (FAR) clause authorizing the government to terminate the contract for its convenience, 48 C.F.R. §52.249-2 (Alternate I), which states, in pertinent part:

> (d) After termination, the Contractor shall submit a final termination settlement proposal to the Contracting Officer in the form and with the certification prescribed by the Contracting Officer....

> (e) Subject to paragraph (d) above, the Contractor and the Contracting Officer may agree upon the whole or any part of the amount to be paid because of the termination....

(f) If the Contractor and the Contracting Officer fail to agree on the whole amount to be paid the Contractor because of the termination of work, the Contracting Officer shall pay the Contractor the amounts determined as follows, but without duplication of any amounts agreed upon under paragraph (e)....

* * *

(i) The Contractor shall have the right of appeal, under the Disputes clause, from any determination made by the Contracting Officer under paragraph (d) [or] (f).... If the Contracting Officer has made a determination of the amount due under paragraph (d) [or] (f)..., the Government shall pay the Contractor (1) the amount determined by the Contracting Officer... if no timely appeal has been taken, or (2) the amount finally determined on appeal.

On July 28, 1988, the agency issued Ellett a partial notice to proceed, which authorized the construction of just 4,000 feet of the road, because of pending legislation to limit entry into the area. The agency then terminated the remainder of the contract for convenience on September 30, 1988.

By letter dated November 17, 1988, the stated purpose of which was "to file formal notice of claim pursuant to the Contract Disputes Act of 1978 [(CDA)]," Ellett sought to recover $545,157.19 from the agency. Specifically, the company claimed: (1) a $136,964.81 equitable adjustment for government-ordered changes; (2) $32,036.50 for "unforeseen and unexpected security costs" that were "not disclosed in the prospectus"; and (3) $376,155.88 in lost profits. Although not submitted on the forms the FAR requires for settlement proposals, see 48 C.F.R. §49.206-1(c) (1995) ("Settlement proposals must be on the forms prescribed in 49.602...."), Ellett says this letter, like a termination settlement proposal, was intended to recover all money due under the contract. The contracting officer responded by letter of December 2, 1988, that FAR Part 49 governs "the settlement of termination proposals and requests for contract modification." The letter said Ellett needed to submit a settlement proposal on Standard Forms (SF) 1436 (Settlement Proposal (Total Cost Basis)) and 1439 (Schedule of Accounting Information), which were enclosed.

On March 3, 1989, Ellett submitted a settlement proposal on the required forms, requesting a net payment of $494,826. It admits that the amount sought in this request was largely duplicative of its November 17, 1988 submission, although different in some respects because of the requirements of the forms and unspecified intervening events. The parties then began to negotiate a mutually agreeable settlement.

In a January 12, 1990 letter to the contracting officer, Ellett observed that it had been "nearly 14 months" since the November 17, 1988 CDA "claim" and one year since the settlement proposal. Consequently, it said that unless the "outstanding claim" were resolved satisfactorily within thirty days, it would file suit in the United States Court of Federal Claims. The agency responded with a settlement offer of $120,649, which Ellett rejected in a March 31, 1990 letter, which also said that unless the agency agreed to a settlement of $250,000 within two weeks, it would file suit.

The government rejected the $250,000 settlement offer, and the contracting officer prepared a document styled "Contracting Officer's Findings and Determination," dated June 25, 1990. There he evaluated the termination settlement proposal and concluded that Ellett was entitled to termination costs of $416,144.01, less progress payments the agency had already made, for a net of $22,779.01.

On July 13, 1990, Ellett filed a complaint in the Court of Federal Claims, seeking $451,084 plus interest, costs, and attorneys fees. The government moved to dismiss * * *

because the November 17, 1988 letter * * * was not properly certified. The court agreed that the letter was not properly certified and dismissed the suit. James M. Ellett Constr. Co. v. United States, No. 90-641 C (Cl.Ct. Feb. 6, 1991). We reversed. James M. Ellett Constr. Co. v. United States, No. 91-5071, 1992 WL 82447 (Fed.Cir. Apr. 24, 1992).

On remand, the government renewed its motion to dismiss, arguing that Ellett had not yet submitted a claim to the contracting officer for purposes of the CDA. * * * The court held that because there was not an existing dispute on November 17, 1988, Ellett's letter of that date was not a "claim"; it was a "unilateral cost (i.e. settlement) proposal." Slip op. at 11. The court also said that the November 17, 1988 letter did not request a final determination by the contracting officer, but was only an invitation to enter negotiations. It concluded that Ellett's March 3, 1989 termination settlement proposal was not a claim because it did not seek a final decision from the contracting officer. This appeal followed.

Discussion

* * *

A. The Termination Settlement Proposal

Ellett does not contend that its March 1989 settlement proposal was a CDA claim. Rather, it argues simply that once the contracting officer reviewed the proposal and unilaterally determined that it was due a net termination settlement of $22,779.01, it was entitled, under the terms of its contract and the FAR, to appeal that determination directly to the court.

This argument is not enough, however, for us to conclude that the court had jurisdiction * * *

Under the FAR, there are three requirements a nonroutine submission must meet to be a "claim." It must be: (1) a written demand or assertion, (2) seeking as a matter of right, (3) the payment of money in a sum certain. 48 C.F.R. §33.201 (1995); Reflectone, 60 F.3d at 1575. Ellett's contract required nothing more. A routine request for payment, on the other hand, must also be "in dispute" when submitted to meet the definition of a "claim." 48 C.F.R. §33.201; Reflectone, 60 F.3d at 1576.

Our threshold inquiry, therefore, is whether Ellett's termination settlement proposal was a routine submission. See Reflectone, 60 F.3d at 1577 ("[T]he critical distinction in identifying a 'claim' is...between routine and non-routine submissions."). In that regard, a "demand for compensation for unforeseen or unintended circumstances cannot be characterized as 'routine.'" Id. (request for an equitable adjustment is "anything but a 'routine request for payment'"). On the other hand, vouchers, invoices, and similar requests for payment are "submitted for work done or equipment delivered by the contractor in accordance with the expected or scheduled progression of contract performance." Id.

Using these beacons as guides, it is difficult to conceive of a less routine demand for payment than one which is submitted when the government terminates a contract for its convenience. Such a demand, which occurs only in a fraction of government contracts is certainly less routine than a request for an equitable adjustment, several of which a contractor might submit on any one contract. Indeed, in concluding that a request for an equitable adjustment is not routine in Reflectone, we pointed to Supreme Court precedent equating a request for an equitable adjustment with an assertion of a breach of contract. That analogue is even more appropriate here, where, but for the convenience termination clause, the government's action would be a breach of contract, and it would be liable for resulting damages. See G. L. Christian and Assocs. v. United States, 160 Ct.Cl. 1, 312 F.2d 418, 423 (1963). A request for payment submitted after the government has terminated the contract during its performance is a far cry from a request submitted in accordance with the expected or scheduled progression of contract performance.

It is beyond serious dispute that the parties intended that Ellett construct the entire 2.7 mile logging road. Because of the unforeseen legislation, however, the government decided to invoke its right to terminate the contract. Ellett's demand for compensation arising from such circumstances can hardly be considered routine. If it were routine, like a voucher or invoice, there would be no need to negotiate. However, the FAR contemplates that only after the amount a contractor is owed because of a convenience termination is determined, whether by agreement, determination, or appeal, shall a contractor submit a voucher or invoice for that amount. 48 C.F.R. § 49.112-2(a)-(b) (1995).

Relying on a dictionary, the government argues that a termination settlement proposal is a routine request for payment because the FAR and the contract establish procedures for submitting one. * * * Once the government terminates for convenience, the procedures used to determine a contractor's recovery could be perceived as routine, in the sense that the same ones are followed each time. However, that does not make them routine in the overall scheme of the contract and the parties' expectations.

* * * So, as a written assertion seeking, as a matter of right under the termination for convenience clause, the payment of $451,084 plus interest, costs, and attorneys fees, it met the FAR's requirements of a valid claim.

As we said in Reflectone, however, not every nonroutine submission constitutes a CDA claim. See 60 F.3d at 1577 n. 7. Besides meeting the FAR definition of a claim, the CDA also requires that all claims be submitted to the contracting officer for a decision. 41 U.S.C. § 605(a) (1994); see also 48 C.F.R. § 33.206; * * *

When a contractor submits a termination settlement proposal, it is for the purpose of negotiation, not for a contracting officer's decision. A settlement proposal is just that: a proposal. See 48 C.F.R. § 49.001 (1995) ("a proposal for effecting settlement of a contract terminated in whole or in part, submitted by a contractor or subcontractor in the form, and supported by the data, required by this part"). Indeed, it is a proposal that Ellett contractually agreed to submit in the event of a convenience termination. The parties agreed that they would try to reach a mutually agreeable settlement. If they were unable to do so, however, it was agreed, consonant with the FAR's requirements, that the contracting officer would issue a final decision, see id. §§ 52.249-2(f) (Alternate I), 49.103, 49.105(a)(4), which Ellett could appeal to the court or to the Department of Agriculture Board of Contract Appeals, id. § 52.249-2(i). Consequently, while Ellett's termination settlement proposal met the FAR's definition of a claim, at the time of submission it was not a claim because it was not submitted to the contracting officer for a decision.

Once negotiations reached an impasse, the proposal, by the terms of the FAR and the contract, was submitted for decision; it became a claim. In other words, in accordance with the contract's prescribed method of compensating Ellett for a convenience termination, a request that the contracting officer issue a decision in the event the parties were unable to agree on a settlement was implicit in Ellett's proposal. After ten months of fruitless negotiations, Ellett explicitly requested that the contracting officer settle its claim. This demand is tantamount to an express request for a contracting officer's decision. Hence, after the subsequent exchange of offers and counteroffers, the contracting officer settled Ellett's proposal by determination and Ellett filed suit.

That the termination settlement proposal would ripen into a claim requiring the contracting officer to issue a unilateral settlement determination was contemplated by the contract and the FAR. They provide explicitly that Ellett had the right to appeal the contracting officer's decision on its proposal. 48 C.F.R. §52.249-2(i); see also id. §49.109-7(d) (a contracting officer's settlement determination "shall advise the contractor that the determination is a final decision from which the contractor may appeal under the Disputes clause"). The FAR implicitly includes termination settlement proposals within the operative definition of a claim to the extent they are not favorably resolved by a contracting officer's decision. The government responds that Ellett's termination settlement proposal was not an appealable claim for three reasons: (1) once negotiations reached an impasse, Ellett was required to submit a new claim or convert its termination settlement proposal into a claim, detailing what issues were in dispute, an act it failed to perform; (2) because the FAR prohibits the payment of interest on a settlement agreement or a settlement by determination, a settlement proposal cannot be a CDA claim; and (3) Ellett's certification was defective because it had to be but was not made after the parties' negotiations stalled.

On the first argument, after negotiations reached an impasse, the contracting officer issued a unilateral decision on the settlement proposal pursuant to paragraph (f) of the termination for convenience clause. 48 C.F.R. §52.249-2(f) (Alternate I); see also id. §49.109-7 (governing settlements by determination). Ellett points out that under section (i) of that clause, "[t]he contractor shall have the right of appeal, under the Disputes clause, from any determination made by the Contracting Officer under paragraph (d) [or] (f)...." Id. §52.249-2(i).

The right of appeal in the Disputes clause provides that "[t]he Contracting Officer's decision [on a claim] shall be final unless the Contractor appeals or files a suit as provided in the Act." Id. §52.233-1(f). Under "the Act," a contractor may appeal a contracting officer's final decision to the appropriate agency board of contract appeals, 41 U.S.C. §§606- 607 (1994), or to the Court of Federal Claims, id. §609(a)(1). Indeed, the FAR grants contractors a right to appeal "from" a contracting officer's determination on a settlement proposal. 48 C.F.R. §52.249-2(i). It does not speak of appealing that decision back "to" the contracting officer by submitting a new claim, a futile act. * * *

Nor is there a requirement that the settlement proposal be converted into a claim. To the contrary, the FAR envisions a direct appeal of the contracting officer's determination. In the cover letter the contracting officer identified the settlement determination as the "final decision of the Contracting Officer," and provided the notice of appeal rights required by the FAR to be included in a contracting officer's final decision on a claim. 48 C.F.R. §33.211(a)(4)(v) (1995). As further evidence of Ellett's appeal rights, 48 C.F.R. §49.109-7(g) ("Decision on the contractor's appeal" (emphasis added)) instructs the contracting officer to "give effect to a decision of the [Court of Federal Claims] or a board of contract appeals, when necessary, by an appropriate modification to the contract."

* * *

B. The November 17, 1988 Submission

Ellett also argues that it was entitled to submit its November 17, 1988 "claim" independently of its termination settlement proposal. If this is correct, then it would be entitled to extra interest under the CDA. 41 U.S.C. §611.

We need not strain to conclude that the November 17, 1988 submission, which we have already held was properly certified, met the requirements of a valid, nonroutine claim under Reflectone. The claim included requests for equitable adjustments for government-ordered changes in the work performed and for a constructive change because of the government's failure to disclose its superior knowledge. See Petrochem Servs., Inc. v. United States, 837 F.2d 1076, 1078-79 (Fed.Cir.1988). Requests for an equitable adjustment submitted in response to contract changes, like these, are precisely the type of claims we held were nonroutine in Reflectone. It is without question a written demand pursuant to the CDA; it seeks a sum certain of $545,157.19; and it does so as a matter of right under the Changes clause of the contract.

We disagree that Ellett's submission, which was identified as a claim under the CDA, failed because it closed with the remark that Ellett would be happy to meet with the government to discuss the adjustment of the claim. * * * The government argues that when it terminates a contract for convenience, all claims a contractor might have, including equitable adjustments, are subsumed within the termination settlement proposal. Ellett, on the other hand, argues that there is no authority in the CDA or the FAR "for simply eliminating valid contractor claims by terminating the contract." We agree with Ellett. * * * *

Our conclusion is buttressed by the FAR. If a contract is completely terminated, the termination contracting officer is required to settle all "related unsettled contract changes" as part of the final settlement. 48 C.F.R. §49.114(a) (1995). An unsettled contract change is "any contract change or contract term for which a definitive modification is required but has not been executed." Id. §49.001. On the other hand, if "a part, but not all, of the work that has not been completed and accepted under a contract" is terminated, id. §49.001, the prime contractor must perform the continued portion of the contract and promptly submit any request for an equitable adjustment of price for that portion. Id. §49.104(d). The contracting officer is required to address these claims unless that responsibility is delegated to the termination contracting officer. Id. §49.114(b); see also id. §49.208(b) (requiring termination contracting officers to ensure that no portion of costs included in an equitable adjustment made after partial termination are included in the termination settlement).

It is unclear from our record whether all of the work Ellett had completed at the time of termination had been accepted. Thus, we are unable to determine whether the termination was partial or complete. Regardless, the regulations anticipate the submission of claims independently of the termination settlement proposal.

Therefore, Ellett was entitled to submit a claim for the increased costs it incurred due to contract changes the government made on the work it performed, notwithstanding its termination settlement proposal. It submitted a claim for such costs, which was either constructively denied in the contracting officer's settlement determination or deemed denied because the contracting officer did not directly address the merits. Either way, the trial court had jurisdiction.

Conclusion

Accordingly, the judgment of the United States Court of Federal Claims is reversed, and the case is remanded for further proceedings consistent with this opinion.

Notes and Questions

1. The opinion illustrates that the contractor's inability to contest whether the government will terminate for convenience only begins, not ends, the lawyering role in such a termination. In effect, by seeking equitable adjustments as part of a termination settlement proposal, the contractor and the contractor's lawyer take the offensive

against the government. They can, and do, contend that the government has engaged in what would have been called, a century ago, a breach of contract, and that therefore the terminated contractor deserves a large measure of damage relief.

2. Procedurally, the termination settlement proposal itself comes across as a combination of a contested proceeding, and a negotiation. The FAR offers separate guidance - for negotiated termination settlements, and for termination settlements imposed by the contracting officer to which the contractor may contest. Is this like an early form of alternative dispute resolution, in which the government and the contractor simply treat negotiation as a possible way to resolve their difference without litigating? Or, given the great variety of termination situations, should it be expected that in many types of situation, a comparatively amicable settlement can occur, and only occasionally need there by a contested proceeding about the size of the payment?

3. The goal after Termination for Convenience remains fair compensation to the contractor, and the FAR provides that business judgment be used in negotiating a settlement agreement - as opposed to rigid measures of cost and accounting data, which should be no more than a guide in reaching an agreement. FAR 49.201 (a). Nonetheless, the FAR provides for specific limitations to costs that may be claimed for settlement by the contractor. Logically, all FAR sections prohibit payment of termination costs that would exceed the total contract price. Then, the FAR addresses allowable and prohibited costs based on the type of contract and the nature of termination (by default or for convenience).

Generally, costs categorized as overhead may not be included in a settlement. For example, when a contract for commercial items is terminated for convenience, the settlement cannot include costs associated with unabsorbed overhead (FAR 252.211-7000). Allocable portions of costs attributed to facilities acquired for the work in a multi-year contract may be claimed, so long as the costs have not been charged to the contract through overhead (FAR 52.217-2). Settlement costs may include charges associated with the "storage, transportation, and other costs incurred...for the preservation, protection, or disposition of the termination inventory" (FAR 52.249-2), but undelivered items in the contractor's stock which are readily marketable cannot be claimed (FAR 252.211-7000).

2. Defense

The grounds for contesting a termination for convenience have interest in the abstract, making up somewhat for the lack of practical significance. While the contract boards and courts rarely invalidate a termination for convenience, they do discuss in a highly sophisticated and illuminating way what they consider the standard to be. This gives the distinct impression that the standard has changed over time, something which the *Krygoski* opinion both describes, as to prior opinions, and exemplifies, as to how its own statement of the standard varies from prior ones.

Each of the two types of standard discussed in *Krygoski* warrant separate consideration. First, as *Krygoski* describes, the contracting officer cannot properly terminate in bad faith or as an abuse of discretion. This reflects the role of reviewing tribunals in checking abuses of official power. The deferential standard applied, that contractors have a heavy burden of proof to show bad faith, reflects that the system contemplates a broad grant of power to terminate for convenience.

Second, a more unclear standard has applied to whether and when a contracting officer can terminate for reasons that, at the time of contracting, were anticipated, or knowable, rather than for an unforeseen later change in circumstances. This reflects, in part, the contrast between government contracting and basic (private) contracting. On purely economic grounds, a private contractor who possessed the power to cancel unilaterally, without needing any cause, would take simple advantage of shifts in the market of a kind fully anticipated at the time of contracting. For example, a buyer who contracted to buy widgets for delivery six months hence, with a power to cancel unilaterally without needing any cause, would cancel if the market price of widgets went down and not if the price went up. Such concerns underlie the serious question, at common law, whether a contract with such a power to cancel unilaterally without cause would be deemed no contract at all, an "illusory" contract without valid consideration because of the buyer's having a "free way out." The *Torncello* opinion, which has been discussed, interpreted, and reinterpreted in all the subsequent contested termination for convenience opinions, including *Krygoski*, reflects this fundamental concern.

G. L. CHRISTIAN AND ASSOCIATES
v. The UNITED STATES. Court of Claims
312 F.2d 418 No. 56—59. Jan. 11, 1963.
Opinion is in Chapter I.

Notes and Questions

1. Observe how the G. L. Christian opinion refers back to the history of the power of termination for convenience as justification for the government's ability to provide a limited remedy. Why did government contract law diverge early from contract law in this regard? Why has the divergence continued?

2. In previous parts of this subchapter, the detailed wording of the termination for convenience clause has mattered greatly, sometimes for the government's benefit, sometimes for the contractor's benefit. Why is the court able, for purposes of this case, to get past the absence of that clause from the text of the contract?

Charles Tiefer, Forfeiture by Cancellation
or Termination
54 Mercer Law Review 1031 (2003)

Termination for convenience by the government provides a valuable field in which to study the doctrines of termination powers, for it allows a look back at almost a century and a half of readily examined development. During that time, vigorous debate has occurred between two positions: the position that public policy warrants the government terminating its contracts by paying for the contractors' reliance interest but not full expectation damages, and the opposition position of contractors, often backed by sympathetic commentators, that such termination transgresses their legitimate contract rights to full expectation damages. * * *

Federal government termination of contracts for convenience doctrine dates back to seminal Supreme Court cases following the Civil War. During World War I, Congress provided legislatively for government termination for convenience, producing two signal Supreme Court rulings. In the first, the Court reasoned that, given the prospect of government termination of contracts at war's end, "[t]he possible loss of profits [from this] must be regarded as within the contemplation of the parties," and the remedy for the canceled contractor could just compensate the reliance interest without also compensating for the contractor's lost anticipated profits. Second, in *College Point*, the Court created the doctrine of constructive termination for convenience, allowing the government to compensate just for the reliance interest in diverse situations.[1]

The concept of termination for convenience received extensive use during and after World War II. In 1982, the Court of Claims, hearing a major case en banc, heeded criticisms by commentators in an important ruling that produced extensive debate over the following fourteen years: *Torncello v. United States*. An opinion for three of the six judges of the en banc court traced the history of termination for convenience in detail, suggested that without greater protection for contractors the government contract would be illusory, and concluded that the refusal to allow expectation damages could not be so generally justified.

During the following decade and a half, *Torncello* drew extensive attention in subsequent cases[2] and commentary. The Federal Circuit, the newly-created successor court to the Court of Claims, although generally adhering to Claims Court precedents, began visibly undermining *Torncello* in 1990, and sent a second major signal in 1995. The Federal Circuit delivered the coup de grace against *Torncello* in 1996 in *Krygoski Construction Co. v. United States*. *Krygoski* culminated in what might be called a public policy analysis of how government officials could be trusted not to abuse a termination power * * *.

Krygoski Construction Company, Inc., Plaintiff-Appellee, v. The United States, Defendant-Appellant.

No. 95-5136. United States Court of Appeals,
Federal Circuit. 94 F.3d 1537. Aug. 1, 1996.

Before RICH, RADER, and BRYSON, Circuit Judges.

RADER, Circuit Judge.

The United States Court of Federal Claims determined that the United States Army Corps of Engineers (Corps) had no justification for terminating a demolition contract with Krygoski Construction Company, Inc. (Krygoski) for the Government's convenience. Krygoski Constr. Co. v. United States, No. 214- 89C (Fed.Cl. March 2, 1993). To remedy the breach, the trial court awarded Krygoski $1,456,851.10 in damages plus interest pending payment. Krygoski Constr. Co. v. United States, No. 214-89C (Fed.Cl.

---

1. The government could limits its compensation to the reliance interest even in situations where it had not considered itself to be, or notified that it was, terminating for convenience. As Justice Brandeis contrasted in one of his classic analyses of government contracting, in an ordinary contract, "the ordinary liability of one who, having contracted...without cause, gives notice that he will not accept delivery...[is] for the prospective profits." However, since the government's "right to cancel....[was a] continuing right of cancellation, which was asserted later.....Prospective profits were not recoverable." * * *

2. By 1996, "Torncello has been cited for various legal propositions in 90 board of contract appeals decisions, 46 Claims Court and Court of Federal Claims decisions, and 12 Federal Circuit decisions." * * *

May 19, 1995). Because the trial court incorrectly relied on Torncello v. United States, 231 Ct.Cl. 20, 681 F.2d 756 (1982), this court reverses and remands.

BACKGROUND

In 1985, the Corps undertook demolition of an abandoned U.S. Air Force airfield and missile site near Raco, Michigan. During surveys of the site, the Corps found asbestos contamination. Based on blueprints and its survey, the Corps estimated that two buildings at the site contained asbestos contamination in 1600 linear feet of pipe insulation and 650 square feet of tank and duct insulation. The survey also revealed that extensive vandalism may have spread asbestos debris on the floors of the buildings.

On August 12, 1985, the Corps issued an invitation for bids on the demolition project. The solicitation noted that bids should range between $500,000 and $1,000,000. Eight bidders bid on the contract. Krygoski won the contract with the low bid of $414,696. On or about September 30, 1985, Krygoski and the United States through the Detroit District of the Army Corps of Engineers entered into Contract No. DACA35-85-C-0001. This contract required removal and disposal of the asbestos during restoration of the site.

* * *

The contract contained a Variations in Estimated Quantities (VEQ) Clause for items 1, 2, 4, and 5 above:

> Variation from the estimated quantity in the actual work performed under any second or subsequent sub-item...will not be the basis for an adjustment in contract unit price.

This VEQ Clause anticipated variations in asbestos quantities for these four items at the Raco site. The VEQ Clause, however, did not contemplate quantity variations for asbestos removal in other areas.

Krygoski conducted a predemolition survey. Just ten days after Krygoski acknowledged receipt of the notice to proceed with the contract, Mr. Phillips, Krygoski's counsel, informed the Corps of asbestos in the vinyl flooring and roof insulation of the Raco buildings. Krygoski proposed to remove the tile for a unit price of $8.78 per square foot—the cost of removing additional duct insulation under item 2 of the VEQ Clause. The Corps requested Thermo Analytical, Inc. to take samples at potential new locations of asbestos contamination. The tests showed asbestos in the tile and the flashing at the Composite building, but not in the roof insulation.

From examining the drawings, the Corps' Area Office estimated asbestos removal needs at 36,340 square feet. At Krygoski's removal price of $8.78 per square foot, this amount of removal yielded an additional cost of about $320,000 for the floor tile. The Corps did not, however, actually test each tile. The Corps derived its estimate from the drawings.

The contracting officer, Lieutenant Colonel Phillip Johnson (LTC Johnson), considered a price increase of this dimension a cardinal change in the contract. LTC Johnson reached this conclusion because this increase exceeds 33% of the total contract cost. For a change of this magnitude, the Corps followed a general policy of terminating the contract for the convenience of the Government and reprocuring the work competitively under the Competition in Contracting Act. LTC Johnson also considered that Krygoski had not started work on the contract. In fact, Krygoski had done little beyond transporting four pieces of equipment to the Raco site. In light of these circumstances, the Corps terminated the contract for the convenience of the Government on September 5, 1986.

Following the termination, the Corps resolicited bids for the Raco site demolition. The Corps revised its specifications to reflect the additional asbestos removal work as well as other changes. The Corps received eight offers on this new solicitation, DACA35-87-B-001. Krygoski was the sixth lowest bidder at $1,200,000. Anderson Excavating & Wrecking Co. (Anderson) won the bidding at $443,200. Due to modifications to the contract, the Corps eventually paid Anderson a total of $542,861.60 to complete the contract.

Krygoski sued in the Court of Federal Claims alleging that the Corps breached its original contract. Relying on Torcello, 681 F.2d at 772 (reading the termination for convenience clause to require some change in the circumstances of the bargain or in the expectations of the parties), the trial court found the Government improperly terminated Krygoski's contract. In the alternative, the trial court found the Government abused its discretion in terminating the contract under the Kalvar standard. Kalvar Corp. v. United States, 211 Ct.Cl. 192, 543 F.2d 1298, 1301-02 (1976), cert. denied, 434 U.S. 830, 98 S.Ct. 112, 54 L.Ed.2d 89 (1977). Accordingly, the trial court awarded Krygoski $1,456,851.20 in damages plus interest. This amount included anticipatory lost profits. The Government appeals.

DISCUSSION

This court reviews Court of Federal Claims decisions for errors of law and clearly erroneous findings of fact. Cooper v. United States, 827 F.2d 762, 763 (Fed.Cir.1987) (citing Milmark Servs., Inc. v. United States, 731 F.2d 855, 857 (Fed.Cir.1984)).

The trial court thoroughly analyzed the factual circumstances and legal principles of this case. Its careful work properly framed the issues for this appeal. As the trial court perceived, the case law governing the decision to terminate a contract for convenience has not always set a clear, unambiguous standard. See Torcello, 681 F.2d at 764-72 (recounting history of terminations for convenience). An examination of termination for convenience law from several decades ago discloses mixed signals about limiting terminations under the bad faith/abuse of discretion standard in Kalvar, 543 F.2d at 1301-06, or the change of circumstances test in Torcello, 681 F.2d at 772. A full review of more recent case law, coupled with recent enactments, however, discloses a clear signal for implementation of termination for convenience clauses.

I.

At the outset, this court traces some of the history leading up to articulation of two tests for convenience terminations. The Government always possessed the power to terminate its contracts; such action, however, constituted a contract breach. * * * Terminations for the Government's convenience developed as a tool to avoid enormous procurements upon completion of a war effort. Because public policy counselled against proceeding with wartime contracts after an end to hostilities, the Government, under certain circumstances, began to terminate contracts and settle with the contractor for partial performance. In 1863, the Army, for example, promulgated Rule 1179 in the Army Regulations concerning contracting for subsistence stores. Rule 1179 expressly "provide[d] for [subsistence contract] termination at such time as the Commissary-General may direct." United States v. Speed, 75 U.S. (8 Wall.) 77, 78, 19 L.Ed. 449 (1868). The Supreme Court has acknowledged the Government's authority to settle breach claims after a convenience termination. Cf. United States v. Corliss-Steam Engine Co., 91 U.S. 321, 323, 23 L.Ed. 397 (1875) (finding the Navy Department had authority to suspend work under a contract and enter into a breach settlement for partial performance); see also Cibinic & Nash, at 1073-74.

After World War I, the Government terminated contracts in large numbers. New statutory authority provided for settlement of the claims from those terminations. See Dent Act, 40 Stat. 1272 (1919). When World War II started, the Contract Settlement Act of 1944, 58 Stat. 649, provided further statutory and regulatory provisions for contract termination. See Cibinic & Nash, at 1074.

In 1964, the first edition of the Federal Procurement Regulation (FPR) included optional termination for convenience clauses. FPR 1-8.700-2. By 1967, the FPR required termination for convenience clauses in most procurement contracts. 32 Fed.Reg. 9683 (1967). Thus, termination for convenience—initially developed for war contracts—evolved into a principle for Government contracts of far-ranging varieties, both civilian and military. See 48 C.F.R. §49.502 (1995). The exigencies of war no longer limited the Government's ability to terminate a contract for convenience. Although wartime situations no longer limit use of the practice, the Government's authority to invoke a termination for convenience has, nonetheless, retained limits. A contracting officer may not terminate for convenience in bad faith, for example, simply to acquire a better bargain from another source. Torncello, 681 F.2d at 772. When tainted by bad faith or an abuse of contracting discretion, a termination for convenience causes a contract breach. See Allied Materials & Equip. Co. v. United States, 215 Ct.Cl. 902, 905-06, 1977 WL 9596 (1977); National Factors, Inc. v. United States, 204 Ct.Cl. 98, 492 F.2d 1383, 1385 (1974); Keco Indus., Inc. v. United States, 203 Ct.Cl. 566, 492 F.2d 1200, 1203-04 (1974); John Reiner & Co. v. United States, 163 Ct.Cl. 381, 325 F.2d 438, 442 (1963), cert. denied, 377 U.S. 931, 84 S.Ct. 1332, 12 L.Ed.2d 295 (1964).

The contractor's burden to prove the Government acted in bad faith, however, is very weighty. Kalvar, 543 F.2d at 1301 ("Any analysis of a question of Governmental bad faith must begin with the presumption that public officials act 'conscientiously in the discharge of their duties.'" (quoting Librach v. United States, 147 Ct.Cl. 605, 612 (1959))). Due to this heavy burden of proof, contractors have rarely succeeded in demonstrating the Government's bad faith. See Cibinic & Nash, at 1078; Kalvar, 543 F.2d at 1301; Librach, 147 Ct.Cl. at 612.

II.   *Torcello*

In 1982, this court's predecessor articulated in dicta another test for the sufficiency of convenience terminations. Torncello, 681 F.2d at 758. In Torncello, the Navy awarded a requirements contract, but then purchased some work covered by the contract from a competing bidder at a lower price. Id. In an earlier case, Colonial Metals Co. v. United States, 204 Ct.Cl. 320, 494 F.2d 1355 (1974), the Court of Claims had allowed a termination for convenience under these circumstances. In Colonial Metals, the Navy terminated a contract for copper ingot solely to obtain a better price. In fact, the Navy knew of the better price at the time of contract award. The Court of Claims permitted this termination because "such a motive [contracting for a lower price elsewhere] is not improper." 494 F.2d at 1359.

Torncello offered the opportunity to revisit and overrule the Colonial Metals case. Indeed Colonial Metals was inconsistent with the Kalvar bad faith limit on terminations for convenience. Even factoring in Kalvar's presumption of good faith actions by public officials, 543 F.2d at 1301, the Navy in Colonial Metals contracted in bad faith. At the time of award, the Navy knew of the better price it later terminated the contract to obtain.

In Torncello, the Navy—knowing it could acquire the same services at a lower price from another contractor—again contracted with Torncello and Soledad Enterprises in an exclusive requirements contract. The Navy then began satisfying its requirements from that cheaper source. Torncello claimed the Navy breached the requirements contract. The Armed Services Board of Contract Appeals found the contract constructively terminated for the Government's convenience, disallowing Torncello contract breach damages. This court's predecessor overruled Colonial Metals because the Navy used the termination for convenience clause to escape a promise it never had an intention to keep. Torncello, 681 F.2d at 772. Indeed, then Chief Judge Friedman concurred with that narrow understanding of the court's action:

> As I understand the court's opinion, the court holds only that when the government enters into a requirements contract, knowing that it can obtain an item the contract covers for less than the contract price and intending to do so, there cannot be a constructive termination for convenience of the government when the government follows that course. On that basis, I join in the opinion.

Id. at 773;[1] see also Salsbury Indus. v. United States, 905 F.2d 1518, 1521 (Fed.Cir.1990), cert. denied, 498 U.S. 1024, 111 S. Ct. 671, 112 L.Ed.2d 664 (1991) (construing the Torncello holding).

Despite the adequate justification to overrule Colonial Metals under the existing Kalvar test, a plurality of judges in Torncello proceeded to articulate in dicta a broader test for gauging the sufficiency of a convenience termination. The plurality stated that the Navy could not invoke a convenience termination unless some change in circumstances between the time of award of the contract and the time of termination justified the action. Torncello, 681 F.2d at 772. As in this case, trial courts and boards have occasionally vacillated between applying the long-standing Kalvar test or the Torncello test.

III.   *Reason distinguish Torncello*

Recent enactments, however, have underscored rules of Government contracting which render the plurality's dicta in Torncello inapplicable to the present regime of contract administration. Recent statutes fully address the concerns of the Torncello plurality regarding the Government's shopping for lower prices after contract award. The Competition in Contracting Act (CICA), Pub.L. No. 98-369, 98 Stat. 1175 (codified as amended in scattered sections of 10, 31 and 41 U.S.C.), compels the promulgation of regulations and procedures to ensure full and open competition. See 41 U.S.C. §§401, 405(a) and 416 (1994).

In 1984, CICA articulated significant factors addressing a contracting officer's decision to terminate a contract for the Government's convenience. CICA requires executive agencies, when procuring property or services, to "obtain full and open competition through use of competitive procedures." 41 U.S.C. §253(a)(1)(A) (1994). Thus, CICA ensures that contracting officers receive bids at competitively low prices. For each solicitation, a contracting officer must maintain full and open competition in the procurement process, unless one of the limited exceptions applies. See 10 U.S.C. §2304 (1994). CICA mandates impartial, fair, and equitable treatment for each contractor. See 10 U.S.C. §§2304 and 2305 (1994).

---

1. Six judges participated in the en banc Torncello opinion. A plurality of three judges joined the reasoning that postulated a broad alternative "change of circumstances" test for convenience terminations. The remaining three judges, then Chief Judge Friedman and Circuit Judges Davis and Nichols, each concurred separately under much narrower reasoning. Judge Davis stated: "I do not agree that 'abuse of discretion' is an inadequate or unsatisfactory general standard for gauging the contracting officer's use of the termination clause." Torncello, 681 F.2d at 773. * * *

This competitive fairness requirement, with its bid protest remedies, restrains a contracting officer's contract administration. If, for instance, a contracting officer discovers that the bid specifications inadequately describe the contract work, regulations promulgated under CICA may compel a new bid. See 10 U.S.C. §2305; 48 C.F.R. §1.602-2. Thus, to accommodate CICA's fairness requirements, the contracting officer may need to terminate a contract for the Government's convenience to further full and open competition. 48 C.F.R. §§1.602-2(b); see 41 U.S.C. §414 (1994). Thus, to further its full competition objective, CICA permits a lenient convenience termination standard.

Not every necessary alteration of the contract scope, however, requires a new bid procedure. See 41 U.S.C. §§423(e)(1), 423(e)(2) (1994) (providing procedures for certifications before a contract modification or extension). Only "modifications outside the scope of the original competed contract fall under the statutory competition requirement." AT & T Communications, Inc. v. WilTel, Inc., 1 F.3d 1201, 1205 (Fed.Cir.1993). CICA does not fully define a "standard for determining when modification of an existing contract requires new competition or falls within the scope of the original competitive procurement." Id. This court, nonetheless, has stated that a "cardinal change" is a drastic modification beyond the scope of the contract:

> Under established case law, a cardinal change is a breach. It occurs when the government effects an alteration in the work so drastic that it effectively requires the contractor to perform duties materially different from those originally bargained for. By definition, then a cardinal change is so profound that it is not redressable under the contract, and thus renders the government in breach.

Id. (citing Allied Materials & Equip. Co. v. United States, 215 Ct. Cl. 406, 569 F.2d 562, 563-64 (1978)); see also Air-A-Plane Corp. v. United States, 187 Ct. Cl. 269, 408 F.2d 1030, 1032-33 (1969). In WilTel, the question was not whether the Government modifications breached a contract, but was "whether Government modifications changed the contract enough to circumvent the statutory requirement of competition." 1 F.3d at 1205. In other words, the court inquired whether the modification was within the scope of the competition for the original contract. Id.

IV. *Reason to Return to Torncello.*

In the wake of CICA, with its protections for competition, this court has revisited the dicta in the Torncello plurality opinion. Salsbury, 905 F.2d at 1518. * * *

Again, more recently, this court has confronted an invitation to apply the reasoning and test of the Torncello plurality. Caldwell & Santmyer, Inc. v. Glickman, 55 F.3d 1578 (Fed.Cir.1995). * * *

In sum, on two recent occasions after enactment of CICA, this court has expressly repeated the narrow applicability of Torncello. Id. at 1582; Salsbury, 905 F.2d at 1521. Indeed this court's recent pronouncements are fully consistent with the policy goals of CICA and other Government procurement statutes. Under these policies, contracting officers have no incentive to terminate a contract for convenience except to maintain full and open competition under CICA. With an adequate contractor in place, the contracting officer has no interest to reprocure. Moreover, where an officer must choose between modifying or terminating a contract, ease of administration usually imparts a bias in favour of modification. Thus Salsbury and Caldwell suggest that this court will avoid a finding of abused discretion when the facts support a reasonable inference that

the contracting officer terminated for convenience in furtherance of statutory requirements for full and open competition.

V.

Turning now to this case, the termination for convenience clause of the contract
provided:

> The Government may terminate performance of work under this contract in
> whole or, from time to time, in part if the Contracting Officer determines that
> a termination is in the Government's interest.

See 48 C.F.R. §52.249-2 (1995). This contract language governs the legal relations of
the parties. Under the discretion conferred by this contract language, Contracting Officer LTC Johnson decided to terminate the contract with Krygoski because removing
the asbestos-containing vinyl tile would constitute a cardinal change from the originally competed contract. The contracting officer felt that a change increasing the total
contract price between 25% and 33% warranted resolicitation. The trial court stated
that LTC Johnson cited "no authority for his definition of cardinal change." Because
the Government ultimately removed only 9,000 square feet of tile, not 36,000 square
feet, the trial court concluded that the Corps arbitrarily and capriciously miscalcu-
lated the scope of asbestos abatement. To the contrary, the contracting officer had a
reasonable basis for terminating the contract for the Government's convenience. Asbestos removal was originally estimated to cost about $40,000 out of an estimated
$415,000 demolition contract. Thus asbestos removal accounted for about 10% of the
total cost of the contract. At that point, the contracting officer's experts increased the
cost of asbestos removal by about $320,000. After this change, the total asbestos re-
moval cost was about $360,000 on a contract near $775,000 — just under 50% of the
total contract. Asbestos removal, originally about 10%, became about 50% of the contract work.

Under these circumstances, the contracting officer had ample justification for
conducting a reprocurement competitively under CICA. With this change in the
scope of contract work, different bidders, like asbestos removal firms, may have entered the competition on the contract. See 48 C.F.R. §§14.203-1, 14.203-2 (1995)
(enumerating the methods of soliciting bids where invitations for bids or presolicitation notices are mailed to prospective bidders or are displayed in public places, like
trade journals).

In determining whether a modification falls within CICA's competition requirement,
this court in WilTel examined whether the contract as modified materially departs from
the scope of the original procurement. WilTel, 1 F.3d at 1205. In this case, the contracting officer, LTC Johnson, determined that the removal of the asbestos-contaminated
floor tile amounted to a cardinal change, a modification outside the scope of the original
competed contract. The contract has no provision to increase the cost of the contract
under the VEQ Clause for removal of asbestos-contaminated floor tile. In fact, if the removal of floor tile was within the scope of the contract, Krygoski may have the obligation to remove the tile without increasing the contract price. The contracting officer, recognizing the equities of this situation, terminated the contract for convenience to comply
with CICA.

The trial court erred by invoking and relying upon the Torncello plurality test. The
trial court improperly found no change of circumstances sufficient to justify terminating the contract for the Government's convenience. Although arguably the Govern-

ment's circumstances had sufficiently changed to meet even the Torncello plurality standard, this court declines to reach this issue because Torncello applies only when the Government enters a contract with no intention of fulfilling its promises. Salsbury, 905 F.2d at 1521.

LTC Johnson's decision to terminate is analogous to that made in Caldwell. LTC Johnson terminated the contract to preserve full and open competition. He decided to avoid any prospect of prejudice to other bidders. Unlike the Torncello situation, this record shows no evidence that the Corps intended from the outset to void its promises. Thus, Torncello does not apply. Accordingly, this court finds that LTC Johnson did not abuse his discretion, act arbitrarily or capriciously or in bad faith in terminating the contract for the Government's convenience.

This court reverses and remands for termination for convenience damages which are to include costs of performance prior to termination, profits on that performance and termination costs. No anticipatory profits are to be awarded. Reversed and remanded to calculate these costs.

COSTS

Each party shall bear its own costs.

REVERSED AND REMANDED.

Notes and Questions

1. *Krygoski* gives a glimpse back into the historic mists of termination for convenience, including the unusual spectacle of a current clause's origin in Army Regulations of the Civil War. Congress enacted fresh statutory authority in connection with World War I and World War II. What is so fundamental about termination for convenience that it arose so early and has been important so long? See Joseph J. Petrillo & William E. Conner, From Torncello to Krygoski: 25 Years of the Government's Termination for Convenience Power, 7 Fed. Circuit B.J. 337 (1997).

2. This opinion also combines with the issue of termination for convenience another venerable concept, the difference between modifications within the scope of the original competed contract and cardinal changes. That distinction has been discussed elsewhere, in connection with equitable adjustments. What is the conceptual link among these various matters?

3. The opinion makes strong use of CICA to explain its downgrading of the Torncello opinion. Is this simply the instinct of a court, seeking to overcome a troublesome but high-profile precedent, to emphasize whatever basis it has to say that legal circumstances, specifically legislation, changed after that precedent? Or, did CICA in fact seek to transform the role of the contracting officer into more active promoter of competitive contracting, significantly affecting the tools such an officer can use, like termination of previously awarded contracts to allow their recompetition?

4. In the facts of this case, who set whom up here? Could the contractor Krygoski fairly complain that the government had set it up to take the loss if its bid had turned out to be a good deal for the government, but for the government to withhold the gain when its bid turned out to be a good deal for the contractor? Or could the government fairly complain that it had correctly estimated the cost of performance as high, and the contractor set it up by bidding low and then demanding a high figure?

E. Governmental Breach

The government has another way to end a contract: breach. As the government, it can breach in ways a private buyer would not, such as by a new statute or program effectively frustrating completion of existing contracts. This topic has a long history in the law, such as the seminal 1925 case when the United States was sued for breach for dishonoring a contract involving a sale of silk. The government defended successfully on the ground the breach resulted from a subsequent embargo on such transactions, notwithstanding that the government itself had imposed that embargo. *Horowitz v. United States*, 267 U.S. 458 (1925). In recent years, the topic received renewed attention focusing upon the interesting but exceedingly complex opinions in *United States v. Winstar*, 518 U.S. 839 (1996). Cases since *Winstar* now appear to have clarified somewhat the contemporary law Accordingly, this section provides a post-*Winstar* case, *Mobil*, followed by notes.

MOBIL OIL EXPLORATION & PRODUCING SOUTHEAST, INC., Petitioner, v. UNITED STATES.

Supreme Court of the United States Nos. 99-244, 99-253.
Argued March 22, 2000., Decided June 26, 2000.

Justice delivered the opinion of the Court.

Two oil companies, petitioners here, seek restitution of $156 million they paid the Government in return for lease contracts giving them rights to explore for and develop oil off the North Carolina coast. The rights were not absolute, but were conditioned on the companies' obtaining a set of further governmental permissions. The companies claim that the Government repudiated the contracts when it denied them certain elements of the permission-seeking opportunities that the contracts had promised. We agree that the Government broke its promise; it repudiated the contracts; and it must give the companies their money back.

I

A

A description at the outset of the few basic contract law principles applicable to this action will help the reader understand the significance of the complex factual circumstances that follow. "When the United States enters into contract relations, its rights and duties therein are governed generally by the law applicable to contracts between private individuals." *United States v. Winstar Corp.*, 518 U.S. 839, 895, 116 S.Ct. 2432, 135 L.Ed.2d 964 (1996) (plurality opinion) (internal quotation marks omitted). The Restatement of Contracts reflects many of the principles of contract law that are applicable to this action. As set forth in the Restatement of Contracts, the relevant principles specify that, when one party to a contract repudiates that contract, the other party "is entitled to restitution for any benefit that he has conferred on" the repudiating party "by way of part performance or reliance." (hereinafter Restatement). The Restatement explains that "repudiation" is a "statement by the obligor to the obligee indicating that the obligor will commit a breach that would of itself give the obligee a claim for damages for total breach." *Id.*, § 250. And "total breach" is a breach that "so substantially impairs the value of the contract to the injured party at the time of the breach that it is just in the circumstances to allow him to recover damages based on all his remaining rights to performance." *Id.*, §243.

* * *

B

In 1981, in return for up-front "bonus" payments to the United States of about $156 million (plus annual rental payments), the companies received 10- year renewable lease contracts with the United States. In these contracts, the United States promised the companies, among other things, that they could explore for oil off the North Carolina coast and develop any oil that they found (subject to further royalty payments) provided that the companies received exploration and development permissions in accordance with various statutes and regulations to which the lease contracts were made "subject." App. to Pet. for Cert. in No. 99-253, pp. 174a-185a.The statutes and regulations, the terms of which in effect were incorporated into the contracts, made clear that obtaining the necessary permissions might not be an easy matter. In particular, the Outer Continental Shelf Lands Act (OCSLA), 67 Stat. 462, as amended, *et seq.* (1994 ed. and Supp. III), and the Coastal Zone Management Act of 1972 (CZMA), 86 Stat. 1280, *et seq.*, specify that leaseholding companies wishing to explore and drill must successfully complete [various] procedures. * * * *

C

The events at issue here * * * are the following:

1. In 1981, the companies and the Government entered into the lease contracts. The companies paid the Government $156 million in up-front cash "bonus" payments.

2. In 1989, the companies, Interior, and North Carolina entered into a memorandum of understanding. In that memorandum, the companies promised that they would submit an initial draft Exploration Plan to North Carolina before they submitted their final Exploration Plan to Interior. * * *

4. On August 20, 1990, the companies submitted both their final Exploration Plan and their CZMA "consistency certification" to Interior.

5. Just two days earlier, on August 18, 1990, a new law, the Outer Banks Protection Act (OBPA), §6003, 104 Stat. 555, had come into effect.* * *

6. About five weeks later, and in light of the new statute, Interior wrote a letter to the Governor of North Carolina with a copy to petitioner Mobil. It said that the final submitted Exploration Plan "is deemed to be approvable in all respects." * * * But, it noted, the new law, the "Outer Banks Protection Act (OBPA) of 1990...prohibits the approval of any Exploration Plan at this time." It concluded, "because we are currently prohibited from approving it, the Plan will remain on file until the requirements of the OBPA are met." In the meantime a "suspension has been granted to all leases offshore the State of North Carolina." *Ibid.* * * *

7. In November 1990, North Carolina objected to the companies' CZMA consistency certification on the ground that Mobil had not provided sufficient information about possible environmental impact. A month later, the companies asked the Secretary of Commerce to override North Carolina's objection.

8. In 1994, the Secretary of Commerce rejected the companies' override request, relying in large part on the fact that the new [OBPA-created] Panel had found a lack of adequate information in respect to certain environmental issues.

9. In 1996, Congress repealed OBPA. § 109, 110 Stat. 1321-177.

D

In October 1992, after all but the two last-mentioned events had taken place, petitioners joined a breach-of-contract lawsuit brought in the Court of Federal Claims. On motions for summary judgment, the court found that the United States had broken its contractual promise to follow OCSLA's provisions * * * A panel of the Court of Appeals for the Federal Circuit reversed, one judge dissenting. * * * We granted certiorari to review the Federal Circuit's decision.

II

* * *[T]he Government denies that it must refund the companies' money.This is because, in the Government's view, it did not breach the contracts or communicate its intent to do so; [and] any breach was not "substantial" * * *

A

The Government's "no breach" arguments depend upon the contract provisions that "subject" the contracts to various statutes and regulations. * * * [After analyzing these,] [w]e conclude, for these reasons, that the Government violated the contracts. * * *

The dissent argues that only the statements contained in the letter from Interior to the companies may constitute a repudiation because "the enactment of legislation is not typically conceived of as a 'statement' of anything to any one party in particular," and a repudiation requires a "statement by the obligor to the obligee indicating that the obligor will commit a breach." *Post,* at 2441, n. 4 (opinion of STEVENS, J.) (quoting Restatement). * * * If the dissent means to invoke a special exception such as the "sovereign acts" doctrine, which treats certain laws as if they simply created conditions of impossibility, see Winstar, *518 U.S.,* at 891-899, 116 S.Ct. 2432 *(principal opinion of SOUTER, J.); id.,* at 923-924, 116 S.Ct. 2432 (SCALIA, J., concurring in judgment), it cannot do so here. The Court of Federal Claims rejected the application of that doctrine to this action, see Cl., at 334-336, and the Government has not contested that determination here. Hence, under these circumstances, the fact that Interior's repudiation rested upon the enactment of a new statute makes no significant difference.We do not say that the changes made by the statute were unjustified. We say only that they were changes of a kind that the contracts did not foresee. They were changes in those approval procedures and standards that the contracts had incorporated through cross-reference. The Government has not convinced us that Interior's actions were authorized by any other contractually cross- referenced provision. Hence, in communicating to the companies its intent to follow OBPA, the United States was communicating its intent to violate the contracts.

B

The Government next argues that any violation of the contracts' terms was not significant; hence there was no "substantial" or "material" breach that could have amounted to a "repudiation." In particular, it says that OCSLA's 30-day approval period "does not function as the 'essence' of these agreements." Brief for United States 37. The Court of Claims concluded, however, that timely and fair consideration of a submitted Exploration Plan was a "necessary reciprocal obligation," indeed, that any "contrary interpretation would render the bargain illusory." Cl., at 327. We agree. * * *

The Government's modification of the contract-incorporated processes was not technical or insubstantial. It did not announce an (OBPA-required) approval delay of a few days or weeks, but of 13 months minimum, and likely much longer. The delay turned out to be at least four years. And lengthy delays matter, particularly where several successive agency approvals are at stake. * * *

The upshot is that, under the contracts, the incorporated procedures and standards amounted to a gateway to the companies' enjoyment of all other rights. To significantly narrow that gateway violated material conditions in the contracts. The breach was "substantia[l]," depriving the companies of the benefit of their bargain. Restatement § 243. And the Government's communication of its intent to commit that breach amounted to a repudiation of the contracts.

* * *

D

Finally, the Government argues that repudiation could not have hurt the companies. Since the companies could not have met the CZMA consistency requirements, they could not have explored (or ultimately drilled) for oil in any event. * * * This argument, however, misses the basic legal point. The oil companies do not seek damages for breach of contract. They seek restitution of their initial payments. Because the Government repudiated the lease contracts, the law entitles the companies to that restitution * * * If a lottery operator fails to deliver a purchased ticket, the purchaser can get his money back—whether or not he eventually would have won the lottery. And if one party to a contract, whether oil company or ordinary citizen, advances the other party money, principles of restitution normally require the latter, upon repudiation, to refund that money. Restatement § 373. * * *

* * And therefore the Government must give the companies their money back. For these reasons, the judgment of the Federal Circuit is reversed. We remand the cases for further proceedings consistent with this opinion.

It is so ordered.

Justice STEVENS, dissenting.

Since the 1953 passage of the Outer Continental Shelf Lands Act (OCSLA), 43 U.S.C. § 1331 *et seq.*, the United States Government has conducted more than a hundred lease sales of the type at stake today, and bidders have paid the United States more than $55 billion for the opportunity to develop the mineral resources made available under those leases. The United States, as lessor, and petitioners, as lessees, clearly had a mutual interest in the successful exploration, development, and production of oil in the Manteo Unit pursuant to the leases executed in 1981. * * *

From the outset, however, it was apparent that the Outer Banks project might not succeed for a variety of reasons. Among those was the risk that the State of North Carolina would exercise its right to object to the completion of the project. That was a risk that the parties knowingly assumed. They did not, however, assume the risk that Congress would enact additional legislation that would delay the completion of what would obviously be a lengthy project in any event. I therefore agree with the Court that the Government did breach its contract with petitioners in failing to approve, within 30 days of its receipt, the plan of exploration petitioners submitted. As the Court describes, *ante,* at 2430, the leases incorporate the provisions of the OCSLA into their terms, and the OCSLA, correspondingly, sets down this 30-day requirement in plain language. 43 U.S.C. § 1340(c).

I do not, however, believe that the appropriate remedy for the Government's breach is for petitioners to recover their full initial investment. When the entire relationship between the parties is considered, with particular reference to the impact of North Carolina's foreseeable exercise of its right to object to the project, it is clear that the remedy ordered by the Court is excessive. I would hold that petitioners are entitled at best to damages resulting from the delay caused by the Government's failure to approve the plan within the requisite time. * * *

Notes and Questions

1. After this case, it makes sense to touch briefly on the highlights of its complex predecessor, *United States v. Winstar*, 518 U.S. 839 (1996). In *Winstar*, a federal lending agency dealing with the savings and loan crisis induced healthy financial entities to take over ailing ones by agreeing to permit their intangible "goodwill" to satisfy capital reserve requirements. Congress thereafter enacted new legislation that, among other matters, forbid this practice, and the acquiring entities sued for breach of their contract with the federal agency. The Supreme Court, with badly divided opinions, held the government liable for breach. A plurality opinion by Justice Souter held the lending agency's agreement with the acquiring entities constituted a promise to indemnify them from losses from future legal changes.

Notably, *Winstar* addressed several special defenses the government may raise in such cases, including the "sovereign acts" defense that the government is not liable for the "public and general acts" it adopts in its sovereign capacity. The different opinions had different reasoning about why the sovereign acts defense did not apply, but, however they were to synthesize, they evidently downgraded new legislation as a complete government defense, in some circumstances, to a breach suit. Although the Court in *Mobil* took the sovereign acts defense as having been resolved in the court below, the issues that Mobil did address, reflect somewhat the post-*Winstar* sense downgrading new legislation as a complete government defense in breach cases. For further discussion of *Winstar*, see Richard E. Speidel, *Contract Excuse Doctrine and Retrospective Legislation: The* Winstar *Case*, 2001 Wisc. L. Rev. 795; Joshua I. Schwartz, *Assembling* Winstar: *Triumph of the Ideal of Congruence in Government Contracts Law?*, 26 Pub. Cont. L.J. 481 (1997); Joshua I. Schwartz, *Liability for Sovereign Acts: Congruence and Exceptionalism in Government Contracts Law*, 64 Geo. Wash. L. Rev. 633 (1996); Gilliam Hadfield, *Of Sovereignty and Contract: Damages for Breach of Contract by Government*, 8 S. Cal. Interdisciplinary L.J. 467 (1999).

2. *Winstar* and *Mobil* arise in contexts distinct from the goods and services government agreements under the Federal Acquisition Regulations. However, agreements of that kind can raise related issues. How do you think the following two disputes should come out? (1) After defense contractors enter into cost-reimbursement contracts, Congress enacts a cap on executive pay that can be charged to such contracts, applying to pay subsequently incurred under contracts already made. A contractor challenges this cap as unconstitutional. (2) Cost-reimbursement contracts include government reimbursement of the costs of contractor employee pension plan contributions. These receive elaborate regulation pursuant to the Cost Accounting Standards. In 1995, revisions of the relevant standards were promulgated. These may be triggered, after 1995, by contractor restructurings affecting government reimbursements before 1995. Contractors challenge such triggering. As to both of these, see Charles Tiefer, Did *Eastern Enterprises* Send Enterprise Responsibility South?, 51 Ala. L. Rev. 1305 (2000). As to is-

sues in this context, see Bernard W. Bell, *In Defense of Retroactive Laws*, 78 Tex. L. Rev. 235 (1999); Jill E. Fisch, *Retroactivity and Legal Change: The Equilibrium Model*, 110 Harv. L. Rev. 1055 (1997).

3. How much does *Mobil* turn on the specific circumstances - how the statutes and regulations that existed or were contemplated at the time of the lease, as which the lessee "assumed the risk" for how they would operate, compared in effect with those, particularly the OBPA, that later came into existence? How much does *Mobil* reflect a general view coming down either from the spirit of the age, or that of the Supreme Court, about the government being less exceptional as a sovereign and more like other non-sovereign contracting parties? For an analysis that *Mobil* does not weaken sovereign defenses, see Seon J. Lee, Note, *Does* Mobil Oil *Weaken the Sovereign Defenses of Government Breach of Contract Claims? An Analysis of the Unmistakability Doctrine and the Sovereign Acts Doctrine*, 31 Pub. Cont. L.J. 559 (2002); Deena B. Bothello, Note, *An Unequal Balance: Repudiation and Restitution in* Mobil Oil Exploration & Producing Southeast, Inc. v. United States, 80 Ore. L. Rev. 1469 (2001).

4. How does the outcome in *Mobil* compare with the remedy given to a contractor terminated for convenience pursuant to the FAR?

5. Suppose the feedback from cases like *Winstar* and *Mobil* arms opponents in Congress of new proposed legislation affecting existing contracts with new ammunition to forestall enactment. Is that good, because it makes the enactment of legislation depend upon full awareness and acceptance of its costs? Or is it bad, because of the one-way direction in which it operates? Namely, the public gets set back by the prospect it must pay the business world for the burdens bestowed by some new legislation. But, the public does not get correspondingly encouraged by any similar prospect to recover other windfall benefits bestowed on the business world.

Chapter 11

Remedy Procedures

To someone familiar with the remedy procedures for basic (private) contract law, the remedy procedures for government contract law come as a shock. Rarely does the government allow cases with contractors to proceed like simple private contract cases, with aggrieved contractors and the government suing each other in the nearest court of general jurisdiction. On the contrary, government contract remedy procedures seem more the product of elaborate administrative law, with its many special aspects designed to channel and shape the controversies between private and public actors.

This area of law starts with the existence of an array of highly specialized tribunals, like the General Accounting Office and the boards of contract appeals. Cases cannot begin without a series of required preliminary steps commonly referred to in administrative law as tests of ripeness and "exhaustion," a technical word for the requisite sequence of actions which, coincidentally, expresses well the litigants' likely state of mind before they are through. Specially shaped procedures govern those tribunals, such as the complex procedures regarding when the award of a contract gets stayed to await decision of a protest. Also, unique types of remedies exist both for and against the contractor, such as debarment, a remedy for the government to protect itself from some contractors by preventing them from contracting again.

Moreover, the remedy procedures for government contract law derive from a long and tortuous history, having been changed frequently and radically by Congressional enactments, some quite recent. Those specialized tribunals do not exist because someone sat down and developed a structured master plan, nor by some teleologically purposeful evolution of the common law, but by a series of historical accidents as repaired by the intermittent intervention of statutory alterations. Thus, the General Accounting Office decides most protests by disappointed bidders, in part because of a long, almost accidental, historical development of its willingness to be the giver of incidental advice on the spending of government funds, and in part by the major surgery Congress wrought on the government contract system by the Competition in Contracting Act of 1984. The False Claims Act creates a unique procedure by which whistleblowers can recover from fraudulent contractors on behalf of the government, owing partly to a hoary old mechanism known to the Framers and first enacted as to government contracts in 1863, and in part to the Congressional reaction in 1986 to modern defense procurement scandals and the active construction of the 1986 Act by federal appellate judges in the 1990s.

This chapter starts with protest mechanisms for disappointed bidders. Some general sense of this procedure undoubtedly came from the cases in the early chapters about sealed bidding and negotiated procurement, but in those chapters the focus was on the substantive law rather than on how the protest procedures worked. Here, the interest lies in the mechanisms of protests. One section addresses the General Accounting Office ("GAO"), which decides most contract protests. A particular subject of interest concerns whether and how a disappointed bidder or a pleased but challenged awardee wage their struggle if the protest of the award halts proceeding with the contract. Another section addresses the courts, including the Court of Federal Claims which is a specialized court with a major role in government contract cases, such as protests.

Next, the chapter looks at the mechanisms for aggrieved contractors to litigate their claims against the government through the disputes process. The Contract Disputes Act of 1978 imposes an array of constraints on contractors as to what claims, when, and how they can present. Moreover, the disputes process provides for claims to receive a decision from contracting officers and then constrains all subsequent proceedings in the boards of contract appeals and the Court of Federal Claims by the content of that contracting officer decision.

Thereafter, a section is devoted to perhaps the most important type of court case about government contracts occurring outside of the protest and dispute processes, namely, the civil False Claims Act case. This Act creates a unique set of standards and procedures, exposing contractors who engage in fraud to penalties. Moreover, it provides for suits by whistleblowers as "relators," who can sue contractors for recoveries on behalf of the government even though they are themselves mere private citizens holding no government office. The chapter then addresses suits against the government.

For further discussion of the subjects of this chapter, see: the periodic surveys such as the annual *Year in Review: Analysis of Significant Federal Circuit Government Contracts Decisions* in the Public Contract Law Journal, the *Contract and Fiscal Law Developments—The Year in Review* in the Army Lawyer, and the *Cases and Recent Developments* in the Federal Circuit Bar Journal; Peter Verchinski, Note, *Are District Courts Still a Viable Forum for Bid Protests?*, 32 Pub. Cont L.J. 393 (2003); Steven L. Schooner, *Fear of Oversight: The Fundamental Failure of Businesslike Government*, 50 Am. U. L. Rev. 627 (2001); Richard H. Seamon, *Separation of Powers and the Separate Treatment of Contract Claims Against the Federal Government for Specific Performance*, 43 Vill. L. R. 155 (1998); Michael J. Davidson, *10 U.S.C. §2408: An Unused Weapon in the Procurement Fraud Wars*, 26 Pub. Cont. L.J. 181 (1997); Paul Frederic Kirgis, *Section 1500 and the Jurisdictional Pitfalls of Federal Government Litigation*, 47 Am. U. L. Rev. 301 (1997).

A. Protests

The protest remedy provides the crucial procedural machinery for many of the previously discussed myriad of statutes and regulations applicable to the government's acquiring of goods and services. Those statutes and regulations, numbering in the thousands of pages, set forth how government personnel are to spend the hundreds of billions of tax dollars with which they are entrusted for both Department of Defense and civilian agency acquisitions. The statutes and regulations are intended to ensure that federal procurements are conducted fairly by both mandating certain activity (e.g., providing for full and open competition whenever possible) and prohibiting other activity (e.g., the disclosure of contractor proprietary information prior to award).

There is no doubt that the federal procurement system benefits from the active participation of firms and businesses in a competitive marketplace. Furthermore, Congress views the fair opportunity for their constituents to compete for government contracts as an overall positive aspect of government spending. As a result, Congress and the courts have ensured that bidders or others interested in government procurements have forums in which to raise concerns about contracts that have been or are about to be awarded improperly or illegally or to respond to complaints that a particular entity has been unfairly denied the opportunity to compete for the government's business.

Unfortunately (or some may say fortunately) for the government contractor and the government contract practitioner, the number of different forums in which "bid protests" may be raised include: (1) the Court of Federal Claims; (2) the General Accounting Office; and (3) the actual Contracting Agency. While having four different forums in which to pursue a bid protest provides the government contractor with the opportunity to do a bit of forum shopping, it also presents the practitioner with the need to be familiar with the various jurisdictional and procedural requirements of each. What follows is a brief description of each such forum, in reverse order as presented above.

For further discussions of the subject of this section, see:

Peter Verchinski, Note, *Are District Courts Still a Viable Forum for Bid Protests?*, 32 Pub. Cont L.J. 393 (2003);

Jonathan R. Cantor, *Bid Protests and Procurement Reform: The Case for Leaving Well Enough Alone*, 27 Pub. Cont. L.J. 155 (1997);

Michael F. Mason, *Bid Protests and the U.S. District Courts-Why Congress Should Not Allow the Sun to Set on This Effective Relationship*, 26 Pub. Cont. L.J. 567 (1997).

Richard D. Lieberman, *Bid Protests at the Court of Federal Claims and the General Accounting Office: A Comparison*, 67 Fed. Cont. Rep. (BNA) 382 (Mar. 31, 1997).

George M. Coburn, *Enlarged Bid Protest Jurisdiction of the United States Court of Federal Claims*, 33 Procurement Law., Fall 1997, at 16.

Michael R. Golden & John Van Schaik, *Bid Protests from a GAO Perspective*, 32 Procurement Law., Fall 1996, at 8.

William E. Kovacic, *Procurement Reform and the Choice of Forum in Bid Protest Disputes*, 9 Admin. L.J. 461 (1995).

Thomas K. Gump, *Rationalizing the Procurement Dispute Process: The Case for Consolidating Federal Court Bid Protest Fora. 42-FEB Fedrl Law 20 (1995).*

Richard D. Lieberman, *Scorekeeping Bid Protests in Six Forums*, 63 Fed. Cont. Rep. (BNA) No. 8 (Feb. 27, 1995).

Alexander J. Brittin, *The Comptroller General's Dual Statutory Authority to Decide Bid Protests*, 22 Pub. Cont. L.J. 636 (1993).

Mark A. Riordan, *Federal Court Actions Challenging Agency Overrides of the CICA Stay*, 23 Pub. Cont. L.J. 397 (1994).

1. The Contracting Agency

Although many agencies have had very informal procedures for resolving contractor disputes about the manner in which their contracts were awarded since 1991, the FAR has set forth slightly more formalized procedures for pursuing agency level protests. *See* FAR 33.103. Agency level protests received a further boost in 1995, when President Clinton issued Executive Order 12979 for the purpose of ensuring "effective and efficient expenditures of public funds and fair and expeditious resolution of protests to the award of Federal procurement contracts...." The order mandated that each agency prescribe administrative procedures for the resolution of protests as an alternative to the various other available forums.

The procedures required by the Executive Order are to:

(a) emphasize that whenever conduct of a procurement is contested, all parties should use their best efforts to resolve the matter with agency contracting officers;

(b) to the maximum extent practicable, provide for inexpensive, informal, procedurally simple, and expeditious resolution of protests, including, where appropriate and as permitted by law, the use of alternative dispute resolution techniques, third party neutrals, and another agency's personnel;

(c) allow actual or prospective bidders or offerors whose direct economic interests would be affected by the award or failure to award the contract to request a review, at a level above the contracting officer, of any decision by a contracting officer that is alleged to have violated a statute or regulation and, thereby, caused prejudice to the protester; and

(d) except where immediate contract award or performance is justified for urgent and compelling reasons or is determined to be in the best interest of the United States, prohibit award or performance of the contract while a timely filed protest is pending before the agency. To allow for the withholding of a contract award or performance, the agency must have received notice of the protest within either 10 calendar days after the contract award or 5 calendar days after the bidder or offeror who is protesting the contract award was given the opportunity to be debriefed by the agency, whichever date is later.

The FAR guidance for agency level protests now includes the procedures mandated by the Executive Order as well as additional details. FAR 33.103. In order to ensure that alleged disputes are dealt with and resolved on a timely basis, protests based on alleged improprieties in a solicitation must be filed before bid opening or the closing date for receipt of proposals. In all other cases, protests must be filed no later than ten days after the basis of protest is known or should have been known, whichever is earlier. Protests that do not meet these time deadlines for filing will almost always be rejected no matter how meritorious their grounds of protest, although the agency is allowed to consider an untimely protest for "good cause shown" or if it raises issues significant to the agency's acquisition system.

There is no particular form or style for preparing a protest. The regulatory guidance provides that protests shall be concise and logically presented to facilitate review by the agency. The protest document, filed either directly with the government contracting officer or other designated agency official must include the following:

(1) Name, address, and fax and telephone numbers of the protester.

(2) Solicitation or contract number.

(3) Detailed statement of the legal and factual grounds for the protest, to include a description of resulting prejudice to the protester.

(4) Copies of relevant documents.

(5) Request for a ruling by the agency.

(6) Statement as to the form of relief requested.

(7) All information establishing that the protester is an interested party for the purpose of filing a protest.

(8) All information establishing the timeliness of the protest.

As part of the protest, the protester may request an independent review of the protest at a level above the contracting officer. That official should be someone that has not had previous personal involvement in the particular procurement at issue.

Agencies are to delay award of a contract when a protest is received prior to award unless the agency makes a written determination that there are "urgent and compelling reasons" or that proceeding with award would be "in the best interest of the Government." Agencies are to delay performance of a contract when a protest is received within ten days after contract award or within five days after a debriefing date is offered by the contracting officer, whichever is later. Performance may, however, proceed if the agency makes the written determination of "urgent and compelling reasons" or "best interest of the Government."

There are no document discovery rules or rights, although the parties to the protest may exchange information to the extent permitted by law. An agency decision on the protest is due thirty-five days after the protest is filed, although that date is not a mandatory requirement and may be unilaterally extended by the agency.

Agency level protests are the least expensive and procedurally simplest protests to be filed and decided. It is, however, difficult for the protester to obtain the necessary government documents it may need to successfully pursue its protest. There are no provisions for a hearing or taking of depositions or testimony and the protest decision is made by an official of the agency alleged to have engaged in improper or illegal activity. It is a forum that provides some semblance of the possibility of obtaining an adequate remedy in protest situations, but one that does not provide for full development of a protest issue and record.

2. The General Accounting Office

As part of the Competition in Contracting Act of 1984 ("CICA"), the Comptroller General of the General Accounting Office ("GAO"), part of the legislative branch of government, was given statutory authority to decide a protest concerning an alleged violation of a procurement statute or regulation. 31 U.S.C. §3552. Notwithstanding the fairly recent specific statutory grant of protest authority, GAO has been hearing and deciding such protests for almost seventy-five years as part of the Comptroller General's role as auditor of the government for Congress with the power to "settle and adjust" claims against the United States. As a result, there is a well developed set of case law and decisions involving protests of procurement actions that have been relied upon by Congress, the courts, and executive branch agencies. Today, GAO remains a popular forum at which to file a bid protest, with over 3,000 protests being filed each year.

In deciding bid protests, GAO considers whether federal agencies have complied with statutes and regulations controlling government procurements. As explained in "Bid Protests at GAO: A Descriptive Guide" published by the Office of General Counsel for GAO, an overview of the bid protest process at GAO is as follows:

> The bid protest process at GAO begins with the filing of a written protest. Unless the protest is dismissed because it is procedurally or substantively defective

(e.g., the protest is untimely or the protest fails to clearly state legally sufficient grounds of protest), the contracting agency is required to file with GAO an agency report responding to the protest and to provide a copy of that report to the protester. The protester then has an opportunity to file written comments on the report. Other parties may be permitted to intervene, which means that they will also receive a copy of the report and will be allowed to file written comments on the report.

During the course of a GAO protest, as appropriate, GAO may schedule status or other informal types of conferences to resolve procedural matters and to obtain information material to the disposition of the protest. GAO also may find that a hearing is necessary to resolve factual and legal issues raised in the protest. If it decides to hold a hearing, GAO will usually conduct a pre-hearing conference to decide the issues that will be considered at the hearing, to identify the witnesses who will testify at the hearing, and to settle procedural questions. After the hearing, all parties will be allowed to submit written comments on the hearing.

After the record is complete, GAO will consider the facts and legal issues raised and will issue a decision, a copy of which will be sent to all parties participating in the protest. GAO may sustain the protest (that is, find that the agency violated a procurement statute or regulation and that the violation prejudiced the protester), in which case GAO will recommend appropriate corrective action. Alternatively, GAO may deny the protest or may dismiss the protest without reviewing the matter. GAO will issue its decision not later than 100 days from the date the protest was filed. The exact date on which GAO issues the decision depends on the urgency of the procurement, the complexity of the factual and legal issues raised in the protest, and GAO's work load.

"Bid Protests at GAO: A Descriptive Guide" published by the Office of General Counsel, United States General Accounting Office, GAO/OCG-96-24, Sixth Edition 1996 at 7-8.

GAO has promulgated fairly detailed regulations that govern the procedures of filing and pursuing a protest. *See* 4 CFR Part 21. The failure to follow the regulations will almost certainly result in a protest being summarily dismissed by GAO and the opportunity for corrective action being taken by the contracting agency will then be lost.

In order to file a protest at GAO, a person, represented either by himself or herself or by counsel, must be an "interested party" which means being an actual or prospective bidder or offeror with a direct economic interest in the procurement. Note that only bidders or offerors have standing to protest—subcontractors to a bidder to be prime contractor do not have standing.

Most GAO protests challenge the acceptance or rejection of a bid or proposal and the award or proposed award of a contract. GAO will also consider protests that allege defects in the solicitation such as unduly restrictive specifications that prevent a competitor from competing, omissions of required provisions, or ambiguous evaluation factors. GAO will not consider protests involving matters of: (1) contract administration; (2) Small Business Administration issues such as challenges as to whether a particular company qualifies as a small business concern; (3) procurements under section 8(a) of the Small Business Act involving the award of subcontracts to small disadvantaged businesses; (4) affirmative determinations of responsibility of the proposed or actual contractor; (5) violations of the procurement integrity laws; and (6) procurement actions taken by agencies other than those defined by section 3 of the Federal Property and Administrative Services of 1949, 40 U.S.C. §472, such as the U.S. Postal Service, the Federal Deposit Insurance Corporation, and non-appropriated fund activities.

As is the case with an agency level protest, there is no particular prescribed form for filing a protest at GAO. The requirements for such a written protest follow those now established for agency level protests and include the following:

(1) The name, address, and telephone and fax numbers of the protester or its representative;

(2) The signature of the protester or its representative;

(3) The identification of the contracting agency and the solicitation and/or contract number;

(4) A detailed statement of the legal and factual grounds of protest, including copies of relevant documents;

(5) Information establishing that the protester is an interested party for the purposes of filing a protest;

(6) Information establishing the timeliness of the protest;

(7) The specific request for a ruling by the Comptroller General; and

(8) The form of relief requested.

In addition, the protest should identify any agency documents requested by the protester that are relevant to the protest grounds, a request for a protective order if documents that contain proprietary or confidential information are either submitted by the protester or requested from the agency, and a request for a hearing if the protester believes that there is a sufficient reason for having one.

Again, as is now the case with agency level protests, GAO follows very strict requirements for the filing of a timely protest. Protests alleging defects in the solicitation must be filed prior to the due date for bids or offers. All other protests must be filed not later than ten days after the basis for the protest is known except in the case of protests challenging a procurement conducted on the basis of competitive proposals. In that case, when a debriefing is requested and offered, the protest is to be filed within ten days after the date on which the debriefing was offered.

After a protest is filed, GAO will immediately notify the contracting agency of the protest. If the contracting agency receives notice of the protest from GAO either prior to contract award or within ten days of contract award, the contracting agency is directed by 31 U.S.C. §3553(c) to either withhold award or suspend award, unless the agency makes a written determination of "urgent and compelling" reasons for proceeding with the contract or a written determination that proceeding with the contract is in the best interests of the government. Once the contracting agency has received notice of the protest it will in turn, give notice of the protest to the awardee or if no award has been made, to all bidders or offerors which have a reasonable chance of receiving award. Those parties may advise GAO that they wish to intervene in the protest in order to have an opportunity to comment on the basis of the protest.

After receiving notice of a protest, the contracting agency is required to prepare an "agency report" that responds to the issues raised in the protest. The agency report is to be submitted within thirty days of the filing of the protest. The protester and each intervenor are then given ten days to file comments on the findings and determinations and legal arguments made in the agency report.

Once the record is complete, GAO will consider the protest and decide the case by means of a written decision issued by the Comptroller General. The decision must be issued within one hundred days of the protest being filed. As is often the case, supplemental protests are often filed by protesters after receipt of agency documents or the agency report that reveals additional grounds for alleged improprieties. GAO attempts to resolve these additional protests within the same one hundred day period, but may extend the decision date for the supplemental protests if necessary.

If GAO concludes in its written decision that the protested agency action does not comply with statute or regulation, GAO will recommend to the contracting agency any combination of the following remedies:

(1) Refrain from exercising options under the contract;

(2) Terminate the contract;

(3) Recompete the contract;

(4) Issue a new solicitation;

(5) Award a contract consistent with statute and regulation; or

(6) Such other recommendation(s) as GAO determines necessary to promote compliance.

The GAO decision sustaining the protest contains only *recommendations* to the agency for corrective action. As a result, although the vast majority of GAO recommendations are accepted, the contracting agency retains the right to take whatever corrective action it believes is necessary in order to correct defects found by GAO. This broad discretionary authority granted to contracting agencies by virtue of their position in the executive branch of government with the ultimate authority for spending money appropriated to them by Congress means that the protester may be successful in winning its battle that an agency violated procurement statutes or regulations, but more often than not will lose the war of actually being awarded the contract in dispute. Typically, the agency takes corrective action that either simply corrects a defect and permits the same outcome or recompetes the contract and makes an award decision consistent with its initial decision. This "winning the battle and losing the war" scenario should make pursuing a protest at GAO the consequence of a thoughtful process where all possibilities are presented by counsel and examined by the potential protester.

The following case illustrates the workings of the GAO system, focusing on when the automatic stay is lifted by agency decision or reinstated by judicial action.

Dairy Maid Dairy, Inc., Plaintiff, v. The United States of America et al. Defendants

Civ. No. 2:93CV260. United States District Court,
E.D. Virginia, 1993, 837 F.Supp. 1370.

PAYNE, District Judge.

Dairy Maid Dairy, Inc. ("Dairy Maid") filed this action seeking declaratory and injunctive relief as the consequence of alleged violations of the Competition in Contracting Act ("CICA") by the United States Army (the "Army"). Following an evidentiary hearing and upon consideration of the affidavits and pleadings, the court entered a temporary restraining order. Upon agreement of the parties, the trial of the action on its merits was advanced and consolidated with the hearing on Dairy Maid's application for preliminary injunctive relief, see Fed. R. Civ. P. 65(a)(2). After reviewing the affidavits, the exhibits, the testimony presented at trial and the briefs and arguments of counsel, the court issued an order on April 13, 1993 deciding the case on the merits and granting permanent injunctive relief. The reasons supporting that decision and order are set forth fully below.

STATEMENT OF FACTS

This action arises out of the solicitation, award and resulting protests of a contract for the operation of the Eighth U.S. Army Milk Plant, located at the K-16 Air Base, Songnam, Republic of Korea. The milk plant is a Government Owned-Contractor Operated ("GOCO") facility. As its name implies, the facility is owned by the Army and, pursuant to contract, the contractor is obligated to operate the milk plant, to maintain the operating equipment and to produce and deliver milk and other dairy products for consumption by United States military personnel and their dependents. By law, the contract must be awarded to an American company, but the milk plant is actually operated by a staff of approximately 75 Korean nationals who work under the supervision of the contractors' American employees.

The milk plant is the only source in the Republic of Korea of veterinary- approved milk and other dairy products for 61 dining facilities used by United States military personnel and by Army civilian employees. It also is the sole source of supply of milk and other dairy products to Army hospitals, the enlisted and officer club systems, the military exchange outlets and the schools operated for dependents of military personnel. It is undisputed that there are no approved local dairies in the Republic of Korea which could constitute an alternate source for milk and dairy products. It is also undisputed that supplies of extended shelf life milk from the continental United States are not available in quantities sufficient to meet demand.

The Historical Setting for the Current Dispute

At the time this action was filed, Dairy Maid was operating the milk plant under contract no. DAJB03-92-C-3216 (the "3216 Contract") which originally was to expire on September 30, 1992, but was extended twice by mutual agreement. Before the 3216 Contract was awarded to Dairy Maid, the milk plant was operated by Contact International, Inc. ("CIC") under contract no. DAJB03-89-C-1001 (the "1001 Contract").

Near the end of the 1001 Contract, CIC and Dairy Maid competed for award of the 3216 Contract and, after the 3216 Contract was awarded to Dairy Maid, CIC filed a protest with the Comptroller General of the United States ("GAO") under 31 U.S.C. §3552 (Supp.1993). As required by 31 U.S.C. §3553(c)(1), the award of the 3216 Contract to Dairy Maid was stayed pending a decision by the GAO on CIC's protest. In order to maintain the status quo and an uninterrupted supply of milk and other dairy products, CIC and the Army mutually agreed to extend the 1001 Contract until the GAO decided the merits of CIC's protest of the 3216 Contract. In fact, the 1001 Contract, the terms and conditions of which are the same as the 3216 Contract insofar as they pertain to contract extensions, previously had been extended by mutual agreement three times.

The 0002 Solicitation and Protests

On November 23, 1992, the Army issued solicitation no. DAJB03-93-R-0002 ("0002 Solicitation") for a follow-on contract to the 3216 Contract. In December 1992, Dairy

Maid filed two protests of the 0002 Solicitation, alleging numerous defects therein. Those protests were consolidated and set for hearing on their merits by the GAO. However, by letter dated January 21, 1993, the Army requested dismissal of the consolidated protests as moot because the Army had considered the protests and taken corrective action. * * *

Subsequently, by letter dated January 28, 1993, Phillip A. Grace, the Army's contracting officer in Korea, advised Dairy Maid that the government was prepared to extend the 3216 Contract by mutual agreement through September 30, 1993, and solicited a proposal from Dairy Maid. Dairy Maid responded on February 11, 1993, by submitting two alternate proposals for a six-month contract extension.

* * *

On February 16, 1993, five days after submitting the proposals solicited by the Army on January 28, Dairy Maid received a letter from Mr. Grace, stating that a new solicitation, which would be identical to the 0002 Solicitation except as to the provisions governing duration of the contract and the guaranteed minimums, was being issued for a six-month extension of the 3216 Contract. Dairy Maid was requested to prepare a proposal by February 26, 1993. Confused by these developments and by the inconsistent instructions from the Army, Dairy Maid's counsel posed six questions to the contracting officer by letter dated February 18, 1993. One of those inquiries asked whether the government intended to negotiate with Dairy Maid a six-month extension to the 3216 Contract. The Army responded to that inquiry on February 25, 1993, stating that:

> It was the Government's desire to negotiate for a six-month extension to the current contract. However, the Government is now able to obtain competitive prices under solicitation DAJB03-93-R-0002 in compliance with procurement regulations. Therefore an extension to the current contract for six months may not be necessary.

The 0072 Solicitation

On February 23, 1993, Dairy Maid received solicitation DAJB03-93-R-0072 (the "0072 Solicitation," which subsequently became the "0072 Contract"). The next day, Dairy Maid filed a protest with the GAO challenging numerous improprieties and defects in the 0072 Solicitation. The Army partially revised the 0072 Solicitation * * * On March 22, 1993, Dairy Maid informed the contracting officer that, as a consequence of the Army's amendment of the 0072 Solicitation, Dairy Maid would require ten working days to reprice its proposal.

The 0072 Protests and The Stays Here At Issue

The filing of a timely protest of the 0072 Solicitation, automatically stays an award of the 0072 Contract pending resolution of the protest by the GAO, unless the head of the procuring activity decides to override the stay after making a written finding pursuant to 31 U.S.C. §3553(c)(2) that:

> urgent and compelling circumstances which significantly affect interests of the United States will not permit waiting for the [GAO decision on the merits of the protest].

On March 19, 1993, Major General Scott, the head of the procuring agency, acting pursuant to staff recommendations dated March 18, 1993, and March 17, 1993, decided to override the automatic pre-award stay and award the 0072 Contract to CIC.

The stated basis of General Scott's determination was that "... delay in awarding a contract shall have a devastating impact on all dining facilities in Korea as well as on hospitals, club system, and AAFES." This conclusion was based on the fact that the milk plant was the sole source of supply of important dairy products. General Scott's determination did not address the potential availability of Dairy Maid to continue performance of the contract pending a decision by the GAO on Dairy Maid's protest. Nor did the determination explain why the Army could not extend the 3216 Contract as it had when CIC protested the award of the 3216 Contract, and the Army extended the 1001 Contract to allow CIC to continue operation of the milk plant while its protest of the award of the 3216 Contract was pending before GAO. On March 22, 1993, the Deputy Secretary of the Army signed the document authorizing the override of the automatic stay.

On March 23, 1993, Dairy Maid received a copy of a letter from the contracting officer announcing that the 0072 Contract had been awarded to CIC, notwithstanding that CIC's contract price for the first six-month period of the contract exceeded the price that would be obtained under the 3216 Contract if it were extended pending resolution of Dairy Maid's pre-award protest of the 0072 Solicitation. The next day, Dairy Maid filed a post-award protest with GAO challenging the award of the 0072 Contract to CIC. Dairy Maid requested that the award and performance of the contract to CIC be stayed pending a decision by GAO on the protests, and also offered to continue to supply milk and dairy products under the terms of the 3216 Contract until the protests were resolved.

Upon receipt of Dairy Maid's timely post-award protest, the Army was obligated under 31 U.S.C. §3553(d)(1) to direct CIC to suspend performance of the 0072 Contract and to refrain from engaging in any related activities that might result in additional obligations being incurred by the government pending resolution of Dairy Maid's post-award protest, unless the head of the procuring activity decided to override the stay by making a written finding pursuant to 31 U.S.C. §3553(d)(2)(A)(ii):

> that urgent and compelling circumstances that significantly affect interest of the United States will not permit waiting for the decision of the Comptroller General concerning the protest....

No such determination was made.

Dairy Maid instituted this action challenging the Army's decision to override the pre-award protest of the 0072 Solicitation and seeking to enjoin the Army's action in proposing to allow CIC to proceed with the 0072 Contract without making the requisite finding under CICA to override the automatic stay pending resolution of the post-award protest. For the reasons set forth below, the court finds that Dairy Maid's challenges to the Army's conduct are well-taken and that Dairy Maid is entitled to permanent injunctive relief.

* * *

DISCUSSION

CICA "was enacted to remedy a major loophole in the longstanding GAO [procurement] review procedure: by the time the GAO reviewed most bid protests, the protests had become moot because either the contract had been let or the contractor was engaged in performing the contract." Ameron, Inc. v. United States Army Corps. of Engrs., 787 F.2d 875, 878 (3d Cir.1986). Congress enacted CICA, and incorporated the stay provisions here at issue, in an attempt to provide effective and meaningful review of procurement challenges before the protested procurements become "faits accomplis." Id. at 879. For this reason, the filing of a protest with GAO automatically stays the award or performance of the challenged contract until (1) the GAO decides the protest on the merits, or (2) the head of the procuring activity or agency certifies in writing that the statutory requirements for overriding the stay have been met. 31 U.S.C. §3553; Ameron, Inc., 787 F.2d at 879.

The statutory requirements for overriding a stay pending resolution of a pre- award protest differ from the requirements for overriding a stay pending resolution of a post- award protest. Compare 31 U.S.C. §3553(c)(2) with 31 U.S.C. §3553(d)(2). In order to override an automatic stay pending resolution of a pre-award protest, the head of the procuring activity must make "a written finding that urgent and compelling circum- stances which significantly affect interests of the United States will not permit waiting for the [GAO decision on the merits of the protest]." 31 U.S.C. §3553(c)(2). An auto- matic stay pending resolution of a post-award protest may be overridden only if the head of the procuring activity makes a written finding:

> (i) that performance of the contract is in the best interests of the United States; or

> (ii) that urgent and compelling circumstances that significantly affect interests of the United States will not permit waiting for the decision of [GAO] concern- ing the protest;...

31 U.S.C. §3553(d)(2) (emphasis added). Although these statutory requirements are substantially similar, the "best interests of the United States" factor only comes into consideration in situations where the procuring agency is seeking to override a post- award stay.

Thus, except in those circumstances where a stay is properly overridden, CICA pre- serves the status quo by preventing the award or performance of a challenged govern- ment contract until after the GAO has resolved the merits of any protests concerning that contract. Further, CICA is clear in what findings must be made in order to justify a departure from the norm established by the stay requirements.

Mindful of this statutory framework, of the congressional purposes for enacting CICA and of the applicable standard of review, the court now considers the Army's de- cision to override the automatic stay pending resolution of Dairy Maid's pre-award protest of the 0072 Solicitation and the Army's decision to allow performance of the 0072 Contract without overriding the automatic stay pending resolution of Dairy Maid's timely protest of the award of the 0072 Contract to CIC.

I. The Pre-Award Protest

The Army's position is that it made the requisite finding under 31 U.S.C. §3553(c)(2) before overriding Dairy Maid's pre-award protest and awarding the 0072 contract to CIC. Dairy Maid asserts that the Army's finding did not comport with the statutory re- quirements or the decision interpreting the statute. After reviewing the administrative record and the applicable decisions, the court concludes that the Army failed to make the requisite statutory findings, and that therefore the Army's decision to override Dairy Maid's pre-award protest was arbitrary, capricious and not in accordance with law.

As required by 31 U.S.C. §3553(c)(2)(A), the Army issued on March 19, 1993 a written "Determination and Findings" ("D & F") setting forth its rationale for lifting the stay of the award of the 0072 contract to CIC. The D & F and its supporting docu- ments comprise the record to be examined in determining whether the Army's find- ings satisfied the requirements of the statute. The D & F noted a number of reasons why the continued production of milk at the facility was of critical importance, and carefully explained that there were no means of supplying the Army's requirements for dairy products if the plant was not operating. Having fully and adequately documented those findings, which are not disputed, the Army concluded that there existed urgent and compelling circumstances which significantly affected the United States, and that, accordingly, there should be an override of the stay imposed by Dairy Maid's protest.

The D & F did not explain, however, why the award of the 0072 Contract could not abide the resolution of Dairy Maid's protest by the GAO. The statute is clear that the automatic stay must not be overridden unless there is a finding that urgent and compelling circumstances which are found to significantly affect the interests of the United States "will not permit waiting" for the GAO's decision on the protest. This language requires that the Army must find: (1) the existence of urgent and compelling circumstances; (2) that those circumstances significantly affect the United States; and (3) that those circumstances are such as to preclude waiting for the procedure prescribed by statute to run its course. The decision to override a stay must be based on all three components set by the statute. If not, the decision is defective.

Here the Army did not explain why, under the circumstances of this case, award of the 0072 Contract could not await a decision by the GAO. This defect is extremely significant where, as here, the history of the administration of the contract respecting operation of this plant was replete with instances of contract extensions and reflected that the Army in fact had previously stayed the award of a virtually identical contract under substantially similar circumstances. The Army's findings completely ignored the availability of Dairy Maid to continue production under the terms of the 3216 Contract while its protest was pending before the GAO. In like fashion, the Army did not explain why it considered performance by CIC, rather than Dairy Maid, to have been essential. These factors are both among the circumstances which must be considered under the facts of this case if the requirements of the statute are to be satisfied.

Several courts have held that CICA requires the agency to explain why performance by a specific proposed contractor presents urgent and compelling circumstances, and that it is insufficient for the agency to rely solely on the fact that performance of the contract itself is urgent and compelling. D.T.H. Management Group v. Kelso, No. 93-439-CIV-5-D (E.D.N.C. Aug. 4, 1993) (Dupree, J.) (granting preliminary injunction to current contractor where D & F failed to explain why specific contractor was required to do job); Ace Fed. Reporter v. Federal Energy Regulatory Comm'n, No. 90- 2396, 1990 U.S.Dist. LEXIS 13823, at *11-*12 (D.D.C. October 16, 1990) (Penn, J.) (granting preliminary injunction in favor of current contractor to stay performance until resolution of a pending protest because agency's failure to consider fact that current contractor was able to perform contract in interim before GAO's determination was contrary to purpose of the CICA to preserve status quo); Samson Tug & Barge Co. v. United States, 695 F.Supp. 25, 29 (D.D.C.1988) (Oberdorfer, J.) (granting current contractor's motion for a preliminary injunction because agency's failure to consider the availability of continuing its services while the GAO decided protest was likely to prove arbitrary, capricious and contrary to law); Universal Shipping Co. v. United States, 652 F.Supp. 668, 675-76 (D.D.C.1987), (Richey, J.) (granting permanent injunction in favor of current contractor and staying award of contract until resolution of pending protest before GAO because agency's failure to consider ability of contractor to continue services in interim in determining whether to lift stay was not rational or reasonable).

The underlying rationale of these decisions is that CICA requires the agency to make findings that performance of the contract by the particular proposed contractor is urgent and compelling. They also instruct that adopting the contrary view, which is what the Army proposes here, "would eviscerate the purpose and effect of the stay provision of the CICA because performance of almost any government contract could conceivably be deemed 'urgent and compelling circumstances.'" D.T.H. v. Kelso, (slip op. p. 11). Indeed, the Army's interpretation would allow the exception for lifting the automatic stay provided in 31 U.S.C. §3553(c)(2)(A) to swallow the general provision in 31 U.S.C. §3553(c)(1) imposing an automatic stay pending resolution of the protest on its merits.

* * *

Taken as a whole, the record provides no rational basis for the decision to override the automatic stay. Moreover, on the facts of this record, the court finds that the decision to override the stay was a clear and prejudicial violation of the applicable law. For these reasons, the decision to override the pre-award stay was arbitrary, capricious and otherwise not in accordance with law.

II. The Post-Award Protest

Pursuant to 31 U.S.C. §3553(d)(1), once the Army received notice from GAO of Dairy Maid's timely post-award protest it was required to direct CIC to (1) cease performance of the 0072 contract, and (2) suspend any activities which might result in the United States incurring any additional costs. The statute provides:

> If a federal agency receives notice of a protest under this section after the contract has been awarded but within 10 days of the date of the contract award, the federal agency (except as provided under paragraph (2)) shall, upon receipt of that notice, immediately direct the contractor to cease performance under the contract and to suspend any related activities that may result in additional obligations being incurred by the United States under that contract. Performance of the contract may not be resumed while the protest is pending.

31 U.S.C. §3553(d)(1) (emphasis added). The provisions of the statute are mandatory and hence the Army was required to direct CIC to cease performance under the 0072 Contract unless and until a finding was made pursuant to 31 U.S.C. §3553(d)(2).

The undisputed record shows that the Army neither made the requisite finding under 31 U.S.C. §3553(d)(2) nor directed CIC to cease performance of the 0072 Contract pending resolution by GAO of Dairy Maid's post-award protest. The Army asserts that it was not required to make a finding under 31 U.S.C. §3553(d)(2), because it already had made a finding of urgent and compelling circumstances under 31 U.S.C. §3553(c)(1) in order to override the automatic stay created by Dairy Maid's pre-award protest. This argument does not pass muster.

The Army's position is based on the Comptroller General's decision in In re: Southern California Roofing Co., B-236631, 89-2 CPD ¶594 (December 26, 1989). In that case, the Comptroller General held that when a post-award protest merely reiterated positions advanced in a pre-award protest which had been properly overridden, it was not necessary for the procuring activity to make a new finding of urgent and compelling circumstances to override the stay imposed by the post-award protest. The reasoning of that case is not persuasive for two reasons. First, Southern California is factually distinguishable from this action because Dairy Maid's post-award protest advances positions and arguments which were not asserted in its consolidated pre-award protests. In fact, Dairy Maid advanced arguments in its post-award protest, such as its assertion that CIC's bid was unbalanced, which could not have been raised until after the 0072 Contract was awarded to CIC. Second, Southern California reads into the clearly mandatory language of 31 U.S.C. §3553(d) an exception to the requirement of a finding of urgent and compelling circumstances which is not found in the text of the statute, and which, if adopted, would render 31 U.S.C. §3553(d)(2) meaningless in all cases where a protestor files both pre-award and post-award protests.

* * *

Considering the clear and mandatory language of 31 U.S.C. §3553(d)(2) in light of the principal purpose for which CICA was enacted, the court finds that the complete failure to comply with the statute cannot be remedied by characterizing it as "a mere technical violation" of CICA. Rather, the Army's complete failure to comply with 31 U.S.C. §3553(d)(2) constitutes "a clear and prejudicial violation of the applicable statutes or regulations" and, accordingly, the Army's override of the automatic stay imposed by Dairy Maid's post-award protest was arbitrary, capricious and otherwise not in accordance with law. See Shoals Am. Ind., Inc. v. United States, 877 F.2d 883, 887 (11th Cir.1989); 5 U.S.C. §706(2)(A).

* * *

It is so ordered.

Notes and Questions

1. Given the very large number of protests filed at the GAO, attention to the GAO procedure is warranted. *Dairy Maid* focuses on the automatic CICA stay pending GAO decision of a protest, the contracting agency's power to override the CICA stay, and judicial review of the agency's override. Plainly, the stay matters greatly, as agency award of contracts largely obviates GAO recommendations against award. The opinion traces judicial analysis of the CICA stay back to the *Ameron* decision, a key decision upholding the constitutionality of the CICA stay. At the time, the Department of Justice contended the stay was unconstitutional on separation of power grounds, and so the constitutionality of the stay was defended, successfully as it turned out, by counsel for Congress, namely, then-House Solicitor and Deputy General Counsel Charles Tiefer. For discussion, see *Ameron, Inc. v. United States Army Corps. of Engrs.*, 787 F.2d 875, 878 (3d Cir.1986). Why would the Executive branch challenge the statutory stay, and why would the courts uphold it?

2. As mentioned, the GAO has procedures, codified in 4 C.F.R. §21, for its bid protests. Section 21.1 details what agency actions may be protested, as well as the requirements for filing: specifically, that the protest be undertaken by an "interested party"(§21.1(a)), and be in writing (§21.1(b)). While the section disclaims the need for "formal briefs or...technical forms of pleading or motion...." (§21.1(f)), there are numerous mandatory recitations regarding such elements as: legal and factual basis for the protest with copies of any relevant documents (§21.1(c)(4)); establishment of the interested party status of the protestor (§21.1(c)(5)); timeliness of the protest (§§21.1(c)(6), 21.2); the requirement for a specific request for a ruling from the Comptroller General (§21.1(c)(7)); and for a statement of the form of relief requested (§21.1(c)(8)).

All protestors are required to provide a copy of the protest and attachments to the agency's designee not later than one day after GAO filing (§21.1(e)). Omission of any of these is grounds for dismissal (§21.1(i)), except that dismissal is not permitted in cases where the contract officer "has actual knowledge of the basis of protest," or where the agency was not prejudiced in the preparation of its report by the protestor's noncompliance. Intervenors may join, such as awardees. Why should an intervenor retain counsel and join the protest, considering that the agency can, and will, defend the award?

3. GAO procedure includes the important step of the "agency report" which provides much of the record in the matter. After the filing of a protest, the GAO requires the procuring agency to submit a report which must include the key documents on the matter (§21.3(c); 31 U.S.C. §3553 (b)(2)). Why, and how, would skillful counsel for a protester demand specific documents and otherwise expand the "protest file"? Access to documents may, in turn, lead protesters to realize that they could raise additional issues, sometimes leading to the filing of supplemental protests. Why? What would be the timeliness constraints? Note the reliance on document discovery and the absence of the procedure, regular in judicial cases, of power for the parties to depose witnesses. Between the absence of witness discovery and the relative rarity of hearings, GAO protests are much less burdensome to agencies and less expensive for protesters than court cases. Does this suit the nature of the bid protest process and, if so, why?

4. Another important aspect of GAO protest procedure consists of the arrangements for confidential handling of some information. Although most protests are assumed to be public record "unless precluded by law," §21.1(g) provides for withholding confidential information. Protestors making such requests must so advise on the front page of the document, and provide redacted copies to both GAO and the agency within one day of the initial GAO filing. An agency report may also receive confidential treatment: the GAO will issue a protective order to limit access to the report's confidential information (§§21.3(h), 21.4(a)-(d)). Why would protests regarding the evaluation of negotiated offers ("competitive proposals") call for protective orders fairly urgently, much more than protests of sealed bids or of agency solicitations? Ticklish points of much complexity concern the admission under a protective order of awardees' or bidders outside counsel, in-house counsel, and consultants. What would the arguments be for and against admission of each of these categories?

5. While the documentary record may suffice, the GAO may conduct a hearing with oral testimony where there is a factual dispute necessitating it (§21.7). Although this occurs in a relatively small percentage of all protests, at the GAO it is a moment of comparative excitement. It is like a trial, but the GAO attorney, and likely the counsel for the protester and the government, have collectively a good deal of sophistication about government contract issues. Within one hundred days, the GAO issues its decision with the remedy of a recommendation of agency action (31 U.S.C. §3554(a)-(b)). The GAO sustains only a fraction of the cases considered on the merits (13% by count at one point). Agencies usually follow GAO recommendations, but have the option, shared by protestors and intervenors, of requesting reconsideration (§21.14). The Comptroller General must report annually to Congress a summary of each case from the preceding year in which the Comptroller General determined that the solicitation, award, or proposed award did not comply with applicable statutes or regulations, and the agency failed to implement GAO recommendations. (31 U.S.C. §3554(e)(2)).

6. The GAO dismisses a sizable fraction of protests without reaching the merits. Its associate general counsel for procurement law published an insightful study of the 110 protests filed in one particular month (October 2000). Of these, 34 had been dismissed as untimely, 28 had been dismissed because the protesters withdrew them, and five were dismissed because the protesters failed to comment on agency reports. While that may sound like a high percentage of fruitless wheel-spinning, the author notes that some of these withdrawals or other dismissals may have occurred in response to agencies taking corrective action or to alternative dispute resolution. Daniel I. Gordon, Dismissals of Bid Protests at the General Accounting Office, Procurement Lawyer, Winter 2002, at 1.

7. For a discussion of standing to protest, see Jennifer Gartner, The Meaning of "Interested Party" under 28 U.S.C. § 1491, 29 Pub. Cont. L. J. 739 (2000).

3. The U.S. Court of Federal Claims

The third available forum for bid protests is the U.S. Court of Federal Claims (previously named the U.S. Claims Court and U.S. Court of Claims), physically located in Washington, D.C., but with the authority to "ride circuit" and hear claims throughout the United States. The court's authority to hear and decide bid protests had been somewhat confusing in the 1980s and 1990s, although the enactment of the Administrative Dispute Resolution Act of 1996, 28 U.S.C. §1491, clarified the court's authority. It is an active participant in the complete bid protest process, affording protesters the opportunity for a more comprehensive review of bid protest allegations by independent judges that regularly hear cases involving the standard federal procurement statutes and regulations. The following case reflects an important historic point in the court's authority over bid protests.

HEYER PRODUCTS COMPANY, Inc.,
v. The UNITED STATES.

United States Court of Claims, 1956.
140 F.Supp. 409

Before JONES, Chief Judge, and LITTLETON, WHITAKER, MADDEN and LARAMORE, Judges.

WHITAKER, Judge.

This case is before the court on defendant's motion to dismiss plaintiff's petition on the ground that it does not state a cause of action.

The material allegations of the petition are as follows: On March 17, 1952, the Ordnance Tank Automotive Center, Ordnance Corps, United States Army (hereinafter referred to as OTAC) advertised for bids on 5,500 low-voltage circuit testers. On April 15, 1952, plaintiff submitted a bid, together with a sample unit and a letter of explanation, a photograph of the completed unit, a schematic diagram showing the circuit connections, and a specification describing the unit in detail. It alleges that its bid of $205,975 was the low bid, and that it was and is a responsible bidder; but that the Government, nevertheless, awarded the contract to a bidder whose bid was higher than the bids of six other bidders, including the plaintiff, and $190,043 higher than plaintiff's low bid of $205,975.

Plaintiff alleges that the failure of defendant to award it the contract 'was the result of a deliberate artifice to retaliate against plaintiff for testifying against OTAC at a Senate hearing in 1952; that defendant deliberately and in violation of law wished to favor the successful bidder, and that defendant's action throughout the entire transaction was arbitrary, capricious, and taken in bad faith.'

As a result, plaintiff says it not only lost the $7,000 which it spent in preparing its bid, but also lost its anticipated profit on the contract of $38,000, for which amounts it sues.

Defendant moves to dismiss plaintiff's petition on the ground that it does not state a cause of action.

Plaintiff's allegation of arbitrary and capricious action and of bad faith in awarding the contract was not a reckless averment. Facts are alleged that tend to support the allegation. The very fact that the bid was awarded to a bidder whose bid was higher than the bids of six other bidders, and that it was awarded at a price almost twice the low bid, put in by a responsible bidder, makes one strongly suspect discrimination and favoritism and a failure to accept that bid which was most advantageous to the Government, as OTAC was required to do under the Armed Services Procurement Act of 1947, 62 Stat. 21, 41 U.S.C.A. § 151 et seq. This suspicion grows stronger in the light of the further facts alleged.

Three months elapsed between the opening of the bids and the award of the contract. In the meantime, plaintiff's president had appeared before the Select Committee on Small Business of the United States Senate in connection with the rejection of a prior bid of the Heyer Products Company for 3,000 low- voltage circuit testers, and in that hearing he had testified that that contract had been awarded to Weidenhoff Company, who was higher than six other bidders and whose bid was $116,730 higher than plaintiff's low bid of $134,100. It is further alleged that after hearing this testimony, the Committee, to quote from its report (Senate Report 1092, 83d Cong., 2d sess.), which is incorporated in plaintiff's petition,—

> '* * * sought to ascertain what procurement policies and procedures in use at OTAC could possibly result in passing up the Heyer low bid to award this contract to the seventh high bidder at almost double the low bid price. This was of particular interest to your committee as the evidence revealed that Heyer had built thousands of low-voltage testers for commercial use, and some 52,000 for military use during World War II, and that Heyer had been a well-known manufacturer of automotive test equipment for 25 years, having built equipment for many of the leading companies in the automotive field, including Ford, Goodyear, Goodrich, Firestone, Willard, Exide, Atlas, Autolite.'

After hearing testimony of representatives of the Ordnance Corps, the Select Committee on Small Business made a report (Senate Report 2070, 82d Cong., 2d sess., p. 13), released April 28, 1952, quoted in the petition, in which it said:

> 'The representatives of Army Ordnance who appeared before your committee to explain * * * why the Heyer bids had been rejected did not give convincing explanations.'

After his testimony and the report of the Select Committee, the petitioner alleges that, in retaliation for his appearance before the Select Committee, the award of the present contract in suit was again made to the same Weidenhoff Company, whose bid again was higher than the bid of six other bidders, and $190,043 higher than plaintiff's low bid of $205,975. Plaintiff alleges that this was done in brazen defiance of the provisions of the Armed Services Procurement Act of 1947, requiring the acceptance of that bid which was most advantageous to the Government.

After the rejection of its bid on July 3, 1952, and the award of the contract to Weidenhoff Company, plaintiff alleges he again appeared before the Select Committee on Small Business, which conducted further hearings and made Report No. 1092, 83d Cong., 2d sess., which plaintiffs sets out in its petition. In its report the Committee set out the prior history of plaintiff's dealings with the Ordnance Department, as detailed above, and stated:

> 'This incredible coincidence (that both on November 3, 1950 and on April 16, 1952, the contract should have been awarded to the Weidenhoff Company, whose bid in both instances was higher than the bids of six other bidders and nearly double that of the lowest bidder) would seem to indicate that the officials in charge of OTAC have no wish or will to abide by the spirit and purpose of the Armed Services Procurement Act of 1947.'

* * *

From all of this the Committee concluded: 'Your committee can only conclude that for some reason unknown to it, OTAC wished to favor Weidenhoff, or to eliminate Heyer. The evidence adduced above permits no other inference, unless it be attributed to gross incompetence.' And finally the Committee said: 'All in all, this is a shameful story.'

It will thus be seen that plaintiff's petition contains sufficient allegations to make out a case of discrimination against it, and of favoritism toward Weidenhoff Company, at a loss to the Government of several hundred thousand dollars. If the allegations are true, it would seem impossible to conclude that that bid had been accepted which was most advantageous to the Government.

Notwithstanding all this, defendant says that plaintiff has no legal capacity to sue, and that its petition should be dismissed.

It has been settled beyond controversy that most statutes governing the awarding of bids by governmental agencies are enacted for the benefit of the public who are served by these agencies, and not for the benefit of the bidders, and, therefore, that bidders have no right to sue on the ground that the provisions of such an Act have been violated, in that the contract had not been let to the lowest bidder. United States v. New York & Puerto Rico Steamship Co., 239 U.S. 88, 36 S.Ct. 41, 60 L.Ed. 161; American Smelting & Refining Co. v. United States, 259 U.S. 75, 42 S.Ct. 420, 66 L.Ed. 833; Perkins v. Lukens Steel Co., 310 U.S. 113, 60 S.Ct. 869, 84 L.Ed. 1108; Colorado Paving Co. v. Murphy, 8 Cir., 78 F. 28, 37 L.R.A. 630, and other cases cited in Perkins v. Lukens Steel Co., supra.

It is true that one of the purposes of the Act of February 19, 1948, the 'Armed Services Procurement Act of 1947,' was to induce the letting of a fair proportion of Government contracts to small business concerns; indeed, this was declared to be the 'policy of Congress' in the beginning of the Act; but the main purpose of the Act was to give directions for the conduct of Government agents in making contracts, and this was for the purpose of protecting the public, and not the bidders. Clearly, section 3(b), which plaintiff says was violated, was enacted for the benefit of the public, and not for the benefit of bidders. This section reads:

> 'All bids shall be publicly opened at the time and place stated in the advertisement. Award shall be made with reasonable promptness by written notice to that responsible bidder whose bid, conforming to the invitation for bids, will be most advantageous to the Government, price and other factors considered: Provided, That all bids may be rejected when the agency head determines that it is in the public interest so to do.'

41 U.S.C.A. § 152(b).

So, if an award is made to a bidder whose bid was not 'most advantageous to the Government, price and other factors considered', and the Act was, therefore, violated, it is only the public who has a cause for complaint, and not an unsuccessful bidder.

The advertisement for bids was, of course, a request for offers to supply the things the Ordnance Department wanted. It could accept or reject an offer as it pleased, and no contract resulted until an offer was accepted. Hence, an unsuccessful bidder cannot recover the profit he would have made out of the contract, because he had no contract.

But this is not to say that he may not recover the expense to which he was put in preparing his bid.

It was an implied condition of the request for offers that each of them would be honestly considered, and that that offer which in the honest opinion of the contracting officer was most advantageous to the Government would be accepted. No person would have bid at all if he had known that 'the cards were stacked against him.' No bidder would have put out $7,000 in preparing its bid, as plaintiff says it did, if it had known the Ordnance Department had already determined to give the contract to the Weidenhoff Company. It would not have put in a bid unless it thought it was to be honestly considered. It had a right to think it would be. The Ordnance Department impliedly promised plaintiff it would be. This is what induced it to spend its money to prepare its bid.

The OTAC knew it would involve considerable expense to prepare models, photographs, diagrams and specifications and other things necessary to comply with the invitation, and so, when it invited plaintiff to incur this expense, it must necessarily be implied that it promised to give fair and impartial consideration to its bid, having in mind only the interest of the Government and not the interest of some favorite bidder.

That promise was broken, shamefully broken, if plaintiff's petition states the facts. If the facts there stated are true, the conclusion seems inescapable that the Ordnance Department knew from the beginning they were going to give Weidenhoff the contract. The advertisement for bids was a sham, done only to appear to comply with the law, to clothe their apparently dishonest purpose with the habiliments of legality. If these allegations are true, they practiced a fraud on plaintiff and on all other innocent bidders. They induced them to spend their money to prepare their bids on the false representation that their bids would be honestly considered.

This implied contract has been broken, and plaintiff may maintain an action for damages for its breach. ***

It goes without saying that not every unsuccessful bidder is entitled to recover the cost of putting in his bid. Recovery can be had in only those cases where it can be shown by clear and convincing proof that there has been a fraudulent inducement for bids, with the intention, before the bids were invited or later conceived, to disregard them all except the ones from bidders to one of whom it was intended to let the contract, whether he was the lowest responsible bidder or not. In other words, it must be shown that bids were not invited in good faith, but as a pretense to conceal the purpose to let the contract to some favored bidder, or to one of a group of preferred bidders, and with the intent to wilfully, capriciously, and arbitrarily disregard the obligation to let the contract to him whose bid was most advantageous to the Government.

Defendant's motion to dismiss plaintiff's petition is denied.

It is so ordered.

JONES, Chief Judge, and LITTLETON, Judge, concur.

MADDEN, Judge (dissenting in part)[omitted].

LARAMORE, Judge (dissenting).

While I cannot condone the wrong done plaintiff, as alleged, I must respectfully dissent.

If the officer acting on behalf of the Government was guilty of the acts alleged in the petition, it would amount to fraud. A suit founded on fraud would sound in tort, and it is clear that this court has no original jurisdiction of tort actions. Martilla v. United States, 118 Ct. Cl. 177.

The plaintiff, in order to recover, must show that he has a contract that he shall receive fair consideration of his bid, or that a statute by its own terms authorizes his recovery in the event his bid does not receive fair consideration. Neither the facts nor the statutes involved justify a conclusion that the Government made a contract with plaintiff to give him fair consideration. On the other hand, there is nothing in the statute which, by its own terms, would authorize the plaintiff to receive a judgment if the contracting officials had not given his bid fair consideration. Without one or the other basis, I cannot see how the court can render judgment for the plaintiff.

I would dismiss the petition.

Notes and Questions

1. Historically, this opinion constituted the origin of the modern law of courts entertaining bid protests. The opinion itself acknowledges that previously, it had been "settled beyond controversy" that "bidders have no right to sue." Why did the Court of Claims create the new right of protest? By inventing the theory of the "implied contract" to consider a bid honestly? By seizing upon a set of established facts, exposed in Congressional investigations, that provided a stronger case for bid protests than anything seen before? By taking advantage of a historical moment - the period of vigorous government contracting legal development of the decade following the ASPA of 1947 and the FPASA of 1949 - when the law was ready to take on a set of proceedings it could not have in wartime and had not previously seen the need to in peacetime?

2. The theory of the contract made by a unilateral offer to consider a bid honestly uses some concepts - like unilateral offers and implied contracts - that may well make more sense to the law student for whom the introductory contracts course is fresh in memory, than to anyone else. Is the theory a real one that grows out of norms of fairness that somehow survive even in the strictly formal, statutory- and regulation- based government contract legal world, or just a fiction to get around legal barriers? Note the dissent. Does the majority's theory still matter anymore, now that bid protests both before the GAO and the courts have statutory charters?

3. Bidders receive an extremely minimal remedy under this theory, merely their bid costs. Is what gave the bid protest its significance that they received that remedy? Does the smallness of the remedy deprive the procedure of significance? Or are awarded bid costs merely the symbol that the bidder has rights, that procurement officials operate under law, and that the courts pass judgment even on such seemingly sovereign and discretionary acts of the government, with the symbolic significance quite important even without a lot of money?

Enlarged Bid Jurisdiction of the United States Court of Federal Claims

From: The Procurement Lawyer, Fall 1997,
at 16 by George M. Coburn

The 104th Congress repealed the bid protest jurisdiction of the General Services Board of Contract Appeals in information technology procurements and just ten months later greatly expanded the bid protest jurisdiction of the U.S. Court of Federal Claims for all procurement protests. Section 12 of the Administrative Dispute Resolution Act of 1996, enacted on October 19, 1996, amended 28 U.S.C. §1491 by adding a new subsection (b) and thereby extending the jurisdictional authority of the U.S. Court of Federal Claims to include both pre- and postaward bid protests:

(b)(1) Both the United States Court of Federal Claims and the district courts of the United States shall have jurisdiction to render judgment on an action by an interested party objecting to a solicitation by a Federal agency for bids or proposals for a proposed contract or to a proposed award of a contract or any alleged violation of statute or regulation in connection with a procurement or proposed procurement. Both theUnited States Court of Federal Claims and the district courts of the United States shall have jurisdiction to entertain such an action without regard to whether suit is instituted before or after the contract is awarded.

(b)(2) To afford relief in such an action, the courts may award any relief the court considers proper, including declaratory and injunctive relief except that any monetary relief shall be limited to bid preparation and proposal costs.

(b)(3) In exercising jurisdiction under this subsection, the courts shall give due regard to the interests of national defense and national security and the need for expeditious resolution of the action.

(b)(4) In any action under this subsection, the courts shall review the agency's decision pursuant to the standards set forth in section 706 of title 5.

Subsection (b) applies to all bid protests filed in the U.S. Court of Federal Claims and in the U.S. District courts on and after December 31, 1996.

Origins of the Law

This analysis examines (1) the origins of the law, (2) the broadened bid protest jurisdiction of the Court of Federal Claims, (3) the scope of review of agency procurement decisions, (4 the extent of discovery including depositions, (5) the availability of stays of procurement pending decision on the merits of the protest, and (6) a comparison with the GAO protest remedy and the potential for expansion of the protest remedy in the Court of Federal Claims and in the district courts.

In passing the House bill to extend the Administrative Dispute Resolution Act of 1996, the Senate added a new section 12 at the administration's request. It appeared essentially as quoted above, but with the difference that the Court of Federal Claims would have exclusive jurisdiction in the federal courts over all protests. Under pressure from the House and the U.S. Chamber of Commerce to protect district courts' *Scanwell* jurisdiction in bid protests, the Senate rewrote section 12 to make the bid protest jurisdiction of the district courts concurrent with that of the Court of Federal Claims, but with a sunset of January 1, 2001, for the district court protest jurisdiction unless extended by Congress.

The new section 12 also provides that starting no earlier than October 1998, the GAO "shall undertake a study regarding the concurrent jurisdiction of the district courts... and the Court of Federal Claims to determine whether concurrent jurisdiction is necessary" and "shall specifically consider the effect of any proposed change on the ability of small businesses to challenge violations of Federal procurement law." This study is to be completed no later than December 31, 1999. The House accepted this compromise on October 4, 1996, and sent the bill to the president.

Enlarged Bid Protest Jurisdiction of the Court of Federal Claims

The Federal Courts Improvement Act of 1982 first conferred limited bid protest jurisdiction on the Court of Federal Claims (then called the U.S. Claims Court). Section 133(a) amended the court's jurisdictional statute to confer exclusive jurisdiction to grant declaratory judgment and other equitable relief on any contract claim brought before the contract is awarded.

This new preaward protest jurisdiction was soon narrowly interpreted by the Court of Appeals for the Federal Circuit to require the existence of an implied-in-fact contract, formed by the submission of a bid or proposal in a response to an agency procurement solicitation, thereby foreclosing suits challenging solicitations prior to receipt of bids or proposals. Under this implied-in-fact contract jurisdiction, the court's standard of review was "extremely limited." * * *

These jurisdictional limits are now swept aside by the new section 12. Under subsection (b)(1), a solicitation, a proposed award or award may be protested "by an interested party" as well as "any alleged violation of statute or regulation in connection with a procurement or proposed procurement." This latter phrase was added in the Senate redrafting of its original version of section 12 to preserve the district court protest jurisdiction. The extent of the additional jurisdiction it confers on the courts remains to be determined. Examples may include protests of awards made without full and open competition, reverse protests by awardees challenging contract termination following a protest, protests of elimination from the competitive range, protests against the cancellation of solicitations, and protests of failure to compete prior to contract modifications or the exercise of purchase options. It may also cover protests such as those of agency overrides of procurement stays, debarments and suspensions, and any violation of any other statute or regulation in connection with a procurement or proposed procurement. Thus subsection (b)(1) would seem to reach every imaginable kind of protest. As such, it goes well beyond the GAO bid protest jurisdiction and the prior narrow preaward jurisdiction of the Court of Federal Claims. In addition, at least for the next four years, the federal district courts for the first time will have explicit statutory jurisdiction over bid protests, jurisdiction that is fully concurrent with that of the Court of Federal Claims.

Subsection (b)(2) first repeats the substance of the prior Claims Court authority to award any relief the court considers proper including declaratory and injunctive relief. It then adds "except that any monetary relief shall be limited to bid preparation and proposal costs". As before, this rules out the award of protest costs such as may be recovered in GAO protests or by small business firms under the Equal Access to Justice Act. Under the prior law, protest costs were not recoverable either in the Court of Federal Claims or the federal district courts. The recovery of bid and proposal costs for prevailing protesters dates back to 1956 when the Court of Claims interpreted its contract jurisdiction under 28 US.C §1491 to confer standing on a disappointed offeror to recover damages for breach of the Government's implied contractual duty to consider its bid in good faith. The measure of damages for the breach was viewed as the recovery of bid and proposal costs. Heretofore recovery of these costs in federal district court bid protests was subject to a jurisdictional limit of $10,000, a limit that subsection (b)(2) may now eliminate.

The admonition in subsection (b) (3) for the courts when exercising this jurisdiction to give due regard to the interests of national defense and security also repeats the prior law but then adds that the due regard includes "the need for expeditious resolution of the action." * * *

Scope of Review of Agency Procurement Decisions

The scope of review of agency decisions is covered by subsection (b) (3), which provides that the courts shall review the agency's decision "pursuant to the standards set forth in section 706 of title 5." This reference to the scope of review section of the Administrative Procedure Act of 1946 incorporates the following:

> To the extent necessary to decision and when presented, the reviewing court shall decide all relevant questions of law, interpret constitutional and statutory provisions, and determine the meaning or applicability of the terms of an agency action. The reviewing court shall —
>
> compel agency action unlawfully withheld or unreasonably delayed; and
>
> hold unlawful and set aside agency action, findings, and conclusions found to be —
>
> arbitrary, capricious, an abuse of discretion, or otherwise not in accordance with law;
>
> contrary to constitutional right, power, privilege, or immunity;
>
> in excess of statutory jurisdiction, authority, or limitations, or short of statutory right;
>
> without observance of procedure required by law;
>
> unsupported by substantial evidence in a case subject to sections 556 and 557 of this title or otherwise reviewed on the record of an agency hearing provided by statute; or
>
> unwarranted by the facts to the extent that the facts are subject to trial de novo by the reviewing court.

In making the foregoing determinations, the court shall review the whole record or those parts of it cited by a party, and due account shall be taken of the rule of prejudicial error.

Most protests will be decided under clause (2)(A) of the APA, reviewing whether the agency procurement action or decision is prejudicially "arbitrary, capricious, an abuse of discretion, or otherwise not in accordance with law." According to Supreme Court precedent, the review is ordinarily based on the full administrative record before the Contracting Officer or other decision maker at the time of the challenged action. Although the agency action or decision is "entitled to a presumption of regularity," that presumption does not shield that action or decision "from a thorough, probing, in-depth review." This review, except on questions of law, is not de novo in the sense that the court may not substitute its judgment for that of the agency.

When the protest in the Court of Federal Claims or a district court follows an unsuccessful GAO protest, the administrative record before the court will also include the agency report to the GAO and the GAO decision on the protest, as required by 31 U.S.C- §3556. That section further provides that the GAO does not have exclusive jurisdiction over protests and specifically authorizes protests to be filed with the contracting agency, with the GAO, or with the federal courts, either initially or after an unsuccessful GAO protest. In the latter event, the court does not review the GAO decision. It may nevertheless "rely upon such a decision for general guidance to the extent it is reasonable and persuasive in light of the administrative record."

* * *

Extent of Permitted Discovery

The court of Federal Claims, like the district courts, ordinarily permits limited and expedited discovery by the protester to establish whether the administrative record should be supplemented or the decision-making process was materially flawed. If the protester can make either showing, the court may permit further limited and expedited discovery. Deposition of the Contracting Officer or other source selection official and the two or three principals in the proposal evaluations ordinarily is the most productive means of discovery to establish any prejudicial abuse of discretion or violation of law or regulation in the agency action or decision protested. If the discovery fails to establish a basis for supplementing the administrative record, the discovery will not be received in evidence and the protest will be decided on the administrative record.

Availability of Stays

Perhaps the most critical element in obtaining meaningful relief in a bid protest is obtaining a stay of the procurement pending the decision on the protest. In protests timely filed with the GAO, the procurement is automatically stayed subject to override authority in the procuring agency. In the Court of Federal Claims as well as in the district courts, protesters ordinarily must litigate to obtain injunctive relief through a temporary restraining order (TRO), a preliminary injunction, or a permanent injunction under varying criteria.

* * *

Comparison with the GAO Protest Remedy

The GAO now ordinarily decides protests within 100 days after filing. Before its protest jurisdiction was repealed, the GSBCA was directed to decide IT protests within sixty-five days. The GAO procedures provide for protective orders and for limited documentary discovery to supplement the agency report, but do not provide for depositions; an evidentiary hearing may be granted when GAO is persuaded that material issues of fact are disputed. In the GSBCA protective orders and documentary discovery and depositions were routinely permitted. Both the GAO and the GSBCA would grant relief if the protester established that the challenged agency action or decision prejudicially violated a statute or regulation or was an abuse of discretion. However, in deciding whether to grant relief, the GAO determined the facts primarily on the basis of the administrative record, occasionally supplemented by a hearing record, while the GSBCA routinely determined the facts de novo based on the record of an evidentiary hearing.

This difference produced much criticism of the GSBCA. Although much of this criticism was unwarranted and there is much to be said for de novo fact finding to provide an effective protest remedy, Congress abolished the protest jurisdiction of the GSBCA, effective August 8, 1996.

Although the judges of the Court of Federal Claims will be mindful of this history, they will find facts de novo only to the extent necessary to supplement the administrative record after the protester has established the need to supplement the record on the basis of one or more of the factors discussed above. Nevertheless, with an expedited filing of the administrative record, the reasonable availability of expedited limited discovery, protective orders, and temporary stays of the procurement pending an expeditious decision on merits of the protest, and above all, with the removal of the prior jurisdictional barriers to an adequate protest remedy, protesters should now find a hospitable forum for fair and effective bid protest adjudication in both the Court of Federal Claims and the federal district courts. Now that protests under section 1491(b)(1) may also be based on "any alleged violation of a statute or regulation in connection with a procurement or proposed procurement" that may not be protested in the GAO or to even the contracting agency, this opens the way to an expanded range of protestable matters in the federal courts.

IMPRESA CONSTRUZIONI GEOM. DOMENICO GARUFI, Plaintiff-Appellant, v. UNITED STATES, Defendant-Appellee.

United States Court of Appeals, Federal Circuit,
2001 238 F.3d 1324, Opinion in Chapter 2

Notes and Questions

1. What do protesters lose and what do they gain by suing in the Court of Federal Claims? They may face a much more expensive proceeding, for one thing. Yet, they gain a much bigger procedural opportunity with much fuller discovery and a greater opportunity for an evidentiary trial. For an example, see *United International Investigative Services Inc. v. United States and MVM, Inc.*, 1998 WL 378878 (Fed. Cl.). A protester won in challenging an award on the ground that the agency had engaged in illegal re-scoring and downgrading of its technical proposal. Discussing the outcome, counsel for the successful protester gave much credit to the court's permitting discovery and hearing testimony in a three-day trial. See "Proposal Evaluation: Agency Illegally Allowed One Evaluator to Re-Score, Downgrade Proposal, Court Says," 70 BNA Fed. Cont. Rep. 87 (July 20, 1998).

2. Discussion of Congress' ability to alter Article III jurisdiction of federal courts has obviously much greater meaning in the government contracting context than in some other contexts. In regard to the federal courts' ability to hear controversial cases about constitutional rights, there have been far more threats and debates in recent decades than actual completed instances of Congress using its power to reduce federal court jurisdiction, tartly described as "court-curbing." Why is Congress willing and able, with little political controversiality, to alter the government contract jurisdiction of the Court of Federal Claims and to abolish that jurisdiction of the district courts?

3. Formerly, another forum for filing and prosecuting bid protests was in a U.S. District Court. District courts did not have an active role in adjudicating bid protests until

the D.C. Circuit decided the landmark case of *Scanwell Laboratories, Inc. v. Shaffer*, 424 F.2d 850 (D.C. Cir. 1970). Thirty years later, district court jurisdiction over bid protest was sunsetted on January 1, 2001 pursuant to section 12 of the Administrative Dispute Resolution Act of 1996, Public Law 104-320. *See* Peter Verchinski, Note, *Are District Courts Still a Viable Forum for Bid Protests?*, 32 Pub. Cont L.J. 393 (2003).

B. Disputes

After contract award and during performance, the government has a dispute process which has evolved to channel the variety of disagreements over contracts into an orderly procedure for resolution. While the contractor continues to perform and the government continues to pay, the contractor makes a certified claim and obtains from the contracting officer a final decision rejecting that claim. Then, the contractor who disagrees with the decision chooses whether to take the matter to the agency board of contract appeals or to the Court of Federal Claims.

Historically, the disputes process goes back a long way, but it received a comprehensive restructuring in the Contract Disputes Act ("CDA") of 1978. The CDA put all the boards of contract appeals on a uniform statutory footing. It gave structure to the contracting officer's powers, the types of claims subject to the disputes process, the time limits for the process, and the respective appeal rights of the government and the contractors. The CDA works together with the standard Disputes Clause in government contracts (FAR 52.233) to create a remarkably uniform government-wide process.

Perhaps the single highest set of goals of the disputes process resembles that of the exhaustion requirement in administrative law. The disputes process makes the contractor give full notice to the government so that it can take early remedial action. This process pushes the contractor to negotiation with contracting officers to resolve the disagreement at the administrative level. Moreover, the disputes process prevents the contractor from rushing prematurely into the contract appeals boards or the courts, overloading those tribunals with unnecessary matters.

Besides such general exhaustion purposes, the disputes process has specific aspects that confine what might otherwise be a difficult mess of a disagreement's paperwork, centered around two important documents: the certified claim and the final decision. On the contractor's side, the claim, if above the threshhold, must be "certified." This requires the contractor, instead of making loose, vague, or overbroad claims, to assert a quite specific sum. It takes considerable legal judgment to gauge just how much support a claim needs in order for certification to be proper. This contrasts with, say, the relatively free hand with which a tort plaintiff might pick the figure in her complaint's damages clause.

On the government's side, the contracting officer must issue a final decision. This insures careful thought on both sides, since the contractor must usually make a deliberate, considered effort to get the contracting officer beyond simply rejecting the contractor's request and instead to formally issue a final decision, and since the contracting officer anticipates the prospect of the subsequent challenge in another forum to that final decision. The FAR defines the contents of the final decision, which should cover such points as describing the claim, referring to the pertinent contract provisions, stating the factual areas of agreement or disagreement, and giving the supporting rationale for the decision. It formally notifies the contractor of its appeal rights.

The student familiar with basic (private) contract law will recognize that the disputes process ties in to the orderly processes for handling uncertainty or partial breach. That is, there are ways besides cancellation or repudiation for the parties to a private contract to handle a disagreement. Basic contracts courses today often treat the procedure under UCC §2-609 for seeking assurances of performance, as a way of handling uncertainty or partial breach while giving a chance for the completion of the contract if satisfactory assurances of performance are, in fact, forthcoming. Still, it is far from routine in the context of private contracts for major disagreements to get resolved without at least a threat, if not the actuality, of one side or the other cancelling or repudiating.

In contrast, by the disputes process, the law of government contracts has raised to a high and elaborate art the handling of disagreement in the course of continuing performance of a contract. On the contractor's side, the Disputes Clause of a government contract sternly forbids a refusal to perform. On the government's side, the very fact that the government has not chosen to resort to termination (either for convenience or for default) signals the government's desire to continue mutual performance and payment. Thus, the disputes process takes the disagreement off for slow, thorough adjudication, while performance continues as though there were no disagreement at all.

An important procedural issue has concerned the extent to which formal dispute is necessary to support an appeal. Of course, in most contracts a stream of demands for payment occur in the form of routine vouchers or invoices and the FAR precludes considering these routine demands to amount, in themselves, to sufficient "claims" to support a formal dispute. Making every routine demand into a "claim" would sacrifice all the value of exhaustion, as neither the contractor nor the government would be making the efforts they should prior to the matter heading on down the formal disputes path. On the other hand, an experiment by the Federal Circuit in the 1990s with creating new, higher requirements for what constituted enough formal disagreement to be a "claim" was ended with the *Reflectone* decision. Accordingly, that decision is the proper starting point for understanding the balance in the disputes process between requiring enough exhaustion and enough pointed disagreement and asking too much exhaustion and disagreement before taking a billing controversy up to the litigating level.

For further discussion of the issues in this section, see: Michael Davidson, *Claims Involving Fraud: Contracting Officer Limitations During Procurement Fraud Investigations*, Army Lawyer, Sept. 2002, at 21; Eric R. Fish, *Note: When a Termination for Convenience Settlement Proposal Constitutes a Claim under the Contract Disputes Act*, 26 Pub. Cont. L.J. 423 (1997); Matthew S. Foss, *U.S. Government Printing Office Board of Contract Appeals: The First Decade*, 24 Pub. Cont. L.J. 579 (1995); Michael R. Finke, *The Burden of Proof in Government Contract Schedule Delay Claims*, 22 Pub. Cont. L.J. 125 (1992); Peter C. Latham, Government Contract Disputes (2d ed. 1986).

DISPUTES CLAUSE
(Oct 1995)

(a)   This contract is subject to the Contract Disputes Act of 1978, as amended (41 U.S.C. 601-613).

(b) Except as provided in the Act, all disputes arising under or relating to this contract shall be resolved under this clause.

(c) "Claim," as used in this clause, means a written demand or written assertion by one of the contracting parties seeking, as a matter of right, the payment of money in a sum certain, the adjustment or interpretation of contract terms, or other relief arising under or relating to this contract. A claim arising under a contract, unlike a claim relating to that contract, is a claim that can be resolved under a contract clause that provides for the relief sought by the claimant. However, a written demand or written assertion by the Contractor seeking the payment of money exceeding $100,000 is not a claim under the Act until certified as required by subparagraph (d)(2) of this clause. A voucher, invoice, or other routine request for payment that is not in dispute when submitted is not a claim under the Act. The submission may be converted to a claim under the Act, by complying with the submission and certification requirements of this clause, if it is disputed either as to liability or amount or is not acted upon in a reasonable time.

(d)   *certification requirement*

(1) A claim by the Contractor shall be made in writing and, unless otherwise stated in this contract, submitted within 6 years after accrual of the claim to the Contracting Officer for a written decision. A claim by the Government against the Contractor shall be subject to a written decision by the Contracting Officer.

(2)

(i) Contractors shall provide the certification specified in subparagraph (d)(2)(iii) of this clause when submitting any claim—

  (A) Exceeding $100,000 * * *

(ii) The certification requirement does not apply to issues in controversy that have not been submitted as all or part of a claim.

(iii) The certification shall state as follows: "I certify that the claim is made in good faith; that the supporting data are accurate and complete to the best of my knowledge and belief; that the amount requested accurately reflects the contract adjustment for which the Contractor believes the Government is liable; and that I am duly authorized to certify the claim on behalf of the Contractor."

(3) The certification may be executed by any person duly authorized to bind the Contractor with respect to the claim.

(e) For Contractor claims of $100,000 or less, the Contracting Officer must, if requested in writing by the Contractor, render a decision within 60 days of the request. For Contractor-certified claims over $100,000, the Contracting Officer must, within 60 days, decide the claim or notify the Contractor of the date by which the decision will be made.

(f) The Contracting Officer's decision shall be final unless the Contractor appeals or files a suit as provided in the Act.

(g) If the claim by the Contractor is submitted to the Contracting Officer or a claim by the Government is presented to the Contractor, the parties, by mutual consent, may agree to use ADR. * * *

(h) The Government shall pay interest on the amount found due and unpaid * * *

(i) The Contractor shall proceed diligently with performance of this contract, pending final resolution of any request for relief, claim, appeal, or action arising under the contract, and comply with any decision of the Contracting Officer.

Reflectone, Inc., Appellant, v. John H. Dalton, Secretary of the Navy, Appellee.

United States Court of Appeals,
Federal Circuit, 1995., 60 F.3d 1572

Before ARCHER, Chief Judge, SKELTON, Senior Circuit Judge, NIES, NEWMAN, MAYER, MICHEL, PLAGER, LOURIE, CLEVENGER, RICH, RADER, SCHALL and BRYSON, Circuit Judges.

Opinion for the court filed by Circuit Judge MICHEL. Concurring opinion filed by Circuit Judge NIES.

MICHEL, Circuit Judge.

Reflectone, Inc. (Reflectone) appeals from the decision of the Armed Services Board of Contract Appeals (Board) dismissing Reflectone's appeal for lack of subject matter jurisdiction. Reflectone, Inc., ASBCA No. 43081, 93- 1 BCA ¶25,512, 1992 WL 302847 (1992). The Board held that Reflectone had not submitted a "claim" within the meaning of the Contract Disputes Act of 1978 (CDA), 41 U.S.C. §§601-13 (1988 & Supp. V 1993), as interpreted in the Federal Acquisition Regulation (FAR), because a dispute over the amount of money Reflectone asserted it was owed did not predate Reflectone's June 1, 1990 Request for Equitable Adjustment (REA), the purported claim. Board jurisdiction is grounded in the CDA which authorizes Board review only of a contracting officer's final decision on a "claim." The CDA, however, does not define "claim." Because we conclude that FAR 33.201 (1988), which alone defines "claim" for purposes of the CDA, does not require a pre-existing dispute as to either amount or liability when, as here, a contractor submits a non-routine "written demand...seeking, as a matter of right, the payment of money in a sum certain," FAR 33.201, we hold that Reflectone's REA was a CDA "claim" and, therefore, the Board has jurisdiction. Accordingly, we reverse the dismissal and remand for adjudication of Reflectone's appeal from the contracting officer's decision on its merits.

BACKGROUND

On April 15, 1988, Reflectone entered into a $4,573,559 fixed price contract with the Naval Training Systems Center in Orlando, Florida, requiring Reflectone to update helicopter weapon system trainers. The contract called for delivery of the first trainer on February 15, 1989, with the other three trainers to follow at three-month intervals. In a letter dated December 14, 1988, Reflectone advised the contracting officer (CO) that delivery of certain equipment was being delayed by late, unavailable or defective government- furnished property. In response, the Navy denied responsibility for the delay and issued a cure notice warning Reflectone that unless the condition endangering timely delivery of the equipment was eliminated within thirty days, the Navy might terminate the contract for default.

On January 17, 1989, Reflectone again wrote the CO that the delays were the fault of the government and requested an extension of the contract delivery schedule. Subsequently, the Navy modified two of the original four delivery dates but reserved its right to seek additional compensation for delay. After Reflectone advised the Navy that it would be unable to meet even the extended delivery dates due to faulty government-furnished property, the CO indicated on May 5, 1989, that Reflectone was delinquent on the contract and that the Navy would seek compensation for the delay. Between May

1989 and April 1990, the contract delivery schedule was modified at least three more times and each time the Navy reserved the right to make a claim against Reflectone for delay. In response, Reflectone continued to inform the Navy that it considered the government to have caused all delays and that it would claim relief once the full economic impact of the delay was known.

On June 1, 1990, Reflectone submitted an REA to the CO demanding $266,840 for costs related to government-caused delay with respect to twenty- one enumerated items. Reflectone's President and CEO certified the REA and requested a decision from the CO. In the initial review of the REA, completed on January 15, 1991, the CO denied sixteen of the twenty-one items in their entirety, estimated entitlement in the remaining five items at $17,662, and advised Reflectone that a counterclaim and set-off, exceeding the amount requested by Reflectone, was being prepared. On March 19, 1991, the CO rendered a final decision indicating that the government's position remained the same and advising Reflectone of its right to appeal to the Board.

Reflectone appealed the CO's final decision to the Board, which held that the REA was not a "claim" within the meaning of the Contract Disputes Act and, therefore, it did not have jurisdiction over the appeal. The Board relied on language from Dawco Constr., Inc. v. United States, 930 F.2d 872, 878 (Fed.Cir.1991), stating, "A contractor and the government contracting agency must already be in dispute over the amount requested." Dawco also states "The [CDA] and its implementing regulation require that a 'claim' arise from a request for payment that is 'in dispute.' " Id. The Board interpreted Dawco as holding that no demand for payment could be a claim unless the amount of the payment had been put in dispute. The Board reasoned that because Reflectone first requested a specific amount from the government in the REA, no dispute over the amount existed prior to the REA and, therefore, the REA could not be a claim according to its interpretation of Dawco.

* * *

On appeal to this court, a divided, three-judge panel affirmed the Board's dismissal decision, accepting its interpretation of Dawco and its rationale, in an opinion dated September 1, 1994, now vacated. Reflectone, Inc. v. Kelso, 34 F.3d 1031 (Fed.Cir.) (withdrawn from bound volume), vacated, 34 F.3d 1039 (Fed.Cir.1994). Due to the exceptional public importance of the issue of first impression presented by this case concerning the proper definition of a CDA "claim," we granted Reflectone's Suggestion for Rehearing In Banc.Fed. Cir.R. 35.

* * *

ANALYSIS

I

A. FAR 33.201 Does Not Require That A Payment Demanded In A Non-Routine Submission Be In Dispute Before The Submission To A Contracting Officer Can Be A "Claim"

Under the CDA, a final decision by a CO on a "claim" is a prerequisite for Board jurisdiction. Sharman Co. v. United States, 2 F.3d 1564, 1568-69 (Fed.Cir.1993) (reviewing jurisdictional scheme of CDA). Because the CDA itself does not define the term "claim,"[1] we must assess whether a particular demand for payment constitutes a claim,

---

1. The CDA, 41 U.S.C. §605(a) (1988), states in relevant part:
All claims by a contractor against the government relating to a contract shall be in writing and

based on the FAR implementing the CDA, the language of the contract in dispute, and the facts of the case. Garrett v. General Elec. Co., 987 F.2d 747, 749 (Fed.Cir.1993). The FAR defines "claim" as:

> [1] a written demand or written assertion by one of the contracting parties seeking, as a matter of right, the payment of money in a sum certain, the adjustment or interpretation of contract terms, or other relief arising under or relating to the contract.... [2] A voucher, invoice, or other routine request for payment that is not in dispute when submitted is not a claim. [3] The submission may be converted to a claim, by written notice to the contracting officer as provided in 33.206(a), if it is disputed either as to liability or amount or is not acted upon in a reasonable time.

FAR (48 C.F.R. §) 33.201 (emphasis added). The issue is whether sentence [2] adds a requirement to those stated in sentence [1] that applies to all submissions.

The government and the Board would require that before Reflectone's REA can qualify as a claim, it be preceded by a dispute over entitlement to and the amount of a demand for payment. According to the government, this requirement is mandated by the language of FAR 33.201. In order to explore whether a CDA "claim" requires a dispute which pre-dates the submission to the CO, we requested that the following question be addressed by the in banc briefs.

> Did Dawco Constr., Inc. v. United States, 930 F.2d 872 (Fed.Cir.1991), properly conclude that a Contract Disputes Act (CDA) "claim" as defined in FAR 33.201 requires a pre-existing dispute between a contractor and the government when the claim is in the form of a "written assertion...seeking, as a matter of right, the payment of money in a sum certain" or other contract relief per the first sentence of the FAR definition, or does that requirement only apply when the claim initially is in the form of a "routine request for payment"?

We answer the first half of this question in the negative and the second half in the affirmative. We hold that sentence [1] of FAR 33.201 sets forth the only three requirements of a non-routine "claim" for money: that it be (1) a written demand, (2) seeking, as a matter of right, (3) the payment of money in a sum certain. That sentence simply does not require that entitlement to the amount asserted in the claim or the amount itself already be in dispute when the document is submitted. The subsequent sentence does not add another requirement to a non-routine submission.

FAR 33.201 does not mention a dispute until the fourth sentence, sentence [2], which provides, "[a] voucher, invoice, or other routine request for payment that is not in dispute when submitted is not a claim." Routine requests for payment, too, are "written demand[s]...seeking, as a matter of right, payment of money in a sum certain" and, therefore, appear to fall within the definition of claim recited in sentence [1] of FAR 33.201. However, the FAR explicitly excludes from the definition of "claim" those "routine request[s] for payment" that are not in dispute when submitted to the CO.[2] Nevertheless, nothing in the definition suggests that other written demands seeking

---

shall be submitted to the contracting officer for a decision. All claims by the government against a contractor relating to a contract shall be the subject of a decision by the contracting officer.

2. The distinction excluding routine requests for payment from the definition of "claim" relieves COs from the requirement of issuing a CDA final decision on each and every voucher that the government is obligated to pay under the express terms of the contract during its ordinary progression, including "progress payments." The process for converting such routine requests, if disputed, into claims assures that only those submissions that need final decisions will require them.

payment of a sum certain as a matter of right, i.e., those demands that are not "routine request[s] for payment," also must be already in dispute to constitute a "claim." Moreover, that the regulation specifically excludes only undisputed routine requests for payment from the category of written demands for payment that satisfy the definition of "claim" implies that all other written demands seeking payment as a matter of right are "claims," whether already in dispute or not. The inclusion of only one exception to the definition of "claim"—undisputed, routine requests—implies the exclusion of any others. See United States v. Koonce, 991 F.2d 693, 698 (11th Cir.1993) (applying canon of statutory construction inclusio unius est exclusio alterius).

Our holding today that the FAR requires a "claim" to be a written demand seeking a sum certain (or other contract relief) as a matter of right, but not necessarily in dispute, is consistent with the ordinary meaning of the term "claim": "a demand for something due or believed to be due." Webster's Ninth New Collegiate Dictionary 244 (1990). That the demand is made as a matter of right constitutes the essential characteristic of a "claim" according to both the FAR and the dictionary definitions. See Essex Electro Eng'rs, Inc. v. United States, 960 F.2d 1576, 1580-81 (Fed.Cir.) ("[T]he dictionary definition of 'claim' supports the reasonableness of the requirement that the money be sought as a matter of right."), cert. denied, 506 U.S. 953, 113 S.Ct. 408, 121 L.Ed.2d 333 (1992). Nothing in the common definition of "claim," however, requires a pre-existing dispute before a demand as a matter of right can be a claim. Indeed, everything suggests the contrary.

Moreover, as Reflectone points out, it is illogical to require a dispute before a demand for payment rightfully due can be a "claim" because to have a dispute the contractor first must make a demand as a matter of right, i.e., a claim, that is then refused. Furthermore, neither the CDA, its legislative history, nor the FAR, nor its history, suggests that a dispute must pre-date the contractor's submission of the claim to the CO when the claim is in the form of a non-routine demand as of right.

The government argues, nevertheless, that a close reading of the regulation demonstrates that a "claim" always requires a pre-existing dispute. The government's analysis begins correctly by acknowledging that sentence [1] of the FAR, defining "claim" as "a written demand...seeking, as a matter of right, the payment of money in a sum certain" appears to include vouchers, invoices and other routine requests for payment. According to the government, because the regulation later makes clear that the drafters intended to exclude routine requests for payment from the definition of "claim" unless they are in dispute, the question becomes one of distinguishing between non- routine written demands seeking the payment of a sum certain as a matter of right and "routine request[s] for payment." The government next asserts, incorrectly, that it is the existence of a dispute which distinguishes a non- routine "claim" from a routine request for payment and, therefore, every "claim" must involve a pre-existing dispute.

The government's interpretation of the FAR must fail, as a matter of logic, because it recognizes only two categories of potential claims, undisputed routine requests for payment, which do not satisfy the definition, and disputed non-routine written demands seeking payment as a matter of right, which do. This interpretation ignores a third category, undisputed, non-routine written demands seeking payment as a matter of right. Under the literal language of the FAR, however, the critical distinction in identifying a "claim" is not between undisputed and disputed submissions, but between routine and non- routine submissions.

To read the dispute requirement of sentence [2] of FAR 33.201 as applying to all submissions for payment, as the government suggests, one would have to construe every demand for payment as a matter of right as a "routine request for payment." However, this is clearly not so. For instance, an REA is anything but a "routine request for payment." It is a remedy payable only when unforeseen or unintended circumstances, such as government modification of the contract, differing site conditions, defective or late-delivered government property or issuance of a stop work order, cause an increase in contract performance costs. Pacific Architects and Eng'rs Inc. v. United States, 491 F.2d 734, 739, 203 Ct.Cl. 499 (1974). A demand for compensation for unforeseen or unintended circumstances cannot be characterized as "routine." The Supreme Court has confirmed the non-routine nature of an REA by equating it with assertion of a breach of contract. Crown Coat Front Co. v. United States, 386 U.S. 503, 511, 87 S.Ct. 1177, 1181, 18 L.Ed.2d 256 (1967) ("With respect to claims arising under the typical government contract, the contractor has agreed in effect to convert what otherwise might be claims for breach of contract into claims for equitable adjustment."). Thus, an REA provides an example of a written demand for payment as a matter of right which is not "a routine request for payment" and, therefore, it satisfies the FAR definition of "claim" whether or not the government's liability for or the amount of the REA was already disputed before submission of the REA to the CO.[3]

A routine request for payment, on the other hand, is made under the contract, not outside it. For example, a voucher or invoice is submitted for work done or equipment delivered by the contractor in accordance with the expected or scheduled progression of contract performance. Similarly, progress payments are made by the government when the contractor completes predetermined stages of the contract. An REA can hardly be compared to an invoice, voucher or progress payment.

Thus, we hold that FAR 33.201 does not require that "a written demand . . . seeking, as a matter of right, the payment of money in a sum certain" must already be in dispute when submitted to the CO to satisfy the definition of "claim," except where that demand or request is a "voucher, invoice or other routine request for payment." * * * FAR 33.201, viewed as a whole, establishes a framework in which written demands seeking a sum certain as a matter of right are CDA "claims" with the only exception of "routine request[s] for payment" which may be converted to claims by the existence of a dispute and compliance with other requirements of conversion in FAR 33.206(a). Routine requests are a subset of all written demands for payment. Special requirements apply to the subset, but not to the rest of the set.

Reflectone's REA is clearly "a written demand or written assertion by one of the contracting parties seeking, as a matter of right, the payment of money in a sum certain." Reflectone, a contracting party, submitted a written document to the CO demanding the payment of $266,840 which it asserted the government owed for delaying performance of the contract by furnishing defective goods. The submission was certified and requested a CO decision. Consequently, Reflectone's REA satisfies all the requirements listed for a CDA "claim" according to the plain language of the first sentence of FAR 33.201. The REA is not a "routine request for payment" and, therefore, the fourth sentence of the FAR definition does not apply here to require, inter alia, a pre-existing dispute as to either liability or amount. Because we conclude that Reflectone's REA is a

---

3. We do not hold, however, that every non-routine submission constitutes a "claim" under the FAR. Those submissions which do not seek payment as a matter of right are not claims, a definition which excludes, for example, cost proposals for work the government later decides it would like performed. See Essex Electro Eng'rs, 960 F.2d at 1581-82 (excluding cost proposals and inspection reports from the FAR definition of a CDA "claim").

"claim" according to the FAR, we further conclude that the Board has jurisdiction to review the CO's denial of Reflectone's REA.

* * *

CONCLUSION

We hold that properly construed for its plain meaning, the language of FAR 33.201 does not require that a payment demand contained in a purported CDA claim be in dispute before being submitted for decision to the CO unless that demand is a "voucher, invoice or other routine request for payment." To the extent that Dawco and cases relying on Dawco can be read to suggest otherwise, they are overruled. We further hold that Reflectone's REA satisfies the definition of "claim," and, therefore, we reverse the Board's dismissal for lack of jurisdiction and remand this case to the Board for further proceedings on Reflectone's appeal consistent with this opinion.

[Concurring opinion omitted.]

Notes and Questions

1. *Reflectone* focuses on the existence of a "claim" that is ripe enough in terms of the amount of agency consideration and rejection. In some respects, the government's arguments as recited in the opinion sound phrased almost in delicate euphemisms. Do you understand the government's legitimate arguments for requiring a high level of agency consideration and rejection for a "claim," as hinted at when the government says that it would help for the contracting officer to have more opportunities to request clarification? How does it affect the power relationship of contracting officer and contractor not to require that highly formal level of agency consideration and rejection as a predicate for appeal? What happens to the contracting officer's power when the contractor has both the right and the temptation to appeal over her head that much faster?

2. Another requirement for a dispute under the Contract Disputes Act (41 U.S.C. sec. 601 et seq.) is that an asserted demand exceeding $100,000 must be certified. The submitting contractor is required to certify that the claims are made in good faith, are based on accurate and complete data, and that the sum certain requested accurately reflects the adjustment for which the party seeks payment (sec. 605(a)(1)). Certification can be effected by anyone with authority to bind the contractor regarding the claim, which must be submitted within six years of accrual. See *H. L. Smith, Inc. v. Dalton*, 49 F.3d 1563 (Fed. Cir. 1995); *Newport News Shipbuilding and Dry Dock Co. v. Garrett*, 6 F.3d 1547 (Fed. Cir. 1993); *Reliance Insurance Co v. United States*, 27 Fed. Cl. 815 (1993); *Mediax Interactive Technologies, Inc.*, ASBCA No. 43961 (1993).

3. The concept of what constitutes a "claim" remains elusive. The Contract Disputes Act, 41 U.S.C. §§601-613, simply requires that claims be written and submitted to the contract officer for a decision. 41 U.S.C. §605(a). The FAR specifies further that

> Claim, as used in this clause, means a written demand or written assertion by one of the contracting parties seeking, as a matter of right, the payment of money in a sum certain, the adjustment or interpretation of contract terms, or other relief under or relating to the contract. FAR 52.233.1 (April 1984).

The contractor is further required to include details of the relevant facts of the contract at issue, as well as the basis and amount of the claim, to give the contract officer sufficient information upon which to render a decision. *Appeal of Automated Power Systems*,

DOTCAB No. 2928 (1998). There is no need, however, for the contractor to specifically demand the contract officer's final decision. The subjective intent of the claimant in making the submission will suffice to meet the CDA claim test. *D.C. Cab and Taxi Dispatch*, VABCA No. 5482 (1998).

For a case illustrating the application of *Reflectone*, see *James M. Ellett Construction Co., Inc. v. United States*, 93 F.3d 1537 (Fed. Cir. 1996), provided in the chapter on Terminations.

For further discussions of the subject of disputes, see, in the Summer 1999 issue of the Public Contracts Law Journal, the Contract Disputes Act of 1978 Twentieth Anniversary Essays. These included Eric Bruggink, *A Modest Proposal*, 28 Pub. Cont. L.J. 529 (1999); C. Stanley Dees, *The Future of the Contract Disputes Act: Is It Time to Roll Back Sovereign Immunity?*, 28 Pub. Cont. L. J. 545 (1999); Steven L. Schooner, *What Next? A Heuristic Approach to Revitalizing the Contract Disputes Act of 1978*, 28 Pub. Cont. L.J. 635 (1999); and Martin P. Willard, *Contracting Out of the CDA*, 28 Pub. Cont. L.J. 665 (1999).

BONNEVILLE ASSOCIATES, Plaintiff,
v. The UNITED STATES, Defendant,
v. CAMCO CONSTRUCTION CO.,
Third Party Defendant.

No. 92-21C. 30 Fed.Cl. 85 United States Court of Federal Claims.
Nov. 22, 1993.

MARGOLIS, Judge.

This government contracts case comes before the court on defendant's motion to dismiss for lack of subject matter jurisdiction. The plaintiff, Bonneville Associates ("Bonneville"), contracted with the defendant, acting through the General Services Administration ("GSA"), for the repair and sale of an office building. Disputes arose regarding certain contractual obligations of Bonneville. After receiving a final decision of the contracting officer and filing a notice of appeal with the General Services Administration Board of Contract Appeals ("GSBCA"), plaintiff withdrew its notice of appeal and brought an action involving the same operative facts in this court.

Defendant argues that the contract is subject to the Contract Disputes Act, 41 U.S.C. §§ 601 *et seq.*, because it involved both the repair and sale of real property. Defendant further argues that 41 U.S.C. § 609 and the Election Doctrine bind plaintiff to its decision to appeal the final decision of the contracting officer to the GSBCA, and that this court lacks jurisdiction to hear plaintiff's claim. * * *

After a careful review of the record and after hearing oral argument, this court grants defendant's motion to dismiss for lack of subject matter jurisdiction.

FACTS

The material facts are uncontested. On September 30, 1987, Bonneville entered into a contract with GSA for the repair and sale of an office building in Las Vegas, Nevada. GSA purchased the building for $9,908,452. The parties agreed that $1,708,452 of the contract price would be withheld for improvements to the building by Bonneville. These funds were to be paid to Bonneville as the repair work was completed. Of the amount withheld by GSA, $500,000 remains unpaid.

The parties disputed certain mechanical and structural improvements to the building to be performed by plaintiff. Specifically, Bonneville and GSA attempted to resolve disputes concerning floor strengthening and leveling, additional cooling capacity, duct work and acoustical insulation, and certain warranty issues. Inability to resolve the disputes led to an August 21, 1991 final decision of the contracting officer demanding $5,195,069 from Bonneville, allegedly representing the cost to defendant of correcting deficiencies in the building.

The contracting officer's final decision notified Bonneville of its right to appeal the decision to either the GSBCA within 90 days, or to the United States Court of Federal Claims within twelve months. Bonneville filed a notice of appeal with the GSBCA on November 19, 1991. The GSBCA docketed the appeal on November 26, 1991. Bonneville filed a motion to withdraw its GSBCA appeal on January 8, 1992, and the GSBCA dismissed the appeal without prejudice on January 17, 1992. On January 13, 1992, Bonneville filed this action.

DISCUSSION

The issue is whether the Contract Disputes Act ("Act") covers the contract between Bonneville and GSA, thus binding plaintiff to the Act's procedural rules and conferring jurisdiction on the GSBCA. If this case is subject to the Contract Disputes Act, 41 U.S.C. § 609[1] and the Election Doctrine require dismissal of plaintiff's case for lack of subject matter jurisdiction. Conversely, if this case is not covered by the Contract Disputes Act, then defendant's motion must be denied because the GSBCA was without jurisdiction over plaintiff's claim.

The contract was a dual-purpose agreement for both the repair and sale of an office building. The disputes concern the plaintiff's obligations under the repair and construction clauses of the contract.

Section 8(d) of the Act provides that the boards of contract appeals "shall have jurisdiction to decide any appeal from a decision of a contracting officer...relative to a contract." 41 U.S.C. § 607(d). Section 3 of the Act limits the types of contracts to which the statute applies:

§ 602. Applicability of law

(a) Executive agency contracts

Unless otherwise specifically provided herein, this chapter applies to any express or implied contract (including those of the nonappropriated fund activities described in sections 1346 and 1491 of title 28) entered into by an executive agency for—

(1) the procurement of property, *other than real property in being;*

(2) the procurement of services;

(3) *the procurement of construction, alteration, repair or maintenance of real property;* or,

(4) the disposal of personal property.

41 U.S.C. § 602 (emphasis added).

Plaintiff contends that this case clearly fits within the section 602(a)(1) exception for the procurement of real property and that the Act does not apply. * * *

---

1. Section 609 provides that a contractor may bring an action on a claim in the Court of Federal Claims in lieu of appealing the decision of a contracting officer to an agency board. 41 U.S.C. § 609(a)(1).

Assuming, *arguendo*, that the section 602(a)(1) exception excludes all contracts for procurement of real property in being from the Act's coverage, this court's inquiry is not ended. The contract was not merely for the procurement of real property in being; it was for the *repair* and sale of an office building. Section 602(a)(3) of the Act expressly brings contracts for the "construction, alteration, repair or maintenance of real property" within the statute. Therefore, one purpose of the dual-purpose contract is specifically covered by the Act. * * * *

* * * [T]his court finds that the plaintiff's claim is covered by the Act. Accordingly, this court next considers the applicability of the Election Doctrine.

> The Court of Claims recognized that, although the Contract Disputes Act provides a contractor with a choice of forums in which to contest an adverse decision by the contracting officer, the contractor is precluded by the Contract Disputes Act from pursuing its claim in both forums. Once a contractor makes a binding election under the Election Doctrine to appeal the contracting officer's adverse decision to the appropriate board of contract appeals, that election must stand and the contractor can no longer pursue its claim in the alternate forum. Under the Election Doctrine, the binding election of forums is an "either-or" alternative, and, as such, does not provide a contractor with dual avenues for contesting a contracting officer's adverse decision.

National Neighbors, Inc. v. United States, 839 F.2d 1539, 1542 (Fed.Cir.1988). Once this court finds that a plaintiff appealed a contracting officer's final decision to a board, "the only remaining issue is whether that election was 'informed, knowing and voluntary.'" *Mark Smith Constr. Co., Inc. v. United States*, 10 Cl.Ct. 540, 544 (1986) (citations omitted).

Plaintiff was advised that the contracting officer's decision was a final decision and that plaintiff had a right to appeal the decision to the GSBCA within 90 days or to the Court of Federal Claims within 12 months. *See* 41 U.S.C. § 609(a). Bonneville filed a timely notice of appeal with the GSBCA and its decision was "informed, knowing and voluntary." Under these circumstances, this court dismisses plaintiff's case pursuant to the Election Doctrine. *See, e.g., Prime Constr. Co., Inc. v. United States*, 231 Ct.Cl. 782, 784, 1982 WL 25226 (1982).

CONCLUSION

Because the contract is covered by the Contract Disputes Act, this court is without subject matter jurisdiction. The case must be dismissed pursuant to the Election Doctrine. The defendant's motion to dismiss is granted. The clerk will dismiss the complaint without prejudice. No costs.

Notes and Questions

1. This case points to some of the implicit realities of the dispute litigation system after the contracting officer has denied what the contractor wants, and the contractor has a "claim" (in *Reflectone* terms). At that point, the CDA gives the contractor an important choice, to appeal to the Board of Contract Appeals for that department, or to the Court of Federal Claims. Most contractors prefer the boards, but some prefer the court, and either way, each has its weighty reasons for making that choice of forum. In some respects procedure before the boards is a little more informal and, hence, can be less expensive. Once the contractor chooses, an "Election Doctrine" precludes their changing their mind and going to the other forum.

Any number of questions can arise, such as the one in this case about mixed contracts involving real estate and construction. Other potentially complex questions concern the procedures for when a contracting officer delays ruling on a claim; the government's claims against the contractor, and the government's ability to counterclaim.; and interest on claims.

2. Another issue consists of how the rules of the contract appeals board, like, say, the Federal Rules of Civil Procedure, establish an entire procedural system. A brief description follows, largely applicable to all contract appeals boards, but specifically drawn from the Armed Services Board of Contract Appeals, with its Rules of Practice (e.g., "ASBCA R. 1").

An appeal to a contract appeals board begins with the filing of a Notice of Appeal by the contractor. The board then dockets the appeal. Most appellants are represented by attorneys, but some appellants proceed pro se. The appellant files a complaint, followed by the government filing an answer. ASBCA Rule 4 provides for the contracting officer to assemble and transmit an appeal file pulling together the pertinent documents, known popularly as the "Rule 4 file." Discovery can occur, such as depositions and requests for documents. Other features include subpoenas, motions, and small claims procedures.

Ultimately, a hearing can occur, the functional equivalent of a trial that produces a verbatim transcript though conducted informally. Nearly 75% of all ASBCA hearings are held outside of the Washington area. After the hearing, the parties submit posthearing briefs. The presiding judge prepares a draft opinion, but two other judges participate and if disagreements occur, even more judges may participate. Appeals go to the U.S. Court of Appeals for the Federal Circuit. An alternative path consists of the contractor taking an appeal from the final decision of the contracting officer to the Court of Federal Claims. Procedures in that court resemble, generally, those governing civil litigation in the U.S. District Courts, though trial is to a judge without a jury.

C. Alternative Dispute Resolution

Alternative Dispute Resolution ("ADR") in government contracting law consists of using methods such as mediation and arbitration, among others, to resolve protests and disputes without the full-scale proceedings previously described. For example, a protester and a contracting officer might agree to attempt to resolve the protest through mediation, i.e., working with a neutral third party who facilitates negotiation or even evaluates the two sides' proposals, thereby hopefully obviating the need for a decision by the agency, or GAO, or a court, on the protest. Or, a contractor and a contracting officer might agree to resolve a dispute through arbitration, a binding decision by a neutral arbitrator, rather than go through the disputes process up to the boards of contract appeals or the courts

In the 1990s, there was a marked increase in the use of ADR to resolve protests and disputes. Partly, Congress and senior levels of the contracting agencies encouraged greater use of ADR. Partly, both contracting officers and contractors found that ADR sometimes works better than litigation.

The trend toward ADR began with the Administrative Dispute Resolution Act ("ADRA") of 1990, Pub. L. 101-552, 104 Stat. 2736 (1990), a statute initially set to expire but subsequently reauthorized. FAR provisions implement ADRA. ADRA's fostering of ADR for disputes got implemented by the boards of contract appeals giving procedural instructions to the parties whenever an appeal is docketed, as well as by encouragement of ADR by the Court of Federal Claims and most of the federal district courts. More encouragement came by Executive Order 12979 (Oct. 25, 1995), and by agency policy statements.

ADR methods include partnering, which is just a better relationship between the parties; mediation, which can be either facilitative or evaluative; minitrials, which are truncated but moderately formal adversarial information exchanges heard by the parties' representatives as a way of fostering settlement; and arbitration, in which neutral third parties make binding decisions. Until the 1990s, the government had resisted arbitration, raising constitutional issues since arbitrators make decisions without receiving appointments pursuant to the Appointments Clause (the way, say, judges or agency heads do). However, the Department of Justice issued a legal memorandum, subsequently followed by a decision of the Court of Federal Claims, which upheld arbitration provided certain criteria were present. *Tenaska Washington Partners II, L.P. v. United States*, 34 Fed. Cl. 434 (1995).

In the course of a solicitation that produces a protest or a contract disagreement that produces a dispute, the decisive moment comes when the two sides decide to use an ADR method to resolve the protest or dispute and carry out that deicsion by an ADR Agreement. The ADR Agreement selects the method and the neutral participant (mediator or arbitrator), provides for information exchange and procedures, protects confidentiality, and may anticipate settlement. Once a disagreement gets resolved, the neutral participant prepares a written instrument setting forth the resolution. The parties must then carry out those terms.

For further discussion, see: Robert J. MacPherson, *In Your Face ADR: New York City's Construction Contract Dispute Procedure*, 25 Pub. Cont. L.J. 301 (1996); Laurence J. Zielke, *Arbitrating Miller Act Claims and Problems in Enforcing an Award Under the Federal Arbitration Act*, 24 Pub. Cont. L.J. 401 (1995); Stephen G. Lee, *Hiring the Cheapest Piper: Arbitration of Subcontract Disputes by Boards of Contract Appeals*, 23 Pub. Cont. L.J. 105 (1993); Alexander J. Brittin, *Alternative Dispute Resolution in Government Contract Appeals*, 19 Pub. Cont. L.J. 210 (1990); Reba Page & Frederick J. Lees, *Roles of Participants in the Mini-Trial*, 18 Pub. Cont. L.J. 54 (1988); Kirby Behre, *Arbitration: A Permissible or Desirable Method for Resolving Disputes Involving Federal Acquisition and Assistance Contracts?*, 16 Pub. Cont. L.J. 66 (1986).

D. False Claims Act/Qui Tam

The government faces an overwhelming challenge in contractor fraud resulting in a highly significant subfield of law particularly as to one procedural mechanism, the civil false claims act suit. Contract fraud derives part of its significance from its large scale. On the health care procurement side, it has been estimated that fraud and waste amount to 10% of government spending, or $25 billion. Just as important, fraud represents an open-ended threat. The nature of fraud adapts and changes to circumvent the government's efforts at control; it undermines the government's programs over and above the sheer loss of funding; and, as one of the key components of public corruption, it undermines the legitimacy and capacity to function of any government in general and of a democratic government in particular since fraud, like other corruption, reduces faith in the constitutionally and popularly legitimated officials. In an era in which numerous governments, from the Soviet Union to the Suharto regime in Indonesia, have fallen in part due to the undermining and paralyzing effects of state corruption, government contract fraud represents a threat far beyond even its large numbers.

Of course, the government has many procedural responses to fraud. Many are preventive measures, like open competition in acquisition decisions, inspection of delivered supplies, and active auditing of claims for payment. Others are fairly straightforward variations on familiar procedures, namely, criminal prosecutions for violations of the criminal fraud statute and terminations for contractors behaving fraudulently.

What is most worthy of attention in the fraud context is the unique civil litigation channel established by the False Claims Act. The False Claims Act has two aspects: the aspects common to all cases, regardless of who brings them; and, the unique "qui tam" aspect that a case can be initiated and even pursued to completion by a private party, such as a whistleblower, seeking a recovery on behalf of the government. These two aspects deserve separate treatment and each is represented by an important case in this section: *Aerodex*, illustrating the aspects common to all false claim cases, and *Becton Dickinson*, illustrating the special aspects of a whistleblower suit.

Historically, the False Claims Act was first enacted in 1863 as a response to rampant contractor fraud during the Civil War, and many major cases, including *Aerodex*, proceeded under the law as it existed in 1863-1986. However, the explosive growth in importance of the Act occurred through its amendments in 1986, somewhat as part of the reaction of the mid-1980s to defense procurement scandals. After its initial employment predominantly against defense fraud, the 1990s saw a rapid growth of the statute's use against fraud in government health care contracting. This casebook uses a number of additional False Claims Act opinions in other chapters, notably in the chapter on specialized contracting, precisely because the False Claims Act has had such importance for government health care contracting.

The False Claims Act cases may seem like a sharp break from other aspects of government contracting. Other cases about contractor performance typically arise through the disputes process, following the orderly path of claims presented to contracting officers, final decisions by contracting officers, appeals, and consideration on a record largely created out of the regular documentation of the contracting process. The government personnel who present the government's side typically have a regular participating role in the contracting process, representing further continuity between the contracting process and the disputes case. In sum, the disputes case is an appeal from the contracting process, but deferential toward it and largely shaped by it.

In contrast, the False Claims Act case is a distinct break from the contracting process, not an effort to keep continuity with it, but a deliberate effort to respond to an apparent breakdown in the ordinary contracting process by mounting a highly independent response. The False Claims Act case proceeds only in federal district court, a deliberately independent, nonspecialized tribunal without any particular institutional sympathy toward the folkways of contracting officers and contractors. Moreover, the False Claims Act creates its own record, concerned with keeping sharp the tools for piercing through ingenious deception rather than taking on faith the contractor's adherence to basic norms. A sharp change also occurs in the personnel who participate: representing the government's interests are either Justice Department attorneys or even whistleblower's attorneys, who view the contracting officers as witnesses rather than clients.

The rough treatment received by contractors in this process has led them as a class to fight back politically against civil fraud enforcement. Defense contractors and health care providers have waged somewhat distinct struggles over the years against the fraud enforcement process in general and the civil fraud statute in particular. Such contractors argue that the civil fraud procedure exposes them to harsh penalties - both high damages and the label of defrauder - for what they contend are often relatively innocent mistakes.

Given the many uncertainties of government contracting, contractors urge, it is unfair to subject them to a punitive procedure that breaks so sharply with the ordinary contracting context. Contractors argue that they must often act in reliance on one form or another of informal or unspoken government guidance, or on common sense or commercial practicality, that affords them inadequate protection in the unforgiving procedures used in a civil fraud case. Moreover, they urge, it is inefficient as well, for it separates the government contracting sector from the general commercial marketplace. They argue such government-unique burdens make government contracting an area in which only a limited number of contractors prepared to operate in more self-protective, more defensive, more expensive ways, will take on work. This situation makes not only for interesting policy debates, but, of course, for a great deal of litigation for government contract lawyers.

For further discussions of the subject of this section, see:

Michael Davidson, *Claims Involving Fraud: Contracting Officer Limitations During Procurement Fraud Investigations*, Army Lawyer, Sept. 2002, at 21;

Charles Tiefer & Heather Akehurst-Krause, *Risky Business: Medicare's Vulnerability to Selection Games of Managed Care Providers*, 28 U. Balt. L. Rev. 319 (1999);

William E. Kovacic, *Whistleblower Lawsuits As Monitoring Devices in Government Contracting*, 29 Loy. L.A. L. Rev. 1799 (1996).

Neal A. Cooper, *Third Party Liability or the False Claims Act: It Is Time for Consultants To Pay the Price For Their Bad Advice*, 29 J. Marshall L. Rev. 923 (1996).

Ann M. Lininger, *The False Claims Act and Environmental Law Enforcement*, 16 Va. Envtl. L.J. 577 (1997).

Kara Nicole Schmidt, *Privatizing Environmental Enforcement: The Bounty Incentives of the False Claims Act*, 9 Geo. Int'l Envtl. L. Rev. 663 (1997).

C. Stanley Dees and Christopher C. Bouquet, *Beyond "Diminished Value": New Challenges in the Law of Civil False Claims Act Damages*, 25 Pub. Cont. L.J. 597 (1996).

Robert L. Vogel, *Eligibility Requirements for Relators Under* Qui Tam *Provisions of the False Claims Act*, 21 Pub. Cont. L.J. 593 (1992).

Robert L. Vogel, *The Public Disclosure Bar Against* Qui Tam *Suits*, 24 Pub. Cont. L.J. 477 (1995).

1. Civil False Claims Act

The Civil False Claims Act, 31 U.S.C. 3719, has a number of prongs. Its most important one subjects to liability a person who knowingly presents a false or fraudulent claim to the government. Another important prong subjects a person who knowingly uses a false record or statement to get a false or fraudulent claim paid (a "false record") case. This removes the defense that the person did not directly and personally submit a claim to the government, for example, a fraudulent borrower of a government-guaranteed loan, whose only direct dealings are with the lending bank.

A false claim has three key elements: (1) a claim, that is (2) false and fraudulent, and (3) a level of intent. From the previous discussions in other contexts of what a "claim" is, it will come as no surprise that there is much law on this subject, with an important distinction being that mere bids or proposals to contract are not "claims." What is "false and fraudulent" has much in common with fraud in private contracting. However, many disputes have occurred over the extent to which contractors can raise as a defense that government officials had knowledge of or even approved what they did, with the government insisting that its officials cannot excuse fraud, and the contractors arguing that something is not fraudulent if it could not and did not mislead government officials. As for the intent level, the use of the term "knowingly" in the statute suggests a higher intent requirement than actually exists. The 1986 amendments made recklessness sufficient, so that an official who takes what the legislative history calls a "head-in-the-sand" attitude when submitting false claims is liable.

Contractors found guilty of a false claim pay double damages. Moreover, even if the actual damages were low or nominal, the statute imposes liability to statutory damages.

The first case, *Aerodex*, is a classic illustration of how the False Claims Act empowers the government once it uncovers a deliberate falsehood, to overcome a number of seemingly plausible contractor defenses to liability and to high damage figures.

United States of America, Plaintiff-Appellee, v. Aerodex, Inc., et al., Defendants-Appellants

No. 71-2801. United States Court of Appeals,
Fifth Circuit. 469 F.2d 1003, Nov. 2, 1972.

Before PHILLIPS, THORNBERRY and RONEY, Circuit Judges.

RONEY, Circuit Judge:

This case is about aircraft engine bearings. In 1962 Aerodex, Inc. contracted to sell certain aircraft parts to the Navy Department. Three hundred master rod bearings for the Curtiss-Wright R1820 engine were included in the sale. The bearings delivered were not those specified in the contract. The district court, 327 F.Supp. 1027, held that the invoices submitted by Aerodex for payment for these bearings were "false claims for payment" within the meaning of the Federal False Claims Act, 31 U.S.C.A. §231 (1970). The government was awarded $381,838.36 with interest. We reverse as to Defendant Tonks and remand with directions to modify the amount of the judgment against Aerodex and Crawford.

At the time pertinent to this lawsuit, the Commercial Division of Aerodex, Inc. was engaged in the purchase and sale of spare aircraft parts. Defendant Raymond Tonks was president and general manager of Aerodex, and defendant Frank J. Crawford was vice president in charge of the Commercial Division.

On September 18, 1962, Crawford submitted to the U.S. Navy Aviation Supply Office a bid by Aerodex to sell 300 master rod bearings, Curtiss-Wright part number 171815, at a price of $90.00 each. This bid was accepted and was incorporated as a part of a contract entered into between Aerodex and the Aviation Supply Office on October 6, 1962.

As several of the contract provisions are crucial to this appeal, we set them out in full:

SPECIFICATIONS

Articles furnished from stocks of surplus material are acceptable under this contract provided that the articles so furnished meet the following requirements:

1. All articles furnished must be identified by the applicable Curtiss Wright Corporation, Wright Aeronautical Division part numbers...and must conform to the requirements of the respective drawings for said articles.

* * *

3. All articles furnished...must be in new, unused condition.

INSPECTION AND ACCEPTANCE

* * *

At destination all delivered articles shall be subjected to 100% final inspection by the O & R shop for conformance to the applicable data, drawings and specifications required in the manufacture of said articles. Inspection shall include magnaflux or Zyglo or the equivalent thereof. * * *

UNSATISFACTORY MATERIAL

Any articles delivered which have been determined by the receiving activity to have failed to conform to the applicable specifications and drawings or which are otherwise considered unsuitable for intended use shall be returned, at the Contractor's expense, for replacement. The necessary replacement articles shall then be shipped, all transportation charges paid, to the destinations specified herein. If any of the articles returned to the Contractor are not replaced, the total amount due to be paid under this contract shall be reduced by the contract value of the returned article or articles.

The bearings supplied by Aerodex to the Navy under this contract were not P/N [part number] 171815 bearings. They were P/N 117971 and 117971Y10 bearings which had been reworked by Aerodex employees. The rework consisted of replacing the metallic overlay on the inside diameter of each bearing. After reworking, each bearing was reidentified with P/N 171815. To the naked eye, the reworked bearings were indistinguishable from new, unused P/N 171815 bearings.

Aerodex' reworked bearings were received and accepted at the Jacksonville Naval Air Station without the "100% final inspection" required by the contract. A number of them were installed in aircraft engines. When the Navy subsequently discovered that the bearings were not the ones contracted for, it removed and replaced those which had been installed. This "retrofit" operation cost $160,919.18. That amount was added to the contract price of $27,000 and the total doubled as provided in the False Claims Act. This, together with the $2,000 statutory penalty for each of the three invoices, resulted in the $381,838.36 judgment for the government.

I. Liability Under the False Claims Act

The defendants make a two-pronged attack on the district court's finding of liability under the False Claims Act. They allege that the evidence was (1) legally insufficient in that it did not show the necessary element of scienter, and (2) factually insufficient in that it did not demonstrate the individual defendants' personal knowledge and participation in the alleged fraudulent performance of the contract. The law is settled in this Circuit that to show a violation of the False Claims Act the evidence must demonstrate "guilty knowledge of a purpose on the part of [the defendant] to cheat the Government," United States v. Priola, 272 F.2d 589, 594 (5th Cir. 1959), or "knowledge or guilty intent," United States v. Ridglea State Bank, 357 F.2d 495, 498 (5th Cir. 1966).

The test is easily stated but difficult to apply in the circumstances of this case.

(a) The Mislabeled Parts

A master rod bearing for the R1820 engine is a cylindrical sleeve approximately 3 1/4 inches in length and 3 1/4 inches in diameter. The bearing is composed of steel, with a silver plating material on both the inside and outside surfaces. The inside of the bearing is further coated with a microscopically thin metallic overlay. The inside diameter of the bearing performs the function of a bearing surface which permits the free rotation of the crankshaft within the master rod bearing. This permits the crankshaft to rotate, turning the propellor. Failure of the bearing causes complete engine failure.

The bearing denominated P/N 117971 is impossible to distinguish visually from bearing P/N 171815 but has two basic differences. One difference is hardness of the steel in the shell backing; the P/N 117971 is made of a low carbon steel, while P/N 171815 is made of a harder, high carbon steel. The other difference lies in the composition of the metallic overlay used to line the inside diameter of the bearings: bearing P/N 117971's overlay consists of a lead and indium composition, while the overlay used in P/N 171815 is a lead-tin composition. Aerodex replaced the lead-indium overlay with lead-tin prior to renumbering the P/N 117971 bearings. This reworking did not change the hardness or composition of the bearings' steel shell.

Defendants do not deny that the bearings they sold to the Navy were reworked and renumbered. They argue, nevertheless, that their actions constituted no violation of the False Claims Act. They allege that all military and factory publications available to them showed that both P/N 117971 and P/N 171815 were approved for use in the R1820 engine and that the entire aviation industry at that time considered the two bearings to be interchangeable. Defendants argue, therefore, that they could not have had the requisite intent to "cheat" the government.

We think this argument requires too restrictive a reading of the False Claims Act. The mere fact that the item supplied under contract is as good as the one contracted for does not relieve defendants of liability if it can be shown that they attempted to deceive the government agency. In United States v. National Wholesalers, 236 F.2d 944 (9th Cir. 1956), cert. denied, 353 U. S. 930, 77 S.Ct. 719, 1 L.Ed.2d 724 (1957), the defendant contracted to deliver to the Army a number of Delco-Remy generators. Unable to procure these generators, National Wholesalers had substitutes manufactured and attached spurious "Delco-Remy" labels to them. Although the substitute generators performed according to contract specifications, liability under the False Claims Act was held to attach because of the deliberate misbranding.

We think that the deliberate mislabeling in the case at bar, coupled with the fact that the parts delivered did not actually meet the specifications of the contract, compels a finding of liability under the Act. If defendants had, in fact, believed that the reworked P/N 117971 bearings were interchangeable with the P/N 171815 bearings that they had contracted to deliver, they could easily have requested permission from the Navy to deliver the substitute parts or, at least, could have disclosed to the Navy the manner in which they thought they could comply with the contract. The failure to do so indicates nothing less than an intention to deceive.

II. Failure to Inspect

The government admits that the Navy did not perform the "100% final inspection" called for by the contract. Defendants proved at trial that a simple and inexpensive nondestructive test, the Rockwell Hardness Test, would have shown that the bearings did not meet contract specifications.

The inspection clause in the contract does not, however, insulate appellants from liability for fraud. First, a reading of the clause shows that it is for the government's benefit and imposes no duty on the government in favor of the appellants. Second, Article 5, the inspection article, provides that inspection is not conclusive "as regards latent defects, fraud, or such gross mistakes as to amount to fraud." This provision embodies the established rule that, even where final inspection is the obligation of the government, such obligation does not absolve a contractor on liability for fraud. * * *

In addition, appellants failed to prove that 100% inspection would necessarily have included a Rockwell Hardness Test. Since hardness of the steel used in the bearing is controlled at the manufacturing level and is the same for all bearings of a given part number, the appearance of that part number on the bearing gives notice of the bearing's hardness. Thus, only upon suspicion of fraudulent misnumbering would an inspector conduct a Rockwell Hardness Test.

The lower court was correct in holding that the contract "could not be relied upon by the defendants to escape liability because such an interpretation would allow a supplier to escape liability for any deception where the inspection was not made but the deception discovered by other means-an obviously unfair and unintended result." This holding also applies to the defendants' reliance on the regulations.

III. Measure of Damages

The question raised on this appeal as to the measure of damages applied by the district court is difficult to resolve because there appears to be no precedent against which to judge the facts of this case.

The district court computed damages by first adding the contract price of the bearings, $27,000.00, to the $160,919.18 cost incurred in removing and replacing the P/N 117971 bearings which had been installed in aircraft engines. This sum, $187,919.18, was then doubled under the statutory formula in the False Claims Act which imposes liability for the submission of a false claim in "double the amount of damages which the United States may have sustained by reason of doing or committing such act..." 31 U.S.C.A. §231 (1970).

The cases that have considered the application of this statute's double damage provision have generally been of two kinds. One line of cases involves an overpricing for what was sold and delivered to the government. Here the damage sustained by the United States is the difference between the reasonable cost of the goods sold and the price the government actually paid for the goods, and recovery is double that amount. See, e. g., United States v. Foster Wheeler Corp., 447 F.2d 100 (2d Cir. 1971); United States v. Ben Grunstein & Sons Co., 137 F.Supp. 197 (D. N.J. 1956); United States v. American Packing Corp., supra.

In the other line of cases, the government has been billed and has paid for a greater quantity of goods or services than it has received. The basis for the double damage recovery is then the amount it paid for the goods that were short in delivery. See, e. g., United States v. Koenig, 144 F.Supp. 22 (E.D. Pa. 1956).

These cases all differ somewhat from this one because they involve a quantitative measure, a difference between what the government paid and what it should have paid for goods that were acceptable. None involved consequential damages incurred as a result of defective goods.

Upon careful analysis, we hold that the language of the False Claims Act does not include consequential damages resulting from delivery of defective goods. The statute assesses double damages attributable to the "act," which in this case is the submission of the false vouchers. The submission of these vouchers was not the cause of the government's consequential damages. The delivery and installation of the bearings in the airplanes, not the filing of the false claim, caused the consequential damages.

In a case of this kind, damages under the False Claims Act must be measured by the amount wrongfully paid to satisfy the false claim. United States v. Woodbury, 359 F.2d 370 (9th Cir. 1966); United States v. American Packing Corp., supra.

Toepleman v. United States, 263 F.2d 697 (4th Cir.), cert. denied sub nom. Cato Bros., Inc. v. United States, 359 U. S. 989, 79 S.Ct. 1119, 3 L.Ed.2d 978 (1959), relied upon by the government, is not authority to the contrary, in Toepleman, the defendants had obtained crop support loans from the Commodity Credit Corporation by fraudulently representing that the cotton collateral of the pledged promissory notes had been produced by the makers of the notes. The government had sold the collateral for less than the total amount of the loans, and the Fourth Circuit permitted the government to recover double the foreclosure deficiency under the False Claims Act. Toepleman's reasoning is inapposite here, because the damages were in no way consequential, i. e., additional losses incurred as proximate results of the act of submitting a fraudulent loan application. Rather, the government was permitted to double the amount still owing on the fraudulently obtained loans. In this respect, Toepleman closely resembles both lines of False Claims Act cases, as an example of the government being either overcharged for the correct quantity of goods or charged for goods short in delivery.

We think that a proper application of the double damage provision limits the government's claim to the amount that was paid out by reason of the false claim. We treat the matter as if the claims for $27,000 for P/N 171815 bearings were false because those bearings were never delivered. The government paid $27,000 for bearings it did not receive. This amount must be doubled, and the $2,000 statutory penalty must be added for each of the three invoices. The correct amount recoverable under the False Claims Act, consequently, is $60,000.00, and the judgment for $381,838.36 is reversed.

IV. Breach of Warranty

The consequential damage award to the government can be sustained on another theory. The district court found that Aerodex committed a breach of warranty in delivering to the government bearings which were at variance with those required by the contract. The issue is whether Aerodex has an adequate defense to the recovery of damages for that breach of warranty.

The warranty provisions of the contract are contained in Clause 33, which reads in pertinent part:

(a) Notwithstanding inspection and acceptance by the Government of articles furnished under this contract or any provision of this contract concerning the conclusiveness thereof, the Contractor warrants that at the time of delivery (i) all materials delivered under this contract will be free from defects in material or workmanship and will conform with the specifications, and all other requirements of this contract;....

(b) Within one year after the delivery of any article under this contract, written notice may be given by the Government to the Contractor of any breach of the warranties in paragraph (a) of this clause as to such article. Within a reasonable time after such notice, the Contracting Officer may either (i) require the prompt correction or replacement of any article or part thereof (including preservation, packaging, packing, and marking) that did not at the time of its delivery conform with the requirements of this contract within the meaning of paragraph (a) of this clause, or thereafter does not so conform in consequence of any such breach; or (ii) retain such article, whereupon the contract price thereof shall be reduced by an amount equitable under the circumstances and the Contractor shall promptly make appropriate repayment....

* * *

(e) The remedies afforded the Government by paragraph (b) of this clause shall be exclusive as to any breach of the warranties in paragraph (a) of this clause, except any such breach involving latent defects, fraud, or such gross mistakes as amount to fraud.

The government did not pursue either of the remedies afforded by subparagraph (b) of Clause 33. This omission does not provide Aerodex with a defense to the breach of warranty claim, however, because cases of fraud are specifically excepted from exclusivity under subparagraph (e).

Aerodex' main contention is that the government's failure to conduct the "100% final inspection" precludes it from any remedy for the breach of warranty.

Aerodex makes the following arguments to support its position:

[a] The damages were not foreseeable, since Aerodex could not have known that the government would not make the required inspections;

[b] The government cannot recover damages which it could have avoided by the exercise of reasonable diligence;

[c] The language of the "inspection" and "unsatisfactory material" clauses of the contract is repugnant to the warranty clause, and since the former are typed while the latter is printed, the former clauses must be given precedence, making rejection and return of nonconforming bearings the government's exclusive remedy; and

[d] The Christian doctrine required the government to perform tests required by specific Armed Services regulations.

These arguments are irrelevant because the breached warranty was an express one. Aerodex expressly warranted that the delivered bearings were of a specific serial number, when in truth they were not. The general rule is that a buyer is entitled to rely upon the express warranty of the seller, especially where the warranty is descriptive and the defects are not readily apparent, and the buyer's failure to inspect constitutes no defense for the seller. 8 S. Williston on Contracts §973 (1964); 46 Am.Jur. Sales §330 (1943); 77 C. J.S. Sales §311(b) (1952); Refinery Equipment, Inc. v. Wickett Refining Co., 158 F.2d 710 (5th Cir. 1947). The government was therefore entitled to rely solely upon Aerodex' express warranty describing the bearings, and its failure to inspect the delivered bearings is of no legal consequence.

* * *

Reversed and remanded with directions.

Notes and Questions

1. Note the high penalties. A contract price of $27,000 yielded fraud penalties over $381,000, reduced on remand. Did you follow how they were calculated and, in particular, the existence of a $2,000 statutory penalty? In effect, the False Claims Act deals with the problem of the financial attractiveness of government contract fraud by arranging a lot of monetary punishment for those who are caught.

Over the years, the Supreme Court has devoted much attention to the issues posed by statutory penalties. It upheld such penalties under a statute akin to the False Claims Act against a challenge under the Fifth Amendment in *Rex Trailer Co. v. United States*, 350 U.S. 148 (1956). At one point, the Court temporarily established that civil penalties under the False Claims Act, imposed upon a defendant already sanctioned in a criminal fraud case could run afoul of the Double Jeopardy Clause. *United States v. Halper*, 490 U.S. 435 (1989). However, the Court subsequently disavowed the analysis in that case, finding that the Double Jeopardy Clause only dealt with successive criminal punishments. *Hudson v. United States*, 522 U.S. 93 (1997). Still, the Supreme Court found in criminal contexts that too high a forfeiture could violate the Excessive Fines Clause of the Constitution. *United States v. Bakajakian*, 524 U.S. 321 (1998).

This tension between the high and sometimes multiple penalties that the Civil False Claims Act allows, and the circumstances which in one respect or another contractors argue to be relatively benign, adds extra drive to the many debates about the False Claims Act.

2. One of those debates has concerned whether an element of False Claims Act liability is that there be some injury to the government. In this case, the contractor made the argument it supplied bearings that, although mislabeled, were interchangeable with the ones specified in the contract. Why does the court reject that argument? While the argument that the fraud did not injure the government fails when made in the unappealing circumstances of deliberate mislabeling, that by no means laid the argument to rest. For example, suppose a contractor building missiles creates false inspection records. Assume, for purposes of argument, that the missiles themselves are perfectly adequate and would have passed the most rigorous inspection, and the contractor misbehaved, not in the making of the missiles, but only in the inspecting. What does the government buy: the product or the inspection records? Consider this analysis:

> An economic analysis of the "false testing" cases is that the Government loses the "insurance" value, a concretely valuable aspect of quality control, inherent in a fully operative product testing and certification system. The Govern-

ment loses something it pays competing producers to provide; the fraudulent producer frees itself from something its competitors would have counted as one of their costs to provide. Another way, more of a regulatory analysis, for understanding the "false testing" cases is that they involve loss of the governmental interest expressed by the FAR's contractor self-inspection clauses....

Charles Tiefer & Michael Blumenfeld, *Qui Tam Recovery Without "Actual Damages,"* 6 FCA & Qui Tam Q. Rev., July 1996, at 23, 25.

3. Another of the debates has concerned the defense that the contracting officers themselves in one way or another participated in, approved, knew of, or at least allowed the allegedly fraudulent activity. In this case, that argument takes the form that mandatory government inspections should have caught the mislabeling. That sounds like a weak form of the argument, but it catches the contractor's essential sense that government contracting is not a distant, formal, arms-length activity, but a close-knit activity. Higher management in the government contractor may well consider it a service to both sides to take off excessive layers of controls of the lower levels of production, and to depend on a known form of government inspection to do the policing, or on some other known government form of supervision or advice to provide guidance. The argument is certainly made, in a stronger form than in this case, by hospitals whose alleged fraud consists of how their billing personnel describe medical procedures: if the reviewers of those bills for the government are giving advice about proper billing, why cannot the hospitals rely on it?

4. Yet another of the debates has concerned the False Claims Act's burden of proof. In a criminal fraud case, the government must prove fraud beyond a reasonable doubt; and, in some civil situations, plaintiffs must prove accusations by the standard of clear and convincing evidence. However, the False Claims Act only imposes on the government the burden of proof by a preponderance of the evidence. 31 U.S.C. sec. 3731(c). For this as for other effective aspects of the Act, its proponents cite the peculiar problem that fraud, particularly fraud on the government, is self-concealing and that the ability of contractors to avoid or to disguise evidence of fraud necessitates a not-too-high burden of proof.

2. "Qui Tam" Provisions

The most unique and dynamic feature of the False Claims Act consists of its provision for whistleblowers to initiate lawsuits on behalf of the government. If Jane Q. Citizen knows of fraud by Government Contractor Inc., she files a suit as a relator, captioned "United States ex rel. Jane Q. Citizen v. Government Contractor Inc." ("Ex rel." stands for "ex relator," signifying that Ms. Citizen is filing on behalf of the United States.) Congress has given her the incentive of a share of the recovery. This mechanism, newly envigorated by the Act's 1986 Amendments, brought forth hundreds of qui tam lawsuits with extensive recoveries for the Treasury.

For government contracts lawyers, the challenge comes in understanding the unusual aspects of the qui tam mechanism which can be loosely separated into two parts: the mechanics of how a relator suit works and the particular "public disclosure" jurisdictional barrier by which the FCA limits such suits.

Starting with the mechanics, suppose Ms. Citizen works for GC, Inc., and discovers that the company was doing what Aerodex was found to be doing, mislabeling aircraft parts. Ms. Citizen goes to a lawyer who evaluates whether the case has enough merit to bring. If so, the lawyer files a complaint presenting the case against GC, Inc., under seal, with Ms. Citizen as the "relator." The FCA requires that the lawyer furnish the complaint together with a disclosure statement of useful evidence of the fraud to the Civil Division of the Department of Justice. A public interest group that promotes the use of the Act, Taxpayers Against Fraud, the False Claims Act Legal Center, in Washington, D.C., has published a description of this process, entitled "Qui Tam Practitioner's Guide: Evaluating and Filing a Case," May 1997.

With the complaint and disclosure statement in hand, the Justice Department decides whether it will intervene. Often it tasks the agency inspector general or auditors to evaluate the claim, and makes its decision from a calculation of whether the case merits the investment of the government's limited resources for handling such suits. If the Justice Department decides to intervene, typically the case then goes forward largely the way a false claims case proceeds that had no relator at all, namely, the Justice Department takes the lead in discovery and trial. If the government successfully obtains a recovery through settlement or judgment, the relator receives a share of the proceeds between 15 and 25%, plus reasonable attorney's fees and costs.

If the Justice Department decides not to intervene, the relator, Ms. Citizen, can still proceed with the case. This time, the relator and her attorney themselves conduct discovery and trial. In this situation, if she obtains a recovery by settlement or judgment, that recovery still goes to the Treasury, but she gets a larger share, between 25 and 30%. 31 U.S.C. §3730(d)(2).

The other part of the unique aspects of the qui tam case consists of the "public disclosure" jurisdictional barrier that limits such suits. In a word, if a fraud has already been publicly disclosed, a qui tam relator cannot sue regarding it. This barrier does not apply to the government; a fraud could receive national headlines and the government can still sue. However, a private qui tam relator could not initiate a suit on such a famous fraud, regardless of the merit of the case, because of the statutory barrier. Congress wanted to encourage more relators to uncover fraud, not simply more relators to sue about frauds that had already been uncovered before they sued. The "public disclosure" barrier has an exception for the "original source" of the information, so that if Ms. Citizen first disclosed her company's fraud, then even after the disclosure she can file suit.

Extensive litigation has occurred over the "public disclosure" rule. Contractors prize it as a defense, since it focuses on the relators, a group that contractors consider as having pronounced shortcomings. On the other hand, as a defense it has nothing to do with whether the allegations of fraud have merit, so relators scorn it as a mere technicality. Because of its importance as the special defense against relators, the "public disclosure" barrier has taken on some of the controversiality of all the other previously noted issues surrounding the False Claims Act, such as those concerning the measure of damages and the burden of proof, even though those issues concern relator-initiated and government-issued cases alike.

VERMONT AGENCY OF NATURAL RESOURCES, Petitioner, v. UNITED STATES ex rel. STEVENS.

No. 98-1828. Supreme Court of the United States, 529 U.S. 765,
Argued Nov. 29, 1999. Decided May 22, 2000.

Justice SCALIA delivered the opinion of the Court.

This case presents the question whether a private individual may bring suit in federal court on behalf of the United States against a State (or state agency) under the False Claims Act, 31 U.S.C. §§ 3729-3733.

I

Originally enacted in 1863, the False Claims Act (FCA) is the most frequently used of a handful of extant laws creating a form of civil action known as *qui tam*. As amended, the FCA imposes civil liability upon "[a]ny person" who, *inter alia,* "knowingly presents, or causes to be presented, to an officer or employee of the United States Government... a false or fraudulent claim for payment or approval." 31 U.S.C. § 3729(a). The defendant is liable for up to treble damages and a civil penalty of up to $10,000 per claim. *Ibid.* An FCA action may be commenced in one of two ways. First, the Government itself may bring a civil action against the alleged false claimant. § 3730(a). Second, as is relevant here, a private person (the "relator") may bring a *qui tam* civil action "for the person and for the United States Government" against the alleged false claimant, "in the name of the Government." § 3730(b)(1). If a relator initiates the FCA action, he must deliver a copy of the complaint, and any supporting evidence, to the Government, § 3730(b)(2), which then has 60 days to intervene in the action, §§ 3730(b)(2), (4). If it does so, it assumes primary responsibility for prosecuting the action, § 3730(c)(1), though the relator may continue to participate in the litigation and is entitled to a hearing before voluntary dismissal and to a court determination of reasonableness before settlement, § 3730(c)(2). If the Government declines to intervene within the 60-day period, the relator has the exclusive right to conduct the action, § 3730(b)(4), and the Government may subsequently intervene only on a showing of "good cause," § 3730(c)(3). The relator receives a share of any proceeds from the action—generally ranging from 15 to 25 percent if the Government intervenes (depending upon the relator's contribution to the prosecution), and from 25 to 30 percent if it does not (depending upon the court's assessment of what is reasonable)—plus attorney's fees and costs. §§ 3730(d)(1)-(2).

Respondent Jonathan Stevens brought this *qui tam* action in the United States District Court for the District of Vermont against petitioner Vermont Agency of Natural Resources, his former employer, alleging that it had submitted false claims to the Environmental Protection Agency (EPA) in connection with various federal grant programs administered by the EPA. Specifically, he claimed that petitioner had overstated the amount of time spent by its employees on the federally funded projects, thereby inducing the Government to disburse more grant money than petitioner was entitled to receive. The United States declined to intervene in the action.* * * *

II

We first address the jurisdictional question whether respondent Stevens has standing under Article III of the Constitution to maintain this suit. See *Steel Co. v. Citizens for a Better Environment,* 523 U.S. 83, 93-102, 118 S.Ct. 1003, 140 L.Ed.2d 210 (1998).

As we have frequently explained, a plaintiff must meet three requirements in order to establish Article III standing. See, *e.g., Friends of Earth, Inc. v. Laidlaw Environmental Services (TOC), Inc.,* 528 U.S. 167, ——, 120 S.Ct. 693, 704, 145 L.Ed.2d 610 (2000). First, he must demonstrate "injury in fact"—a harm that is both "concrete" and "actual or imminent, not conjectural or hypothetical." *Whitmore v. Arkansas,* 495 U.S. 149, 155, 110 S.Ct. 1717, 109 L.Ed.2d 135 (1990) (internal quotation marks and citation omitted). Second, he must establish causation—a "fairly...trace[able]" connection between the alleged injury in fact and the alleged conduct of the defendant. *Simon v. Eastern Ky. Welfare Rights Organization,* 426 U.S. 26, 41, 96 S.Ct. 1917, 48 L.Ed.2d 450 (1976). And third, he must demonstrate redressability—a "substantial likelihood" that the requested relief will remedy the alleged injury in fact. *Id.,* at 45, 96 S.Ct. 1917. * * * *

Respondent Stevens contends that he is suing to remedy an injury in fact suffered by the United States. It is beyond doubt that the complaint asserts an injury to the United States—both the injury to its sovereignty arising from violation of its laws (which suffices to support a criminal lawsuit by the Government) and the proprietary injury resulting from the alleged fraud. But "[t]he Art. III judicial power exists only to redress or otherwise to protect against injury *to the complaining party.*" *Warth v. Seldin,* 422 U.S. 490, 499, 95 S.Ct. 2197, 45 L.Ed.2d 343 (1975) (emphasis added); see also *Sierra Club v. Morton,* 405 U.S. 727, 734-735, 92 S. Ct. 1361, 31 L.Ed.2d 636 (1972). It would perhaps suffice to say that the relator here is simply the statutorily designated agent of the United States, *in whose name* (as the statute provides, see 31 U.S.C. §3730(b)) the suit is brought—and that the relator's bounty is simply the fee he receives *out of the United States' recovery* for filing and/or prosecuting a successful action on behalf of the Government. This analysis is precluded, however, by the fact that the statute gives the relator himself an interest *in the lawsuit,* and not merely the right to retain a fee out of the recovery. Thus, it provides that "[a] person may bring a civil action for a violation of section 3729 *for the person and for the United States Government,*" §3730(b) (emphasis added); gives the relator "the right to continue as a party to the action" even when the Government itself has assumed "primary responsibility" for prosecuting it, §3730(c)(1); entitles the relator to a hearing before the Government's voluntary dismissal of the suit, §3730(c)(2)(A); and prohibits the Government from settling the suit over the relator's objection without a judicial determination of "fair[ness], adequa[cy] and reasonable[ness]," §3730(c)(2)(B). For the portion of the recovery retained by the relator, therefore, some explanation of standing other than agency for the Government must be identified.

There is no doubt, of course, that as to this portion of the recovery—the bounty he will receive if the suit is successful—a *qui tam* relator has a "concrete private interest in the outcome of [the] suit." *Lujan, supra,* at 573, 112 S.Ct. 2130. But the same might be said of someone who has placed a wager upon the outcome. An interest unrelated to injury in fact is insufficient to give a plaintiff standing. * * * *

We believe, however, that adequate basis for the relator's suit for his bounty is to be found in the doctrine that the assignee of a claim has standing to assert the injury in fact suffered by the assignor. The FCA can reasonably be regarded as effecting a partial assignment of the Government's damages claim. Although we have never expressly recognized "representational standing" on the part of assignees, we have routinely entertained their suits, see, *e.g., Poller v. Columbia Broadcasting System, Inc.,* 368 U.S. 464, 465, 82 S. Ct. 486, 7 L.Ed.2d 458 (1962); *Automatic Radio Mfg. Co. v. Hazeltine Research, Inc.,* 339 U.S. 827, 829, 70 S. Ct. 894, 94 L.Ed. 1312 (1950); *Hubbard v. Tod,* 171 U.S. 474, 475, 19 S.Ct. 14, 43 L.Ed. 246 (1898)—and also suits by subrogees, who have been described as "equitable assign[ees]," L. Simpson, Law of Suretyship 205 (1950), see, *e.g.,*

Vimar Seguros y Reaseguros, S.A. v. M/V Sky Reefer, 515 U.S. 528, 531, 115 S.Ct. 2322, 132 L.Ed.2d 462 (1995); *Musick, Peeler & Garrett v. Employers Ins. of Wausau,* 508 U.S. 286, 288, 113 S. Ct. 2085, 124 L.Ed.2d 194 (1993). We conclude, therefore, that the United States' injury in fact suffices to confer standing on respondent Stevens.

We are confirmed in this conclusion by the long tradition of *qui tam* actions in England and the American Colonies. * * * *

Qui tam actions appear to have originated around the end of the 13th century, when private individuals who had suffered injury began bringing actions in the royal courts on both their own and the Crown's behalf. * * * *

Qui tam actions appear to have been as prevalent in America as in England, at least in the period immediately before and after the framing of the Constitution. * * * *

We think this history well nigh conclusive with respect to the question before us here: whether *qui tam* actions were "cases and controversies of the sort traditionally amenable to, and resolved by, the judicial process." *Steel Co.,* 523 U.S., at 102, 118 S. Ct. 1003. When combined with the theoretical justification for relator standing discussed earlier, it leaves no room for doubt that a *qui tam* relator under the FCA has Article III standing.[8]

We hold that a private individual has standing to bring suit in federal court on behalf of the United States under the False Claims Act, 31 U.S.C. §§ 3729-3733 * * * *

It is so ordered.

[Separate opinions on other issues are omitted.]

Notes and Questions

1. The *Stevens* case resolved a persistent controversy during the fourteen years following the strengthening of the False Claims Act and its qui tam mechanism by 1986 amendments. Initially, the Supreme Court granted certiorari in the case on a relatively narrow federalism issue, and then suddenly, ten days before argument, informed counsel to address the broad Article III issue unanimously resolved in this opinion. Combined this with Justice Scalia, who has elaborated his own views on Article III, deciding to write this opinion, and there are many tea leaves to read. Some observers believe he positioned himself to write the upholding of qui tam standing as an occasion to limit other kinds of standing, such as that of citizen plaintiffs pursuant to the environmental laws. For discussion, see Charles Tiefer, "Surprise Order in Qui Tam Case May Foretell a Scalia Surprise," Legal Times, Nov. 29, 1999, at 52; Myriam E. Gilles, *Representational Standing: U.S. ex rel. Stevens and the Future of Public Law Litigation,* 89 Cal. L. Rev. 315 (2001).

2. Note how the opinion refers to the injury of the United States that is partially assigned to the suing relator as a "proprietary injury resulting from the alleged fraud." The word proprietary is used in a non-narrow sense, since this case, like many similar cases, occurred regarding a federal grant rather than a federal contract. Even so, the opinion sets off the field of government contract (and grant) law - the realm of such "proprietary injury" - from other fields, like securities or consumer protection law, in which the United States has no proprietary interest. Government contract law thereby becomes a field in which the

---

8. In so concluding, we express no view on the question whether *qui tam* suits violate Article II, in particular the Appointments Clause of § 2 and the "take Care" Clause of § 3. * * * *

government's special "proprietary" injury meant, at least in this instance, greater constitutional flexibility in devising remedial systems, a point of interest in the rest of this chapter.

3. *Stevens* obviously took some, but not all, the steam out of the constitutional opposition to qui tam. What is the meaning of the Article II issue set apart in footnote 8? How would Article II challenges to the qui tam statute fare after an Article III challenge was unanimously rejected? For a case illustrating the application of the False Claims Act, see United States ex rel. Plumbers and Steamfitters Local Union No. 38 v. C. W. Roen Construction Co., 183 F.3d 1088 (9th Cir. 1999), provided in the chapter on Policies, subchapter on Labor Standards.

United States of America, ex rel. David R. Siller, Plaintiff-Appellant, et al., Plaintiff, v. Becton Dickinson, etc., Defendant-Appellee.

Nos. 93-1275, 93-1459. United States Court of Appeals,
Fourth Circuit. Decided April 18, 1994.

Before LUTTIG, Circuit Judge, CHAPMAN, Senior Circuit Judge, and WILSON, United States District Judge for the Western District of Virginia, Sitting by Designation.

Reversed in part, vacated in part, and remanded by published opinion.

LUTTIG, Circuit Judge:

We interpret in this appeal several provisions of the qui tam section of the False Claims Act, 31 U.S.C. §3729 et seq.

Appellant David Siller, the brother and employee of a former distributor of Becton Dickinson & Company products, brought a civil qui tam action under 31 U.S.C. §3730 against Becton Dickinson & Company, alleging that the company had a practice of overcharging the government. The government ultimately elected to intervene in and proceed with the case pursuant to 31 U.S.C. §3730(b)(2)-(b)(4). * * * The district court also dismissed Siller's action under section 3730(e)(4), holding that it was "based upon" publicly disclosed allegations. * * * For the reasons that follow, we vacate the district court's dismissal order and remand for further proceedings with the government and Siller reinstated as plaintiffs. 813 F. Supp. 410 (1993).

I.

From January 1986 until the filing of this lawsuit in January 1991, David Siller was employed at various times, and in various capacities by Scientific Supply, Inc. (SSI), a San Antonio, Texas, distributor of health care products whose president was Siller's brother, Ruben Siller. SSI was an authorized distributor of medical device products manufactured by Becton Dickinson & Company (BD) until BD canceled its distributorship agreement in 1987.

In 1989, SSI filed suit against BD in Texas state court, asserting various causes of action arising from BD's allegedly wrongful termination of its distributorship agreement. The thrust of SSI's complaint was that BD canceled SSI's distributorship because it feared that SSI, which was seeking to sell BD products to the federal government at prices below those quoted by BD itself, would disclose that BD was overcharging the government. See J.A. at 91-99. BD ultimately settled with SSI in September 1989. As part of the settlement agreement, Ruben Siller agreed to keep the existence and terms of the settlement confidential. David Siller, however, Ruben's brother and employee, was not similarly bound by the settlement agreement.

David Siller filed the instant qui tam suit against BD in January 1991. According to Siller, he originally learned that BD overcharged the government through his employment with SSI, not as a result of SSI's suit against BD. In fact, Siller asserts, he obtained this knowledge before the SLS and SSI complaints were filed and had not read those complaints until BD filed its motion to dismiss in January 1993. Siller contends that he learned about the False Claims Act (FCA) and its qui tam provisions in the spring of 1990, after his brother's company's suit against BD was settled, and that he subsequently conducted his own investigation which uncovered evidence revealing how BD overcharged the government and attempted to conceal those overcharges. Siller then retained counsel and, on December 27, 1990, as required by section 3730(b)(2), voluntarily disclosed the evidence he had garnered regarding BD's overcharging practices to the Office of Inspector General for the Department of Veterans' Affairs, the agency BD allegedly overcharged. Siller filed his lawsuit against BD on January 4, 1991. Pursuant to the FCA's requirements, see id., Siller's complaint remained under seal until the government decided whether to proceed with the case.

II.

[The court dealt with the government's claim that the district court erred in dismissing it as a party plaintiff, and reversed that portion of the district court's order dismissing the government as a party plaintiff and dismissing the government's complaint.]

III.

We next address Siller's contention that the district court erred in holding that his action was "based upon" publicly disclosed allegations, and thus barred under section 3730(e)(4).

By 1986, when section 3730(e)(4) was enacted, Congress had come to the conclusion that "fraud against the Government was apparently so rampant and difficult to identify that the Government could use all the help it could get from private citizens with knowledge of fraud," United States ex rel. LaValley v. First Nat'l Bank of Boston, 707 F.Supp. 1351, 1355 (D.Mass.1988) (summarizing sentiments motivating 1986 amendments to FCA); see S.Rep. No. 345, 99th Cong.2d Sess. 2-4 (1986), and consequently amended the FCA to, inter alia, "encourage more private enforcement suits." Id. at 23-24, U.S.Code Cong. & Admin.News 1986, at 5288, 5289. At the same time, however, Congress sought to prevent "parasitic" qui tam actions in which relators, rather than bringing to light independently-discovered information of fraud, simply feed off of previous disclosures of government fraud. See, e.g., United States ex rel. Stinson v. Prudential Ins. Co., 944 F.2d 1149, 1154 (3d Cir.1991) (collecting sources). Congress sought to strike this balance largely through the enactment of section 3730(e)(4), which provides in relevant part that—

> (A) No court shall have jurisdiction over an action under this section based upon the public disclosure of allegations or transactions in a criminal, civil, or administrative hearing...unless...the person bringing the action is an original source of the information.

> (B) For purposes of this paragraph, "original source" means an individual who has direct and independent knowledge of the information on which the allegations are based and has voluntarily provided the information to the

Government before filing an action under this section which is based on the information.

31 U.S.C. 3730(e)(4).

Under the terms of section 3730(e)(4), Siller's action was properly dismissed only if (1) it was "based upon" the allegations against BD in the SSI suit; (2) the SSI suit's disclosure of these allegations constituted a "public disclosure" in a "civil...hearing"; and (3) Siller was not an "original source," either because he did not have "direct and independent knowledge of the information on which the allegations were based" or had not "voluntarily provided the information to the Government" before he brought his suit. We address these issues, each of which raises unsettled questions of statutory construction, seriatim.

A.

The district court held that Siller's action was barred under section 3730(e)(4)(A) because it was "based upon" the disclosures in the complaint filed in SSI's action against BD. Siller contends that a qui tam action is only "based upon" a public disclosure where the relator has actually derived from that disclosure the knowledge of the facts underlying his action. Under this reading of section 3730(e)(4)(A), Siller argues, his complaint, even if substantially similar to that in the SSI litigation, was not "based upon" the disclosures in the SSI complaint because he actually learned of BD's overcharging practices independently of the SSI complaint. BD responds that any qui tam complaint, such as Siller's, that "echoes" previously disclosed allegations is "based upon" those disclosures, regardless of whether those disclosures are actually the source from which the qui tam plaintiff derived his information.

We agree that Siller's reading of "based upon" as meaning "derived from" is the only fair construction of the statutory phrase. Section 3730(e)(4)(A)'s use of the phrase "based upon" is, we believe, susceptible of a straightforward textual exegesis. To "base upon" means to "use as a basis for." Webster's Third New International Dictionary 180 (1986) (definition no. 2 of verb "base"). Rather plainly, therefore, a relator's action is "based upon" a public disclosure of allegations only where the relator has actually derived from that disclosure the allegations upon which his qui tam action is based. Such an understanding of the term "based upon," apart from giving effect to the language chosen by Congress, is fully consistent with section 3730(e)(4)'s indisputed objective of preventing "parasitic" actions, see, e.g., Stinson, supra, at 1154, for it is self-evident that a suit that includes allegations that happen to be similar (even identical) to those already publicly disclosed, but were not actually derived from those public disclosures, simply is not, in any sense, parasitic.

We are aware, as BD points out, that other circuits have not embraced this interpretation of the phrase, assuming instead that an action is based upon a public disclosure of allegations if its allegations are identical or similar to those already publicly disclosed. However, only one court of appeals has actually held that a relator need not have derived his knowledge from a public disclosure in order for his action to have been based upon that disclosure, and that court summoned neither reasoning nor supportive case authority in defense of its holding. In John Doe Corp., the Second Circuit held that a qui tam plaintiff's action is "based upon" a public disclosure where the relator's allegations are "the same as those that ha[ve] been publicly disclosed....regardless of where the relator obtained his information." 960 F.2d at 324.

* * *

We recognize that other courts of appeals seem implicitly to have accepted the position, contrary to ours, that qui tam actions are "based upon" a public disclosure whenever the factual basis for the action has been disclosed into the public domain, regardless of whether the relator actually derived his knowledge of those facts from that disclosure. See United States ex rel. Springfield Terminal Ry. Co. et al. v. Quinn, 14 F.3d 645, 652- 55 (D.C.Cir.1994) (Congress sought to prohibit qui tam actions when allegation of fraud or critical elements of fraudulent transaction "were in public domain."); United States ex rel. Kreindler & Kreindler v. United Technologies Corp., 985 F.2d 1148, 1158 (2d Cir.) (quoting John Doe with approval), cert. denied, 508 U.S. 973, 113 S.Ct. 2962, 125 L.Ed.2d 663 (1993); United States ex rel. Precision Co. v. Koch Industries Inc., 971 F.2d 548, 552 (10th Cir.1992) (" 'based upon' is properly understood to mean 'supported by'"), cert. denied, 507 U.S. 951, 113 S.Ct. 1364, 122 L.Ed.2d 742 (1993). * * * Preferring the plain meaning of the words enacted by Congress over our sister Circuits' as-yet unconsidered assumptions as to the meaning of those words, and over the Second Circuit's considered but unsupported interpretation, we hold that Siller's action was only "based upon" the disclosures in the SSI lawsuit if Siller actually derived his allegations against BD from the SSI complaint.

It is not clear to us that the district court found that Siller actually derived the allegations in his qui tam action from the SSI complaint. The district court found that the SSI suit publicly disclosed allegations that "derive[d] from exactly the same core of operative facts...that form[ ] the basis for" Siller's qui tam complaint. J.A. at 14. That the facts that were disclosed in the SSI complaint and the facts that "form[ed] the basis for" Siller's action were the same does not, however, mean that Siller actually derived his allegations from the allegations in the SSI complaint. It is certainly possible that, as Siller contends, Siller actually learned of BD's alleged fraud entirely independently of the SSI suit, and derived his allegations from that independent knowledge. Therefore, because the district court made no finding on whether Siller actually derived his allegations from the SSI suit, a finding necessary to the conclusion that Siller's action was "based upon" that suit, we also vacate the portion of the district court's order dismissing Siller's action so as to enable the court to address this factual question on remand.

In doing so, however, we do not upset the district court's express finding that the same essential facts underlay both the SSI suit and Siller's qui tam action. Id. We are not persuaded by Siller's argument that the SSI complaint failed to allege a fact (i.e., BD's failure to disclose its overcharges) critical to his present action. Contrary to Siller's assertion, it appears to us that the allegation in SSI's complaint that BD charged the government more than its other customers, in violation of its contractual (and statutory, see 41 U.S.C. §253e(b)) obligation, see J.A. at 95, is essentially the same allegation that Siller has made against BD.

B.

The district court also held that the disclosure of allegations in SSI's complaint that BD charged the Government more than its other customers constituted a "public disclosure of allegations" in a civil "hearing." The district court's interpretation is supported by the holding of every court of appeals to have addressed the question, that any information disclosed through civil litigation and on file with the clerk's office should be considered a public disclosure of allegations in a civil hearing for purposes of section 3730(e)(4)(A). See Quinn, 14 F.3d at 651; Kreindler, 985 F.2d at 1158; Precision, 971 F.2d at 554 n. 5; Stinson, 944 F.2d at 1154-56. Siller argues that, even if his action is deemed to be "based upon" the allegations in the SSI complaint, the action is not barred because the term "hearing" does not encompass the mere filing of a complaint. While we believe this presents a closer question of statutory construction, we affirm the district court's interpretation of this part of section 3730 (e)(4)(A).

A civil complaint is unquestionably a "public disclosure of allegations." The difficult issue is whether a disclosure in a complaint constitutes a disclosure in a "civil hearing." Because a disclosure in a complaint is a disclosure in a civil proceeding, the ultimate resolution of this issue turns on whether the term "hearing" can be understood as including a "civil proceeding." We concede, as Siller argues, that a "hearing" is ordinarily understood as an event that occurs within a civil proceeding, rather than as an entire civil proceeding itself. We do not believe, however, that the definition of the term "hearing" is so fixed that it cannot possibly refer to (or at least include) an entire civil proceeding. See United States v. Florida East Coast Ry. Co., 410 U.S. 224, 239, 93 S.Ct. 810, 818, 35 L.Ed.2d 223 (1973) (term " 'hearing' in its legal context undoubtedly has a host of meanings" that will vary depending on the context); see also Black's Law Dictionary 721 (hearing "frequently used...to describe whatever takes place before magistrates clothed with judicial functions and sitting without jury at any stage of the proceedings subsequent to its inception") (emphasis added) (1990). We are also unpersuaded by Siller's contention that, as a practical matter, Congress might have meant to include live hearings but exclude civil complaints and other court filings because disclosures in a public hearing between private parties are more likely to come to the government's attention than are disclosures in filings, and we can imagine no other reason why Congress would have intended a meaning of "hearing" that excluded civil proceedings. Given the fluidity in the meaning of the term "hearing," and the fact that we can discern no reason why Congress might have intended otherwise, we agree with our sister Circuits (albeit somewhat reluctantly) that an entire civil proceeding can constitute a "hearing" for purposes of section 3730(e)(4)(A). See Quinn, supra, at 651 (" 'hearing' is roughly synonymous with 'proceeding.' "); cf. Anchorage Assoc. v. Virgin Islands. Bd. of Tax Review, 922 F.2d 168, 176 (3d Cir.1990) ("hearing" under Rule 56(d) does not require oral hearing or live, formal judgment). We therefore do not disturb the district court's holding that the allegations in the SSI complaint were, for purposes of section 3730(e)(4)(A), publicly disclosed in a civil "hearing."

C.

In addition to its holding that Siller's action was based upon previously disclosed public allegations in a civil hearing within the meaning of section 3730(e)(4)(A), the district court also held that Siller was not an "original source" within section 3730(e)(4)'s exception to its jurisdictional bar. In so holding, the court expressly adopted the standard fashioned by the Second Circuit in Long Island Lighting Co., 912 F.2d at 16; accord Wang v. FMC Corp., 975 F.2d 1412, 1418 (9th Cir.1992). That standard requires that, in order to be considered an "original source," a qui tam plaintiff must not only have direct and independent knowledge of the information on which his allegations are based, and have provided that information to the government, but also must have "been a source to the entity that publicly disclosed the allegations on which a suit is based." Long Island Lighting, 912 F.2d at 16 (emphasis added). Finding that Siller was not a source to SSI, the "entity that publicly disclosed the allegations" on which Siller's suit was found to be based, id., the district court held that Siller was not an "original source" under section 3730(e)(4).

We reject the Second Circuit's standard, and the district court's adoption of that standard, as imposing an additional, extra-textual requirement that was not intended by Congress. Reading sub-paragraph (B), as we are directed by the statute, as the definition of "original source" applicable to sub-paragraph (A), sub-paragraph (A) is properly read as providing that,

[n]o court shall have jurisdiction over an action...based upon the public disclosure of allegations...in a...civil...hearing...unless...the person bringing
the action...has direct and independent knowledge of the information on
which the allegations are based and has voluntarily provided the information
to the Government before filing an action under this section which is based on
the information.

31 U.S.C. §3730(e)(4) (emphasis added). Under this reading of section 3730(e)(4), the
provision unambiguously does not require, as the Second Circuit has held that it does,
that a relator be a source to the original disclosing entity in order to be an "original
source." Rather it requires only that the relator have direct and independent knowledge
of the information underlying the allegations of a false claim and voluntarily provide
the information to the government before filing his qui tam action.

The Second Circuit's attempt to portray its holding that a relator must also be a
source to the disclosing entity as one derived from the provision's text is not merely unpersuasive, but implausible. The Second Circuit essentially holds that sub-paragraphs
(A) and (B) each provides distinct and cumulative requirements for being an "original
source." Thus, it reasons, sub-paragraph (A) requires that the relator be an original
source to the entity that made the public disclosure, and sub-paragraph (B) additionally
requires that the relator have direct and independent knowledge of the allegations underlying his qui tam action and that he provide his information to the government.
Long Island Lighting, 912 F.2d at 16-17; see also id. at 17 ("¶(4)(B) does not contain the
exclusive requirements in order for one to be an 'original source' and that an additional
requirement is to be found in ¶(4)(A).").

The Second Circuit's interpretation of section 3730(e)(4) to require that the putative
plaintiff provide his information to the disclosing entity might at least be tenable were
there not a definition of "original source" in sub-paragraph (B). But the term "original
source" as it is used in sub-paragraph (A) is expressly defined in sub-paragraph (B).
Sub-paragraph (B) necessarily, therefore, sets forth that which the Second Circuit holds
it does not — "the exclusive requirements that a qui tam plaintiff must satisfy to be an
'original source.'" Id. at 17.

The Second Circuit's "close textual analysis," id. at 16, that yields this interpretation
is wholly indefensible. The essence of the Second Circuit's textual reasoning is that the
word "information" in sub-paragraph (A) refers to the information publicly disclosed,
whereas the "information" in sub- paragraph (B) refers to the information that supplies
the basis for the qui tam action itself. This "slight difference in meaning" between these
two uses of the word "information," suggests the Second Circuit, "permits the interpretation that ¶(4)(B) does not contain the exclusive requirements in order for one to be
an 'original source' and that an additional requirement is to be found in ¶(4)(A)." Id.
Besides the fact that a "slight difference" between the meaning of "information" in the
two paragraphs cannot justify a holding that sub-paragraph (B)'s definition of "original
source" is not the entire definition of that term, the reasoning that underlies the Second
Circuit's conclusion that the word "information" means something different in the two
provisions is demonstrably incorrect.

* * *

The Ninth Circuit premised its holding almost entirely on the fact that one of the
principal objectives of the 1986 amendments was to ensure that, contrary to the holding of decisions such as United States ex rel. State of Wisconsin v. Dean, 729 F.2d 1100,
1104 (7th Cir.1984), a plaintiff who had himself provided the government with the in-

formation of fraud prior to bringing his action would not be barred because the government (as a result of the plaintiff's effort) possessed the information on which the action was based. 975 F.2d at 1419 (citing S.Rep. 345, 99th Cong., 2d Sess. 4 (1986)). That Congress sought to "correct" Dean provides no support whatsoever for the conclusion, see 975 F.2d at 1419, that Congress intended to require a putative plaintiff to have provided his information to the "disclosing entity" in order to be an "original source."

The jurisdictional provision in effect at the time Dean was decided did not even purport to bar qui tam suits based upon prior public disclosures; it barred only suits "based upon evidence or information in the possession of the United States...at the time such suit was brought." 31 U.S.C. §232(C) (1982) (superseded) (emphasis added). The Seventh Circuit in Dean simply held that section 232(C) barred the qui tam suit in that case because the information was "in the possession of" the government, having been provided to it by the plaintiff. To "correct" Dean only required that Congress adopt language that would ensure that a plaintiff who had provided his information to the government would not be barred from bringing a qui tam action on the ground that the government already possessed the information. This it did in section 3730(e)(4)(B), by providing that a plaintiff who produces his independently-obtained information to the government is excepted from section 3730(e)(4)(A)'s jurisdictional bar. The Ninth Circuit's error is in its unexplained assumption that, to remedy Dean, Congress had to require a plaintiff to provide information to the disclosing entity, as opposed merely to the government. 975 F.2d at 1419.

* * *

Accordingly, we hold that a qui tam plaintiff need not be a source to the entity that publicly disclosed the allegations on which the qui tam action is based in order to be an original source under section 3730(e)(4)(B). In addition to having direct and independent knowledge of the information on which the allegations in the public disclosure is based, he need only provide his information to the government before instituting his qui tam action, as the provision unambiguously states.

IV.

For the reasons discussed, we reverse that portion of the district court's order dismissing the government as a party-plaintiff and dismissing the government's complaint, and vacate that portion of its order dismissing Siller's complaint as "based upon" the allegations in the lawsuit by SSI against BD. The case is remanded for further proceedings consistent with this opinion.

Notes and Questions

1. *Becton Dickinson* makes clear that the various federal appellate circuits have taken quite different positions in construing the "public disclosure" barrier. Decisions after *Becton Dickinson* continued the split. *U.S. ex rel. Biddle v. Board of Trustees of the Leland Stanford, Jr. University*, 147 F.3d 821 (9th Cir. 1998); *United States ex rel. Springfield Railway Terminal Co. v. Quinn*, 14 F.3d 645 (D.C. Cir. 1994). When the Supreme Court granted certiorari for its first case under the 1986 Amendments, it seemed as though the Court would clarify the issues, but then the Court only held that the 1986 Amendments were not retroactive and did not go on to clarify them in the least. *Hughes Aircraft Co. v. U.S. ex rel. Schumer*, 520 U.S. 939 (1997). For an ex-

pression of the disappointment felt at that narrow decision, see Charles Tiefer, "Justices Ducked Major Issue in 'Hughes,'" National Law Journal, July 14, 1997. For a review of the arguments regarding the public disclosure barrier, see Charles Tiefer & Michael Blumenfeld, "Investigators as Qui Tam Relators," 7 FCA & Qui Tam Q.R. (April 1997).

Should the barrier be high or low? How one answers that question often seems to depend on how, generally, one views the False Claims Act and the qui tam mechanism. Proponents champion qui tam as summoning forth additional help from whistleblowers in the fight against fraud and want a low threshold barrier; opponents decry the mechanism as subjecting government contractors to unnecessary attacks by fee-seeking lawyers and want a high barrier. Is there a fundamental tension built into the public disclosure barrier because it does not make the merits (or lack thereof) of the relator's allegations an element of the jurisdictional test? Or, does that tension get resolved because the Justice Department evaluates, in at least some sense, the merits of the relator's allegations in deciding whether to intervene, and such intervention obviates application of the jurisdictional test?

2. *Becton Dickinson* also makes clear that the various federal appellate circuits have taken quite different positions in construing the "original source" exception. Just how "direct" and "independent" does an original source's knowledge have to be? For example, could a union investigator qualify, who hears from a union member about contractor fraud? *U.S. ex. rel. Barth v. Ridgedale Electric, Inc.*, 44 F.3d 699 (8th Cir. 1995)(no). Can a government employee who brings a suit qualify as an original source? *U.S. ex rel. Fine v. Chevron, U.S.A.*, 39 F.3d 957 (9th Cir. 1994)(yes).

3. For some of the large literature reflecting upon these and related questions, see Emily R.D. Pruisner, Comment, *The Extent of a Corporation's Ability to Constitute an Original Source Under the False Claims Act*, 87 Minn. L. Rev. 1247 (2003); Katherine Zimmerer, Note, *The Revitalization of Qui Tam Actions*, Note, J. of Na. Res. & Env'tal L. 43 (2002); James Roy Moncus III, Note, *The Marriage of the False Claims Act and the Freedom of Information Act: Parasitic Potential or Positive Synergy?*, 55 Vand. L. Rev. 1549 (2002); Daniel J. Powell, *Using the False Claims Act as a Basis for Institutional Review Board Liability*, 69 U. Chi. L. Rev. 1399 (2002); James B. Helmer, Jr., *ow Great Is They Bounty: Realtor's Share Calculations Pursuant to the False Claims Act*, 68 U. Cin. L. Rev. 737 (2000).

E. Liquidated Damages

DJ MANUFACTURING CORPORATION,
Plaintiff-Appellant, v. The UNITED STATES, Defendant-Appellee.

No. 95-5128. United States Court of Appeals,
Federal Circuit. 86 F.3d 1130, June 12, 1996.

Before CLEVENGER, Circuit Judge, NIES, Senior Circuit Judge, and BRYSON, Circuit Judge.

BRYSON, Circuit Judge.

DJ Manufacturing Corporation (DJ) appeals from a decision of the United States Court of Federal Claims granting summary judgment to the government. DJ argued that the liquidated damages clause in the contract between the parties was unenforceable as a penalty. The trial court rejected that argument, DJ Mfg. Corp. v. United States, 33 Fed. Cl. 357 (Fed.Cl.1995), as do we.

I

In January 1991, the government solicited an offer from DJ for 283,695 combat field packs to support troops who were then participating in Operation Desert Storm. The solicitation documents set forth a delivery schedule, sought accelerated delivery if possible, and provided for liquidated damages for late delivery. The parties negotiated a contract, which became effective on February 14, 1991. Like the underlying solicitation documents, the contract provided that, for each article delivered after the date fixed in the contract, liquidated damages would be assessed at 1/15 of one percent of the contract price for each day of delay.

DJ missed several delivery deadlines. In accordance with the liquidated damages clause, the government withheld payment in the amount of $663,266.92, a reduction of about 8 percent of the total contract price of $8,493,828.

DJ filed suit in the Court of Federal Claims to recover the withheld amount, contending that the liquidated damages clause constituted an unenforceable penalty. The government moved for summary judgment. In support of its motion, the government submitted a declaration by an Army logistics management specialist, who stated that possession of the field packs was essential to the troops' combat readiness. In addition, the government submitted a declaration from the contracting officer, who stated that all contracts for items to be used in Operation Desert Shield/Desert Storm contained liquidated damages clauses for late delivery because of the need to get war items to the soldiers quickly.

In response to the government's motion, DJ produced an affidavit of its president, who stated that the rate set forth in the liquidated damages clause "does not seem related to any specific need with respect to the item in question or the time-frame, but, rather, seems to be a fairly standard rate used in many solicitations for many different items." The affidavit listed several other government contracts and solicitations that allegedly contained clauses setting liquidated damages at the same rate. DJ argued that there was therefore a disputed issue of material fact as to whether the contracting officer had "used a standard rate, historically employed by [the agency]" and had made "no attempt to forecast just compensation."

The Court of Federal Claims granted the government's motion. At the outset, the court held that DJ bore the burden of establishing that the liquidated damages clause was unenforceable, and that in order to avoid summary judgment DJ had to point to evidence raising a triable question of fact with respect to that issue. The court then recited the rule that a liquidated damages clause is enforceable if the harm that would be caused by a breach is difficult to estimate and the amount or rate fixed as liquidated damages is a reasonable forecast of the loss that may be caused by the breach.

As to the first element, the court characterized this case as presenting "a paradigmatic example of a situation where accurate estimation of the damages resulting from delays in delivery is difficult, if not impossible." As to the second element, the cdama rejected DJ's argument that in order to determine the reasonableness of the liquidated damages, it was necessary to inquire into the process that the contracting officer followed in reaching the amount that was inserted into the contract. The inquiry, the court explained, is an objective one. "The proper inquiry focuses on whether the amount itself is a reasonable forecast, not whether, as [DJ] seems to suggest, the individual responsible for proposing the rate engaged in a reasonable attempt to forecast damages." Because DJ failed to offer any evidence that the liquidated damages rate agreed upon in the contract was "greater than that which the government could reasonably suffer as a result of the delayed delivery of the field packs," the court granted the government's motion and ordered DJ's complaint to be dismissed.

II

By fixing in advance the amount to be paid in the event of a breach, liquidated damages clauses save the time and expense of litigating the issue of damages. Such clauses "serve a particularly useful function when damages are uncertain in nature or amount or are unmeasurable," Priebe & Sons v. United States, 332 U.S. 407, 411, 68 S.Ct. 123, 126, 92 L.Ed. 32 (1947), which is often the case when there is a delay in the completion of a contract for the government. Id.; United States v. Bethlehem Steel Co., 205 U.S. 105, 120, 27 S.Ct. 450, 455-56, 51 L.Ed. 731 (1907); Jennie-O Foods, Inc. v. United States, 580 F.2d 400, 413, 217 Ct.Cl. 314 (1978) ("Costs to the public convenience and the temporary thwarting of the public goals... are hard to measure with precision.").

When damages are uncertain or difficult to measure, a liquidated damages clause will be enforced as long as "the amount stipulated for is not so extravagant, or disproportionate to the amount of property loss, as to show that compensation was not the object aimed at or as to imply fraud, mistake, circumvention or oppression." Wise v. United States, 249 U.S. 361, 365, 39 S.Ct. 303, 304, 63 L.Ed. 647 (1919); see United States v. Bethlehem Steel Co., 205 U.S. at 121, 27 S.Ct. at 456 ("The amount is not so extraordinarily disproportionate to the damage which might result from the [breach], as to show that the parties must have intended a penalty and could not have meant liquidated damages."). With that narrow exception, "[t]here is no sound reason why persons competent and free to contract may not agree upon this subject as fully as upon any other, or why their agreement, when fairly and understandingly entered into with a view to just compensation for the anticipated loss, should not be enforced." Wise v. United States, 249 U.S. at 365, 39 S.Ct. at 304; see also Sun Printing & Publishing Ass'n v. Moore, 183 U.S. 642, 674, 22 S.Ct. 240, 253, 46 L.Ed. 366 (1902) (except where "the sum fixed is greatly disproportionate to the presumed actual damages," a court "has no right to erroneously construe the intention of the parties, when clearly expressed, in the endeavor to make better contracts for them than they have made for themselves").

A party challenging a liquidated damages clause bears the burden of proving the clause unenforceable. See Jennie-O Foods, Inc. v. United States, 580 F.2d at 414; Farmers Export Co. v. M/V Georgis Prois, Etc..799 F.2d 159, 162 (5th Cir.1986). That burden is an exacting one, because when damages are uncertain or hard to measure, it naturally follows that it is difficult to conclude that a particular liquidated damages amount or rate is an unreasonable projection of what those damages might be. See Restatement (Second) of Contracts § 356 cmt. b (1981) ("The greater the difficulty either of proving that loss has occurred or of establishing its amount with the requisite certainty... the easier it is to show that the amount fixed is reasonable."); 5 Samuel Williston, A Treatise on the Law of Contracts § 783 (W. Jaeger ed. 1961).

While some state courts are hostile to liquidated damages clauses, federal law "does not look with disfavor upon 'liquidated damages' provisions in contracts." Priebe & Sons, Inc. v. United States, 332 U.S. at 411, 68 S.Ct. at 126. The few federal cases in which liquidated damages clauses have been struck down provide some indication of how rare it is for a federal court to refuse to enforce the parties' bargain on this issue.

For example, in Priebe & Sons, Inc. v. United States, the Supreme Court struck down a liquidated damages clause when it was "certain when the contract was made" that the breach in question "plainly would not occasion damage." 332 U.S. at 413, 68 S.Ct. at 126. The contract in Priebe contained two liquidated damages clauses: one for delay in the delivery of eggs and a second for failure to have the eggs inspected and ready for delivery by a specific time prior to the delivery date. The contractor was late in meeting the inspection requirement, but delivered the eggs on time. Thus, only the second liquidated damages clause was at issue in the case. As the Court viewed that clause, a delay in inspection that did not result in a delay in delivery could not cause any loss to the government. At the same time, however, the Court stated that if the breach had involved "failure to get prompt performance when delivery was due," the Court would have had "no doubt of the validity of the provision for 'liquidated damages' when applied under those circumstances." Id. at 412, 68 S.Ct. at 126.

Another case, equally unusual, involved a liquidated damages clause in a lease. In that case, Kothe v. R.C. Taylor Trust, 280 U.S. 224, 50 S.Ct. 142, 74 L.Ed. 382 (1930), the lessee agreed that the filing of a petition for bankruptcy against him would be deemed a breach, and that the lessor would be entitled to recover damages for the breach in an amount equal to the rent due for the remaining term of the lease. The Court held that the amount stipulated "is so disproportionate to any damage reasonably to be anticipated in the circumstances disclosed that we must hold the provision is for an unenforceable penalty." 280 U.S. at 226, 50 S.Ct. at 143. In reaching that conclusion, the Court made clear that it was influenced by the fact that the clause would take effect only in the event of the lessee's bankruptcy, and thus that the parties "were consciously undertaking to contract for payment to be made out of the assets of a bankrupt estate—not for something which the lessee would be required to discharge" and that enforcing the clause would be contrary to the purposes of the Bankruptcy Act. Id. at 226-27, 50 S.Ct. at 143.

In more conventional cases, when the amount of prospective damages are difficult to determine at the outset and the parties agree upon a fixed amount or rate to pay in the event of a breach, thereby bypassing the trouble and expense of litigating the damages issue, federal courts have regularly upheld liquidated damages clauses. ***

III

In light of these principles, the trial court was correct to grant summary judgment to the government. DJ argues that the government should bear the burden of proving the clause enforceable and that the evidence before the trial court did not establish the government's right to recovery as a matter of law. That argument, however, flies in the face of settled law regarding the burden of proof and the standards for granting summary judgment.

As noted above, it was DJ's burden to prove that the liquidated damages clause was unenforceable. When a party moves for summary judgment on an issue as to which the other party bears the burden of proof, the moving party need not offer evidence, but may obtain summary judgment merely by pointing out to the court "that there is an absence of evidence to support the nonmoving party's case." Celotex Corp. v. Catrett, 477 U.S. 317, 325, 106 S.Ct. 2548, 2554, 91 L.Ed.2d 265 (1986); see Conroy v. Reebok Int'l, Ltd., 14 F.3d 1570, 1575, 29 USPQ2d 1373, 1377 (Fed.Cir.1994); Avia Group Int'l, Inc. v. L.A. Gear Calif., Inc., 853 F.2d 1557, 1560, 7 USPQ2d 1548, 1551 (Fed.Cir.1988).

The only evidence that DJ produced at the summary judgment stage was the affidavit of its president, which alleged that the liquidated damages rate was a "standard" rate, rather than a rate selected specifically for the field pack contract. In addition, DJ relies on the declaration of the contracting officer, which stated that the liquidated damages clause was put into the field pack contract, as well as other contracts for items to be used in Operations Desert Shield/Desert Storm "due to the almost overwhelming need to get war items, such as field packs, into the soldiers' possession as soon as possible."

Neither of those two items of evidence raises an issue of material fact requiring a trial. DJ argues that the contracting officer's statement about the need to get war items into the soldiers' possession quickly shows that the liquidated damages clause was designed to be a "spur to performance" and thus was an unenforceable penalty. That assertion, however, is at odds with several Supreme Court decisions, which make clear that a liquidated damages clause is not rendered unlawful simply because the promisee hopes that it will have the effect of encouraging prompt performance by the promisor. In Robinson v. United States, for example, the Court explained that in the case of construction contracts, "a provision giving liquidated damages for each day's delay is an appropriate means of inducing due performance, or of giving compensation, in case of failure to perform." 261 U.S. at 488, 43 S.Ct. at 421 (emphasis added). Similarly, in Wise v. United States, the Court stated that courts should "look with candor, if not with favor," on liquidated damages clauses "as promoting prompt performance of contracts and adjusting in advance, and amicably, matters the settlement of which through courts would often involve difficulty, uncertainty, delay and expense." 249 U.S. at 366, 39 S.Ct. at 304 (emphasis added). And in United States v. Bethlehem Steel Co., the Court held that a liquidated damages clause may provide "security for the proper performance of the contract as to time of delivery" unless the amount of the liquidated damages is "extraordinarily disproportionate to the damage which might result from the [breach]." 205 U.S. at 121, 27 S.Ct. at 456 (emphasis added).

In support of its assertion that an intention to "spur performance" converts a liquidated damages clause into an unenforceable penalty, DJ cites Priebe & Sons, Inc. v. United States. That case, however, does not stand for such a broad proposition. As noted above, the liquidated damages clause at issue in Priebe & Sons served no compensatory function at all, since there was no possibility that the breach at issue would result in any compensable loss. Thus, the liquidated damages clause was struck down because it served "only as an added spur to performance," and because it constituted "an exaction of punishment for a breach which could produce no possible damage." 332 U.S. at 413, 68 S.Ct. at 127 (emphasis added).

There is no inconsistency in a promisee's seeking assurance of performance through a guarantee of fair compensation for breach. As Williston noted with respect to standard (and legitimate) liquidated damages provisions, "there can be no doubt that these provisions are intended not merely as a provision for an unfortunate and unexpected contingency but also to secure the promisee in the performance of the main obligation and to make the promisor more reluctant to break it." 5 Samuel Williston, supra, § 778, at 692. In this respect, at least, Corbin was in agreement. See 5 Arthur J. Corbin, Corbin on Contracts § 1058, at 339-40 (1964 ed.) ("The purpose of providing for a money payment in case of breach, whether it be called a penalty, a forfeiture, liquidated damages, or merely a sum of money, is primarily to secure the performance promised.... Penalties are said to be in terrorem to induce performance as promised; in large measure the same is true of liquidated damages."). What the policy against penalties is designed to prevent is a penal sanction that is so disproportionate to any damage that could be anticipated that it seeks "to enforce performance of the main purpose of the contract by the compulsion of this very disproportion." 5 Samuel Williston, supra, § 776, at 668 (emphasis added). Nothing that DJ offered or pointed to in the evidence before the trial court remotely suggested that the liquidated damages clause in this case is of that character.

DJ's second argument is that the evidence before the trial court raised a triable issue of fact as to whether the contracting officer set the liquidated damages rate based on a particularized assessment of the facts of this contract. In making that argument, DJ relies on 48 C.F.R. § 12.202(b), which directs that the "rate of liquidated damages used must be reasonable and considered on a case-by-case basis since liquidated damages fixed without any reference to probable actual damages may be held to be a penalty, and therefore unenforceable."

Contrary to DJ's assertion, section 12.202(b) does not create a rule of substantive law requiring a liquidated damages clause to be struck down unless the liquidated damages rate is specially tailored to the particular contract in advance. Section 12.202(b) merely recognizes that a court may refuse to enforce a liquidated damages clause if the liquidated damages amount or rate is shown not to be reasonably related to the actual damages that the promisee could suffer as a result of a breach, and it advises that care should be taken to ensure that the rate or amount is not unreasonable in light of the possible actual damages that could flow from breach. The regulation thus appears to be designed for internal guidance rather than to create rights in contracting parties. In any event, our predecessor court has held that the language on which DJ relies does not require that liquidated damages clauses be "tailor-made for each individual contract." Young Assocs., Inc. v. United States, 471 F.2d at 622 (construing an identically worded predecessor to 48 C.F.R. § 12.202(b) and rejecting the plaintiff's argument that liquidated damages clause is invalid because "no 'case-by-case' consideration was given to the rate of liquidated damages"). Instead, the test is objective; regardless of how the liquidated damage figure was arrived at, the liquidated damages clause will be enforced "if the amount stipulated is reasonable for the particular agreement at the time it is made." Young Assocs., Inc. v. United States, 471 F.2d at 622. See also Higgs v. United States, 546 F.2d at 377 (standard five percent earnest money forfeiture upheld as reasonable liquidated damages, even though not specifically tailored to a particular contract); Hughes Bros., Inc. v. United States, 134 F.Supp. 471, 474, 133 Ct.Cl. 108 (1955) (liquidated damages clause that provided for uniform liquidated damages for a variety of breaches upheld, even though "it had the result that in individual instances there were discrepancies between the stipulated damages and the damages that may actually have been anticipated"). The trial court was therefore correct in holding that it is unnecessary to inquire into the process that the contracting officer followed in arriving at the liquidated damages figure that was put forth in the solicitation and agreed to in the contract.

Finally, DJ argues that there was a triable issue as to whether the liquidated damages rate that the parties agreed upon in the field pack contract was unreasonable. Once again, DJ bore the burden of pointing to evidence establishing a material factual dispute on that issue, and the trial court correctly held that DJ failed to carry that burden.

The damages that are likely to flow from delays in the delivery of goods is often difficult to assess, particularly when the goods are to be produced in the uncertain setting of wartime. See Priebe & Sons, Inc. v. United States, 332 U.S. at 412, 68 S.Ct. at 126; United States v. Bethlehem Steel Co., 205 U.S. at 120-21, 27 S.Ct. at 455-56; Young Assocs., Inc. v. United States, 471 F.2d at 621 ("The Government's damages stemming from delayed receipt of the supplies or construction it ordered are normally hard to measure, and it is usually reasonable to establish some fixed monetary substitute for calculation by trial."). As the Third Circuit put the matter in United States v. Le Roy Dyal Co., 186 F.2d 460, 463 (3d Cir.1950), cert. denied, 341 U.S. 926, 71 S.Ct. 797, 95

L.Ed. 1357 (1951), "[i]n dealing with some matters pertaining to governmental activities, the question of ascertaining how much pecuniary loss is caused by failure of one contracting with the government to keep his promise is especially difficult." To illustrate the point, that court cited a colorful English case that is closely analogous here (id.):

> But how much damage could accrue to the Spanish government because a shipyard failed to deliver, at the time agreed upon, four torpedo-boat destroyers? This question was involved in testing the validity of a provision for liquidated damages for delay in the House of Lords decision in Clydebank Engineering and Shipbuilding Co., Ltd. v. Castaneda. How could the damages be accurately determined? As Lord Halsbury said in an opinion upholding the provision..."in order to do that properly and to have any real effect upon any tribunal determining that question, one ought to have before one's mind the whole administration of the Spanish Navy."

See also 5 Arthur L. Corbin, supra, § 1072, at 402 ("Since the injury caused by [delay in performance] is nearly always difficult to determine, the courts strongly incline to accept the estimate [in a liquidated damages clause] as reasonable and to enforce it").

In this case, not only did DJ fail to raise a triable question with respect to the difficulty of forecasting damages at the outset, but it also failed to raise any factual issue casting doubt on the reasonableness of the stipulated damages rate. Nor is there anything inherently unreasonable about that rate—a reduction in the contract price of 1/15 of one percent per day, or two percent per month, on a contract that was supposed to be completed within a period of only a few months. In fact, the decision of our predecessor court in Pacific Hardware & Steel Co. v. United States, 49 Ct.Cl. 327, 1914 WL 1416 (1914), provides strong support for the reasonableness of the liquidated damages rate selected in this case. The military supply contract at issue in Pacific Hardware contained a liquidated damages clause providing for a deduction of 1/10 of one percent of the contract price for each day of delay after the scheduled delivery date (a slightly higher rate than the liquidated damages rate at issue in this case). Noting that a month's delay would result in the withholding of only three percent of the contract price, the court ruled (49 Ct.Cl. at 334):

> This basis of ascertaining the damages, if we are to treat it as such, does not appear to be unreasonable or oppressive. It indicates, we think, that the parties had in mind the inherent difficulty of proving actual damages and the differences that might arise between the parties in making settlements if there were delays in delivery. The representatives of the Government on the one hand could reason that it was desirable to have a provision in the contract which would render unnecessary any differences in settlement; while the contractor on the other hand could reason that such a course was preferable, because if for no other reason it would eliminate the delays incident to lawsuits brought to secure settlements.

In addition to being of roughly the same dimension as the liquidated damages rate in this case, the rate in Pacific Hardware also appears to have been a "standard" rate, as there were at least two other contemporaneous Court of Claims decisions upholding liquidated damages clauses containing the same liquidated damages rate of 1/10 of one percent per day. See Morris v. United States, 50 Ct.Cl. 154 (1915); Crane Co. v. United States, 46 Ct.Cl. 343 (1911). Despite the "standard" nature of the rate, the Court of Claims found the rate to be reasonable in all three cases. In this case, likewise, DJ has failed to point to any reason to believe that the liquidated damages rate of

1/15 of one percent per day agreed upon by the parties is so exorbitant in light of the prospective injury to the government that it is plainly penal in nature and therefore may not be enforced.

AFFIRMED.

Notes and Questions

1. The opinion fairly reflects the very low level of success that government contractors have in challenging liquidated damage clauses. Clearly a contractor gets nowhere simply by complaining that the liquidated damage clause was boilerplate in no way tailored to an estimate, crude or otherwise, of the actual damages. What would it take for a contractor to get at least a hearing? Suppose the contractor had a declaration from the functional equivalent of the government's declarant, e.g., a former Army logistics management specialist who stated that late delivery could be expected to produce actual damage of well under one percent per month owing (hypothetically) to the Army having stockpiles of what it was procuring. Or suppose the contractor's president declared, from a market survey, that the Army could hire contractors to produce faster than scheduled by paying one percent more per month, showing that the Army could put a ceiling on any actual damage that way. Would either of these suffice?

2. In contrast to sanctions like termination for default or debarment, liquidated damages seems more non-normative in its straightforwardly monetary quality. Could it be argued that liquidated damages permit - as private contract law remedies do, but government contract law penalties do not - the operation of the doctrine of efficient breach? That is, could DJ, as it fell behind schedule, make the rational judgment that it was more efficient to breach and to pay liquidated damages than to cancel some other (hypothetical) more lucrative private contract it was fulfilling? Moreover, from the government's perspective, note how much easier it is to administer liquidated damages - simply by the contracting officer doing a calculation and making a withholding from payment - that it is to timplnate for default or to debar. So, to either side, does it matter that much how uneven or disproportionate the liquidated damages are to estimated actual damages, so long as they give clear guidance to the contractor and administrative simplicity to the government?

F. Suits Against the United States

The previous sections of this chapter discuss the main regular channels for remedies in government contracting cases. Of course, cases occur in various postures outside these main channels, raising the question of what regulates jurisdiction for such cases. For the cases seeking against the United States, the general bar to suit, which regulates jurisdiction, consists of sovereign immunity. This principle, handed down from English common law, holds that the United States, as sovereign, is immune from suit except when it consents to be sued, meaning, when Congress enacts a statute conferring jurisdiction over such suits. The Contract Disputes Act of 1978 exemplifies such statutory consent to suit, by allowing a contractor to sue the United States in what has been renamed the Court of Federal Claims - but only on the precise terms of the statute.

Periodically, a case that does not follow the regular channels of government contract litigation tests the nature of the exceptions to sovereign immunity. The *Blue Fox* opinion describes what happens in one such case.

DEPARTMENT OF THE ARMY, Petitioner,
v. BLUE FOX, INC. 525 U.S. 255

Supreme Court of the United States, 1999

Chief Justice REHNQUIST delivered the opinion of the Court.

An insolvent prime contractor failed to pay a subcontractor for work the latter completed on a construction project for the Department of the Army. The Department of the Army having required no Miller Act bond from the prime contractor, the subcontractor sought to collect directly from the Army by asserting an equitable lien on certain funds held by the Army. The Court of Appeals for the Ninth Circuit held that § 10(a) of the Administrative Procedure Act (APA), 5 U.S.C. § 702, waived the Government's immunity for the subcontractor's claim. We hold that § 702 did not nullify the long settled rule that sovereign immunity bars creditors from enforcing liens on Government property.

Participating in a business development program for socially and economically disadvantaged firms run by the Small Business Administration (SBA), the Department of the Army contracted with Verdan Technology, Inc., in September 1993, to install a telephone switching system at an Army depot in Umatilla, Oregon. Verdan, in turn, employed respondent Blue Fox, Inc., as a subcontractor on the project to construct a concrete block building to house the telephone system and to install certain safety and support systems.

Under the Miller Act, 40 U.S.C. §§ 270a-270d, a contractor that performs "construction, alteration, or repair of any public building or public work of the United States" generally must post two types of bonds. § 270a(a). First, the contractor must post a "performance bond...for the protection of the United States" against defaults by the contractor. § 270a(a)(1). Second, the contractor must post a "payment bond...for the protection of all persons supplying labor and material." § 270a(a)(2). The Miller Act gives the subcontractors and other suppliers "the right to sue on such payment bond for the amount, or the balance thereof, unpaid at the time of institution of such suit and to prosecute said action to final execution and judgment for the sum or sums justly due him." § 270b(a). Although the Army's original solicitation in this case required the contractor to furnish payment and performance bonds if the contract price exceeded $25,000, the Army later amended the solicitation, treated the contract as a "services contract," and deleted the bond requirements. Verdan therefore did not post any Miller Act bonds.

Blue Fox performed its obligations, but Verdan failed to pay it the $46,586.14 that remained due on the subcontract. After receiving notices from Blue Fox that it had not been fully paid, the Army nonetheless disbursed a total of $86,132.33 to Verdan as payment for all work that Verdan had completed. In January 1995, the Army terminated its contract with Verdan for various defaults and another contractor completed the Umatilla project. Blue Fox obtained a default judgment in tribal court against Verdan. Seeing that it could not collect from Verdan or its officers, it sued the Army for the balance due on its contract with Verdan in Federal District Court.

Predicating jurisdiction on and the APA, Blue Fox sought an "equitable lien" on any funds from the Verdan contract not paid to Verdan, or any funds available or appropriated for completion of the Umatilla project, and an order directing payment of those funds to it. Blue Fox also sought an injunction preventing the Army from paying any more money on the Verdan contract or on the follow-on contract until Blue Fox was paid. By the time of the suit, however, the Army had paid all amounts due on the Verdan contract, Blue Fox failed to obtain any preliminary relief, and the Army subsequently paid the replacement contractor the funds remaining on the Verdan contract plus additional funds.

On cross-motions for summary judgment, the District Court held that the waiver of sovereign immunity provided by the APA did not apply to respondent's claim against the Army. * * * In a split decision, the Court of Appeals for the Ninth Circuit reversed in relevant part. * * * The majority held that under this Court's decision in *Bowen v. Massachusetts*, 487 U.S. 879 (1988), the APA waives immunity for equitable actions. Based in part on its analysis of several of our cases examining a surety's right of subrogation, the majority held that the APA had waived the Army's immunity from Blue Fox suit to recover the amount withheld by the Army. The majority concluded that the lien attached to funds retained by the Army but owed to Verdan at the time the Army received Blue Fox notice that Verdan had failed to pay. The majority stated that "[t]he Army cannot escape Blue Fox equitable lien by wrongly paying out funds to the prime contractor when it had notice of Blue Fox unpaid claims." * * * "Absent a waiver, sovereign immunity shields the Federal Government and its agencies from suit." *FDIC v. Meyer*, 510 U.S. 471 (1994). Congress, of course, has waived its immunity for a wide range of suits, including those that seek traditional money damages. Examples are the Federal Tort Claims Act, 28 U.S.C. § 2671 *et seq.*, and the Tucker Act, 28 U.S.C. § 1491[3]

They are not involved here. Respondent sued the Army under § 10(a) of the APA, which provides in relevant part:

> "A person suffering legal wrong because of agency action, or adversely affected or aggrieved by agency action within the meaning of a relevant statute, is entitled to judicial review thereof. An action in a court of the United States seeking relief *other than money damages* and stating a claim that an agency or an officer or employee thereof acted or failed to act in an official capacity or under color of legal authority shall not be dismissed nor relief therein be denied on the ground that it is against the United States or that the United States is an indispensable party." (emphasis added).

Respondent asks us to hold, as did the court below, that this provision, which waives the Government's immunity from actions seeking relief "other than money damages," allows subcontractors to place liens on funds held by the United States Government for work completed on a prime contract. We have frequently held, however, that a waiver of sovereign immunity is to be strictly construed, in terms of its scope, in favor of the sovereign. See, *e.g., Lane v. Peña*, 518 U.S. 187, 192, 116 S.Ct. 2092, 135 L.Ed.2d 486 (1996) (citing cases); *Library of Congress v. Shaw*, 478 U.S. 310, 318, 106 S.Ct. 2957, 92 L.Ed.2d 250 (1986). Such a waiver must also be "unequivocally expressed" in the statutory text. See *Lane, supra*, at 192, 116 S.Ct. 2092. Respondent's claim must therefore meet this high standard.Respondent argues, and the court below held, that our analysis of § 702 in *Bowen* compels the allowance of respondent's lien. We disagree. * * *

---

3. The Federal Tort Claims Act provides that, subject to certain exceptions, "[t]he United States shall be liable, respecting the provisions of this title relating to tort claims, in the same manner and to the same extent as a private individual under like circumstances." 28 U.S.C. § 2674. The Tucker Act grants the Court of Claims jurisdiction "to render judgment upon any claim against the United States founded either upon the Constitution, or any Act of Congress or any regulation of an executive department, or upon any express or implied contract with the United States, or for liquidated or unliquidated damages in cases not sounding in tort." 28 U.S.C. § 1491(a)(1). The Tucker Act also gives federal district courts concurrent jurisdiction over claims founded upon the same substantive grounds for relief but not exceeding $10,000 in damages. See § 1346(a)(2).

* * *Bowen's interpretation of § 702 * * * hinged on the distinction between specific relief and substitute relief, not between equitable and nonequitable categories of remedies. * * *

It is clear from Bowen that the equitable nature of the lien sought by respondent here does not mean that its ultimate claim was not one for "money damages" within the meaning of . Liens, whether equitable or legal, are merely a means to the end of satisfying a claim for the recovery of money. Indeed, equitable liens by their nature constitute substitute or compensatory relief rather than specific relief. * * *

We accordingly hold that the sort of equitable lien sought by respondent here constitutes a claim for "money damages"; its goal is to seize or attach money in the hands of the Government as compensation for the loss resulting from the default of the prime contractor. As a form of substitute and not specific relief, respondent's action to enforce an equitable lien falls outside of § 702's waiver of sovereign immunity. * * *

Instead, recognizing that sovereign immunity left subcontractors and suppliers without a remedy against the Government when the general contractor became insolvent, Congress enacted the Miller Act * * *. But the Miller Act by its terms only gives subcontractors the right to sue on the surety bond posted by the prime contractor, not the right to recover their losses directly from the Government.

Respondent contends that in several cases examining a surety's right of equitable subrogation, this Court suggested that subcontractors and suppliers can seek compensation directly against the Government. See, e.g., Prairie State Bank v. United States, 164 U.S. 227, 32 Ct.Cl. 614, 17 S.Ct. 142, 41 L.Ed. 412 (1896); Henningsen v. United States Fidelity & Guaranty Co., 208 U.S. 404, 410, 28 S.Ct. 389, 52 L.Ed. 547 (1908); Pearlman v. Reliance Ins. Co., 371 U.S. 132, 141, 83 S.Ct. 232, 9 L.Ed.2d 190 (1962) (stating that "the laborers and materialmen had a right to be paid out of the fund [retained by the Government]" and hence a surety was subrogated to this right); but see Munsey Trust Co., supra, at 241, 67 S.Ct. 1599 ("[N]othing is more clear than that laborers and materialmen do not have enforceable rights against the United States for their compensation"). None of the cases relied upon by respondent involved a question of sovereign immunity, and, in fact, none involved a subcontractor directly asserting a claim against the Government. Instead, these cases dealt with disputes between private parties over priority to funds which had been transferred out of the Treasury and as to which the Government had disclaimed any ownership. They do not in any way disturb the established rule that, unless waived by Congress, sovereign immunity bars subcontractors and other creditors from enforcing liens on Government property or funds to recoup their losses.

The judgment of the Court of Appeals is reversed, and the case is remanded for proceedings consistent with this opinion.

It is so ordered.

Notes and Questions

1. Many different visions of sovereign immunity have come forth over the years. It started as the principle that "the King can do no wrong," a sentiment about the government that obviously did not fit the democratic ideals of the United States about government of, by, and for the people rather than ruling over it. At times, it has fallen into disfavor, seen as a hoary old notion just being used to close the courthouse doors. The court below drew on such views, by citing the Administrative Procedure Act's broad

waiver of sovereign immunity as part of a general thrust to tear down much-criticized barriers surrounding the federal government and the courts, and the jurisprudence of the Warren and (to a somewhat lesser but still significant extent) Burger Courts, epitomized by Justice Brennan's decision in *Bowen*, also aimed to open up the federal government and the courts. At other times - this opinion reflects one of them - those believing in firmly closing the courthouse doors have revived sovereign immunity and raised it up as a sturdy barrier wall with only narrow, limited, well-defined exceptions. Do you believe this closed-door view will endure, or, can the pendulum swing back yet again?

2. No brief discussion can do justice to the immense and complex structure of reasoning surrounding sovereign immunity and its exceptions. The opinion mentions that the Tucker Act creates an exception for cases founded on "express or implied contract." A distinction between "implied-in-fact" contracts, for which the act waives sovereign immunity, and "implied-in-law" contracts, for which it does not, by itself has spawned countless cases and further distinctions. See *Hercules, Inc. v. United States*, 516 U.S. 417 (1996). Do you know that distinction from basic first year contract law?

3. Suppose Blue Fox asserted its rights before the payment by the United States reached the prime contractor. Do its rights depend on precisely where that payment is, on the continuum between funds still completely within the general Treasury and funds completely in the pocket of the prime contractor? Or does the discussion of the Miller Act's policy basically mean that Congress intended subcontractors should find any and all relief only against either the contractor itself or a Miller Act bond?

Chapter 12

Ethics and Debarment

The topic of integrity in government contract law has become increasingly important over time. From the beginning of the republic, the contracting system has wrestled with the diverse ill-effects of this tension, namely, how that quest for gain can undermine the sacred public trust, and induce corruption, collusion, favoritism, conflicts of interest, and as many other noisome impairments of integrity as the imagination can conjure. The remedies began with some relatively narrow criminal provisions and the associated common-law questions. Scandals at each stage in procurement history, especially the Civil War, the defense expansion of the 1950s and 1960s, and the renewed defense expansion of the 1980s, have brought statutory and regulatory refinements in the control of such impairments of integrity. Somewhat in parallel, a system of suspension and debarment of contractors lacking in responsibility has also developed, as protection of the procurement system from the troubles expected in further dealings with particular contractors.

Broadly speaking, the subject of ethics in government contracting encompasses a wide array of ethical or normative restrictions imposed on government officials or businesses involved in such contracting. These restrictions concern a fundamental polarity. On the one hand, the public has high expectations for a system of public officials engaged in the dispensing of official funds, a sacred public trust. On the other hand, the public does not, as a general matter, impose the same level of expectations on private contractors, for which an unmitigated self-interested quest for gain, pursued by every allowed means, is tolerated as the route to overall economic efficiency.

At various times, and notably in the 1990s and 2000s, a somewhat countervailing set of considerations has also come into play. Contractors argue that too much of the wrong kinds of ethical restrictions not only accomplish little, but do particular harm to a procurement system. Such restrictions may clog the system with red tape and paperwork, limit desirable competition, and create a higher-cost, lower-efficiency enclave separated from the general marketplace. Moreover, both ethical and debarment rulings can have such stigmatizing and otherwise deleterious impact, as to necessitate a high measure of procedural rights before their imposition lest they become unfair instruments of oppression.

In any event, the life of the law is the clash of attack and defense, and if the lawyers for the government (or, sometimes, for protesting non-awardees) hurl charges about integrity in the thunderous tone of the aroused public conscience, the lawyers for the contractor in the defendant's posture must answer back with the equally righteous call for fairness and due process.

This chapter can only provide an introduction to the numerous complex aspects of procurement integrity. It starts with a section on the basic prohibited forms of rank corruption, bribery, gratuities, and kickbacks. Next, it discusses conflicts of interest and restrictions, and access to information, in procurement. Finally, it addresses debarment, which the tension between the government's need to protect itself from the irresponsible contractor, and the contractor's potentially facing a shut-off, if business from the government really matters, of what sustains its very existence.

For further discussion of the subject of this section, see: Richard J. Bednar, *GThe Fourteenth Major Frank B. Creekmore Lecture*, 175 Mil. L. Rev. 286 (2003)(largely concerning integrity and fraud issues); Christopher R. Yukins, *Ethics in Procreuement: New Challenges After a Decade of* Reform, 38 Procurement Lawyer, Spring 2003, at 3; Michael Davidson, *Claims Involving Fraud: Contracting Officer Limitations During Procurement Fraud Investigations*, Army Lawyer, Sept. 2002, at 21; Steven L. Schooner, *Fear of Oversight: The Fundamental Failure of Businesslike Government*, 50 Am. U. L. Rev. 627 (2001); Julian S. Greenspun, *1988 Amendments to Federal Procurement Policy Act: Did the "Ill Wind" Bring an Impractical Overreaction that May Run Afoul of the Constitution?*, 19 Pub. Cont. L. J. 393 (1990); Paul G. Dembling & Herbert E. Forrest, *Government Service and Private Compensation—Conflict of Interests*, 20

A. Bribery, Gratuities, and Kickbacks

Of course, concerns about basic forms of public corruption date back into English law, and Congress established criminal prohibitions against those basic forms in the 1800s. In basic terms, officials take bribes in taking a payment as the quid pro quo for an official act. Officials take gratuities in taking a payment for or because of an official act, e.g., a payment after a decision as an expression of gratitude, a "tip" or gratuity, for it. The decisions of procurement officers constitute quintessential official acts, potential magnets for bribes or gratuities because they offer such concrete profit as a motivation for such payments. Prime contractors take kickbacks in taking back a payment from a subcontractor for favorable treatment..

The case law on the basic forms of public corruption offers a number of illuminating lessons. Defending or prosecuting basic corruption law cases does not provide that large a part of the practice of the typical government or private procurement lawyer. However, such law creates a foundation for the rest of the often subtle and complex public integrity rules, and these can pop up at any point in procurement. By advising on those more complex public integrity rules, procurement lawyers can help contractors strive hard for profits without crossing the line into wrongdoing.

Moreover, these cases shed a particular light upon the difficult questions of the distinctions and boundaries between public and private in the realm of procurement. Although corrupt practices involving public officials seems both morally offensive and highly dangerous to responsible government, comparatively less concern, either moral or practical, attends similar practices involving private figures. Just why is that? Suppose a salesman for ordinary medical supplies pays off the buying officers for two hospitals and gets caught. Since it is just a minor offense to do so at the private hospital, why does the exact same behavior, with the same effect, become, at the public one, a serious felony?

Each of the particular cases in this section also has its own special illumination of the procurement world. In the first case, the Air Force has largely privatized the functions involved in the procurement itself where the bribery occurs. Hence, the case illustrates just how privatization of procurement works in contemporary practice.

In the second case, regarding a kickback scheme, the Supreme Court dissects elaborately the intermeshed workings of private contracting and subcontracting. Hence, the case illustrates how subcontracting, although not itself contracting with the government, comes to an important degree under government contracting law. Also, the case addresses, when Congress enacts a criminal provision to punish lapses in integrity, the provision's civil implications for the government's rights vis-a-vis violators. This is particularly important as to large government contractors, where the management at some level may credibly dispute any involvement or awareness in an integrity lapse, and the government must decide, not only how to punish the lapse, but what to do about the contract.

UNITED STATES of America, Plaintiff-Appellee, v. Ronnie Brunson KENNEY, Defendant-Appellant.

United States Court of Appeals for the Eleventh Circuit
No. 98-2128. 185 F.2d 1217 Aug. 26, 1999.

Before ANDERSON, Chief Judge, BLACK, Circuit Judge, and FORRESTER , District Judge.

PER CURIAM:

Ronnie Brunson Kenney appeals his conviction for soliciting a gratuity as a public official in violation of 18 U.S.C. § 201(c)(1)(B).* * * *. We conclude that Appellant's assignments of error are unavailing and therefore affirm his conviction.

I. PROCEDURAL BACKGROUND

Appellant was charged in a three-count indictment arising out of the United States District Court for the Northern District of Florida, Panama City Division. In the indictment, Appellant was charged with three separate counts of soliciting a bribe as a public official in violation of 18 U.S.C. § 201(b)(2)(A). * * * * On August 25, 1997, a jury was impaneled and trial began. * * * *

On August 29, 1997, the jury returned verdicts of guilty of the lesser included offense of soliciting a gratuity under Counts 1 and 3 and not guilty as to Count 2. Appellant was sentenced on January 13, 1998 before Judge Hinkle. Appellant was sentenced to two concurrent terms of eighteen months of probation, ten months of which are to be served in home detention. In addition, Appellant was fined $40,000 and ordered to pay a $200.00 special assessment. The imposition of sentence was stayed pending appeal, and Appellant filed a timely notice of appeal on January 26, 1998.

II. FACTS

A. *The Edge-Marker Contract and Appellant's Duties with Respect to it*

Appellant was an employee of BDM International, Inc. ("BDM"), and his official job title was "Manager, Rapid Runway Repair Branch." BDM is a large publicly traded company that, among other things, does extensive government contract work with the Department of Defense. In 1988, BDM received a Systems Integration Support Contract from the United States Air Force. Pursuant to this contract, BDM provided manpower to supplement Air Force Functions. As part of the support provided, BDM supplied acquisition management and engineering personnel to assist the Air Force Civil Engineering Services Agency in procuring and approving materials and equipment. Pursuant to this general contract, BDM employees were assigned to assist in specific ongoing Air Force projects, or tasks.

In September of 1992, officials at Tyndall Air Force Base in Florida awarded a contract to Starflite Boats of Niceville, Florida, pursuant to which Starflite would provide the Air Force with a runway edge-marker system for its runway repair program. An edge marker is used to mark runway damage on a combat zone airfield and consists of a Styrofoam reflector mounted on top of a thirty inch by forty-eight inch rubber mat. Also, as part of the contract, Starflite was to ship the edge markers in wooden shipping containers intended to last fifteen years. As part of its bid, Starflite suggested the possibility of manufacturing more durable and less expensive boxes out of fiberglass.

After the contract was awarded, a post-award conference was held. Among other things, the purpose of this meeting was to finalize the details of the performance of the contract, introduce the principal of Starflite, Mr. Brown, to the people with whom he would be working during the administration of the contract, and establish channels of communication. The minutes from this conference show that it was chaired by Sue Harris, the Air Force contract administrator. These minutes also show that the contracting officer for this contract was Larry G. Edwards, the project manager was Douglas A. Orlando, and Lt. Col. Michael C. Chatham was the officer in charge of the project. All of these individuals were Air Force employees. In addition, pursuant to the BDM-Air Force contract, Appellant was assigned by BDM to serve as its Acquisition Manager to support the performance of this contract.

At the post-award conference, Appellant was introduced to Mr. Brown as the day-to-day contact on the project, and Mr. Brown was told that if anything came up, he should contact Appellant. (R2-47.) Mr. Brown was also informed that Appellant would serve as the "eyes and ears" of the Air Force during the administration of the contract and would report the status of the contract, progress made, and any problems encountered by Starflite. As a result, Mr. Brown believed that Appellant was the engineer on the project and had the authority to approve or disapprove most anything concerning the project. (R2-46.)

In reality, as Acquisition Manager Appellant did not have final decision-making authority and could not bind the government. He did, however, advise decision makers with respect to certain technical issues involved in the edge-marker contract. According to the task description for this project, Appellant's job responsibilities included the provision of "program management, field test support, technical reviews and support for technical meetings when requested by the Chief, Airfield Systems Branch in support of the MOS Marking program." *See* Record Excerpt 773A. In addition, testimony at trial described Appellant's role, variously, as: Providing "technical data...to the people in the government who were making decisions regarding the procurement" and to provide advice based upon that information (R4-489-91; R5-636); processing or evaluating information for use by others in making official government decisions (R4-492; R5-636); functioning as the "eyes and ears" for the Air Force throughout the performance of the contract (R4-519; R3-238); ensuring that the contractor used specified products in the prescribed manner to get the prescribed product, or, in other words, managing the performance of the contract (R2-47); and providing technical advice to support the government in their acquisition of civil engineering systems for the Air Force. (R3-342). Ms. Harris also testified that Appellant held a position of official federal trust. (R3-269.)

In addition, the testimony indicates that Appellant's recommendations and advice were given great weight by those Air Force officials in the position to make procurement decisions. (R3-238; R3-331; R4-512-13.) The evidence shows that, on at least one occasion, Ms. Harris adopted Appellant's recommendation. Appellant had input in at least two decisions to substitute equivalent components. (R2-71; R3-329-30.) Also, Mr. Brown testified that when he spoke to Ms. Harris and Mr. Edwards about substituting an equivalent rubber mat for that specified in the contract, both stated that the approval of the equivalent would be Appellant's decision. Finally, although Appellant's salary was not paid by Air Force, testimony indicates that his salary is paid by BDM directly from funds it receives from the government in payment for services under the contract. (R3-352.)

B. *The Solicitations*

It is alleged in the indictment that in November of 1992, Appellant suggested to Mr. Brown that Mr. Brown could cut costs by using a different brand of rubber mats than that specified in the contract. Appellant offered to approve the change if Mr. Brown would pay him one-half of the cost savings. In addition, in March of 1992, Appellant and Mr. Brown discussed Mr. Brown's preference for using cheaper fiberglass shipping boxes rather than the wooden ones specified in the contract. Again, Appellant told Mr. Brown he could have the contract modified if Mr. Brown would pay him $100.00 per box. At a later date, the contract was in fact modified to allow for the use of the fiberglass boxes. Further, an equivalent mat was eventually used, although not the original equivalent sought by Mr. Brown. Mr. Brown, however, never paid the above-described sums. Instead, he reported Appellant's solicitations to Air Force officials.

After Mr. Brown's report, the Federal Bureau of Investigation (FBI) and the Air Force conducted a joint investigation and on May 24, 1993 recorded an incriminating conversation between Mr. Brown and Appellant on both video and audio tape. Thereafter, the investigation was put on hold for the duration of the contract because law enforcement officials wanted to observe Appellant actually receiving illegal payments. The investigation was also delayed due to health problems suffered by Appellant. Eventually, however, investigators closed the investigation in late 1996 and Appellant was indicted on June 26, 1997. Count one of the indictment related to the change in the contract specifications regarding rubber mats; count two alleged a general promise by Appellant to direct Air Force business to Starflite Boats in return for cash payments; and count three pertained to the change in the contract specifications regarding fiberglass boxes.

III. DISCUSSION

Appellant's first and third enumerations of error regarding the pre-indictment delay and the failure of the government to prove an allegation in the indictment are meritless and may be disposed of without discussion. Appellant's contentions regarding his motion to dismiss and the jury instructions, however, require a bit more attention.

A. *Denial of the Motion to Dismiss*

As stated above, in his first enumeration of error, Appellant contends that the district court improperly denied his motion to dismiss on the grounds that he is not a "public official" as defined by the statute under which he was convicted.

18 U.S.C. § 201 provides that it is unlawful for a "public official" to, among other things, demand, seek, or accept anything of value in return for being influenced in an official act. *See* 18 U.S.C. § 201(b)(2). This statute also makes it illegal to seek, receive,

or accept anything of value for or because of an official act performed or to be performed. *See* 18 U.S.C. § 201(c)(1)(B). The term "public official" is defined as:

> Member of Congress, Delegate, or Resident Commissioner, either before or after such official has qualified, or an officer or employee or person acting for or on behalf of the United States, or any department, agency or branch of Government thereof, including the District of Columbia, in any official function, under or by authority of any such department, agency, or branch of Government, or a juror.

18 U.S.C. § 201(a)(1).

In *Dixson v. United States,* 465 U.S. 482, 104 S.Ct. 1172, 79 L.Ed.2d 458 (1984), the Supreme Court held that this definition extends beyond merely government employees and contractors to include private individuals who "occupy a position of public trust with official federal responsibilities." *Id.* at 496, 104 S.Ct. 1172. Such an individual, however, "must possess some degree of official responsibility for carrying out a federal program or policy" to be considered a public official. *Id.* at 499, 104 S.Ct. 1172.

In the instant case, Appellant contends that he did not occupy a position of public trust with official federal responsibilities. Appellant bases this contention on the fact that his job merely consisted of "making non-binding recommendations based on technical data." Appellant's Brief at 30. In addition, Appellant points out that he was not in a position to authorize changes in the contract or make decisions binding on the government and relies upon internal Department of Defense Policies that identify "inherently governmental functions" that may not be delegated to private contractors such as himself.

Although this circuit has not addressed the scope of the term "public official" in circumstances such as these, the findings of several of our sister circuits are instructive. In *United States v. Hang,* 75 F.3d 1275 (8th Cir.1996), the Eighth Circuit found that an eligibility technician for an independent public corporation organized under Minnesota law and established for the purpose of administering federal programs and funds was a public official. The defendant's duties in *Hang* included screening applications to verify whether the applicants were entitled to preferences for low-income housing and placing them on a waiting list. The defendant did not, however, have authority actually to rent an apartment. In affirming the defendant's conviction for receiving bribes in exchange for accelerating the application process, the Eighth Circuit found that the defendant occupied a position of public trust in that he was "on the front line in the effort to provide affordable housing to eligible families." *Id.* at 1280. In addition, the court held that the defendant's job involved official federal responsibilities in that the agency he worked for was organized for the exclusive purpose of implementing federal programs; was subject to federal oversight; and the defendant himself had a great deal of responsibility in determining who would receive available housing in that he was ultimately responsible for the accuracy of the applicants' files and the approval of his recommendations were largely *pro forma. Id.*

Similarly, in *United States v. Madeoy,* 912 F.2d 1486 (D.C.Cir.1990), *cert. denied,* 498 U.S. 1105, 111 S.Ct. 1008, 112 L.Ed.2d 1091 (1991), the District of Columbia Circuit upheld the conviction of a VA-approved fee appraiser for accepting bribes as a public official. The defendant in *Madeoy* conducted real estate appraisals for the purpose of obtaining Federal Housing Administration-insured loans. Despite the existence of a VA regulation stating generally that appraisers are not agents of the government and had no authority to bind the government, the court found the defendant to be a public official.

In so finding, the court noted that it was on the defendant's recommendation, subject to only limited review, that the government guaranteed loans. *See also United States v. Velazquez,* 847 F.2d 140 (4th Cir.1988) (applying the statute to a county deputy sheriff who was responsible for supervising federal inmates); *United States v. Strissel,* 920 F.2d 1162, 1165–66 (4th Cir.1990) (finding the executive director of a local housing authority to be a public official); *United States v. Ricketts,* 651 F.Supp. 283 (S.D.N.Y.1987) (applying the statute to a supervisor in an organization that contracted with the Bureau of Prisons).

These cases make it clear that in order to be considered a public official a defendant need not be the final decision maker as to a federal program or policy. Rather, it appears to be sufficient that the defendant is in a position of providing information and making recommendations to decision makers as long as the defendant's input is given sufficient weight to influence the outcome of the decisions at issue. Based upon such reasoning, this court finds that Appellant was indeed acting as a public official.

Appellant's position was one of public trust in that his advice and the information he provided was relied upon by officers of the Air Force in making decisions pertaining to the procurement of equipment. In addition, it is clear from the record that Appellant acted as the primary liaison between Starflite and the Air Force and could not have done so without some federal responsibility. Appellant's job also included federal responsibilities in that he was responsible for monitoring and providing information regarding the technical aspects of the edge-marker contract. In providing such information, the evidence shows that his opinion was highly regarded, the decision makers relied upon his technical expertise and deferred to him on many day-to-day decisions. Like the defendants in *Hang* and *Madeoy,* although Appellant did not exercise the final judgment on contracting decisions, the information and recommendations he provided served as the basis for many of those decisions. As a result, it is clear that, in the performance of his duties, Appellant had some official responsibility for the carrying out of a government program.

Nor does the existence of the Department of Defense policies relied upon by Appellant alter this conclusion. These policies do not purport to define what is an official responsibility as that term is used in § 201. Rather, they merely provide guidance as to what functions must be performed by government employees and those that may be out-sourced to contractors such as Appellant. Therefore, they do not provide any guidance as to whether the functions performed by Appellant can be seen as including federal responsibility. As a result, the court hereby AFFIRMS the district court's denial of Appellant's motion to dismiss.

B. *Jury Instructions*

Appellant's final enumeration of error alleges that the jury instructions inaccurately stated the law with respect to the definition of "public official." * * * * The district judge in the instant case drafted jury instructions on the definition of a public official that combine some aspects from the statutory definition of the term with elements from the case law and hypothetical examples. Specifically, the jury was instructed:

> A "public official" … is any person who acts for or on behalf of the United States, that is, a person who possesses some degree of official responsibility for carrying out a federal program or policy. This includes someone who, acting for or on behalf of the government, either (a) makes official governmental decisions himself or herself, or (b) makes recommendations regarding official governmental decisions, or (c) processes or evaluates information for use by others in the making of official governmental decisions.

A "public official" need not be an employee of the federal government or of any government at all; a person who acts for or on behalf of the federal government pursuant to a contract or other business relationship can be a "public official," just as a government employee can be a "public official." The term "public official" thus includes an employee of a private corporation who acts for or on behalf of the federal government pursuant to a contract.

Record Excerpt 26 at 10.

Appellant asserts that examples (b) and (c) above are vague, open-ended, and left the jury no choice but to find him to be a public official. We concede that these examples could be construed as overbroad. When read in conjunction with the preceding language requiring the jury to find that Appellant possessed some official responsibility, however, we find that they accurately reflect the meaning of "public official" as we have construed that term above. Accordingly, although the jury instructions may not be as precise as we would like, we cannot say that the district judge abused his discretion in this regard.

IV. CONCLUSION

After careful consideration of the arguments presented on appeal, we conclude that Appellant is not entitled to relief. Accordingly, we AFFIRM the findings of the district court.

Notes and Questions

1. On first glance, the offering of the corrupt payment itself seems so reprehensible and debilitating that any kind of legal defense constitutes mere pettifoggery about technicalities. However, the line of cases that started with *Dixson* and extends to this case brings out forcefully some real tensions on this issue. The same "corrupt payment" to persons who perform some mundane task in a private setting does not trigger heavy penalties or major law enforcement efforts. If this defendant had been a purchasing manager, performing the exact same task at a private airfield, much less severe penalties and lesser law enforcement efforts would have attended the sam private airfielm for baksheesh.

Looking at some of the examples in the cases this opinion cites as precedents. Had those receiving payments as tenant application-screeners or mortgage appraisers been in the private sector, again, much less severe penalties and lesser law enforcement efforts would have attended the same behaviors. What justifies coming down so hard, yet so selectively, on payments to the public procurement managers, tenant application screeners, or property appraisers, and not private one's-practical considerations about the institutional vulnerability of public government and spending, or, moral ones about the distinctive nature of the public trust?

2. On the other hand, before one scoffs at how arbitrarily these laws work or the historical accidents that generated them, consider that many of the world's countries find themselves plagued with corrupt governments, which they can neither shake off nor cleanse, and which drag down not just their governance but their whole society. The United States is blessed that, compared to many other countries, its procurement stays relatively honest. Does the lack of corruption owe to the legal system or to something in the societal culture - or does that distinction have anymeaning?

3. The bribery and gratuities laws arose historically not so much from some logical systematic reasoning effort as might occur in the perfect creation of a fresh system, but from public and

UNITED STATES, Petitioner,
v. ACME PROCESS EQUIPMENTCOMPANY

Supreme Court of the United States
385 U.S.183. Decided Dec. 5, 1966

Mr. Justice BLACK delivered the opinion of the Court.

The respondent, Acme Process Equipment Company, brought this action against the United States in the Court of Claims to recover damages for breach of a contract under which Acme undertook through itself and subcontractors to manufacture 2,751 75-mm. recoilless rifles for about $337 per rifle. Among other defenses, the United States alleged that it had rightfully canceled its contract with Acme because three of Acme's principal employees had accepted compensation for awarding subcontracts in violation of the Anti-Kickback Act set out in part below.[1] The Court

I.

In October 1952, Acme hired Harry Tucker, Jr., and his associate, James Norris, for the purpose of establishing and managing a new division of the company to handle government contracts. Norris was made general manager of production with authority to submit bids, sign government contracts, and award subcontracts. Tucker was placed in charge of sales, government contracts, and expediting subcontract operations. Prior to this time Tucker had entered into a contract with All Metals Industries, Inc., under which he was to receive a commission for all sales to customers, including Acme, procured by him. Tucker's employment contract with Acme specifically stated that he represented and would continue to represent firms in other lines of business, but Acme did not consult with any of his other clients at the time Tucker was hired.

Late in October, Tucker advised his superiors at Acme of the proposed Army contract for rifles, and at Tucker's suggestion, Acme submitted a bid of $337 per rifle. Since Acme's bid was the lowest, the Army began negotiations with Acme culminating in the award of the contract in January 1953. The negotiations were handled by Tucker and Norris for Acme. Since it was contemplated that the project would be largely subcontracted, leaving to Acme only the final finishing and assembly of components, the Army expressed a keen interest in Acme's proposed subcontractors. Not only did it review Acme's subcontracting plans and require Acme to notify it of

---

1. Section 1 of the Anti-Kickback Act, 60 Stat. 37, as amended, 74 Stat. 740, 41 U.S.C. s 51, provides in pertinent part:

'That the payment of any fee, commission, or compensation of any kind or the granting of any gift or gratuity of any kind, either directly or indirectly, by or on behalf of a subcontractor, * * * (1) to any officer, partner, employee, or agent of a prime contractor holding a negotiated contract entered into by any department, agency, or establishment of the United States for the furnishing of supplies, materials, equipment or services of any kind whatsoever * * * as an inducement for the award of a subcontract or order from the prime contractor * * * is hereby prohibited. The amount of any such fee, commission, or compensation * * * shall not be charged, either directly or indirectly, as a part of the contract price charged by the subcontractor to the prime contractor * * *. The amount of any such fee, cost, or expense shall be recoverable on behalf of the United States from the subcontractor the recipient thereof by setoff * * * or by an action in an appropriate court of the United States. * * *'

Section 4 of the Act, 41 U.S.C. s 54, provides:

'Any person who shall knowingly, directly or indirectly, make to receive any such prohibited payment shall be fined not more than $10,000 or be imprisoned for not more than two years, of both.'

changes in those plans during the final stages of negotiation, but the contract eventually awarded required government approval of all subcontracts in excess of $25,000. All Metals, because its proposed subcontract amounted to one-third of the amount of the prime contract, actually participated in the negotiations between Acme and the Army.

During this period of negotiation two other developments took place. Tucker obtained agreements from two other potential subcontractors to pay him commissions on any orders he could procure from Acme. Army contracting officers warned Acme's president, Joshua Epstein, that Tucker was suspected of having engaged in contingent-fee arrangements with other government contractors.

Finally, Acme was awarded the prime contract. Although the price was fixed at $337 per rifle, the contract contained a price redetermination clause under which, after 30% of the rifles were delivered, the parties could negotiate the price on past and future shipments upward or downward, with an upper limit of $385 per rifle. Within a few weeks after the prime contract was awarded, All Metals and the other two companies with which Tucker had prior kickback arrangements obtained subcontracts from Acme. Tucker was paid his kickbacks, but, apparently unsatisfied with the amount of his payoff, he got Jack Epstein, the superintendent of the chief Acme plant and the son of Acme's president and principal stockholder, to join the kickback conspiracy. Together Epstein and Tucker threatened to cancel All Metals' subcontract unless it paid $25,000 to a dummy corporation owned by Tucker, Norris, and Epstein for fictitious consulting services. All Metals reluctantly acceded to the shakedown. The amount paid to Tucker, Norris, and Epstein was charged to Acme through an increase in the subcontract price.

Although they knew that Tucker was representing other companies and had been notified of the Army's suspicions of Tucker's involvement in contingent fee arrangements, other officials of Acme were not aware of the kickback activities of Tucker, Norris, and Epstein until late in 1953. At that time, Acme's president caused the resignation of the three suspected officials.

In 1956 Tucker, Norris, and Epstein were indicted for violation of the then Anti-Kickback Act, 60 Stat. 37. After presentation of the Government's case, the District Court granted the defendants' motion for acquittal on the ground that the Act—which at that time embraced only 'cost-plus-a-fixed-fee or other cost reimbursable' government contracts—did not apply to Acme's contract, a fixed-price contract with a provision for limited price redetermination. The court found the defendants' actions 'despicable and morally reprehensible, but unfortunately within the narrow letter of the law.' The court recommended that Congress amend the Anti-Kickback Act 'to include as a crime the vicious and immoral type of conduct that has been exhibited in this case.' United States v. Norris, Crim. No. 18535 (D.C.E.D.Pa.), April 14, 1956.

The District Court's opinion did indeed spur the Comptroller General to recommend amendatory legislation and in 1960 the Anti-Kickback Act was amended to apply to all 'negotiated contracts.' The civil provision of the amended Act was made retroactive to allow government recovery of kickbacks 'whether heretofore or hereafter paid or incurred by the subcontractor.'

II.

The Anti-Kickback Act, as originally passed in 1946 and as amended in 1960, provides two express sanctions for its violation: (1) fine or imprisonment for one who makes or receives a kickback, and (2) recovery of the kickback by the United States. The

Court of Claims held, and it is argued here, that had Congress wanted 'to provide the additional remedy of contract annulment, it could have done so' by express language, 347 F.2d, at 521, 171 Ct.Cl. 343, and of course it could have. But the fact that it did not see fit to provide for such a remedy by express language does not end the matter. The Anti-Kickback Act not only 'prohibited' such payments, but clearly expressed a policy decidedly hostile to them. They were recognized as devices hurtful to the Government's procurement practices. Extra expenditures to get subcontracts necessarily add to government costs in cost-plus-a-fixed-fee and other cost reimbursable contracts. And this is also true where the prime contract is a negotiated fixed-price contract with a price redetermination clause, such as the prime contract is here. The kickbacks here are passed on to the Government in two stages. The prime contractor rarely submits his bid until after he has tentatively lined up his subcontractors. Indeed, as here, the subcontractors frequently participate in negotiation of the prime contract. The subcontractor's tentative bid will, of course, reflect the amount he contemplates paying as a kickback, and then his inflated bid will be reflected in the prime contractor's bid to the Government. At the renegotiation stage, where the prime contractor's actual cost experience is the basis for price redetermination, any kickbacks, paid by subcontractors and passed on to the prime contractor after the prime contract is awarded, will be passed on to the Government in the form of price redetermination upward.[5]

Acme argues, however, that the express provision for recovery of kickbacks is enough to protect the Government from increased costs attributable to them. But this argument rests on two false assumptions. The first is that kickbacks can easily be detected and recovered. This is hardly the case. Kickbacks being made criminal means that they must be made—if at all—in secrecy. Though they necessarily inflate the price to the Government, this inflation is rarely detectable. This is particularly true as regards defense contracts where the products involved are not usually found on the commercial market and where there may not be effective competition. Such contracts are generally negotiated and awarded without formal advertising and competitive bidding, and there is often no opportunity to compare going prices with the price negotiated by the Government. Kickbacks will usually not be discovered, if at all, until after the prime contract is let. The second false assumption underlying Acme's argument is that the increased cost of the Government is necessarily equal to the amount of the kickback which is recoverable. Of course, a subcontractor who must pay a kickback is likely to include the amount of the kickback in his contract price. But this is not all. A subcontractor who anticipates obtaining a subcontract by virtue of a kickback has little incentive to stint on his cost estimates. Since he plans to obtain the subcontract without regard to the economic merits of his proposal, he will be tempted to inflate that proposal by more than the amount of the kickback. And even if the Government could isolate and recover the inflation attributable to the kickback, it would still be saddled with a subcontractor who, having obtained the job other than on merit, is perhaps entirely unreliable in other ways. This unreliability in turn undermines the security of the prime contractor's performance—a

---

5. This is precisely what happened here before the Government canceled Acme's contract. Acme in 1953 submitted cost data for price redetermination purposes that included the charges of the five subcontractors which had paid kickbacks to Acme's employees. These subcontracting charges in turn included the amounts paid as kickbacks. Had the kickbacks not been discovered and the contract not been canceled, Acme would have been able to use these costs to renegotiate the price per rifle from $337 to $385. Such price redetermination could have cost the Government about $132,000 more on the entire contract.

result which the public cannot tolerate, especially where, as here, important defense contracts are involved.

III.

In *United States v. Mississippi Valley Co.*, 364 U.S. 520, 563, 81 S.Ct. 294, 316, 5 L.Ed.2d 268, the Court recognized that 'a statute frequently implies that a contract is not to be enforced when it arises out of circumstances that would lead enforcement to offend the essential purpose of the enactment.' The Court there approved the cancellation of a government contract for violation of the conflict-of-interest statute on the ground that 'the sanction of nonenforcement is consistent with and essential to effectuating the public policy embodied in' the statute. Ibid. We think the same thing can be said about cancellation here. * * * *

There is likewise no merit to the Court of Claims' distinction of the Mississippi Valley Co. case on the ground that there the criminal provision of the conflict-of-interest statute was violated whereas here the kickback conspirators were acquitted of violating the Anti-Kickback Act as it existed when the kickbacks occurred, prior to 1960. As we have seen, Acme's employees were acquitted on the technical ground that Acme's prime contract was not a 'cost reimbursable' contract to which the Act then expressly applied. It is unnecessary for us to decide whether this holding was correct.[7] For whether the kickbacks here contravened the narrow letter of the criminal law, strictly construed, they clearly were violative of the public policy against kickbacks first expressed by Congress in 1946. If Congress then limited the reach of the Act to cost reimbursable contracts, it was only because other types of negotiated contracts were rarely in use then. Though the recent extensive use of other forms of negotiated contracts led Congress in 1960 to amend the Act to cover clearly these types of contracts and to close the technical loophole opened by the acquittal of Acme's employees, the congressional policy against all kickbacks was not changed. Congress merely reiterated its recognition of the evil and sought to correct the letter of the law to effectuate its long-standing policy. In making the civil remedy of the 1960 Act retroactive, Congress clearly indicated that there had been no basic change in the public policy against kickbacks.

* * *

The judgment of the Court of Claims is reversed with directions to sustain the United States' right to cancel the prime contract.

It is so ordered.

Notes and Questions

1. Whereas the bribery and gratuity statutes apply, in the procurement context, to those directly involved in contracting between the government and its prime contractor, the anti-kickback law applies centrally to the relations between the contractor and its subcontractors. Recall that the government leaves most of the price relationship between fixed-price contractors, and their subcontractors, as to commercial items, to the ways of the private market, including what are understood as its relaxed standards as to formalities and incentives. Why treat this part of subcontracting differently?

---

7. *See United States v. Barnard*, 255 F.2d 583, cert. denied, 358 U.S. 919, 79 S.Ct. 287, 3 L.Ed.2d 238, holding that a fixed-price contract with provision for unlimited price redetermination is a 'cost reimbursable' contract.

2. As with bribes, on first glance, the corrupt payment itself seems so reprehensible and debilitating as described in this opinion that any kind of legal defense constitutes mere pettifoggery about technicalities. However, part of that owes to the loaded term, "kickback." In fact, fee — or commission-splitting in complex ways during teaming and joint venturing are common in the commercial world. Keep in mind that a typical setting for what contractors might call complex payment-sharing, and prosecutors would call kickbacks, would be construction work. Is it worth the federal government's scarce enforcement resources, or a complex system of regulations and prohibitions, to corral those who continue local norms about routine minor construction when they perform federal projects?

3. The Warren Court decided this case in 1966. It followed its own seminal *Missisppi Valley* opinion in 1961, and Congressional reforms of the early 1960s, all pushing ethics and procurement reform. Also, the Court ruled at the peak of its general willingness, throughout its legislative interpretation cases, to find additional causes of action and remedies against business in order to fill in, expansively, what it considered as gaps left by Congress in statutory schemes. The Supreme Court of the 1990s and thereafter has had much less eagerness to infer the existence of implied causes of action and to create implied remedies. Now the Justices tend to say that if federal law enforcers want more authority, they can ask Congress for it. Would today's Supreme Court, deciding this case on a blank slate, read the statute the way the 1966 Court did?

4. The case identifies some of the history up to that point of the anti-kickback law. In 1986, Congress passed a new Anti-Kickback Act to close up loopholes and revitalize controls on kickbacks. It broadly defined kickbacks. And, it extended to any type of government contract, obviating the previous question of whether what the opinion says would apply equally to fixed-price commercial contracting and subcontracting. See United States v. Kruse, 101 F. Supp. 2d 410 (E.D. Va. 2000)(providing of interest-free loans is an illegal kickback). Now, it applies even without proof the kickbacking subcontractor knew any of what it did, would go towards a federal contract. United States v. Purdy, 144 F.2d 241 (2d Cir. 1998). In the context of health care, an even strongers set of provisions, the Stark Acts, apply, from fear that medical providers' judgments - for example, whether to order lucrative but unnecessary tests - will be distorted by the conflicts of interest from participation in payments made for their provision.

B. Conflicts of Interest, Restricted Information

Congress and executive authorities have created a structure of procurement ethics considerably beyond the age-old concerns with corrupt payments. Contemporary law also concerns conflicts of interest, such as can arise when today's government officials involved in procurement become tomorrow's government contractor employees, and vice-versa. On the one hand, critics fear that a "revolving door" means sweetheart deals provided to contractors because of connections, favors, the anticipation of favors, and other undermining of independence. On the other hand, in some sectors like sophisticated defense contracting, there are values other than independence. A degree of rotation between the defense contractors and the military, some would argue, promotes a coordination that produces a more effective and workable procurement. Denying those with experience the ability to move back and forth would deprive both the government and the private sector of what may be the largest and best pools of personnel with useful, perhaps even essential, experience, capacities, and attitudes.

Another set of issues concerns the question of information obtained by contractors. Naturally, contractors strive to learn all they legitimately can about what the government wants or their competitors have to offer. On the other hand, the famous "Ill Wind" law enforcement project after the defense buildup of the 1980s uncovered extensive and shocking rings of contractors, consultants, and government employees sharing information that made a mockery out of the competitive system. Congress reacted by enacting a first, strict version of the Procurement Integrity Act, which it amended it in 1996 to relax some of the aspects that had come to seem excessive

UNITED STATES of America, Plaintiff-Appellee, v. Eugene Donald SCHALTENBRAND, Defendant-Appellant.

United States Court of Appeals, Eleventh Circuit.
930 F.2d 1554. May 13, 1991.

ON PETITION FOR REHEARING

Before TJOFLAT, Chief Judge, KRAVITCH, Circuit Judge, and GODBOLD, Senior Circuit Judge.

KRAVITCH, Circuit Judge:

* * *

Defendant-Appellant Colonel Eugene Schaltenbrand appeals his conviction of two violations of the government employee conflict of interest statutes. Specifically, he was convicted under § 208(a), which prohibits government employees from working on projects in which they have a financial interest, and § 207(a), which prohibits former government employees from representing private parties before the government on matters in which they previously worked for the government. We affirm the conviction and reverse the conviction.

FACTS

In early 1987, the United States Air Force was engaged in a program to sell certain C-130 aircraft to friendly countries. These aircraft were being phased out of the American fleet because they were no longer cost effective to keep as a means of primary defense. One aspect of the program was to develop a system of maintenance and support for the aircraft through a private defense contractor.

Colonel Carl McPherson served as the System Program Manager of the project. To assist him on the project, McPherson requested the activation of Schaltenbrand, a reserve officer who was available at the time for extended service. From February 17, 1987 through May 1, 1987, Schaltenbrand was activated nine times for short periods of duty, usually lasting two to five days, with one period of sixteen days. Air Force records show that some of these periods were designated "active" duty, while some were designated "inactive" duty. During periods of inactive duty, Schaltenbrand was not paid, but was required to wear his uniform and received credit towards retirement.

In March 1987, Schaltenbrand was sent to Peru to do a site survey, the purpose being to determine the needs of that country so that the Air Force could better tailor a package of aircraft and support for it. While Schaltenbrand was in Peru, discussions between the Air Force and Mexico were progressing rapidly, and McPherson sent Schaltenbrand to Mexico to perform a site survey there also. Shortly after Schaltenbrand's return from Mexico, McPherson requested that Schaltenbrand be activated for a sixty-day period to work exclusively on the Air Force's deal with Mexico (the "Mexican Project"). McPherson made this request on March 25, 1987, but the sixty-day period did not actually begin until May 3, 1987. According to McPherson, Schaltenbrand was to be his "right-hand man" on the Mexican Project.

In early April 1987, Schaltenbrand attended a meeting concerning the Mexican Project. The purpose of the meeting was to discuss the Mexican site survey and to hear a proposal from Teledyne Brown Engineering ("TBE"), a private contractor that had been selected by the Mexican government as the likely provider of support for the aircraft being sold to Mexico. At that time, TBE's contract for the project had not been finalized. Following the meeting, Schaltenbrand spoke with Harold Timmons, TBE's vice president and representative at the meeting. Schaltenbrand informed Timmons that he was interested in working for TBE after his duty with the Air Force ended. Schaltenbrand told Timmons that he thought he was well qualified to assist TBE with its potential contract for the Mexican Project, and Timmons suggested that Schaltenbrand fill out an application and send it to TBE's personnel department. He also mentioned that Schaltenbrand should discuss with the Air Force any potential conflicts of interest that might arise.

Schaltenbrand sent a resume to TBE's personnel department and also travelled to TBE's offices in Huntsville, Alabama to further discuss the possibility of employment. On the day of his visit to TBE, Schaltenbrand apparently was listed on Air Force records as on "inactive" duty. Schaltenbrand spoke with Timmons about his qualifications, and Timmons explained what TBE was looking for. TBE had done some advertising for the position and was seeking someone to lead TBE's Mexican team. In addition to flight experience, TBE wanted someone who could speak Spanish. Schaltenbrand told Timmons that he had thought about that, and that he would take a course in Spanish in order to be qualified. No salary discussions took place at that time.

Schaltenbrand's sixty-day period of duty ended on July 1, 1987, but he was activated for short periods on several occasions throughout August and September. Although the record is unclear as to the description of his duties during these later periods, it does not appear that he was significantly involved in the Mexican Project. On or about September 21, 1987, Schaltenbrand contacted TBE and informed it that he had another offer of employment, and therefore needed to know whether TBE was going to offer him a job. On September 21, TBE offered him the position that he had discussed with Timmons in April. * * *

Schaltenbrand accepted TBE's offer on September 25 and began work on September 28.

In his new capacity as a TBE employee, Schaltenbrand attended a meeting at the Air Force base on November 4, 1987 concerning the Mexican Project. The meeting was considered a "status conference." At this time, TBE still had not formalized its contract on the project. Dale Weaver was the TBE spokesperson at the meeting and requested that Schaltenbrand accompany him because Schaltenbrand would be responsible for implementing the plans discussed at the meeting. Aside from discussing some delivery schedules, there is no evidence that Schaltenbrand made any other contributions to the meeting. * * *

DISCUSSION
Section 208

Schaltenbrand first challenges his conviction under § 208(a). That section provides:

> [W]hoever, being an officer or employee of the executive branch of the United States Government,... participates personally and substantially... in a... particular matter in which, to his knowledge, he,... or any person or organization with whom he is negotiating or has any arrangement concerning prospective employment, has a financial interest... [shall be guilty of a felony].

The parties do not dispute that Schaltenbrand was an officer of the executive branch or that he participated personally and substantially in the Mexican Project. Thus, the only issue with respect to is whether or not his conduct in obtaining his position with TBE amounted to "negotiation" under the statute. Unfortunately, this term is not defined in the statute.

This court recently addressed the definition of "negotiation" under and stated that "the terms 'negotiating' and 'arrangement' are not exotic or abstruse words requiring detailed etymological study or judicial analysis. They are common words of universal usage. People of ordinary intelligence would have fair notice of the conduct proscribed by the statute." United States v. Hedges, *912 F.2d 1397, 1403 (11th Cir.1990) (quoting United States v. Conlon, 628 F.2d 150, 154 (D.C.Cir.1980), cert. denied, S.Ct. 1015, 71 L.Ed.2d 304 (1982)).

Not surprisingly, Schaltenbrand urges a rather rigid definition of negotiation. He points to the language in *Black's Law Dictionary,* which states:

> Negotiation is process of submission and consideration of offers until acceptable offer is made and accepted. The deliberation, discussion, or conference upon the terms of a proposed agreement; the act of settling or arranging the terms and conditions of a bargain, sale, or other business transaction.

Black's Law Dictionary 934 (5th ed. 1979) (citations omitted). * * * Schaltenbrand argues that he had submitted an application to TBE, but TBE did not make him an offer until after he was finished with the Mexican Project. Stating that "[n]egotiating is like doing the Tango—there may be some dispute over who is going to lead, but it still takes two," he argues that no negotiations took place because TBE had not yet shown interest on its side.

Schaltenbrand contends that *Hedges* supports his argument that "negotiation" cannot take place until an offer is made. Although the *Hedges* court found that negotiation had taken place, Schaltenbrand notes that in that case the employer had proposed a salary for the prospective employee, and the prospective employee had countered with a higher salary proposal. *See Hedges,* 912 F.2d at 1403.

Contrary to the interpretation urged by Schaltenbrand, we conclude his actions were not only consistent with the definitions quoted above, but were also consistent with the reasoning in *Hedges.* As an Air Force reserve officer, Schaltenbrand approached TBE about the possibility of employment. TBE responded that he should fill out an application. After submitting an application, he was invited by TBE to come to its offices for an interview. During the interview, Schaltenbrand and TBE discussed the necessary qualifications to fill a particular position. TBE stressed that they needed someone who spoke Spanish. Schaltenbrand replied that he would learn to speak Spanish. Some months later, he received the exact position he had discussed at the interview.

The above circumstances clearly indicate active interest on both sides. The two parties were not engaged in mere general discussions, but had a specific position in mind and discussed the qualifications of the position in detail. Moreover, when TBE suggested that Schaltenbrand did not meet all of the qualifications, he responded that he would remedy that problem. Schaltenbrand contends that because *TBE* did not make a formal offer, no negotiations took place. Here, Schaltenbrand seems to forget his own argument that negotiations "take two"—clearly if it takes two to negotiate, there should not be a requirement as to who must make their offer first. Schaltenbrand initiated the dialogue, and TBE invited him to its offices and pursued the matter further. To require that the statute does not apply until the moment when a formal offer is made is to read the statute too narrowly. * * *

This reading of the term "negotiate" is consistent with the purpose of the statute. In discussing the history of the statute, the *Hedges* court stated:

> In the seminal case of the *United States v. Mississippi Valley Generating Co.*, 364 U.S. 520, 548, 81 S.Ct. 294, 308-10, 5 L.Ed.2d 268, 288–89 (1961), in considering 's predecessor statute, §434, the Supreme Court reviewed the legislative history of the conflict of interest statute. It observed that "[t]he obvious purpose of the statute is to insure honesty in the Government's business dealings by preventing federal agents who have interests adverse to those of the Government from advancing their own interests at the expense of the public welfare." Although the statute, enacted in 1863, has been reenacted several times, "the broad prohibition contained in the original statute has been retained throughout the years."

Hedges, 912 F.2d at 1401-02. Despite the Supreme Court's broad reading of the statute, Congress amended the statute in 1962 with the intent to make it even broader. *See United States v. Irons*, 640 F.2d 872, 878 (7th Cir.1981). With regard to the specific term "negotiate," the *Hedges* court found that "[t]he term is to be broadly construed." *Hedges*, 912 F.2d at 1403. Other courts have also reached this conclusion. *See Conlon* 628 F.2d at 155.

Schaltenbrand also argues that if his definition of negotiation is not adopted, the court should at least hold that the term is ambiguous and apply the rule of lenity. Schaltenbrand relies on the recent Supreme Court case of *United States v. Crandon*, 494 U.S. 152, 110 S.Ct. 997, 108 L.Ed.2d 132 (1990), which applied the rule of lenity to another government conflict of interest provision. We simply note that *Hedges*, which was decided several months after *Crandon*, specifically addressed the issue of lenity with respect to the term "negotiate" and found that the term was not ambiguous. Our reasoning above is clearly consistent with the *Hedges* holding on this issue.

Section 207

Schaltenbrand also was convicted under 18 U.S.C. §207(a). Section 207(a) prohibits former officers of the executive branch from knowingly acting "as agent or attorney for, or otherwise represent[ing], any other person (except the United States), in any formal or informal appearance before" any department of the United States in connection with any contract in which the former government employee participated personally and substantially while employed by the government. Again, there is no dispute that Schaltenbrand had been an officer of the executive branch or that he was involved personally and substantially in the Mexican Project.

Although the statute prohibits acting as "agent or attorney for, or otherwise represent[ing]," the indictment in this case stated only that Schaltenbrand "did act as agent" for TBE and failed to allege that he "otherwise represent [ed]" TBE. Based on the language in the indictment, Schaltenbrand could only be convicted of a violation of 207(a) if the government proved beyond a reasonable doubt that he acted as an agent at the November 4, 1987 meeting. *See United States v. Figueroa, 666 F.2d 1375 (11th Cir.1982).* The term "agent" is not defined in the statute, and we have discovered no cases interpreting the term as it pertains to the statute.

Agency is defined as "the fiduciary relation which results from the manifestation of consent by one person to another that the other shall act on his behalf and subject to his control, and consent by the other so to act." Restatement (Second) of Agency § 1(1) (1958). The "principal" is "[t]he one for whom action is to be taken," *id.* § 1(2), and the "agent" is "[t]he one who is to act." *Id.* § 1(3). This court has stated that "an essential characteristic of an agency is the power of the agent to commit his principal to business relationships with third parties...." *Griffin v. United States,* 588 F.2d 521, 528 (5th Cir.1979). * * *

The above evidence shows only that Schaltenbrand attended the November 4 meeting as an employee of TBE, and that he did not participate other than to discuss delivery schedules. The government produced no evidence to show that TBE had given Schaltenbrand authority to make any binding decisions on its behalf. Moreover, the government produced no evidence to show that TBE had held out Schaltenbrand as one who could make binding commitments on its behalf or that it had permitted Schaltenbrand to so hold himself out. The government's evidence on this point is especially meager in light of the other stipulations indicating that TBE's spokesperson at the meeting was Weaver, and that Weaver had asked Schaltenbrand to accompany him to the meeting "in order to listen." Based on this record, we reject the government's argument that Schaltenbrand acted as "agent" at the meeting. In light of this holding, we need not address Schaltenbrand's other arguments with respect to section 207(a) .

* * *

CONCLUSION

In accordance with the above discussion, we AFFIRM the conviction for Count I. We REVERSE the conviction for Count II, direct entry of acquittal, and VACATE the sentence imposed as to that count.

Notes and Questions

1. It is a challenge for those studying procurement integrity to keep in mind the historical contexts in which the laws, rules, and doctrines arose, but, a sense of the context of origin helps. This opinion looks back at the 1961 *Mississippi Valley* case about conflicts of interest, which, like the *Acme* about kickbacks, construed the pre-1960 statutory system. Then, it construes the Congressional reforms pushed by the Kennedy Administration in 1962, from a reaction to the national sense that the 1950s had been a period of insensitivity to ethical considerations by the federal government in general, and by pro-

curement, particularly military procurement, in particular. Ironically, no one at the time had expressed this out more forcefully than President Eisenhower—himself the great military leader of World War II — in his famous 1960 warning of a "military-industrial complex" with undue influence. Conversely, because the case deals with the 1962 Act, it does not involve the further wave of statutory reforms from the mid-1980s, like the Procurement Integrity Act, responding to the scandals of the defense buildup of the 1980s.

2. What do you think of the way the court upholds the conviction for Schaltenbrand's participation when negotiating for a job, but reverses the second count about his then being an agent of his employer after taking that job? Did the court reach a sort of compromise verdict of partial conviction and partial acquittal, or do you accept its reasoning that he was proven to commit one offense and not the other?

3. Two different gray areas came together here: the former (or reserve) military officer going to work for the military contractor, and the American military contractor in a government-approved sale of military items to foreign countries. Given how common both situations and others like them are, so that public and private clients of the procurement lawyer will want and expect to go right up to the line on them, could you give advice that would enable them to do so without crossing over that line?

NKF ENGINEERING, INC., Appellee/Cross-Appellant, v. The UNITED STATES, Appellant/Cross-Appellee, and Weidlinger Associates, Intervenor.

United States Court of Appeals,
Federal Circuit., 805 F.2d 372. Nov. 5, 1986.

Before RICH and BALDWIN, Circuit Judges, and MILLER, Senior Circuit Judge.

BALDWIN, Circuit Judge.

This is an appeal from an order of the United States Claims Court, 9 Cl.Ct. 585, enjoining the government agency involved from awarding a contract to a contractor other than appellee NKF Engineering, Inc. ("NKF"). The order requires the injunction to remain in effect until the contracting officer ("CO") on remand either (1) reexamines NKF's original disqualification after ascertaining whether NKF's bid was tainted by inside information or (2) puts aside the offers received and calls for another round of best and final offers.

* * *

We vacate that portion of the order enjoining the agency from awarding the contract to someone other than NKF. That in effect allows the agency to pursue its original award to Weidlinger Associates ("Weidlinger") and moots the government's challenge to the remand instructions as well as NKF's cross-appeal.

Background

* * * * In March, 1983, the Naval Sea Systems Command ("NAVSEA") issued a Request For Proposals N00024-83-R-4175(Q) ("RFP 4175"). The request called for technical and cost proposals to provide engineering services in support of Navy ships and ship systems. It originated in a subgroup of NAVSEA identified "SEA 55X."

In May, 1983, five proposals were submitted, including those of NKF and Weidlinger, two small business concerns. The proposals were evaluated both technically and on the basis of cost. RFP 4175 was conducted by negotiation rather than by formal advertised bidding.

SEA 55X had as its deputy director a Mr. Yip Park—a civilian employee of the Navy with approximately 30 years of experience in the field of weapons effects and ship survivability and protection. Mr. Park was designated the CO's Technical Representative ("COTR") for RFP 4175. In addition, he chaired the Contract Award Review Panel ("CARP"), the group charged with overseeing the contractor selection process. In those dual capacities, Mr. Park's responsibilities included development of the following matters pertaining to RFP 4175: the evaluation plan pursuant to which the offerors' initial technical proposals were to be evaluated, the government's estimates of the "labor mix" and the range of costs it considered reasonable, and the technical vs. cost weighting formula. In his role as CARP chairman, Mr. Park learned the number of offerors who had chosen to participate in the procurement effort and their relative rankings following initial evaluation. Mr. Park knew that of the five offerors involved, two—NKF and Weidlinger—had received nearly identical rankings on their technical proposals but NKF was more than $2.5 million higher on cost.

In late August, 1984, roughly one year after the initial round of proposals had been received and evaluated by the government, Mr. Park contacted NKF and several other private companies concerning possible employment with them.

During the interviewing process, Mr. Amir (the president of NKF) asked Mr. Park to check with appropriate NAVSEA officials to verify that NKF's employment of Mr. Park would not create a conflict of interest. Although he in fact never checked, Mr. Park later informed Mr. Amir that he had received assurances from NAVSEA legal counsel. With that confirmation, Mr. Amir offered Mr. Park a non-exclusive consulting job, and they soon signed an employment agreement. At that time, neither Mr. Amir nor anyone else at NKF was aware that Mr. Park had involvement with RFP 4175 beyond having knowledge of its technical requirements as stated in the contract's "Scope of Work." Mr. Park nevertheless maintained his dual status as CARP chairman and COTR until his retirement from government service on September 30, 1984.

Some three months after Mr. Park began work with NKF, the contracting officer (Mr. Lloyd) requested (in January, 1985) the submission of best and final offers. Included as part of that request was an amendment to the solicitation, "Amendment 5," which revised the Statement of Work contemplated. Amendment 5 increased the importance of a particular low-cost technical area of the work statement, and necessarily decreased the relative importance of the high cost technical areas. NKF and Weidlinger viewed Amendment 5 as requiring a revision of their initial proposals. Also included in the request for a best and final offer sent to NKF was an attachment in which the government identified aspects of NKF's initial cost proposal judged to be in need of reevaluation and improvement.

NKF re-costed its proposal, an effort that led to a price reduction from $16.7 million initially to $11.2 million—a downward revision of approximately 33 percent—and gave NKF the lowest cost proposal. The other offerors also reduced their final price, but none by more than 19 percent.

In the technical evaluations of the best and final offers, Weidlinger received the highest score; NKF was rated second. However, when the CARP met and applied its predetermined weighting formula to both the technical and cost criteria, NKF received the highest overall score. Accordingly, on July 2, 1985, the CARP issued its final report recommending an award to NKF.

Shortly after that report, the contract negotiator (Mr. Dennard) voiced his concern about a possible conflict of interest involving NKF. He discussed the problem with Mr. Mills, head of the contracts division responsible for RFP 4175 and supervisor of the contracting officer (Mr. Lloyd). Mr. Mills then reviewed the situation with CARP members and, with the concurrence of Mr. Lloyd, Mr. Saul (legal advisor), Mr. Dennard, and another, decided to disqualify NKF on the ground of conflict of interest.

Mr. Mills had never before seen a price swing as extreme as NKF's 33 percent decrease. Because of Mr. Park's prior involvement in RFP 4175 as a NAVSEA employee, Mr. Mills considered the decrease suspicious, *i.e.,* that it was probably the result of Mr. Park's having passed on "inside" information to NKF. Mr. Mills concluded that this appearance of and potential for an unfair competitive advantage so tainted the procurement process that the integrity of the process had been damaged. In his view, the only way to eliminate the harm was to disqualify NKF. The determination to disqualify was reviewed by the Deputy Commander for Contracts, NAVSEA, and the Commander of NAVSEA. Subsequently, the contracting officer announced a proposed award to Weidlinger, the second-highest bidder, by notice dated August 19, 1985.

On August 26, 1985, NKF filed a protest of the proposed award to Weidlinger with the General Accounting Office (GAO). On December 9, 1985, GAO denied NKF's protest, and on the following day NKF filed suit in the Claims Court.

Preliminarily, the Claims Court rejected Weidlinger's arguments that NKF had "unclean hands" based on an alleged violation of the Ethics in Government Act, particularly 18 U.S.C. § 208(a). That section, *inter alia,* imposes criminal liability on one participating "personally and substantially" as a government employee in a contract in which, to his knowledge, any organization with whom he is negotiating prospective employment has a financial interest. The Claims Court found no violation because Park was not "substantially and personally" involved with RFP 4175 during his employment negotiations (August-September 1984) with NKF. It also rejected Weidlinger's argument of waiver based on NKF's failure to acquire the government's written approval before hiring Park; the Claims Court ruled that no such requirement existed.

The Claims Court posited the critical issue as whether NKF proved that the agency's procurement decision was irrational in fact or erroneous in law. The Claims Court read the agency's decision as resting on both the appearance of an impropriety (appearance of exchange of price information) and an actual impropriety (exchange of price information). It concluded that (1) appearance of impropriety, alone, is an insufficient basis to disqualify a bidder and (2) the CO's decision that an actual impropriety occurred was not based on all relevant facts and, hence, was arbitrary and capricious. The Claims Court ordered that no contractor but NKF should be awarded the contract. Nevertheless, it remanded to the CO. It said that NKF could still be disqualified * * * *

Opinion

* * *

The Claims Court * * * determined that the bid rejection, to the extent based on an appearance of impropriety, was unreasonable because *CACI, Inc.-Federal,* though allowing bid rejections based on actual improprieties, prohibits a bid rejection based merely on the *appearance* of impropriety. We reject that view of *CACI, Inc.-Federal.*

In CACI, Inc.-Federal, the Claims Court enjoined the agency's award of a contract to the successful bidder based on a conflict of interest, but this Court reversed. After noting that "a major thrust of the decision of the Claims Court was that there were both the opportunity for and the appearance of impropriety in that process," this Court concluded "that there was no appearance of or opportunity for impropriety that would warrant enjoining the award." *Id.* at 1575. It added that:

> the Claims Court ruling that the Department's award of the contract to Sterling would be 'arbitrary, capricious, and an abuse of discretion' because of the possibility and appearance of impropriety is not supported by the record and therefore is not a proper basis for enjoining the award of the contract.

Id. at 1581–82. It added that the Claims Court "based its inferences of actual or potential wrongdoing by the Department on suspicion or innuendo, not on hard facts" and its analysis "was clearly erroneous and did not justify an injunction against the government's award of the contract." *Id.* at 1582.

We read *CACI, Inc.-Federal* as merely prohibiting the agency from rejecting the relevant bidder where the facts of the case do not support a finding of an appearance of impropriety. That is not to say that such prohibition applies in all cases—the result would depend upon the circumstances in each case. Indeed, our vacating the Claims Court order in this case is consistent with the reversal in *CACI, Inc.-Federal.* In both cases, this Court finds the agency award to be based on a rational ground and Claims Court interference with the normal procurement process to be error.

Under the facts at issue here, we cannot say that the agency's conclusion, that there was an appearance of impropriety, was unreasonable or irrational. Mr. Park had been actively involved in the procurement process on RFP 4175 and, before the contract was awarded, took a job with one of the bidders. Then, and although the proposal was changed in part by the agency necessitating cost revisions by all bidders, NKF submitted the winning bid that included a price revision of 33 percent where no other offeror decreased its bid by more than 19 percent. Whether or not inside information was actually passed from Mr. Park to NKF, the appearance of impropriety was certainly enough for the CO to make a rational decision to disqualify NKF.

NKF argues that Mr. Park was not "substantially" participating in the contract at the time he was negotiating for employment. Though that may matter for determining a violation of 18 U.S.C. §208, it does not make irrational the agency's conclusion that an appearance of impropriety existed. Mr. Park had been a major cog in the bid process, with access to much relevant information. The drastic bid reduction followed by award of the contract to a company with whom he accepts employment has a certain aroma that is hard to purify. Certainly, announcing his retirement prior to negotiating—assuming that occurred—does not purify it. The CO was sensitive, as common sense compels him to be, to the integrity of the bidding process—an integrity attached not only to RFP 4175 but also to the bidding procedure of the entire government. That sensitivity is by no means irrational.

NKF argues that neither the terms of the solicitation nor any regulation or statute authorize its disqualification "to protect the integrity of the procurement process from the appearance of and the potential for an unfair competitive advantage." The Claims Court responded:

> Despite the seeming absence of any authority expressly authorizing the actions that were taken in this case the court is of the view that the contracting officer's responsibility of 'safeguarding the interests of the United States in its contractual relationships', 48 C.F.R. § 1.602-2 (1985), is sufficient to support the exer-

cise of authority that was asserted. What persuades us to this view is the latitude the courts have historically shown with respect to the contracting officer's basic authority to enter into, administer, or terminate contracts, *see, e.g.,* *Arthur Venneri Co. v. United States,* 180 Ct.Cl. 920, 924–25, 381 F.2d 748, 750 (1967); *Sperry Flight Systems Division v. United States,* 212 Ct.Cl. 329, 339–40, 548 F.2d 915, 921 (1977), and the overriding importance of the Government's need to insure full and fair competition in the conduct of its procurements. A procurement system powerless to rid itself of an unfair competitive advantage gained through inside information would soon lose every vestige of competitiveness. There can be no question, therefore, that the contracting officer had authority to act upon his concerns and, in an appropriate case, to cause the disqualification of a bidder.

Though the Claims Court erroneously limited that power to cases involving actual, but not the appearance of, impropriety, we do not repeat that mistake here.

NKF argues that Congress, in creating the Ethics in Government Act, established the standards of conduct to be followed by former government employees and that the broadening of post-employment restrictions beyond the intent of Congress would have adverse effects. However, there is no indication in the Act or its legislative history that Congress intended the Act to be the exclusive means for dealing with all ethical problems. Indeed, certain areas of potential conflict—receipt of gifts and coercive use of office to name two—were not covered by the Act. *See The New Federal Conflict-of-Interest Law,* 76 Harv.L.Rev. 1113, 1162–65 (1963). Hence, when a CO perceives a strong appearance of impropriety in a situation not precisely covered by the Act, it would undermine Congressional concern in the conflict of interest area to tie the hands of the CO.

NKF argues that the government's formal decision to disqualify was not received by NKF until after the decision was made, violating due process. The Claims Court correctly points out, however, that "there surely was no want of due process at the administrative level." Recognizing as a fundamental due process requirement the opportunity to be heard "at a meaningful time and in a meaningful manner," the Claims Court correctly stated that "[t]he protest procedures before the General Accounting Office to which NKF resorted before coming here were certainly sufficient to satisfy any due process requirements inherent in plaintiff's disqualification. *See* 31 U.S.C.A. §§ 3551-3556 (West Supp.1985) (providing for automatic stay of award and subsequent administrative review upon filing of protest with GAO)."

* * *

Conclusion

The CO's decision to disqualify NKF because of an appearance of impropriety was not irrational, arbitrary or capricious. Consequently, the Claims Court order overturning that decision was erroneous and is vacated.

VACATED

ATTACHMENT

Excerpt from agency's formal determination to disqualify

NKF's proposed cost decreased by 33% between their original proposal and their Best and Final Offer. NKF's proposed costs are now at the low end of the Government's internal estimate of the range of costs it considered reasonable.

NAVSEA was concerned about the potential impact of Mr. Park's employment by NKF. * * * *

The Contracting Office must also be concerned about maintaining the integrity of the competitive process. Recent Congressional and media attention has focused on the perception that the Government's source selection process may at times be biased as well as that certain Government employee's [sic] may make certain decisions or take certain actions in their official capacity to enhance their post-Government employment prospects. Under the circumstances of this acquisition, it is not possible to make award to NKF without causing such an appearance. Award to NKF would seriously harm the integrity of the competitive system because of the strong appearance of impropriety. 'Each individual contracting situation should be examined on the basis of its particular facts and the nature of the proposed contract. The exercise of common sense, good judgement, and sound discretion is required in both the decision on whether a signifi-cant potential conflict exists and, if it does, the development of an appropriate means for resolving it' (FAR 9.504). One of the underlying principles is preventing an unfair competitive advantage. The fact that NKF hired the Chairman of the CARP during the source selection process, and then dropped their cost so drastically, much more than they would have been expected to under normal circumstances, indicates a strong pos-sibility that they were aware of information which gave them an unfair competitive ad-vantage and therefore damages the integrity of the proposal system.

* * *

JACK R. MILLER, Senior Circuit Judge, concurring.

I agree with the result suggested by the majority, but consider it unnecessary to de-cide whether the "appearance of impropriety," alone, is adequate ground to disqualify a successful bidder. The facts of this case establish both a possible conflict of interest *and* an unusual pattern in bidding. These, together, provide a rational basis for the contract-ing officer's decision.

Notes and Questions

1. Notice the entirely different mode of enforcement. This is not a prosecution or a civil enforcement suit; it arises in the regular course of decisions on contract award, fol-lowed by protest from disappointed bidders. That means a different role for lawyers as well. The further the contractor gets into the subtler areas of conflicts in hiring, and of suspicions during the acquisition process, where the issue will arise in protests, the more the lawyer has extensive advisory work and regular protest-type litigation work rather than criminal or civil defense. On the other hand, when the case involves what the court calls a "certain aroma that is hard to purity," was anyone really likely to lay the matter out to attorneys in time to receive advice, or is the attorney called in afterwards for what might be called "aromatherapy"?

2. The court brushes aside that the behavior arguably did not violate the prohibition in 18 U.S.C. 208 on postemployment participation in matters where there had been prior substantial involvement. Then, who decides the rules of postemployment restrictions: Congress, the agency ethics officers, or the protest tribunals? Can the rule, after this case, get distilled into a precise, or even an imprecise rule? Consider that a standard as vague as that of the "appearance of propriety" may generate endless debate, uncertainty, and protests. This particular former government employee may not be a model citizen. Yet oth-ers may work hard for the government, acquire valuable experience, and have every reason

to want to put it to work - wanting nothing more than bright-line guidance about when they can, and cannot, properly do with their talents. On the other hand, as in the context of corrupt payments, are rulings like this a necessary party of having a clean procurement system and avoiding the fate of the countries with endemic corruption problems?

Matter of: Loral Western Development Labs
General Accounting Office
B-256066. May 5, 1994

Loral Western Development Labs protests the award of a cost-plus-award fee, level-of-effort contract to HRB Systems, Inc. under request for proposals (RFP) No. MDA904-93-R-I001, issued by the National Security Agency (NSA), Maryland Procurement Office, for the agency's Worldwide Software Lifecycle Support Program. Loral asserts that NSA * * * failed to consider that HRB violated the procurement integrity provisions of the Office of Federal Procurement Policy Act.

We deny the protest.

BACKGROUND

The RFP contemplated award of the Worldwide Software Lifecycle Support contract (WSLSC) for a base year and 3 option years. The contractor is required to provide specified labor categories and associated hours necessary to perform highly-skilled support services at locations inside the continental United States (CONUS) and outside the continental United States (OCONUS). The services include professional engineering, software support and maintenance, technical support, configuration management, and documentation required to supervise and support the performance of these services.

* * *

The RFP provided for award to the responsible offeror which submitted the proposal most advantageous to the government and stated that proposals would be evaluated against the following criteria: technical/personnel, management, and cost. Technical was weighted 50 percent, management 15 percent, and cost 35 percent. Under the technical factor, personnel qualifications and personnel availability were listed as subfactors and each was worth 25 percent of the evaluation score. Under the cost factor, the RFP stated that the evaluation would consider evaluated cost, worth 15 percent, and cost realism, worth 20 percent.

NSA received proposals from Loral and HRB. After evaluating the offers, conducting discussions with both offerors and receiving and evaluating best and final offers (BAFO), NSA determined that the RFP did not accurately reflect its needs and issued amendment No. 4 to the solicitation which deleted the phase-in plan, changed the basis of award, decreased the level-of-effort and provided HRB and Loral with written discussion questions. After evaluating the responses to the discussion questions, NSA provided Loral with additional cost and technical questions and requested both offerors to submit second BAFOs by November 23. NSA received, evaluated, and scored the BAFOs * * * * The evaluation board recommended award to HRB based on the difference in point scores and, consistent with the RFP, recognized that the point scores took into account the technical/management evaluation factors and cost. The source selection authority reviewed the evaluation results and agreed that HRB should be selected for award. The contract was awarded to HRB and this protest followed.

* * *

PROCUREMENT INTEGRITY

Loral protests that NSA failed to follow applicable procurement regulations in awarding the contract to HRB in the face of an alleged violation of the procurement integrity provisions of the Office of Federal Procurement Policy Act, 41 U.S.C. § 423 (1988 and Supp. IV 1992). Loral explains that in September 1993, after the first BAFOs had been evaluated, a Loral employee informed Loral management that an HRB employee stated that he had been told by HRB management that Loral's proposal was approximately $8 million lower than HRB's and that a second round of BAFOs would be requested. Loral states that it informed the agency of this "rumor" and was told that the alleged violation was being investigated by the Inspector General.

Loral complains that the agency improperly made award to HRB before the investigation was completed. Loral further complains that even if the agency could properly award the contract to HRB while the investigation was pending, it failed to obtain approval from a level higher than the contracting officer before doing so as required by the Federal Acquisition Regulation (FAR). Finally, Loral argues that since its proposal was in fact about $8 million lower in cost than HRB's and since a second round of BAFOs was requested, it is clear that there was a violation of the act and that HRB had Loral proprietary information. According to Loral, HRB thus should not have received the award because HRB was able to use this information to revise its cost and technical proposals to offset Loral's lower cost.

Under FAR § 3.104.11(a), if the contracting officer learns of a violation or possible violation of the procurement integrity provisions of the act, he or she must determine if the violation has an impact on the pending award. If the contracting officer determines that there is no impact, he or she may proceed with the procurement with the concurrence of a designated official. FAR § 3.104.11(a)(1). The designated official must then refer the matter to the head of the contracting agency who reviews all available information and determines what action to take, including whether to advise the contracting officer to continue with the procurement, initiate an investigation, refer the matter for criminal investigation, or determine if a violation occurred. FAR § 3.104.11(b). If the head of the contracting agency determines that a violation occurred before an award was made, he or she may cancel the procurement, disqualify an offeror, or take other appropriate action. FAR § 3.104.11(d). If the head of the contracting agency decides that a violation occurred after an award has been made, he or she may void the contract, effect appropriate contractual remedies, or refer the matter to the debarment official. Id.

The regulations specifically provide the head of the contracting agency with a number of options when a possible violation is reported. These include advising the contracting officer to continue with the procurement and initiating an investigation.

We find that the agency acted consistently with the FAR in conducting the procurement once it was aware of the alleged violation. When Loral informed the agency that it had heard a rumor that HRB knew its cost was $8 million lower than Loral's and that a second round of BAFOs would be requested, the agency referred the matter to the Chief of the Maryland Procurement Office, an official higher than the contracting officer. The chief instructed the contracting officer to request both offerors to execute special procurement integrity certificates stating that they were not aware of any violations of the procurement integrity provisions of the act.

Finally, he determined that there was no reason to stop the procurement because at the time the alleged violations were classified only as rumors. Thus, as required by FAR § 3.104.11(a)(1), the contracting officer continued with the procurement only after being advised by a higher level official to do so. Also as required by the FAR, the matter was referred to the head of the contracting agency who considered the matter before the contract was awarded to HRB. Before the award was made, the head of the contracting agency, with the contracting officer and the Chief of the Maryland Procurement Office, reviewed the issue and determined, as permitted by FAR § 3.104.11(b), that there was no basis to conclude that there was a violation of the act. They reached this conclusion because HRB had not acted on the information—that is, HRB did not raise its price, because Loral never provided any further information, and because the offerors executed the special procurement integrity certificates. They also considered that the issue was still under investigation. Thus, the agency followed the requirements of the FAR in deciding to award the contract.

Finally, while Loral argues that the facts show that there was a procurement integrity violation, NSA reports that the investigation is still pending before the Defense Criminal Investigation Service. Accordingly, we will not consider this issue further.

The protest is denied.

Robert P. Murphy
Acting General Counsel

Notes and Questions

1. The opinion deals with aspects of the regulations pursuant to the Procurement Integrity Act (PIA). See 41 U.S.C. sec. 423. This act grew out of the "Ill Wind" scandal, in which contractors benefitted from inside information. The original version of the PIA in 1988 was amended in 1996. It targets two things, information disclosure, and contacts about post-employment As to the first, it circumscribes the disclosure or receipt of procurement information. Chiefly, it seeks to prevent disclosure of contractor proposal information or source selection information, like rankings or evaluation of proposals. That is the issue in NKF.

2. Second, it restricts acceptance of employment by former agency officials with, or employment contacts between agency officials and government contractors. It has mandatory reporting requirements for officials with personal and substantial participation in acquisitions. And, it bans certain persons, like those deeply involved in source selection, for a year from compensation by an awardee. In this respect, it is part of the controls on conflicts of interests in the 1962 legislation.

3. In contrast to the indignant and tough response in some opinions on integrity matters, this opinion reacts coolly and declines to interfere with a procurement award. What does this opinion tell about the possibility that integrity rules might get pushed so far that they do as much harm as good? If the integrity rules at issue here had gotten pushed to extreme strictness, would the government lose out on the ordinary criteria for deciding on awardees - price and technical factors - and instead ended up having to accept inferior bidders who behave in a nicer way?

C. Suspension and Debarment

Suspension and debarment constitute a mechanism by which the government formally decides not to do business with particular contractors for a period of time. This may arise either out of ethical issues of the kinds just discussed, or issues demonstrating contractor irresponsibility that may not involve a primarily ethical dimension, e.g., heavy-duty incompetent failures to perform. However, a debarment does involve the public imposition of a particular status upon a contractor, so that it kicks in some of the legal constraints that apply to normative judgments. Moreover, the procurement lawyer uses an understanding of suspension and debarment in two ways: to handle such cases, and to advise on how not to end up in that situation.

For the government, this constitutes a radical, but sometimes necessary, decision to deny itself the benefits of doing business with a particular contractor. For the contractor, this constitutes a very serious change of status, particularly if much or most of its economic activity comes from government sources. On both sides, apart from the economic impact, suspension and debarment constitute a major normative statement by the government against a contractor who has engaged in wrongdoing. Resort to that sanction signifies a strong governmental and societal stance against such wrongdoing, which may, depending on one's perspective and the pertinent factors, be considered either just and right to obtain respect for the law, or harsh and oppressive in its impact.

Suspension and debarment follow government-wide procedures laid down in FAR Part 9.4. A classic situation occurs when a contractor faces a fraud investigation. The government may immediately suspend the contractor to await the results of the investigation. Suspension can occur on limited evidence, such as the mere indictment (without adjudication) on the criminal fraud charges. The government may or may not give advance notice of a proposed suspension, and there may or may not be a hearing at which the contractor can oppose the suspension. While there are no hard and fast rules about duration, suspension would often, in the absence of debarment proceedings, be a matter of weeks or months, not more.

Suppose that the fraud investigation produces strong evidence of serious wrongdoing by a contractor, such as suffices for the contractor to plead guilty to felony fraud charges. The government may follow up that criminal conviction by initiating a debarment proceeding, seeking to preclude a contractor from receiving new contract awards for a specified time, usually not more than three years. In that proceeding, the government puts forth its basis for debarment and the contractor may both counter that basis and raise mitigating factors.

Government contracting lawyers obviously have a large role in fashioning, or defending, suspension and debarment proceedings. Moreover, awareness of these ultimate sanctions influences all the preliminary steps taken in situations of potentially serious charges against contractors. For example, counsel for a contractor may urge that it implement compliance procedures, make voluntary disclosures, cooperate with investigations, admit wrongdoing, and negotiate civil settlements and even criminal pleas, all with an eye to persuading the government not to push hard in the end for suspension and debarment.

For further discussions of the subject of this section, see: Gary Krump, *The VA's Suspension/Debarment Program*, 33 Procurement Law., Spring 1998, at 10; Paul Griffin, *Debarment for Federal Contractors Who Knowingly Hire Unauthorized Alien Workers*, 10 Geo. Immgr. L.J. 532 (1996); Steven D. Gordon, *Suspension and Debarment from Federal Programs*, 23 Pub. Cont. L.J. 573 (1994); Edwin J. Tomko & Kathy C. Weinberg, *After the Fall: Conviction, Debarment, and Double Jeopardy*, 21 Pub. Cont. L.J. 355 (1992); Brian D. Shannon, *The Government-wide Debarment and Suspension Regulations After a Decade*, 21 Pub. Cont. L.J. 370 (1992).

United States of America, Plaintiff-Appellee, v. Fred L. Hatfield, Sr., d/b/a HVAC Construction Company, Incorporated, Defendant-Appellant

United States Court of Appeals, Fourth Circuit.
108 F.3d 67. Decided March 7, 1997.

Before MURNAGHAN and NIEMEYER, Circuit Judges, and HARVEY, Senior United States District Judge for the District of Maryland, sitting by designation.

Affirmed and remanded by published opinion.

NIEMEYER, Circuit Judge:

This case presents the question of whether a debarred government contractor may be prosecuted criminally for the same fraudulent conduct that led to the debarment. The defendant, arguing that his debarment constituted punishment, asserts that the Double Jeopardy Clause of the Fifth Amendment bars his subsequent criminal prosecution. Because we conclude that debarment is civil and remedial, we reject the argument and affirm the district court's order refusing to dismiss his indictment.

In a twelve-count indictment, the government charges that over a period of several years beginning in September 1990, Fred L. Hatfield, Sr., doing business as HVAC Construction Company, made false and fraudulent statements to the government. The indictment charges that on several occasions when bidding for government work, Hatfield fraudulently misrepresented that he had never had a government contract terminated for default. It also charges that in performing government contracts, Hatfield had on various occasions made certifications for payment that fraudulently stated that work had been performed and that payments had been made to his subcontractors. The government further charges that on one occasion Hatfield presented a false subcontractor invoice.

This conduct alleged in the government's indictment was also the basis for Hatfield's earlier debarment from government contracting. In July 1994, the Department of the Army debarred Hatfield and his companies from all government contracting for a period of 26 months. That debarment, Hatfield claims, cost Hatfield and his company $1,147,227 in attorneys fees, lost profits, and out-of-pocket expenses. He attributes the majority of that assessment to lost profits and his own unpaid compensation.

Hatfield filed a motion to dismiss the indictment, arguing that under United States v. Halper, 490 U.S. 435, 109 S.Ct. 1892, 104 L.Ed.2d 487 (1989), his debarment constituted punishment because it caused him far more loss than the loss sustained by the government. Accordingly, he argued, his current prosecution would result in a second punishment in violation of the Double Jeopardy Clause. From the district court's order denying Hatfield's motion to dismiss the indictment, this interlocutory appeal followed.

The Double Jeopardy Clause, which provides, "nor shall any person be subject for the same offence to be twice put in jeopardy of life or limb," U.S. Const. amend. V, prohibits not only successive criminal prosecutions but also successive punishments for the same offense. Thus, if the government's debarment of Hatfield and his companies constituted punishment for double jeopardy purposes, he is entitled to have his subsequent criminal prosecution dismissed. As Hatfield argues, it does not matter whether the debarment preceded or succeeded the criminal prosecution. If both are punishment, the second proceeding is barred. See United States v. Reed, 937 F.2d 575, 576 n. 3 (11th

Cir.1991); United States v. Bizzell, 921 F.2d 263, 267 (10th Cir.1990). If, on the other hand, debarment is a civil proceeding, it does not implicate the Double Jeopardy Clause because that clause prohibits "two criminal trials [or] two criminal punishments." One Lot Emerald Cut Stones v. United States, 409 U.S. 232, 235, 93 S.Ct. 489, 492, 34 L.Ed.2d 438 (1972). To determine whether debarment is civil or criminal, we look to (1) whether the procedure was designed to be remedial, and (2) whether the remedy provided, even if designated as civil, "is so unreasonable or excessive that it transforms what was clearly intended as a civil remedy into a criminal penalty." Id. at 237, 93 S.Ct. at 493; see also United States v. Ursery,— U.S —,—, 116 S.Ct. 2135, 2147, 135 L.Ed.2d 549 (1996); United States v. One Assortment of 89 Firearms, 465 U.S. 354, 362, 104 S.Ct. 1099, 1104–05, 79 L.Ed.2d 361 (1984).

Debarment is the action taken against a contractor to exclude it from government contracting for a specified period. See 48 C.F.R. §9.403. The action is an agency proceeding which is "as informal as is practicable, consistent with the principles of fundamental fairness." 48 C.F.R. §9.406-3(b)(1). The cause for debarment, if not based on a conviction or judgment, must be established by "a preponderance of the evidence." 48 C.F.R. §9.406-3(d)(3). Finally, debarment cannot be imposed to punish but only to serve the remedial goal of protecting the government. See 48 C.F.R. §9.402(b).

There can be little doubt that debarment was designed to be a civil proceeding. By its own procedural rules, it may not be imposed for punishment, but only to protect the government in its dealings with contractors. See id. Moreover, its procedures are informal and the proof demanded is by a preponderance of the evidence. See 48 C.F.R. §9.406-3(b)(1), (d)(3). Finally, the remedial purpose is linked to specific conduct that relates to the protection of the government from fraud, neglect, nonperformance, or other conduct lacking integrity, with a focus on the "present responsibility" of the contractor. 48 C.F.R. §9.406-2; see also United States v. Bizzell, 921 F.2d 263, 267 (10th Cir.1990) ("debarment constitutes the rough remedial justice permissible as a prophylactic governmental action" (internal quotation marks omitted)); cf. Ursery,— U.S. at—, 116 S.Ct. at 2148 (even though in rem civil forfeiture has "certain punitive aspects," it is designed to serve important nonpunitive goals and is, therefore, a remedial sanction).

We also believe that debarment for 26 months is not so "unreasonable or excessive" as to transform what is designed as a civil remedy into a criminal penalty. Hatfield is accused of fraudulently misrepresenting material facts on numerous occasions over a span of years, and of overstating a subcontractor's billing by more than $10,000. These facts raise a serious question about his "present responsibility" as an honest and dependable contractor to the government. In United States v. Glymph, 96 F.3d 722 (4th Cir.1996), where the facts are strikingly similar—Glymph was debarred for knowingly supplying the government with parts that did not conform to purchase order specifications—we rejected the argument that a four-year debarment was "overwhelmingly disproportionate" where the government paid more than $40,000 for nonconforming parts. See id. at 725–26. We so held even though the regulations provide that generally debarment should not exceed three years. See 48 C.F.R. §9.406-4; see also Glymph, 96 F.3d at 725 n. *. We believe the holding of Glymph controls the disposition of this case. The government estimates that Hatfield caused direct losses between $40,000 and $60,000, which does not take into account victims and losses sustained by subcontractors and suppliers whom Hatfield did not pay. In these circumstances, the 26-month debarment was not so unreasonable or excessive as to transform the remedial sanctions into a criminal penalty.

For the same reasons given in Ursery, we believe that debarment here is not subject to the same type of "particularized assessment" which Halper requires for fixed-amount penalties. That is, the government does not seek the return of a particular quantity of funds but instead seeks to protect the quality of its acquisition programs. Of course, the debarred contractor may quantify its losses in terms of potential profits, and the government may even be able to attach a number to much of the reason for debarment. For instance, we identified a $40,000 loss in nonconforming parts in Glymph. See 96 F.3d at 726. But the government may also debar a contractor for nonmonetary causes such as those affecting the responsibility of a contractor or for disreputable business practices. See 48 C.F.R. §9.406-2(a)(5), (c). Where the sanction and the purposes it seeks to achieve are qualitative rather than merely quantitative, the Halper inquiry is inapplicable. Instead, the question becomes the one raised in Ursery — whether the debarment is in effect so unreasonable and excessive, i.e. so punitive, that we must, from the "clearest proof" conclude that the proceeding is not civil but criminal in nature. See Ursery, — U.S. at— —, 116 S.Ct. at 2148–49.

In the case before us, Hatfield has not carried the burden of demonstrating with clearest proof that his 26-month debarment is disproportionate to the benefits received by the government in protec ting it against the effects of willful failures to perform in accordance with the terms of government contracts, the effects of a history of failures to perform, and the adverse effect of having the government contract with an irresponsible contractor. See 48 C.F.R. §9.406-2(b)(1), (c); §9.402(b); see also Glymph, 96 F.3d at 725–26. Indeed, we doubt that any debarment within the three-year guideline established in the regulations, see 48 C.F.R. §9.406-4, could present a case sufficiently punitive to implicate the Double Jeopardy Clause. Cf. Glymph, 96 F.3d at 725 n. * (holding a four-year debarment not to be of constitutional significance).

Accordingly, we affirm the district court's order denying Hatfield's motion to dismiss the indictment in this case. The case is remanded for further proceedings.

Notes and Questions

1. Is it a fair comparison, as to proportionality that the government estimates that Hatfield caused losses of $40,000-$60,000, while Hatfield pegs the cost of debarment over $1 million? Or is that a comparison of apples and oranges? What Hatfield loses in lost profits, presumably some other contractor gains.

2. While the opinion explains that the government does not inflict (criminal) punishment, surely debarment has a normative dimension and a deterrant effect on potential wrongdoers. So, how much due process shold be provided? Enough to match the potent effect it has on the contractor? Or less so as not to clog the wheels of efficient government action to safeguard the fisc from plainly bad contractors?

3. There came a time at the end of the big 1980s defense buildup, when quite a large percentage of the top 100 Defense Department contractors were under investigation for crimes or had even been convicted. At the time, the Defense Department, with some support from the Justice Department, successfully argued that to debar many of these would hurt the government. So instead, the government put an emphasis on foregoing debarment when contractors would develop an internal control system for abuse. Critics in public interest groups and in Congress regarded this as a sellout. Was it?

4. A contractor's criminal conviction is cause for debarment, but even a convicted contractor still has a due process opportunity to oppose debarment and may succeed in

doing so. *Present* responsibility (lack of which may be inferred from past acts) is the applicable test. In making debarment determinations, the FAR obliges the debarring official to consider the following factors: What self-policing and internal control mechanisms were put in place by the contractor prior to the government investigation; whether the contractor itself alerted the government agency to the cited conduct; the degree of cooperation between the government and the contractor; any restitution agreements; whether appropriate disciplinary actions were taken with respect to wrongdoers; implementation of remedial steps; overhaul of review and control procedures and ethics training programs; whether the contractor has had time to eliminate the circumstances that led to cause for debarment; and whether the contractor acknowledges the severity of the misconduct.

5. Once the government has notified the contractor of a debarment determination, the burden shifts to the contractor to establish that the decision was arbitrary or capricious, or that mitigating factors (including but not limited to those described above) were not considered. See 10 USC §2393; FAR 9.403 (definitions); 9.406-1(lists mitigating factors); *S.D. Carruthers Sons, Inc.*, DBCA No. 95-A-124-D17, 1996 WL 368751 (Debarment vacated on review of mitigating factors) ; Brian D. Shannon, *Debarment and Suspension Revisited: Fewer Eggs in the Basket?* 44 Cath. U. L. Rev. 363 (1995); Steven D. Gordon, *Suspension and Debarment From Federal Programs*, 23 Pub. Cont. L.J. 573 (1994).

SAMEENA INC., an Oregon corporation dba Samtech Research; Sameena Ali; Mirza Ali, Plaintiffs-Appellants, v. UNITED STATES AIR FORCE; V. Carol Moore; Steve Bangs; Alan Schoenberg; Maxwell Air Force Base; Pilson; Mike Thomason, Defendants-Appellees.

No. 97-15252. United States Court of Appeals, Ninth Circuit.
147 F.3d 1148 Decided July 6, 1998.

Before: D. W. NELSON, BOOCHEVER, and REINHARDT, Circuit Judges.

D.W. NELSON, Circuit Judge:

This case arises from a contractor's alleged attempts to defraud the government and the government's efforts to bar the contractor from bidding on future government projects. The appellants bring civil rights and common-law tort claims against a number of individual employees of the United States Air Force (the "Air Force") and argue that the Air Force's decision to debar them for a period of fifteen years was arbitrary and capricious, in violation of the Administrative Procedure Act ("APA"), codified in pertinent part at 5 U.S.C. §704. The district court dismissed the claims against the individual defendants and granted summary judgment in favor of the Air Force on the APA claims. We have jurisdiction pursuant to 28 U.S.C. §1291. Although we affirm the dismissal of the claims against the individual defendants, we reverse the district court's summary judgment because we conclude that the Department of the Air Force (the "Air Force") violated the appellants' constitutional right to due process when it denied them an evidentiary hearing, as required by 48 C.F.R. §9.406-3(b)(2).

FACTUAL AND PROCEDURAL BACKGROUND

In February 1992, the Social Security Administration ("SSA") solicited bids from computer suppliers for a quantity of microcomputer workstations. University Systems, Inc. ("USI"), a California-based corporation of which Appellant Mirza Ali was Chief Executive Officer, submitted a proposal to the SSA in April 1992. USI's bid was deemed competitive, and USI provided the SSA with samples of its products for further evaluation.

During this process, questions arose regarding whether a mouse device included in the proposal was manufactured in compliance with the Trade Agreements Act of 1979, 19 U.S.C. §§ 2501-2582. While this matter was being investigated, it was discovered that two USI officers had submitted a fraudulent letter to the SSA. The SSA consequently eliminated USI from consideration for the workstation contract.

Subsequently, the United States Department of Health and Human Services ("HHS"), of which the SSA is part, commenced "debarment" proceedings against USI and four of its officers, including Mirza Ali, seeking to disqualify them from submitting government contract proposals for three years. On February 2, 1994, USI, Mirza Ali, and the other USI officers were debarred from government contracting through February 18, 1996.

Mirza Ali's wife, Appellant Sameena Ali, is president and sole director of Appellant Sameena Inc. ("Sameena"), which was incorporated in February 1993 by Keith Griffen, a USI officer. Each of the appellants uses aliases: Sameena Ali sometimes goes by "Sameena Ikbal." Mirza Ali sometimes goes by "Zulfiqar Eqbal." Sameena Inc. operates under the assumed name "Samtech Research, Inc." ("Samtech").

Like USI, Samtech supplied computer workstations to government agencies. In June 1995, an Alabama-based contracting squadron of the Air Force issued a contract solicitation for laptop computers. An amendment to the solicitation indicated that the buyer was V. Carol Moore.

Samtech submitted a proposal to Moore in July 1995. Included in Samtech's proposal was a certification that neither Samtech nor any of its principals was debarred or proposed for debarment at that time. The certification defined "principals" as "officers; directors; owners; partners; and persons having primary management or supervisory responsibilities within a business entity." Because the Air Force solicitation required that bidders have at least three years of experience as a government contractor, Samtech's proposal also included a list of "Government Contract Awards." Among them was a contract with the United States Department of Energy (the "DoE contract") that Sameena had obtained in 1994 through a novation from USI.

In response to a query, Samtech sent Moore a letter in September 1995 explaining that Samtech "started doing business with the Federal Government by acquiring a contract for the supply of ADP equipment to the United States Department of Energy in 1992." On further investigation, Moore discovered that the contract actually had been awarded to USI in 1992 and had only been novated to Samtech in 1994. Moore also obtained bank documents indicating that "Sameena Ikbal" and "Zulfiqar Eqbal" were authorized to make withdrawals from Samtech's accounts and were, respectively, "President/Secretary" and "Vice President" of the corporation. This information appeared to Moore to contradict the statements made in Samtech's contract proposal.

On the basis of these apparent misrepresentations, Samtech was deemed ineligible for the Air Force contract. Moreover, in December 1995, the Air Force Contracting Officer, Gladys McBride, submitted a recommendation that Samtech be debarred.

McBride appended the entire administrative file to her recommendation, including an affidavit by Moore describing her investigations.

On December 26, 1995, Sameena Inc., Samtech, Sameena Ali, and Mirza Ali ("the appellants") were notified that they had been proposed for debarment (and, in Mirza Ali's case, an "extension" of debarment). The notices were accompanied by memoranda setting forth the grounds for the proposed debarments. The notices also invited the appellants to submit information and argument in opposition to the debarment.

The appellants included in their response a letter dated February 21, 1996, from an official at Samtech's bank. The letter stated that the document indicating that Zulfiqar Eqbal was Vice President of Samtech—a bank signature card—had been "corrected" after the bank was informed "that Eqbal was not a corporate officer" of Sameena or Samtech. The submission also included copies of checks written on Sameena's bank accounts. A number of these checks were signed by "Zulfiqar Eqbal" and were made out to a variety of payees, including physicians, a sports club, and Eqbal (Mirza Ali) himself. The appellants' submission also requested an evidentiary hearing on the issue of Mirza Ali's role at Samtech. Notwithstanding the submission, and without an evidentiary hearing, the Air Force issued a final decision in June 1996 to debar Sameena/Samtech and Sameena Ali—and to extend Mirza Ali's debarment—until December 2010. The debarment was based on findings that the appellants had (1) made false statements regarding Samtech's experience as a contractor, (2) provided false certifications that none of Samtech's principals was debarred, and (3) participated in a scheme to avoid the effects of USI's debarment.

On August 30, 1996, the appellants filed two complaints in the United States District Court for the Northern District of California. The first complaint, brought by Mirza Ali against HHS and against six agency employees in their individual capacities, focused on Ali's initial debarment and sought declaratory relief and damages. The second complaint, brought by Mirza Ali, Sameena Ali, and Sameena/Samtech against the Air Force and seven Air Force employees in their individual capacities, focused both on the debarment of Sameena/Samtech and Sameena Ali and on the extension of Mirza Ali's debarment.

This second complaint made substantially the same allegations as the first, even though it was directed at entirely different defendants. The appellants alleged (1) that the individual Air Force officials had conspired to violate their civil rights and had committed several common-law torts and (2) that the Air Force's decision to debar them was arbitrary and capricious and should be set aside pursuant to the APA.

In an order filed December 11, 1996, the district court dismissed the claims against the individual defendants for lack of personal jurisdiction and, alternatively, on the grounds that the appellants had failed either to plead conspiracy with sufficient particularity or to comply with the Federal Tort Claims Act, 28 U.S.C. §§ 1346(b), 2671-2680. The court also granted summary judgment to the Air Force on the APA claims. The appellants timely appeal. We affirm the district court's dismissal of the claims against the individual defendants but reverse the summary judgment in favor of the Air Force.

* * *

ANALYSIS

* * * The Supreme Court has long recognized that a federal agency is obliged to abide by the regulations it promulgates. See Vitarelli v. Seaton, 359 U.S. 535, 545, 79 S.Ct. 968, 3 L.Ed.2d 1012 (1959); Service v. Dulles, 354 U.S. 363, 372, 77 S.Ct. 1152, 1 L.Ed.2d 1403 (1957); Accardi v. Shaughnessy, 347 U.S. 260, 267, 74 S.Ct. 499, 98 L.Ed.

681 (1954). An agency's failure to follow its own regulations "tends to cause unjust discrimination and deny adequate notice" and consequently may result in a violation of an individual's constitutional right to due process. NLRB v. Welcome-American Fertilizer Co., 443 F.2d 19, 20 (9th Cir.1971); see also United States v. Newell, 578 F.2d 827, 834 (9th Cir.1978). Where a prescribed procedure is intended to protect the interests of a party before the agency, "even though generous beyond the requirements that bind such agency, that procedure must be scrupulously observed." Vitarelli, 359 U.S. at 547, 79 S.Ct. 968 (Frankfurter, J., concurring); see also Note, Violations by Agencies of Their Own Regulations, 87 Harv. L. Rev. 629, 630 (1974) (observing that agency violations of regulations promulgated to provide parties with procedural safeguards generally have been invalidated by courts).

The Federal Acquisition Regulation ("FAR") establishes a system of uniform policies and procedures governing acquisitions by all executive agencies. See 48 C.F.R. § 1.101. In recognition of the "serious nature of debarment," see 48 C.F.R. § 9.402, the FAR sets out detailed procedures to ensure that this sanction, which is intended to safeguard the integrity of the acquisitions process, itself is applied in conformity with "principles of fundamental fairness." 48 C.F.R. § 9.406-3(b). Accordingly, the FAR provides:

> [I]f it is found that the contractor's submission in opposition raises a genuine dispute over facts material to the proposed debarment, agencies shall also—(i) Afford the contractor an opportunity to appear with counsel, submit documentary evidence, and confront any person the agency presents.

48 C.F.R. § 9.406-3(b)(2). Thus, in the event of a genuine factual dispute, the FAR clearly establishes that a contractor facing debarment is entitled to an evidentiary hearing.

The appellants claim that they raised a genuine issue of material fact with regard to Mirza Ali's position at Sameena/Samtech. They contend that Ali was mistakenly listed as Vice President of the company on the bank signature card discovered by Moore and that the February 1996 letter from the bank supports that contention. Accordingly, they claim that they were entitled under the FAR to an evidentiary hearing on the matter.

The district court rejected the appellants' claims on two grounds. First, the court found the letter from the bank to be inconclusive. The court pointed out that the letter merely acknowledged that the bank had issued a new signature card deleting Eqbal's name, and that it had made this "correction" after being informed that Zulfiqar Eqbal was not a corporate officer. The district court suggested that the letter had little probative value because it was sent after debarment proceedings against the appellants already had commenced.

Second, the district court observed that the operative factual question informing the debarment decision was not whether Ali/Eqbal was Vice President of Sameena/Samtech but, rather, whether he exercised control over the business. As the court noted, the Debarring Official found that Ali had written business-related and personal checks on Samtech's account and had stated on the telephone that he was project manager for government solicitations. Based on that evidence, the Debarring Official concluded, "[I]t is clear that Mr. Eqbal had full authority to expend Samtech's resources and bind the company." Because the district court found that "[n]othing plaintiffs submitted created a dispute as to this issue," it concluded that they were not entitled to an evidentiary hearing.

The district court failed, however, to acknowledge evidence submitted by the appellants that calls into question whether Ali/Eqbal was a principal of Sameena/Samtech. The appellants submitted evidence that Ali/Eqbal was Vice President of a Hong Kong corporation also called Samtech and that his position there had likely caused the confusion involving the signature cards. The appellants also submitted evidence indicating that Ali/Eqbal held no official position with Sameena/Samtech other than bookkeeper and that the writing of checks was consistent with that position. The appellants denied that Ali/Eqbal had represented himself to be a project manager or any other type of corporate officer. They explained that the checks made out to and signed by Eqbal were not for his personal use and were not issued at his discretion. Finally, the appellants challenged the government to produce any document indicating that Ali/Eqbal had actually acted in the capacity of a principal with regard to control over the company's decisionmaking process. Thus, although the appellants' submission does not establish that the Debarring Official acted arbitrarily or capriciously in determining that Ali/Eqbal was a principal of Samtech/Sameena, it does raise a genuine factual dispute regarding the issue.

The appellants requested an evidentiary hearing to address this question. The Debarring Official decided, however, that a hearing was unwarranted, finding the appellants' denials of the charges against them to be "unsupported by credible evidence." We do not doubt that the Air Force is in a better position than this Court to assess the credibility of the evidence offered by the appellants. We are convinced, however, that an evidentiary hearing would have been the appropriate forum in which to make such an assessment, particularly in view of the serious consequences attaching to a debarment of 15 years. The FAR states unambiguously that such a hearing "shall" be afforded if genuine factual disputes arise. Accordingly, we conclude that the Air Force violated the appellants' constitutional right to due process in failing to comply with binding regulations and that the appellants are entitled to such a hearing on remand. As Justice Frankfurter observed in a similar context, "He that takes the procedural sword shall perish with that sword." Vitarelli, 359 U.S. at 547, 79 S.Ct. 968 (Frankfurter, J., concurring).

CONCLUSION

For the foregoing reasons, we AFFIRM the district court's dismissal of the appellants' claims against the individual defendants. However, we REVERSE the summary judgment in favor of the Air Force and REMAND to the district court with instructions to remand this matter to the Air Force. The Air Force should hold an evidentiary hearing, pursuant to 48 C.F.R. §9.406-3(b)(2), to address whether Mirza Ali/Zulfiqar Eqbal was a principal of Sameena/Samtech.

AFFIRMED in part, REVERSED in part and REMANDED. Each party shall bear its own costs.

Notes and Questions

1. This case is a triumph of procedure. How would it look to someone who cared more about results than procedure. Suppose you were the Air Force officer who had put together the case against Ali/Eqbal. Would you view a Ninth Circuit reversal and the need for an evidentiary proceeding as wonderful triumphs of justice or as rewarding culpable parties for hiring lawyers to come up with delaying tactics?

2. Note the total lack of deference. The Ninth Circuit reaches past the district court's affirmance to an intense review of the Air Force Debarring Official that accords him no respect at all. A driving force is the sense that a fifteen year debarment is so intense that

it raises serious due process concerns. Note the contrast with the *Hatfield* case, where the court upheld (against a different kind of challenge, to be sure) a debarment of 26 months. Also, the Air Force tried to do this debarment on the quick and easy with just a paper record. Within the government, it presumably seemed virtuous to move swiftly to debar Ali/Eqbal as a repeat offender who had resumed offending before his previous debarment even ended. Outside the government, doing it just on a paper record looked to the Ninth Circuit more indolent than virtuous. For a further discussion of this issue, see Gary Krump, *The VA's Suspension/Debarment Program*, 33 Procurement Lawyer, Spring 1998, at 10.

Index

(Page references indicate either that a note is found on the page or
that a case or other multi-page item begins on the page.)